American Government

FREEDOM AND POWER

Third Edition

American Government

FREEDOM AND POWER

Third Edition

THEODORE J. LOWI

CORNELL UNIVERSITY

AND

BENJAMIN GINSBERG

THE JOHNS HOPKINS UNIVERSITY

W. W. NORTON & COMPANY

NEW YORK • LONDON

Copyright © 1994, 1993, 1992, 1990 by W. W. Norton & Company, Inc.

The text of this book is composed in Bembo
with the display set in Bembo italic.
Composition by TSI Graphics
Manufacturing by Maple-Vail Book Manufacturing Group.
Book design by Suzanne Bennett.

Library of Congress Cataloging-in-Publication Data
Lowi, Theodore J.
    American government : freedom and power / Theodore J. Lowi and
Benjamin Ginsberg. — 3rd ed.
        p.   cm.
    Includes bibliographical references and index.
    1. United States—Politics and government.   I. Ginsberg,
Benjamin.   II. Title.
JK274.L647   1994
320.973—dc20   93-17522

ISBN 0-393-96465-5

W. W. Norton & Company, Inc., 500 Fifth Avenue, New York, N.Y. 10110
W. W. Norton & Company Ltd., 10 Coptic Street, London WC1A 1PU

3 4 5 6 7 8 9 0

For our families:
  Angele, Anna, and Jason Lowi
  Sandy, Cindy, and Alex Ginsberg

Contents

PART 2
INSTITUTIONS

CHAPTER 5

CHAPTER 6

PART 3
POLITICS

CHAPTER 9

Public Opinion   361

CHAPTER 10

Elections   405

PART 4
GOVERNANCE

Preface

In the two years since the publication of the second edition of *American Government: Freedom and Power,* the world has changed in a number of surprising ways. Symbolized by the destruction of the Berlin Wall, the Soviet Union has collapsed, Russia has been compelled to seek economic aid from the West, and the Cold War that once seemed to threaten the survival of civilization has come to an end. In the Middle East, the United States fought a short but decisive war against Iraq and is now leading a diplomatic initiative that may, after fifty years of violence, bring about some solution to the problems of the Middle East. In South Africa, the hated system of *apartheid* has weakened in the face of domestic opposition and international pressure. The nations of Western Europe have taken giant steps toward economic and political integration.

Against this backdrop of dramatic political change throughout the world, American domestic politics seems almost to be frozen in time. When we wrote the first and second editions, the United States was plagued by a divided government, huge budget deficits, and lack of popular political participation. Today, as we shall see in the third edition, government is no longer divided after Democrat Bill Clinton's victory in the 1992 presidential election. However, budget deficits are larger than ever and Americans participate less than ever before.

But, in a changing world it is more important than ever to understand the politics of the United States. More than at any time since the Second World War, the world is looking to America for leadership and for an example of popular government in action. Throughout the world, America—despite its problems and faults—symbolizes the combination of freedom and power to which so many now aspire. This makes the task of our book all the more important.

The collaboration on this book began nearly ten years before its publication, and the book is in every way a product of collaboration in teaching, research, and writing. Each author has taught other courses—for thirty-five and twenty-one years respectively—and has written other books; but we agree that no course has been more challenging than the introductory course, and no book has been more difficult to write. Someone once asked if it is difficult for scholars to "write down" to introductory students. No. It is difficult to "write up" to them. Introductory students, of whatever age or reading level, need more, require more, and expect more of a book.

A good teaching book, like a good novel or play, is written on two levels. One is the level of the narrative, the story line, the characters in action. The second is the level of character development, of the argument of the book or play. We would not be the first to assert that theater is an aspect of politics, but our book may be unusual to the extent that we took that assertion as a guide. We have packed it full of narrative—with characters and with the facts about the complex situations in which they find themselves. We have at the same time been determined not to lose sight of the second level, yet we have tried to avoid making the second level so prominent as to define us as preachers rather than teachers.

The book is only one product of our collaboration. The other important product is about 5,000 Cornell and Johns Hopkins students who took the courses out of which this book grew. There is no way to convey adequately our appreciation to those students. Their raw intelligence was not satisfied until the second level could provide a logic linking the disparate parts of what we were asserting was a single system of government. And these linkages had to be made in ordinary language. We hope we brought this to the book.

We hope also that we brought over from our teaching experience a full measure of sympathy for all who teach the introductory course, most particularly those who are obliged to teach the course from departmental necessity rather than voluntarily as a desired part of their career. And we hope our book will help them appreciate the course as we do—as an opportunity to make sense of a whole political system, one's own, and one of the largest, most durable, and most consequential ever. Much can be learned about the system from a reexamination of the innumerable familiar facts, under the still more challenging condition that the facts be somehow interesting, significant, and, above all, linked.

This points to what must be the most troublesome, sometimes the most embarrassing, problem for this course, for this book, and for political science in general: All Americans are to a great extent familiar with the politics and government of their own country. No fact is intrinsically difficult to grasp, and in such an open society, facts abound. In America, many facts are commonplace that are suppressed elsewhere. The ubiquity of political commonplaces is indeed a problem, but it can be turned into a virtue. These very commonplaces give us a vocabulary that is widely shared, and such a vocabulary enables us to communicate effectively at the first level of the book, avoiding abstract concepts and professional language (jargon). Reaching beyond the commonplaces to the second level also identifies what is to us the single most important task of the teacher of political science—to confront the million commonplaces and to choose from among them the small number of really significant concepts. Students give us proportion; we must in turn give the students priorities. Virtually everything we need to know about the institutions and processes of government and politics is readily at hand. But to choose a few commonplaces from the millions: there's the rub.

We have tried to provide a framework to help the teacher make choices among commonplaces and to help the students make some of the choices for themselves. This is good political science, and it is good citizenship, which means more than mere obedience and voting; it means participation through constructive criticism, being able to pierce through the periphery of the great information explosion to the core of lasting political reality.

Our framework is freedom and power. To most Americans that means freedom *versus* governmental power, because Americans have been raised to believe that every expansion of the government's power involves a contraction of personal freedom. Up to a point we agree with this traditional view. The institutions of Amer-

ican government are in fact built on a contradiction: Popular freedom and governmental power *are* contradictory, and it is the purpose of our Constitution to build
a means of coping with that contradiction. But as Supreme Court justices sometimes say to their colleagues, "We concur, dissenting in part." For in truth, freedom and power are related to each other as husband and wife—each with some
conflicting requirements, but neither able to produce, as a family, without the
other.

Just as freedom and power are in conflict, so are they complementary. *There can
be little freedom, if any, without governmental power.* Freedom of any one individual depends fundamentally on the restraints of everyone else in their vicinity. Most of
these restraints are self-imposed. We call that *civility*, respect for others borne of
our awareness that it is a condition of their respect for us. Other restraints vital to
personal freedom are imposed spontaneously by society. Europeans call those restraints *civil society;* sociologists call them *institutions.* Institutions exist as society's
means of maintaining order and predictability through routines, customs, shared
values. But even in the most stable society, the restraints of civility and of civil society are incomplete and insufficient; there remains a sphere of deliberate restraint
that calls for the exercise of public control (public power). Where society falls
down, or where new events and new technologies produce new stresses, or where
even the most civil of human beings find their basic needs in conflict with others,
there will be an exercise of public control, or public power. Private property, that
great bastion of personal freedom in the Western world, would disappear without
elaborate government controls over trespass.

If freedom were only a matter of the absence of control, there would be no
need for a book like ours. In fact, there would be little need for political science at
all. But politics, however far away in the national or the state capital, is a matter of
life and death. It can be as fascinating as any good novel or adventure film if the
key political question is one's own survival or the survival of one's society. We have
tried to write each chapter of this book in such a way that the reader is tempted to
ask what that government institution, that agency, this committee or that election,
this group or that amendment has to do with *me* and *us,* and how has it come to be
that way? That's what freedom and power are all about—my freedom and your restraint, my restraint and your freedom.

Having chosen a framework for the book there was also a need for a method.
The method must be loyal to the framework; it must facilitate the effort to choose
which facts are essential, and it must assist in evaluating those facts in ways that not
only enlighten students but enable them to engage in analysis and evaluation for
themselves. Although we are not bound exclusively to a single method in any scientific or philosophic sense, the method most consistently employed is one of history, or history as development: First, we present the state of affairs, describing the
legislature, the party, the agency, or policy, with as many of the facts as are necessary to tell the story and to enable us to reach the broader question of freedom versus governmental power. Next, we ask how we have gotten to where we are. By
what series of steps, and when by choice, and when by accident? To what extent
was the history of Congress or of the parties or the presidency a fulfillment of constitutional principle, and when were the developments a series of dogged responses
to economic necessity? History is our method because it helps choose which facts

are significant. History also helps those who would like to try to explain why we are where we are. But more important even than explanation, history helps us make judgments. In other words, we look less to causes and more to consequences. Political science cannot be satisfied with objective description, analysis, and explanation. Political science would be a failure if it did not have a vision about the ideal as well as the real. What is a good and proper balance between freedom and governmental power? What can a constitution do about it? What can enlightened people do about it?

Evaluation makes political science worth doing but also more difficult to do. Academics make a distinction between the hard sciences and the soft sciences, implying that hard science is the only real science: laboratory, people in white coats, precision instruments making measurements to several decimal points, testing hypotheses with "hard data." But as medical scientist Jared Diamond observes, that is a recent and narrow view, considering that science in Latin means knowledge and careful observation. Diamond suggests, and we agree, that a better distinction is between hard (i.e., difficult) science and easy science, with political science fitting into the hard category, precisely because many of the most significant phenomena in the world cannot be put in a test tube and measured to several decimal points. We must nevertheless be scientific about them. And more: unlike physical scientists, social scientists have an obligation to judge whether the reality could be better. In trying to meet that obligation, we hope to demonstrate how interesting and challenging political science can be.

THE DESIGN OF THE BOOK

The objective we have taken upon ourselves in writing this book is thus to advance our understanding of freedom and power by exploring in the fullest possible detail the way Americans have tried to balance the two through careful crafting of the rules, through constructing balanced institutions, and by maintaining moderate forms of organized politics. The book is divided into four parts, reflecting the historical process by which freedom and governmental power are (or are not) kept in balance. Part I, "Foundations," comprises the chapters concerned with the writing of the rules of the contract. The founding of 1787–1789 put it all together, but that was actually a second effort after a first failure. The original contract, the Articles of Confederation, did not achieve an acceptable balance—too much freedom, and not enough power. The second founding, the Constitution ratified in 1789, was itself an imperfect effort to establish the rules, and within two years new terms were added—the first ten amendments, called the Bill of Rights. And for the next century and a half following their ratification in 1791, the courts played umpire and translator in the struggle to interpret those terms. Chapter 1 introduces our theme. Chapter 2 concentrates on the founding itself. Chapters 3 and 4 chronicle the long struggle to establish what was meant by the three great principles of limited government, *federalism, separation of powers,* and *individual liberties and rights.*

Part II, "Institutions," includes the chapters sometimes referred to as the "nuts and bolts." But none of these particles of government mean anything except in the larger context of the goals governments must meet and the limits, especially of procedure, that have been imposed upon them. Chapter 5 is an introduction to the fundamental problem of *representative government* as this has been institutionalized in Congress. Congress, with all its problems, is the most creative legislative body in the world. But how well does Congress provide a meeting ground between consent and governing? How are society's demands taken into account in debates on the floor of Congress and deliberations by its committees? What interests turn out to be most effectively "represented" in Congress? What is the modern Congress's constituency?

Chapter 6 explores the same questions for the presidency. Although Article II of the Constitution provides that the president should see that the laws made by Congress are "faithfully executed," the presidency was always part of our theory of representative government, and the modern presidency has increasingly become a law *maker* rather than merely a law implementor. What, then, does the strong presidency do to the conduct and the consequences of representative government? Chapter 7 treats the executive branch as an entity separate from the presidency, but ultimately it has to be brought back into the general process of representative government. That, indeed, is the overwhelming problem of what we call "bureaucracy in a democracy." After spelling out the organization and workings of "the bureaucracy" in detail, we then turn to an evaluation of the role of Congress and the president in imposing some political accountability on an executive branch composed of roughly five million civilian and military personnel.

Chapter 8 on the judiciary should not be lost in the shuffle. Referred to by Hamilton as "the least dangerous branch," the judiciary truly has become a co-equal branch, to such an extent that if Hamilton were alive today he would probably eat his words.

Part III we entitle simply "Politics" because politics encompasses all the efforts by any and all individuals and groups inside as well as outside the government to determine what government will do and on whose behalf it will be done. Our chapters take the order of our conception of how politics developed since the Age of Revolution and how politics works today: Chapter 9, "Public Opinion"; Chapter 10, "Elections"; Chapter 11, "Political Parties"; Chapter 12, "Groups and Interests"; and Chapter 13, "The Media." But we recognize that, although there may be a pattern to American politics, it is not readily predictable. One need only contemplate the year-long nomination of presidential candidates to recognize how much confusion, downright disorder, there is in what we political scientists blithely call "political process." Chapter 14 is an evaluation of that process. We ask whether our contemporary political process is consistent with good government. Unfortunately, the answer is not entirely positive.

Part IV is entitled "Governance." These are chapters primarily about public policies, which are the most deliberate and goal-oriented aspects of the still-larger phenomenon of "government in action." Chapter 15 is virtually a handbook of public policy. Since most Americans know far less about policies than they do about institutions and politics, we felt it was necessary to provide a usable, common vocabulary of public policy. Since public policies are most often defined by the goals that the government establishes in broad rhetorical terms and since there can be an uncountable number of goals, we have tried to get beyond and behind goals by looking at the "techniques of control" that any public policy goal must embody if the goal is even partially to be fulfilled. We also look at how the selection of a particular technique of control can actually shape the political process just as much as the political process shapes the policy choice. These "techniques of control" are the analytic units of the succeeding policy chapters. Chapter 16, "Government and the Economy," looks at a limited slice of policies that are concerned with the conduct of businesses, the obligations of employers, the rights and limits of workers to organize, and the general ability of the economy to operate without flying apart. Chapter 17, "Government and Society" looks at similar "techniques of control" as these are utilized to affect conduct in the society at large, outside and beyond the economic marketplace. Since we are a commercial society, many policies aimed at the society have direct economic consequences. For example, many aspects of what we call the welfare state are social policies, but they have a profound effect on the economy, because welfare, as we put it, "changes the rules governing who shall be poor." Chapter 18, "Foreign Policy and World Politics," turns to the international realm and America's place in it. Our concern here is to understand American foreign policies and why we have adopted the policies that we have. Given the traditional American fear of "the state" and the genuine danger of international involvements to domestic democracy, a chapter on foreign policies is essential to a book on American government and also reveals a great deal about America as a culture.

Chapter 19 is a summation. We are not debaters, and we are not lawyers writing a brief for the defense of freedom or power. Our brief is for the balance. It is not, as some popular authors would put it, "that delicate balance." It is for us a very *in*delicate balance." Nearly 160 years ago, Alexis de Tocqueville wrote that Americans would eventually permit their government to become so powerful that elections and representative processes would come to be ironic interludes providing citizens with little more than the opportunity to wave the chains by which the government had bound them. Can we have both popular freedom and governmental power in a nation of 250 million people making up a nation-state with historic obligations and historic vulnerabilities to 200 other nation-states? To what extent can we continue to depend upon and benefit from governmental power while retaining our liberties? These are the questions every generation must ask for itself—if it is fortunate enough to be able to do so.

ACKNOWLEDGMENTS

Our students at Cornell and Johns Hopkins have already been identified as an essential factor in the writing of this book. They have been our most immediate intellectual community, a hospitable one indeed. Another part of our community, perhaps a large suburb, is the discipline of political science itself. Our debt to the scholarship of our colleagues is scientifically measurable, probably to several decimal points, in the footnotes of each chapter. Despite many complaints that the field is too scientific or not scientific enough, political science is alive and well in the United States. It is an aspect of democracy itself, and it has grown and changed

in response to the developments of government and politics that we have chroni-
cled in our book. If we did a "time line" on the history of political science as we
have done in each chapter of the book, it would show a close association with developments in "the American state." Sometimes the discipline has been out of
phase and critical; at other times, it has been in phase and perhaps apologetic. But
political science has never been at a loss for relevant literature, and without it, our
job would have been impossible.

There have, of course, been individuals on whom we have relied in particular.
Of all writers, living and dead, we find ourselves most in debt to the writing of
two—James Madison and Alexis de Tocqueville. Many other great authors have
shaped us as they have shaped all political scientists. But Madison and Tocqueville
have stood for us not only as the bridge to all timeless political problems; they represent the ideal of political science itself—that political science must be steadfastly
scientific in the search for what is, yet must keep alive a strong sense of what ought
to be, recognizing that democracy is neither natural nor invariably good, and must
be fiercely dedicated to constant critical analysis of all political institutions in order
to contribute to the maintenance of a favorable balance between individual freedom and public power.

We are pleased to acknowledge our debt to the many colleagues who had a
direct and active role in criticism and preparation of the manuscript. The first
edition was read and reviewed by: Gary Bryner, Brigham Young University; James
F. Herndon, Virginia Polytechnic Institute and State University; James W. Riddlesperger, Jr., Texas Christian University; John Schwarz, University of Arizona;
Toni-Michelle Travis, George Mason University; and Lois Vietri, University of
Maryland. Their comments were enormously helpful.

For subsequent editions, we relied heavily on the thoughtful manuscript
reviews we received from Russell Hanson, University of Indiana; William
Keech, University of North Carolina; Donald Kettl, University of Wisconsin;
William McLauchlan, Purdue University; J. Robert Baker, Wittenberg University; James Lennertz, Lafayette College; and Allan McBride, Grambling State
University. The advice we received from these colleagues was especially welcome
because all had used the book in their own classrooms. Other colleagues who offered helpful comments based upon their own experience with the text included
Douglas Costain, University of Colorado; Robert Hoffert, Colorado State University; Mark Silverstein, Boston University; and Norman Thomas, University of
Cincinnati.

We also want to reiterate our thanks to the four colleagues who allowed us
the privilege of testing a trial edition of our book by using it as the major text in
their introductory American Government courses. Their reactions, and those of
their students, played an important role in our first edition. We are grateful to
Gary Bryner, Brigham Young University; Allan J. Cigler, University of Kansas;
Burnet V. Davis, Albion College; and Erwin A. Jaffe, California State University-
Stanislaus.

We owe a special debt to Robert J. Spitzer, State University of New York-
College at Cortland for preparing most of the essays profiling important individuals that appear throughout all three editions of the book. By linking concepts and
events to real people, these essays help to make this a more lively and interesting

book and thus one that students will be more likely to read and remember. Professor Spitzer also helped develop the new "Debating the Issues" boxes, in which core concepts are debated by political thinkers.

One novel feature is a series of "Process Boxes" that illustrate the actual operation of a major political institution or procedure. Several individuals, all leading figures in their own fields, were generous enough to contribute their time and expertise to helping us develop what we know will be a useful pedagogic tool. Our thanks to Thomas Edsall, the *Washington Post;* Kathleen Francovic, CBS News; Benjamin L. Ginsberg, Republican National Committee; and Ray Rist, U.S. General Accounting Office.

We also are grateful for the talents and hard work of several research assistants, whose contribution can never be adequately compensated: Douglas Dow and John Forren prepared the test bank. Brenda Holzinger helped to develop the study questions. Steve McGovern prepared the film guide and the annotated bibliographies. Others who gave us significant help with the book are Melody Butler, Nancy Johnson, Noah Silverman, Rebecca Fisher, Michael Harvey, David Lytell, Dennis Merryfield, Rachel Reiss, Nandini Sathe, Rob Speel, Jennifer Waterston, and Daniel Wirls (now a member of the Politics faculty at the University of California at Santa Cruz).

Jacqueline Discenza not only typed several drafts of the manuscript, but also helped to hold the project together. We thank her for her hard work and dedication.

Theodore Lowi would like to express his gratitude to the French-American Foundation and the Gannett Foundation whose timely invitations helped him prepare for his part of this enterprise.

Perhaps above all, we wish to thank those who kept the production and all the loose ends of the book coherent and in focus. Roby Harrington has been an extremely talented editor. Through three editions, Roby has kept careful track of all the details while maintaining a clear vision of the text as a whole. Nancy Yanchus devoted the better part of a year to the third edition. She prepared many of the photo essays and spent countless hours making certain that all the pieces of the manuscript were in place. For two editions, Margie Brassil, as both our manuscript editor and project editor, has kept us from making too many mistakes. Jean Yelovich also prepared a number of excellent photo essays. Stephen Dunn and Sandra Smith helped out on many editorial and marketing questions. Ruth Dworkin was our efficient production manager. We also want to reiterate our thanks to Amy Cherry and Sandy Lifland for their marvelous work on the first edition. Finally, our thanks to Donald Lamm, Norton's president, for his continuing commitment to the project.

We are, however, more than happy to absolve all these contributors from any flaws, errors, and misjudgments that will inevitably be discovered. We wish the book could be free of all production errors, grammatical errors, misspellings, misquotes, missed citations, etc. From that standpoint, a book ought to try to be perfect. But substantively we have not tried to write a flawless book; we have not tried to write a book to please everyone. We have again tried to write an effective book, a book that cannot be taken lightly. Our goal was not to make every reader a political scientist. Our goal was to restore politics as a subject matter of vigorous and enjoyable discourse, recapturing it from the bondage of the thirty-second news bite and the thirty-page technical briefing. Every person can be knowledgeable because everything about politics is accessible. One does not have to be an anchor person to profit from political events. One does not have to be a philosopher to argue about the requisites of democracy, a lawyer to dispute constitutional interpretations, an economist to debate a public policy. We would be very proud if our book contributes in a small way to the restoration of the ancient art of political controversy.

Theodore J. Lowi
Benjamin Ginsberg
August 1993

Part 1
Foundations

1

Freedom and Power: An Introduction to the Problem

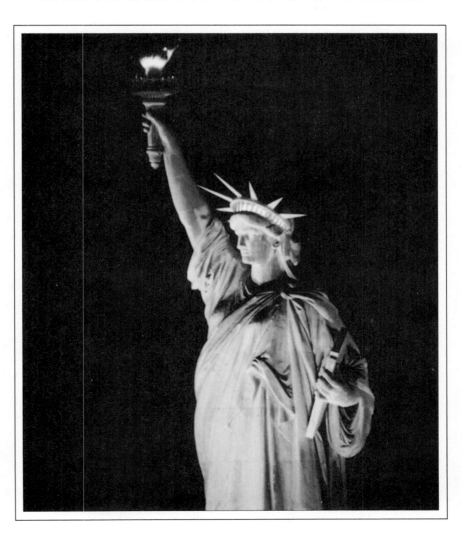

A story often told by politicians concerns a voter from the Midwest who, upon returning home from military service in Korea, took advantage of his federal educational benefits under the G.I. Bill to complete college. After graduation, this individual was able to obtain a government loan from the Small Business Administration (SBA) to help him start a business, and a mortgage subsidized by the Federal Housing Administration (FHA) to purchase a home. Subsequently, he received medical care in a Veteran's Administration Hospital, including treatment with drugs developed by the National Institutes of Health. This voter drove to work every day on a four-lane highway built under the federal interstate highway program, frequently used Amtrak to travel to a nearby city and, though he was somewhat nervous about air travel, relied on the Federal Aviation Administration (FAA) to make certain that the aircraft he depended on for business and vacation trips were safe. When this voter's children reached college age, they obtained federal student loans to help pay their expenses. At the same time, his aging parents were happy to begin receiving monthly Social Security checks and, when his father unexpectedly required major surgery, financial disaster was averted because the federal government's Medicare program paid the bulk of the cost. What was our midwestern friend's response to all of this? Well, in both 1980 and 1984, he strongly supported Ronald Reagan's presidential candidacy because of Reagan's promise to get the federal government off people's backs. In 1988, our friend voted for George Bush because he believed that Bush would continue Reagan's efforts to hold the line on federal domestic spending. But in 1992, disgusted by Bush's failure to adhere to his pledge not to raise taxes, this Midwesterner supported Ross Perot. During this entire period, meanwhile, he also voted for the re-election of his congressman, a staunch Democrat, who steadfastly opposed any cuts in the government's domestic programs. This is an example of the love-hate relationship between Americans and their government.

Government has become a powerful and pervasive force in the United States. In 1789, 1889, and even in 1929, America's national government was limited in size, scope, and influence, and most of the important functions of government were provided by the states. By 1933, however, the influence of the government expanded to meet the crises created by the stock market crash of 1929, the Great Depression, and the run on the banks of 1933. Congress passed legislation that brought the government into the business of home mortgages, farm mortgages, credit, and relief of personal distress. Whereas in 1933 people tried to withdraw their money from the banks only to find that their savings had been wiped out, sixty years later, most are confident that although many savings and loan institutions may be insolvent, their money is still safe because it is guaranteed by the government. Today, the national government is an enormous institution with programs and policies reaching into every corner of American life. It oversees the nation's economy; it is the nation's largest employer; it provides citizens with a host of services; it controls a formidable military establishment; and it regulates a wide range of social and commercial activities in which Americans engage. The founding fathers never dreamed the government could take on such obligations; we today can hardly dream of a time when the government was not so large a part of our lives.

Freedom and Power: The Enduring Debate

*S**triking the right balance between freedom and power is the essential paradox of governing. One could select any point in American history and find a vigorous debate between those who want a stronger government and those who believe that individual freedom is endangered by an encroaching state. This debate was a central feature of the early struggle to establish a permanent, stable, yet limited national government in America.*

Thomas Jefferson was an eloquent spokesman for a government of sharply limited powers. He laid his trust in majority will and personal freedom. In fact, he considered regular revolts by the people to be healthy for a democracy, not unlike the way the physicians of his time viewed bloodletting. "The tree of liberty must be refreshed from time to time, with the blood of patriots and tyrants."

Opposing him was Alexander Hamilton, an avowed elitist, who recognized the failings of weak government (such as the country had experienced under the Articles of Confederation). Hamilton argued that the national government had to possess the power to enforce its decisions in order to ensure the political and economic well-being of its citizenry.

Jefferson

I own, I am not a friend to a very energetic government. It is always oppressive. It places the governors indeed more at their ease, at the expense of the people. The late rebellion in Massachusetts [Shays's Rebellion] has given more alarm, than I think it should have done. Calculate that one rebellion in thirteen States in the course of eleven years, is but one for each State in a century and a half. No country should be so long without one. Nor will any degree of power in the hands of government, prevent insurrections. . . . And say . . . whether peace is best preserved by giving energy to the government, or information to the people. This last is the most certain, and the most legitimate engine of government. Educate and inform the whole mass of the people. Enable them to see that it is their interest to preserve peace and order, and they will preserve them. And it requires no very high degree of education to convince them of this. They are the only sure reliance for the preservation of our liberty. After all, it is my principle that the will of the majority should prevail.[1]

Hamilton

If it be possible at any rate to construct a federal government capable of regulating the common concerns, and preserving the general tranquillity, it must be founded . . . upon the reverse of the principle contended for by the opponents of the proposed Constitution [that is, a confederacy]. It must carry its agency to the persons of the citizens. It must stand in need of no intermediate legislations, but must itself be empowered to employ the arm of the ordinary magistrate to execute its own resolutions. The majesty of the national authority must be manifested through the medium of the courts of justice. The government of the Union, like that of each State, must be able to address itself immediately to the hopes and fears of individuals; and to attract to its support those passions which have the strongest influence upon the human heart. It must, in short, possess all the means, and have a right to resort to all the methods, of executing the powers with which it is entrusted, that are possessed and exercised by the governments of the particular States.[2]

[1]Thomas Jefferson, Letter to James Madison, December 20, 1787, in *Jefferson's Letters,* arr. by Willson Whitman (Eau Claire, WI: E. M. Hale, 1950), p. 85.
[2]*The Federalist Papers,* Clinton Rossiter, ed., (New York: New American Library, 1961), No. 16, p. 116.

The growth of government in the United States has been accompanied by a change in the way Americans perceive government. In the nineteenth century, Americans generally were wary of government, especially the national government. Government meant control, and control meant reduction in individual liberties. National government was a still greater threat because it was remote. The best government, as Thomas Jefferson put it, was the one that governed least. Many Americans today continue to pay lip service to this early view of government, but a new theory of democratic government has gradually come to dominate modern American perceptions. From the perspective of this new theory, if government could be made less of a threat and less remote by the development of elections, representative bodies, and other mechanisms of popular control and if government could be made to pay attention to its citizens' needs and wishes, then a more powerful government would be a government with greater capacity to serve the people. In other words, government control of the people would be more acceptable if people, in turn, controlled the government.[1]

Today, the consensus favoring a large and active government is so broad that even self-styled "conservatives" differ more with their "liberal" counterparts over the proper character of government than over its ultimate desirability. Ronald Reagan, our most conservative president in more than half a century, began his successful 1980 presidential campaign not by promising to curtail government activity but rather by vowing "to restore to the federal government the capacity to do the people's work." In his first inaugural address, President Reagan pledged to curb the growth of the federal establishment but at the same time declared, "Now so there will be no misunderstanding, it is not my intention to do away with government. It is, rather, to make it work."[2] Reagan repeated this sentiment in his 1985 inaugural. In 1992, in his speech accepting the Democratic presidential nomination, Bill Clinton noted correctly that "the Republicans have campaigned against big government for a generation. . . . But have you noticed? They've run this big government for a generation and they haven't changed a thing."[3]

[1]For examples, see Richard Wollheim, "A Paradox in the Theory of Democracy," in *Philosophy, Politics and Society,* ed. Peter Laslett and W. G. Runciman (Oxford: Blackwell, 1962).

[2]"President Reagan's Inaugural Address," *New York-Times,* 21 January 1981, p. B1.

[3]E.T. Dionne, "Beneath the Rhetoric, an Old Question," *Washington Post,* 31 August 1992, p. 1.

TABLE 1.1

Some Activities of the U.S. Government in 1993

Beneficiary and Program	Cost	Beneficiary and Program	Cost
Business		**Farmers**	
Department of Energy, *Energy Supply, Research & Dev. Activities*	2,576,000,000	Department of Agriculture, *Commodity Credit Corporation*	9,745,000,000
Export-Import Bank of U.S.	2,236,385,000	Department of Agriculture, Farmers Home Administration, *Agriculture Credit Insurance Fund*	4,043,000,000
Needy Children			
Department of Agriculture, Food & Nutrition Science, *Child Nutrition Program*	5,577,000,000	**Homeowners**	
Department of Health & Human Services, *Health Resources & Human Services*	1,862,000,000	HUD, *Federal Housing Administration Fund*	1,937,300,000
		Labor Unions	
College Students and Universities		Department of Labor, *Training & Employment Services*	4,079,000,000
Department of Education, Office of Postsecondary Education, *Pell Grants*	6,715,000,000	**The Sick and Disabled**	
Department of Education, Office of Postsecondary Education, *Guaranteed Student Loans*	1,956,402,000	Department of Education, Office of Special Education & Rehabilitation Services, *Education for the Handicapped*	2,467,000,000
The Elderly		HHS, National HIV Program	1,760,000,000
HSS, *Supplemental Security Income Program*	14,234,000,000	HSS, *Supplemental Security Income Program*	14,234,000,000
HHS, *Federal Old-Age & Survivors Insurance*	286,487,968,000	HHS, Social Security, *Federal Disability Insurance*	29,158,000,000
Law Enforcement		**Veterans**	
FBI	1,699,000,000	Veterans Administration, *Compensation*	16,397,000,000
Drug Enforcement Admin.	696,000,000	VA, *Pensions*	3,989,000,000
		VA, *Medical Care*	12,335,000,000

Source: Executive Office of the President, Office of Management and Budget, *Budget of the United States, Fiscal Year 1993* (Washington, DC: Government Printing Office, 1992).

According to the polls, Americans want to keep the political and economic benefits they believe they derive from government (see Table 1.1). Indeed, many Americans want the government not only to continue its present involvement but actually to do more in a variety of areas. According to the polls, many would be willing to pay higher taxes to maintain government services and programs and to keep the government solvent.

How did government come to play such an important role in our lives? How did Americans come to lose some of their fear of remote government and to perceive government as a valuable servant rather than a threat to freedom?

To answer these questions, this chapter will first assess the meaning and character of government as a phenomenon and will describe some of the alternative forms government can take and the key differences among them. Second, the chapter will examine the factors that led to one particular form of government—representative democracy—in western Europe and the United States. Finally, we will begin to address the question central not only to our book but also to the most fundamental and enduring problem of democratic politics—the relationship between government and freedom.

GOVERNMENT AND CONTROL

Government is the term generally used to describe the formal institutions through which a land and its people are ruled. To govern is to rule. *Government is comprised of institutions and processes that rulers establish to strengthen and perpetuate their power or control over a territory and its inhabitants.* A government may be as simple as a tribal council that meets occasionally to advise the chief, or as complex as our own vast establishment with its forms, rules, and bureaucracies. This more complex government is sometimes referred to as "the state," an abstract concept referring to the source of all public authority.

Foundations of Government

Whatever their makeup, governments historically have included two basic components: a means of coercion, such as an army or police force, and a means of collecting revenue. These two components have been the essential foundations of government—the building blocks that all individuals and groups who ever sought to rule have been compelled to construct if they were to secure and maintain a measure of control over their territory and its people. Groups aspire to govern for a variety of reasons. Some have the most high-minded aims, while others are little more than ambitious robbers. But whatever their motives and character, those who aspire to rule must be able to secure obedience and fend off rivals as well as collect the revenues needed to accomplish these tasks.[4] Some governments, including many of the less-developed nations today, have consisted of little more than an army and a tax-collecting agency. Other governments, especially those in the developed nations, have attempted to provide services as well as to collect taxes in order to secure popular consent and control. For some, power is an end in itself. For most, power is necessary for the maintenance of public order.

---

[4]For an excellent discussion, see Charles Tilly, "Reflections on the History of European State-Making," in *The Formation of National States of Western Europe,* ed. Charles Tilly (Princeton, NJ: Princeton University Press, 1975), pp. 3–83. See also Charles Tilly, "War Making and State Making as Organized Crime," in *Bringing the State Back In,* ed. Peter Evans, Dietrich Rueschemeyer, and Theda Skocpol (New York: Cambridge University Press, 1985), pp. 169–91.

TABLE 1.2
The Means of Coercion in 1990

Forms	Amount	Level of Government
Arrests	11.2 million	Federal and state
Criminal cases	47,335	Federal
Imprisonments	23,450	Federal
Fines	4,482	Federal
Executions	23	State

Source: Timothy J. Flanagan and Kathleen Maguire (eds.) *Sourcebook of Criminal Justice Statistics 1991* (Washington, D.C.: U.S. Department of Justice, Bureau of Justice Statistics, 1992.)

The Means of Coercion   Government must have the power to order people around, to get people to obey its laws, and to punish them if they do not. Coercion takes many different forms, and each year millions of Americans are subject to one form of government coercion or another. Table 1.2 is an outline of the uses of coercion by federal and state governments in America. Chapter 15 will bring these into the context of public policy in its discussion of "the techniques of control."

One aspect of coercion is **conscription,** whereby government requires certain involuntary services of citizens. The best-known example of conscription is military conscription, which is called "the draft." Although there has been no draft since 1974, there were drafts during the Civil War, World War I, World War II, and the wars in Korea and Vietnam. With these drafts, our government compelled millions of men to serve in the armed forces; one-half million of these soldiers made the ultimate contribution by giving their lives in their nation's service. If the need arose, military conscription would undoubtedly be reinstituted. Eighteen-year-old males are required to register today, just in case.

Military conscription, however, is not the only form of involuntary service that government can compel Americans to perform. We can, by law, be compelled to serve on juries, to appear before legal tribunals when summoned, to file a great variety of official reports, including income tax returns, and to attend school or to send our children to school.

The Means of Collecting Revenue   Each year American governments collect enormous sums from their citizens to support their institutions and programs. Taxation has grown steadily over the years. In 1989, the national government alone collected $516 billion in individual income taxes, $117 billion in corporate income taxes, $337 billion in social insurance taxes, $26 billion in excise taxes, and another $18 billion in miscellaneous revenue. The grand total amounted to more than $1 trillion or more than $4,000 from every living soul in the United States. And of course, while some groups receive more in benefits from the government than they pay in taxes, others get less for their tax dollar. One of the perennial issues in American politics is the distribution of tax burdens versus the distribution of program benefits. Every group would like more of the benefits while passing more of the burdens of taxation onto others.

Governments vary in their institutional structure, in their size, and in their modes of operation. Two questions are of special importance in determining how governments differ from each other: Who governs? How much government control is permitted?

In some nations, governing is done by a single individual—a king or dictator, for example. This state of affairs is called **autocracy.** Where a small group of landowners, military officers, or wealthy merchants control most of the governing decisions, that government is said to be an **oligarchy.** If more people participate, and if the populace is deemed to have some influence over their actions, that government is tending toward **democracy.**

Governments also vary considerably in terms of how they govern. In the United States and a small number of other nations, governments are severely limited as to *what* they are permitted to control (substantive limits), as well as *how* they go about it (procedural limits). Governments that are so limited are called **constitutional,** or liberal governments. In other nations, including many in Europe as well as in South America, Asia, and Africa, though the law imposes few real limits, a government is nevertheless kept in check by other political and social institutions that the government is unable to control but must come to terms with—such as autonomous territories, an organized church, organized business groups, or organized labor unions. Such governments are generally called **authoritarian.** In a third group of nations, including the Soviet Union under Joseph Stalin, Nazi Germany, and perhaps prewar Japan and Italy, governments not only are free of legal limits but in addition seek to eliminate those organized social groupings that might challenge or limit their authority. These governments typically attempt to dominate or control every sphere of political, economic, and social life and, as a result, are called **totalitarian** (see Box 1.1).

Influencing the Government: Politics

In its broadest sense, the term "politics" refers to conflicts over the character, membership, and policies of any organization to which people belong. As Harold Lasswell, a famous political scientist, once put it, politics is the struggle over "who gets what, when, how."[5] Although politics is a phenomenon that can be found in any organization, our concern in this book is more narrow. Here, politics will be used to refer only to conflicts and struggles over the leadership, structure, and policies of *governments.* The goal of politics, as we define it, is to have a share or a say in the composition of the government's leadership, how the government is organized, or what its policies are going to be. Having a share is called *power* or *influence.*

As we shall see throughout the book, not only does politics influence government, but the character and actions of government also influence a nation's politics. A constitutional government is actually an effort to gain more popular consent by opening channels for political expression. People are moved to accept these

[5]Harold Lasswell, *Politics: Who Gets What, When, How* (New York: Meridian Books, 1958).

BOX 1.1

Constitutional, Authoritarian, and Totalitarian Governments

Most Western democracies have constitutions that actually define the limits and scope of governmental power. But the mere existence of a constitution does not, by itself, define a regime as constitutional. Some governments have constitutions that they ignore. At least until recently, this was the case in such Eastern European nations as Romania and Bulgaria. In the true constitutional setting, the actual processes of government follow the forms prescribed by the constitution, and groups in society have sufficient freedom and power to oppose efforts by the government to overstep these limits. The governments in the United States and Western Europe provide the best examples.

Authoritarian governments must sometimes be responsive to a small number of powerful social groups and institutions such as the army, but such governments recognize no formal obligations to consult their citizens or to respect limits on their actions. Examples of authoritarian governments in the recent past included Spain under the leadership of General Francisco Franco and Portugal under Prime Minister Antonio Salazar.

Totalitarian governments can be distinguished from both democratic and authoritarian governments by the lack of any distinction between the government and other important social institutions. Indeed, totalitarian governments generally seek to destroy all other social institutions—for example, churches, labor unions, and political parties—that may function as rival sources of power. Examples of totalitarian governments include the Third Reich in Germany under Adolf Hitler in the 1930s and 1940s and the government of the Soviet Union under Marshall Joseph Stalin between the 1930s and 1950s.

In recent years, a number of authoritarian regimes in Eastern Europe, including the Soviet Union and its satellite states, faced severe economic hardship and popular discontent. Most of these regimes, including Czechoslovakia, Poland, Hungary, East Germany, and the Soviet Union, itself, collapsed and were replaced by new governments.

channels in the hope that they can make the government more responsive to their demands. These channels can be *democratic politics,* through election of candidates to fill the top governing positions; or they can be *mass politics,* through voting on proposed government actions one at a time, as in a **referendum** or a **plebiscite.** When the political channels are indirect, through methods of selecting representatives, that system is usually called *republican politics,* or **representative democracy.** When politics is provided or sought by competition among leaders or among powerful groups outside the government, we call this **pluralistic politics.** Sometimes politics does not take place through formal channels but through direct action. Direct action politics can be either violent politics or **civil disobedience**—both of which attempt to shock rulers into behaving more responsibly. Or direct action politics can be revolutionary politics, which rejects the system entirely and attempts to replace it with a new ruling group that has a new set of rules. But all of these are politics—some of it encouraged by the rulers themselves, some of it accepted begrudgingly by rulers, and some brutally suppressed by rulers.

FROM COERCION TO CONSENT

Americans have the good fortune to live in a nation in which limits are placed on *what* governments can do and *how* governments can do it. But such constitutional democracies are relatively rare in today's world—it is estimated that only 20 or so of the world's nearly 200 governments could be included in this category. And constitutional democracies were unheard of before the modern era. In many areas of the world today, governments have little interest in the views of their citizens and recognize few formal limits on the scope of their power.

The Extraction-Coercion Cycle

Many Americans truly believe that governments originate from a general agreement entered into by individuals trying to address common problems. This is called the *contract model* of the origins of the state, and some governments actually come close to fitting that model. The Mayflower Compact is one of the few such efforts, and our Constitution may be considered another (see Box 1.2). But most governments begin with efforts by a small group to subdue all their rivals and to

---

BOX 1.2
The Mayflower Compact

The Mayflower Compact, written and signed on November 11, 1620, was the first agreement for self-government ever enforced in America. Having landed at a place outside the jurisdiction of their original royal charter, the Pilgrim leaders sought to develop their own guidelines for governing the colony. They drafted a compact, or agreement, which called upon the Pilgrims to unite under a single government and to abide by any laws that were passed "for the general good of the colony."

> In the name of God, Amen. We whose names are underwritten, the loyal subjects of our dread sovereign lord, King James, by the grace of God, of Great Britain, France, and Ireland, King, Defender of the Faith, etc.
>
> Having undertaken for the glory of God, and advancement of the Christian faith and honor of our king and country, a voyage to plant the first colony in the northern parts of Virginia, do by these present, solemnly and mutually, in the presence of God and one of another, covenant and combine ourselves together into a civil body politic, for our better ordering and preservation and furtherance of the ends aforesaid; and by virtue hereof to enact, constitute, and frame such just and equal laws, ordinances, acts, constitutions, offices from time to time as shall be thought most meet and convenient for the general good of the colony; unto which we promise all due submission and obedience. In witness whereof we have hereunder subscribed our names, Cape Cod, 11th of November, in the year of the reign of our sovereign lord, King James, of England, France, and Ireland 18, and of Scotland 54. Anno Domini 1620.

THE HISTORY OF COMPACTS

The Magna Carta of 1215 was one of the earliest attempts at a compact drawn up between citizens and rulers. Weakened by recent defeats in France and desperately in need of financing, King John of England, pictured here in a thirteenth-century tapestry, reluctantly signed the charter. Its main purpose was to ensure the feudal rights of the barons and church and prohibit the king from encroaching on baronial privileges. While the charter was actually a failure at creating a governmental system, it became over the years a symbol of the rights of people for a greater voice in government.

By 1787, the United States government was in disarray. The Articles of Confederation, which had been written during the Revolution, were not forceful enough to hold the independent-minded states together. Congress faced increasing opposition from the states on crucial matters such as the nation's budget. The Constitutional Convention that met in Philadelphia devised a new constitution with a strong central government. By balancing power between the three branches of government, ensuring a Bill of Rights, and leaving the document flexible enough for adaptation, the "assembly of demi-gods" created a constitution that remains strong two hundred years later.

The Declaration of the Rights of Man and Citizen was written at the outset of the French Revolution in 1789 and became the preamble to the first French constitution completed in 1791. It was strongly influenced by the American Declaration of Independence, listing "inalienable rights" and asserting the equality of man and the sovereignty of the people. Promising to liberate individuals from the tyranny of the monarchy, it called for religious tolerance, representative government, and freedom of expression.

Following Japan's surrender on September 2, 1945, after the bombing of Hiroshima and Nagasaki, an eleven-member Allied Council occupied Japan under the command of General Douglas MacArthur. Under their guidance, a constitution was written retaining the emperor as the symbolic head of state while placing sovereignty with the people by giving power to a popularly elected prime minister and diet. The constitution was overwhelmingly embraced by popular vote and signed by the emperor on May 3, 1947. Japan did not gain full sovereignty until 1952.

The 1989 Velvet Revolution marked the end of Communist rule in Czechoslovakia. In 1992, with the ratification of a new constitution in sight, the country split into two separate republics: the Czech Republic and Slovakia, each with a different system of government. The Czech Republic adopted a parliament system similar to Britain's. However, the language used to describe citizens' rights was markedly different from Western constitutions. It clearly stated the liberties to be provided by the government instead of the limits on the government to preserve individual rights. This difference is attributed to attitudes developed under communism when the government was seen as a provider of services as opposed to a threat to the pursuit of liberty. The Czech constitution was ratified in 1993.

institutionalize their power and their privileges. Often, of course, such efforts fail. But, in general, those governments that survive and flourish do so because their leaders are able to set in motion a process that Samuel Finer, the famous British political scientist, called the *extraction-coercion cycle*. This means that rulers initially use what force they can muster to collect taxes and to compel military service. Whatever revenues and services they initially acquire increase their capacity to extract more revenues and services, which in turn makes possible larger armies and bureaucracies, which enables them to extract more revenues and services.

The cycle of extraction and coercion was at the heart of state building in western Europe. In 1640, when Frederick William succeeded as the elector of Brandenburg-Prussia, he commanded a military force consisting of a mere 1,300 mercenary troops, his government had virtually no central administrative machinery, and he was at the mercy of the Estates, the assembly of provincial nobles, for tax revenues. In stages over the next forty years, Frederick William used his troops to acquire more funds, with which he in turn enforced the collection of more taxes. By the conclusion of Frederick William's reign in 1688, Brandenburg-Prussia boasted a standing army of 30,000 men and an elaborate administrative machinery. This cycle was continued by his successors, particularly by Frederick William I, King of Prussia, who was able to construct what, on a *per capita* basis, was the largest standing army in Europe in the early eighteenth century. This permanent force of 80,000 troops both supported and was supported by an extensive bureaucracy and tax collection apparatus.

For many centuries, even in nations such as Britain where constitutional democracy and democratic forms of rule eventually developed, rulers relied almost exclusively on force to maintain their power and to secure the compliance of their subjects. This style of rule can eventually bring on riots and insurrections, but civil disturbances usually posed no real challenge to these early governments. Indeed, given the local character of governmental administration, rioting and disorder also tended to be local and usually did not disrupt affairs elsewhere in that country.

Limits and Democratization

Prior to the eighteenth and nineteenth centuries, governments seldom sought—and rarely received—the support of their ordinary subjects. The available evidence strongly suggests that the ordinary people had little love for the government or for the social order. After all, they had no stake in it. They equated government with the police officer, the bailiff, and the tax collector.[6]

Beginning in the seventeenth century, in a handful of Western nations, two important changes began to take place in the character and conduct of government. First, governments began to acknowledge formal limits upon their power. Second, a small number of governments began to provide the ordinary citizen with a formal voice in public affairs through the vote. Obviously, the desirability of limits on government and the expansion of popular influence on government were at the heart of the American Revolution of 1776. "No taxation without representation,"

---

[6]See Eugen Weber, *Peasants into Frenchmen* (Stanford, CA: Stanford University Press, 1976), Chapter 5.

as we shall see in Chapter 2, was hotly debated beginning with the American Revolution and through the founding in 1789. But even before the American Revolution, there was a tradition of limiting government and expanding participation in the political process all over western Europe. Thus, to understand how the relationship between rulers and the ruled was transformed, we must broaden our focus to take into account events in Europe as well as those in America. We will have to divide the transformation into its two separate parts. The first is the effort to put limits on government. The second is the effort to expand the influence of the people through politics.

Limiting Government   The key force behind the imposition of limits on government power was a new social class, the "bourgeoisie." *Bourgeoisie* is a French word for freeman of the city, or bourg. Being part of the bourgeoisie later became associated with being "middle class" and with being in commerce or industry. In order to gain a share of control of government—to join the kings, aristocrats, and gentry who had dominated governments for centuries—the bourgeoisie sought to change existing institutions—especially parliaments—into instruments of real political participation. Parliaments had existed for centuries, controlling from the top and not allowing influence from below. The bourgeoisie embraced parliament as the means by which they could exert the weight of their superior numbers and growing economic advantage against their aristocratic rivals. At the same time, the bourgeoisie sought to place checks on the capacity of governments to threaten these economic and political interests by placing formal or constitutional limits on governmental power. The three bourgeois (also called liberal) philosophers with the strongest influence on American thinking were John Locke, Adam Smith, and John Stuart Mill (see Box 1.3).

Although motivated primarily by the need to protect and defend their own interests, the bourgeoisie advanced many of the principles that became the central underpinnings of individual freedom for all citizens—freedom of speech, of assembly, of conscience, and freedom from arbitrary search and seizure. It is important to note here that the bourgeoisie generally did not favor democracy as such. They were advocates of electoral and representative institutions, but they favored property requirements and other restrictions so as to limit participation to the middle classes. Yet, once these institutions of politics and the protection of the right to engage in politics were established, it was difficult to limit them just to the bourgeoisie. We will see time after time that principles first advanced to justify a selfish interest tend to take on a life of their own and to be extended to those for whom the principles were not at first designed.

The Expansion of Democratic Politics   Along with limits on government came an expansion of democratic government. Three factors explain why rulers were forced to give ordinary citizens a greater voice in public affairs: the first is internal conflict, the second is external threat, and the third is national unity and development.[7]

---

[7]For a fuller account, see Benjamin Ginsberg, *The Captive Public* (New York: Basic Books, 1986), Chapter 1.

BOX 1.3

The Philosophical Basis of Limited Government

Three liberal philosophers had a particularly strong influence on American political thought: John Locke (1632–1704), Adam Smith (1723–1790), and John Stuart Mill (1806–1873). These three thinkers espoused the liberal philosophy that placed limits on government.

John Locke argued for limited government because of his belief that, just as a person had a right to his own body, he had a right to his own labor and the fruits of that labor. From that he argued that people formed a government to protect their property, lives, and liberty, and that this government could not properly act to harm or take away that which it had been created to protect. According to Locke in his *Second Treatise on Government* (1690), government could only properly function with the consent of the governed through their representatives; if the government acted improperly, it would have broken its contract with society and would no longer be a legitimate government. The people would have the right to revolution and the right to form a new government.

Adam Smith supported a severely limited government as a protection for the economic freedom of the individual. In his *Wealth of Nations* (1776), he argued for private enterprise as the most efficient means of production, leading to the growth of national wealth and income. He believed that freedom for individual economic and social advancement was only possible in a competitive free market, unhindered by government intervention. Nonetheless, he argued that government must protect the economic freedoms—free trade, free choice of individuals to do what they wanted, to live where they wished, and to invest and spend as they saw fit—by ensuring that the market remains competitive and honest through such governmental actions as the regulation of standard weights and measures, the prevention of the formation of monopolies, and the defense of the community.

John Stuart Mill believed that government should be limited so as not to interfere with the self-development of the individual. In order for individuals to fully develop their faculties, Mill believed that they need as large a sphere of freedom as possible, including freedom of thought and discussion. In *On Liberty* (1859), Mill argued that any restrictions on individuals ought to be based on recognized principles rather than on the preferences of the majority. He believed that social control should be exercised only to prevent harm to others. He maintained that when thoughts are suppressed, if they are right, individuals are deprived of truth; if the ideas are wrong, they are deprived of that better understanding of truth that comes out of conflict with error.

First, during the eighteenth and nineteenth centuries, every nation was faced with intense conflict among the landed gentry, the bourgeoisie, lower-middle-class shopkeepers and artisans, the urban working class, and farmers. Many governments came to the conclusion that if basic class and group conflicts were not dealt with in some constructive way, disorder and revolution might well result. One of the most effective ways of responding to such conflict was to extend the rights of political participation, especially voting rights, to each new group as it grew more powerful. Such a liberalization was sometimes followed by suppression, as rulers began to fear that their calculated risk was not paying off. This was true even in

the United States. The Federalists, who were securely in control of the government after 1787, began to fear the emergence of an opposition party being led by Thomas Jefferson (see Box 1.4). Fearing Jefferson as leader of a vulgar and dangerous democratic party, the Federalist majority in Congress adopted an infamous law, the Alien and Sedition Acts of 1798, which, among other things, declared any opposition to or criticism of the government to be a crime. Hamilton and other Federalist leaders went so far as to urge that the opposition be eliminated by force, if necessary. The failure of the Federalists to suppress their Republican opposition was, in large measure, attributable to the fact that the Federalists lacked the mili-

---

BOX 1.4

The Federalists and the Jeffersonian Republicans

The first two distinct political parties formed in the United States were the Federalists and the Jeffersonian Republicans. The two parties agreed on many basic principles of governance: they agreed that the proper end of government was to advance individual self-interest, that governmental authority could be exercised only with the consent of the governed, and that only a republican government with limited authority could achieve these ends.

Fundamentally, however, the parties disagreed over the means by which these ends could be achieved and the conditions under which a republican government could flourish. The Jeffersonians believed that republicanism could succeed only when there was close contact between the electors and their elected representatives and only when there was a high degree of homogeneity among those represented. For these reasons, the Jeffersonians resisted the delegation of power to a central government, preferring to locate the greatest degree of governmental power in the smaller and more homogeneous states.

The Federalists attempted to answer the concerns of their critics with the argument advanced by James Madison in *The Federalist Papers,* No. 10. Madison had argued that factionalism was inevitable in any civil society and that it could best be handled by accommodating a diversity of interest groups within the same governmental framework. The struggle between these groups would eventually result in compromises securing the public good. This concept of struggle and accommodation pervaded Federalist thought. The potential for abuse of governmental authority was checked under the new Constitution, the Federalists argued, not only by separating powers and functions among the legislative, executive, and judicial branches of the federal government, but by dividing governmental sovereignty itself between the states and the federal government.

The struggle between the Jeffersonians and the Federalists had a distinct class basis. The Jeffersonians were led by wealthy southern landowners, while the Federalists were led by wealthy northern merchants. These two groups had been allied during the colonial period and cooperated to write the Constitution. But conflicts over economic matters and foreign policy, as well as personal clashes, led to bitter disputes during the 1790s. Thomas Jefferson's victory in 1800 marked the beginning of the end for the Federalist party. But the forces that supported the Federalists regrouped and reemerged as the Whig party during the late 1820s and early 1830s.

tary and political means of doing so. Their inability to crush the opposition eventually led to acceptance of the principle of the "Loyal Opposition."[8]

Another form of internal threat is social disorder. Thanks to the Industrial Revolution, societies had become much more interdependent and therefore much more vulnerable to disorder. As that occurred, and as more people moved from rural areas to cities, disorder had to be managed, and one important approach to that management was to give the masses a bigger stake in the system itself. As one supporter of electoral reform put it, the alternative to voting was "the spoliation of property and the dissolution of social order."[9] In the modern world, social disorder helped compel East European regimes to take steps toward democratic reform. The most notable example is the territory formerly called the German Democratic Republic (DDR or East Germany) which, in 1990, was absorbed into the Federal Republic of Germany. The DDR had been created in the portion of Germany occupied by Soviet troops after World War II, and became one of the most ruthless authoritarian regimes in eastern Europe. In the late 1980s, this regime was faced with massive popular demonstrations as well as the spectacle of hundreds of thousands of citizens fleeing across the border to the West. The government, at first, responded with force. However the Soviet Union, which exercised considerable control over the DDR's military and security forces, was anxious to improve its relations with the West and to reduce its military commitments. As a result, the Soviets refused to permit the East German government to use its military and police forces to curb disorder. The government of the DDR was forced to introduce a variety of reforms and concessions including, of course, the dramatic opening of the Berlin Wall that had divided the two Germanys for two generations. In 1990, the citizens of the DDR voted to abolish their government, altogether, and join the Federal Republic.

External Threat The main external threat to governments' power is the existence of other nation-states. During the past three centuries, more and more tribes and nations—people tied together by a common culture and language—have formed into separate principalities, or "nation-states," in order to defend their populations more effectively. But as more nation-states formed, there was a vastly increased probability that external conflicts would take place. War and preparation for war became constant rather than intermittent facts of national life, and the size and expense of military forces increased dramatically with the size of the nation-state and the size and number of its adversaries.

The cost of defense against external threats forced rulers to seek popular support to maintain military power. Huge permanent armies of citizen-soldiers could be raised more easily and could be induced to fight more vigorously and to make greater sacrifices if imbued with enthusiasm for cause and country. The turning point was the French Revolution in 1789. The unprecedented size and commitment and the military success of the French citizen-army convinced the rulers of all European nations that military power was forevermore closely linked with mass

[8]See Richard Hofstadter, *The Idea of a Party System* (Berkeley, CA: University of California Press, 1969).

[9]Quoted in John Cannon, *Parliamentary Reform 1640–1832* (Cambridge, England: Cambridge University Press, 1973), p. 216.

Tom Paine
Voice of Revolution

Thomas Paine (1737–1809)

All revolutions have their sloganeers who coalesce and articulate dissent. The American Revolution's principal popular voice was Thomas Paine. Born in England in 1737 into a struggling Quaker family, lacking the rudiments of a formal education, Paine worked at many jobs as a young man, from schoolteacher to tobacconist.

England held little for him, so Paine left for America. Before doing so, however, he chanced to meet Ben Franklin, who was sufficiently impressed with Paine to write him a letter of recommendation, referring to Paine as an "ingenious, worthy young man." Arriving in Philadelphia in 1774, Paine fell into journalism, contributing articles to many publications. Among other causes, he trumpeted that of the abolition of slavery as early as 1775.

His most famous and compelling work, *Common Sense,* was published in Philadelphia on January 10, 1776. Beyond simply urging American independence, the two-shilling, forty-seven-page pamphlet viewed American independence as a moral obligation—an opportunity to be seized while the society was still democratic and uncorrupted. Paine also stressed the necessity for a strong federal union.

The success of *Common Sense* was astonishing. According to Paine, 120,000 copies were sold in less than three months. In all, as many as 500,000 copies were sold. Paine's authorship of the piece soon became known, and his fame spread. When war came, Paine enlisted and rallied public support by writing about the war in a series of sixteen pamphlets called *The Crisis.* The opening sentence of one of his essays heartened many when he wrote that "These are the times that try men's souls."

Returning to England after the war, Paine felt the need to cultivate the spread of the revolutionary spirit. In 1791 and 1792, he published *The Rights of Man,* written in response to Edmund Burke's criticism of the French Revolution, *Reflections on the Revolution in France.* Paine's criticism of English institutions (including an appeal to the English that they overthrow their monarchy) led to his prosecution for treason, whereupon he went to France in 1792. There, he took an active part in French affairs, but he found himself imprisoned when the more radical Jacobins took power. Paine was released in 1793 at the urging of the American ambassador, James Monroe. In the meantime, however, he had written his famous deistic, antibiblical work, *The Age of Reason.*

Paine returned to America in 1802, and again he immersed himself in political controversy. Poverty, social ostracism, and declining health, however, marked his final days, and he died in 1809.

Source: W.M. Van der Weyde, ed., *The Life and Works of Thomas Paine* (New Rochelle, NY: Thomas Paine National Historical Association, 1925).

support. The expansion of participation and representation were key tactics in the effort of European regimes to convince citizens that they should be willing to contribute to the defense of the nation. Throughout the nineteenth century, war and the expansion of the suffrage went hand in hand.

National Unity and Development   The expansion of popular participation often has been associated with efforts to promote national unity and development. In some instances, governments seek to subvert local or regional popular loyalties by linking citizens directly to the central government via the ballot box. America's founding fathers saw direct popular election of members of the House of Representatives as a means through which the new federal government could compete with the states for popular allegiance.

In addition, many governments have conceived the expansion of popular participation to be a way of persuading citizens to be more willing to provide the taxes and services sometimes associated with large-scale economic development or political change, and to build popular support for attacks on entrenched elites or bureaucracies that are resistant to change. While he was the Soviet premier, Mikhail Gorbachev, for example, initiated more democratic forms of participation primarily to generate greater popular support for economic development and for his campaigns against opponents in the Communist party and the state bureaucracy. Gorbachev was able to win the support of many professionals and intellectuals, the nearest Eastern European equivalent of the eighteenth-century Western European bourgeoisie.

The Great Transformation: Tying Democracy to Strong Government

The construction of democratic electoral institutions and popular representative bodies had two historic consequences. First, democratization opened up the possibility that citizens might now use government for their own benefit rather than simply watching government being used for the benefit of others. This consequence is widely understood. But the second is not so well understood: Once citizens perceived that governments could operate in response to their demands, citizens *became increasingly willing to support the expansion of government.* The public's belief in its capacity to control the government's actions is only one of the many factors responsible for the growth of government. But at the very least, this linkage of democracy and government set into motion a wave of governmental growth in the West that began in the middle of the nineteenth century and has continued to this day.

The U.S. government appears at first to be an exception to this pattern because the national government, as we observed at the outset, remained so weak and small throughout the nineteenth century, and well into the twentieth century. But as we shall see, particularly in Chapter 3, that is a misleading impression. There was in fact a great deal of governmental growth during the nineteenth century, but most of that growth took place in the state governments, as provided for by our federal Constitution. Thus, we have a very different system, but it does not exempt us from the general pattern in which democracy and the support of the people for

stronger government are related.

FREEDOM AND POWER: THE PROBLEM

Ultimately, the growth of governmental power poses the most fundamental threat to the liberties Americans have so long enjoyed. Because ours is a limited government subject to democratic control, we often see government as simply a powerful servant. However, the growth of governmental power continues to raise profound questions about the future.

First, expansion of governmental powers inevitably reduces popular influence over policy making. The enormous scope of national programs in the twentieth century has required the construction of a large and elaborate state apparatus and the transfer of considerable decision-making power from political bodies like Congress to administrative agencies. As a consequence, the development and implementation of today's public policies are increasingly dominated by bureaucratic institutions, rules, and procedures that are not so easily affected by the citizen in the voting booth. Can citizens use the power of the bureaucracies we have created, or are we doomed simply to become their subjects?

Second, as government has grown in size and power, the need for citizen cooperation has diminished. In the eighteenth and nineteenth centuries, rulers sought popular support and became responsive to mass opinion because of the fragility of state power. Rulers lacked the means to curb disorder, collect taxes, and maintain their military power without popular support. In an important sense, the eighteenth and nineteenth centuries in the West represented a "window of opportunity" for popular opinion. A conjunction of political and social circumstances compelled those in power to respond to public opinion to shore up their power. To the extent that they think about such matters at all, westerners tend to assume that this commitment on the part of the eighteenth- and nineteenth-century rulers forever binds their successors to serve public opinion. It is true that the institutional linkages—elections, representative bodies and so on—between government and opinion developed during the eighteenth and nineteenth centuries and have flourished for nearly 200 years. But what has generally gone unnoticed is that the underlying conditions—the window of opportunity—that produced these institutions have, in many respects, closed behind them. Unlike their predecessors, many Western states today may now have sufficiently powerful administrative, military, and police agencies that they now *could* curb disorder, collect taxes, and keep their foes in check without necessarily depending upon popular support and approval. Will government necessarily continue to bow to the will of the people even though favorable public opinion may not be as crucial as it once was?

Finally, because Americans view government as a servant they believe that they can have both the blessings of freedom and the benefits of government. Even most self-proclaimed conservatives have learned to live with Big Brother. In today's America, agencies of the government have considerable control over who may enter occupations, what may be eaten, what may be seen and heard over the air waves, what forms of education are socially desirable, what types of philanthropy serve the public interest, what sorts of business practices are acceptable, as well as citizens' marital plans, vacation plans, child-rearing practices, and medical care. Is this government still a servant? Of course, we continue to exert our influence through elections, representation and referenda. But do even these processes mean that we can control the government? One hundred fifty years ago, Alexis de Tocqueville predicted that Americans would eventually permit their government to become so powerful that elections, representative processes, and so on would come to be ironic interludes providing citizens little more than the opportunity to wave the chains by which the government had bound them. Can we have both freedom and government? To what extent can we continue to depend upon and benefit from the state's power while still retaining our liberties? These are questions that every generation of Americans must ask.

FOR FURTHER READING

Bendix, Reinhard. *Kings or People: Power and the Mandate to Rule.* Berkeley: University of California Press, 1978.

Bendix, Reinhard. *Nation-Building and Citizenship.* New York: Wiley, 1964.

Binder, Leonard, et al., eds. *Crises and Sequences in Political Development.* Princeton: Princeton University Press, 1971.

Dahl, Robert A. *Polyarchy: Participation and Opposition.* New Haven: Yale University Press, 1971.

Grant, Ruth W. *John Locke's Liberalism.* Chicago: University of Chicago Press, 1987.

Hartz, Louis. *The Liberal Tradition in America.* New York: Harcourt, Brace, 1955.

Higgs, Robert. *Crisis and Leviathan: Critical Episodes in the Growth of American Government.* New York: Oxford University Press, 1987.

Huntington, Samuel P. *American Politics: The Promise of Disharmony.* Cambridge: Harvard University Press, 1981.

Keller, Morton. *Affairs of State: Public Life in Late Nineteenth Century America.* Cambridge: Harvard University Press, 1977.

Moore, Barrington. *Social Origins of Dictatorship and Democracy.* Boston: Beacon Press, 1966.

Schumpeter, Joseph A. *Capitalism, Socialism and Democracy.* New York: Harper, 1942.

Skocpol, Theda. *States and Social Revolutions.* New York: Cambridge University Press, 1979.

Strayer, Joseph R. *On the Medieval Origins of the Modern State.* Princeton: Princeton University Press, 1970.

Tilly, Charles, ed. *The Formation of Nation-States in Western Europe.* Princeton: Princeton University Press, 1975.

Tocqueville, Alexis de. *Democracy in America.* Translated by Phillips Bradley. New York: Knopf, Vintage Books, 1945; orig. published 1835.

Weber, Max. *The Theory of Social and Economic Organization.* Translated by Talcott Parsons. New York: Oxford University Press, 1947.

2

Constructing a Government: The Founding and the Constitution

TIME LINE ON THE FOUNDING

EVENTS		INSTITUTIONAL DEVELOPMENTS
	1750	
		Albany Congress calls for colonial unity (1754)
French defeated in North America (1760)		
Stamp Act enacted (1765)		Stamp Act Congress attended by delegates from all colonies (1765)
Townshend duties enacted (1767)		
Boston Massacre (1770)	**1770**	
Tea Act; Boston Tea Party (1773)		
British adopt Coercive Acts to punish colonies (1774)		First Continental Congress rejects plan of union, but adopts Declaration of American Rights denying Parliament's authority over internal colonial affairs (1774)
Battles of Lexington and Concord (1775)		Second Continental Congress assumes role of revolutionary government (1775); adopts Declaration of Independence (1776)
		New state constitutions adopted after ties with Britain severed (1776–1784)
		Congress adopts Articles of Confederation as constitution for new government (1777)
	1780	
British surrender at Yorktown (1781)		Annapolis Convention calls for consideration of government revision (1786)
Shays's Rebellion (1786)		
		Constitutional Convention drafts blueprint for new government (1787)
Federalist Papers (1788)		Constitution ratified by states (1788–1790)
	1790	

"No taxation without representation" were words that stirred a generation of Americans long before they even dreamed of calling themselves Americans rather than Englishmen. Reacting to new English attempts to extract tax revenues to pay for the troops that were being sent to defend the colonial frontier, protests erupted throughout the colonies against the infamous Stamp Act of 1765. This act created revenue stamps and required that they be affixed to all printed and legal documents, including newspapers, pamphlets, advertisements, notes and bonds, leases, deeds, and licenses. To show their displeasure with the act, the colonists conducted mass meetings, parades, bonfires, and other demonstrations throughout the spring and summer of 1765. In Boston, for example, a stamp agent was hanged and burned in effigy. Later, the home of the lieutenant-governor was sacked, leading to his resignation and that of all of his colonial commission and stamp agents. By November 1765, business proceeded and newspapers were published without the stamp; in March 1766, Parliament repealed the detested law. Through their protest, the nonimportation agreements that the colonists subsequently adopted, and the Stamp Act Congress that met in October 1765, the colonists took the first steps that ultimately would lead to war and a new nation.

The people of every nation tend to glorify their own history and especially their nation's creation. Americans are no exception. To most contemporary Americans, the revolutionary period represents a heroic struggle by a determined and united group of colonists against British oppression. The Boston Tea Party, the battles of Lexington and Concord, the winter at Valley Forge—these are the events that we emphasize in our history. Similarly, the American Constitution—the document establishing the system of government that ultimately emerged from this struggle—is often seen as an inspired, if not divine, work, expressing timeless principles of democratic government. These views are by no means false. During the founding era, Americans did struggle against misrule. Moreover, the American Constitution did establish the foundations for over two hundred years of democratic government.

To really understand the character of the American founding and the meaning of the American Constitution, however, it is essential to look beyond the myths and rhetoric, and to explore the conflicting interests and forces at work during the revolutionary and constitutional periods. Thus, we will first assess the political backdrop of the American Revolution, and then we will examine the Constitution that ultimately emerged as the basis for America's government.

THE FIRST FOUNDING: INTERESTS AND CONFLICTS

Competing ideals and principles often reflect competing interests, and so it was in revolutionary America. The American Revolution and the American Constitution were outgrowths and expressions of a struggle among economic and political forces within the colonies. Five sectors of society had interests that were important in colonial politics: (1) the New England merchants; (2) the southern planters; (3) the "royalists"—holders of royal lands, offices, and patents (licenses to engage in a profession or business activity); (4) shopkeepers, artisans, and laborers; and (5) small farmers. Throughout the eighteenth century, these groups were in conflict over issues of taxation, trade, and commerce. For the most part, however, the southern planters, the New England merchants, and the royal office and patent holders—groups that together made up the colonial elite—were able to maintain a political alliance that held in check the more radical forces representing shopkeepers, laborers, and small farmers. After 1750, however, by seriously threatening the interests of New England merchants and southern planters, British tax and trade policies split the colonial elite, permitting radical forces to expand their political influence, and set into motion a chain of events that culminated in the American Revolution.[1]

British Taxes and Colonial Interests

Beginning in the 1750s, the debts and other financial problems faced by the British government forced it to search for new revenue sources. This search rather quickly led to the Crown's North American colonies which, on the whole, paid remarkably little in taxes to the mother country. The British government reasoned that a sizable fraction of its debt was, in fact, attributable to the expenses it had incurred in defense of the colonies during the recent French and Indian wars, as well as to the continuing protection that British forces were giving the colonists from Indian attacks and that the British navy was providing for colonial shipping. Thus, during the 1760s, England sought to impose new, though relatively modest, taxes upon the colonists.

Like most governments of the period, the British regime had at its disposal only limited ways to collect revenues. The income tax, which in the twentieth century has become the single most important source of governmental revenues, had not yet been developed. For the most part, in the mid-eighteenth century, governments relied on tariffs, duties, imposts, and other taxes on commerce, and it was to such taxes, including the Stamp Act, that the British turned during the 1760s.

The Stamp Act and other taxes on commerce, such as the Sugar Act of 1764, which taxed sugar, molasses, and other commodities, most heavily affected the two groups in colonial society whose commercial interests and activities were most extensive—the New England merchants and southern planters. Under the famous slogan "no taxation without representation," the merchants and planters together sought to organize opposition to the new taxes. In the course of their struggle against British tax measures, the planters and merchants broke with their royalist allies and turned to their former adversaries—the shopkeepers, small farmers, laborers, and artisans—for help. With the assistance of these groups, the merchants and planters organized demonstrations and a boycott of British goods that

---

[1]The social makeup of colonial America and some of the social conflicts that divided colonial society are discussed in Jackson Turner Main, *The Social Structure of Revolutionary America* (Princeton, NJ: Princeton University Press, 1965).

BOX 2.1
The Road to Revolution

The road that led the American colonies to break with England was long, indirect, and by no means inevitable. Most rebel leaders hoped for reform; few spoke openly of revolution. Yet dissatisfaction, misunderstanding, and violence spread, yielding what in many ways was an eighteenth-century American guerrilla war against the world's preeminent superpower of the day.

The first American casualties of the Revolution came on a frosty March day in 1770. Massachusetts had been a hotbed of dissent against various British actions, including impressment (forced military conscription) and various economic measures. Boston was the center of colonial smuggling that proliferated as Americans sought to avoid what they considered unfair and oppressive levies and taxes. Among the many repugnant economic measures were the Townshend Acts, enacted in 1767, which levied duties on colonial imports and created a Board of Customs Commission in Boston to oversee the collection of revenue.

In 1769, the British stationed 2,000 soldiers in Boston to quell the rising tide of disturbances. The presence of the troops, however, merely provided a focal point for local discontent. Moreover, the British "lobster backs" began to take the jobs of local people at a time when jobs were scarce, driving up unemployment.

On March 5, a crowd that included ropemakers who had lost their jobs to British soldiers gathered in front of the Boston Customhouse (where the hated customs commissioners did their work). At the head of the crowd was a runaway slave named Crispus Attucks, who had worked for several years on ships out of Boston. The crowd taunted the sentry on duty, who called for help. Nine other soldiers appeared, and they soon found themselves being taunted and pelted with snowballs, clamshells, and sticks by the growing crowd. In the fear and confusion of the moment, one soldier was knocked to the ground. He rose and fired. The other soldiers then fired into the belligerent but unarmed crowd. When the smoke cleared, five were dead, and eight wounded. The first to be shot and mortally wounded was Attucks. Thus it was that the first casualty of the Revolutionary War was a black man.

The resistance cause had its first real martyrs, and resistance leaders lost no time in capitalizing on the propaganda value of the incident. After the "Boston Massacre," as it was dubbed by pamphleteers, the Massachusetts governor ordered the troops withdrawn from Boston to avoid further incidents. Six British soldiers were tried for murder. Four were acquitted, and two were punished by having their thumbs branded and being discharged from the army.

Despite a subsequent lull in direct confrontations, anti-British sentiment escalated, as did the cycle of violence. As with many revolutions to follow, few anticipated where the cycle of repression and violence would lead. But leaders were quick to seize as symbols those actions deemed unjust and pernicious. Indeed, the facts of the day were in a real sense less important than the symbols they generated.

Source: Robert A. Divine, et al., *American Past and Present* (Glenview, IL: Scott, Foresman, 1984).

ultimately forced the Crown to rescind most of its new taxes. It was in the context of this unrest that a confrontation between colonists and British soldiers in front of the Boston customs house on the night of March 5, 1770, resulted in what came to be known as the Boston Massacre. Nervous British soldiers opened fire on the mob surrounding them, killing five colonists and wounding eight others. News of this event quickly spread throughout the colonies as was used by radicals to fan anti-British sentiment.

From the perspective of the merchants and planters, however, the British government's decision to eliminate most of the hated taxes represented a victorious end to their struggle with the mother country. They were anxious to end the unrest they had helped to arouse, and they supported the British government's efforts to restore order. Indeed, most respectable Bostonians supported the actions of the British soldiers involved in the Boston Massacre. In their subsequent trial, the soldiers were defended by John Adams, a pillar of Boston society and a future president of the United States. Adams asserted that the soldiers' actions were entirely justified, provoked by, "a motley rabble of saucy boys, Negroes and mulattos, Irish teagues and outlandish Jack tars." All but two of the soldiers were acquitted.[2]

Despite the efforts of the British government and the better-to-do strata of colonial society, it proved difficult to bring an end to the political strife. The more radical forces representing shopkeepers, artisans, laborers, and small farmers, who had been mobilized and energized by the struggle over taxes, continued to agitate for political and social change within the colonies. These radicals, led by individuals like Samuel Adams, cousin of John Adams, began to assert that British power supported an unjust political and social structure within the colonies, and began to advocate an end to British rule.[3]

Political Strife and the Radicalizing of the Colonists

The political strife within the colonies was the background for the events of 1773–1774. In 1773, the British government granted the politically powerful East India Company a monopoly on the export of tea from Britain, eliminating a lucrative form of trade for colonial merchants. To add to the injury, the East India Company sought to sell the tea directly in the colonies instead of working through the colonial merchants. Tea was an extremely important commodity in the 1770s, and these British actions posed a mortal threat to the New England merchants. Together with their southern allies, the merchants once again called upon their radical adversaries for support. The most dramatic result was the Boston Tea Party of 1773, led by Samuel Adams.

This event was of decisive importance in American history. The merchants had hoped to force the British government to rescind the Tea Act, but they did not support any demands beyond this one. They certainly did not seek independence

[2]George B. Tindall and David E. Shi, *America: A Narrative History,* Third Edition (New York: W. W. Norton, 1992), p. 194.

[3]For a discussion of events leading up to the Revolution, see Charles M. Andrews, *The Colonial Background of the American Revolution* (New Haven, CT: Yale University Press, 1924).

Samuel Adams
Career Politician

Samuel Adams (1722–1803)

Unlike other revolutionary political leaders, Samuel Adams resembled many of the career politicians we see today. Born in Boston in 1722 and educated at Harvard, he quickly established his propensity for politics over other occupations. His family's brewery business failed shortly after he took it over, and he secured an appointment as a tax collector in Boston in 1756.

Adams thrived on public life, developing his early constituency in the taverns, clubs, and fire companies of eighteenth-century Boston, and becoming the epitome of an early republican. He was adept at manipulating information and not at all averse to engaging in extralegal acts to attain his goals when he thought his actions would be supported by public opinion. He was elected to the Massachusetts House of Representatives in 1762. As a member of that body, he was instrumental in securing a colony-wide boycott of British goods after the British Parliament passed a new series of taxes, the Townshend Acts. This boycott was so successful that Parliament repealed these acts altogether in 1770. Adams subsequently chaired the Boston committee of correspondence, which proved a highly effective means of mobilizing popular support to protest British attempts to control commerce in the colonies. He is best remembered for organizing and managing the Boston Tea Party in 1773 in response to Parliament's restrictions on the tea trade in the colonies. Adams participated in the Continental Congress and signed the Declaration of Independence.

After the Revolutionary War, he remained active in Massachusetts politics, serving as both lieutenant governor and governor. He was well into his sixties by that time, and his views on national politics were becoming dated. Receding into the background, he remained a political observer until his death in 1803.

from Britain. Samuel Adams and the other radicals, however, hoped to induce the British government to take actions that would alienate its colonial supporters and pave the way for a rebellion. This was precisely the purpose of the Boston Tea Party, and it succeeded. By dumping the East India Company's tea into Boston Harbor, Adams and his followers goaded the British into enacting a number of harsh reprisals. Within five months after the incident in Boston, the House of Commons passed a series of acts that closed the port of Boston to commerce, changed the provincial government of Massachusetts, provided for the removal of accused persons to England for trial, and most important, restricted movement to the West—further alienating the southern planters who depended upon access to new western lands. These acts of retaliation confirmed the worst criticisms of England and helped radicalize Americans. Radicals like Samuel Adams and Christopher Gadsden of South Carolina had, at least since 1770, been agitating for more violent measures to deal with England. But ultimately they needed Britain's political repression to create widespread support for independence.

Thus, the Boston Tea Party set into motion a cycle of provocation and retaliation that in 1774 resulted in the convening of the First Continental Congress—an assembly consisting of delegates from all parts of the country—that called for a total boycott of British goods and, under the prodding of the radicals, began to consider the possibility of independence from British rule. The eventual result was the Declaration of Independence.

The Declaration of Independence

In 1776, the Second Continental Congress appointed a committee consisting of Thomas Jefferson of Virginia, Benjamin Franklin of Pennsylvania, Roger Sherman of Connecticut, and Robert Livingston of New York to draft a statement of American independence from British rule. The Declaration of Independence, written by Jefferson and adopted by the Second Continental Congress, was an extraordinary document both in philosophical and political terms. Philosophically, the Declaration was remarkable for its assertion that certain rights, called "unalienable rights"—including life, liberty, and the pursuit of happiness—could not be abridged by governments. In the world of 1776, a world in which some kings still claimed to rule by divine right, this was a dramatic statement. Politically, the Declaration was remarkable because, despite the differences of interest that divided the colonists along economic, regional, and philosophical lines, the Declaration identified and focused on problems, grievances, aspirations, and principles that might unify the various colonial groups. The Declaration was an attempt to identify and articulate a history and set of principles that might help to forge national unity.[4]

The Articles of Confederation

Having declared their independence, the colonies needed to establish a governmental structure. In November 1777, the Continental Congress adopted the Articles of Confederation and Perpetual Union—the United States's first written constitution. Although it was not ratified by all the states until 1781, it was the country's operative constitution for almost twelve years, until March 1789.

The Articles of Confederation was a constitution concerned primarily with limiting the powers of the central government. The central government, first of all, was based entirely in Congress. Since it was not intended to be a powerful government, it was given no executive branch. Execution of its laws was to be left to the individual states. Second, Congress had little power. Its members were not much more than delegates or messengers from the state legislatures. They were chosen by the state legislatures, their salaries were paid out of the state treasuries, and they were subject to immediate recall by state authorities. In addition, each state, regardless of its size, had only a single vote.

Congress was given the power to declare war and make peace, to make treaties and alliances, to coin or borrow money, and to regulate trade with the Native Americans. It could also appoint the senior officers of the United States Army. But

[4]See Carl Becker, *The Declaration of Independence* (New York: Vintage, 1942).

it could not levy taxes or regulate commerce among the states. Moreover, the
army officers it appointed had no army to serve in because the nation's armed forces were composed of the state militias. Probably the most unfortunate part of the Articles of Confederation was that the central government could not prevent one state from discriminating against other states in the quest for foreign commerce.

In brief, the relationship between Congress and the states under the Articles of Confederation was much like the contemporary relationship between the United Nations and its member states, a relationship in which virtually all governmental powers are retained by the states. It was properly called a "confederation" because, as provided under Article II, "each state retains its sovereignty, freedom and independence, and every power, jurisdiction, and right, which is not by this confederation expressly delegated to the United States, in Congress assembled." Not only was there no executive, there was also no judicial authority and no other means of enforcing Congress's will. If there was to be any enforcement at all, it would be done for Congress by the states.[5]

THE SECOND FOUNDING: FROM COMPROMISE TO CONSTITUTION

The Declaration of Independence and the Articles of Confederation were not sufficient to hold the nation together as an independent and effective nation-state. From almost the moment of armistice with the British in 1783, moves were afoot to reform and strengthen the Articles of Confederation.

International Standing and Balance of Power

There was a special concern for the country's international position. Competition among the states for foreign commerce allowed the European powers to play the states off against each other, which created confusion on both sides of the Atlantic. At one point during the winter of 1786–1787, John Adams of Massachusetts, a leader in the independence struggle, was sent to negotiate a new treaty with the British, one that would cover disputes left over from the war. The British government responded that, since the United States under the Articles of Confederation was unable to enforce existing treaties, it would negotiate with each of the thirteen states separately.

At the same time, well-to-do Americans—in particular the New England merchants and southern planters—were troubled by the influence that "radical" forces exercised in the Continental Congress and in the governments of several of the states. The colonists' victory in the Revolutionary War had not only meant the end of British rule, but it had also significantly changed the balance of political power within the new states. As a result of the Revolution, one key segment of the

[5]See Merrill Jensen, *The Articles of Confederation* (Madison, WI: University of Wisconsin Press, 1963).

colonial elite—the royal land, office, and patent holders—was stripped of its economic and political privileges. In fact, many of these individuals, along with tens of thousands of other colonists who considered themselves loyal British subjects, left for Canada after the British surrender. And while the pre-revolutionary elite was weakened, the pre-revolutionary radicals were now better organized than ever before, and were the controlling forces in such states as Pennsylvania and Rhode Island, where they pursued economic and political policies that struck terror into the hearts of the pre-revolutionary political establishment. In Rhode Island, for example, between 1783 and 1785, a legislature dominated by representatives of small farmers, artisans, and shopkeepers had instituted economic policies, including drastic currency inflation, that frightened businessmen and property owners throughout the country. Of course, the central government under the Articles of Confederation was powerless to intervene.

The Annapolis Convention

The continuation of international weakness and domestic economic turmoil lead many Americans to consider whether their newly adopted form of government might not already require revision. In the fall of 1786, many state leaders accepted an invitation from the Virginia legislature for a conference of representatives of all the states. Delegates from five states actually attended. This conference, held in Annapolis, Maryland, was the first step toward the second founding. The one positive thing that came out of the Annapolis Convention was a carefully worded resolution calling on Congress to send commissioners to Philadelphia at a later time "to devise such further provisions as shall appear to them necessary to render the Constitution of the Federal Government adequate to the exigencies of the Union."[6] This resolution was drafted by Alexander Hamilton, a thirty-four-year-old New York lawyer who had played a significant role in the Revolution as Washington's secretary and who would play a still more significant role in framing the Constitution and forming the new government in the 1790s. But the resolution did not necessarily imply any desire to do more than improve and reform the Articles of Confederation.

Shays's Rebellion

It is quite possible that the Constitutional Convention of 1787 in Philadelphia would never have taken place at all except for a single event that occurred during the winter following the Annapolis Convention: Shays's Rebellion.

Daniel Shays, a former army captain, led a mob of farmers in a rebellion against the government of Massachusetts. The purpose of the rebellion was to prevent foreclosures on their debt-ridden land by keeping the county courts of western Massachusetts from sitting until after the next election. The state militia dispersed the mob, but for several days, Shays and his followers terrified the state govern-

---

[6]Reported in Samuel E. Morison, Henry Steele Commager, and William Leuchtenberg, *The Growth of the American Republic,* vol. 1 (New York: Oxford University Press, 1969), p. 244.

ment by attempting to capture the federal arsenal at Springfield, provoking an appeal to Congress to help restore order. Within a few days, the state government re-
gained control and captured fourteen of the rebels (all were eventually pardoned).
In 1787, a newly elected Massachusetts legislature granted some of the farmers'
demands.

Although the incident ended peacefully, its effects lingered and spread. Washington summed it up: "I am mortified beyond expression that in the moment of
our acknowledged independence we should by our conduct verify the predictions
of our transatlantic foe, and render ourselves ridiculous and contemptible in the
eyes of all Europe."[7]

Congress under the Confederation had been unable to act decisively in a time
of crisis. This provided critics of the Articles of Confederation with precisely the
evidence they needed to push Hamilton's Annapolis resolution through the Congress. Thus, the states were asked to send representatives to Philadelphia to discuss
constitutional revision. Delegates were eventually sent by every state except
Rhode Island.

The Constitutional Convention

Fifty-five delegates selected by the state governments convened in Philadelphia in
May 1787, with political strife, international embarrassment, national weakness,
and local rebellion fixed in their minds. Recognizing that these issues were symp-
toms of fundamental flaws in the Articles of Confederation, the delegates soon
abandoned the plan to revise the Articles and committed themselves to a second
founding—a second, and ultimately successful, attempt to create a legitimate and
effective national system. This effort occupied the convention for the next five
months.

A Marriage of Interest and Principle   Scholars have for years disagreed about the
motives of the founders in Philadelphia. Among the most controversial views of
the framers' motives is the "economic" interpretation put forward by historian
Charles Beard and his disciples.[8] According to Beard's account, America's founders
were a collection of securities speculators and property owners whose only aim
was personal enrichment. From this perspective, the Constitution's lofty principles
were little more than sophisticated masks behind which the most venal interests
sought to enrich themselves.

Contrary to Beard's approach is the view that the framers of the Constitution
were concerned with philosophical and ethical principles. Indeed, the framers
sought to devise a system of government consistent with the dominant philosophical and moral principles of the day. But, in fact, these two views belong together;
the founders' interests were reinforced by their principles. The convention that
drafted the American Constitution was chiefly organized by the New England
merchants and southern planters. Though the delegates representing these groups

[7]Ibid., p. 242.
[8]Charles A. Beard, *An Economic Interpretation of the Constitution of the United States* (New York: Macmillan, 1913).

The Constitution: Property versus Pragmatism

Throughout the second half of the nineteenth century, the prevailing attitude toward the country's founders was increasingly that of veneration, even worship. Like Moses receiving the Ten Commandments, the founders came to be viewed as messengers from God who had received the Constitution intact and whole rather than creating it through a messy political process. Historian Charles Beard helped shatter this myth in the early twentieth century when he argued that the founders were members of the social and economic elite, little interested in democracy and more motivated by a desire to protect their property and wealth, and that the Constitution was their instrument to achieve this end.

Many have examined Beard's work, and found fault with his arguments and facts. Notably, political scientist John P. Roche, writing in the 1960s, argued that the founders, even if they were elite, were excellent politicians who were simply trying to forge a government that would be more effective than the Articles of Confederation. Still, Beard's impact was great, in that he helped move constitutional analysis away from uncritical worship and much closer to viewing the political realities of the late eighteenth century.

Beard

The Constitution was essentially an economic document based upon the concept that the fundamental private rights of property are anterior to government and morally beyond the reach of popular majorities.

The major portion of the members of the [Constitutional] Convention are on record as recognizing the claim of property to a special and defensive position in the Constitution.

In the ratification of the Constitution, about three-fourths of the adult males failed to vote on the question, having abstained from the elections at which delegates to the state conventions were chosen, either on account of their indifference or their disfranchisement by property qualifications.

The Constitution was ratified by a vote of probably not more than one-sixth of the adult males.

It is questionable whether a majority of the voters participating in the elections for the state [ratifying] conventions in New York, Massachusetts, New Hampshire, Virginia, and South Carolina, actually approved the ratification of the Constitution. . . .

In the ratification, it became manifest that the line of cleavage for and against the Constitution was between substantial personalty interests on the one hand and the small farming and debtor interests on the other.

The Constitution was not created by "the whole people" as the jurists have said; neither was it created by "the states" as Southern nullifiers long contended; but it was the work of a consolidated group whose interests knew no state boundaries and were truly national in their scope.[1]

[1] Charles Beard, *An Economic Interpretation of the Constitution of the United States* (New York: Macmillan, 1935), pp. 324–25.

The Constitution. . . was not an apotheosis of "constitutionalism," a triumph of architectonic genius; it was a patch-work sewn together under the pressure of both time and events by a group of extremely talented democratic politicians. They refused to attempt the establishment of a strong, centralized sovereignty on the principle of legislative supremacy for the excellent reason that the people would not accept it. They risked their political fortunes by opposing the established doctrines of state sovereignty because they were convinced that the existing system was leading to national impotence and probably foreign domination. For two years, they worked to get a convention established. For over three months, in what must have seemed to the faithful participants an endless process of give-and-take, they reasoned, cajoled, threatened, and bargained amongst themselves. The result was a Constitution which the people, in fact, by democratic processes, did accept, and a new and far better national government was established.[2]

[2]John P. Roche "The Founding Fathers: A Reform Caucus in Action," *American Political Science Review* 55 (December 1961), pp. 815–16.

did not all hope to profit personally from an increase in the value of their securities, as Beard would have it, they did hope to benefit in the broadest political and economic sense by breaking the power of their radical foes and establishing a system of government more compatible with their long-term economic and political interests. Thus, the framers sought to create a new government capable of promoting commerce and protecting property from radical state legislatures. At the same time, they hoped to fashion a government less susceptible than the existing state and national regimes to populist forces hostile to the interests of the commercial and propertied classes.

The Great Compromise   The proponents of a new government fired their opening shot on May 29, 1787, when Edmund Randolph of Virginia offered a resolution that proposed corrections and enlargements in the Articles of Confederation. The proposal, which showed the strong influence of James Madison, was not a simple motion. It provided for virtually every aspect of a new government. Randolph later admitted it was intended to be an alternative draft constitution, and it did in fact serve as the framework for what ultimately became the Constitution. (There is no verbatim record of the debates, but Madison was present during virtually all of the deliberations and kept full notes on them.)[9]

The portion of Randolph's motion that became most controversial was the "Virginia Plan." This plan provided for a system of representation in the national legislature based upon the population of each state or the proportion of each state's

[9]Madison's notes along with the somewhat less complete records kept by several other participants in the convention are available in a four-volume set. See Max Farrand, *The Records of the Federal Convention of 1787,* 4 vols., rev. ed. (New Haven, CT: Yale University Press, 1966).

revenue contribution, or both. (Randolph also proposed a second branch of the legislature, but it was to be elected by the members of the first branch.) Since the states varied enormously in size and wealth, the Virginia Plan was thought to be heavily biased in favor of the large states.

While the convention was debating the Virginia Plan, additional delegates were arriving in Philadelphia and were beginning to mount opposition to it. Their resolution, introduced by William Patterson of New Jersey and known as the "New Jersey Plan," did not oppose the Virginia plan point for point. Instead, it concentrated on specific weaknesses in the Articles of Confederation, in the spirit of revision rather than radical replacement of that document. Supporters of the New Jersey Plan did not seriously question the convention's commitment to replacing the Articles. But their opposition to the Virginia Plan's scheme of representation was sufficient to send its proposals back to committee for reworking into a common document. In particular, delegates from the less populous states, which included Delaware, New Jersey, Connecticut, and New York, asserted that the more populous states, such as Virginia, Pennsylvania, North Carolina, Massachusetts, and Georgia, would dominate the new government if representation were to be determined by population. The smaller states argued that each state should be equally represented in the new regime regardless of its population.

The issue of representation was one that threatened to wreck the entire constitutional enterprise. Delegates conferred, factions maneuvered, and tempers flared. James Wilson of Pennsylvania told the small-state delegates that if they wanted to disrupt the union they should go ahead. The separation could, he said, "never happen on better grounds." Small-state delegates were equally blunt. Gunning Bedford of Delaware declared that the small states might look elsewhere for friends if they were forced. "The large states," he said, "dare not dissolve the confederation. If they do the small ones will find some foreign ally of more honor and good faith, who will take them by the hand and do them justice." These sentiments were widely shared. The union, as Oliver Ellsworth of Connecticut put it, was "on the verge of dissolution, scarcely held together by the strength of a hair."

The outcome of this debate was the Connecticut Compromise, also known as the Great Compromise. Under the terms of this compromise, in the first branch of Congress—the House of Representatives—the representatives would be apportioned according to the number of inhabitants in each state. This, of course, was what delegates from the large states had sought. But in the second branch—the Senate—each state would have an equal vote regardless of its size; this was to deal with the concerns of the small states. This compromise was not immediately satisfactory to all the delegates. Indeed, two of the most vocal members of the small-state faction, John Lansing and Robert Yates of New York, were so incensed by the concession that their colleagues had made to the large-state forces that they stormed out of the convention. In the end, however, both sets of forces preferred compromise to the breakup of the union, and the plan was accepted.

The Question of Slavery: The "Three-fifths" Compromise   The story so far is too neat, too easy, and too anticlimactic. If it were left here, it would only contribute to American mythology. After all, the notion of a bicameral (two-chambered) legislature was very much in the air in 1787. Some of the states had had this for years.

The Philadelphia delegates might well have gone straight to the adoption of two

chambers based on two different principles of representation even without the dramatic interplay of conflict and compromise. But a far more fundamental issue had to be confronted before the Great Compromise could take place: the issue of slavery.

Many of the conflicts that emerged during the Constitutional Convention were reflections of the fundamental differences between the slave and the nonslave states—differences that pitted the southern planters and New England merchants against one another. This was the first premonition of a conflict that was almost to destroy the Republic in later years. In the midst of debate over large versus small states, Madison observed:

> The great danger to our general government is the great southern and northern interests of the continent, being opposed to each other. Look to the votes in Congress, and most of them stand divided by the geography of the country, not according to the size of the states.[10]

Over 90 percent of all slaves resided in five states—Georgia, Maryland, North Carolina, South Carolina, and Virginia—where they accounted for 30 percent of the total population. In some places, slaves outnumbered nonslaves by as much as ten to one. If the Constitution were to embody any principle of national supremacy, some basic decisions would have to be made about the place of slavery in the general scheme. Madison hit on this point on several occasions as different aspects of the Constitution were being discussed. For example, he observed:

> It seemed now to be pretty well understood that the real difference of interests lay, not between the large and small but between the northern and southern states. The institution of slavery and its consequences formed the line of discrimination. There are five states on the South, eight on the northern side of this line. Should a proportional representation take place it was true, the northern side would still outnumber the other, but not in the same degree at this time, and every day would tend towards an equilibrium.[11]

Northerners and southerners eventually reached agreement through the "Three-fifths Compromise." The seats in the House of Representatives would be apportioned according to a "population" in which five slaves would count as three persons. The slaves would not be allowed to vote, of course, but the number of representatives would be apportioned accordingly. This arrangement was supported by the slave states, which obviously included some of the biggest and some of the smallest states at that time. It was also accepted by many delegates from nonslave states who strongly supported the principle of property representation, whether that property was expressed in slaves or in land, money, or stocks. The concern exhibited by most delegates was over how much slaves would count toward a state's representation rather than whether the institution of slavery would continue. The Three-fifths Compromise, in the words of political scientist Donald

[10]Ibid., vol. 1, p. 476.
[11]Ibid., vol 2, p. 10.

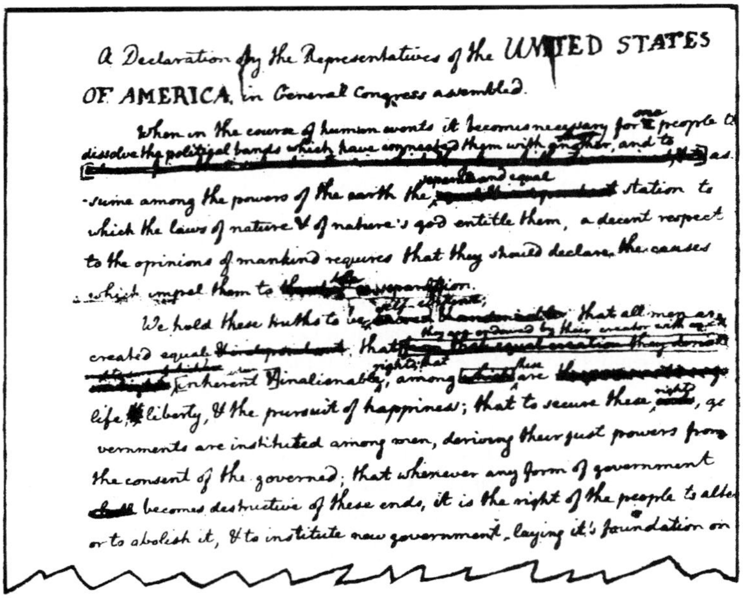

No longer under the auspices of British rule, the American colonies had the task of officially declaring their independence and forming their own government. Filled with a vision that reached beyond the realms of kings and kingdoms, Thomas Jefferson, Benjamin Franklin, Robert Sherman, and Robert Livingston put into words the sentiment and ideals that would eventually help bind the colonies together to form the United States of America. Here is Thomas Jefferson's draft of the *Declaration of Independence*.

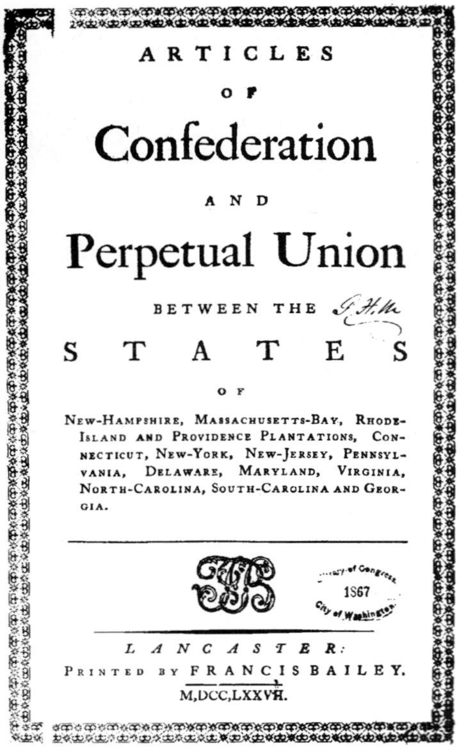

ARTICLES

OF

Confederation

AND

Perpetual Union

BETWEEN THE *J.H.M*

S T A T E S

OF

NEW-HAMPSHIRE, MASSACHUSETTS-BAY, RHODE-ISLAND AND PROVIDENCE PLANTATIONS, CONNECTICUT, NEW-YORK, NEW-JERSEY, PENNSYLVANIA, DELAWARE, MARYLAND, VIRGINIA, NORTH-CAROLINA, SOUTH-CAROLINA AND GEORGIA.

1867

LANCASTER:
PRINTED BY FRANCIS BAILEY.
M,DCC,LXXVII.

The Articles of Confederation created a decentralized form of federal government. Under the Articles, the government had no power to raise revenue, nor could it ratify amendments without unanimous consent of Congress. The federal government was too weak to govern the nation, and the Articles were eventually abandoned. However, the Articles did contribute several crucial cornerstones to the foundation of the new government: the establishment of the first executive department and the general principle of land distribution that helped the nation expand westward.

The war left the new nation deeply in debt, but the Articles restricted the power of the federal government to offer the states any assistance. In the winter of 1787, when the Massachusetts legislature levied heavy taxes that hit the poor particularly hard, three counties revolted. Daniel Shays, a poor farmer and war veteran, led a makeshift army against the federal arsenal at Springfield in protest. Shays's group was easily routed, but they did get the legislature to grant some of their demands. The inability of the federal government to take any action during the crisis convinced many of the necessity of revising the Articles.

The delegates to the Constitutional Convention who met in Philadelphia in the Spring of 1787 quickly agreed to abandon the Articles in favor of constructing a stronger federal system. The result: a bicameral Congress, an independent presidency, and a supreme court, with a system of checks and balances to prevent the abuse of power, became the main features of the Constitution of the United States.

George Washington was the obvious choice to fill the new post of president designated in the Constitution. With Congress divided as to how much ritual should surround the office, Washington satisfied the lovers of show but dismayed those who wished to put royalty in the past. Thus, he decked himself and his carriage out ostentatiously and ceremoniously refused to visit anyone until they had paid a visit to him first. Here he rides his horse to his inauguration.

Robinson, "gave Constitutional sanction to the fact that the United States was composed of some persons who were 'free' and others who were not, and it established the principle, new in republican theory, that a man who lives among slaves had a greater share in the election of representatives than the man who did not. Although the Three-fifths Compromise acknowledged slavery and rewarded slave owners, nonetheless, it probably kept the South from unanimously rejecting the Constitution."[12]

The issue of slavery was the most difficult faced by the framers and nearly destroyed the Union. Although some delegates believed slavery to be morally wrong, an evil and oppressive institution that made a mockery of the ideals and values espoused in the Constitution, morality was not the issue that caused the framers to support or oppose the Three-fifths Compromise. Whatever they thought of the institution of slavery, most delegates from the northern states opposed counting slaves in the distribution of congressional seats. Wilson of Pennsylvania, for example, argued that if slaves were citizens they should be treated and counted like other citizens. If on the other hand, they were property, then why should not other forms of property be counted toward the apportionment of Congress? But southern delegates made it clear that if the northerners refused to give in, they would never agree to the new government. William R. Davie of North Carolina heatedly said that it was time "to speak out." He asserted that the people of North Carolina would never enter the Union if slaves were not counted as part of the basis for representation. Without such agreement, he asserted ominously "the business was at an end." Even southerners like Edward Randolph of Virginia, who conceded that slavery was immoral, insisted upon including slaves in the allocation of congressional seats. This conflict between the southern and northern delegates was so divisive that many came to question the possibility of creating and maintaining a union of the two. Pierce Butler of South Carolina declared that the North and South were as different as Russia and Turkey. Eventually, the North and South compromised on the issue of slavery and representation. Indeed, northerners even agreed to permit a continuation of the odious slave trade to keep the South in the union. But, in due course, Butler proved to be correct, and a bloody war was fought when the disparate interests of the North and South could no longer be reconciled.

THE CONSTITUTION

The political significance of the Great Compromise and Three-fifths Compromise was to reinforce the unity of the mercantile and planter forces, which sought to create a new government. The Great Compromise reassured those who feared that the importance of their own local or regional influence would be reduced by the new governmental framework. The Three-fifths Compromise temporarily defused the rivalry between the merchants and planters. Their unity secured, members of

[12]Donald Robinson, *Slavery in the Structure of American Politics,* 1765–1820 (New York: Harcourt Brace Jovanovich, 1971), p. 201.

the alliance supporting the establishment of a new government moved to fashion a constitutional framework consistent with their economic and political interests.

In particular, the framers sought a new government that, first, would be strong enough to promote commerce and protect property from radical state legislatures such as Rhode Island's. This became the constitutional basis for national control over commerce and finance, as well as the establishment of national judicial supremacy and the basis for the effort to construct a strong presidency. Second, the framers sought to prevent what they saw as the threat posed by the "excessive democracy" of the state and national governments under the Articles of Confederation. This led to such constitutional principles as bicameralism (division of the Congress into two chambers), checks and balances, staggered terms in office, and indirect election (selection of the president by an electoral college rather than voters directly). Third, the framers, lacking the power to force the states or the public-at-large to accept the new form of government, sought to identify principles that would help to secure support. This became the basis of the constitutional provision for direct popular election of representatives and, subsequently, for the addition of the Bill of Rights to the Constitution. Finally, the framers wanted to be certain that the government they created did not use its power to pose even more of a threat to its citizens' liberties and property rights than did the radical state legislatures they feared and despised. To prevent the new government from abusing its power, the framers incorporated principles such as the separation of powers and federalism into the Constitution. Let us assess the major provisions of the Constitution's seven articles to see how each relates to these broad objectives.

The Legislative Branch

The Constitution provided in Article I, Sections 1–7, for a Congress consisting of two chambers—a House of Representatives and a Senate. Members of the House of Representatives were given two-year terms in office and were to be elected directly by the people. Members of the Senate were to be appointed by the state legislatures (this was changed in 1913 by the Seventeenth Amendment, providing for direct election of senators) for six-year terms. These terms, moreover, were staggered so that the appointments of one-third of the senators would expire every two years. The Constitution assigned somewhat different tasks to the House and Senate. Though the approval of each body was required for the enactment of a law, the Senate alone was given the power to ratify treaties and approve presidential appointments. The House, on the other hand, was given the sole power to originate revenue bills.

The character of the legislative branch was directly related to the framers' major goals. The House of Representatives was designed to be directly responsible to the people in order to encourage popular consent for the new Constitution and, as we saw in Chapter 1, to help enhance the power of the new government. At the same time, to guard against "excessive democracy," the power of the House of Representatives was checked by the Senate, whose members were to be appointed for long terms rather than be elected directly by the people. The purpose of this provision, according to Alexander Hamilton, was to avoid, "an unqualified complaisance to every sudden breeze of passion, or to every transient impulse which the people may receive."[13] Staggered terms of service in the Senate, moreover, were intended to make that body even more resistant to popular pressure. Since only one-third of the senators would be selected at any given time, the composition of the institution would be protected from changes in popular preferences transmitted by the state legislatures. This would prevent what James Madison called "mutability in the public councils arising from a rapid succession of new members."[14] Thus, the structure of the legislative branch was designed to contribute to governmental power, to promote popular consent for the new government, and at the same time to place limits on the popular political currents that many of the framers saw as a radical threat to the economic and social order.

The Powers of Congress and the States The issues of power and consent were important throughout the Constitution. Section 8 of Article I specifically listed the powers of Congress, which include the authority to collect taxes, to borrow money, to regulate commerce, to declare war, and to maintain an army and navy. By granting it these powers, the framers indicated very clearly that they intended the new government to be far more influential than its predecessor. At the same time, by defining the new government's most important powers as powers of Congress, the framers sought to promote popular acceptance of this critical change by reassuring citizens that their views would be fully represented whenever the government exercised its new powers.

As a further guarantee to the people that the new government would pose no threat to them, the Constitution implied that any powers not listed were not granted at all. This is the doctrine of **expressed power.** The Constitution grants only those powers specifically *expressed* in its text. But the framers intended to create an active and powerful government, and so they included the "necessary and proper clause," sometimes known as the **elastic clause,** which signified that the enumerated powers were meant to be a source of strength to the national government, not a limitation on it. Each power could be used with the utmost vigor, but no new powers could be seized upon by the national government without a constitutional amendment. In the absence of such an amendment, any power not enumerated was conceived to be "reserved" to the states (or the people).

If there had been any doubt at all about the scope of the necessary and proper clause, it was settled by Chief Justice John Marshall in one of the most important constitutional cases in American history, *McCulloch* v. *Maryland* (see Box 2.2), which dealt with the question of whether states could tax the federally charted Bank of the United States.[15] This bank was largely under the control of the Federalist party and was extremely unpopular in the West and South. A number of states, including Maryland, imposed stiff taxes on the bank's operations, hoping to weaken or destroy it. When the bank's Baltimore branch refused to comply with Maryland law and pay state taxes, the state brought a suit that was eventually heard by the U.S. Supreme Court (see also Chapter 3). Writing for the Court, Chief Jus-

[13]E.M. Earle, ed., *The Federalist* (New York: Modern Library, 1937), No. 71.

[14]Ibid., No. 62.

[15]McCulloch v. Maryland, 4 Wheaton 316 (1819).

BOX 2.2
McCulloch v. Maryland

. . . [A constitution's] nature . . . requires that only its great outlines should be marked, its important objects designated, and the minor ingredients which compose those objects be deduced from the nature of the objects themselves.

. . . [I]t may with great reason be contended that a government, entrusted with such ample powers, on the due execution of which the happiness and prosperity of the nation so vitally depends, must also be entrusted with ample means for their execution.

. . . [T]he Constitution of the United States has not left the right of Congress to employ the necessary means for the execution of the powers conferred on the government to general reasoning. To its enumerated powers is added that of making "all laws which shall be necessary and proper, for carrying into execution the foregoing powers and all other powers vested by this Constitution, in the government of the United States, or in any department thereof."

We admit, as all must admit, that the powers of the government are limited, and that its limits are not to be transcended. But we think the sound construction of the Constitution must allow to the national legislature that discretion, with respect to the means by which the powers it confers are to be carried into execution, which will enable that body to perform the high duties assigned to it, in the manner most beneficial to the people. Let the end be legitimate, let it be within the scope of the Constitution, and all means which are appropriate, which are plainly adapted to that end, which are not prohibited, but consist with the letter and spirit of the Constitution, are constitutional.

Source: McCulloch v. Maryland, 41 ed. 579 (1819).

tice John Marshall ruled that states had no power to tax national agencies. Moreover, Marshall took the opportunity to give an expansive interpretation of the "necessary and proper" clause of the Constitution by asserting that Congress clearly possessed the power to charter a bank even though this was not explicitly mentioned in the Constitution. Marshall argued that so long as Congress was passing acts pursuant to one of the enumerated powers, then any of the means convenient to such an end were also legitimate. As he put it, any government "entrusted with such ample powers . . . must also be entrusted with ample means for their execution." It was through this avenue that the national government could grow in power without necessarily taking on any powers that were not already enumerated.

Limits on the National Government and the States   The Constitution listed in Section 9 a number of important limitations on the national government, which are in the nature of a mini-bill of rights. These included the right of *habeas corpus,* which means, in effect, that the government cannot deprive a person of liberty without explaining the reason to a court. These limitations are part of the reason that most delegates at the Constitutional Convention felt no urgent need to add a full-scale bill of rights to the Constitution. Some provisions were clearly designed to prevent the federal government from threatening important property interests.

For example, Congress was prohibited from giving preference to the ports of one state over those of another. Furthermore, neither Congress nor the state legislatures could require American vessels to pay duty as they entered the ports of any state, thereby preventing the states from charging tribute. All this was part of the delegates' effort to clear away major obstructions to national commerce.

The framers also included restrictions on the states because of their fear of the capacity of the state legislatures to engage in radical action against property and creditors. There are few absolutes in the Constitution, and most of them are found in Article I, Section 10, among the limitations on state powers in matters of commerce. The states were explicitly and absolutely denied the power to tax imports and exports and to place any regulations or other burdens on commerce outside their own borders. They were also explicitly prohibited from issuing paper money or from the payment of debts in any form except gold and silver coin. Finally, and of greatest importance, they were not allowed to impair the obligation of contracts. This was almost sufficient by itself to reassure commercial interests because it meant that state legislatures would not be able to cancel their contracts to purchase goods and services. Nor would they be able to pass any laws that would seriously alter the terms of contracts between private parties. All the powers that the states were in effect forbidden to exercise came to be known as the "exclusive powers" of the national government.

The Executive Branch

The Constitution provided for the establishment of the presidency in Article II. As Alexander Hamilton commented, the presidential article aimed toward "energy in the Executive." It did so in an effort to overcome the natural stalemate that was built into the bicameral legislature as well as into the separation of powers among the legislative, executive, and judicial branches. The Constitution afforded the president a measure of independence from the people and from the other branches of government—particularly the Congress.

In line with the framers' goal of increased power to the national government, the president was granted the unconditional power to accept ambassadors from other countries; this amounted to the power to "recognize" other countries. He was also given the power to negotiate treaties, although their acceptance required the approval of the Senate. The president was given the unconditional right to grant reprieves and pardons, except in cases of impeachment. And he was provided with the power to appoint major departmental personnel, to convene Congress in special session, and to veto congressional enactments. (The veto power is formidable. But it is not absolute, since Congress can override it by a two-thirds vote.)

The framers hoped to create a presidency that would make the federal government rather than the states the agency capable of timely and decisive action to deal with public issues and problems. This was the meaning of the "energy" that Hamilton hoped to impart to the executive branch.[16] At the same time, however, the framers sought to help the president withstand (excessively) democratic pres-

[16]*The Federalist*, No. 70.

sures by making him subject to indirect rather than direct election (through his se- lection by a separate electoral college). The extent to which the framers' hopes were actually realized will be the topic of Chapter 7.

The Judicial Branch

In establishing the judicial branch in Article III, the Constitution reflected the framers' preoccupations with nationalizing governmental power and checking radical democratic impulses, while guarding against potential interference with liberty and property from the new national government itself.

Under the provisions of Article III, the framers created a court that was to be literally a supreme court of the United States, and not merely the highest court of the national government. The most important expression of this intention was granting the Supreme Court the power to resolve any conflicts that might emerge between federal and state laws. In particular, the Supreme Court was given the right to determine whether a power was exclusive to the federal government, concurrent with the states, or exclusive to the states. The significance of this was noted by Justice Oliver Wendell Holmes, who observed:

> I do not think the United States would come to an end if we lost our power to declare an act of Congress void. I do think the union would be imperilled if we could not make that declaration as to the laws of the several states.[17]

In addition, the Supreme Court was assigned jurisdiction over controversies between citizens of different states. The long-term significance of this was that as the country developed a national economy, it came to rely increasingly on the federal judiciary, rather than on the state courts for resolution of disputes.

Judges were given lifetime appointments in order to protect them from popular politics and from interference by the other branches. This, however, did not mean that the judiciary would actually remain totally impartial to political considerations, or to the other branches, for the president was to appoint the judges, and the Senate to approve the appointments. Congress would also have the power to create inferior (lower) courts, to change the jurisdiction of the federal courts, to add or subtract federal judges, even to change the size of the Supreme Court.

No direct mention is made in the Constitution of *judicial review*—the power of the courts to render the final decision when there is a conflict of interpretation of the Constitution or of laws between the courts and Congress, the courts and the executive branch, or the courts and the states. Scholars generally feel that judicial review is implicit in the very existence of a written Constitution and in the power given directly to the federal courts over "all Cases . . . arising under this Constitution, the Laws of the United States and Treaties made, or which shall be made, under their Authority" (Article III, Section 2). The Supreme Court eventually assumed the power of judicial review. Its assumption of power, as we shall see in Chapter 9, was not based on the Constitution itself but on the politics of later decades and the membership of the Court.

[17]Oliver Wendell Holmes, *Collected Legal Papers* (New York: Harcourt Brace, 1920), pp. 295–96.

National Unity and Power

Various provisions in the Constitution addressed the framers' concern with national unity and power, including Article IV's provisions for comity (reciprocity) among states and among citizens of all states. They were extremely important, for without them there would have been little prospect of unobstructed national movement of persons and goods. Both "comity clauses," the ***full faith and credit*** clause and the ***privileges and immunities*** clause, were taken directly from the Articles of Confederation. The first clause provided that each state had to give "full faith and credit" to the official acts of all other states. The second provided that the citizens of any state were guaranteed the "privileges and immunities" of every other state, as though they were citizens of that state.

Each state was prohibited from discriminating against the citizens of other states in favor of its own citizens, with the Supreme Court charged with deciding in each case whether a state had discriminated against goods or people from another state. The Constitution restricted the power of the states in favor of ensuring enough power to the national government to give the country a free-flowing national economy.

The Constitution also contained the infamous provision that obliged persons living in free states to capture escaped slaves and return them to their owners. This provision, repealed in 1865 by the Thirteenth Amendment, was a promise to the South that it would not have to consider itself an economy isolated from the rest of the country.

The Constitution provided for the admission of new states to the union and guaranteed existing states that no territory would be taken from any of them without their consent. The Constitution provided that the United States "shall guarantee to every State . . . a Republican Form of Government." Although this may sound at first like an open invitation to the national government to intervene in the affairs of any of the states, the provision has worked in exactly the opposite manner because of the clause that states that the federal government can intervene in matters of domestic violence only when invited to by a state legislature or the state executive when the legislature is not in session or when necessary to enforce a federal court order. This has left the question of national intervention in local disorders almost completely to the discretion of local and state officials.

The framers' concern with national supremacy was also expressed in Article VI, in the "supremacy clause," which provided that national laws and treaties "shall be the supreme law of the land." This meant that all laws made under the "authority of the United States" would be superior to all laws adopted by any state or any other subdivision, and the states would be expected to respect all treaties made under that authority. This was a direct effort to keep the states from dealing separately with foreign nations or businesses. The supremacy clause also bound the officials of all state and local as well as federal governments to take an oath of office to support the national Constitution. This meant that every action taken by the United States Congress would have to be applied within each state as though the action were in fact state law.

To found the nation on a solid economic base, the Constitution also provided that all debts entered into under the Articles of Confederation were to be continued as valid debts under the new Constitution. The question of whether "all debts" included debts incurred by state governments during the Revolution was deliberately left unsettled and became one of the first great issues to be dealt with in the First Congress after 1789. The decision to have the national government assume all the state debts was a major victory for holders of these obligations. This action secured the allegiance of the mercantile class within the country, because most of the debts incurred by the national and state governments during and after the Revolution were held by wealthy Americans concerned about the dependability of their government. It was one of the most important assurances to the commercial interests that the Constitution favored commerce. It also assured foreign countries, especially France and England, that the United States could be trusted in matters of trade, treaties, defense, and credit. Repudiation of debts at the very outset would have endangered the country's sovereignty, since sovereignty depends on the credibility a nation enjoys in the eyes of other nations.

Amending the Constitution

The Constitution established procedures for its own revision in Article V. Its provisions are so difficult that Americans have availed themselves of the amending process only seventeen times since 1791, when the first ten amendments were adopted. Many other amendments have been proposed in Congress, but fewer than forty of them have even come close to fulfilling the Constitution's requirement of a two-thirds vote in Congress, and only a fraction have gotten anywhere near adoption by three-fourths of the states. (A breakdown of these figures and further discussion of amending the Constitution appear in Chapter 3.) The Constitution could also be amended by a constitutional convention. Occasionally, proponents of particular measures, such as a "balanced-budget amendment," have called for a constitutional convention to consider their proposals. Whatever the purpose for which it was called, however, such a convention would presumably have the authority to revise America's entire system of government.

Ratifying the Constitution

The rules for the ratification of the Constitution of 1787 made up Article VII of the Constitution. This provision actually violated the amendment provisions of the Articles of Confederation. For one thing, it adopted a nine-state rule in place of the unanimity among the states required by the Articles of Confederation. For another, it provided that ratification would occur in special state conventions called for that purpose rather than in the state legislatures. All the states except Rhode Island eventually did set up state conventions to ratify the Constitution, and none seemed to protest very loudly the extralegal character of the procedure.

Constitutional Limits on the National Government's Power

As we have indicated, though the framers sought to create a powerful national government, they also wanted to guard against possible misuse of that power. To that end, the framers incorporated two key principles into the Constitution—the *separation of powers* and *federalism* (see Chapter 3). A third set of limitations, in the form of a *bill of rights* was added to the Constitution to help secure its ratification when opponents of the document charged that it paid insufficient attention to citizens' rights.

The Separation of Powers　No principle of politics was more widely shared at the time of the 1787 founding than the principle that power must be used to balance power. The French political theorist Montesquieu (1689–1755) believed that this balance was an indispensable defense against tyranny, and his writings, especially his major work, *The Spirit of the Laws,* "were taken as political gospel" at the Philadelphia Convention.[18] The principle of the separation of powers is nowhere to be found explicitly in the Constitution, but it is clearly built on Articles I, II, and III, which provide for:

1. Three separate and distinct branches of government.
2. Different methods of selecting the top personnel, so that each branch is responsible to a different constituency. This is supposed to produce a "mixed regime," in which the personnel of each department will develop very different interests and outlooks on how to govern, and different groups in society will be assured some access to governmental decision making.
3. *Checks and balances*—a system under which each of the branches is given some power over the others. Familiar examples are the presidential veto power over legislation, the power of the Senate to approve presidential appointments, and judicial review of acts of Congress.

One clever formulation of the separation of powers is that of a system not of separated powers but of "separated institutions sharing power,"[19] and thus diminishing the chance that power will be misused.

Federalism　Compared to the confederation principle of the Articles of Confederation, federalism was a step toward greater centralization of power. The delegates agreed that they needed to place more power at the national level, without completely undermining the power of the state governments. Thus, they devised a system of two sovereigns—the states and the nation—with the hope that competition between the two would be an effective limitation on the power of both.

The Bill of Rights　Late in the Philadelphia Convention, a motion was made to include a bill of rights in the Constitution. After a brief debate in which hardly a word was said in its favor and only one speech was made against it, the motion to include it was almost unanimously turned down. Most delegates sincerely believed that since the federal government was already limited to its expressed powers, further protection of citizens was not needed. The delegates argued that the states should adopt bills of rights because their greater powers needed greater limitations. But almost immediately after the Constitution was ratified, there was a movement

---

[18]Max Farrand, *The Framing of the Constitution of the United States* (New Haven, CT: Yale University Press, 1962), p. 49.

[19]Richard E. Neustadt, *Presidential Power* (New York: Wiley, 1960), p. 33.

to adopt a national bill of rights. This is why the Bill of Rights, adopted in 1791,
comprises the first ten amendments to the Constitution rather than being part of
the body of it. We will have a good deal more to say about the Bill of Rights in
Chapter 3.

THE FIGHT FOR RATIFICATION

The first hurdle faced by the new Constitution was ratification by state conventions of delegates elected by the people of each state. This struggle for ratification was carried out in thirteen separate campaigns. Each involved different men, moved at a different pace, and was influenced by local as well as national considerations. Two sides faced off throughout all the states, however, taking the names of Federalists and Antifederalists. The Federalists (who more accurately should have called themselves "Nationalists," but who took their name to appear to follow in the revolutionary tradition) supported the Constitution and preferred a strong national government. The Antifederalists opposed the Constitution and preferred a federal system of government that was decentralized; they took on their name by default, in reaction to their better-organized opponents. The Federalists were united in their support of the Constitution, while the Antifederalists were divided as to what they believed the alternative to the Constitution should be.

Under the name of "Publius," Alexander Hamilton, James Madison, and John Jay wrote eighty-five articles in the New York papers supporting ratification of the Constitution. These *Federalist Papers,* as they are collectively known today, defended the principles of the Constitution and sought to dispel the fears of a national authority. The Antifederalists, on the other hand, men like Richard Henry Lee and Patrick Henry of Virginia, and George Clinton of New York, argued that the new Constitution betrayed the Revolution and was a step toward monarchy. They accused the Philadelphia Convention of being a "Dark Conclave," which had worked under a "thick veil of secrecy" to overthrow the law and spirit of the Articles of Confederation.

By the end of 1787 and the beginning of 1788, five states had ratified the Constitution. Delaware, New Jersey, and Georgia ratified it unanimously; Connecticut and Pennsylvania ratified by wide margins. (Although in Pennsylvania, both the Federalists and Antifederalists resorted to tricks in their attempts to win the struggle, beginning with the meeting of the legislature to send the Constitution to the ratifying convention. Antifederalists refused to meet on the floor of the legislature, and in response a mob of Federalists virtually dragged two reluctant legislators onto the floor from their lodgings, thereby making a quorum and enabling the supporters of the Constitution to send it to the ratifying convention for the state.) Opposition was overcome in Massachusetts after Sam Adams and John Hancock were converted to the Federalist position and by the inclusion of nine recommended amendments to the Constitution to protect human rights. Ratification by Maryland and South Carolina followed. In June 1788, New Hampshire became the ninth state to ratify. With nine states approving, the Constitution could be put into effect, but for the new national government to have real power, the approval of both Virginia and New York would be needed. After impassioned debate and a

James Madison and George Clinton
A Federalist and an Antifederalist Who
Built a Nation

James Madison is best known as the man who, more than any other, shaped the U.S. Constitution, forged in Philadelphia in 1787. George Clinton, who served as a popular New York governor from 1777 to 1795 and again from 1801 to 1804, is little remembered by history except for his opposition to the Constitution. Yet Clinton's contribution as an Antifederalist was nearly as significant to the new government as Madison's.

As a member of Congress under the Articles of Confederation Madison was convinced that a new system of government was necessary. At the Constitutional Convention, he was the primary architect of the Virginia Plan, the original constitutional blueprint, and even though some of Madison's most cherished ideas were defeated by the convention (such as the idea that Congress should have an absolute veto over all state laws), he is credited with being the "father" of the Constitution. After the convention, Madison worked tirelessly for the document's ratification; with Alexander Hamilton and John Jay, he wrote *The Federalist* essays, which were published in newspapers around the country to persuade the nation to accept the Constitution.

George Clinton was among the prominent figures who opposed Madison's efforts. Like many Antifederalists, Clinton was suspicious of the enhanced powers of this new central government, fearing that a single government ruling a large population would be too quick to deprive the people of their

James Madison

great number of recommendations for future amendment of the Constitution, especially for a bill of rights, the Federalists barely mustered enough votes for approval of the Constitution by Virginia in June and New York in July of 1788. North Carolina would join the new government in 1789, after a bill of rights actually was submitted to the states by Congress, and Rhode Island would hold out until 1790 before finally becoming part of the new union.

REFLECTIONS ON THE FOUNDING

The final product of the Constitutional Convention would have to be considered an extraordinary victory for the groups that had most forcefully called for the cre-

liberties. Unlike Madison, who opposed too much government by the people, Clinton believed that government should be founded on the consent of the governed. His opinions on direct representation based on geographically small districts buttressed arguments on behalf of retaining a "popular house" in Congress—that is, the House of Representatives.

When the new Constitution was sent to the states for ratification, it met a chilly reception in New York, a hotbed of Antifederalist sentiment. When the state's ratification convention met in the summer of 1788, Antifederalists outnumbered Federalists 2 to 1. The convention selected Governor Clinton to preside, but in doing so, silenced his eloquent voice (since he had to concern himself with conducting the meetings). Led by Alexander Hamilton, the Federalists decided to stall the proceedings in the hope that other key states would ratify the new document in the meantime, thereby increasing the pressure on New York. News of Virginia's ratification—the tenth state to do so—forced the collapse of Antifederalist resistance, and New York ratified by the closest vote of any state, 30 to 27.

Despite Clinton's silence at the state convention, once the Constitution was approved, his was a leading voice on behalf of the addition of a Bill of Rights to safeguard individual liberties against governmental encroachment. In 1791, the first ten amendments were added to the Constitution, thanks in part to the key guidance of Congressman James Madison. Despite enduring personal animosities, when Madison became president, in 1808, he chose George Clinton for his vice-president.

Source: Stephen L. Schechter, ed., *The Reluctant Piller* (Troy, NY: Russel Sage College, 1985).

George Clinton

ation of a new system of government to replace the Articles of Confederation. The new Constitution laid the groundwork for a government that would be sufficiently powerful to promote trade, to protect property, and to check the activities of radical state legislatures. Moreover, this new government was constructed through internal checks and balances, indirect selection of officeholders, lifetime judicial appointments, and other similar provisions intended to preclude the "excessive" democracy feared by many of the founding fathers. Some of the framers, of course, favored limits on popular influence, but the general consensus at the convention was that a thoroughly undemocratic document would never receive the popular approval needed to be ratified by the states.[20]

[20]See Farrand, *The Records of the Federal Convention*, vol. 1, p. 132.

Yet, while the Constitution sought to lay the groundwork for a powerful government, the framers struggled to reconcile government power with freedom. The framers surrounded the powerful institutions of the new regime with a variety of safeguards—a continual array of checks and balances—designed to make certain that the power of the national government could not be used to undermine the states' power and their citizens' freedoms. Thus, the framers were the first Americans to confront head-on the dilemma of freedom and power. Whether their solutions to this dilemma were successful is, of course, the topic of the remainder of our story.

SUMMARY

Political conflicts between the colonies and England, and among competing groups within the colonies led to the first founding as expressed by the Declaration of Independence. The first constitution, the Articles of Confederation, was adopted one year later (1777). Under this document, the states retained their sovereignty. The central government, composed solely of Congress, had few powers and no means of enforcing its will. The national government's weakness soon led to the Constitution of 1787, the second founding.

In this second founding the framers sought, first, to fashion a new government sufficiently powerful to promote commerce and protect property from radical state legislatures. Second, the framers sought to bring an end to the "excessive democracy" of the state and national governments under the Articles of Confederation. Third, the framers introduced mechanisms that helped secure popular consent for the new government. Finally, the framers made certain that their new government would not itself pose a threat to liberty and property.

The Constitution consists of seven articles. Articles I provides for a Congress of two chambers (Sections 1–7), defines the powers of the national government (Section 8), interprets the national government's powers as a source of strength rather than a limitation (necessary and proper clause), places specific restrictions on the national government (Section 9), and limits state powers (Section 10). Article II describes the presidency and establishes it as a separate branch of government. Article III is the judiciary article. While there is no direct mention of judicial review in this article, the Supreme Court eventually assumed that power. The main provisions of Article IV are the full faith and credit clause and the privileges and immunities clause. Article V describes the procedures for amending the Constitution. Article VI establishes that national laws and treaties are "the supreme law of the land." And finally, Article VII specifies the procedure for ratifying the Constitution of 1787.

FOR FURTHER READING

Andrews, Charles M. *The Colonial Background of the American Revolution*. New Haven: Yale University Press, 1924.

Bailyn, Bernard. *The Ideological Origins of the American Revolution*. Cambridge: Harvard University, 1967.

Beard, Charles. *An Economic Interpretation of the Constitution of the United States*. New York: Macmillan, 1913.

Becker, Carl L. *The Declaration of Independence*. New York: Vintage, 1942.

Cohler, Anne M. *Montesquieu's Politics and the Spirit of American Constitutionalism*. Lawrence: University Press of Kansas, 1988.

Farrand, Max, ed. *The Records of the Federal Convention of 1787*. New Haven: Yale University Press, 1966.

Hamilton, Alexander, James Madison, and John Jay. *The Federalist Papers*. Edited by Isaac Kramnick. New York: Viking Press, 1987.

Jensen, Merrill. *The Articles of Confederation*. Madison: University of Wisconsin Press, 1963.

Lipset, Seymour M. *The First New Nation: The United States in Historical and Comparative Perspective*. New York: Basic Books, 1963.

McDonald, Forrest. *The Formation of the American Republic*. New York: Penguin, 1967.

Main, Jackson Turner. *The Social Structure of Revolutionary America*. Princeton: Princeton University Press, 1965.

Palmer, R.R. *The Age of the Democratic Revolution*. Princeton: Princeton University Press, 1964.

Rossiter, Clinton. *1787: Grand Convention*. New York: Macmillan, 1966.

Storing, Herbert, ed. *The Complete Anti-Federalist*. Chicago: University of Chicago Press, 1980.

Walker, Samuel. *In Defense of American Liberties—A History of the ACLU*. New York: Oxford University Press, 1990.

Wills, Gary. *Explaining America*. New York: Penguin, 1982.

Wood, Gordon S. *The Creation of the American Republic*. New York: W. W. Norton, 1982.

3

The Constitutional Framework: Federalism and the Separation of Powers

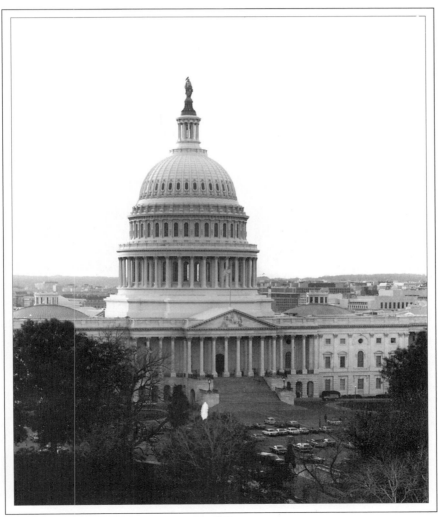

TIME LINE ON FEDERALISM

EVENTS		INSTITUTIONAL DEVELOPMENTS
National Bank established; national excise tax on whiskey enacted (1791); Jay's Treaty with Great Britain approved by Senate (1795)		Congress establishes national economic power, power to tax, power over foreign policy (1791–1795)
	1800	Epoch of Dual Federalism: Congress promotes commerce; states possess unchallenged police power (1800–1937)
Hartford Convention—New England states threaten secession from Union (1814)		Secession from Union first threatened by some states (1814)
States attempt to resist national economic power (early 1800s)		*McCulloch* v. *Maryland* (1819) and *Gibbons* v. *Ogden* (1824) reaffirm national supremacy
President Andrew Jackson decisively deals with South Carolina's threat to the Union (1833)		Supremacy of the Union is upheld during the Nullification Crisis (1833)
Attempt to use U.S. Bill of Rights to restrict state power (1830s)		*Barron* v. *Baltimore*—State power not subject to the U.S. Bill of Rights (1833)
Territorial expansion; slaves taken into territories (1800s)	**1850**	*Dred Scott* v. *Sandford*—Congress may not regulate slavery in the territories (1857)
Secession of southern states (1860–1861)		Union destroyed (1860–1861)
Civil War (1861–1865)		Union restored (1865)
Reconstruction of South (1867–1877)	**1870**	Constitution amended: XIII (1865), XIV (1868), XV (1870) Amendments
Compromise of 1877—self-government restored to former Confederate states (1877)		Reestablishment of South's full place in the Union (1877)
Consolidation of great national industrial corporations (U.S. Steel, AT&T, Standard Oil) (1880s and 1890s)		Interstate Commerce Act (1887) and Sherman Antitrust Act (1890) provide first national regulation of monopoly practices
Franklin D. Roosevelt's first New Deal programs for national economic recovery enacted by Congress (1933)	**1930**	Supreme Court upholds expanded powers of president in *U.S.* v. *Curtiss-Wright* (1936); and of Congress in *Stewart Machine* v. *Davis* (1937) and *NLRB* v. *Jones & Laughlin Steel* (1937)

TIME LINE ON FEDERALISM

EVENTS		INSTITUTIONAL DEVELOPMENTS
Blacks reject segregation after World War II (1950s)	**1950**	Supreme Court holds that segregation is "inherently unequal" in *Brown* v. *Board of Ed.* (1954)
Registration drive to register southern blacks to vote (1965)		Voting Rights Act (1965)
Black protests against segregation in South (1950s and 1960s)		National power expanded to reach discrimination, poverty, education, and poor health (1960s)
Republicans take control of the White House (1968)	**1970**	Revenue sharing under Nixon to strengthen state governments (1972)
Election of Ronald Reagan (1980)		States' rights reaffirmed by Reagan and Bush administrations (1980–1990s)
Election of George Bush (1988)	**1990**	Americans with Disabilities Act (1990); Civil Rights Act (1991)
Election of Bill Clinton; Democrats control Congress and Executive (1992)		

Replacement of the Articles of Confederation by the Constitution is a classic case study of political realism. As an instrument of government, the Articles of Confederation had many virtues. It may be the *second* greatest constitution ever drafted. But since it created or tolerated limits on the new economic interests seeking larger national and international markets, the Articles would have to go. The god-like men we call the founding fathers were nothing more nor less than a group of enlightened politicians breaking down barriers to economic progress. One sophisticated analyst has referred to the founding fathers as "a reform caucus in action."[1]

To a point, political realists are correct. Everything in politics revolves around interests; a constitution must satisfy those interests or it will not last long as a governing instrument. But just as pure force is an inadequate foundation for government, so is pure interest, despite its immediate importance. Interests must be

[1]John P. Roche, "The Founding Fathers: A Reform Caucus in Action," *American Political Science Review* 55 (December 1961), pp. 799–816. Roche's political realism is close to but still to be contrasted with the economic realism of Charles Beard, as discussed in Chapter 2. Also see "Debating the Issues" in Chapter 2.

translated into higher principles, and there will be no loyalty or support for any government unless most of the powerful as well as the powerless accept the principles as *legitimate*. Acceptance of the interests will follow.

Legitimacy can be defined as *the next best thing to being good*. Legitimacy is not synonymous with popularity. A government can be considered legitimate when its actions appear to be consistent with the highest principles that people already hold. In most countries, governments have attempted to derive their legitimacy from *religion* or from a common past of shared experiences and sacrifices that are called *tradition*. Some governments, or their rulers, have tried to derive their legitimacy from the *need for defense against a common enemy*. The American approach to legitimacy contained parts of all of these factors but with a unique addition: *contract*. A contract is an exchange, a deal. The contract we call the American Constitution was simply this: *the people would give their consent to a strong national government if that government would in turn accept certain strict limitations on its powers*. In other words, power in return for limits.

Three fundamental limitations were the principles involved in the contract between the American people and the framers of the Constitution: *federalism, the separation of powers, and individual rights*. Nowhere in the Constitution were these mentioned by name, but we know from the debates and writings that they were the primary framework of the Constitution. We can call them the *framework* because they were to be the structure, the channel through which governmental power would flow.

The principle of *federalism* sought to limit the national government by creating a second layer of state governments in opposition to it. American federalism recognized two sovereigns in the original Constitution and reinforced the principle in the Bill of Rights by granting a few "expressed powers" to the national government and reserving all the rest to the states.

The principle of the *separation of powers* sought to limit the power of the national government by dividing it against itself—by giving the legislative, executive, and judicial branches separate functions, thus forcing them to share power.

The principle of *individual rights* sought to limit government by defining the people as separate from it—granting to each individual an identity in opposition to the government itself. Individuals are given rights, which are claims to identity, to property, and to personal satisfaction or "the pursuit of happiness," that cannot be denied except by extraordinary procedures that demonstrate beyond doubt that the need of the government or the "public interest" is more compelling than the claim of the citizen. The principle of individual rights implies also the principle of *representation*. If there is to be a separate private sphere, there must be a set of procedures, separate from judicial review of individual rights, that somehow takes into account the preferences of citizens before the government acts.

Political realists treat these three great principles as a mere front for the economic interests that were dominant in Philadelphia in 1787 and in the state legislatures during ratification. But that would be only half the truth. The other half is that *principles themselves are an aspect of political realism*. Although a principle may first be stated to promote self-interests, once the principle has been expressed, it tends to take on a life of its own. Thus, a principle like federalism may serve one interest best at one point and cut against that interest later. To be a source of legitimacy, principles in a constitution must be consistent with interests yet must transcend those interests and connect with higher, more universal values. This is why a constitution cannot last if it is written for the present only; it cannot last unless it is written with a keen sense of history and philosophy. Chief Justice John Marshall was being the political realist when in 1819 he observed that "a constitution [is] intended to endure for ages to come and, consequently, to be adapted to the various crises of Human Affairs."[2]

This chapter will be concerned with the first two principles—federalism and the separation of powers. The purpose here is to look at the evolution of each principle in order to understand how we got to where we are and what the significance of each principle in operation is. After that we will look briefly at how and why the constitutional framework can be changed through the process of constitutional amendment. The third key principle, individual rights, will be the topic of the next chapter. But all of this is for introductory purposes only. All three principles form the background and the context for every chapter in the book.

THE FEDERAL FRAMEWORK

Few will disagree that the Constitution has had its most fundamental influence on American life through federalism. *Federalism* can be defined with misleading ease and simplicity as the division of powers and functions between the national government and the state governments. Tracing out the influence of federalism is not so simple, but we can make the task easier by breaking it down into three distinctive forms.

First, federalism sought to limit national power by creating two sovereigns—the national government and the state governments. It was called "dual federalism." At the time of our nation's founding, the states already existed as former colonies and, for nearly thirteen years, as virtually autonomous units of a confederacy under the Articles of Confederation. The Constitution imposed a stronger national government on the states. But even after the ratification of the Constitution, the states continued to be more important than the national government. For nearly a century and a half, virtually all of the fundamental policies governing the lives of American citizens were made by the state legislatures, not by Congress. (See Table 3.1.)

Second, that same federalism specifically restrained the power of the national government over the economy. The Supreme Court's definition of "interstate commerce" was so restrictive that Congress could only legislate as to the actual flow of goods across state lines; local conditions were protected from Congress by the contrary doctrine called "intrastate" commerce. As we shall see later in this chapter and again in Chapters 16 and 17, the federalism of strong states and weak national government was not changed until 1937, when the Supreme Court in *NLRB* v. *Jones & Laughlin Steel Corporation* reversed itself and redefined "interstate

---

[2]McCulloch v. Maryland, 4 Wheaton 316 (1819).

TABLE 3.1

The Federal System: Specialization of Governmental Functions in the Traditional System (1800–1933)

National Government Policies (Domestic)	State Government Policies	Local Government Policies
Internal improvements	Property laws (including	Adaptation of state laws
Subsidies	slavery)	to local conditions
Tariffs	Estate and inheritance	("variances")
Public lands disposal	laws	Public works
Patents	Commerce laws	Contracts for public
Currency	Banking and credit laws	works
	Corporate laws	Licensing of public
	Insurance laws	accommodations
	Family laws	Assessible improvements
	Morals laws	Basic public services
	Public health laws	
	Education laws	
	General penal laws	
	Eminent domain laws	
	Construction codes	
	Land-use laws	
	Water and mineral laws	
	Criminal procedure laws	
	Electoral and political	
	parties laws	
	Local government laws	
	Civil service laws	
	Occupations and	
	professions laws	

commerce" to permit the national government to regulate local economic conditions.

Third, since federalism freed the states to make so many important policies according to the wishes of their own citizens, states were therefore also free to be different from each other. Federalism allowed a great deal of variation from state to state in the rights enjoyed by citizens, in the roles played by governments, and in definitions of crime and its punishment. During the past half century, we have moved toward greater national uniformity in state laws and in the rights enjoyed by citizens. Nevertheless, as we shall see, federalism continues even today to permit significant differences among the states.

Each of these consequences of federalism will be considered in its turn. The first two—the creating of two sovereigns and the restraining of the economic power of the national government—will be treated in this chapter. The third, even though it is an aspect of federalism, will be an important part of the next chapter, because it is that part of federalism that relates to the framework of individual rights and liberties.

The Constitution created two layers of government: the national government and the state governments. This two-layer system can be called dual federalism or dual sovereignty. Even though there have been many changes since 1937, the consequences of dual sovereignty are fundamental to the American system of government in theory and in practice.

Table 3.1 is a listing of the major types of public policies by which Americans were governed for the first century and a half under the Constitution. We call it the "traditional system" because it prevailed for three-quarters of our history and because it closely approximates the intentions of the framers of the Constitution.

Under the traditional system, the federal government was quite small by comparison both to the state governments and to the governments of other Western nations. Not only was it smaller than most governments of that time, it was actually very narrowly specialized in the functions it performed. Our national government built or sponsored the construction of roads, canals, and bridges ("internal improvements"). It provided cash subsidies to shippers and ship builders and free or low-priced public land to encourage western settlement and business ventures. It placed relatively heavy taxes on imported goods (tariffs), not only to raise revenues but to protect "infant industries" from competition from the more advanced European enterprises. It protected patents and provided for a common currency, also to encourage and facilitate enterprises and to expand markets.

These functions of the national government reveal at least two additional insights. First, virtually all the functions of the national government were aimed at assisting commerce. It is quite appropriate to refer to the traditional American system as a "commercial republic." Second, virtually none of the national government's policies directly coerced citizens. The emphasis of governmental programs was on assistance, promotion, and encouragement—the allocation of land or capital where they were insufficiently available for economic development. Some historians would go a step further by arguing that the national government was instrumental in the development of American capitalism. But this is inaccurate. National policies contributed significantly to American economic development, but they were incidental to the development of capitalism as such. Capitalism actually took the form as we know it from *state* laws and state court decisions. There are no national property laws; there are no national corporate laws; in the nineteenth century, there were almost no national banking laws. Even where the national government had a constitutional mandate—as in bankruptcy regulation—Congress chose not to act. And although Article I, Section 8, expressly delegates to Congress the power "to regulate Commerce with foreign Nations, and among the several States . . . ," the only laws Congress passed directly regulating commerce were those concerning foreign commerce or commerce in and around the ports. Actions by the national government in the domestic economy were aimed at the promotion rather than regulation of economic activity.

Meanwhile, state legislatures were actively involved in economic regulation during the nineteenth century. In the United States, then and now, private prop-

BOX 3.1
The Iroquois League: Native American Model

The origins of the Iroquois League, which united the great Indian tribes of the Northeast, are shrouded in Indian myth and legend. Nonetheless, experts seem to agree that an Indian of the Onondaga tribe named Hiawatha (although popularized by Henry Wadsworth Longfellow in the nineteenth century, Longfellow's Hiawatha bears no resemblance to Iroquois legend) was instrumental in breaking the revenge-motivated cycle of killing that marked neighboring tribal relations. The result was establishment of the "Great Peace," a mutual nonagression pact, probably consummated around 1500. The agreement brought together the Onondaga, Mohawk, Oneida, Cayuga, and Seneca tribes (the Tuscaroras joined later) to form the Iroquois League.

While the agreement brought peace to the five nations, its members still faced aggression from other Indian nations, impelling them to work together in concert to face common foes. The Iroquois eventually came to dominate the Northeast. A system of league representation was established, whereby each of the five nations was represented by league chiefs (sachems). Within each nation, the chiefs were selected by clans. Within each clan, chief assignments were made by senior women descended from dominant family lines. Decisions made by league chiefs had to be unanimous, so as to facilitate consensus building; junior chiefs spoke first, and more senior chiefs last.

At least one clear link between the Iroquois and European settlers (who struggled to form their own political bonds) is known. In the summer of 1754, representatives from seven northern colonies met in Albany, New York, for the purposes of buttressing local defense against the French and hostile Indians, and promoting other mutual interests. Pennsylvania delegate Benjamin Franklin compared the colonists' then-fruitless efforts to unite with the successful efforts of the six Iroquois nations: "It would be a strange thing if six nations of ignorant savages should be capable of forming such a union and . . . it has subsisted for ages and appears indissolvable, and yet . . . a like union should be impractical for ten or a dozen English colonies." Despite the failure of the Albany Congress, it provided a blueprint for subsequent successful self-governing efforts. And the Iroquois model was clearly known to colonial leaders.

The power of the Iroquois Confederacy waned as the result of British-French struggles, and the Revolutionary War. In part, the Iroquois Confederacy suffered for the same reason as America's first constitution, the Articles of Confederation: neither governing system included any mechanism to enforce compliance, and both were paralyzed when they could not achieve unanimous agreement. Nevertheless, the Iroquois governing system rules the six tribes to this day.

Source: E. Tooker, "The League of the Iroquois: Its History, Politics, and Ritual," in *Handbook of North American Indians,* vol. 15, ed. B. G. Trigger (Washington, DC: Smithsonian Institution, 1978), pp. 418–41; Dean R. Snow, "Hiawatha: Constitution-maker," *New York Notes* (Albany, NY: New York State Bicentennial Commission, 1987).

erty exists only in state laws and state court decisions regarding property, trespass, and real estate. It bears repeating that American capitalism took its actual form from state property and trespass laws, as well as state laws and court decisions regarding contracts, markets, credit, banking, incorporation, and insurance. Laws

concerning slavery were a subdivision of property law in states where slavery existed. State law regulated the practice of important professions such as law and medicine. The birth or adoption of a child, marriage, and divorce have all been controlled by state law. To educate or not to educate a child has been a decision governed more by state laws than by parents, and not at all by national law. It is important to note also that virtually all the criminal laws—regarding everything from trespass to murder—have been state laws. Most of the criminal laws adopted by Congress are concerned with the District of Columbia and other federal territories.

All this (and more, as shown in Column 2 of Table 3.1) demonstrates without any question that most of the fundamental governing in this country was done by the states. The contrast between national and state policies, as shown by the table, demonstrates the difference in the power vested in each. The list of items in Column 2 could actually have been made much longer. Moreover, each item on the list is only a category of law that fills many volumes of statutes and court decisions for each state.

This contrast between national and state governments is all the more impressive because it is basically what was intended by the framers of the Constitution. There is probably no better example in world history of consistency between formal intentions and political reality.[3] Since the 1930s, the national government has expanded into local and intrastate matters, far beyond what anyone would have foreseen in 1890 or even in 1914. But this significant expansion of the national government did not alter the basic framework. The national government has become much larger, but the states have continued to be central to the American system of government. Since the 1930s, the national government has had a wide range of laws and agencies dealing with corporations, capital investment, the value of money, the level of interest, and other such issues. But most people are not large corporations or interstate investors, and therefore most people still have their primary government experience with state government and state laws. The national government has expanded, *but only minimally at the expense of the states.* (The exceptions, where states have lost some powers, will be identified below, as will the place of local government.)

And here lies probably the most important point of all: The fundamental impact of federalism on the way the United States is governed comes not from any particular provision of the Constitution but from the framework itself, which has determined the flow of government functions and, through that, the political developments of the country. By allowing state governments to do most of the fundamental governing, the Constitution saved the national government from many policy decisions that might have proven too divisive for this large but very young country. There is no doubt that if the Constitution had provided for a unitary

---

[3]Alexander Hamilton, the founder most famous for favoring a strong national government, came up with a list of extremely bold proposals for the national government when he was the first secretary of the treasury under President Washington; but when these are examined, they turn out to be nothing more than a detailed set of proposals very like the policies Congress ultimately adopted. Hamilton's proposals are contained in his *Report on Manufactures* (1791), one of the most important state papers ever written.

Dred Scott
When Persons Were Property

Dred Scott (1795?–1858)

Slave life for Dred Scott was not as gruelling as it was for most. Born in Virginia about 1795, Scott was originally owned by the Blow family. In 1833, he was sold to an army surgeon living in St. Louis, Dr. John Emerson. In 1834, Scott was taken along as a personal servant to Rock Island, Illinois, and then to Fort Snelling in the Wisconsin Territory (what is now Minnesota), returning to St. Louis in 1838.

When Dr. Emerson died in 1843, Scott attempted to buy his freedom. But instead, he was transferred to Emerson's widow, who then moved to New York, leaving Scott in the care of his previous owners, the Blow family. At least one member of the Blow family felt some sympathy for Scott. Opposed to the extension of slavery into the West, Henry Blow (who later helped found the antislavery Free Soil party) provided financial support to Scott to test in court whether his residence on free soil in Illinois and the Wisconsin territory would provide a basis for declaring Scott a free man.

A suit was brought in Missouri in 1846 on this basis, where a jury ruled in Scott's favor. On appeal to the state supreme court, this verdict was overturned. The Missouri court ruled in 1852 that under state law Scott continued to be a slave. The case eventually made its way to the Supreme Court.

In a 7-to-2 ruling handed down in 1857, the Court ruled against Scott. Speaking for the majority, Chief Justice Roger Taney said that blacks such as Scott were not meant to be considered citizens as the term was used in the Constitution, and that blacks "were never thought of or spoken of except as property." This was, without doubt, a crushing defeat for Scott and other blacks. Yet, the Court went even further in its pronouncement than the law or the particulars of the case required, and by doing so, it unintentionally hastened the bloody war that marked the demise of slavery.

At the urging of President James Buchanan, Justice Taney attempted to carve out a broad Court ruling that he hoped would resolve the issue of slavery by providing clear protection for it. In particular, he ruled that Congress lacked the constitutional authority to bar slavery in the territories. For the first time since *Marbury v. Madison,* the Court declared an act of Congress—the Missouri Compromise—unconstitutional. These bold steps enraged much of the country.

As for Scott himself, his life had been marked by frail health. His owners freed him a few weeks after the Court decision, but Scott died in St. Louis on September 17, 1858, of tuberculosis. His funeral expenses were paid by Henry Blow.

Source: Bruce Catton, "The Dred Scott Case," in *Quarrels That Have Shaped the Constitution,* ed. John A. Garraty (New York: Harper & Row, 1964); Dred Scott v. Sandford, 19 How. 393 (1857).

rather than a federal system, the war over slavery would have come in 1789 or
1809 rather than 1860; and if it had come that early, the South might very well have seceded and established a separate and permanent slaveholding nation. In helping the national government remain small and aloof from the most divisive issues of the day, federalism contributed significantly to the political stability of the nation even as the social, economic, and political systems of many of the states and regions of the country were undergoing tremendous and profound, and sometimes violent, change.[4] As we shall see, some important aspects of federalism have changed, but the federal framework has survived two centuries and a devastating civil war.

Federalism as a Limitation on the National Government's Power

Having created the national government, and recognizing the potential for abuse of power, the states sought through federalism to constrain the national government. The "traditional system" of weak national government prevailed for over a century despite economic forces favoring its expansion and despite Supreme Court cases giving a pro-national interpretation to Article I, Section 8.

That article delegates to Congress the power "to regulate commerce with foreign nations, and among the several States and with the Indian tribes," and this clause was consistently interpreted *in favor* of national power by the Supreme Court for most of the nineteenth century. The first and most important case favoring national power over the economy was *McCulloch* v. *Maryland* (1819).[5] As mentioned in Chapter 2, the case involved the Bank of the United States and the question of whether Congress had the power to charter a bank, since such an explicit grant of power was nowhere to be found in Article I, Section 8. Chief Justice John Marshall answered that the power could be "implied" from other powers that were expressly delegated to Congress such as the "powers to lay and collect taxes; to borrow money; to regulate commerce; and to declare and conduct a war." The constitutional authority for the implied powers doctrine is a clause in Article I, Section 8, which enables Congress "to make all laws which shall be necessary and proper for carrying into Execution the foregoing powers." By allowing Congress to use the "necessary and proper" clause to interpret its delegated powers, the Supreme Court created the potential for an unprecedented increase in national government power.

A second historic question posed by *McCulloch* was whether a state had the power to tax the Baltimore branch of the U.S. Bank, since it was a national agency. Here Marshall again took the side of national supremacy, arguing that an agency created by a legislature representing all the people (Congress) could not be put out of business by a state legislature (Maryland) representing only a small portion of

---

[4]For a good treatment of the contrast between national political stability and social instability, see Samuel P. Huntington, *Political Order in Changing Societies* (New Haven, CT: Yale University Press, 1968), Chapter 2.

[5]McCulloch v. Maryland, 4 Wheaton 316 (1819). See also Chapter 2.

PROCESS BOX 3.1

How the National Government Actually Governs—
There Is More to American Government than Federalism

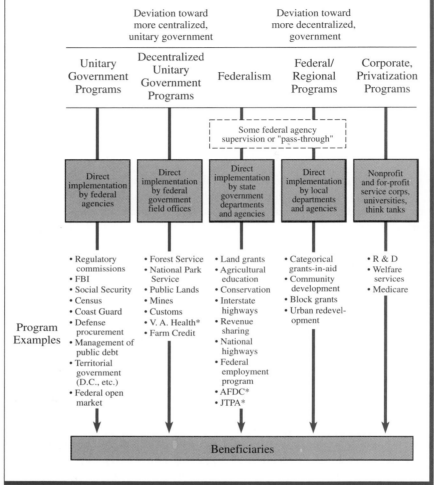

*V.A. = Veterans Administration; AFDC = Aid to Family with Dependent Children; JTPA = Job Training Partnership Act

Source: My thanks to Randall Ripley, Gary Bryner, and Donald Kettl for help in adapting a General Accounting Office diagram. See also Randall Ripley and Grace Franklin, *Policy Implementation and Bureaucracy* (Homewood, IL: Dorsey Press, 1986), p. 69.

the people (since "the power to tax is the power to destroy"). Marshall concluded that whenever a state law conflicted with a federal law, the state law would be deemed invalid since "the laws of the United States . . . 'shall be the supreme law of the land.'" Both parts of this great case were "pro-national," yet Congress did not immediately seek to expand the policies of the national government.

This nationalistic interpretation of the Constitution was reinforced by another major case, that of *Gibbons* v. *Ogden* in 1824. The important but relatively narrow

issue was whether the state of New York could grant a monopoly to Robert Fulton's steamboat company to operate an exclusive service between New York and New Jersey. Ogden had secured his license from Fulton's company, while Gibbons, a former partner, secured a competing license from the U.S. government. Chief Justice Marshall argued that Gibbons could not be kept from competing because the state of New York did not have the power to grant this particular monopoly. In order to reach this decision, it was necessary for Chief Justice Marshall to define what Article I, Section 8, meant by "commerce among the several states." Marshall insisted that the definition was "comprehensive," extending to "every species of commercial intercourse." He did say that this comprehensiveness was limited "to that commerce which concerns more states than one," giving rise to what later came to be called "interstate commerce." *Gibbons* is important because it established the supremacy of the national government in all matters affecting interstate commerce.[6] What would remain uncertain during several decades of constitutional discourse was the precise meaning of interstate commerce, notwithstanding John Marshall's expansive reading of "commerce among the several states."

Article I, Section 8, backed by the "implied powers" decision in *McCulloch* and by the broad definition of "interstate commerce" in *Gibbons,* was a source of power for the national government as long as Congress sought to improve commerce through subsidies, services, and land grants. But later in the nineteenth century, when the national government sought to use those powers to *regulate* the economy rather than merely to promote economic development, federalism, and the concept of interstate commerce, began to operate as a restraint on rather than as a source of national power (see Chapter 15). Any effort of the federal government to regulate commerce in such areas as fraud, the production of impure goods, the use of child labor, or the existence of dangerous working conditions or long hours was declared unconstitutional by the Supreme Court as a violation of the concept of interstate commerce. Such legislation meant that the federal government was entering the factory and workplace, and these areas were considered inherently local, because the goods produced there had not yet passed into commerce. Any effort to enter these local workplaces was an exercise of police power—the power reserved to the states for the protection of the health, safety, and morals of their citizens. No one questioned the power of the national government to regulate certain kinds of businesses, such as railroads, gas pipelines, and waterway transportation, because they intrinsically involved interstate commerce.[7] But well into the twentieth century, most other efforts by the national government to regulate commerce were blocked by the Supreme Court's interpretation of the meaning of federalism, which used the concept of interstate commerce as a barrier against most efforts by Congress to regulate local conditions. Congress occasion-

---

[6]Gibbons v. Ogden, 9 Wheaton 1 (1824).

[7]In Wabash, St. Louis, and Pacific Railway Company v. Illinois, 118 U.S. 557 (1886), the Supreme Court struck down a state law prohibiting rate discrimination by a railroad; in response, Congress passed the Interstate Commerce Act of 1887 creating the Interstate Commerce Commission (ICC), which was the first federal administrative agency.

ally tried to get around the Supreme Court's defense of federalism by passing laws that said in effect, "you can produce substandard or adulterated goods, or provide unhealthy working conditions, but you cannot put goods made under such conditions into interstate commerce." But the Supreme Court rejected most of these efforts by looking behind the law to Congress's motivation, which was to regulate the local situation. The Court was of course not perfectly consistent. Or let us say it made a few rather peculiar exceptions; for example, the Court agreed that Congress had the power to keep sawed-off shotguns, prostitutes, lottery tickets, kidnapped children, oleomargarine, and dangerous food and drugs out of interstate commerce, but it held that the Congress could not keep out of interstate commerce goods that had been produced by companies employing children under sixteen. It allowed for the regulation of a few specific goods, but it would not permit regulation of manufacturing in general.

Although the logical flaw in the Supreme Court's effort to distinguish between interstate and intrastate commerce was almost universally understood, it was not until 1937 (in response to New Deal legislation) that the Court finally decided to throw out the old distinction altogether and start with a clean slate. In *West Coast Hotel Co.* v. *Parrish,* it upheld a Washington minimum wage law; in *National Labor Relations Board* v. *Jones & Laughlin Steel Corporation,* it upheld the Wagner Act, which sought to protect labor's efforts to organize into unions and to engage in collective bargaining; in *Associated Press* v. *National Labor Relations Board,* it held that the labor relations of newspapers and press associations were also subject to the Labor Relations Act; and in *Steward Machine Company* v. *Davis,* it upheld the Social Security Act.[8] After these cases, the Court essentially ceased trying to restrict the efforts of the national government to reach local conditions. Although the Court has not abdicated its power to review acts of Congress, it will probably never again use "interstate commerce" as a means of limiting national power. But note that this particular aspect of federalism worked consistently as a restraint on national regulatory power until 1937, and it gave the American economy a freedom from federal government control that closely approximated the ideal of "free enterprise."

The economy was, of course, never entirely free; in fact, entrepreneurs themselves did not want complete freedom from government. They needed law and order. They needed a stable currency. They needed courts and police to enforce contracts and prevent trespass. They needed roads, canals, and railroads. But federalism, as interpreted by the Supreme Court for seventy years after the Civil War, made it possible for business to have its cake and eat it too. Entrepreneurs enjoyed the benefits of national policies facilitating commerce and were protected by the Courts from policies regulating commerce.[9] In 1937, the Supreme Court changed

[8]West Coast Hotel v. Parrish, 300 U.S. 379 (1937); NLRB v. Jones & Laughlin Steel Corp., 301 U.S. 1 (1937); Associated Press v. NLRB, 301 U.S. 103 (1937); Steward Machine Co. v. Davis, 301, U.S. 548 (1937). The case holding unconstitutional Congress's effort to outlaw goods produced by child labor was Hammer v. Dagenhart, 247 U.S. 251 (1918); it was reversed by U.S. v. Darby, 312 U.S. 100 (1941).

[9]The Sherman Antitrust Act, adopted in 1890, for example, was enacted, not to restrict commerce, but rather to protect it from monopolies, or trusts, so as to prevent unfair trade practices, and to enable the market again to become *self-regulating.* Moreover, the Supreme Court sought to uphold liberty of con-

the framework by permitting Congress to adopt a whole series of policies regulat- ing commerce: laws protecting the rights of employees to organize and engage in collective bargaining, laws regulating the amount of farm land in cultivation, laws extending low-interest credit to small businesses and farmers, laws restricting the activities of corporations dealing in the stock market, and a host of laws, which, when taken together, created the "welfare state." In effect, the Supreme Court converted the commerce clause from a source of limitations to a source of power.[10] This has been referred to as the First Constitutional Revolution. (A Second Constitutional Revolution will be identified and discussed in Chapter 4.)

The Continuing Influence of Federalism: State and Local Government Today

State Government National government policies since the First Constitutional Revolution have been add-ons; there is simply more government than there used to be. The states are now more constrained by these policies and by limits imposed on their powers by the Supreme Court, especially in the area of civil rights and civil liberties. But in most areas of traditional state policy, the states still reign supreme (as shown on Table 3.1, page 62).

No better demonstration of the continuing significance of the federal framework can be offered than Column 2 of Table 3.1, which is still an accurate portrayal of state government, even in the 1990s. To be sure, Column 1 has grown much longer; the "traditional system" of *national* government has evolved in many nontraditional directions. But Column 2 remains today essentially as it was in the nineteenth century. Of course, states can no longer pass laws making property out of human beings; nor can states, in the name of morality or the family or public order, make laws segregating the races, requiring religious observances in schools, or "outlawing" abortion (although some of this may be changing, as we shall see in Chapter 4). Otherwise, however, Column 2 holds up very well today.

Local Government and the Constitution The continuing vitality of the federal framework and of state government can be seen in still another area: local government. Local government occupies a peculiar but very important place in the American system. In fact, the status of American local government is probably unique in world experience.

Local governments became administratively important in the early years of the

---

tract to protect businesses. For example, in Lochner v. New York, 198 U.S. 45 (1905), the Court invalidated a New York law regulating the sanitary conditions and hours of labor of bakers on the grounds that the law interfered with liberty of contract.

[10]One of the most interesting examples is Congress's use of its new commerce power to improve the status of blacks and other minorities. Civil rights laws seek, among other things, to regulate the employment practices of businesses in order to reduce the freedom of employers to discriminate in their hiring on the basis of race, ethnic considerations, and gender. The Court permitted Congress to use the commerce power to regulate discrimination of *private employers* and businesses. The Court itself has used the Fourteenth Amendment to restrict the powers of the *states* to discriminate against minorities. The relevant provision of the Fourteenth Amendment is as follows: "Nor shall any State . . . deny to any person within its jurisdiction the equal protection of the laws." See Chapters 4 and 17.

TABLE 3.2
82,341 Governments in the United States

Type	Number
National	1
State	50
County	3,041
Municipal	19,076
Townships	16,734
School districts	14,851
Other special districts	28,588

Source: Department of Commerce, *Statistical Abstract of the United States, 1986* (Washington, DC: Government Printing Office, 1986).

Republic because the states possessed little administrative capability, and they relied on local governments to implement the laws of the state. Local government was an alternative to a statewide bureaucracy. The states created two forms of local government: territorial and corporate. The basic territorial unit is the county; every resident of the state is also a resident of a county (except in Rhode Island and Connecticut, which do not have county governments). Traditionally, counties existed only for handling state obligations, whether these were administrative, legislative, or judicial, whether the job was building roads or collecting state taxes or catching bootleggers.

The second, or corporate unit, is the city, town, or village. These are called corporate because each holds an actual corporate charter granted it by the state government; they are formed ("incorporated") by residents of an area as these residents discover that their close proximity and common problems can be more effectively and cheaply dealt with cooperatively. Not everyone lives in a city or town; many rural areas are "unincorporated."

Although cities, especially larger cities, develop their own unique political and government personalities, they are nevertheless like the counties in being units of state administration. We associate police forces, fire fighting companies, public health and zoning agencies with the very essence of local government. But all of those functions and agencies are operating under state laws. The state legislature and courts allow cities to adapt state laws to local needs, and out of that discretion cities can develop their own political personalities. But they remain under state authority, applying state laws to local conditions.[11]

Changes in the traditional place of local government began to take place in the latter part of the nineteenth century with the adoption of **home rule.** Beginning in Missouri in 1875, the states one after another changed their constitutions to permit cities (and eventually a few counties) of a certain size and urban density to

[11]A good discussion of the constitutional position of local governments is in York Willbern, *The Withering Away of the City* (Bloomington, IN: Indiana University Press, 1971). For more on the structure and theory of federalism see Thomas R. Dye, *American Federalism: Competition among the States* (Lexington, MA: Lexington Books, 1990), Chapter 1; and Martha Derthick, "Up-to-Date in Kansas City: Reflections on American Federalism" (the 1992 John Gaus Lecture), *PS: Political Science & Politics* (December 1992), pp. 671–75.

frame and adopt local charters. By the beginning of the twentieth century, home

rule was adopted in many of the states and the provisions were extended until
home rule came to mean giving cities the right of ordinary corporations to change
their government structures, to hold property, to sue and be sued, and most importantly, to be guaranteed that state legislatures would not pass legislation concerning the "local affairs, property, and government" of cities except by laws of
statewide application. This was a guarantee within the state constitution that no
city would be subjected to special legislation imposed on that city alone by the
state legislature. As part of this movement, many states began to allow cities to
make the basic laws for themselves rather than administering laws passed by the
state legislature. Cities were given the power to make their own laws ("ordinances") to regulate slaughterhouses, to regulate and establish public transportation
services and facilities, to regulate local markets and trade centers, to set quality and
safety standards for the construction of apartments and other private buildings, and
to control properties for administering fire prevention.

After such powers were delegated from state governments to many cities, it was
inevitable that people would come to the conclusion that cities constituted a third
level of sovereignty, and that some cities, such as New York City, were the constitutional equal of a state. But these conclusions are distinctly untrue. There are only
two levels of sovereignty in the United States, the national government and the
state government. Local governments, important as they have become in this
urban nation, remain exactly what they always have been: creatures of state government.

Updating Federalism—Grants-in-Aid As the national government has expanded, state and local governments have become stronger, not weaker. Since
1937, the national government has exerted more and more influence over the
states and localities, but thanks to American federalism, the form of that influence
is quite peculiar. Some of this new federal influence is direct, imposed by statutory
command and administrative control—as for occupational health and safety, air
pollution control, and voting rights. Most of the influence of the national government, however, is through **grants-in-aid.** A grant-in-aid is really a kind of bribe,
or inducement, whereby Congress appropriates money for state and local governments but on condition that the money be spent for a particular purpose as defined by Congress. Congress uses grants-in-aid because it does not have the
political or constitutional power to command cities to do its bidding. When you
can't command, a monetary inducement becomes a viable alternative.

The principle of the grant-in-aid goes back to the nineteenth-century land
grants to states for the improvement of agriculture and farm-related education.
Since farms were not in "interstate commerce," it was unclear whether the Constitution would permit the national government to provide direct assistance to
agriculture. Grants-in-aid to the states, earmarked to go to farmers, presented a
way of avoiding the constitutional problem while pursuing what was recognized in
Congress as a national goal.

This same approach was applied to cities beginning in the late 1930s. Congress
set national goals such as public housing and assistance to the unemployed and provided grants-in-aid to meet these goals. World War II temporarily stopped the

TABLE 3.3

Historical Trend of Federal Grants-in-Aid

(Fiscal years; dollar amounts in billions)

Fiscal Year	Amount of grants-in-aid	Total*	Domestic programs†	State and local expenditures‡	Gross National Product‡
Five-year intervals:					
1950	$2.3	5.3%	11.6%	10.4%	0.8%
1955	3.2	4.7	17.2	10.1	0.8
1960	7.0	7.6	20.6	14.6	1.4
1965	10.9	9.2	20.3	15.2	1.6
1970	24.1	12.3	25.3	19.2	2.4
1975	49.8	15.0	23.1	22.7	3.3
Annually:					
1980	91.5	15.5	23.3	25.8	3.4
1981	94.8	14.0	21.6	24.6	3.2
1982	88.2	11.8	19.0	21.6	2.8
1983	92.5	11.4	18.6	21.3	2.8
1984	97.6	11.5	19.6	20.9	2.6
1985	105.9	11.2	19.3	20.9	2.7
1986	112.4	11.3	19.8	20.5	2.7
1987	108.4	10.8	19.0	18.3	2.4
1988	115.4	10.8	19.0	NA	2.4
1989	122.0	10.7	18.7	NA	2.4
1990	136.9	10.9	17.0	18	2.5
1991 estimate	158.6	11.2	17.0	NA	2.8
1992 estimate	171.0	11.8	18.0	NA	2.9
1993 estimate	184.1	12.7	19.0	NA	2.9
1994 estimate	162.0	11.6	17.1	NA	2.2
1995 estimate	169.2	11.5	NA	NA	2.2

*Federal grants as percentage of federal outlays. Includes off-budget outlays; all grants are on-budget.
†As a percentage of federal outlays for domestic programs. Excludes outlays for national defense, international affairs, and net interest.
‡As a percentage of state and local expenditures, and as a percentage of GNP.
NA = Not available.
Source: Executive Office of the President, Office of Management and Budget, *Budget of the United States Government, Fiscal Year 1991* (Washington, DC: Government Printing Office, 1991), p. A321.

distribution of these grants. But after the war, Congress resumed providing grants for urban development and lunches in the schools. The value of such ***categorical grants-in-aid*** increased from $2.3 billion in 1950, to $7 billion in 1960, $24 billion in 1970, $94.8 billion in 1981, to roughly $119 billion in 1989 (see Table 3.3). Sometimes Congress requires the state or local government to match the national contribution dollar for dollar, but for some programs, such as the interstate highway system, the congressional grant-in-aid provides 90 percent of the cost of the program. The nation-wide speed limit of 55 mph was not imposed on individual drivers by an act of Congress. Instead, Congress bribed the state legislatures

by threatening to withdraw the federal highway grants-in-aid if the states did not
set the 55 mph speed limit. In the early 1990s, Congress began to ease up on the
states, permitting them, under certain conditions, to go back to the 65 mph speed
limit.

On more than one occasion, the number of such specific categorical grants-in-aid and the amount of money involved in them have come under criticism, by Democrats as well as Republicans, ultra-liberals as well as ultra-conservatives. But there is general agreement that grants-in-aid helped to reduce disparities of wealth between rich states and poor states. And although some critics have asserted that grants encouraged state and local governments to initiate programs merely because "free money from Washington" was available, the fact is that when federal grants were reduced by the Reagan administration, most states and localities continued funding the same programs with their own revenues. Daniel Elazar, an authority on federalism, has observed that "Despite many protestations to the contrary, only in rare situations have federal grant programs served to alter state administrative patterns in ways that did not coincide with already established state policies."[12]

Federalism has not stood still. If the traditional system of two separate sovereigns performing highly different functions could be called **dual federalism,** historians of federalism suggest that the system since the New Deal era could be called *cooperative federalism,* through which grants-in-aid have been used strategically to encourage states and localities (without commanding them) to pursue nationally defined goals. The most important student of the history of federalism, Morton Grodzins, characterized this as a move from "layer cake federalism" to "marble cake federalism,"[13] in which intergovernmental cooperation and sharing have blurred the distinguishing line, making it difficult to say where the national government ends and the state and local governments begin. Figure 3.1 demonstrates the financial basis of the marble cake idea. At the high point of grant-in-aid policies in 1977–1978, federal aid contributed an average of 25 percent of the operating budgets of all the state and local governments in the country. The numbers in Table 3.4 present some of the more extreme examples.

Developments in the past twenty years moved well beyond marble cake federalism to what might be called "regulated federalism."[14] In some areas the national government has actually tried to regulate the states, by threatening to withhold grant money unless state and local governments conformed to national standards. The most notable instances of this regulation are in the areas of civil rights and poverty programs. More recently, the national government has set national standards of conduct or has required the states to set standards that meet national

[12]Daniel Elazer, *American Federalism: A View from the States,* 3rd ed. (New York: Harper & Row, 1984), p. 110. For a view from the cities, see Paul Kantor, *The Dependent City: The Changing Political Economy of Urban America* (Glencoe, IL: Scott Foresman, 1988).

[13]Morton Grodzins, "The Federal System," in *Goals for Americans* (Englewood Cliffs, NJ: Prentice-Hall, 1960), p. 265. In a marble cake, the white cake is distinguishable from the chocolate cake, but the two are streaked rather than in distinct layers.

[14]The concept and the best discussion of this modern phenomenon will be found in Donald F. Kettl, *The Regulation of American Federalism* (Baltimore: Johns Hopkins University Press, 1983 and 1987), especially pp. 33–41.

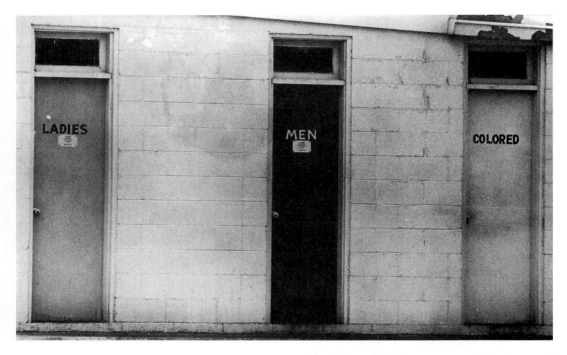

The division of legislative power among federal, state, and local authorities has been, and continues to be, a fundamental debate in American government. For many years, states codified racial discrimination by enacting laws that called for separate schools, drinking fountains, seats on buses, and restroom facilities. The Warren Court's unanimous decision in *Brown* led the way for a review of all state laws promoting such discrimination.

Through poll taxes and literacy tests, southern states had barred blacks from registering to vote and from voting. With the passage of the Voting Rights Act in 1965, Congress prohibited states from making any laws that limited a person's right to vote. These people were part of a crowd of 500 attempting to register to vote in a national election. Only 72 people succeeded by the end of the day, because of the willfully slow processing of applicants by the officials inside the courtroom.

In 1976 the Burger Court, in *Gregg* v. *Georgia*, gave back to the states the right to impose the death penalty. Thirty-seven states have enacted capital punishment statutes, but the methods of execution vary by state. The electric chair is used for execution by the state of Florida. California uses the gas chamber, Idaho the firing squad, and Texas uses lethal injection. On January 5, 1993, using a split-level room with a trap door and an Army execution manual dating from the nineteenth century, Washington became the first state since 1965 to hang a convicted murderer.

Left: During the oil crises of the 1970s, the federal government restricted highway driving to 55 miles per hour both to cut fuel consumption and to reduce the incidence of fatalities on the roads. As oil prices plummeted in the early 1980s, states began lobbying to raise the speed limit. *Right:* Their efforts resulted in a law that allowed cars on certain rural stretches of highway to travel 65 miles per hour. The law has come into widest use on the open straightaways in the western half of the country.

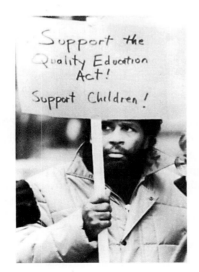

Each state is responsible for organizing and regulating its own system of education, supported financially by local, state, and federal taxes. This has lead to inequalities between school districts: those with higher-valued property taxes being able to afford a higher quality education system. In New Jersey, a Quality Education Act, originally intended to make the system more equitable by redistributing the tax moneys, was considerably watered down by the legislature, provoking protests such as this one.

FIGURE 3.1
The Rise and Decline of Federal Aid

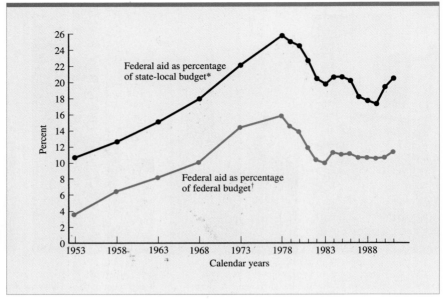

*Federal aid as a percentage of state-local expenditures after transfers.
†Federal aid as a percentage of federal expenditures from own funds.

Source: Advisory Commission on Intergovernmental Relations, *Significant Features of Fiscal Federalism* (Washington, DC: Government Printing Office, September 1992).

guidelines. Important cases of such efforts are in the field of environmental protection, in interstate highway use, in social services standards, and in education. The net effect of these national standards is that state and local policies are more uniform from coast to coast.

There has also been an expansion of national policies that reach individuals directly with no state or local involvement at all (as in direct benefit payments for welfare), or that use state and local agencies merely as conduits, with an administrative role but no direct policy-making role.

Yet there have been countertrends, attempting to reverse this nationalization and reestablish traditional policy making and implementation. Presidents Nixon and Reagan called their efforts the "new federalism," by which national policies attempted to return more discretion to the states. This was the purpose of Nixon's revenue sharing and the goal of Reagan's block grants, which consolidated a number of categorical grants into one larger category leaving the state (or the local) government to decide how to use the grant. Presidents Nixon and Reagan, as well as President Bush, were sincere in wanting to return somewhat to a traditional notion of freedom of action for the states. They called it "new federalism," but their concept and their goal was really much closer to the older, traditional federalism that pre-dated Franklin Roosevelt.

Although President Reagan succeeded in reducing national appropriations for grants-in-aid during his first term, he could not prevent increases for his second

TABLE 3.4

79

THE SECOND
PRINCIPLE: THE
SEPARATION OF
POWERS

Federal Aid as a Percentage of General Annual Expenditure

City	1977	1990	City	1977	1990
Buffalo	31%	8%	Oakland	39%	5%
Cleveland	29%	15%	Oklahoma City	39%	8%
Detroit	31%	8%	Portland	28%	5%
Honolulu	30%	9%	San Antonio	28%	6%
Louisville	41%	9%	Tulsa	24%	2%

Source: Department of Commerce, *Statistical Abstract of the United States, 1992* (Washington, DC: Government Printing Office, 1992).

term. Both he and Bush were only able to hold the line sufficiently to keep these outlays from increasing faster than the overall increase in the national budget. Note on Figure 3.1 that federal aid as a percentage of total federal outlays has been close to constant since 1984.

Thus, despite the inexorable march of national power, despite the rise of regulated federalism by mandates and by threats of withholding federal grants, and despite some virtual unitary government that eliminates the state/local role altogether, federalism remains a vital part of the American system of government. States and cities clamor (and lobby) for a larger share of the national budget, and state and local leaders have shown a willingness to cooperate with the national standards embodied in environmental protection laws and civil rights laws, but states continue to hold on jealously to the maximum freedom of action that is embodied in the historic concept of federalism.

THE SECOND PRINCIPLE: THE SEPARATION OF POWERS

James Madison is best qualified to speak to Americans of the separation of powers:

> There can be no liberty where the legislative and executive powers are united in the same person . . . [or] if the power of judging be not separated from the legislative and executive powers.[15]

Using this same reasoning, many of Madison's contemporaries argued that there was not *enough* separation among the three branches, and Madison had to do some backtracking to insist that the principle did not require complete separation:

> . . . unless these departments [branches] be so far connected and blended as to give each a constitutional control over the others, the degree of separation which the maxim requires, as essential to a free government, can never in practice be duly maintained.[16]

[15]Clinton Rossiter, ed., *The Federalist Papers* (New York: New American Library, 1961), No. 47, p. 302.

[16]Ibid., No. 48, p. 308.

This is the secret of how we have made the separation of powers effective: We made the principle self-enforcing by giving each branch of government the means to participate in, and partially or temporarily to obstruct, the workings of the other branches.

Checks and Balances

The means by which each branch of government interacts is known informally as "checks and balances." The best-known examples are: the presidential power of veto over legislation passed by Congress; the power of Congress to override the veto by a two-thirds majority vote, to impeach the president, and (of the Senate) to approve presidential appointments; the power of the president to appoint the members of the Supreme Court and the other federal judges with Senate approval; and the power of the Supreme Court to engage in judicial review (to be discussed below). The best-known examples are shown graphically in Table 3.5. The framers sought to guarantee that the three branches would in fact use the checks and balances as weapons against each other by giving each branch a different political constituency: direct, popular election of the members of the House; indirect election of senators (until the Seventeenth Amendment, adopted in 1913); indirect election of the president (which still exists, at least formally, today); and appointment of federal judges for life. All things considered, the best characterization of the separation of powers principle in action is, as we said in Chapter 2, "separated institutions sharing power."[17]

Legislative Supremacy

Although each branch was to be given adequate means to compete with the other branches, it is also clear that within the system of separated powers the framers provided for **legislative supremacy.** It may appear to be paradoxical or downright illogical to combine "co-equal branches" with legislative supremacy, but that is the case. And legislative supremacy made the provision of checks and balances in the other two branches all the more important.

The most important indication of the intention of legislative supremacy was made by the framers when they decided to place the provisions for national powers in Article I, the legislative article, and to treat the powers of the national government as powers of Congress. In a system based on the "rule of law," the power to make the laws is the supreme power. Section 8 provides in part that "*Congress* shall have Power . . . to lay and collect taxes . . . to borrow money . . . to regulate commerce . . ." [emphasis added]. The founders also provided for legislative supremacy in their decision to give Congress the sole power over appropriations and to give the House of Representatives the power to initiate all revenue bills.

[17]Neustadt, *Presidential Power,* p. 33.

TABLE 3.5
Checks and Balances

	Legislative branch can be checked by:	Executive branch can be checked by:	Judicial branch can be checked by:
Legislative branch can check:	NA	Can overrule veto (2/3 vote) Controls appropriations Controls by statute Impeachment of president Senate approval of appointments and treaties Committee oversight	Controls appropriations Can create inferior courts Can add new judges Senate approves appointments Impeachment of judges
Executive branch can check:	Can veto legislation Can convene special session Can adjourn Congress when chambers disagree Vice-president presides over Senate and votes to break ties	NA	President appoints judges
Judicial branch can check:	Judicial review of legislation Chief justice presides over Senate during proceedings to impeach president	Judicial review over presidential actions Power to issue warrants Chief justice presides over impeachment of president	NA

NA = Not applicable

Madison recognized legislative supremacy as part and parcel of the separation of powers:

> . . . It is not possible to give each department equal power of self defense. In republican government, the legislative authority necessarily predominates. The remedy for this inconvenience is to divide the legislature into different branches; and to render them, by different modes of election and different principles of action, as little connected with each other as the nature of their common functions and their common dependence on the society will admit.[18]

In other words, Congress was so likely to dominate the other branches that it would have to be divided against itself, into House and Senate. One could say that the Constitution provided for four branches, not three.

Legislative supremacy became a fact soon after the founding decade was over. National politics centered on Congress. Undistinguished presidents followed one another in a dreary succession. Even Madison—so brilliant as a constitutional theorist, so loyal as a constitutional record keeper, and so effective in the struggle for the founding—was a weak president. Jackson and Lincoln are the only two who stand out in the entire nineteenth century, and their successors dropped back out of sight; except for these two, the other presidents operated within the accepted framework of legislative supremacy (see Chapter 6).

The development of political parties, and in particular the emergence in 1832 of the national convention method of nominating presidential candidates (which replaced the congressional "King Caucus" method), saved the presidency from complete absorption into the orbit of legislative power by giving the presidency a base of power independent of Congress. But although this preserved the presidency and salvaged the separation of powers, it did so only in a negative sense. That is to say, presidents were more likely (after 1832 when the national conventions were established) to veto congressional enactments than before, or to engage in a military action, but they were not more likely to present programs for positive legislation or to attempt to lead Congress in the enactment of legislation.[19] This will underscore the significance of the shift to presidential supremacy when it came after 1937 (see also Chapter 6).

The role of the judicial branch in the separation of powers has depended upon the power of judicial review, a power not provided for in the Constitution but asserted by Chief Justice Marshall in 1803:

> If a law be in opposition to the Constitution; if both the law and the Constitution apply to a particular case, so that the Court must either decide that case conformable to the law, disregarding the Constitution, or conformable to the Constitution, disregarding the law; the Court must determine which of these conflicting rules governs the case: This is of the very essence of judicial duty.[20]

---

[18]*The Federalist,* No. 51, p. 322.

[19]For a good review of the uses of the veto, see Raymond Tatalovich and Byron Daynes, *Presidential Power in the United States* (Monterey, CA: Brooks/Cole, 1984), pp. 148–51; and Robert Spitzer, *The Presidential Veto: Touchstone of the American Presidency* (Albany: SUNY Press, 1988).

[20]Marbury v. Madison, 1 Cranch 137 (1803).

The Supreme Court has exercised the power of judicial review with caution, as
though to protect its power by using it sparingly. Indeed, the Court has developed at least three rules to minimize the use of judicial review: (1) Avoid constitutional questions unless it is absolutely necessary in deciding a case. (2) Do not deal with constitutional issues if there are other grounds upon which a case may be decided. (3) Even where an act of Congress raises severe questions of constitutionality, first attempt an interpretation of the statute that might avoid the constitutional question. Through these and other escapes, the Supreme Court has kept its confrontations with the president and Congress minimal and manageable. The reputation of the Supreme Court for activism is based almost entirely upon the frequency of judicial review of *state* actions.

Review of the constitutionality of acts of the president or Congress is in fact very rare.[21] In the fifty years since the rise of big government and strong presidents, no important congressional enactment has been invalidated on constitutional grounds.[22] During the same time, there have been only two important judicial confrontations with the president. One was the so-called *Steel Seizure* case of 1952. The second case was *U.S.* v. *Nixon* in 1974, where the Court declared unconstitutional President Nixon's refusal to respond to a subpoena to make available the infamous White House tapes as evidence in a criminal prosecution. The Court argued that although executive privilege did protect the confidentiality of communications to and from the president, this did not extend to data in presidential files or tapes bearing upon criminal prosecutions.[23]

[21]In response to New Deal legislation, the Supreme Court struck down eight out of ten New Deal statutes. For example, in Panama Refining Co. v. Ryan, 293 U.S. 388 (1935), the Court ruled against a section of the National Industrial Recovery Act, as being an invalid delegation of legislative power to the executive branch. And in Schechter Poultry Co. v. U.S., 295 U.S. 495 (1935), the Court found the National Industrial Recovery Act itself to be invalid for the same reason. But since 1935, the Supreme Court rarely confronts the president or Congress on constitutional questions.

[22]Compare with Lawrence Tribe, *American Constitutional Law* (Mineola, NY: Foundation Press, 1978), p. 234. Since 1937, only two cases of any significance whatsoever can be identified where the Court actually invalidated an act of Congress on constitutional grounds. The first of these was INS v. Chada, 462 U.S. 919 (1983); the Supreme Court declared unconstitutional the so-called legislative veto, whereby Congress had required certain regulatory agencies to submit proposed regulations to Congress for approval prior to implementation. The regulation would assume the force of law if Congress failed to pass a resolution vetoing the proposed regulation within a set period of time, thirty or sixty days. The second case, Bowsher v. Synar, 92 L. Ed. 583 (1986), struck down the Gramm-Rudman Act mandating a balanced federal budget. Only one part of the act was declared unconstitutional, the part delegating to the comptroller general the power to direct the president to reduce the budget by a specified amount if the budget deficit provided by Congress exceeded a certain set amount. The Court argued that since the comptroller general could be removed only by Congress, it was unconstitutional for Congress to give the comptroller general "executive" powers. It is thus interesting and probably quite significant that the only two cases where congressional enactments were declared unconstitutional by the Supreme Court were cases where the Court was actually defending the principle of the separation of powers. In a third case, National League of Cities v. Usery, 426 U.S. 833 (1976), the Court invalidated a congressional act applying wage and hour regulations to state and local governments. Even the Court conceded it was not a fundamental issue and then proceeded to reverse itself nine years later in Garcia v. San Antonio Metropolitan Transit Authority, 469 U.S. 528 (1985). Further discussion of these cases will be found in Chapter 6, because they have had a significant influence on Congress's powers today in the epoch of presidential supremacy.

[23]The official name of the *Steel Seizure* case is Youngstown Sheet & Tube Co. v. Sawyer, 343 U.S. 579 (1952). U.S. v. Nixon, 418 U.S. 683 (1974). For more on the relation of "executive privilege" to the separation of powers, see Raoul Berger, *Executive Privilege: A Constitutional Myth* (Cambridge, MA: Harvard University Press, 1974).

All in all, the separation of powers has had an uneven history. Although "presidential government" seemed to supplant legislative supremacy after 1937, the relative power position of the three branches has not been static. The degree of conflict between the president and Congress has varied with the rise and fall of political parties—being especially intense when one party controls the White House and another controls the Congress, as has been the case almost solidly since 1969.

Since Watergate, Congress has tried to get back some of the power it had delegated to the president (see Chapter 6). One of the methods it seized upon was the Ethics in Government Act of 1978, which established a "special prosecutor" (later called "independent counsel") with the authority to investigate allegations of wrongdoing by executive branch officials. The statute provides for a special panel of federal judges to appoint an independent counsel. To guard against any conflict of interest on the part of the attorney general, the act also provided that the independent counsel could be removed by the attorney general only for causes specified in the statute. In 1988 the Court of Appeals declared the act unconstitutional on the grounds that it violated the separation of powers, because it gave some law enforcement powers to an officer not appointed by the president. Had it been upheld by the Supreme Court, the investigations of many of the key figures in the Iran-Contra affair would have been terminated. A reversal might well have been expected, because seven of the nine justices were Republican appointees, and Rehnquist had received his promotion from justice to chief justice from Ronald Reagan. Thus it was surprising to many when an extraordinary majority of seven to one rejected the Justice Department's argument that the executive should control all administrative matters. The Court reversed the Court of Appeals decision and restored to Congress the power to provide as it wishes for the investigation of the executive branch.[24]

Some will argue that the lower court was correct in its argument that Congress was violating the separation of powers by infringing on executive hierarchy and administrative responsibility to the president. Others could argue that the Supreme Court decision was the one that strengthened the separation of powers, by restoring to Congress a weapon for use in its competition with presidential power. Either way, the very effort of Congress to provide by law for competition with the executive branch suggests that the separation of powers is still very much alive. And the judiciary is very much a part of the continuing vitality of the separation of powers. Although they rarely question the constitutionality of a statute, the federal courts are constantly involved in judicial review of statutes and administrative orders because agencies have to get court orders to enforce their decisions. This gives the judiciary a regular opportunity to influence executive as well as legislative actions (see Table 3.5 on page 81). In other words, in order to apply a statute, the court has to first interpret it; and to interpret a statute is to have the power to change it. (See also Chapter 8.) This offers more evidence of the continuing vitality of the separation of powers.

---

[24]*Morrison v. Olson*, 108 S. Ct. 2597 (1988). For a lively account of this case and the issues involved in it, see David G. Savage, *Turning Right—The Making of the Rehnquist Supreme Court* (New York: Wiley, 1992), pp. 194–203. See also Louis Fisher, *American Constitutional Law* (New York: McGraw-Hill, 1990), p. 225 and pp. 263–71.

CHANGING THE FRAMEWORK: CONSTITUTIONAL AMENDMENT

The Constitution has endured for two centuries as the framework of government. But is has not endured without change. Without change, the Constitution might have become merely a sacred text, stored under glass.

Amendments: Many Are Called, Few Are Chosen

The need for change was recognized by the framers of the Constitution, and the provisions for amendment incorporated into Article V were thought to be "an easy, regular and Constitutional way" to make changes, which would occasionally be necessary because members of Congress "may abuse their power and refuse their consent on the very account . . . to admit to amendments to correct the source of the abuse."[25] Madison made a more balanced defense of the amendment procedure in Article V: "It guards equally against that extreme facility, which would render the Constitution too mutable; and that extreme difficulty, which might perpetuate its discovered faults."[26]

Experience since 1789 raises questions even about Madison's more modest claims. The Constitution has proven to be extremely difficult to amend. In the history of efforts to amend the Constitution, the most appropriate characterization is "many are called, few are chosen." Between 1789 and 1993, 9,746 amendments were formally offered in Congress. Of these, Congress officially proposed only 29, and 27 of these were eventually ratified by the states. But the record is even more severe than that. Since 1791, when the first 10 amendments, the Bill of Rights, were added, only 17 amendments have been adopted. And 2 of them—Prohibition (Eighteenth) and its repealer (Twenty-first)—cancel each other out, so that for all practical purposes, only 15 amendments have been added to the Constitution since 1791. Despite the vast changes in American society and its economy, only 12 amendments have been adopted since the Civil War amendments in 1868.

One amendment is noteworthy for its history alone. On May 7, 1992, Michigan and New Jersey became the thirty-eighth and thirty-ninth states to ratify the Twenty-seventh Amendment, which bans pay raises for Congress "until an election of Representatives shall have intervened." The first state to ratify it was Maryland, on December 19, 1789. It had been proposed by James Madison as one of the twelve original amendments, of which ten were immediately ratified to become the Bill of Rights. Only six states ratified this amendment at that time, but since there was no provision for a deadline, the Madison amendment did not die. The proposed amendment was revived in 1978 by Wyoming's ratification, and then a trickle of other states followed in the mid-1980s. Once the thirty-eighth state came in, the U.S. archivist had no choice but to certify the amendment and

---

[25]Observation by Colonel George Mason, delegate from Virginia, early during the convention period, quoted in Max Farrand, *The Records of the Federal Convention of 1787,* vol. 1, rev. ed. (New Haven, CT: Yale University Press, 1966), pp. 202–3.

[26]*The Federalist,* No. 43, p. 278.

PROCESS BOX 3.2

How the Constitution Is Amended: Four Possible Routes

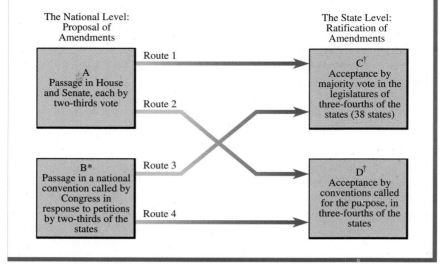

*This method of proposal has never been employed. Thus amendment routes 3 and 4 have never been attempted.

†In each amendment proposal, Congress has the power to choose the method of ratification, the time limit for consideration by the states, and other conditions of ratification.

to publish it in the *Federal Register,* making it official. Speaker of the House Tom Foley begrudgingly accepted it: "I think as a practical matter, it will be considered a part of the Constitution."[27]

As Process Box 3.2 illustrates, four methods of amendment are provided for in Article V:

1. Passage in House and Senate by two-thirds vote; then ratification by majority vote of the legislature of three-fourths (thirty-eight) of the states.
2. Passage in House and Senate by two-thirds vote; then ratification by conventions called for the purpose in three-fourths of the states.
3. Passage in a national convention called by Congress in response to petitions by two-thirds of the states; ratification by majority vote of the legislatures of three-fourths of the states.
4. Passage in a national convention, as in (3); then ratification by conventions called for the purpose in three-fourths of the states.

Since no amendment has ever been proposed by national convention, however, methods (3) and (4) have never been employed. And method (2) has only been employed once (the Twenty-first Amendment, which repealed the Eighteenth, or Prohibition, Amendment). Thus, method (1) has been used for all the others. An

[27]"Madison's 1789 Pay Raise Amendment Is Approved," *Congressional Quarterly Guide to Current American Government* (Washington, DC: Congressional Quarterly, 1992), pp. 2–3. Thanks also to Peter Belej of Rochester Institute of Technology.

effort was made in 1978–79 to use method (3) or (4) by getting two-thirds of the states to petition for a national convention in order to propose an amendment requiring a balanced federal budget. This effort caused a good deal of controversy and alarm. Some critics opposed the amendment itself. Many others, however, were opposed for a much more interesting reason: If such a convention were called, it would not necessarily be required to hold itself to consideration of the specific matters for which it was convened. It might be able to consider any and all sorts of amendments. A "runaway" convention could end up being like the one held in Philadelphia in 1789 and could, like that one, change our entire system of government.

Now we should be better able to explain why it has been so difficult to amend the Constitution. The main reason is the requirement of a two-thirds vote in the House and the Senate, which means that any proposal for an amendment in Congress can be killed by only 34 senators *or* 136 members of the House. What is more, if the necessary two-thirds vote is obtained, the amendment can still be killed by the refusal or inability of only thirteen state legislatures to ratify it. Since each state has an equal vote regardless of its population, the thirteen hold-out states may represent a very small fraction of the total American population.

The Case of the Equal Rights Amendment

The Equal Rights Amendment (ERA) is a case study of a proposed amendment that almost succeeded. In fact, ERA is one of the very few proposals that got the necessary two-thirds vote in Congress and then failed to obtain the ratification of the requisite thirty-eight states.

On October 12, 1971, the U.S. House of Representatives approved the Equal Rights Amendment by the required two-thirds majority; the Senate followed suit on March 22, 1972. The amendment was very simple:

Sec. 1. Equality of rights under the law shall not be denied or abridged by the United States or by any State on account of sex.
Sec. 2. The Congress shall have the power to enforce, by appropriate legislation, the provisions of this article.
Sec. 3. This amendment shall take effect two years after the date of ratification.

The congressional resolution provided for the accustomed method of ratification through the state legislatures rather than by state conventions—method (1) rather than method (2) on Process Box 3.2—and that it had to be completed within seven years, by March 22, 1979.

Since ERA had received the necessary two-thirds vote in Congress, it did not require the president's signature and was therefore forwarded directly to each state legislature. If thirty-eight states had ratified the amendment, it would have become the Twenty-seventh Amendment to the Constitution of the United States.

Since the amendment was the culmination of nearly a half-century of efforts, and since the women's movement had spread and intensified its struggle for several years prior to 1971, the amendment was ratified by twenty-eight state legislatures during the very first year. But opposition forces quickly organized into the "Stop ERA" movement. By the end of 1974, five more states had ratified the amend-

Phyllis Schlafly and Gloria Steinem
The Battle over Equal Rights

Phyllis Schlafly and Gloria Steinem have carved out leadership roles on opposing sides of many issues that have dominated the American political scene in recent decades, including abortion, family values, sexuality, and equal rights. The fight to ratify the Equal Rights Amendment was among their most public struggles.

Phyllis Schlafly has long been active in Republican and conservative politics, even running for Congress herself three times (unsuccessfully). She attracted national attention for defending the presidential candidacy of Barry Goldwater in 1964 in a book called *A Choice Not an Echo.* Schlafly is best known, however, for her opposition to the proposed Equal Rights Amendment (ERA).

As head of the Eagle Forum and Stop-ERA, she has argued that efforts such as the ERA are not only unnecessary but even harmful to women. Women are "extremely well treated," she has asserted. "The women's liberationist is imprisoned by her own negative view of herself and of her place in the world around her." Schlafly's alternative is "the Positive Woman," who "rejoices in the creative capability within her body and . . . understands that men and women are different, and that those very differences provide the key to her success as a person and fulfillment as a woman."

As a prominent conservative Republican, Schlafly has exerted pressure within the party to maintain traditional values. In 1992, for example, she successfully fought for wording in the Republican party platform that called for a ban on all abortions, even including instances in which the woman's life is in danger.

Gloria Steinem, credited with being one of the founders of the modern women's movement, is the granddaughter of a pioneering feminist. After graduating *magna cum laude* from Smith College, she became a journalist and helped found the National

Phyllis Schlafly

ment, but three states that had ratified it in 1973—Idaho, Nebraska, and Tennessee—had afterwards voted to rescind their ratification. This posed an unprecedented problem, whether a state legislature had the right to rescind its approval. The Supreme Court steadfastly refused to deal with this question, insisting that it was a "political question" to be settled by Congress. If ERA had been ratified by the thirty-eight state minimum, Congress would have had to decide whether to respect the rescissions or to count them as ratifications.

This point was rendered moot by events. By the end of 1978, thirty-five state legislatures had ratified ERA—counting the three rescinding legislatures as rati-

Organization for Women (NOW) and *Ms.* magazine. Steinem believes that women's contributions to society have been undervalued; that popular images of women perpetuate stereotypes harmful to women; and that historical patterns of sexism and discrimination against women require remedies such as the ERA and legislation to protect a woman's rights.

The text of the ERA says that "equality of rights under the law shall not be denied or abridged by the United States or by any state on account of sex." The initial efforts of Steinem and her allies to get the amendment ratified were very successful. ERA easily passed Congress in 1972 and was quickly ratified by twenty-eight states, thanks to coordinated state-by-state campaigns designed to sway state legislatures. But Schlafly (sometimes labeled "the Gloria Steinem of the Right") and her allies mounted a comparable state-by-state counterattack, and although the ratification deadline was extended to 1982, it fell three states short of the necessary thirty-eight for ratification. Charges from Schlafly and others that the ERA would require the drafting of women into military service and legitimize homosexual marriages had helped defeat it.

Despite periodic calls to revive the ERA, most proponents consider it a dead issue for the immediate future. Instead, Steinem and her allies have increased pressure on state governments, the national government, and the courts to realize ERA-type protections. For example, congressional passage of a family leave bill, and the Clinton administration's decision to allow women to fly military combat missions, both enacted in 1993, represented important changes consistent with the goals of ERA.

Gloria Steinem

Sources: Phyllis Schlafly, *The Power of the Positive Woman* (New Rochelle, NY: Arlington House, 1977); Gloria Steinem, *Outrageous Acts and Everyday Rebellions* (New York: Signet, 1986).

fiers. But even counting them, the three additional state ratifications necessary to reach thirty-eight became increasingly difficult to get. Among the remaining fifteen states, the amendment had already been rejected at least once. The only hope of the ERA forces was that the 1978 elections would change the composition of some of those state legislatures. Pinning their hopes on that, the ERA forces turned back to Congress and succeeded in getting an extension of the ratification deadline to June 30, 1982. This was an especially significant victory, because it was the first time Congress had extended the time limit since it began placing time restrictions on ratification in 1917. But this victory in Washington failed to impress any of the fifteen hold-out legislatures. June 30, 1982, came and went, and the ERA was, for the time being at least, laid to rest. It was beaten by the efforts of the "Stop ERA" group and by the emergence of conservatism generally, which had culminated in Ronald Reagan's election as president.[28]

If the ERA was a defeat for liberal forces, conservatives have done no better. Constitutional amendments were high on the agenda of the Republican party from the beginning of their presidential victories in the 1980s, and had the blessings of Presidents Reagan and Bush. The School Prayer Amendment sought to restore power to the states to require selected religious observances, thereby reversing a whole series of earlier Supreme Court decisions.[29] The Pro-Life Amendment sought to reverse *Roe* v. *Wade* in order to restore to the states the power to outlaw abortions. Two other efforts of less social but of great economic significance were the amendment proposed to require a balanced budget and the amendment proposed to give the president the "line-item veto" power. A more recent proposal was for an amendment to protect the flag, to outlaw flag burning or other flag desecration. President Bush had supported such a law in the 1988 election campaign and went on to become the leading supporter of the constitutional amendment for the same purpose. None of these efforts got very close to being adopted by Congress for submission to the states for ratification. No genuinely serious effort was made by the Left or by the Right between 1989 and 1993 to amend the Constitution.

Which Were Chosen? An Analysis of the Twenty-seven

There is, however, more to the amending difficulties than the politics of campaigning and voting. It would appear that only a limited number of changes needed by society can actually be made through the Constitution. Although we shall see that the ERA fit the pattern of successful amendments, most efforts to amend the Constitution failed because they were simply attempts to use the Constitution as an alternative to legislation for dealing directly with a public problem. A review of the successful amendments will provide two insights: First, it will give us some understanding of the conditions underlying successful amendments; and second, it will reveal a great deal about what constitutionalism means.

The purpose of the ten amendments in the Bill of Rights was basically structural, *to give each of the three branches clearer and more restricted boundaries* (see Table 3.6). The First Amendment clarified the jurisdiction of Congress. Although the powers of Congress under Article I, Section 8, would not have justified laws regulating religion, speech, and the like, the First Amendment made this

---

[28]Marcia Lee, "The Equal Rights Amendment—Public Policy by Means of a Constitutional Amendment," in *The Politics of Policy-Making in America,* ed. David Caputo (San Francisco: W.H. Freeman, 1977); Jane Mansbridge, *Why We Lost the ERA* (Chicago: University of Chicago Press, 1986); and Donald Mathews and Jane Sherron DeHart, *Sex, Gender, and the Politics of the ERA* (New York: Oxford University Press, 1990).

[29]For judicial action see Engel v. Vitale, 370 U.S. 421 (1926). For the efforts of states to get around the Supreme Court requirement that public schools be secular, see John A. Murley, "School Prayer: Free Exercise of Religion or Establishment of Religion?" in *Social Regulatory Policy,* ed. Raymond Tatalovich and Byron Daynes (Boulder, CO: Westview Press, 1988), pp. 5–40.

TABLE 3.6
The Bill of Rights: Analysis of Its Provisions

Amendment	Purpose
I	*Limits on Congress:* Congress is not to make any law establishing a religion or abridging speech, press, assembly, or petition freedoms.
II, III, IV	*Limits on Executive:* The executive branch is not to infringe on the right of people to keep arms (II), is not to arbitrarily take houses for a militia (III), and is not to engage in the search or seizure of evidence without a court warrant swearing to belief in the probable existence of a crime (IV).
V, VI, VII, VIII	*Limits on Courts:* The courts are not to hold trials for serious offenses without provision for a grand jury (V), a petit (trial) jury (VII), a speedy trial (VI), presentation of charges, confrontation of hostile witnesses (VI), immunity from testimony against oneself (VI), and immunity from trial more than once for the same offense (V). Neither bail nor punishment can be excessive (VIII), and no property can be taken without just compensation (V).
IX, X	*Limits on National Government:* All rights not enumerated are reserved to the states or the people.

limitation explicit: "Congress shall make no law . . ." The Second, Third, and Fourth Amendments similarly spelled out limits on the executive branch, a necessity given the abuses of executive power Americans had endured under British rule.

The Fifth, Sixth, Seventh, and Eighth Amendments contain some of the most important safeguards for individual citizens against the arbitrary exercise of government power. And these amendments sought to accomplish their goal by defining the judicial branch more concretely and clearly than had been done in Article III of the Constitution.

Five of the seventeen amendments adopted since 1791 are directly concerned with expansion of the electorate (see Table 3.7). Occasional efforts to expand the

TABLE 3.7
Amending the Constitution to Expand the Electorate

Amendment	Purpose	Year Proposed	Year Adopted
XV	Extended voting rights to all races	1869	1870
XIX	Extended voting rights to women	1919	1920
XXIII	Extended voting rights to residents of the District of Columbia	1960	1961
XXIV	Extended voting rights to all classes by abolition of poll taxes	1962	1964
XXVI	Extended voting rights to citizens aged 18 and over	1971	1971*

*The Twenty-sixth Amendment holds the record for speed of adoption. It was proposed on April 23, 1971, and adopted on July 5, 1971. The only other other adoption time that comes close is the Prohibition repealer (XXI), proposed February 20, 1933, and adopted December 5, 1933.

electorate were made necessary by the fact that the founders were unable to establish a national electorate with uniform voting qualifications. Stalemated on that issue, the delegates decided to evade it by providing in the final draft of Article I, Section 2, that eligibility to vote in a national election would be the same as "the Qualification requisite for Elector of the most numerous branch of the state Legislature." Article I, Section 4, added that Congress could alter state regulations as to the "Times, Places, and Manner of holding Elections for Senators and Representatives," but this meant that any important *expansion* of the American electorate, would almost certainly require a constitutional amendment.

Six more are also electoral in nature, although not concerned directly with voting rights and the expansion of the electorate. These six amendments are concerned with the elective offices themselves or with the relationship between elective offices and the electorate (see Table 3.8).

Another five have sought to expand or to delimit the powers of the national and state governments (see Table 3.9).[30] The Eleventh Amendment protected the states from suits by private individuals and took away from the federal courts any power to take suits by private individuals of one state (or a foreign country) against another state. The other three amendments in Table 3.9 are obviously designed to reduce state power (Thirteenth), to reduce state power and expand national power (Fourteenth), and to expand national power (Sixteenth). The Twenty-seventh put a moderate limit on Congress's ability to raise its own salary.

The one missing amendment underscores the meaning of the rest: the Eigh-

TABLE 3.8
Amending the Constitution to Change the Relationship between Elected Offices and the Electorate

Amendment	Purpose	Year Proposed	Year Adopted
XII	Separate ballot for vice-president in the electoral college	1803	1804
XIV	(Part 1) Provided a national definition of citizenship*	1866	1868
XVII	Provided direct election of senators	1912	1913
XX	Eliminated "lame duck" session of Congress	1932	1933
XXII	Limited presidential term	1947	1951
XXV	Provided presidential succession in case of disability	1965	1967

*In defining *citizenship*, the Fourteenth Amendment actually provided the constitutional basis for expanding the electorate to include all races, women, and residents of the District of Columbia. Only the "eighteen-year-olds' amendment" should have been necessary, since it changed the definition of citizenship. The fact that additional amendments were required following the Fourteenth suggests that voting is not considered an inherent right of U.S. citizenship. Instead it is viewed as a privilege.

[30]The Fourteenth Amendment is included in this table as well as in Table 3.8 because it seeks not only to define citizenship but *seems* to intend also that this definition of citizenship included, along with the right to vote, all the rights of the Bill of Rights, regardless of the state in which the citizen resided. A great deal more will be said about this in the next chapter.

TABLE 3.9

93
CHANGING THE
FRAMEWORK

**Amending the Constitution to Expand or Limit the
Power of Government**

Amendment	Purpose	Year Proposed	Year Adopted
XI	Limited jurisdiction of federal courts over suits involving the states	1794	1798
XIII	Eliminated slavery and eliminated the right of states to allow property in persons	1865*	1865
XIV	(Part 2) Applied due process of Bill of Rights to the states	1866	1868
XVI	Established national power to tax incomes	1909	1913
XXVII	Limited Congress's power to raise its own salary	1789	1992

*The Thirteenth Amendment was proposed January 31, 1865, and adopted less than a year later, on December 18, 1865.

teenth, or Prohibition, Amendment. This is the only instance in which the country tried to *legislate* by constitutional amendment. In other words, it is the only amendment that was designed to deal directly with some substantive social problem. And it was the only amendment ever to have been repealed. Two other amendments—the Thirteenth, which abolished slavery, and the Sixteenth, which established the power to levy an income tax—can be said to have had the effect of legislation. But the purpose of the Thirteenth was to restrict the power of the states by forever forbidding them to treat any human being as property. As for the Sixteenth, it is certainly true that income tax legislation followed immediately; nevertheless, the amendment concerns itself strictly with establishing the power of Congress to enact such legislation. The legislation came later; and if down the line a majority in Congress had wanted to abolish the income tax, they could also have done this by legislation rather than through the arduous path of a constitutional amendment repealing the income tax.

All of this points to the principle underlying the twenty-five existing amendments: all are concerned with the structure or composition of government. This is consistent with the dictionary, which defines *constitution* as the make-up or composition of a thing, anything. And it is consistent with the concept of a constitution as "higher law," because the whole point and purpose of a higher law is to establish *a framework within which government and the process of making ordinary law can take place.* Even those who would have preferred more changes in the Constitution would have to agree that there is great wisdom in this principle. A constitution ought to enable legislation and public policies to take place, but it should not attempt to determine what that legislation or those public policies ought to be.

For those whose hopes for change center on the Constitution, it must be emphasized that the amendment route to social change is, and always will be, extremely limited. Through a constitution it is possible to establish a working

Is the Separation of Powers Obsolete?

*T*he separation of governmental powers among three branches of government is a
cornerstone of the political system constructed by the Constitution's framers in
1787. In recent years, however, the separation of powers has come under increasing attack by many who feel that this political arrangement is a root cause of many of the difficulties of modern governing. Political gridlock, governmental paralysis, and a seeming
inability of government to create a coherent policy are all problems seen as resulting from
the separation of powers.

*In 1987, a distinguished group of academics and former government officials issued a
report calling for extensive changes in a system they believe is no longer suited to resolving pressing American problems. The historian Arthur M. Schlesinger, Jr., among others, argues that the virtues of the separation of powers continue to outweigh its
drawbacks.*

Committee on the Constitutional System

The separation of powers, as a principle of constitutional structure, has served
us well in preventing tyranny and the abuse of high office, but it has done so
by encouraging confrontation, indecision and deadlock, and by diffusing accountability for the results. . . . Because the separation of powers encourages
conflict between the branches and because the [political] parties are weak, the
capacity of the federal government to fashion, enact and administer coherent
public policy has diminished and the ability of elected officials to avoid accountability for governmental failures has grown. More specifically, the problems include: Brief Honeymoons. Only the first few months of each four-year
presidential term provide an opportunity for decisive action on domestic
problems. . , . Divided Government. We have had divided government (one
party winning the White House and the other a majority in one or both
houses of Congress). . . . Lack of Party Cohesion in Congress. Even in times
of united government, disunity persists between the branches. . . . Loss of Accountability. Divided government and party disunity also lead to diffused accountability. . . . Lack of a Mechanism for Replacing Failed or Deadlocked
Government. Presently there is no way between our fixed election dates to resolve basic disagreements between the President and Congress by referring
them to the electorate.[1]

Schlesinger

Is the difficulty we encounter these days in meeting our problems really the
consequence of defects in the structure of our government? After all, we have
had the separation of powers from the beginning of the republic. This has not
prevented competent presidents from acting with decision and dispatch. The
separation of powers did not notably disable Jefferson or Jackson or Lincoln or
Wilson or the Roosevelts. . . . Why are things presumed to be so much worse
today?

It cannot be that . . . we face tougher problems than our forefathers.
Tougher problems than slavery? the Civil War? the Great Depression? World
War II? . . .

The real difference is that the presidents who operated the system successfully *knew what they thought should be done*—and were able to persuade Congress and the nation to give the remedies a try. . . . Our problem is not at all that we know what to do and are impeded from doing it by some structural logjam in the system. Our problem—let us face it—is that we do not know what to do. . . .

If we don't know what ought to be done, efficient enactment of a poor program is a dubious accomplishment. . . . What is the great advantage of acting with decision and dispatch when you don't know what you are doing? . . .

When the country is not sure what ought to be done, it may be that delay, debate and further consideration are not a bad idea. . . .

I believe that in the main our Constitution has worked pretty well. It has ensured discussion when we have lacked consensus and has permitted action when a majority can be convinced that the action is right. . . .

My concern is that this agitation about constitutional reform is a form of escapism. Constitution-tinkering is a flight from the hard question, which is the search for remedy.[2]

[1]Committee on the Constitutional System, *A Bicentennial Analysis of the American Political Structure: Report and Recommendations of the Committee on the Constitutional System,* (January, 1987), pp. 3–7.
[2]Arthur M. Schlesinger, Jr., "Leave the Constitution Alone," in *Reforming American Government: The Bicentennial Papers of the Committee on the Constitutional System,* ed. Donald L. Robinson (Boulder, CO: Westview Press, 1985), pp. 53–54.

structure of government; and through a constitution it is possible to establish basic rights of citizens by placing limitations and obligations on the powers of that government. Once these things have been accomplished, the real problem is how to extend rights to those people who do not already enjoy them. Of course, the Constitution cannot enforce itself. But it can and does have a real influence on everyday life because a right or an obligation set forth in the Constitution can become a *cause of action* in the hands of an otherwise powerless person.

Private property is an excellent example. Property is one of the most fundamental and well-established rights in the United States; but it is well established not because it is recognized in so many words in the Constitution, but because legislatures and courts have made it a crime for anyone, including the government, to trespass or to take away property without compensation.

A constitution is good if it produces the *cause of action* that leads to good legislation, good case law, appropriate police behavior. A constitution cannot eliminate power. But its principles can be a citizen's dependable defense against the abuse of power.

SUMMARY

In this chapter we have had two objectives. The first was to trace out the development of two of the three basic principles of the U.S. Constitution—federalism and the separation of powers. Federalism involves a division between two layers of government, national and state. The separation of powers involves the division of the national government into three branches. These principles are limitations on the powers of government; Americans made these compromises as a condition of giving their consent to be governed. And these principles became the framework within which the government operates. The persistence of local government and of reliance of the national government on grants-in-aid to coerce local governments into following national goals was used as a case study to demonstrate the continuing vitality of the federal framework. Examples were also given of the intense competition between the president, Congress and the courts to dramatize the continuing vitality of the separation of powers.

The second goal was to gain an appreciation of constitutionalism itself. In addition to describing how the Constitution is formally amended, we analyzed the twenty-seven amendments in order to determine what they had in common, contrasting them with the hundreds of amendments that were offered but never adopted. We found that with the exception of the two Prohibition Amendments, the amendments were oriented toward some change in the framework or structure of government. The Prohibition Amendment was the only adopted amendment that sought to legislate by constitutional means.

Our conclusion was that the purpose of a constitution is to organize the makeup or the composition of the government, the *framework within which* government and politics, including actual legislation, can take place. A country does not require federalism and the separation of powers to have a real constitutional government. And the country does not have to approach individual rights in the same manner as the American Constitution. But to be a true constitutional government, a government must have some kind of framework, which consists of a few principles that cannot be manipulated by people in power merely for their own convenience. This is the essence of constitutionalism—principles that are above the reach of everyday legislatures, executives, bureaucrats, and politicians, yet that are not so far above their reach that they cannot under some conditions be adapted to changing conditions.

FOR FURTHER READING

Anton, Thomas. *American Federalism and Public Policy*. Philadelphia: Temple University Press, 1989.

Bensel, Richard. *Sectionalism and American Political Development: 1880–1980*. Madison: University of Wisconsin Press, 1984.

Berger, Raoul. *Executive Privilege: A Constitutional Myth*. Cambridge, MA: Harvard University Press, 1974.

Bowman, Ann O'M., and Richard Kearny. *The Resurgence of the States.* Englewood Cliffs, NJ: Prentice-Hall, 1986.

Crovitz, L. Gordon, and Jeremy Rabkin, eds. *The Fettered Presidency: Legal Constraints on the Executive Branch.* Washington, DC: American Enterprise Institute, 1989.

Dye, Thomas R. *American Federalism: Competition Among Governments.* Lexington, MA: Lexington Books, 1990.

Elazar, Daniel. *American Federalism: A View from the States.* New York: Harper & Row, 1984.

Ginsberg, Benjamin, and Martin Shefter. *Politics by Other Means: Institutional Conflict and the Declining Significance of Elections in America.* New York: Basic Books, 1990.

Grodzins, Morton. *The American System.* Chicago: Rand McNally, 1974.

Kelley, E. Wood. *Policy and Politics in the United States: The Limits of Localism.* Philadelphia: Temple University Press, 1987.

Kettl, Donald. *The Regulation of American Federalism.* Baltimore: Johns Hopkins University Press, 1987.

Palley, Marian Lief, and Howard Palley. *Urban America and Public Policies.* Lexington, MA: D. C. Heath, 1981.

Peterson, Paul, Barry Rabe, and Kenneth K. Wong. *When Federalism Works.* Washington, DC: Brookings Institution, 1986.

Robinson, Donald L. *To the Best of My Ability.* New York: W. W. Norton, 1986.

Wright, Deil S. *Understanding Intergovernmental Relations.* Monterey, CA: Brooks/Cole, 1982.

4

The Constitutional Framework and the Individual: Civil Liberties and Civil Rights

EVENTS		INSTITUTIONAL DEVELOPMENTS
Bill of Rights sent to states for ratification (1789)		States ratify U.S. Bill of Rights (1791)
Undeclared naval war with France (1798–1800); passage of Alien and Sedition Acts (1798)	**1800**	Alien and Sedition Acts limiting free speech, press, and aliens, disregarded and not renewed (1801)
Maine admitted to Union as free state (1820); Missouri admitted as slave state (1821)		Missouri Compromise regulates expansion of slavery into territories (1820)
		Barron v. *Baltimore* confirms dual citizenship (1833)
Slaves taken into territories (1800s)		*Dred Scott* v. *Sandford* invalidates Missouri Compromise; perpetuates slavery (1857)
Civil War (1861–1865)	**1860**	Emancipation Proclamation (1863); Thirteenth Amendment prohibits slavery in the U.S. (1865)
Southern blacks now vote but Black Codes in South impose special restraints (1865)		Civil Rights Act (1866)
Reconstruction (1867–1877)		Fourteenth Amendment ratified (1868)
"Jim Crow" laws spread throughout the South (1890s)		*Plessy* v. *Ferguson* upholds doctrine of "separate but equal" (1896)
World War I (1914–1918)		
Postwar pacifist and anarchist agitation and suppression (1920s and 1930s)	**1920**	*Gitlow* v. *N.Y.* (1925) and *Near* v. *Minnesota* (1931) apply First Amendment to states
U.S. enters World War II (1941–1945)		
Civil Rights Movement, e.g., Montgomery bus boycott (1955); lunch counter sit-ins (1960); freedom riders (1961)	**1950**	*Brown* v. *Board of Education* overturns *Plessy,* invalidates segregation (1954); federal use of troops to enforce court order to integrate schools (1957)

TIME LINE ON CIVIL LIBERTIES AND CIVIL RIGHTS

EVENTS		INSTITUTIONAL DEVELOPMENTS
March on Washington, largest civil rights demonstration in American history (1963)		Civil Rights Act outlaws segregation (1964)
		Katzenbach v. *McClung* upholds use of commerce clause to bar segregation (1964)
Spread of movement politics—students, women, environment, right to life (1970s)	**1970**	*Roe* v. *Wade* prohibits states from outlawing abortion (1973)
Affirmative action plans enacted in universities and corporations (1970s and 1980s)		Court orders to end malapportionment and segregation (1970s and 1980s)
		Georgia law upheld in *Bowers* v. *Hardwick* allowing states to regulate homosexual activity (1986)
Challenges to affirmative action plans continue (1980s–1990s)		Court accepts affirmative action on a limited basis—*Regents of Univ. of Calif.* v. *Bakke* (1978), *Wards Cove* v. *Atonio* (1989), *Martin* v. *Wilks* (1989)
States adopt restrictive abortion laws (1990–91)	**1990**	Missouri law restricting abortion upheld in *Webster* v. *Reproductive Health Services* (1989)
Bush signs civil rights bill favoring suits against employment discrimination (1991)		Court permits school boards to terminate busing (1991)
Roe v. *Wade* upheld; prisoner rights expanded (1992)		Clinton positions on abortion and gay rights revives civil rights activity (1993)

*W*hen the First Congress under the new Constitution met in late April of 1789 (having been delayed since March 4 by lack of a quorum because of bad winter roads), the most important item of business was consideration of a proposal to add a bill of rights to the Constitution. Such a proposal by Virginia delegate George Mason had been turned down with little debate in the waning days of the Philadelphia Constitutional Convention in September 1787, not because the delegates were too tired or too hot or against rights, but because of arguments by

102
THE
CONSTITUTIONAL
FRAMEWORK
AND THE
INDIVIDUAL

Hamilton and other Federalists that a bill of rights was irrelevant in a constitution providing the national government with only delegated powers. How could the national government abuse powers not given to it in the first place? But when the Constitution was submitted to the states for ratification, Antifederalists, most of whom had *not* been delegates in Philadelphia, picked up on the argument of Thomas Jefferson (who also had not been a delegate) that the omission of a bill of rights was a major imperfection of the new Constitution. Whatever the merits of Hamilton's or Jefferson's positions, in order to gain ratification, the Federalists in Massachusetts, South Carolina, New Hampshire, Virginia, and New York made an "unwritten but unequivocal pledge" to add a bill of rights and a promise to confirm (in what became the Tenth Amendment) the understanding that all powers not delegated to the national government or explicitly prohibited to the states were reserved to the states.[1]

James Madison, who had been a delegate at the Philadelphia Convention and later became a member of Congress, may still have agreed privately that a bill of rights was not needed. But in 1789, recognizing the urgency of obtaining the support of the Anti-federalists for the Constitution and the new government, he fought for the bill of rights arguing that the principle it embodied would acquire "the character of fundamental maxims of free Government, and as they become incorporated with the national sentiment, counteract the impulses of interest and passion."[2]

"After much discussion and manipulation . . . at the delicate prompting of Washington and under the masterful prodding of Madison," the House adopted seventeen amendments; the Senate adopted twelve of these. Ten of the amendments were ratified by the states on December 15, 1791, which from the start were called the Bill of Rights.[3]

The Bill of Rights—its history and the controversy of interpretation surrounding it—can be usefully subdivided into two categories: civil liberties and civil rights. This chapter will be divided accordingly. *Civil liberties* comes first because civil liberties are defined as *protections of citizens from improper government action.* When adopted in 1791, the Bill of Rights was seen as a private sphere of personal liberty free of governmental restrictions.[4] As Jefferson had put it, a bill of rights "is what people are entitled to *against every government on earth* . . . " Note the emphasis—citizen *against* government. In this sense, we could call the Bill of Rights a "bill of liberties" because the amendments focus on what government must *not* do. For example (with emphasis added):

---

[1]Clinton Rossiter, *1787: The Grand Convention* (New York: W. W. Norton, Norton Library Edition, 1987), p. 302.

[2]Quoted in Milton Konvitz, "The Bill of Rights: Amendments I–X," in *An American Primer,* ed. Daniel J. Boorstin (Chicago: University of Chicago Press, 1966), p. 159.

[3]Rossiter, *1787: The Grand Convention,* p. 303, where he also reports that "In 1941 the States of Connecticut, Massachusetts, and Georgia celebrated the sesquicentennial of the Bill of Rights by giving their hitherto withheld and unneeded assent."

[4]Lest there be confusion in our interchangeable use of the words "liberty" and "freedom," treat them as synonyms. "Freedom" is from the German, *Freiheit.* "Liberty" is from the French, *liberté.* Both have to do with the absence of restraints on individual choices of action.

1. "Congress shall make *no* law . . . "(I)
2. "The right to . . . bear Arms, shall *not* be infringed," (II)
3. "*No* soldier shall . . . be quartered . . . " (III)
4. "*No* warrants shall issue, but upon probable cause . . ." (IV)
5. "*No* person shall be held to answer . . . unless on presentment or indictment of a Grand Jury. . . " (V)
6. "Excessive bail shall *not* be required . . . *nor* cruel and unusual punishments inflicted." (VIII)

Thus, the Bill of Rights is a series of "thou shalt nots"—restraints addressed to government. Some of these restraints are *substantive,* putting limits on *what* the government shall and shall not have power to do—such as establishing a religion, quartering troops in private homes without consent, or seizing private property without just compensation. Other restraints are *procedural,* dealing with *how* the government is supposed to act. For example, even though the government has the substantive power to declare certain acts to be crimes and to arrest and imprison persons who violate its criminal laws, it may not do so except by fairly meticulous observation of procedures designed to protect the accused person. The best-known procedural rule is that "a person is presumed innocent until proven guilty." This rule does not question the government's power to punish someone for committing a crime; it questions only the way the government determines *who* committed the crime. Substantive and procedural restraints together identify the realm of civil liberties.

We define **civil rights** as obligations imposed on government to take *positive (or affirmative) action to protect citizens from the illegal actions of other private citizens and other government agencies.* Civil rights did not become part of the Constitution until 1868 with the adoption of the Fourteenth Amendment, which addressed the issue of who was a citizen and provided for each citizen "the equal protection of the laws." From that point on, we can see more clearly the distinction between civil liberties and civil rights, because civil liberties issues arise under the "due process of law" clause, and civil rights issues arise under the "equal protection of the laws" clause.

We turn first to civil liberties and to the long history of the effort to make personal liberty a reality for every citizen in America. The struggle for freedom against arbitrary and discriminatory actions by governments has continued to this day. And inevitably it is tied to the continuing struggle for civil rights, to persuade those same governments to take positive actions. We shall deal with that in the second section of this chapter, but we should not lose sight of the connection in the real world between civil liberties and civil rights. We should also not lose sight of the connection between this principle and the constitutional framework established in Chapter 3. Although the principle of individual liberties and rights was identified in Chapter 3 as comprising the third of the three most important principles in the Constitution, the third cannot be understood except in the context of the other two, especially federalism. Americans are forever fearful about their individual autonomy, and American history is filled with discourse about how to protect and expand individual freedom. This has given Americans a love/hate relationship with government, because the individual recognizes the need to be pro-

104

THE
CONSTITUTIONAL
FRAMEWORK
AND THE
INDIVIDUAL

tected *from* government and at the same time recognizes that an active government is needed to protect and to advance the individual's opportunity to enjoy liberty.[5]

CIVIL LIBERTIES: NATIONALIZING THE BILL OF RIGHTS

The First Amendment provides that "Congress shall make no law respecting an establishment of religion . . . or abridging freedom of speech, or of the press; or the right of [assembly and petition]." But this is the only amendment in the Bill of Rights that addresses itself exclusively to the national government. For example, the Second Amendment provides that "the right of the people to keep and bear Arms shall not be infringed." The Fifth Amendment says, among other things, that *"no person* shall . . . be twice put in jeopardy of life or limb" for the same crime; that *no person* "shall be compelled in any Criminal Case to be a witness against himself"; that *no person* shall "be deprived of life, liberty, or property, without due process of law"; and that private property cannot be taken "without just compensation."[6] Since the First Amendment is the only part of the Bill of Rights that is explicit in its intention to put limits on the national government, a fundamental question inevitably arises: *Do the remaining amendments of the Bill of Rights put limits on state governments or only on the national government?*

Dual Citizenship

The question concerning whether the Bill of Rights also limits state governments was settled in 1833 in a way that seems odd to Americans today. The 1833 case was *Barron* v. *Baltimore,* and the facts were simple. In paving its streets, the city of Baltimore had disposed of so much sand and gravel in the water near Barron's wharf that the value of the wharf for commercial purposes was virtually destroyed. Barron brought the city into court on the grounds that it had, under the Fifth Amendment, unconstitutionally deprived him of his property. Barron had to take his case all the way to the Supreme Court, despite the fact that the argument made by his attorney seemed airtight. The following is Chief Justice Marshall's characterization of Barron's argument:

> The plaintiff [Barron] . . . contends that it comes within that clause of the Fifth Amendment of the Constitution which inhibits the taking of private property for

---

[5]For some recent scholarship on the Bill of Rights and its development, see: Geoffrey Stone, Richard Epstein, and Cass Sunstein, eds., *The Bill of Rights and the Modern State* (Chicago: University of Chicago Press, 1992); and Michael J. Meyer and William A. Parent, eds., *The Constitution of Rights* (Ithaca, NY: Cornell University Press, 1992).

[6]It would be useful at this point to review all the provisions of the Bill of Rights (in the Appendix) to confirm this distinction between the wording of the First Amendment and the rest. Emphasis in the example quotations was not in the original. For a spirited and enlightening essay on the extent to which the entire Bill of Rights was about equality, see Martha Minow, "Equality and the Bill of Rights," in Meyer and Parent, *The Constitution of Rights,* pp. 118–28.

public use without just compensation. He insists that this amendment, being in favor of the liberty of the citizen, ought to be so construed as to restrain the legislative power of a State, as well as that of the United States.[7]

Then Marshall, in one of the most significant Supreme Court decisions ever handed down, disagreed:

> The Constitution was ordained and established by the people of the United States for themselves, for their own government, and not for the government of the individual States. Each State established a constitution for itself, and in that constitution provided such limitations and restrictions on the powers of its particular government as its judgment dictated . . . . If these propositions be correct, *the fifth amendment must be understood as restraining the power of the general government, not as applicable to the States.*[8]

In other words, if an agency of the *national* government had deprived Barron of his property, there would have been little doubt about Barron's winning his case. But if the constitution of the state of Maryland contained no such provision protecting citizens of Maryland from such action, then Barron had no legal leg to stand on against Baltimore, an agency of the state of Maryland.

Barron v. *Baltimore* confirmed "dual citizenship," that is, that each American was a citizen of the national government and *separately* a citizen of one of the states. This meant that the Bill of Rights did not apply to decisions or to procedures of state (or local) governments. Even slavery could continue, because the Bill of Rights could not protect anyone from state laws treating people as property. In fact, the Bill of Rights did not become a vital instrument for the extension of civil liberties for anyone until after a bloody Civil War and a revolutionary Fourteenth Amendment intervened. And even so, as we shall see, nearly a second century would pass before the Bill of Rights would truly come into its own.

The Fourteenth Amendment

From a constitutional standpoint, the defeat of the South in the Civil War settled one question and raised another. It probably settled forever the question of whether secession was an option for any state. After 1865 there was to be more "united" than "states" to the United States. But this left unanswered just how much the states were obliged to obey the Constitution, in particular, the Bill of Rights. Just reading the words of the Fourteenth Amendment, anyone might think it was almost perfectly designed to impose the Bill of Rights on the states and thereby to reverse *Barron* v. *Baltimore*. The very first words of the Fourteenth Amendment point in that direction.

> All persons born or naturalized in the United States, and subject to the jurisdiction thereof, are citizens of the United States and of the State wherein they reside.

This provides for a *single national citizenship,* and at a minimum that means that civil

[7]Barron v. Baltimore, 7 Peters 243 (1833).

[8]Ibid., p. 246. [Emphasis added.]

106

THE
CONSTITUTIONAL
FRAMEWORK
AND THE
INDIVIDUAL

liberties should not vary drastically from state to state. That would seem to be the spirit of the Fourteenth Amendment: *to nationalize the Bill of Rights by nationalizing the definition of citizenship.*

This interpretation of the Fourteenth Amendment is reinforced by the next clause of the Amendment:

> *No state* shall make or enforce any law which shall abridge the privileges or immunities of citizens of the United States; nor shall any state deprive any person of life, liberty, or property, without due process of law. [Emphasis added.]

All of this sounds like an effort to extend the Bill of Rights in its *entirety* to citizens *wherever* they might reside.[9] But this was not to be the Supreme Court's interpretation for nearly a hundred years. Within five years of ratification of the Fourteenth Amendment, the Court was making decisions as though it had never been adopted. The shadow of *Barron* grew longer and longer. Table 4.1 outlines the major developments in the history of the Fourteenth Amendment against the backdrop of *Barron,* citing the particular provisions of the Bill of Rights as they

TABLE 4.1
Incorporation of the Bill of Rights into the Fourteenth Amendment

Selected Provisions and Amendments	*Not "Incorporated" Until*	*Key Case*
Eminent domain (V)	1897	*Chicago, Burlington, and Quincy R.R.* v. *Chicago*
Freedom of speech (I)	1925	*Gitlow* v. *New York*
Freedom of press (I)	1931	*Near* v. *Minnesota*
Freedom of assembly (I)	1939	*Hague* v. *CIO*
Freedom from warrantless search and seizure (IV) ("exclusionary rule")	1961	*Mapp* v. *Ohio*
Right to counsel in any criminal trial (VI)	1963	*Gideon* v. *Wainwright*
Right against self-incrimination and forced confessions (V)	1964	*Malloy* v. *Hogan* *Escobedo* v. *Illinois*
Right to counsel and to remain silent (VI)	1966	*Miranda* v. *Arizona*
Right against double jeopardy (V)	1969	*Benton* v. *Maryland*
Right to privacy (III, IV, & V)	1973	*Roe* v. *Wade* *Doe* v. *Bolton*

[9]The Fourteenth Amendment also seems designed to introduce civil rights. The final clause of the all-important Section 1 provides that no state can "deny to any person within its jurisdiction the equal protection of the laws." It is not unreasonable to conclude that the purpose of this provision was to obligate the state governments as well as the national government to take *positive* actions to protect citizens from arbitrary and discriminatory actions, at least those based on race. This will be explored in the second half of the chapter.

were incorporated by Supreme Court decisions into the Fourteenth Amendment
as limitations on all the states. This is a measure of the degree of "nationalization" of civil liberties. In an important 1873 decision, known as the *Slaughterhouse Cases,* the Supreme Court determined that the federal government was under no obligation to protect the "privileges and immunities" of citizens of a particular state against arbitrary actions by that state's government. The case had its origins in 1867, when a corrupt Louisiana legislature conferred upon a single corporation a monopoly of all the slaughterhouse business in the city of New Orleans. The other slaughterhouses, facing bankruptcy, all brought suits claiming, like Mr. Barron, that this was a taking of their property in violation of Fifth Amendment rights. But unlike Mr. Barron, they believed that they were protected now because, they argued, the Fourteenth Amendment incorporated the Fifth Amendment, applying it to the states. The suits were all rejected. The Supreme Court argued, first, that the primary purpose of the Fourteenth Amendment was to protect "Negroes as a class." Second, and more to the point here, the Court argued, without trying to prove it, that the framers of the Fourteenth Amendment could not have intended to incorporate the entire Bill of Rights.[10] Yet, when the Civil Rights Act of 1875 attempted to protect blacks from discriminatory treatment by proprietors of hotels, theaters, and other public accommodations, the Supreme Court disregarded its own primary argument in the previous case and held the act unconstitutional, declaring that the Fourteenth Amendment applied only to discriminatory actions by state officials, "operating under cover of law," and not to discrimination against blacks by private individuals, even though these private individuals were companies offering services to the public.[11] Such narrow interpretations raised the inevitable question of whether the Fourteenth Amendment had incorporated *any* of the Bill of Rights. The Fourteenth Amendment remained shadowy until the mid-twentieth century. The shadow was *Barron* v. *Baltimore* and the Court's reluctance to nationalize civil liberties.

The only change in civil liberties during the first sixty years following the adoption of the Fourteenth Amendment came in 1897, when the Supreme Court held that the due process clause of the Fourteenth Amendment did in fact prohibit states from taking property for a public use without just compensation.[12] This effectively overruled *Barron,* because it meant that the citizen of Maryland or any state was henceforth protected from a "public taking" of property (eminent domain) even if the state constitution did not provide such protection. However, in a broader sense, *Barron* still cast a shadow, because the Supreme Court had "incorporated" into the Fourteenth Amendment only the property protection provision of the Fifth Amendment and no other clause, let alone the other amendments of the Bill of Rights. In other words, although "due process" applied to the taking of life and liberty as well as property, only property was incorporated into the Fourteenth Amendment as a limitation on state power.

No further expansion of civil liberties through incorporation occurred until 1925, when the Supreme Court held that freedom of speech is "among the

[10]The Slaughterhouse Cases, 16 Wallace 36 (1883).

[11]The Civil Rights Cases, 109 U.S. 3 (1883).

[12]Chicago, Burlington and Quincy Railroad Company v. Chicago, 166 U.S. 226 (1897).

108
THE
CONSTITUTIONAL
FRAMEWORK
AND THE
INDIVIDUAL

fundamental personal rights and 'liberties' protected by the due process clause of the Fourteenth Amendment from impairment by the states."[13] In 1931, the Court added freedom of the press to that short list of civil rights protected by the Bill of Rights from state action; in 1939, it added freedom of assembly.[14] But that was as far as the Court was willing to go. As late as 1937, the Supreme Court was still loathe to nationalize civil liberties beyond the First Amendment. In fact, the Court in that year took one of its most extreme turns backward toward *Barron* v. *Baltimore.* The state of Connecticut had indicted a man named Palko for first-degree murder, but a lower court had found him guilty of only second-degree murder and sentenced him to life in prison. Unhappy with the verdict, the state of Connecticut appealed the conviction to its highest court, won the appeal, got a new trial, and then succeeded in getting Palko convicted of first-degree murder. Palko appealed to the Supreme Court on what seemed an open and shut case of double jeopardy—being tried twice for the same crime. Yet, though the majority of the Court agreed that this could indeed be considered a case of double jeopardy, they decided that double jeopardy was *not* one of the provisions of the Bill of Rights incorporated in the Fourteenth Amendment as a restriction on the powers of the states. Justice Benjamin Cardozo, considered one of the most able Supreme Court justices of this century, rejected the argument made by Palko's lawyer that "whatever is forbidden by the Fifth Amendment is forbidden by the Fourteenth also." Cardozo responded tersely, "There is no such general rule." As far as Cardozo was concerned (and he was speaking for the majority), the only rights from the Bill of Rights that ought to be incorporated into the Fourteenth Amendment as applying to the states as well as to the national government were those that were "implicit in the concept of ordered liberty." He asked the question: Does double jeopardy subject Palko to a "hardship so acute and shocking that our polity will not endure it? Does it violate those 'fundamental principles of liberty and justice which lie at the base of all our civil and political institutions?' . . . The answer must surely be 'no.'"[15] Palko was eventually executed for the crime, because he lived in the state of Connecticut rather than in some state whose constitution included a guarantee against double jeopardy.

Cases like *Palko* extended the shadow of *Barron* into its second century, despite adoption of the Fourteenth Amendment. The Constitution, as interpreted by the Supreme Court, left standing the framework in which the states had the power to determine their own law on a number of fundamental issues. It left states with the power to pass laws segregating the races—and everyone knows that the thirteen southern states chose to exercise that power. The constitutional framework also left states with the power to engage in search and seizures without a warrant, to indict accused persons without benefit of a grand jury, to deprive persons of trial by jury, to deprive persons of their right not to have to testify against themselves, to deprive accused persons of their right to confront adverse witnesses, and as we have seen, to prosecute accused persons more than once for the same crime.[16] Few

---

[13]Gitlow v. New York, 268 U.S. 652 (1925).

[14]Near v. Minnesota, 283 U.S. 697 (1931); Hague v. C.I.O., 307 U.S. 496 (1939).

[15]Palko v. Connecticut, 302 U.S. 319 (1937).

[16]All of these were implicitly identified in the *Palko* case as "not incorporated" into the Fourteenth Amendment as a limitation on the powers of the states.

states chose the option to use that kind of power, but some states did, and the power to do so was there for any state whose legislative majority so chose.

The Second Constitutional Revolution

For nearly thirty years following the *Palko* case,[17] the nineteenth-century framework was sustained, but signs of change in the framework could be detected after World War II, and virtually everyone could see the writing on the wall after 1954, in *Brown* v. *Board of Education,* when the Supreme Court overturned the infamous *Plessy* v. *Ferguson.*[18] *Plessy* was a civil rights case involving the "equal protection" clause of the Fourteenth Amendment and was not an issue of applying the Bill of Rights to the states. (It will be dealt with in the next section.) Nonetheless, *Brown* indicated that the new Warren Court was going to be expansive about civil liberties as well. In retrospect, one could say that the Second Constitutional Revolution began with or soon after the *Brown* decision.[19] This can be seen in Table 4.1 by the number of civil liberties incorporated after 1954.

As with the First, the Second Constitutional Revolution was a movement toward nationalization. But the two revolutions required opposite motions on the part of the Supreme Court. In the area of commerce (the first revolution), the Court had to decide to assume a *passive* role by not trying to interfere as Congress expanded the meaning of the commerce clause of Article I, Section 8. This expansion has been so extensive that the national government can now constitutionally reach a single farmer growing twenty acres of wheat or a small neighborhood restaurant selling barbecues to local "whites only" without being anywhere near interstate commerce routes. In the second revolution—involving the Bill of Rights through the Fourteenth Amendment rather than the commerce clause—the Court had to assume an *active* role, which required close review not of Congress but of the laws of state legislatures and decisions of state courts, in order to apply a single national Fourteenth Amendment standard to the rights and liberties of all citizens.

Until 1961, only the First Amendment had been fully and clearly incorporated into the Fourteenth Amendment.[20] After 1961, several other important provisions of the Bill of Rights were incorporated. Of the cases that expanded the Fourteenth Amendment's reach, the most famous was *Gideon* v. *Wainwright* because it became the subject of a best-selling book and movie.[21] By 1969, the Supreme Court had come full circle, explicitly reversing the *Palko* ruling and thereby incorporating double jeopardy. And then, as one important study of constitutional history put it,

[17]*Palko* was explicitly reversed in Benton v. Maryland, 395 U.S. 784 (1969), in which the Court said that double jeopardy was in fact incorporated in the Fourteenth Amendment as a restriction on the states.

[18]Plessy v. Ferguson, 163 U.S. 537 (1896).

[19]The First Constitutional Revolution, beginning with NLRB v. Jones & Laughlin Steel Corp. (1937), was dealt with in Chapter 3.

[20]The one exception was the right to public trial (the Sixth Amendment), but the 1948 case did not actually mention the right to public trial as such; it was cited in a 1968 case as a case establishing the right to public trial as part of the Fourteenth Amendment. The 1948 case was In re Oliver, 33 U.S. 257, where the issue was put more generally as "due process" and public trial itself was not actually mentioned. Later opinions, such as Duncan v. Louisiana, 391, U.S. 145 (1968), cited the *Oliver* case as the precedent for incorporating public trials as part of the Fourteenth Amendment.

[21]Gideon v. Wainwright, 372 U.S. 335 (1963).

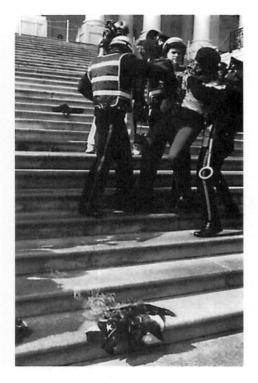

The right to free speech. In 1931, the Supreme Court acknowledged that symbols and symbolic speech may receive First Amendment protection. Over the years, though, individuals have been tried and convicted by state law for desecrating and mutilating the American flag. The Supreme Court, in a 5–4 decision, overturned the state conviction of Gregory Johnson, who was found guilty of flag desecration and mutilation in violation of a Texas statute *(Texas v. Johnson 1989)*. The Court, in keeping with the 1939 decision, ruled that the desecration of the flag is symbolic speech and is therefore protected under the First Amendment. In 1989, Congress tried and failed to pass a Constitutional amendment against flag desecration; it fell thirty-four votes short of the required two-thirds majority vote in the House and nine votes short in the Senate. Pictured here on October 30, 1989, is a man identifying himself as "Dred Scott and a revolutionary artist" after he ignited an American flag on the steps of the Capitol.

The right to free assembly. From the Ku Klux Klan and neo-Nazis to antiwar protesters and antinuclear activists, the Constitution gives us the right to raise our voices and to make our views known, whether or not we agree with the majority of other Americans.

The right to freedom of religion. The Constitution guarantees people the right to practice their religion without government intervention. The Amish, for example, set themselves apart from the rest of society, dressing in styles dating back to nineteenth-century Germany. They will not use most modern inventions, nor will they bear arms. Since their ways are not harmful to others, they may exercise their religious precepts fully.

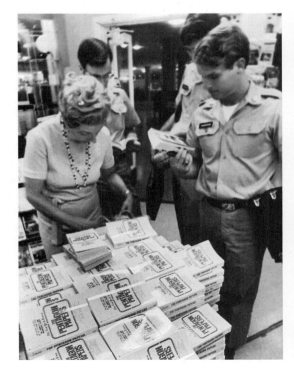

The right to a free press. The U.S. Constitution guarantees its citizens access to an uncensored press. This right exists even in times of political turmoil as evidenced by the publication of the Pentagon Papers, secret Defense Department documents regarding U.S. policy in Vietnam that were illegally obtained by the *New York Times* in 1971 at the height of that unpopular war.

112

THE
CONSTITUTIONAL
FRAMEWORK
AND THE
INDIVIDUAL

"The final step in nationalizing the Bill of Rights was taken by Congress. In the Civil Rights Act of 1968 it extended the guarantees of the first eight amendments to Indians living under tribal authority on reservations. Thus, all governments in the United States—federal, state, local, and Indian tribal—were restricted by the Bill of Rights."[22] The first eight amendments really are the true Bill of Rights. The Ninth Amendment confirms that the enumeration of rights in the Constitution is not supposed to mean that other rights cannot be added later. The Tenth Amendment, as observed earlier, reassures the states that the powers not delegated to the national government (and not explicitly prohibited to the states) are reserved to the states or the people.

Even today, however, the spirit of *Barron* v. *Baltimore* has not been entirely put to rest. Many have urged the Supreme Court to take the final step by declaring as a matter of constitutional law that the *entire* Bill of Rights was incorporated by the Fourteenth Amendment. But the Court has not been willing to do so. In fact, a court with the power to expand the Bill of Rights has the power to contract it.[23]

From Warren through Burger to Rehnquist

Table 4.1 is virtually a history of the Warren Court. When Warren retired in 1969, he was replaced by Chief Justice Warren Burger, a conservative upon whom many, including President Nixon, pinned their hopes for a more traditional interpretation, or "strict construction," of the Constitution. Those hopes were strengthened by President Nixon's opportunity to appoint three additional justices—Harry Blackmun, Lewis Powell, and William Rehnquist. Nevertheless, the directions set by the Warren Court and the Second Constitutional Revolution *were not reversed.* There were two broad areas of civil liberties in which the Burger Court did chart its own course. The first was the Burger Court's conservative redirection of the Warren Court's liberal emphasis on protecting the procedural rights of criminal defendants; the Burger Court instead strengthened the hands of state and local police and prosecutors. In the second area, the Burger Court actually *extended* Warren Court rulings regarding women, their power over their own bodies, and the general right to privacy. Each of these areas deserves closer examination.

Civil Liberties and the Police—Burger Conservatism Two of the most important decisions handed down by the Warren Court, *Mapp* and *Miranda,*[24] put severe restrictions on the ability of local police and prosecutors to deal with suspects, prisoners, and all persons accused of crimes. In *Mapp,* the Court held that evidence obtained in violation of the Fourth Amendment ban on unreasonable searches and seizures would be excluded from trial. This "exclusionary rule" was particularly irksome to the police and prosecutors because it meant that patently guilty defendants sometimes go free because the evidence that clearly damned them could not

---

[22]Alfred Kelly et al., *The American Constitution: Its Origins and Development,* 6th ed. (New York: W. W. Norton, 1983), p. 647.

[23]For a lively and readable treatment of the possibilities of restricting provisions of the Bill of Rights, without actually reversing Warren Court decisions, see David G. Savage, *Turning Right: The Making of the Rehnquist Supreme Court* (New York: Wiley, 1992).

[24]Mapp v. Ohio, 367 U.S. 643 (1961); Miranda v. Arizona, 384 U.S. 436 (1966).

PROCESS BOX 4.1

113

CIVIL LIBERTIES:
NATIONALIZING
THE BILL OF
RIGHTS

Free Speech: Protection by the First Amendment

		From protected speech →	Through Supreme Court →	To unprotected speech
Content of Speech	**True**	All speech protected by First Amendment when it is the truth.	Speech is a "preferred freedom" and every effort to regulate or punish speech is given "strict scrutiny" by the Supreme Court.	Speech can be regulated *only* • If it fails the "clear & present danger" test, or • If it falls below community standards, of obscenity/ pornography.
	False	Defamatory speech is protected when: • Spoken or written by a public official in the course of official business, or • Spoken or written by a citizen or press against people in the public eye.		Speech can be regulated or punished *only* when it can be demonstrated there was a reckless disregard for the truth. (as in libel/slander).

*For instance, if a speech calls for an armed and violent overthrow of the government, it is not protected.

be used. In *Miranda,* the Court's ruling required that arrested persons be informed of the right to remain silent and to have counsel present during interrogation. This is the basis of the "Miranda rule" of reading persons their rights made famous on TV police shows.

Decisions like these gave rise to the "law and order" movement that failed in its efforts to get Congress to "impeach Earl Warren" but succeeded in influencing the Nixon 1968 campaign, which emphasized law and order. The Burger Court could have been called the Nixon Court. Yet, it disappointed the law and order forces, as most courts disappoint their political supporters. The Burger Court refused to reverse either the *Mapp* or *Miranda* decisions or, for that matter, any of the major civil liberties decisions. But, while disappointing to the law and order movement, the Burger Court did give those decisions a more conservative interpretation. In *U.S. v. Harris,*[25] Chief Justice Burger, writing for the majority, argued that mere technical violations of search and seizure ought not to be used to free known criminals. Several other cases also strengthened the position of the police. For example, the Burger Court held that the professional judgment of police ought to be sufficient for warrants, that warrantless searches can under certain circumstances be

[25]U.S. v. Harris, 403 U.S. 924 (1971).

114

THE
CONSTITUTIONAL
FRAMEWORK
AND THE
INDIVIDUAL

accepted, and that illegally seized evidence might be presented to a grand jury even when it was not presentable to the trial jury.[26] The Burger Court revised *Miranda* by holding that although a statement was inadmissible (if the Miranda warning wasn't given), the prosecutor could nonetheless use it to impeach the defendant's testimony if the defendant took the stand.[27] Yet, this same Burger Court *extended* the liberal position toward right to counsel in one respect by requiring counsel not only for those accused of felonies but also for those accused of misdemeanors.[28]

Women and the "Right to Privacy"—Burger Liberalism   To the surprise of many, the Burger Court significantly expanded (and nationalized) an important area of civil liberties with its 1973 decision in *Roe v. Wade,* rendering unconstitutional all state laws making abortion a crime.[29] This brought the Second Constitutional Revolution to women, mainly through the discovery or establishment of a new right, the right of privacy. Nowhere can such a right of privacy be found in the Bill of Rights or the Fourteenth Amendment. But from early in the Warren era, the Court had been developing a concept of a "right of privacy" that went well beyond mere incorporation of clauses in the first eight amendments. New rights in the area of civil liberties were actually anticipated by the Ninth Amendment: "The enumeration in the Constitution, of certain rights, shall not be construed to deny or disparage others retained by the people." In that spirit, the Court concluded that there was in particular a right of privacy (that is, to be left alone) that could be derived from a combination of other more specific constitutional provisions. In 1958, the Supreme Court recognized "privacy in one's association" in its argument protecting the NAACP from the state of Alabama using its membership list.[30] This argument would be combined with the Third, Fourth, and Fifth Amendments, thereby creating a "zone of privacy" beyond the reach of government.

In the first new privacy case, the Court held that this privacy right included the right of marital privacy in regard to married persons' use of contraceptives and the circulation of birth control information.[31] In 1972, the Court extended that right to unmarried women.[32] This right of privacy was confirmed and extended in the most important of all the privacy cases, *Roe v. Wade,* to support the Court's ruling that the states had no constitutional power to make abortion a criminal act. Note again that the essence of civil liberties involves rights to be free of government interference. And note also that the preference for privacy and for its extension to include the rights of women to control their own bodies was not something invented by the Supreme Court in a political vacuum. According to Table 4.2,

[26]An excellent treatment of these cases will be found in Kelly et al., *The American Constitution,* pp. 718–19.

[27]Harris v. New York, 401 U.S. 222 (1971).

[28]Argersinger v. Hamlin, 407 U.S. 25 (1972).

[29]Roe v. Wade, 410 U.S. 113 (1973).

[30]NAACP v. Alabama ex rel. Patterson, 357 U.S. 449 (1958).

[31]Griswold v. Connecticut, 381 U.S. 479 (1965).

[32]Eisenstadt v. Baird, 405 U.S. 438 (1972).

TABLE 4.2

115

CIVIL LIBERTIES:
NATIONALIZING
THE BILL OF
RIGHTS

Abortion Regulation and Deregulation

1. States adopt anti-abortion laws

	Number of States
1820–1900	43
1900–1965	7

2. States permit therapeutic abortions

Year	*States*
1966–1968	MS, CO, CA, NC, GA, MD
1969	AR, DE, KS, NM, OR
1970–1972	SC, VA, FL

3. States repeal anti-abortion laws

Year	*States*
1970	AL, HI, NY, WA

4. Supreme Court declares all state abortion laws invalid

Year	*Decision*
1973	*Roe* v. *Wade*

5. States adopt new anti-abortion laws

Year	*States*
1980	MO, OH, IL, MN

6. Supreme Court re-opens the way for state regulation of abortion

Year	*Decision*
1989	*Webster* v. *Repro. Health Serv.*
1991	*Rust* v. *Sullivan*
1992	*Planned Parenthood of Southwestern Penn.* v. *Casey*

7. States adopt new laws restricting abortions[*]

Year	*States*
1989	PA
1990	SC, OH, MN, Guam, LA, MI
1991	UT, MS, KS

[*]Other states with serious efforts in legislature that were defeated, vetoed, or still incomplete at the end of 1992: ID, IN, FL, SD, ND, VA. Two states, CT and MD, passed abortion rights laws to protect women's access to abortion in the event that *Roe* was overturned. At the end of 1992, MA was considering a similar bill.

Source: Raymond Tatalovich and Byron Daynes, *The Politics of Abortion* (New York: Praeger, 1981), p. 18. Copyright © 1981 by Praeger Publishers. Used with permission. Updated by data from the *New York Times,* 4–6 July 1989.

116

THE
CONSTITUTIONAL
FRAMEWORK
AND THE
INDIVIDUAL

Norma McCorvey and Randall Terry
From *Roe* v. *Wade* to
"Operation Rescue"

Abortion is perhaps the most potent and explosive issue of the last two decades. Norma McCorvey (known to most as Jane Roe) and Randall Terry demonstrate the power of this issue to bring average people into the political fray in a highly personal way. Each in their own way, McCorvey and Terry have sought to redefine the constitutional interpretation surrounding abortion.

In 1969, Norma McCorvey was a twenty-one-year-old carnival worker, divorced with a five-year-old daughter, and living on the edge of poverty. She was in Texas with the carnival when she discovered she was pregnant. Seeking an abortion, McCorvey found she was in a state that only allowed abortions to save the life of the woman. In her words, "I found one doctor who offered to abort me for $500. Only he didn't have a license, and I was scared to turn my body over to him. So there I was—pregnant, . . . alone and stuck."

McCorvey bore her child and gave it up for adoption, but in the process she met two recent law school graduates, Sarah Weddington and Linda Coffey. These three women decided to challenge the Texas abortion law in court. In order to avoid personal stigma, McCorvey's name was changed to Jane Roe. The defendant was Henry Wade, a district attorney for Dallas County, Texas. The result of the challenge was the controversial landmark Supreme Court case *Roe* v. *Wade* (1973), in which a seven-member majority of the court affirmed a constitutional right to abortion under most circumstances.

That case stunned and mobilized abortion opponents, including Randall Terry, a used-car salesman. A native of upstate New

Norma McCorvey

over half of the states in existence at the time did not regulate abortion until the second half of the nineteenth century, and the state legislatures began to "decriminalize" and "deregulate" abortion well before the 1973 Supreme Court decision. In the wake of the Court's 1989 decision in the case of *Webster* v. *Reproductive Health Services,* however, a number of states moved to write or reinstate restrictive statutes (see below).

Like any important principle, once privacy was established as an aspect of civil liberties protected by the Bill of Rights through the Fourteenth Amendment, it took on a life all its own. In a number of important decisions, the Supreme Court

York, Terry and his wife settled in Binghamton, where they began to stand in front of abortion clinics to try to talk women out of getting abortions. By 1988, Terry quit his job and devoted his full-time energies to his organization Operation Rescue. Led by Terry, the group has sought to close down doctors' offices, clinics, and other places where abortion is discussed or practiced. His means have been highly controversial. At the Southern Tier Women's Services office near Binghamton, for example, Terry was arrested for the first of many times for spreading nails in the office's parking lot and for gluing the office doors shut.

Terry has led large-scale protests in such cities as Wichita, Kansas, and Buffalo, New York, where his followers have attempted to forcibly block entrances, harass physicians as well as clients, and otherwise disrupt abortion-related activities. Terry has been repeatedly cited and tried for trespass, destruction of property, harassment, and other violations. During the Democratic National Party Convention in 1992, an associate of Terry's attempted to present Democratic presidential nominee Bill Clinton with an aborted fetus. Terry's motivation for the action was his belief that "to vote for Bill Clinton is to sin against God." He also accused Clinton of "actively promoting rebellion against the Ten Commandments."

To the members of Operation Rescue, such illegal activities are justifiable as a

means to discourage abortions. Yet the extreme tactics of Operation Rescue, while receiving much publicity, have served to alienate many Americans. In the midst of this charged political atmosphere, the Supreme Court (dominated by Reagan and Bush appointees) ruled in the 1992 case of *Planned Parenthood* v. *Casey* that the constitutional right to privacy continued to support the "essence" of the right to abortion as established in *Roe.*

Source: Marian Faux, *Roe v. Wade* (New York: Dutton, 1989).

Randall Terry

and the lower federal courts sought to protect rights that could not be found in the text of the Constitution but could be discovered through the study of the philosophic sources of fundamental rights. Through this line of reasoning, the federal courts sought to protect sexual autonomy, lifestyle choices, sexual preferences, procreational choice, and various forms of intimate association.

Criticism mounted with every extension of this line of reasoning. The federal courts were accused of creating an uncontrollable expansion of rights demands. The Supreme Court, the critics argued, had displaced the judgments of legislatures and state courts with its own judgment of what is reasonable, without regard to

118

THE
CONSTITUTIONAL
FRAMEWORK
AND THE
INDIVIDUAL

local popular majorities and without regard to specific constitutional provisions. This is virtually the definition of what came to be called "judicial activism" in the 1980s, and it was the basis for a more strongly critical label, "the imperial judiciary."[33]

Rehnquist: A De-nationalizing Trend? Controversy over judicial power will extend well into the 1990s. Burger's successor is a guarantee of that. As an associate justice, William Rehnquist was the leading critic of "judicial activism" as it related to privacy and other new rights, such as the right to be represented in districts of numerically equal size,[34] and the right not to be required to participate in prayers in school.[35] Although it is difficult to determine just how much influence Rehnquist has had as Chief Justice, the Court has in fact been moving in a more conservative, de-nationalizing direction. Constitutional scholar David O'Brien has made the following comparison: Between 1961 and 1969, more than 76 percent of the Warren Court's rulings from term to term tended to be liberal—that is, tending toward nationalizing the Bill of Rights to protect individuals and minorities mainly against the actions of state government. During the Burger years, 1969–1986, the liberal tendency dropped on the average below 50 percent. During the first four years of the Rehnquist Court (the extent of O'Brien's research), the average liberal "score" dropped to less than 35 percent.[36] For example, he reports that in the 1990 term, the Court ruled against prisoner's claims in twenty-three out of thirty-one cases, leaving more power over prisoners in state and local hands. The direction was equally conservative on the burning issue of abortion and freedom of choice. The Court actually upheld *Roe* v. *Wade* in a 5-to-4 decision in July 1992 but, in so doing, nevertheless refused to invalidate a Pennsylvania law that significantly restricts freedom of choice. The majority of the Court was willing to recognize the right of a woman to choose an abortion, but defined it as a "limited or qualified" right subject to regulation by the states as long as the regulation does not impose an "undue burden." As one constitutional authority concluded from this case, "Until there is a Freedom of Choice Act, and/or a U.S. Supreme Court able to wean *Roe* from its respirator, state legislatures will have significant discretion over the access that women will have to legalized abortions."[37]

[33]A good discussion will be found in Paul Brest and Sanford Levinson, *Processes of Constitutional Decision-Making: Cases and Materials,* 2nd ed. (Boston: Little, Brown, 1983), p. 660. See also Chapter 8.

[34]Baker v. Carr, 369 U.S. 186 (1962).

[35]Engel v. Vitale, 370 U.S. 421 (1962), on the Court's striking down a state-composed prayer for recitation in the schools. Of course, a whole line of cases followed *Engel,* as states and cities tried various ways and means of getting around the Court's principle that any organized prayer in the public schools violated the First Amendment rights of the individual.

[36]David M. O'Brien, *Supreme Court Watch—1991,* Annual Supplement to *Constitutional Law and Politics* (New York: W. W. Norton, 1991), p. 6 and Chapter 4.

[37]Gayle Binion, "Undue Burden? Government Now Has Wide Latitude to Restrict Abortions," *Santa Barbara News-Press,* 5 July 1992, p. A13. The case being referred to is Planned Parenthood of Southeastern Pennsylvania v. Casey 112 S.Ct. 2791 (1992). A case three years earlier had already significantly narrowed the scope of the *Roe* precedent. Webster v. Reproductive Health Services 109 S.Ct. 3040 (1989). In this 5-to-4 decision, written by Rehnquist, the Court upheld a Missouri law that restricted the use of public medical facilities for abortion, thus opening the way for other states to limit the availability of

But the question remains: Will a Supreme Court, even with a majority of conservatives, reverse the nationalization of the Bill of Rights? Possibly, but not necessarily. First of all, the Rehnquist Court has not actually reversed any of the decisions made by the Warren or Burger Courts nationalizing most of the clauses of the Bill of Rights. As we have seen, the Rehnquist Court has given narrower and more restrictive interpretations of the earlier decisions, but it has not literally reversed any, not even *Roe* v. *Wade*. Second, President Clinton will have an opportunity to affect the balance of the Court. When Justice Byron White retired in 1993, Clinton chose Ruth Bader Ginsburg, a moderate, to replace him. With the probable retirement during his term of Justice Harry Blackmun, the oldest sitting justice, Clinton will have at least one more chance to change the Court's direction. Unquestionably, expansion or contraction of the Bill of Rights and the Fourteenth Amendment will be in the forefront of political debate for a long time to come.

CIVIL RIGHTS

The very simplicity of the "civil rights clause" of the Fourteenth Amendment left it open to interpretation:

> No State shall make or enforce any law which shall . . . deny to any person within its jurisdiction the equal protection of the laws.

But in the very first Fourteenth Amendment case to come before the Supreme Court, the majority gave it a distinct meaning:

> . . . it is not difficult to give meaning to this clause ["the equal protection of the laws"]. The existence of laws in the States . . . which discriminated with gross injustice and hardship against [Negroes] as a class, was the evil to be remedied by this clause, and by it such laws are forbidden.[38]

Beyond that, contemporaries of the Fourteenth Amendment understood well that private persons offering conveyances, accommodations, or places of amusement to the public incurred certain public obligations to offer them to one and all—in other words, these are *public* accommodations, such that arbitrary discrimination in their use would amount to denial of equal protection of the laws—unless a government took action to overcome the discrimination.[39] This puts governments

---

abortions. The first to act was the Pennsylvania legislature, which adopted in late 1989 a law banning all abortions after pregnancy had passed 24 weeks, except to save the life of the pregnant woman or to prevent irreversible impairment of her health. In 1990, the pace of state legislative action increased, with new statutes being passed in South Carolina, Ohio, Minnesota, and Guam. In 1991, the Louisiana legislature adopted the strictest law yet, over the governor's veto. The Louisiana law prohibits all abortions, except when the mother's life is threatened or when rape or incest victims report these crimes immediately.

[38]The Slaughterhouse Cases, 16 Wallace 36 (1873).

[39]See Civil Rights Cases, 109 U.S. 3 (1883), where the Supreme Court affirmed this position even as it was holding against the black plaintiffs by declaring the Civil Rights Act of 1875 unconstitutional.

120

THE
CONSTITUTIONAL
FRAMEWORK
AND THE
INDIVIDUAL

under obligation to take positive actions to extend to each citizen the opportunities and resources necessary to their proper enjoyment of freedom. A skeptic once observed that "the law, in its majestic equality, forbids the rich as well as the poor to sleep under bridges, to beg in the streets, and to steal bread." The purpose of civil rights principles and laws is to use government in such a way as to give equality a more substantive meaning than that.

Discrimination refers to the use of any unreasonable and unjust criterion of exclusion. Of course, all laws discriminate, including some people while excluding others; but some discrimination is considered unreasonable. Now, for example, it is considered reasonable to enforce twenty-one as the legal drinking age, thereby excluding all persons younger than twenty-one; for these purposes, the age criterion is considered reasonable discrimination. But is age a reasonable distinction when seventy (or sixty-five or sixty) is selected as the age for compulsory retirement? In the mid-1970s, Congress answered this question by making old age a new civil right; except for a few jobs, such as university faculty, compulsory retirement at seventy is now an unlawful, unreasonable, discriminatory use of age.[40]

Plessy *v.* Ferguson: *"Separate but Equal"*

Following its initial decisions making "equal protection" a civil rights clause, the Supreme Court turned conservative, no more ready to enforce the civil rights aspects of the Fourteenth Amendment than it was to enforce the civil liberties provisions. As we have seen, the Court declared the Civil Rights Act of 1875 unconstitutional on the ground that the act sought to protect blacks against discrimination by *private* businesses, while the Fourteenth Amendment, according to the Court's interpretation, was intended to protect individuals from discrimination only against actions by *public* officials of state and local governments.

In 1896, the Court went still further, in the infamous case of *Plessy* v. *Ferguson,* by upholding a Louisiana statute that *required* segregation of the races on trolleys and other public carriers (and by implication in all public facilities, including schools). Plessy, a man defined as "one-eighth black," had violated a Louisiana law that provided for "equal but separate accommodations" on trains and a $25 fine for any white passenger who sat in a car reserved for blacks or any black passenger who sat in a car reserved for whites. The Supreme Court held that the Fourteenth Amendment's "equal protection of the laws" was not violated by racial distinction as long as the facilities were equal. People generally pretended they were equal as long as some accommodation existed. The Court said that although "the object of the [Fourteenth] Amendment was undoubtedly to enforce the absolute equality of the two races before the law, . . . it could not have intended to abolish distinctions based on color, or to enforce social, as distinguished from political, equality, or a commingling of the two races upon terms unsatisfactory to either."[41] What the Court was saying in effect was that the use of race as a criterion of exclusion in public matters was not unreasonable.

[40]The best recent analysis will be found in Lawrence M. Friedman, *Your Time Will Come: The Law of Age Discrimination and Mandatory Retirement* (New York: Russell Sage Foundation, 1984).

[41]Plessy v. Ferguson, 163 U.S. 537 (1896).

The shame of discrimination against black military personnel during World War II, plus revelation of Nazi racial atrocities, moved President Harry S. Truman finally to bring the problem to the White House and national attention, with the appointment in 1946 of a President's Committee on Civil Rights. In 1948, the committee submitted its report, *To Secure These Rights*, which laid bare the extent of the problem of racial discrimination and its consequences. The report also revealed the success of experiments with racial integration in the armed forces during World War II to demonstrate to southern society that it had nothing to fear. But the committee recognized that the national government had no clear constitutional authority to pass and implement civil rights legislation. The committee proposed tying civil rights legislation to the commerce power, although it was clear that discrimination was not itself part of the flow of interstate commerce.[42] The committee even suggested using the treaty power as a source of constitutional authority for civil rights legislation.[43]

As for the Supreme Court, it had begun to change its position regarding racial discrimination ever so slightly before World War II by being stricter about what the states would have to do to meet the criterion of equal facilities in the "separate but equal" rule. In 1938, the Court rejected Missouri's policy of paying the tuition of qualified blacks to out-of-state law schools rather than admitting them to the University of Missouri Law School.[44] After the war, modest progress resumed. In 1950, the Court rejected Texas's claim that its new law school for Negroes afforded education equal to that of the all-white University of Texas Law School; without confronting the "separate but equal" principle itself, the Court's decision anticipated *Brown* v. *Board* by opening the question of whether *any* segregated facility could be truly equal.[45]

---

[42]The prospect of a Fair Employment Practices law tied to the commerce power produced the Dixiecrat break with the Democratic party in 1948. The Democratic party organization of the States of the Old Confederacy seceded from the national party and nominated their own candidate, the then Democratic governor of South Carolina, Strom Thurmond, who is now a Republican senator. This almost cost President Truman the election.

[43]This was based on the little appreciated provision in Article VI of the Constitution, the famous "supremacy clause," which provides that in addition to the Constitution and the laws, "all treaties made, . . . under the authority of the United States," shall be the "supreme law of the land." The committee recognized that if the U.S. Senate ratified the Human Rights Covenant of the United Nations—a treaty—then it would become a source of power for the U.S. Congress, even if that power did not otherwise exist under other constitutional provisions. This proposal, however, caused such a special furor that it led to a serious effort to amend the Constitution. The proposed amendment provided that "a treaty [or executive agreement] shall become effective as internal law only through legislation which would be valid in the absence of the treaty." This amendment failed by only one vote in the Senate, and this only after President Dwight D. Eisenhower and Secretary of State John Foster Dulles announced their opposition to it. But it was a sign that it would be politically impossible to use the treaty power as the constitutional umbrella for effective civil rights legislation. The Supreme Court had recognized in Missouri v. Holland, 252 U.S. 416 (1920), that a treaty could enlarge federal power at the expense of the states. A later court recognized that executive agreements have the same status as treaties, despite the fact that they do not require the "advice and consent" of the Senate. This meant that executive agreements would have the same status as treaties in being a source of power for Congress, United States v. Pink, 315 U.S. 203 (1942).

[44]Missouri ex rel. Gaines v. Canada, 305 U.S. 337 (1938).

[45]Sweatt v. Painter, 339 U.S. 629 (1950).

122
THE
CONSTITUTIONAL
FRAMEWORK
AND THE
INDIVIDUAL

Dennis Banks
America's First Americans

Dennis Banks (b. 1932)

Broken promises, broken treaties, and savage treatment followed by neglect were all experienced by the first people to occupy the American continent. Even though the Indian Wars ended long ago, Native Americans continue to struggle for their rights as they face poverty, discrimination, alcoholism, and widespread hopelessness on their reservations. Native American activist Dennis Banks has struggled for over twenty years to dramatize these problems and improve the lives of his people.

A member of the Chippewa, or Ojibwa, Banks was born in Minnesota but was sent to boarding schools in North and South Dakota run by the Bureau of Indian Affairs (BIA), where the students were forbidden to speak their native language. Banks joined the Air Force in 1953. With no job opportunities after his discharge, he took to drinking and petty crime, for which he went to prison. After his release from prison, he decided to devote his life to his people, and in 1968 he co-founded the American Indian Movement (AIM). AIM first made national headlines in 1969 when 200 Indians, including Banks, took over the abandoned federal prison, Alcatraz, just off the coast of California, saying they were reclaiming it for the Indians. The occupation lasted over eighteen months, but in the end accomplished nothing. In 1972, the group staged a march on Washington, called the Trail of Broken Treaties, which converged on the offices of the BIA. After a scuffle with police, some of the marchers took over the building, occupying it for five days. The occupation resulted in a leadership shakeup at BIA, but again no real policy changes.

In a move that garnered considerable national attention, Banks and other AIM members took over the town of Wounded Knee in 1971, the site of the last major battle and massacre of Indians in 1890. Periodic gunfire was exchanged between the Indians and federal agents during the seventy-one-day standoff. The occupation finally ended by negotiation, with promises from the federal government to investigate Indian complaints. Banks and other leaders were eventually convicted for their involvement in the takeover. Later investigations revealed that the government had falsified evidence against Banks and another activist, Russell Means, and the charges were eventually dropped. Still facing prison time for another crime, Banks fled to California, where he served for a time as chancellor of D-Q University, in Davis, California, a two-year college for Indian students. In 1984, however, Banks gave himself up to South Dakota officials and served a year in prison.

Returning to a South Dakota reservation, Banks switched to less confrontational and more local activities, working as an alcohol counselor. He also persuaded Honeywell and other companies to locate plants in the area, which provided hundreds of jobs to formerly unemployed Indians. He has continued to serve as a leader and spokesman for Indian causes.

Banks and other AIM members have turned away from the militancy of the 1970s. Yet that militancy, and the extensive press coverage, especially of the Alcatraz and Wounded Knee incidents, served to focus national attention on the plight of America's first Americans.

Source: Dee A. Brown, *Bury My Heart at Wounded Knee* (New York: Pocket Books, 1981).

But the Supreme Court, in ordering the admission of blacks to all-white state
law schools, did not directly confront the principle of the "separate but equal" rule
of *Plessy* because the Court needed only to recognize the absence of any law
school for blacks. The same was true in 1944, when the Supreme Court struck
down the southern practice of "white primaries," which legally excluded blacks
from participation in the nominating process. Here the Court simply recognized
that primaries could no longer be regarded as the private affairs of the parties but
were an integral aspect of the electoral process. This made parties "an agency of
the State," and therefore any practice of discrimination against blacks was "state action within the meaning of the Fifteenth Amendment."[46] The most important
pre-1954 decision was probably *Shelley v. Kraemer,*[47] in which the Court ruled
against the widespread practice of "restrictive covenants," whereby the seller of a
home added a clause to the sales contract requiring the buyer to agree not to sell
the home later to any non-Caucasian, non-Christian, etc. The Court ruled that although private persons could sign such restrictive covenants, they could not be judicially enforced since the Fourteenth Amendment prohibits any organ of the
state, including the courts, from denying equal protection of its laws.

Although none of those pre-1954 cases confronted "separate but equal" and the
principle of racial discrimination as such, they were extremely significant to black
leaders in the 1940s, giving them encouragement enough to believe that there was
at last an opportunity and enough legal precedent to change the constitutional
framework itself. Until then, lawyers working for the Legal Defense Fund of the
National Association for the Advancement of Colored People (NAACP) concentrated on winning small victories within that framework. Then in 1948, the Legal
Defense Fund upgraded their approach by simultaneously filing suits in different
federal districts and through each level of schooling from unequal provision of
kindergarten for blacks to unequal sports and science facilities in all-black high
schools. After nearly two years of these mostly successful equalization suits, the
lawyers decided the time was ripe to confront *Plessy* head on, but they felt they
needed some heavier artillery to lead the attack. Their choice was Thurgood Marshall, who had been fighting, and mainly winning, equalization suits since the
early 1930s. Marshall was pessimistic about the readiness of the Supreme Court for
a full confrontation with segregation itself and the constitutional principle sustaining it. But the unwillingness of Congress after the 1948 election to consider fair
employment legislation seems to have convinced Marshall that the courts were the
only hope.

The Supreme Court must have come to the same conclusion because, during
the four years following 1948, there emerged a clear impression that the Court was
willing to take more civil rights cases on appeal. Yet, this was no guarantee that the
Court would reverse *on principle* the separate but equal precedent of *Plessy* v. *Ferguson*. All through 1951 and 1952, as cases like *Brown* v. *Board* and *Bolling* v. *Sharpe*
were winding slowly through the lower court litigation maze, there were intense
discussions and disagreements among NAACP lawyers as to whether a full-scale
assault on *Plessy* was good strategy or whether it might not be better to continue
with specific cases alleging unequal treatment and demanding relief with a Court-

[46]Smith v. Allwright, 321 U.S. 649 (1944).
[47]Shelley v. Kraemer, 334 U.S. 1 (1948).

124

THE
CONSTITUTIONAL
FRAMEWORK
AND THE
INDIVIDUAL

Cause and Effect in the Civil Rights Movement:
Interactions between Government Action and Political Action

Judicial and Legal Action	Political Action
1954 *Brown* v. *Board of Education*	
1955 *Brown* II—Implementation of *Brown* I	**1955** Montgomery Bus Boycott
1956 Federal courts order school integration, especially one ordering Autherine Lucy admitted to University of Alabama, with Governor Wallace officially protesting	
1957 Civil Rights Act creating Civil Rights Commission; President Eisenhower sends paratroops to Little Rock, Arkansas, to enforce integration of Central High School	**1957** Southern Christian Leadership Conference (SCLC) formed, with King as president
1960 First substantive Civil Rights Act, primarily voting rights	**1960** Student Nonviolent Coordinating Committee formed to organize protests, sit-ins, freedom rides
1961 Interstate Commerce Commission orders desegregation on all buses, trains, and in terminals	
1961 JFK favors executive action over civil rights legislation	
1963 JFK shifts, supports strong civil rights law; assassination; LBJ asserts strong support for civil rights	**1963** Nonviolent demonstrations in Burmingham, Alababma, lead to King's arrest and his "Letter from the Birmingham Jail"
	1963 March on Washington
1964 Congress passes historic Civil Rights Act covering voting, employment, public accommodations, education	
1965 Voting Rights Act	**1965** King announces drive to register 3 million blacks in the South
1966 War on Poverty in full swing	Movement dissipates: part toward litigation, part toward Community Action Programs, part toward war protest, part toward more militant "Black Power" actions

imposed policy of equalization.[48] But for some lawyers like Marshall, these kinds of victories could amount to a defeat. South Carolina, for example, under the leadership of Governor James F. Byrnes, a former Supreme Court Justice, had undertaken a strategy of equalization of school services on a large scale in order to satisfy the *Plessy* rule and to head off or render moot litigation against the principle of separate but equal.

In the fall of 1952, the Court had on its docket cases from Kansas, South Carolina, Virginia, Delaware, and the District of Columbia challenging the constitutionality of school segregation. Of these, the Kansas case became the chosen one. It seemed to be ahead of the pack in its district court, and it had the special advantage of being located in a state outside the Deep South.[49]

Oliver Brown, the father of three girls, lived "across the tracks" in a low-income, racially mixed Topeka neighborhood. Every school-day morning, Linda Brown took the school bus to Monroe School for colored children about a mile away. In September 1950, Oliver Brown took Linda to the all-white Sumner School, which was actually closer to home, to enter her into the third grade in defiance of state law and local segregation rules. When they were refused, Brown took his case to the NAACP, and soon thereafter *Brown* v. *Board of Education of Topeka* was born. In mid-1953, the Court announced that the several cases on their way up would be re-argued within a set of questions having to do with the intent of the Fourteenth Amendment. Almost exactly a year later, the Court responded to those questions in one of the most important decisions in its history.

In deciding the case, the Court, to the surprise of many, basically rejected as inconclusive all the learned arguments about the intent and the history of the Fourteenth Amendment and committed itself to considering only the consequences of segregation:

> Does segregation of children in public schools solely on the basis of race, even though the physical facilities and other "tangible" factors may be equal, deprive the children of the minority group of equal educational opportunities? We believe that it does. . . . We conclude that in the field of public education the doctrine of "separate but equal" has no place. Separate educational facilities are inherently unequal.[50]

The *Brown* decision altered the constitutional framework in two fundamental respects. First, after *Brown,* the states would no longer have the power to use race as a criterion of discrimination in law. Second, the national government would from then on have the power (and eventually the obligation) to intervene with strict regulatory policies against the discriminatory actions of state or local governments, school boards, employers, and many others in the private sector (see Chapters 15 and 17).

---

[48]Kermit L. Hall, *The Magic Mirror—Law in American History* (New York: Oxford University Press, 1989), pp. 322–24. See also Richard Kluger, *Simple Justice,* (New York: Random House, Vintage Edition, 1977), pp. 530–37.

[49]The District of Columbia case came up too, but since the District of Columbia is not a state, this case did not directly involve the Fourteenth Amendment and its "equal protection" clause. It confronted the Court on the same grounds, however, that segregation is inherently unequal. Its victory in effect was "incorporation in reverse," with equal protection moving from the Fourteenth Amendment to become part of the Bill of Rights (Bolling v. Sharpe, 347 U.S. 497 [1954]).

[50]Brown v. Board of Education of Topeka, Kansas, 347 U.S. 483 (1954).

Rights for blacks. In the mid-1950s, black people began organizing against the Jim Crow laws, which kept them segregated from white people in public facilities, including restaurants, washrooms, buses, trains, and, most importantly, schools. An early nonviolent form of protest was the sit-in, during which blacks would enter a segregated facility and break the law by sitting in a "whites only" space.

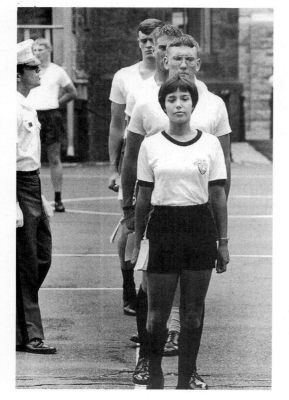

Rights for women. Although the women's movement dates back to the 1800s, the latest surge of activity came in the 1970s. Women sought equal opportunity and equal pay for their work, whether as heads of corporations, as journalists, or as soldiers. This woman was among the first group to go to West Point in the mid-1970s. Women served actively in the Persian Gulf War and have increased their efforts to be involved in combat duty.

Rights for homosexuals. Gay men, lesbians, and their supporters struggle to end discrimination based on sexual orientation. Their movement has sought to abolish both *de facto* prejudice by changing negative perceptions of homosexuals and *de jure* prejudice that has restricted their right to equal opportunities in employment and housing.

Rights for the handicapped. President Bush signed into law the Discrimination against Disabilities Act on July 26, 1990. The bill prohibits discrimination against those with a physical or mental condition "that substantially limits a major life activity" such as seeing or walking. It reaches into the areas of employment, public accommodations, telecommunications, and transportation.

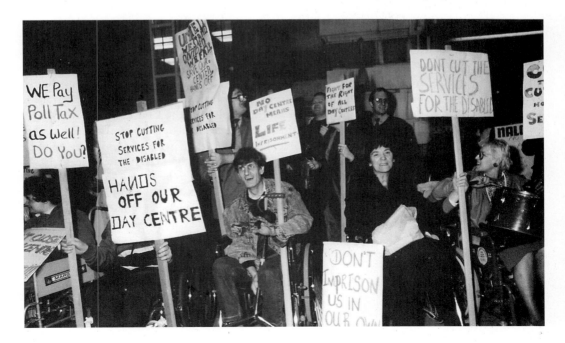

128
THE
CONSTITUTIONAL
FRAMEWORK
AND THE
INDIVIDUAL

Simple Justice: *The Courts, the Constitution, and Civil Rights after* Brown *v.* Board of Education

Although *Brown v. Board of Education* withdrew all constitutional authority to use race as a criterion of exclusion, this historic decision was merely a small opening move.[51] First, the Court ruling "to admit to public schools on a racially nondiscriminatory basis with all delibrate speed," which came a year later, [52] was directly binding only on the five school boards that had been defendants in the cases appealed to the Supreme Court. Rather than fall into line, as most parties do when a new judicial principle is handed down, most states refused to cooperate until sued, and many ingenious schemes were employed to delay obedience (such as paying the tuition for white students to attend newly created "private" academies). Second, even as southern school boards began to cooperate by eliminating their legally enforced (*de jure*) school segregation, there remained extensive actual (*de facto*) school segregation in the North as well as the South, as a consequence of racially segregated housing that could not be reached by the 1954–1955 *Brown* principles. Third, discrimination in employment, public accommodations, juries, voting, and other areas of social and economic activity were not directly touched by *Brown*.

A decade of frustration following *Brown* made it fairly obvious to all that adjudication alone would not succeed. The goal of "equal protection" required positive, or affirmative, action by Congress and by administrative agencies. And given massive southern resistance and a generally negative national public opinion toward racial integration, progress would not be made through courts, Congress, *or* agencies without intense, well-organized support. Table 4.3 shows the increase in civil rights demonstrations for voting rights and public accommodations. It shows that there were virtually no significant, organized civil rights demonstrations prior to *Brown v. Board of Education* and that the frequency of these demonstrations mounted slowly but surely until the 1960s. At that time, political action and congressional action culminated in a series of stunning majorities in congressional votes for enactment of fundamental new civil rights laws. An important insight to be drawn from Table 4.3 is that the constitutional action by the Supreme Court in 1954–1955 actually *produced* the civil rights movement as it came to be known in the late 1950s. Adding Table 4.4 to Table 4.3 brings forth still another insight into the political relationships among the three branches of the national government. Just as *political* agitation to expand rights followed the Court's formal recognition of their existence, so did greatly expanded *judicial* action follow the success of political action in Congress. Table 4.4 confirms this with the enormous jump in NAACP-sponsored civil rights cases brought in the federal courts, from 107 in 1963 to 145 in 1964 and 225 in 1965, continuing to move upward thereafter. The number of actual cases brought by the Legal Defense Fund of the NAACP actually continued to go up at a significant rate even as the number of individuals defended by these cases dropped. This suggests how strongly the NAACP was interested in

---

[51]The heading for this section is drawn from the title of Richard Kluger's important book, *Simple Justice.*

[52]Brown v. Board of Education of Topeka, 349 U.S. 294 (1955), often referred to as *Brown II.*

TABLE 4.3

129
CIVIL RIGHTS

Peaceful Civil Rights Demonstrations,* 1954–1968

Year	Total	For Public Accommodations	For Voting
1954	0	0	0
1955	0	0	0
1956	18	6	0
1957	44	9	0
1958	19	8	0
1959	7	11	0
1960	173	127	0
1961	198	122	0
1962	77	44	0
1963	272	140	1
1964	271	93	12
1965	387	21	128
1966	171	15	32
1967	93	3	3
1968	97	2	0

*This table is drawn from a search of the *New York Times Index* for all references to civil rights demonstrations during the years the table covers. The table should be taken simply as indicative, for the data—news stories in a single paper—are very crude. The classification of the incident as peaceful or violent and the subject area of the demonstration are inferred from the entry in the *Index,* usually the headline from the story. The two subcategories reported here—public accommodations and voting—do not sum to the total because demonstrations dealing with a variety of other issues (e.g., education, employment, police brutality) are included in the total.
Source: Jonathan D. Casper, *The Politics of Civil Liberties* (New York: Harper & Row, 1972), p. 90.

using the cases to advance the principles of civil rights rather than to improve the prospects of individual black litigants.

School Desegregation, Phase One Although the District of Columbia and some of the school districts in the border states began to respond almost immediately to court-ordered desegregation, the states of the Deep South responded with a well-planned delaying tactic commonly called "massive resistance" by the more dema-

TABLE 4.4
Activity of NAACP Legal Defense and Educational Fund (LDF), 1963–1967

Year	Individuals Defended by the LDF	Cases on LDF Docket
1963	4,200	107
1964	10,400	145
1965	17,000	225
1966	14,000	375
1967	13,000	420

Source: Data from *Report 66,* published in 1967 by the NAACP Legal Defense and Educational Fund, Inc., New York. Reprinted from Jonathan D. Casper, *The Politics of Civil Liberties* (New York: Harper & Row, 1972), p. 91. Reprinted by permission of the NAACP Legal Defense and Educational Fund, Inc.

130

THE
CONSTITUTIONAL
FRAMEWORK
AND THE
INDIVIDUAL

gogic southern leaders and "nullification" and "interposition" by the centrists. Either way, southern politicians stood shoulder to shoulder to declare that the Supreme Court's decisions and orders were without effect. The legislatures in these states enacted statutes ordering school districts to maintain segregated schools and state superintendents to terminate state funding wherever there was racial mixing in the classroom. Some southern states violated their own long tradition of local school autonomy, and they centralized public school authority under the governor or the state board of education, giving them power to close the schools and to provide alternative private schooling wherever local school boards might be tending to obey the Supreme Court.

Most of these plans of "massive resistance" were tested in the federal courts and were struck down as unconstitutional.[53] But southern resistance was not confined to legislation. For example, in Arkansas in 1957, Governor Orval Faubus mobilized the National Guard to intercede against enforcement of a federal court order to integrate Central High School of Little Rock, and President Eisenhower was forced to deploy U.S. troops and literally place the city under martial law. The Supreme Court considered the Little Rock confrontation so historically important that the opinion they rendered in that case was not only agreed to unanimously but was, unprecedentedly, signed personally by each and every one of the justices.[54] The end of massive resistance, however, became simply the beginning of still another southern strategy, "pupil placement" laws, which authorized school districts to place each pupil in a school according to a whole variety of academic, personal, and psychological considerations, never mentioning race at all. This put the burden of transferring to an all-white school on the nonwhite children and their parents, making it almost impossible for a single court order to cover a whole district, let alone a whole state. This delayed desegregation a while longer.[55]

As new devices were invented by the southern states to avoid desegregation, the federal courts followed with cases and decisions quashing them. Ten years after *Brown,* less than 1 percent of black school-age children in the Deep South were attending schools with whites.[56] It had become unmistakably clear well before that time that the federal courts could not do the job alone. The first modern effort to legislate in the field of civil rights was made in 1957; but the law contained only a federal guarantee of voting rights, without any powers of enforcement, although it did create the Civil Rights Commission to study abuses. Much more important

[53]The two most important cases were Cooper v. Aaron, 358 U.S. 1 (1958), which required Little Rock, Arkansas, to desegregate; and Griffin v. Prince Edward County School Board, 377 U.S. 218 (1964), which forced all the schools of that county to reopen after five years of closing to avoid desegregation.

[54]In *Cooper,* the Supreme Court ordered immediate compliance with the lower court's desegregation order and went beyond that with a stern warning that it is "emphatically the province and duty of the judicial department to say what the law is."

[55]Shuttlesworth v. Birmingham Board of Education, 358 U.S. 101 (1958). This decision upheld a "pupil placement" plan purporting to assign pupils on various bases, with no mention of race. This case interpreted *Brown* to mean that school districts must stop explicit racial discrimination but were under no obligation to take positive steps to desegregate. For awhile black parents were doomed to case-by-case approaches.

[56]For good treatments of that long stretch of the struggle of the federal courts to integrate the schools, see Brest and Levinson, *Processes of Constitutional Decisionmaking,* pp. 471–80; and Kelly et al., *The American Constitution,* pp. 610–16.

Martin Luther King, Jr.
A Drum Major for Justice

No advocate for civil rights could lay greater claim to having advanced the standards of justice and equality for blacks than this highly educated, charismatic minister from Georgia.

Martin Luther King, Jr., received his Ph.D. in theology from Boston University in 1955. His studies of philosophy and religion shaped his approach to the struggle for civil rights. In his words, "From my Christian background I gained my ideals, and from [Mohandas K.] Gandhi my operational technique."

King first received national attention for his leadership of the Montgomery Improvement Association, an organization formed in 1955 to integrate the Alabama city's segregated bus system. During the 382-day boycott, King's home was firebombed and he was arrested for the first of many times. Yet he urged positive, nonviolent action, a strategy borrowed from Gandhi's successful effort to free India from British rule, and Christian forgiveness of one's enemies. The strategy worked in Montgomery, and throughout the South.

In 1957, King co-founded the Southern Christian Leadership Conference, becoming president and leader of efforts to eliminate racial discrimination in transportation facilities, public accommodations, hiring practices, and voting. In 1957 alone, King traveled 780,000 miles and delivered 208 speeches. In succeeding years, King met with presidents, world leaders, and countless thousands of fellow Americans to advance the rights and dignity

Martin Luther King, Jr. (1929–1968)

of all Americans. Repeatedly beaten, arrested, and threatened with death, King and his followers continued to employ the tactics of civil disobedience and passive resistance in the face of guns, fire hoses, and police dogs.

King galvanized national opinion as a leader of the March on Washington in August 1963. Addressing the over 250,000 participants from the steps of the Lincoln Memorial, he delivered his prophetic and moving "I Have a Dream" speech. The following year, King was awarded the Nobel Peace Prize, becoming at thirty-five the youngest-ever recipient. This and other efforts stirred the nation's conscience, contributing directly to the enactment of landmark civil rights legislation in the 1960s.

Despite rising violence in the mid-1960s, King continued to urge nonviolence. The cycle of violence eventually snared the Georgia preacher, as he was shot and killed by an assassin's bullet outside of a Memphis, Tennessee, motel on April 4, 1968. The previous February when asked what he wanted as a eulogy, King had responded "Say that I was a drum major for justice. Say that I was a drum major for peace. Say that I was a drum major for righteousness."

Source: Juan Williams, *Eyes on the Prize* (New York: Penguin, 1988).

132

THE
CONSTITUTIONAL
FRAMEWORK
AND THE
INDIVIDUAL

legislation for civil rights followed, especially the Civil Rights Act of 1964. These acts will be discussed in Chapter 17, but it is important to observe again here the mutual dependence of the courts and legislatures—not only the need of the legislatures for constitutional authority to act, but the need of the courts for legislative and political assistance, through the power of the purse, the power to organize administrative agencies to implement court orders, and through the focusing of political support. Consequently, even as the U.S. Congress finally moved into the field of school desegregation (and other areas of "equal protection"), the courts continued to exercise their powers, not only by placing court orders against recalcitrant school districts, but also by extending and reinterpreting aspects of the "equal protection" clause to support legislative and administrative actions.

School Desegregation: Busing and Beyond   The most important judicial extension of civil rights in education after 1954 was probably the *Swann* decision, which held that state-imposed desegregation could be brought about by "busing," indeed busing of children across school districts even where relatively long distances were involved:

> If school authorities fail in their affirmative obligations judicial authority may be invoked. Once a right and a violation have been shown, the scope of a district court's equitable powers to remedy past wrongs is broad. . . . *Bus transportation [is] a normal and accepted tool of educational policy.*[57]

But the decision went beyond that, adding that under certain limited circumstances even racial quotas could be used as the "starting point in shaping a remedy to correct past constitutional violations," and that pairing or grouping of schools and reorganizing school attendance zones would also be acceptable.

Three years later, however, the *Swann* case was severely restricted when the Supreme Court determined that only cities found guilty of deliberate and *de jure* racial segregation (segregation in law) would have to desegregate their schools.[58] This was the 1974 case of *Milliken* v. *Bradley* involving the city of Detroit and its suburbs. The *Milliken* ruling had the effect of exempting most northern states and cities from busing because school segregation in northern cities is generally *de facto* segregation (segregation in fact) that follows from segregated housing and from thousands of acts of private discrimination against blacks and other minorities.

Detroit and Boston provide the best illustrations of the agonizing problem of making further progress in civil rights in the schools under the constitutional framework established by the *Swann* and *Milliken* cases. Following *Swann,* the federal district court and the court of appeals had found that Detroit had engaged in deliberate segregation and that, since Detroit schools were overwhelmingly black, the only way to provide a remedy was to bus students between Detroit and the white suburbs beyond the Detroit city boundaries. The Supreme Court in *Swann* had approved a similar "interdistrict" integration plan for Charlotte, North Carolina, but it refused to do so in Detroit. Although Detroit's segregation had been deliberate, the city and suburban boundary lines had not been drawn deliberately

---

[57]Swann v. Charlotte-Mecklenburg Board of Education, 402 U.S. 1 (1971). [Emphasis added.]
[58]Milliken v. Bradley, 418 U.S. 717 (1974).

to separate the races. Therefore, the remedy had to take place within Detroit. That same year, and no doubt influenced by the Detroit decision as well as by President Nixon, Congress amended Title VI of the 1964 Civil Rights Act, reducing the authority of the federal government to withhold monetary assistance only in instances of proven *de jure,* state government–imposed segregation. This action was extremely significant in taking the heat off most northern school districts.

In Boston, school authorities were found guilty of deliberately building school facilities and drawing school districts "to increase racial segregation." After vain efforts by Boston school authorities to draw up an acceptable plan, federal Judge W. Arthur Garrity ordered an elaborate desegregation plan of his own involving busing between the all-black ghetto of Roxbury and the nearby white working-class community of South Boston. Opponents of this plan were organized and eventually took the case to the Supreme Court, where *certiorari* (the Court's device for accepting appeals) was denied; this had the effect of approving Judge Garrity's order (see Chapter 8). The facts were that the city's schools were so segregated and uncooperative that even the conservative Nixon administration had already initiated a punitive cutoff of funds. But many liberals also criticized Judge Garrity's plan as being badly conceived, because it involved two neighboring communities with a history of tension and mutual resentment. The plan worked well at the elementary school level but proved so explosive at the high school level that it generated a continuing crisis for the entire city and for the whole nation over court-ordered, federally directed desegregation in the North.[59]

Additional progress in the desegregation of schools is likely to be extremely slow unless the Supreme Court decides to permit federal action against *de facto* segregation and against the varieties of private schools and academies that have sprung up for the purpose of avoiding integration. The prospects for further school integration diminished with the Supreme Court decision handed down January 15, 1991. The opinion, written for the Court by Chief Justice Rehnquist, held that lower federal courts could end supervision of local school boards if those boards could show compliance "in good faith" with court orders to desegregate and could show that "vestiges of past discrimination" had been eliminated "to the extent practicable." It will not necessarily be easy for a school board to prove that the new standard has been met, but this is the first time since *Brown* and the 1964 Civil Rights Act that the Court has opened the door at all to retreat.

Outlawing Discrimination in Employment   Despite the agonizingly slow progress of school desegregation, there was some progress in other areas of civil rights during the 1960s and 1970s. Voting rights were established and fairly quickly began to revolutionize southern politics. Service on juries was no longer denied to minorities. But progress in the right to participate in politics and government dramatized the relative lack of progress in the economic domain. This became the new frontier in the civil rights struggle, and with it came the historic joining of women's rights to the civil rights cause.

---

[59]For a good evaluation of the Boston effort, see Gary Orfield, *Must We Bus? Segregated Schools and National Policy* (Washington: Brookings Institution, 1978) pp. 144–46. See also Bob Woodward and Scott Armstrong, *The Brethren: Inside the Supreme Court* (New York: Simon and Schuster, 1979), pp. 426–27; and J. Anthony Lukas, *Common Ground* (New York: Random House, 1986).

134
THE
CONSTITUTIONAL
FRAMEWORK
AND THE
INDIVIDUAL

The federal courts and the Justice Department entered this area through Title VII of the Civil Rights Act of 1964 (see also Chapter 17), which outlawed job discrimination by all private and public employers, including governmental agencies (such as fire and police departments), that employed more than fifteen workers. We have already seen that the Supreme Court gave "interstate commerce" such a broad definition that Congress had the constitutional authority to cover discrimination by virtually any local employers.[60] Title VII makes it unlawful to discriminate in employment on the basis of color, religion, sex, and national origin, as well as race.

The first problem with Title VII was that the complaining party had to show that deliberate discrimination was the cause of the failure to get the job or the training opportunity. Rarely does an employer explicitly admit discrimination on the basis of race, sex, or any other illegal reason. Recognizing the rarity of such an admission, the courts have allowed aggrieved parties (the plaintiffs) to make their case if they can show that an employer's hiring practices had the *effect* of exclusion. A leading case in 1971 involved a "class action" by several black employees in North Carolina attempting to show with statistical evidence that blacks had been relegated to only one department in the Duke Power Company, which involved the least desirable, manual-labor jobs, and that they had been kept out of contention for the better jobs because the employer had added high school education and the passing of specially prepared aptitude tests as qualifications. The Supreme Court held that although the statistical evidence did not prove intentional discrimination, and although the requirements were race-neutral in appearance, their effects were sufficient to shift the burden of justification to the employer to show that his requirements were a "business necessity" that bore "a demonstrable relationship to successful performance."[61] The ruling in this case was subsequently applied to other hiring, promotion, and training programs.[62]

The Politics of Rights: Affirmative Action

Even before equal employment laws were beginning to have a positive effect on the economic situation of blacks, something far more dramatic was already happening—the *universalization* of civil rights. That is, the right not to be discriminated against was being successfully claimed by the other groups listed in Title VII,

[60]See especially Katzenbach v. McClung, 379 U.S. 294 (1964). Almost immediately after passage of the Civil Rights Act of 1964, a case was brought challenging the validity of Title II, which covered discrimination in public accommodations. Ollie's Barbecue was a neighborhood restaurant in Birmingham, Alabama, located eleven blocks away from an interstate highway and even farther from railroad and bus stations. Its table service was for whites only; there was only a take-out service for blacks. The Supreme Court agreed that Ollie's was strictly an intrastate restaurant, but since a substantial proportion of its food and other supplies were bought from companies outside the state of Alabama, there was a sufficient connection to interstate commerce; therefore, racial discrimination at such restaurants would "impose commercial burdens of national magnitude upon interstate commerce." Although this case involved Title II, it had direct bearing on the constitutionality of Title VII.

[61]Griggs v. Duke Power Company, 401 U.S. 24 (1971). See also Allan Sindler, *Bakke, DeFunis, and Minority Admissions* (New York: Longman, 1978), pp. 180–89.

[62]For a good treatment of these issues, see Charles O. Gregory and Harold A. Katz, *Labor and the Law* (New York: W. W. Norton, 1979), Chapter 17.

those defined by religion, sex, or national origin—and eventually by still other groups defined by age and by sexual preference. Any group or individual can try, and in fact is encouraged to try, to convert their goals and grievances into questions of rights and the deprivation of their rights. What they have to establish is that any important choice based upon their membership in a group is an unreasonable basis for discrimination unless it can be proven to be "job-related" or otherwise clearly reasonable and relevant.

The politics of rights not only spread to increasing numbers of groups in the society, it also expanded its goal. The relatively narrow goal of equalizing opportunity by eliminating discriminatory barriers had been developing toward the far broader goal of **affirmative action**—compensatory action to overcome the consequences of past discrimination. An affirmative action policy tends to involve two novel approaches: (1) positive or benign discrimination in which race or some other status is actually taken into account, but for compensatory action rather than mistreatment; and (2) compensatory action to favor members of the disadvantaged group who themselves may never have been the victims of discrimination. (Quotas may be but are not necessarily involved in affirmative action policies.)

In 1965, President Johnson attempted to inaugurate affirmative action by executive orders directing agency heads and personnel officers to pursue vigorously a policy of minority employment in the federal civil service and in companies doing business with the national government. But affirmative action did not become a prominent goal until the 1970s.

As this movement spread, it also began to divide civil rights activists and their supporters. The whole issue of qualification versus minority preference was addressed formally in the case of Allan Bakke. Bakke, a white male with no minority affiliation, brought suit against the University of California at Davis Medical School on the ground that in denying him admission the school had discriminated against him on the basis of his race (that year the school had reserved 16 of 100 available slots for minority applicants). He argued that his grades and test scores had ranked him well above many students who had been accepted at the school and that the only possible explanation for his rejection was that those others accepted were black or Hispanic while he was white. In 1978, Bakke won his case before the Supreme Court and was admitted to the medical school, but he did not succeed in getting affirmative action declared unconstitutional. The Court rejected the procedures at the University of California because its medical school had used both a quota *and* a separate admissions system for minorities. The Court agreed with Bakke's argument that racial categorizations are suspect categories that place a severe burden of proof on the state to show a "compelling public purpose." The Court went on to say that achieving "a diverse student body" was such a public purpose, but the method of a rigid quota of student slots assigned on the basis of race was incompatible with the equal protection clause. Thus, the Court permitted universities (and presumably other schools, training programs, and hiring authorities) to continue to take minority status into consideration but limited severely the use of quotas to situations in which (1) previous discrimination had been shown, and (2) it was used more as a *guideline* for social diversity than as a mathematically defined ratio.[63]

[63]Regents of the University of California v. Bakke, 438 U.S. 265 (1978).

136
THE
CONSTITUTIONAL
FRAMEWORK
AND THE
INDIVIDUAL

Affirmative Action

*T*he principle of equality has long been a bedrock value of the American political *system. Yet the devotion to equality has contrasted sharply with the fact that Americans have not all been treated equally. Women, African Americans, Latinos, Native Americans, and other groups rightly claim that they have suffered historical patterns of discrimination that have deprived them of basic rights. African Americans in particular believe that hundreds of years of slavery and savage treatment cannot simply be wiped away by the proclamation that all are now equal.*

This belief has prompted the government to promote affirmative-action programs designed to provide an added advantage for minorities in areas such as college admissions and employment, based on the principle that past discrimination against African Americans and others can be rectified only by tilting the scales more in their favor now. Advocates of affirmative action, such as Supreme Court Justice Thurgood Marshall, have argued that equal treatment of unequals merely perpetuates inequality. Opponents to such programs, such as law professor Stephen L. Carter, contend that such preferential treatment is inconsistent with American values and may actually harm those it tries to help.

Marshall

Three hundred and fifty years ago, the Negro was dragged to this country in chains to be sold into slavery. Uprooted from his homeland and thrust into bondage for forced labor, the slave was deprived of all legal rights. It was unlawful to teach him to read; he could be sold away from his family and friends at the whim of his master; and killing or maiming him was not a crime. The system of slavery brutalized and dehumanized both master and slave.

The denial of human rights was etched into the American colonies' first attempts at establishing self-government. . . . The self-evident truths and the unalienable rights were intended . . . only to apply to white men. . . . The implicit protection of slavery embodied in the Declaration of Independence was made explicit in the Constitution. . . . The status of the Negro as property was officially erased by his emancipation at the end of the Civil War. But the long awaited emancipation, while freeing the Negro from slavery, did not bring him citizenship or equality in any meaningful way. Despite the passage of the Thirteenth, Fourteenth, and Fifteenth Amendments, the Negro was systematically denied the rights those amendments were supposed to secure. . . . In light of the sorry history of discrimination and its devastating impact on the lives of Negroes, bringing the Negro into the mainstream of American life should be a state interest of the highest order. To fail to do so is to ensure that America will forever remain a divided society. . . . We now must permit the institutions of this society to give consideration to race in making decisions about who will hold the positions of influence, affluence and prestige in America. For far too long, the doors to those positions have been shut to Negroes.[1]

If we as a people were not defeated by slavery and Jim Crow, we will not be defeated by the demise of affirmative action. Before there were any racial preferences, before there was a federal antidiscrimination law with any teeth, our achievements were already on the rise: our middle class was growing, as was our rate of college matriculation—both of them at higher rates than in the years since. Black professionals, in short, should not do much worse without affirmative action than we are doing with it, and thrown on our own resources and knowing that we have no choice but to meet the same tests as everybody else, we may do better.

We must be about the business of defining a future in which we can be fair to ourselves and demand opportunities without falling into the trap of letting others tell us that our horizons are limited, that we cannot make it without assistance. . . . The likely demise, or severe restriction, of racial preferences will also present for us a new stage of struggle, and we should treat it as an opportunity, not a burden. It is our chance to make ourselves free of the assumptions that too often underlie affirmative action, assumptions about our intellectual incapacity and other competitive deficiencies. It is our chance to prove to a doubting, indifferent world that our future as a people is in our hands.[2]

[1]Regents of the University of California v. Bakke, 438 U.S. 265, 387 (1978).

[2]Stephen L. Carter, *Reflections of an Affirmative Action Baby* (New York: Basic Books, 1991), as excerpted in George McKenna and Stanley Feingold, eds., *Taking Sides: Clashing Views on Controversial Political Issues,* 8th ed. (Guilford, CT: Dushkin, 1993), pp. 192–93.

For nearly a decade after *Bakke,* the Supreme Court was tentative and permissive about efforts by corporations and governments to experiment with affirmative action programs in employment.[64] But in 1989, the Court returned to the *Bakke* position that any "rigid numerical quota" is suspect. In *Wards Cove* v. *Atonio,* the Court backed away further from affirmative action by easing the way for employers to prefer white males, holding that the burden of proof of unlawful discrimination should be shifted from the defendant (the employer) to the plaintiff (the person claiming to be the victim of discrimination).[65] This decision virtually over-

[64]United Steelworkers v. Weber, 443 U.S. 193 (1979); and Fullilove v. Klutznick, 100 S.Ct. 2758 (1980).

[65]City of Richmond v. J. A. Croson Co., 109 S.Ct. 706 (1989); Ward's Cove v. Atonio, 109 S.Ct. 2115 (1989).

138

THE
CONSTITUTIONAL
FRAMEWORK
AND THE
INDIVIDUAL

ruled the Court's prior holding in *Griggs*. That same year the Court ruled that any affirmative action program already approved by federal courts could be subsequently challenged by white males who alleged that the program discriminated against them.[66]

In 1991, after a lengthy battle with the White House, Congress enacted a piece of legislation designed to undo the effects of these decisions. Under the terms of the Civil Rights Acts of 1991, the burden of proof in employment discrimination cases was shifted back to employers, overturning the *Wards Cove* decision. In addition, the act made it more difficult to mount later challenges to consent decrees in affirmative action cases, reversing the *Martin* v. *Wilkes* decision. Despite Congress's actions, however, the federal judiciary will have the last word when cases under the new law reach the courts. In a 5-to-4 decision in 1993, the Court ruled that employees had to prove their employers intended discrimination, again placing the burden of proof on employees.[67] Until the 1992 election, there had been little reason to expect that the federal courts would be sympathetic to Congress's efforts. But that could change. President Clinton began his term with nearly fifty federal judgeships to appoint, Congress will almost certainly expand the number of federal judicial posts, and other vacancies will occur at all levels, including that of the Supreme Court, where Clinton has already had one vacancy to fill. (See also Chapter 8.)

Affirmative action efforts have contributed to the polarization of the politics of civil rights. At the risk of grievous oversimplification, we can divide up the sides by two labels: liberals and conservatives.[68] The conservatives' disagreements can be reduced to two major points. The first is that rights in the American tradition are innately individual, and affirmative action violates this concept by concerning itself with "group rights," an idea that they say is alien to the American tradition. The second point has to do with quotas. Conservatives would argue that the Constitution is "color blind," and that any discrimination, even if it is called positive or benign discrimination, ultimately violates the equal protection clause and the American way.

The liberal side agrees that rights ultimately come down to individuals. But since the essence of discrimination is the use of unreasonable and unjust criteria of exclusion to deprive *an entire group* of access to something valuable the society has to offer, then the phenomenon of discrimination itself has to be attacked on a group basis. Liberals can also use Court history to support their side, because the first definitive interpretation of the Fourteenth Amendment by the Supreme Court in 1873 stated explicitly:

[66]Martin v. Wilks, 109 S.Ct. 2180 (1989). In this case, some white fire fighters in Birmingham challenged a consent decree mandating goals for hiring and promoting blacks. This was an affirmative action plan that had been worked out between the employer and aggrieved black employees and had been accepted by a federal court. Such agreements become "consent decrees" and are subject to enforcement. Chief Justice Rehnquist held that the white fire fighters could challenge the legality of such programs, even though they had not been parties to the original litigation.

[67]St. Mary's Honor Center v. Hicks.

[68]There are still many genuine racists in America, but with the exception of a lunatic fringe, made up of neo-Nazis and members of the Ku Klux Klan, most racists are too ashamed or embarrassed to take part in normal political discourse. They are not included in either category here.

The existence of laws in the state where the newly emancipated Negroes resided, which discriminated with gross injustice and hardship against them *as a class,* was the evil to be remedied by this clause.[69]

Liberals also have a response to the other conservative argument concerning quotas. The liberal response is that the Supreme Court has already accepted ratios—a form of quota—that are admitted as evidence to prove a "pattern of practice of discrimination" sufficient to put the burden of proof on the employer to show that there was *not* an intent to discriminate. Liberals can also argue that benign quotas have often been used by Americans both to compensate for some bad action in the past or to provide some desired distribution of social characteristics—sometimes called diversity. For example, a long and respected policy in the United States is "veterans preference," on the basis of which the government automatically adds a certain number of points on civil service examinations to persons who have served the country in the armed forces. The justification is that ex-servicemen deserve compensation for having made sacrifices for the good of the country. And the goal of social diversity has justified "positive discrimination," especially in higher education, the very institution where the conservatives have most adamantly argued against positive quotas for blacks and women. For example, all of the Ivy League schools and many other private colleges and universities regularly and consistently reserve places in their student admissions for some students whose qualifications in a strict academic sense are somewhat below others who are not admitted. These schools not only recruit a few students from minority groups, but they set aside places for the children of loyal alumni and of their own faculty, even when, in a pure competition solely and exclusively based on SAT scores and high school records, many of those same children would not have been admitted. These practices are not conclusive justification in themselves, but they certainly underscore the liberal argument that affirmative or compensatory action for minorities who have been unjustly treated in the past is not alien to American experience.

Although the problems of rights in America are agonizing, they can be looked at optimistically. The United States has a long way to go before it constructs a truly just, "equally protected" society. But it also has come very far in a relatively short time. All explicit *de jure* (legal) barriers to minorities have been dismantled. Many *de facto* barriers have also been dismantled, and thousands upon thousands of new opportunities have been opened. Perhaps the greatest promise, however, is in fact the rise of the "politics of rights." The American people are now accustomed to interest groups—conservative and liberal—who call themselves "public interest groups" and accept their efforts to translate their goals in vigorous and eloquent statements about their rights to their goals. Few people now fear that such a politics of rights will produce violence. Deep and fundamental differences have polarized many groups, but political and governmental institutions have proven themselves capable of maintaining balances between them. This kind of balancing can be done without violence so long as everyone recognizes that policy choices, even about rights, cannot be absolute and final.

Finally, the most important contribution to be made by the politics of rights is

[69]Slaughterhouse Cases, 16 Wallace 36 (1873). [Emphasis added.]

140

THE
CONSTITUTIONAL
FRAMEWORK
AND THE
INDIVIDUAL

probably to the American conscience. Whatever compromises have to be made in order to govern without violence, Americans cannot afford to be satisfied. Injustices do exist. We cannot eliminate them all, but we must maintain our sense of shame for all the injustices that persist. This is precisely why the constitutional framework is so important in the real world and not just in theory. It establishes a context of rights, defined both as limits on the power of the government (civil liberties) and as rightful claims to particular opportunities or benefits (civil rights). Without that framework, rights would remain in the world of abstract philosophy; with that framework, in the United States, they remain now as they did two hundred years ago, real *causes of action*.

SUMMARY

Although freedom and power are inextricably intertwined, they had to be separated for purposes of analysis. *Civil liberties* and *civil rights* are two quite different phenomena and have to be treated legally and constitutionally in two quite different ways. We have defined *civil liberties* as that sphere of individual freedom of choice created by restraints on governmental power. When the Constitution was ratified, it was already seen as inadequate in the provision of protections of individual freedom and required the addition of the Bill of Rights. The Bill of Rights explicitly placed a whole series of restraints on government. Some of these were *substantive,* regarding *what* government could do; and some of these restraints were *procedural,* regarding *how* the government was permitted to act. The rights in the Bill of Rights we call civil liberties because they are rights to be free from arbitrary government interference.

But *which* government? This was settled in the *Barron* case in 1833 when the Supreme Court held that the restraints in the Bill of Rights were applicable only to the national government, and not to the stares. The Court was recognizing "dual citizenship." At the time of its adoption in 1868, the Fourteenth Amendment was considered by many as a deliberate effort to reverse *Barron*, to put an end to dual citizenship, and to nationalize the Bill of Rights, applying its restrictions to state governments as well as to the national government. But the post–Civil War Supreme Court interpreted the Fourteenth Amendment otherwise. Dual citizenship remained almost as it had been before the Civil War, and the shadow of *Barron* extended across the rest of the nineteenth century and well into the twentieth century. The slow process of nationalizing the Bill of Rights began in the 1920s, when the Supreme Court recognized that at least the restraints of the First Amendment had been "incorporated" into the Fourteenth Amendment as restraints on the state governments. But it was not until the 1960s that most of the civil liberties in the Bill of Rights were incorporated into the Fourteenth Amendment. Almost exactly a century after the adoption of the Fourteenth Amendment, the Bill of Rights was nationalized. Citizens now enjoy close to the same civil liberties regardless of the state in which they reside.

As for the second aspect of protection of the individual, *civil rights,* stress has been put upon the expansion of governmental power rather than restraints upon it.

If the constitutional base of civil liberties is the "due process" clause of the Four-

teenth Amendment, the constitutional base of civil rights is the "equal protection"
clause. This clause imposes a positive obligation on government to advance civil
rights, and its original motivation seems to have been to eliminate the gross injustices suffered by "the newly emancipated Negroes . . . as a class." But as with civil
liberties, there was little advancement in the interpretation or application of the
"equal protection" clause until after World War II. The major breakthrough came
in 1954 with *Brown* v. *Board of Education of Topeka,* and advancements came in fits
and starts during the succeeding ten years.

After 1964, Congress finally supported the federal courts with effective civil
rights legislation that outlawed a number of discriminatory practices in the private
sector and provided for the withholding of federal grants in aid to any local government, school, or private employer as a sanction to help enforce the civil rights
laws. This legislation will be dealt with in Chapter 17. From that point, civil rights
developed in two ways. First, the definition of civil rights was expanded to include
victims of discrimination other than blacks. Second, the definition of civil rights
became increasingly positive; affirmative action has become an official term. Judicial decisions, congressional statutes, and administrative agency actions have all
moved beyond the original goal of eliminating discrimination toward creating new
opportunities for minorities and, in some areas, compensating present minority individuals for the consequences of discriminatory actions not directly against them
but against members of their group in the past. Because compensatory civil rights
action has sometimes relied upon quotas, there has been intense debate over the
constitutionality as well as the desirability of affirmative action.

The story has no end and is not likely to. The politics of rights will remain an
important part of American political discourse.

FOR FURTHER READING

Abraham, Henry. *Freedom and the Court: Civil Rights and Liberties in the United States.* 4th ed.
New York: Oxford University Press, 1982.

Baer, Judith A. *Equality under the Constitution: Reclaiming the Fourteenth Amendment.* Ithaca,
NY: Cornell University Press, 1983.

Brigham, John. *Civil Liberties and American Democracy.* Washington, DC: Congressional
Quarterly Press, 1984.

Eisentein, Zillah. *The Female Body and the Law.* Berkeley: University of California Press,
1988.

Forer, Lois G. *A Chilling Effect: The Mounting Threat of Libel and Invasion of Privacy Actions to
the First Amendment.* New York: W. W. Norton, 1987.

Friendly, Fred W. *Minnesota Rag: The Dramatic Story of the Landmark Supreme Court Case
That Gave New Meaning to Freedom of the Press.* New York: Vintage, 1982.

Garrow, David J. *Bearing the Cross: Martin Luther King and the Southern Christian Leadership
Conference: A Personal Portrait.* New York: William Morrow, 1986.

Glindon, Marianne. *Rights Talk: The Impoverishment of Political Discourse.* New York: Free
Press, 1991.

142

THE
CONSTITUTIONAL
FRAMEWORK
AND THE
INDIVIDUAL

Hentoff, Nat. *The First Freedom: The Tumultuous History of Free Speech in America.* New York: Delacorte, 1980.

Kelly, Alfred, Winfred A. Harbison, and Herman Beltz. *The American Constitution: Its Origins and Development.* 7th ed. New York: W. W. Norton, 1991.

Levy, Leonard. *Freedom of Speech and Press in Early America: Legacy of Suppression.* New York: Harper, 1963.

Lewis, Anthony. *Gideon's Trumpet.* New York: Vintage, 1964.

Minow, Martha. *Making All the Difference—Inclusion, Exclusion, and American Law.* Ithaca, NY: Cornell University Press, 1990.

Randall, Richard S. *Censorship of the Movies.* Madison: University of Wisconsin Press, 1970.

Silberman, Charles. *Criminal Violence, Criminal Justice.* New York: Random House, 1978.

Silverstein, Mark. *Constitutional Faiths.* Ithaca, NY: Cornell University Press, 1984.

Sunstein, Cass. *After the Rights Revolution.* Cambridge, MA: Harvard University Press, 1990.

Thernstrom, Abigail M. *Whose Votes Count? Affirmative Action and Minority Voting Rights.* Cambridge, MA: Harvard University Press, 1987.

Thurow, Sarah, ed. *E Pluribus Unum: Constitutional Principles and the Institutions of Government.* Washington, DC: University Press of America, 1988.

Part 2
Institutions

5

Congress: The First Branch

EVENTS		INSTITUTIONAL DEVELOPMENTS
New Congress of U.S. meets for first time (1789)		Creation of House Ways and Means Committee (1789)
Jeffersonian party born in Congress (1792)		House committees develop. First procedural rules adopted—Jefferson's Rules (1790s)
	1800	
		Congressional party caucuses control presidential nominations (1804–1828)
		Congressional committees take control of legislative process. Rise of congressional government (1820s)
Andrew Jackson renominated for president by Democratic party convention (1832)		Presidential nominating conventions replace caucuses (1831–1832)
Abraham Lincoln elected president (1860)	1860	No longer blocked by southerners, Congress adopts protective tariff, transcontinental railroad, Homestead Act, National Banking Act, Contract Labor Act (1861–1864)
South secedes. Its delegation leaves Washington (1860–1861) period of Republican leadership (1860s)		
Congress impeaches but does not convict Andrew Johnson (1868)		
Long era of Republican ascendancy begins (1897)		Filibuster develops as a tactic in the Senate (1880s)
	1900	
Theodore Roosevelt makes U.S. a world power (1901–1909)		House revolt against power of Speaker; rise of seniority system in House (1910)
Democratic interlude with election of Woodrow Wilson (1913)		Seventeenth amendment ratified; authorizes direct election of senators (1913)
		Senate cloture rule (1917)
		Budget and Accounting Act—development of presidential budget (1921)
Democrats take charge; Franklin Delano Roosevelt elected president (1932)	1930	Rise of presidential government as Congress passes FDR's New Deal legislation (1930s)
		Legislative Reorganization Act (1946)
		Regulation of lobbyists (1949)

EVENTS		INSTITUTIONAL DEVELOPMENTS
	1950	Democratic Congresses expand Social Security and federal expenditures for public health (1954–1959)
McCarthy hearings (1950s)		Use of legislative investigations as congressional weapon against executive (1950s—1980s)
Watergate hearings (1973–1974)		
Richard Nixon resigns presidency (1974)		Growing importance of incumbency (1960s–1980s)
		Code of ethics adopted (1971)
		Campaign Finance Act (1974)
		Filibuster reform (1975)
		Enactment of statutory limits on presidential power—War Powers Resolution (1973), Budget and Impoundment Control Act (1974), Amendments to Freedom of Information Act (1974), Ethics in Government Act (1978)
		Revival of party caucus and weakening of seniority rules (1970s–1980s)
Ronald Reagan elected president (1980)	**1980**	President's big deficits impose budgetary limits on Congress; period of intense conflict between legislative and executive branches (1980s and 1990s)
Republicans temporarily take control of Senate (1980–1986)		
Iran-Contra hearings damage Reagan administration (1987)		Gramm-Rudman-Hollings Act (1985)
George Bush elected president (1988)		
Congress scores victory over Bush administration in budget crisis (1990)	**1990**	
President Bush wins congressional authorization to attack Iraq (1991)		
Democrats control Congress and White House for first time in 12 years; Republicans rely on Senate filibuster threat to influence Clinton program (1993)		Congress enacts new tax and deficit reduction programs (1993)

The U.S. Congress is the "first branch" of government under Article I of our Constitution and is also among the world's most important representative bodies. Throughout American history, the Congress has initiated, fashioned, and implemented programs in all areas of American domestic and foreign policy. Prior to the twentieth century, the Congress, not the executive, was the central policy-making institution in the United States. Congressional leaders like Henry Clay, Daniel Webster, and John C. Calhoun were the dominant political figures of their time and often treated mere presidents with disdain. But during the twentieth century, although Congress continues to be important, its influence has waned relative to that of the executive branch. The presidency has become the central institution of American government. Members of Congress may support or oppose, but they are seldom free to ignore presidential leadership. Moreover, the bureaucracies of the executive branch have—often with the encouragement of Congress—usurped a good deal of legislative power.

Despite this decline in influence, however, the U.S. Congress is still the only national representative assembly that can actually be said to govern. Many of the world's representative bodies only represent. That is, their governmental functions consist mainly of affirming and legitimating the national leadership's decisions, tying local activists more firmly to the central government by allowing them to take part in national political affairs, and giving all citizens the impression that popular views actually play a role in the decision-making process. For example, before the collapse of the U.S.S.R., its national representative body, the Supreme Soviet, included deputies representing every locality, as well as every ethnic, religious, and occupational group in Soviet society. The Supreme Soviet, however, only possessed the power to say "yes" to leadership proposals. Its visible approval of policies and programs was seen by the Communist party hierarchy as a useful way of convincing citizens that their interests were taken into account at some point in the national decision-making process.

While many of the world's representative bodies possess only the right to say "yes," a second, smaller group of representative institutions—most notably Western European parliaments—also have the power to say "no" to the proposals of executive agencies. Such institutions as the British Parliament have the power to reject programs and laws sought by the government, although the use of this power is constrained by the fact that the rejection of an important governmental proposal can lead to Parliament's dissolution and the need for new elections. While they can and sometimes do say "no," Western European parliaments generally do not have the power to modify governmental proposals or, more important, to initiate major programs. The only national representative body that actually possesses such powers is the U.S. Congress.

POWER AND REPRESENTATION

In this chapter, we shall try to understand how the U.S. Congress is able to serve simultaneously as a representative assembly and a powerful agency of government. Unlike most of its counterparts around the world, Congress controls a formidible battery of powers that it uses to shape policies and, when necessary, defend its prerogatives against the executive branch. We shall examine each of these powers in its turn.

As we shall see, however, congressional power cannot be separated from congressional representation. Indeed, there is a reciprocal relationship between the two. Without the important governmental powers that we shall examine below, Congress would be a very different sort of representative body. Americans might feel some sense of symbolic representation if they found that Congress contained members of their own race, religion, ethnic background, or social class. They might feel some sense of gratification if members of Congress tried to help them with their problems. But without this array of powers, Congress could do little to represent effectively the views and interests of its constituents. Power is necessary for effective congressional representation. At the same time, the power of Congress is ultimately a function of its capacity to effectively represent important groups and forces in American society. This can best be understood by looking at the relationship between Congress and the executive branch over the course of American history.

Because they feared both executive and legislative tyranny, the framers of the Constitution pitted Congress and the president against one another. But for more than one hundred years, the contest was unequal. During the first century of American government, Congress was the dominant institution. American foreign and domestic policy was formulated and implemented by Congress and generally the most powerful figures in American government were the Speaker of the House and the leaders of the Senate—not the president. The War of 1812 was planned and fought by Congress. The great sectional compromises prior to the Civil War were formulated in Congress, without much intervention from the executive branch. Even during the Civil War, an extraordinary period of presidential leadership, a joint congressional committee on the conduct of the war played a role in formulating war plans and campaign tactics, and even in the promotion of officers. After the Civil War, when President Andrew Johnson sought to interfere with congressional plans for Reconstruction, he was summarily impeached, and saved from conviction by only one vote. Subsequent presidents understood the moral and did not attempt to thwart Congress.

This congressional preeminence began to diminish after the turn of the century, so that by the 1960s, the executive had, at least temporarily, become the dominant branch of American government. The major domestic policy initiatives of the twentieth century—Franklin Roosevelt's "New Deal," Harry Truman's "Fair Deal," John F. Kennedy's "New Frontier," and Lyndon Johnson's "Great Society"—all included some congressional involvement but were essentially developed, introduced, and implemented by the executive. In the area of foreign policy, though Congress continued to be influential during the twentieth century, the focus of decision-making power clearly moved into the executive branch. The War of 1812 may have been a congressional war, but in the twentieth century, American entry into World War I, World War II, Korea, Vietnam, and a host of lesser conflicts was essentially a presidential—not congressional—decision. What accounts for this decline of congressional power?

A key factor in understanding the power of any political institution, be it Congress, the executive, or the judiciary, is its representative character. If a political institution is able to link itself to important groups and forces in the society by serving their interests and meeting their needs, then these forces can generally be expected, in turn, to support that institution in its struggles with other agencies or against any public opposition to its programs. On the other hand, if a political institution is unable to link itself to a political constituency, then it may find itself without defenses if it comes under attack. During the nineteenth century, Congress—particularly the House of Representatives—was the most accessible and permeable institution of American government. Turnover in the House was rapid, and new groups and forces in American society generally found it easy to obtain access to the House and to find members of Congress to support their aims and aspirations. In other words, Congress was the most representative governmental institution. This led various groups in society to support Congress in its battles with the executive branch and the courts. For example, during the 1830s, many merchants and bankers found Congress very receptive to their interests and became a strong constituency for congressional power vis-à-vis what they called the "usurpations" of the executive branch under President Andrew Jackson, in particular his attack on the Bank of the United States, an institution that business interests saw as essential to their well-being.

During the twentieth century, the executive branch became far more accessible than Congress and important national political forces began more and more to turn to the executive with their problems.[1] To the extent that they found the executive to be hospitable to them, these forces began to support executive or presidential rather than congressional power. The critical juncture in the congressional–executive balance was the period of the New Deal. In the 1930s, President Franklin Delano Roosevelt succeeded, through major innovations in programs and policies, in linking a number of important social and political forces—organized labor, urban political machines, farmers, blacks, key sectors of American industry—to the executive branch. These forces were the beneficiaries of the programs developed by the Roosevelt administration and its successors. In turn, these forces formed a constituency for executive power.[2] The upshot was that during the Roosevelt era, powerful groups, forces, and interests in American society came to see the executive branch as more representative—as the agency most likely to be open to their demands. This perception helped greatly to enhance executive power at the expense of congressional power.

Thus, power and representation have been closely linked in congressional history. Congress was most powerful when it was most representative, least powerful when it was least accessible to important groups in society. In the last thirty years, there has been a good deal of resurgence of congressional power vis-à-vis the executive. This has occurred mainly because Congress has sought to represent many

---

[1]See Samuel Huntington, "Congressional Responses to the Twentieth Century," in *Congress and America's Future,* ed. David Truman (Englewood Cliffs, NJ: Prentice-Hall, 1965), Chapter 1.

[2]See Thomas Ferguson, "From Normalcy to New Deal: Industrial Structure, Party Competition and American Public Policy in the Great Depression," *International Organization,* 38 (Winter 1984), pp. 42–94.

Carol Moseley-Braun
Breaking Into the Club

Carol Moseley-Braun (b. 1947)

One of the most distinctive milestones of the 1992 elections was the first election of an African American woman to the United States Senate.

Carol Moseley-Braun grew up on Chicago's South Side, attended the public schools, graduated from the University of Illinois, and received her law degree from the University of Chicago. She began her career as an assistant attorney general and then won election to the Illinois state legislature, where she served for ten years. She was serving as Recorder of Deeds for Cook County in 1991 when, along with millions of other TV viewers, she became outraged at what she saw as the unfair treatment of Anita Hill by the all-white, all-male Senate judiciary committee during the Clarence Thomas nomination hearings. That outrage focused on Illinois's senior senator, Democrat Alan Dixon, when he decided to vote in favor of Thomas's confirmation. The night after the Senate confirmation vote, Moseley-Braun was deluged with phone calls from friends urging her to mount a Senate campaign.

Moseley-Braun decided to enter the race against Dixon, despite the fact that the two-term senator had proven himself one of the state's biggest vote-getters; even the Republicans considered a challenge to Dixon all but futile. Despite the fact that she began with no budget, organization, or political backing, she launched a grass-roots campaign aimed at tapping into popular disaffection with a Senate viewed by many as, in Moseley-Braun's words, "an elitist club made up of mostly white male millionaires over fifty." In a stunning upset, the unknown Moseley-Braun defeated Dixon and another challenger in the March Democratic primary by capitalizing on the nation's anti-incumbent disposition and by criticizing Dixon for his key support for Thomas. The primary victory catapulted Moseley-Braun into the national spotlight.

Moseley-Braun's candidacy was in keeping with the feeling that 1992 was the year of the outsider. She became an instant national celebrity and dominated the fall campaign, raising $5 million to finance her efforts and attracting large crowds in appearances around the state. She was careful to broaden her appeal in order to reach beyond the ethnic constituencies of Chicago, spending much of her time in predominantly white suburbs. Moseley-Braun's appeal was especially strong to women in a campaign year dubbed "the year of the woman." A record number of women sought congressional seats in 1992: eleven women sought Senate seats (six were elected), and 108 sought seats in the House (47 were elected).

Yet Moseley-Braun's campaign stumbled in early October when she was accused of mishandling a large sum of money that her ailing mother had received from the sale of some land. Moseley-Braun's Republican opponent, former Reagan administration aide Richard Williamson, sought to exploit the issues of ethics and credibility. Despite losing some support, Moseley-Braun won a decisive victory in November. Moseley-Braun promised to remain responsive to her constituents: "Elected officials have to be very clear that they are not leaders, but servants of the people."

important political forces, such as the civil rights, feminist, environmental, consumer, and peace movements, which in turn, became constituencies for congressional power.

We shall return to the relationship between power and representation at the conclusion of this chapter. Before we do this, however, let us look more carefully at each individual part of the equation. First, let us examine some of the ways in which Congress can be said to "represent" the American people. Second, let us examine the institutional structure of Congress and how congressional powers are organized and used. Finally, we will assess the contemporary connection between congressional power and congressional representation.

Representation

Assemblies and the idea of representation have been around in one form or another for centuries. But until the eighteenth century—with the American and French revolutions—assemblies were usually means used by monarchs for gaining or regaining the support of local leaders. According to political theorist Carl Friedrich, the king's calling of assemblies "was necessary because the undeveloped state of central administrative systems and the absence of effective means of coercion rendered the collection of . . . war taxes impossible without local cooperation."[3]

Eventually, the regional lords and lesser barons, joined by the rising merchant classes, began to see the assembly as a place where they could state their case against the monarch, rather than merely receive his messages to take back to their regions. Through their efforts, the assembly was slowly converted from part of the monarch's regime to an institution that could be used against the monarchy and, later, used by the middle classes against the aristocracy. But the original function of the assembly—getting obedience through consent—never disappeared. It was simply joined by new functions. Once the assembly had evolved into a place where demands could be made, it became a "parliament"—a place where people could come together to talk. ("Parliament" is derived from the French *parler*—to talk.) The French and many other Europeans gave their national assemblies the name "parliament" because they felt that talk was its essential feature. Although the U.S. Congress does not share that name, talk is still one of its essential ingredients, built into its very structure. Talk is facilitated by the fact that each member of the House and Senate is, in principle, equal to all the other members. Although the committee structure of Congress gives some members more power than others, a measure of equality in Congress exists by virtue of the fact that membership is determined entirely by election from districts defined as absolutely equal. Each member's primary responsibility is to the district, not to the congressional leadership, a party, or even the institution. Another important support for the parliamentary aspect of Congress is a provision in the Constitution that exempts members of Congress from arrest for any except the most serious crimes while conducting congressional business. This provision of Article I, Section 6, has generally freed members of

[3]Carl Friedrich, *Constitutional Government and Democracy,* 4th ed. (Boston: Ginn, 1968), p. 274.

Congress from the fear of libel and slander suits and therefore from the fear of any
negative consequences from things they might say in the heat of debate or else- where. Supreme Court decisions have extended this immunity to their activities as members of committees.

We have become so accustomed to the idea of representative government that we tend to forget what a peculiar concept representation really is. A representative claims to act or speak for some other person or group. But how can one person be trusted to speak for another? How do we know that those who call themselves our representatives are actually speaking on our behalf, rather than simply pursuing their own interests?

There are two circumstances under which one person reasonably might be trusted to speak for another. The first of these occurs if the two individuals are so similar in background, character, interests, and perspectives that anything said by one would very likely reflect the views of the other as well. This principle is at the heart of what is sometimes called *sociological representation*—the sort of represen- tation that takes place when representatives have the same racial, ethnic, religious, or educational backgrounds as their constituents. The assumption is that sociolog- ical similarity helps to promote good representation, and thus, the composition of a properly constituted representative assembly should mirror the composition of society.

The second circumstance under which one person might be trusted to speak for another occurs if the two are formally bound together so that the representative is in some way accountable to those he or she purports to represent. If representa- tives can somehow be punished or held to account for failing to speak properly for their constituents, then we know they have an incentive to provide good represen- tation even if their own personal backgrounds, views, and interests differ from those they represent. This principle is called *agency representation*—the sort of representation that takes place when constituents have the power to hire and fire their representatives.

Both sociological and agency representation play a role in the relationship be- tween members of Congress and their constituencies.

The Social Composition of the U.S. Congress

The extent to which the U.S. Congress is representative of the American people in a sociological sense can be seen from the following tables, which give some indica- tion of the distribution of important social characteristics in the House and Senate today. It comes as no surprise that the religious affiliations of members of both the House and Senate (Table 5.1) are overwhelmingly Protestant—the distribution is very close to the proportion in the population at large—although the Protestant category is composed of more than fifteen denominations. Catholics continue to comprise the second largest category of religious affiliation, and Jews a much smaller third category. Nonetheless, since most policies that cut along religious lines are dealt with by state legislatures, the religious affiliations of members of Congress are almost entirely symbolic. The same is true of their ethnic back- grounds. Statistics on ethnic or national background are difficult to get and gener-

TABLE 5.1

Religious Affiliations of the Members of the 103rd Congress*
(1993–1994)

	House			Senate			Congress
	D	R	Total	D	R	Total	Total
African Methodist Episcopal	4	0	4	0	0	0	4
Apostolic Christian	0	1	1	0	0	0	1
Baptist	38	13	51	4	7	11	62
Christian Church	1	0	1	0	0	0	1
Christian Reformed Church	0	2	2	0	0	0	2
Christian Scientist	0	4	4	0	0	0	4
Church of Christ	4	1	5	0	0	0	5
Disciples of Christ	1	0	1	0	0	0	1
Episcopalian	18	17	35	4	11	15	50
French Huguenot	0	1	1	0	0	0	1
Greek Orthodox	0	4	4	1	0	1	5
Jewish	26	5	32†	9	1	10	42†
Lutheran	9	8	17	3	1	4	21
Methodist	31	23	54	7	4	11	65
Mormon	2	7	9	1	2	3	12
Presbyterian	20	26	46	5	3	8	54
Roman Catholic	77	41	118	15	8	23	141
Seventh-Day Adventist	0	2	2	0	0	0	2
Unitarian	4	1	5	0	2	2	7
United Church of Christ and Congregationalist	5	2	7	4	3	7	14
Unspecified	9	0	9	1	0	1	10
Unspecified Protestant	10	17	27	2	0	2	29

*Statistics based on apparent winners as of November 6, 1992.
†Includes Sanders, I-VT.
Source: *Congressional Quarterly Weekly Report,* 7 November 1992. Used by permission.

ally unreliable. Individual members of Congress may make a point of their ethnic backgrounds, but an actual count has not been done. Occasionally, an issue like support for Israel or for the Greek community in Cyprus may activate members of Congress along religious or ethnic lines. But these exceptions actually underscore the essentially symbolic nature of these social characteristics.

African Americans, women, Hispanic Americans, and Asian Americans have increased their congressional representation somewhat in the past two decades. Indeed, in 1992, forty-eight women were elected to the House of Representatives (up from only twenty-nine in 1990). Six women were elected to serve in the Senate (up from only two in the previous Congress). California became the first state ever to be represented by two women in the Senate when it elected Diane Feinstein and Barbara Boxer, both Democrats.

Even now, however, representation of women and minorities in Congress is still not comparable to the proportions in the general population. Since many impor-

TABLE 5.2

**Occupational Background of the Members of the 103rd Congress*
(1993–1994)**

| | House | | | Senate | | | Congress |
	D	R	Total	D	R	Total	Total
Acting/Entertainment	0	1	1	0	0	0	1
Aeronautics	0	2	2	1	0	1	3
Agriculture	7	12	19	3	5	8	27
Business or Banking	56	75	131	12	12	24	155
Clergy	1	1	2	0	1	1	3
Education	45	20	66†	6	5	11	77†
Engineering	2	3	5	0	0	0	5
Homemaking	0	1	1	0	0	0	1
Journalism	11	12	24†	7	2	9	33†
Labor Officials	2	0	2	0	0	0	2
Law	122	59	181	33	25	58	239
Law Enforcement	8	2	10	0	0	0	10
Medicine	4	2	6	0	0	0	6
Military	0	0	0	0	1	1	1
Professional Sports	0	1	1	1	0	1	2
Public Service	51	36	87	8	2	10	97
Real Estate	9	17	26	2	3	5	31

*Statistics based on apparent winners as of November 6, 1992.
†Includes Sanders, I-VT.
Source: *Congressional Quarterly Weekly Report,* 7 November 1992. Used by permission.

tant contemporary national issues do cut along racial and gender lines, a considerable amount of clamor for reform in the representative process is likely to continue until these groups are fully represented.

The occupational backgrounds of members of Congress have always been a matter of interest because so many issues cut along economic lines that are relevant to occupations and industries. A fair, although incomplete, mix of occupations is presented in Table 5.2. The legal profession is the dominant career of most members of Congress prior to their election to Congress. Public service and politics is also a significant background. In addition, many members of Congress also have important ties to business and industry. One composite portrait of a typical member of Congress has been that of "a middle-aged male lawyer whose father was of the professional or managerial class; a native-born 'white,' or—if he cannot avoid being an immigrant—a product of Northwestern or Central Europe or Canada, rather than of Eastern or Southern Europe, Latin America, Africa or Asia."[4] This is not a portrait of the United States's population. Congress is not a sociological microcosm of our society, and it probably can never become one. One obvious reason is that the skills and resources needed to achieve political success in the United States are much more likely to be found among well-educated and relatively well-

[4]Marian D. Irish and James Prothro, *The Politics of American Democracy,* 5th ed. (Englewood Cliffs, NJ: Prentice-Hall, 1971), p. 352.

TABLE 5.3

Representation of Ethnic Minorities in the 103rd Congress (1993–1994)

Blacks

House (39)

Alabama: Earl F. Hilliard, D
California: Ronald V. Dellums, D; Julian C. Dixon, D; Maxine Waters, D; Walter R. Tucker, D
Connecticut: Gary Franks, R
District of Columbia: Eleanor Holmes Norton, D*
Florida: Corrine Brown, D; Carrie Meek, D; Alcee L. Hastings, D
Georgia: Sanford Bishop, D; John Lewis, D; Cynthia McKinney, D
Illinois: Bobby L. Rush, D; Mel Reynolds, D; Cardiss Collins, D
Louisiana: William J. Jefferson, D; Cleo Fields, D
Maryland: Albert R. Wynn, D; Kweisi Mfume, D
Michigan: John Conyers Jr., D; Barbara-Rose Collins, D

Mississippi: Mike Espy, D
Missouri: William L. Clay, D; Alan Wheat, D
New Jersey: Donald M. Payne, D
New York: Floyd H. Flake, D; Edolphus Towns, D; Major R. Owens, D; Charles B. Rangel, D
North Carolina: Eva Clayton, D; Melvin Watt, D
Ohio: Louis Stokes, D
Pennsylvania: Lucien E. Blackwell, D
South Carolina: James E. Clyburn, D
Tennessee: Harold E. Ford, D
Texas: Craig Washington, D; Eddie Bernice Johnson, D
Virginia: Robert C. Scott, D

Senate (1)
Illinois: Carol Moseley-Braun, D

Hispanics

House (19)

Arizona: Ed Pastor, D
California: Xavier Becerra, D; Matthew G. Martinez, D; Lucille Roybal-Allard, D; Esteban E. Torres, D
Florida: Ileana Ros-Lehtinen, R; Lincoln Diaz-Balart, R
Illinois: Luis V. Gutierrez, D
New Jersey: Robert Menendez, D

New Mexico: Bill Richardson, D
New York: Nydia M. Velázquez, D; Jose E. Serrano, D
Puerto Rico: Antonio Colorado, D*
Texas: E. "Kika" de la Garza, D; Henry B. Gonzalez, D; Henry Bonilla, R; Solomon P. Ortiz, D; Frank Tejeda, D
Virgin Islands: Ron de Lugo, D*

Asians and Pacific Islanders

House (7)

American Samoa: Eni F.H. Faleomavaega, D*
California: Robert T. Matsui, D; Norman Y. Mineta, D; Jay C. Kim, R Mark A. Takano, D

Guam: Ben Blaz, R*
Hawaii: Patsy T. Mink, D

Senate (2)
Hawaii: Daniel K. Inouye, D; Daniel K. Akaka, D

American Indian

Senate (1)
Colorado: Ben Nighthorse Campbell, D

*Non-voting delegate

Source: *Congressional Quarterly Weekly Report,* 7 November 1992. Used by permission.

TABLE 5.4
Representation of Women in the 103rd Congress
(1993–1994)

House (48)

Arkansas: Blanche Lambert, D

Arizona: Karan English, D

California: Lynn Woolsey, D; Nancy
Pelosi, D; Anna G. Eshoo, D;
Lucille Roybal-Allard, D;
Maxine Waters, D; Jane Harman, D;
Lynn Schenk, D

Colorado: Patricia Schroeder, D

Connecticut: Barbara B. Kennelly, D;
Rosa DeLauro, D; Nancy L. Johnson, R

District of Columbia: Eleanor Holmes
Norton, D*

Florida: Corrine Brown, D;
Tillie Fowler, R; Karen L. Thurman, D;
Carrie Meek, D; Ileana Ros-Lehtinen, R

Georgia: Cynthia McKinney, D

Hawaii: Patsy T. Mink, D

Illinois: Cardiss Collins, D

Indiana: Jill L. Long, D

Kansas: Jan Meyers, R

Maine: Olympia J. Snowe, R

Maryland: Helen Delich Bentley, R;
Constance A. Morella, R

Michigan: Barbara-Rose Collins, D

Missouri: Pat Danner, D

North Carolina: Eva Clayton, D

Nevada: Barbara F. Vucanovich, R

New Jersey: Marge Roukema, R

New York: Nydia M. Velázquez, D; Susan
Molinari, R; Carolyn B. Maloney, D;
Nita M. Lowey, D; Louise M. Slaughter, D

Ohio: Marcy Kaptur, D;
Deborah Pryce, R

Oregon: Elizabeth Furse, D

Pennsylvania: Marjorie Margolies
Mezvinsky, D

Tennessee: Marilyn Lloyd, D

Texas: Eddie Bernice Johnson, D

Utah: Karen Shepherd, D

Virginia: Leslie L. Byrne, D

Washington: Maria Cantwell, D;
Jolene Unsoeld, D; Jennifer Dunn, R

Senate (6)

California: Dianne Feinstein, D;
Barbara Boxer, D

Illinois: Carol Moseley-Braun, D

Kansas: Nancy Landon Kassebaum, R

Maryland: Barbara A. Mikulski, D

Washington: Patty Murray, D

*Non-voting delegate

Source: *Congressional Quarterly Weekly Report,* 7 November 1992. Used by permission.

to-do Americans than among members of minority groups and the poor. Take money, for example. As we shall see in Chapter 11, successful congressional candidates must be able to raise hundreds of thousands of dollars to finance their campaigns. Poor people from the inner city are much less likely to be able to convince corporate political action committees to provide them with these funds.

Is Congress still able to legislate fairly or to take account of a diversity of views and interests if it is not a sociologically representative assembly? There is ample reason to believe it can. Representatives, as we shall see shortly, can serve as the faithful agents of their constituents, even if they do not precisely mirror their sociological attributes. Yet, sociological representation is a matter of some interest, even if it is not a prerequisite for fair legislation on the part of members of the House and Senate. The social composition of a representative assembly is very important for symbolic purposes—to demonstrate to groups in the population that they are taken seriously by the government. Concern about the proportion of women, African Americans, and ethnic minorities in Congress and elsewhere in government would exist whether or not these social characteristics influenced the outcomes of laws and policies. It is rare to find a social group whose members do not feel short-changed if someone like themselves is not a member of the assembly. Thus, the symbolic composition of Congress is ultimately important for the political stability of the United States. If Congress is not representative symbolically, then its own authority and indeed that of the entire government would be reduced.[5]

Representatives as Agents

A good deal of evidence indicates that whether or not members of Congress share their constituents' sociological characteristics, they *do* work very hard to speak for their constituents' views and serve their constituents' interests in the governmental process. The idea of representative as agent is similar to the relationship of lawyer and client. True, the relationship between the member of Congress and as many as 550,000 "clients" in the district, or the senator and millions of clients in the state, is very different from that of the lawyer and client. But the criteria of performance are comparable. One expects at the very least that each representative will constantly be seeking to discover the interests of the constituency and will be speaking for those interests in Congress and in other centers of government.[6]

There is constant communication between constituents and congressional offices. For example, each year the House and Senate post offices handle nearly 100 million pieces of incoming mail, and in recent years, members of Congress have sent out nearly 400 million pieces of mail.[7]

The seriousness with which members of the House attempt to behave as representatives can be seen in the amount of time spent on behalf of their constituents. Well over a quarter of their time and nearly two-thirds of the time of their staff members is devoted to constituency service (termed "case work"). This service is not merely a matter of writing and mailing letters. It includes talking to constituents, providing them with minor services, presenting special bills for them, and attempting to influence decisions by regulatory commissions on their behalf.[8] One example of the lengths to which congressional offices have been prepared to go on behalf of constituents is given in the following case:

> A shipyard worker had been severely crippled in an on-the-job accident. Because of technicalities in his former employment status, he had been three times ruled ineligible for disability compensation. A "Catch 22" interpretation also made welfare unavailable. By the time the constituent sought help at his Congressman's field office

[5]For a discussion, see Benjamin Ginsberg, *The Consequences of Consent* (New York: Random House, 1982), Chapter 1.

[6]For some interesting empirical evidence, see Angus Campbell, Philip Converse, Warren Miller, and Donald Stokes, *Elections and the Political Order* (New York: Wiley, 1966) Chapter 11.

[7]Congressional Quarterly, *Guide to the Congress of the United States,* 2nd ed. (Washington, DC: Congressional Quarterly Press, 1976), p. 588.

[8]John S. Saloma, *Congress and the New Politics* (Boston: Little, Brown, 1969), pp. 184–85. A 1977 official report using less detailed categories came up with almost the same impression of Congress's workload. Commission on Administrative Review, *Administrative Reorganization and Legislative Management,* House Doc. #95–232 (28 September 1977), vol. 2, especially pp. 17–19.

the situation was desperate. He had been unable to work for several years, medical and other bills had piled up, the family budget was in shambles, home utilities were about to be shut off, the family car had been repossessed and a bank was about to foreclose on the home mortgage.

Resolving this case required several months and more than a hundred caseworker manhours. Eventually the shipyard (federal agency) was persuaded to reclassify the former employee. That enabled the constituent to qualify (following more appeals by the caseworker) for disability compensation (state agency) as well as for welfare (county agency—more appeals). Meanwhile, the caseworker and the AA (the congressman's administrative assistant) used their patron's good offices to persuade the constituent's banker (private), automobile credit agency (private), hospital (county) and utility company (city) to accept delayed debt-repayment schedules. Finally, the caseworker went to the constituent's home to give advice on home economics and family budgeting.[9]

Although no members of Congress are above constituency pressures (and they would not want to be), on many issues constituents do not have very strong views and representatives are free to behave as they think best. Foreign policy issues often have this character. But in many districts there are two or three issues on which constituents have such pronounced opinions that representatives feel that they have little freedom of choice. For example, representatives from wheat, cotton, or to-bacco districts probably will not want to exercise a great deal of independence on relevant agricultural legislation. In the oil-rich states (such as Oklahoma, Texas, and California), the senators and members of the House are likely to be leading advocates of oil interests. For one thing, they are probably fearful of voting against their district interests; for another, the districts are unlikely to elect representatives who would want to vote against them.

The influence of constituencies is so pervasive that both parties have strongly embraced the informal rule that nothing should be done to endanger the re-election chances of any member. Party leaders obey this rule fairly consistently by not asking any member to vote the party line whenever it might conflict with a district interest.

Direct Patronage

Members of Congress often have an opportunity to provide direct benefits for their constituents. The most important of these opportunities for direct patronage is in legislation that has been described half-jokingly as the "pork barrel." This type of legislation specifies both the projects or other authorizations and the location within a particular district. Many observers of Congress argue that pork-barrel bills are the only ones that some members are serious about moving toward actual passage because they are seen as so important to members' reelection.

[9]John D. MacCartney, "Political Staffing: A View from the District" (Ph.D. dissertation, University of California, Los Angeles, 1975), pp. 113–14. Quoted in Bruce Cain, John Ferejohn, and Morris Fiorina, "Constituency Service in the United States and Great Britain," in Lawrence Dodd and Bruce J. Oppenheimer, eds., *Congress Reconsidered,* 3rd ed. (Washington, DC: Congressional Quarterly Press, 1985), p. 116.

Often, congressional leaders will use pork-barrel projects in exchange for votes on other matters. For example, while serving as Senate majority leader in 1957, Lyndon Johnson won crucial support for civil rights legislation by awarding water projects to Senators Margaret Chase Smith of Maine and Frank Church of Idaho. Some members of Congress appear to seek immortality through pork. For example, the Mark Hatfield Marine Science Center in Oregon was built with funds obtained by Oregon's Senator Mark Hatfield. The Mildred and Claude Pepper fountain is the centerpiece of a Miami park project that had been strongly supported by the late representative Claude Pepper. Federal dollars secured by Pennsylvania representative Bud Shuster helped to build the Bud Shuster Byway, a four-lane highway serving Everett, Pennsylvania. The most important rule of pork-barreling is that any member of Congress whose district receives a project as part of a bill must support all the other projects on the bill. This cuts across party and ideological lines (see Box 5.1). Thus, the same 1984 appropriations bill that was supported by conservative Republican senator Ted Stevens of Alaska because it provided funds for Blackhawk helicopters for the Alaska National Guard was also supported by liberal Democrat Ted Kennedy who had won a provision for $2 million for a lighthouse at Nantucket. Though some members of Congress oppose the principle of pork-barreling, the prevailing view was epitomized by former Democratic representative Kenneth Gray of Illinois, who declared, "I have been called the 'Prince of Pork.' I would rather be called the 'King of Pork.'"[10]

A limited amount of other direct patronage exists. One important form of this constituency service is intervening with federal administrative agencies on behalf of their constituents. Members of the House and Senate spend a great deal of time on the telephone and in administrative offices seeking to secure favorable treatment for constituents and supporters. A small but related form of patronage is getting an appointment to one of the military academies for the child of a constituent. Traditionally, these appointments are allocated one to a district.

Sometimes patronage can go too far. The case of the so-called Keating Five, raised serious questions about the extent to which members of Congress could properly and legitimately seek to intervene with regulating agencies on a constituent's behalf. In this case, five senators—Alan Cranston (D-Calif.); Dennis DeConcini (D-Ariz.); John Glenn (D-Ohio); John McCain (R-Ariz.); and Donald Riegle (D-Mich.)—came under the scrutiny of the Senate Ethics Committee, because of charges that they sought to pressure the Federal Home Loan Bank Board to give lenient regulatory treatment to the Lincoln Savings and Loan Association, headed by Charles Keating, a wealthy political contributor. The bank later failed, at a cost to the government of more than $2 billion. Keating was charged with improperly using $1.1 billion in deposits for personal purposes and for company contributions.[11] The Senate Ethics Committee recommended that the Senate censure Cranston for his role in the Keating affair, and he retired from the Senate when his term ended in 1992. The four other senators received only

---

[10]See Paul Starubin, "Pork: A Time-Honored Tradition Lives On," *Congressional Quarterly Weekly Report,* 24 October 1987, p. 2581.

[11]*Congressional Quarterly Weekly Report,* 27 January 1990, pp. 211–16.

BOX 5.1

The Federal Pork Barrel

Public Law 101–101
101st Congress

An Act

Making appropriations for energy and water development for the fiscal year ending September 30, 1990, and for other purposes.

Be it enacted by the Senate and House of Representatives of the United States of America in Congress assembled, That the following sums are appropriated, out of any money in the Treasury not otherwise appropriated, for the fiscal year ending September 30, 1990, for energy and water development, and for other purposes, namely:

For the prosecution of river and harbor, flood control, shore protection, alteration and removal of obstructive bridges, and related projects authorized by laws; and detailed studies, and plans and specifications, of projects (including those for development with participation or under consideration for participation by States, local governments, or private groups) authorized or made eligible for selection by law (but such studies shall not constitute a commitment of the Government to construction), $997,400,000, of which such sums as are necessary pursuant to Public Law 99–662 shall be derived from the Inland Waterways Trust Fund, to remain available until expended: *Provided,* That with funds herein appropriated the Secretary of the Army, acting through the Chief of Engineers, is directed to undertake the following projects in fiscal year 1990 in the amounts specified:

Beaver Lake, Arkansas (Water Quality Enhancement), $1,100,000;

Red River Emergency Bank Protection, Arkansas and Louisiana, $2,000,000;

Westwego to Harvey Canal, Louisiana, Hurricane Protection, $1,100,000;

Atlantic Coast of Maryland, Maryland, $8,200,000;

Cape Girardeau-Jackson, Missouri, $500,000;

Missouri National Recreation River, Nebraska and South Dakota, $620,000;

Papillion Creek and Tributaries, Nebraska, $2,500,000;

Great Egg Harbor Inlet and Peck Beach, New Jersey, $250,000;

Shinnecock Inlet, New York, $5,300,000;

Roanoke River Upper Basin, Virginia, $200,000;

Kissimmee River, Florida, $4,000,000;

Sarasota County, Florida, $2,000,000;

Roseau River (Duxby Levee), Minnesota, $200,000;

Trimble Wildlife Area, Smithville Lake, Little Platte River, Missouri, $1,570,000;

Acequias Irrigation System, New Mexico, $2,000,000.

Grays Harbor, Washington, $13,000,000;

Small Boat Harbor, Buffalo Harbor, New York, $1,000,000:

[And many other projects.]

PROCESS BOX 5.1
How Members of Congress Represent Their Districts

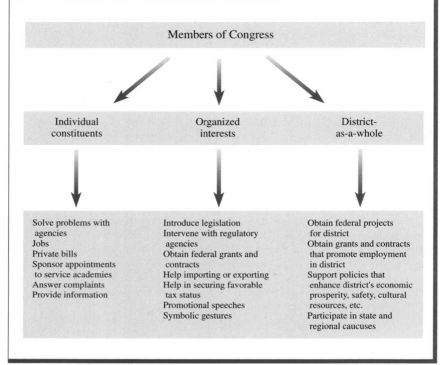

Members of Congress

Individual constituents	Organized interests	District-as-a-whole
Solve problems with agencies Jobs Private bills Sponsor appointments to service academies Answer complaints Provide information	Introduce legislation Intervene with regulatory agencies Obtain federal grants and contracts Help importing or exporting Help in securing favorable tax status Promotional speeches Symbolic gestures	Obtain federal projects for district Obtain grants and contracts that promote employment in district Support policies that enhance district's economic prosperity, safety, cultural resources, etc. Participate in state and regional caucuses

mild rebukes. Critics of the Senate process charged that the Ethics Committee had not gone nearly far enough in its investigations or recommendations for punishment.

A different form of patronage is the private bill—a proposal to grant some kind of relief, special privilege, or exemption to the person named in the bill (Box 5.2). The private bill is a type of legislation, but it should be distinguished from a public bill, which is supposed to deal with general rules and categories of behavior, people, and institutions.

As many as 75 percent of all private bills introduced (and one-third of the ones that pass) are concerned with providing relief for foreign nationals who cannot get permanent visas to the United States because the immigration quota for their country is filled or because of something unusual about their particular situation. The majority of private bills not concerned with immigration problems are introduced to provide monetary relief for individual citizens because of injuries allegedly received from a public action or because of a meritorious act that would have otherwise gone unrewarded. About 20 percent of those bills become law.[12]

---

[12]Congressional Quarterly, *Guide to the Congress of the United States*, pp. 229–310.

> ### BOX 5.2
> **Private Law**
>
> Private Law 99–19
> 99th Congress
>
> #### An Act
> For the relief of Sueng Ho Jang and Sueng Il Jang.
>
> *Be it enacted by the Senate and House of Representatives of the United States of America in Congress assembled,* That, (a) for the purposes of the Immigration and Nationality Act, Sueng Ho Jang and Sueng Il Jang shall be considered to have been lawfully admitted to the United States for permanent residence as of the date of the enactment of this Act if, within two years after such date, Sueng Ho Jang and Sueng Il Jang apply to the Attorney General for adjustment to such status and pay the required visa fees.
>
> (b) Upon the granting of permanent residence to Sueng Ho Jang and Sueng Il Jang pursuant to this Act, the Secretary of State shall instruct the proper officer to deduct two numbers from the total number of immigrant visas which are made available to natives of the country of the aliens' birth under section 203(a) of the Immigration and Nationality Act and, if applicable, from the total number of immigrant visas which are made available to such natives under section 202(e) of such Act.
>
> Approved October 21, 1986.

Private legislation is a congressional privilege that is often abused, but it is impossible to imagine members of Congress giving it up completely. It is one of the easiest, cheapest, and most effective forms of patronage available to each member. It can be defended as an indispensable part of the process by which members of Congress seek to fulfill their role as representatives. And obviously they like the privilege because it helps them win re-election.

House and Senate: Differences in Representation

The framers of the Constitution provided for a **bicameral legislature**—that is, a legislative body consisting of two chambers. As we saw in Chapter 2, the framers intended each of these chambers, the House and Senate, to serve a different constituency. Members of the Senate, appointed by state legislatures for six-year terms, were to represent the elite members of society and to be more attuned to the interests of property than of population. Today, members of the House and Senate are both elected directly by the people. The 435 members of the House are elected from districts apportioned according to population; the 100 members of the Senate are elected by state, with 2 senators from each. Senators continue to have much longer terms in office and usually represent much larger and more diverse constituencies than do their counterparts in the House (Table 5.5).

The House and Senate play different roles in the legislative process. In essence, the Senate is the more deliberative of the two bodies—the forum in which any

TABLE 5.5

Differences Between The House And The Senate

	House	Senate
Minimum age of member	25 years	30 years
U.S. citizenship	at least 7 years	at least 9 years
Length of term	2 years	6 years
Number per state	Depends on population 1 per 30,000 in 1789 now 1 per 550,000	2 per state
Constituency	Tends to be local	Both local and national

and all ideas can receive a thorough public airing. The House is the more central-ized and organized of the two bodies—better equipped to play a routine role in the governmental process. In part, this difference stems from the different rules governing the two bodies. These rules give House leaders more control over the legislative process and provide for House members to specialize in certain legisla-tive areas. The rules of the much smaller Senate give the leadership relatively little power and discourage specialization.

Both formal and informal factors contribute to differences between the two chambers of Congress. Differences in the length of terms and requirements for holding office specified by the Constitution in turn generate differences in how members of each body develop their constituency and exercise their powers of of-fice. The result is that members of the House most effectively and frequently serve as the agents of well-organized local interests with specific legislative agendas—for instance, used-car dealers seeking relief from regulation, labor unions seeking more favorable legislation, farmers looking for higher subsidies. The small size and relative homogeneity of their constituencies and the frequency with which they must seek re-election make House members more attuned to these well-organized local interests with individual legislative needs.

Senators, on the other hand, serve larger and more heterogeneous constituen-cies. As a result, they are somewhat better able than members of the House to serve as the agents for groups and interests organized on a statewide or national basis. Moreover, with longer terms in office, senators have the luxury of consider-ing "new ideas" or seeking to bring together new coalitions of interests, rather than simply serving existing ones.

Thus, the House and Senate represent somewhat different forces in American political life. The House is more likely to represent entrenched local interests; the Senate is better able to serve new or emergent national forces. In recent years, as a result, it has been the Senate that has been most friendly to new social movements, such as feminism and gay rights.

MAKING LAW

The United States Congress is not only a representative assembly. It is also a legislative body. For Americans, representation and legislation go hand in hand. As we saw earlier, however, many parliamentary bodies are representative without the power to legislate. It is no small achievement that the U.S. Congress both represents *and* governs.

It is extraordinarily difficult for a large, representative assembly to formulate, enact, and implement laws. The internal complexities of conducting business within Congress—the legislative process—alone are complicated. In addition, there are many individuals and institutions that have the capacity to influence the legislative process. For example, legislation to raise the salaries of members of the House of Representatives received input from congressional leaders of both parties, special legislative task forces, the president, the national chairmen of the two major parties, public interest lobbyists, the news media, and the mass public before it became law in 1989. Since successful legislation requires the confluence of so many distinct factors, it is little wonder that most of the thousands of bills considered by Congress each year are defeated long before they reach the president.

Before an idea or proposal can become a law, it must pass through a complex set of organizations and procedures in Congress. Collectively, these are called the policymaking process, or the legislative process. Understanding this process is central to understanding why some ideas and proposals eventually become the law of the land while most do not. Although the supporters of legislative proposals often feel that the formal rules of the congressional process are deliberately designed to prevent their own deserving proposals from ever seeing the light of day, these rules allow Congress to play an important role in lawmaking. If it wants to be more than simply a rubber stamp for the executive branch, like so many other representative assemblies around the world, a national legislature like the Congress must develop a division of labor, set an agenda, maintain order through rules and procedures, and place limits on discussion. Equality among the members of Congress must give way to hierarchy—ranking people according to their function within the institution.

To exercise its power to make the law, Congress must first bring about something close to an organizational miracle. We will now examine the organization of Congress and the legislative process, particularly, the basic building blocks of congressional organization: political parties, the committee system, congressional staff, the caucuses, and the parliamentary rules of the House and Senate. Each of these factors plays a key role in the organization of Congress and in the process through which Congress formulates and enacts laws. We will then look at other powers Congress has in addition to lawmaking and explore the future role of Congress in relation to the powers of the executive. Once we review the organization and powers of Congress, we can reconnect them to congressional representation to understand the role of Congress in modern America.

POLITICAL PARTIES: CONGRESS'S OLDEST HIERARCHY

The Constitution makes only one provision for the organization of business in Congress. In Article I, it gives each chamber a presiding officer. In the Senate, this officer is known as the president, and the office is held ex officio by the vice-president of the United States. The Constitution also allows the Senate to elect a president pro tempore—a temporary president—to serve in the absence of the vice-president. In the House of Representatives, the presiding officer is known as the Speaker and is elected by the entire House membership.

Article I of the Constitution gives little guidance for how to conduct congressional business. Even during the first Congress (1789–1791), it was the political parties that provided the organization needed by the House and Senate. For the first century or more of the Republic, America had literally a party government in Congress.[13]

Party Leadership in the House and the Senate

Every two years, at the beginning of a new Congress, the members of each party gather to elect their House leaders. This gathering is traditionally called the ***caucus,*** or ***conference.*** The elected leader of the majority party is later proposed to the whole House and is automatically elected to the position of Speaker, with voting along straight party lines. The House majority caucus then also elects a majority leader. The minority party goes through the same process and selects the minority leader. Both parties also elect whips to line up party members on important votes and relay voting information to the leaders.

In December 1992, prior to the opening of the 103rd Congress, Democrats designated Thomas Foley of Washington to continue as Speaker, Richard Gephardt of Missouri to remain the majority leader, and David Bonior of Michigan to continue as whip. Republicans reelected Robert Michel of Illinois to the position of minority leader and Newt Gingrich of Georgia to serve as minority whip. In a victory for the GOP's conservative wing, House Republicans unseated the Republican conference chair, Jerry Lewis of California, and replaced him with Richard Armey of Texas. Armey, like Gingrich, is an advocate of confrontational politics. His selection to the House Republican leadership put Democrats on notice that Republican opposition was likely to become more vocal and more intense than ever.

Next in line of importance for each party after the Speaker and majority or minority leader is its Committee on Committees (called the Steering and Policy Committee by the Democrats), whose tasks are to assign new legislators to committees and to deal with the requests of incumbent members for transfers from one committee to another. The Speaker serves as chair of the Democratic Steering and Policy Committee, while the minority leader chairs the Republican Committee

---

[13] *Origins and Development of Congress* (Washington DC: Congressional Quarterly Press, 1982).

167

POLITICAL
PARTIES:
CONGRESS'S
OLDEST
HIERARCHY

TABLE 5.6
House and Senate Leadership in the 103rd Congress

The Senate

Democratic Leadership

Majority Leader: George J. Mitchell (ME)
Majority Whip: Wendell H. Ford (KY)
Chief Deputy Whip[*]: John Breaux (LA)
Democratic Senatorial Campaign Committee Chair: Bob Graham (FL)
Democratic Policy Committee: Mitchell and Thomas A. Daschle (SD)

New Committee Chairs

(All are Democrats)
Environmental and Public Works: Max Baucus (MT)
Ethics: Richard Bryan (NV)
Finance: Daniel Patrick Moynihan
Intelligence: Dennis DeConcini (AZ)
Veterans Affairs: John D. "Jay" Rockefeller IV (WV)

Republican Leadership

Minority Leader: Robert J. Dole (KS)
Minority Whip: Alan K. Simpson (WY)
Republican Conference Chair: Thad Cochran (MS)
Republican Policy Committee Chair: Don Nickles (OK)
National Republican Senatorial Committee Chair: Phil Gramm (TX)
Republican Conference Secretary: Trent Lott (MS)

The House

Democratic Leadership

Speaker: Thomas S. Foley (WA)
Majority Leader: Richard A. Gephardt (MO)
Majority Whip: David E. Bonior (MI)
Democratic Caucus Chair: Steny H. Hoyer (MD)
Democratic Congressional Campaign Committee Chair: Vic Fazio (CA), who is also Democratic Caucus vice-chair.
Chief Deputy Whips: Butler Derrick (SC), Barbara V. Kennelly (CT), John Lewis (GA), and Bill Richardson (NM).[*]

New Committee Chairs

(All are Democrats)
Appropriations: William H. Natcher (KY)
Armed Services: Ronald V. Dellums (CA)
Budget: Martin O. Sabo (MN)
District of Columbia: Fortney "Pete" Stark (CA)
Foreign Affairs: Lee H. Hamilton (IN)
Public Works and Transportation: Norman Y. Mineta (CA)

Republican Leadership

Minority Leader: Robert H. Michel (IL)
Minority Whip: Newt Gingrich (GA)
Republican Conference Chair[*]: Richard K. Armey (TX)
Republican Conference Vice-Chair: Bill McCollum (FL)
Republican Conference Secretary: Tom DeLay (TX)
Republican Policy Committee Chair: Henry J. Hyde (IL)
Republican Research Committee Chair: Duncan Hunter (CA)
National Republican Congressional Committee Chair: Bill Paxon (NY)

[*]Indicates positions that have changed hands since last session.
Source: *Washington Post,* 5 January 1993, p. A6.

FIGURE 5.1

Majority Party Structure in the House of Representatives

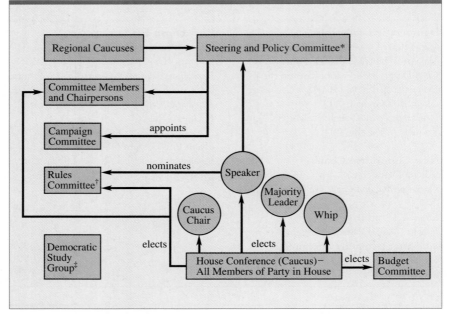

*Includes Speaker (chair), majority leader, chief and deputy whips, caucus chair, four members appointed by Speaker, and twelve members elected by regional caucuses. Created by caucus to assist party leaders in making committee assignments, ordering legislation, and developing policy.
†Speaker nominates members, ratified by caucus, elected by House. Official committee for determining the order of business in the House.
‡Similar to Republicans' Wednesday Club. Both serve as self-conscious, policy-oriented voting blocs. The Democratic Study Group is the larger and is thought to be the more effective of the two.

on Committees. (The Republicans have a separate Policy Committee.) At one time party leaders strictly controlled committee assignments, using them to enforce party discipline. Today, in principle, representatives receive the assignments they want. But assignments on the most important committees are often sought by several individuals, which gives the leadership an opportunity to cement alliances (and, perhaps, make enemies) as it resolves conflicting requests.

Generally, representatives seek assignments that will allow them to influence decisions of special importance to their districts. Representatives from farm districts, for example, may request seats on the Agriculture Committee.[14] Seats on powerful committees such as Ways and Means, which is responsible for tax legislation, and Appropriations are especially popular. In order to integrate the extraordinarily large freshman class elected in 1992 into the congressional process, and to win their loyalty, the House Democratic leadership made a special effort to give them significant committee appointments. As a result, Democratic freshmen received coveted appointments to Appropriations, Ways and Means, and other key committees at the start of the 103rd Congress.

[14]Richard Fenno, Jr., *Home Style: House Members in Their Districts* (Boston: Little, Brown, 1978).

169

POLITICAL
PARTIES:
CONGRESS'S
OLDEST
HIERARCHY

FIGURE 5.2
Majority Party Structure in the Senate

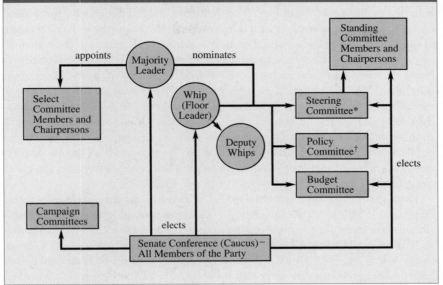

*Chaired by majority leader. Members nominated by majority leader and whip to reflect a geographical and philosophical balance.
†Schedules legislative activity.

Most freshmen had campaigned on platforms calling for congressional reform and had entered Congress pledging to cut congressional expenditures, to reduce the perquisites of office, and, in general, to make Congress a more open and democratic body. Partly as a result of the leadership's efforts, however, even the most reform-minded Democratic freshmen gradually accepted the rules and traditions of the Congress. Some Democratic freshmen did not want to make demands that might impede the passage of President Clinton's program. Others, particularly representatives from districts with heavy Democratic majorities quickly realized that the congressional seniority system would eventually make them influential figures in the Congress. This realization reduced their enthusiasm for reforms that might someday reduce their own power.[15]

Within the Senate the president pro tempore exercises mainly ceremonial leadership. Usually, the majority party designates a member with the greatest seniority to serve in this capacity. Real power is in the hands of the majority leader and minority leader, each elected by party caucus. Currently, George Mitchell of Maine is majority leader and Robert Dole of Kansas serves as minority leader. Together they control the Senate's calendar or agenda for legislation. In addition, the senators from each party elect a whip. Each party also selects a Policy Committee, which advises the leadership on legislative priorities. The majority party structures for the House and Senate are shown in Figures 5.1 and 5.2.

[15]See Clifford Krauss, "Leaders Blunt Lances of Quixotic Freshmen," *New York Times,* 4 April 1993, p. 26.

Party Discipline

In both the House and Senate, party leaders have a good deal of influence over the behavior of their party members. This influence, sometimes called "party discipline," was once so powerful that it dominated the lawmaking process. At the turn of the century, party leaders could often command the allegiance of more than 90 percent of their members. A vote on which 90 percent or more of the members of one party take a particular position while at least 90 percent of the members of the other party take the opposing position is called a ***party vote.*** At the beginning of the twentieth century, nearly half of all roll-call votes in the House of Representatives were party votes. Today, this type of party-line voting is rare in Congress. It is, however, fairly common to find at least a majority of the Democrats opposing a majority of the Republicans on any given issue. This display of party unity has increased in recent sessions of Congress as a result of the intense partisan struggles during the Reagan and Bush years (see Figure 5.3).

During the first session of the 103rd Congress, straight, party-line voting reemerged briefly in the House of Representatives. House Democrats were virtually unanimous in their support of a number of President Clinton's policy proposals. For their part, House Republicans were united in their opposition to Clinton. In the March 18, 1993, House vote on Clinton's proposed tax increases and spending cuts, the president was supported by 96 percent of the Democratic members and opposed by 100 percent of the Republicans. The next day, Clinton's economic stimulus package was supported by 91 percent of the Democrats and opposed by 98 percent of the Republicans.

FIGURE 5.3

Party Unity Scores by Chamber[*]

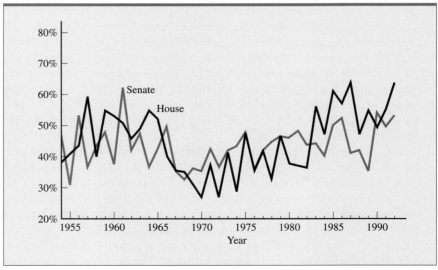

[*]The percentage of times that members voted with the majority of their party, based on recorded votes on which a majority of one party voted against the majority of the other party.
Source: *Congressional Quarterly Weekly Report,* 19 December 1992. Used by permission.

Most political observers attributed this high level of party unity to the fervent desire of congressional Democrats to contribute to the success of the first Democratic administration in twelve years. Many Democrats, particularly members of the large group of congressional newcomers, considered their own political futures to be tied, at least in part, to Clinton's success or failure.

171
POLITICAL
PARTIES:
CONGRESS'S
OLDEST
HIERARCHY

Republicans were equally as determined to make certain that any future blame for Clinton's programs should fall entirely upon the shoulders of the Democrats. Republicans also deeply resented what they saw as Democratic "steamroller" tactics that completely ignored the views of GOP legislators. "For two months they acted like we weren't even around" complained one Republican aide.[16]

Given the many long-term factors working against party discipline in the United States, few observers expected this situation to continue for long.[17] The early show of Democratic party unity was achieved only after an intense debate within the Democratic camp. Conservative Democrats, led by Representative Charles Stenholm of Texas, supported Clinton's economic package only after insisting on $55 billion in spending cuts beyond the president's request. To maintain the support of western Democratic senators for his economic package, Clinton was forced to give in to demands that he drop his proposal to charge fees for the use of public lands by western ranchers and mining interests.[18] By the summer, Democratic unity in the House had once again diminished. In June, thirty-eight conservative Democrats broke ranks with the president and voted against his budget package. Eleven of the defectors chaired subcommittees and loyal Democrats demanded they be stripped of their positions. The House leadership, however, balked at such a divisive step.

Typically, party unity is greater in the House than in the Senate. House rules grant greater procedural control of business to the majority party leaders, giving them more influence over their members. In the Senate, the leadership has few sanctions over its members. Senator Tom Daschle (D-S.D.), co-chair of the Democratic Policy Committee, observed that a Senate leader seeking to influence other senators has "a bushel full of carrots and a few twigs."[19] Even so, during President Clinton's spring 1993 "honeymoon" with Congress, Senate Democrats also gave him almost unanimous support, producing extraordinary, straight party-line voting. The one exception was Senator Richard Shelby of Alabama, who strongly opposed the president's economic program and responded to its introduction by saying, "The taxman cometh." Democratic unity eroded still further in June, when the president's economic package came up for a vote. Six Democrats joined the Republicans to vote against it, leaving Gore to cast the necessary tie-breaking vote.

In August 1993, Republicans in both the House and Senate again voted unani-

[16]David Broder, "Republicans Turn Democrats' Hardball Tactics Into Rallying Point," *Washington Post,* 3 April 1993, p. 1.

[17]David Broder, "Hill Democrats Vote as One: New Era of Unity or Short-term Honeymoon?" *Washington Post,* 14 March 1993, p. A1. See also, Adam Clymer, "All Aboard: Clinton's Plan Gets Moving," *New York Times,* 21 March 1993, sec. 4, p. 1.

[18]Adam Clymer, "Single-Minded President," *New York Times,* 3 April 1993, p. 1.

[19]Holly Idelson, "Signs Point to Greater Loyalty on Both Sides of the Aisle," *Congressional Quarterly Weekly Report,* 19 December 1992, p. 3849.

CONGRESSIONAL DISILLUSIONMENT

During the four years of the Bush administration, Congress was plagued by scandal and inertia. In 1989, House Speaker Jim Wright was forced to resign after being accused of evading income limits by transforming extra money received for campaign contributions into book royalties. The House bank "bad check" scandal, combined with news of perks and health care benefits available to members of Congress at taxpayers' expense, further alienated a nation mired in a lingering recession.

Governmental gridlock was reinforced by an almost perfect record of presidential vetoes by Bush—forty-six total, with only one overridden by Congress. This standoff reached disturbing new levels after Bush vetoed legislation proposed to aid urban areas hurt by the recession because it included new taxes that would hurt him politically.

On Capitol Hill, frustration with Congress's inability to enact legislation caused a record number of incumbents to retire. Most notable was Senator Warren Rudman (R.-N.H.), best known for co-authoring the Gramm-Rudman-Hollings Act to help balance the budget. He had been a member of Congress since 1980 and was respected by members of both parties as well as by his constituents. He cited his frustration with the logjam caused by partisan bickering and presidential vetoing as his reasons for returning to the private sector. In spite of these problems within Congress, very few incumbents were defeated in the 1992 election although many had close, bitter re-election battles.

The public elected Democrat Bill Clinton, hoping he and a Democratic Congress would be more cooperative. The vacancies created by retirements and redistricting put many new faces on Capitol Hill, and Congress slowly began to represent the nation's ethnic and gender diversity. Nydia M. Velásquez (D.-N.Y.) became the first Puerto Rican American female elected to Congress. Jay C. Kim (R.-Calif.), a former Republican mayor of Diamond Bar, California, became the first Korean American elected to Congress. These new members, guided into office by voter disgruntlement, promised change and an end to "politics as usual."

mously in opposition to President Clinton's budget proposals. While Clinton was supported by a solid core of Democrats in both houses, defections by conservative Democrats made his victory razor thin. Clinton won in the House by a mere two votes, 218 to 216. In the Senate, Vice-President Gore again cast a tie-breaking vote to give the Clinton budget a 51-to-50 edge. A number of congressional Democrats in the end only supported the president's program in exchange for specific services or benefits for their own constituents or interest group backers. The process leading to the budget's enactment was aptly characterized by Democratic Senator Bill Bradley of New Jersey as a "giant bazaar," rather than a "principled debate."[20]

To some extent, party unity is based on ideology and background. Republican members of Congress are more likely than Democrats to be drawn from rural or suburban areas. Democrats are likely to be more liberal on economic and social questions than their Republican colleagues. These differences certainly help to explain roll-call divisions between the two parties. Ideology and background, however, are only part of the explanation of party unity. The other part has to do with party organization and leadership. Although party organization has weakened since the turn of the century, today's party leaders still have some resources at their disposal: (1) committee assignments, (2) access to the floor, (3) the whip system, (4) logrolling, and (5) the presidency. These resources are regularly used and are often effective in securing the support of party members.

Committee Assignments   Leaders can create debts among members by helping them get favorable committee assignments. These assignments are made early in the congressional careers of most members and cannot be taken from them if they later balk at party discipline. Nevertheless, if the leadership goes out of its way to get the right assignment for a member, this effort is likely to create a bond of obligation that can be called upon without any other payments or favors. This is one reason the leadership worked so hard to give freshmen favorable assignments in the 103rd Congress.

Access to the Floor   The most important everyday resource available to the parties is control over access to the floor. With thousands of bills awaiting passage and most members clamoring for access in order to influence a bill or to publicize themselves, floor time is precious. In the Senate, the leadership allows ranking committee members to influence the allocation of floor time—who will speak for how long; in the House, the Speaker, as head of the majority party (in consultation with the minority leader), allocates large blocks of floor time. Thus, floor time is allocated in both houses of Congress by the majority and minority leaders. More importantly, the Speaker of the House and the majority leader in the Senate possess the power of recognition. Although this power may not appear to be substantial, it is a formidable authority, and it can be used to stymie a piece of legislation completely or to frustrate a member's attempts to speak on a particular issue. Be-

[20]Lloyd Grove, "Rebel Senator Faces White House Wrath," *Washington Post,* 4 April 1993, p. 1. See also David Rogers and John Harwood, "No Reasonable Offers Refused as Administration Bargained to Nail Down Deficit Package in House," *Wall Street Journal,* 6 August 1993, p. A12; and Hobart Rowan, "It's Not Much of a Budget," *Washington Post,* 12 August 1993, p. A27.

cause the power is significant, members of Congress usually attempt to stay on *175*
POLITICAL
PARTIES:
CONGRESS'S
OLDEST
HIERARCHY good terms with the Speaker and the majority leader in order to ensure that they will continue to be recognized.

Some House members, Republicans in particular, have also taken advantage of "special orders," under which members can address the floor after the close of business. These addresses are typically made to an empty chamber, but are usually carried live by C-Span, a cable channel. Democrats control the House floor and tend to have ample time to present their positions during the day. Republicans, however, have often used "special orders" to present their views effectively to national audiences. Representative Newt Gingrich, for example, launched a televised after-hours attack on House Speaker Jim Wright in 1988 that ultimately led to Wright's resignation.[21]

The Whip System   Some influence accrues to party leaders through the whip system, which is primarily a communications network. Between twelve and twenty assistant and regional whips are selected by zones to operate at the direction of the majority or minority leader and the whip. They take polls of all the members in order to learn their intentions on specific bills. This enables the leaders to know if they have enough support to allow a vote as well as whether the vote is so close that they need to put pressure on a few swing votes. Leaders also use the whip system to convey their wishes and plans to the members, but only in very close votes do they actually exert pressure on a member. In those instances, the Speaker or a lieutenant will go to a few party members who have indicated they will switch if their vote is essential. The whip system helps the leaders limit pressuring members to a few times per session.

The whip system helps maintain party unity in both houses of Congress, but it is particularly critical in the House of Representatives because of the large number of legislators whose positions and votes must be accounted for. The majority and minority whips and their assistants must be adept at inducing compromise among legislators who hold widely differing viewpoints. The whips' personal styles and their perception of their function significantly affect the development of legislative coalitions and influence the compromises that emerge.

Logrolling   An agreement between two or more members of Congress who have nothing in common except the need for support is called logrolling. The agreement states, in effect, "You support me on bill X and I'll support you on another bill of your choice." Since party leaders are the center of the communications networks in the two chambers, they can help members create large logrolling coalitions. Hundreds of logrolling deals are made each year, and while there are no official record-keeping books, it would be a poor party leader whose whips did not know who owed what to whom.

The Presidency   Of all the influences that maintain the clarity of party lines in Congress, the influence of the presidency is probably the most important. Indeed,

---

[21]See Beth Donovan, "Busy Democrats Skirt Fights to Get House in Order," *Congressional Quarterly Weekly Report,* 12 December 1992, p. 3778.

Tom Foley and Newt Gingrich
The Traditional and Modern Styles of Congress

The careers and styles of congressional leaders Tom Foley and Newt Gingrich closely mirror the opposing forces that shape the modern Congress.

Tom Foley was first elected to the House of Representatives as a Democrat from Washington state in 1964. Quiet, hard-working, known for his fairness and integrity, Foley rose in the ranks of his party rapidly. In 1972, he was chosen to chair the Democratic Study Group, a policy oriented group of House Democrats. After the 1974 elections, Foley was selected to chair the Agriculture Committee after the Democratic Caucus pushed aside the committee's aged chair, Robert Poage. Although the chairing of a committee is normally a highly sought-after privilege, Foley had actually backed Poage.

After the 1980 elections, House speaker Tip O'Neill and Majority Leader Jim Wright chose Foley to serve as majority whip. (Foley was the last to obtain this post by leader appointment; thereafter, the position became elective.) When O'Neill retired in 1986, Foley moved up to majority leader; when the new Speaker, Jim Wright, resigned his seat in the wake of ethics violations charges in 1989, Foley became the Speaker. Without question, the rise of this highly respected leader would not have occurred had competition for the whip position been opened up to all House Democrats, as is now the case. Yet Foley's calm, conciliatory, almost non-partisan style raised questions in 1993 about whether he could be tough and ruthless enough to impose the discipline necessary to win enactment of President Clinton's ambitious legislative program. Responding to these criticisms, Foley said "You don't get support for these programs by routine arm-twisting. It's mythical to think members can be forced to do something they don't want to do."

In contrast, the rise of Georgia's Newt Gingrich reflects the more wide-open, competitive process increasingly seen in Congress in recent years. First elected to the House in 1978, this conservative Republi-

Tom Foley

it is a touchstone of party discipline in Congress. Since the late 1940s, under President Truman, presidents each year have identified a number of bills to be considered part of their administration's program. By the mid-1950s, both parties in Congress began to look to the president for these proposals, which became the most significant part of Congress's agenda. The president's support is a criterion for party loyalty, and party leaders are able to use it to rally some members.

can quickly became known for his brash, contentious, abrasive style. In an environment in which collegiality, respect, and deference were considered necessary to win advancement, Gingrich waged what was labeled "guerrilla warfare against the Democrats." For example, he and fellow conservative Republicans used C-SPAN (the televised proceedings of Congress) to harshly criticize the Democrats and even some Republican party leaders in a manner designed to be highly public and therefore highly embarrassing. Gingrich was among the first to criticize Speaker Wright for alleged ethics problems. Gingrich himself summed up his tactics as, "conflict equals exposure equals power."

In 1989, a sudden vacancy for the position of House minority whip opened up. Despite an unimpressive legislative record and lack of service in a leadership role either on a committee or for the party, Gingrich won a narrow vote among House Republicans and became the Republican Whip. Gingrich's surprise victory underscored the discontent of many Republicans who were no longer satisfied with accepting the Republicans' seemingly permanent status as minority party (the Republicans have not held a majority in the House since 1954). In Gingrich's words, "We had a choice of being attack dogs or lapdogs. We decided attack dogs are more useful."

Many feared that Gingrich's aggressive style would only further reduce Republican influence in the House. But Gingrich toned down his rhetoric and began to practice the kind of congressional leadership skills so ably employed by Speaker Foley. Still, on some issues, such as the 1990 deficit-reduction package, Gingrich has been a strident and vocal critic of the Democrats and some Republican leaders. Gingrich's "conflict" style maintains a certain appeal, but it is also clear that the low-key, bargaining style epitomized by Foley is still vital to an effective Congress.

Source: Roger H. Davidson and Walter J. Oleszek, 3rd ed., *Congress and Its Members* (Washington, DC: Congressional Quarterly Press, 1990).

Newt Gingrich

THE COMMITTEE SYSTEM: THE CORE OF CONGRESS

The committee system provides Congress with its second organizational structure, but it is more a division of labor than a hierarchy of power. Committee and subcommittee chairs have a number of important powers, but their capacity to discipline committee members is limited. Ultimately, committee members are hired and fired by the electorate not by the leadership.

Congress had only a few standing committees during the first twenty-five years of its existence. As the national government expanded, however, Congress expanded these committees. The committee system has been reformed, reorganized, and streamlined on several occasions.

Six fundamental characteristics define the congressional committee system:

1. *Each committee is a standing committee.* It is given a permanent status by the official rules, with a fixed membership, officers, rules, staff, offices, and, above all, a jurisdiction that is recognized by all other committees and usually the leadership as well.
2. *The jurisdiction of each standing committee is defined by the subject matter of legislation.* Except for the House Rules Committee, all the important committees receive proposals for legislation and process them into official bills. The House Rules Committee decides the order in which bills come up for a vote and determines the specific rules that govern the length of debate and opportunity for amendments.
3. *Committees' jurisdictions usually parallel those of the major departments or agencies in the executive branch.* There are important exceptions—Appropriations (House and Senate) and Rules (House), for example—but by and large, the division of labor is self-consciously designed to parallel executive branch organization.
4. *Bills are assigned to committees on the basis of subject matter, but the Speaker of the House and the Senate's presiding officer have some discretion in the allocation of bills to committees.* Most bills "die in committee"—that is, they are not reported out favorably. Ordinarily this ends a bill's life. There is only one way for a legislative proposal to escape committee processing: A bill passed in one chamber may be permitted to go directly on to the calendar of the other chamber. Even here, however, the bill has received the full committee treatment before passage in the first chamber.
5. *Each committee is unique.* No effort is made to compose the membership of any committee to be representative of the total House or Senate membership. In both the House and the Senate, each party has established a Committee on Committees, which determines the committee assignments of new members and of established members who wish to change committees. Ordinarily, members can keep their committee assignments as long as they like.
6. *Each committee's hierarchy is based on seniority.* Seniority is determined by years of continuous service on a particular committee, not years of service in the House or Senate. In general, each committee is chaired by the most senior member of the majority party. Although the power of committee chairs is limited, they help determine scheduling hearings, select subcommittee members, and appoint committee staff. Because Congress has a large number of subcommittees and has given each representative a larger staff, the power of committee chairs has been diluted. Democrats elect committee chairs by secret ballot, rather than permit seniority to determine the outcome automatically. However, seniority has been followed in all but a handful in recent years.

Seniority can sometimes result in odd outcomes. In 1993, Representative Les Aspin of Wisconsin, chair of the House Armed Services Committee, was named secretary of defense by President Bill Clinton. The most senior Democrat eligible

to replace Aspin was Representative Ron Dellums of California. Dellums, who
represented Berkeley, California, was a self-described socialist who advocated substantial cuts in defense spending. Dellums reportedly cried when he learned that American forces had attacked Iraq in 1991.[22] Thus, ironically, the seniority system has placed a pacifist in the chair of the House Armed Services Committee.

At the opening of the 103rd Congress, House Democrats partially reversed the decentralizing reforms of the 1970s by opting to abolish 16 of the 137 subcommittees. Under the rubric of congressional cost saving, four select committees were also eliminated. These had dealt with hunger, children, the elderly and illegal drugs. The Democrats also established a party policy council to set a legislative agenda. This twenty-member group was selected by the Speaker, with half of its members coming from the Steering and Policy Committee.With these reforms, Democrats increased the power of the House leadership, paving the way for more efficient enactment of new programs and policies.

For their part, House Republicans weakened seniority by limiting their members to six consecutive years in any committee's top position. Under the new rule, there would be a complete turnover of every committee's ranking Republican spot in 1996. The major purpose of the rule was to embarrass the Democrats, who had declined to adopt term limits for committee chairs. Most observers predicted that the Republicans would rescind the rule before it took effect in 1996.

THE STAFF SYSTEM: STAFFERS AND AGENCIES

A congressional institution second in importance only to the committee system is the staff system. Every member of Congress employs a large number of staff members, whose tasks include handling constituency requests and, to a large and growing extent, dealing with legislative details and the activities of administrative agencies. Increasingly, staffers bear the primary responsibility for formulating and drafting proposals, organizing hearings, dealing with administrative agencies, and negotiating with lobbyists. Indeed, legislators typically deal with one another through staff, rather than through direct, personal contact. Representatives and senators together employ nearly eleven thousand staffers in their Washington and home offices. Today, staffers even develop policy ideas, draft legislation, and in some instances, have a good deal of influence over the legislative process.

In addition to the personal staffs of individual senators and representatives, Congress also employs roughly three thousand committee staffers. These individuals comprise the permanent staff, who stay regardless of turnover in Congress, attached to every House and Senate committee, and who are responsible for organizing and administering the committee's work, including research, scheduling, organizing hearings, and drafting legislation. Congressional staffers can come to

[22]Pat Towell, "Dellums Will Bring Savvy, Not Just Anger to Chair," *Congressional Quarterly Weekly Report,* 2 January 1993, p. 33.

play key roles in the legislative process. For example, according to informal accounts, important pieces of legislation such as the Clean Air Act of 1963, the Mass Transportation Act of 1964, and the Budget and Impoundment Act of 1974 were actually shaped by congressional staffers with only cursory supervision from their bosses.[23] In some cases, staffers have enormous influence over the behavior and thinking of the senators and representatives for whom they work. For example, Senator Warren Magnuson (D-Wash.) served as chair of the Senate Commerce Committee for twenty-three years (1955–1978). During this period, under the influence of staffers Gerald Grinstein and Michael Pertschuk, Magnuson shifted from a conservative political stance to become a liberal activist on such national issues as consumer affairs.[24] The influence of congressional staff was summarized by Senator Robert Morgan (D-N.C.), who said, "This country is basically run by the legislative staffs of the Senate and House of Representatives."[25]

Not only does Congress employ personal and committee staff, but the Congress has also established four staff agencies designed to provide the legislative branch with resources and expertise independent of the executive branch. Thus they enhance Congress's capacity to oversee administrative agencies and to evaluate presidential programs and proposals. These staff agencies are the Congressional Research Service, which performs research for legislators who wish to know the facts and competing arguments relevant to policy proposals or other legislative business; the General Accounting Office, through which Congress can investigate the financial and administrative affairs of any government agency or program; the Office of Technology Assessment, which provides Congress with analyses of any scientific or technical issues that may be relevant to national programs; and the Congressional Budget Office, which assesses the economic implications and likely costs of proposed federal programs.

INFORMAL ORGANIZATION: THE CAUCUSES

In addition to the formal organization of Congress, there also exists an informal organizational structure—the caucuses. Caucuses are groups of senators or representatives who share certain opinions, interests, or social characteristics. There are ideological caucuses such as the liberal Democratic Study Group, the conservative Democratic Forum (popularly known as the "boll weevils"), and the moderate Republican Wednesday Group. At the same time, there are a large number of caucuses composed of legislators representing particular economic or policy interests such as the Travel and Tourism Caucus, the Steel Caucus, the Mushroom Caucus, and the Concerned Senators for the Arts. Legislators who share common back-

---

[23]See Harrison W. Fox and Susan W. Hammond, *Congressional Staffs: The Invisible Force in American Lawmaking* (New York: Free Press, 1977).

[24]Michael Malbin, *Unelected Representatives* (New York: Basic Books, 1980), pp. 29–30.

[25]*Congressional Record,* 8 September 1976, S15432. Quoted in Fox and Hammond, *Congressional Staffs,* p. 3.

grounds or social characteristics have organized caucuses such as the Congressional
Black Caucus, the Congressional Caucus for Women's Issues, and the Hispanic
Caucus. All these caucuses seek to advance the interests of the groups they repre-
sent by promoting legislation, encouraging Congress to hold hearings, and pressing administrative agencies for favorable treatment. The Congressional Black
Caucus, for example, which now includes thirty-eight representatives and one
senator, is expected to increase its role in the 103rd Congress. Representative
Kweisi Mfume (D-M.D.), elected to chair the caucus, has become an important
and effective congressional advocate for economic development in the African
American community.[26] The policy-making role of the caucuses has become
important enough to make them a "third force," rivaling, though not equaling,
committees and parties.

RULES OF LAWMAKING: HOW A BILL BECOMES A LAW

The institutional structure of Congress is one key factor that helps to shape the
legislative process. A second and equally important set of factors are the rules of
congressional procedures (see Box 5.3). These rules govern everything from the
introduction of a bill through its submission to the president for signing. Not only
do these regulations influence the fate of each and every bill, they also help to determine the distribution of power in the Congress.

Committee Deliberation

Even if a member of Congress, the White House, or a federal agency has spent
months developing and drafting a piece of legislation, it does not become a bill
until it is submitted officially by a senator or representative to the clerk of the
House or Senate and referred to the appropriate committee for deliberation. No
floor action on any bill can take place until the committee with jurisdiction over it
has taken all the time it needs to deliberate. During the course of its deliberations,
the committee typically refers the bill to one of its subcommittees, which may
hold hearings, listen to expert testimony, and amend the proposed legislation before referring it to the full committee for its consideration. The full committee
may accept the recommendation of the subcommittee or hold its own hearings
and prepare its own amendments. Or, even more frequently, the committee and
subcommittee may do little or nothing with a bill that has been submitted to
them. Many bills are simply allowed to "die in committee" with little or no serious consideration given to them. Often, members of Congress introduce legislation that they neither expect nor desire to see enacted into law merely to please a
constituency group. These bills die a quick and painless death. Other pieces of leg-

[26]See Jeffrey Katz, "Mfume to Chair Caucus," *Congressional Quarterly Weekly Report,* 12 December
1992, p. 3780.

BOX 5.3
A Selection Of Important Congressional Rules

Rules Governing Deliberation	*Comments*
1. Most of the rules of each chamber, especially since 1946, define the jurisdictions of the standing committees, one rule for each.	1. The Speaker's power over committees is limited since there is little discretion on where to assign bills.
2. All proposals are read once and referred immediately to committee.	2. A committee can be bypassed only when a bill has already been passed by the other chamber.
3. Public bills cannot go to calendar (be put on the agenda) until reported out of committee.	3. Again, the only exception is when the bill has already been passed by the other chamber.
4. Committees may be given the power to subpoena witnesses and compel testimony, as a type of grand jury.	4. A limitation on this rule is that the committee questions must have a legislative purpose when citizens other than administrators of agencies and departments are subpoenaed.
5. Bills remain in committee until the committee is ready to report them out.	5. This power of life and death over bills is mainly a result of the great difficulty of discharging bills from committee.
6. Discharge and Calendar Wednesday are the only two meaningful exceptions to the power of a committee to retain and deliberate on bills as long as it chooses.	6. In the House, a discharge petition must be signed by an absolute majority (218). Then the bill goes on calendar, after which it can be debated only on the second or fourth Monday of each month. In the Senate, a discharge motion requires only a simple majority but is subject to debate and therefore to the cloture rule. Calendar Wednesday is even more limited.

islation have ardent supporters and die in committee only after a long battle. But, in either case, most bills are never reported out of the committees to which they are assigned. In a typical congressional session, 95 percent of the roughly eight thousand bills introduced die in committee—an indication of the power of the congressional committee system.

The relative handful of bills that are reported out of the committee to which they were originally referred must, in the House, pass one additional hurdle within the committee system—the Rules Committee. This powerful committee determines the rules that will govern action on the bill on the House floor. In particular, the Rules Committee allots the time for debate and decides to what extent amendments to the bill can be proposed from the floor. A bill's supporters generally prefer what is called a ***closed rule,*** which puts severe limits on floor debate and

183

RULES OF
LAWMAKING:
HOW A BILL
BECOMES A
LAW

Rules Governing Debate	*Comments*
1. Rule and tradition give unlimited power of recognition to the presiding officer, especially the Speaker of the House.	1. Senate presiding officers try to play down this power, attempting to work through agreements between majority and minority committee leaders.
2. While in session, Congress must meet every day except Sunday.	2. There rarely are weekend sessions. Occasionally, the leadership threatens such sessions to discourage casual attendance or diversionary tactics.
3. To encourage talk, House rules allow the House to adjourn into the "Committee of the Whole House on the State of the Union."	3. A quorum is 100 instead of 218, and rules governing debate are less strict than formal House rules.
4. In both House and Senate, actual debate time is controlled by the committee responsible for handling the bill.	4. The "floor managers" are the chairperson and the top ranking minority member of the committee whose bill is up for debate. They can designate another committee member as floor manager.
5. House rules severely limit the power of a member to offer amendments to bills. These limits are policed by the Rules Committee and chairpersons. The Senate sets no serious limit on the right of senators to offer amendments and to speak for them.	5. Even in the Senate, there is a long distance between offering an amendment and getting it adopted as part of a bill. Amendments not agreed to in advance by the bill's sponsors have a low probability of acceptance.
6. When the House sits as the House again, it hears the Report of the Committee of the Whole. Amendments rejected by the Committee of the Whole cannot be reconsidered, and debate on the bill is usually closed very quickly. The Senate allows amendments at any time.	6. A Senate rule requires germaneness, but unless someone makes a point of order that the rule is being violated, it is not seriously observed.

amendments. Opponents of a bill usually prefer an "open rule," which permits potentially damaging floor debate and makes it easier to add amendments that may cripple the bill or weaken its chances for passage. Thus, the outcome of the Rules Committee's deliberations can be extremely important and the committee's hearings can be an occasion for sharp conflicts.

In 1988, House Republicans lashed out at the Rules Committee, claiming that restrictive rules barring floor amendments had seriously weakened their power. Since House committees are currently controlled by the Democrats, bills reported out of committees generally reflect a Democratic bias, and Republicans consider themselves disadvantaged when they cannot propose amendments on the floor. At least one Republican charged that the Rules Committee had relegated Republicans to second-class status. In the last decade under Democratic control, the number of bills issuing from committees with "open" rules has dropped from 88 percent to 56 percent.

The Calendar

Once reported out of a "subject matter" committee and the Rules Committee, a bill must be placed on a calendar—Congress's name for its agenda. There are several calendars, each of which indicates the status as well as the stature of a bill. The House has five legislative calendars: the *Union Calendar* for revenue, appropriations, and other public bills to be considered by the whole House; the *House Calendar* for public bills not included in the Union Calendar; the *Consent Calendar* for noncontroversial bills likely to be passed without objections or debate; the *Private Calendar* for all private bills; and the *Discharge Calendar* for motions to discharge bills from committees. The Senate has only two calendars: the *Executive Calendar* for treaties and nominations, and the *Calendar of Business* for all legisltion.

Some bills, even if favorably reported by a committee, may stay on a calendar through one or both sessions of Congress, while others go on the calendar and off to the floor for debate after only a brief wait. In both chambers, each week's business is drawn from the calendar according to decisions made by majority and minority party leaders who have consulted with appropriate committee chairs, the White House, and leaders from the other chamber. Usually, a program of floor activities is posted on Friday for the following week so members can plan accordingly.

Debate

Party control of the agenda is reinforced by the rule giving the Speaker of the House and the president of the Senate the power of recognition during debate on a bill. Usually the chair knows the purpose for which a member intends to speak well in advance of the occasion. Spontaneous efforts to gain recognition are often foiled. For example, the speaker may ask "For what purpose does the member rise?" before deciding whether to grant recognition.

Virtually all of the time allotted by the Rules Committee for debate on a given bill is controlled by the bill's sponsor and by its leading opponent. In almost every case, these two people are the committee chair and the ranking minority member of the committee that processed the bill—or those they designate. These two participants are, by rule and tradition, granted the power to allocate most of the debate time in small amounts to members who are seeking to speak for or against the measure. Preference in the allocation of time goes to the members of the committee whose jurisdiction covers the bill.

In the Senate, the leadership has much less control over floor debate. Indeed, the Senate is unique among the world's legislative bodies for its commitment to unlimited debate. Once given the floor, a senator may speak as long as he or she wishes. On a number of memorable occasions, senators have used this right to prevent action on legislation that they opposed. Through this tactic, called the ***fili-***

185
RULES OF
LAWMAKING:
HOW A BILL
BECOMES A
LAW

PROCESS BOX 5.2
How a Bill Becomes a Law

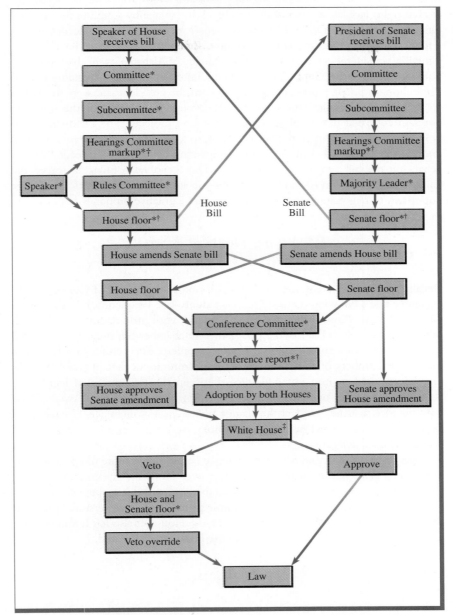

*Points at which bill can be amended.
†Points at which bill can die.
‡If the president neither signs nor vetoes the bill within ten days, it automatically becomes law.

buster, small minorities or even one individual in the Senate can force the majority to give in to their demands. During the 1950s and 1960s, for example, opponents of civil rights legislation often sought to block its passage by adopting the tactic of filibuster. The votes of three-fifths of the Senate, or sixty votes, are needed to end a filibuster. This procedure is called *cloture.* In April 1993, Senate Republicans, joined by one Democrat, Senator Richard Shelby of Alabama, were able to use the filibuster to block the adoption of President Clinton's proposal to spend more than $16 billion on public works and other programs the president said were needed to create jobs and stimulate the economy. Republicans claimed that the spending program consisted mainly of wasteful pork-barrel projects. The Democrats held only a 57-to-43 majority in the Senate. Thus, so long as the Republicans remained unified, the Democrats had no hope of mustering the sixty votes needed to end debate on the bill and bring it to a vote. The Republican filibuster forced the Clinton administration to modify its economic stimulus package and, even more important, to negotiate with the GOP on future legislative proposals.[27]

Reconciling House and Senate Versions of an Act

Getting a bill out of committee and through one of the houses of Congress is no guarantee that a bill will eventually be enacted into law. Frequently, bills that began with similar provisions in both chambers emerge with little resemblance to each other. Alternatively, a bill may be passed by one chamber but undergo substantial revision in the other chamber. In such cases, a conference committee composed of the senior members of the committees or subcommittees that initiated the bills may be required to iron out differences between the two pieces of legislation. Sometimes members or leaders will let objectionable provisions pass on the floor with the idea that they will get the change they want in conference. Usually, conference committees meet behind closed doors. Agreement requires a majority of each of the two delegations.

Legislation that emerges from a conference committee is more often a compromise than a clear victory of one set of forces over another. For example, in 1993, House and Senate negotiators had considerable difficulty reconciling their differing versions of President Clinton's economic plan. The Senate version eliminated the energy tax, which had been approved by the House. It also left less money for expanding domestic social programs than the House had allocated.

The Budget Process

The budget is handled a bit differently from other pieces of legislation. The budget process is designed to allow Congress to consider the overall relationship between

[27]Ruth Marcus and Helen Dewar, "Partisan Strategy on Stimulus Was Clinton Gamble," *Washington Post,* 4 April 1993, p. 1. See also, Michael Wines, "Truly Modern Filibuster," *New York Times,* 4 March 1993, p. 26.

anticipated revenues and expenditures during any given year. The first step in the *187*
RULES OF
LAWMAKING:
HOW A BILL
BECOMES A
LAW process is the adoption of a budget resolution by the House and Senate. This resolution stipulates the amount of money that will be spent and the amount of revenue that will be raised each year. Subsequently, the House and Senate appropriations committees work to develop a plan for discretionary spending whose total level—enacted into law in a series of thirteen appropriations bills (one for each of thirteen functional areas, such as defense, commerce, transportation)—cannot exceed the overall limit stated by the budget resolution.

At the same time, congressional authorization and tax-writing committees must produce legislation to meet the revenue targets and any savings goals embodied in the budget resolution. Such legislation includes changes in tax policy and, where necessary, adjustments in entitlement programs. All such changes are ultimately bundled together in a reconciliation bill. In the Senate, the reconciliation bill is considered under special rules that make it immune to filibusters. This is designed to prevent senators from blocking the entire bill while they seek to compel the enactment (or deletion) of a specific item. In addition, nongermane amendments are prohibited to prevent "killer amendments"—provisions added deliberately to reduce the bill's chance of passing.

In 1993, President Clinton and his allies in Congress secured the enactment of a federal budget providing for spending cuts and substantial tax increases. Clinton asserted that his budget would trim the nation's enormous budget deficit by nearly $500 billion over a five-year period. Republicans argued that Clinton's estimates were based on optimistic projections and that the president should have cut spending more and raised taxes less.

Vetoes

Once adopted by the House and Senate, a bill goes to the president, who may choose to sign the bill into law or veto it. To veto a bill, the president returns it within ten days to the house of Congress in which it originated, along with his objections to the bill. If Congress adjourns during the ten-day period, and the president has taken no action, the bill is also considered to be vetoed. This latter method is known as the "pocket veto." The veto is the president's constitutional power to reject a piece of legislation. The possibility of a presidential veto affects how willing members of Congress are to push for different pieces of legislation at different times. If they think a proposal is likely to be vetoed they might shelve it for a later time.

A presidential veto may be overridden by a two-thirds vote in both the House and Senate. A veto override says much about the support that a president can expect from Congress, and it can deliver a stinging blow to the executive branch. Bush used his veto power on forty-six occasions during his four years in office and, in all but one instance, was able to defeat or avoid a congressional override of his action. Bush's frequent resort to the veto power was one indicator of the struggle between the White House and the Congress over domestic and foreign policy that took place during his term.

BEYOND LEGISLATION: ADDITIONAL CONGRESSIONAL POWERS

In addition to the power to make the law, Congress has at its disposal an array of other instruments through which to influence the process of government. The Constitution gives the Senate the power to approve treaties and appointments. And Congress has drawn to itself a number of other powers through which it can share with the other branches the capacity to administer the laws. The powers of Congress can be called "weapons of control" to emphasize the fact of Congress's power to govern and to call attention to what government power means.

Oversight

Oversight, as applied to Congress, refers not to something neglected but to the effort to oversee or to supervise. Congress sometimes finds it difficult to pass statutes that are clear in wording and intent. That is why the lawmaking branch relied increasingly on legislative oversight of administrators.

Individual senators and members of the House can engage in a form of oversight simply by calling or visiting administrators, sending out questionnaires, or talking to constituents about programs. But in a more formal sense, oversight is carried out by committees or subcommittees of the Senate or House, which conduct hearings and investigations. Congress delegates to these committees or subcommittees the power to subpoena witnesses, take oaths, cross-examine, compel testimony, and bring criminal charges for contempt (refusing to cooperate) and perjury (lying). Hearings and investigations resemble each other in many ways, but they differ on one fundamental point. A hearing is usually held on a specific bill, and the questions asked there are usually intended to build a record with regard to that bill. In an investigation, the committee or subcommittee does not begin with a particular bill, but examines a broad area or problem and then concludes its investigation with one or more proposed bills. An example of an investigation is the congressional inquiry into the Reagan administration's shipment of arms to the government of Iran.

Committees and subcommittees can subpoena any government official or any other citizen as a witness to testify on the behavior of individual administrators or as an expert to analyze and evaluate agencies and the effectiveness of their programs. The purpose may be to locate inefficiencies, to explore the relationship between what an agency does and what a law intended, or to change or abolish a program. Most programs and agencies are subject to some oversight every year during the course of hearings on appropriations, the funding of agencies and government programs. Both the House and Senate have an appropriations committee, which is divided into subcommittees to cover one or more departments and major agencies. Regular standing committees also have opportunities to engage in oversight of past agency behavior, even while considering bills proposing new agency responsibilities. Thus, for example, the House and Senate Intelligence Committees seek to monitor the actions of the Central Intelligence Agency (CIA) and other U.S. intelligence agencies on an ongoing basis.

Investigating committees occasionally run into trouble when they start subpoenaing ordinary citizens rather than administrative officials. No one would deny Congress the ability to subpoena citizens as witnesses in evaluating a specific agency or bill or in defining or evaluating a general problem in an investigation. But when a committee seeks to investigate individual wrongdoing, it has converted itself into a combination grand jury and trial court. In that role, it can easily jeopardize the rights of citizens involved in its investigation, as often happened with the infamous House Unamerican Activities Committee (HUAC) during the 1950s. To address this problem, the Supreme Court has required that each question the committee asks in such a situation be shown to serve a "legislative purpose" before the witness must respond to it.[28]

Advice and Consent: Special Senate Powers

The Constitution has given the Senate a special power, one that is not based on lawmaking. The president has the power to make treaties and to appoint top executive officers, ambassadors, and federal judges—but only "with the Advice and Consent of the Senate" (Article II, Section 2). For treaties, two-thirds of those present must concur; for appointments, a majority is required.

The power to approve or reject presidential requests also involves the power to set conditions. The Senate only occasionally exercises its power to reject treaties and appointments, and usually that is when opposite parties control the Senate and White House. During the final two years of President Reagan's term, Senate Democrats rejected Judge Robert Bork's Supreme Court nomination and gave clear indications that they would reject a second Reagan nominee, Judge Douglas Ginsburg, who withdrew his nomination before the Senate could act. During the first year of the Bush administration, the Senate rejected President Bush's nominee for defense secretary, John Tower. These instances, however, actually underscore the restraint with which the Senate usually uses its power to reject presidential requests. For example, only nine judicial nominees have been rejected by the Senate during the past century, while hundreds have been approved.

Most presidents make every effort to take potential Senate opposition into account in treaty negotiations and will frequently resort to "executive agreements" with foreign powers instead of treaties. The Supreme Court has held that such agreements are equivalent to treaties, but they do not need Senate approval.[29] In the past, presidents sometimes concluded secret agreements without informing Congress of the agreements' contents, or even their existence. For example, American involvement in the Vietnam War grew in part out of a series of secret arrangements made between American presidents and the South Vietnamese dur-

---

[28]McGrain v. Dougherty, 273 U.S. 135 (1927).

[29]U.S. v. Pink, 315 U.S. 203 (1942). For a good discussion of the problem, see James W. Davis, *The American Presidency* (New York: Harper & Row, 1987). Chapter 8.

Patty Murray
"Just a Mom in Tennis Shoes"

Patty Murray (b. 1951)

The political experts and pundits gave Patty Murray, Washington state mother and housewife, no chance to win election to the U.S. Senate in 1992. That verdict did not deter Murray, however.

Murray launched her campaign against incumbent Democratic senator Brock Adams in the fall of 1991. The motivation for her race began in 1980, when Democrat Murray went to Washington's state capital, Olympia, to lobby against proposed budget cuts for the state's community colleges. One male member of the state legislature dismissed Murray by saying, "You can't do anything; you're just a mom in tennis shoes." A community college teacher by training, Murray then became involved in various neighborhood political groups, served on the local school board, and won election to the Washington state senate.

The "mom in tennis shoes" theme became the basis of her U.S. Senate campaign; one of her political advertisements even featured a re-enactment of the incident, and one of her campaign gimmicks included handing out sets of shoelaces with her name on them. Murray won the open senatorial primary in September 1992, outpolling the Democratic and Republican contenders. (Washington holds blanket primaries, where candidates from both parties compete on the same ballot.) By this time, Adams had decided to withdraw from the race, in the wake of accusations of sexual misconduct against him.

Murray's campaign avoided labels like "feminist" or "liberal" and emphasized her average middle-class roots and outsider status. Yet she took strong stands on issues during the campaign, including support for abortion rights, the environment, and an array of educational and family issues. Even during the campaign, she continued to take care of her elderly parents and her two children, for whom she still prepared meals several times a week. In Murray's words, "What I am is a different role model. This mom in tennis shoes is really what I am." Referring to the event that drove many women into politics in 1992, she added, "I didn't see anything like me during the Clarence Thomas hearings."

Murray won a solid victory over a better-financed conservative Republican congressman. Her win was built on support from both rural and urban areas around the state. She relied heavily for campaign finance support from a national organization specializing in financing women candidates called Emily's List. Harriet Woods, head of the National Women's Political Caucus, explained Murray's success this way: "Here is a woman who has none of the lofty credentials, but she represents just what the voters are looking for: an outsider, who is close to them and understands their lives."

Source: Gary Jacobson, *The Politics of Congressional Elections* (New York: Harper Collins, 1992).

ing the 1950s and 1960s. Congress did not even learn of the existence of these agreements until 1969. In 1972, Congress passed the Case Act, which required that the president inform Congress of any executive agreement within sixty days of its having been reached. This provides Congress with the opportunity to cancel agreements that it opposes. In addition, Congress can limit the president's ability to conduct foreign policy through executive agreement by refusing to appropriate the funds needed to implement an agreement. In this way, for example, executive agreements to provide American economic or military assistance to foreign governments can be modified or even canceled by Congress.

191
BEYOND
LEGISLATION:
ADDITIONAL
CONGRES-
SIONAL POWERS

Direct Committee Government

Direct committee government refers to the practice of delegating certain congressional powers from the whole Congress to one of its committees. Each chamber can grant a committee the power to approve a proposed agency project without having to return to Congress for authorization and appropriation. This device was widely used during the 1950s and early 1960s, when a great deal of money was spent on public works facilities for defense and space exploration. It was Congress's way of guaranteeing itself a role in handing out some choice projects to favored constituents.

The Legislative Veto

The **legislative veto** is a technique through which Congress grants the president the authority to act, but reserves the right to reject or override his actions if it is not satisfied with what he does. In 1932 and 1933, Congress granted the president the power to reorganize administrative agencies and departments. The president was required to submit a reorganization plan to Congress, and if it took no action within sixty days, the plan would go into effect. The law granting this power of overriding presidential action expired in 1973, but it was revived early in the Carter administration. Subsequently, the legislative veto was incorporated in a number of other statutes. In the 1983 case of *Immigration and Naturalization Service* v. *Chadha,* however, the Supreme Court held that the legislative veto was unconstitutional, primarily because it seemed to reverse the usual relationship between the president and Congress. That is, Congress was vetoing the executive branch rather than the other way around.[30] Despite this Supreme Court decision, Congress has continued to enact—and the president to sign—statutes incorporating a modified legislative veto, the "committee veto," where presidential actions must be approved by a congressional committee. Because Congress sees the legislative veto as an important source of power, and the executive branch is willing to accept statutes containing the veto so long as the statute also delegates to the executive powers it seeks, Congress and the president have essentially ignored the Supreme Court on this question.

[30]Immigration and Naturalization Services v. Chadha, 462 U.S. 919 (1983).

THE FALL AND RISE OF
CONGRESSIONAL POWER

Since Franklin D. Roosevelt expanded the power of the presidency at the time of the Depression, scholars have been proclaiming the era of presidential government and the demise of congressional power. Indeed, in 1965 one influential political scientist suggested that Congress consider abandoning its legislative efforts altogether, to focus more fully on constituency service and oversight.[31] Subsequent events, however, have shown that obituaries for congressional power were premature. Congress has been more than able to cope with presidential efforts to dominate the governmental process.

From the 1930s through the administration of Lyndon Johnson, the presidency seemed to be the dominant institution in American politics and government. Events that took place during the 1960s and 1970s, however, set the stage for a reassertion of congressional power. In this period, a number of new groups and forces emerged in American society and sought to change the focus and direction of American foreign and domestic policy. These groups, which formed "public interest" lobbies, included blacks, women, upper-middle-class professionals (dubbed "yuppies" by the media and the "new class" by conservative sociologists). On such issues as the Vietnam War, civil rights, and women's rights, as well as environmental and consumer affairs, these new groups were intensely opposed to the policies and aims of the older coalition of forces—including organized labor, heavy industry, organized agriculture, and urban political machines—that had been closely linked to the presidency since the 1930s.

To counter their foes' links with the executive branch, the new forces of the 1960s and 1970s sought to use the Congress as an institutional base. The Senate, in particular, proved to be receptive to these forces. Senators saw civil rights, antiwar, environmental, and consumer groups as potentially important sources of support for their own re-election efforts—and, perhaps, presidential bids. A number of senators became prominent spokespersons for these groups. Senate hearings on the Vietnam War, on threats to the environment, and on other issues gave the new political forces a forum in which to assert their claims.

As the Congress began to serve these forces, they in turn became supporters of congressional power, ready to defend the powers of Congress—"their branch" of government—against executive encroachments. This development greatly enhanced the potential power of Congress, and as Congress continued to serve its new constituencies, it came into sharp conflict with the presidency and those groups in American society that supported presidential programs.

During the course of this conflict, which began during the Johnson administration and continues to this day, Congress sought to reassert some of the authority it lost to the executive branch during the previous thirty years. The most dramatic illustration of this reassertion of power was, of course, the congressional investiga-

---

[31]Samuel Huntington, "Congressional Responses to the Twentieth Century," in David Truman, ed., *The Congress and America's Future* (Englewood Cliffs, NJ: Prentice-Hall, 1965), pp. 5–31.

tion that led to President Nixon's resignation from office.[32] Congress also enacted
legislation and adopted practices designed to enhance its role in government and
to diminish the power of the executive. For example, Congress adopted the War
Powers Resolution (1973), intended to limit the president's ability to make unilateral foreign and military policy decisions by giving Congress a broader formal role
in these areas. At the same time, Congress began writing laws that gave the
executive branch very little discretion in its exercise of power. For example, the
Endangered Species Act, the Campaign Finance Act (1974), and the various environmental and consumer safety acts adopted by Congress during the 1970s contain
clear and specific instructions to the executive branch and leave little room for administrators to act on their own.

Congress also sought to strengthen its budgetary powers. The budget is always a
central arena of conflict between Congress and the executive branch. Several presidents, most notably President Nixon, refused to spend money appropriated by
Congress for programs they opposed—a tactic called ***impoundment***. Congress responded with the Budget and Impoundment Control Act of 1974. This act was
designed not only to inhibit the practice of impoundment but also to expand
congressional budgetary powers more generally. The act limited the use of impoundment by requiring the president to spend any funds appropriated by Congress unless that body specifically agreed to cancel the expenditure.

The 1974 act also established two budget committees, one in the House and
one in the Senate. The function of these committees was to allow Congress to coordinate the appropriations recommendations made by the other standing committees and to assess the relationship between expenditures and revenues. Prior to
1974, appropriations had been the domain of the Appropriations Committees,
while revenue came under the supervision of the House Ways and Means and Senate Finance Committees. By coordinating these functions, Congress hoped to acquire more control over the budget and more influence over presidential budget
requests.

Finally, the 1974 act created the Congressional Budget Office (CBO) to give
Congress expertise in economic analysis and forecasts. Before 1974, the Office of
Management and Budget (OMB) in the executive branch had given the president
a virtual monopoly over "the facts" upon which economic policy decisions were
based. Under the terms of the Budget and Impoundment Control Act, Congress
established a new, two-part budgetary process. First, each budget committee was
to set target figures for taxing and spending. Second, the sum of the appropriations
enacted by all other congressional committees was to be reconciled with the initial
targets. Through this process, Congress sought to force itself to deal with national
priorities in a coordinated way rather than merely succumbing to the pleas of an
array of constituents.

As its creators had intended, this budget process gave Congress more power. Indeed, Congress, rather than the president, was the dominant budgetary actor during the Ford and Carter administrations. In the area of budgets, however, as in a
number of other areas, the Reagan administration was initially able to block the

[32]See James L. Sundquist, *The Decline and Resurgence of Congress* (Washington, DC: Brookings
Institution, 1981).

Congressional Term Limits: Remedy or Snake Oil?

Τ*he idea of limiting by law or constitutional amendment the number of terms that a member of Congress may serve is not new, but in the 1990s it gained considerable momentum. In the 1992 elections, for example, fourteen states enacted some kind of measure to limit the terms of their national representatives.*

Editorial-page writer John H. Fund argues that term limits will break the hold of political professionals and curtail the power of incumbency. Political scientist Charles R. Kesler asserts that such a move will only serve to make new members of Congress even more dependent on Washington professionals and will divert attention away from the real problems of Washington governance.

Fund

Not since Proposition 13 created a national tidal wave of tax protest has a political idea caught on with such speed. Polls show that over 70 percent of Americans back a limit on terms for elected officials . . . .

Term limits will encourage different people to run for office and pave the way for passage of other reforms—including rules to make legislative districts more competitive and reduce incumbent advantages in campaign financing . . . .

Franking privileges, huge staffs, liberal travel funds, easy access to the news media, and unfair campaign finance laws have all provided incumbents with a grossly unfair advantage . . . . The playing field must be made more level than it is now.

A limit on elected congressional and state legislative tenure would reduce the incentive for such abuses of power by eliminating congressional careerism. No longer would those political offices be held by longtime incumbents. They would be held by citizen-legislators, who would be more disposed to represent the will of the people and rein in the out-of-control bureaucracy that now substitutes for a federal government.

The idea of citizen-representatives serving a relatively short time is not new or radical. Although the writers of the Constitution did not see fit to include a term limitation, perhaps that was because the public-service norm of those days did not include careerist senators and representatives. Instead, the attitude of that time can be seen in the decision of George Washington to voluntarily serve only two terms as president.

Term limitation is a traditional and uniquely American concept. Now it must be made mandatory instead of voluntary because the spirit of voluntary service limitation has obviously been lost.[1]

Kesler

Limiting congressional terms to 12 years will do little or nothing to remedy the situation [of problems with Congress]. Any new faces that are brought to Washington as the result of such an amendment will find themselves up against the same old incentives. They will still be eligible for reelection five times. How will they ensure their continued political prosperity without seeing to constituents' administrative needs? If anything, these new congressmen will find themselves confronting bureaucrats rendered more powerful by the representatives' own ignorance of the bureaucracy; for in the administrative state, knowledge is power. It is likely, therefore, that the new congressmen will initially be at a disadvantage relative to the agencies. To counter this they will seek staff members and advisers who are veterans of the Hill, and perhaps larger and more district-oriented staffs to help ward off challengers who would try to take advantage of their inexperience. Is it wise to increase the already expansive power of bureaucrats and congressional staff for the sake of a new congressman in the district every half-generation or so?

. . . [Term limits] could deprive the country of the experience and wisdom gained by an incumbent, perhaps just when that experience is needed most. This is particularly true for senators, whose terms would be limited even though Senate races are frequently quite competitive . . . . The pursuit of a constitutional amendment to limit congressional terms would act as a colossal distraction from the serious work of politics that needs to be done.[2]

[1]John H. Find, "Term Limitation: An Idea Whose Time Has Come," Policy Analysis No. 141, Cato Institute, reprinted in Gerald Benjamin and Michael J. Malbin, eds., *Limiting Legislative Terms,* (Washington, DC: Congressional Quarterly Press, 1992), pp. 225, 235–37.

[2]Charles R. Kesler, "Bad Housekeeping: The Case against Congressional Term Limits," *Policy Review* (Summer 1990), reprinted in Benjamin and Malbin, eds., *Limiting Legislative Terms,* pp. 247–49.

reassertion of congressional power and to force Congress back on the defensive. Reagan's enormous budget deficits made it impossible for Congress to propose new spending programs, and his promise to veto any tax increases made it impossible to enact new tax programs. In essence, congressional control of the budget had become meaningless. At the same time, the Reagan administration undermined Congress's new foreign policy powers through *faits accomplis* such as the invasion of Grenada and the bombing of Libya. Not only was Congress ignored but it could not even oppose the president, because his actions turned out to be enormously popular. At the beginning of the Reagan era, the balance of power shifted back toward the executive branch.

But presidential power began to wane dramatically as Congress began to investigate the 1986 Iran-Contra affair, in which the Reagan administration had sold weapons to Iran in exchange for the release of several American hostages held in Lebanon. The profits from this sale were then illegally funneled to the Nicaraguan Contra rebels whom the administration supported in their campaign against the leftist Sandinista government in Nicaragua. Over the next several years, Lawrence

E. Walsh, the independent counsel appointed by the attorney general to investigate the administration's dealings with Iran, was able to secure indictments against a number of important Reagan administration officials, charging them with withholding information from Congress. However, all were pardoned by President George Bush in December 1992, just before he left office.

Undaunted, Walsh vowed that he would focus his investigation on charges that while serving as Reagan's vice-president, Bush had participated in discussions of the arms sales to Iran and then lied to Congress about his involvement. Thus, six years later, the Iran-Contra investigation launched by Congress continued to remind officials in the executive branch that the days of their unquestioned supremacy in the area of foreign policy were long past.

On the domestic front, when George Bush entered the White House in 1989, he inherited a massive deficit and a weakening economy, and Congress appeared to be in the driver's seat. In the fall of 1990, Bush and the congressional Democratic leadership engaged in a pitched battle over the 1991 federal budget. At the outset, President Bush insisted that deficit reduction be accomplished entirely through spending cuts. This was consistent with his 1988 campaign pledge of "no new taxes." Congressional leaders insisted on tax increases that would permit them to maintain or increase spending levels for domestic programs supported by the Democratic party. When negotiations failed to produce a budget by October 1 (the end of the fiscal year), President Bush refused to sign a continuing resolution that would have allowed federal agencies to maintain 1990 spending levels into the next fiscal year. For one weekend the federal government was shut down. Subsequently, Congress enacted and the president signed a continuing resolution that permitted the government to operate until a new budget was adopted.

In the end, Bush was forced to renege on his campaign pledge—a pledge that had been a cornerstone of the Republican electoral strategy. The budget adopted for 1991 included tax increases that especially affected wealthier taxpayers, which permitted congressional Democrats to present themselves as friends of the common people and to depict the Republicans as protectors of millionaires. The budget compromise represented virtually a total victory for Congress and a major defeat for the president.

Following on the heels of its budget victory, Congress sought to challenge President Bush's Persian Gulf policies. Most members of Congress had initially expressed support for the president's decision to dispatch massive American forces to the Persian Gulf following Iraq's invasion of Kuwait in August 1990. By the end of the year, however, congressional leaders sought to constrain the president's ability to use these forces in combat, urging him instead to rely on diplomacy and economic sanctions to compel Iraq to withdraw from Kuwait. Congressional criticism, especially televised Senate hearings in December 1990, helped erode Bush's popular standing, almost undermining the president's power to act in the crisis.

In January 1991, however, President Bush sought and received congressional approval for the use of military force against Iraq if it failed to honor the United Nations deadline of January 15 for an Iraqi withdrawal from Kuwait. This approval came by a very narrow margin in the Senate and a somewhat more comfortable margin in the House, as enough moderate and conservative Democrats deserted their party's leadership to pass resolutions authorizing the use of force.

The complete success of the American military effort led to a surge of public support for President Bush. In the immediate aftermath of the war the president's popularity topped the 90 percent mark. Most members of Congress were compelled to declare their support for the president's war policies. Those who had opposed Bush before the war were left to explain their actions to suddenly hawkish constituents.

By the end of April, however, congressional Democrats began to turn public attention away from the Persian Gulf and back to domestic issues, such as health care and civil rights. Congress rejected the president's budgetary proposals and demanded higher levels of spending for domestic social programs. As the 102nd Congress resumed its work in the spring of 1991, Congress and the president continued to be locked in a struggle over control of the government. Congress had succeeded in stalemating presidential power without, however, developing a set of responses of its own to the nation's problems. Although Congress defeated President Bush on the 1991 budget, it really did nothing to solve the nation's deficit problem. The 1991 budget deficit grew to about $250 billion, and the 1992 deficit exceeded $300 billion.

In the last year of the Bush administration, Republicans attacked Congress's Democratic leadership on several fronts. First, led by the minority whip, Newt Gingrich, House Republicans spearheaded charges that the Democratic leadership had permitted abuses at the House bank and House post office. As the scandals unfolded, a number of senior members of Congress were embarrassed when it was revealed that they had frequently written bad checks at the House bank. Though the revelations hurt Republicans as well as Democrats, the Democrats stood to lose more because they controlled the House. Gingrich and his allies, in effect, calculated that a bomb thrown into the primarily Democratic House would inevitably do more damage to the Democrats than to the GOP. For similar reasons, Republicans supported investigations into the management of the House post office, particularly charges that some representatives had used the post office to launder campaign contributions. The Republicans' chief target was Daniel Rostenkowski (D-Ill.), the powerful chair of the House Ways and Means committee.

At the same time, Republicans gave their enthusiastic support to a national movement to enact congressional term-limit legislation. Here again Republicans calculated that the Democrats, with their bevy of powerful, entrenched incumbents and a seemingly perpetual control of Congress, had much more to lose than the GOP from legislation that would limit congressional terms. Fourteen states have enacted some form of term-limit legislation. It is, however, by no means clear that such state legislation is binding since the terms of members of Congress are set by the U.S. Constitution.

As will be discussed in Chapter 9, Republicans also worked to create "minority districts," following the 1990 census. These were districts whose heavy concentration of minority voters virtually ensured the election of African American or Hispanic American representatives. Though these representatives were almost certain to be Democrats, Republicans were speculating that the concentration of minority voters into fewer districts would help the GOP overall. This strategy did result in the ouster of several powerful Democrats, including Steven Solarz of New York.

After Bill Clinton's victory in 1992, congressional Democrats moved both to attack their Republican foes and to make certain that they were not overshadowed by an activist White House. To accomplish both these ends, Democratic leaders sought to increase their power over the congressional lawmaking process. In particular, as we saw, the House leadership sought to enhance its power by streamlining the House committee structure and winning the allegiance of the large class of freshmen by giving them desirable committee assignments. Providing these freshmen, which included minorities and women, with significant posts was also seen as a way of maintaining the power of Congress by linking it more closely to the groups and forces in society that these members represented. The relationship between power and representation was also understood by Clinton, who emphasized social diversity in the creation of his cabinet.[33] Congress could certainly not afford to be less representative in its leadership structure than the White House if it was to maintain its power vis-à-vis the executive branch. House Democrats also opted to give limited voting rights to the delegates from the District of Columbia and the U.S. territories—all Democrats who previously had only served as observers. Republicans managed to beat off an effort by the House leadership to reduce their access to the floor.

Congressional Democrats hoped that with a Democrat in the White House, they would finally be in a position to enact programs and policies that would strengthen the Congress, their party, and the nation as a whole. Of course, congressional leaders were not prepared to permit an activist president—even a fellow Democrat—to run roughshod over them. The House and Senate leaders greeted Bill Clinton's request for the line-item veto, which would permit the president to veto portions of bills rather than accept or reject the entire bill, with the same lack of enthusiasm they had shown when Bush and Reagan made the same request.

Nevertheless, at the start of the Clinton administration, Congress seemed prepared to cooperate with the White House. For his part, Clinton signaled that he wanted to work closely with members of Congress by appointing Senator Lloyd Bentsen of Texas as treasury secretary, Representative Mike Espy of Mississippi as agriculture secretary, Representative Leon Panetta of California as director of the Office of Management and Budget, and Representative Les Aspin of Wisconsin as defense secretary. These appointments represented Clinton's strongest possible acknowledgment that support on Capitol Hill would be critical to the success of his administration.

Thus, at the beginning of a new Congress and a new presidency, members of both institutions seemed ready for a truce in their long struggle. Given the governmental framework created by the nation's founders, however, we should not expect this truce to last very long.

[33]David Broder, "Diversity Was Paramount in Building the Cabinet," *Washington Post,* 25 December 1992, p. 1.

CONGRESS: FREEDOM AND POWER

The struggle between Congress and the White House is one more illustration of the dilemma that lies at the heart of the American system of government. The framers of the Constitution checked and balanced a powerful Congress with a powerful executive. This was seen as a way of limiting the potential for abuse of governmental power and of protecting freedom. No doubt, it has this effect. Certainly, a vigilant Congress was able to curb presidential abuse of power during the Nixon era. Similarly, the executive branch under the leadership of President Eisenhower played a role in curbing congressional witch hunts ostensibly aimed at uncovering communist agents in the federal government, conducted by Senator Joseph McCarthy (R–Wis.) during the 1950s.

At the same time, however, the constant struggle between Congress and the president can hinder stable and effective governance. Over the past quarter century, in particular, Republican presidents and Democratic Congresses often seemed to be more interested in undermining one another than in promoting the larger public interest. On issues of social policy, economic policy, and foreign policy, Congress and the president have been at each other's throats while the nation suffered. As noted above, this struggle between the White House and Capitol Hill is one reason that the United States presently faces a deficit crisis of unprecedented magnitude. We shall return to this point in Chapter 14.

Thus, we face a fundamental dilemma. A political arrangement designed to preserve freedom can undermine the government's power. Indeed, it can undermine the government's very capacity to govern. Must we always choose between freedom and power? Can we not have both? Let us turn now to the second branch of American government, the presidency, to view this dilemma from a somewhat different angle.

SUMMARY

The U.S. Congress is one of the few national representative assemblies that actually governs. Members of Congress take their representative function seriously. They devote a significant portion of their time to constituent contact and service. Representation and power go hand in hand in congressional history.

The legislative process must provide the order necessary for legislation to take place amid competing interests. It is dependent on a hierarchical organizational structure within Congress. Six basic dimensions of Congress affect the legislative process: (1) the parties, (2) the committees, (3) the staff, (4) the caucuses, (5) the rules, and (6) the presidency.

Since the Constitution provides only for a presiding officer in each house, some method had to be devised for conducting business. Parties quickly assumed the responsibility for this. In the House, the majority party elects a leader every two years. This individual becomes Speaker. In addition, a majority leader and a minority leader (from the minority party) and party whips are elected. Each party has a committee whose job it is to make committee assignments. Party structure in the Senate is similar, except that the vice-president of the United States is the Senate president.

While party voting regularity remains strong, party discipline has declined. Still, parties do have several means of maintaining discipline: (1) Favorable committee assignments create obligations. (2) Floor time in the debate on one bill can be allocated in exchange for a specific vote on another. (3) The whip system allows party leaders to assess support for a bill and convey their wishes to members. (4) Party leaders can help members create large logrolling coalitions. (5) The president, by identifying pieces of legislation as his own, can muster support along party lines. In most cases, party leaders accept constituency obligations as a valid reason for voting against the party position.

The committee system surpasses the party system in its importance in Congress. In the early nineteenth century, standing committees became a fundamental aspect of Congress. They have, for the most part, evolved to correspond to executive branch departments or programs and thus reflect and maintain the separation of powers.

The Senate has a tradition of unlimited debate, on which the various cloture rules it has passed have had little effect. Filibusters still occur. The rules of the House restrict talk and support committees; deliberation is recognized as committee business. The House Rules Committee has the power to control debate and floor amendments. The rules prescribe the formal procedure through which bills become law. Generally, the parties control scheduling and agenda, but the committees determine action on the floor. Committees, seniority, and rules all limit the ability of members to represent their constituents. Yet, these factors enable Congress to maintain its role as a major participant in government.

The power of the post–New Deal presidency does not necessarily signify the decline of Congress and representative government. During the 1970s Congress again became the "first branch" of government. During the early years of the Reagan administration, some of the congressional gains of the previous decade were diminished, but in the last two years of Reagan's second term, and in President Bush's term, Congress reasserted its role. At the start of the Clinton era, congressional leaders promised to cooperate with the White House rather than confront it.

FOR FURTHER READING

Arnold, R. Douglas. *The Logic of Congressional Action.* New Haven, CT: Yale University Press, 1990.

Baker, Ross K. *House and Senate.* New York: W. W. Norton, 1989.

Burnham, James. *Congress and the American Tradition.* Chicago: Henry Regnery, 1965.

Clem, Alan L. *Congress: Powers, Processes and Politics.* Pacific Grove, CA: Brooks/Cole, 1989.

Congressional Quarterly, Inc. *Origins and Development of Congress.* Washington, DC: Congressional Quarterly Press, 1982.

Congressional Quarterly, Inc. *Powers of Congress.* Washington, DC: Congressional Quarterly Press, 1976.

Davidson, Roger, ed. *The Postreform Congress.* New York: St. Martin's Press, 1991.

Dodd, Lawrence, and Bruce J. Oppenheimer, eds. *Congress Reconsidered.* Washington, DC: Congressional Quarterly Press, 1988.

Fenno, Richard F. *Congressmen in Committees.* Boston: Little, Brown, 1973.

Fenno, Richard F. *Homestyle: House Members in Their Districts.* Boston: Little, Brown, 1978.

Fiorina, Morris. *Congress: Keystone of the Washington Establishment.* New Haven, CT: Yale University Press, 1977.

Fisher, Louis. *The Politics of Shared Power: Congress and the Executive.* Washington, DC: Congressional Quarterly Press, 1981.

Foreman, Christopher. *Signals from the Hill: Congressional Oversight and the Challenge of Social Regulation.* New Haven, CT: Yale University Press, 1988.

Fowler, Linda, and Robert McClure. *Political Ambition: Who Decides to Run for Congress?* New Haven, CT: Yale University Press, 1989.

Jacobson, Gary. *The Politics of Congressional Elections.* Boston: Little, Brown, 1983.

Leloup, Lance T. *Budgetary Politics.* Brunswick, Ohio: King's Court, 1986.

Light, Paul. *Forging Legislation.* New York: W. W. Norton, 1991.

Malbin, Michael. *Unelected Representatives: Congressional Staff and the Future of Representative Government.* New York: Basic Books, 1970.

Mayhew, David R. *Congress: The Electoral Connection.* New Haven, CT: Yale University Press, 1974.

Oleszek, Walter J. *Congressional Procedures and the Policy Process.* Washington, DC: Congressional Quarterly Press, 1983.

Ornstein, Norman, and Shirley Elder. *Interest Groups, Lobbying and Policymaking.* Washington, DC: Congressional Quarterly Press, 1978.

Ornstein, Norman, et al. *Vital Statistics on Congress.* Washington, DC: Congressional Quarterly Press, 1987.

Peabody, Robert L. *Leadership in Congress.* Boston: Little, Brown, 1976.

Price, David. *Who Makes the Laws?: Creativity and Power in Senate Committees.* Cambridge, MA: Schenkman, 1972.

Rieselbach, Leroy. *Congressional Reform.* Washington, DC: Congressional Quarterly Press, 1986.

Ripley, Randall. *Congress: Process and Policy.* New York: W. W. Norton, 1988.

Schick, Allen, ed. *Making Economic Policy in Congress.* Washington, DC: American Enterprise Institute, 1983.

Sinclair, Barbara. *Majority Leadership in the U.S. House.* Baltimore: Johns Hopkins University Press, 1983.

Sinclair, Barbara. *The Transformation of the U.S. Senate.* Baltimore: Johns Hopkins University Press, 1989.

Smith, Steven S., and Christopher Deering. *Committees in Congress.* Washington, DC: Congressional Quarterly Press, 1984.

Strahan, Randall. *New Ways and Means: Reform and Change in a Congressional Committee.* Chapel Hill, NC: University of North Carolina Press, 1990.

Sundquist, James L. *The Decline and Resurgence of Congress.* Washington, DC: Brookings Institution, 1981.

6

The President: From Chief Clerk to Chief Executive

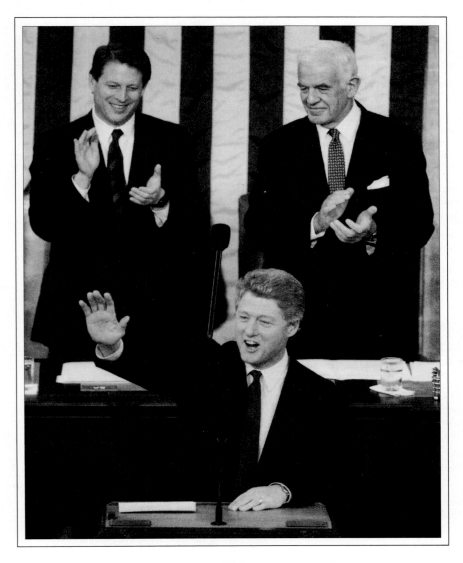

TIME LINE ON THE PRESIDENCY

EVENTS		INSTITUTIONAL DEVELOPMENTS
George Washington elected first president (1789)		President establishes powers in relation to Congress (1789)
Thomas Jefferson elected president (1800)	**1800**	Orderly transfer of power from Federalists to Jeffersonian Republicans (1801)
"Midnight judicial appointments" by John Adams before he leaves office (1801)		*Marbury* v. *Madison* holds that Congress and the president are subject to judicial review (1803)
Republican caucus nominates James Madison, who is elected president (1808)		Congress dominates presidential nominations through "King Caucus" (1804–1831)
Andrew Jackson elected president (1828)		Strengthening of presidency; nominating conventions intro- duced; broaden president's base of support (1830s)
Period of weak presidents (Martin Van Buren, William Harrison, James Polk, Zachary Taylor, Franklin Pierce, James Buchanan) (1837–1860)		
Abraham Lincoln elected president (1860)	**1860**	"Constitutional dictatorship" during Civil War and after (1861–1865)
Impeachment of President Andrew Johnson (1868)		Congress takes back initiative for action (1868–1933)
Industrialization, big railroads, big corporations (1860s–1890s)		*In re Neagle*—Court holds to expansive inference from Consti- tution on rights, duties, and obligations of president (1890)
World War I (1914–1918)		
Congress fails to approve Wilson's League of Nations (1919–1920)	**1920**	Budget and Accounting Act; Congress provides for an executive budget (1921)
FDR proposes New Deal programs to achieve economic recovery from the Depression (1933)		Congress adopts first New Deal programs: epoch of presidential government (1930s)
U.S. enters World War II (1941–1945)		*U.S.* v. *Pink*—Court confirms legality of executive agreements in foreign relations (1942)
Korean War without declaration (1950–1953)	**1950**	*Steel Seizure* case holds that president's power must be author- ized by statute and is not inherent in the presidency (1952)

TIME LINE ON THE PRESIDENCY

EVENTS		INSTITUTIONAL DEVELOPMENTS
Gulf of Tonkin Resolution (1964); U.S. troop buildup begins in Vietnam (1965)		Great Society program enacted; president sends troops to Vietnam without consulting Congress (1965)
Watergate affair (1972); Watergate cover-up revealed (1973–1974)	**1970**	Congressional resurgence begins—War Powers Act (1973); Budget and Impoundment Act (1974)
Nixon becomes first president to resign; Gerald Ford succeeds after Nixon's resignation (1974)		
Reagan's election begins new Republican era of "supply side" economics, deregulation, and military build-up (1980–1988)		*INS* v. *Chadha*—Court holds legislative veto to be unconstitutional (1983)
Iran-Contra affair (1986–1987)		Gramm-Rudman Act seeks to contain deficit spending (1985)
Bush elected on "no new taxes" pledge (1988)		End of Cold War puts new emphasis on foreign policy (1989)
Clinton's election ends "divided government" (1993)	**1990**	Military actions in Iraq and Somalia may define post–Cold War foreign policy (1992)
		Clinton gains adoption of first deficit-reduction budget (1993)

On the front cover of its January 7, 1991 issue, *Time* magazine gave the world something new. Rather than its usual Man of the Year, *Time* presented its "Men of the Year," a double exposure of the same person, George Bush. As *Time* explained it, "One was a foreign policy profile that was a study in resoluteness and mastery, the other a domestic visage just as strongly marked by wavering and confusion."[1] The first impressions of President Clinton in 1993 seemed to be almost the reverse, with mastery in the domestic field and timidity in the foreign policy field. Yet, there was never any doubt that foreign policy would be Clinton's alone to succeed or fail at while domestic policy was a joint endeavor with Congress.

[1]George J. Church, "A Tale of Two Bush's," *Time*, 7 January 1991, p. 20.

President Clinton demonstrated mastery in getting his $1.52 trillion budget package through Congress quickly and without a hitch. But this was about all the honeymoon he was able to get. The details of actual budgetary authorization would come later, with each item requiring debates and votes in the House and the Senate, and with identical results before the president would have a budget-reduction bill to sign into law. Meanwhile, Republican opposition in Congress stood at 100 percent, and Democratic support, though strong, weakened at the margins as Clinton's poll ratings dropped. Compromise was in the air. Although Clinton looked to FDR as his role model, he was looking more like JFK, whose bold vision of a New Frontier moved slowly even after two years in office.

President Clinton's restraint toward the violent civil war in Bosnia was almost certainly in accord with prevailing American public opinion in the spring of 1993. But, as we shall see later in the chapter, only actions influence public opinion, not inactions. The bombing of Bagdad in retaliation for the Iraqi attempt to assassinate former President Bush during his visit to Kuwait boosted President Clinton's poll ratings momentarily, as did his first summit meeting in Tokyo with leaders of the other industrialized nations in July. But these actions were not important enough to outweigh the depressing effects of the presidential actions necessary to push Clinton's domestic proposals through Congress to reduce the deficit and strengthen the economy. Thus, although the power to succeed or fail in foreign policy is recognized as a presidential power, the consequences of presidential foreign policy actions heavily influence presidential power in domestic politics. In this sense, "all politics in America is local politics," as one professional politician put it. But not all politics is the same politics.

All of this points to the dual nature of the presidency. And that duality has been the source of consternation and dispute since the founding itself, kept alive by an army of scholars puzzling out the intent of the framers. The framers, wanting "energy in the Executive," provided for a single-headed office with an electoral base independent of Congress. But by giving the presidency no explicit powers independent of Congress, each president would have to provide that energy by asserting powers beyond the Constitution itself and inherent in the presidency as head of state. Or, as Theodore Roosevelt so eloquently expressed it: "My belief was that it was not only [the president's] right but his duty to do anything that the needs of the nation demanded unless such action was forbidden by the Constitution or by the law."[2] John F. Kennedy echoed Roosevelt decades later:

> The Constitution is a very wise document. It permits the president to assume just about as much power as he is capable of handling. . . . I believe that the president should use whatever power is necessary to do the job unless it is expressly forbidden by the Constitution.[3]

A tug of war between formal constitutional provisions for a president who is little more than chief clerk and a theory of necessity favoring a real chief executive

[2] Theodore Roosevelt, *An Autobiography* (New York: Charles Scribner's Sons, 1931), p. 388.

[3] Quoted in James MacGregor Burns, *John Kennedy—A Political Profile* (New York: Harcourt, Brace, 1959), p. 275. It is interesting that Kennedy made these remarks nearly two years prior to his election to the presidency.

has persisted for over two centuries. President Jefferson's acquisition of the Louisiana Territory in virtual defiance of the Constitution seemed to establish the chief executive presidency; yet, he was followed by three chief clerks, James Madison, James Monroe, and John Quincy Adams. Presidents Andrew Jackson and Abraham Lincoln believed in and acted on the theory of the strong president with power transcending the formal Constitution, but neither of them institutionalized the role, and both were followed by a series of chief clerks. Theodore Roosevelt and Woodrow Wilson were also considered genuine chief executives. But it was not until Franklin Roosevelt that the tug of war seems to have been won for the chief executive presidency, because after FDR, as we shall see, every president has been strong whether he was committed to the strong presidency or not. Harry Truman, following the great FDR and having almost no political resources, was nevertheless a dominating presence, especially after election to a full term in 1948. Eisenhower opposed the strong presidency, but Congress literally insisted he act the part. Although Gerald Ford was in the weakest position of all presidents—having been appointed to the job as a result of the worst scandal in the history of the office—he stood above all but two or three nineteenth-century presidents in institutional strength. And although George Bush spent eight years in the vice-presidency as "yes man" to President Reagan, he became a strong chief executive after winning the 1988 election, and he continued to be a strong president even through his seventy-nine days as a "lame duck" following his defeat on November 3, 1992. During that time he committed over 25,000 U.S. troops to Somalia and secured U.N. sponsorship, in addition to the contributions of troops and supplies from thirty-four other countries.

Thus, a strong executive, a genuine chief executive, has been institutionalized in the twentieth century. But it continues to operate in a schizoid environment: as the power of the presidency has increased, popular expectations of presidential performance have increased at an even faster rate, requiring more leadership than was ever exercised by any but the greatest presidents in the past. The growth of the presidency has created a "dilemma of power":[4] How can we provide enough presidential power without providing too much? This dilemma of power is part of our past and will no doubt continue to be part of our future.

Our focus in this chapter will be on the development of the institutional character of the presidency, the power of the presidency, and the relationship between the two. The chapter is divided into three sections. First, we shall review the constitutional origins of the presidency. In particular, this will involve an examination of the constitutional basis for the president's foreign and domestic roles. Second, we shall review the history of the American presidency to see how the office has evolved from its original status under the Constitution. We will look particularly at the ways in which Congress has augmented the president's constitutional powers by deliberately delegating to the presidency, many of its own responsibilities. Finally, we shall assess both the formal and informal means by which presidents seek to enhance their own ability to govern.

---

[4]The idea of a "dilemma of power" comes from Barrington Moore, *Soviet Politics: The Dilemma of Power* (Cambridge, MA: Harvard University Press, 1951).

THE CONSTITUTIONAL BASIS OF
THE PRESIDENCY

Article II of the Constitution, which establishes the presidency, does not solve the dilemma of power. Although Article II has been called "the most loosely drawn chapter of the Constitution,"[5] the framers were neither indecisive nor confused. They held profoundly conflicting views of the executive branch, and Article II was probably the best compromise they could make. The formulation the framers agreed upon is magnificent in its ambiguity: "The executive power shall be vested in a President of the United States of America" (Article II, Section 1, first sentence). The meaning of "executive power," however, is not defined except indirectly in the very last sentence of Section 3, which provides that the president "shall take Care that the Laws be faithfully executed."[6]

One very important conclusion can be drawn from these two provisions. The office of the president was to be an office of ***delegated powers.*** Since, as we have already seen, all of the powers of the national government are defined as powers of Congress and incorporated into Article I, Section 8, then the "executive power" of Article II, Section 3, must be understood to be defined as the power to execute faithfully the laws *as they are adopted* by Congress. This does not doom the presidency to weakness. Presumably, Congress can pass laws delegating almost any of its powers to the president. But presidents are not free to discover sources of executive power completely independent of the laws as passed by Congress. In the 1890 case of *In re Neagle,* the Supreme Court did hold that the president could be bold and expansive in the inferences he drew from the Constitution as to "the rights, duties and obligations" of the presidency; but the powers of the president would have to come from that Constitution and laws, not from some independent or absolute idea of executive power.[7]

Immediately following the first sentence of Section 1, Article II defines the manner in which the president is to be chosen. This is a very odd sequence, but it does say something about the struggle the delegates were having over how to provide great power of action or energy to the executive and at the same time to balance that power with limitations. The struggle was between those delegates who wanted the president to be selected by, and thus responsible to, Congress and those delegates who preferred that the president be elected directly by the people. Direct

---

[5]E. S. Corwin, *The President: Office and Powers,* 3d rev. ed. (New York: New York University Press, 1957), p. 2.

[6]Article II, Section 3. There is a Section 4, but all it does is to define impeachment.

[7]In re Neagle, 135 U.S. 1 (1890). Neagle, a deputy U.S. marshall, had been authorized by the president to protect a Supreme Court justice whose life had been threatened by an angry litigant. When the litigant attempted to carry out his threat, Neagle shot and killed him. Neagle was then arrested by the local authorities and tried for murder. His defense was that his act was "done in pursuance of a law of the United States." Although the law was not an act of Congress, the Supreme Court declared that it was an executive order of the president, and the protection of a federal judge was a reasonable extension of the president's power to "take care that the laws be faithfully executed." See Chapter 8 for a more detailed account of the bizarre facts underlying *In re Neagle.*

popular elections would create a more independent and more powerful presidency.

With the adoption of a scheme of indirect election through an electoral college in which the electors would be selected by the state legislatures (and close elections would be resolved in the House of Representatives), the framers hoped to achieve a "republican" solution: a strong president responsible to state and national legislators rather than directly to the electorate.

The heart of presidential power as defined by the Constitution, however, is found in Sections 2 and 3, where the several clauses define the presidency in two dimensions: the president as head of state and the president as head of government. Although these will be given separate treatment, the presidency can be understood only by the summation of the two.

The President as Head of State: Some Imperial Qualities

The constitutional position of the president as head of state is defined by three constitutional provisions, which are the source of some of the most important powers on which presidents can draw. The areas can be classified as:

1. *Military.* Article II, Section 2, provides for the power as "Commander in Chief of the Army and Navy of the United States, and of the Militia of the several States, when called in to the actual Service of the United States."
2. *Judicial.* Article II, Section 2, also provides the power to "grant reprieves and pardons for Offenses against the United States, except in Cases of impeachment."
3. *Diplomatic.* Article II, Section 3, provides the power to "receive Ambassadors and other public ministers."

Military　First, the position of commander in chief makes the president the highest military authority in the United States, giving him control of the entire military establishment. No American president, however, would dare put on a military uniform for a state function—not even a former general like Eisenhower—even though the president is the highest military officer in war and in peace. The president is also the head of the secret intelligence hierarchy, which includes not only the Central Intelligence Agency (CIA) but also the National Security Council (NSC), the National Security Agency, the Federal Bureau of Investigation (FBI), and a host of less well-known but very powerful international and domestic security agencies. But of course, care must be taken not to conclude too much from this—as some presidents have done. Although Article II, Section 1, does provide that all the executive power is vested in the president, and Section 2 does provide that the president shall be commander in chief of all armed forces, including state militias, these impressive provisions must be read in the context of Article I, wherein seven of the eighteen clauses of Section 8 provide particular military and foreign policy powers to Congress, including the power to declare wars that presidents are responsible for. Presidents have tried to evade this at their peril. In full awareness of the woe visited upon President Johnson for evading and misleading Congress at the outset of the Vietnam War, President Bush sought congressional authorization for the Gulf War in January 1991.

Richard Nixon
The Imperial President

Richard Nixon (1913–1994)

For both friend and foe, Richard Milhous Nixon was a dominant political figure for more than a quarter of a century. And his presidency was pivotal for the institution and the country.

Born in California in 1913, Nixon graduated from Whittier College and Duke University Law School. After military service in World War II, he ran for and was elected to the House of Representatives in 1946 as a Republican. In four short years, he was elected to the Senate. Two years later, he was chosen by Dwight Eisenhower to run for vice-president.

Nixon's role as vice-president was relatively active, and in 1960 Nixon became the Republican party's presidential nominee. In the election that followed, Nixon lost narrowly to John F. Kennedy. Two years later, Nixon attempted a comeback by running for California governor, but he was defeated by Pat Brown in an election marred by charges of campaign impropriety. Nixon's resentment surfaced when he said to the press after his defeat on election night that they "wouldn't have Dick Nixon to kick around any more." Nonetheless, Nixon did again run for the presidency, capturing the office in a close race in 1968. This time, however, Nixon's public image was more carefully controlled. Yet, it was an incomplete victory, as Nixon became the first president since Zachary Taylor (1848) not to carry at least one house of Congress with him.

As president, Nixon scored some important achievements, including improved relations with the Soviet Union and China, and a slow winding down of the Vietnam War (although Vietnam continued to divide the country). In 1972, Nixon won re-election by a landslide, yet again he failed to carry either house of Congress.

Despite his electoral victories, the Nixon administration became ever more concerned with "enemies"—political opponents who became the targets of Nixon's ire. Political opponents found themselves being audited by the IRS, wiretapped, or subjected to other investigation. Lists of enemies were drawn up, including journalists, politicians, entertainers, and academics. This mentality spread to the 1972 campaign, culminating in the White House-inspired break-in of the Democratic National Committee Headquarters in June 1972. This plot, and its subsequent cover-up, led to the unraveling of the Nixon administration, the formulation of impeachment charges, and the first resignation of a president from office, in August 1974.

To students of the presidency, the Nixon years brought home the simple, yet unappreciated fact that an ever-stronger presidency opened the door to an ever-greater potential for abuse of power.

Source: Larry Berman, *The New American Presidency* (Boston: Little, Brown, 1987).

Judicial   The presidential power to grant reprieves, pardons, and amnesties involves the power of life and death over all individuals who may be a threat to the security of the United States. Presidents may use this power on behalf of a particular individual, as did Gerald Ford when he pardoned Richard Nixon in 1974 "for all offenses against the United States which he . . . has committed or may have committed." Or they may use it on a large scale, as did President Andrew Johnson in 1868, when he gave full amnesty to all southerners who had participated in the "Late Rebellion," and President Carter in 1977, when he declared an amnesty for all the draft evaders of the Vietnam War. George Bush used this power before relinquishing office when he pardoned former secretary of defense Caspar Weinberger and five other participants in the Iran-Contra affair. Although not required by the Constitution to give reasons, President Bush published an elaborate statement on Christmas Day providing among other reasons, that "whether they were right or wrong," they had acted out of patriotism, they did not profit from their conduct, they each had already paid a heavy price by the revelations and accusations, and they were victims of what President Bush called "the criminalization of policy differences [which] should be addressed in . . . the voting booth, not the courtroom."[8] This power of life and death over others helped elevate the president to the level of earlier conquerors and kings by establishing him as the person before whom supplicants might come to make their pleas for mercy.

Diplomatic   When President Washington received Edmond Genêt ("Citizen Genêt") as the formal emissary of the revolutionary government of France in 1793 and had his cabinet officers and Congress back his decision, he established a greatly expanded interpretation of the power to "receive Ambassadors and other public ministers," extending it to the power to "recognize" other countries. That power gives the president the almost unconditional authority to review the claims of any new ruling groups to determine if they indeed control the territory and population of their country, so that they can commit it to treaties and other agreements. Critics questioned the wisdom of President Franklin Roosevelt's exchange of ambassadors with the Soviet Union fifteen years after the Russian Revolution in 1917. They also questioned the wisdom of President Nixon's recognition of the People's Republic of China and of President Carter's recognition of the Sandinista government in Nicaragua. But they did not question the president's authority to make such decisions. Because the breakup of the Soviet bloc countries was generally perceived as a positive event, no one criticized President Bush for his quick recognition of the several former Soviet and Yugoslav republics as soon as they declared themselves independent states. And few would not approve of President Clinton recognizing the two new republics that came into being on January 1, 1993, when Czechoslovakia was officially split into the Czech Republic and Slovakia.

---

[8]*New York Times,* 25 December 1992, p. A22. For a briefer view of the factors that produced the Iran-Contra scandal and the allegations and indictments that produced the presidential pardon, see Joel Brinkley, "Birth of a Scandal and Mysteries of Its Parentage," *New York Times,* 25 December 1992, p. A23. For a comparison of the Bush decision to other pardons, see R.W. Apple, "The President as Pardoner: A Calculated Gamble," *New York Times,* 25 December 1992, p. A23.

Have presidents used these three constitutional powers—military, judicial, and diplomatic—to make the presidency too powerful, indeed "imperial?"[9] Debate over the answer to this question has produced an unusual lineup, with presidents and the Supreme Court on one side and Congress on the other. The Supreme Court supported the expansive view of the presidency in three historically significant cases. The first was *In re Neagle,* discussed above. The second was the 1936 *Curtiss-Wright* case in which the Court held that Congress may delegate a degree of discretion to the president in foreign affairs that might violate the separation of powers if it were in a domestic arena.[10] In the third case, *U.S. v. Pink,* the Supreme Court upheld the president's power to use executive agreements to conduct foreign policy.[11] An **executive agreement** is exactly like a treaty because it is a contract between two countries; but an executive agreement does not require a two-thirds vote of approval by the Senate. Ordinarily, executive agreements are used to carry out commitments already made in treaties, or to arrange for matters well below the level of policy. But when presidents have found it expedient to use an executive agreement in place of a treaty, the Court has gone along. This verges on an imperial power.

Many recent presidents have even gone beyond formal executive agreements to engage in what amounts to unilateral action. They may seek formal congressional authorization, as in 1965 when President Lyndon Johnson convinced Congress to adopt the Gulf of Tonkin Resolution authorizing him to expand the American military presence in Vietnam. Johnson interpreted the resolution as a delegation of discretion to use any and all national resources according to his own judgment. Or they may not even bother with the authorization but merely assume it, as President Nixon did when he claimed to need no congressional authorization at all to continue or to expand the Vietnam War. In keeping with this claim, Nixon's top legal adviser, William Rehnquist, now chief justice of the Supreme Court, testified before Congress that the president's unilateral invasion of Cambodia was no more than a "valid exercise of his constitutional authority as commander in chief to secure the safety of American forces."[12] Mr. Rehnquist has been called a "strict constructionist"—someone who believes that Congress and the president ought to be held to a narrow interpretation of constitutional provisions, and who feels that any expansive interpretation of the Constitution should be viewed with suspicion. Yet,

[9]Arthur Schlesinger, Jr., *The Imperial Presidency* (Boston: Houghton Mifflin, 1973).

[10]U.S. v. Curtiss-Wright Corp., 299 U.S. 304 (1936). In 1934, Congress passed a joint resolution authorizing the president to prohibit the sale of military supplies to Bolivia and Paraguay, who were at war, if the president determined that the prohibition would contribute to peace between the two countries. When prosecuted for violating the embargo order by President Roosevelt, the defendants argued that Congress could not constitutionally delegate such broad discretion to the president. The Supreme Court disagreed. Previously, however, the Court had rejected the National Industrial Recovery Act precisely because Congress had delegated too much discretion to the president in a domestic policy, see Schechter Poultry Corp. v. U.S., 495 (1936).

[11]In United States v. Pink, 315 U.S. 203 (1942), the Supreme Court confirmed that an executive agreement is the legal equivalent of a treaty, despite the absence of Senate approval. This case approved the executive agreement that was used to establish diplomatic relations with the Soviet Union in 1933. An executive agreement, not a treaty, was used in 1940 to exchange "fifty over-age destroyers" for ninety-nine-year leases on some important military bases.

[12]Senate Foreign Relations Committee, 92nd Congress, 1st Session, *War Powers Legislation: Hearings* (Washington, DC: Government Printing Office, 1971), pp. 827–28.

on a profoundly important issue of presidential power in foreign affairs, Mr. Rehnquist favored a bold rather than a strict interpretation.

These presidential claims and actions led to a congressional reaction. In 1973, Congress passed the War Powers Resolution over President Nixon's veto. This resolution asserted that the president could send American troops into action abroad only in the event of a declaration of war or other statutory authorization by Congress, or if American troops were attacked or directly endangered. This was an obvious effort to revive the principle that the presidency is an office of *delegated* powers—that is, powers granted by Congress—and that there is no blanket prerogative. But this resolution has not prevented presidents from using force when they deemed it necessary. In May 1975, without consulting with Congress, President Ford sent a number of American troops into Cambodia to rescue the crew of the *Mayaguez,* a U.S. freighter that had been captured by Cambodian forces in the Gulf of Thailand. In 1980, President Carter sent troops to Iran to try to rescue the American hostages there. And President Reagan took at least four military actions that could be seen as violations of the War Powers Resolution. The first was the 1983 stationing of troops in Beirut. Although the original purpose had been to remain neutral while lending support to the U.N. peace efforts, President Reagan redefined their mission as one of supporting President Gemeyal's government in Lebanon, thereby taking sides and putting American troops at risk, which ultimately led to 230 deaths. The second action was the 1983 Grenada invasion, again introducing American armed forces into situations where "imminent involvement in hostilities is clearly indicated . . . " without consulting Congress. The third was the 1986 surprise bombing of Libya in response to the alleged participation of the Libyan government in international terrorism. The fourth was the diversion of profits from arms sales to Iran to finance the Contra rebels in Nicaragua, as revealed in November 1986. These Iran-Contra actions not only violated the spirit of the War Powers Resolution but also violated the precise letter of the Boland Amendment, which had been adopted by Congress to prohibit military assistance to the Contras.

These experiences were not lost on President Bush. He disregarded Congress in the Panama incursion but was fortunate in bringing the affair to a successful conclusion quite quickly. In contrast, once he saw that the situation in Kuwait was tending toward protracted military involvement, he submitted the issue to Congress. President Clinton did not need to seek congressional approval for ordering the launch of twenty-three Tomahawk cruise missiles against Iraqi intelligence headquarters on the evening of June 26, 1993, because it was a single act, and because it was deemed to be a retaliation for an attack against the United States itself.

More important than any single case of a president's disregard for congressional authority is the attitude toward presidential involvement in secret diplomacy that seems to be shared by every modern president. Ronald Reagan was probably speaking for his successors as well as his predecessors in the following encounter, which was reported only in 1992 on the basis of newly revealed documents: At one point in the midst of the arms-for-hostages negotiation with Iran, Secretary of Defense Caspar Weinberger bluntly warned the president that the arms transfers were almost certainly illegal under the Arms Export Control Act. According to Secretary of State George Shultz's eyewitness account, President Reagan responded that "Well, the American people would never forgive me if I failed to get these hostages out over this legal question." As to potential violation of an act of Congress, the president quipped, "Visiting hours are on Thursday."[13] What emerges from all these cases is a clear sense that no piece of legislation can end, once and for all, the struggle over questions of presidential power that is virtually lodged in our Constitution.

The Domestic Presidency: The President as Head of Government

The constitutional basis of the domestic presidency also has three parts. And here again, although real power grows out of the combination of the parts, the analysis is greatly aided by examining the parts separately:

1. *Executive.* The "executive power" is vested in the president by Article II, Section 1, to see that all the laws are faithfully executed by Section 3, and under Article II, Section 2, to appoint, remove, and supervise all executive officers and to appoint all federal judges.
2. *Military.* This power is derived from Article IV, Section 4, which stipulates that the president has the power to protect every state "against Invasion; . . . and against domestic Violence."
3. *Legislative.* The president is given the power under various provisions to participate effectively and authoritatively in the legislative process.

Executive Power   The most important basis of the president's power as chief executive is to be found in Article II, Section 3, which stipulates that the president must see that all the laws are faithfully executed, and Section 2, which provides that the president will appoint, remove, and supervise all executive officers, and appoint all federal judges. The *Neagle* case has already demonstrated the degree to which Article II, Section 1, is a source of executive power. Further powers do indeed come from the appointing power, although at first this may not seem to be very impressive. But the power to appoint the "principal executive officers" and to require each of them to report to the president on subjects relating to the duties of their departments makes the president the true chief executive officer (CEO) of the nation. In this manner, the Constitution focuses executive power and legal responsibility upon the president. The famous sign on President Truman's desk, "The buck stops here," was not a mere assertion of President Truman's personal sense of responsibility but was in fact recognition by him of the legal and constitutional responsibility of the president. The president is subject to some limitations, because the appointment of all such officers, including ambassadors and ministers and federal judges, is subject to a majority approval by the Senate. But these appointments are at the discretion of the president, and the loyalty and the responsibility of each appointment are presumed to be directed toward the president.

Although the Constitution is silent on the power of the president to remove

---

[13]Murray Waas and Craig Unger, "Annals of Government. In the Loop: Bush's Secret Mission," *The New Yorker,* 2 November 1992, p. 73.

such officers, the federal courts have filled this silence with a series of decisions

which grant the president this power. In certain instances—for example, the commissioners appointed to the independent regulatory commissions (see Chapter 7) —Congress has by law limited the president's removal power. But in all other such instances, removal of the top administrative officials is "at the pleasure of the president," and this does indeed give the president a great deal of management power.[14] Although the United States has no cabinet in the parliamentary sense of a collective decision-making body or board of directors with collective responsibilities (discussed later in this chapter), the Constitution nevertheless recognizes departments with department heads, and that recognition establishes the lines of legal responsibility up and down the executive hierarchy, culminating in the presidency (See Figure 6.1).

Military Sources of Domestic Presidential Power   Although Article IV, Section 4, provides that the "United States shall protect every State . . . against Invasion and . . . domestic Violence," Congress has made this an explicit presidential power through statutes directing the president as commander-in-chief to discharge these obligations.[15] The Constitution restrains the president's use of domestic force by providing that a state legislature (or governor when the legislature is not in session) must request federal troops before the president can send them into the state to provide public order. Yet, this proviso is not absolute. First, presidents are not obligated to deploy national troops merely because the state legislature or governor makes such a request. And more important, the president may deploy troops in a state or city without a specific request from the state legislature or governor if he considers it necessary in order to maintain an essential national service, in order to enforce a federal judicial order, or in order to protect federally guaranteed civil rights.

The most famous instance of the president's unilateral use of this power to protect every state "against domestic violence" is probably its use during the Pullman Strike of 1894. In 1893, the Pullman Palace Car Company imposed a 20 percent wage cut on all its employees (exempting its executives) in response to the business depression. In response to this and the firing of three members of a grievance committee, several thousand Pullman workers, organized by the American Railway Union under the leadership of Eugene V. Debs, went on strike in May 1894 against the Pullman Company and against all the railroads hauling Pullman cars. A great deal of violence ensued, especially in and around the city of Chicago. President Cleveland immediately sought and got a federal court to issue a blanket in-

---

[14]The Supreme Court defined the president's removal power very broadly in Myers v. U.S., 272 U.S. 52 (1926). Later, in Humphrey's Executor v. U.S., 295 U.S. 62 (1935), the Court accepted Congress's effort to restrict presidential removal powers as they applied to heads of independent regulatory commissions. In those instances, the president can remove officers only "for cause." Two later cases restricted presidential power a bit further by providing that he could not remove at his pleasure certain other officers whose tasks require independence from the executive: Weiner v. U.S., 357 U.S. 349 (1958); and Bowsher v. Synar, 478 U.S. 714 (1986). In another, more tricky case, the Court held that the attorney general, not the president, could remove a special prosecutor because of the power and obligation of the prosecutor to investigate the president: Morrison v. Olson, 108 S.Ct. 2597 (1988).

[15]These statutes are contained mainly in Title 10 of the United States Code, Sections 331, 332, and 333.

FIGURE 6.1
The Institutional Presidency*

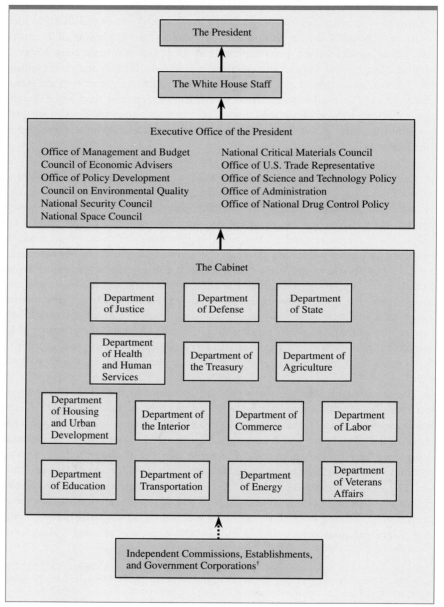

*Note: Arrows are used to indicate lines of legal responsibility.

†There are fifty-six independent regulatory commissions in the executive branch, but they are legally responsible to Congress, not directly to the president (see Chapter 7).

Source: *U.S. Government Organization Manual, 1991–1992* (Washington, DC: Government Printing Office, 1991), p. 88.

junction against all the strikers to cease their striking and go back to work. When

they persisted, in contempt of the court order, President Cleveland called out federal troops and assigned 5,000 deputy marshalls, sworn in for the occasion, to restore order. Eugene V. Debs was arrested and put on trial for his role. President Cleveland's justification, and the defense used in the *Debs* case, was that "the strong arm of the national government may be put forth to brush away all obstructions to the freedom of interstate commerce or the transportation of the mails."[16]

A second historic example of the unilateral use of presidential power to protect the states against domestic disorder, even when the states don't request it, was the decision by President Eisenhower in 1957 to send troops into Little Rock, Arkansas, literally against the wishes of the state of Arkansas, to enforce court orders to integrate Little Rock's Central High School (see Chapter 4). Arkansas Governor Orval Faubus had actually posted National Guardsmen at the entrance of the Central High School to prevent the court-ordered admission of nine black students. After an effort to negotiate with Governor Faubus failed, President Eisenhower reluctantly sent a thousand paratroopers to Little Rock, who stood watch while the black students took their places in the all-white classrooms. These cases make quite clear that the president does not have to wait for a decision of a state legislature or governor before acting as a domestic commander in chief.[17]

However, in most instances of domestic disorder—whether from human or from natural causes—presidents tend to exercise unilateral power by declaring a "state of emergency," thereby making available federal grants, insurance, and direct assistance. In 1992, in the aftermath of the devastating riots in Los Angeles and the hurricanes in Florida, American troops were very much in evidence—but in the role more of Good Samaritans than of military police.

The President's Legislative Power   The president plays a role not only in the administration of government but also in the legislative process. Two constitutional provisions are the primary sources of the president's power in the legislative arena. The first of these is the provision in Article II, Section 3, providing that the president "shall from time to time give to the Congress Information of the State of the Union, and recommend to their consideration such measures as he shall judge necessary and expedient." The second of the president's legislative powers is of course the "veto power" assigned the president by Article I, Section 7.[18]

---

[16]In re Debs, 158 U.S. 564 (1895).

[17]The best study covering all aspects of the domestic use of the military is that of Adam Yarmolinsky, *The Military Establishment* (New York: Harper & Row, 1971).

[18]There is a third source of presidential power implied from the provision for "faithful execution of the laws." This is the president's power to impound funds—that is, to refuse to spend money Congress has appropriated for certain purposes. One author referred to this as a "retroactive veto power." (Robert E. Goosetree, "The Power of the President to Impound Appropriated Funds," *American University Law Review,* January 1962.) This impoundment power was used freely and to considerable effect by many modern presidents, and Congress occasionally delegated such power to the president by statute. But reacting to the Watergate scandal, Congress adopted the Budget and Impoundment Control Act of 1974 and designed this act to circumscribe the president's ability to impound funds by requiring that the president must spend all appropriated funds unless both Houses of Congress consent to an impoundment within forty-five days of a presidential request. Therefore, since 1974, the use of impoundment has declined significantly. Presidents have either had to bite their tongues and accept unwanted appropriations or to revert to the older and more dependable but politically limited method of vetoing the entire bill.

The Veto
How a Bill Is Born, Dies, Is Reborn,
and Becomes Law (or Doesn't)

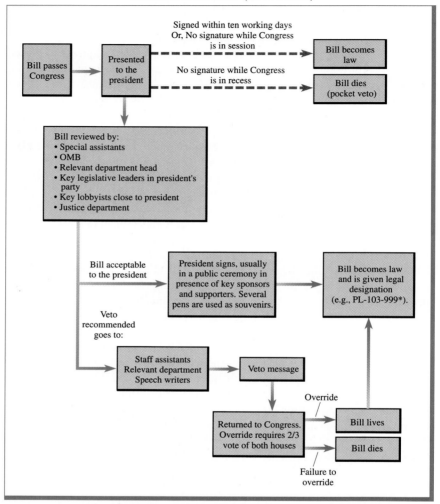

*PL = Public Law; 103 = Number of Congress (103rd is 1993–94); 999 = the number of the actual law.

The first of these does not at first appear to be of any great import. It is a mere obligation on the part of the president to make recommendations for Congress's consideration. But as political and social conditions began to favor an increasingly prominent role for presidents, each president, especially since Franklin Delano Roosevelt, began to rely upon this provision to become the primary initiator of proposals for legislative action in Congress and the principal source for public awareness of national issues as well as the most important single individual participant in legislative decisions. Few today doubt that the president and the executive branch together are the primary source for important congressional actions.[19]

Finally, the veto power alone makes the president the most important single legislative leader.[20] No bill vetoed by the president can become law unless both the House and the Senate override the veto by a two-thirds vote. Taking these two sources of power together—the president's constitutional duty to address Congress on the state of the union and the president's veto power—it is remarkable that it took so long—well over a century—for these constitutional powers to be fully realized. Let us see how this happened as well as why it took so long.

THE RISE OF PRESIDENTIAL GOVERNMENT

Most of the real power of the modern presidency comes from the powers granted by the Constitution and the laws made by Congress.[21] Thus, any person properly elected and sworn in as president will possess almost all of the power held by the strongest presidents in American history. Even when they are "lame ducks," presidents still possess all the power of the office. In 1974, as President Nixon was declining to the point where he was forced to resign or be impeached, he could still veto legislation, recognize a new government, order troops, or "push the button" in response to an armed attack. His successor, Gerald Ford, was the only person ever to occupy the presidency without being elected president or vice-president— having been appointed by President Nixon to fill the office of vice-president before moving up to succeed President Nixon himself. Yet, Gerald Ford was a genuine president and not a mere caretaker for the two and a half years he served as president. And, as a lame duck during the weeks after his electoral defeat on November 3, 1992, President Bush committed troops to Somalia and conducted a series of air strikes against Iraq.

These cases illustrate an extremely important fact about the presidency: *The popular base of the presidency is important less because it gives the president power than because it gives him consent to use all the powers already vested by the Constitution in the office.* Anyone installed in the office could exercise most of its powers.

The presidency is a democratic institution. Although the office is not free from the powerful interests in society, neither is it a product or a captive of any one set

---

[19]For a different perspective, see William F. Grover, *The President as Prisoner: A Structural Critique of the Carter and Reagan Years* (Albany: State University of New York Press, 1989).

[20]Although the veto power is the most important legislative resource in the hands of the president, it can often end in frustration, especially when the presidency and Congress are held by opposing parties. George Bush vetoed forty-six congressional enactments during his four years, and only one was overridden. Ronald Reagan vetoed thirty-nine in his eight years, and nine were overridden. This compares to thirty-one during Jimmy Carter's four years, with two overridden. For more on the veto, see Chapter 5 and Robert J. Spitzer, *The Presidential Veto—Touchstone of the American Presidency* (Albany, NY: State University of New York Press, 1988).

[21]This very useful distinction between pow*er* and pow*ers* is inspired by Richard Neustadt, *Presidential Power* (New York: Wiley, 1960), p. 28.

of interests. Its broad popular base is a great resource for presidential power. *But resources are not power.* They must be converted to power, and as in physics, energy is expended in the conversion. It took more than a century, perhaps as much as a century and a half, before presidential government came to replace congressional government. A bit of historical review will be helpful in understanding how presidential government arose.

The Legislative Epoch, 1800–1933

In 1885, political science professor Woodrow Wilson entitled his general textbook *Congressional Government* because American government was just that, "congressional government." This characterization seemed to fly in the face of the separation of powers principle that three separate branches were and ought to be equal. Nevertheless, there is ample evidence that Wilson's description of the national government was not only consistent with nineteenth-century reality but also with the intentions of the framers. Within the system of three separate and competing powers, the clear intent of the Constitution was for *legislative supremacy.*

The strongest evidence of original intent is the fact that the powers of the national government were not placed in a separate article of the Constitution, but they were instead listed in Article I, the legislative article. Madison had laid it out explicitly in *The Federalist* No. 51: "In republican government, the legislative authority necessarily predominates." President Washington echoed this in his first inaugural address in 1789:

> By the article establishing the Executive Department, it is made the duty of the President "to recommend to your consideration, such measures as he shall judge necessary and expedient."—The circumstances under which I now meet you, will acquit me from entering into that subject, farther than to refer to the Great Constitutional Charter . . . which, in defining your powers, designates the objects to which your attention is to be given.—It will be more consistent with those circumstances . . . to substitute, in place of a recommendation of particular measures, the tribute that is due . . . the characters selected to devise and adopt them.

The first decade was of course unique precisely because it was first; everything was precedent making, and nothing was secure. It was a state-building decade in which relations between president and Congress were more cooperative than they were going to be at any time thereafter. The First Congress of 1789–1791 accomplished an incredible amount. In seven short months following Washington's inauguration, Congress provided for the organization of the executive and judicial branches, established a first system of national revenue, and worked through the first seventeen amendments proposed to the Constitution, ten of which were to be ratified to become the Bill of Rights.[22]

One of the last actions of the First Congress, First Session, was to authorize the secretary of the treasury, Alexander Hamilton, to develop a policy to establish a system for national credit. In January 1790, during the Second Session, Hamilton

---

[22]See Richard Buel, Jr., *Securing the Revolution: Ideology in American Politics, 1789–1815* (Ithaca, NY: Cornell University Press, 1972), Part I and see Chapter 4.

DEBATING THE ISSUES

Presidential Power: Broad or Narrow?

Presidents and pundits have debated the proper scope of presidential power since the founding of the Republic. Some have argued that the Constitution provides broad latitude for presidents to act as they think best; others have asserted that presidents must be mindful of constitutional and political limitations in a three-branch system of government. In the twentieth century, the argument for a strong presidency has carried more weight. Yet in the face of such abuses of presidential power as Watergate and Iran-Contra, some have argued for a return to a more limited view of the presidency.

The first elected president of this century, Theodore Roosevelt, described in his autobiography his support for expansive presidential authority. Roosevelt's successor, William Howard Taft, summarized the arguments for presidential restraint. Their views are as timely today as a century ago.

Roosevelt

My view was that every executive officer, and above all every executive officer in high position, was a steward of the people bound actively and affirmatively to do all he could for the people, and not to content himself with the negative merit of keeping his talents undamaged in a napkin. . . . My belief was that it was not only his right but his duty to do anything that the needs of the nation demanded unless such action was forbidden by the Constitution or by the laws. Under this interpretation of executive power I did and caused to be done many things not previously done by the president and the heads of the departments. I did not usurp power, but I did greatly broaden the use of executive power. In other words, I acted for the public welfare, I acted for the common well-being of all our people, whenever and in whatever manner was necessary, unless prevented by direct constitutional or legislative prohibition.[1]

Taft

The true view of the executive functions is, as I conceive it, that the president can exercise no power which cannot be fairly and reasonably traced to some specific grant of power or justly implied and included within such express grant as proper and necessary to its exercise. Such specific grant must be either in the federal Constitution or in an act of Congress passed in pursuance thereof. There is no undefined residuum of power which he can exercise because it seems to him to be in the public interest, and there is nothing in the . . . law of the United States, or in other precedents, warranting such an inference. . . . [His] jurisdiction must be justified and vindicated by affirmative constitutional or statutory provision, or it does not exist.[2]

[1]Theodore Roosevelt, *An Autobiography* (New York: Scribner's, 1958), pp. 197–200.
[2]William Howard Taft, *Our Chief Magistrate and His Powers* (New York: Columbia University Press, 1916), pp. 138–45.

Andrew Jackson
"King Andrew the First"

Andrew Jackson (1767–1845)

If the Constitution that took effect in 1789 provided the forms of democracy, many of the realities of democracy were not realized until forty years later with the election of the seventh president. Andrew Jackson did not set out to remake American politics, yet that is what he did.

Born in the South Carolina backwoods, the son of Irish immigrants, Jackson fought in a Revolutionary War battle at the young age of twelve. Jackson acquired important legal and political connections that led him to government service when Tennessee was admitted as a state in 1796, culminating in his election to the House of Representatives that year. The following year, he served briefly in the Senate. In 1802, Jackson became head of the state militia, and established his military reputation by defeating hostile Indians, and then by successfully defending New Orleans from British assault during the War of 1812 (although the battle was fought after the war had ended).

Jackson then turned his ambitions to national politics. In the election of 1824, he outpolled his three rivals, but since no candidate received a majority of electoral college votes, the election was thrown into the House of Representatives where the election swung to John Quincy Adams. Four years later, Jackson swept into office as the first non-aristocrat from a state other than Massachusetts or Virginia by arousing mass sentiment against the Washington cabals and thus quadrupling his popular vote. During the next four years, Jackson and his allies persuaded the states to eliminate property qualifications for voting, establishing universal white male suffrage.

In addition to the extension of voting rights, the spread of "Jacksonian democracy" was marked by adoption of the more open political party nominating convention, by which Jackson was renominated in 1832 (eliminating the more elitist caucus method of nomination). He succeeded in dismantling the Bank of the United States, regarded by common people as an institution to serve the privileged. He challenged the ascendence of Congress and waged political war by using his veto to block the bank and internal improvement projects. He opened government service to outsiders by giving many government jobs to political newcomers.

Jackson's actions caused an uproar in Washington but fanned his popularity in the country. Viewing the election of 1832 as a referendum on his policies, Jackson won handily, carrying the electoral votes of 17 of 24 states. In 1834, the Senate formally voted to censure Jackson for actions taken to dismantle the bank. Yet, Jackson continued to challenge congressional control over executive agencies and national policy, winning him the sarcastic nickname "King Andrew the First." Jackson successfully used his popularity as a lever to expand the power of the presidential office, establishing precedents that would open the door to the modern strong presidency. Jackson retired from office in 1836, and died in 1845.

Source: Arthur M. Schlesinger, Jr., *The Age of Jackson* (Boston: Little, Brown, 1945).

submitted to Congress such a proposal; his *Report on Public Credit* is one of the

great state papers in the history of American public policy. In 1791, Hamilton presented the second of the reports ordered by Congress, the *Report on Manufactures,* probably of even greater significance than the first, because its proposals for internal improvements and industrial policies influenced Congress's agenda for years to come. Thus, it was Congress that ordered that a policy agenda be prepared by the president or his agent. In creating the executive departments, however, Congress (in particular the House) was so fearful of the powers to be lodged in the Treasury Department that it came close to adopting the three-man board that many Antifederalists favored. The compromise sought to make the Treasury Department an agent of Congress rather than simply a member of the independent executive branch.[23] This kind of cooperation resembles the British parliamentary system, but it was not to last.

Before the Republic was a decade old, Congress began to develop a strong organization, including its own elected leadership, the first standing committees, and the party hierarchies. By the second term of President Jefferson (1805), the executive branch was beginning to play the secondary role anticipated by the Constitution. The quality of presidential performance and then of presidential personality and character declined accordingly. The president during this era was seen by some observers as little more than America's "chief clerk." Of President James Madison, who had been principal author of the Constitution, it was said that he knew everything about government except how to govern. Indeed, after Jefferson and until the beginning of this century, most historians agree that Presidents Jackson and Lincoln were the only exceptions to what had been the rule of weak presidents; and those two exceptions can be explained, since one was a war hero and founder of the Democratic party and the other was a wartime president and first leader of the newly founded Republican party. In his 1888 essay, "Why Great Men Are Not Chosen Presidents," the great British observer Lord Bryce wrote:

> In America, which is beyond all other countries the country of a "career open to talents" . . . it might be expected that the highest place would also be won by a man of brilliant gifts. But from the time when the heroes of the Revolution died out . . . no person except General Grant . . . would have been remembered had he not been president, and no president except Abraham Lincoln had displayed rare or striking qualities. Of James K. Polk or Franklin Pierce, the only thing remarkable about them is that being so commonplace they should have climbed so high.[24]

Thirty-five years later, in his third and last edition, the same chapter appeared without revision, except for the disclaimer in a footnote that "of presidents since 1900 it is not yet time to speak."[25]

One of the reasons that so few great men became presidents in the nineteenth century is that there was only occasional room for greatness in such a weak of-

---

[23]See, for example, Forrest McDonald, *The Presidency of George Washington* (Lawrence, KS: The University Press of Kansas, 1974), pp. 36–42.

[24]Bryce, *The American Commonwealth,* 2nd ed. (London: MacMillan & Company, 1889), p. 73.

[25]Bryce, *The American Commonwealth,* new edition, 1924, p. 84.

fice.[26] As Chapter 3 indicated, the national government of that period was not a particularly powerful entity. Moreover, most of the policies adopted by the national government were designed mainly to promote the expansion of commerce. These could be directed and administered by the congressional committees and political parties without much reliance on an executive bureaucracy.

Another reason for the weak presidency of the nineteenth century is that during this period the presidency was not closely linked to major national political and social forces. Indeed, there were few important *national* political or social forces to which presidents could have linked themselves even if they had wanted to. Federalism had taken very good care of this by fragmenting political interests and diverting the energies of interest groups toward the state and local levels of government, where most key decisions were being made.

The presidency was strengthened somewhat in the 1830s with the introduction of the national convention system of nominating presidential candidates. Until then, presidential candidates had been nominated by their party's congressional delegates. This was the "caucus" system of nominating candidates, and it was derisively called "King Caucus" because any candidate for president had to be beholden to his party's leaders in Congress if he was to succeed in getting the party's nomination and the support of the party's congressional delegation in the election. The national nominating convention arose outside Congress in order to provide some representation for a party's voters who lived in districts where they weren't numerous enough to elect a member of Congress. The political party in each state made its own provisions for selecting delegates to attend the presidential nominating convention, and in virtually all states the selection was dominated by the party leaders (called "bosses" by the opposition party). It is only in recent decades that state laws have intervened to regularize the selection process and to provide (in all but a few instances) for open election of delegates. The convention system quickly became the overwhelmingly most popular method of nominating candidates for all elective offices and remained so until well into the twentieth century when it succumbed to the criticism that it was a nondemocratic method dominated by a few leaders in a "smoke-filled room." But in the nineteenth century, it was seen as a victory for democracy against the congressional elite. And the national convention gave the presidency a base of power independent of Congress.

This additional independence did not immediately transform the presidency into the office we recognize today because the parties disappeared back into their states and Congress once the national election was over. But the national convention did begin to open the presidency to larger social forces and newly organized interests in society. In other words, it gave the presidency a constituency base that would eventually support and demand increased presidential power. Improvements in telephone, telegraph, and mass communications allowed individuals to share their complaints and allowed national leaders—especially presidents and presidential candidates—to reach out directly to people to ally themselves with, and even sometimes to create, popular groups and forces. Eventually, though more slowly, the presidential selection process began to be further democratized, with the adop-

[26]For a related appraisal, see Jeffrey Tulis, *The Rhetorical Presidency* (Princeton, NJ: Princeton University Press, 1988).

tion of primary elections through which millions of ordinary citizens were given

an opportunity to take part in the presidential nominating process by popular selection of convention delegates.

The Democrats went still further to democratize the nominating process after
their 1968 election loss, with new rules requiring that any candidate receiving at
least 15 percent of the vote in a state primary, caucus or convention must receive
the same percentage of the delegates from that state to the national convention.
Still other rules required half of each state's delegation to be female, and also required at least genuine, good faith efforts to select delegates for ethnic, racial, and
other diversity. These changes did help democratize the Democratic party's presidential nomination process in the extreme but also almost certainly made it much
more difficult for the Democrats to nominate a candidate who could stage an effective national campaign. As a result of their second successive loss in 1984, the
Democrats created a new category of "super delegate" to be chosen by congressional caucuses and state conventions from among elected public officials, in order
to give the party leadership a greater voice at the convention. However, the experiences of 1988 and 1992 do not indicate that this produced any real influence over
the nominating process, since super delegates voted the way of the regularly
elected delegates. Thus, although Clinton decisively won the Democratic nomination in 1992, the Democratic party was no better organized than it had been before. This helps explain why President Clinton continued to reach out directly to
the American people as though he were still campaigning.

Despite political and social conditions favoring the enhancement of presidential
power, however, the development of presidential government as we know it today
did not mature until the middle of our own century. For a long period, even as the
national government began to grow, Congress was careful to keep tight reins on
the president's power. For example, when Congress began to make its first efforts
to exert power over the economy (beginning in 1887 with the adoption of the
Interstate Commerce Act and in 1890 with the adoption of the Sherman Antitrust
Act), it sought to keep this power away from the president and the executive
branch by placing these new regulatory policies in "independent regulatory commissions" responsible to Congress rather than to the president (see also Chapter 7).

The real turning point in the history of American national government came
during the administration of Franklin Delano Roosevelt. The New Deal was a response to the political forces that had been gathering national strength and focus
for fifty years. What is remarkable is not that they gathered but that they were so
long gaining influence in Washington—and even then it took the Great Depression to bring about the new national government.

The New Deal and the Presidency

The "First Hundred Days" of the Roosevelt administration in 1933 had no parallel in U.S. history. But this period was only the beginning. The policies proposed
by President Roosevelt and adopted by Congress during the first thousand days so
changed the size and character of the national government that they constitute a
moment in American history equivalent to the founding or to the Civil War. The

president's constitutional obligation to see "that the laws be faithfully executed" became virtually a responsibility to shape the laws before executing them.

New Programs Expand the Role of National Government   Many of the New Deal programs were extensions of the traditional national government approach, which was described already in Chapter 3 (see especially Table 3.1). The New Deal extensions of these traditional types of policies are shown in Table 6.1 and labeled the "traditional state." But the New Deal went well beyond that, adopting types of policies never before tried on a large scale by the national government. (The highlights of these are in Table 6.1 and labeled the "regulatory state" and the "redistributive state." There were always some policies like those listed under the "organizational state." More will be said about the organizational state in Chapters 7 and 15.) The New Deal began intervening into economic life in ways that had hitherto been reserved to the states. In other words, the national government discovered that it, too, had "police power" and could directly regulate individuals as well as provide roads and other services.

The new programs were such dramatic departures from the traditional policies of the national government that their constitutionality was in doubt. The Supreme Court in fact declared several of them unconstitutional, mainly on the grounds that in regulating the conduct of individuals or their employers the national government was reaching beyond "*inter*state," into "*intra*state," essentially local, matters. Most of the New Deal remained in constitutional limbo until 1937, five years after Roosevelt was first elected and one year after his landslide 1936 re-election.

The turning point came with *National Labor Relations Board* v. *Jones & Laughlin Steel Corporation*. At issue was the National Labor Relations Act, or Wagner Act, which prohibited corporations from interfering with the efforts of employees to organize into unions, to bargain collectively over wages and working conditions, and under certain conditions, to go on strike and engage in picketing. The newly formed National Labor Relations Board (NLRB) had ordered Jones & Laughlin to reinstate workers fired because of their union activities. The appeal reached the Supreme Court because Jones & Laughlin had made a constitutional issue over the fact that its manufacturing activities were local and therefore beyond the national government's reach. The Supreme Court rejected this argument with the response that a big company with subsidiaries and suppliers in many states was innately in interstate commerce:

> When industries organize themselves on a national scale, making their relation to interstate commerce the dominant factor in their activities, how can it be maintained that their industrial labor relations constitute a forbidden field into which Congress may not enter when it is necessary to protect interstate commerce from the paralyzing consequences of industrial war?[27]

---

[27]NLRB v. Jones & Laughlin Steel Corporation, 301 U.S. 1 (1937). Congress had attempted to regulate the economy before 1933, as with the Interstate Commerce Act and Sherman Antitrust Act of the late nineteenth century and with the Federal Trade Act and the Federal Reserve in the Wilson period. But these were rare attempts, and each, very carefully, was restricted to a narrow and acceptable definition of "interstate commerce." The big break did not come until after 1933.

TABLE 6.1
The Political Economy of the New Deal

Program	Acronym	Year
Traditional State		
Civil Works Administration	CWA	1933
Public Works Administration	PWA	1933
Civilian Conservation Corps	CCC	1933
Works Progress Administration	WPA	1933
Tennessee Valley Authority	TVA	1933
Rural Electrification Administration	REA	1933
Soil Conservation Service	SCS	1935
Regulatory State		
Agricultural Adjustment Administration	AAA	1933
National Recovery Administration	NRA	1933
Securities & Exchange Commission	SEC	1933
Public Utility Holding Company Act		1935
National Labor Relations Act and Board	NLRB	1935
Fair Labor Standards Act	FLSA	1938
Civil Aeronautics Act and Board	CAB	1938
Redistributive State		
Federal Deposit Insurance Corporation	FDIC	1933
Bank Holiday		1933
Home Owners Loan Corporation	HOLC	1933
Devaluation		1934
Federal Housing Administration	FHA	1934
Federal Reserve Reforms	FED	1935
Social Security Act	SSA	1935
Farm Security Administration	FSA	1935
Internal Revenue Tax Reforms	IRS	1935
Organizational State (Constituent Policies)		
Judiciary Reform		1937
Executive Office of the President	EOP	1939
Budget Bureau	OMB	1939
White House Staff		1930s
Administrative Law		1930s
Federal Bureau of Investigation	FBI	1940s
Joint Chiefs of Staff	JCOS	1940s

Since the end of the New Deal, the Supreme Court has never again questioned the constitutionality of an important act of Congress authorizing the executive branch to intervene into the economy or society.[28]

Delegation of Power   The most important constitutional effect of Congress's actions and the Supreme Court's approval of those actions during the New Deal was the enhancement of *presidential power.* Most major acts of Congress in this period involved significant exercises of control over the economy. But few programs specified the actual controls to be used. Instead, Congress authorized the president or, in some cases, a new agency to determine what the controls would be. Some of the new agencies were independent commissions, responsible to Congress. But most of the new agencies and programs of the New Deal were placed in the executive branch directly under presidential authority.

Technically, this form of congressional act is called the "delegation of power." In theory, the delegation of power works as follows: (1) Congress recognizes a problem; (2) Congress acknowledges that it has neither the time nor expertise to deal with the problem; and (3) Congress therefore sets the basic policies and then delegates to an agency the power to "fill in the details." But in practice, Congress was delegating not merely the power to "fill in the details," but actual and real *policy-making powers,* that is, real legislative powers, to the executive branch. For example, the president through the secretary of agriculture was authorized by the 1938 Agricultural Adjustment Act (AAA) to determine the amount of acreage each and every farmer could devote to crops that had been determined to be surplus commodities, in order to keep prices up and surpluses down. Authority extended, for example, from growers of thousands of acres of wheat for market to farmers cultivating twenty-five acres of feed for their own livestock.[29]

This authority continues today in virtually the same form, covering many commodities and millions of acres. Lest this is thought to be a power delegated to the president only during emergencies like the 1930s, take the example of environmental protection laws passed by Congress in the 1960s and 1970s. Under the president, the Environmental Protection Agency was given the authority to "monitor the conditions of the environment," "establish quantitative base lines for pollution levels," and "set and enforce standards of air and water quality and for individual pollutants."[30]

---

[28]Some will argue that there are at least two exceptions to this statement. One was the 1976 case declaring unconstitutional Congress's effort to supply national minimum wage standards to state and local government employees (National League of Cities v. Usery, 426 U.S. 833 [1976]). But the Court reversed itself nine years later, in 1985 (Garcia v. San Antonio Metropolitan Transit Authority, 469 U.S. 528 [1985]). The second was the 1986 case declaring unconstitutional the part of the Gramm-Rudman law authorizing the comptroller general to make "across the board" budget cuts when total appropriations exceeded legally established ceilings (Bowsher v. Synar, 92 L. Ed. 583 [1986]). But cases such as these are few and far between, and they only touch on part of a law, not the constitutionality of the entire program.

[29]See Wickard v. Filburn, 317 U.S. 111 (1942).

[30]Environmental Reorganization Plan of July 9, 1970, reprinted from Government Printing Office in *Congressional Quarterly Almanac,* 1970, pp. 119a–120a. Other examples of broad delegations of power to the president will be found in Theodore J. Lowi, *The End of Liberalism* (New York: W. W. Norton, 1979), Chapter 5. See also Sotirios Barber, *The Constitution and the Delegation of Congressional Power* (Chicago: The University of Chicago Press, 1975).

No modern government can avoid the delegation of significant legislative powers to the executive branch. But the fact remains this delegation produced a very fundamental shift in the American constitutional framework. *During the 1930s, the growth of the national government through acts delegating legislative power tilted the American national structure away from a Congress-centered government toward a president-centered government.*[31] Congress continues to be the constitutional source of policy, and Congress can rescind these delegations of power or can restrict them with later amendments, committee oversight, or budget cuts. But we can say that presidential government has become an established fact of American life.

PRESIDENTIAL GOVERNMENT

There was no great mystery in the shift from Congress-centered government to president-centered government. As already observed in Chapter 5, Congress simply delegated its own powers to the executive branch. Congress committed legiscide—or at least partial legiscide. These delegated powers were the link from congressional dominance to presidential dominance, and they became the main resources for presidential government.

Congressional delegations of power, however, are not the only resources available to the president. Presidents have at their disposal a variety of other formal and informal resources that have important implications for their ability to govern. Indeed, without these other resources, presidents would lack the ability—the tools of management and public mobilization—to make much use of the power and responsibility given to them by Congress. Let us first consider the president's formal or official resources and then, in the section following, turn to the more informal resources that affect a president's capacity to govern, in particular the president's base of popular support.

Formal Resources of Presidential Power

Patronage as a Tool of Management   The first tool of management available to most presidents is the choice of high-level political appointees. These appointments allow the president to fill top management positions with individuals who will attempt to carry out his agenda. But he must appoint individuals who have experience and interest in the programs that they are to administer and who share the president's goals with respect to these programs. At the same time, presidents use the appointment process to build links to powerful political and economic

---

[31]The Supreme Court did in fact *dis*approve broad delegations of legislative power by declaring the National Industrial Recovery Act of 1933 unconstitutional on the grounds that Congress did not accompany the broad delegations with sufficient standards or guidelines for presidential discretion (Panama Refining Co. v. Ryan, 293 U.S. 388 [1935], and Schechter Poultry Corp. v. United States, 295 US. 495 [1935]). The Supreme Court has never reversed those two decisions, but it has also never really followed them. Thus, broad delegations of legislative power from Congress to the executive branch can be presumed to be constitutional.

constituencies by giving representation to important state political party organizations, the business community, organized labor, the scientific and university communities, organized agriculture, and certain large and well-organized religious groups.

When President Clinton took office, he had literally about four thousand appointments he could make "at the pleasure of the president."[32] Virtually all of these appointments were genuine plums, nearly half of them very ripe plums with salaries ranging from $60,000 to $100,000 a year. This is why the general directory of exempt positions, *Policy and Supporting Positions,* is affectionately referred to as the *Plum Book.*[33] At the top are the roughly seven hundred cabinet and top White House positions. Next are roughly eight hundred Senior Executive Service (SES) positions that can be appointed outside the career service; these are called noncareer appointees in the SES. Their salaries can range from $45,000 to $100,000 a year. Then there are more than two thousand "schedule C" positions. A schedule C position is defined as a "position of a confidential or policy determining character . . . to which appointments may be made without examination by [the Office of Personnel Management]."[34] Salaries for these positions can run as high as $80,000 a year. In addition, the president can appoint up to 25 percent more schedule C personnel to assist with the transition for the first 240 days (eight months) of office, and after that, many of these people can be moved into other positions if they do not wish to return to the private sector.

Now, four thousand plums are far too many appointments for the president to make personally. But, as a person committed to being a "strong president," President Clinton supervised a large percentage of these appointments, even when he did not make them himself. One expert observer on the presidential appointment process reports that the increasing trend of distrust of the federal bureaucracy, coupled with the tendency of presidential candidates to run against Washington, has led each president in recent times to increase the centralization of the appointment process.[35] Most presidents have been particularly attentive to the 1,500 or 2,000 higher-level appointees.

Table 6.2 presents a thirty-year overview of presidential appointees and their backgrounds. However, it masks a big difference between the first half and the second half of the epoch. Up until the 1970s, beginning before 1961, modern presidents showed a distinct preference for outsiders—men (with a sprinkling of women) whose experience prior to top presidential appointment had been outside government altogether and outside the campaign organization of the president. In

---

[32]All of these are exempted from the competitive career service requirements. Some may have to meet a qualification standard as set by law or by an agency head, but they are otherwise discretionary and do not have to meet the general legal standards of the Office of Personnel Management in the career service.

[33]Committee on Post Office and Civil Service, House of Representatives, *United States Government, Policy and Supporting Positions* (Washington, DC: Government Printing Office, 1992).

[34]*Policy and Supporting Positions,* p. v.

[35]James P. Pfiffner, "Political Appointees and Career Executives: The Democracy-Bureaucracy Nexus," in Patricia Ingraham and Donald Kettl, eds., *Agenda for Excellence—Public Service in America* (Chatham, NJ: Chatham House, 1992), pp. 48–50.

particular, few of the top appointees had any significant experience in the administrative processes of the agencies they were to be responsible for managing. Presidents tended to draw their top appointees from among business executives, state
governors, and interest group leaders, with an occasional former senator and
member of Congress, and university professor. Many appointees hardly knew the
president before they were chosen, few had a long working relationship with the
president, and still fewer had any working relationship with other members of the
president's administration.

The figures on Table 6.2 show higher average national government and Washington administrative experience because of the significant increase of such appointees in the second half of the period covered by the table. President Carter,
despite his claim to being himself an outsider to Washington, drew liberally from
among people who had served Johnson and Kennedy in the 1960s. President
Reagan drew from the Nixon administration. President Bush appointed a still
higher percentage of Washington insiders, and President Clinton has established a
similar pattern. Bush's preference for appointees with national government experience could be attributed to the fact that he himself was an insider with a long and
varied experience in Washington. Clinton's preference for choosing people with

TABLE 6.2
Previous Career Experience of the Top Executive Officials, by Party*
(1961–1992)

Previous Experience	Inner Cabinet			Outer Cabinet			Executive Office of the President			White House Staff		
	All	Dem	Rep	All	Dem	Rep	All	Dem	Rep	All	Dem	Rep
National Government (all)	85%	80%	87%	65%	61%	67%	79%	68%	85%	69%	50%	80%
National Administration	78%	73%	81%	56%	52%	58%	74%	57%	83%	61%	46%	69%
U.S. Congress	15%	7%	19%	14%	12%	15%	8%	7%	8%	10%	0%	15%
State and Local Government	28%	20%	32%	37%	48%	32%	17%	18%	17%	16%	9%	20%
Private Business	48%	40%	52%	48%	36%	54%	38%	29%	42%	44%	32%	51%
Attorney	59%	73%	52%	39%	52%	33%	25%	32%	21%	34%	36%	33%
Academics	26%	33%	23%	26%	33%	23%	23%	36%	15%	23%	36%	15%
Political Party Office	11%	7%	13%	16%	9%	20%	12%	7%	15%	15%	14%	15%
No Government Experience	11%	20%	6%	18%	18%	18%	15%	21%	12%	23%	41%	13%
N=	46	15	31	99	33	66	80	28	52	61	22	39

*Entries are the percentage of appointees to Cabinet, Executive Office of the President, and White
House Staff positions by the party of the appointing president with experience in the positions and professions listed.

Source: James W. Riddlesperger and James D. King, "Presidential Appointments to the Cabinet, Executive Office, and White House Staff," *Presidential Studies Quarterly* 16, no. 4 (1986), p. 695. Courtesy
Center for the Study of the Presidency. This is a new table extending the data from 1985 to 1992, provided courtesy of the authors. Our thanks to Professors Riddlesperger and King.

PRESIDENTIAL POWER: ITS USE AND MISUSE

Early in the Civil War, Abraham Lincoln used his presidential power to suspend the writ of *habeas corpus*, a constitutional right that safeguards against unlawful imprisonment by ensuring due process of law. The Constitution allows it to be suspended only "in Cases of Rebellion or Invasion." Of the more than 14,000 arrests made during the Civil War, the case of Clement L. Vallandigham, a Democrat radical from Ohio arrested in 1863, became well known because he was a prominent political opponent of Lincoln's. This outright suppression of a political foe angered the public, forcing Lincoln to later drop this method of control.

During the Korean War, negotiations between the United Steel Workers union and the steel industry became deadlocked and the USW called for a nationwide strike. Believing that as president he had the power to take action, Truman ordered the federal government to seize the steel mills on April 8, 1952. He was concerned that a decrease in steel production would hurt the U.S. effort in the Korean War as well as the economy. Outraged, the steel industry took Truman to court, comparing his tactics to those of Hitler and Mussolini. In a landmark decision on June 2, 1952, *(Youngstown Sheet & Tube Co. v Sawyer)*, the Supreme Court declared Truman's action invalid: he did not have the constitutional authority nor the necessary congressional authority to take such action.

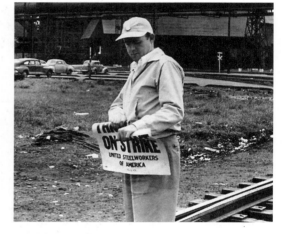

The Constitution sets up the president to be commander in chief of the armed forces, in effect placing a civilian at the head of the military. Even when a former general—such as Jackson, Grant, or Eisenhower—is elected president, he does not govern as a general, but as a civilian. Truman made the point clearly when he fired General Douglas MacArthur for insubordination during the Korean War: "It is fundamental that military commanders must be governed by the policies and directives issued to them in the manner provided by our laws and constitution," and the military must be controlled by civilian authority. Truman's decision proved to be unpopular. Protests, such as lowering flags to mourn symbolically the death of an outstanding military career, were common across the country. However, no one disputed the fact that Truman had the right to take such action.

After being directly linked to the Watergate scandal and facing probable impeachment by Congress, Richard M. Nixon became the first United States president to resign from office. Until his resignation was official on August 9, 1974, Nixon retained full presidential powers. When Gerald Ford took office, he initially deplored the previous administration's actions. However, on September 8, 1974, using his constitutional power to "grant Reprieves and Pardons for Offenses against the United States," Ford gave Nixon "full, free, and absolute pardon" from his involvement in Watergate. The nation felt betrayed by his decision, which greatly hindered his quest for a second term.

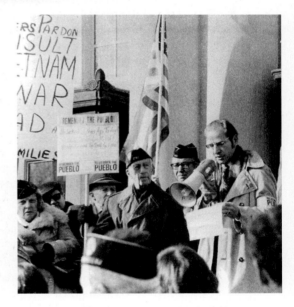

On January 21, 1977, President Jimmy Carter used the power of presidential pardon when he signed the Proclamation of Presidential Pardon for those who had evaded military service from August 4, 1964, through March 28, 1973, in an attempt to soothe the country's lingering disenchantment over the Vietnam War. Public response echoed the divided attitude toward the war, with both praise and protest for his decision. Veterans demonstrated against Carter's pardon, claiming it devalued the lives sacrificed by those who had dutifully served.

In 1990, using his presidential power to "receive Ambassadors and other public Ministers," President Bush received Russian president Boris Yeltsin at the White House, having officially recognized the independence of the new states that had been members of the former Soviet Union.

Washington experience has been attributed to his determination to be a strong and active president. This interpretation has been certainly confirmed by the prominence of members of Congress among the top appointees—not the retired or defeated member going on to his higher reward, but active members of Congress who were powerful in the realms over which they were appointed to serve in the cabinet. Other appointees had been members of previous administrations, and they, along with the former governors, mayors, campaign officials, and other public officials tell a story of Clinton's genuine commitment to the value and effectiveness of experience in public office as a qualification for high appointment in his administration.

The Cabinet   In the American system of government, the **cabinet** is the traditional but informal designation for the heads of all the major federal government departments. The cabinet has no constitutional status. Unlike England and many other parliamentary countries, where the cabinet *is* the government, the American cabinet is not a collective body. It meets but makes no decisions as a group. Each appointment must be approved by the Senate but is not responsible to the Senate or to Congress at large. Cabinet appointments help build party and popular support, but the cabinet is not a party organ. The cabinet is made up of directors but is not a board of directors.

Time and time again, presidents have tried to make the cabinet more of a board of directors, but this has never taken hold. President Carter was more serious about doing so than most presidents. He criticized the Republicans for being secretive and isolated in the White House, and he sought true "cabinet government" from the start by meeting frequently with cabinet members and permitting them to make many of the high-level appointments within their own departments. But White House journalists soon detected a change of heart and of practice. The frequency of cabinet meetings was soon cut in half, and Carter became less and less accessible to individual cabinet members, relying increasingly on his White House staff. President Reagan also came out early in favor of cabinet government, and he even organized "cabinet councils" of subgroups of cabinet members to develop his policies. Yet, by the end of his first term, the policy recommendations made by these cabinet councils were virtually all reshaped by a White House group led by President Reagan's then-key special assistants, James Baker (later appointed secretary of the treasury) and Edwin Meese (later appointed attorney general). One heard less and less about these cabinet councils later in the Reagan administration.[36]

President Bush never made any pretense of "cabinet government." In fact, although his cabinet appointees brought more than the average government experience, Bush took sixty-five days to complete his cabinet selections, and there is no better way to denigrate cabinet status than to start an administration without it.

[36]For good appraisals of efforts to create cabinet government, see Dom Bonafede, "Carter Sounds Retreat from 'Cabinet Government,'" *National Journal,* 18 November 1978; Dick Kirschten, "Reagan's Cabinet Council May Have Less Influence Than Meets the Eye," *National Journal,* 11 July 1981; and Benjamin Page and Mark Petracca, *The American Presidency* (New York: McGraw-Hill, 1983), pp. 188–93.

Bush had intended apparently to continue the Reagan practice of cabinet councils;

however, the cabinet councils and the cabinet as a whole were both undercut by Bush's own preference for dealing directly with each cabinet member on an individual basis, usually by telephone, and for allowing cabinet members a good deal of latitude to act in their own capacity as department heads.[37]

Although President Clinton is similar to Bush in his preference for a cabinet with a lot of Washington experience in particular and public service experience in general, the resemblance seems to end there. First, Clinton completed his cabinet selections nearly a month prior to his inauguration. Second, he made his appointments in clusters, with a foreign policy team announced together, an economic team, a natural resources team, etc. Third, the cabinet-level appointments were all in place before subcabinet appointments were made, to presumably give the top appointees a role in the selection of their deputy secretaries and undersecretaries. All of this tended to give the Clinton appointees a bit more stature as department heads, to stand a bit taller as chief executive officers in managing the affairs of their department. But none of this promises to bring these appointees together to act as a genuine cabinet, as a board of directors.

Why hasn't a president had a real cabinet that serves collectively as a board of directors? After all, we speak collectively of the Bush administration or the Clinton administration. And we call it a cabinet, and all the members (with an occasional exception) are members of the same party, which will be subjected to the judgment of the electorate after four years. Why, then, have we never developed a cabinet with a concept of collective responsibility—a cabinet with members who share the president's political responsibilities and help diffuse and divert some of the heavy burden of the president's personal responsibilities? The explanation lies deep in the American system of national politics, which catches the cabinet and each member of it in a web of three basic interacting forces:

1. Each presidential candidate must build a winning electoral coalition, state by state. Winning primaries and collecting delegates for the party convention and then building a coalition to win the general election requires that the candidate build a direct, personal relationship with the public. Expectations of national government performance come to focus *personally* on the candidate who must as president produce or give the appearance of making things happen. His responsibilities are personal and immediate, and he is under too much personal pressure once he gets the nomination to stop and create a viable cabinet. In fact, by the time a president is inaugurated, it is too late to create cabinet government. Presidents don't even know personally some of their appointees, and many appointees don't know each other.

2. Cabinet members have their own constituencies and are usually selected by the president because of the support they can bring him. But these constituencies do not automatically transfer to the president, and they may continue to be at odds with him. For the same reason, it is extremely difficult to remove a cabinet member or other high-level official.

[37]James P. Pfiffner, "Establishing the Bush Presidency," *Public Administration Review,* January/February 1990, pp. 66–67.

3. Each cabinet member heads a department that is composed of a large bureaucracy with a momentum of its own. Career administrators consider political executives birds of passage. Very often an order from a political executive is seen as in conflict with the judgment and expectations of their profession. Thus, career administrators do not easily fall into line with each new administration. Cabinet members often face a choice between giving loyalty to the president or gaining the loyalty of their department.

Being aware of this web of forces, the president tends to develop a burning impatience with and a mild distrust of cabinet members; he seeks to make the cabinet a rubber stamp for actions already decided on; and he demands results, or the appearance of results, more immediately and more frequently than most department heads can provide. Since cabinet appointees generally have not shared political careers with the president or with each other, and since they have been brought together literally for the first time after their selection, the formation of an effective, governing group out of this motley collection of appointments is very unlikely. While President Clinton's insistence on a cabinet diverse enough to resemble American society itself could be considered an act of political wisdom, it virtually guaranteed that few of his appointees would ever have spent a lot of time working together or would even know the policy positions or beliefs of the other appointees.[38] While they can find out this information quickly enough, that is still unlikely to produce a cabinet capable of making collective decisions. And there was every indication that President Clinton didn't particularly want this. David Broder's interviews for the *Washington Post* indicated that although Clinton's top appointees were to be commended for "intellectual firepower," the pattern showed that Clinton "wants this to be a very personal and very powerful presidency [with] the policy reins firmly in his own hands."[39] Clinton, like most of his predecessors, is likely to work with each individual member of his cabinet when the decision at issue involves the department of that member.

Some presidents have relied more heavily on an "inner cabinet," the National Security Council (NSC). The NSC, established by law in 1947, is composed of the president, the vice-president, the secretaries of state, defense, and the treasury, the attorney general, and other officials invited by the president. It has its own staff of foreign policy specialists run by the special assistant to the president for national security affairs (see Chapter 18 for details). Table 6.3 suggests that for these highest appointments, presidents turn to people from outside Washington, usually longtime associates. A counterpart, the Domestic Council, was created by law in 1970, but no specific departments were designated for it. President Clinton hit upon his own version of the Domestic Council, entitled the National Economic Council, which may or may not end up with a status higher than the original Domestic Council's. But it will operate in competition with the Council of Economic Advisers.

Presidents have obviously been uneven and unpredictable in their reliance on

[38] *New York Times,* 23 December 1992, p. 1.

[39] David Broder, "Clinton's Eclectic Cabinet," *Washington Post, National Weekly Edition,* 4–10 January 1993, p. 13.

TABLE 6.3
Backgrounds of Appointees to Inner Cabinet* (1961–1993)

Republicans	Democrats

Secretary of State

William Rogers (RMN) Law practice, att. gen.	Dean Rusk (JFK-LBJ) Foreign service, foundation executive
Henry Kissinger (RMN-GF) Professor	
Alexander Haig (RR) General, assistant to the president, NATO command	Cyrus Vance (JC) International law, department of defense official
George Shultz (RR) Professor, secretary of treasury (RMN), corporate executive	Edmund Muskie (JC) Senator
James Baker (GB) Texas corporate law, chief of staff, secretary of treasury (RR)	Warren M. Christopher (BC) Corporate law, Department of State official

Secretary of the Treasury

David Kennedy (RMN) Banking and finance	Douglas Dillon (JFK-LBJ) Securities and finance, state department
John Connally (RMN) Governor, law practice	
George Shultz (RMN) Professor	Henry Fowler (LBJ) Banking, law practice
William Simon (RMN-GF) Securities and investments	Joseph Barr (LBJ) Mayor, state government official
Donald Regan (RR) Securities executive	Michael Blumenthal (JC) Corporate executive
James Baker (RR) Texas corporate law, chief of staff	William Miller (JC) Corporate executive, Federal Reserve Board
Nicholas Brady (RR-GB) Investment banker	Lloyd M. Bentsen (BC) Financier, Senator

Secretary of Defense

Melvin Laird (RMN) Congressman	Robert McNamara (JFK-LBJ) Corporate executive
Elliot Richardson (RMN) State lieutenant governor, secretary of HEW	Clark Clifford (LBJ) Law practice
James Schlesinger (RMN-GF) Professor, science administrator, head of CIA, head of OMB	Harold Brown (JC) Air Force secretary, college president
Donald Rumsfeld (GF) Congressman, NATO official	Les Aspin (BC) Chair, House Armed Services Committee
Caspar Weinberger (RR) Secretary of HEW (RMN), head of OMB, corporate official	
Frank Carlucci (RR) Career government official	
Richard Cheney (GB) Wyoming congressman, White House chief of staff (GF)	

Attorney General

John Mitchell (RMN) Law practice, securities adviser	Robert Kennedy (JFK-LBJ) Counsel for Senate investigatory committee
Richard Kleindienst (RMN) Law practice	Nicholas Katzenbach (LBJ) Professor
Elliot Richardson (RMN) State official, lieutenant governor, secretary of defense (RMN)	Ramsey Clark (LBJ) Law practice
William Saxbe (RMN-GF) Senator, state att. gen.	Griffin Bell (JC) Law practice
Edward Levi (GF) Law professor, college president	Benjamin Civiletti (JC) Law practice
William French Smith (RR) Lawyer, adviser to president	Janet Reno (BC) Dade County (Miami) Prosecutor
Edwin Meese (RR) Lawyer, aide to president	
Richard Thornburgh (RR-GB) Governor, lawyer	

*These are the four cabinet posts that legally comprise the National Security Council.

JFK=John F. Kennedy; LBJ=Lyndon B. Johnson; RMN=Richard M. Nixon; GF=Gerald Ford; JC=Jimmy Carter; RR=Ronald Reagan; GB=George Bush; BC=Bill Clinton.

Sources: *Congress and the Nation,* vol. 4 (Washington DC: Congressional Quarterly, 1977), pp. 1107–11; *Who's Who in American Politics* (New York: Bowker, 1973, 1977); and *Who's Who in America* (Chicago: Marquis, various years).

the NSC and other subcabinet bodies, because executive management is inherently a personal matter. However, despite all the personal variations, one generalization can be made: presidents have increasingly preferred the White House staff to the cabinet as their means of managing the gigantic executive branch.

The White House Staff[40]   It is not accidental that journalists have come to popularize the staff of each president with such names as the "Irish Mafia" (Kennedy), the "Georgia Mafia" (Carter), and the "California Mafia" (Reagan). President Bush's inner staff was characterized less as a "mafia" and more as a "club," composed of "camaraderie, humor, and male bonding."[41] Like every modern president, Bush gathered around him people who fought most of the battles with him during his long struggle for ultimate political success. President Clinton's appointments indicated that his White House staff would be even more traditional than that of President Bush. His chief of staff, Thomas McLarty, has been a close friend from Clinton's childhood, and that relationship, combined with a very successful business career, put McLarty in a position to be brutally frank with the president and to provide him at every moment with a genuine sense of political reality. McLarty lacked the political stature or "clout" of such predecessors as John Sununu or James Baker or Donald Regan, but he had the close personal relationship and reputation for good instinct most occupants of that position have possessed. The rest of the White House staff has been much the same—lacking in independent political stature but long on direct experience with President Clinton, good political instinct, and strong personal loyalty. As one seasoned White House watcher reported, "The Clintons [note the plural] essentially have selected people of long-standing loyalty to them, and of little or no independent standing in Washington, or nationally. The two most striking features of the staff are its lack of towering, or intimidating figures, and its intensely political nature."[42] Thus, although President Clinton may ultimately behave as a "different kind of Democrat" (as he had defined his search for top appointments) his White House staff is quite conventional. But for someone who wants to be a strong president and who wants advice he can depend upon, a staff of this nature is justifiable.

The White House staff is composed mainly of analysts and advisers. Although many of the top White House staffers are given the title "special assistant" for a particular task or sector, the types of judgments they are expected to make and the kinds of advice they are supposed to give are a good deal broader and more generally political than that which comes from the Executive Office of the President (see below) or from the cabinet departments. Table 6.4 gives an indication of the size and nature of work in the White House. Table 6.5 shows how much more closely associated the White House staff appointees have been to the president than are most cabinet members and Executive Office staff.

---

[40]A substantial portion of this section is taken from Theodore J. Lowi, *The Personal President* (Ithaca, NY: Cornell University Press, 1985), pp. 141–50.

[41]Ann Reilly Dowd, "How Bush Manages the Presidency," *Fortune,* 27 August 1990, p. 74.

[42]Elizabeth Drew, "For Clinton, the Clock Is Ticking," *Washington Post National Weekly Edition,* 25–31 January 1993, p. 25.

TABLE 6.4

Size and Specialization in the White House, 1992
The White House Staff

Chief of Staff to the President
Assistant to the President and Deputy Chief of Staff
Assistant to the President and Staff Secretary
Assistant to the President and Secretary of the Cabinet
Assistant to the President and Deputy for National Security Affairs
Counsel to the President
Associate Counsels to the President (5)
Press Secretary
Executive Secretary of the National Security Council
Physician to the President

Assistants to the President (10)

Assistant to the President for Science and Technology
Assistant to the President for Communications
Assistant to the President and Press Secretary
Assistant to the President for Legislative Affairs
Assistant to the President and Director, Office of
National Service

Assistant to the President for Economic and Domestic
Policy
Assistant to the President for National Security Affairs
Assistant to the President for Public Events and
Initiatives
Assistant to the President for Presidential Personnel
Assistant to the President for Media Affairs

Deputy Assistants to the President (19)

Deputy Assistant to the President and Director,
Office of Intergovernmental Affairs
Deputy Assistant to the President for Management
and Director, Office of Administration
Deputy Assistant to the President and Director,
Office of Cabinet Affairs
Deputy Assistant to the President for Legislative
Affairs (House)
Deputy Assistant to the President for Appointments
and Scheduling
Deputy Assistant to the President for Legislative
Affairs (Senate)
Deputy Assistant to the President for Political Affairs
Deputy Assistant to the President and Deputy
Director of Presidential Personnel

Deputy Assistant to the President for Public Liaison (2)
Deputy Assistant to the President for Policy Planning
Deputy Assistant to the President and Deputy Press
Secretary
Deputy Assistant to the President
Deputy Assistant to the President and Executive
Assistant to the Chief of Staff
Deputy Assistant to the President for Domestic Policy
Deputy Assistant to the President and Chief of Staff
to the First Lady
Deputy Counsel to the President
Deputy Assistant to the President for Cabinet Liaison
Deputy Assistant to the President for Communications
and Director of Speechwriting
Deputy Assistant to the President and Director of
White House Operations

Special Assistants to the President (42)

Special Assistant to the President for Communications
Special Assistant to the President for Legislative
Affairs (House) (2)
Special Assistant to the President for National Security
Affairs (9)
Special Assistant to the President for
Intergovernmental Affairs (3)
Special Assistant to the President and Director,
Office of Political Affairs
Special Assistant to the President for Political Affairs
Special Assistant to the President for Policy
Development (4)
Special Assistant to the President and Associate
Director of Presidential Personnel (4)
Special Assistant to the President for Presidential Press
Advance
Special Assistant to the President and Assistant Staff
Secretary
Special Assistant to the President and Deputy Press
Secretary (2)
Special Assistant to the President and Senior Director
for European And Soviet Affairs

Special Assistant to the President and Executive
Secretary for Cabinet Liaison
Special Assistant to the President for Presidential
Messages and Correspondence
Special Assistant to the President and Deputy Director,
Office of Administration
Special Assistant to the President and Executive
Secretary, Economic Policy Counsel
Military Assistant to the President and Director,
White House Military Office
Special Assistant to the President for Legislative Affairs
(Senate) (1)
Special Assistant to the President for Public Liaison
Special Assistant to the President and Director of
Presidential Advance
Special Assistant to the President for Legislative
Affairs (3)
Special Assistant to the President and Executive
Secretary, Domestic Policy Council

Source: *U.S. Government Manual, 1991–1992* (Washington, DC: Government Printing Office, 1991), pp. 89–92.

TABLE 6.5

**Appointees Who Had a Close Association with the President,
Prior to Selection (1961–1992)**

Appointees in	All	Democrats	Republicans
Inner Cabinet* (State, Defense, Treasury, Attorney General)	33%	20%	39%
Outer Cabinet (all other cabinet posts)	20%	9%	26%
Executive Office of the President (EOP)	38%	50%	31%
White House Staff	62%	86%	49%

*This generally refers to the top four cabinet posts that legally comprise the National Security Council (see Table 6.3).

Source: James W. Riddlesperger and James D. King, "Presidential Appointments to the Cabinet, Executive Office, and White House Staff," *Presidential Studies Quarterly* 16, no. 4 (1986), pp. 696–97. Courtesy of the Center for the Study of the Presidency. This is a new table extending the data from 1985 to 1992, provided courtesy of the authors. Our thanks to Professors Riddlesperger and King.

From an informal group of fewer than a dozen people (popularly called the "Kitchen Cabinet"), and no more than four dozen at the height of the domestic Roosevelt presidency in 1937, the White House staff has grown substantially with each successive president (see Table 6.6).[43] Richard Nixon employed 550 staffers in 1972. President Carter, who found so many of the requirements of presidential power distasteful, and who publicly vowed to keep his staff small and decentralized, built an even larger and more centralized staff. President Clinton promised during the campaign to reduce the White House staff by 25 percent and announced in February 1993 that he was proceeding to carry out his promise. It is highly probable, however, that the staff will eventually expand back to earlier levels, because a large White House staff has become essential.

The biggest variation among presidential management practices lies not in the size of the White House staff but in its organization. President Reagan went to the extreme in delegating important management powers to his chief of staff, and he elevated his budget director to an unprecedented level of power in *policy* making rather than merely *budget* making. President Bush went to still more staff centralization under his chief of staff, John Sununu. At the same time, President Bush continued to deal directly with his cabinet heads, the press, and key members of Congress. President Clinton showed a definite preference for competition among equals in the cabinet and among senior White House officials, obviously liking the competition and conflict among staff members, for which FDR was also famous.

[43]All the figures since 1967, and probably 1957, are understated, because additional White House staff members were on detached service from the military and other departments (some secretly assigned) and are not counted here because they were not on the White House payroll.

TABLE 6.6
The Expanding White House Staff

Year	President	Full-time employees*
1937	Franklin D. Roosevelt	45
1947	Harry S. Truman	190
1957	Dwight D. Eisenhower	364
1967	Lyndon B. Johnson	251
1972	Richard M. Nixon	550
1975	Gerald R. Ford	533
1980	Jimmy Carter	488
1984	Ronald Reagan	575
1992	George Bush	605**
1993	Bill Clinton	543**

*The vice-president employs over 20 staffers, and there are at least 100 on the staff of the National Security Council. These work in and around the White House and Executive Office but are not included in the above totals.

**These figures are made up of the staffs of the Office of the President, the Executive Residence, and the Office of the Vice President. None of the figures include the employees temporarily detailed to the White House from outside agencies (approximately 50 to 75 in 1992 and 1993). While not precisely comparable, these figures convey a sense of scale.

Source: Thomas E. Cronin, "The Swelling of the Presidency: Can Anyone Reverse the Tide?" by Peter Woll, ed., *American Government: Readings and Cases,* 8th ed. (Boston: Little Brown, 1984), p. 347. Copyright © 1984 by Thomas E. Cronin. Reproduced with the permission of the author. Figures for 1992 and 1993 provided by the Office of Management and Budget and the White House.

But rather than making President Carter's mistake "micromanaging" his administration, President Clinton ultimately had to settle on some degree of hierarchy. Politics by pluralism is one thing. Government by pluralism, in the age of the CEO, is quite another matter.

The Executive Office of the President The development of the White House staff can be appreciated only in its relation to the still larger Executive Office of the President (EOP). Created in 1939, the EOP is what is often called the "institutional presidency"—the permanent agencies that perform defined management tasks for the president. The most important and the largest EOP agency is the Office of Management and Budget (OMB). Its roles in preparing the national budget, designing the president's program, reporting on agency activities, and overseeing regulatory proposals make OMB personnel part of virtually every conceivable presidential responsibility. The staff of the Council of Economic Advisers (CEA) constantly analyzes the economy and economic trends and attempts to give the president the ability to anticipate events rather than to wait and react to events. The Council on Environmental Quality (CEQ) was designed to do the same for environmental issues as CEA does for economic issues. The National Security Council (NSC) is composed of designated cabinet officials who meet regularly with the president to advise him on the large national security picture. The staff of

FIGURE 6.2

Executive Office of the President

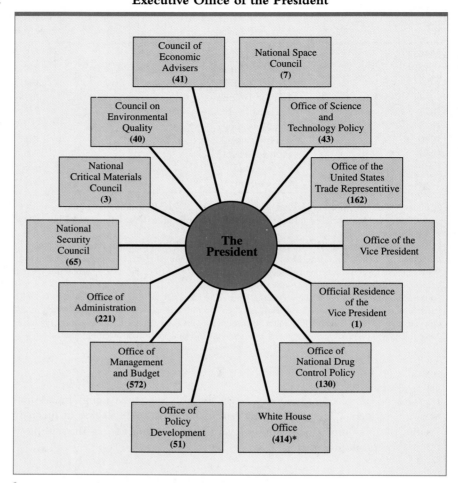

*See Table 6.4 for a full picture of the White House staff.

Source: *The United States Government Manual 1987–1988* (Washington, DC: Government Printing Office, 1987), p. 88. Figures are for 1988; more recent figures are unavailable but not significantly different.

the NSC, headed by the assistant to the president for national security affairs, assimilate and analyze data from all intelligence-gathering agencies (CIA, etc.). Other EOP agencies perform more specialized tasks for the president.

Somewhere between fifteen hundred and two thousand highly specialized people work for EOP agencies.[44] Numbers in parentheses on Figure 6.2 are the

[44]The actual number is difficult to estimate because, as with White House staff, some EOP personnel, especially in national security work, are detached to EOP from outside agencies.

official numbers of employees in each agency. However, these do not include a
substantial but variable number of key specialists detached on assignment to EOP
agencies from outside agencies, especially from the Pentagon to the staff of NSC.
The importance of each agency in EOP varies according to the personal orientations of each president. For example, the NSC staff was of immense importance
under President Nixon, especially because it served essentially as the personal staff
of presidential assistant Henry Kissinger. But it was of less importance to President
Bush, who looked outside the EOP altogether for military policy matters, much
more to the Joint Chiefs of Staff and its chairman, General Colin Powell.

The status and power of one agency within EOP has, however, not varied in
importance but has in fact grown in importance from president to president until,
under President Reagan, the director of OMB (the budget director) was granted
actual cabinet status. Presidents Bush and Clinton continued the practice, but even
if they had not chosen to make the budget director a virtual prime minister, circumstances would have imposed the choice upon them. In 1974, Congress passed
the Budget and Impoundment Act, to impose upon itself a more rational approach
to the budget. Up until 1974, congressional budget decisions were decentralized
(to put it gently), with budget decisions made by the appropriations committees
and subcommittees in the House and Senate, and with revenue decisions made independently by the House Ways and Means Committee and by the Senate Finance
Committee. The primary purpose of the 1974 act was to impose enough discipline on congressional budget decision making to enable Congress as a whole to
confront the presidency more effectively. New budget committees were created to
establish in a single "comprehensive budget resolution" a ceiling for the total of
authorized spending, including spending priorities within that ceiling. That was to
be accomplished by April 15 each year, and by June 15 of each year, Congress was
required to pass a "budget reconciliation bill" that would adjust individual appropriations bills to the ceiling and make some stab at connecting the whole thing to
estimated revenues.

This reconciliation process was not very important until 1981, when President
Reagan and his budget director David Stockman turned it into an opportunity for
presidential power. Reagan and Stockman included in their budget virtually the
entire Reagan program, including increases in defense and massive cuts in most
domestic programs. By using the reconciliation resolution, President Reagan, with
the help of his leaders in Congress, was able to force Congress to consider all the
Reagan proposals in one package rather than in separate bills. The Reagan 1981
success made Democrats more watchful and produced a budget stalemate in 1982.
Although Congress approved the president's version of a reconciliation bill, with
all its cuts in domestic programs and increases in defense expenditures, within two
months Congress passed a series of "supplementary appropriation bills," that broke
the president's hold on them and destroyed the whole principle of deficit control.
This kind of mutual frustration between president and Congress continued, with
deadlines being broken, ceilings being broken, and with government having to
function under "continuing resolutions" that simply extended current spending
into the next fiscal year. All that began to resemble pre-1974 practices.

By 1985, confronting the very deficits and fragmented decision making that the
1974 act and the Reagan presidency had been dedicated to controlling, Congress

PROCESS BOX 6.2

The Budget and Deficit Process Set by Law for 1992–1995

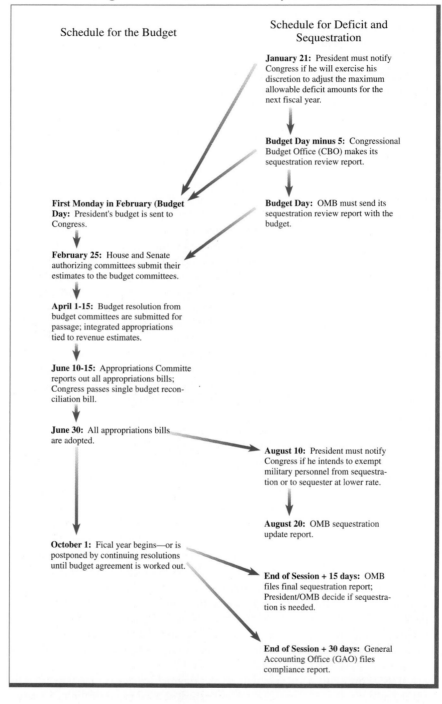

Schedule for the Budget

Schedule for Deficit and Sequestration

January 21: President must notify Congress if he will exercise his discretion to adjust the maximum allowable deficit amounts for the next fiscal year.

Budget Day minus 5: Congressional Budget Office (CBO) makes its sequestration review report.

First Monday in February (Budget Day: President's budget is sent to Congress.

Budget Day: OMB must send its sequestration review report with the budget.

February 25: House and Senate authorizing committees submit their estimates to the budget committees.

April 1-15: Budget resolution from budget committees are submitted for passage; integrated appropriations tied to revenue estimates.

June 10-15: Appropriations Committe reports out all appropriations bills; Congress passes single budget reconciliation bill.

June 30: All appropriations bills are adopted.

August 10: President must notify Congress if he intends to exempt military personnel from sequestration or to sequester at lower rate.

August 20: OMB sequestration update report.

October 1: Fical year begins—or is postponed by continuing resolutions until budget agreement is worked out.

End of Session + 15 days: OMB files final sequestration report; President/OMB decide if sequestration is needed.

End of Session + 30 days: General Accounting Office (GAO) files compliance report.

adopted the Gramm-Rudman-Hollings Act.[45] (Hollings's name is usually dropped
from everyday reference.) This act requires the president and budget director to
meet with congressional leaders and to reach spending and taxing agreements that
are virtually like treaties in their legal weight. Gramm-Rudman required that the
budget be set in such a way that the annual deficits would be reduced year by year
until they were wiped out entirely and a "balanced budget" achieved. If in any
year the deficit goal was not met, an across-the-board spending cut—known as sequestration—had to be imposed, such that the FBI and the IRS were to be cut
equally with the Mining and Mineral Resources Research Institute. (Social Security and some other mandatory programs were exempted.)

Gramm-Rudman requirements boosted still further the role of OMB and its
director because the director was made responsible for keeping all the details in
each and every appropriation bill in line with presidential goals and congressional
understandings. This is why such directors as David Stockman under Reagan and
Richard Darman under Bush earned a reputation not only for power but for genius, since their power rested heavily upon their knowledge of every detail.

In 1986, the Supreme Court ruled Gramm-Rudman's enforcement provisions
unconstitutional, on the grounds that since the General Accounting Office (GAO)
was an agent of Congress, it could not be given the power to make the Gramm-
Rudman cuts and to decide when and how to sequester funds, because these are
executive functions.[46] The 1987 revision of Gramm-Rudman met the constitutional issue created by the Court by transferring responsibility from GAO to
OMB, and it gave OMB still more power by giving the director (for the president)
more discretion regarding the estimates on which the cuts are to be based, more
discretion on the kinds of programs and commitments whose expenditures can be
exempted from the budget calculations, and more discretion about whether to sequester funds at all. The still newer provisions adopted by Congress in 1990 provide that OMB look beyond the overall budget deficit to a bill-by-bill evaluation
of appropriations. According to the semi-official *Congressional Quarterly*, "This had
the effect of involving [OMB] even more directly than it already is in congressional law-making."[47] In effect, these recent actions gutted Gramm-Rudman but
left OMB with far more power than it had before 1987 or in fact before 1974.
Added presidential power? These recent actions come as close as one can get to
"line-item veto" power over the budget without a constitutional amendment
granting the president such power.

This also explains why OMB directors have tended to be cordially hated on
Capitol Hill. Budgeting is no longer "bottom up," with expenditure and program
requests passing from the lowest bureaus through the departments to "clearance"
in OMB and hence to Congress, where each agency could be called in to reveal
what its "original request" had been before OMB got hold of it. The process be-

---

[45]The official title of the Gramm-Rudman-Hollings Act is the Balanced Budget and Emergency
Deficit Control Act of 1985. A good account of the transition from 1981 to the Gramm-Rudman era
will be found in David Price, "The House: A Report from the Field," in *Congress Reconsidered,*
ed. Lawrence Dodd and Bruce Oppenheimer (Washington, DC: Congressional Quarterly Press, 1989),
pp. 413–41.

[46]Bowsher v. Synar, 92 L. Ed. 583 (1986).

[47]*Congressional Quarterly Weekly Report,* 1 December 1990, p. 4034.

came one of "top down," with OMB setting the terms of discourse for agencies as well as for Congress. Bush and Darman were a particularly powerful budget duo. Bush could make demands on Congress and then threaten to use his veto power, since he had so few commitments to new domestic policies. Darman gave Bush added leverage because he had complete command of the budgetary details and could use these details, particularly warnings about their contribution to greater deficits, to discourage members of Congress from making the kinds of log-rolling agreements that break budgetary ceilings. President Clinton's budget director, Leon Panetta, is comparable in knowledge and clout to Richard Darman. Listed second only to the secretary of the treasury in Clinton's "economic team," a long-term member of the House of Representatives, and chair of the Budget Committee, Panetta was from the start a "master of the arcane budget process."[48] However, President Clinton and Leon Panetta have had a more difficult time from the start, despite Democratic majorities in both House and Senate, because Clinton's program required more statutes and therefore needed more positive congressional cooperation. For Bush, a veto was a kind of success, and "divided government" was virtually an advantage, given his genuine commitment to "smaller government." For President Clinton, a veto would be a sign of failure, and Panetta's details will have to serve a more delicate balance between fighting the deficit and stimulating the economy.

The Vice-Presidency The vice-presidency is a constitutional anomaly even though the office was created along with the presidency by the Constitution. The vice-president exists for two purposes only: to succeed the president in case of a vacancy and to preside over the Senate. First, under the Constitution, if a president dies or resigns or becomes hopelessly disabled, the vice-president becomes president. This provision was clarified and strengthened by the Twenty-Fifth Amendment (1967), which provides that the president (with majority confirmation of both houses of Congress) must appoint someone to fill the office of vice-president if it is vacated. In 1947, Congress had already established a line of succession in case both president and vice-president are unable to serve: the Speaker of the House, the president pro tempore of the Senate, and after them, the secretaries of state, the treasury, defense, and so on down the line. The Twenty-fifth Amendment has been invoked twice. When Vice-President Spiro Agnew resigned in 1973, President Nixon immediately nominated Gerald Ford, who was quickly confirmed as vice-president. When Ford became president, he moved as quickly as possible to fill the vice-presidential vacancy with Nelson Rockefeller.

It is with regard to the second formal purpose that the office of vice-president is a constitutional anomaly. Although they preside over the Senate, providing the tie-breaking vote when necessary,[49] vice-presidents are much more a part of the executive branch. Some vice-presidents, such as Henry Wallace (1940), Spiro Agnew (1968), and Nelson Rockefeller (1974), have actually never served in the Senate at all. Most recent vice-presidents were senators before their election to the

---

[48]Quoted characterization from *New York Times,* 27 December 1992, p. 22.

[49]Article I, Section 3, provides that "The Vice-President . . . shall be President of the Senate, but shall have no Vote, unless they be equally divided." This is the only vote the vice-president is allowed.

vice-presidency: Alben Barkley (1948), Richard Nixon (1952), Lyndon Johnson

(1960), Hubert Humphrey (1964), Walter Mondale (1976), Dan Quayle (1988), and Al Gore (1992). For three of them—Johnson, Humphrey, and Gore—the vice-presidency was a demotion, in that they had been very powerful members of the Senate prior to their election as vice-president.

The main value of the vice-presidency as a political resource for the president is electoral. Traditionally, a presidential candidate's most important rule for the choice of a running mate is that he or she bring the support of at least one state (preferably a large one) not otherwise likely to support the ticket. Another rule holds that the vice-presidential nominee should provide some regional balance and, wherever possible, some balance among various ideological or ethnic subsections of the party. It is very doubtful that John Kennedy would have won in 1960 without his vice-presidential candidate, Lyndon Johnson, and the contribution Johnson made to carrying Texas. It is equally doubtful that Jimmy Carter would have been elected if his running mate had not been someone like Walter Mondale from Minnesota. It was for virtually the same reason that Walter Mondale designated Geraldine Ferraro, a representative from New York, as his running mate. The emphasis however, has recently shifted away from geographical to ideological balance. In 1980, Ronald Reagan probably could have carried Texas without George Bush, a Texan, as his running mate; nonetheless, Reagan selected him because he needed someone like Bush from the moderate mainstream of the party to help unite the party; Bush's second-place finish in the primaries also made him an attractive candidate who would help Reagan reunify the party. In 1988, both presidential candidates went for ideological balance. Democrat Michael Dukakis, a Massachusetts liberal, selected as his running mate Senator Lloyd Bentsen, whose record put him at the conservative, opposite extreme of the party. Since Republican Bush was not fully embraced by the conservative wing of his party, despite his eight years of loyal service to President Reagan, he chose arch-conservative Indiana Senator J. Danforth Quayle as his running mate. Quayle's youth and Midwest location may have helped marginally, but ideological balance was the key to Bush's choice. Bill Clinton combined considerations of region and ideology in his selection of a vice-presidential running mate. The choice of Al Gore signaled that Bill Clinton was solidly on the right wing of the Democratic party and would also remain steadfastly a southerner. Democratic strategists had become convinced that Clinton could not win without carrying a substantial number of southern states.

Presidents have constantly promised to give their vice-presidents more responsibility, but they almost always break their promise, indicating that they are unable to utilize the vice-presidency as a management or political resource after the election. No one can explain exactly why. Perhaps it is just too much trouble to share responsibility. Perhaps the president as head of state feels unable to share any part of that status. Perhaps, like many adult Americans who do not draw up their wills, presidents may simply dread contemplating their own death. But management style is certainly a factor. George Bush, as vice-president, was "kept within the loop" of decision making because President Reagan delegated so much power. A copy of virtually everything made for Reagan was made for Bush, especially during the first term when Bush's close friend James Baker was chief of staff. But, as

Dan Quayle and Al Gore
Is the Vice-Presidency Still the
"Most Insignificant Office"?

The office of vice-president has long been a dead-end, powerless, thankless job. Yet the office has been highly sought after in recent decades, and recent vice-presidents, including Dan Quayle and Al Gore, have played key roles in their administrations.

Indiana native Dan Quayle grew up in a prosperous publishing family that owned a chain of newspapers. After graduating from college and law school, Quayle worked as an associate publisher of the *Huntington Herald-Press,* which stimulated his interest in politics. In 1976, he stunned the experts by winning a seat in Congress against a nine-term incumbent. Four years later, he again surprised doubters by winning a Senate seat. In 1988, Republican presidential nominee George Bush picked the then-unknown senator for his running mate, hoping to strengthen and "balance" his ticket by choosing a young conservative from the Midwest. (Bush claimed Texas as his home state.) Despite some political embarrassments during the campaign, such as revelations that his family connections had helped Quayle gain entrance to law school and avoid military service in Vietnam, the Bush-Quayle ticket defeated Democratic rivals Michael Dukakis and Lloyd Bentsen.

As vice-president, Quayle was a part of Bush's inner decision-making circle, playing an active role in such key issues as America's response to the military revolt in the Philippines and the Persian Gulf War of 1991. A staunch conservative, Quayle also served as a key administration liaison to Christian fundamentalists and other conservative constituencies. He rallied conservative sympathies but outraged other constituencies during the 1992 presidential campaign when he argued that the fictional television character, Murphy Brown, offered a poor role model to Americans when she bore a child out of wedlock. Conservatives hailed the criticism as a just rebuke to those who opposed what they labeled "family values." Liberals responded that Quayle's attack of a fictional character (who had decided against

Dan Quayle

one observer put it, that situation "can hardly be compared with that of the Bush White House, from which a torrent of notes and phone calls to world figures and people around the country routinely goes forth. Keeping Vice-President Quayle in the loop just wouldn't be possible."[50]

[50]John Newhouse, "Profiles," *The New Yorker,* 7 May 1990, p. 70.

the abortion option) revealed the poverty of the Bush administration's commitment to assistance for single mothers.

Al Gore grew up in a political family: his father, Al Gore, Sr., was a three-term senator from Tennessee. Both Gore and his father had opposed the Vietnam War, yet, following his graduation from college, he felt a strong duty to serve his country (he was also concerned about harming his father's reputation if he avoided service). Gore entered the military and served a tour of duty in Vietnam, finishing in 1971. After leaving the service, Gore wrote for a Tennessee newspaper and then entered divinity school.

In 1976, Gore decided almost on impulse to pursue the family business, seeking and winning a Tennessee congressional seat. In 1984, he captured a vacant Senate seat. Gore's first foray into national politics came four years later when he unsuccessfully sought the Democratic presidential nomination. In 1992, Bill Clinton picked Gore as his running mate, hoping to strengthen his ticket with Gore's experience and knowledge of foreign policy and environmental issues. This decision was criticized, not because of questions about Gore's credentials, but because the two were so much alike—young southerners, considered liberal on domestic social policy and conservative on defense. Despite violating the unwritten rule that a running mate should be selected to "balance" the ticket by region or ideology, the two proved to be highly compatible and a strong campaign team.

As vice-president, Gore continued to play an active role in Clinton's inner circle. His expertise on nuclear and military strategy and environmental and family issues placed him in a leadership position in the administration. Like his most recent predecessor, Gore's vice-presidency has been active in both policy formulation and political advocacy.

John Adams once labeled the vice-presidency "the most insignificant office that ever the invention of man contrived." Quayle and Gore may have made this dictum obsolete.

Source: Richard F. Fenno, Jr., *The Making of a Senator: Dan Quayle* (Washington, D.C.: CQ Press, 1989); Al Gore, *Earth in the Balance* (New York: Houghton Mifflin, 1992).

Al Gore

Vice-President Gore shows promise of enjoying relatively enhanced status, considering that President Clinton kept him ostentatiously present at all public appearances during the transition and during the vital public and private efforts to present and campaign for the president's program early in 1993. However, this laying on of hands during the early part of an administration guarantees nothing about the status or power of the office later on.

Elections as a Resource   Although we emphasized earlier that any ordinary citizen, legitimately placed in office, would be a very powerful president, there is no denying that a decisive presidential election translates into a more effective presidency. Some presidents claim that a landslide election gives them a "mandate," by which they mean that the electorate approved the programs offered in the campaign and that Congress ought to therefore go along. And Congress is not unmoved by such an appeal. The Johnson and Reagan landslides of 1964 and 1980 gave them real strength during their honeymoon year. In contrast, the close elections of Kennedy in 1960, Nixon in 1968, and Carter in 1976 seriously hampered their effectiveness. Although Bush was elected decisively in 1988, he had no legislative commitments that would have profited from any claim to an electoral mandate.

President Clinton, an action-oriented president, was nevertheless seriously hampered by having been elected by a minority of the popular vote, a mere 43 percent. He was further burdened by the 19.7 million (19 percent) votes cast for Ross Perot, in fact, so much so that he adopted a substantial portion of Perot's program. At the height of his effort to get his budget package through Congress, President Clinton said publicly, in exasperation, that he was "interested [in] why my economic program, which is 85 percent what Ross Perot recommended in the campaign . . . hasn't been endorsed since it is almost identical to the one he ran on."[51] President Clinton obviously had felt that it was necessary to build as much as possible on the Perot constituency, even if it meant some adulteration of his own program. In the days following announcement of his dramatic program on February 7, 1993, President Clinton, along with Vice-President Gore and most of the members of his cabinet, traveled around the country to build the base of public support that had not been captured adequately in the November 1992 election.

Initiative as a Presidential Resource   "To initiate" means to originate, and in government that can mean power. The framers of the Constitution clearly saw this as one of the keys to executive power. The president as an individual is able to initiate decisive action, while Congress as a relatively large assembly must deliberate and debate before it can act. Initiative also means ability to formulate proposals for important policies. There is power in this too.

Over the years, Congress has sometimes deliberately and sometimes inadvertently enhanced the president's power to seize the initiative. Curiously, the most important congressional gift to the president seems the most mundane, namely, the Office of Management and Budget, known until 1974 as the Bureau of the Budget.

In 1921, Congress provided for an "executive budget," and turned over to a new Bureau of the Budget in the executive branch the responsibility for maintaining the nation's accounts. In 1939, this bureau was moved from the Treasury De-

---

[51]Quoted in Ann Devroy, "Clinton Reciprocates Perot's Criticism—The President Questions Why Texan Has Not Endorsed Plan," *Washington Post,* 2 April 1993, p. A7.

partment to the newly created Executive Office of the President. The purpose of
this move was to permit the president to make use of the budgeting process as a management tool. Through the new budgeting process, the president could keep better track of what was going on among all of the executive branch's hundreds of agencies and hundreds of thousands of civil servants. In this respect, the budget is simply a good investigative and informational tool for management. But in addition to that, Congress provided for a process called *legislative clearance,* defined as the power given to the president to require all agencies of the executive branch to submit to him through the budget director all requests for new legislation along with estimates of their budgetary needs. Thus, heads of agencies must submit budget requests to the White House so that the requests of all the competing agencies can be balanced. Although there are many violations of this rule, it is usually observed.

At first, legislative clearance was a defensive weapon, used mainly to allow the president to avoid the embarrassment of having to oppose or veto legislation originating in his own administration. But eventually, legislative clearance became far more important. It became the starting point for the development of comprehensive presidential programs.[52] As noted earlier, recent presidents have also used the budget process as a method of gaining tighter "top down" management control.

Presidential proposals fill the congressional agenda and tend to dominate congressional hearings and floor debates, not to speak of the newspapers. Everyone recognizes this, but few appreciate how much of this ability to maintain the initiative is directly and formally attributable to legislative clearance. Through this seemingly routine process, the president is able to review the activities of his administrators, to obtain a comprehensive view of all legislative proposals, and to identify those that are in accord with his own preferences and priorities. This is why the whole process of choice has come to be called "planning the president's program." Professed anti-government Republicans, such as Reagan and Bush, as well as allegedly pro-government Democrats, such as Clinton, are alike in their commitment to central management, control, and program planning. This is precisely why all three presidents have given the budget director cabinet status.

Presidential Use of the Media Although a more adequate treatment will have to await our chapter on the media (see Chapter 13), let it be said here that the president is able to take full advantage of his access to the communications media mainly because of the legal and constitutional bases of initiative. In the media, reporting on what is new sells newspapers. The president has at his command the thousands of policy proposals that come up to him through the administrative agencies; he can feed these to the media as being newsworthy initiatives. Consequently, virtually all newspapers and television networks habitually look to the White House as the chief source of news about public policy. They tend to assign one of their most important and skillful reporters to the White House "beat." And

[52]Although dated in some respects, the best description and evaluation of budgeting as a management tool and as a tool of program planning is still found in Richard E. Neustadt's two classic articles, "Presidency and Legislation: Planning the President's Program," and "Presidency and Legislation: The Growth of Central Clearance," in *American Political Science Review,* September 1954 and December 1955.

since news is money, they need the president as much as he needs them in order to meet their mutual need to make news. Presidents have successfully gotten from Congress significant additions to their staff to take care of press releases and other forms of communications. In this manner, the formal and the informal aspects of initiative tend to reinforce each other: The president's formal resources put him at the center of policy formulation; this becomes the center of gravity for all buyers and sellers of news, which in turn requires the president to provide easy access to this news. Members of Congress, especially senators, are key sources of news. But Congress is an anarchy of sources. The White House has more control of what and when. That's what initiative is all about.

Presidential personalities make a difference in how these informal factors are used. For example, different presidents use the media in quite different ways. The press conference as an institution probably got its start in the 1930s, when Franklin Roosevelt gave several a month. But his press conferences were not recorded or broadcast "live"; direct quotes were not permitted. The model we know today got its start with Eisenhower and was put into final form by Kennedy. Since 1961, the presidential press conference has been a distinctive institution, available to every president when he wants to dominate the news. Between 300 and 400 certified reporters attend and file their accounts within minutes of the concluding words, "Thank you, Mr. President." But despite the importance of the press conference, its value to each president has varied. Although the average from Kennedy through Carter was about two press conferences a month, Johnson dropped virtually out of sight for almost half of 1965 when Vietnam was warming up, and so did Nixon for over five months in 1973 during the Watergate hearings. Moreover, Johnson and Ford preferred to call impromptu press conferences with only a few minutes' notice. President Reagan single-handedly brought the average down by holding only seven press conferences during his entire first year in office and only sporadically thereafter. In great contrast, President Bush held more conferences during his first seventeen months than Reagan held in eight years. Moreover, Bush shifted them from elaborate prime-time affairs in the ornate East Room to less formal gatherings in the White House briefing room. Fewer reporters and more time for follow-up questions permitted media representatives to "concentrate on information for their stories, rather than getting attention for themselves."[53] President Clinton has tended to take both Reagan and Bush approaches, combining Reagan's high profile—elaborate press conferences and prime-time broadcasts—with the more personal one-on-one approach generally preferred by Bush. But, thanks to Ross Perot, there is now a third approach, for which President Clinton has shown a certain amount of aptitude—the informal and basically nonpolitical talk shows, such as that of Larry King, Arsenio Hall, MTV, and Oprah Winfrey. Low-key, laid back, no time pressure, no concerted message. Just the personal touch.

Of course, in addition to the presidential press conference there are other routes from the White House to news prominence.[54] For example, President Nixon pre-

[53]David Broder, "Some Newsworthy Presidential CPR," *Washington Post National Weekly Edition,* 4–10 June 1990, p. 4.

[54]See George Edwards III, *At the Margins—Presidential Leadership of Congress* (New Haven, CT: Yale University Press, 1989), Chapter 7; and Robert Locander, "The President and the News Media," in *Dimensions of the Modern Presidency,* ed. Edward Kearney (St. Louis: Forum Press, 1981), pp. 49–52.

ferred direct television addresses, and President Carter tried to make the initiatives
more homey with a television adaptation of President Roosevelt's "fireside chats."
President Reagan made unusually good use of prime-time television addresses and
his more informal but regular Saturday afternoon radio broadcasts.

Party as a Presidential Resource Although on the decline, the president's party is far from insignificant as a political resource for him (see Chapter 11). Figure 6.3 dramatically demonstrates the point. Figure 6.3 gives a thirty-six-year history of the "presidential batting average" in Congress—the percentage of winning roll-call votes in Congress on bills publicly supported by the president. Note, for example, that President Eisenhower's "batting average" started out with a very impressive .900 but declined to .700 by the end of his first term and to little more than half his starting point by the end of his administration. The single most important explanation of this decline was President Eisenhower's loss of a Republican party majority in Congress after 1954, the recapture of some seats in 1956, although short of majority, and then a significant loss of seats to the Democrats after the election of 1958.

The presidential batting average went back up and stayed consistently higher through the Kennedy and Johnson years, mainly because these two presidents enjoyed Democratic party majorities in the Senate and in the House. Even so, Johnson's batting average in the House dropped significantly during his last two years, following a very large loss of Democratic seats in the 1966 election. Note how much higher Carter's success rate was than that of Ford or of Nixon during his last

FIGURE 6.3

The Presidential Batting Average: Presidential Success on Congressional Votes[*] (1953–1992)

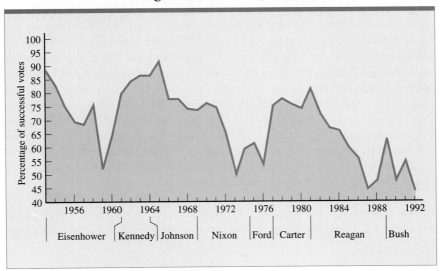

[*]Percentages based on votes on which presidents took a position.
Source: *Congressional Quarterly Weekly Report,* 19 December 1992, p. 3842.

two years in office. Note also the significant decline in President Reagan's batting average, which reached a low point in 1987–88. President Bush fared a bit better than Reagan during his honeymoon year of 1989 but was otherwise less successful than Reagan during his four years.

These low batting averages for Republican presidents are clearly attributable to *the political party as a presidential resource.* Democrats support Democratic presidents and Republicans support Republican presidents. Since Democrats have held the majority in the House of Representatives for all but the 1952–54 Congress and in the Senate except for 1952–54 and 1980–86, it is to be expected that the averages for Democratic presidents would be higher than they would be for Republican presidents. As Figure 6.3 shows clearly, the political party is the key factor.

At the same time, party has its limitations as a resource. The more unified the president's party is behind his legislative requests, the more unified the opposition party is also likely to be. Unless the president's party majority is very large, he must also appeal to the opposition to make up for the inevitable defectors within the ranks of his own party. Consequently, the president often poses as being above partisanship in order to win "bipartisan" support in Congress. But to the extent he pursues a bipartisan strategy, he cannot throw himself fully into building the party loyalty and party discipline that would maximize the value of his own party's support in Congress. This is a dilemma for every president, especially Republicans because they have been the consistent minority in Congress, and a Republican president has to draw in Democratic votes to get a majority. For example, during his first two years, President Reagan depended so heavily upon the votes of conservative Democrats in Congress, especially the southern Democrats, called "boll weevils," to get his first budget and tax cuts adopted, that he neglected campaigning for Republican congressional candidates in 1984, when there was an outside chance to elect a Republican majority in the House. Robert Michel (R-Ill.), House minority leader, responded in frustration after the election, "He [Reagan] never really, in my opinion, joined the issue of what it really means to have the numbers in the House. . . . Here the son-of-a-buck ended up with 59 percent [for himself] and you bring in [a mere] 15 seats." Although President Clinton has enjoyed clear Democratic majorities in the House and the Senate, he has had to move carefully because the Republicans are voting so close to 100 percent in opposition that a few Democratic defectors can beat him. Clinton won the Senate vote on the deficit-reduction plan by a margin of 50-to-49, with Vice-President Gore having to cast the tie-breaking vote in late June 1993. He lost on his $16 billion stimulus package because he could not muster four Republican votes to break a Republican filibuster in the Senate. And he lost on the renewal of the Hyde Amendment (forbidding Medicaid reimbursement for abortions) because many House Democrats joined the Republicans to pass it.

Groups as a Presidential Resource   The classic case in modern times of groups as a resource for the presidency is the Roosevelt or New Deal coalition.[55] The New

---

[55]A wider range of group phenomena will be covered in Chapter 12. In that chapter the focus is on the influence of groups *upon* the government and its policy-making processes. Here our concern is more with the relationship of groups to the presidency and the extent to which groups and coalitions of groups become a dependable resource for presidential government.

Deal coalition was composed of an inconsistent, indeed contradictory, set of interests. Some of these interests were not organized interest groups, but were regional
interests, such as southern whites, or residents of large cities in the industrial
Northeast and Midwest, or blacks who later succeeded in organizing as an interest
group. In addition to these sectional interests that were drawn to the New Deal,
there were several large, self-consciously organized interest groups. The most important in the New Deal coalition were organized labor, agriculture, and the
financial community.[56] All of the parts were held together by a judicious use of patronage—not merely patronage in jobs but patronage in policies. Many of the
groups virtually were permitted to write their own legislation. In exchange, the
groups supported President Roosevelt and his successors in their battles with opposing politicians.

Republican presidents have had their group coalition base also. The most important segments of organized business have tended to support Republican presidents. They have most often been joined by upper-income groups, as well as by
some ethnic groups. In recent years, Republican presidents have expanded their
interest coalition base. President Reagan, for example, won the support of traditionally Democratic southern white and northern blue-collar voters. This expanded base of support served him well in his struggles with Congress. When the
Reagan/Republican coalition began to loosen toward the end of the Bush administration, the astute Bill Clinton was quick to sense it. His 1992 campaign succeeded in part because he brought back together many of the original interests that
had made up the New Deal coalition. But he attempted to go even beyond those
interests by holding an unprecedented "economic summit" in Little Rock,
Arkansas, less than a month after his election. It was a very public meeting of some
three hundred bankers, corporate executives, interest-group representatives,
prominent economists, and a sprinkling of average citizens—with Clinton himself
presiding for almost the entire forty-eight hours of speech-making and serious
discussion. It was indeed an extraordinary effort to expand the president's coalition base.

Mass Popularity as a Resource (and a Liability)   As presidential government
grew, a presidency developed whose power is linked directly to the people.[57] We
call it the "plebiscitary" presidency—drawing from the practice of some Roman
rulers to present themselves to the Roman public—the plebs—for expression of
approval and affection.

Even with the help of all other formal and informal resources, successful presidents have to be able to mobilize mass opinion in their favor in order to keep

[56]For a more detailed review of the New Deal coalition in comparison with later coalitions, see
Thomas Ferguson and Joel Rogers, *Right Turn: The Decline of the Democrats and the Future of American
Politics* (New York: Hill & Wang, 1986), Chapter 2. For updates on the group basis of presidential pol-
itics, see Thomas Ferguson, "Money and Politics," in *Handbooks to the Modern World—the United States,*
vol. 2, ed. Godfrey Hodgson (New York: Facts on File, 1992), pp. 1060–84; and Lucius J. Barker, ed.,
"Black Electoral Politics," *National Political Science Review,* vol. 2, (New Brunswick, NJ: Transaction
Publishers, 1990).

[57]For a book-length treatment of this shift, see Lowi, *The Personal President.* For an analysis of the character of mass democracy, see Benjamin Ginsberg, *The Captive Public* (New York: Basic Books, 1986).

FIGURE 6.4

Presidential Performance Ratings from Truman to Reagan
Nationwide responses to the question: "Do you approve of the way
the president is handling his job?"*

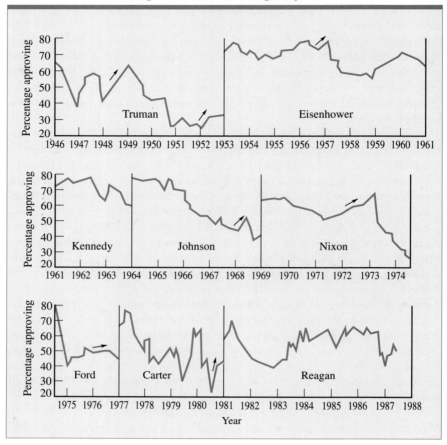

*Note: Arrows indicate pre-election upswings.

Source: Data from the Gallup Poll and the Harris Survey through regular press releases. Courtesy of the Gallup Organization and Louis Harris & Associates.

Congress in line. But as we shall see, each president tends to *use up* his mass resources as he *uses* them. Virtually everyone is aware that presidents are constantly making appeals to the public over the heads of Congress and the Washington community. But the mass public does *not* turn out to be made up of fools. The American people react to presidential *actions* rather than mere speeches or other image-making devices.

The public's sensitivity to presidential actions can be seen in the tendency of all presidents *to lose popular support*. Despite the twists and turns shown on Figure 6.4, the percentage of positive responses to "Do you approve of the way the president is handling his job?" starts out at a level significantly higher than the percentage of votes the president got in the previous national election and then declines throughout his administration. Though the shape of the line differs, the destination is the same.

This general downward tendency is to be expected if American voters are rational, inasmuch as almost any action taken by the president can be divisive, with some voters approving and other voters disapproving. Take, for example, the enormous drop in President Ford's initially high approval rating in 1974 following his decision to pardon President Nixon. President Carter took a similar beating in April 1979, despite his already low ratings, after gas rationing was imposed throughout the country. President Reagan's approval history shows one of the biggest drops in the history of approval rating questions (15 percentage points) following revelation late in 1986 that his national security staff had been involved in selling arms to Iran. President Bush took similar losses in several instances, especially in 1990 following his breach of promise on "no new taxes." And President Clinton's ratings dropped from an initial 57 percent to 49 percent in April 1993, largely in response to his domestic package of tax increases and spending cuts.[58]

The general downward tendency in approval ratings is interrupted from time to time by upward "blips." Table 6.7 puts these blips under the microscope, revealing that although Americans respond negatively to most *domestic* issues, they consistently respond positively to *international actions or events associated with the president*. Analysts call this reaction the "rallying effect."

This rallying effect explains why President Reagan's approval ratings between 1983 and 1986 moved upward when the experience of his predecessors would have led us to expect it to be downward. (See Figure 6.4.) This was largely in response to a series of international events beginning in September 1983 when the Soviets shot down a South Korean airliner, 2,000 marines were sent to Lebanon, a terrorist attack killed 230 of those marines, and Grenada was successfully invaded. President Reagan's performance began to drop toward the end of 1986, when serious arms reduction negotiations reduced his ability to "go it alone" and to choose international events at will to associate with.

Figure 6.5 demonstrates in more detail the same pattern with President Bush. No president had ever enjoyed such consistently high ratings so far into his term. But note the remarkable sequence of international events, as shown by the annotations on Figure 6.5. Each of these is what the late Republican party chairman Lee Atwater called a "political jackpot." But, having reached an historic high of 91 percent in January 1991 Bush's ratings plunged to among the lowest for any president in recent history.

Why? Surely the persistent recession hurt him, but economists disagreed on just how grave the recession was; and some were asserting in 1993 that the recession was already over in 1991, well before the 1992 presidential campaign ever began. Ross Perot's candidacy could well have hurt President Bush. But here again, many analysts argued in 1992 and continued to argue in 1993 that Perot took away votes about equally from both candidates, not from Bush alone. What is most striking

---

[58]For data on the regularity of the loss of presidential support following domestic policy actions, see Theodore J. Lowi, *Incomplete Conquest: Governing America,* 2nd ed. (New York: Holt, Rinehart and Winston, 1981), pp. 310–17; and Raymond Tatalovich and Byron W. Daynes, *Presidential Power in the United States* (Monterey, CA: Brooks/Cole Publishing Co., 1984), pp. 102–106.

TABLE 6.7

The President in the Eyes of the Public—A History of International Events and Popular Reaction

Nature of Presidential Action at Issue	Percent of Sample Group Who Approved of Presidential Actions	
	Before the Action	After the Action
Nixon announces Vietnam withdrawal plan	October 1969 53%	November 1969 68%
Nixon's trip to China	December 1971 49%	February 1972 56%
Vietnam Peace Agreement	December 1972 53%	January 1973 67%
Mayaguez incident	May 1975 40%	June 1975 51%
Camp David Summit on the Middle East	September 1978 42%	September 1978 56%
American hostage crisis in Iran/Iranian assets frozen	November 1979 32%	December 1979 61%
Hostage rescue attempt	April 1980 39%	April 1980 43%
Korean airliner shot down by Soviets	September 1983 45%	September 1983 55%
Terrorist attack on U.S. Marine barracks, killing 230/Successful invasion of Grenada	October 1983 48%	November 1983 56%
TWA airliner hijacked by Shiites	June 1985 63%	July 1985 63%
U.S. bombs Libya	March 1986 63%	April 1986 69%
Tiananmen Square demonstrations	April 1989 60%	June 1989 74%
Authorization for use of armed forces against Iraq/Beginning of war	October 1990 57%	January 1991 91%
Cruise missile attack on Iraq intelligence headquarters	June 1993 39%	June 1993 50%

Source: Courtesy of Roper Opinion Research Center, Storrs, CT. A more detailed examination of 1989–1992 will be found on Figure 6.5.

about the period of Bush's decline in 1991 and 1992 is the absence of *international events associated with the president* after the Gulf War. President Bush had a reputation for dealing face-to-face with heads of state throughout the world, using personal diplomacy to very good affect in putting together the U.N.-sponsored coalition in the Gulf War. But it is quite probable that the success of Bush's personal diplomacy contributed to his political undoing in the last eighteen months of his presidency. He was unable, in brief, to give himself a "foreign policy fix."

Reference to a "foreign policy fix" does not reflect well on the presidency of

FIGURE 6.5
A Profile of Bush's Presidential Popularity, 1989–1992
Nationwide responses to the question: "Do you approve of the job George Bush is doing as president?"

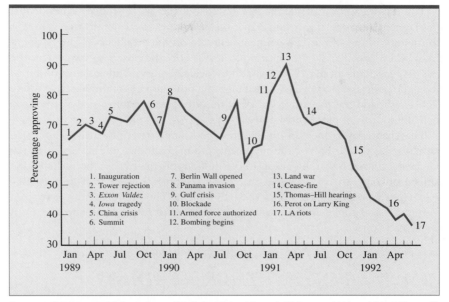

Source: NBC News/Wall Street Journal Poll, in *National Journal,* 19 January 1991, p. 184; Gallup polls, various years.

the United States, nor does the reference by Atwater to the military invasion of Panama as a "political jackpot," or of White House Chief of Staff John Sununu to the Persian Gulf War as a "political goldmine." Americans may indeed be rational when they rally to the president in response to a foreign policy event. But it is not a healthy situation in a democracy for a president to have to decide *between* popularity and diplomacy.

We will return to the president at the end of Chapter 7, where we will be confronting the 5 million employees in the U.S. federal service, "the bureaucracy." All the president's resources, including the rallying effect, have to be summoned to achieve a minimum of bureaucratic accountability. But even with the help of Congress, presidential power is rarely enough. The story continues.

SUMMARY

The foundations for presidential government were laid in the Constitution by providing for a unitary executive who is head of state as well as head of government. The first section of the chapter reviewed the powers of each: The head of state with its military, judicial, and diplomatic powers, the head of government with its executive, military, and legislative powers. But this section noted that the presidency was subordinated to congressional government during the nineteenth century and part of the twentieth, when the national government was small for domestic functions and inactive or sporadic in foreign affairs.

The second section of the chapter traced out the rise of modern presidential government after the much longer period of congressional dominance. There is no mystery in the shift to government centered on the presidency. Congress built the modern presidency by delegating to it not only the power to implement the vast new programs of the 1930s but also by delegating its own legislative power to make the policies themselves. The cabinet, the other top appointments, the White House staff, and the Executive Office of the President are some of the impressive formal resources of presidential power.

The chapter then focused on the president's impressive informal resources, in particular his political party, the supportive group coalitions, and his access to the media and, through that, his access to the millions of Americans who make up the general public. But it was noted that these resources are not cost-free or risk-free. The chapter concluded on a special problem: The president's direct relation with the mass public is his most potent modern resource, but also the most problematic one.

FOR FURTHER READING

Barber, James David. *The Presidential Character.* Englewood Cliffs, NJ: Prentice-Hall, 1985.

Corwin, Edward S. *The President: Office and Powers.* New York: New York University Press, 1957.

Greenstein, Fred I. *The Hidden-Hand Presidency: Eisenhower as Leader.* New York: Basic Books, 1982.

Grover, William F. *The President as Prisoner—A Structural Criticism of the Carter and Reagan Years.* Albany, NY: SUNY Press, 1989.

Heard, Alexander, with Scarlett Graham and Kay L. Hancock. *Made in America—Improving the Nomination and Election of Presidents.* New York: HarperCollins, 1991.

Hinckley, Barbara and Paul Brace. *Follow the Leader: Opinion Polls and Modern Presidents.* New York: Basic Books, 1992.

Kearns, Doris. *Lyndon Johnson and the American Dream.* New York: Harper & Row, 1965.

Kernell, Samuel. *Going Public: New Strategies of Presidential Leadership.* Washington, DC: Congressional Quarterly Press, 1986.

Lowi, Theodore J. *The Personal President: Power Invested, Promise Unfulfilled.* Ithaca, NY: Cornell University Press, 1985.

McKay, David. *Domestic Policy and Ideology: Presidents and the American State, 1964–1987.* New York: Cambridge University Press, 1989.

Mann, Thomas E., ed. *A Question of Balance: The President, Congress, and Foreign Policy.* Washington, D.C.: Brookings Institution, 1991.

Nelson, Michael, ed. *The Presidency and the Political System.* 3rd ed. Washington, DC: Congressional Quarterly Press, 1990.

Neustadt, Richard E. *Presidential Power: The Politics of Leadership from Roosevelt to Reagan,* rev. ed. New York: The Free Press, 1990.

Pfiffner, James P., ed. *The Managerial Presidency.* Pacific Grove, CA: Brooks/Cole Publishing, 1991.

Polsby, Nelson and Aaron Wildavsky. *Presidential Elections: Contemporary Strategies of American Electoral Politics.* 8th ed. New York: Free Press, 1991.

Rockman, Bert A. *The Leadership Question: The Presidency and the American System.* New York: Praeger, 1984.

Spitzer, Robert. *The Presidential Veto: Touchstone of the American Presidency.* Albany, NY: State University of New York Press, 1988.

Tulis, Jeffrey. *The Rhetorical Presidency.* Princeton: Princeton University Press, 1987.

Watson, Richard A., and Norman Thomas. *The Politics of the Presidency.* Washington, DC: Congressional Quarterly Press, 1988.

Willner, Ann Ruth. *The Spellbinders: Charismatic Political Leadership.* New Haven: Yale University Press, 1984.

7

The Executive Branch: Bureaucracy in a Democracy

EVENTS		INSTITUTIONAL DEVELOPMENTS
Washington appoints Jefferson (state), Knox (war), Hamilton (treasury) to the first cabinet (1789)	**1789**	Congress creates first executive departments (state, war, treasury) (1789)
Jackson elected president; "rule of the common man" (1828)		Jackson supports "party rotation in office" and "spoils system" (1829–1836)
President Garfield assassinated by disappointed office seeker; President Arthur allies himself with civil service reformers (1881)	**1880**	Pendleton Act sets up Civil Service Commission and merit system for filling "classified services" jobs (1883)
Conflict between railroads and farmers over freight rates (1880s)		Interstate Commerce Commission (ICC) created to regulate railroads; first independent regulatory commission (1887)
Progressive attack parties and advance civil service reforms (1901–1908)	**1900**	Department of Commerce and Labor created (1903)
World War I (1914–1918)		Federal Reserve Board (1913); Federal Trade Commission (1914)
Postwar labor unrest, race riots, Red Scare (1919–1920)		General Accounting Office and Budget Bureau created; Congress turns over budget to the executive branch (1921)
Teapot Dome scandal (1924)		Classification Act (1923); Corrupt Practices Act (1925)
Franklin Roosevelt and the New Deal (1930s)	**1930**	New Deal "alphabetocracy" created (1930s)
		Administrative Reorganization Act creates Executive Office of the President (EOP) (1939)
World War II begins (1939)		Hatch Act restricts political activity of executive branch employees (1939)
U.S. involvement in World War II (1941–1945)		Veterans preference for civil service jobs (1944)
Red Scare and Cold War (1945 and 1960s)	**1950**	National Security Act creates Department of Defense, National Security Council (NSC), CIA (1947); Truman and Eisenhower loyalty programs (1947–1954)

TIME LINE ON THE BUREAUCRACY

EVENTS		INSTITUTIONAL DEVELOPMENTS
Civil Rights Movement (1950s and 1960s)		Equal Employment Opportunity Commission created (1964)
Growth of government (1962–1974)		New welfare and social regulatory agencies (1965); Department of Housing and Urban Development; Dept. of Transportation (1966)
President Nixon enlarges the managerial presidency (1969–1974)	**1970**	Executive Office reorganized; Office of Management and Budget (OMB)(1970)
Watergate cover-up revealed (1973–1974)		
President Carter attempts to make bureaucracy more accountable (1977–1980)		Civil Service Reform Act (1978); creation of new departments: Energy (1977); Education (1980); Health and Human Services (1980)
President Reagan fires over 10,000 air traffic controllers; centralizes presidential management (1981–1988)		OMB is given power to review all proposed agency rules and regulations (1984)
Reagan and Bush tighten presidential control of all top political appointees (1982–92)	**1990**	Supreme Court declares political patronage unconstitutional except for top political positions (1990)
Clinton decentralizes somewhat by appointing cabinet first and giving them share of subcabinet selection (1993)		Federal civilian employment up from 2.8 million (1982) to 3.1 million (1992)
		Clinton proposes 25 percent cut in executive branch: 100,000 jobs cut plus 14 percent costs cut (1993)

*D*uring his 1980 campaign, Ronald Reagan promised to dismantle the Departments of Energy and Education as part of the "Reagan Revolution" commitment to "get the government off our backs." Reagan claimed that abolishing the Department of Energy (DOE) would not only save $250 million over a three-year period, but would also permit the free market to develop a much better system of energy production and distribution. At the same time, Republicans criticized President Carter for having created the Department of Education (ED) mainly to repay a debt he owed the powerful National Education Association for its political support. After his election, in keeping with his cam-

266

THE EXECUTIVE
BRANCH:
BUREAUCRACY
IN A
DEMOCRACY

paign promises, President Reagan appointed as the new heads of these two departments individuals publicly committed to eventually eliminating their departments and therefore their own jobs.

Even though the Departments of Energy and Education had only been established in 1977 and 1979 respectively, they had powerful allies. Strong support for both agencies developed in Congress, including support from some members who were otherwise favorable to the Reagan program of tax cuts, domestic budget cuts, and defense budget increases. By 1984, President Reagan seemed to have changed his mind, indicating he had "no intention of recommending abolition of the Department of Education at this time." Plans for abolishing the Energy Department and turning over a few of its remaining functions to other departments were relegated to the dead end of "further discussion." President Reagan actually did cut some employees after his inauguration and tried strenuously to continue cutting, but despite his commitment to this, the number of federal employees actually grew by about 18,000 during his first year in office. Although the president continued to denounce "big government," by 1984, President Reagan seemed to give up his efforts to do something about it.[1]

What is this bureaucratic phenomenon that seems to expand despite policies to keep it in check? What is this structure that is the frustration of every president? Why does it seem to have a life of its own despite every presidential effort to make it respond to voters and public opinion? How is it possible for agencies that are composed of highly dependent employees to resist pointed efforts to reorganize or abolish their positions?

In this chapter, we will focus on the federal bureaucracy—the administrative structure that on a day-to-day basis *is* the American government. We will, first, seek to answer these questions by defining and describing bureaucracy as a social and political phenomenon. Second, we will look in detail at American bureaucracy in action by examining our major administrative agencies, their role in the governmental process, and their political behavior. These details of administration are the very heart and soul of modern government and will provoke the question of the third and final section of the chapter: Can bureaucracy and democracy coexist? Can bureaucracy be made accountable to the president and Congress?

THE BUREAUCRATIC PHENOMENON

Despite widespread and consistent complaints about "bureaucracy," most Americans recognize that the maintenance of order in a large society is impossible without a large governmental apparatus of some sort. When we approve of what a

---

[1] A good assessment of Reagan's approach and a comparison with his predecessors will be found in Harold Seidman and Robert Gilmour, *Politics, Position and Power*, 4th ed. (New York: Oxford University Press, 1986), Chapter 6. The best update on the status of the federal service is Patricia Ingraham and Donald Kettl, eds., *Agenda for Excellence—Public Service in America* (Chatham, NJ: Chatham House, 1992).

TABLE 7.1
The Six Primary Characteristics of Bureaucracy

Characteristic	Explanation
Division of labor	Workers are specialized. Each worker develops a skill in a particular job and performs the job routinely and repetitively, thereby increasing productivity.
Allocation of functions	Each task is assigned. Division of labor is of little use unless each worker sticks to the assigned task. No one makes a whole product; each worker depends on the output of other workers.
Allocation of responsibility	Each task becomes a personal responsibility—a contractual obligation. No task can be changed without permission.
Supervision	Some workers are assigned the special task of watching over other workers rather than contributing directly to the creation of the product. Each supervisor watches over a few workers (a situation known as span of control), and communications between workers or between levels move in a prescribed and orderly fashion (known as chain of command).
Purchase of full-time employment	The organization controls all the time the worker is on the job, so each worker can be assigned and held to a task. Some part-time and contracted work is tolerated, but it is held to a minimum.
Identification of career within the organization	Workers come to identify with the organization as a way of life. Seniority, pension rights, and promotions are geared to this relationship.

government agency is doing, we give the phenomenon a positive name, *administration;* when we disapprove of what it is doing, we call the phenomenon *bureaucracy.*[2]

Although the terms "administration" and "bureaucracy" are often used interchangeably, it is useful to distinguish between the two. Administration is the more general of the two terms; it refers to all the ways human beings might rationally coordinate their efforts to achieve a common goal. This applies to private as well as public organizations. **Bureaucracy** refers to the actual offices, tasks, and principles of organization that are employed in the most formal and sustained administration. Table 7.1 defines bureaucracy by identifying its six basic characteristics.

Bureaucratic Organization

The core of bureaucracy is the *division of labor.* The key to bureaucratic effectiveness is coordination of experts performing complex tasks. If each job is specialized

---

[2] The title of this section is drawn from an important sociological work by Michel Crozier, *The Bureaucratic Phenomenon* (Chicago: University of Chicago Press, 1964).

268

THE EXECUTIVE
BRANCH:
BUREAUCRACY
IN A
DEMOCRACY

"Boss" Tweed and George Pendleton
The Spoils System vs. the Merit System

Most federal government employees today earn their jobs through competitive service examinations—that is, applicants must take an examination that tests their merit for a position. Only a handful of top-level appointments are exempted from this system. In the nineteenth century, however, most government employees obtained their jobs through political favoritism, a practice known as the spoils system. The king of the spoils system in the nineteenth century was William Marcy "Boss" Tweed. The demise of the spoils system is traced to George Pendleton.

Tweed's political career began with his service as a volunteer fireman in New York City. Always a shrewd organizer, Tweed used his fire company leadership to acquire greater power by bargaining with the Democratic party machine, Tammany Hall. After winning several local elections, Tweed gradually gained control of Tammany and the vast patronage resources of the city government, including thousands of jobs and millions of dollars in contracts, fees, and other government-controlled benefits.

In 1864, for example, Tweed acquired a printing business, which he then required local companies to use if they wanted business with the city. Insurance companies, construction companies, and the railroads all had to use his printer or lose their lucrative contracts with the city. Even though he had virtually no knowledge of the law, Tweed opened a law firm and required businesses working with the city to pay the firm exorbitant legal fees. Tweed filled local and state elected and appointed offices with his cronies. In 1869, Tammany leaders inflated all expenses charged to the city or county of New York by 50 percent, and the extra money was pocketed by Tweed and other top Tammany leaders (they later increased the overcharging to 85 percent).

Finally, mounting public pressure, fanned by the biting political cartoons of Thomas Nast, resulted in criminal charges against

William Marcy "Boss" Tweed

in order to gain efficiencies, then each worker must depend upon the output of other workers, and that requires careful *allocation* of jobs and resources. Inevitably, bureaucracies become hierarchical, often approximating a pyramid in form. At the base of the organization are workers with the fewest skills and specializations; one supervisor can deal with a relatively large number of these workers. At the next level of the organization, where there are more highly specialized workers, the supervision and coordination of work involves fewer workers per supervisor. Toward the top of the organization, there is a very small number of high-level executives engaging in the "management" of the organization, meaning the organization and

Tweed and his cronies. By some accounts, the Tweed organization had bilked the city and state governments of as much as $200 million.

The federal civil service was not nearly as corrupt as New York's, but public sentiment and the cries of reformers put increasing pressure on Congress to end the federal spoils system. By the 1880s, presidents filled 200,000 federal jobs with political friends and supporters. Writing in 1881, President James Garfield wrote that "my day is frittered away with the personal seeking of people when it ought to be given to the great problems which concern the whole country." Garfield was assassinated that year by a disappointed office seeker.

Leading the call for civil service reform was Ohio senator George Pendleton. He was raised in a prominent Virginia family and ran as the vice presidential candidate for the Democratic party in 1864. In the 1880s Pendleton chaired the Senate committee on civil service. Following Garfield's assassination, he won enactment of his bill, the Civil Service Act of 1883, also known as the Pendleton Act. It established a civil service commission and placed under their control about 14 percent of all federal government jobs. Labeled "classified services," these jobs could only be obtained by competitive examination. Presidents were also given the power to enlarge the base of classified services and, indeed, the next several presidents did.

Pendleton's reward for pushing through the civil service reform was to be denied his party's nomination for a second Senate term in 1884 by Democrats who favored the spoils system. The following year, Pendleton was appointed ambassador to Germany.

The corruption of the spoils system in New York and elsewhere gave reformers the necessary ammunition to change the nature of public service. National reform, in turn, prodded civil service reform in the states. Although many today complain about government run by faceless bureaucrats insulated from politics, the merit system of civil service has professionalized and regularized government service.

Source: Leonard D. White, *The Republican Era* (New York: Free Press, 1958).

George H. Pendleton

reorganization of all the tasks and functions, plus the allocation of the appropriate supplies, and the distribution of the outputs of the organization to the market (if it is a "private sector" organization) or to the public.

The Size of the Federal Service

Americans like to complain about bureaucracy. Americans don't like Big Government because Big Government means Big Bureaucracy, and bureaucracy means *the*

270

THE EXECUTIVE
BRANCH:
BUREAUCRACY
IN A
DEMOCRACY

FIGURE 7.1

**Employees in the Federal Service—
Total Number as a Percentage of the Work Force**

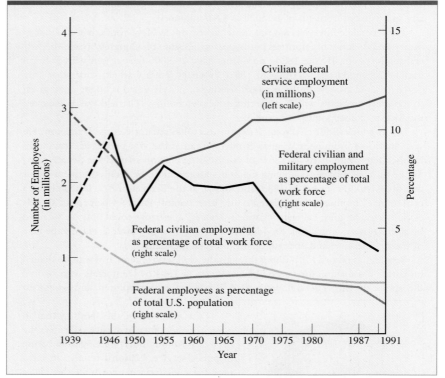

Source: Tax Foundation: *Facts & Figures on Government Finance,* 1990 Edition. Baltimore: Johns Hop-kins University Press, 1990, pp. 22 and 44; and U.S. Office of Personnel Management, *Employment and Trends as of January 1991* (Washington, DC: Government Printing Office, 1991), p. 13. Lines between 1939 and 1946 are broken for the obvious reason that they connect the last pre-war year with the first post-war year, disregarding the temporary ballooning of federal employees, especially military, during the war years.

federal service—almost 3 million civilian and 2.4 million military employees.[3] Promises to cut the bureaucracy are popular campaign appeals; "cutting out the fat" with big reductions in the number of federal employees is held out as a sure-fire way of cutting the deficit. Reducing the size of the bureaucracy was not high on President Bush's agenda, perhaps because he followed Ronald Reagan. But President Clinton pushed it back up again, even though the Democratic party has traditionally been the pro-growth party. Immediately after his inauguration, he cut the personnel in his own executive office by 25 percent. Even though this would

---

[3] This is just under 99 percent of all national government employees. About .7 percent work for the legislative branch and .4 percent work for the federal judiciary. See United States Office of Personnel Management, *Federal Civilian Workforce Statistics:* Employment and Trends as of January 1990 (Washington, DC: Government Printing Office, January 1990), pp. 9-11; also U.S. Bureau of the Census, *Statistical Abstract of the United States, 1989* (Washington, DC: Government Printing Office, 1989).

FIGURE 7.2

271

THE
BUREAUCRATIC
PHENOMENON

Total Federal Outlays and Outlays as a Percentage of GNP

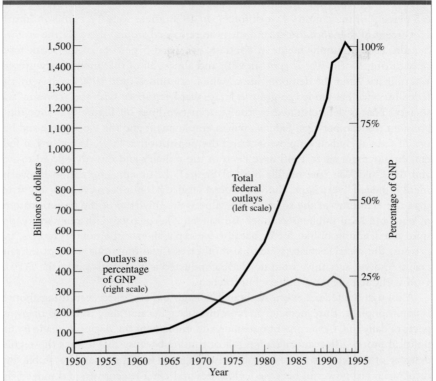

Sources: U.S. Office of Management and Budget, *U.S. Budget in Brief,* Fiscal Year 1981 (Washington, DC: Government Printing Office, 1980), pp. 2 and 14; U.S. Bureau of the Census, *Statistical Abstract of the United States, 1986* (Washington, DC: Government Printing Office, 1986), p. 262; and *The World Almanac, 1987* (New York: Pharos Books, 1987), p. 119.

amount to a savings of only around $10 million per year, it was a gesture of no small importance, accompanied by a genuine commitment to cut military personnel by numbers that could amount to as much as $10 *billion* of savings per year.

Despite fears of bureaucratic growth getting out of hand, however, the federal service has hardly grown at all during the past twenty-five years. As shown on Figure 7.1, the federal service reached its peak postwar level in 1968 with 2.9 million civilian employees plus an additional 3.6 million military personnel (swollen by Vietnam). Since that time the number of civilian federal employees has remained close to that figure. The growth of the federal service is even less imposing when placed in the context of the total work force and when compared to the size of state and local public employment.. Figure 7.1 indicates that since 1950 the ratio of federal service employment to the total work force has been steady and in fact has declined slightly in the past fifteen years. Another useful comparison is to be found in Figure 7.2. Although the dollar increase in federal spending looks very

272

THE EXECUTIVE
BRANCH:
BUREAUCRACY
IN A
DEMOCRACY

impressive, the lower line indicates that even here the national government has simply kept pace with the growth of the economy.

In 1950, there were 4.3 million state and local civil service employees (about 6.5 percent of the country's work force). In 1978, there were 12.7 million (nearly 15 percent of the work force), and the ratio remained around there for the ensuing decade. Federal employment, in contrast, exceeded 5 percent of the work force only during World War II (not shown), and almost all of that momentary growth was military. After the demobilization, which continued until 1950 (as shown), the federal service has tended to grow at a rate that keeps pace with the economy and society. That is demonstrated by the bottom two lines on Figure 7.1, showing a constant relation between federal civilian employment and the work force and between federal civilian employment and the population at large. Variations in federal employment since 1946 have been in the military and directly related to war and the Cold War (the middle line on Figure 7.1). In sum, the national government is indeed "very large," but the federal service has not been growing any faster than the economy or the society. The same is roughly true of the growth pattern of state and local public personnel. Bureaucracy keeps pace with our society, despite our seeming dislike for it, because we can't operate the control towers, the prisons, the social security system, and other essential functions without bureaucracy. And we certainly could not have conducted a successful war in the Persian Gulf without a gigantic military bureaucracy.

Although the federal executive branch is large and complex, everything about it is commonplace. Bureaucracies are commonplace because they touch so many aspects of daily life. Government bureaucracies implement the decisions made by the political process. Bureaucracies are full of routine because that assures the regular delivery of the services and ensures that each agency fulfills its mandate. Public bureaucracies are powerful because legislatures and chief executives, and indeed the people, delegate to them vast power to make sure a particular job is done—enabling the rest of us to be more free to pursue our private ends. And for the same reason, bureaucracies are a threat to freedom, because their size, their momentum, and the interests of the civil servants themselves in keeping their jobs impel bureaucracies and bureaucrats to resist any change of direction.

AGENCIES AND THEIR POLITICS

Although Figure 7.3 is an "organization chart" of the Department of Agriculture, any other department could have been used as an illustration. At the top is the head of the department, who in the United States is called the "secretary" of the department. Below the department head are several top administrators, such as the general council and the judicial officer, whose responsibilities cut across the various departmental functions and provide the secretary with the ability to manage the entire organization. Of equal status are the assistant secretaries, each of whom has management responsibilities for a group of operating agencies, which are arranged vertically below each of the assistant secretaries.

FIGURE 7.3

273

AGENCIES AND
THEIR POLITICS

Organization Chart of the Department of Agriculture

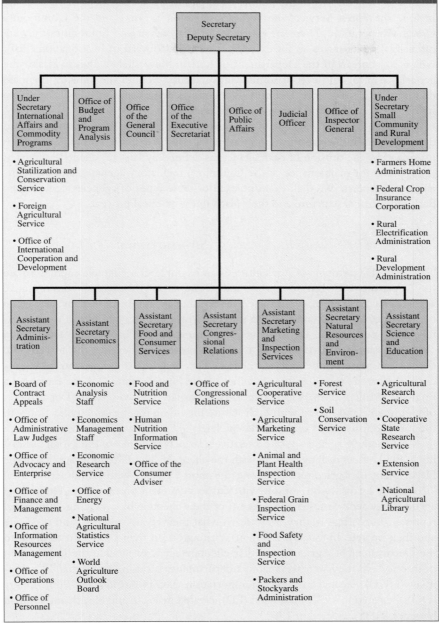

Source: *U.S. Government Manual,* 1992–1993 (Washington, DC: Government Printing Office, 1992), p. 113.

274

THE EXECUTIVE
BRANCH:
BUREAUCRACY
IN A
DEMOCRACY

The third tier, generally called the "bureau level," is the highest level of responsibility for specialized programs. The names of these "bureau-level agencies" are often very well known to the public. Examples in the Department of Agriculture include the Forest Service, the Soil Conservation Service, and the Commodity Credit Corporation. These are examples of "line agencies." Sometimes they are officially called bureaus, as for example the Federal Bureau of Investigation (FBI), which is a bureau in the Department of Justice. Nevertheless, bureau is also the generic term for this level of administrative agency. Within the bureaus, there are divisions, offices, services, and units—sometimes designating agencies of the same status, sometimes designating agencies of lesser status.

There are too many agencies in the executive branch to identify, much less to describe, so a simple classification of agencies will be helpful. This classification is organized by the mission of each agency, as defined by law: (1) clientele agencies, (2) agencies for maintenance of the Union, (3) regulatory agencies, and (4) redistributive agencies. We shall examine each of these types of agencies, focusing on both their formal structure and their place in the political process.

The Clientele Agencies: Structures and Politics

The entire Department of Agriculture is an example of a clientele agency. So are the Departments of Interior, Labor, and Commerce. Although all administrative agencies have clientele, certain agencies are singled out and called by that name because they are directed by law to foster and promote the interests of their clientele. For example, the Departments of Commerce and Labor were founded in 1903 as a single department "to foster, promote, and develop the foreign and domestic commerce, the mining, the manufacturing, the shipping, and fishing industries, and the transportation facilities of the United States."[4] They remained a single department until 1913, when the law created the two separate Departments of Commerce and Labor, with each statute providing for the same obligation—to support and foster their respective clienteles.[5]

Most clientele agencies locate a relatively large proportion of their total personnel in field offices dealing directly with the clientele. The Extension Service of the Department of Agriculture is among the most familiar, with its numerous local "extension agents" who consult with farmers on farm productivity. These same agencies also seek to foster the interests of their clientele by providing "functional representation"; that is, they try to learn what their clients' interests and needs are and then operate almost as a lobby in Washington on their behalf. In addition to the Department of Agriculture, other clientele agencies include the Department of Interior and the five newest cabinet departments: Housing and Urban Development (HUD), created in 1966; Transportation (DOT), created in 1966; Energy (DOE), created in 1977; Education (ED), created in 1980; and Health and Human Services (HHS), created in 1980.

---

[4] 32 Stat. 825; 15 USC 1501.

[5] For a detailed account of the creation of the Department of Commerce and Labor and its split into two separate departments, see Theodore J. Lowi, *The End of Liberalism*, (New York: W. W. Norton, 1979), pp 78–84.

Donna Shalala
"Power Is Fun"

Donna Shalala (b. 1941)

No cabinet official embodied the energy and exuberance of the early Clinton administration more fully than Donna Shalala. Appointed by President Clinton in 1993 to serve as secretary of Health and Human Services (HHS), Shalala faced perhaps the most difficult test of managerial skills of any cabinet member with a department of 125,000 employees and a budget of $540 billion.

Ambitious from an early age, Shalala received her B.A. in urban studies from Western College, served a tour in the Peace Corps, and then went on to earn a master's and doctorate degree in political science from Syracuse University. After brief teaching stints at Baruch College and Columbia University, she was appointed to New York City's Municipal Assistance Corporation in 1975, a body designed to steer the city through its fiscal difficulties. She was both the youngest member of the committee and its only woman. Two years later, she joined the Carter administration as assistant secretary of the Department of Housing and Urban Development. Unprepared for the aggressive bureaucratic infighting typical of national administrative politics, Shalala found her first year on the job to be the toughest of her professional life. "I got chewed up," she said. While at HUD, her key projects included a program to expand home mortgage opportunities to women and funding for shelters for battered women.

Shalala returned to the academic world in 1980, becoming president of Hunter College in New York City. She quickly won attention and praise for her high energy, progressive leadership, and personal involvement in campus affairs. In 1987, she became chancellor of the University of Wisconsin at Madison, a campus of 42,000 students with an annual budget of $1 billion. She acted quickly to stem racial tensions on campus, hire more minority faculty, recruit more ethnic students, and diversify the curriculum. Falling short of some of her goals, Shalala nevertheless won praise for her dynamism.

As HHS secretary, Shalala faced her most daunting administrative challenge. Health care reform, a primary issue pressed by Clinton during the presidential campaign, fell under her responsibility. In addition, she faced major initiatives to improve the Head Start program (providing pre-school education), escalate the battle against AIDS, implement a nation-wide child immunization program, and charter science and technology policy. Another Clinton campaign priority, welfare reform, awaited longer-term action.

Shalala's greatest skill is considered to be her ability to cut through bureaucratic red tape—a skill that is necessary for successful management. Shalala's antidote for bureaucracy? "I learned you have to get a fast start, and you have to have sharp elbows."

Shalala is a woman proud of her accomplishments who has not been reluctant to display her ambition and pride. Some questioned the wisdom of Shalala's appointment to HHS, given her limited background in welfare issues. But she was quick to point out her diverse management experiences, diligent work habits, and academic training. And, as Shalala has often noted, she does not shrink from the exercise of power. "Power is fun," she observed.

Source: Martin Shefter, *Political Crisis/Fiscal Crisis* (New York: Basic Books, 1987).

276

THE EXECUTIVE
BRANCH:
BUREAUCRACY
IN A
DEMOCRACY

Since clientele agencies exist to foster the interests of clients, it is no wonder that clients support the agency when it is in jeopardy of being abolished, reorganized, or cut back. Thus, it is not surprising to learn that client-supported agency resistance finally wore down President Reagan's resolve to abolish the Department of Energy, an entire clientele department. When created by President Carter, the Department of Energy had 18,000 employees and a $10 billion budget. The agencies in the new department were mainly pre-existing agencies drawn from other departments on the theory that agencies with related programs can be better managed within a common department. But each brought its own supportive clientele along. Imagine the resistance to abolition that arose from all the universities and corporations whose research labs depended on a piece of the DOE's multi-billion-dollar energy research budget.

The Department of Education is another case in point. Although President Reagan failed in his effort to abolish the department, as reported earlier, he did manage to cut its budget. For example, the Office of Education, the oldest and most important bureau within ED, was cut by President Reagan from $15 billion in 1981 (Carter's last budget) to $14.1 billion in 1982, and its personnel was cut from 7,364 employees in 1980 to 5,343 employees in 1984. Yet, by 1987, the Office of Education and the entire Department of Education was back up to its pre-Reagan size. Unless a president wants to drop everything else and concentrate alone on this department, its constituency is just too much for a president to handle on a part-time basis. First, the "constituency" of the Department of Education includes the departments of education in all the fifty states, and all the boards and school systems in the thousands of counties and cities; there are also the teacher's colleges, and the major unions of secondary school teachers. One of the most formidable lobbies in the United States is the National Education Association (NEA), and there is a state chapter of NEA in every state in the country. It was their access to Carter that led to the creation of the Department of Education, and it is their continuing support of the department that frustrates efforts to change, much less to abolish it. The department gained an entirely new lease on life with the election of President Clinton. His Secretary of Education, Richard Riley, had been a governor of South Carolina and a close associate of Clinton when he was governor of Arkansas. Riley had gained a reputation as a top governor largely on the basis of his support of school and pre-school programs in South Carolina, and, although he was to the center/right on the matter of linking teacher salary increases with merit, he was clearly a proven pro-growth supporter for the department. His deputy secretary, Madeline Kunin, had also been a state governor, of Vermont, and had been a prominent supporter of Clinton during the presidential campaign. Her ardent support of education programs was a virtual certainty. All of this added up to a mighty impressive base of political support for the department.

These examples and those in Figure 7.4 point to what is known as an *iron triangle,* a pattern of stable relationships between an agency in the executive branch, a congressional committee or subcommittee, and one or more organized groups of agency clientele. Other configurations are of course possible. One of those might be called an iron rectangle or a network because in recent years the federal courts have entered the process, sometimes on the side of clientele groups against the

FIGURE 7.4

277
AGENCIES AND
THEIR POLITICS

Iron Triangles, Complexes, and Networks
These diagrams are classic uses of "iron triangles"; in fact, these are three of the cases observers had in mind when they invented the concept of "iron triangles."

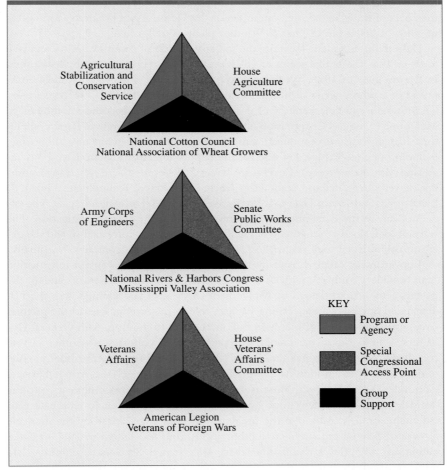

Agricultural Stabilization and Conservation Service — House Agriculture Committee — National Cotton Council / National Association of Wheat Growers

Army Corps of Engineers — Senate Public Works Committee — National Rivers & Harbors Congress / Mississippi Valley Association

Veterans Affairs — House Veterans' Affairs Committee — American Legion / Veterans of Foreign Wars

KEY

Program or Agency

Special Congressional Access Point

Group Support

Source: Adapted from U.S. Congress, House of Representatives, *Report of the Subcommittee for Special Investigations of the Committee on Armed Services,* 86 Congress, 1st session (Washington, DC: Government Printing Office, 1960), p. 7. Reprinted from Theodore J. Lowi, *Incomplete Conquest: Governing America,* 2nd ed. (New York: Holt, Rinehart and Winston, 1981), p. 139.

agency. But even so, the result reinforces the program against drastic change or abolition by a hostile president.[6]

[6] Martin Shapiro, "The Presidency and the Federal Courts," in *Politics and the Oval Office,* ed. Arnold Meltsner (San Francisco: Institute for Contemporary Studies, 1981), Chapter 8; and Hugh Heclo, "Issue Networks and the Executive Establishment," in *The New American Political System,* ed. A. King (Washington, DC: American Enterprise Institute, 1978), Chapter 3.

278

THE EXECUTIVE
BRANCH:
BUREAUCRACY
IN A
DEMOCRACY

Another related concept is the *complex,* as in military-industrial complex, coined by President (and former general) Eisenhower himself in his farewell address in 1961. When he warned against "the acquisition of unwarranted influence, whether sought or unsought, by the military-industrial complex," he had in mind the relationships of mutual support between such major contractors as GE or Pratt & Whitney, the air force officers developing a new fighter plane, and the key members of the Defense Subcommittee of the House Appropriations Committee in whose districts GE or Pratt & Whitney plants were located.[7]

Despite this eloquent warning, the military-industrial complex is alive and well today and on a scale that seems to grow as the Defense Department budget grows. In the summer of 1988, Washington was the scene of a Pentagon scandal comprised of a whole series of iron triangles and networks. In 1987, Melvyn Paisley left his post as assistant secretary of the navy for research to become a consultant to McDonnell Douglas Corporation and several other large private defense contractors. FBI investigation produced more than two hundred grand jury subpoenas, including one for Paisley and one for the deputy director of tactical weapons acquisition for the air force. Warrants for secret FBI searches were issued for a number of very large defense contractors, including United Technologies, Teledyne Electronics, and Litton Data Systems, as well as for McDonnell Douglas. The offices of at least three members of Congress were also part of the investigation. The warrants described a "scheme [for] the illegal disclosure of information and the exertion of influence with respect to Department of Defense contracts . . . [involving] government officials receiving bribes or gratuities" since inside information "can provide a company with an unfair advantage over its competitors and/or the government." Amid denials by McDonnell Douglas of any wrongdoing, the FBI demanded documents concerning Paisley's role in the foreign sales of the premier navy warplane, the F-18, plus a $4 billion contract to develop, with General Dynamics, a new Advanced Tactical Aircraft. Paisley's cohort was another private consultant, retired Rear Admiral James "Ace" Lyons, former commander in chief of the Pacific Fleet. Within days of the FBI revelations, the House Armed Services Committee jumped in with the first of a series of congressional inquiries into the scandal, ostensibly to determine how to reform the Pentagon to eliminate procurement scandals. Although the problem had been exacerbated by the dramatic growth of defense procurement appropriations from $35 billion in 1980 to $96.8 billion in 1985 (leveling off after that), the Armed Services Committee had jumped into this scandal as though it was something new. Yet, the scandal centering on Paisley arose out of reforms already brought to the Pentagon by Reagan and Defense Secretary Caspar Weinberger in response to the procurement problems and scandals of previous administrations! It seems that the more things change at the Pentagon, the more the triangles and rectangles remain the same.[8]

These iron triangles, rectangles, and complexes make the clientele agencies the most difficult to change or to coordinate. Generally, these agencies are able to re-

---

[7] Randall B. Ripley and Grace A. Franklin, *Bureaucracy and Policy Implementation* (Homewood, IL.: Dorsey Press, 1982), pp. 118–19.

[8] The fact and quote are taken from *Congressional Quarterly Weekly Report,* 18 June 1988, p. 1696; 25 June 1988, pp. 1723–24; 2 July 1988, p. 1814.

sist external demands or pressures for change and vigorously defend their own prerogatives and institutional integrity. Congress, in fact, felt compelled to adopt the Whistleblower Act in 1989, to encourage civil servants to report abuses of trust and to protect them from retaliations from within their own agencies. Because of their power of resistance, Congress and the president have frequently discovered that it is far easier to create new clientele agencies than to compel an existing agency to implement programs that it opposes. This has produced a strong tendency in the United States toward duplication, waste, and collusion. The scandal that hit the Pentagon in mid-1988 was a mere exaggeration of normal triangular trading patterns. If President Eisenhower had been alive in the summer of 1988, he would have said, "I told you so."

Agencies for Maintenance of the Union

These agencies could be called public order agencies were it not for the fact that our Constitution entrusts so many of the vital functions of public order, such as the police, to the state governments. This is a remarkable feature of the American system, the more so because it is taken for granted that we have no national police force and little national criminal law. But some agencies vital to maintaining *national* bonds do exist in the national government, and they can be grouped for convenience into three categories: (1) agencies for control of the sources of government revenue, (2) agencies for control of conduct defined as a threat to internal national security, and (3) agencies for control of conduct threatening to external security. Most revenue control is housed in the Treasury Department. Agencies for defending internal national security are housed mainly in the Department of Justice. Some such agencies are also in the Departments of Defense and State, but the law is careful to limit these to external threats to security.

Revenue Agencies One of Congress's first actions in President Washington's administration was to create the Department of the Treasury. Soon thereafter, the House of Representatives created the first standing committee, the Committee on Ways and Means, in order to maintain its ability to supervise the Treasury. Probably the oldest function of the Treasury Department is the collection of revenues on imports, called tariffs. Now housed in the United States Customs Service, federal customs agents are located at every seaport and international airport to oversee the collection of "duties" on imported goods. Tariffs were far more important in the nineteenth century, when they were our most important source of revenue. Tariffs have also been used for a purpose other than revenue collection. When the tariff rate on an imported commodity is set very high and beyond mere revenue needs, it causes the price of that commodity to rise higher than the same commodity produced at home, giving the home product a competitive advantage. This is called a *protective tariff.* Protective tariffs are still in use, although Democrats as well as Republicans oppose them in principle. The Clinton administration came to power in 1993 with a commitment to impose protective tariffs on selected Japanese goods in retaliation against their trade restrictions and to impose similar tariffs or trade regulations in retaliation against European Common Market subsidies of certain

280

THE EXECUTIVE
BRANCH:
BUREAUCRACY
IN A
DEMOCRACY

agricultural exports. Democratic support in Congress makes such threats credible, but they are more likely to lead to renewed negotiations over reduced tariffs and freer trade. Tariffs are no longer the significant contributor to federal revenues that they were in the days before the income tax.

The Internal Revenue Service (IRS) is also a bureau within the Department of Treasury, and one experience with the IRS is enough to remind anyone of the very close relationship between taxation and control. Control is justified on the grounds of necessity, but there is a thin line between necessary control and abusing the rights guaranteed to all citizens since, for example, a citizen's privacy can be invaded if there is a suspicion of fraud or nonreporting. Indeed, persons accused in tax cases bear the burden of proving their own innocence—the reverse of the normal rule that a person accused of a crime is presumed innocent until proven guilty. Al Capone, the infamous gangland figure, was convicted in 1931 of federal income tax evasion and sentenced to eleven years in prison, served eight years, and was released in 1939 because he was dying. Although Capone was universally recognized as a leading crime figure, all other efforts to convict Capone had failed, and the tax approach was utilized because it was the only way to apprehend him. Although Capone was a disreputable person, his case is an example of the conflict between freedom and power. The power to tax is very close to the police power, since governments must rely on police power to collect taxes. But to use personal income tax records to imprison someone even like Capone, only when there was insufficient evidence to convict him on the relevant crimes of which he had been accused, can undermine the legitimacy of the tax system and instill fear in ordinary citizens that their privacy if not their freedom could be in danger.

The IRS is one of the federal government's largest bureaus. Its 125,000 professional and clerical employees are spread throughout seven regions, sixty-five districts, ten service centers, and hundreds of local offices.[9] In 1991, the IRS processed 203.7 million tax returns and supplemental documents—a one percent increase over 1990. Nearly 20,000 IRS employees are engaged in auditing tax returns, and in 1991 they recommended additional tax and penalties on 1,123,522 individual returns. The IRS is not unresponsive to political influences, given its close working relationships with Congress through the staffs as well as the members of the House Ways and Means Committee and Senate Finance Committee. But the political patterns of the IRS are virtually opposite those of a clientele agency; as one expert puts it, "probably no organization in the country, public or private, creates as much clientele *dis*favor as the Internal Revenue Service. The very nature of its work brings it into an adversary relationship with vast numbers of Americans every year."[10] Despite many complaints about the Internal Revenue Service, however, it has for the most part been evenhanded in its administration of the "tax code," and surprisingly few scandals have soiled its record.

The broad principles of American tax policy are set by summit agreements between the president, the Treasury Department, the chairs of the two tax commit-

---

[9] These are 1987 employment figures from the IRS Office of Public Information, *Information on Regional and Districts from the Government Manual, 1985–1986,* pp. 453–56. Also *The 1993 Information Please Almanac* (Boston: Houghton Mifflin, 1992), pp. 73–74.

[10] George E. Berkley, *The Craft of Public Administration* (Boston: Allyn & Bacon, 1975), p. 417.

tees, a few other congressional leaders, and a few leading corporate interests with

close ties to the party in power. These principles are concerned first with how "progressive" the tax structures should be—that is, whether the rate of taxation should go up at a disproportionate rate with each bracket of income. A related question is what kinds of "relief" taxpayers should get, such as deductions for business expenses, charity, and medical services (see Chapter 16). There are widespread suspicions that influential tax lobbyists can get personal advantages included in the tax code with obscure, technical, and undetected provisions. There are also fears of abuse of IRS powers by unethical politicians. President Nixon admitted to having tried to use confidential IRS data to blackmail his enemies.[11] But unfair deductions are introduced by Congress, *not* by the IRS; and as for use of the IRS for blackmail, although Nixon admits to having tried, "All he could manage to achieve was a few simple audits, something that almost any citizen could engineer with a well-worded letter to his regional IRS representative."[12]

Agencies for Internal Security   As long as the country is not in a state of insurrection, most of the task of maintaining the Union takes the form of legal work, and the main responsibility for that lies in the Department of Justice. It is indeed a luxury, and rare in the world, when national unity can be maintained by routines of civil law instead of imposed by martial law.

A strong connection exists between Justice and Treasury, because a major share of the responsibility for protecting national revenue sources is held by the Tax Division of the Justice Department. This agency handles the litigation arising out of actions taken by the IRS against delinquency, fraud, and dispute over interpretation of the Internal Revenue Code—the source of the tax laws and court interpretations.

In tax cases and in most other legal matters coming before agencies in the Justice Department, the United States itself is the sole party, as it is considered the legal representative of the American people as a whole and thus a legal individual (a legal fiction) that can sue and be sued. The Civil Division of the Justice Department (a bureau) deals with all litigation in which the United States is the *defendant* being sued by plaintiffs for injury and damage allegedly inflicted by the government or one of its officials. The agency also handles the occasional admiralty cases involving all disputes as to navigable waters or concerning shippers and workers on the ships. The work of several other agencies in the Justice Department involves cases where the United States is the *plaintiff.* The largest and most important of these is the Criminal Division, which is responsible for enforcing all the federal criminal laws, except for a few specifically assigned to other divisions. Criminal litigation is actually done by the U.S. Attorneys. There is a presidentially appointed U.S. Attorney assigned to each federal judicial district, and he or she supervises the work of assistant U.S. Attorneys. (See Chapter 8 for details.) The work or jurisdic-

---

[11] Richard M. Nixon, *Memoirs of Richard Nixon* (New York: Grosset & Dunlap, 1978), p. 996.

[12] Berkley, *The Craft of Public Administration,* pp. 214–15. The most fascinating insights into the difference between broad tax policies and the narrower tax deductions, incentives, and "tax break ornaments" will be found in David Stockman, *The Triumph of Politics* (New York: Harper & Row, 1986), Chapter 9 and *passim.*

282

THE EXECUTIVE
BRANCH:
BUREAUCRACY
IN A
DEMOCRACY

tion of the Antitrust, Civil Rights, and Internal Security Divisions is described by their official names.

Although it looms so very large in American folklore, the Federal Bureau of Investigation (FBI), is nothing more nor less than another bureau of the Department of Justice. The FBI handles no litigation, but instead it serves as the information-gathering agency for all the other divisions. Established in 1908, the FBI expanded and advanced in stature during the 1920s and 1930s under the early direction of J. Edgar Hoover. Although it is only one of the fifteen bureaus and divisions in the department, and although it officially has no higher legal status than any of the others, its political importance is greater than that of the others. It is also the largest, taking over 40 percent of the appropriations allocated to the Department of Justice. Since the FBI is responsible only for crimes under federal law, and as our knowledge of the federal system informs us (Chapters 3 and 4), most crimes come under state laws, the FBI ought to be a relatively small bureau. The FBI does not even have responsibility for investigating tax crimes. (Those investigations come under the IRS and the Justice Department's Tax Division.)

In the 1930s, the FBI was in fact of minor importance; its so-called G–Men and Untouchables became important folk heroes because of newsreels, movies, and radio shows about a few spectacular cases of kidnapping and bootlegging, and because J. Edgar Hoover was a master at public relations. Some growth of the bureau can be attributed to laws authorizing the FBI to enter cases involving presumption of "interstate flight to avoid crime." But the FBI did not grow significantly in size or importance until World War II, when the president assigned the bureau responsibility for uncovering "fifth columnists"—Nazi spies and saboteurs. After the war, this grew into the Loyalty and Security Programs, giving the FBI jurisdiction over millions of government personnel as well as suspected Communist agents, the members of the American Communist party and the members of a large and expanding list of organizations declared by the FBI as "subversive" or "fellow travelers." To this was added responsibility in the 1960s for "the Mafia" and organized crime in general. Initially, Hoover and the FBI resisted taking on this assignment, and recent biographies have alleged that Hoover was actually being blackmailed by the Mafia. But as an organization, the FBI gets much less credit for underground and unreported surveillance assignments than it does for the occasional spectacular apprehension of such famous criminals as John Dillinger, "Machine Gun" Kelley, and Bonnie and Clyde, or for dramatic events such as the Waco, Texas, standoff.[13]

Despite its professionalism and its fierce pride in its autonomy, the FBI has not been unresponsive to the partisan commitments of Democratic and Republican administrations. This helps explain Hoover's longevity as director. However, other units of the Justice Department are a good deal more systematically responsive to political controls. The Justice Department is headed by the attorney general, who, with the second in command, the deputy attorney general, supervises the legal activities of the department and renders legal advice to the president and the heads of executive departments. The second most important officer in the Justice Depart-

---

[13] The best source of information on the history, the organization, and the control functions of the FBI will be found in William Keller, *The Liberals and J. Edgar Hoover* (Princeton, NJ: Princeton University Press, 1989).

ment, however, is the solicitor general, who decides what cases the government should appeal to the Supreme Court and supervises case preparations. (See Chapter 8 for more detailed discussion.)

Four times this century, serious political scandals have involved the attorney general. In fact, John Mitchell, President Nixon's attorney general, served a term in prison. During the past thirty years, attorneys general have been close friends as well as loyal party associates of the president. Robert Kennedy was John Kennedy's brother; John Mitchell had been President Nixon's personal attorney and friend, as well as a big party financier; Griffin Bell had held a similar relationship to Carter, as did Edwin Meese with Reagan. Toward the end of his term, Reagan appointed Richard Thornburgh as attorney general, mainly because of Thornburgh's close association with George Bush, who then retained Thornburgh as attorney general after his election. President Clinton's experience appeared exceptional, but only at first glance. His third choice for attorney general, Janet Reno, was indeed a departure from the close personal and political relationships of most appointees to the office. But President Clinton had appointed two close personal friends from Little Rock to be deputy attorney general and associate attorney general. As the *New York Times* put it, by appointing the two of them, the president may have felt "no need to pick a close political or personal ally as Attorney General, as presidents have often done." Thus, the overall pattern suggests why it is not surprising that the Justice Department has been generally more responsive to political direction from the White House than many of the other agencies.

For example, after two years of President Reagan's commitment to deregulation, the Antitrust Division so relaxed its vigil that the number of corporate mergers jumped dramatically and continued to mount during most of the 1980s. One knowledgeable Democratic party leader at the time complained that "as record-shattering merger activity has increased, record-low merger enforcement has followed in its wake. We have also seen a virtual disappearance of antitrust enforcement in entire categories of anticompetitive conduct."[14] Even some members of Reagan's own camp were embarrassed by the "unnerving parallels between the Wall Street raiders of the 1980s and the takeover pools of the 1920s."[15] Still more embarrassing to these Republican critics was the contribution of deregulation to the Savings and Loan crisis, which surfaced just toward the end of the Reagan administration and came to its culmination in the Bush administration. Kevin Phillips, an ardent Reagan supporter, quoted Edwin Gray, a major Reagan economic advisor, in his observation that deregulation helped turn the S&L problem into a crisis.[16]

The Criminal Division is another bureau that has been responsive to presidential preferences, the most famous example being its response to President Johnson's desire to suppress dissenters against the Vietnam War by engaging in extensive trials against them on charges of conspiracy to cause riots. Even the FBI, the most in-

---

[14] Congressman Peter Rodino, former chairman of the House Judiciary Committee, quoted in Kevin Phillips, *The Politics of the Rich and Poor* (New York: Random House, 1990), p. 96.

[15] Phillips, *The Politics of Rich and Poor*, p. 97.

[16] Ibid., p. 97; See also Perry D. Quick, "Businesses—Reagan's Industrial Policy," in *The Reagan Record,* ed. John L. Palmer and Isabel Sawhill (Cambridge: Ballinger Publishing Co., 1984), pp. 304–306.

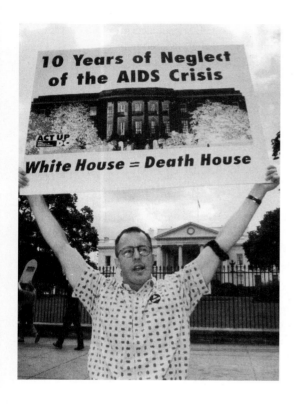

Although AIDS began to reach epidemic proportions during Reagan's first term, a unified governmental policy has yet to be formulated, twelve years later. Before disbanding, the National Commission on AIDS urged the Clinton administration to take action to combat the epidemic. It estimated that over 300,000 people in the United States had AIDS, and that number was increasing by 50,000 a year. In April 1993, Clinton appointed the first White House AIDS coordinator, Kristine Gebbie, and gave the position cabinet-level status.

These pages are from a brochure that the Public Health Service mailed to every American household in an effort to alert people about the dangers of AIDS and to try to eliminate some of the popular misconceptions.

Under-standing AIDS

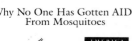

What Do You Really Know About AIDS?

Are You At Risk?

AIDS And Sex

Why No One Has Gotten AIDS From Mosquitoes

OTIS R. BOWEN, M.D.,
Secretary
U.S. Department of Health and Human Services

AMERICA RESPONDS TO AIDS

ROBERT E. WINDOM, M.D.,
Assistant Secretary for Health
U.S. Department of Health and Human Services

This brochure has been prepared by the Surgeon General and the Centers for Disease Control,
U.S. Public Health Service. The Centers for Disease Control is the government agency
responsible for the prevention and control of diseases, including AIDS, in the United States.

U.S. GOVERNMENT PRINTING OFFICE: 1988 — 555-923

Understanding AIDS

A Message From The Surgeon General

This brochure has been sent to you by the Government of the United States. In preparing it, we have consulted with the top health experts in the country.

I feel it is important that you have the best information now available for fighting the AIDS virus, a health problem that the President has called "Public Enemy Number One."

Stopping AIDS is up to you, your family and your loved ones.

Some of the issues involved in this brochure may not be things you are used to discussing openly. I can easily understand that. But now you must discuss them. We all must know about AIDS. Read this brochure and talk about it with those you love. Get involved. Many schools, churches, synagogues, and community groups offer AIDS education activities.

I encourage you to practice responsible behavior based on understanding and strong personal values. This is what you can do to stop AIDS.

C. Everett Koop, M.D., Sc.D.
Surgeon General

Este folleto sobre el SIDA se publica en Español.
Para solicitar una copia, llame al 1 800 344-SIDA.

U.S. Department of Health
& Human Services
Public Health Service
Centers for Disease Control
P.O. Box 6003
Rockville, MD 20850

Official Business

HHS Publication No. (CDC) HHS-88-8404. Reproduction of the contents of this brochure is encouraged.

Bureaucracies at all levels of government have joined in the AIDS battle. This poster is one of numerous public appeals made by the New York City Department of Health. It appeared in subways and on buses.

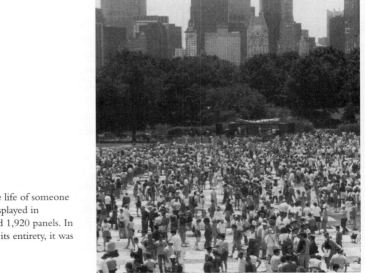

Each panel of the AIDS quilt honors the life of someone who has died from AIDS. When first displayed in Washington, D.C., in 1987, the quilt had 1,920 panels. In October 1992, when it was displayed in its entirety, it was made up of 20,000 panels.

286

THE EXECUTIVE
BRANCH:
BUREAUCRACY
IN A
DEMOCRACY

dependent of the bureaus, responded to President Kennedy's wish to extend the fight against the Mafia and to significantly extend the fight against southern whites who opposed the civil rights laws.[17] And in response to President Reagan, pro-civil rights activity by the Civil Rights Division dropped to an all-time low.[18]

With this sort of responsiveness to political authorities, it is no wonder that leaders of opposing political parties, citizens subject to these agencies, and the federal courts watch with intense vigilance the conduct of Justice Department officials. This confirms the earlier observation that the politics of these revenue and national security agencies are the reverse of the politics of the clientele agencies.

Agencies for External National Security   Two departments occupy center stage here, State and Defense. There are a few key agencies outside State and Defense that have external national security functions. They will be treated in this chapter only as bureaucratic phenomena and for the political problems relevant to administration. Although it is difficult to draw a clear line between policy and administration, the policy questions will be held over until Chapter 18.

State. The constitutional center of all foreign affairs is the Department of State. It has been in continuous operation since 1789, when Thomas Jefferson was appointed secretary of state. Although diplomacy is generally considered the primary task of the department, diplomatic missions are only one of its tasks. The State Department is composed of thirteen bureau-level units, each under the direction of an under secretary or an assistant secretary, with most of the top positions held by career foreign service officers. Eight of the thirteen are "functional" bureaus, handling international economic affairs, scientific and technological affairs, and intelligence. Five are regional bureaus concerned with all of the problems within defined geographic subdivisions of the world. Since these bureaus overlap in their jurisdictions and compete with each other, every president and every secretary of state has delicate diplomatic tasks *within* the department as well as with other countries.

These bureaus are managed by and exist to support the responsibilities of the elite of foreign affairs, the foreign service officers (FSOs). Recruited at a young age under rigorous competitive conditions, FSOs literally represent the United States abroad and share in the responsibility for sending home information and insights about the countries in which they serve. They serve abroad for periods of two to four years, preceded by intense training in the language of that country, and then return for a term of management of analysis back at State, affectionately or derisively called "Foggy Bottom." But although FSOs are part of the solution to the management of the bureaus, they are also part of the problem. The FSOs are part of a "career system," with slow and often painful promotion through the ranks. But there is a second career system at State, composed of ordinary civil servants. Expert observers consistently report jealousy and distrust between the two

---

[17] Victor Navasky, *Kennedy Justice* (New York: Athenaeum, 1971), Chapter 2, and p. 8. The FBI probably went a good deal farther than Presidents Kennedy, Johnson, and Nixon had wanted, by infiltrating the Ku Klux Klan and the various civil rights organizations. But even so, it was responding literally to what each of those presidents had wanted. See also Keller, *The Liberals and J. Edgar Hoover.*

[18] See Keller, *The Liberals and J. Edgar Hoover.*

career systems, exacerbated by the fact that although the FSOs represent only 15
percent of the department's total employees, they hold virtually all the most powerful positions below the rank of ambassador, as well as some of the ambassadorships themselves.[19]

Management of foreign affairs is complicated all the more by the existence of many agencies in the external national security business outside the authority of the State Department. Fewer than 20 percent of all U.S. government employees working abroad are directly under the authority of the State Department. Another 12 percent are State Department employees attached to some other agency.

By far the largest number of career government professionals working abroad are under Defense Department authority. Although many of these people are attached to diplomatic missions and are expected to cooperate with the ambassador, they owe their primary loyalty to the Pentagon. This "pluralism" in the conduct of foreign affairs is a management nightmare. (For more on this, see Chapter 18.) For example, the three most important agencies for collecting and evaluating strategic information (called "intelligence") are the FBI, the Central Intelligence Agency (CIA), and the National Security Agency (NSA). Although precise figures on the personnel and scale of activities of the latter two cannot be gathered, they are known to be extensive. For example, in 1968, at the height of the Vietnam War, journalist Stuart Alsop (generally considered a "hawk" in foreign affairs) reported that the "intelligence community" was spending $3 billion a year and employing about 160,000 people. Accounts coming out of 1975 investigations suggested it was by that time up to $6 billion and employing more than 200,000 people spread throughout ten regular agencies.[20] The estimated CIA budget was $10 billion in 1981, and by the end of the decade it had tripled to nearly $30 billion.[21] Senator Daniel Patrick Moynihan (D–N.Y.), speaking as chairman of the Senate Committee on Intelligence, whose oversight jurisdiction includes the CIA, put the 1992–1993 CIA budget at close to $50 billion.

The Iran-Contra affair of 1986–1987 gave the American public its most recent impression of the character and scope of CIA activities, and the extensive testimony of Secretary of State George Shultz before the special Senate-House Investigating Committee revealed three important organizational facts: (1) that the State Department has no legal authority over the CIA, (2) that the CIA is more politically responsive to the White House and the president's national security adviser than to the secretary of state, and (3) that laws and customs do not even require that the secretary of state be informed of the covert activities of the CIA, despite the effect of these activities on the conduct of diplomacy.

Defense. The creation of the Department of Defense by legislation from 1947 to 1949 was an effort to unify the two historic military departments, the War Depart-

---

[19] For more details, consult John E. Harr, *The Professional Diplomat* (Princeton, NJ: Princeton University Press, 1969).

[20] Data in this paragraph are from I. M. Destler, *Presidents, Bureaucrats and Foreign Policy* (Princeton, NJ: Princeton University Press, 1972), p. 11: and Nicholas Horrock, "The CIA Has Neighbors in the 'Intelligence Community,'" *New York Times*, 29 June 1975, pp. IV–2.

[21] Roger Morris, "C. I. A.—Costly, Inept, Anachronistic," *New York Times*, June 10, 1990, sec. 4, p. 23. Morris was a member of the National Security Council during the Johnson and Nixon administrations.

288

THE EXECUTIVE
BRANCH:
BUREAUCRACY
IN A
DEMOCRACY

ment and the Navy Department and to integrate with them a new department, the Air Force Department. Real unification, however, did not occur. Rather, the Defense Department adds more pluralism to national security.

The American military, following worldwide military tradition, is organized according to "chain of command," a tight hierarchy of clear responsibility and rank, made clearer by uniforms, special insignia, and detailed organizational charts and rules of order and etiquette (see Figure 7.5). The "line" agencies are the military commands, distributed geographically by divisions and fleets. "Staff" agencies, serving each military region, are logistics, intelligence, personnel, research and development (R&D), quartermaster, and engineering. At the top of the military chain of command is a chief of staff (called chief of naval operations in the navy, and commandant in the marines), of four-star rank. These chiefs of staff are *ex officio* (by virtue of their office) members of the Joint Chiefs of Staff—the center of military policy.

Each of the armed forces is truly a career service. The top elite of officers are produced by the three military academies, with top officers occasionally also coming out of such civilian military colleges as the Virginia Military Institute or the Citadel in South Carolina. Entry into top command out of even the most eminent of relevant civilian careers (called "lateral entry") is unthinkable. Yet, movement of top military officers into high civilian jobs is accepted and in fact increasing because of the liberalization of the curriculum at the academies and the incentives in recent years for young officers to attend graduate school. The new military professional has become the equal of the foreign service officer and is often used in foreign service and other management functions. In 1993, four of the five members of the Joint Chiefs of Staff had earned advanced degrees in management or political science, and all five of them had degrees outside military science.

Here is another case where the solution becomes part of the problem. The professionalized (and in many respects civilianized) military is not only a competitor of the FSO; it also has to compete with a second administrative system within Defense: the civilian system. This is comparable to the second system at State except that it reaches higher, all the way to the civilian heads, the secretaries of the Departments of the Army, Navy, and Air Force. Even the law itself separates them from real command authority: "The chain of command . . . extends from the president to the secretary of defense through the Joint Chiefs of Staff, to the commanders of the unified and specified commands."[22] The civilian secretaries have one important job to do, and that is a staff job, mainly supplying personnel and procuring equipment. As one military reporter put it, a secretary of the navy can be responsible for the development of a missile-launching submarine costing billions of dollars but has little to say on whether the submarine is needed or how it should be used.[23]

Thus, two systems plus three departments at Defense, plus two systems at State, plus several important independent agencies equals rampant pluralism in the poli-

---

[22] *United States Government Manual, 1978–1979* (Washington, DC: Government Printing Office, 1978), p. 173.

[23] John W. Finney, "Service Secretaries Have the Title But Little Else," *New York Times,* 24 July 1973, p. 4. See also Adam Yarmolinsky, *The Military Establishment* (New York: Harper & Row, 1971), p. 17.

FIGURE 7.5

The Chain of Command in the Department of Defense

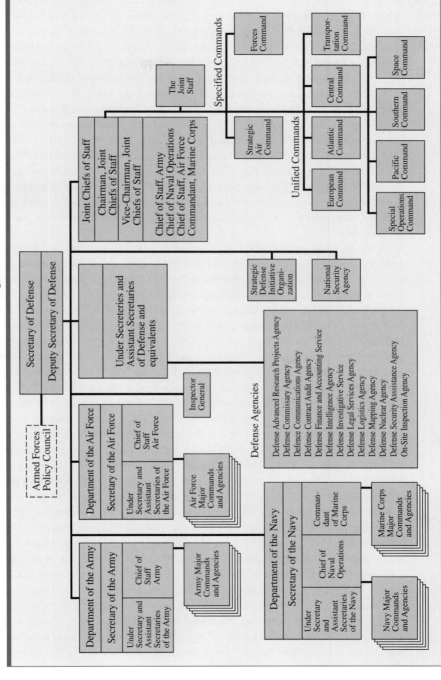

Source: Office of the Federal Register, *U.S. Government Manual, 1992–1993* (Washington, DC: Government Printing Office, 1992), p. 184.

290

THE EXECUTIVE
BRANCH:
BUREAUCRACY
IN A
DEMOCRACY

tics of management of U. S. external national security. There is no better example of this extreme pluralism than the Iran-Contra affair, where the ability to disregard coordination with other agencies and routines enabled "rogues" and "loose cannons" on the National Security Council Staff to draw the United States into embarrassing inconsistencies in policy with several countries. Yet, matters could be worse if the military looked upon itself as an institution equal to and independent of civilian authority. A brief glance at the historic problem of civil-military relations in Latin America or at times in France and Germany will remind Americans of their good luck in having a military that stresses subordination to civilian political authority. For example, all armed services commanders cooperated after World War II when Congress reduced their forces from 3.5 million to 400,000 troops, with equivalent cuts in air force and navy strength. They adjusted just as quickly to the demobilization after the Korean War. Almost no criticism or public opposition came out of the military leadership when President Truman fired the great military hero General Douglas MacArthur for his insubordination during the Korean War.

Actually, and perhaps ironically, America's primary political problem with its military has not been the historic one of how to keep the military out of the politics of governing—a problem that has plagued so many countries in Europe and Latin America. The American military problem is one of the lower politics of the "pork barrel." The 1988 Pentagon scandal, involving several high-tech companies and an assistant secretary of the navy (see p. 278), was a dramatic but not unique example, because a very large portion of the military budget is invested in research and development (R&D), in procurement and stockpiling of strategic resources, and in the production of finished military hardware. Recent examples of military pork barrel abound. In the heat of the presidential campaign, in September 1992, President Bush made a gift stop in Fort Worth, where he announced his approval of the sale to Taiwan of up to 150 new F-16 fighter planes, worth an estimated 11,000 jobs saved for 1995–1999; and he stopped in St. Louis to announce approval of the sale to Saudi Arabia of F-15 fighter planes, again saving a significant number of jobs in the St. Louis economy. These broke his policy against nonproliferation of high-tech weapons. He also broke his reduced-spending pledge in Michigan, where "$9 billion in pork went out the window in one campaign week" with his renewal of M-1 tank production. As one senior member of the Senate Armed Services Committee asserted, "We already have more tanks than we will ever need."[24] President Clinton's long list of proposed military base closings, a major part of his budget-cutting drive for 1993, caused a firestorm of opposition even within his own party, including a number of members of Congress who were otherwise prominently in favor of significant reductions in the Pentagon budget. Emphasis on jobs rather than strategy and policy means pork barrel—use of the military for political purposes. President Eisenhower's warning about the "military-industrial complex" deserves to be kept in mind here, because it helps explain why there will probably be no "peace dividend" in the wake of the ending of the Cold War.

---

[24] Quoted in William Safire, "Bush's Gamble," *New York Times Magazine,* 18 October 1992, p. 60.

The best way to understand the military in American politics is to study it within the same bureaucratic framework used to explain the domestic agencies. The everyday political efforts of American military personnel seem largely self- defensive.

The Regulatory Agencies

As we saw in Chapter 4, our national government did not even begin to get involved in the regulation of economic and social affairs until the late nineteenth century. Until then, regulation was strictly a state and local affair. The federal regulatory agencies are, as a result, relatively new, most dating from the 1930s. But they have come to be extensive and important. In this section, we will look at these regulatory agencies as an administrative phenomenon, with its attendant politics. We defer the policies to Chapters 15 and 16.

The United States has no Department of Regulation but has many regulatory agencies. Some of these are bureaus within departments, such as the Food and Drug Administration (FDA) in the Department of Health and Human Services, the Occupational Safety and Health Administration (OSHA) in the Department of Labor, and the Agricultural Stabilization and Conservation Service (ASCS) in the Department of Agriculture. Other regulatory agencies are independent regulatory commissions. Examples include the Interstate Commerce Commission (ICC), the Federal Trade Commission (FTC), and the Environmental Protection Agency (EPA). But whether departmental or independent, an agency or commission is regulatory if Congress delegates to it relatively broad powers over a sector of the economy or a type of commercial activity and authorizes it to make rules governing the conduct of people and businesses within that jurisdiction. Rules made by regulatory agencies have the force and effect of legislation. And when these agencies make decisions or orders settling disputes between parties or between the government and a party, they are really acting like courts. Box 7.1 contains an example of an administrative rule (or regulation) that could have been an act of Congress and an example of an administrative order that could have been a federal court decision.

Since regulatory agencies exercise a tremendous amount of influence over the economy, and since their rules are a form of legislation, Congress was at first loath to turn them over to the executive branch as ordinary agencies under the control of the president. Consequently, most of the important regulatory programs were delegated to independent commissions with direct responsibility to Congress rather than to the White House. This is the basis of the 1930s reference to them as the "headless fourth branch."[25] With the rise of presidential government, most recent presidents have supported more regulatory programs but have successfully opposed the expansion of regulatory independence. The 1960s and 1970s witnessed adoption of an unprecedented number of new regulatory programs but only four new independent commissions.

---

[25] Final Report of the President's Committee on Administrative Management (Washington, DC: Government Printing Office, 1937). The term "headless fourth branch" was invented by a member of the committee staff, Cornell government professor Robert Cushman.

292

THE EXECUTIVE
BRANCH:
BUREAUCRACY
IN A
DEMOCRACY

BOX 7.1
Administrative Legislation
and Adjudication

An exerpt from a single administrative rule

Sec. 917,448 Pear regulation 8

(a) . . . no handler shall ship:
(2) any box or container of Bartlett or Max Red . . . varieties of pears unless such pears are of a size not smaller than the size known commercially as size 165;
(3) any box or container of Bartlett or Max Red . . . varieties of pears unless such box or container is stamped or otherwise marked, in plain sight and in plain letters, on one outside end with the name of the variety; . . .
(5) Bartlett or Max Red . . . varieties of pears, when packed in other than a closed container, unless such pears do not vary more than 3/8 inch in their transverse diameter for counts 120 or less, and 1/4 inch for counts 135–165, inclusive: *Provided* that 10 percent of the containers in any lot may fail to meet the requirements of this paragraph . . .*

An exerpt from a single administrative order

. . . in representation cases, [employer may not] litigate the issue of whether a union has engaged in race or sex discrimination . . . [because] "the Employer's purpose is to delay the onset of bargaining, rather than to protect the minority or female employees from actual discrimination by the bargaining representative."**

Federal Register, Vol. 43, no. 145, Thursday, 27 July 1978, pp. 32430–31. Taken from David Rosenbloom, *Public Administration* (New York: Random House, 1986), pp. 43–44.

**National Labor Relations Board, *Handy Andy, Inc.* (1977), quoted in *Labor and Law,* 3rd. ed. edited by Charles O. Gregory and Harold A. Katz (New York: W. W. Norton, 1979), p. 448.

The political patterns of these agencies arise from their ability to play the president against the Congress. But this tends to throw the agencies into a more direct struggle with the interests they are regulating. And even though many of the regulatory programs were enacted over the opposition of the regulated groups, these groups often have succeeded in turning the programs to their advantage. Thus, for example, during the years when the airlines were being regulated by the Civil Aeronautics Board (CAB), they were able to protect themselves from competition from each other and to prevent new and more competitive transportation companies from entering the airlines market. Even organized labor found security within the CAB regulatory umbrella; regulation permitted the companies not only to charge exorbitant fares but to yield to pressure from airline unions for wage escalation far out of line with the rest of the work force. Consequently, in 1978, both airlines and organized labor within the airlines industry strongly opposed congressional efforts to deregulate the airlines by eliminating CAB.[26]

[26] See Walter Adams and James Brock, *The Business Complex—Industry, Labor, and Government in the American Economy* (New York: Pantheon Books, 1986), pp. 229–31 and 322–23.

Three factors in particular have enabled regulated companies to turn the programs to their advantage: First, the top agency personnel are often drawn from the regulated industries themselves or from related law firms. Second, throughout its life, the regulatory agency has to depend on the regulated industries for important data about whether the industry is complying with the laws and rules. Third, regulated industries and their trade associations provide a preponderance of expert witnesses at agency hearings where new regulations are formulated. These factors encourage not only interdependence but interpenetration between regulators and regulated.[27]

During the 1970s there were two reactions. First, many citizens and members of Congress began to learn that regulatory agencies weren't necessarily regulating on behalf of what they considered to be the public interest. They formed "public interest groups" or "public interest lobbies" and began to agitate to get regulatory agencies to maintain a more adversarial relation with the regulated companies. These groups even brought hundreds of lawsuits in federal courts to try to force agencies to be more zealous in regulating their part of the economy or society (see also Chapters 8 and 12). The second reaction was from many of the regulated interests themselves, who became convinced that they could do better without the safety of protective regulation; deregulation and the resulting more competitive market would, after a period of adjustment, be better for their entire industry. Moreover, the globalization of the economy provided new and vigorous international sources of competition in many industries, making the need for domestic regulation of these industries less compelling than when they had enjoyed virtual monopoly power within their domestic borders.[28]

Thus, the "new politics" movement and the "deregulation movement" started at about the same time, the first coming mainly from the liberal side of the political spectrum, and the second coming from some liberals as well as libertarians and conservatives. Nevertheless, all this pressure for both deregulation and for more regulation neither invigorated regulatory programs nor terminated them.

These movements did favor President Reagan's efforts to deregulate, however. First he was able to reduce agency size and cut down on the number of rules and regulations they issued. Table 7.2 demonstrates his success in cutting the size of regulatory agencies—counting budgets as well as personnel, the estimated cut in size was between 20 and 30 percent. Another effort he made was to restrict his appointments of heads of the regulatory agencies to those who agreed with him on the need to deregulate. Third, and most importantly, Reagan extended and strengthened the power of the Office of Management and Budget to review and evaluate all proposed agency rules and regulations prior to their being printed in the *Federal Register* and taking on the force of law. He established within OMB an Office of Information and Regulatory Affairs (OIRA) "to provide for presidential oversight of the regulatory process." This was to be accomplished by subjecting every rule with an estimated annual impact of $100 million or more to a cost-benefit test. (Oversight by OIRA is required of all regulatory agencies directly under the president's authority and is obligatory but not mandatory for the independent commissions.) Although OIRA has recommended rejection of fewer than

[27] Lowi, *The End of Liberalism*, especially Chapters 5 and 11.

[28] Alfred C. Aman, Jr., *Administrative Law in a Global Era* (Ithaca, NY: Cornell University Press, 1992).

294

THE EXECUTIVE
BRANCH:
BUREAUCRACY
IN A
DEMOCRACY

TABLE 7.2

Deregulation: Reagan and Bush Compared*

Agency	Reagan Years 1980	1984	1987	Bush Years 1989	1991
Civil Rights Commission	304	25	66	66	72
Consumer Product Safety Commission	871	558	456	487	511
Environmental Protection Agency	10,951	13,048	13,488	14,088	16,323
Equal Employment Opportunity Commission	3,515	3,168	3,052	3,170	2,796
Federal Communications Commission	2,244	2,027	1,855	1,835	1,743
Federal Election Commission	251	225	230	245	254
Federal Emergency Management Commission	3,427	2,691	2,465	2,529	2,434
Federal Labor Relations Authority	349	323	277	261	236
Federal Mediation and Conciliation Service	503	350	323	338	310
Federal Trade Commission	1,846	1,318	918	860	926
Food and Drug Administration	7,419	7,168	6,949	7,330	8,398
Interstate Commerce Commission (planned abolition by Oct. 1990)	1,998	1,071	706	675	664
National Labor Relations Board	2,936	2,720	3,000	3,000	2,227
National Transportation Safety Board	384	348	324	324	325
Nuclear Regulatory Commission	3,283	3,678	3,218	3,209	3,188
Occupational Safety and Health Administration	3,015	2,355	2,141	2,415	2,472
Securities and Exchange Commission	2,056	1,959	2,086	2,278	2,130

*This table shows staff cuts and increases in employment in selected regulatory agencies.

Source: Office of Management and Budget, *Budget of the U.S. Government* (Washington, DC: Government Printing Office, various fiscal years), Appendix.

5 percent of the rules submitted to it, this review process added significant delays
to the time it takes to develop a new rule and influenced the care with which agencies draft their proposed rules.[29]

President Bush, being less ideological and more pragmatic, did in fact reverse the Reagan trend, albeit moderately. Fears of "creeping re-regulation" were confirmed fairly early in his administration, first by moderate increases in personnel in several important regulatory agencies, as shown on Table 7.2. Re-regulation also manifested itself at the Environmental Protection Agency and the Transportation Department with new and tougher automobile safety and automobile mileage requirements, resisted for years by Reagan-appointed officials. Passage of a whole series of amendments to the Clean Air Act of 1990 provided further visible proof of a new posture toward regulation. The Occupational Safety and Health Administration (OSHA) under Bush showed a willingness to lay heavier fines on corporations violating OSHA rules, and in February 1990, the Supreme Court declared the OMB had no authority to block an OSHA policy of disclosing occupational health and safety data to employees or to the public.

Two civil rights acts that would also lead to significant government regulation were also adopted with President Bush's cooperation. The Americans with Disabilities Act of 1990 adds significant power to the national government to regulate employers by applying general discrimination laws to the disabled. President Bush proudly took some credit for that one, and the second one, the Civil Rights Act of 1991, was adopted with Bush's signature after he had vetoed an earlier version which he claimed was a "quota bill." The revised act reversed 1989 Supreme Court rulings that had made it more difficult for women and minorities to win job discrimination suits. Following the S&L scandals, President Bush also went along with the tightening of regulations on banks.

On the other hand, President Bush was responsible for reducing the regulatory activities of many of the established regulatory agencies. He went even further than President Reagan by making his own vice-president, Dan Quayle, head of "regulatory review." The Office of Information and Regulatory Affairs (OIRA) remained in OMB, but it became the servant of Dan Quayle's presidentially appointed Council on Competitiveness, whose purpose was to provide more regulatory relief to individual companies as well as to clarify and reduce the number of regulatory rules.

Since Clinton has put himself in the moderate wing of the Democratic party, there is little chance that he will add new regulatory programs during his term. On the other hand, as a Democrat, President Clinton has no ideological opposition to regulating—as so many Republicans do—and he will almost certainly encourage many if not all regulatory agencies to pursue their regulatory responsibilities with more vigor. The first indication of his direction was probably his decision in July 1993 to protect the forests in the northwest by requiring loggers to scale back the number of trees cut by nearly two-thirds. In return, he promised approximately $1.2 billion in aid for displaced workers and economic development.

---

[29] Murray L. Weidenbaum, "Regulatory Reform under the Reagan Administration," in *The Reagan Regulatory Strategy*, ed. George Eads and Michael Fix (Washington, DC: The Urban Institute, 1984), pp. 23–25; and Seidman and Gilmour, *Politics, Position and Power*, pp. 128–31.

296

THE EXECUTIVE
BRANCH:
BUREAUCRACY
IN A
DEMOCRACY

Redistributive Administration—Fiscal-Monetary and Welfare Agencies

Welfare agencies and monetary agencies seem at first to be too far apart to belong to the same category, but they are related in a very special way. They are responsible for the transfer of literally hundreds of billions of dollars annually between the public and the private sphere, and through such transfers these agencies influence how people and corporations spend and invest trillions of dollars annually. We call them agencies of redistribution because they influence the amount of money in the economy and because they directly influence who has money, who has credit, and whether people will want to invest or save their money rather than spend it. The best generic term for government activity affecting or relating to money is "fiscal" policy. The *fisc* was the Roman imperial treasury; fiscal can refer to anything and everything having to do with public finance. However, we in the United States choose to make a further distinction, reserving *fiscal* for taxing and spending policies and using *monetary* for policies having to do with banks, credit, and currency. And the third, *welfare,* deserves to be treated as an equal member of this redistributive category.

Administration of fiscal policy is primarily in the Treasury Department. It is no contradiction to include the Treasury here as well as with the agencies for maintenance of the Union. This indicates (1) that the Treasury is a complex department performing more than one function of government, and (2) that traditional controls have had to be adapted to modern economic conditions and new technologies.

Today, in addition to administering the income tax and other taxes, the Treasury is also responsible for managing the enormous federal debt—$4 trillion as of 1992 and growing by $250–$300 billion a year. (The debt was a mere $914 billion in 1980.) But debt is not simply something the country *has;* it is something a country has to *manage* and *administer.* Those thousands of billions of dollars of debt are in bonds, deposits, and obligations spelled out in contracts with industries in the public sector. The scale of the problem was probably best captured by Ross Perot in his call to arms during the 1992 presidential campaign: "Today we have a four-trillion dollar debt. By 2000 we could well have an eight-trillion dollar debt. Today all the income taxes collected from the states west of the Mississippi go to pay the interest on that debt. By 2000 we will have to add to that all the income tax revenues from Ohio, Pennsylvania, Virginia, North Carolina, New York, and six other states just to pay the interest on the eight trillion dollars."[30]

The Treasury Department is also responsible for printing the currency that we use, but of course currency represents only a tiny proportion of the entire money economy. Most of the trillions of dollars used in the transactions that comprise the private and public sectors of the U.S. economy exist on printed accounts and computers, not in currency.

---

[30] Ross Perot, *United We Stand—How We Can Take Back Our Country* (New York: Hyperion, 1992), p. 6. In case there is any confusion, the federal *debt* is the total amount of money the national government owes. Most of the debt is held by the American people and American corporations and other institutions in the form of long-term and short-term bonds and other IOU's. The federal *deficit* is the annual difference between expenditures and revenues. The annual deficit is added annually to the public debt.

Another important fiscal agency (although for technical reasons it is called an agency of monetary policy) is the Federal Reserve System, headed by the Federal Reserve Board. The Federal Reserve System (the Fed) has authority over the credit rates and lending activities of the nation's most important banks. Established by Congress in 1913, the Fed is responsible for adjusting the supply of money to the needs of banks in the different regions and of the commerce and industry in each. The Fed helps shift money from where there is too much to where it is needed. It also ensures that the banks do not overextend themselves by too liberal a lending policy, out of fear that if there is a sudden economic scare, a run on a few banks might be contagious and cause another terrible crash like the one in 1929. The Federal Reserve Board sits at the top of the pyramid of twelve district Federal Reserve Banks, which are "bankers' banks," serving the monetary needs of the hundreds of member banks in the national bank system (see also Chapter 16).

Welfare agencies seem at first glance to be just another set of clientele agencies. But there is a big difference between welfare agencies and clientele agencies: welfare agencies operate under laws that discriminate between rich and poor, old and young. Access to welfare agencies is restricted to those individuals who fall within some legally defined category. Those who fall outside the relevant legal category would not be entitled to access even if they sought it. In contrast, people come under the jurisdiction of traditional clientele agencies either through self-selection or by coincidence. Access to a clientele agency is open to just about anyone.

The most important and expensive of the welfare programs are the insurance programs, traditionally called Social Security, where all employed persons contribute during their working years and receive benefits as a matter of right when in need.[31] Two other programs come closer to what is popularly understood as welfare—Aid to Families with Dependent Children (AFDC) and Supplemental Security Income (SSI). Although no contributions are required for access, each program is "means-tested,"—that is, applicants for benefits must demonstrate that their total annual cash earnings fall below the officially defined poverty line.

There is a third category of welfare, called "in-kind programs," which includes food stamps and Medicaid. These two programs are also means-tested, and people who fall within the minimum-income category qualify for the noncash benefits of food stamps and the noncash services of hospital and doctor care. Cash is involved in the Medicaid program, but it does not go directly to the person on welfare; the government is the "third party," guaranteeing to pay the doctor or hospital for the services rendered. Another welfare program with very large fiscal significance is Medicare, an extension of Social Security for the elderly, not means-tested.

There is no single government department responsible for all of the programs that comprise "the social security system" or the "welfare state." The largest of all the agencies in this field is the Social Security Administration (SSA), which manages the social insurance aspects of Social Security and SSI. SSA is by far the largest bureau in the Department of Health and Human Services, which is also responsible for the administration of AFDC and Medicaid. The Department of Agriculture is responsible for the food stamp program.

---

[31] These are called insurance because people pay premiums; however, the programs are not fully self-sustaining, and people do not receive benefits in proportion to the size of their premiums. For actual expenditures on these and other welfare programs, see Chapter 17.

298

THE EXECUTIVE
BRANCH:
BUREAUCRACY
IN A
DEMOCRACY

Our concern in the first two sections of this chapter has been to present a picture of bureaucracy, its necessity as well as its scale, and the particular uses to which the bureaucracies are being put by the national government. But it is clearly impossible to present these bureaucracies merely as organizations when in fact they exist to implement actual public policies. We will have a great deal more to say directly about those public policies in later chapters (Chapters 15–18). What remains for this chapter is to explore how the American system of government has tried to accommodate this vast apparatus to the requirements of representative democracy. The title of the chapter "Bureaucracy in a Democracy"[32] was intended to convey the sense that the two are contradictory. We cannot live without bureaucracy, because it is the most efficient way to organize people and technology to get a large collective job done. But we can't live comfortably with bureaucracy either. Bureaucracy requires hierarchy, appointed authority, and professional expertise. Those requirements make bureaucracy the natural enemy of representation, which requires discussion among equals, reciprocity among equals, and a high degree of individualism. Yet, the task is not to retreat from bureaucracy but to try constantly to take advantage of its strengths while trying to make it more *accountable* to the demands made upon it by democratic politics and representative government. That is the focus of the remainder of this chapter.

BUREAUCRACY IN A DEMOCRACY: ADMINISTRATIVE ACCOUNTABILITY

Two hundred years, millions of employees, and billions of dollars after the founding, we must return to James Madison's observation that "You must first enable the government to control the governed; and in the next place oblige it to control itself."[33] Today the problem is the same, but the form has changed. Our problem today is bureaucracy and our inability to keep it accountable to elected political authorities. We conclude this chapter with a review of the presidency and Congress as institutions for keeping the bureaucracy accountable. Some of the facts from Chapters 5–7 are repeated, but in this important context. We will then look at the special role of the federal courts in Chapter 8.

President as Chief Executive

Making the Managerial Presidency[34] The rise of "presidential government" means above all that our system depends upon the president to establish and main-

---

[32] The title was inspired by an important book by Charles Hyneman, *Bureaucracy in a Democracy* (New York: Harper, 1950). For a more recent effort to describe the federal bureaucracy and to provide some guidelines for improvement, see Patricia W. Ingraham and Donald F. Kettl, eds., *Agenda for Excellence— Public Service in America* (Chatham, NJ: Chatham House, 1992).

[33] *The Federalist*, No. 51.

[34] Title inspired by Peri Arnold, *Making the Managerial Presidency* (Princeton, NJ: Princeton University Press, 1986).

tain a connection between popular aspirations and day-to-day administration.

Congress and the American people have shown a consistent willingness to delegate to the president almost any powers he seeks to enable him to meet this primary obligation. But there is no guarantee that the pow*ers* granted, no matter how many, will be sufficient pow*er* to do the job. In 1937, President Roosevelt, through his President's Committee on Administrative Management, made the plea that "the president needs help." Each president since that time has found it necessary to make the same plea, because *presidents have great power to commit but much less power to guide.* In other words, the president can summon up popular opinion and congressional support to impose a new program and a new agency on the bureaucracy—even to impose an unwanted new responsibility on the FBI. But since the president can never have enough time and staff to watch over more than a few high-priority agencies, all the others can take advantage of their obscurity and go their merry way—until some scandal or dissatisfied client turns on the light.

The story of the modern presidency can be told largely as a series of responses to the rise of big government. *Each expansion of the national government in the twentieth century has been accompanied by a parallel expansion of presidential management authority,* that is, the expansion of the presidency as a real chief executive officer. Table 7.3 provides a sketch of this pattern over most of the twentieth century. The table shows, for example, that the first sustained expansion of the national government in the twentieth century, the Wilson period, was followed by one of the most important executive innovations in U.S. history, the Budget and Accounting Act of 1921. By this act, Congress turned over this prime legislative power, the budget, to the executive branch. Moving on to FDR, expansions of government during the 1930s were so large and were sustained over such a long period of time that reactions to control government growth occurred under the same president, producing some of the most important innovations in executive branch management.

After World War II, the "managerial presidency" was an established fact, but its expansion continued, with each president trying to keep pace with the continually growing bureaucracy. And the purpose of the struggle remained the same: to react to every expansion with another mechanism of popular control. For example, as shown on Table 7.3, the two presidents most supportive of big government since Roosevelt were Kennedy and Johnson, but they were also equally committed to expanding the managerial and oversight powers to control the expanded government. Management reform had become a regular and frequent activity.

President Nixon also greatly enlarged the managerial presidency. Nixon's approach to presidential reorganization can be attributed in part to his own boldness and confidence as president and in part to the great need of the Republicans at that time to impose their own brand of control on an executive branch that had been tremendously enlarged by the "pro-government" Democrats who had controlled the White House for twenty-eight of the previous thirty-six years.[35]

---

[35]For the story of Nixon's effort to transform the cabinet as a means of improving the management capacities of the chief executive, see Richard Nathan, *The Plot That Failed: Nixon and the Administrative Presidency* (New York: Wiley, 1975), pp. 68–76. To the secretary of state, there would be added three super secretaries, who were also to be appointed "counsellors to the president" and also to serve in the chair of each of three Domestic Council Committees, enabling them to supervise not only their own

TABLE 7.3
Government Expansions and Reform Responses to Them

Period of Government Expansion	*Responses of the Presidency to Expansion*
Wilson (1914–1918): World War I; budget up from average $800 million to over $18 billion in 1919; agencies expanded.	Budget and Accounting Act, 1921; (1) Bureau of the Budget in executive branch; (2) General Accounting Office (GAO) as agent of Congress.
Roosevelt (1933–1936): New Deal period; budget growth; addition of many new agencies, the "alphabetocracy."	Executive Office of the President, including Budget Bureau; reorganization powers, 1939.
Roosevelt (1940–1944): World War II; total mobilization.	Council of Economic Advisers, 1946; Secretary of Defense, National Security Council, Joint Chiefs of Staff, 1947.
Truman (1947–1951): Postwar, Korean War mobilization.	Emergence of "president's program," 1948+; emergence of White House staff, 1950+.
Eisenhower (1953–1960): Cold War; reaction against domestic government.	Formalizing of White House staff; enhancement of the National Security Council; effort to coordinate and control social agencies; Hoover Commission.
Kennedy (1961–1963): Comprehensive program; increased taxing power; direct pressure to control wages and prices.	Specialized White House staff; applied central budgeting (Planning Programming Budgeting System, PPBS) to Defense Department; upgraded Council of Economic Advisers.
Johnson (1964–1966): Great expansion of domestic social programs—Medicare and Medicaid, civil rights laws and agencies; expansion of war powers.	Applied PPBS to domestic agencies; created Organization for Economic Opportunity (OEO) to coordinate welfare programs: with "participatory democracy" established two departments (HUD and Transportation) to coordinate common activities.
Nixon (1969–1973): Increased Social Security benefits; expansion of diplomacy; price controls; many new regulatory programs.	Centralization and further specialization of White House staff; Office of Management and Budget (OMB) created; revenue sharing to decentralize urban and welfare programs; "indexing" of Social Security to eliminate annual legislative adjustments; cabinet-level coordinating councils on wages and prices and domestic policy; enhanced use of FBI surveillance of administrators.
Carter (1977–1980): Post-Watergate.	New Departments of Energy and Education; reform of U.S. Civil Service; zero-base budgeting; vast effort to reduce paperwork; first to impose cost-benefit analysis on regulation; first major effort to "deregulate."
Reagan (1981–1985): Dramatic expansion of defense budget; great expansion of national trade deficit.	Director of OMB promoted to cabinet status; expansion of OMB power of regulatory review; cabinet councils; expanded cost-benefit test for regulations.
Bush (1989–1991): Decision to put costs of Gulf War and S&L bail-out "off-budget," outside deficit-control calculations.	More power given to OMB over total budget deficits, along with broad discretion to adjust agency budget targets to economic conditions.

President Carter was probably more preoccupied with administrative reorganization than any Democratic president in this century. Responding to Watergate,
his 1976 campaign was filled with plans to make the bureaucracy more accountable as well as more efficient. His reorganization of the civil service will long be
recognized as one of his more significant contributions. The Civil Service Reform
Act of 1978 was the first major revamping of the federal civil service since its in-
ception in 1883. The 1978 act abolished the century-old Civil Service Commission (CSC) and replaced it with three agencies, each designed to take on one part
of the old CSC's functions on the theory that combining these functions had given
the CSC an "identity crisis." A new Merit System Protection Board (MSPB) was
created to defend merit recruitment and promotion from political encroachment
and individual abuses. Merit in the U.S. Civil Service is defined as objective ratings
in open competition through testing and personal records for specific and officially
classified jobs. Officials are given very little discretion in choosing from the eligibility list to fill vacancies, to make promotions, or to decide on transfers or firings
of personnel. A separate Federal Labor Relations Authority (FLRA) was set up to
administer collective bargaining and individual personnel grievances. The third
new agency, the Office of Personnel Management (OPM), was set up to manage
the testing, training, and retirement systems. An entirely new Senior Executive
Service was created to recognize and foster "public management" as a profession
and to facilitate the movement of top, "supergrade" career officials across agencies
and departments.[36]

Carter also tried to impose a stringent budgetary process on all executive agencies. Called "zero-base budgeting" (ZBB), it was a "bottom-up" method of budgeting, wherein each agency was required to justify its entire mission rather than
merely next year's request. ZBB did not succeed, but the effort was not lost on
President Reagan. Although Reagan gave the impression of being a "laid-back"
president, he actually centralized management to an unprecedented degree. From
Carter's "bottom-up" approach, Reagan went to a "top-down" approach whereby
a White House budgetary decision would be made first and the agencies would be
required to fit within it. The effect of this process was to convert OMB into an
agency of policy determination and presidential management. As one expert put
it, the Reagan management strategy was "centralization in the service of decen-
tralization."[37] President Reagan brought the director of OMB into the cabinet and

---

department but one or two other departments in their area. The secretary of agriculture would head a
group called Natural Resources; the secretary of the then Department of Health, Education, and Welfare would head a committee supervising other departments in the area of Human Resources, and the
secretary of housing and urban development would head other departments in a general area called
Community Development. This would have been a much more hierarchical approach to executive
management, but it was a perfectly logical effort that failed largely because of the mounting distrust
during the Watergate turmoil.

[36]For more details and evaluations, see David Rosenbloom, *Public Administration* (New York: Random
House, 1986) pp. 186–221; and Charles H. Levine and Rosslyn S. Kleeman, "The Quiet Crisis in
American Public Service," and Patricia Ingraham and David Rosenbloom, "The State of Merit in the
Federal Government," both in Ingraham and Kettl, eds., *Agenda for Excellence,* Chapters 10 and 11.

[37] Lester Salamon and Alan Abramson, "Governance: The Politics of Retrenchment," in *The Reagan
Record,* ed. John Palmer and Isabel Sawhill (Cambridge, MA: Ballinger, 1984), p. 40.

302

THE EXECUTIVE
BRANCH:
BUREAUCRACY
IN A
DEMOCRACY

The Federal Bureaucracy: Who Should Control It?

Every modern president has entered office faced with the daunting task of developing meaningful and effective strategies for dealing with the federal government's sprawling bureaucracy. Presidents have alternately viewed the bureaucracy as a lion to be tamed or as a vast resource pool.

Political scientists Richard P. Nathan and Norton E. Long both recognize the role of politics in administrative actions. But Nathan argues that presidents should seek political control of the bureaucracy by pursuing an "administrative presidency" strategy. Long notes that the dispersal of power in government impels administrators to develop their own sources of power, including support from special interests outside of government, and that efforts by presidents to enforce administrative conformity are not only likely to fail but are undesirable as well.

Nathan

. . . Such officials [as the president] should organize their office—appoint, assign, and motivate their principal appointees—in a way that *penetrates* the administrative process. The reason is that in a complex, technologically advanced society in which the role of government is pervasive, much of what we would define as policymaking is done through the execution of laws in the management process . . . .

. . . Ronald Reagan among recent presidents appears to have the best handle on the need for an administrative strategy. He avoided the pitfalls of Nixon's heavy-handedness, Johnson's grand design, and Carter's atomic-submarine approach to management. . . . The five main ingredients of an administrative presidency strategy . . . are: (1) selecting cabinet secretaries whose views are closely in line with those of the president; (2) selecting subcabinet officials who also share the president's values and objectives; (3) motivating cabinet and subcabinet officials to give attention to agency operations and administrative processes; (4) using the budget process as the central organizing framework for public policy-making; and, finally, (5) avoiding over-reliance on centralized White House clearance and control systems. . . .

I believe a managerial strategy is appropriate for the American presidency. Even if we assume that the president is successful in establishing a greater measure of managerial cohesion and control over the federal bureaucracy, there still exists an abundance of ways in which the president's power in this area and in others can be checked and balanced. . . . The exercise of a greater measure of . . . control over the executive branch of the American national government . . . is fully consistent with democratic values.[1]

Long

It is clear that the American political system of politics does not generate enough power at any focal point of leadership to provide the conditions for an even partially successful divorce of politics from administration. Subordinates [i.e., administrators] cannot depend on the formal chain of command to deliver enough political power to permit them to do their jobs. Accordingly they must supplement the resources available throughout the hierarchy with those they can muster on their own, or accept the consequences in frustration—a course itself not without danger. Administrative rationality demands that objectives be determined and sights set in conformity with a realistic appraisal of power position and potential. . . . The weakness in party structure both permits and makes necessary the . . . political activities of the administrative branch. . . . Agencies and bureaus . . . are in the business of building, maintaining, and increasing their political support. They lead and in large part are led by the diverse groups whose influence sustains them. . . . A major and most time-consuming aspect of administration consists of the wide range of activities designed to secure enough "customer" acceptance to survive and, if fortunate, develop a consensus adequate to program formulation and execution. . . .

The task of the Presidency lies in feeling out the alternatives of policy which are consistent with the retention and increase of the group support on which the Administration rests. . . . Like most judges, the Executive needs to hear argument for his own instruction. The alternatives presented by subordinates in large part determine the freedom and the creative opportunity of their superiors. . . . Reorganization of the executive branch to centralize administrative power in the Presidency . . . may effect improvement, but in a large sense it must fail.[2]

[1]Richard P. Nathan, *The Administrative Presidency* (New York: Wiley, 1983), pp. 82, 88, 93.
[2]Norton E. Long, "Power and Administration," *Public Administration Review* 9 (Autumn 1949), pp. 257–64.

centralized the budget process as well as the process of regulatory review, as referred to earlier.

President Bush went even further than President Reagan in using the White House staff instead of cabinet secretaries in management. But although he concentrated things in the White House, his management style was actually less centralized than Reagan's because of his preference for informality, for telephone calls and personal relationships, leading one president-watcher to summarize his management style as the "Let's Deal President."[38]

President Clinton projected his approach to management in his 1993 Man of the Year interview with *Time:*

[38] Colin Campbell, "The White House and the Presidency Under the 'Let's Deal' President," in Colin Campbell and Bert A. Rockman, *The Bush Presidency—First Appraisals* (Chatham, NJ: Chatham House, 1991), pp. 185–222.

304

THE EXECUTIVE
BRANCH:
BUREAUCRACY
IN A
DEMOCRACY

One of the things that struck me since I won this election is that there are a huge number of people who work for the Federal Government . . . devoted people who ought to be given a chance to hook into this future we are trying to build . . . . I believe that if you look at the most successful organizations in this country, that's what they do.[39]

In other words, more of actual management should, in his view, be delegated to the responsible administrators "on the line."

The Problem of Management Control by the White House Staff   The cabinet's historic failure to perform as a board of directors, and the inability of any other agency to perform that function, has left a vacuum. OMB has met part of the need, and the management power of the director seems to go up with each president. But the need for executive management control goes far beyond what even the boldest of OMB directors can do. The White House staff has filled the vacuum to a certain extent precisely because in the past thirty years, the "special assistants to the president" have been given relatively specialized jurisdictions over one or more departments or strategic issues. These staffers have additional power and credibility beyond their access to the president because they also have access to confidential information. Since information is the most important bureaucratic resource, White House staff members gain management power by having access to the CIA for international intelligence and the FBI and the Treasury for knowledge about agencies, not only beyond what the agencies report but on matters that are likely to make agency personnel fearful and respectful. The FBI has exclusive knowledge about the personal life of each bureaucrat, since each one has to go through a rigorous FBI security clearance procedure prior to being appointed and promoted.

Responsible bureaucracy, however, is not going to come simply from more presidential power, more administrative staff, and more management control. All this was, for example, inadequate to the task of keeping the National Security Staff from seizing the initiative to run its own policies toward Iran and Nicaragua for at least two years (1985–1986) after Congress had restricted activities on Nicaragua and the president had forbidden negotiations with Iran. The Tower Commission, appointed to investigate the Iran-Contra Affair, concluded that although there was nothing fundamentally wrong with the institutions involved in foreign policy making—State, Defense, White House, and their relation to Congress—there had been a "flawed process" and "a failure of responsibility," and a thinness of the president's personal engagement in the issues. The Tower Commission found that "at no time did [Reagan] insist upon accountability of performance review."[40]

No particular management style is guaranteed to work. Each White House management innovation, from one president to the next shows only the inadequacy of the approaches of previous presidents. And as the White House grows and the Executive Office of the President grows, the management bureaucracy itself becomes a management problem. Something more and different is obviously needed.

[39] *Time,* 4 January 1993, p. 37.

[40] Quoted in I. M. Destler, "Reagan and the World: An 'Awesome Stubbornness,'" in Charles O. Jones, ed., *The Reagan Legacy—Promise and Performance* (Chatham, NJ: Chatham House, 1988), p. 244 and p. 257. The source of the quote is *Report of the President's Special Review Board,* 26 February 1987.

Congress is constitutionally essential to responsible bureaucracy because the key to bureaucratic responsibility is legislation. When a law is passed and its intent is clear, then the president knows what to "faithfully execute" and the responsible agency understands what is expected of it. In our modern age, legislatures rarely make laws directly for citizens; most laws are really instructions to bureaucrats and their agencies. But when Congress enacts vague legislation, agencies are thrown back upon their own interpretations. The president and the federal courts step in to tell them what the legislation intended. And so do the intensely interested groups. But when everybody, from president to courts to interest groups, gets involved in the actual interpretation of legislative intent, to whom is the agency responsible? Even when it has the most sincere desire to behave responsibly, how shall this be accomplished?

The answer is ***oversight.*** The more legislative power Congress has delegated to the executive, the more it has sought to get back into the game through committee and subcommittee oversight of the agencies. The standing committee system in Congress is well-suited for oversight, inasmuch as most of the congressional committees and subcommittees are organized with jurisdictions roughly parallel to one or more executive departments or agencies. Appropriations committees as well as authorization committees have oversight powers—as do their respective subcommittees. In addition to these, there is a committee on government operations in the House and in the Senate, each with oversight powers not limited by departmental jurisdiction.

The best indication of Congress's oversight efforts is the use of public hearings, before which bureaucrats and other witnesses are summoned to discuss and defend agency budgets and past decisions. The data drawn from systematic studies of congressional committee and subcommittee hearings and meetings show quite dramatically that Congress has tried through oversight to keep pace with the expansion of the executive branch. Between 1950 and 1980, the annual number of committee and subcommittee meetings in the House of Representatives rose steadily from 3,210 to 7,022 and in the Senate from 2,607 to 4,265 (in 1975–76). Beginning in 1980 in the House and 1978 in the Senate, the number of committee and subcommittee hearings and meetings slowly began to decline, reaching 4,222 in the House and 2,597 in the Senate by the mid-1980s. This pattern of rise and decline in committee and subcommittee oversight activity strongly suggests that congressional vigilance toward the executive branch is responsive to long-term growth in government rather than to yearly activity or to partisan considerations.[41]

Oversight can also be carried out by individual members of Congress. Such inquiries addressed to bureaucrats are considered standard congressional "case work"

---

[41]Data from Norman Ornstein et al., *Vital Statistics on Congress, 1987–88* (Washington, DC: Congressional Quarterly Press, 1987), pp. 161–62. Lawrence Dodd and Richard Schott, counting only hearings and not all hearings and meetings, report the same pattern for a shorter period. Between 1950 and 1970, the annual number of public hearings grew from about 300 in the Senate and 350 in the House to 700 in the Senate and 750 in the House. *Congress and the Administrative State* (New York: Wiley, 1979), p. 169. For a valuable and skeptical assessment of legislation oversight of administrations, see James W. Fesler and Donald F. Kettl, *The Politics of the Administration Process,* (Chatham, NJ: Chatham House, 1991), Chapter 11.

306

THE EXECUTIVE
BRANCH:
BUREAUCRACY
IN A
DEMOCRACY

and can turn up significant questions of public responsibility even when the motivation is only to meet the demand of an individual constituent. Oversight also takes place very often through communications between congressional staff and agency staff. Congressional staff has been enlarged tremendously since the Legislative Reorganization Act of 1946, and the legislative staff, especially the staff of the committees, is just as professionalized and specialized as the agency staff. In addition, Congress has created for itself four quite large agencies whose obligations are to engage in constant research on problems taking place in the executive branch. These are the General Accounting Office, the Congressional Research Service, the Office of Technology Assessment, and the Congressional Budget Office. Each is designed to give Congress information independent of the information it can get through hearings and other communications directly from the executive branch.[42]

The better approach is for Congress to spend more of its time clarifying its legislative intent and spend less of its time on oversight activity. If its original intent in the law were clearer, Congress could then afford to defer to presidential management to maintain bureaucratic responsibility. Bureaucrats are more responsive to clear legislative guidance than to anything else. But when Congress and the president are at odds, bureaucrats have an opportunity to evade responsibility by playing one branch off against the other.

Bureaucracy is here to stay. There is no ultimate or sure solution to the problem of bureaucracy in a democracy. The national bureaucracy will not suddenly become smaller or more malleable. Congress will not suddenly change its practice of loose and vague legislative draftsmanship. Presidents will not suddenly discover new reserves of power or vision to draw more tightly the reins of responsible management. No solution will be found in quick fixes. As in all complex social and political problems, the solution lies mainly in a sober awareness of the nature of the problem. This awareness enables people to avoid fantasies and myths about the abilities of a democratized presidency or the virtues of a professionalism or the magical powers of the computer.

SUMMARY

Most American citizens possess less information and more misinformation about bureaucracy than about any other feature of government. We therefore began the chapter with an elementary definition of bureaucracy, identifying its key characteristics and demonstrating the extent to which bureaucracy is not only a phenome-

---

[42] Until 1983, there was still another tool of legislative oversight, the legislative veto. Each agency operating under such provisions was obliged to submit to Congress every proposed decision or rule. It was to lie before both houses for thirty to sixty days; then if Congress took no action by one-house or two-house resolution explicitly to veto the proposed measure, it became law. The legislative veto was declared unconstitutional by the Supreme Court in 1983 on the grounds that it violated the separation of powers because the resolutions Congress passed to exercise their veto were not subject to presidential veto, as required by the Constitution, Immigration and Naturalization Service v. Chadha 462 U.S. 919 (1983).

non but an American phenomenon. In the second section of the chapter we sought to show how all essential government services and controls were carried out by bureaucracies—or to be more objective, administrative agencies. Following a very general description of a typical department of the executive branch—the Agriculture Department—we divided up the agencies of the executive branch into four categories, because there are too many agencies to deal with them individually. The four are: (1) the clientele agencies, (2) the agencies for maintaining the Union, (3) the regulatory agencies, and (4) the agencies for redistribution. These illustrate the varieties of administrative experience in American government. Although the bureaucratic phenomenon is universal, not all the bureaucracies are the same in the way they are organized, in the degree of their responsiveness, or in the way they participate in the political process.

Finally, the chapter concluded with a review of all three of the chapters on "representative government" (Chapters 5, 6, and 7) in order to assess how well the two political branches (the legislative and the executive) do the toughest job any government has to do: making the bureaucracy accountable to the people it serves and controls. "Bureaucracy in a Democracy" was the subtitle and theme of the chapter not because we have succeeded in democratizing bureaucracies but because it is the never-ending task of politics in a democracy.

FOR FURTHER READING

Arnold, Peri E. *Making the Managerial Presidency: Comprehensive Organization Planning.* Princeton: Princeton University Press, 1986.

Bryner, Gary. *Bureaucratic Discretion.* New York: Pergamon Press, 1987.

Dodd, Lawrence C., and Richard L. Schott. *Congress and the Administrative State.* New York: Wiley, 1979.

Downs, Anthony. *Inside Bureaucracy.* Boston: Little, Brown, 1966.

Fesler, James W., and Donald F. Kettl. *The Politics of the Administrative Process.* Chatham, NJ: Chatham House, 1991.

Frederickson, H. George, ed. *Ethics and Public Administration.* Armonk, NY: M.E. Sharpe, 1993.

Fry, Bryan R. *Mastering Public Administration—From Max Weber to Dwight Waldo.* Chatham, NJ: Chatham House, 1989.

Heclo, Hugh. *A Government of Strangers.* Washington, DC: Brookings Institution, 1977.

Hill, Larry B., ed. *The State of Public Bureaucracy.* Armonk, NY: M.E. Sharpe, 1992.

Lynn, Naomi B., and Aaron Wildavsky. *Public Administration—The State of the Discipline.* Chatham, NJ: Chatham House, 1990.

Nachmias, David, and David H. Rosenbloom. *Bureaucratic Government USA.* New York: St. Martin's Press, 1980.

Nathan, Richard. *The Plot That Failed: Nixon's Administrative Presidency.* New York: Wiley, 1975.

Ripley, Randall B., and Grace A. Franklin. *Congress, the Bureaucracy and Public Policy.* Homewood, IL: Dorsey Press, 1991.

308

THE EXECUTIVE
BRANCH:
BUREAUCRACY
IN A
DEMOCRACY

Rohr, John. *To Run a Constitution: The Legitimacy of the Administrative State.* Lawrence, KS: The University Press of Kansas, 1986.

Rourke, Francis E. *Bureaucracy, Politics and Public Policy.* Boston: Little, Brown, 1984.

Rubin, Irene S. *The Politics of Public Budgeting.* Second Edition. Chatham, NJ: Chatham House, 1993.

Skowronek, Stephen. *Building a New American State: The Expansion of National Administrative Capacities, 1877–1920.* New York: Cambridge University Press, 1982.

Weiss, Carol H., and Allen H. Barton, eds. *Making Bureaucracies Work.* Beverly Hills, CA: Sage Publications, 1980.

Wildavsky, Aaron. *The New Politics of the Budget Process.* Second Edition. New York: HarperCollins, 1992.

Wilson, James Q. *Bureaucracy: What Government Agencies Do and Why They Do It.* New York: Basic Books, 1989.

8

The Federal Courts: Least Dangerous Branch or Imperial Judiciary?

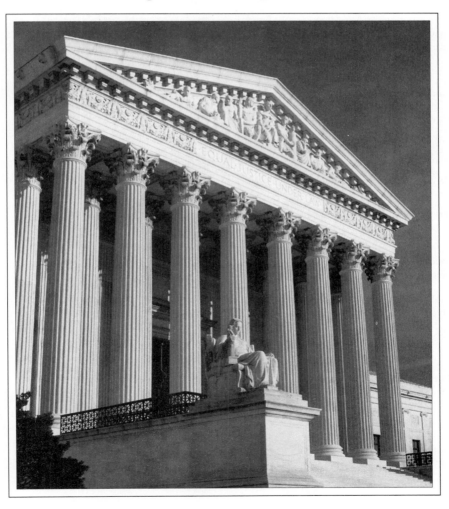

TIME LINE ON THE JUDICIARY

EVENTS		INSTITUTIONAL DEVELOPMENTS
George Washington appoints John Jay chief justice (1789–1795)	**1800**	Judiciary Act creates federal court system (1789)
John Marshall appointed chief justice (1801)		*Marbury* v. *Madison* provides for judicial review (1803)
States attempt to tax the second Bank of the U.S. (1818)		*McCulloch* v. *Maryland*—Court upholds supremacy clause, broad construction of necessary and proper clause; denies right of states to tax federal agencies (1819)
Andrew Jackson appoints Roger Taney chief justice; Taney Court expands power of states (1835)		*Barron* v. *Baltimore*—Court rules that only the federal government and not the states are limited by the U.S. Bill of Rights (1833)
Period of westward expansion; continuing conflict and congressional compromises over slavery in the territories (1830s–1850s)	**1850**	*Dred Scott* v. *Sanford*—Court rules that federal government cannot exclude slavery from the territories (1857)
Civil War (1861–1865)		*Slaughterhouse Cases*—Court limits scope of Fourteenth Amendment to newly freed slaves; states retain right to regulate state businesses (1873)
Reconstruction (1866–1877)		
Self-government restored to former Confederate states (1877)		
"Jim Crow" laws spread throughout southern states (1890s)	**1890**	*Plessy* v. *Ferguson*—Court upholds doctrine of "separate but equal" (1896)
World War I; wartime pacifist agitation in U.S. (1914–1919)		*Abrams* v. *U.S.* (1919) to *Gitlow* v. *N.Y.* (1925) apply First Amendment to states and limit free speech by "clear and present danger"
Red Scare; postwar anarchist agitation (1919–1920)		
FDR's New Deal (1930s)	**1930**	Court invalidates many New Deal laws, e.g., *Schechter Poultry Co.* v. *U.S.* (1935)
Court-packing crisis—proposal to increase the number of Supreme Court justices defeated by Congress (1937)		Court reverses position, upholds most of New Deal, e.g., *NLRB* v. *Jones & Laughlin Steel* (1937)
U.S. enters World War II (1941–1945)		*Korematsu* v. *U.S.*—Court approves sending Japanese-Americans to internment camps (1944)

EVENTS		INSTITUTIONAL DEVELOPMENTS
Korean War (1950–1953)	**1950**	*Youngstown Sheet & Tube Co.* v. *Sawyer*—Court rules that president's steel seizure must be authorized by statute (1952)
Earl Warren appointed chief justice (1953)		
Civil Rights Movement (1950s and 1960s)		*Brown* v. *Board of Ed.*—Court holds that school segregation is unconstitutional (1954)
		Court begins nationalization of the Bill of Rights—*Baker* v. *Carr* (1962); *Gideon* v. *Wainwright* (1963); *Escobedo* v. *Ill.* (1964); *Miranda* v. *Arizona* (1966), etc.
Warren Burger appointed chief justice (1969)		*Flast* v. *Cohen*—Court permits class action suits (1968)
Right-to-life movement (1970s and 1990s)	**1970**	*Roe* v. *Wade*—Court strikes down state laws making abortion illegal (1973)
Affirmative action programs (1970s–1990s)		*Univ. of Calif.* v. *Bakke*—Court holds that race may be taken into account but limits use of quotas (1978)
Court arbitrates conflicts between Congress and president (1970s and 1980s)		*U.S.* v. *Nixon*—Court limits executive privilege (1974); *Bowsher* v. *Synar*—Court invalidates portion of Gramm-Rudman Act (1986); *Morrison* v. *Olson*—Court upholds constitutionality of special prosecutor (1988)
William Rehnquist appointed chief justice (1986)		
Bush appoints David Souter (1990), Clarence Thomas (1991) to the Supreme Court	**1990**	Reagan and Bush appointees create a Republican Court (1980–1991)
Clinton appoints Ruth Bader Ginsburg to the Supreme Court (1993)		

*E*very year nearly 25 million cases are tried in American Courts and one American in every nine is directly involved in litigation. Cases can arise from disputes between citizens, from efforts by government agencies to punish wrongdoing, or from citizens' efforts to prove that a right provided them by law has been infringed upon as a result of government action—or inaction. Many critics of the

American legal system assert that we have become much too litigious (ready to use the courts for all purposes), and perhaps we have. But the heavy use that Americans make of the courts is also an indication of the extent of conflict in American society. And given the existence of social conflict, it is far better that Americans seek to settle their differences through the courts rather than by fighting or feuding.

In this chapter, we will first examine the judicial process, including the types of cases that the federal courts consider and the types of law with which they deal. Second, we will assess the organization and structure of the federal court system as well as the flow of cases through the courts. Third, we will consider judicial review and how it makes the Supreme Court a "lawmaking body." Fourth, we will examine various influences on the Supreme Court. Finally, we will analyze the role and power of the federal courts in the American political process, looking in particular at the growth of judicial power in the United States.

The framers of the American Constitution called the Court the "least dangerous branch" of American government. Today, it is not unusual to hear friends and foes of the Court alike refer to it as the "imperial judiciary."[1] Before we can understand this transformation and its consequences, however, we must look in some detail at America's judicial process.

THE JUDICIAL PROCESS

Originally, a "court" was the place where a sovereign ruled—where the king and his entourage governed. Settling disputes between citizens was part of governing. According to the Bible, King Solomon had to settle the dispute between two women over which of them was the mother of the child both claimed. Judging is the settling of disputes, a function that was slowly separated from the king and the king's court and made into a separate institution of government. Courts have taken over from kings the power to settle controversies by hearing the facts on both sides and deciding which side possesses the greater merit. But since judges are not kings, they must have a basis for their authority. That basis in the United States is the Constitution and the law. Courts decide cases by hearing the facts on both sides of a dispute and applying the relevant law or principle to the facts. (See Table 8.1 for an explanation of the various types of laws and disputes.)

Cases and the Law

Most cases in the United States arise under common law and civil law, types of law that overlap. **Common law** has no statutory basis. It is established by judges who apply previous case decisions to present cases. The previous cases are called **precedents;** they are applied under the doctrine of **stare decisis** ("let the decision stand"). Common law cases are always state and local cases; there is no federal common

---

[1]See Richard Neely, *How Courts Govern America* (New Haven, CT: Yale University Press, 1981).

TABLE 8.1

313
THE JUDICIAL
PROCESS

Types of Laws and Disputes

Type of Law	Type of Case or Dispute	Form of Case
Judge–made law		
Common law	Previous decisions (precedents) applied by judges to current cases. Basis of large proportion of disputes between private citizens over contracts, property, divorce, injuries, and so on. Always state and local cases (there is no federal common law).	*Smith v. Jones*
Equity	Cases where applicable precedents are considered too rigid or inadequate.	*Smith v. Jones*
Statutory law		
Civil law	"Private law," involving disputes between citizens or between government and citizen where no crime is alleged. Two general types are contract and tort. *Contract cases* are disputes that arise over voluntary actions. *Tort cases* are disputes that arise out of obligations inherent in social life. Negligence and slander are examples of torts.	*Smith v. Jones* *New York v. Jones* *U.S. v. Jones* *Jones v. New York*
Criminal law	Cases arising out of actions that violate laws protecting the health, safety, and morals of the community. The government is always the plaintiff.	*U.S. (or state) v. Jones* *Jones v. U.S. (or state), if Jones lost and is appealing*
Public law	All cases where the powers of government or the rights of citizens are involved. The government is the defendant. *Constitutional law* involves judicial review of the basis of a government's action in relation to specific clauses of the Constitution as interpreted in Supreme Court cases. *Administrative law* involves disputes over the statutory authority, jurisdiction, or procedures of administrative agencies.	*Jones v. U.S. (or state)* *In re Jones* *Smith v. Jones, if a license or statute is at issue in their private dispute*

law. Lawyers representing each side in a dispute attempt to show to their own client's advantage that a previous case is or is not a binding precedent for the case at hand. For example, did Smith's failure to deliver the goods on time constitute a breach of contract, or did certain circumstances relieve Smith of the obligation? Was Jones's injury in Johnson's swimming pool due to Johnson's negligence (tort), or did Jones contribute to it by drinking or horseplay (contributory negligence)? The one who brings a complaint is the plaintiff; the one against whom the complaint is brought is the defendant. In the twentieth century, more of these "civil" (noncriminal) cases have risen under laws adopted by legislatures rather than under common law. These legislative enactments are known as *civil law.*

The second category of law is *criminal law.* The government is the plaintiff and alleges that someone has committed a crime. Most of these cases arise in state courts. But there is a large body of federal criminal law and a growing number of federal criminal cases in such areas as tax evasion, mail fraud, false advertising, and sale of narcotics.

A case becomes a matter of the third category, *public law,* if a plaintiff or a defendant can show that the government has the constitutional or statutory authority to take action. For example, one vitally important public law case was *Berman* v. *Parker,* decided by the U.S. Supreme Court in 1954.[2] In this case, which involved a government effort to clear slum properties in the nation's capital to make way for new housing, the Court held that the government had a very broad constitutional sanction, under the concept of "eminent domain," to declare that the public interest required the taking of land from a private owner. Eminent domain is a right of the government to seize private property for public purposes. In such cases, the government is, in a sense, always the defendant, because the court has to be convinced that the government does have the constitutional power or that the agency does have the statutory authority to take the action it seeks against a citizen. Public law cases include those in which a citizen claims that a government action violates his or her civil rights, as well as instances in which citizens charge that administrative agencies are conducting their activities in a manner inconsistent with the law—failing to file an environmental impact statement for a proposed project, for example.

Another kind of case is an *equity* case. This is a court proceeding in which an applicable law is either too rigid or too limited to provide a just as well as a legal remedy. For example, a common law principle or a statute may provide for monetary compensation for damage or injury, but a court may consider this compensation insufficient and increase the amount. An equity case may also seek to prevent damage rather than to provide compensation after the damage is done. An *injunction* is an equity concept. Sometimes called an "extraordinary remedy," it is a court order protecting the rights or interests of the plaintiff. For example, injunctions were often used to prevent strikes when employers claimed that the damage caused by a strike would be irreparable so that after-the-fact compensation would be worthless.

[2]Berman v. Parker, 348 U.S. 26 (1954).

Courts of original jurisdiction are the courts that are responsible for discovering
the facts in a controversy and creating the record upon which a judgment is based.
Although the Constitution gives the Supreme Court original jurisdiction in several types of cases, such as those affecting ambassadors and those in which a state is
one of the parties, most original jurisdiction goes to the lowest courts—the trial
courts. (In courts that have appellate jurisdiction, judges receive cases after factual
record is determined by the trial court. Ordinarily, new facts cannot be presented
before appellate courts.)

Disputes between Parties   Article III of the Constitution and Supreme Court decisions define judicial power as extending only to "cases and controversies." This
means that the parties to any case must have a substantial stake in the outcome of
the case and that the issues cannot be hypothetical. Unless these criteria are met,
the litigant does not have **standing** to sue and the court will not accept the dispute
as a *bona fide* case (see Box 8.1). The courts have consistently refused to give advisory opinions to legislatures or agencies about the constitutionality of proposed
laws or regulations.

Even after a law is enacted, the courts will generally refuse to consider its constitutionality until it is actually applied. The major exception to this rule is the so-
called declaratory judgment, by which a statute is deemed to be unconstitutional
on its face. In the case of *Ada* v. *Guam Society of Obstetricians and Gynecologists,* for
example, a federal appeals court in San Francisco struck down a 1990 Guam
statute that made performing an abortion a felony.[3] The statute was challenged
immediately after its enactment, and before it could actually be enforced, by Guam
physicians who feared prosecution for performing abortions. The federal appeals
court declared that the statute, on its face, represented a violation of the constitutional protection of the right to abortion established in *Roe* v. *Wade.* In November
1992, the U.S. Supreme Court, with three justices dissenting, refused to give the
case further consideration. One of the dissenters, Justice Antonin Scalia, argued
vehemently that the appeals court should not have rendered a decision before the
Guam statute was actually applied.

The courts also refuse to take the initiative. Cases must be formulated from disputes between parties and must be brought to court. The other side of the principle is that the courts cannot, in theory, refuse to take real cases or controversies
even when they fear serious repercussions in the community. Often, however, the
appellate courts do dodge real cases and controversies by returning cases to the
lower court for retrial or by holding that a case should be settled by the electoral
process and the legislature rather than the courts. For example, the Supreme Court
refused to hear cases challenging the constitutionality of American intervention in
Vietnam, holding that the issue was a political question that should be resolved by
Congress and the president.

[3]See *Congressional Quarterly Weekly Report,* 5 December 1992, p. 3751.

BOX 8.1
Access to the Courts: The Rules of Standing

Over the years, the Supreme Court has developed rules governing which cases it can and cannot properly hear. The rules of access can be broken down into three major categories: (1) case or controversy, (2) standing, and (3) mootness.

(1) *Case or controversy:* The Constitution provides the judiciary with the power to decide various "cases" and "controversies," and the Court has from the very first taken this language to mean that it does not have the power to render advisory opinions. In *Muskrat v. United States* (1911), the Court extended the rule to eliminate feigned controversy. The case before the court must be a real controversy, with two truly adversarial parties; if one side is a straw man, the adversary system cannot work.

(2) *Standing:* To have standing is to be the proper person to bring a suit, and the basic requirement for standing is to show injury to oneself. In order for a group or class of people to have standing (as in class action suits), each member must show injury. The Court's definition of injury has changed over the years; it has expanded from the narrow reading of the term—personal and/or economic harm—to include such values as "aesthetic and environmental well-being" (*Sierra Club* v. *Morton* [1972]). It should be noted, however, that a general interest in the environment does not provide a group with sufficient basis for standing; the members must be among those specifically injured (*United States* v. *S.C.R.A.P.* [1973]). In short, standing requires specific, personal, and substantial harm.

(3) *Mootness:* There are two time-factor requirements that must be met for the Court to hear a case. One is the question of ripeness. The Court must feel that the issue is ready to be heard—that the issue is still not too abstract, that all other possible remedies have been exhausted, that the matter has been absorbed into the national consciousness. Conversely, it is necessary that the case not be moot—that the particular problem has not already been resolved by other means. The Court began to relax its rules on mootness in cases where the situation was likely to come up again. For example, under the original definition of mootness, it was usually impossible to challenge election rules since the election was almost sure to be over by the time the case reached the appellate courts. But the Court began to hear some such cases if the issue was likely to be repeated in later elections (*Moore* v. *Ogilvie* [1969]). And as the Court pointed out in *Roe* v. *Wade* (1973), the major abortion case, questions relating to pregnancy could never be appealed if the older standards of mootness were to be applied, since the case would surely take longer than the pregnancy. It was equally true that the issue was likely to recur, not only for the particular woman bringing suit but for many other women as well, and issues "capable of repetition yet evading review" should be heard.

The Role of the Judiciary   The purpose of the judiciary is to judge, and thus, the courts settle the disputes brought before them. The rulings made by judges in individual cases are studied by lawyers who seek to derive principles to apply in future cases.

The judicial process is filled with formalities, rituals, and procedures designed to protect the interests of all individuals and, short of that, to impress all individuals with the wisdom of settling disputes in court rather than taking matters into

their own hands. So elaborate are the judicial rituals that specialists in them—
lawyers—are indispensable. But the rituals should not mask the basic purpose of
the judiciary. Judges exist to make choices. They may or may not listen carefully to
evidence. They may or may not give full respect to both sides in a dispute or to the
procedures available to protect people's interests. But they do choose who gets the
money or who is to be punished and how. Their decisions can determine life and
death, or resolve questions such as who receives certain property or whether or
not strikers are trespassing. Such decisions can even validate calling out the armed
forces to deliver the property or disperse the trespassers.

The Role of Juries   In courts of original jurisdiction, judges may be provided
with juries to help them make their decisions. The Constitution requires juries for
all criminal prosecutions (unless the defendant waives the right to a jury) and the
right of trial by jury for all civil actions where the value in controversy exceeds
$20. The jury brings community values to bear in the trial, and it helps weigh ev-
idence and decide who gets the money or who is culpable and to what degree.
The jury's role in the legal process, however, is quite circumscribed, and is heavily
dependent upon the judge. The judge defines what the facts are, which of them
are admissible, and which are relevant. The judge also defines the alternative verdicts open for a jury to reach. Jury decisions may also be reversed or altered by appeals courts when an error of procedure is deemed to have been made, even when
the appeals court sympathizes with the original verdict. It will, for example, reverse the conviction of a proven criminal if illegally gained evidence was used in
the trial. Often appeals courts reverse the verdict or substantially reduce the award
in negligence suits when juries presumably have gotten carried away with sympa-

PROCESS BOX 8.1
How a Jury Trial Is Conducted

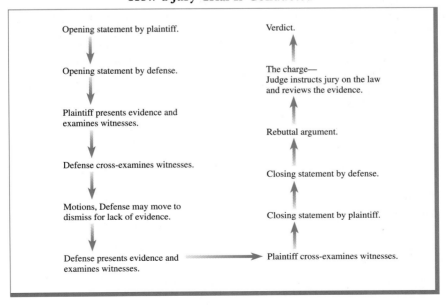

thy for the individual or for a small business suing a giant corporation. For example, in 1978 a jury in federal district court awarded $120 million to a small photographic company to compensate it for damages attributable to the "monopolistic practices" of Eastman Kodak. The trial judge cut the award to $87 million. In 1979, a court of appeals cut the award to $900,000 and returned the case to the lower court for a new trial on whether further damages were warranted.[4] Such reversals are good reminders of the limited place of juries within the judicial system.

Adversary Proceedings   A basic assumption underlying the American judicial process is that the best way to provide judges and juries with the materials necessary to make wise choices is to allow each side in a dispute to present those arguments most favorable to it. In the words of an old adage: "When two people argue, as unfairly as possible, on opposite sides, it is certain that no important considerations will altogether escape notice." No one can prove that the adversary process produces the truth. A good argument could in fact be made that judges might provide themselves with a better basis for decision by dispensing with both lawyers and the adversary process, investigating the situation for themselves, interrogating witnesses for themselves, and so on. This so-called "inquisitorial process" is the typical procedure in Western Europe. Everyone is aware that lawyers' abilities can vary greatly. Why assume that an adversary process will produce the truth if one side of the case is better presented than the other?

Although the adversary process provides no guarantee that trials will produce truth, it possesses two virtues that enormously facilitate judging and increase the legitimacy of the judicial process. The first virtue is the presumption of innocence in criminal cases. People give lip service to the idea that the accused is innocent until proven guilty. But the adversary process reinforces this presumption by compelling the government to prove the guilt of the accused despite the best efforts of a skilled advocate to prevent it from so doing.

The second virtue of the adversary process is that it helps preserve the equality of the contending parties in criminal as well as civil cases. In criminal cases, because of the adversary process, government is simply one of the contending forces. The defendant can face accusers and cross-examine them and can present contrary evidence. There are many flaws in the theory and practice of equality between the parties, but the routine of adversary proceedings does help keep the judge in the middle rather than on the side of the government.

FEDERAL JURISDICTION

The overwhelming majority of court cases are tried not in federal courts but in state and local courts under state common law, state statutes, and local ordinances. Of all the cases heard in the United States in 1990, federal district courts (the lowest federal level) received 266,000 (see Box 8.2). Although this number is up sub-

---

[4]Berkey Photo, Inc. v. Eastman Kodak Co., 457 F. Supp. 400 (D.N.Y. 1979), *aff'd in part, rev. in part* 603 F2d. 263; *cert den.* 444 U.S. 1093.

BOX 8.2
Federal Laws and Federal Cases

S ince all common law and most statutory laws in the American federal system are
of state and local origin, it is not surprising that over 99 percent of all cases are
tried in state and local courts. The relatively few federal cases can be grouped into
three categories:

1. *Civil cases involving "diversity of citizenship."* The Constitution provides for federal
   jurisdiction whenever a citizen of one state brings suit against a citizen of another
   state. Congressional legislation requires that the amount at issue be more than
   $10,000. Otherwise the case is handled by a regular state court in the state where
   the grievance occurs.
2. *Civil cases where an agency of the federal government is seeking to enforce federal laws that
   provide for civil, not criminal, penalties.* These laws can range from bankruptcy laws
   to admiralty and maritime laws to occupational and consumer safety laws, environmental protection laws, and energy conservation and development laws.
3. *Cases where federal criminal statutes are involved or where issues of public law have been
   made of state criminal cases.* State prisoner petitions alleging mistreatment, unfair
   trial, or abridgment of civil rights represent the largest source of criminal cases
   coming before the federal appellate courts.

stantially from the 87,000 cases heard in 1961, it still constitutes under 1 percent of
the judiciary's business. The federal courts of appeal listened to 40,898 cases in
1990, and the U.S. Supreme Court reviewed 6,316 in its 1989–1990 term. Only
125 cases were given full-dress Supreme Court review (the nine justices actually
sitting *en banc*—in full court—and hearing the lawyers argue the case).[5]

The Lower Federal Courts

Most of the more than 200,000 annual cases of original federal jurisdiction are
handled by the federal district courts (see Figure 8.1 for the organization of all the
U.S. courts). The federal district courts are trial courts of general jurisdiction and
their cases are, in form, indistinguishable from cases in the state trial courts.

There are eighty-nine district courts in the fifty states, plus one in the District
of Columbia and one in Puerto Rico, and four territorial courts. In an effort to
deal with the greatly increased court workload of recent years, in 1978 Congress
increased the number of district judgeships from 400 to 517. District judges are assigned to district courts according to the workload; the busiest of these courts may

[5]Data were drawn from the National Court Statistical Project, Department of Justice, Law Enforce-
ment Assistance Administration, *State Court Caseload Statistics; Annual Report 1977* (Washington, DC:
Government Printing Office, 1979); Administrative Office of the U.S. Courts, *Federal Judicial Workload
Statistics, 1979* (Washington, DC: Government Printing Office, 1980); and Administrative Office of
U.S. Courts, *Annual Report of the Director 1979* (Washington, DC: Government Printing Office, 1980);
U.S. Bureau of the Census, *Statistical Abstract of the United States* (Washington, DC: Government Print-
ing Office, 1992).

FIGURE 8.1

Organization of the Courts

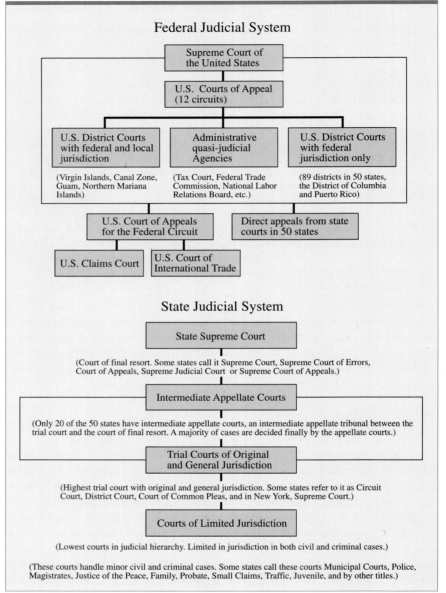

Federal Judicial System

Supreme Court of
the United States

U.S. Courts of Appeal
(12 circuits)

U.S. District Courts
with federal and local
jurisdiction

Administrative
quasi-judicial
Agencies

U.S. District Courts
with federal
jurisdiction only

(Virgin Islands, Canal Zone,
Guam, Northern Mariana
Islands)

(Tax Court, Federal Trade
Commission, National Labor
Relations Board, etc.)

(89 districts in 50 states,
the District of Columbia
and Puerto Rico)

U.S. Court of Appeals
for the Federal Circuit

Direct appeals from state
courts in 50 states

U.S. Claims Court

U.S. Court of
International Trade

State Judicial System

State Supreme Court

(Court of final resort. Some states call it Supreme Court, Supreme Court of Errors,
Court of Appeals, Supreme Judicial Court or Supreme Court of Appeals.)

Intermediate Appellate Courts

(Only 20 of the 50 states have intermediate appellate courts, an intermediate appellate tribunal between the
trial court and the court of final resort. A majority of cases are decided finally by the appellate courts.)

Trial Courts of Original
and General Jurisdiction

(Highest trial court with original and general jurisdiction. Some states refer to it as Circuit
Court, District Court, Court of Common Pleas, and in New York, Supreme Court.)

Courts of Limited Jurisdiction

(Lowest courts in judicial hierarchy. Limited in jurisdiction in both civil and criminal cases.)

(These courts handle minor civil and criminal cases. Some states call these courts Municipal Courts, Police,
Magistrates, Justice of the Peace, Family, Probate, Small Claims, Traffic, Juvenile, and by other titles.)

Source: Congressional Quarterly, *Guide to the Congress of the United States,* 3rd ed. (Washington, DC:
Congressional Quarterly Press, 1982). Used by permission.

have as many as twenty-seven judges. Only one judge is assigned to each case, except where statutes provide for three-judge courts to deal with special issues. (Cases involving constitutional issues are appealed from district courts directly to the Supreme Court.) The routines and procedures of the federal district courts are

essentially the same as those of the lower state courts, except that federal procedural requirements tend to be stricter. States, for example, do not have to provide
a grand jury, a twelve-member trial jury, or a unanimous jury verdict. Federal
courts must provide all these things.

Besides the district courts, there are also some federal courts with original jurisdiction over specific classes of cases. The U.S. Court of Claims has jurisdiction over disputes about compensation when property has been taken for a public use, cases alleging that a government agency has not properly observed its contracts, and claims by employees for back pay. The U.S. Tax Court handles cases arising out of enforcement of the Internal Revenue (income tax) Code. The Customs Court also handles tax cases, but mainly those involving tariffs. The disputes are most often over the value that ought to be put on imported merchandise for tariff purposes. Original jurisdiction over patent infringement cases is given to an administrative agency, the U.S. Patent and Trademark Office.

Indeed, many administrative agencies enjoy the status of federal district courts in that their decisions go directly to a court of appeals and are not further tried by the district courts. Regulatory agencies whose decisions are appealed over the district courts directly to the appeals courts include the Securities and Exchange Commission, the National Labor Relations Board, the Federal Trade Commission, and the Interstate Commerce Commission. In 1990, the various U.S. appeals courts handled 40,898 cases. Of this total, 38,323 came directly from the U.S. district courts, and 2,578 came from the administrative agencies, boards, and commissions whose appeals go directly to the appeals courts, bypassing the district courts.

The Appellate Courts

Roughly 10 percent of all lower court and agency cases are accepted for review by the federal appeals courts and by the Supreme Court in its capacity as an appellate court. The country is divided into eleven judicial circuits, each of which has a U.S. Court of Appeals. Every state and the District of Columbia is assigned to the circuit in the continental United States that is closest to it. Prior to the establishment of the appellate courts in 1891, each Supreme Court justice, in addition to his duties in Washington, was expected to act as the presiding judge of a circuit. This involved the arduous task of traveling from city to city within a circuit to review all cases appealed from the district courts.

One of the more colorful stories of Supreme Court justices "riding circuit" in the nineteenth century derives from the case of *In re Neagle* (1890). While sitting as a circuit justice in California, Justice Stephen Field ruled against a litigant, Mrs. Terry, who thereby lost a claim involving title to over a million dollars. Dismayed by the result, Mrs. Terry and her husband accused Justice Field of corruption and vowed to kill him if he should ever return to California. The next time Justice Field was obligated to ride circuit in California, he was assigned a bodyguard, Neagle, by the U.S. attorney general. Undaunted and determined to execute his murderous threat, Mr. Terry confronted Justice Field in a restaurant one day. But just as Mr. Terry was about to pull out his knife, Neagle shot and killed him. Neagle was arrested for murder, but he was acquitted. The Supreme Court held that he had acted pursuant to a valid executive order. (See Chapter 6 for a discus-

sion of the broader constitutional issues raised by the case.) In 1891, Congress enacted a law creating a network of appellate courts to relieve Justice Field and other
Supreme Court justices of having to ride circuit. Each justice is still chief of a circuit but is no longer required to be present as its presiding judge.

Except for cases selected for review by the Supreme Court, decisions made by
the appeals courts are final. Because of this finality, certain safeguards have been
built into the system. The most important is the provision of more than one judge
for every appeals case. Each court of appeals has from three to fifteen permanent
judgeships, depending on the workload of the circuit. Although normally three
judges hear appealed cases, in some instances a larger number of judges sit together
en banc.

Another safeguard is provided by the assignment of a Supreme Court justice as
the circuit justice for each of the eleven circuits. Since the creation of the appeals
court in 1891, the circuit justice's primary duty has been to review appeals arising
in the circuit in order to expedite Supreme Court action. The most frequent and
best-known action of circuit justices is that of reviewing requests for stays of execution when the full Court is unable to do so—mainly during the summer, when
the Court is in recess.

The Supreme Court

The Supreme Court is without question the top court of the entire U.S. judiciary—local, state, and federal. Article III of the Constitution vests "the judicial
power of the United States" in the Supreme Court, and this court is supreme in
fact as well as form. It has the power of judicial review—the power and the obligation to review any lower court decision where a substantial issue of public law is
involved. The disputes can be over the constitutionality of federal or state laws,
over the propriety or constitutionality of the court procedures followed, and over
whether public officers are exceeding their authority.

Congress and the state legislatures do have the power virtually to overturn
Court decisions by remedial legislation. An example of this kind of legislation
occurred in 1978, when Congress effectively overturned a 1976 Supreme Court
ruling that had permitted pregnancy leaves to be treated differently from other
temporary disability leaves in employee health plans. In amending Title VII of the
1964 Civil Rights Act, Congress required employers to provide benefits for pregnancy leaves similar to those for other temporary disability leaves.[6] The initial
Court ruling had found no legislative requirement that pregnancy leaves be treated
identically to other disability leaves. By enacting such a requirement, Congress reversed the Court. In 1991, Congress overturned a series of 1989 Supreme Court
decisions that limited the ability of members of minority groups to prove that they
had been victims of employment discrimination by passing the Civil Rights Act
of 1991.

Most of the time, however, state legislators and members of Congress have
found it extremely difficult to summon up the majorities necessary to react against

---

[6]PL 95-955 amended Title VII of the 1964 Civil Rights Act. The 1976 Supreme Court ruling came in
the case of G.E. v. Gilbert, 429 U.S. 126 (1976).

John Marshall
The Great Chief Justice

John Marshall (1755–1835)

John Marshall was sworn in as chief justice of the Supreme Court on February 4, 1801. Appointed in the waning days of the administration of John Adams, Marshall was a die-hard Federalist at a time when the Federalist party was losing power. Adam's successor, Thomas Jefferson, was an archenemy, and the two often found themselves at opposite ends of political quarrels. Moreover, Marshall came to the Court with marginal legal credentials. His formal education consisted of attending a few months' worth of lectures at the College of William and Mary. In short, Marshall's appointment seemed to resemble little more than the elevation of a political hack to the nation's highest court.

Yet, in his thirty-four years on the Supreme Court, John Marshall would win the admiration of friends and foes alike. He would help elevate the status of the judiciary to its rightful position among the three branches of government, and he would craft some of the most important decisions in the Court's history.

Although his formal training was limited, Marshall was admitted to the bar in 1780, and practiced law in western Virginia, his native state. Marshall earned a reputation as brilliant in constructing arguments, and became one of his state's most renowned lawyers. Marshall was a delegate to the Virginia Ratifying Convention, convened in 1788 to consider the new Constitution, where he staunchly defended the document.

Marshall viewed the Constitution as the central instrument of national unity and federal power. He considered the Constitution to be a precise document articulating specific powers, yet also as a living document open to broad interpretation for the purpose of affirming appropriate federal authority. He established for posterity the right of the Court to rule on the constitutionality of federal and state laws in the landmark case of *Marbury* v. *Madison*. In the *Dartmouth College* case and many others, he elevated the inviolability of contract and property rights. He gave teeth to the federal government's interstate commerce power in *Gibbons* v. *Ogden* by affirming that the federal government alone could regulate trade, travel, and navigation between the states.

In these and many other cases, Marshall exhibited an extraordinarily adept sense not only of law, but also of the political and the possible. He recognized early that the courts had very limited power resources (neither purse nor sword). They would thus have to rely on procedure, precedent, respect for the law, and the avoidance of direct political confrontations. The shroud of constitutional legitimacy that today envelops the courts was, in all probability, more the product of John Marshall than of any other jurist.

Source: Robert McCloskey, *The American Supreme Court* (Chicago: University of Chicago Press, 1960).

a Supreme Court decision. As Justice Robert Jackson once put it, "The Court is not final because it is infallible; the Court is infallible because it is final."[7]

JUDICIAL REVIEW

The Supreme Court's power of judicial review has come to mean review not only of lower court decisions but also of state legislation and acts of Congress. For this reason, if for no other, the Supreme Court is more than a judicial agency—it is also a major lawmaking body.

The Supreme Court's power of judicial review over lower court decisions has never been at issue. Nor has there been any serious quibble over the power of the federal courts to review administrative agencies in order to determine whether their actions and decisions are within the powers delegated to them by Congress. There has, however, been a great deal of controversy occasioned by the Supreme Court's efforts to review acts of Congress and the decisions of state courts and legislatures.

Judicial Review of Acts of Congress

Since the Constitution does not give the Supreme Court the power of judicial review of congressional enactments, the Court's exercise of it is something of a usurpation. Various proposals were debated at the Constitutional Convention. Among them was the proposal to create a council composed of the president and the judiciary that would share the veto power over legislation. Another proposal would have routed all legislation through the Court as well as through the president; a veto by either one would have required an overruling by a two-thirds vote of the House and Senate. Each proposal was rejected by the delegates, and no further effort was made to give the Supreme Court review power over the other branches.

This does not prove that the framers of the Constitution opposed judicial review, but it does indicate that "if they intended to provide for it in the Constitution, they did so in a most obscure fashion."[8] Disputes over the intentions of the framers were settled in 1803 in the case of *Marbury* v. *Madison*.[9] Though Congress and the president have often been at odds with the Court, its legal power to review acts of Congress has not been seriously questioned since 1803 (see Box 8.3). One reason is that judicial power has been accepted as natural, if not intended. Another reason is that the Supreme Court has rarely reviewed the constitutionality of the acts of Congress, especially in the past fifty years. When such acts do come up for review, the Court makes a self-conscious effort to give them an interpretation that will make them constitutional.

[7]Brown v. Allen, 344 U.S. 443 (1952).

[8]C. Herman Pritchett, *The American Constitution* (New York: McGraw-Hill, 1959), p. 138.

[9] Marbury v. Madison, 1 Cr. 137 (1803).

BOX 8.3
Marbury v. Madison

The 1803 Supreme Court decision handed down in *Marbury* v. *Madison* established the power of the Court to review acts of Congress. The case arose over a suit filed by William Marbury and seven other people against Secretary of State James Madison to require him to approve their appointments as justices of the peace. These had been last-minute ("midnight judges") appointments of outgoing President John Adams. Chief Justice John Marshall held that although Marbury and the others were entitled to their appointments, the Supreme Court had no power to order Madison to deliver them, because the relevant section of the first Judiciary Act of 1789 was unconstitutional—giving the Courts powers not intended by Article III of the Constitution.

Marshall reasoned that constitutions are framed to serve as the "fundamental and paramount law of the nation." Thus, he argued, with respect to the legislative action of Congress, the Constitution is a "superior...law, unchangeable by ordinary means." He concluded that an act of Congress that contradicts the Constitution must be judged void.

As to the question of whether the Court was empowered to rule on the constitutionality of legislative action, Marshall responded emphatically that it is "the province and duty of the judicial department to say what the law is." Since the Constitution is the supreme law of the land, he reasoned, it is clearly within the realm of the Court's responsibility to rule on the constitutionality of legislative acts and treaties. This principle has held sway ever since.

Sources: Gerald Gunther, *Constitutional Law* (Mineola, NY: Fountain Press, 1980), pp. 9–11; and *Marbury* v. *Madison*, 1 Cr. 137 (1803).

Judicial Review of State Actions

The power of the Supreme Court to review state legislation or other state action and to determine its constitutionality is neither granted by the Constitution nor inherent in the federal system. But the logic of the "supremacy clause" of Article VI of the Constitution, which declares it and laws made under its authority to be the supreme law of the land, is very strong. Furthermore, in the Judiciary Act of 1789, Congress conferred on the Supreme Court the power to reverse state constitutions and laws whenever they are clearly in conflict with the U.S. Constitution, federal laws, or treaties.[10] This power gives the Supreme Court jurisdiction over all of the millions of cases handled by American courts each year.

The supremacy clause of the Constitution not only established the federal Constitution, statutes, and treaties as the "supreme law of the land," but also provided that "the Judges in every State shall be bound thereby, any Thing in the Constitution or Laws of the State to the Contrary notwithstanding." Under this authority, the Supreme Court has frequently overturned state constitutional provisions or

---

[10]This review power was affirmed by the Supreme Court in Martin v. Hunter's Lessee, 1 Wheaton 304 (1816).

statutes and state court decisions it deems to contravene rights or privileges guaranteed under the federal Constitution or federal statutes.

The civil rights area abounds with examples of state laws that were overturned because the statutes violated guarantees of due process and equal protection contained in the Fourteenth Amendment to the Constitution. For example, in the 1954 case of *Brown* v. *Board of Education,* the Court overturned statutes from Kansas, South Carolina, Virginia, and Delaware that either required or permitted segregated public schools, on the basis that such statutes denied black school children equal protection of the law.[11] In 1967, in *Loving* v. *Virginia,* the Court invalidated a Virginia statute prohibiting interracial marriages.[12]

State statutes in other subject matter areas are equally subject to challenge. In *Griswold* v. *Connecticut,* the Court invalidated a Connecticut statute prohibiting the general distribution of contraceptives to married couples on the basis that the statute violated the couples' rights to marital privacy.[13] In *Brandenburg* v. *Ohio,* the Court overturned an Ohio statute forbidding any person from urging criminal acts as a means of inducing political reform or from joining any association that advocated such activities on the grounds that the statute punished "mere advocacy" and therefore violated the free speech provisions of the federal Constitution.[14]

Judicial Review and the Administration of Justice

Given the millions of disputes that arise every year, the job of the Supreme Court would be impossible if it were not able to control the flow of cases and its own case load (see Process Box 8.2). Its original jurisdiction is only a minor problem. The original jurisdiction includes: (1) cases between the United States and one of the fifty states, (2) cases between two or more states, (3) cases involving foreign ambassadors or other ministers, and (4) cases brought by one state against citizens of another state or against a foreign country. The most important of these cases are disputes between states over land, water, or old debts. Generally, the Supreme Court deals with these cases by appointing a "special master," usually a retired judge, to actually hear the case and present a report. The Supreme Court then allows the states involved in the dispute to present arguments for or against the master's opinion.[15]

The Supreme Court's major problem is actually the same as that of the head of any large organization—that of keeping most decisions at the lower level and bringing to the top only the few disputes that involve high-level policy. To do this, the Court must keep tight control over the number and type of cases it accepts for review.

Decisions handed down by lower courts can today reach the Supreme Court in

---

[11]Brown v. Board of Education, 347 U.S. 483 (1954).

[12]Loving v. Virginia, 388 U.S. 1 (1967).

[13]Griswold v. Connecticut, 381 U.S. 479 (1965).

[14]Brandenburg v. Ohio, 395 U.S. 444 (1969).

[15]Walter F. Murphy, "The Supreme Court of the United States," in *Encyclopedia of the American Judicial System,* ed. Robert J. Janosik (New York: Scribner's, 1987).

How Cases Reach the Supreme Court

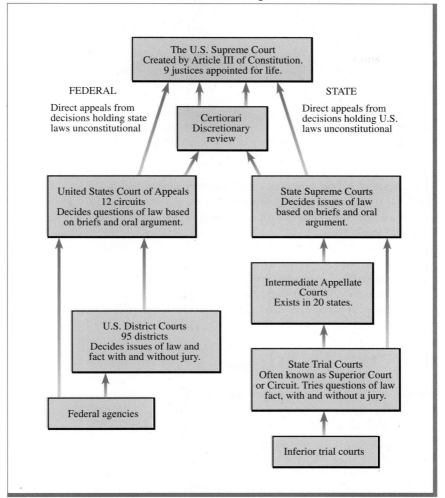

one of two ways: through a writ of *certiorari,* or, in the case of convicted state prisoners, through a writ of *habeas corpus.* A *writ* is a court document conveying an
order of some sort. In recent years, an effort has been made to give the Court
more discretion regarding the cases it chooses to hear. Before 1988, the Supreme
Court was obligated to review cases on what was called a writ of appeal. This has
since been eliminated, and the Court now has virtually complete discretion over
what cases it will hear.

Most cases reach the Supreme Court through the ***writ of certiorari,*** which is
granted whenever four of the nine justices agree to review a case. The Supreme
Court was once so inundated with appeals that in 1925 Congress enacted

laws giving it some control over its case load with the power to issue writs of *certio-rari*. Rule 10 of the Supreme Court's own rules of procedure defines *certiorari* as "not a matter of right, but of sound judicial discretion . . . granted only where there are special and important reasons therefor." The reasons provided for in Rule 10 are:

1. Where a state has made a decision that conflicts with previous Supreme Court decisions.
2. Where a state court has come up with an entirely new federal question.
3. Where one court of appeals has rendered a decision in conflict with another.
4. Where there are other inconsistent rulings between two or more courts or states.
5. Where a single court of appeals has sanctioned too great a departure by a lower court from normal judicial proceedings (a reason rarely given).

The **writ of habeas corpus** is a fundamental safeguard of individual rights (see Box 8.4). Its historical purpose is to enable an accused person to challenge arbitrary detention and to force an open trial before a judge. But in 1867, Congress's distrust of southern courts led it to confer on federal courts the authority to issue writs of *habeas corpus* to prisoners already tried or being tried in state courts of proper jurisdiction, where the constitutional rights of the prisoner were possibly being violated. This writ gives state prisoners a second channel toward Supreme Court review in case their direct appeal from the highest state court fails. The writ of *habeas corpus* is discretionary; that is, the Court can decide which cases to review.

Judicial Review and Lawmaking

When courts of original jurisdiction apply existing statutes or past cases directly to citizens, the effect is the same as legislation. Lawyers study judicial decisions in order to discover underlying principles, and they advise their clients accordingly. Often the process is nothing more than reasoning by analogy; the facts in a particular case are so close to those in one or more previous cases that the same decision should be handed down. Because of the legitimacy and adaptability of common law, Anglo-Saxon countries (England and its former colonies) got by for a long time without much legislation at all.

The appellate courts, however, are in another realm. When an appellate court hands down its decision, it accomplishes two things. First, of course, it decides who wins—the person who won in the lower court or the person who lost in the lower court. But at the same time, it expresses its decision in a manner that provides guidance to the lower courts for handling future cases in the same area. Appellate judges try to give their reasons and rulings in writing so the "administration of justice" can take place most of the time at the lowest judicial level. They try to make their ruling or reasoning clear, so as to avoid confusion, which can produce a surge of litigation at the lower levels. These rulings can be considered laws, but they are laws governing the behavior only of the judiciary. They influence citizens' conduct only because, in the words of Justice Oliver Wendell Holmes, who served

BOX 8.4
Habeas Corpus

A writ of *habeas corpus* is an order issued by a court directing the release of an individual in custody, which is obtained by filing a petition alleging that the detention of the individual is improper for reasons specific to each case, from allegations that the person in custody is not the person who committed the crime to allegations that technical errors have denied the accused certain constitutional rights. Petitions for writs of *habeas corpus* may take many forms. Petitions may be filed by an attorney on behalf of an individual in custody, but they are as frequently filed by the person in custody. In fact, most jails and prisons have at least one "jailhouse lawyer"—an inmate who spends the majority of his or her time preparing petitions for writs of *habeas corpus* for other inmates. If a court decides the petition should be granted, it will issues a writ of *habeas corpus* (order of release) citing the reasons set forth in the petition. A petition for a writ of *habeas corpus* generally takes the following form:

John Jones

   v.

People of the State
of North Carolina

John Jones respectfully states that:

1. He is imprisoned at the Doe County Jail in Doe, North Carolina.

2. He has been imprisoned by Jim Smith, Sheriff of Doe County, North Carolina.

3. He has been imprisoned as the result of a conviction of theft entered in Doe County on January 1, 1988.

4. This imprisonment is illegal because the court failed to provide John Jones with assistance of counsel.

5. John Jones has not previously applied for a writ of *habeas corpus* (or, if a previous writ has been filed, the circumstances under which the writ was filed are stated here).

6. John Jones has not filed an appeal (or if an appeal has been filed, the disposition of the appeal is stated here).

    Accordingly, John Jones asks that a writ of *habeas corpus* directed to Jim Smith, Sheriff of Doe County, be issued inquiring into the propriety of this imprisonment and ordering his release from custody, pursuant to law.

on the Court from 1900–1932, lawyers make "prophecies of what the courts will do in fact."[16]

    The written opinion of an appellate court is about halfway between common law and statutory law. It is judge-made and draws heavily on the precedents of pre-

---

[16]Oliver Wendell Holmes, Jr., "The Path of the Law," *Harvard Law Review* 10 (1897), p. 457.

Thurgood Marshall and Clarence Thomas
From Helping Others to Self-Help

As the first and second African Americans to serve on the Supreme Court, Thurgood Marshall and Clarence Thomas both claimed humble origins rooted in America's troubled racial past. Marshall was the great-grandson of a slave; Thomas was a sharecropper's grandson. Yet their public careers represent diametrically opposed views on how the law should treat disadvantaged citizens.

Born and raised in a Baltimore family of modest means but grand ambitions, Marshall graduated from Howard Law School and began a legal practice specializing in cases defending blacks mistreated by the legal system. In 1938, he became head of Legal Services for the National Association for the Advancement of Colored People (NAACP). In the 1940s and 1950s, he spearheaded legal efforts to end discrimination, arguing thirty-two cases before the Supreme Court (including *Brown* v. *Board of Education*). After Marshall had served on the U.S. Court of Appeals and as President Lyndon Johnson's solicitor general, he was elevated by Johnson to the Supreme Court in 1967.

Clarence Thomas's appointment to the high court by President George Bush in 1991 reinforced the Court's more conservative tendencies. His early education in a Catholic seminary had instilled in Thomas the belief that hard work and individual initiative could overcome racial discrimination and other adversities. Ironically, Thomas won admission to Yale Law School on a program aimed at recruiting blacks and others from disadvantaged backgrounds. His rapid rise included service in the Missouri attorney general's office. In his early work, Thomas carefully avoided working on race-related issues, but the Reagan administration

Thurgood Marshall

vious cases. But it tries to articulate the rule of law controlling the case in question and future cases like it. In this respect, it is like a statute. But it differs from a statute in that a statute addresses itself to the future conduct of citizens, whereas a written opinion addresses itself mainly to the willingness or ability of courts in the future to take cases and render favorable opinions. Decisions by appellate courts affect citizens by giving them a cause of action or by taking it away from them. That is, they open or close access to the courts.

A specific case may help clarify the distinction. Before the Second World War, one of the most insidious forms of racial discrimination was the "restrictive covenant," a clause in a contract whereby the purchasers of a house agreed that if

tapped him to become head of the Equal Employment Opportunity Commission, the agency that enforces laws against discrimination. Thomas then served briefly on the Court of Appeals before his ascension to the Supreme Court.

In his many opinions from the bench, Marshall championed government efforts to eliminate discrimination through such means as busing to achieve racial balance in schools and the implementation of affirmative action programs designed to provide educational and employment opportunities for those who had been historically closed out of such areas. Thomas has been a strong critic of such programs. In a 1987 law journal article, for example, Thomas criticized the landmark *Brown* case; later he sharply attacked Marshall himself, saying that it was wrong for Marshall to dwell on slavery during the commemoration of the Constitution's bicentennial.

Thomas himself ran afoul of the nation's heightened sensitivity to discrimination and fair treatment when a former employee, law school professor Anita Hill, leveled charges of sexual harassment against him that riveted the nation's attention.

On the Court, Thomas's conservative philosophy has stood in stark contrast to Marshall's liberal philosophy. Unlike the man he succeeded, Thomas favors the death penalty (including limiting death penalty appeals) and limiting the rights of the accused, opposes abortion rights, and in general has sided with the conservative activist wing of the Court.

Justice Marshall sought to focus the powers of government to assist those who have benefited least from the American system. Justice Thomas argues that self-help and limited government interference provide the most appropriate remedy for injustice. Both of these arguments will continue to find support in American courts.

Source: Richard Kluger, *Simple Justice* (New York: Vintage Books, 1975).

Clarence Thomas

they later decided to sell it, they would sell only to a Caucasian. When a test case finally reached the Supreme Court in 1948, the Court ruled unanimously that citizens had a right to discriminate with restrictive covenants in their sales contracts but that the courts could not enforce these contracts. Its argument was that enforcement would constitute violation of the Fourteenth Amendment provision that no state shall "deny to any person within its jurisdiction equal protection under the law."[17] The Court was thereby predicting what it would and would not

[17]Shelley v. Kraemer, 334 U.S. 1 (1948).

THE SUPREME COURT'S MOST CONTROVERSIAL DECISION: ROE V. WADE

On January 22, 1973, *Roe* v. *Wade*, its most controversial ruling ever, the Supreme Court declared that women had a constitutional right to abortion. Justice Harry Blackmun wrote the Court's 7-to-2 opinion: "[the] right of privacy, whether it be founded in the Fourteenth Amendment's concept of personal liberty and restrictions upon state action . . . or in the Ninth Amendment's reservation of rights to the people, is broad enough to encompass a woman's decision whether or not to terminate her pregnancy. . . . The Court has held that regulation limiting these rights may be justified only by a 'compelling state interest.' " States were only allowed to regulate abortions after the first trimester of pregnancy or when a woman faced greater risk of injury or death during an abortion than in delivery.

The 1973 Burger Court. Seated in the front row are, from left to right: Potter Stewart; William O. Douglas; Chief Justice Warren Burger; William Brennan; and Byron White. Standing are, from left to right: Lewis F. Powell, Jr.; Thurgood Marshall; Harry A. Blackmun; and William Rehnquist.

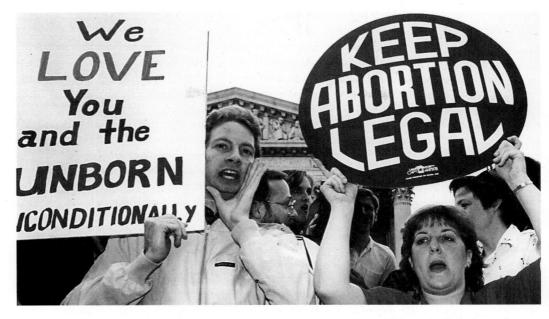

In the years following *Roe,* the Court heard twenty more cases concerning the issue of abortion and mostly struck down statutes that made an abortion difficult to obtain. *Webster* v. *Reproductive Health Services* (1989) marked a turning point. While only two justices joined in Rehnquist's opinion, two others concurred in part, a reflection of the bitter division on the Court over this issue by the late 1980s. This decision enabled states and localities to begin passing restrictions on the availability of abortions.

Meanwhile, outside the Court, public opinion has coalesced on opposite sides of the issue. The pro-choice movement—made up of women's and civil rights groups—supports a woman's fundamental right to control her reproductive decisions. The pro-life movement—supported by the Roman Catholic church and fundamentalist religious groups—believes in preserving life at all stages of fetal development. These groups both try to get their views heard in court, mounting challenges to any ruling or state law that does not go their way.

Following *Webster,* four states immediately passed more restrictive legislation whose constitutionality was also immediately challenged. In 1991, the first challenge reached the Supreme Court in *Planned Parenthood of Southeastern Pennsylvania* v. *Casey.* This case further fragmented the Court. In a narrow 5-to-4 vote, the Court upheld most of the state's restrictions. While not overturning *Roe,* a definite majority abandoned *Roe's* assertion of a "fundamental right of women to choose abortion." Phyllis Schlafly *(below left),* representing the pro-life groups, and Patricia Ireland *(below middle),* representing the women's rights groups, each claimed partial victory in the ruling.

do in future cases of this sort. Most states have now forbidden homeowners to place such covenants in sales contracts.

Gideon v. *Wainwright* extends the point. When the Supreme Court ordered a new trial for Gideon because he had been denied the right to legal counsel, it was saying to all trial judges and prosecutors that henceforth they would be wasting their time if they cut corners in trials of indigent defendants. It was also inviting thousands of prisoners to appeal their convictions.

Many areas of civil law have been constructed in the same way—by judicial messages to other judges, some of which are codified eventually into legislative enactments. An example of great concern to employees and employers is that of liability for injuries sustained at work. Courts have sided with employees so often that it has become virtually useless for employers to fight injury cases. It has become "the law" that employers are liable for such injuries, without regard to negligence. But the law in this instance is simply a series of messages to corporate lawyers that they should advise their corporate clients not to appeal injury decisions.

The appellate courts cannot decide what behavior will henceforth be a crime. They cannot directly prevent the police from forcing confessions or intimidating witnesses. In other words, they cannot directly change the behavior of citizens or eliminate abuses of power. What they can do, however, is make it easier for mistreated persons to gain redress.

Technically, the Court's refusal to hear a case challenging a statute does not constitute an endorsement of existing law. Because of the constitutional obligation of the federal courts to take all real cases or controversies, however, even a refusal to deal with a case can, in effect, create law. For example, if the Supreme Court had continued to avoid taking school segregation cases in the 1950s, its avoidance would have amounted to a reaffirmation of established laws and practices in the southern states. The Court had to take a case if it wanted to convey a different impression. Once it did so, it made litigation much easier for African Americans.

Thus, every Supreme Court decision, in reality if not in legal theory, including the decision to deny review, makes law; and every decision affects the distribution of power in American society. When litigants have standing to sue, judicial review cannot be avoided. This does not mean that all litigants will get a satisfactory response, but it does mean that they will get a meaningful one.

Faced with an appeal, an appellate court can review it negatively either by dismissing it or by hearing it and holding against the appellant. In both instances, the court is refusing to change established legal principles. Thus, since an appeal always involves an established legal principle, that principle will be reinforced, weakened, or changed altogether by the review.

The alternative is that the appellate court can review the appeal positively by hearing it and holding for the appellant. In that event, the court is asserting a new legal principle and is at the same time almost certainly altering the litigants' positions in society. If the decision by the appellate court is then appealed to the Supreme Court, the Supreme Court will be confronted with the same alternatives.

Each response therefore makes law. The higher up the appeal goes, the more law is made (since the higher courts have more status and their decisions have wider applicability). The appellate courts can limit the scope of the law they make by writing opinions that lay out precise legal principles, but they cannot avoid making law.

The impact of "judge-made law" often favors the status quo. Two of the three appellate court options, for example, favor it. Rejecting the constitutional or legal argument of the appellant is an explicit embrace of the status quo. Avoidance of the issue by dismissing the appeal or by reversing it on technical grounds is an implicit embrace of the status quo because it leaves power relationships where they were.

Yet, the appellate courts—and even the Supreme Court itself—sometimes accept the third option, holding in favor of the litigant who is calling for a radical change in legal principle. Acceptance of this option can have extremely important consequences. Changes in race relations, for example, would probably have taken a great deal longer if the Supreme Court had not rendered the 1954 *Brown* decision that redefined the rights of African Americans.

Similarly, the Supreme Court interpreted the separation of church and state doctrine so as to alter significantly the practice of religion in public institutions. For example, in a 1962 case, *Engel* v. *Vitale,* the Court declared that a once widely observed ritual—the recitation of a prayer by students in a public school—was unconstitutional under the establishment clause of the First Amendment. Almost all the dramatic changes in the treatment of criminals and of persons accused of crimes have been made by the appellate courts, especially the Supreme Court. The Supreme Court brought about a veritable revolution in the criminal process with three cases over less than five years: *Gideon* v. *Wainwright,* in 1963, was discussed earlier in the chapter. *Escobedo* v. *Illinois,* in 1964, gave suspects the right to remain silent and the right to have counsel present during questioning. But the decision left confusions that allowed differing decisions to be made by lower courts. In *Miranda* v. *Arizona,* in 1966, the Supreme Court cleared up these confusions by setting forth what is known as the **Miranda rule:** arrested people have the right to remain silent, the right to be informed that anything they say can be held against them, and the right to counsel before and during police interrogation (see Box 8.5).[18]

One of the most significant changes brought about by the Supreme Court was the revolution in legislative representation unleashed by the 1962 case of *Baker* v. *Carr.*[19] In this landmark case, the Supreme Court held that it could no longer avoid reviewing complaints about the appointment of seats in state legislatures. Following that decision, the federal courts went on to force reapportionment of all state, county, and local legislatures in the country (see Box 8.6).

Many experts on court history and constitutional law criticize the federal appellate courts for being too willing to introduce radical change, even when these experts agree with the general direction of the changes. Often they are troubled by the courts' (especially the Supreme Court's) willingness to jump into such cases prematurely—before the constitutional issues are fully clarified by many related

[18]Engel v. Vitale, 370 U.S. 421 (1962); Gideon v. Wainwright, 372 U.S. 335 (1963); Escobedo v. Illinois, 378 U.S. 478 (1964); and Miranda v. Arizona, 384 U.S. 436 (1966).

[19]Baker v. Carr, 369 U.S. 186 (1962).

BOX 8.5
Miranda v. Arizona

Throughout the 1950s and 1960s, increasingly vocal critics decried what they viewed as an alarming rise in "judicial activism" on the part of the Supreme Court. In a series of controversial rulings, the Court, led by Chief Justice Earl Warren, handed down sweeping rulings in controversial areas such as racial discrimination, school prayer, reapportionment, and rights of the accused. Few cases aroused more ire than that of the 1966 case of *Miranda* v. *Arizona.*

Ernesto Miranda was a poorly educated indignent of limited mental capabilities who had confessed to kidnapping and raping an eighteen-year-old woman. Miranda's confession provided key evidence of his complicity, but his conviction was challenged on the grounds that he had not been informed of his constitutional rights to remain silent and to have counsel during police questioning, as stated in the Fifth and Sixth Amendments, respectively.

By a 5-to-4 vote, the Supreme Court overturned Miranda's conviction, ruling that his confession was inadmissible in the absence of prior warnings from the police. "Prior to any questioning," the Court said, "the person must be warned that he has a right to remain silent, that any statement he does make may be used against him, and that he has a right to the presence of an attorney, either retained or appointed." The decision was based on the understanding that custodial interrogation of suspects not allowed to have lawyers present made it extremely difficult for a suspect to assert the right to avoid self-incrimination.

Critics raged that these new rules amounted to judicial invasion of local police houses, that they tied the hands of law enforcement officials. and balanced the scales of justice too heavily in favor of criminals. But the Supreme Court and others noted that the FBI had followed these procedures for years without a problem. Indeed, suspects often waived their rights and confessed. Studies of police behavior and criminal prosecutions after *Miranda* indicated that police were not prevented from doing their jobs.

Still, the *Miranda* decision did not sit well with many who felt that an individual who probably belonged in jail could be freed on a "technicality." President Richard Nixon won election in 1968 in part on a campaign of "law and order" that was based partially on Court rulings like *Miranda*. In the same year, Congress passed the Omnibus Crime Control and Safe Streets Act, Title II of which was aimed at curtailing suspect rights by allowing submission of confessions and other incriminating evidence if offered voluntarily but without Miranda warnings.

Despite protracted controversy and the appointment to the Supreme Court of more conservative justices, the Miranda principle has become an integral part of the law enforcement process, and an essential means for protecting basic rights, including the presumption of innocence, for all suspects. What some labeled derisively as legal "technicalities" are basic procedural safeguards that provide protection from the exercise of arbitrary government power.

As for Miranda himself, the hand of ironic fate intervened when he was killed in a barroom brawl in 1976, Miranda's assailant was, of course, read his Miranda rights.

Source: Liva Baker, *Miranda: Crime, Law and Politics* (New York: Athenaeum, 1983).

> BOX 8.6
> **Baker v. Carr**
>
> The issue of reapportionment of state and federal election districts was a ticklish one for the Supreme Court, as it was reluctant to issue a ruling that would adversely affect most of the legislators in state and federal offices. In many states, rural areas were considerably over-represented in both state and federal legislatures because election district boundaries were not being revised to reflect demographic changes as the nation's population moved from rural to urban areas. In *Colegrove* v. *Green* (1946), the Court had avoided ruling on the issue as it related to the election of federal House and Senate members, declaring that the case was not "justiciable." In other words, the Court declared that the question was not suited to judicial resolution because it raised a political question about what constituted adequate political representation—an issue which, under the separation of powers doctrine, was better left to the determination of the legislatures. Legislators, however, had a vested interest in maintaining district lines, and they were not likely to freely engage in re-districting. As a result, the Court was forced to face the issue in *Baker* v. *Carr* (1962).
>
> *Baker* v. *Carr* was a case brought to compel the Tennessee legislature to reapportion its state election district boundaries. Tennessee had last apportioned its election districts in 1901, and by 1962, there was significant imbalance among the districts; 37 percent of the voters elected 60 percent of the Tennessee Senate, while 40 percent of the voters of Tennessee elected 64 percent of its House of Representatives. In this case, the Court held that the issue of malapportionment raised a justiciable claim under the Equal Protection Clause of the Fourteenth Amendment to the Constitution. The effect of the case was to force the reapportionment of nearly all federal, state, and local election districts nationwide.
>
> Source: Baker v. Carr, 369 U.S. 186 (1962).

cases through decisions by district and appeals courts in various parts of the country.[20] But from the perspective of the appellate judiciary, especially the Supreme Court, the situation is probably one of choosing between the lesser of two evils: They must take the cases as they come and then weigh the risks of opening new options against the risks of embracing the status quo.

INFLUENCES ON SUPREME COURT DECISIONS

The judiciary is conservative in its procedures, but its impact on society can be radical. That impact depends on a variety of influences, three of which stand out above the rest. The first influence is the individual members of the Supreme

---

[20]See Philip Kurland, *Politics, the Constitution and the Warren Court* (Chicago: University of Chicago Press, 1970).

Court, their attitudes, and their relationships with each other. The second is the Justice Department, especially the solicitor general, who regulates the flow of cases involving public law issues. The third is the pattern of cases.

The Supreme Court Justices

If any individual judges in the country influence the federal judiciary, they are the Supreme Court justices. Many presidents have assumed that they can gain influence over the Court through the justices they appoint. That influence is usually overrated. Each justice is, after all, only one of nine, and each has the protection of lifetime tenure (see Table 8.2).

During the presidency of Richard Nixon, four vacancies on the Supreme Court gave him an opportunity to make enough appointments potentially to have an effect on Supreme Court decisions. Nixon's appointees were Chief Justice Warren Burger and Justices Harry Blackmun, Lewis Powell, and William Rehnquist. Some of the decisions of his Court—known as the Burger Court after its chief justice—went in the directions that Nixon would have desired. First, Nixon's appointees persuaded the Supreme Court to soften its stand on the rights of accused persons. For example, while the Warren Court had been virtually absolute on the right of defendants to legal counsel, the Burger Court identified circumstances under which counsel need not necessarily be present.[21] The Burger Court handed down other conservative decisions in this general area as well. For example, it gave police and prosecuting attorneys more power and flexibility in arrests

TABLE 8.2

Supreme Court Justices, 1993 (in order of seniority)

Name	Year of Birth	Prior Experience	Appointed By	Year of Appointment
William H. Rehnquist Chief Justice	1924	Assistant Attorney General	Nixon[*]	1972
Harry A. Blackmun	1908	Federal Judge	Nixon	1970
John Paul Stevens	1916	Federal Judge	Ford	1975
Sandra Day O'Connor	1930	State Judge	Reagan	1981
Antonin Scalia	1936	Law Professor, Federal Judge	Reagan	1986
Anthony Kennedy	1937	Federal Judge	Reagan	1988
David Souter	1940	Federal Judge	Bush	1990
Clarence Thomas	1948	Federal Judge	Bush	1991
Ruth Bader Ginsburg	1933	Federal Judge	Clinton	1993

[*]Appointed chief justice by Reagan in 1986.

[21]Scott v. Illinois, 440 U.S. 367 (1979).

and in searches and seizures by loosening the restrictions on how evidence may be obtained.[22]

The second area in which the Nixon appointees influenced Supreme Court decisions was civil rights. In the 1978 *Bakke* case, the Court held (by a 5-to-4 vote) that the University of California had violated Title VI of the 1964 Civil Rights Act when it set aside a specific number of places for minority group members wanting admission to the medical school.[23] The Court, however, softened its own *Bakke* position in 1979 in the *Weber* case by permitting voluntary affirmative action or quota programs in areas of work that had traditionally been closed to minorities.[24] Nevertheless, the Burger Court was less activist than the Warren Court in these areas. The lawyer for a black family in a school desegregation case or the lawyer for a prisoner in a civil liberties case at one time would automatically have appealed to the Supreme Court. The Burger Court began to send out the message that it was probably better for such litigants to pursue remedies as far as possible in the state courts.

But despite these decisions, the Nixon appointees did not point the Court in a dramatically new direction. The Burger Court overturned very few Warren Court decisions, although it restricted and weakened a number of them. It even took a liberal position on some new issues. For example, the Burger Court was the first Supreme Court to recognize the unconstitutionality of discrimination against women. Until 1971, gender lines in the law were considered legitimate. In 1971, in a case entitled *Reed* v. *Reed,* the Supreme Court invalidated an Idaho probate statute that required courts to give preference to males over females as administrators of estates.[25] That decision was soon followed by significant cases in a number of different areas. In *Frontiero* v. *Richardson* the Court rendered an important decision relating to the economic status of women when it held that the armed services could not deny married women fringe benefits (housing allowances and health care) that were automatically granted to married men.[26] In 1981, in *Kirchberg* v. *Fenestra,* the Court invalidated Louisiana's "head and master" rule that gave married men the sole right to dispose of property held jointly by both spouses.[27] The Court's 1973 decision in *Roe* v. *Wade,* limiting the ability of states to prohibit voluntary abortions, was another decision significantly affecting the status of women.[28]

On the issue of capital punishment, the Burger Court was not as strongly conservative as Nixon had hoped it would be. It continued to review capital punishment cases carefully rather than leaving the states with the absolute power over executions. Most important of all, the Nixon appointees to the Supreme Court made unanimous the decision against President Nixon on the question of whether

[22]See Stone v. Powell, 428 U.S. 465 (1976); Nix v. Williams, 467 U.S. 431 (1984); and U.S. v. Leon, 468 U.S. 897 (1984).

[23]Regents of the University of California v. Bakke, 438 U.S. 265 (1978).

[24]United Steelworkers v. Weber, 443 U.S. 193 (1979)

[25]Reed v. Reed, 404 U.S. 71 (1971).

[26]Frontiero v. Richardson, 411 U.S. 677 (1973).

[27]Kirchberg v. Fenestra, 450 U.S. 455 (1981).

[28]Roe v. Wade, 410 U.S. 113 (1973).

executive privilege extended to the famous White House tapes in the Watergate case.[29]

Both Republican presidents Ronald Reagan and George Bush assigned a high priority to the creation of a judiciary more sympathetic to conservative ideas and interests. Reagan made three significant appointments to the Supreme Court. First, he named Sandra Day O'Connor to be the first woman to serve as a Supreme Court justice. Second, after Chief Justice Warren Burger announced his resignation in 1986, Reagan promoted Justice William Rehnquist to the position of chief justice. This shift seemed certain to move the Court a bit further to the conservative end of the political spectrum. Third, Reagan designated Circuit Court Justice Antonin Scalia to fill the position vacated by Rehnquist. Scalia, a brilliant conservative, became an intellectual leader of the Court and strengthened the hold of conservative principles upon it. Finally, Reagan nominated Judge Anthony Kennedy, who was promptly confirmed by the Senate. As we shall see below, Kennedy and O'Connor proved to take more moderate positions than Reagan had hoped. Nevertheless, the Reagan appointments gave the Court a much more conservative cast than it has had at any time since the New Deal.

Of course, like Nixon, Reagan discovered that judicial appointments do not guarantee judicial decisions favored by the administration. For example, in the 1988 case of *Morrison* v. *Olson,* the Supreme Court by a 7-to-1 vote (the newly appointed Justice Kennedy did not participate in the case) upheld the constitutionality of the special prosecutor law, which allows the attorney general to recommend that a panel of federal judges appoint an independent counsel to investigate alleged wrongdoing by officials of the executive branch. In the majority opinion, conservative Chief Justice Rehnquist rejected the Reagan administration's argument that the law unconstitutionally impinged upon an exclusively executive branch function—the power to initiate and conduct criminal prosecutions.[30]

In a series of 5-to-4 decisions in 1989, however, President Reagan's appointees were able to swing the Court to a more conservative position on civil rights and abortion. In the case of civil rights, the Rehnquist Court's most important decision came in the case of *Wards Cove* v. *Atonio,* which shifted the burden of proof from employers to employees in hiring and promotion discrimination suits. (This decision was subsequently reversed by Congress in the 1991 Civil Rights Act.)[31] In 1993, the Library of Congress made public the papers of the late Justice Thurgood Marshall, long a champion of the civil rights cause. Marshall's papers reveal not only his disappointment at the Court's change of direction, but also the key role played by President Reagan's appointees in bringing about this change.[32] The Court did uphold some affirmative action programs, most notably in the 1990 case of *Metro Broadcasting* v. *FCC,* which upheld two federal programs aimed at increasing minority ownership of broadcast licenses.[33]

[29]U.S. v. Nixon, 418 U.S. 683 (1974).

[30]Morrison v. Olson, 108 S. Ct. 2597 (1988).

[31]Wards Cove v. Atonio, 109 S. Ct. 2115 (1989).

[32]Joan Biskupic, "The Marshall Files: How an Era Ended in Civil Rights Law," *Washington Post,* 24 May 1993, p. 1.

[33]Metro Broadcasting v. *FCC,* 110 S. Ct. 2997 (1990).

Sandra Day O'Connor
Swing Vote on the Court

Sandra Day O'Connor (b. 1930)

In 1950, Sandra Day O'Connor graduated *magna cum laude* from Stanford University; two years later, she graduated third in her Stanford Law class. Her law school friend and future Supreme Court chief justice William Rehnquist graduated first. Desiring to practice law, she applied to a variety of California law firms, only to meet a stone wall of prejudice against a female lawyer. This experience caused her to shift her interest to public service.

In 1959, she began private practice and became involved in Republican party politics, but spent much of her time caring for her family and raising three children. In 1965, she returned to full-time public service, becoming Arizona assistant attorney general. In 1969, O'Connor was appointed to fill a vacant seat in the Arizona state senate, a position to which she was reelected twice. In 1972, she was elected majority leader of her party in the senate—the first woman to hold such a post in the nation. In 1974, she moved to the state judiciary by being elected to a county superior court. In 1979, the state's governor appointed her to the state court of appeals.

Two years later, President Reagan fulfilled a campaign pledge by nominating O'Connor as the first woman to serve on the U.S. Supreme Court. Sidestepping specific questions concerning her views on abortion and other controversial matters, she did offer herself as an advocate of judicial restraint compatible with Reagan's philosophy. Despite some protests from right-wing groups, O'Connor was unanimously confirmed by the Senate.

While she has participated in hundreds of decisions, O'Connor's tenure on the Court has been seemingly dogged by the quintessential woman's issue, abortion. Right-wing objections to her nomination stemmed in large part from suggestions of pro-choice sympathy during her time with the state senate. Yet, after joining the Court, O'Connor sided with the growing court minority that sought to cut back, or even overrule, the landmark *Roe* v. *Wade* (1973) court case that had made abortions legal under most circumstances. In 1989, she helped form a five-member majority in voting to uphold a series of restrictive abortion regulations in Missouri (*Webster* v. *Reproductive Health Services*). O'Connor differed from her other four colleagues, however, in that they strongly hinted that they would like to overturn *Roe* entirely. O'Connor seemed to indicate that she would not go that far, writing that "a regulation imposed on a lawful abortion is not unconstitutional unless it unduly burdens the right to seek an abortion."

On abortion as on most issues, O'Connor has articulated a conservative position that stopped short of embracing the positions of the most conservative Court members. Her role in this and other issues will keep attention focused on her as the Court grapples with similarly controversial topics.

Source: Marian Faux, *Roe v. Wade* (New York: New American Library, 1988).
Photo Credit: José R. Lopez/*The New York Times*.

The Rehnquist Court's key abortion decision came in the case of *Webster* v. *Reproductive Health Services.* Justice Marshall's papers reveal that the Court actually came very close to overturning *Roe*. Rehnquist's early drafts of the decision would have effectively overturned *Roe*. He was able to win the support of only three other justices, Scalia, Kennedy, and White, for this course of action. A fourth justice, Sandra O'Connor, wavered for several weeks. Had O'Connor joined Rehnquist, of course, the Chief Justice would have had the five votes needed for a majority. Ultimately, O'Connor decided not to support overturning *Roe,* and Rehnquist was forced to write a narrower ruling, which did, however, open the way for new state regulation of abortion. Subsequently, in the 1990 cases of *Hodgson* v. *Minnesota* and *Ohio* v. *Akron Center for Reproductive Health,* the Court upheld state laws requiring parental notification before an abortion could be performed on a woman under the age of eighteen.[34]

In addition to these areas, the Rehnquist Court also eased restriction on the use of capital punishment, allowing states to execute mentally retarded murderers *(Penry* v. *Lynaugh)* and murderers who were as young as sixteen at the time of the crime *(Stanford* v. *Kentucky).*[35]

Reagan also had a good deal of influence on appointments to the federal district and appellate courts. By the end of his second term, retirements and deaths had given President Reagan the opportunity to fill more than one-third of the positions on these courts. Reagan sought to name at least some judges who were not only conservative but who also possessed the talent, background, and personality to serve as intellectual leaders who would set the intellectual and jurisprudential tones of their courts. Thus, whatever President Reagan's ultimate impact on the Supreme Court, these appointments will certainly influence the temperament and behavior of the district and circuit courts for years to come.

With the election of George Bush, the Republicans were given another four years in which to attempt to shape the composition and character of the courts. Bush continued to appoint conservative district and appellate court judges. By the end of Bush's term in office, he and Reagan together had appointed nearly half of all federal judges (see Table 8.3). President Bush's first opportunity to appoint a justice to the Supreme Court came in 1990 with the retirement of Justice William Brennan, perhaps the most important liberal activist in the Court's modern history. Bush chose David Souter, a conservative federal appeals court judge from New Hampshire.

In June 1991, liberal Justice Thurgood Marshall, the first black justice on the Supreme Court, announced his resignation. President Bush nominated federal judge Clarence Thomas, a prominent black conservative who had formerly chaired the Equal Employment Opportunity Commission, to replace Marshall. The Thomas nomination was severely criticized by liberal Democrats and was bit-

[34]Benjamin Weiser and Bob Woodward, "Roe's Eleventh-Hour Reprieve: 89 Drafts Show Court Poised to Strike Abortion Ruling," *Washington Post,* 23 May 1993, p. 1. Webster v. Reproductive Health Services, 109 S. Ct. 3040 (1989); Hodgson v. Minnesota, 110 S. Ct. 2926 (1990); Ohio v. Akron Center for Reproductive Health, 110 S. Ct. 2972 (1990).

[35]Penry v. Lynaugh, 109 S. Ct. 2934 (1989); Stanford v. Kentucky, 109 S. Ct. 2969 (1989).

TABLE 8.3
Presidential Impact on the Federal Courts

President	Supreme Court	Court of Appeals[1]	District Courts[2]	Total	Total Judgeships[3]
Roosevelt (1933–45)	9	52	136	197	262
Truman (1945–53)	4	27	102	133	292
Eisenhower (1953–61)	5	45	127	177	322
Kennedy (1961–63)	2	20	102	124	395
Johnson (1963–69)	2	41	125	168	449
Nixon (1969–74)	4	45	182	231	504
Ford (1974–77)	1	12	52	65	504
Carter (1977–81)	0	56	206	262	657
Reagan (1981–89)	3	83	292	378	740
Bush (1989–92)	2	27	95	124	825

[1]Does not include the appeals court for the Federal Circuit
[2]Includes district courts in the territories
[3]Total judgeships authorized in president's last year in office. Does not include Supreme Court.
Source: Administrative Office of the U.S. Courts, reported in *Congressional Quarterly Weekly Report*, 19 January 1991, p. 173.

terly attacked by the congressional black caucus because of Thomas's opposition to affirmative action. This nomination sparked one of the most bitter struggles in recent American political history. During his lengthy confirmation hearings, Thomas refused to discuss his views on abortion, particularly refusing to indicate how he viewed the Supreme Court's landmark decision in the case of *Roe* v. *Wade*. The day before the Senate was to vote on his confirmation, however, with a favorable vote virtually certain, opponents of the nomination revealed that a University of Oklahoma law professor, Anita Hill, had claimed that Thomas had sexually harassed her when she worked for him at the EEOC and, previously, at the Department of Education. This charge led to two days of dramatic, nationally televised Senate hearings marked by charges of racism, sexual misconduct, and perjury. Ultimately, Thomas was confirmed by the Senate by the narrow vote of 52-to-48, allowing President Bush to strengthen the Court's conservative bloc.

From 1990 to 1992 the Court made a number of decisions in the areas of civil rights, abortion, property rights, and criminal procedure that suggested some shift to the political right under the influence of the Reagan and Bush appointees.

For example, in the case of *Board of Education of Oklahoma City* v. *Dowell*,[36] the Court restricted the use of judicially mandated busing plans to achieve school integration. In the case of *Rust* v. *Sullivan*,[37] the Court held that employees of federally financed family planning programs could be forbidden to discuss abortion with their clients. In *Arizona* v. *Fulminante*,[38] the Court found that the use of a coerced confession in a trial did not automatically invalidate a conviction. In *Coleman* v.

[36]Board of Education of Oklahoma City v. Dowell, 111 S. Ct. 630 (1991).
[37]Rust v. Sullivan, 89–1391 (1991).
[38]Arizona v. Fulminante, 89–839 (1991).

Thompson,[39] the Court restricted the ability of state prison inmates to pursue appeals in the federal courts. In *Lucas* v. *South Carolina Coastal Council,* the Court gave a sympathetic hearing to a property owner's claim that state restrictions on land development constituted a seizure of property without compensation in violation of the Constitution's Fifth Amendment.[40] In the case of *Payne* v. *Tennessee,*[41] the Court allowed the introduction of evidence pertaining to the character of a murder victim and the grief of the family in a capital case.

Efforts by Reagan and Bush to reshape the federal judiciary, however, were only partially successful. Often in American history, judges have surprised and disappointed the presidents who named them to the bench and the Reagan/Bush appointees were no exception. A number of recent cases have suggested the development of a moderate bloc on the Supreme Court consisting of Justices O'Connor, Kennedy, and Souter. Though all three were seen as conservatives at the time of their appointments, these justices have opposed the views of forces on the political right, particularly in the areas of school prayer and abortion.

Led by the moderate bloc, the Court has refused to weaken limitations on school prayer. For example, in the 1992 case of *Lee* v. *Weisman* the Court, by a 5-to-4 vote, held that the use of a prayer at a high school graduation was impermissible.[42] As to abortion, in the important 1992 case of *Planned Parenthood of Southeastern Pennsylvania* v. *Casey,* the court upheld state regulations requiring that women seeking abortions wait twenty-four hours after being provided with the information about the process and parental consent for minors.[43] The Court, however, reaffirmed the constitutional right to an abortion established by *Roe* v. *Wade.* Indeed, in their unusual joint opinion, Justices O'Connor, Kennedy, and Souter expressed irritation at the White House for its ceaseless pressure on the Court to strike down *Roe* v. *Wade.*[44] The Court's moderate bloc felt that this pressure represented a threat to the institutional integrity of the Supreme Court.

Bill Clinton's election in 1992 reduced the possibility of any further rightward drift on the part of the Court. During Clinton's first year in office, Justice Byron White, the conservative bloc's lone Democrat, announced his desire to retire from the bench. After a long search, the president nominated a Federal Appeals Court judge, Ruth Bader Ginsburg, a moderate liberal, to succeed White. She had a long record of support for abortion rights and women's rights. However, as a federal appeals court judge, she often sided with the government in criminal cases and did not hesitate to vote against affirmative action plans she deemed to be too broad. Most observers viewed Ginsburg as a probable addition to Kennedy, Souter, and O'Connor in the Court's moderate bloc.[45]

Opinion Writing   The assignment to write the majority opinion in an important constitutional case is an opportunity for the chosen justice to exercise great influ-

---

[39]Coleman v. Thompson, 89–7662 (1991).

[40]Lucas v. South Carolina Coastal Council, 112 S. Ct. 2886 (1992).

[41]Payne v. Tennessee, 90–5721 (1991).

[42]Lee v. Weisman, 112 S. Ct. 2649

[43]Planned Parenthood of Southeastern Pennsylvania v. Casey, 112 S. Ct. 2791

[44]Joan Biskupic, "New Term Poses Test for Alliance at Center of Conservative Court," *Wall Street Journal,* 4 October 1992, p. A12.

ence on the Court. But in some ways it also severely limits that influence. The assignment is made by the chief justice or by the senior associate justice in the majority when the chief justice is a dissenter. But it is not a simple procedure. Serious thought has to be given to the impression the case will make on lawyers and on the public and to the probability that one justice's opinion will be more widely accepted than another's.

One of the more dramatic instances of this tactical consideration occurred in 1944, when Chief Justice Harlan F. Stone chose Justice Felix Frankfurter to write the opinion in the "white primary" case, *Smith v. Allwright.* The chief justice believed that this sensitive case, which overturned the southern practice of prohibiting black participation in nominating primaries, required the efforts of the most brilliant and scholarly jurist on the Court. But, the day after Stone made the assignment, Justice Robert H. Jackson wrote a letter to Stone urging a change of assignment. In it Jackson argued that Frankfurter, a foreign-born Jew from New England, would not win the South with his opinion, regardless of its brilliance. Stone accepted the advice and substituted Justice Stanley Reed, an American-born Protestant from Kentucky, who was a southern Democrat in good standing.[46]

Biographical and scholarly records of the Court show that the drafting of opinions requires not only good reasoning but the formulation of arguments that will keep and expand the support of a majority of the justices as well as the public. Sometimes the effort to bring one of the dissenting justices over to the majority involves a significant change in the reasoning of the majority opinion. For instance, Chief Justice Stone brought Justice James F. Byrnes from dissent to majority support in an important case arising out of the Depression. The California legislature had erected legal barriers against the migration of thousands of persons displaced from the midwestern Dust Bowl (popularly known in the 1930s as "Okies"). The Court had already voted 8-to-1 in conference, with Byrnes dissenting, to reverse the California laws. Chief Justice Stone convinced Byrnes to join the other justices and thereby make the vote unanimous when Stone agreed with Byrnes to switch the legal ground for the decision from the Constitution's privileges and immunities clause, which Byrnes felt supported California's claim, to the interstate commerce clause. Byrnes agreed that the broad grant of federal power in this clause might provide a more valid basis for rejecting the California statutes.[47]

Dissent Ironically, the most dependable way an individual justice can exercise a direct and clear influence on the Court is to write a dissenting opinion. Because there is no need to please a majority, dissenting opinions can be more eloquent and less guarded than majority opinions (see Box 8.7). Some of the greatest writing in the history of the Court is found in dissents, and some of the most famous justices, such as Oliver Wendell Holmes and Louis D. Brandeis earlier in this century, and liberal Justice William O. Douglas in more recent years, were notable dis-

[45]See Richard L. Berke, "Clinton Names Ruth Ginsburg, Advocate for Women, to Court: Centrist Role Cited," *New York Times,* 15 June 1993, p. 1; See also, Joan Biskupic, "Judge Ruth Ginsburg Named to High Court: Nominee's Philosophy Seen Strengthening the Center," *Washington Post,* 15 June 1993, p. 1.

[46]Smith v. Allwright, 321 U.S. 649 (1944).

[47]Edwards v. California, 314 U.S. 160 (1941). See Henry J. Abraham, *The Judicial Process,* (New York: Oxford University Press, 1962), p. 191.

BOX 8.7
Dissenting Opinion

Dissenting opinions differ significantly in form from majority opinions. A dissenting opinion points out the fallacies in the majority's reasoning and attempts to lay the groundwork for limiting or overruling the majority opinion in the future. Because a dissenting judge need not hold together a majority of the Court, such an opinion is often quite direct in its criticism of the majority. For example, in *New York* v. *Quarles* (1984), Justice Thurgood Marshall began his dissent with the observation that "[t]he majority's treatment of the legal issues presented in this case is no less troubling than its abuse of the facts."

In *Bowers* v. *Hardwick* (1986), the Supreme Court was asked to decide whether a Georgia statute prohibiting sodomy violated a constitutional right to privacy. Hardwick, a Georgia male, had been cited for violating the statute by engaging in consensual sexual activity with another male in Hardwick's home. The majority of the Court upheld the Georgia statute, ruling that the constitutional right of privacy protected the traditional family unit and did not protect conduct between homosexuals when that conduct offended "traditional Judeo–Christian values." The following passage is excerpted from the dissenting opinion of Justice Harry Blackmun:

> This case is no more about "a fundamental right to engage in homosexual sodomy," as the Court purports to declare . . . than *Stanley* v. *Georgia* was about a fundamental right to watch obscene movies, or *Katz* v. *United States* was about a fundamental right to place interstate bets from a telephone booth. Rather, this case is about "the most comprehensive of rights and the right most valued by civilized men," namely, "the right to be let alone" (*Olmstead* v. *United States*).
>
> ***
>
> Like Justice Holmes, I believe that "[i]t is revolting to have no better reason for a rule of law than that it was laid down in the time of Henry IV. It is still more revolting if the grounds upon which it was laid down have vanished long since, and the rule simply persists from blind imitation of the past" (Holmes, *The Path of the Law*). I believe we must analyze respondent's claim in the light of the values that underlie the constitutional right to privacy. If that right means anything, it means that, before Georgia can prosecute its citizens for making choices about the most intimate aspects of their lives, it must do more than assert that the choice they have made is an "abominable crime not fit to be named among Christians" (*Herring* v. *State*).
>
> ***
>
> I can only hope that . . . the Court soon will reconsider its analysis and conclude that depriving individuals of the right to choose for themselves how to conduct their intimate relationships poses a far greater threat to the values most deeply rooted in our Nation's history than tolerance of noncomformity could ever do. Because I think the Court today betrays those values, I dissent.

senters. In the single 1952–53 Court term, Douglas wrote thirty-five dissenting opinions. In the 1958–59 term, he wrote eleven dissents. During the latter term, Justices Frankfurter and Harlan wrote thirteen and nine dissents, respectively.

Dissent plays a special role in the work and impact of the Court because it amounts to an appeal to lawyers all over the country to keep bringing cases of the sort at issue. Therefore, an effective dissent influences the flow of cases through the Court as well as the arguments that will be used by lawyers in later cases. Even more important, dissent emphasizes the fact that, although the Court speaks with a single opinion, it is the opinion only of the majority—and one day the majority might go the other way.

Individual Supreme Court justices thus have a certain amount of influence by virtue of their participation in choosing cases and in constituting a majority—or a dissenting minority—on the decisions. Since four justices must vote to grant *certiorari,* however, there are only three ways a single justice can significantly influence the judicial process: (1) by writing an eloquent dissenting opinion, (2) by issuing a stay of execution pending full Court review, and (3) by issuing a writ of *habeas corpus,* temporarily removing a criminal case from state jurisdiction until the Court can determine its merits. The latter two powers lead to temporary stoppages pending review by the full Court.

Controlling the Flow of Cases—The Role of the Solicitor General

If any single person has greater influence than the individual justices over the work of the Supreme Court, it is the solicitor general of the United States. The solicitor general is third in status in the Justice Department (below the attorney general and the deputy attorney general) but is the top government lawyer in almost all cases before the appellate courts where the government is a party. Although others can regulate the flow of cases, the solicitor general has the greatest control, with no review of his actions by any higher authority in the executive branch. More than half the Supreme Court's total work load consists of cases under his direct charge. Even the bland description in the *U.S. Government Manual* cannot mask the extraordinary importance of the solicitor general:

> The Solicitor General is in charge of representing the Government in the Supreme Court. He decides what cases the Government should ask the Supreme Court to review and what position the Government should take in cases before the Court; he supervises the preparation of the Government's Supreme Court briefs and other legal documents and the conduct of the oral arguments in the Court and argues most of the important cases himself. The Solicitor General's duties also include deciding whether the United States should appeal in all cases it loses before the lower courts.[48]

The influence of the solicitor general is especially strong because he screens cases long before they approach the Supreme Court, and the justices rely on him to "screen out undeserving litigation and furnish them with an agenda to govern-

---

[48]*United States Government Organization Manual* (Washington, DC: Government Printing Office, 1985).

ment cases that deserve serious consideration."[49] Agency heads may lobby the president or otherwise try to circumvent the solicitor general, and a few of the independent agencies have a statutory right to make direct appeals, but these are almost inevitably doomed to *per curiam* rejection—rejection through a brief, unsigned opinion by the whole Court—if the solicitor general refuses to participate. Congress has given only the Interstate Commerce Commission, the Federal Communications Commission, the Federal Maritime Commission, and in some cases, the Department of Agriculture (even though it is not an independent agency) the right to appeal directly to the Supreme Court without going through the solicitor general.

The solicitor general can enter a case even when the federal government is not a direct litigant by writing an *amicus curiae* ("friend of the court") brief. A "friend of the court" is not a direct party to a case but has a vital interest in its outcome. Thus, when the government has such an interest, the solicitor general can file as *amicus curiae,* or the Court can invite him to file a brief because it wants his opinion in writing. The solicitor general also has the power to invite others to enter cases as *amici curiae.*

In addition to exercising substantial control over the flow of cases, the solicitor general can shape the arguments used before the Court. Indeed, the Court tends to give special attention to the way the solicitor general characterizes the issues. The solicitor general is the person appearing most frequently before the Court and, theoretically at least, the most disinterested. He is known to reject more requests for appeals than he accepts, and his credibility is not hurt when several times each year he comes to the Court to withdraw a case with the admission that the government has made an error.

The solicitor general's sway over the flow of cases does not, however, entirely overshadow the influence of the other agencies and divisions in the Department of Justice. The solicitor general is counsel for the major divisions in the department, including the Antitrust, Tax, Civil Rights, and Criminal Divisions. Their activities generate a great part of the agenda with which he must deal. This is particularly true of the Criminal Division, whose cases come before him on appeal every day. These cases are generated by initiatives taken by the United States Attorneys and the district judges before whom they practice.

The FBI's Role   Another important influence on the flow of cases through the appellate judiciary comes from the Federal Bureau of Investigation (FBI), one of the bureaus of the Department of Justice. Its work provides data for numerous government cases against businesses, individual citizens, and state and local government officials. Its data are the most vital source of material for cases in the areas of national security and organized crime.

The FBI also has the important function of linking the Justice Department very closely to cases being brought by state and local government officials. Since the FBI has a long history of cooperation with state and local police forces, the solici-

---

[49]Robert Scigliano, *The Supreme Court and the Presidency* (New York: Free Press, 1971), p. 162. For an interesting critique of the solicitor general's role during the Reagan administration, see Lincoln Caplan, "Annals of the Law," *The New Yorker,* 17 August 1987, pp. 30–62.

tor general often finds himself joining (as *amicus curiae*) appeals involving state criminal cases.

The Case Pattern

The Supreme Court has discretion over which cases will be reviewed. The solicitor general can influence the Court's choice by the advice he gives and by his encouragement of particular cases and his discouragement or suppression of others. But, neither the court nor the solicitor general can suppress altogether the kinds of cases that individuals bring to court. Each new technology, such as computers and communications satellites, produces new disputes and the need for new principles of law. Newly awakened interest groups, such as the black community after World War II or the women's and the environmental movements in the 1970s, produce new legislation, new disputes, and new cases. Lawyers are professionally obligated to appeal their clients' cases to the highest possible court if an issue of law or constitutionality is involved.

The litigation that breaks out with virtually every social change produces a pattern of cases that eventually is recognized by the state and federal appellate courts. Appellate judges may at first resist trying such cases by ordering them remanded (returned) to their court of original jurisdiction for further trial. They may reject some appeals without giving any reason at all *(certiorari* denied *per curiam)*. But eventually, one or more of the cases from the pattern may be reviewed and may indeed make new law.

Although some patterns of cases emerge spontaneously as new problems produce new litigation, many interest groups try to set a pattern as a strategy for expediting their cases through the appeals process. Lawyers representing these groups have to choose the proper client and the proper case, so that the issues in question are most dramatically and appropriately portrayed. They also have to pick the right district or jurisdiction in which to bring the case. Sometimes they even have to wait for an appropriate political climate.

Group litigants have to plan carefully when to use and when to avoid publicity. They must also attempt to develop a proper record at the trial court level, one that includes some constitutional arguments and even, when possible, errors on the part of the trial court. One of the most effective litigation strategies used in getting cases accepted for review by the appellate courts is bringing the same type of suit in more than one circuit, in the hope that inconsistent treatment by two different courts will improve the chance of a Supreme Court review.

As we shall see more fully in Chapter 12, Congress will sometimes provide interest groups with legislation designed to facilitate their use of litigation. One important recent example is the 1990 Americans with Disabilities Act (ADA), enacted after intense lobbying by public interest and advocacy groups which, in conjunction with the 1991 Civil Rights Act, opens the way for disabled individuals to make extremely effective use of the courts to press their interests.

The two most notable users of the pattern of cases strategy in recent years have been the National Association for the Advancement of Colored People (NAACP) and the American Civil Liberties Union (ACLU). For many years, the NAACP (and its Defense Fund organization—now a separate group) has worked through local chapters and with many individuals to encourage litigation on issues of racial discrimination and segregation. Sometimes it distributes petitions to be signed by parents and filed with local school boards and courts, deliberately sowing the seeds of future litigation. The NAACP and the ACLU often encourage private parties to bring suit and then join the suit as *amici curiae.*

One illustration of an interest group employing a carefully crafted litigation strategy to pursue its goals through the judiciary was the Texas-based effort to establish a right to free public school education for children of illegal aliens. The issue arose in 1977 when the Texas state legislature, responding to a sudden wave of fear about illegal immigration from Mexico, enacted a law permitting school districts to charge undocumented children a hefty tuition for the privilege of attending public school. A public interest law organization, the Mexican-American Legal Defense Fund, prepared to challenge the law in court after determining that public opposition precluded any chance of persuading the legislature to change its own law.

Part of the defense fund's litigation strategy was to bring a lawsuit in the northwest section of Texas, far from the Mexican border, where illegal immigration would be at a minimum. Thus, in Tyler, Texas, where the complaint was initially filed, the trial court found only sixty undocumented alien students in a school district composed of 16,000. This strategy effectively contradicted the state's argument that the Texas law was necessary to reduce the burdens on educational resources created by masses of incoming aliens. Another useful litigation tactic was to select plaintiffs who, although illegal aliens, were nevertheless clearly planning to remain in Texas even without free public education for their children. Thus, all of the plaintiffs came from families that had already lived in Tyler for several years and included at least one child who was an American citizen by virtue of birth in the United States. By emphasizing the stability of such families, the defense fund argued convincingly that the Texas law would not motivate families to return to the poverty in Mexico from which they had fled, but would more likely result in the creation of a subclass of illiterate people who would add to the state's unemployment and crime rates. Five years after the lawsuit on behalf of the Tyler children began, the U.S. Supreme Court in the case of *Plyler* v. *Doe* held that the Texas law was unconstitutional under the equal protection clause of the Fourteenth Amendment.[50]

In many states, it is considered unethical and illegal for attorneys to engage in "fomenting and soliciting legal business in which they are not parties and have no pecuniary right or liability."[51] The NAACP was sued by the state of Virginia in the late 1950s in an attempt to restrict or eliminate its efforts to influence the pattern of cases. The Supreme Court reviewed the case in 1963, recognized that the strategy was being utilized, and held that it was protected by the First and Fourteenth Amendments, just as other forms of speech and petition are protected.[52]

Thus, regardless of the wishes of the Justice Department or the Supreme Court, many path-breaking cases are eventually granted *certiorari,* because continued re-

[50]Plyler v. Doe, 457 U.S. 202 (1982).

[51]NAACP v. Button, 371 U.S. 415 (1963).

[52]Ibid.

fusal to review one or more of them would amount to a rule of law just as much as
if the courts had handed down a written opinion. In this sense, the flow of cases, especially the pattern of significant cases, influences the behavior of the appellate judiciary.

JUDICIAL POWER AND POLITICS

One of the most important institutional changes to occur in the United States during the past half century has been the striking transformation of the role and power of the federal courts, those of the Supreme Court in particular. Understanding how this transformation came about is the key to understanding the contemporary role of the courts in America.

Traditional Limitations on the Federal Courts

For much of American history, the power of the federal courts was subject to five limitations.[53] First, courts were constrained by judicial rules of standing that limited access to the bench. Claimants who simply disagreed with governmental action or inaction could not obtain access. Access to the courts was limited to individuals who could show that they were particularly affected by the government's behavior in some area. This limitation on access to the courts diminished the judiciary's capacity to forge links with important political and social forces. Second, courts were traditionally limited in the character of the relief they could provide. In general, courts acted only to offer relief or assistance to individuals and not to broad social classes, again inhibiting the formation of alliances between the courts and important social forces. Third, courts lacked enforcement powers of their own and were compelled to rely upon executive or state agencies to ensure compliance with their edicts. And if the executive or state agencies were unwilling to assist the courts, judicial enactments could go unheeded, as when President Andrew Jackson declined to enforce Chief Justice John Marshall's 1832 order to the state of Georgia to release two missionaries it had arrested on Cherokee lands. Marshall asserted that the state had no right to enter the Cherokee's lands without their assent.[54] Jackson is reputed to have said, "John Marshall has made his decision, now let *him* enforce it."

Fourth, federal judges are, of course, appointed by the president (with the consent of the Senate). As a result, the president and Congress can shape the composition of the federal courts and ultimately, perhaps, the character of judicial decisions. Finally, Congress has the power to change both the size and jurisdiction of the Supreme Court and other federal courts. In many areas, federal courts obtain their jurisdiction not from the Constitution but from congressional statutes.

[53]For limits on judicial power, see Alexander Bickel, *The Least Dangerous Branch* (Indianapolis, IN: Bobbs-Merrill, 1962).

[54]Worcester v. Georgia, 6 Peters 515 (1832).

On a number of occasions, Congress has threatened to take matters out of the Court's hands when it was unhappy with the Court's policies.[55] For example, on one memorable occasion, presidential and congressional threats to expand the size of the Supreme Court—Franklin Roosevelt's "court packing" plan—encouraged the justices to drop their opposition to New Deal programs. As a result of these five limitations on judicial power, through much of their history the chief function of the federal courts was to provide judicial support for executive agencies and to legitimate acts of Congress by declaring them to be consistent with constitutional principles. Only on rare occasions did the federal courts actually dare to challenge Congress or the executive.[56]

Two Judicial Revolutions

Since the Second World War, however, the role of the federal judiciary has been strengthened and expanded. There have actually been two judicial revolutions in the United States since World War II. The first and most visible of these was the substantive revolution in judicial policy. As we saw earlier in this chapter and in Chapter 4, in policy areas, including school desegregation, legislative apportionment, and criminal procedure, as well as obscenity, abortion, and voting rights, the Supreme Court was at the forefront of a series of sweeping changes in the role of the U.S. government, and ultimately, in the character of American society.[57]

But at the same time that the courts were introducing important policy innovations, they were also bringing about a second, less visible revolution. During the 1960s and 1970s, the Supreme Court and other federal courts instituted a series of changes in judicial procedures that fundamentally expanded the power of the courts in the United States. First, the federal courts liberalized the concept of standing to permit almost any group to bring its case before the federal bench. Indeed, Congress helped to make it even easier for groups dissatisfied with government policies to bring their cases to the courts by adopting Section 1983 of the U.S. Code, which permits the practice of "fee shifting." Section 1983 allows citizens who successfully bring a suit against a public official for violating their constitutional rights to collect their attorneys' fees and costs from the government. Thus, Section 1983 encourages individuals and groups to bring their problems to the courts rather than to Congress or the executive branch.

Second, the federal courts broadened the scope of relief to permit themselves to act on behalf of broad categories or classes of persons in "class action" cases, rather than just on behalf of individuals.[58] A class action suit is a procedural device that permits large numbers of persons with common interests to join together under a representative party to bring or defend a lawsuit. One recent example is the case

---

[55]See Walter Murphy, *Congress and the Court* (Chicago: University of Chicago Press, 1962).

[56]Robert Dahl, "The Supreme Court and National Policy Making," *Journal of Public Law* 6 (1958), p. 279.

[57]Martin Shapiro, "The Supreme Court: From Warren to Burger," in *The New American Political System,* ed. Anthony King (Washington, DC: American Enterprise Institute, 1978).

[58]See "Developments in the Law—Class Actions," *Harvard Law Review* 89 (1976), p. 1318.

of *In re Agent Orange Product Liability Litigation,* in which a federal judge in New
York certified Vietnam War veterans as a class with standing to sue a manufacturer
of herbicides for damages allegedly incurred from exposure to the defendants'
product while in Vietnam.[59] The class potentially numbered in the tens of
thousands.

Third, the federal courts began to employ so-called structural remedies, in effect retaining jurisdiction of cases until the court's mandate had actually been implemented to its satisfaction.[60] The best-known of these instances was Federal Judge W. Arthur Garrity's effort to operate the Boston school system from his bench in order to ensure its desegregation. Between 1974 and 1985, Judge Garrity issued fourteen decisions relating to different aspects of the Boston school desegregation plan that had been developed under his authority and put into effect under his supervision.[61] In another recent case, Federal Judge Leonard B. Sand imposed fines that would have forced the city of Yonkers, New York, into bankruptcy if it had refused to accept his plan to build public housing in white neighborhoods. After several days of fines, the city gave in to the judge's ruling. In its 5-to-4 decision in the 1990 case of *Missouri* v. *Jenkins,* the Court held that federal judges could actually order local governments to increase taxes to remedy such violations of the Constitution as school segregation.[62] This decision upheld an order by a federal district judge, Russel G. Clark, to the Kansas City, Missouri, school board to adopt a "magnet" school plan that would lessen segregation in the schools. Judge Clark also ordered the school district to double the local property tax from $2.05 to $4.00 per $100 of assessed valuation. Potentially, this decision claims for the judiciary the power to levy taxes—a power normally seen as belonging to elected legislatures.

Through these three judicial mechanisms, the federal courts paved the way for an unprecedented expansion of national judicial power. In essence, liberalization of the rules of standing and expansion of the scope of judicial relief drew the federal courts into linkages with important social interests and classes, while the introduction of structural remedies enhanced the courts' ability to serve these constituencies. Thus, during the 1960s and 1970s, the power of the federal courts expanded in the same way the power of the executive expanded during the 1930s—through links with constituencies, such as civil rights, consumer, environmental, and feminist groups, that staunchly defended the Supreme Court in its battles with Congress, the executive, or other interest groups.

The Reagan and Bush administrations, of course, sought to end this relationship between the Court and liberal political forces. As we have seen, the conservative judges appointed by these Republican presidents modified the Court's position in areas such as abortion, affirmative action, and judicial procedure, though not as completely as some conservatives had hoped. Interestingly, however, the Court has not been eager to surrender the expanded powers carved out by its lib-

---

[59]In re Agent Orange Product Liability Litigation, 100 F.R.D. 718 (D.C.N.Y. 1983).

[60]See Donald Horowitz, *The Courts and Social Policy* (Washington, DC: The Brookings Institution, 1977).

[61]Moran v. McDonough, 540 F. 2nd 527 (1 Cir., 1976; *cert denied* 429 U.S. 1042 [1977]).

[62]Missouri v. Jenkins, 110 S. Ct. 1651 (1990).

Interpreting the Constitution and Original Intent

*J*udges bear the responsibility of interpreting the meaning and applicability of the Constitution, written over two hundred years ago, to modern society. The application of
constitutional principles to modern problems is inherently difficult because of disagreements over what the founders intended and over how the Constitution's words ought to
apply to issues and problems unimagined in the eighteenth century.

 *Former federal judge Robert H. Bork argues in favor of the "original intent" ap-
proach, urging judges to stick as closely to the Constitution's text and original meaning
as possible. Constitutional scholar Leonard W. Levy counters that original intent, even
if it could be divined, is an inadequate and inappropriate way to deal with constitutional
interpretation.*

Bork

What was once the dominant view of constitutional law—that a judge is to
apply the Constitution according to the principles intended by those who ratified the document—is now very much out of favor among the theorists of
the field. . . .

 In truth, only the approach of original understanding meets the criteria
that any theory of constitutional adjudication must meet in order to possess
democratic legitimacy. Only that approach is consonant with the design of the
American Republic. . . .

 . . . The original understanding is . . . manifested in the words used and in
secondary materials, such as debates at the conventions, public discussion,
newspaper articles, dictionaries in use at the time, and the like.

 The search for the intent of the lawmaker is the everyday procedure of
lawyers and judges when they apply a statute, a contract, a will, or the opinion
of a court. . . . Lawyers and judges should seek in the Constitution what they
seek in other legal texts: the original meaning of the words. . . .

 A judge, no matter on what court he sits, may never create new constitutional rights or destroy old ones. Any time he does so, he violates the limits of
his own authority and, for that reason, also violates the rights of the legislature
and the people. . . .

 The role of a judge committed to the philosophy of original understanding
is not to "choose a level of abstraction." Rather, it is to find the meaning of a
text—a process which includes finding its degree of generality, which is part
of its meaning—and to apply that text to a particular situation. . . . The equal-
protection clause [for example] was adopted in order to protect freed slaves,
but its language, being general, applies to all persons.[1]

Levy

James Madison, Father of the Constitution and of the Bill of Rights, rejected
the doctrine that the original intent of those who framed the Constitution
should be accepted as an authoritative guide to its meaning. "As a guide in
expounding and applying the provisions of the Constitution . . . the debates and incidental decisions of the Convention can have no authoritative

character.". . . . We tend to forget the astounding fact that Madison's Notes were first published in 1840, fifty-three years after the Constitutional Convention had met. . . . What mattered to them [the founders] was the text of the Constitution, construed in the light of conventional rules of interpretation, the ratification debates, and other contemporary expositions. . . . Original intent is an unreliable concept because it assumes the existence of one intent. . . . The entity we call "the Framers" did not have a collective mind. . . . In fact, they disagreed on many crucial matters. . . .

Fifty years ago . . . Jacobus tenBroek asserted, rightly, that "the intent theory . . . inverts the judicial process." . . . Original intent . . . makes the judge "a mindless robot whose task is the utterly mechanical function" of using original intent as a measure of constitutionality. In the entire history of the Supreme Court . . . no Justice employing the intent theory has ever written a convincing and reliable study.

The Court has the responsibility of helping regenerate and fulfill the noblest aspirations for which the nation stands. It must keep constitutional law constantly rooted in the great ideals of the past yet in a state of evolution in order to realize them. . . . Chief Justice Earl Warren . . . declared, "We serve only the public interest as we see it, guided only by the Constitution and our own consciences." That, not the original intent of the Framers, is our reality.[2]

[1]Robert H. Bork, "The Case against Political Judging," *National Review,* 8 December 1989, pp. 23–28.
[2]Leonard W. Levy, *Original Intent and the Framers' Constitution* (New York: Macmillan, 1988), pp. 1–2, 294, 388, 396, 398.

eral predecessors. In a number of decisions during the 1980s and 1990s, the Court was willing to make use of its expanded powers on behalf of interests it favored.[63]

In the important 1992 case of *Lujan* v. *Defenders of Wildlife,* the Court seemed to retreat to a conception of standing more restrictive than that affirmed by liberal activist jurists.[64] Rather than representing an example of judicial restraint, however, the *Lujan* case was actually a direct judicial challenge to congressional power. The case involved an effort by an environmental group, the Defenders of Wildlife, to make use of the 1973 Endangered Species Act to block the expenditure of federal funds being used by the governments of Egypt and Sri Lanka for public works projects. Environmentalists charged that the projects threatened the habitats of several endangered species of birds and, therefore, that the expenditure of federal funds to support the projects violated the 1973 act. The Interior Department claimed that the act affected only domestic projects.[65]

[63]Mark Silverstein and Benjamin Ginsberg, "The Supreme Court and the New Politics of Judicial Power," *Political Science Quarterly* 102 (Fall 1987), pp. 371–88.
[64]Lujan v. Defenders of Wildlife, 112 S. Ct. (1992).
[65]Linda Greenhouse, "Court Limits Legal Standing in Suits," *New York Times,* 13 June 1992, p. 12.

The Endangered Species Act, like a number of other pieces of liberal environmental and consumer legislation enacted by Congress, encourages citizen suits—suits by activist groups not directly harmed by the action in question—to challenge government policies they deem to be inconsistent with the act. Justice Scalia, however, writing for the Court's majority, reasserted a more traditional conception of standing, requiring those bringing suit against a government policy to show that the policy is likely to cause *them* direct and imminent injury.

Had Scalia stopped at this point, the case might have been seen as an example of judicial restraint. Scalia, however, went on to question the validity of any statutory provision for citizen suits. Such legislative provisions, according to Justice Scalia, violate Article III of the Constitution which limits the federal courts to consideration of actual "cases" and "controversies." This interpretation would strip Congress of its capacity to promote the enforcement of regulatory statutes by encouraging activist groups not directly affected or injured to be on the lookout for violations that could provide the basis for lawsuits. This enforcement mechanism—which conservatives liken to bounty hunting—was an extremely important congressional instrument and played a prominent part in the enforcement of such pieces of legislation as the 1990 Americans with Disabilities Act (see Chapter 10). Thus, the *Lujan* case offers an example of judicial activism rather than of judicial restraint. It remains to be seen, however, whether an activist conservative Court can mobilize sufficient political support to prevail in struggles against a Democratic Congress *and* White House. But it also remains to be seen what effect a Democratic president will have on the composition of the Court. If President Clinton has his way, in a few years, conservatives may be complaining again about judicial liberalism.

SUMMARY

Millions of cases come to trial every year in the United States. The great majority—nearly 99 percent—are tried in state and local courts. The types of law are common law, civil law, criminal law, and public law. In addition, equity proceedings permit courts to take into account special situations and conditions when rigid literal adherence to precedents and statutes would not serve the interests of justice.

There are three kinds of federal cases: (1) civil cases involving diversity of citizenship, (2) civil cases where a federal agency is seeking to enforce federal laws that provide for civil penalties, and (3) cases involving federal criminal statutes or where state criminal cases have been made issues of public law. Judicial power extends only to cases and controversies. Litigants must have standing to sue, and courts neither hand down opinions on hypothetical issues nor take the initiative. Sometimes appellate courts even return cases to the lower courts for further trial. They may also decline to decide cases by invoking the doctrine of political questions.

Juries and adversary proceedings help define the American judicial process. In courts of original jurisdiction, juries are constitutionally required in all criminal prosecutions and, when requested by the defendants, in all civil actions where the

value in controversy exceeds $20. The adversary process is important because:
(1) it underscores the presumption that the accused is innocent until proven guilty,
and (2) it helps maintain the equality of the contending parties.

Judge-made law is like a statute in that it articulates the law as it relates to future controversies. It differs from a statute in that it is intended to guide judges rather than the citizenry in general.

The organization of the federal judiciary provides for original jurisdiction in the federal district courts, the U.S. Court of Claims, the U.S. Tax Court, the Customs Court, and federal regulatory agencies.

Each district court is in one of the eleven appellate districts, called circuits, presided over by a court of appeals. Appellate courts admit no new evidence; their rulings are based solely on the records of the court proceedings or agency hearings that led to the original decision. Appeals court rulings are final unless the Supreme Court chooses to review them.

The Supreme Court has some original jurisdiction, but its major job is to review lower court decisions involving substantial issues of public law. Supreme Court decisions can be reversed by Congress and the state legislatures, but this seldom happens. There is no explicit constitutional authority for the Supreme Court to review acts of Congress. Nonetheless, the 1803 case of *Marbury* v. *Madison* established the Court's right to review congressional acts. The supremacy clause of Article VI and the Judiciary Act of 1789 give the Court the power to review state constitutions and laws. Cases reach the Court mainly through the writ of *certiorari*. The Supreme Court controls its case load by issuing few writs and by handing down clear leading opinions that enable lower courts to resolve future cases without further review.

Both appellate and Supreme Court decisions, including the decision not to review a case, make law. The impact of such law usually favors the status quo. Yet, many revolutionary changes in the law have come about through appellate court and Supreme Court rulings—in the criminal process, in apportionment, and in civil rights.

The judiciary as a whole is subject to three major influences: (1) the individual members of the Supreme Court, who have lifetime tenure; (2) the Justice Department—particularly the solicitor general, who regulates the flow of cases; and (3) the pattern of cases.

The influence of the individual member of the Supreme Court is limited when the Court is polarized, and close votes in a polarized Court impair the value of the decision rendered. Writing the majority opinion for a case is an opportunity for a justice to influence the judiciary. But the need to frame an opinion in such a way as to develop majority support on the Court may limit such opportunities. Dissenting opinions can have more impact than the majority opinion; they stimulate a continued flow of cases around that issue. The solicitor general is the most important single influence outside the Court itself because he controls the flow of cases brought by the Justice Department; he also shapes the argument in those cases. But the flow of cases is a force in itself, which the Department of Justice cannot entirely control. Social problems give rise to similar cases that ultimately must be adjudicated and appealed. Some interest groups attempt to develop such case patterns as a means of gaining power through the courts.

In recent years, the importance of the federal judiciary—the Supreme Court in particular—has increased substantially as the courts have developed new tools of judicial power and forged alliances with important forces in American society.

FOR FURTHER READING

Abraham, Henry. *The Judicial Process.* New York: Oxford University Press, 1986.

Bickel, Alexander. *The Least Dangerous Branch.* Indianapolis: Bobbs–Merrill, 1962.

Blasi, Vincent. *The Burger Court: The Counter-Revolution That Wasn't.* New Haven: Yale University Press, 1983.

Bryner, Gary, and Dennis L. Thompson. *The Constitution and the Regulation of Society.* Provo, UT: Brigham Young University, 1988.

Carp, Robert, and Ronald Stidham, *The Federal Courts.* Washington, DC: Congressional Quarterly Press, 1985.

Davis, Sue. *Justice Rehnquist and the Constitution.* Princeton: Princeton University Press, 1989.

Faulkner, Robert K. *The Jurisprudence of John Marshall.* Princeton: Princeton University Press, 1968.

Goldman, Sheldon, and Thomas P. Jahnige, *The Federal Courts as a Political System.* New York: Harper & Row, 1985.

Graber, Mark A. *Transforming Free Speech: The Ambiguous Legacy of Civil Libertarianism.* Berkeley: University of California Press, 1991.

Hamilton, Charles V. *The Bench and the Ballot: Southern Federal Judges and Black Voters.* New York: Oxford University Press, 1973.

Haskins, George L., and Herbert A. Johnson. *History of the Supreme Court of the United States.* New York: Macmillan, 1981.

Maveety, Nancy. *Representation Rights and the Burger Years.* Ann Arbor: University of Michigan Press, 1991.

Melnick, R. Shep. *Regulation and the Courts: The Case of the Clean Air Act.* Washington, DC: Brookings Institution, 1983.

Mezey, Susan G. *No Longer Disabled: The Federal Courts and the Politics of Social Security Disability.* New York: Greenwood, 1988.

Nardulli, Peter F., James Eisenstein, and Roy B. Fleming. *The Tenor of Justice: Criminal Courts and the Guilty Plea.* Urbana, IL: University of Illinois Press, 1988.

Neely, Richard. *How Courts Govern America.* New Haven: Yale University Press, 1981.

O'Brien, David M. *Storm Center: The Supreme Court in American Politics,* 2nd ed. New York: W. W. Norton, 1990.

Rosenberg, Gerald. *The Hollow Hope: Can Courts Bring about Social Change?* Chicago: University of Chicago Press, 1991.

Rubin, Eva. *Abortion, Politics and the Courts.* Westport, CT: Greenwood Press, 1982.

Scigliano, Robert. *The Supreme Court and the Presidency.* New York: The Free Press, 1971.

Stimson, Shannon C. *The American Revolution in the Law: Anglo-American Jurisprudence before John Marshall.* (Princeton, NJ: Princeton University Press, 1990.

Tribe, Lawrence. *Constitutional Choices.* Cambridge, MA: Harvard University Press, 1985.

Wolfe, Christopher. *The Rise of Modern Judicial Review.* New York: Basic Books, 1986.

Part 3
Politics

9

Public Opinion

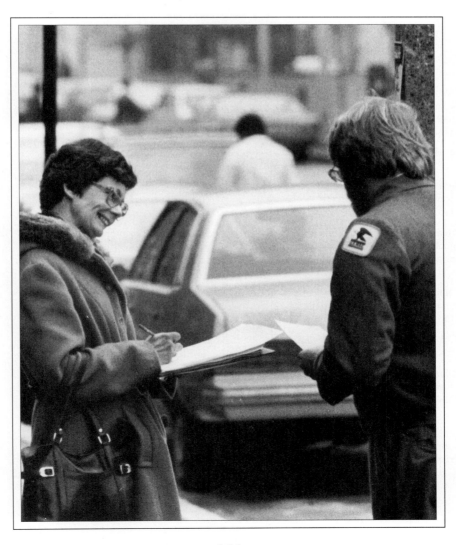

EVENTS		INSTITUTIONAL DEVELOPMENTS
Congressional investigation of Gen. St. Clair's conduct of war against Indians (1792)		George Washington begins policy of executive secrecy in regard to congressional investigations (1792)
Territorial expansion (1800s)	**1800**	Straw polls and other impressionistic means of measuring opinion (1830s–1890s)
Civil War (1861–1865)		
		Urban school systems—development of civic education programs (1880s)
		Birth of advertising industry—scientific manipulation of public opinion (1880s)
Democrats denounce polling as a Republican plot; they instruct their voters not to answer questions (1896)		
World War I (1914–1919)	**1900**	Creel Committee tries to "sell" WW I to American public (1917)
Literary Digest poll predicts Hoover will defeat Roosevelt (1932)		Beginning of routine governmental efforts to manage opinion (1930s)
Media used to defeat Upton Sinclair in California campaign for governor (1934)		Media experts manipulate public opinion through negative campaign using newspapers, leaflets, and radio (1934)
Gallup and Roper use sample surveys in national political polls (1936)		Introduction of sample surveys to predict winners of national elections (1936)
Chicago Tribune poll shows Dewey victory over Truman (1948)		Growth of national polls (1930s–1950s)
Kennedy campaign uses computers to analyze polls and bellwether districts (1959–1960)	**1950**	Emergence of computer analysis of polls and bellwether districts (1959–1960)
CBS uses computer bellwether system to correctly forecast winner of California Republican primary (1964)		

TIME LINE ON PUBLIC OPINION

EVENTS		INSTITUTIONAL DEVELOPMENTS
		Emergence of exit polls (1960s)
CBS airs "Selling of the Pentagon" (1971)	**1970**	Media attack government opinion manipulation (1960s and 1970s)
Exit polls used to predict presidential election outcome before polls close on West Coast (1976, 1980, 1984, 1988)		Expansion of mass media; nationalization of public opinion (1960s–1980s)
Daily polls on public support for Persian Gulf War (1991)	**1990**	Politicians create new media formats to pitch themselves and their programs; era of permanent campaign (1992)
President Clinton uses town meetings and media appeals to bolster popular support for programs; lobbies Congress by mobilizing popular pressure (1993)		Members of presidential campaign staffs become part of White House staff to bolster public support for programs (1993)

*I*n January 1991, after American-led U.N. coalition forces achieved a swift victory over Iraq, President George Bush's level of public approval soared to an unprecedented 91 percent. Many commentators assumed that Bush would be reanointed, rather than merely re-elected, in 1992. Indeed, several leading Democratic presidential aspirants decided there would be no point in challenging Bush in the upcoming presidential race. Only a year later, however, Bush's poll standing had fallen below the 50 percent approval level. By the late summer of 1992, the Democratic presidential candidate, Bill Clinton, had opened a commanding lead in the polls over Bush, who by then could barely muster a 40 percent popular approval rating.

After his election to the presidency, Clinton, too, found that public opinion could be quite fickle. By May 1993, only one hundred days after his inauguration, Clinton's approval ratings had fallen sharply. For example, according to a May 4–6 New York Times/CBS News poll, 50 percent of Americans disapproved of the way Clinton was handling the economy while only 38 percent approved.[1] Only a month earlier, nearly half of all respondents to the same poll had approved of Clinton's economic performance, while only 37 percent had disapproved. Consistent with the pattern discussed in Chapter 6, Clinton's public approval rating briefly increased by 11 points, to nearly 50 percent, in June 1993, after he ordered

---

[1]Gwen Ifill, "As Ratings Stall, Clinton Tries Tune-Up," *New York Times*, 10 May 1993, p. A16; Richard Morin and Ann Devroy, "President's Popularity Continues to Weaken," *Washington Post,* 30 June 1993, p. 1.

a cruise missile attack on Iraqi intelligence headquarters. The attack was in retaliation for an alleged Iraqi plot to assassinate former president George Bush. Clinton himself attributed his improved poll standing to what he termed better public understanding of his economic program. Within a few days, however, Clinton's approval rating had dropped back to its previous 38 percent level.

Commentators and social scientists, of course, carefully plotted these massive changes in public opinion and pondered their causes. Significantly, no analyst charting these shifts in popular sentiment was so bold as to ask whether public opinion was right or wrong—whether it made sense or nonsense. Rather, opinion was viewed as some sort of natural force which, like the weather, affected everything but was itself impervious to human intervention and immune to criticism.

Public opinion has become the ultimate standard against which the conduct of contemporary governments is measured. In the democracies, especially in the United States, both the value of government programs and the virtue of public officials are typically judged by the magnitude of their popularity. Twentieth-century dictatorships, for their part, are careful at least to give lip service to the idea of popular sovereignty, if only to bolster public support at home and to maintain a favorable image abroad.

In this chapter, we will examine the role of public opinion in American politics. First, we will look at the institutions and processes that help to shape public opinion in the United States, most notably the "marketplace of ideas" where opinions compete for acceptance. Second, we will assess the government's role in shaping American public opinion. Third, we will address the problem of measuring opinion. Finally, we will consider the issue of governmental responsiveness to citizens' opinions.

THE MARKETPLACE OF IDEAS

Opinions are products of individuals' personalities, social characteristics, and interests. But opinions are also shaped by institutional, political, and governmental forces that make it more likely that citizens will hold some beliefs and less likely that they will hold others. In the United States and the other Western democracies, opinions and beliefs compete for acceptance in what is sometimes called the "marketplace of ideas." In America, it is mainly the "hidden hand" of the market that determines which opinions and beliefs will flourish and which will fall to the wayside. Thus, to understand public opinion in the United States, it is important to understand the origins and operations of this "idea market."

Origins of the Idea Market

Prior to the nineteenth century, each of the various regional, religious, ethnic, linguistic, and economic strata generally possessed their own ideas and beliefs based upon their own experiences and life circumstances. The members of different primary groups generally had little contact with one another, and they knew remarkably little about the history, customs, or character—much less the opinions—of

their nominal countrymen.

In every European nation and in America, city was separated from countryside and region from region by the lack of usable roads, the unavailability of effective communications media, and, in many nations in Europe, by the absence of even a common national language. Language barriers could be formidable. For example, before the nineteenth century, Parisians traveling just a few days from the capital often reported that it was impossible to understand the "patois" of the local populace and that outside of the larger towns it was difficult to find anyone who spoke even a few words of French.[2] Equally significant was the matter of class. The members of the different social classes, even when living near each other, existed in very different worlds. Often, each class spoke its own language, adhered to its own religious beliefs, maintained its own cultural orientations, and manifested distinct conceptions of the political and social universe.

The autonomy of the various regions, groups, and classes began to diminish in the nineteenth century. During this period, every European regime initiated the construction of what came to be called a "marketplace of ideas"—a national forum in which the views of all strata would be exchanged. Westerners often equate freedom of opinion and expression with the absence of state interference. Western freedom of opinion, however, is not unbridled freedom, rather, it is the structured freedom of a public forum constructed and maintained by the state. The creation and maintenance of this forum, this "marketplace of ideas," has required nearly two centuries of extensive governmental effort in the areas of education, communication, and jurisprudence.

First, in the nineteenth century, most Western nations engaged in intense efforts to impose a single national language upon their citizens. In the United States, massive waves of immigration during the nineteenth century meant that millions of residents spoke no English. In response, the American national government, as well as state and local governments, made vigorous efforts to impose the English language upon these newcomers. Schools were established to provide adults with language skills. At the same time, English was the only language of instruction permitted in the public elementary and secondary schools. Knowledge of English became a prerequisite for American citizenship. With some exceptions, the efforts of the United States and other Western nations to achieve linguistic unification succeeded by the twentieth century.

Second, and closely related to the effort to achieve linguistic unity, was the matter of literacy. Prior to the nineteenth century, few ordinary people were able to read or write. Possession of these skills was, for the most part, limited to the upper strata. Widespread illiteracy in a pre-technological era meant that communication depended upon word of mouth, a situation hardly conducive to the spread of ideas across regional, class, or even village or neighborhood boundaries. During the nineteenth and twentieth centuries, however, all Western governments actively sought to expand popular literacy. With the advent of universal, compulsory education, children were taught to read and write the mother tongue. Together with literacy programs for adults, including extensive efforts by the various national mil-

[2] Eugen Weber, *Peasants into Frenchmen* (Stanton, CA: Stanford University Press, 1976).

itary services to instruct uneducated recruits, this educational process led to the gradual reduction of illiteracy in the industrial West. Like the imposition of a common language, the elimination of illiteracy opened the way for the communication of ideas and information across primary group lines.[3]

A third facet of the construction of the marketplace of ideas was the development of communications mechanisms. This process involved a number of elements. During the early nineteenth century, governments built hundreds of thousands of miles of roads, opening lines of communication among the various regions and between cities and the countryside. Road building was followed later in the century by governmental promotion of the construction of rail and telegraph lines, further facilitating the exchange of goods, persons, and, not least important, ideas and information among previously disparate and often isolated areas. Such "internal improvements" constituted the single most important activity undertaken by the American central government both before and after the Civil War. During the twentieth century, all Western regimes promoted the development of radio, telephone, television, and of the complex satellite-based communications networks that today link the world.

The final key component of the construction of a free market of ideas was, and is, legal protection for free expression of ideas. This last factor is, of course, what most clearly distinguished the construction of the West's idea market from the efforts of authoritarian regimes. Obviously, the development of communication networks, linguistic unification, and universal literacy were goals pursued just as avidly by autocratic nation-builders in the East as by the more liberal regimes of the West.

During the early portion of the nineteenth century, Western governments began to lift some of the traditional legal restrictions upon the exchange of ideas. For example, during the 1830s, Britain rescinded the newspaper taxes that had limited papers' circulation.[4] Subsequently, all Western regimes, to a greater or lesser extent, developed principles of jurisprudence that protected and encouraged the production and promotion of ideas. These principles include the prohibition of prior restraint on publication; the disallowance of many, if not all, forms of censorship; protection of speakers and writers from assault by hostile audiences; restriction of the scope of libel law; and the protection of copyrights.

The cumulative result of all these governmental efforts was the gradual destruction of internal barriers to communication in every Western nation, and the construction of a forum in which the views of all groups and strata could easily be exchanged. In most Western nations, at the present time, there are few physical or legal impediments to the transmission of ideas and information across municipal, regional, class, ethnic, or other primary group boundaries. All groups are, to a greater or lesser extent, linked by a common language, mass communications media, and transportation networks. In the United States, for example, the newspapers, wire services, radio, television, and news magazines present a common core of ideas and information to virtually the entire citizenry. Every region of the country can be reached by mail, phone, and broadcast media; virtually no area is inaccessible by road, rail, or air transport; and persons, ideas, and information can

[3] See Richard Hoggart, *The Uses of Literacy* (Oxford, England: Oxford University Press, 1970).
[4] See Joel Wiener, *The War of the Unstamped* (Ithaca, NY: Cornell University Press, 1969).

The Idea Market Today

The operation of the idea market in the United States today has continually exposed individuals to concepts and information originating outside their own region, class, or ethnic community. It is this steady exposure that over time leads members of every social group to acquire at least some of the ideas and perspectives embraced by the others. Given continual exposure to the ideas of other strata, it is virtually impossible for any group to resist some modification of its own beliefs.

Common Fundamental Values Today most Americans share a common set of political beliefs and opinions. First, Americans generally believe in *equality of opportunity.* That is, they assume that all individuals should be allowed to seek personal and material success. Moreover, Americans generally believe that such success should be linked to personal effort and ability rather than family "connections" or other forms of special privilege. Second, Americans strongly believe in *individual freedom.* They typically support the notion that governmental interference with individuals' lives and property should be kept to the minimum consistent with the general welfare (although in recent years Americans have grown accustomed to greater levels of governmental intervention than would have been deemed appropriate by the founding fathers of liberal theory). Third, most Americans believe in *democracy.* They presume that every person should have the opportunity to take part in the nation's governmental and policy-making processes and to have some "say" in determining how they are governed.[5]

One indication of the extent to which Americans of all political stripes share these fundamental values is shown by a comparison of the acceptance speeches delivered by Bill Clinton and George Bush upon receiving their parties' presidential nominations in 1992. Clinton and Bush differed on many specific issues and policies. Yet, the political visions they presented reveal an underlying similarity. The fundamental emphasis of both candidates was on equality of opportunity. Clinton, in his speech declared:

> Somewhere at this very moment another child is born in America. . . . Let it be our cause to see that child has the chance to live to the fullest of her God-given capacities. Let it be our cause to see that child grow up strong and secure, braced by her challenges but never struggling alone; with family and friends and a faith that in America, no one is left out; no one is left behind.

And George Bush concluded his acceptance speech by proclaiming:

> And the world changes for which we've sacrificed for a generation have finally come to pass, and with them a rare and unprecedented opportunity to pass the sweet cup of

[5] For a discussion of the political beliefs of Americans, see Harry Holloway and John George, *Public Opinion* (New York: St. Martin's, 1986). See also Paul R. Abramson, *Political Attitudes in America* (San Francisco: W. H. Freeman, 1983).

prosperity around our American table. . . . As I travel our land I meet veterans who once worked the turrets of a tank and can now master the keyboards of a high-tech economy.

Thus, however much the two candidates differed on means and specifics, their understanding of the fundamental goals of government was quite similar.

Agreement on fundamental political values, though certainly not absolute, is probably more widespread in the United States than anywhere else in the Western world. During the course of Western political history, competing economic, social, and political groups put forward a variety of radically divergent views, opinions, and political philosophies. America was never socially or economically homogeneous. But two forces that were extremely powerful and important sources of ideas and beliefs elsewhere in the world were relatively weak or absent in the United States. First, the United States never had the feudal aristocracy that dominated during so much of European history. Second, for reasons including America's prosperity and the early availability of political rights, no Socialist movements comparable to those that developed in nineteenth-century Europe were ever able to establish themselves in the United States. As a result, during the course of American history, there existed neither an aristocracy to assert the virtues of inequality, special privilege, and a rigid class structure, nor a powerful American Communist or Socialist party to seriously challenge the desirability of limited government and individualism.[6]

Agreement and Disagreement on Issues Agreement on fundamentals, however, by no means implies that Americans do not differ with one another on a wide variety of issues. American political life is characterized by vigorous debate on economic, foreign policy, and social policy issues; race relations; environmental affairs; and a host of other matters. Factors such as income, education, and occupation have a great deal of influence upon political opinions. Similarly, factors such as race, gender, ethnicity, age, religion, and region, which not only influence individuals' interests but also shape their experiences and upbringing, have enormous influence upon their beliefs and opinions.

For example, individuals whose incomes differ substantially have rather different views on the desirability of a number of important economic and social programs. In general, the poor—who are the chief beneficiaries of these programs—support them more strongly than do those whose taxes pay for the programs. Similarly, blacks and whites have rather different views on questions of civil rights and civil liberties—presumably reflecting differences of interest and historical experience. In recent years, many observers have begun to take note of a number of differences between the views expressed by men and those supported by women, especially on foreign policy questions, where women appear to be much more concerned with the dangers of war, and on social welfare issues, where women show more concern than men for the problems of the poor and unfortunate. Quite conceivably these differences—known collectively as the "gender gap"—reflect the results of differences in the childhood experiences and socializa-

[6] See Louis Hartz, *The Liberal Tradition in America* (New York: Harcourt, Brace, 1955).

tion of men and women in America.

To say that individuals' opinions are related to their economic interests or social characteristics is not to say that it is always easy or even possible to predict opinions from these factors. Some individuals resolutely hold views that seem to run counter to their obvious economic interests. Wealthy Socialists are an example. Moreover, the same set of interests or social characteristics can reasonably give rise to any number of opinions and viewpoints, depending upon the circumstances of the time. Opinions grow out of the interaction of individual interests, personalities, and experiences with the particular issues, events, and problems of the day. Thus, the views of "the rich," "women," or "young people" are hardly fixed and immutable attributes of these groups, but instead depend upon and often change as the interests and experiences of these groups interact with changing economic, social, and political realities.

Liberalism and Conservatism   Many Americans describe themselves as either liberal or conservative in political orientation (see Box 9.1 and Box 9.2). Historically these terms were defined somewhat differently than they are today. As recently as the nineteenth century, a liberal was an individual who favored freedom from state control, while a conservative was someone who supported the use of governmental power and favored continuation of the influence of church and aristocracy in national life.

Today, the term *liberal* has come to imply support for political and social reform; support for extensive governmental intervention in the economy; the expansion of federal social services; more vigorous efforts on behalf of the poor, minorities, and women; and greater concern for consumers and the environment. In social and cultural areas, liberals generally support abortion rights, are concerned with the rights of persons accused of crime, support decriminalization of drug use, and oppose state involvement with religious institutions and religious expression. In international affairs, liberal positions are usually seen as including

---

BOX 9.1
Profile of a Liberal: Jesse Jackson

Advocates increasing taxes for corporations and for the wealthy.
Advocates a "Right to Food Policy" to make available a nutritionally balanced diet for all U.S. citizens.
Advocates the establishment of a national health care program for all citizens.
Advocates higher salaries for teachers, more college grants and loans, a doubling of the federal education budget.
Favors increasing the minimum wage.
Advocates the use of $500 billion in pension funds to finance public works programs, including the construction of a "national railroad."
Calls for the reimposition of sanctions against South Africa.
Favors foreign assistance programs designed to wipe out hunger and starvation throughout the world.
Advocates dramatic expansion of federal social and urban programs.

BOX 9.2

Profile of a Conservative: Patrick Buchanan

Wants to trim the size of the federal government and to transfer power to state and local governments.

Wants to diminish government regulation of business.

Favors prayer in the public schools.

Opposes gay rights legislation.

Supports programs that would allow children and parents more flexibility in deciding what school to attend.

Supports strict regulation of pornography.

Favors making most abortions illegal.

Would eliminate some environmental regulations.

Supports harsher treatment of criminals.

Opposes affirmative action programs.

Opposes allowing women to serve in military combat units.

support for arms control, opposition to the development and testing of nuclear weapons, support for aid to poor nations, opposition to the use of American troops to influence the domestic affairs of Third World nations, opposition to South Africa's system of apartheid, and support for international organizations such as the United Nations.

By contrast, the term *conservative* today is used to describe those who generally support the social and economic status quo and are suspicious of efforts to introduce new political formulae and economic arrangements. Conservatives believe strongly that a large and powerful government poses a threat to citizens' freedom. Thus, in the domestic arena, conservatives generally oppose the expansion of governmental activity, asserting that solutions to social and economic problems can be developed in the private sector. Conservatives particularly oppose efforts to impose government regulation on business, pointing out that such regulation is frequently economically inefficient and costly and can ultimately lower the entire nation's standard of living. As to social and cultural positions, many conservatives oppose abortion, support school prayer, are more concerned for the victims than the perpetrators of crimes, oppose school busing, and support traditional family arrangements. In international affairs, conservatism has come to mean support for the maintenance of American military power.

Often political observers search for logical connections among the various positions identified with liberalism or with conservatism, and they are disappointed or puzzled when they are unable to find a set of coherent philosophical principles that define and unite the several elements of either of these sets of beliefs. On the liberal side, for example, what is the logical connection between opposition to U.S. intervention in Asia and Africa and demands that the United States seek to force South Africa to end apartheid? Surely the latter is a call for the sort of intervention that liberals claim to deplore. On the conservative side, what is the logical relationship between opposition to governmental regulation of business and support for a ban on abortion? Indeed, the latter would seem to be just the sort of regulation of private conduct that conservatives claim to abhor.

Frequently, the relationships among the various elements of liberalism or the
several aspects of conservatism are *political* rather then *logical*. One underlying basis of liberal views is that all or most represent criticisms of or attacks on the foreign and domestic policies and cultural values of the business and commercial strata that have been prominent in the United States for the past century. In some measure, the tenets of contemporary conservatism represent this elite's defense of its positions against its enemies, who include organized labor, minority groups, and some intellectuals and professionals. Thus, liberals attack business and commercial elites by advocating more governmental regulation, including consumer protection and environmental regulation, opposition to military weapons programs, and support for expensive social programs. Conservatives counterattack by asserting that governmental regulation of the economy is ruinous, that military weapons are needed in a changing world, and they seek to stigmatize their opponents for showing no concern for the rights of "unborn" Americans.[7]

Of course, it is important to note that many people who call themselves liberals or conservatives accept only part of the liberal or conservative ideology. During the 1980s, many political commentators asserted that Americans were becoming increasingly conservative. Indeed, it was partly in response to this view that the Democrats in 1992 selected a presidential candidate drawn from the party's moderate wing. Although it appears that Americans have adopted more conservative outlooks on some issues, their views in most areas have remained largely unchanged or even have become more liberal in recent years (see Table 9.1). Thus, there are many individuals who are liberal on social issues but conservative on eco-

TABLE 9.1
Have Americans Become More Conservative?

	1972	1978	1980	1982	1984	1986	1988
Percentage responding "yes" to the following questions:							
Should the government help minority groups?	30%	25%	16%	21%	27%	26%	13%
Should the government see to it that everyone has a job and a guaranteed standard of living?	27	17	22	25	28	25	24
Should abortion never be permitted?	9	10	8	13	13	13	12
Should the government provide fewer services and reduce spending?	NA	NA	27	32	28	24	25

NA = Not asked
Source: Center for Political Studies of the Institute for Social Research, University of Michigan. Data were made available through the Inter-University Consortium for Political and Social Research.

---

[7] For a discussion of this conflict, see Benjamin Ginsberg and Martin Shefter, "A Critical Realignment? The New Politics, the Reconstituted Right, and the Election of 1984," in *The Elections of 1984*, ed. Michael Nelson (Washington, DC: Congressional Quarterly Press, 1985), pp. 1–26.

nomic issues. There is certainly nothing illogical about these mixed positions. They indicate the relatively open and fluid character of American political debate.

The idea market thus has created a common ground for Americans in which discussion of issues is encouraged and based on common understandings. Despite the many and often sharp divisions that exist in the twentieth century—between liberals and conservatives, different income groups, different regional groups— most Americans see the world through similar lenses.

SHAPING PUBLIC OPINION

Public opinion is not some disembodied entity that stands alone and unalterable. Opinion can often be molded, shaped, or manipulated. In many areas of the world, governments determine which opinions their citizens may or may not express. People who assert views that their rulers do not approve of may be subject to imprisonment—or worse. Americans and the citizens of the other Western democracies are fortunate to live in nations where freedom of opinion and expression are generally taken for granted.

Even with freedom of opinion, however, not all ideas and opinions flourish. Both private groups and the government itself today attempt to influence which opinions do take hold in the public imagination. We will first examine how government seeks to shape values that in turn influence public opinion. Then we will discuss the marketing of political issues, both by the government and by private groups.

Enlisting Public Support for Government

All governments attempt to shape or structure citizens' underlying beliefs about the regime, the social and economic structure, and the political process. Governments seek to imbue their citizens with positive feelings toward the established order through the creation of a national ethos, the promotion of property ownership, education, and the opportunity to participate in national politics. Nationalism, property ownership, education, and political participation can be labeled "deadly virtues." These may be forces for good if they help to create a unified and public-spirited citizenry, or forces for evil if they are merely used as instruments of control.

Nationalism   Nationalism is the belief that people who occupy the same territory have something important in common, making them separate from and superior to other people. It is based on myths about the origin and history of the people, their exploits and sufferings as a nation, their heroes, and their mission in the world. Such myths are not necessarily falsehoods. They are simply beliefs that are accepted whether they are true or false.

Nationalism takes root in family, community, and tribal loyalties, but it is strong enough to displace those local ties in favor of the nation. The great virtue of nationalism is precisely that it gives individuals something far larger than themselves with which to identify. It brings out nobility in people, calling on them to sacrifice something of themselves—even their lives—for their society. Nationalism helps

weave the social fabric together with a minimum of coercion.

Nationalism also has a darker side, however. Since it encourages pride in one's own country, it can also produce distrust and hatred of others. This tendency is often encouraged by rulers as a means of whipping up support for a war or other international adventures. There will always be conflicts among nations, but these conflicts are much more likely to escalate toward full-scale war when each country is backed by strong national myths. The paramount example of the misuse of nationalism is the case of Nazi Germany, where nationalistic sentiment was perverted to justify aggression and murder on an unprecedented scale.

Private Property　Property ownership is probably a less universal factor in the manipulation of belief than nationalism but that makes it no less important. Governments regard widespread property ownership to be a good, conservative force in society because it discourages disorder and revolution. The citizen who owns property has a stake in the existing order—a piece of the rock—which he or she will seek to protect.

Many important American leaders have dreamed of creating the ideal polity—political system—around property ownership. Thomas Jefferson, for example, believed that the American Republic ought to be composed of a population of farmers, each with enough property to appreciate social order and to oppose excessive wealth and power. Although the United States did not become a republic of farmers, this idea was certainly behind the federal government's nineteenth-century policy of giving millions of acres of land from the public treasury to persons who were willing to settle and improve it. Squatting and homesteading were the names for this method of gaining property ownership. It was justified—indeed encouraged—by the government in large part as a means of giving people a stake in their country.

Even leaders of some of the least-privileged groups in American society have discovered the importance of property ownership, particularly home ownership. As one African American leader put it:

> Fulfillment can never come through housing efforts which afford people no sense of investment, nor ownership with control of, their immediate environment. Renters tend to be far less responsible than home-owners. Black people, in our urban ghettos, are a renter class, and hence the system tends inevitably to make them into irresponsible people.[8]

Mass industrialization has expanded the meaning of property, but its value has not weakened. For most people, property is no longer a plot of land but instead is a mortgage on a house or a stock certificate that indicates ownership of a tiny proportion of some large corporation.

Another modern form of property is the vested interest in a company. People who work for large companies are often entitled to pensions and other privileges after a minimum period of service. These vested interests give them a heavy stake

[8] Testimony of Dr. Mason Wright, Jr., Chairman of the National Housing Conference on Black Power, in *Housing Legislation of 1967: Hearings before the Subcommittee on Housing and Urban Affairs of the Committee on Banking and Currency* (Washington, DC: Government Printing Office, 1967), p. 865.

in the company until their retirement. Attachment to the company can also be cemented by the option to buy the company's stock at favorable prices.

Education In the United States, education is a multibillion-dollar investment. Few people have questioned the need for the investment because it promises to yield people with high-level skills, problem-solving capacity, and productivity, along with a significant amount of social mobility. This is not to say that a formal education has helped every American child realize the ideal of success. But it does mean that education has made it possible for most children in America to join the work force.

Formal schooling goes beyond skills and training, however. Schools shape values as well. Harry L. Gracey has described school as "academic boot camp." He meant that beginning as early as kindergarten students learn "to go through the routines and to follow orders with unquestioning obedience, even when these make no sense to them. They learn to tolerate and even to prosper in the bureaucratized environment of school, and this is preparation for their later life."[9]

French sociologist Émile Durkheim (1858–1917) said essentially the same thing when he observed matter-of-factly that education "consists of a methodical socialization of the younger generation" and that the education process "is above all the means by which society perpetually recreates the conditions of its very existence."[10] This is usually done at the state and local government levels, where most educational policies in the United States are formulated. The schools themselves are capable of adjusting their curriculums to the occupational needs of their region.

An example of the use of the school system to orient students toward national needs is the reaction of the United States in the late 1950s to the embarrassment of Sputnik, the Soviet Union's triumphal first entry into space. This Soviet triumph convinced many American policy makers that the country's pool of scientific and technical skills was too small. Consequently, within two or three years, mathematics and the sciences were deliberately reorganized throughout the country. They became the "new math" and the "new science" that within half a decade of Sputnik dominated the school curriculums.

Since that time, a reaction against the extremes of the new math and new science has occurred. Many local schools have, for example, gone back to conventional approaches—especially in math. But this change is itself an expression of local efforts to adapt students to national and local needs.

Some of the schools' influences are not in the curriculum, but they are systematic nevertheless. Studies of the elementary textbooks used in many school systems revealed, for example, that various stories showed women choosing inferior roles, low-paying jobs, and service functions, and men choosing more active and important social functions.[11] Thanks to these studies and other criticisms and to efforts

---

[9] Harry L. Gracey, "Learning the Student Role: Kindergarten as Academic Boot Camp," in *The Quality of Life in America,* ed. A. David Hill (New York: Holt, 1973), p. 261.

[10] Emile Durkheim, *Education and Sociology,* trans. Sherwood D. Fox (Glencoe, IL: Free Press, 1956), p. 71.

[11] Lenore J. Weitzman, "Sex-Role Socialization," in *Woman: A Feminist Perspective,* ed. Jo Freeman (Palo Alto, CA: Mayfield Publishing, 1979), pp. 153–216.

to eliminate the stereotypes, sex biases in books and in other school situations are probably diminishing, and the self-esteem of women may be improving. But the studies themselves reveal the importance of the schools in spreading and in changing all sorts of cultural values, including attitudes towards one's own personal qualities as well as general political ideologies.

Participation and Cooptation   To participate is to share, or to take part in. It is an association with others, usually for the purpose of taking joint action and is essential for any kind of democratic government. Even representation is not enough unless there is widespread participation in the choice of representatives. Virtually all political leaders endorse some types of participation, especially voting.

Participation is an instrument of governance because it encourages people to give their consent to being governed. A broad and popularly based process of local consultation, discussion, town meetings, and secret ballots may actually produce a sense of the will of the people. But even when it does not produce a clear sense of that will, the purpose of participation is nonetheless fulfilled because the process itself produces consent. Deeply embedded in people's sense of fair play is the principle that those who play the game must accept the outcome. Those who participate in politics are similarly committed, even if they are consistently on the losing side. Why do politicians plead with everyone to get out and vote? Because voting is the simplest and easiest form of participation by masses of people. Even though it is minimal participation, it is sufficient to commit all voters to being governed, regardless of who wins. (Voting will be discussed in more detail in Chapter 10.)

There are many examples in recent American history of the use of participation to generate more favorable popular beliefs about the government. It is no coincidence, for example, that youths between the ages of eighteen and twenty-one were given the right to vote in the late 1960s just at a time when they were already participating at almost historic levels of sound and fury. Young people were politically active, but they were not participating in the conventional forms, and they were protesting against established authority. Therefore, Congress and the state legislatures ratified the Twenty-sixth Amendment (1971), giving eighteen-year-olds the right to vote. The vote was used to placate young Americans, to provide them with a conventional channel of participation, and to justify suppressing their disorderly activities. The following testimony by the late Senator Jacob Javits of New York is one example of the motivation behind the voting rights amendment:

> We all realize that only a tiny minority of college students on these campuses engaged in unlawful acts. But these deplorable incidents make a point. . . . I am convinced that self-styled student leaders who urged such acts of civil disobedience would find themselves with little or no support if students were given a more meaningful role in the political process. Passage of the [Twenty-sixth Amendment]. . . would give us the means, sort of the famous carrot and the stick, to channel this energy.[12]

[12] U.S. Senate, Committee on the Judiciary, *Hearings before the Subcommittee on Constitutional Amendments on S.J. Res. 8, S.J. Res. 14, and S.J. Res. 78 Relating to Lowering the Voting Age to 18,* May 14, 15, and 16, 1968 (Washington DC: Government Printing Office), p. 12.

The most familiar examples of cooptation through participation are the efforts of political leaders to balance their electoral tickets and their political appointments. Political party leaders in city, state, and national campaigns try their best to select candidates for public office who "represent" each of the important minorities in their constituency. This effort involves balancing ethnic, religious, and regional groups, as well as men and women and any other segments of the constituency. African American, Hispanic American, and women's movement leaders study presidential appointments with considerable interest. They do this not so much because an additional black or Hispanic or female representative would give them much more power but because such appointments are a measure of their current worth in national politics.

Nationalism, property ownership, education, and participation are used by all governments, including our own, to bolster popular support for leaders and their policies. Through these four mechanisms, governments seek to give their citizens a more generally positive orientation toward the political and social order, regardless of their attitudes toward specific programs. Through these techniques, governments hope to convince their citizens voluntarily to obey laws, pay taxes, and serve in the armed forces. Many social scientists believe that if popular support falls below some minimum level, the result could be chaos or even some form of rebellion. This fear was especially manifest during the 1960s and 1970s when diminished levels of popular support did indeed coincide with increases in political violence and unrest.

Marketing Political Issues

Beyond these broad efforts by the government to subtly shape popular attachments to the political regime, both the government and private groups attempt to muster support for different political ideas and programs. Both use public relations to enlist support and shape opinion.

Few ideas spread spontaneously. Usually, whether they are matters of fashion, science, or politics, ideas must be vigorously promoted to become widely known and accepted. For example, the clothing, sports, and entertainment fads that occasionally seem to appear from nowhere and sweep the country before being replaced by some other new trend are almost always the product of careful marketing campaigns by one or another commercial interest, rather than spontaneous phenomena. Even in the sciences, generally considered *the* bastions of objectivity, new theories, procedures, and findings are not always accepted simply and immediately on their own merit. Often, the proponents of a new scientific principle or practice must campaign within the scientific community on behalf of their views. Like their counterparts in fashion and science, successful—or at least widely held—political ideas are usually the products of carefully orchestrated campaigns by government or by organized groups and interests, rather than the results of spontaneous popular enthusiasm.

Government Management of Issues   All governments attempt, to a greater or lesser extent, to influence, manipulate, or manage their citizens' beliefs. In the

United States, some efforts have been made by every administration since the na-

tion's founding to influence public sentiment. But efforts to shape opinion did not
become a routine and formal official function until World War I, when the Wilson
administration created a censorship board, enacted sedition and espionage legislation, and attempted to suppress groups that opposed the war, like the International
Workers of the World (IWW) and the Socialist party. Eugene Debs, a prominent
Socialist and presidential candidate, was arrested and convicted of having violated
the Espionage Law, and he was sentenced to ten years in prison for delivering a
speech that defended the IWW.

At the same time, however, World War I was the first modern industrial war requiring a total mobilization of popular effort on the home front for military
production. The war effort required the government to persuade the civilian population to bear the costs and make the sacrifices needed to achieve industrial and
agricultural, as well as battlefield, success. The chief mechanism for eliciting the
support of public opinion was the Committee on Public Information (CPI),
chaired by journalist and publicist George Creel. The CPI organized a massive
public relations and news management program aimed at promoting popular enthusiasm for the war effort. This program included the dissemination of favorable
news, the publication of patriotic pamphlets, films, photos, cartoons, bulletins, and
periodicals, and the organization of "war expositions" and speakers' tours. Special
labor programs were aimed at maintaining the loyalty and productivity of the work
force. Many of the CPI's staff were drawn from the major public relations firms of
the time.[13]

The extent to which public opinion is actually affected by governmental public
relations efforts is probably limited. The government—despite its size and
power—is only one source of information and evaluation in the United States.
Very often, governmental claims are disputed by the media, by interest groups, and
at times, by opposing forces within the government itself. Thus, for example,
efforts by Presidents Reagan and Bush to convince Americans that we should
provide support for anti-Communist forces in Nicaragua, Afghanistan, and
Mozambique were countered by the public relations efforts of a variety of political
and religious groups, as well as by the publicity campaigns mounted by Reagan's
and Bush's opponents in the Congress. Often, too, governmental efforts to manipulate public opinion backfire when the public is made aware of the government's
tactics. Thus, in 1971, the United States government's efforts to build popular support for the Vietnam War were hurt when CBS News aired its documentary "The
Selling of the Pentagon," which purported to reveal the extent and character of
governmental efforts to sway popular sentiment. In this documentary, CBS
demonstrated the techniques, including planted news stories and faked film
footage, the government had used to misrepresent its activities in Vietnam. These
revelations, of course, had the effect of undermining popular trust in all governmental claims. During the 1991 Persian Gulf War, the U.S. military was very careful about the accuracy of its assertions.

At the start of his new administration in 1993, President Bill Clinton made a

---

[13] See George Creel, *How We Advertised America* (New York: Harper and Brothers, 1920).

James Carville and Mary Matalin
All's Fair in Love, War, and Politics

The tumultuous 1992 presidential campaign contained many dramatic elements, including George Bush's surprising drop in the polls following the Persian Gulf War, and Bill Clinton's phoenix-like rise in the polls in the summer and fall before the election. The candidates' campaign managers labored unceasingly throughout the campaign to swing public sentiment their way. Yet, like a made-for-television movie, this pitched political battle between the Bush and Clinton camps included a melodramatic quality: the real-life romance between Clinton's top strategist, James Carville, and Bush's political director, Mary Matalin.

James Carville began his political career in his home state of Louisiana. A mediocre student at Louisiana State University, Carville completed his undergraduate degree in seven years (interrupted by service in the Marines) and acquired a law degree in 1973. After working on several state political campaigns, Carville struck out on his own as a political consultant in 1982, working for state Democratic candidates around the country. Carville acquired a national reputation in 1991 when he engineered the come-from-behind Pennsylvania Senate victory of unknown Democrat Harris Wofford against former attorney general Richard Thornburgh.

The Clinton campaign posed a similar challenge in that Clinton was little known and given little chance of winning. Carville brought to the campaign two key principles: the campaign should respond immediately to any charges or attacks and the campaign should stay focused on its own core message and not allow itself to forced on the defensive. These tactics were crucial to Clinton's winning effort.

Mary Matalin is also considered a rising young star in the world of campaign management. Brought up on the South Side of Chicago, the daughter of a steel mill worker, Matalin also took seven years to complete her undergraduate degree and then had early experience in Illinois political cam-

James Carville

major effort to shape popular opinion in support of his programs and initiatives. The president had the Democratic National Committee (DNC) hire a "campaign manager" to coordinate a nationwide grassroots effort to mobilize public support for Clinton's health care reform plan.[14] Clinton also turned to the DNC to hire a telemarketing firm to arrange a cascade of phone calls and letters to members of Congress, the media, and pollsters in support of his economic program. He

---

[14] Dana Priest, "White House to Stump for Health Plan," *Washington Post*, 6 February 1993, p. 1.

paigns. In the 1980s, she did political work with the Republican National Committee in Washington, D.C. Her big break came when she was credited with designing Bush's winning strategy in the important Michigan caucuses during the 1988 Republican nominating season. Matalin acknowledges having learned much from Republican campaign wizard Lee Atwater, who was credited with successfully guiding the Reagan and Bush campaigns of the 1980s.

In the race against Clinton, Matalin was considered among the toughest and most loyal campaign leaders in the Bush camp. Despite taking some flak for saying that the Clinton campaign had to control its "bimbo eruptions" (a reference to allegations of womanizing by Clinton), Matalin was one of Bush's most effective campaign operatives. Unlike the Clinton campaign, however, the Bush campaign faced organizational problems, including indecisiveness about which direction the campaign should take.

Both Carville and Matalin are considered tough, quick-witted, plain-speaking, hard-working partisans. Their romantic relationship began after meeting at a Washington dinner party in 1991. In public, both agreed to suspend their relationship during the campaign. Yet gossip columnists reported that they continued to see each other throughout the campaign. When asked if they fought about politics, Matalin responded "In terms of intense disagreements that we've had, politics ranks pretty much in the middle." When Matalin was criticized for the "bimbo" remark, Carville expressed public sympathy for her plight.

After the campaign, the two left for an extended European vacation. On returning, they signed a joint book agreement to publish their campaign memoirs. Love notwithstanding, Carville picked up where he left off, working the re-election of New Jersey Democratic governor Jim Florio, and Matalin resumed her work for the Republican party.

Source: Gerald M. Pomper, et al., *The Election of 1992* (Chatham, NJ: Chatham House, 1993).

Mary Matalin

wanted to make certain that there would be an outpouring of popular support for the plan presented in his February 17, 1993, State of the Union address.[15] Clinton, Vice-President Al Gore, and other key members of the administration also engaged in extensive media campaigning and public appearances to muster support for the administration's programs.

---

[15] Ruth Marcus and Ann Devroy, "Asking Americans to Face Facts, Clinton Presents Plan to Raise Taxes, Cut Deficit," *Washington Post,* 19 February 1993, p. 1.

Indeed, a hallmark of the Clinton administration has been the steady use of campaign techniques like those used in election campaigns to bolster popular enthusiasm for White House initiatives. The president established a "political war room" in the Executive Office Building similar to the one that operated in his campaign headquarters. Representatives from all departments meet in the war room every day to discuss and coordinate the president's public relations efforts. Many of the same consultants and pollsters who directed the successful Clinton campaign have been employed in the selling of the president's programs.[16]

Private Groups and the Shaping of Opinions   The success of a political idea is often determined by the marketing efforts of organized interests. Two examples of successful political ideas—ideas that have attracted millions of adherents—are *right to life,* i.e., the notion that abortions should be severely curtailed or outlawed altogether, and *nuclear freeze,* the argument that the United States should halt the development and production of nuclear weapons either unilaterally or through the negotiation of agreements with other nations with nuclear weapons. These ideas obviously differ in substance and certainly appeal to very distinct subgroups of the population. The notion of the right to life is most popular among Protestant and Catholic social conservatives, while the appeal of the nuclear freeze argument is strongest among liberal urban professionals. But, despite their dissimilarity in subject matter and adherents, these two political ideas are similar in one important respect. Both were developed and successfully promoted by well-financed and well-organized groups using sophisticated public relations techniques. Though each of these ideas can and should be debated on its own merits, it is also important to understand their political origins and implications.

The right-to-life issue was heavily promoted by conservative politicians who saw the issue of abortion as a potential means of uniting Catholic and Protestant conservatives and linking both groups to the Republican coalition. These politicians convinced Catholic and evangelical Protestant leaders that they shared similar views on the question of abortion, and they worked with religious leaders to focus public attention on the negative issues in the abortion debate. To advance their cause, leaders of the movement sponsored well-publicized Senate hearings, where testimony, photographs, and other exhibits were presented to illustrate the violent effects of abortion procedures. At the same time, publicists for the movement produced leaflets, articles, books, and films such as *The Silent Scream,* to highlight the agony and pain ostensibly felt by the unborn when they were being aborted. All this underscored the movement's claim that abortion was nothing more or less than the murder of millions of innocent human beings. Finally, Catholic and evangelical Protestant religious leaders were organized to denounce abortion from their church pulpits and, increasingly, from their electronic pulpits on the Christian Broadcasting Network (CBN) and the various other television forums available for religious programming. Religious leaders also organized demonstrations, pickets, and disruptions at abortion clinics throughout the nation.[17]

[16] Gerald F. Seib and Michael K. Frisby, "Selling Sacrifice," *Wall Street Journal,* 5 February 1993, p. 1.

[17] See Gillian Peele, *Revival and Reaction* (Oxford, England: Clarendon Press, 1985). Also see Connie Paige, *The Right to Lifers* (New York: Summit, 1983).

Like the right-to-life issue, the idea of a nuclear freeze was developed and promoted by organized political forces seeking to further their political interests. In
particular, liberal activists conceived the idea of a nuclear freeze in the early 1980s
as a means of reviving and galvanizing the liberal antiwar coalition that had been
such an important force in American politics during the Vietnam era. To promote
their cause, advocates of the nuclear freeze, like those of right to life, employed the
full gamut of public relations mechanisms. Liberal senators introduced a resolution
supporting the concept of a freeze and conducted well-publicized hearings on the
topic. Rallies were held throughout the nation on behalf of the freeze, including a
gigantic New York City rally in 1982 that attracted several hundred thousand participants. Local organizations were formed, generally on college and university
campuses, to foster local antinuclear activities and to enlist potential student activists. Scientists, entertainers, physicians, politicians, and educators gave speeches
and held press conferences throughout the country on the dangers of nuclear war.
Finally, nuclear freeze advocates helped to promote films that depicted the dangers
of nuclear war, such as *Testament* and, most notably, the television film *The Day
After,* viewed by tens of millions of Americans. The result of the efforts was a substantial increase in popular concern with issues of war and peace and, in particular,
heightened public fear of nuclear war.[18]

In general, the notions that are most successful in the marketplace of ideas are
precisely those advocated and promoted by the nation's more important political
and economic forces. Ideas are marketed best by groups with access to financial resources, public or private institutional support, and sufficient skill or education to
select, develop, and draft ideas that will attract interest and support. Thus, the development and promotion of conservative themes and ideas in recent years has
been greatly facilitated by the millions of dollars that conservative corporations and
business organizations such as the Chamber of Commerce and the Public Affairs
Council spend each year on public information and what is now called in corporate circles "issues management." In addition, conservative businessmen have
contributed millions of dollars to such conservative institutions as the Heritage
Foundation, the Hoover Institution, and the American Enterprise Institute.[19]
Many of the ideas that helped those on the Right influence political debate were
first developed and articulated by scholars associated with these institutions.

Although they do not usually have access to financial assets that match those
available to their conservative opponents, liberal intellectuals and professionals have
ample organizational skills, access to the media, and practice in creating, communicating, and using ideas. During the past three decades, the chief vehicle through
which liberal intellectuals and professionals advanced their ideas has been the
"public interest group," an institution that relies heavily upon voluntary contributions of time, effort, and interest on the part of its members. Through groups like
Common Cause, the National Organization for Women, the Sierra Club, Friends

---

[18] See Adam Garfinkle, *The Politics of the Nuclear Freeze* (Philadelphia: Foreign Policy Research Institute, 1983). Also see Fox Butterfield, "Autonomy of the Nuclear Protest," *New York Times Magazine,*
11 July 1982, pp. 14–39.
[19] See David Vogel, "The Power of Business in America: A Reappraisal," *British Journal of Political Science* 13 (January 1983), pp. 19–44.

HEALTH CARE REFORM:
AN ISSUE FOR THE 1990S

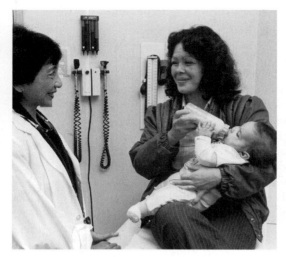

JACK JURDEN
Courtesy Wilmington News-Journal

Occasionally a combination of economic, social, and political forces comes together and generates a truly national debate on a public policy issue. National health care reform is a wonderful example to help us see exactly where issues come from and how public opinion on them is shaped. The debate in the United States over national health insurance has been going on for decades. Although many policy initiatives have been brought before Congress, none have made it into law because of partisan wrangling, lobbying by the health industry, and public uneasiness about the amount of government regulation that would be required to make a national plan work. As a result, the United States—the world leader in medical research and technology, and in the number of top-quality health care providers—is one of only two industrialized countries unable to ensure access to these services for all citizens.

The tremendous increase in medical care costs in the 1980s, due largely to new, expensive medical technologies like the CAT scan, created fertile ground for national health insurance to re-emerge as a crucial issue in the early 1990s. Employers—the major providers of health insurance—began to stagger under enormous health costs and found it necessary to greatly reduce insurance benefits or, particularly for small businesses, cut them completely. Individuals left on their own discovered they were often unable to afford insurance, the annual cost of which could equal or surpass the amount spent on food or a mortgage.

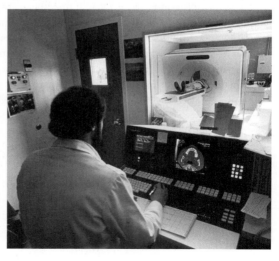

Seizing upon voters' anxieties over obtaining good quality health care in Pennsylvania, political consultant James Carville encouraged political unknown Harris Wofford to make it the centerpiece of his senatorial campaign. The strategy was overwhelmingly successful. Wofford, after campaigning almost exclusively on the need to make quality health care accessible to all Americans, came from far back in the polls to defeat former Attorney General Richard Thornburgh for the position. The Pennsylvania Senate contest catapulted the issue of health care reform into presidential campaign politics, where it then gained the attention and momentum necessary to generate national debate.

National health care finally gained undisputed legitimacy as a crucial issue in the public opinion when it became a focus for the 1992 presidential campaign. Placing the need for national health care alongside standard issues like the economy and education, Bill Clinton defeated incumbent George Bush. By assigning First Lady Hillary Rodham Clinton to head the Health Care Task Force, President Clinton showed his commitment to ensure this issue would finally be resolved.

of the Earth, and Physicians for Social Responsibility, intellectuals and professionals have been able to use their organizational skills and educational resources to develop and promote ideas like the nuclear freeze.[20]

As journalist and author Joe Queenan put it, though political ideas can erupt
spontaneously, they almost never do. Instead,

> issues are usually manufactured by tenured professors and obscure employees of think
> tanks. . . . It is inconceivable that the American people, all by themselves, could in-
> dependently arrive at the conclusion that the depletion of the ozone layer poses a
> dire threat to our national well-being, or that an immediate, across-the-board cut in
> the capital-gains tax is the only thing that stands between us and the economic abyss.
> The American people do not have that kind of sophistication. *They have to have
> help.*[21]

One interesting recent case in which a politician seemed willing to provide the
American people with quite a bit of "help" in arriving at an idea was the 1992 independent presidential candidacy of Ross Perot. After withdrawing from the race
in July 1992, Perot announced in September that he would be willing to reenter
the contest, but only if his supporters across the nation asked him to do so. Indeed,
Perot contrasted his own campaign organization, United We Stand America,
which he described as "driven from the bottom up," with the efforts of other
politicians, which were "driven from the top down by a handful of powerful
people."[22] Ostensibly to learn how his supporters felt about a renewal of his presidential bid, Perot established an 800-number and invited citizens to call with their
advice. During the first week in October, Perot announced his decision to reenter
the presidential race—purely in response to the demands of the American people.

Whatever the actual merits of the Perot candidacy, one thing is clear: the
American people had considerable help in deciding that it was a good idea. According to Federal Election Commission (FEC) records, after nominally withdrawing from the presidential race in July 1992, Perot spent several million dollars
making certain that his name would be on the presidential ballot in all fifty states.
At the same time, according to the FEC and a number of Perot volunteers, United
We Stand volunteer coordinators in several key states were replaced by paid political professionals during the months of August and September, when Perot was
supposedly not a candidate.[23] Moreover, many individuals who called Perot's 800-
number to urge him *not* to enter the presidential race were surprised to learn that
any call to the number was automatically recorded as favoring Perot's candidacy.
Obviously, Perot forces did not want to risk the possibility that ideas "driven from
the bottom up," would fail to coincide with their own.

Whatever their particular ideology or interest, those groups and forces that can
muster the most substantial financial, institutional, educational, and organizational

---

[20] See David Vogel, "The Public Interest Movement and the American Reform Tradition," *Political Science Quarterly* 96 (Winter 1980), pp. 607–27.

[21] Joe Queenan, "Birth of a Notion," *Washington Post,* 20 September 1992, p. C1.

[22] Steven Holmes, "Grass-Roots Drive Shows Hand of Oz," *New York Times,* 30 September 1992,
p. A20.

[23] Ibid.

resources—or, as we shall see later, access to government power—are also best able
to promote their ideas in the marketplace. Obviously, these resources are most readily available to upper- and upper-middle-class groups. As a result, their ideas and concerns are most likely to be discussed and disseminated by books, films, newspapers, magazines, and the electronic media. As we shall see in Chapter 13, upper-income groups dominate the marketplace of ideas, not only as producers and promoters, but also as consumers of ideas. In general, and particularly in the political realm, the print and broadcast media and the publishing industry are most responsive to the tastes and views of the more "upscale" segments of the potential audience.

MEASURING PUBLIC OPINION

As recently as fifty years ago, American political leaders gauged public opinion by people's applause or cheers and by the presence of crowds in meeting places. This direct exposure to the people's views did not necessarily produce accurate knowledge of public opinion. It did, however, give political leaders confidence in their public support—and therefore confidence in their ability to govern by consent.

Abraham Lincoln and Stephen Douglas confronted each other seven times in the summer and autumn of 1858, two years before they became presidential nominees. Their debates took place before audiences in parched cornfields and courthouse squares. A century later, the presidential debates, although seen by millions, take place before a few reporters and technicians in television studios that might as well have been on the moon. The public's response cannot be experienced directly. This distance between leaders and followers is one of the agonizing problems of modern democracy. The new media of communication send information to millions of people, but they are not yet as efficient at getting information back to leaders. Is government by consent possible where the scale of communication is so large and impersonal? In order to compensate for the decline in their ability to experience public opinion for themselves, leaders have turned to science, in particular the science of opinion polling.

It is no secret that politicians and public officials make extensive use of public opinion polls to help them decide whether to run for office, what policies to support, how to vote on important legislation, and what types of appeals to make in their campaigns. President Lyndon Johnson was famous for carrying the latest Gallup and Roper poll results in his hip pocket, and it is widely believed that he began to withdraw from politics as the polls reported losses in public support. All recent presidents and other major political figures have worked closely with polls and pollsters. Yet, even the most scientific measurements of public opinion do not necessarily lighten the burden of ignorance.

Besides measuring public opinion through expensive surveys and polls, politicians and political leaders are also using cheaper and more traditional methods. The range of measures from least to most expensive is:

1. Interpreting mass opinion from measurements of mass behavior.
2. Interpreting mass opinion from impressions of individual opinions gained by *ad*

hoc person-to-person polling, selective personal polling, and intensive polling in a few districts thought to be microcosms of the whole electorate. (These districts, called "bellwether districts," will be discussed later in the chapter.)

3. Using science to try to construct public opinion from random sample surveys of individual opinions.

Interpreting Mass Opinion from Mass Behavior and Mass Attributes

The conduct of business and public affairs would be next to impossible without the ability to interpret mass opinion from mass behavior. Important business decisions are often made on the basis of insights about future consumer preferences that are gained from past consumer behavior. One successful movie about organized crime, for example, will produce a glut of sequels or copies.

Politicians also watch consumer behavior in order to gain insights about people's political opinions. Traditionally, political analysts have assumed that the business cycle produces changes in public opinion and that these changes ultimately express themselves in choices at election time. The most important theory in this area is that people will vote against the party in power during a downturn in the business cycle and will support it during an upswing in that cycle. Thus, for example, Ronald Reagan's victory over incumbent President Jimmy Carter was in part a result of popular dissatisfaction with the Democrats' handling of the economy. Similarly, the electorate's economic concerns undermined George Bush's re-election bid in 1992. Until recent elections (and the development of elaborate methods of polling and computer analysis), better predictions about changes in public opinion were made by observing economic events than by studying polls.

Everyone from government officials to ordinary citizens uses observable behavior as a means of estimating less observable opinions. The FBI studies assaults on police officers to try to understand attitudes toward authority. Social service agencies study the "white flight" from central cities in response to the influx of non-white minorities to improve their understanding of whites' racial attitudes. Many social scientists have tried to develop "social indicators" to enable public and private agencies to locate important changes of attitude in their communities and elsewhere.

For many years, efforts to interpret political opinions from measurable or "objective" data have been an important area of academic social science. This kind of analysis is based on the assumption that opinions are drawn so largely from the environment that they can be predicted by measuring it. Political scientists analyze the relationship between elections and certain characteristics of the population in each of the states, counties, or congressional districts where elections are held.

For each area, the breakdown between Democratic and Republican voting, or yes-no voting on a referendum, or voting for candidates known to be liberal or conservative can be statistically related to certain characteristics of voters. Among these characteristics are their average income, the percent who live in urban or rural communities, and the percent who are black or white. Wherever the relationship between elections and a given population characteristic is repetitive and clear, interpretations have been made about voter opinions and tendencies.

In the past two decades, this kind of aggregate statistical analysis has often been
replaced by the analysis of public opinion polls, which provide data on the opinions and the economic and racial characteristics of individuals. There are some
severe limitations, however, on the extent to which measurements of aggregate
population characteristics can be relied on to produce knowledge about mass
opinions. Information is often needed about the bases of opinions on specific political issues since the insights that can be drawn from mass behavior and aggregate
population characteristics are only about generalized values or tendencies. For example, a study of the socioeconomic characteristics of counties supporting drastic
cuts in property taxes cannot reveal whether a general anti-government ideology is
emerging or whether the anti-tax movement is confined to a more special objec-
tion by property owners to increased taxation on their homes.

Getting Public Opinion Directly from People

Getting public opinion from the study of mass behavior has proved inadequate.
American politicians want rapport with the people; they want to mingle, to shake
hands, to get the feel of the crowd. And where crowds are too large to experience
directly, the substitutes also have to be more direct than those described up to
this point.

Approaches to the direct measurement of public opinion can be divided conve-
niently into two fairly distinct types—the impressionistic and the scientific. The
impressionistic approach can be subdivided into at least three methods—person-
to-person, selective polling, and the use of bellwether districts. The scientific approach may take on several different forms, but they all amount to an effort to use
random sampling techniques and established and psychologically validated survey
questions.

Person-to-Person   Politicians traditionally acquire knowledge about opinions
through direct exposure to a few people's personal impressions—the person-to-
person approach. They attempt to convert these impressions into reliable knowledge by intuition. When they are in doubt about first impressions, they seek
further impressions from other people; but the individuals they rely on the most
heavily are their friends and acquaintances. Presidents have usually relied on associates for political impressions. These few friends occupy an inner circle, which gives
political advice after the experts and special leaders have finished.

The advantage of the person-to-person approach is that it is quick, efficient,
and inexpensive. Its major disadvantage is that it can close off unpleasant information or limit the awareness of new issues. Franklin Roosevelt, for example, was one
of the best-informed presidents, and yet, when he attempted to influence the
Supreme Court by increasing the number of justices on it and when he attempted
to punish some of the opposition leaders in Congress by opposing their renomination in local primaries, he was shocked by the degree of negative public reaction.
His inner circle had simply lost touch with the post-1936 electorate.

President Nixon's downfall from the Watergate scandal has been attributed in
part to the fact that he isolated himself in the White House and relied too heavily
on a few close personal advisers. Consequently, it is argued, he was unaware first of

George Gallup
Polling Pioneer

George Gallup (1901–1984)

George Gallup did not invent public opinion polling, but his name became synonymous with polling to such an extent that in some European languages, the verb, "to poll" became to do "a Gallup." Gallup's own view of polling was that it is "one of the most useful instruments of democracy ever devised."

Gallup's background was in journalism and advertising. He combined his talents in these areas when he formed the American Institute of Public Opinion in 1935. The organization's stated purpose was to measure public opinion on various political, social, and economic issues. Its method was to be scientific polling—that is, based on principles of random selection. Many organizations claimed to have success at plumbing American opinion, but most such efforts were unsystematic and inaccurate. One of the most famous polling mistakes in history occurred in the 1936 presidential election when a prominent magazine, the *Literary Digest*, carried out a straw vote predicting that President Franklin Roosevelt would be defeated by Republican Alf Landon. The magazine poll was badly flawed, as it sent out massive numbers of surveys to citizens whose names were drawn from telephone directories and automobile registration lists. At that time, such sampling lists were, of course, heavily biased toward the wealthy, who were much more likely to vote Republican. After the election, George Gallup's organization was propelled into national attention for correctly predicting FDR's victory.

Gallup developed the now standard presidential popularity ratings, questions to measure the intensity of citizen preferences, and a host of other polling techniques now taken for granted. Yet, despite the connection of the term "scientific" with that of "polling," the measurement of public opinion retains a certain quality of art. The Gallup organization stumbled badly in 1948, for example, when it incorrectly predicted that Thomas E. Dewey would defeat incumbent President Harry Truman. The error was accounted for partly by the fact that polling was stopped too soon before the election. Still, Gallup readily admitted the error, saying that "we are continually experimenting and continually learning."

Gallup often asserted that polling was "merely an instrument for gauging public opinion." Yet, polls have made and broken campaigns, led and misled public perceptions, and changed the course of governmental decisions. Like any tool, a poll can provide important information and insight. But it can also be used to mislead and distort. Gallup's devotion to nonpartisan polling represented an important benchmark for all who would strive to gauge public opinion.

Source: Benjamin Ginsberg, *The Captive Public* (New York: Basic Books, 1986).

How a Poll Is Conducted

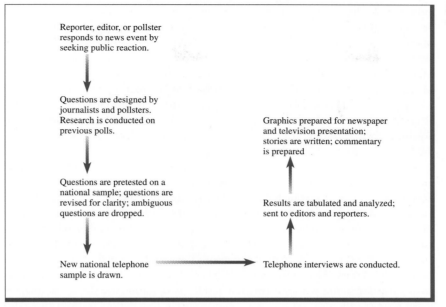

Reporter, editor, or pollster responds to news event by seeking public reaction.

Questions are designed by journalists and pollsters. Research is conducted on previous polls.

Questions are pretested on a national sample; questions are revised for clarity; ambiguous questions are dropped.

New national telephone sample is drawn.

Telephone interviews are conducted.

Results are tabulated and analyzed; sent to editors and reporters.

Graphics prepared for newspaper and television presentation; stories are written; commentary is prepared

the strength of his own position as he approached the 1972 re-election campaign and then of the extent to which his political position had deteriorated because of the scandal. Of course, as we saw in the case of Ross Perot, politicians may seek to delude themselves and others by polling only those whose opinions agree with their own!

Selective Polling   When politicians lack confidence in their own intuition or that of their immediate associates, and especially when they distrust the reports they get from group advocates, they turn to rudimentary forms of polling. They may informally interview a few ordinary citizens from each of the major religious faiths or from different occupations in an effort to construct a meaningful distribution of opinions in a constituency. Many politicians have been successful with such impressionistic methods (although skeptics attribute their success to luck). Moreover, these politicians have used more systematic approaches as soon as they could afford to.

Newspapers have followed suit. Not too long ago, the top journalists on major newspapers, such as the *New York Times,* based many of their political articles on selective, impressionistic polling. But in recent years, their newspapers have, at great expense, become clients of Gallup, Roper, and other large scientific polling organizations. Some newspapers have joined forces with television networks to produce their own polls. The New York Times/CBS News Poll is one example.

Bellwether Districts   The bellwether originally was the lead sheep of a flock, on whose neck a bell was hung. The term now refers to something that is used as an indicator of where a group is heading. A bellwether town or district is assumed to be a good predictor of the attitudes of large segments of the national population. Maine was once an important bellwether state for forecasting national elections (and therefore for plotting national campaign strategies). The old saying "As Maine goes, so goes the nation" was based on two facts. First, the distribution of Maine's votes for presidential candidates was often like that of the national popular two-party votes. Second, for many years, the wintry state of Maine held its general election in September rather than November, which provided a meaningful opportunity for forecasting. (Because Maine now holds its election in November like the rest of the states, it is no longer a bellwether.)

The use of bellwether districts has been brought to greater and greater levels of precision in the past two decades because of advances in methods used by television networks. The three major networks have developed elaborate computerized techniques to predict the outcomes of elections within minutes after the polls close. The networks' news staffs spend months prior to November selecting important districts—especially districts on the East Coast, where the polls close an hour to three hours earlier than in the rest of the country, thereby giving the forecasters a head start. They enter into a large computer the voting history of the selected districts, along with information about the opinions and the economic and social characteristics of the residents. As the voting results flow in from these districts on election night, the computer quickly compares them with prior elections and with other districts in the country in order to make fairly precise predictions about the outcome of the current election.

Large-scale computer analysis of polls and of bellwether districts most likely was done first in 1959–1960 by John Kennedy's campaign organization, but it was quickly picked up by the television networks as an important part of their entertainment program on election day and night. By 1964 it was a spectacular success. In June of that year, Columbia Broadcasting System (CBS) took its bellwether system of forecasting to the all-important California Republican primary and correctly predicted Senator Barry Goldwater's victory within twenty-two minutes of the closing of the polls in Los Angeles. The prediction was made on the basis of reports from 42 precincts out of the more than 32,000 precincts in California.

The commercial and political interests that rely on bellwether district methods closely guard the exact information they plug into the computer and the exact methods of weighing and comparing results in order to make their forecasts. It is nevertheless possible to evaluate the contributions this approach makes to political knowledge. First, the bellwether method is useful when there is an election involving a limited number of candidates. Second, it tends to work well only when the analysis takes place close to the actual day of the election. Third, the lasting knowledge to be gained from it is limited. No matter how accurately the bellwether district method forecasts elections, it is not particularly useful for stating what opinions people are holding, how consistently and with what intensity they hold opinions on various issues, why they hold these opinions, and how their opinions might be changing.

The population in which pollsters are interested is usually quite large. To conduct their polls they choose a sample of the total population. The selection of this sample is important. Above all, it must be representative; the views of those in the sample must accurately and proportionately reflect the views of the whole. To a large extent, the validity of the poll's results depends on the sampling procedure used, several of which are described below.

Quota sampling is the method used by most commercial polls. In this approach, respondents are selected whose characteristics closely match those of the general population along several significant dimensions, such as geographic region, sex, age, and race.

Probability sampling is the most accurate polling technique. By definition, this method requires that every individual in the population must have a known (usually equal) probability of being chosen as a respondent so that the researcher can give equal weight to all segments of society. A requirement, then, is a complete list of the population or a breakdown of the total population by cities and counties. The simplest methods of obtaining a probability sample are *systematic sampling,* choosing every ninth name from a list, and *random sampling,* drawing from a container whose contents have been thoroughly mixed. This latter method, of course, can be simulated by computer-generated random numbers. Both quota sampling and probability sampling are best suited for polls of small populations.

For polls of large cities, states, or the whole nation, the method usually employed when a high level of accuracy is desired is *area sampling.* This technique breaks the population down into small, homogeneous units, such as counties. Several of these units are then randomly selected to serve as the sample. These units are, in turn, broken down into even smaller units. The process may extend even to individual dwellings on randomly selected blocks, for example. Thus, area sampling is very costly and generally used only by academic survey researchers.

Some types of sampling do not yield representative samples and so have no scientific value. Haphazard sampling, for instance, is an unsystematic choice of respondents. A reporter who stands on a street corner and asks questions of convenient passersby is engaging in haphazard sampling. Systematically biased sampling occurs when an error in sampling technique destroys the representative nature of the sample. A systematic error, for example, may cause a sample to include too many old people, too many college students, or too few minority group members.

Even with reliable sampling procedures, problems can occur. Validity can be adversely affected by poor question format, faulty ordering of questions, inappropriate vocabulary, ambiguity of questions, or questions with built-in biases. Occasionally, respondents and pollsters may have very different conceptions of the meaning of the words used in a question. For example, an early Gallup Poll which asked people if they owned any stock found that stock ownership in the Southwest was surprisingly high. It turned out that many of the respondents thought "stock" meant cows and horses rather than securities.[24] Often, apparently minor differ-

---

[24] Charles W. Roll and Albert H. Cantril, *Polls* (New York: Basic Books, 1972), p. 106.

ences in the wording of a question can convey vastly different meanings to respondents and, thus, produce quite different response patterns. For example, prior to World War II, a poll asked Americans if they supported "collaboration" with Great Britain to combat Germany. The overwhelming majority of those surveyed said they were opposed. But when the same poll asked Americans if they supported "cooperation" with Britain against Germany, an equally overwhelming majority of respondents indicated their support.[25] Similarly, for many years the University of Chicago's National Opinion Research Center (NORC) has asked respondents whether they think the federal government is spending too much, too little, or about the right amount of money on "assistance for the poor." Answering the question posed this way, about two-thirds of all respondents seem to believe that the government is spending too little. However, the same survey also asks whether the government spends too much, too little, or about the right amount for "welfare." When the word "welfare" is substituted for "assistance for the poor," about half of all respondents indicate that too much is being spent by the government.[26]

The choice of responses offered by a poll question can also have a major impact on the results. For example, in the summer of 1992, the Gallup Poll asked respondents whether their opinions of George Bush and Bill Clinton were favorable or unfavorable. Respondents were given the opportunity to say they did not know. In the case of Bush, 40 percent of the respondents said they had a favorable impression, 53 percent had unfavorable opinions, and 7 percent said they didn't know. As for Clinton, 63 percent were favorable, 25 percent were unfavorable, and 12 percent didn't know.

During the same week, the New York Times/CBS poll asked the same question. However, this poll gave respondents four options instead of three. Respondents could indicate that their opinion of the candidate was favorable, unfavorable, that they were undecided, or that they had not yet heard enough about the candidate. Providing two non-opinion options produced New York Times/CBS survey results quite different from those reported by the Gallup poll. In Bush's case, only 27 percent of those responding gave him a favorable rating, 49 percent were unfavorable, 22 percent were undecided, and 2 percent said they had not yet heard enough. Clinton's favorable rating dropped to 36 percent, while 24 percent were unfavorable, 31 percent were undecided, and 9 percent indicated that they had not yet heard enough about the candidate.[27]

The degree of precision in polling is a function of sample size, not population size. Just as large a sample is needed to represent a small population as to represent a large population. The typical size of a sample is from 450 to 1,500 respondents. This number, however, reflects a trade-off between cost and degree of precision desired. The degree of accuracy that can be achieved with a small sample can be seen from the polls' success in predicting election outcomes.

Table 9.2 shows how accurate the major national polling organizations have

---

[25] Burns W. Roper, "Are Polls Accurate?" *Annals of the American Academy of Political and Social Science,* no. 472 (March 1984), p. 32.

[26] Michael Kagay and Janet Elder, "Numbers Are No Problem for Pollsters. Words Are," *New York Times,* 9 August 1992, p. E6.

[27] Ibid.

TABLE 9.2

393

MEASURING
PUBLIC
OPINION

The Pollsters and Their Record (1948–1992)

	Harris	Gallup	Actual Outcome
1992			
Clinton	44%	44%	43%
Bush	38	37	38
Perot	17	14	19
1988			
Bush	51%	53%	54%
Dukakis	47	42	46
1984			
Reagan	56%	59%	59%
Mondale	44	41	41
1980			
Reagan	48%	47%	51%
Carter	43	44	41
Anderson		8	
1976			
Carter	48%	48%	51%
Ford	45	49	48
1972			
Nixon	59%	62%	61%
McGovern	35	38	38
1968			
Nixon	40%	43%	43%
Humphrey	43	42	43
G. Wallace	13	15	14
1964			
Johnson	62%	64%	61%
Goldwater	33	36	39
1960			
Kennedy	49%	51%	50%
Nixon	41	49	49
1956			
Eisenhower	NA	59.5%	58%
Stevenson		40.5	42
1952			
Eisenhower	47%	51%	55%
Stevenson	42	49	44
1948			
Truman	NA	44.5%	49.6%
Dewey		49.5	45.1

All figures except those for 1948 are rounded. NA = Not Asked.

Sources: Data from the Gallup Poll and the Harris Survey (New York: Chicago Tribune-New York News Syndicate, various press releases 1964–1992). Courtesy of the Gallup Organization and Louis Harris Associates.

been in predicting the outcomes of presidential elections. In only three instances between 1952 and 1992 did the final October poll predict the wrong outcome; and in all three instances—Roper in 1960 and Harris in 1968 and Gallup in 1976—the actual election was extremely close and the prediction was off by no more than two percentage points.

Even in 1948, when the pollsters were deeply embarrassed by their almost uniform prediction of a Dewey victory over Truman, they were not off by much. For example, Gallup predicted 44.5 percent for Truman, and Truman actually received 49.6 percent. Although Gallup's failure to predict the winner was embarrassing, its actual percentage error would not be considered large by most statisticians.

Since 1948, Gallup has averaged a difference of less than 1 percent between what it predicts and the actual election outcome—and all its predictions have been made on the basis of random samples of not more than 2,500 respondents. In light of a national voting population of more than 60 million, these estimates are impressive.

This ability to predict elections by projecting estimates from small samples to enormous populations validates the methods used in sample survey studies of public opinion: the principles of random sampling, the methods of interviewing, and the statistical tests and computer programming used in data analysis. It also validates the model of behavior by which social scientists attempt to predict voting behavior on the basis of respondents' characteristics rather than on the basis of only their stated intentions. This model of behavior is built on the respondent's voting intention and includes data on (1) the influence of the respondent's place in the social structure, (2) the influence of habit and previous party loyalty, (3) the influence of particular issues for each election, (4) the direction and strength of the respondent's general ideology, and (5) the respondent's occupational and educational background, income level, and so on. Each of these characteristics is treated as a variable in an equation leading to a choice among the major candidates in the election. The influence of the variables, or correlates, is far greater than most respondents realize.

Limits to Assessing Political Knowledge with Polls

The survey, or polling, approach to political knowledge has certain inherent problems. The most noted but least serious of them is the bandwagon effect, which occurs when polling results influence people to support the candidate marked as the probable victor. Some scholars argue that this bandwagon effect can be offset by an "underdog effect" in favor of the candidate who is trailing in the polls.[28]

Other problems with polling are equally more substantial. One, of course, is human error—bad decisions based on poor interpretations of the data. That in itself is a problem of the users of the polls, not of polling itself. But the two most se-

---

[28] See Michael Traugott in, "The Impact of Media Polls on the Public," in *Media Polls in American Politics,* ed. Thomas E. Mann and Gary R. Orren, (Washington, DC: Brookings Institution, 1992), pp. 125–49.

FIGURE 9.1

395

MEASURING
PUBLIC
OPINION

**The Assumption of Centrality Visualized as a Bell–Shaped Curve
When asked to express their attitudes toward a moderately
controversial proposition, members of a sample group
might respond as illustrated by this bell–shaped distribution.**

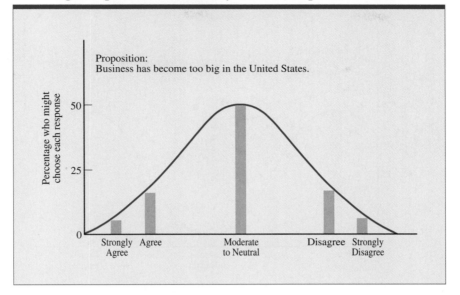

rious problems inherent in polling are the source of most of the human error. They are the illusion of central tendency and the illusion of saliency.

The Illusion of Central Tendency   The assumption that attitudes tend toward the average or center is known as the illusion of central tendency. In any large statistical population, measurements tend to be distributed most heavily toward the middle, or average. Weights, heights, even aptitudes, tend so strongly toward the average that their graphic representation bulges high in the middle and low at each extreme, in the form of a bell–shaped curve. So many characteristics are distributed in the bell shape that it is called a "normal distribution." But are opinions normally distributed also? Some opinions can be. Figure 9.1 shows the distribution for a hypothetical sample of individuals responding to the proposition that business in the United States has become too big. Respondents could agree or disagree, could agree strongly or disagree strongly, or could take a moderate to neutral position. The results shown by the figure indicate a bell–shaped curve.

But not all opinions in the United States are normally distributed. On at least a few issues, opinions are likely to be distributed bimodally, as shown in Figure 9.2. On a bimodal distribution of an issue, the population can be said to be polarized. For example, opinions about the right of women to have an abortion are highly polarized. Very few people are neutral; most are either strongly for or strongly against it.

FIGURE 9.2

**A Polarized Population Visualized as a Bimodal Distribution
When asked to express their attitudes toward a highly
controversial proposition, members of a sample group
might respond as illustrated in this bimodal distribution.**

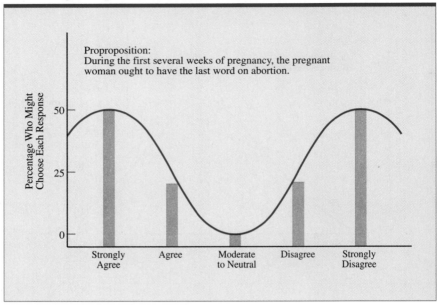

Proproposition:
During the first several weeks of pregnancy, the pregnant
woman ought to have the last word on abortion.

Despite the variation in the actual distribution of opinions, politicians often assume that opinions are distributed more toward neutral and moderate than toward
the extremes; and their assumption of (and wish for) a moderate electorate is reinforced by polling. A good poll can counteract this illusion. And, of course, people
who come to the wrong conclusions on their own are not the responsibility of the
pollsters. But the illusion of central tendency can be produced unintentionally by
polls themselves. Respondents are usually required to express opinions in terms of
five or six prescribed responses on a questionnaire. But this leaves out many of the
issues' complexities. For example, during virtually the entire period of the Watergate affair between 1973 and 1974, the Gallup poll reported that most Americans
were opposed when asked, "Should President Richard Nixon be impeached and
compelled to leave the Presidency?" These findings strengthened the Nixon administration's view that the public supported the president. However, in mid-1974
the Gallup organization changed the wording of the question to ask if respondents,
"think there is enough evidence of possible wrongdoing in the case of President
Nixon to bring him to trial before the Senate, or not?" With this new wording, as
many as two-thirds of those surveyed answered that they favored impeachment.
Apparently, most Americans favored impeaching Nixon, as defined by the second
question. However, they did not want to convict him without a trial, as implied by
the original question. Thus, what had been seen by some as Americans' failure to
respond to the serious charges made against the president, may have actually indi-

cated that respondents' understanding of the impeachment process was more sophisticated than that of the pollsters.[29]

In a similar vein, how does the intelligent person respond to such questions as
"Do you favor busing?" or "Should we spend more money on law and order?" or
"Has business become too big in America?" The more a respondent knows about
a given issue, the more subtleties and considerations have to be suppressed in order
to report a position to the interviewer. Thus, many moderate and neutral responses are actually the result of a balance among extreme but conflicting views
within the individual, called ambivalence.

In response to the proposition that business has become too big in America, a
respondent may disagree because he or she is a Socialist and feels bigger business
can be nationalized more easily by the government, or a person may disagree because big businesses have too much power. The respondent may end up choosing
a moderate or "it all depends" response to the question. Yet, the moderate attitude
is a product of alternatives provided by the interviewer or questionnaire, not a
weighing of real opinions.

Inasmuch as central tendency suggests moderation, and moderation around the
center gives the appearance of consensus, then clearly the consensus reported in
opinion polls is often artificial. This does not mean that the data or the findings are
false. Nor does it mean that they have been deliberately distorted by the pollsters.
Rather, an artificial consensus is the result of mixing different opinions through
the mechanical limits of questionnaires and multiple-choice responses.

Opinion polls can produce an artificial central tendency in still another way.
Each survey asks respondents a whole series of questions about a variety of specific
issues. But since the polling agency's clients are usually interested in the general
mood of the country, the agency summarizes the answers to these questions in
such forms as "tending toward the right" or "generally holding to the Democratic
line." These summaries can help campaigns and can help predict elections, but
they can also betray the actual findings.

Some political advisers have used such summaries to bolster party morale.
Kevin Phillips, for example, helped contribute to the rebuilding of the Republican
party after it suffered its tremendous defeat in 1964. Phillips, a Republican conservative, wrote a book, *The Emerging Republican Majority,* in which he identified the
political and social positions of the American middle class. He saw that in general
they held positions different from those of higher- and lower-income groups and
that in general they were angered by the "softness" and the extravagance of the
Democrats.[30]

The Illusion of Saliency   Salient interests are interests that stand out beyond others, that are of more than ordinary concern to respondents in a survey or to voters
in the electorate. Politicians, social scientists, journalists, or pollsters who assume
something is important to the public when in fact it is not are creating an illusion
of saliency. This illusion can be created and fostered by polls despite careful con-

[29]Kagay and Elder, "Numbers Are No Problem."

[30]Kevin Phillips, *The Emerging Republican Majority* (New Rochelle, NY: Arlington House, 1969).

The Power of Public Opinion

A *central tenet of democratic nations holds that a government's rulers should be guided by the wishes of the people. Yet it is often difficult to discern what people want their government to do; moreover, leaders recognize that they are frequently in a position to shape or mold popular opinion.*

Pollsters Charles W. Roll and Albert H. Cantril argue that public preferences ultimately prevail, even though most people are not well informed about the particulars of important public issues. Political scientist Benjamin Ginsberg argues that public opinion can indeed be shaped and molded by skillful leaders and that, ironically, the very method used to determine public preferences—public opinion polling—may be the very device by which the public is molded and channeled.

Roll and Cantril

What is the competence of public opinion? . . . In our own view, the competence of public opinion is at the "feeling level." The public obviously cannot be expected to be informed and up-to-date in its understanding of complex issues, the implications of alternative courses of action, nor the advantages of specific instrumentalities by which a policy is effected. . . .

However, when it comes to generalized impressions, in two areas the public's judgment usually proves sound and prophetic. The public is quick to spot a phony—the disingenuous politician who is facile and whose transparency soon betrays itself. The public is also very sensitive to the direction and adequacy of policies being pursued by its leaders. While public opinion takes longer to jell with regard to policies, once it becomes clear a policy is unworkable or simply getting too costly, the public will desert its leaders. . . .

Thus, in political research the crucial dimension . . . is the public's sense of trust and confidence in its leaders. . . . What it judges its leaders on, then, is less the substance of policies and programs than the overall impression of whether its leaders "are on top of things." . . .

When events or actions by leaders bring an issue home to the public, public opinion can quickly catch up to events, and when it does, it becomes all powerful. To quote Woodrow Wilson: "Opinion ultimately governs the world."[1]

Ginsberg

Polling fundamentally alters the character of the public agenda of opinion. . . . Opinions elicited by polls . . . mainly concern matters of interest to government, business, or other poll sponsors. Typically, poll questions have as their ultimate purpose some form of exhortation. Businesses poll to help persuade customers to purchase their wares. Candidates poll as part of the process of convincing voters to support them. Governments poll as part of the process of inducing citizens to obey. . . .

In essence, rather than offer governments the opinions that citizens want them to learn, polls tell governments—or other sponsors—what they would like to learn about citizens' opinions. The end result is to change the public expression of opinion from an assertion of demand to a step in the process of persuasion. . . .

Taken together, the changes produced by polling contribute to the transformation of public opinion from an unpredictable, extreme, and often dangerous force into a more docile expression of public sentiment. Opinion stated through polls imposes less pressure and makes fewer demands on government than would more spontaneous or natural assertions of popular sentiment. Though opinion may be expressed more democratically via polls than through alternative means, polling can give public opinion a plebiscitary character—robbing opinion of precisely those features that might maximize its impact on government and policy.[2]

[1] Charles W. Roll and Albert H. Cantril, *Polls: Their Use and Misuse in Politics* (Cabin John, MD: Seven Locks Press, 1972), pp. 143–45.
[2] Benjamin Ginsberg, *The Captive Public: How Mass Opinion Promotes State Power* (New York: Basic Books, 1986), pp. 82–83.

trols over sampling, interviewing, and data analysis. In fact, the illusion is strengthened by the credibility that science gives survey results.

Thus, if a survey includes questions on twenty subjects—because the pollsters or their clients feel they might be important issues—that survey can actually produce twenty salient issues. Although the responses may be sincere, the cumulative impression is artificial, since a high proportion of the respondents may not have concerned themselves with many of the issues until actually confronted with questions by an interviewer. For example, usually not more than 10 percent (rarely more than 20 percent) of the respondents will report that they have no attitude on an issue. Yet, equally seldom will more than 30 percent of a sample spontaneously cite one or more issues as the main reason for their choices. It is nearly impossible to discover how many respondents feel obliged to respond to questions for which they never had any particular concern before the interview.

Similarly, when asked in the early days of a political campaign which candidates they do, or do not, support, the answers voters give often have little significance because the choice is not yet salient to them. Their preference may change many times before the actual election. This is part of the explanation for the phenomenon of the post-convention "bounce" in the popularity of presidential candidates, which was observed after the 1992 Democratic and Republican national conventions.[31] Respondents' preferences reflected the amount of attention a candidate received during the convention rather than strongly held views.

The problem of saliency has become especially acute as a result of the prolifera-

[31] See Richard Morin, "Is Bush's Bounce a Boom or a Bust?" *Washington Post National Weekly Edition,* 31 August–6 September 1992, p. 37.

tion of media polls. The television networks and major national newspapers all make heavy use of opinion polls. Increasingly, polls are being commissioned by local television stations and local and regional newspapers as well.[32] On the positive side, polls allow journalists to make independent assessments of political realities—assessments not influenced by the partisan claims of politicians.

At the same time, however, media polls can allow journalists to make news when none really exists. Polling diminishes journalists' dependence upon news makers. A poll commissioned by a news agency can provide the basis for a good story even when candidates, politicians, and other news makers refuse to cooperate by engaging in newsworthy activities. Thus, on days when little or nothing is actually taking place in a political campaign, poll results, especially apparent changes in candidate margins, can provide exciting news for voters. Several times during the 1992 presidential campaign, for example, small changes in the relative standing of the Democratic and Republican candidates produced banner headlines around the country. Stories about what the candidates actually did or said often took second place to reporting the "horse race."

Interestingly, because rapid and dramatic shifts in candidate margins tend to take place when voters' preferences are least fully formed, horse race news is most likely to make the headlines when it is actually least significant.[33] In other words, media interest in poll results is inversely related to the actual salience of voters' opinions and the significance of the polls' findings.

However, by influencing perceptions, especially those of major contributors, media polls can influence political realities. A candidate who demonstrates a lead in the polls usually finds it considerably easier to raise campaign funds than a candidate whose poll standing is poor. With additional funds, poll leaders can often afford to pay for television time and other campaign activities that will cement their advantage. For example, Bill Clinton's substantial lead in the polls during much of the summer of 1992 helped the Democrats raise far more money than in any previous campaign, primarily from interests hoping to buy access to a future President Clinton. For once, the Democrats were able to outspend the usually better-heeled Republicans. Thus, the appearance of a lead, provided by the polls, helped make Clinton's lead a reality.

The two illusions engendered by polling often put politicians on the horns of a dilemma in which they must choose between a politics of no issues (due to the illusion of central tendency) and a politics of too many trivial issues (due to the illusion of saliency). This has to be at least part of the explanation for why many members of Congress can praise themselves at the end of the year for the hundreds of things they worked on during the past session while not perceiving that they have neglected the one or two overriding issues of the day. Similarly, politicians preparing for major state or national campaigns compose position papers on virtually every conceivable issue—either because they will not make a judgment as to which are the truly salient issues or because they feel that stressing all issues is a way of avoiding a choice among the truly salient ones.

---

[32] See Mann and Orren, eds., *Media Polls in American Politics.*

[33] For an excellent and reflective discussion by a journalist, see Richard Morin, "Clinton Slide in Survey Shows Perils of Polling," *Washington Post*, 29 August 1992, p. A6.

Public Opinion, Political Knowledge, and the
Importance of Ignorance

401
PUBLIC
OPINION AND
GOVERNMENT
POLICY

Many people are distressed to find public opinion polls not only unable to discover public opinion but unable to avoid producing unintentional distortions of their own. No matter how hard they try, no matter how mature the science of opinion polling becomes, politicians forever may remain substantially ignorant of public opinion.

Although knowledge is good for its own sake, and knowledge of public opinion may sometimes produce better government, ignorance also has its uses. It can, for example, operate as a restraint on the use of power. Leaders who think they know what the public wants are often autocratic rulers. Leaders who realize that they are always partially in the dark about the public are likely to be more modest in their claims, less intense in their demands, and more uncertain in their uses of government power. Their uncertainty may make them more accountable to their constituencies because they will be more likely to continue searching for consent.

One of the most valuable benefits of survey research is actually "negative knowledge"—knowledge that pierces through irresponsible claims about the breadth of opinion or the solidarity of group or mass support. Because this sort of knowledge reveals the complexity and uncertainty of public opinion, it can help make citizens less gullible, group leaders less strident, and politicians less deceitful. This alone gives public opinion research, despite its great limitations, an important place in the future of American politics.[34]

PUBLIC OPINION AND GOVERNMENT POLICY

In democratic nations leaders should pay heed to public opinion, and the evidence suggests that indeed they do. There are many instances in which public policy and public opinion do not coincide, but in general the government's actions are consistent with citizens' preferences. One recent study, for example, found that between 1935 and 1979, in about two-thirds of all cases, significant changes in public opinion were followed within one year by changes in government policy consistent with the shift in the popular mood.[35] Other studies have come to similar conclusions.

Despite the evidence of broad agreement between opinion and policy, there are always areas of disagreement. For example, the majority of Americans for years have favored stricter governmental control of handguns—without much result. Similarly, most Americans—blacks as well as whites—oppose school busing to achieve racial balance, which nevertheless continues to be used in many parts of

---

[34]For a fuller discussion of the uses of polling and the role of public opinion in American politics, see Benjamin Ginsberg, *The Captive Public* (New York: Basic Books, 1986)

[35] Benjamin I. Page and Robert Y. Shapiro, "Effects of Public Opinion on Policy," *American Political Science Review* 77 (March 1983), pp. 175–90.

the nation. Most Americans are far less concerned with the rights of the accused than the federal courts seem to be. Most Americans oppose U.S. military intervention in other nations' affairs, yet such interventions continue to take place and often win public approval after the fact.

Several factors can contribute to a lack of consistency between opinion and governmental policy. First, the nominal majority on a particular issue may not be as intensely committed to its preference as the adherents of the minority viewpoint. An intensely committed minority may often be more willing to commit its time, energy, efforts, and resources to the affirmation of its opinions than an apathetic, even if large, majority. In the case of firearms, for example, although the proponents of gun control are by a wide margin in the majority, most do not regard the issue as one of critical importance to themselves and are not willing to commit much effort to advancing their cause. The opponents of gun control, by contrast, are intensely committed, well organized, and well financed, and as a result are usually able to carry the day.

A second important reason that public policy and public opinion may not coincide has to do with the character and structure of the American system of government. The framers of the American Constitution, as we saw in Chapter 2, sought to create a system of government that was based upon popular consent but that did not invariably and automatically translate shifting popular sentiments into public policies. As a result, the American governmental process includes arrangements such as an appointed judiciary that can produce policy decisions that may run contrary to prevailing popular sentiment—at least for a time.

When, however, all is said and done, there can be little doubt that in general the actions of the American government do not remain out of line with popular sentiment for very long. A major reason for this is, of course, the electoral process, to which we shall now turn.

SUMMARY

All governments claim to obey public opinion, and in the democracies politicians and political leaders actually try to do so.

The American government does not directly regulate opinions and beliefs in the sense that dictatorial regimes often seek to do. Opinion is regulated by an institution that the government constructed and that it maintains—the marketplace of ideas. In this marketplace, opinions and ideas compete for support. In general, opinions supported by upper-class groups have a better chance of succeeding than those views that are mainly advanced by the lower classes.

Americans share a number of values and viewpoints but often classify themselves as liberal or conservative in their basic orientations. The meaning of these terms has changed greatly over the past century. Once liberalism meant opposition to big government. Today liberals favor an expanded role for the government. Once conservatism meant support for state power and aristocratic rule. Today conservatives oppose government regulation, at least of business affairs.

Although the United States relies mainly on market mechanisms to regulate opinion, even our government intervenes to some extent, seeking both to influence particular opinions and, more important, the general climate of political opinion. Political leaders' increased distance from the public makes it difficult for them to gauge public opinion. Until recently, public opinion on some issues could be gauged better by studying mass behavior than by studying polls. Population characteristics are also useful in estimating public opinion on some subjects. Another approach is to go directly to the people. Two techniques are used: the impressionistic and the scientific. The impressionistic method relies on person-to-person communication, selective polling, or the use of bellwether districts. A person-to-person approach is quick, efficient, and inexpensive; but because it often depends on an immediate circle of associates, it can also limit awareness of new issues or unpleasant information. Selective polling usually involves interviewing a few people from different walks of life. Although risky, it has been used successfully to gauge public opinion. Bellwether districts are a popular means of predicting election outcomes. They are used by the media as well as by some candidates.

The scientific approach to learning public opinion is random sample polling. One advantage of random sample polling is that elections can be very accurately predicted; using a model of behavior, pollsters are often able to predict how voters will mark their ballots better than the voters themselves can predict. A second advantage is that polls provide information on the bases and conditions of voting decisions. They make it possible to assess trends in attitudes and the influence of ideology on attitudes.

There are also problems with polling, however. An illusion of central tendency can encourage politicians not to confront issues. The illusion of saliency, on the other hand, can encourage politicians to confront too many trivial issues. Even with scientific polling, politicians cannot be certain that they understand public opinion. Their recognition of this limitation, however, may function as a valuable restraint.

FOR FURTHER READING

Asher, Herbert. *Polling and the Public: What Every Citizen Should Know.* Washington, DC: Congressional Quarterly Press, 1988.

Bennett, W. Lance. *Public Opinion in American Politics.* New York: Harcourt Brace Jovanovich, 1980.

Bogart, Leo. *Silent Politics: Polls and the Awareness of Public Opinion.* New York: Wiley, 1972.

Elder, Charles D., and Roger W. Cobb. *The Political Uses of Symbols.* New York: Longman, 1983.

Erikson, Robert S., Norman Luttbeg, and Kent Tedin. *American Public Opinion: Its Origins, Content and Impact.* New York: Wiley, 1980.

Gallup, George. *The Pulse of Democracy.* New York: Simon and Schuster, 1940.

Ginsberg, Benjamin. *The Captive Public: How Mass Opinion Promotes State Power.* New York: Basic Books, 1986.

Herbst, Susan. *Numbered Voices: How Opinion Polling Has Shaped American Politics.* Chicago: University of Chicago Press, 1993.

Holloway, Harry, and John George. *Public Opinion: Coalitions, Elites, and Masses.* New York: St. Martin's, 1986.

Key, V. O. *Public Opinion and American Democracy.* New York: Alfred A. Knopf, 1961.

Lippmann, Walter. *Public Opinion.* New York: Harcourt, Brace and Co., 1922.

Lipset, Seymour M., and William Schneider. *The Confidence Gap: Business Labor and Government in the Public Mind,* rev. ed. Baltimore: Johns Hopkins University Press, 1987.

Margolis, Michael, and Gary A. Mauser. *Manipulating Public Opinion.* Pacific Grove, CA: Brooks/Cole, 1989.

Neuman, W. Russell. *The Paradox of Mass Politics: Knowledge and Opinion in the American Electorate.* Cambridge, MA: Harvard University Press, 1986.

Page, Benjamin, and Robert Y. Shapiro. *The Rational Public: Fifty Years of Trends in Americans' Policy Preferences.* Chicago: University of Chicago Press, 1992.

Roll, Charles W., and Albert H. Cantril. *Polls: Their Use and Misuse in Politics.* New York: Basic Books, 1972.

Stimson, James. *Public Opinion in America: Moods, Cycles, and Swings.* Boulder, CO: Westview, 1991.

Sullivan, John L., James Piereson, and George E. Marcus. *Political Tolerance and American Democracy.* Chicago: University of Chicago Press, 1982.

Sussman, Barry. *What Americans Really Think: And Why Our Politicians Pay No Attention.* New York: Pantheon, 1988.

Tanur, Judith, ed. *Questions about Questions: Inquiries into the Cognitive Bases of Surveys.* New York: Russell Sage, 1992.

Weissberg, Robert. *Public Opinion and Popular Government.* Englewood Cliffs, NJ: Prentice-Hall, 1976.

10
Elections

EVENTS		INSTITUTIONAL DEVELOPMENTS
All electoral votes cast for Washington (1788)		Federalists in control of national government (1789–1800)
Thomas Jefferson elected president (1800)	**1800**	First electoral realignment—Jeffersonian Republicans defeat Federalists (1800)
Andrew Jackson elected president; beginning of party government (1828)		Second realignment—Jacksonian Democrats take control of White House and Congress (1828)
		Presidential nominating conventions introduced (1830s)
Whigs win; William Henry Harrison elected president (1840)		Whig party forms (1830s)
Lincoln elected (1860); South secedes (1860–1861)		Civil War realignment—Republican party founded (1856); Whig party destroyed (1860)
Civil War (1861–1865)		
Reconstruction (1865–1877)		Under Reconstruction Acts, blacks enfranchised in South (1867)
	1870	Fifteenth Amendment forbids states to deny voting rights based on race (1870)
Contested presidential election—Hayes v. Tilden (1876); Republican Rutherford Hayes elected by electoral vote of 185–184 (1877)		Hayes's election leads to end of Reconstruction; voting rights of South restored (1877)
		Southern blacks lose voting rights through poll taxes, literacy tests, grandfather clause (1870s–1890s)
		Progressive reforms—direct primaries, civil service reform, Australian ballot, registration requirements; voter participation drops sharply (1890s–1910s)
Republican William McKinley elected president (1896)		Realignment of 1896; Republican hegemony (1896–1932)
	1900	Seventeenth Amendment authorizes direct election of senators (1913)
		Nineteenth Amendment gives women right to vote (1920)

TIME LINE ON ELECTIONS

EVENTS		INSTITUTIONAL DEVELOPMENTS
Democrat Franklin D. Roosevelt elected president (1932)		Democratic realignment (1930s)
Democrat John F. Kennedy first Catholic elected president (1960)	**1960**	*Baker* v. *Carr*—Supreme Court declares doctrine of "one man, one vote" (1962); period of reapportionment (1960s)
		Voting Rights Act (1965)
Republican Richard Nixon elected president (1968)		Breakdown of Democratic New Deal coalition (1968)
Rise of black voting in the South (1970s)		Twenty-sixth Amendment lowers voting age to eighteen (1971)
Era of new campaign technology and PACS (1970s–1980s)		Federal Elections Campaign Act (1971)
Republican Ronald Reagan elected president (1980)	**1980**	
Geraldine Ferraro first woman on major party national ticket (1984)		Electoral statement; Democrats dominate Congress; Republicans control presidency (1986)
Jesse Jackson first black candidate to become important presidential contender (1988)		
Democrats regain control of Congress (1990)	**1990**	New rules governing voter registration adopted; new campaign finance regulations proposed—Democrats stand to benefit (1993)
Democrat Bill Clinton elected president (1992)		

The peaceful participation of ordinary people in politics is one of the great accomplishments of the United States and the other Western democracies. Its importance cannot be overstated, although it can be misunderstood. Most Americans, including many who seldom vote, are committed to two propositions about elections. First, we believe that elections promote accountability. That is, we believe that elections force those in power to conduct themselves in a responsible manner and to take account of popular interests when they make their decisions. Second, Americans feel that elections facilitate popular influence. Americans assume that the chance to select at least some public officials is also an opportunity to make choices about the policies, programs, and future directions of government action. Accountability and influence are the two key principles underlying the electoral process.

In this chapter, we will look first at what distinguishes voting from other forms of political activity. Second, we will examine the formal structure and setting of American elections. Third, we will see how—and what—voters decide when they take part in elections. Fourth, we will discuss the consequences of elections, especially the phenomenon of electoral realignments, and we shall try to make sense of contemporary American electoral politics. Fifth, we will focus on recent national elections including the 1992 presidential race and congressional contests. Finally, we will assess the place of elections in the American political process.

POLITICAL PARTICIPATION

In the twentieth century, voting is viewed as the normal form of mass political activity. Yet ordinary people took part in politics long before the introduction of the election or any other formal mechanism of popular involvement in political life. If there is any natural or spontaneous form of mass political participation, it is the riot rather than the election. Indeed, the urban riot and the rural uprising were a part of life in western Europe prior to the nineteenth century and in eastern Europe until the twentieth. In eighteenth-century London, for example, one of the most notorious forms of popular political action was the "illumination." Mobs would march up and down the street demanding that householders express support for their cause by placing a candle or lantern in a front window. Those who refused to illuminate in this way risked having their homes put to the torch by the angry crowd. This eighteenth-century form of civil disorder may well be the origin of the expression, "to shed light upon" an issue.

The fundamental difference between voting and rioting is that voting is a socialized and institutionalized form of mass political action.[1] When, where, how, and which individuals participate in elections are matters of public policy rather than questions of spontaneous individual choice. With the advent of the election, control over the agenda for political action passed at least in part from the citizen to the government.

In an important study of participation in the United States, Sidney Verba and Norman Nie define political participation as consisting of "activities 'within the system'—ways of influencing politics that are generally recognized as legal and legitimate."[2] This definition of participation is precisely in accord with most governments' desires. Governments try very hard to channel and limit political participation to actions "within they system." Even with that constraint, however, the right to political participation represents a tremendous advancement in the status

---

[1]For a fuller discussion, see Benjamin Ginsberg, *The Consequences of Consent* (New York: Random House, 1982).

[2]Sidney Verba and Norman Nie, *Participation in America* (New York: Harper & Row, 1972), pp. 2–3.

of citizens on two levels. At one level, it improves the probability that they will

regularly affect the decisions that governments make. On the other level, it reinforces the concept of the individual as independent from the state. It is on the basis
of both dimensions that philosophers like John Stuart Mill argued that popular
government was the ideal form of government.[3]

Those holding power are willing to concede the right to participate in the hope
that it will encourage citizens to give their consent to being governed. This is a
calculated risk for citizens. They give up their right to revolt in return for the right
to participate regularly. They can participate, but only in ways prescribed by the
government. Outside the established channels, their participation can be suppressed or disregarded. It is also a calculated risk for the politician, who may be
forced into certain policy decisions or forced out of office altogether by citizens
exercising their right to participate. This risk is usually worth taking, since in return, governments acquire consent, and through consent citizens become supporters of government action.[4]

The Role of Elections in Society

The introduction of the election as a form of mass political participation has a
number of vitally important consequences. The most obvious of these is a lessening of civil disruption and disorder. By establishing an institutional channel of political activity and convincing citizens of its use, governments reduce the danger
that mass political action poses to the established political and social order. Elections contain and channel away potentially violent and disruptive activities and
protect the government's stability.

Elections also affect the character of mass political involvement in at least two
other crucial respects. Elections can expand and democratize citizen involvement.
In the absence of public mechanisms for its organization, political activity is almost
certain to distort the popular will. Left to their own devices, only relatively small
and unrepresentative segments of the public normally attempt to take part in public affairs. At the same time, however, elections help to limit mass political involvement by prescribing conditions for acceptable participation in political life.

First, elections limit the frequency of citizen participation in politics. In the
United States, elections occur at fixed points in time and grant elected officials the
freedom and authority to govern, without fear of citizen intervention, for a defined term. So long as participation is confined to periodic voting, officials have an
opportunity to overlook public sentiment about the conduct of public affairs at
least some of the time.

Second, elections limit the scope of mass political participation. Elections permit citizens to take part only in the selection of leaders. The mass public does not
directly participate in subsequent policy making (except for an occasional policy
referendum). Although there are links between citizens' choices among candidates

[3]John Stuart Mill, *Considerations on Representative Government* (London: Basil Blackwell, 1948; originally
published in 1859), pp. 141–42.

[4]See Benjamin Ginsberg, *Consequences of Consent.*

Do Elections and Voting Matter?

Most Americans take pride in the country's annual election rituals, pointing out that few nations of the world have mechanisms for transferring power in such a smooth and peaceful fashion. Critics of American elections argue, however, that the differences between the candidates and political parties are marginal, if not nonexistent; that elections and campaigns are more spectacle and show than about real power; and that elections pacify the electorate more than they encourage true citizenship.

Political scientists Gerald M. Pomper and Susan S. Lederman argue that elections in fact do meet the criteria for meaningful political exercises. Political scientist Howard L. Reiter, on the other hand, argues that voting is at best a poor method for translating preferences into policies and, worse, that voting tends to channel citizens toward a relatively harmless political act and away from other more effective methods of political expression.

Pomper and Lederman

The first necessity for meaningful elections is an organized party system. . . . Without a choice between at least two competing parties, the electorate is powerless to exert its influence.

A related vital requirement is for free competition between the parties. The voters must be able to hear diverse opinions and be able to make an uncoerced choice. . . . Nomination and campaigning must be available to the full range of candidates, and the means provided for transmitting their appeals to the electorate. . . .

Elections in the United States do largely meet the standards of meaningful popular decisions; true voter influence exists. The two parties compete freely with one another, and the extent of their competition is spreading to virtually all states. Access to the voters is open to diverse candidates, and no party or administration can control the means of communication. Suffrage is virtually universal, and voters have fairly simple choices to make for regular offices. In the overwhelming number of cases, voting is conducted honestly. . . .

Whatever the future may hold, present conditions in the United States do enable the voters to influence, but not control, the government. The evidence . . . does not confirm the most extravagant expectations of popular sovereignty. Neither are elections demonstrably dangerous or meaningless. Most basically, we have found the ballot to be an effective means for the protection of citizen interests. Elections in America ultimately provide only one, but the most vital, mandate.[1]

Reiter

Most of the major issues in American history have been resolved not by elections but by other historical forces. . . . Elections are not very good ways of expressing the policy views of the people who actually vote. Elections are even less effective as a means of carrying out the policy views of all citizens. . . .

Politics, we are encouraged to believe, occurs once a year in November, and for most adults it occurs only once every four years. We are able to discharge our highest civic function by taking a few minutes to go into a booth and flip a few levers once every four years. Although we are all free to engage in other political activities, such as collective action, writing to officials or working on campaigns, most adults are quite content to limit their political activity to that once-in-a-quadrennium lever flip. And if we think of voting as the crown jewel of our liberties, we will not think that citizenship requires anything else.

All in all, the message that elections sends us is to be passive about politics. Don't take action that involves any effort, don't unite with other citizens to achieve political goals, just respond to the choice that the ballot box gives us. In a strange way, then, elections condition us *away* from politics. A nation which defines its precious heritage in terms of political rights discourages its citizens from all but the *least* social, *least* public, and *least* political form of activity. This should raise the most profound questions for us. Why should we as a society discourage political activism? What is the real role that voting plays in our politics?[2]

[1]Gerald M. Pomper and Susan S. Lederman, *Elections in America: Control and Influence in Democratic Politics,* 2nd ed. (New York: Longman, 1980), pp. 223–25.
[2]Howard L. Reiter, *Parties and Elections in Corporate America* (New York: St. Martin's Press, 1987), pp. 1–3, 9.

for office and choices about the government's actions, elections do not necessarily function as referenda on issues or policies.

Third, elections limit the intensity of political activity. In the absence of formal avenues, political activity serves almost exclusively as a device for the expression of strongly held beliefs and preferences. So long as political involvement is difficult, only those individuals with intense views will normally be motivated to become involved. Elections, however, make it easy for large numbers of citizens to take part despite their relative indifference or apathy about many public questions. Elections can submerge those participants with strongly held views in a generally apathetic mass electorate.

Encouraging Electoral Participation

Americans are free to assert whatever demands, views, and grievances they might have through a variety of different means. Citizens may, if they wish, lobby, petition, demonstrate, or file suit in court. Although there are some legal impediments to many of these forms of participation, relatively few modes of political expression are directly barred by law.

Despite the availability of an array of alternatives, in practice citizen participation in American politics is generally limited to voting and a small number of other electoral activities (for example, campaigning). It is true that voter turnout in the United States is relatively low. But when, for one reason or another, Americans do seek to participate, their participation generally takes the form of voting.

The preeminent position of voting in the American political process is not surprising. The American legal and political environment is overwhelmingly weighted in favor of electoral participation. Probably the most influential forces helping to channel people into the voting booth are law, civic education, and the party system. The availability of the suffrage is, of course, a question of law. But in addition to simply making the ballot available, state legislation in the United States prescribes the creation of an elaborate and costly public machinery that makes voting a rather simple task for individuals. Civic education, to a large extent mandated by law, encourages citizens to believe that electoral participation is the appropriate way to express opinions and grievances. The major parties are legally charged with staffing and operating the normal machinery of elections and in a number of vital ways help directly to induce citizens to participate.

Making it Easy to Vote Despite complicating factors such as registration, the time, energy, and effort needed to vote are considerably less than are required for all but a few other political activities. The relatively low degree of individual effort required to vote, however, is somewhat deceptive. Voting is a simple way for large numbers of citizens to participate only because it is made simple by an elaborate and costly electoral system. The ease with which citizens can vote is a function of law and public policy. The costs of voting are paid mainly by the state.

In the United States, electoral contests are administered principally by states and localities. Although state law is sometimes conceived as only regulating and limiting the suffrage, most states try to facilitate voting by as many citizens as possible. States and localities legally require themselves to invest considerable effort in the facilitation of voting. In every state, the steps needed to conduct an election fill hundreds of pages of statutes. At the state, county, and municipal levels, boards of elections must be established to supervise the electoral process. For every several hundred voters, in each state, special political units—precincts or election districts—are created and staffed exclusively for the administration of elections. During each electoral period, polling places must be set up, equipped with voting machines or ballots, and staffed by voting inspectors. Prior to an election, its date, the locations of polling places, and the names of candidates must be publicized. After each election, returns must be canvassed, tallied, reported, and often recounted.

Although every state makes voting easy by providing for the creation and funding of election machinery, states obviously vary in the precise extent to which they encourage electoral participation. Indeed, until the 1970s, states varied enormously in their voter residence requirements, registration procedures, absentee voting rules, and the hours that polls remained open. Until recent years, literacy tests and poll taxes, often employed in a deliberately discriminatory manner, were also important in producing interstate differences in the ease of voting.

Civic Education Laws, of course, cannot completely explain why most people vote rather than riot or lobby. If public attitudes were completely unfavorable to elections, it is doubtful that *legal* remedies alone would have much impact.

Positive public attitudes about voting do not come into being in a completely spontaneous manner. Americans are taught to equate citizenship with electoral participation. Civic training, designed to give students an appreciation for the American system of government, is a legally required part of the curriculum in every elementary and secondary school. Although it is not as often required by law, civic education usually manages to find its way into college curricula as well.

In the elementary and secondary schools, through formal instruction and, more subtly, through the frequent administration of class and school elections, students are taught the importance of the electoral process. By contrast, little attention is given to lawsuits, direct action, organizing, parliamentary procedures, lobbying, or other possible modes of participation. For example, the techniques involved in organizing a sit-in or protest march are seldom part of an official school course of study.[5]

The New York State first grade social studies curriculum offers a fairly typical case study of the training in political participation given very young children. The State Education Department provides the following guidelines to teachers:

> To illustrate the voting process, present a situation such as: Chuck and John would both like to be the captain of the kickball team. How will we decide which boy will be the captain? Help the children to understand that the fairest way to choose a captain is by voting.
>
> Write both candidates' names on the chalk board. Pass out slips of paper. Explain to the children that they are to write the name of the boy they would like to have as their captain. Collect and tabulate the results on the chalk board.
>
> Parallel this election to that of the election for the Presidency. Other situations which would illustrate the election procedure are voting for:
>
> a game
> an assignment choice
> classroom helpers.[6]

Although secondary-school students periodically elect student government representatives rather than classroom helpers and are given more sophisticated illustrations than kickball team elections, the same principle continues to be taught, in compliance with legal requirements. College students, it must be added, are also frequently given the opportunity to elect senators, representatives, and the like, to serve on the largely ornamental representative bodies that are to be found at most institutions of higher learning. Obviously, civic education is not always completely successful. Rather than relying on the electoral process, people continue to demonstrate, sit in, and picket for various political causes.

Civic education, of course, does not end with formal schooling. Early training is supplemented by a variety of mechanisms, ranging from the official celebration of national holidays to the activities of private patriotic and political organizations.

[5]See Fred Greenstein, *Children and Politics* (New Haven, CT: Yale University Press, 1969). See also Robert Weissberg, *Political Learning, Political Choice and Democratic Citizenship* (Englewood Cliffs, NJ: Prentice-Hall, 1974).

[6]The University of the State of New York, State Education Department, Bureau of Elementary Curriculum Development, *Social Studies-Grade 1, A Teaching System* (Albany, NY: 1971), p. 32.

Election campaigns themselves are occasions for the reinforcement of training to vote. Campaigns and political conventions include a good deal of oratory designed to remind citizens of the importance of voting and the democratic significance of elections. Parties and candidates, even if for selfish reasons, emphasize the value of participation, of "being counted," and the virtues of elections as instruments of popular government. Exposure to such campaign stimuli appears generally to heighten citizens' interest in and awareness of the electoral process.

The Party System   Law and civic education do not directly stimulate voting as much as they create a favorable climate for electoral participation. Within the context of this climate, the major parties, until recent years at least, have been the principal agents responsible for giving citizens the motivation and incentive actually to vote. By law, in most American states, party workers staff the electoral machinery. Indeed, at one time, the parties even printed the ballots used by voters. Although the parties have played a role in both civic education and legal facilitation of voting, their principal efforts have been aimed at the direct mobilization of voters. One of the most interesting pieces of testimony to the lengths to which parties have been willing to go to induce citizens to vote is a list of Chicago precinct captains' activities in the 1920s and 1930s. Among other matters, these party workers helped constituents obtain food, coal, and money for rent; gave advice in dealing with juvenile and domestic problems; helped constituents to obtain government and private jobs; adjusted taxes; aided with permits, zoning, and building-code problems; served as liaisons with social, relief, and medical agencies; provided legal assistance and help in dealing with government agencies; and in addition handed out Christmas baskets and attended weddings and funerals.[7] Obviously, all these services were provided in the hope of winning voters' support at election time.

Party competition has long been known to be a key factor in stimulating voting. As political scientists Stanley Kelley, Richard Ayres, and William Bowen note, competition gives citizens an incentive to vote and politicians an incentive to get them to vote.[8] The origins of the American national electorate can be traced to the competitive organizing activities of the Jeffersonian Republicans and the Federalists. According to historian David Fischer:

> During the 1790s the Jeffersonians revolutionized electioneering. . . . Their opponents complained bitterly of endless "dinings," "drinkings," and celebrations; of handbills "industriously posted along every road"; of convoys of vehicles which brought voters to the polls by the carload; of candidates "in perpetual motion."[9]

The Federalists, although initially reluctant, soon learned the techniques of mobilizing voters: "mass meetings, barbecues, stump-speaking, festivals of many kinds, processions and parades, runners and riders, door-to-door canvassing, the

[7]Harold Gosnell, *Machine Politics, Chicago Model*, rev. ed. (Chicago: University of Chicago Press, 1968), Chapter 4.

[8]Stanley Kelley, Jr., Richard E. Ayres, and William G. Bowen, "Registration and Voting: Putting First Things First," *American Political Science Review* 61 (June 1967), pp. 359–70.

[9]David H. Fischer, *The Revolution of American Conservatism* (New York: Harper & Row, 1965), p. 93.

How a Presidential Campaign Is Conducted

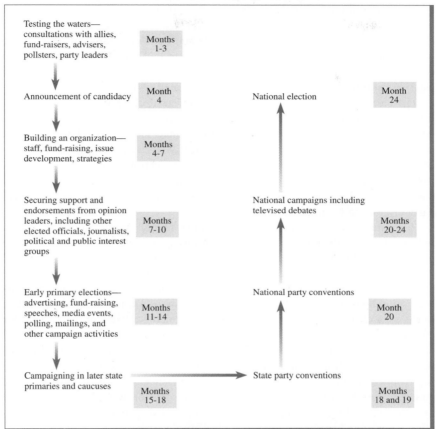

Testing the waters—
consultations with allies,
fund-raisers, advisers,
pollsters, party leaders — Months 1-3

Announcement of candidacy — Month 4

Building an organization—
staff, fund-raising, issue
development, strategies — Months 4-7

Securing support and
endorsements from opinion
leaders, including other
elected officials, journalists,
political and public interest
groups — Months 7-10

Early primary elections—
advertising, fund-raising,
speeches, media events,
polling, mailings, and
other campaign activities — Months 11-14

Campaigning in later state
primaries and caucuses — Months 15-18

National election — Month 24

National campaigns including
televised debates — Months 20-24

National party conventions — Month 20

State party conventions — Months 18 and 19

distribution of tickets and ballots, electioneering tours by candidates, free transportation to the polls, outright bribery and corruption of other kinds."[10]

The result of this competition for votes was described by historian Henry Jones Ford in his classic *Rise and Growth of American Politics*.[11] Ford examined the popular clamor against John Adams and Federalist policies in the 1790s that made government a "weak, shakey affair" and appeared to contemporary observers to mark the beginnings of a popular insurrection against the government.[12] Attempts by the Federalists initially to suppress mass discontent, Ford observed, might have "caused an explosion of force which would have blown up the government."[13]

---

[10]Ibid., p. 109.

[11]Henry Jones Ford, *The Rise and Growth of American Politics* (New York: Da Capo Press, 1967 reprint of the 1898 edition), Chapter 9.

[12]Ibid., p. 125.

[13]Ibid.

What intervened to prevent rebellion was Jefferson's "great unconscious achievement," the creation of an opposition party that served to "open constitutional channels of political agitation."[14] The creation of the Jeffersonian party diverted opposition to the administration into electoral channels. Party competition gave citizens a sense that their votes were valuable and that it was thus not necessary to take to the streets to have an impact upon political affairs. Whether or not Ford was correct in crediting party competition with an ability to curb civil unrest, it is clear that competition between the parties promoted voting.

The parties' competitive efforts to attract citizens to the polls are not their only influence on voting. Individual voters tend to form psychological ties with parties. Although the strength of partisan ties in the United states has declined in recent years, a majority of Americans continue to identify with the Republican or Democratic party. Party loyalty gives citizens a stake in election outcomes that encourages them to take part with considerably greater regularity than those lacking partisan ties.[15] Even where both legal facilitation and competitiveness are weak, party loyalists vote with great regularity.

In recent decades, as we will see in Chapter 11, the importance of party as a political force in the United States has diminished considerably. The decline of party is undoubtedly one of the factors responsible for the relatively low rates of voter turnout that characterize American national elections. To an extent, the federal and state governments have directly assumed some of the burden of voter mobilization once assigned to the parties. Voter registration drives and public funding of electoral campaigns are two obvious ways in which government helps to induce citizens to go to the polls. Another more subtle public mechanism for voter mobilization is the primary election, which can increase voter interest and involvement in the electoral process. It remains to be seen, however, whether government mechanisms of voter mobilization can be as effective as party mechanisms. Of course, a number of private groups like the League of Women Voters, church groups, and civil rights groups have also actively participated in voter registration efforts, but none have been as effective as political parties.

REGULATING THE ELECTORAL PROCESS

Elections allow citizens to participate in political life on a routine and peaceful basis. Indeed, American voters have the opportunity to select and, if they so desire, depose some of their most important leaders. In this way, Americans have a chance to intervene in and to influence the government's programs and policies. Yet, it is important to recall that elections are not spontaneous affairs. Instead, they are formal government institutions. While elections allow citizens a chance to participate in politics, they also allow the government a chance to exert a good deal of control

---

[14]Ibid., p. 126.
[15]See Angus Campbell et al., *The American Voter* (New York: Wiley, 1960).

over when, where, how, and which of its citizens will participate. Electoral

processes are governed by a variety of rules and procedures that allow those in power a significant opportunity to regulate the character—and perhaps also the consequences—of mass political participation.

Thus, elections provide governments with an excellent opportunity to regulate and control popular involvement. Three general forms of regulation have played especially important roles in the electoral history of the Western democracies. First, governments often attempt to regulate the composition of the electorate in order to diminish the electoral weight of groups they deem to be undesirable. Second, governments frequently seek to manipulate the translation of voters' choices into electoral outcomes. Third, virtually all governments attempt to insulate policy-making processes from electoral intervention through regulation of the relationship between electoral decisions and the composition or organization of the government.

Electoral Composition

Perhaps the oldest and most obvious device used to regulate voting and its consequences is manipulation of the electorate's composition. In the earliest elections in western Europe, for example, the suffrage was generally limited to property owners and others who could be trusted to vote in a manner acceptable to those in power. To cite just one illustration, property qualifications in France prior to 1848 limited the electorate to 240,000 of some 7 million men over the age of twenty-one.[16] Of course, no women were permitted to vote. During the same era, other nations manipulated the electorate's composition by assigning unequal electoral weights to different classes of voters. The 1831 Belgian constitution, for example, assigned individuals anywhere from one to three votes depending upon their property holdings, education, and position.[17] But even in the context of America's ostensibly universal and equal suffrage in the twentieth century, the composition of the electorate is still subject to manipulation. Until recent years, some states manipulated the vote by the discriminatory use of poll taxes and literacy tests or by such practices as the placement of polls and the scheduling of voting hours to depress participation by one or another group. Today the most important example of the regulation of the American electorate's composition is our unique personal registration requirements.

Levels of voter participation in twentieth-century American elections are quite low by comparison to those of the other Western democracies.[18] Indeed, voter participation in presidential elections in the United States has barely averaged 50 percent recently. During the nineteenth century, by contrast, voter turnout in the United States was extremely high. Records, in fact, indicate that in some counties as many as 105 percent of those eligible voted in presidential elections. Some pro-

[16]Stein Rokkan, *Citizens, Elections, Parties* (New York: David McKay, 1970), p. 149.

[17]John A. Hawgood, *Modern Constitutions Since 1787* (New York: D. Van Nostrand, 1939), p. 148.

[18]See Walter Dean Burnham, "The Changing Shape of the American Political Universe," *American Political Science Review* 59 (1965), pp. 7–28.

FIGURE 10.1

Voter Turnout in Presidential and Congressional Elections (1892–1992)

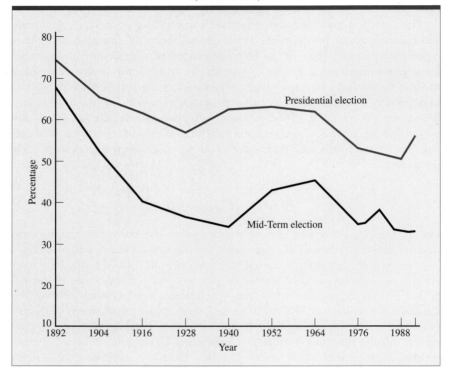

Sources: For 1890 to 1958, Erik Austin and Jerome Clubb, *Political Facts of the United States since 1789* (New York: Columbia University Press, 1986), pp. 378–79; for 1960–1992, *U.S. Statistical Abstract* (Washington, DC: Government Printing Office, 1992).

portion of this total obviously was artificial—a result of the widespread corruption that characterized American voting practices during that period. Nevertheless, it seems clear that the proportion of eligible voters actually going to the polls was considerably larger in nineteenth-century America than it is today.

As Figure 10.1 indicates, the critical years during which voter turnout declined across the United States were between 1890 and 1910. These years coincide with the adoption of laws across much of the nation requiring eligible citizens to appear personally at a registrar's office to register to vote some time prior to the actual date of an election. Personal registration was one of several "Progressive" reforms of political practices initiated at the turn of the century. The ostensible purpose of registration was to discourage fraud and corruption. But to many Progressive reformers, "corruption" was a code word, referring to the type of politics practiced in the large cities where political parties had organized immigrant and ethnic populations. Reformers not only objected to the corruption that surely was a facet of party politics in this period, but they also opposed the growing political power of these urban populations and their leaders.

Personal registration imposed a new burden upon potential voters and altered the format of American elections. Under the registration systems adopted after 1890, it became the duty of individual voters to secure their own eligibility. This duty could prove to be a significant burden for potential voters. During a personal appearance before the registrar, individuals seeking to vote were (and are) required to furnish proof of identity, residence, and citizenship. While the inconvenience of registration varied from state to state, usually voters could register only during business hours on weekdays. Many potential voters could not afford to lose a day's pay in order to register. Second, voters were usually required to register well before the next election, in some states up to several months earlier. Third, since most personal registration laws required a periodic purge of the elections rolls, ostensibly to keep them up-to-date, voters often had to re-register to maintain their eligibility. Thus, although personal registration requirements helped to diminish the widespread electoral corruption that accompanied a completely open voting process, they also made it much more difficult for citizens to participate in the electoral process.

Registration requirements particularly depress the participation of those with little education and low incomes because it requires a greater degree of political involvement and interest than does the act of voting itself. To vote, a person need only be concerned with the particular election campaign at hand. Yet, requiring individuals to register before the next election forces them to make a decision to participate on the basis of an abstract interest in the electoral process rather than a simple concern with a specific campaign. Such an abstract interest in electoral politics is largely a product of education. Those with relatively little education may become interested in political events once the stimuli of a particular campaign become salient, but by that time it may be too late to register. As a result, personal registration requirements not only diminish the size of the electorate but also tend to create an electorate that is, in the aggregate, better educated, higher in income and social status, and composed of fewer African Americans and other minorities than the citizenry as a whole. Presumably this is why the elimination of personal registration requirements has not always been viewed favorably by some conservatives.[19]

Over the years, voter registration restrictions have been modified somewhat to make registration easier. In 1993, for example, Congress approved and President Clinton signed the "motor voter" bill to ease voter registration by allowing individuals to register when they applied for driver's licenses, as well as in public assistance and military recruitment offices.[20] A similar bill had been vetoed by President George Bush in 1992. Republicans objected to the bill because they feared it would increase registration by the poor and minority voters who, generally, tended to support the Democrats. Experience suggests, however, that *any* registration rules, however liberal, tend to depress voting on the part of the poor and uneducated.

[19]See Kevin Phillips and Paul H. Blackman, *Electoral Reform and Voter Participation* (Washington, DC: American Enterprise Institute, 1975).

[20]Helen Dewar, "'Motor Voter' Agreement Is Reached," *Washington Post,* 28 April 1993, p. A6.

With the exception of America's personal registration requirements, contemporary governments generally do not try to limit the composition of their electorates. Instead, they prefer to allow everyone to vote, and then to manipulate the outcome of the election. This is possible because there is no single or automatic way to decide the relationship between individual votes and electoral outcomes. There are any number of possible rules that can be used to determine how individual votes will be translated. Two types of regulations are especially important: the rules that set the criteria for victory and the rules that define electoral districts.

The Criteria for Winning   In some nations, to win a seat in the parliament or other representative body a candidate must receive a majority (50%+1) of all the votes cast in the relevant district. This type of electoral system is called a ***majority system*** and was used in the primary elections of most southern states until recent years. Generally, majority systems have a provision for a second or "runoff" election among the two top candidates if the initial contest drew so many contestants that none received an absolute majority of the votes cast.

In other nations, candidates for office need not receive an absolute majority of the votes cast to win an election. Instead, victory is awarded to the candidate who receives the most votes in a given election regardless of the actual percentage of votes this represents. Thus, a candidate who received 40 percent or 30 percent of the votes case may win the contest so long as no rival receives more votes. This type of electoral process is called a ***plurality system,*** and it is the system used in almost all general elections in the United States.

Most European nations employ still a third form of electoral system, called ***proportional representation.*** Under proportional rules, competing political parties are awarded legislative seats roughly in proportion to their actual percentage of the popular votes cast. For example, a party that won 30 percent of the votes would receive roughly 30 percent of the seats in the parliament or other representative body. In the United States, proportional representation is used by many states in presidential primary elections. In these primaries, candidates for the Democratic and Republican nominations are awarded convention delegates in rough proportion to the percentage of the popular vote they receive in the primary.

Generally, systems of proportional representation work to the electoral advantage of smaller or weaker social groups, while majority and plurality systems tend to help larger and more powerful forces. This is so because in legislative elections, proportional representation reduces, while majority and plurality rules increase, the number of votes that political parties must receive to win legislative seats. For instance, in European parliamentary elections, a minor party that wins 10 percent of the national vote will also receive 10 percent of the parliamentary seats. In American congressional elections, by contrast, a party winning only 10 percent of the popular vote would probably receive no congressional seats at all. Obviously, choices among types of electoral systems can have important political consequences. Competing forces often seek to establish an electoral system they believe will serve their political interests while undermining the fortunes of their opponents. For example, in 1937, New York City council seats were awarded on the

basis of proportional representation. This led to the selection of several Communist party council members. During the 1940s, to prevent the election of
Communists, the city adopted a plurality system. Under the new rule, the tiny
Communist party was unable to muster enough votes to secure a council seat. In a
similar vein, the introduction of proportional representation for the selection of
delegates to the Democratic party's 1972 national convention was designed in part
to maximize the voting strength of minority groups and, not entirely coinciden-
tally, to improve the electoral chances of the candidates they were most likely to
favor.[21]

Electoral Districts   Despite the use of proportional representation and the occasional use of majority voting systems, most electoral contests in the United States
are decided on the basis of plurality rules. Rather than seeking to manipulate the
criteria for victory, American politicians have usually sought to influence electoral
outcomes by manipulating the organization of electoral districts. The manipulation of electoral districts to increase the likelihood of one or another outcome is
called **gerrymandering** in honor of nineteenth-century Massachusetts Governor
Elbridge Gerry, who was alleged to have designed a district in the shape of a sala-
mander to promote his party's interests. The principle is a simple one. Different
distributions of voters among districts produce different electoral outcomes; those
in a position to control the arrangements of districts are also in a position to manipulate the results. For example, until recent years, gerrymandering to dilute the
voting strength of racial minorities was employed by many state legislatures. One
of the more common strategies involved redrawing congressional boundary lines
in such a way as to divide and disperse a black population that would have otherwise constituted a majority within the original district.

This form of racial gerrymandering, sometimes called "cracking," was used in
Mississippi during the 1960s and 1970s to prevent the election of a black congressman. Historically, the black population in Mississippi was clustered in the western
half of the state along the Mississippi Delta. From 1882 until 1966, the delta was
one congressional district. Although blacks constituted a clear majority within the
district (66 percent in 1960), the continuing election of white congressmen was
assured simply because blacks were *denied* the right to register and vote. With
Congress's passage of the Voting Rights Act of 1965, however, the Mississippi state
legislature moved swiftly to minimize the potential voting power of blacks by
redrawing congressional district lines in such a way as to fragment the black population in the delta into four of the state's five congressional districts. Mississippi's
gerrymandering scheme was preserved in the state's redistricting plans in 1972 and
1981 and helped to prevent the election of any black representative until 1986,
when Mike Espy became the first African American since Reconstruction to represent Mississippi in Congress.

In recent years, the federal government has encouraged what is sometimes
called, "benign gerrymandering," designed to increase minority representation in
Congress. The 1982 amendments to the Voting Rights Act of 1965 encourage the
creation of legislative districts with predominantly African American or Hispanic

---

[21]See Nelson Polsby and Aaron Wildavsky, *Presidential Elections* (New York: Scribners, 1980).

PROCESS BOX 10.2
Congressional Redistricting

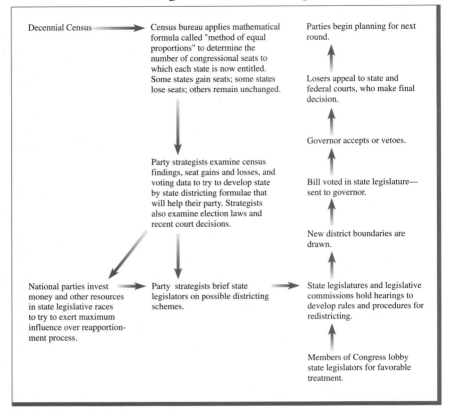

Decennial Census → Census bureau applies mathematical formula called "method of equal proportions" to determine the number of congressional seats to which each state is now entitled. Some states gain seats; some states lose seats; others remain unchanged.

Party strategists examine census findings, seat gains and losses, and voting data to try to develop state by state districting formulae that will help their party. Strategists also examine election laws and recent court decisions.

National parties invest money and other resources in state legislative races to try to exert maximum influence over reapportionment process.

Party strategists brief state legislators on possible districting schemes.

Parties begin planning for next round.

Losers appeal to state and federal courts, who make final decision.

Governor accepts or vetoes.

Bill voted in state legislature—sent to governor.

New district boundaries are drawn.

State legislatures and legislative commissions hold hearings to develop rules and procedures for redistricting.

Members of Congress lobby state legislators for favorable treatment.

American populations by requiring states, when possible, to draw district lines that take account of concentrations of African American and Hispanic American voters. These amendments were initially supported by Democrats who assumed that minority-controlled districts would guarantee the election of Democratic members of Congress. However, Republicans have championed these efforts, reasoning that if minority voters were concentrated in their own districts, Republican prospects in other districts would be enhanced.[22] Moreover, Republicans hoped some Democratic incumbents might be forced from office to make way for minority representatives. This strategy has been somewhat successful. As a result of the creation of a number of new minority districts in 1991, several long-term white Democrats lost their congressional seats. The Supreme Court decision in 1993, in *Shaw* v. *Reno,* however, opened the way for challenges by white voters to the drawing of these districts. In the 5-to-4 majority opinion, Justice O'Connor wrote that if district boundaries were so "bizarre" as to be inexplicable on any

[22]Roberto Suro, "In Redistricting, New Rules and New Prizes," *New York Times,* Sunday, 6 May 1990, sec. 4, p. 5.

ground other than an effort to ensure the election of minority group members to office, white voters would have reason to assert that they had been the victims of unconstitutional racial gerrymandering.[23]

Congressional district boundaries in the United States are redrawn by governors and state legislatures every ten years, after the decennial census determines the number of House seats to which each state is entitled. Because 1990 was a census year, both political parties were especially anxious to win control of as many governorships and state legislative chambers (upper and lower legislative houses) as possible in the 1990 national elections. These elections gave the Democrats control of seventy-two state legislative chambers to the Republicans' twenty-one, with five chambers tied. One state, Nebraska, has a unicameral, nonpartisan legislature. At the gubernatorial level, the Democrats scored a net gain of two states, giving them twenty-eight gubernatorial slots to the Republicans' twenty. Two states, Alaska and Connecticut, elected independent governors. One of the few positive notes for Republicans was Pete Wilson's victory in California's gubernatorial race. As a result of the 1990 census, California gained another seven congressional seats, for a total of fifty-two. Wilson's victory gave the Republicans an opportunity to influence Californias's redistricting plan. After the 1980 census, Democrats had implemented a redistricting plan that gave them twenty-eight of California's congressional seats and left the Republicans with only seventeen. Prior to redistricting, the Democrats had held only a 22–21 advantage. The new post-1990 district boundaries should have left the Republicans in a better position. In the 1992 election, however, with Bill Clinton carrying the state by a fifteen-point margin, Republicans were unable to take full advantage of their opportunity. Republicans won only twenty-one of California's fifty seats. This represented a net gain of four seats, compared to the Democrats' net gain of three seats.

Although governments do have the capacity to manipulate electoral outcomes, this capacity is not absolute. Electoral arrangements conceived to be illegitimate may prompt some segments of the electorate to seek other ways of participating in political life. Moreover, no electoral system that provides universal and equal suffrage can, by itself, long prevent an outcome favored by large popular majorities. Yet, faced with opposition short of an overwhelming majority, governments' ability to manipulate the translation of individual choices into collective decisions can be an important factor in preserving the established distribution of power.

Insulating Decision-Making Processes

Virtually all governments attempt at least partially to insulate decision-making processes from electoral intervention. The most obvious forms of insulation are the confinement of popular election to only some governmental agencies, various modes of indirect election, and lengthy tenure in office. In the United States, the framers of the Constitution intended that only members of the House of Representatives would be subject to direct popular selection. The president and senators

---

[23]Shaw v. Reno (1992); Linda Greenhouse, "Court Questions Districts Drawn to Aid Minorities," *New York Times*, 29 June 1993, p. 1; see also Joan Biskupic, "Court's Conservatism Unlikely to Be Shifted by a New Justice," *Washington Post*, 30 June 1993, p. 1.

were to be indirectly elected for rather long terms to allow them, as the *Federalist* put it, to avoid "an unqualified complaisance to every sudden breeze of passion, or to every transient impulse which the people may receive."[24]

Somewhat less obvious are the insulating effects of electoral arrangements that permit direct, and even frequent, popular election of public officials, but tend to fragment the impact of elections upon the government's composition. In the United States, for example, the constitutional provision of staggered terms of service in the Senate was designed to diminish the impact of shifts in electoral sentiment upon the Senate as an institution. Since only one-third of its members were to be selected at any given point in time, the composition of the institution would be partially protected from changes in electoral preferences. This would prevent what the *Federalist* called "mutability in the public councils arising from a rapid succession of new members."[25]

The division of the nation into relatively small, geographically based constituencies for the purpose of selecting members of the House of Representatives was, in part, designed to have a similar effect. Representatives were to be chosen frequently. And although not prescribed by the Constitution, the fact that each was to be selected by a discrete constituency was thought by Madison and others to diminish the government's vulnerability to mass popular movements.

In a sense, the House of Representatives was compartmentalized in the same way that a submarine is divided into watertight sections to confine the impact of any damage to the vessel. First, by dividing the national electorate into small districts, the importance of local issues would increase. Second, the salience of local issues would mean that a representative's electoral fortunes would be more nearly tied to factors peculiar to his or her own district than to national responses to issues. Third, given a geographical principle of representation, national groups would be somewhat fragmented while the formation of local forces that might or might not share common underlying attitudes would be encouraged. No matter how well-represented individual constituencies might be, the influence of voters on national policy questions would be fragmented. In Madison's terms, the influence of "faction" would thus become "less likely to pervade the whole body than some particular portion of it."[26]

Another example of an American electoral arrangement that tends to fragment the impact of mass elections upon the government's composition is the Australian ballot (named for its country of origin). Prior to the introduction of the official ballot in the 1890s, voters cast ballots composed by the political parties. Each party printed its own ballots, listed only its own candidates for each office, and employed party workers to distribute its ballots at the polls. This ballot format had two important consequences. First, the party ballot precluded secrecy in voting. Because each party's ballot was distinctive in size and color, it was not difficult for party workers to determine how individuals intended to vote. This, of course, facilitated the intimidation and bribery of voters. Second, the format of the ballot prevented

---

[24]Clinton Rossiter, ed., *The Federalist Papers* (New York: New American Library, 1961), No. 71, p. 432.

[25]Ibid., No. 62.

[26]Ibid., No. 10.

split-ticket voting. Because only one party's candidates appeared on any ballot, it was difficult for a voter to cast anything other than a straight party vote.

The official ***Australian ballot*** represented a significant change in electoral procedure. The new ballot was prepared and administered by the state rather than the parties. Each ballot was identical and included the names of all candidates for office. This reform, of course, increased the secrecy of voting and reduced the possibility for voter intimidation and bribery. Because all ballots were identical in appearance, even the voter who had been threatened or bribed might still vote as he wished, without the knowledge of party workers. But perhaps even more important, the Australian ballot reform made it possible for voters to make their choices on the basis of the individual rather than the collective merits of a party's candidates. Because all candidates for the same office now appeared on the same ballot, voters were no longer forced to choose a straight-party ticket. It was indeed the introduction of the Australian ballot that gave rise to the phenomenon of split-ticket voting in American elections.[27] Ticket splitting is especially prevalent in states that use the "office-block" ballot format, which does not group candidates by their partisan affiliations. By contrast, the "party-column" format places all the candidates affiliated with a given party in the same row or column. Figures 10.2 and 10.3 compare the ballots used in New York (party-column) and Maryland (office-block). The former facilitates straight-ticket voting while the latter encourages ticket splitting.

It is this second consequence of the Australian ballot reform that tends to fragment the impact of American elections upon the government's composition. Prior to the reform of the ballot, it was not uncommon for an entire incumbent administration to be swept from office and replaced by an entirely new set of officials. In the absence of a real possibility of split-ticket voting, any desire on the part of the electorate for change could be expressed only as a vote against all candidates of the party in power. Because of this, there always existed the possibility, particularly at the state and local levels, that an insurgent slate committed to policy change could be swept into power. The party ballot thus increased the potential impact of elections upon the government's composition. Although this potential may not always have been realized, the party ballot at least increased the chance that electoral decisions could lead to policy changes. By contrast, because it permitted choice on the basis of candidates' individual appeals, the Australian ballot lessened the likelihood that the electorate would sweep an entirely new administration into power. Ticket splitting led to increasingly divided partisan control of government.

Taken together, regulation of the electorate's composition, regulation of the translation of voters' choices into electoral decisions, and regulation of the impact of those decisions upon the government's composition allow those in power a measure of control over mass participation in political life. These techniques do not necessarily have the effect of diminishing citizens' capacity to influence their rulers' conduct. Rather in the democracies, at least, these techniques are generally used to *influence electoral influence.* They permit governments a measure of control over what citizens will decide that governments should do.

---

[27]Jerold G. Rusk, "The Effect of the Australian Ballot Reform on Split Ticket Voting: 1876 - 1908," *American Political Science Review* 64 (December 1970), pp. 1220–38.

FIGURE 10.2

The Party-Column Ballot: General Election Ballot (November 1992)

	A ★ DEMOCRATIC	B REPUBLICAN	C CONSERVATIVE	D RIGHT TO LIFE	E LIBERAL	F LIBERTARIAN	G NO PARTY	H SWP SOCIALIST WORKERS
1 — Electors for President and Vice-President of the United States / Electores para Presidente y Vice-Presidente de los Estados Unidos	Bill Clinton AND Al Gore 1A	George Bush AND Dan Quayle 1B	George Bush AND Dan Quayle 1C	George Bush AND Dan Quayle 1D	Bill Clinton AND Al Gore 1E	Andre Merrou AND Nancy Lord 1F / John Hagelin AND Mike Tompkins 1I (NATURAL LAW)	Ross Perot AND James B. Stockdale 1G (NO PARTY) / Lenora B. Fulani AND M. Elizabeth Munoz 1J (NEW ALLIANCE)	James Mac Warren AND Estelle DeBates 1H
6 — United States Senator / Senador de los Estados Unidos	Robert Abrams 6A	Alfonse M. D'Amato 6B	Alfonse M. D'Amato 6C	Alfonse M. D'Amato 6D	Robert Abrams 6E	Norma Segal 6F / Stanley Nelson 6I (NATURAL LAW)	Mohammad T. Mahdi 6J (NEW ALLIANCE)	Ed Warren 6H
9 Justices of the Supreme Court	Steven W. Fisher 9A	Thomas V. Polizzi 9B	Thomas V. Polizzi 9C		Steven W. Fisher 9E			
10	Fred T. Santucci 10A	Fred T. Santucci 10B	Fred T. Santucci 10C		Fred T. Santucci 10E			
11	Simeon Golar 11A	Richard J. Wagner 11B	Richard J. Wagner 11C		Simeon Golar 11E			
12	Evelyn L. Braun 12A	Joseph A. Suraci 12B	Evelyn L. Braun 12C		Evelyn L. Braun 12E			
13	Richard Buchter 13A	John G. Lopresto 13B	John G. Lopresto 13C		Richard Buchter 13E			
14	Robert C. Kohm 14A	Kerry J. Katsorhis 14B	Robert C. Kohm 14C		Robert C. Kohm 14E			
15 Judge of the Civil Court (County)	Darrell L. Gavrin 15A		Paul Aronow 15C		Darrell L. Gavrin 15E			
16	Frederick D. Schmidt 16A		Frederick D. Schmidt 16C	Frederick D. Schmidt 16D				
17 Representative in Congress	Nydia M. Velazquez 17A	Angel Diez 17B	Angel Diez 17C	Angel Diez 17D	Ruben Franco 17E		Rafael Mendez 17J (NEW ALLIANCE)	
18 State Senator	Emanuel R. Gold 18A				Emanuel R. Gold 18E			
19 Member of Assembly	Jeffrion L. Aubry 19A				Jeffrion L. Aubry 19E			

Lot Q83

FIGURE 10.3
The Office-Block Ballot: General Election Ballot (November 1992)

CARD A

SIDE 1	SIDE 2

SIDE 1

FRONT
OFFICIAL BALLOT **A**

 Montgomery County, Maryland

GENERAL ELECTION
NOVEMBER 3, 1992

VOTE BOTH SIDES

President and Vice President of the United States	**VOTE FOR NO MORE THAN ONE PAIR**		
BILL CLINTON Little Rock, AR **ALBERT GORE, JR.** Carthage, TN	Democrat ●	x	
GEORGE BUSH Houston, TX **DAN QUAYLE** Huntington, IN	Republican ●	x	
ANDRE MARROU Las Vegas, NV **NANCY LORD** Atlanta, GA	Libertarian ●	x	
LENORA B. FULANI New York, NY **MARIA ELIZABETH MUNOZ** Los Angeles, CA	Alliance ●	x	
ROSS PEROT Dallas, TX **JAMES STOCKDALE** Coronado, CA	Independent ●	x	
	●	x	

United States Senator	**VOTE FOR NO MORE THAN ONE**	
BARBARA A. MIKULSKI Baltimore City	Democrat ●	x
ALAN L. KEYES Montgomery County	Republican ●	x
	●	x

Representative in Congress 8th Congressional District	**VOTE FOR NO MORE THAN ONE**	
EDWARD J. HEFFERNAN	Democrat ●	x
CONSTANCE A. MORELLA	Republican ●	x
	●	x

TURN CARD OVER AND CONTINUE VOTING

A103 —VOTE BOTH SIDES— A

SIDE 2

BACK
OFFICIAL BALLOT **A**

Montgomery County, Maryland

GENERAL ELECTION
NOVEMBER 3, 1992

VOTE BOTH SIDES

Judge of the Circuit Court 6th Judicial Circuit	**VOTE FOR NO MORE THAN ONE**	
JAMES L. RYAN	●	x
	●	x

Judge, Court of Special Appeals At Large	**VOTE YES OR NO FOR EACH JUDGE**		
JOHN J. BISHOP, JR. For continuance in office	YES ●	x	
	NO ●	x	

Judge, Court of Special Appeals At Large	**VOTE YES OR NO FOR EACH JUDGE**		
GLENN T. HARRELL, JR. For continuance in office	YES ●	x	
	NO ●	x	

Board of Education At Large	**VOTE FOR NO MORE THAN ONE**	
SHELDON FISHMAN	●	x
BEATRICE B. GORDON	●	x
	●	x

Board of Education District 2	**VOTE FOR NO MORE THAN ONE**	
STEPHEN N. ABRAMS	●	x
EUGENE M. THIROLF, JR.	●	x
	●	x

Board of Education District 4	**VOTE FOR NO MORE THAN ONE**	
BLAIR G. EWING	●	x
ROBERT NEIL WEISS	●	x
	●	x

CONTINUE VOTING ON NEXT CARD

A102 —VOTE BOTH SIDES— A

HOW VOTERS DECIDE

Thus far, we have focused on the election as an institution. But, of course, the election is also a process in which millions of individuals make decisions and choices that are beyond the government's control. Whatever the capacity of those in power to organize and structure the electoral process, it is these millions of individual decisions that ultimately determine electoral outcomes. Sooner or later the choices of voters weigh more heavily than the schemes of electoral engineers.

The Bases of Electoral Choice

Three types of factors influence voters' decisions at the polls: partisan loyalty, issue and policy concerns, and candidate characteristics.

Partisan Loyalty   Many studies have shown that most Americans identify more or less strongly with one or the other of the two major political parties. Partisan loyalty was considerably stronger during the 1940s and 1950s than it is today. But even now most voters feel a certain sense of identification or kinship with the Democratic or Republican party. This sense of identification is often handed down from parents to children and is reinforced by social and cultural ties. Partisan identification predisposes voters in favor of their party's candidates and against those of the opposing party. At the level of the presidential contest, issues and candidate personalities may become very important, although even here many Americans supported George Bush or Bill Clinton only because of partisan loyalty. But partisanship is more likely to assert itself in the less visible races, where issues and the candidates are not as well known. State legislative races, for example, are often decided by voters' party ties. Once formed, voters' partisan loyalties seldom change. Voters tend to keep their party affiliations unless some crisis causes them to reexamine the bases of their loyalties and to conclude that they have not given their support to the appropriate party. During these relatively infrequent periods of electoral change, millions of voters can change their party ties. For example, at the beginning of the New Deal era between 1932 and 1936, millions of former Republicans transferred their allegiance to Franklin Roosevelt and the Democrats.

Issues   Issues and policy preferences are a second factor influencing voters' choices at the polls. Voters may cast their ballots for the candidate whose position on economic issues they believe to be closest to their own. Similarly, they may select the candidate who has what they believe to be the best record on foreign policy. Issues are more important in some races than others. If candidates actually "take issue" with one another, that is, articulate and publicize very different positions on important public questions, then voters are more likely to be able to identify and act upon whatever policy preferences they may have. In recent American history, the 1964 presidential election, pitting conservative Republican Barry Goldwater against liberal Democrat Lyndon Johnson, was one in which each candidate vigorously promoted a perspective on the role of government and shape of national policy very different from the one asserted by his opponent. Voters elected Johnson,

basing their choice on the issues. The 1980 and 1984 contests, won by Ronald
Reagan, the most conservative American president of the postwar period, were
very heavily issue oriented, with Reagan emphasizing tax policy, social policy, and
foreign policy positions different from prior American governmental commitments. In response, voters in large numbers based their choices on issue and policy
preferences. The 1992 election emphasized economic issues. Voters concerned
with America's continuing economic recession and long-term economic prospects
gave their support to Bill Clinton who called for an end to Reaganomics. Efforts
by Bush to inject other issues, such as "family values," into the race proved generally unsuccessful.

The ability of voters to make choices on the bases of issue or policy preferences
is, however, diminished if competing candidates do not differ substantially or do
not focus their campaigns on policy matters. Very often, candidates deliberately
take the safe course and emphasize topics that will not be offensive to any voters.
Thus, candidates often trumpet their opposition to corruption, crime, and inflation. Presumably, few voters favor these things. While it may be perfectly reasonable for candidates to take the safe course and remain as inoffensive as possible, this
candidate strategy makes it extremely difficult for voters to make their issue or policy preferences the bases for their choices at the polls.

Candidate Characteristics   Candidates' personal attributes always influence voters'
decisions. Some analysts claim that voters prefer tall candidates to short candidates,
candidates with shorter names to candidates with longer names, and candidates
with lighter hair to candidates with darker hair. Perhaps these rather frivolous criteria do play some role. But the more important candidate characteristics that affect voters' choices are race, ethnicity, religion, gender, geography, and social
background. In general, voters prefer candidates who are closer to themselves in
terms of these categories. Voters presume that such candidates are likely to have
views and perspectives close to their own. Moreover, they may be proud to see
someone of their ethnic, religious, or geographic background in a position of leadership. This is why, for many years, politicians sought to "balance the ticket," making certain that their party's ticket included members of as many important groups
as possible. In 1988, for example, Democratic presidential candidate Michael
Dukakis named Texas Senator Lloyd Bentsen as his running mate to balance the
ticket with a conservative southerner. George Bush, in turn, selected Dan Quayle
to appeal to younger voters and ultra-conservatives.

Just as a candidate's personal characteristics may attract some voters, they may
repel others. Many voters are prejudiced against candidates of certain ethnic, racial,
or religious groups. And for many years voters were reluctant to support the political candidacies of women, although this appears to be changing.

Voters also pay attention to candidates' personality characteristics, such as their
"decisiveness," "honesty," and "vigor." In recent years, integrity has become a key
election issue. During the 1992 campaign, George Bush accused Bill Clinton of
seeking to mislead voters about his anti-Vietnam war activities and his efforts to
avoid the draft during the 1960s. This, according to Bush, revealed that Clinton
lacked the integrity required of a president. Clinton, in turn, accused Bush of re-

sorting to mudslinging because of his poor standing in the polls—an indication of Bush's own character deficiencies.

All candidates seek, through polling and other mechanisms, to determine the best image to project to the electorate. At the same time, the communications media—television in particular—exercise a good deal of control over how voters perceive candidates. During the 1992 campaign, as we shall see in Chapters 11 and 14, the candidates developed a number of techniques designed to take control of the image-making process away from the media. Among the chief instruments of this "spin control" was the candidate talk-show appearance used very effectively by both Ross Perot and Bill Clinton. As we shall see, however, no candidate was fully able to circumvent media scrutiny.

ELECTORAL ALIGNMENTS AND REALIGNMENTS

Elections are not only forms of political expression, they also have important consequences. At the very least, elections decide who will govern, and by so doing, they may have consequences for how the government behaves and what policy directions it pursues. In the United States, election outcomes have followed a fascinating pattern (see Figure 10.4). Typically, during the course of American political history, the national electoral arena has been dominated by one party for a period of roughly thirty years. At the conclusion of this period, the dominant party has been supplanted by a new party in what political scientists call a *critical electoral realignment.* The realignment is typically followed by a long period in which the new party is the dominant political force in the United States—not necessarily winning every election but generally maintaining control of the Congress and usually of the White House as well.[28]

Realigning Eras

Although there are some disputes among scholars about the precise timing of these critical realignments, there is general agreement that at least five have occurred since the founding of the American Republic. The first took place around 1800 when the Jeffersonian Republicans defeated the Federalists and became the dominant force in American politics. The second realignment occurred around 1828 when the Jacksonian Democrats took control of the White House and the Congress. The third period of realignment centered on 1860. During this period, the newly founded Republican party led by Abraham Lincoln won power, in the process destroying the Whig party, which had been one of the nation's two major parties since the 1830s. During the fourth critical period, centered on the election

---

[28]See Walter Dean Burnham, *Critical Elections and the Mainsprings of American Electoral Politics* (New York: W. W. Norton, 1970). See also James L. Sundquist, *Dynamics of the Party System* (Washington, DC: Brookings Institution, 1983).

FIGURE 10.4

431

ELECTORAL
ALIGNMENTS
AND REALIGN-
MENTS

The Party Balance: Number of Institutions Controlled*

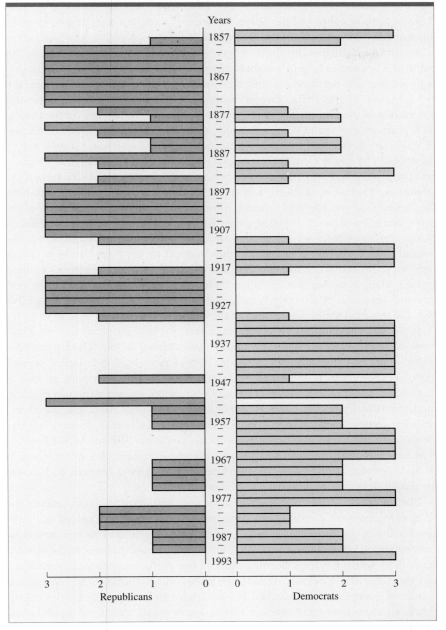

Years

Republicans · Democrats

*A possible three institutions can be controlled: the House, the Senate, and the presidency. The numbers indicate how many of these are controled by each party.

of 1896, the Republicans reasserted their dominance of the national government, which had been weakening since the 1880s. The fifth realignment took place during the period 1932–1936 when the Democrats, led by Franklin Delano Roosevelt, took control of the White House and Congress and, despite sporadic interruptions, maintained control through the 1960s.

Historically, realignments occur when new issues combined with economic or political crises persuade large numbers of voters to reexamine their traditional partisan loyalties and permanently shift their support from one party to another. For example, during the 1850s, diverse regional, income, and business groups supported one of the two major parties, the Democrats or the Whigs, on the basis of their positions on various economic issues, such as internal improvements, the tariff, monetary policy, and banking. This economic alignment was shattered during the 1850s. The newly formed Republican party campaigned on the basis of opposition to slavery and, in particular, opposition to the expansion of slavery into the territories. The issues of slavery and sectionalism produced divisions within both the Democratic and the Whig parties, ultimately leading to the dissolution of the latter, and these issues compelled voters to reexamine their partisan allegiances. Many northern voters who had supported the Whigs or the Democrats on the basis of their economic stands shifted their support to the Republicans as slavery replaced tariffs and economic concerns as the central item on the nation's political agenda. Many southern Whigs shifted their support to the Democrats. The new sectional alignment of forces that emerged was solidified by the trauma of the Civil War and persisted almost to the turn of the century.

In 1896, this sectional alignment was at least partially supplanted by an alignment of political forces based on economic and cultural factors. During the economic crises of the 1880s and 1890s, the Democrats forged a coalition consisting of economically hard-pressed midwestern and southern farmers, as well as small-town and rural economic interests. These groups tended to be native-stock, fundamentalist Protestants. The Republicans, on the other hand, put together a coalition comprising most of the business community, industrial workers, and city dwellers. In the election of 1896, Republican candidate William McKinley, emphasizing business, industry, and urban interests, decisively defeated Democrat William Jennings Bryan, who spoke for sectional interests, farmers, and fundamentalism. Republican dominance lasted until 1932.

These periods of critical realignment are very important to understanding the relationship between elections and American governmental institutions and policies. Critics of the American political process frequently assert that it is very difficult for voting choices to be translated into programs and policies in the United States. Very often, it is true, elections result in one party controlling the presidency and the other the Congress. Frequently, policy initiatives taken by one elected branch of government are blocked by the other—or occasionally by the courts. Often, elections have no discernible consequences for the direction of public policy or the shape of governmental institutions.

Periods of critical realignment in American politics, however, have had extremely important institutional and policy results. Realignments occur when new issue concerns coupled with economic or political crises weaken the established political elite and permit new groups of politicians to create coalitions of forces ca-

pable of capturing and holding the reins of governmental power. The construction
of new governing coalitions during these realigning periods has effected major
changes in American governmental institutions and policies. Each period of realignment represents a turning point in American politics. In effect, the choices
made by the national electorate during these periods have helped shape the course
of American political history for a generation.[29]

Elections in America Today: Factional Struggle without Realignment

The importance of realignments in American political history has led analysts to
search for evidence of contemporary realignments. Ronald Reagan's victory in
1980, followed by his landslide success in the 1984 presidential race, and a solid
victory by Republican George Bush in the 1988 contest suggested to some observers that we had undergone another realignment and were entering a new Republican era in national politics.[30] However, Bush's defeat and the Democrats'
recapture of the White House in 1992 seemed to put an end to thoughts of Republican hegemony. To understand contemporary American electoral politics,
though, we must look back to Roosevelt's New Deal realignment before moving
forward to the Reagan, Bush, and Clinton eras.

The New Deal Coalition and Its Disruption Franklin Roosevelt's New Deal
coalition was composed of unionized labor, members of urban ethnic groups,
southerners, northern blacks, middle-class liberals, and, ultimately, important sectors of the American business community. Roosevelt and his successors won and
maintained the support of these groups by building governmental institutions and
enacting policies that served their needs and interests. For example, New Deal
labor legislation confirmed the support of organized labor for the Democratic
party; Roosevelt's welfare and social service programs won the loyalty of northern
blacks and members of urban ethnic groups; southerners benefitted from New
Deal farm programs; middle-class liberals benefitted from the expansion of white-
collar employment in the public sector as well as from New Deal programs in areas
such as education and the arts; segments of the business community benefitted
from New Deal support for free trade and, later, from the expansion of industrial
production in the World War II and postwar periods.[31]

This New Deal coalition dominated the government and politics of the United
States until the 1960s, when it was shattered by conflicts over race relations, the
Vietnam War, and the government's fiscal and regulatory policies. These conflicts
drove apart the various groups that had made up the New Deal coalition and set

---

[29]Ginsberg, *Consequences of Consent,* Chapter 4.

[30]For a fuller discussion, see Benjamin Ginsberg and Martin Shefter, "A Critical Realignment? The
New Politics, the Reconstituted Right, and the Election of 1984," in *The Elections of 1984*, ed. Michael
Nelson (Washington, DC: Congressional Quarterly Press, 1985).

[31]See Thomas Ferguson, "From Normalcy to New Deal: Industrial Structure, Party Competition and
American Public Policy in the Great Depression," *International Organization* 38 (Winter 1984),
pp. 42–94.

How well a president succeeds in implementing programs to fulfill campaign promises can provide a valuable measure of his effectiveness and ability as a chief executive. At stops along the campaign trail in 1932, Franklin Roosevelt stumped for his vision of a New Deal for the Depression-mired United States. Although vague about the specifics of the New Deal, he promised that under his leadership, the country would try bold, persistent experimentation to create a mature, strong economy.

Roosevelt succeeded in reversing the fortunes of the country in such a dramatic fashion that he won an unprecedented four presidential elections. He is shown here visiting with a Civilian Conservation Corps (CCC) camp in Virginia's Shenandoah Valley. The CCC is considered one of the most successful programs of the New Deal.

Lyndon Johnson escalated U.S. involvement in the war in Vietnam, despite pledging in the 1964 race for president that "we seek no wider war." He defeated Barry Goldwater in a landslide, taking 61 percent of the popular vote, but his victory was based on a pledge that he did not keep.

After his 1964 election, Johnson predicted to his aides, "every day I'm in office, I'm going to lose votes. I'm going to alienate somebody." What alienated most people was the escalation of American involvement in the Vietnam War. Despite a crescendo of protest from his advisers, the press, and the public, Johnson had committed over half a million American troops to the war by 1968. Finally responding to the growing antiwar movement, Johnson decided not to seek re-election, saying he "should not permit the presidency to become involved in the partisan divisions that are developing in this political year."

One of the most spectacular failures to fulfill a campaign promise was Ronald Reagan's handling of the federal budget. In 1980, he assailed Jimmy Carter for the $29 billion deficit (down from the $66 billion that Carter had inherited from Ford) and pledged to eliminate the deficit altogether by 1983. Once in office, Reagan cut taxes and dramatically increased military spending—the result was a series of yearly deficits that have swollen the national debt to over $3 trillion.

In 1988, George Bush campaigned on the theme of "no new taxes." But in 1991, following a deadlock with Congress over the budget, Bush signed a deficit reduction bill that called for a rise in the top tax rate from 28 percent to 31 percent. Bush's decision to raise taxes haunted him during the 1992 presidential campaign when it became apparent that this was one pledge the nation had expected him to keep. The broken campaign promise, combined with a lingering recession, ended his quest for a second term.

the stage for new forces to attempt to reconstruct a governing coalition in the United States. Grouped on one side were middle-class liberals, public-sector professionals, organized labor, and blacks vying for influence within the Democratic party and seeking to use that party as a vehicle through which to secure power on the national level. On the other side, segments of the business community, social and religious conservatives, upper-middle-class suburbanites, southern whites, and many northern blue-collar workers united in a reconstituted coalition of the political Right within the Republican party.

Over the past twenty-six years, segments of the Democratic coalition have pursued a variety of electoral strategies. In 1968, liberal Democrats supported Eugene McCarthy's attempt to win the Democratic presidential nomination. In 1972, Democratic liberals forged an alliance with blacks that succeeded in securing the Democratic presidential nomination for George McGovern but was routed again in the general election by the Republicans. In 1976, liberals, in alliance with organized labor, played a key role in bringing about Jimmy Carter's presidential victory. This alliance between labor and liberals, however, collapsed in 1980, when liberals spurned both Carter and Reagan and essentially boycotted the presidential contest—throwing away their votes in support of John Anderson's hopeless independent candidacy. In 1984, Walter Mondale sought to build a strong and lasting alliance between liberals, blacks, and organized labor. Mondale's political career had been closely linked with the labor and civil rights movements, and he ardently courted the support of liberal groups, promising if elected to press the causes of feminism, environmentalism, and demilitarization. Republicans, however, charged Mondale with pandering to "special interests" and routed him in the election.

In 1988, Massachusetts Governor Michael Dukakis sought to win support from all elements of the party while not offending independents and Republicans. To accomplish this, Dukakis stressed the themes of competence and leadership and sought to eschew commitments on substantive programs. In this way he hoped to avoid the problems faced by Mondale in 1984. Nevertheless, Republicans attacked Dukakis as a "Massachusetts liberal" who would raise taxes, weaken the nation's defense, coddle criminals like furloughed murderer Willie Horton, and be fundamentally out of step with basic American values. For fear of alienating key Democratic constituencies, Dukakis could scarcely disavow his commitments to civil rights, civil liberties, and social programs. Thus, despite Dukakis's efforts to avoid the problems faced by the liberal Mondale, he could not escape being depicted as a politician with commitments to constituencies and causes that could be served only at the expense of the taxpayer and middle America. Some conservative whites even believed Dukakis had secretly agreed to give Jesse Jackson a major role in his administration if he was elected to the White House. Once again, the Democrats lost the presidential contest.

Reagan and the Reconstituted Right   Under the leadership of Ronald Reagan, the Reconstituted Right became the dominant force in American electoral politics during the 1980s. For the 1980 election campaign, Reagan fashioned a set of programs and policies designed to link the disparate forces on the political Right to one another and to his presidential campaign. First, Reagan promised middle-class suburbanites that he would trim social programs, cut taxes, and bring inflation under control—whatever the cost in terms of blue-collar unemployment. Second,

Reagan promised social and religious conservatives that he would support "pro-family," anti-abortion, and school prayer legislation. Third, Reagan promised white southerners and other opponents of the civil rights revolution an end to federal support for affirmative action, minority quotas, and other programs designed to aid blacks. Fourth, Reagan promised American business a relaxation of the environmental rules and other forms of "new regulation" that liberals had succeeded in enacting during the 1970s. Finally, Reagan promised the defense industry greatly increased rates of military spending.

perity at home and strength abroad. Reagan and his successor promised voters that by unleashing the energies of the free marketplace, without the damaging regulation imposed by Democrats, Republicans would bring a new era of prosperity to America. Moreover, Reagan and Bush promised to keep America strong. Only the Republican party, they argued, could be trusted to maintain American power in the face of the "evil empire" controlled by the Soviet Union. Reagan's programs of military buildup and economic stimulation appeared to fulfill both these pledges.

In 1992, these two key elements were gone. First, the nation had become mired in one of the longest economic downturns in recent decades. Second, the Soviet Union had collapsed, bringing an end to the Cold War and diminishing the threat of a nuclear holocaust.

Between 1989 and 1992, virtually every indicator of economic performance told the same story: rising unemployment, declining retail sales and corporate profitability, continuing penetration of American markets by foreign firms and the loss of American jobs to foreigners, a sharp drop in real estate prices followed by a wave of bank collapses, and large numbers of business failures. The poor performance of the American economy during his term in office eroded Bush's popularity and divided the Republican coalition. First, business groups that had supported the Republicans since the 1970s began to desert the GOP. During the 1970s, most businesses had perceived government as a threat, fearing that consumer and environmental legislation, which were supported by the Democrats, would be enormously costly and burdensome. Reagan's call for "deregulation" was a major source of the enthusiastic and virtually united support he received from the business community.

By 1992, however, economic hardship had divided the business community. Some business sectors, especially "big business" and the multinationals, continued to support Republican laissez-faire economics. Republican policies of free trade and unrestricted competition permitted the nation's largest firms to expand their manufacturing base abroad in countries where labor and production costs were cheap, while leaving the American market open to their finished products. These firms favored the North American Free Trade Agreement (NAFTA) negotiated by the Bush administration in 1992, because it would allow them to move much of their production to Mexico.

Small and medium-size firms, though, could not as easily move to Mexico or elsewhere to enjoy the benefits of free trade and cheap labor. These firms had been especially vehement opponents of regulation and thus were enthusiastic supporters of Reaganism in the 1970s. In the 1990s, however, new economic realities compelled them to seek governmental assistance rather than worry about the threat of excessive governmental regulation. In particular, firms facing severe foreign competition in the domestic and world markets sought government aid in the form of protection of their domestic markets coupled with vigorous government efforts to promote their exports. As a result, the political unity of American business brought about by Reagan was shattered and a major prop of the Republican coalition undermined.

Economic hardship also drove away the blue-collar support for the Republican coalition. Blue-collar voters had been tied to the Democratic party since the New Deal on the basis of the party's economic stands. During the 1980s, however, Reagan and Bush won the support of many of these voters in both the North and the South by persuading them to put their economic interests aside and to focus instead on their moral and patriotic concerns.

A major function of the Republican "social agenda" of opposition to abortion, support for prayer in the public schools, and unabashed patriotism was to woo blue-collar voters from the Democratic camp by persuading them to regard themselves as right-to-lifers and patriots rather than as workers. Similarly, Republican opposition to affirmative action and school busing was designed to appeal to blue-collar northerners as well as to traditionally Democratic southerners offended by their party's liberal positions on matters of race.

By 1992, however, the political value of the social agenda had diminished. Faced with massive layoffs in many of their industries, blue-collar voters could no longer afford the luxury of focusing on moral or racial issues rather than on their economic interests. In a number of states, as a result, the racial issues of the 1980s lost their political potency.[33] Indeed, even patriotism gave way to economic concerns as the recession lengthened. This was why George Bush's incredible 91 percent approval rating following the Persian Gulf War fell as much as 50 points in less than one year as pocketbook issues replaced citizens' pride in American military prowess. During the 1980s and early 1990s, millions of working-class voters became unemployed or were forced to find lower-paying jobs. These voters gradually deserted the Republican camp.

Though the constituency for the Republican social agenda shrank, the moral fervor of the groups most fiercely committed to those issues nonetheless grew. When right-to-life forces launched protests and sought to block the doors of abortion clinics across the nation, President Bush saw no choice but to strongly endorse the activities of these loyal Republicans. However, Bush's support for these groups hurt his standing among rank-and-file suburban Republicans. The traditional Republican suburban upper-middle-class constituency had never been enthusiastic about the social agenda or about the sorts of people it had brought into the party. It had been prepared, however, to hold its collective nose so long as the social agenda brought political success and the Republican national leadership did not seem to be working very hard *actually* to bring about the criminalization of abortion, return prayer to the schools, and so forth. Ronald Reagan had been extremely adept at convincing right-to-lifers that he was on their side while reassuring his suburban upper-middle-class constituents that, however much he might talk about abortion, he did not actually plan to *do* anything about it. Because Bush's political base on the Right was weaker than Reagan's, however, he felt compelled to do more to satisfy anti-abortion groups and other social conservatives. This led to a pattern of Supreme Court appointments and legislative initiatives that pleased social conservatives but offended upper-income suburban Republicans—the "country club set"—who had been the party's backbone. As

---

[33]For a discussion of events in one state, see David Broder, "In North Carolina, Racially Coded Wedge Issues No Longer Dominate," *Washington Post*, 13 October 1992, p. A12.

the 1992 campaign approached, Bush suffered a considerable loss of support in this stratum that was only exacerbated by the prominent role assigned to social conservatives at the 1992 Republican convention.

Even more than their dismay over the social agenda, economic hard times eroded Republican support among middle-class urban and suburban voters. Middle-class executives and professionals are usually fairly well insulated from the economic downturns that often devastate blue-collar workers, but the economic crises of the late 1980s and early 1990s had a major impact on them as well. The cumulative effect of the mergers and acquisitions of the 1980s, the failure of hundreds of banks, corporate restructuring and "down-sizing," the massive shift of manufacturing operations out of the country, the decline of the securities industry, the collapse of the housing market, and the end of the defense boom meant at least the possibility of unemployment or income reduction for hundreds of thousands of white-collar, management, and professional employees. Even those whose jobs were secure saw their economic positions eroded by the sharply declining values of their homes.

Economic hard times gave middle-class voters another reason for alarm. One of the inevitable consequences of economic distress and unemployment is an increase in crime rates. During the late 1980s and early 1990s, crime rates throughout the United States soared. In 1980, middle-class taxpayers had responded favorably to Ronald Reagan's call for a cap on social spending coupled with a tough approach to crime. For twelve years, limits on domestic social spending were a cornerstone of the Republican program. In 1992, however, rising crime rates despite Republican "get tough" rhetoric allowed the Democrats to persuade many middle-class voters that the expansion of domestic social spending was a price that had to be paid for the preservation of social peace and public safety.

Thus, the decline of prosperity at home caused cracks in the Reagan coalition. Under the pressure of economic distress, groups that had been enthusiastic supporters of Reaganism in the early 1980s broke away from the GOP in 1992. To compound the Republican party's woes, the unity of its coalition was also undermined by the collapse of the Soviet Union and the end of the Cold War threat.

Strength abroad had been the second cornerstone of Reaganism. Reagan had defined the Soviet Union as an "evil empire" that threatened the security of the world. To confront the Soviets, the Reagan administration embarked on a massive arms buildup that raised American military spending to levels unprecedented for peacetime.

Whatever its strategic purposes, the Reaganite program of hard-line anti-communism and massive increases in arms spending had a number of domestic political functions. First, the Reaganite posture of at least rhetorical confrontation with the Soviet Union cemented the loyalty of political conservatives to the Reagan coalition and the Republican party. This posture also attracted the support of members of various ethnic groups that had reason either to oppose the U.S.S.R. or, as in the case of pro-Israel Jews, to favor increased American military outlays. Moreover, it helped the GOP to appeal to the patriotic sentiments of blue-collar voters who had traditionally supported the Democrats.

Second, the Reaganite military buildup was an enormous boon to the American defense industry and to those regions of the country—primarily the South and

Southwest—where military construction was an important economic factor. During the 1980s, billions of dollars in new military contracts for items ranging from mundane uniforms and supplies to exotic antimissile defenses poured into the coffers of thousands of American corporations. At the same time, hundreds of thousands of workers benefitted from high-paying jobs in the defense industry. This helped boost the prosperity of much of the so-called Sunbelt, and gave voters and industries in this region a strong reason to support the GOP.

Third, the military buildup represented an effort to assert the primacy of national security and international concerns over domestic issues. Since the New Deal, the Democratic party's political advantage had come in the arena of domestic policy. Under Reagan's leadership, the GOP sought to persuade voters that domestic concerns were secondary to the nation's vital security interests, which they claimed were severely threatened by the expansive Soviet empire. In the foreign policy arena, voters tended to have more confidence in Republican leadership. This tendency was reinforced during the Bush administration by the public's overwhelmingly favorable response to the president's handling of the Persian Gulf crisis. The presence of a Soviet threat helped Republicans persuade voters to focus on foreign rather than on domestic policy and therefore to support the GOP.

In a similar vein, the Reaganite call for strengthening America's defenses provided a justification for limiting domestic social expenditures and programs. Domestic programs, and the federal, state, and quasi-public agencies that administered them, had become major elements of the organizational base of the national Democratic party. By asserting an overriding need to preserve the nation's security in a hostile world, the GOP was able to rationalize diverting funds from domestic to military programs and, in this way, to attack the Democratic party's institutional base. Thus, the Soviet threat not only permitted the Republicans to strengthen their own coalition but allowed them to attack their rivals' camp as well.

The collapse of the Soviet Union may have represented a victory for Republican foreign policy, but paradoxically it was a disaster for Republican domestic political strategy. As the Soviet Union weakened and, finally, dissolved, the rationale for a continuation of high levels of military spending disappeared, as did much of the justification for focusing on international rather than domestic problems and priorities. Industries and workers that had benefitted from Republican military spending now began to look to the Democrats, whose call for massive investment in the American economic infrastructure held out the promise of a new array of government contracts to replace those lost by the ending of the Cold War.

At the same time, ethnic groups that had been drawn to the GOP by its anti-Soviet stance no longer had a strong reason to remain in the Republican camp. One group, Jewish Republicans, completely abandoned the GOP. The collapse of the Soviet Union had led the White House to conclude that it could now afford to loosen its military and political links to Israel in order to pursue closer ties to Arab nations. When American Jews protested this shift in U.S. policy, President Bush, during a televised news conference, appeared to question their patriotism. Despite the president's subsequent apologies, few Jewish Republicans returned to the fold.

Finally, especially when coupled with the poor performance of the American economy, the collapse of the Soviet Union made it impossible for the Republicans to continue to insist on the primacy of international and security issues. Now that

Pat Buchanan and Jerry Brown
The Politics of Insurgency

Presidential aspirants Pat Buchanan and Jerry Brown hoped to capitalize on their underdog status during the 1992 primaries in an effort to promote the issues that concerned them, and perhaps to knock off each party's front-runner.

Pat Buchanan challenged incumbent President George Bush in the Republican primaries with the hope of appealing to core Republican voters who viewed Bush as too liberal. An arch-conservative, Buchanan was trained as a journalist and worked as a speech writer for Presidents Nixon and Reagan. He served as Reagan's director of communications from 1985 to 1987. The contentious and combative Buchanan became well known to viewers of such commentary, news, and discussion shows as "The McLaughlin Group," "Crossfire," and "The Capitol Gang."

Buchanan turned his pit-bull style to the political arena in his run against Bush because of his belief that the president had abandoned the conservative legacy of Ronald Reagan. Buchanan advocated deep tax cuts, opposed the Persian Gulf War (he labeled Bush's "quest for global democracy"as "messianic globaloney"), and favored greater American isolationism in foreign policy. While Buchanan never posed a serious threat to Bush's renomination, his candidacy did serve to push Bush closer to the Republican's conservative base; it also overshadowed the presidential candidacy of former American Nazi and Ku Klux Klan leader David Duke.

In a similarly unorthodox style, former California Governor Edmund G. "Jerry" Brown entered the 1992 Democratic presidential contest with little prospect of victory. But Brown, too, sought to promote

Pat Buchanan

the threat of war had receded, Americans were freer than they had been in years to focus on problems at home. As a result, working-class voters who had been persuaded to support the GOP despite economic interests that had historically linked them to the Democrats now began to reassess their positions. Many patriots became workers once again.

Thus, the collapse of the Soviet Union undermined the second key element of the Republican coalition's political success. For twelve years, the Republicans had emphasized prosperity at home and strength abroad. Now, in 1992, the nation was *not* prosperous and its unprecedented military strength now seemed irrelevant.

As the loyalty of the forces brought into the Republican camp by Reaganite appeals began to wane, President Bush found himself increasingly dependent on a

concerns that he believed the mainstream nominees had neglected. Brown sought to appeal to the party's traditional liberal base, including union members, blacks, and environmentalists, in his "We the People" campaign. Ridiculed by some as "Governor Moonbeam" because of his unpredictable and unconventional political style (such as his study of Zen philosophy and the fact that his limousine when he was governor was a beat-up old compact car), Brown ran a shoestring campaign with few paid aides. He refused to accept campaign contributions over $100, and at every opportunity he advertised a toll-free number for those interested in contributing.

Brown argued strenuously for strict campaign contribution limits as well as for a major overhaul of the entire campaign finance process, term limits, a flat 13 percent tax on income, worker rights, and stricter environmental regulations. He also offered to make Jesse Jackson his vice-presidential running mate should he win the nomination. Despite a weak showing in the early primaries, Brown was able to stay in the race because of his economical campaign style and populist appeal, as reflected by his toll-free-number approach to fund-raising. By portraying himself as an outsider in the later primaries, Brown sought to undercut front-runner Bill Clinton and capitalize on the electorate's frustration with the political system, even though he admitted

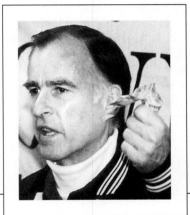

that as chair of the California state Democratic party from 1989 to 1991, he had raised tens of millions of dollars from the same wealthy special interests he was running against in 1992.

Both Buchanan and Brown pursued "outsider" campaigns, hoping to draw on their party's core bases. In the process, both reminded the front-runners that the party core constituents could not be ignored.

Source: Stephen J. Wayne, *The Road to the White House* (New York: St. Martin's Press, 1992).

Jerry Brown

core Republican constituency of hard-line social and political conservatives. Political conservatives had been furious with Bush since 1991 when he broke his "Read my lips" pledge never to raise taxes, in order to reach a budget agreement with congressional Democrats. Bush angered these conservatives even further when he signed the 1991 Civil Rights Act and the Americans with Disabilities Act. The first was seen by conservatives as a "quotas" bill, while the second appeared to be opening the way to a torrent of litigation against business firms.

Bush calculated that he had to maintain his support on the political right in order to have any chance of re-election. For this reason, he gave conservatives, including his nemesis from the presidential primaries, Patrick Buchanan, a prominent role in the 1992 Republican National Convention, allowed their views a place in the Republican platform, and emphasized "family values" in his presidential campaign. All this helped to strengthen Bush's support on the Right. Unfortunately for Bush, his efforts to placate the Right led to unease among moderate Republicans whose support for the president was already wavering under the pressure of economic and world events.

Democratic Opportunity

These cracks in the Republican coalition provided the Democrats with their best opportunity in two decades to capture the White House. First, however, they had to put their own party's house in order. Since the early 1970s, Democratic candidates had been handicapped by problems of a liberal ideology and racial issues. The Democratic party's nominating process had produced candidates and platforms that were seen as too liberal by the general electorate. At the same time, the issue of race had divided the party. Democratic candidates depended heavily on African American voters and thus were compelled to appeal for their support. However, Democratic pledges and programs like affirmative action, designed to win the support of blacks, had the effect of alienating conservative working-class whites in the North and South whose votes the Democrats also needed. Race and a liberal ideology had helped undermine five Democratic candidacies since 1968. In 1992, however, the Democrats were able to handle both these problems successfully.

Since the electoral debacle of 1972, when Richard Nixon won a landslide victory over George McGovern, moderate Democrats had argued that the party needed to present a more centrist image if it hoped to be competitive in national elections. The major organizational vehicle for the centrists was the Democratic Leadership Council (DLC), an organization based in Washington and funded by business firms with ties to the Democratic party. Throughout the Reagan and Bush years, the DLC organized networks of state and local party officials and sought to develop political themes that could both bring about a measure of party unity *and* appeal to the national electorate.[34]

In 1992, the DLC and its moderate allies were able to dominate the Democratic party's presidential nominating processes as well as its national convention. The party chose as its presidential and vice-presidential candidates Governor Bill Clinton and Senator Al Gore, both founding members of the DLC. The platform adopted at the party's national convention was widely perceived to be the most conservative in decades, stressing individual responsibility and private enterprise while implicitly criticizing welfare recipients. Though the platform mentioned the importance of protecting the rights of women, gays, and minorities, gone were the calls for expanded rights for criminals and welfare recipients that had provided Republicans with such convenient political targets in previous years.

Democrats sought to deal with their party's racial divisions by keeping black politicians and racial issues at arm's length and relying upon economic appeals to woo both working-class white and black voters. Democratic strategists calculated

---

[34]For a discussion, see Thomas Edsall, "The Democrats Pick a New Centerpiece," *Washington Post National Weekly Edition,* 24 August, 1992, p. 14.

that black voters and politicians would have no choice but to support the Democratic ticket. Given the nations's economic woes, which afflicted blacks even more
than whites, Democratic leaders reasoned that they had no need to appeal explicitly for black support. This freed the party to seek the votes of conservative whites.
One step in this direction was, of course, the creation of a ticket headed by two
southerners. Democrats hoped that the Clinton/Gore ticket would appeal directly
to the southern white voters who once had been Democratic stalwarts but had
made the Deep South a Republican bastion during the Reagan years.

Clinton went out of his way to assure conservative whites in both the North
and South that, unlike previous Democratic candidates, he would not cater to
blacks. For example, Clinton was careful to avoid any association with America's
most visible African American Democrat, Jesse Jackson. In a similar vein, Clinton
seized an opportunity after the 1992 Los Angeles riots to sharply attack an African
American rap singer, Sister Souljah, for her anti-white comments. Many African
American Democrats were angry about the party's apparent shift to the right on
matters of race and threatened to withhold their backing in the general election.
Jesse Jackson, for example, pointedly remarked, "It takes two wings to fly." There
was, however, little that African American politicians could do, and, ultimately,
Jackson and the others had no choice but to support the Clinton ticket.

Thus, Clinton became the first Democratic presidential candidate in two
decades who was neither burdened by an excessively liberal image nor plagued by
the party's racial division. With Democratic strategists believing they had stabilized
the party's traditional southern, African American, and blue-collar base, Clinton
and his allies moved to expand the Democratic coalition into Republican electoral
territory—business and the middle class. For this purpose, the Democrats fashioned an economic message designed to appeal to business and the middle class
without alienating the party's working-class constituency.

The centerpiece of the Democratic campaign was a call for the development of
a multifaceted "national economic strategy." One major element of this strategy
was support for free trade but with the proviso that America would act against nations deemed to be guilty of unfair trade practices or to have poor labor policies or
deficient environmental programs.[35] A second element increased government
spending to support scientific research and development, as well as strong government backing for new technologies and industries, and tax credits for small and
medium-size businesses. Third, the Democrats' economic strategy envisioned extensive retraining programs for workers to prepare them for jobs in the new, high-
technology industries of the future. Fourth, the Democrats called for massive
federal spending to rebuild America's industrial infrastructure. Finally, their 1992
national economic strategy promised expanded funding for education, health care,
and other social services—to be paid for by tax increases on the wealthy—under
the rubric of investment in the human capital resources needed to improve America's competitive position in the world economy.

Taken as a whole, the Democrats' national economic strategy was a blueprint as
much for political success as for economic recovery. Each element of their plan was

---

[35]Stuart Auerbach, "Bush, Clinton Differ on Government's Role," *Washington Post,* 8 October 1992, p.
A23.

calculated to appeal to the interests of traditional Democratic constituencies or to create a new coalition of forces that would strengthen the Democratic camp. Thus, most obviously, the pledge to invest heavily in research and new technologies, as well as the modernization of America's infrastructure through such means as the creation of high-speed trains and electronic "information highways," was aimed at winning the support of firms in the computer, telecommunications, and aerospace industries threatened by cuts in defense spending and intense foreign competition. The executives of hundreds of high-tech firms responded to this Democratic initiative by announcing their support for Clinton.

Similarly, Democratic caveats on the issue of free trade were designed to reassure firms threatened by foreign competition, or by the competition of American firms utilizing cheap labor in Mexico under the new NAFTA agreement, that a Democratic administration would be sensitive to their needs. Democratic rhetoric suggested that especially troublesome foreigners or Mexican transplants might be charged with unfair labor and trade practices, or even with environmental mismanagement, to protect the market share of American-based businesses.

Democratic support for limits on free trade were also designed to please organized labor, which feared a continuing loss of unionized jobs to foreign countries. Labor had reason, too, to support Democratic calls for infrastructural redevelopment (which would presumably provide public works jobs for unionized workers in a variety of industries) and job retraining programs. Through these initiatives, the Democrats hoped to rebuild their own economic infrastructure as well as the nation's. Under Franklin Roosevelt, the Democratic party had forged coalitions between industry and labor through regulatory, defense, and public employment programs that provided benefits for workers and their firms. These coalitions had been broken during the Reagan-Bush years with damaging consequences for the Democratic party's electoral prospects. With their new economic strategy, the Democrats hoped to reunite business and labor and tie both to the Democratic party.

Finally, the Democrats' national economic strategy identified a new rationale for traditional Democratic social programs and thus pointed the way toward an expansion of domestic social spending for the benefit of Democratic constituencies. The Reaganites had discredited Democratic social programs by charging that they represented transfers of income from the hardworking middle class to the unworthy poor. In 1992, the Democrats redefined social spending. No longer was social spending a transfer to the poor. Rather, it was now to be seen as an investment in resources needed to improve America's competitive position in the world.

This call obviously had enormous appeal not only for the nominal recipients of social services but, even more important, for the millions of public- and quasi-public-sector professionals in the human service, education, health care, mental health, and related fields who provided social services. In recent decades, these public-sector professionals came to be among the most vehement and important supporters of the Democrats and determined foes of the Republicans, who, of course, sought to limit domestic social spending.

With this national economic strategy Clinton and the Democrats accomplished in 1992 what Reagan and the Republicans had achieved in 1980 when they formed a coalition with another political strategy presented as an economic theory—supply-side economics.

Against the backdrop of continuing economic recession and Republican disarray, the Democrats' economic program and new posture of moderation on racial issues and ideology helped the Clinton/Gore ticket take a commanding lead in the polls in August 1992, after the Democratic National Convention. Unable to make effective use of economic issues because of the recession, or of the familiar Republican rallying cries of taxes, race, and regulation because of his own weak record in these areas, Bush fell back upon the theme of "family values" and attacks upon Clinton's character in his attempt to catch up in the polls. For three months, the nation was transfixed by the often bitter campaigning, the renewed candidacy of billionaire populist Ross Perot, and the presidential and vice-presidential debates before casting their vote on November 3.

The Republican ticket's difficulties became fully evident during the nationally televised presidential and vice-presidential debates in October. While the Democratic candidates focused on the nation's economic distress, constantly reminding voters of the need for programs and policies designed to improve the nation's economy, Bush and Quayle, for their part, had considerable difficulty articulating an affirmative message and were left to talk about character. Not surprisingly, the debates attracted few new voters to the Republican camp.

Complicating the debates, and the 1992 campaign more generally, was the peculiar candidacy of Ross Perot. During the spring of 1992, Perot had announced his intention to campaign as an independent presidential candidate if his name was placed on the ballot in every state. With more than a little help from a well-financed and well-organized Perot effort, Perot "volunteers" complied with Perot's stipulation, and his independent candidacy was launched.[36] Initially, Perot's blunt, no-nonsense, can-do style generated considerable enthusiasm among voters apparently tired of mainstream politicians. Perot made extremely effective use of television talk show and call-in programs such as "Larry King Live" to present himself as an ordinary American tired of the inability of the politicians to resolve the nation's many problems. By mid-June, both major-party candidates began to assess the potential damage of a Perot candidacy. For their part, pundits began to discuss the possibility that, for the first time since 1824, an election might be thrown into the House of Representatives if a strong Perot showing prevented either major-party candidate from obtaining the electoral college majority needed to capture the White House.

On the last day of the Democratic National Convention, however, Perot surprised his supporters by withdrawing from the race. Perot never fully explained his decision, though many analysts believed he had grown irritated with the constant media scrutiny to which presidential candidates are subjected. Perot's decision to leave the race gave Clinton a boost. Perot had won the support of many disaffected Republicans not yet ready to back a Democrat. Having gotten their toes wet in the Perot camp, many of these voters were now ready to take the plunge and support Clinton. Perot thus served as a bridge for movements of voters from the Re-

---

[36]Steven Holmes, "Grass-Roots Drive Shows Hand of Oz," *New York Times,* 30 September 1992, p. A20.

H. Ross Perot
Billionaire Populist

H. Ross Perot (b. 1930)

During the 1992 presidential election, Texas businessman and billionaire H. Ross Perot alternately charmed and angered Americans with his plain-speaking, tough-talking independent presidential candidacy.

Born in Texarkana, a town that straddles Texas and Arkansas, in 1930, Perot was raised in a home of modest means during the Depression era. After leaving the Navy in 1957, he worked for a fledgling computer company, IBM. In 1962, he formed his own company modeled after IBM: Electronic Data Systems Corporation. Starting with $1,000, he built the company into a giant by the end of the 1960s, and was soon a multimillionaire himself. His company's success rested primarily on a government program: processing Medicare claims in Texas for the federal Medicare program enacted in 1965. Some later accused Perot of having exercised undue influence to win the contract.

In the 1970s, Perot became heavily involved in the search for American soldiers missing in Southeast Asia, a concern he pursued for the next two decades. In 1979, he traveled personally and under cover to revolution-torn Iran to win the release of two of his employees. It was a move that underscored his personal courage to some and his recklessness to others.

On February 20, 1992, during an appearance on CNN's "Larry King Live," Perot was asked whether he would consider a run for the presidency. After much equivocation, he said he would if citizens put him on the ballot in all fifty states. Thus began the "Perot for President" movement,

with financial support provided by Perot himself (who said that he was prepared to spend as much as $200 million on the campaign if necessary). Perot unofficially launched his candidacy in June and proceeded to make the state of the economy and the ballooning federal deficit his primary issues. By this point, Perot was actually leading Republican incumbent George Bush and Democratic nominee Bill Clinton in some polls.

Yet with increased exposure came increased scrutiny. Critics accused Perot of being short-tempered, intolerant, and unwilling to listen to different points of view. These criticisms received support when Perot abruptly quit the race in mid-July. In still another unexpected move, Perot re-entered the race in October, saying he was merely abiding the wishes of his supporters. Though many of his supporters were by now disenchanted, Perot's popular standing improved dramatically following his performance in all three national television debates. In late October, however, after accusing the Republicans of using various "dirty tricks" against him, none of which he could prove, his standing waned somewhat. He still won nearly 19 percent of the popular vote, but no electoral votes.

Source: Lawrence Wright, "The Man from Texarcana," *New York Times Magazine,* 28 June 1992.

publican to the Democratic coalitions. Third-party and independent candidates

often play this role.[37]

In the fall, however, Perot muddied the political waters once again by reentering the race, supposedly at the behest of the American people. Analysts initially greeted Perot's return with skepticism, believing that he could no longer have much impact on the election. However, Perot soon reestablished himself as a formidable figure, performing extremely well in the three presidential debates and again impressing voters as a plainspoken man of action. Following the debates, Perot presented his ideas and plans during dozens of talk show appearances and in a series of televised thirty- and sixty-minute infomercials, which drew substantial audiences. As Perot spent money freely (an estimated $60 million of his own funds), his standing in the polls rose, and pundits once again began to wonder whether the billionaire could affect the outcome of the election.

The Perot balloon, however, burst in late October. During an appearance on the CBS television program "60 Minutes," Perot asserted that his earlier decision to withdraw from the presidential campaign had been prompted by a Republican "dirty tricks" effort to somehow embarrass his daughter and spoil her wedding with a forged photograph. This strange claim was greeted by indignant Republican denials and general incredulity. Within two days, Perot withdrew the charge. This unusual episode led many voters to conclude that Perot was temperamentally unsuited for the White House. The Perot campaign's momentum waned.

On November 3, Perot captured nearly 19 percent of the popular vote. This was the best showing for an independent presidential bid since Theodore Roosevelt's Bull Moose candidacy in 1912. Perot, however, carried no states and appeared to draw support away from Clinton and Bush in roughly equal percentages. Thus, despite its sound and fury, the Perot campaign ultimately had little effect upon the outcome of the election.

More than anything else, the Perot episode revealed the weakness of America's two-party system. Many voters had grown so disenchanted with established politicians and parties, and so distrustful of their promises, that they were willing to consider electing an enigmatic and mercurial outsider to the nation's highest office. To many Americans, Perot seemed to be the savior on horseback who would somehow end the stalemate, corruption, and ineptitude plaguing the nation. Citizens, of course, look to such saviors when they lose confidence in the political process and even, perhaps, in democratic politics, itself. The strength of the Perot candidacy was a symptom of popular disaffection. America's political leadership must take this disaffection seriously even as its most recent symptom goes away.

Democratic Triumph

After the long and arduous campaign, the result was almost anticlimactic. The Clinton/Gore ticket achieved a comfortable victory, winning 43 percent of the popular vote and 370 electoral votes. Bush and Quayle received 38 percent of

---

[37]See the discussion in James Sundquist, *Dynamics of the Party System* (Washington, DC: Brookings Institution, 1983), chap. 2.

the popular vote and only 168 electoral votes. Economic recession, the end of the Cold War, and the Democrats' newfound moderation on matters of race and ideology combined to oust the Republicans from the White House for the first time in twelve years.

According to national exit-poll results reported by the *Washington Post* immediately after the election, the single issue with the largest impact upon the election's outcome was the economy.[38] Nearly half the voters surveyed cited jobs and the economy as their central concerns, and these voters supported the Democrats by a 2-to-1 margin. Among voters who felt that their own economic prospects were worsening, Clinton won by a 5-to-1 margin.

By contrast, Bush led Clinton by a 2-to-1 margin among voters citing the Republican theme of "family values" as an important issue. However, this major Republican focus was of concern to only one voter in seven. Similarly, against the backdrop of the end of the Cold War and the collapse of the Soviet Union, foreign policy no longer served as a major Republican rallying point. Voters concerned with foreign policy supported Bush by an overwhelming 9-to-1 margin. However, only one voter in twelve cited foreign policy as a major worry. Moreover, the once-powerful Republican tax issue had completely lost its potency in the face of Bush's failure to adhere to his own pledge never to raise taxes. Only one voter in seven cited taxes as an important issue. Twenty percent of those surveyed said that Bush's failure to keep his promise on taxes was "very important."

At the same time, the Democrats' racial strategy was successful. Democratic strategists had opted to ignore blacks and to court conservative whites, calculating that the economic hard times left blacks no choice but to support the Clinton ticket. This calculation proved to be correct. Conservative white voters in the North and South responded positively to Clinton's well-publicized conflicts with Jesse Jackson and other Clinton gestures designed to distance himself from blacks. For their part, African American voters supported the Democratic ticket in overwhelming numbers, helping Clinton carry a number of southern states.

After twelve years, the political coalition formed by Ronald Reagan in 1980 had been shattered. The Republicans' bastions in the South and West had been breached. Many of the blue-collar "Reagan Democrats," lured to the GOP by social, patriotic, foreign policy, and racial issues, had returned to the Democratic fold. Even southern evangelicals—the prime targets for the GOP's family values campaign—were attracted to a Democratic ticket featuring two southern Baptists. At the same time, the GOP's core, upper-middle class and business constituency could muster little enthusiasm for a Republican administration that had failed to hold the line on taxes and had allowed the economy to deteriorate, while devoting its energy and attention to abortion and other social issues. As a result, Clinton even outpolled Bush in the GOP's traditional suburban strongholds. Indeed, according to *New York Times* exit polls, among voters earning more than $75,000 a year, normally the nation's most rock-ribbed Republican group, Bush support fell from 62 percent in 1988 to a meager 48 percent in 1992.[39] Thus, on November 3, 1992, the nation elected a Democratic president. It was time for a change.

[38]Thomas B. Edsall and E. J. Dionne, Jr., "Younger, Lower-Income Voters Spurn GOP," *Washington Post,* 4 November 1992, p. 1.

[39]"Portrait of the Electorate," *New York Times,* 5 November 1992, p. B9.

Even when the Republicans were winning presidential elections, the Democrats maintained a strong grip on Congress. This pattern of divided party control was made possible by the decline of party organization and the rise of split-ticket voting. Three developments over the past three decades have enabled Democrats in Congress to entrench themselves in office even as the Republicans were leading in the arena of presidential elections.

First, during the 1960s and 1970s, Congress enacted a large number of new programs for local economic development, housing, hospital construction, water and air pollution control, education, and social services. These programs made available tens of billions of dollars each year that members of Congress could channel into their constituencies. By using their influence over the allocation of these funds, incumbent representatives and senators could build political support for themselves at home. In this way, incumbents greatly enhanced their prospects for re-election. Since the Democrats held a solid majority in Congress when this process began, it has helped to perpetuate their control.

Second, the flow of billions of federal dollars to state and local governments and nonprofit organizations has expanded the number and influence of individuals associated with the public and not-for-profit sectors throughout the country. These men and women have a strong stake in the continuation of high levels of federal funding for domestic programs and, therefore, in the election of congressional candidates with such a commitment. Although Republicans in Congress can usually be counted upon to pursue existing federal dollars for their districts, Democratic representatives are more likely to support new federal domestic initiatives as well as greater expenditures on current programs. Hence, Democratic congressional candidates throughout the nation—newcomers and incumbents, alike—are usually able to recruit large numbers of talented individuals from the public and nonprofit sectors to work in their campaigns. As a result, the Democrats have a reach and depth and institutional base throughout the nation that is unmatched by the Republicans. In presidential contests, which are fought mainly in the media, campaign workers are not of decisive importance. In lower-visibility congressional, state, and local elections, however, they can be, and so the greater depth of the Democratic party is of particular importance here. Senate races lie somewhere in between, which helps to explain why the Republicans are at less of a disadvantage in Senate than House elections.

Finally, because members of Congress devote so much effort to maximizing the flow of federal benefits to their constituencies, voters have come to judge congressional candidates largely in terms of their ability to deliver these benefits. While voters expect presidential candidates to articulate national interests, they want their own representatives to protect their particular interests. As discussed above, congressional Democrats have, on the whole, been more effective in this respect than their Republican colleagues. Thus, while electing Republican presidential candidates who promise to slash domestic spending, voters have regularly returned congressional Democrats who could be counted upon to fight for more federal dollars for their own favorite programs.

As the 1992 presidential elections approached, Democrats began to hope that voter dissatisfaction with the weak state of the nation's economy would allow them to expand their representatives in Congress as well as to unseat President Bush. Republicans, for their part, hoped that anger over the recent congressional bank and post office scandals, coupled with substantial congressional redistricting, would help the GOP expand its strength in Congress.

Neither side was fully pleased with the results of the 1992 contest. In the Senate, the party balance remained unchanged. The Democrats continued to hold fifty-seven seats while the Republicans controlled forty-three. In the House of Representatives, the Republicans gained ten seats, leaving the Democrats with a 259 to 176 margin.

Thus, Democrats were disappointed because Clinton's victory in the presidential election did not translate into Democratic gains in Congress. In their euphoria following Clinton's victory, however, most Democrats predicted that the new Congress would work effectively with the Clinton administration. For their part, Republicans were sorry that the nation's dismay over congressional scandals and Americans' putative anti-incumbent mood did not result in more Republican victories. However, Republican congressional leaders breathed a sigh of relief that the collapse of the Bush campaign had not undermined their own positions.

Whatever its partisan makeup, the new Congress reflected a number of the changes manifesting themselves in American society during the past decade. Most striking was the large number of women elected to the House and even to the Senate. Women had been mobilized for political action in the wake of the Clarence Thomas confirmation hearings. As a result, forty-seven women won election to the House of Representatives (compared with twenty-eight in the old House) and four to the Senate, where there were now six women. One of these women, Carol Mosely-Braun (D–Ill.), became the first black woman ever elected to serve in the Senate. Two women now represented California: Dianne Feinstein and Barbara Boxer.

African American and Hispanic American representation in Congress also increased in 1992, the former from twenty-five to thirty-seven and the latter from eleven to eighteen. Four Asian Americans were elected to the House. One, Jay C. Kim, former Republican mayor of Diamond Bar, California, became the first Korean American elected to Congress. Increased minority voter registration coupled with the redrawing of congressional district boundaries to enhance minority groups' representation had achieved their purpose.

All in all, Americans elected 11 new senators and 110 new House members in 1992. This was the largest group of congressional freshmen since 1948, larger even than the classes entering with Lyndon Johnson's landslide victory in 1964 or in the post-Watergate 1974 election. Interestingly, though, this huge freshman class could not be said to represent a clear or consistent message from the electorate.

Did the electorate want a Congress that would support Bill Clinton? Perhaps, but 40 percent of the newcomers were Republicans. Was the electorate tired of politics as usual? Perhaps, but three-fourths of the newcomers had previous governmental experience. Did the electorate seek revenge on incumbents? After all, voters in fourteen states had approved congressional term-limit proposals. Nevertheless, most incumbents were reelected. In the House, for example, 75 percent of those elected on November 3 were incumbents. Moreover, only sixteen of the newcomers actually defeated incumbents in the general election. The other ninety-four replaced incumbents who had retired, lost their districts in the decennial redrawing of district boundaries, or, in a few cases, were defeated in primaries. Viewed another way, 95 percent of the House incumbents running in the general election were successful. As usually happens, the electorate's biennial message to Washington was by no means loud and clear. It was left to the new Congress and the new administration to interpret the will of the people according to their own lights.

THE CONSEQUENCES OF CONSENT

Voting choices and electoral outcomes can be extremely important in the United States. Yet, to observe that there can be relationships between voters' choices, leadership composition, and policy outputs is only to begin to understand the significance of democratic elections, rather than to exhaust the possibilities. Important as they are, voters' choices and electoral results may still be less consequential for government and politics than the simple fact of voting itself. The impact of electoral decisions upon the governmental process is, in some respects, analogous to the impact made upon organized religion by individuals being able to worship at the church of their choice. The fact of worship can be more important than the particular choice. Similarly, the fact of mass electoral participation can be more significant than what or how citizens decide once they participate. Thus, electoral participation has important consequences in that it socializes and institutionalizes political action.

First, democratic elections socialize political activity. Voting is not a natural or spontaneous phenomenon. It is an institutionalized form of mass political involvement. That individuals vote rather than engage in some other form of political behavior is a result of national policies that create the opportunity to vote and discourage other political activities relative to voting. Elections transform what might otherwise consist of sporadic, citizen-initiated acts into a routine public function. This transformation expands and democratizes mass political involvement. At the same time, however, elections help to preserve the government's stability by containing and channeling away potentially more disruptive or dangerous forms of mass political activity. By establishing formal avenues for mass participation and accustoming citizens to their use, government reduces the threat that volatile, unorganized political involvement can pose to the established order.

Second, elections bolster the government's power and authority. Elections help to increase popular support for political leaders and for the regime itself. The formal opportunity to participate in elections serves to convince citizens that the government is responsive to their needs and wishes. Moreover, elections help to persuade citizens to obey. Electoral participation increases popular acceptance of taxes and military service upon which the government depends. Even if popular voting can influence the behavior of those in power, voting serves simultaneously as a form of cooptation. Elections—particularly democratic elections—substitute consent for coercion as the foundation of governmental power.

Finally, elections institutionalize mass influence in politics. Democratic elections permit citizens to routinely select and depose public officials, and elections can serve to promote popular influence over officials' conduct. But however effective this electoral sanction may be, it is hardly the only means through which citizens can reward or punish public officials for their actions. Spontaneous or privately organized forms of political activity, or even the threat of their occurrence, can also induce those in power to heed the public's wishes. The behavior of even the most rigid autocrat, for example, can be influenced by the possibility that his policies may provoke popular disobedience, clandestine movements, or riot and insurrection. The alternative to democratic elections is not clearly and simply the absence of popular influence, rather it can be unregulated and unconstrained popular intervention into governmental processes. It is, indeed, often precisely because spontaneous forms of mass political activity can have too great an impact upon the actions of government that elections are introduced. Walter Lippmann, a journalist who helped to pioneer the idea of public opinion voicing itself through the press via the "Opinion/Editorial" page, once observed that "new numbers were enfranchised because they had power, and giving them the vote was the least disturbing way of letting them exercise their power."[40] The vote can provide the "least disturbing way" of allowing ordinary people to exercise power. If the people had been powerless to begin with, elections would never have been introduced.

Thus, although citizens can secure enormous benefits from their right to vote, governments secure equally significant benefits from allowing them to do so.

SUMMARY

Allowing citizens to vote represents a calculated risk on the part of power holders. On the one hand, popular participation can generate consent and support for the government. On the other hand, the right to vote may give ordinary citizens more influence in the governmental process than political elites would like.

Voting is only one of many possible types of political participation. The significance of voting is that it is an institutional and formal mode of political activity. Voting is organized and subsidized by the government. This makes voting both more limited and more democratic than other forms of participation.

All governments regulate voting in order to influence its effects. The most important forms of regulation include regulation of the electorate's composition, regulation of the translation of voters' choices into electoral outcomes, and insulation of policy-making processes from electoral intervention.

Voters' choices, themselves, are based on partisanship, issues, and candidates' personalities. Which of these criteria will be most important varies over time and depends upon the factors that opposing candidates choose to emphasize in their campaigns.

Voters' choices have had particularly significant consequences during periods of critical electoral realignment. During these periods, which have occurred roughly

---

[40]Walter Lippman, *The Essential Lippman,* ed. Clinton Rossiter and James Lare (New York: Random House, 1965), p. 12.

every thirty years, new electoral coalitions have formed, new groups have come to power, and important institutional and policy changes have occurred. The last such critical period was associated with Franklin Roosevelt's New Deal.

Whatever voters decide, elections are important institutions because they socialize political activity, increase governmental authority, and institutionalize popular influence in political life.

FOR FURTHER READING

Andersen, Kristi. *The Creation of a Democratic Majority: 1928–1936.* Chicago: University of Chicago Press, 1979.

Black, Earl, and Merle Black. *The Vital South: How Presidents Are Elected.* Cambridge, MA: Harvard University Press, 1992.

Brady, David. *Critical Elections and Congressional Policymaking.* Stanford: Stanford University Press, 1988.

Burnham, Walter D. *The Current Crisis in American Politics.* New York: Oxford University Press, 1982.

Carmines, Edward G., and James Stimson. *Issue Evolution: The Racial Transformation of American Politics.* Princeton, NJ: Princeton University Press, 1988.

Conway, M. Margaret. *Political Participation in the United States.* Washington, DC: Congressional Quarterly Press, 1985.

Dinkin, Robert J. *Campaigning in America: A History of Election Practices.* Westport, CT: Greenwood Press, 1989.

Ferguson, Thomas, and Joel Rogers. *Right Turn: The Decline of the Democrats and the Future of American Politics.* New York: Hill and Wang, 1986.

Fowler, Linda, and Robert D. McClure. *Political Ambition: Who Decides to Run for Congress.* New Haven, CT: Yale University Press, 1989.

Ginsberg, Benjamin, and Martin Shefter. *Politics by Other Means: Institutional Conflict and the Declining Significance of Elections in America.* New York: Basic Books, 1990.

Jackson, Brooks. *Honest Graft: Big Money and the American Political Process.* New York: Alfred A. Knopf, 1988.

Jamieson, Kathleen H. *Eloquence in an Electronic Age: The Transformation of Political Speechmaking.* New York: Oxford University Press, 1988.

Nie, Norman, Sidney Verba, and John Petrocik. *The Changing American Voter.* Cambridge, MA: Harvard University Press, 1979.

Niemi, Richard, and Herbert Weisberg. *Controversies in American Voting Behavior.* Washington, DC: Congressional Quarterly Press, 1984.

Norrander, Barbara. *Super Tuesday: Regional Politics and Presidential Primaries,* Lexington, KY: University of Kentucky Press, 1992.

Piven, Frances Fox, and Richard A. Cloward. *Why Americans Don't Vote.* New York: Pantheon, 1988.

Pohlmann, Marcus. *Black Politics in Conservative America.* New York: Longman, 1990.

Reed, Adolph. *The Jesse Jackson Phenomenon.* New Haven, CT: Yale University Press, 1987.

Reichley, A. James, ed. *Elections American Style.* Washington, DC: Brookings Institution, 1987.

Sorauf, Frank. *Inside Campaign Finance: Myths and Realities.* New Haven, CT: Yale University Press, 1992.

Stanley, Harold. *Voter Mobilization and the Politics of Race: The South and Universal Suffrage, 1952–1984.* New York: Praeger, 1987.

Wilcox, Clyde. *God's Warriors: The Christian Right in Twentieth-Century America,* Baltimore: Johns Hopkins University Press, 1991.

11

Political Parties

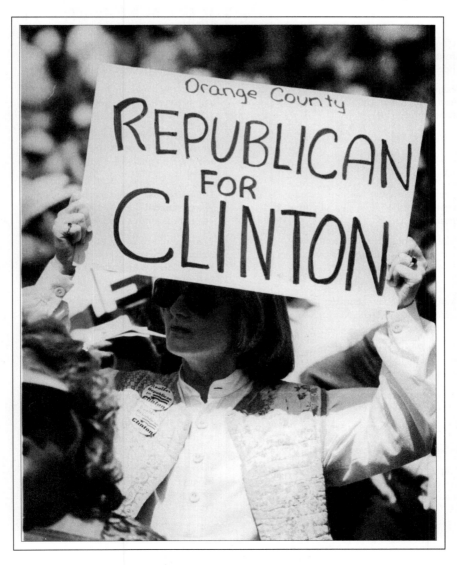

TIME LINE ON POLITICAL PARTIES

EVENTS		INSTITUTIONAL DEVELOPMENTS
Parties form in Congress (1790s)		Washington peacefully assumes the presidency (1789)
Washington's farewell address warns against parties (1796)		First party system—Federalists v. Republicans (1790s)
Republican Thomas Jefferson elected president (1800)	**1800**	Federalists try to retain power by Alien and Sedition Acts (1798) and by appointing "midnight judges" (1801)
Jefferson renominated by congressional caucus; re-elected by a landslide (1804)		Congressional caucuses nominate presidential candidates from each party (1804–1831)
Republican James Monroe re-elected president; no Federalist candidate; no caucuses called (1820)		Destruction of Federalists; period of one partyism; "era of good feelings" (1810s–1830s)
		Republican party splinters into National Republicans (Adams) and Democratic Republicans (Jackson) (1824)
Democrat Andrew Jackson elected president, ushering in "era of common man" (1828)		Democrats use party rotation to replace National Republicans in government positions (1829)
National nominating conventions held by Democrats and National Republicans (1831)	**1830**	National nominating conventions replace caucuses as method of selecting presidential candidates from each party (1830s)
Whig presidential candidates lose to Democratic candidate Martin Van Buren (1836)		Second party system—Whig party forms in opposition to Jackson—Democrats v. Whigs (1830s–1850s)
Whig William Henry Harrison elected president (1840)		Whigs gain presidency and majority in Congress; both parties organized down to the precinct level (1840)
Republican Abraham Lincoln elected president (1860)	**1850**	Third party system; destruction of Whigs; creation of Republicans—Democrats v. Republicans (1850s–1890s)
Civil War (1861–1865)		
Reconstruction (1865–1877)		
Republican William McKinley elected president; Democrats decimated (1896)		Fourth party system; both the Democratic and Republican parties are rebuilt along new lines (1890s–1930s)

TIME LINE ON POLITICAL PARTIES

EVENTS		INSTITUTIONAL DEVELOPMENTS
Era of groups and movements; millions of southern and eastern European immigrants arrive in U.S. (1870s–1890s)		Shrinking electorate; enactment of Progressive reforms, including registration laws, primary elections, the Australian ballot, and civil service reform; decline of party machines; emergence of many one-party states (1890s)
Republican Theodore Roosevelt becomes president (1901)	**1900**	
Democrat Franklin D. Roosevelt elected president (1932)		Fifth party system; period of New Deal Democratic dominance (1930s–1960s)
Democratic convention—party badly damaged; Republican Richard Nixon elected president (1968)	**1960**	Disruption of New Deal coalition; decay of party organizations (1968)
Watergate scandal (1973–1974)		Federal Election Campaign Act regulates campaign finance (1971)
Nixon resigns (1974)		Introduction of new political techniques (1970s and 1980s)
Republican Ronald Reagan elected president. (1980)	**1980**	Efforts by Republicans to build a national party structure (1980s)
Republican George Bush elected president; Democrats continue to control House and Senate (1988 and 1990)		Continuation of divided government, with Democrats controlling Congress and Republicans the White House (1980s–1990s)
Democrat Bill Clinton elected president; Democrats retain control of House and Senate (1992)	**1990**	High levels of congressional party unity and partisan conflict as Democrats seek to strengthen control of government through ambitious program of economic, social, and political reform (1993)

We often refer to the United States as a nation with a "two-party system." By this we mean that in the United States the Democratic and Republican parties compete for office and power. Most Americans believe that party competition contributes to the health of the democratic process. Certainly, we are more than just a bit suspicious of those nations that claim to be ruled by their people but do not tolerate the existence of opposing parties.

The idea of party competition was not always accepted in the United States. In the early years of the Republic, parties were seen as threats to the social order. In his 1796 "Farewell Address," President George Washington warned his countrymen to shun partisan politics:

> Let me warn you in the most solemn manner against the baneful effects of the spirit of party generally. This spirit exists under different shapes in all government, more or less stifled, controlled, or repressed, but in those of the popular form it is seen in its greater rankness and is truly their worst enemy.

Often, those in power viewed the formation of political parties by their opponents as acts of treason that merited severe punishment. Thus, in 1798, the Federalist party, which controlled the national government, in effect sought to outlaw its Jeffersonian Republican opponents through the infamous Alien and Sedition Acts which, among other things, made it a crime to publish or say anything that might tend to defame or bring into disrepute either the president or the Congress (see Box 11.1). Under this law, twenty-five individuals—including several Republican newspaper editors—were arrested and subsequently convicted.[1]

BOX 11.1
Alien and Sedition Acts: A Party's Attempt to Suppress the Opposition

In 1798 war seemed likely to break out between the United States and France. The overt purpose of the Alien and Sedition Acts was to protect the government against subversive activities by foreigners in the country—particularly the French. Their covert purpose, however, was to suppress Jefferson's and Madison's Republican party, which was rapidly gaining strength in its opposition to the Federalists.

The four pieces of legislation collectively referred to as the Alien and Sedition Acts are: (1) the Naturalization Act, passed June 18, 1798; (2) the Act Concerning Aliens, passed June 25, 1798; (3) the Act Respecting Alien Enemies, passed July 6, 1798; and (4) the Act for the Punishment of Certain Crimes (the Sedition Act), passed July 14, 1798.

The Alien Enemies Act never went into effect because it was contingent on the declaration of war. The Alien Act, which gave the president power to order out of the country all aliens he considered a threat to national security, was never enforced. Nonetheless, it is believed to have been responsible for the departure of many of the French. Since most naturalized citizens became Republicans, this act may have functioned to diminish the number of potential Republicans. In extending the period of residence required for naturalization from five to fourteen years, the Naturalization Act was an obvious move to weaken the Republican party.

The Sedition Act had the most serious legal implications. It was designed to suppress critics of the administration by limiting their freedom of speech and of the press. It was used to indict approximately twenty-five persons. While fewer than half of those indicted were ever brought to trial, several prominent Republican journalists were convicted. By 1802 all but the Alien Enemies Act had either expired or been repealed.

---

[1]See Richard Hofstadter, *The Idea of a Party System* (Berkeley: University of California Press, 1969).

Obviously, over the past two hundred years, our conception of political parties has changed considerably—from subversive organizations to bulwarks of democracy. In this chapter, we will examine the realities underlying these changing conceptions. First, we will look at party organization and its place in the American political process. Second, we shall evaluate America's two-party system, and assess the similarities and differences between the parties. Third, we will discuss the functions of the parties. Finally, we will address the significance and changing role of parties in American politics today.

WHAT ARE POLITICAL PARTIES?

Political parties, like interest groups, are organizations seeking influence over government. Ordinarily, they can be distinguished from interest groups on the basis of their orientation. A party seeks to control the entire government by electing its members to office and thereby controlling the government's personnel. Interest groups usually accept government and its personnel as a given and try to influence government policies through them.

Outgrowths of the Electoral Process

Political parties as they are known today developed along with the expansion of suffrage and can be understood only in the context of elections. The two are so intertwined that American parties actually take their structure from the electoral process. The shape of party organization in the United States has followed a simple rule: For every district where an election is held, there should be some kind of party unit. Republicans failed to maintain units in most of the southern counties between 1900 and 1952; Democrats were similarly unsuccessful in many areas of New England. But for most of the history of the United States, two major parties have had enough of an organized presence to oppose each other in elections in most of the nation's towns, cities, and counties. This makes the American party system one of the oldest political institutions in the history of democracy.

Compared to political parties in Europe, parties in the United States have always seemed weak. They have no criteria for party membership—no cards for their members to carry, no obligatory participation in any activity, no notion of exclusiveness. Today, they seem weaker than ever; they inspire less loyalty and are less able to control nominations. Some people are even talking about a "crisis of political parties," as though party politics were being abandoned. But there continues to be at least some substance to party organizations in the United States.

Party Organization: The Committees

In the United States, party organizations exist at virtually every level of government (see Figure 11.1). These organizations are usually committees made up of a number of active party members. State law and party rules prescribe how such

FIGURE 11.1

How American Parties Are Organized

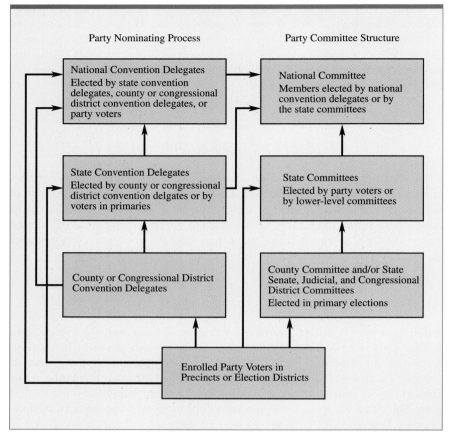

Party Nominating Process

National Convention Delegates
Elected by state convention delegates, county or congressional district convention delegates, or party voters

State Convention Delegates
Elected by county or congressional district convention delgates or by voters in primaries

County or Congressional District Convention Delegates

Party Committee Structure

National Committee
Members elected by national convention delegates or by the state committees

State Committees
Elected by party voters or by lower-level committees

County Committee and/or State Senate, Judicial, and Congressional District Committees
Elected in primary elections

Enrolled Party Voters in Precincts or Election Districts

committees are constituted. Usually, committee members are elected at local party meetings—called caucuses—or as part of the regular primary election. The best-known examples of these committees are at the national level—the Democratic National Committee and the Republican National Committee. Each of the two major parties also has a central committee in each state. The parties traditionally also have county committees and in some instances state senate district committees, judicial district committees, and in the case of larger cities city-wide party committees and local assembly district "ward" committees as well. Congressional districts also may have party committees.

Some cities also have precinct committees. Precincts are not districts from which any representative is elected but instead are legally defined subdivisions of wards that are used to register voters and set up ballot boxes or voting machines. They are typically composed of three hundred to six hundred voters. Well-organized political parties—especially the famous old machines of New York,

Chicago, and Boston—provided for "precinct captains" and a fairly tight group of

party members around them (see Box 11.2). Precinct captains were usually members of long standing in neighborhood party clubhouses, which were important social centers as well as places for distributing favors to constituents.[2] As the old machines declined, so did this level of party organization. Party organizations are now layerings of committees with overlapping boundaries and interlocking memberships. (The causes of party decline are discussed below.)

In this kind of a loosely jointed, multi-layered organization, a strong and centralized political party is exceptional. Nonetheless, many cities and counties and even a few states upon occasion have had such well-organized parties that they were called "machines" and their leaders were called "bosses." Some of the great reform movements in American history were motivated by the excessive powers and abuses of these machines and their bosses. But few, if any, machines are left today, and the current political challenge is strengthening weak parties rather than weakening strong ones.

BOX 11.2
Boss Rule in Chicago

During the 1950s and 1960s, Mayor Richard J. Daley was the absolute ruler of the city of Chicago. Politicians, judges, the police and fire departments, and municipal agencies all were subservient to the Daley "machine." The source of machine power was its control of county and municipal elections. Those who supported Daley's political opponents often found that such heresy could be dangerous. Consider the case of one supporter of Republican Benjamin Adamowski, who opposed Daley in the 1957 mayoral election:

> The owner of a small restaurant at Division and Ashland, the heart of the city's Polish neighborhood put up a big Adamowski sign. The day it went up the precinct captain came around and said, "How come the sign Harry?" "Ben's a friend of mine," the restaurant owner said. "Ben's a nice guy Harry, but that's a pretty big sign. I'd appreciate it if you'd take it down." "No, it's staying up."
>
> The next day the captain came back. "Look, I'm the precinct captain. Is there anything wrong, any problem, anything I can help you with?" Harry said no. "Then why don't you take it down. You know how this looks in my job." Harry wouldn't budge. The sign stayed up.
>
> On the third day, the city building inspectors came. The plumbing improvement alone cost Harry $2,100.

Source: Mike Royko, *Boss: Richard J. Daley of Chicago* (New York: E.P. Dutton, Inc., 1971). Copyright ©1971 by Mike Royko. Reprinted by permission of the publisher, E.P. Dutton, a division of Penguin Books, U.S.A. Inc.

---

[2]See Harold Gosnell, *Machine Politics* (Chicago: University of Chicago Press, 1968, rev. ed.).

THE TWO-PARTY SYSTEM
IN AMERICA

Although George Washington, and in fact, many statesmen of the time. deplored partisan politics, the two-party system emerged early in the history of the new Republic. Beginning with the Federalists and the Jeffersonian Republicans in the late 1780s, two major parties would continue to dominate national politics, although which particular two parties would change with the times and issues, culminating in today's Democrats and Republicans.

Historical Origins

Historically, parties form in one of two ways. The first, which could be called *internal mobilization,* occurs when political conflicts break out and government officials and competing factions seek to mobilize popular support. This is precisely what happened during the early years of the American Republic. Competition in the Congress between northeastern mercantile and southern agrarian factions led first the southerners and then the northeasterners to attempt to organize popular followings. The result was the foundation of America's first national parties—the Jeffersonians, whose primary base was in the South, and the Federalists, whose strength was greatest in the New England states.

The second common mode of party organization, which could be called *external mobilization,* takes place when a group of politicians outside the established governmental framework develop and organize popular support to win governmental power. For example, during the 1850s, a group of state politicians who opposed slavery, especially the expansion of slavery in America's territorial possessions, built what became the Republican party by constructing party organizations and mobilizing popular support in the Northeast and West.

America's two major parties are now, of course, the Democrats and Republicans. Each has had an important place in U.S. history.

The Democrats   When the Jeffersonian party splintered in 1824, Andrew Jackson emerged as the leader of one of its four factions. In 1830, Jackson's group became the Democratic party. This new party had the strongest national organization of its time and presented itself as the party of the common man. Jacksonians supported reduction in the price of public lands and a policy of cheaper money and credit. Laborers, immigrants, and settlers west of the Alleghenies were quickly attracted to it.

From 1828, when Jackson was elected president, to 1860, the Democratic party was the dominant force in American politics. For all but eight of those years, the Democrats held the White House. In addition, a Democratic majority controlled the Senate for twenty-six years and the House for twenty-four years during the same time period. Nineteenth-century Democrats emphasized the importance of

How the Party System Evolved

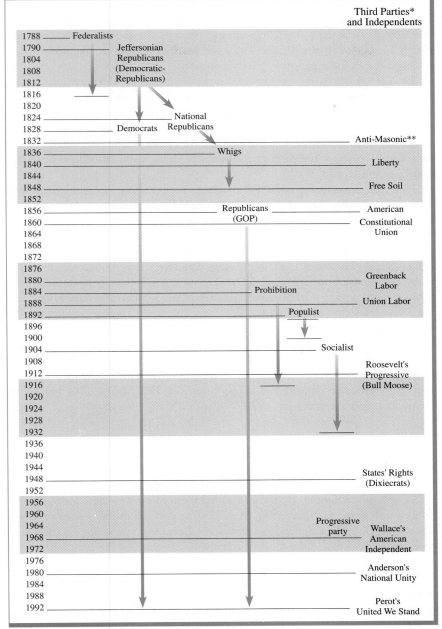

Third Parties*
and Independents

1788	Federalists	
1790	Jeffersonian	
1804	Republicans	
1808	(Democratic-	
1812	Republicans)	
1816		
1820		
1824		National
1828	Democrats	Republicans
1832			Anti-Masonic**
1836		Whigs
1840			Liberty
1844		
1848			Free Soil
1852		
1856	Republicans		American
1860	(GOP)		Constitutional
1864			Union
1868		
1872		
1876			Greenback
1880			Labor
1884	Prohibition	
1888			Union Labor
1892	Populist	
1896		
1900		
1904		Socialist
1908		
1912		Roosevelt's
1916		Progressive
		(Bull Moose)
1920		
1924		
1928		
1932		
1936		
1940		
1944		
1948		States' Rights
1952		(Dixiecrats)
1956		
1960		
1964	Progressive	
	party	Wallace's
1968		American
1972		Independent
1976		
1980		Anderson's
		National Unity
1984		
1988		Perot's
1992		United We Stand

*Or in some cases, fourth party; most of these are one-term parties.
**The Anti-Masonics not only had the distinction of being the first third party, but it was also the first party to hold a national nominating convention and the first to announce a party platform.

interpreting the Constitution literally, upholding states' rights, and limiting federal spending.

In 1860, the issue of slavery split the Democrats along geographic lines. In the South, many Democrats served in the Confederate government. In the North, one faction of the party (the Copperheads) opposed the war and advocated negotiating a peace with the South. Thus, for years after the war, Republicans denounced the Democrats as the "party of treason."

The Democratic party was not fully able to regain its political strength until the Great Depression. In 1932, Democrat Franklin D. Roosevelt entered the White House. Subsequently, the Democrats won control of Congress as well. Roosevelt's New Deal coalition, composed of Catholics, Jews, blacks, farmers, intellectuals, and members of organized labor, dominated American politics until the 1970s and served as the basis for the party's expansion of federal power and efforts to remedy social problems.

The Democrats were never fully united. In Congress, southern Democrats often aligned with Republicans in the so-called "conservative coalition" rather than with members of their own party. But the Democratic party remained America's majority party, usually controlling both Congress and the White House, for nearly four decades after 1932. By the 1980s, the Democratic coalition faced serious problems. The once Solid South often voted for the Republicans, along with many blue-collar northern voters. On the other hand, the Democrats increased their strength among African American voters and women. At the present time, the Democrats continue to be the dominant force in Congress, even while the Republicans had an edge in presidential races. The Democrats also have a strong base in the bureaucracies of the federal government and the states, in labor unions, and in the not-for-profit sector of the economy. During the 1980s and 1990s, moderate Democrats were able to take control of the party nominating process and sought to broaden middle-class support for the Democrats. This helped the Democrats elect a president in 1992.

The Republicans   The 1854 Kansas-Nebraska Act overturned the Missouri Compromise of 1820 and the Compromise of 1850, which had barred the expansion of slavery in the American territories. The Kansas-Nebraska Act gave each territory the right to decide whether or not to permit slavery. Opposition to this policy galvanized antislavery groups and led them to create a new party, the Republicans. It drew its membership from existing political groups—former Whigs, Know-Nothings, Free Soilers, and antislavery Democrats. In 1856, the party's first presidential candidate, John C. Fremont, won one-third of the popular vote and carried eleven states.

The early Republican platforms appealed to commercial as well as antislavery interests. The Republicans favored homesteading, internal improvements, the construction of a transcontinental railroad, and protective tariffs, as well as the containment of slavery. In 1858, the Republican party won control of the House; in 1860, the Republican presidential candidate, Abraham Lincoln, was victorious.

For almost seventy-five years after the North's victory in the Civil War, the Republicans were America's dominant political party. Between 1860 and 1932, Republicans occupied the White House for fifty-six years, controlled the Senate for sixty years, and the House for fifty. During these years, the Republicans came to be closely associated with big business. The party of Lincoln became the party of Wall Street.

The Great Depression, however, ended Republican hegemony. The voters held Republican President Herbert Hoover responsible for the economic catastrophe, and by 1936, the party's popularity was so low that Republicans won only eighty-nine seats in the House and seventeen in the Senate. The Republican presidential candidate, Governor Alfred M. Landon of Kansas, carried only two states. The Republicans won only four presidential elections between 1932 and 1980, and they controlled Congress for only four of those years (1947–1949 and 1953–1955).

The party has widened its appeal over the last four decades. Groups previously associated with the Democratic party—particularly blue-collar workers and southern Democrats—have been increasingly attracted to Republican presidential candidates (for example, Dwight D. Eisenhower, Richard Nixon, Ronald Reagan, and George Bush). Yet, Republicans generally have not done as well at the state and local levels and have had little chance of capturing a majority in either the House or Senate. The Watergate scandal of the Nixon administration was a setback in the party's efforts to increase its political power. In 1980, under the leadership of Ronald Reagan, the Republicans began to mount a new bid to become the nation's majority party, but the Iran-Contra scandal damaged Reagan's popularity. Reagan's successor, George Bush, was voted out of office in 1992, mainly in response to voters' concerns about the economy.

Similarities and Differences Today

One of the most familiar observations about American politics is that the two major parties try to be all things to all people and are therefore indistinguishable from each other. Data and experience give some support to this observation. Even in the late 1960s, when American society was unusually polarized, Democratic and Republican candidates stood for some of the same things. The wide range of interests within the Democratic party today can be represented by liberals such as Mario Cuomo and Tom Harkin, and by conservatives such as Howell Heflin. The 1992 Democratic presidential ticket consisted of two moderates, Bill Clinton and Al Gore, who appealed successfully for the votes of many conservative Democrats and moderate Republicans. A similar spectrum exists within the Republican party, as represented by such liberals as Mark Hatfield and conservatives like Newt Gingrich, although in the Reagan years, liberal Republicans became something of an endangered species.

Parties in the United States are not programmatic or ideological, as they have sometimes been in England or other parts of Europe. But this does not mean there are no differences between them. During the Reagan era, important differences emerged between the positions of Democratic and Republican party leaders on a number of key issues, and these differences are still apparent today. For example,

Comparing the 1992 Republican and Democratic Platforms: Close on Economics, Distant on Social Issues

Political cynics often criticize America's political parties by saying that "there's not a dime's worth of difference between them." If this claim is true, it lends fuel to the fires of critics who say that the political parties have failed in their purpose of offering the voters a real choice. While there are indeed similarities, an examination of the party platforms from the 1992 presidential election reveals a few differences.

Both parties focused much attention on the role of government and economic issues. The Republican platform claimed proudly that it "cut taxes, reduced red tape, put people above bureaucracy. And . . . we vanquished the idea of the almighty state as the supervisor of our daily lives." While the Democratic platform took a similar anti-government stand, it noted the "anguish and the anger of the American people . . . directed . . . at Government itself," and it called for "a revolution in Government—to take power away from entrenched bureaucracies and narrow interests in Washington and put it back in the hands of ordinary people."

Both parties emphasized the need to create jobs. The Republicans stressed promoting economic growth to expand job opportunities. The Democrats took a similar tack by urging job creation in both the private and the public sector. Both parties addressed the problem of the federal budget deficit; the Republicans emphasized tax cuts to stimulate economic growth, while the Democrats stressed cuts in government spending levels.

The parties echoed similar themes on another spending issue—welfare. The Repub-

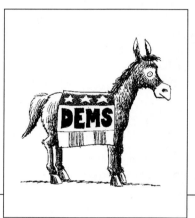

the national leadership of the Republican party supports maintaining high levels of military spending, cuts in social programs, tax relief for middle- and upper-income voters, tax incentives to business, and the "social agenda" backed by members of conservative religious denominations. The national Democratic leadership, on the other hand, supports expanded social welfare spending, cuts in military spending, increased regulations of business, and a variety of consumer and environmental programs. In 1990, most Republicans supported President Bush's policies in the Persian Gulf, while most Democrats opposed the use of American military force against Iraq—at least until the president's policies succeeded.

These differences reflect differences in philosophy as well as differences in the core constituencies to which the parties seek to appeal. The Democratic party at the national level seeks to unite organized labor, the poor, members of racial minorities, and liberal upper-middle-class professionals. The Republicans, by con-

licans claimed, "Today's welfare system is anti-work and anti-marriage." Departing from past platforms, the Democrats also adopted a strict tone: "Welfare should be a second chance, not a way of life. We want to break the cycle of welfare."

The greatest differences between the party platforms appeared in the realm of social issues. For example, the Republicans advocated a constitutional amendment prohibiting abortion under all circumstances, even including instances in which the life of the woman is at stake. (President Bush himself continued to favor abortion in such cases and in cases of rape or incest.) The Republican platform also opposed gay rights and birth control counseling; it favored school prayer, the construction of a barrier along the country's southern border to keep illegal immigrants out, and tuition tax credits for parents wishing to send their children to private and parochial schools.

In contrast, the Democrats supported abortion rights, including the enactment of protective national legislation. In addition, the platform also supported an end to the military's ban on gay soldiers and expanded health care and family planning efforts.

On the environment, the Republican platform emphasized development by saying, "Our public lands should not be arbitrarily locked up and put off limits to re-

sponsible uses." The Democratic platform emphasized conservation: "We will protect our old-growth forests, preserve critical habitats . . . wetlands . . . soil, water, air, oppose new offshore oil drilling and mineral exploration." The Democrats expressed similar concerns about global warming, ozone depletion in the air, and biodiversity.

While parties seemed to lean in the same more conservative direction in 1992, both still sought to emphasize their differences in order to woo voters.

trast, appeal to business, upper and upper-middle-income groups in the private sector, and social conservatives.

American Third Parties

Although the United States is said to possess a two-party system, we have always had more than two parties. Typically, third parties in the United States have represented social and economic protests that, for one or another reason, were not given voice by the two major parties.[3] Such parties have had a good deal of influ-

---

[3]For a discussion of third parties in the United States, see Daniel Mazmanian, *Third Parties in Presidential Election* (Washington, DC: Brookings Institution, 1974).

ence on ideas and elections in the United States. The Populists, a party centered in the rural areas of the West and Midwest, and the Progressives, spokesmen for the urban middle classes in the late nineteenth and early twentieth centuries, are the most important examples in the past hundred years. More recent examples include New York's American Labor party, Liberal party, and Conservative party. The Farmer-Labor party has occasionally dominated the politics of the state of Minnesota. The segregationist Dixiecratic party made an important challenge in national politics in 1948, and its descendant, Alabama Governor George Wallace's American Independent party, made a challenge in the late 1960s. This challenge ended when Wallace was shot and seriously wounded during the 1972 campaign. Illinois Congressman John Anderson's National Unity party polled several million voters in 1980 but quickly disappeared from the political scene. In 1992, Ross Perot, running as an independent, impressed voters with his folksy style in the presidential debates and garnered almost 19 percent of the votes cast in the presidential election. Other parties, such as the Socialists, have influenced political ideas even when they have had no chance of winning elections.

Table 11.1 is a listing of all the parties that offered candidates in one or more states in 1992 as well as independent candidates who ran. With the exception of Ross Perot, the third party and independent candidates together polled hardly more than one million votes. They gained no electoral votes for president, and most of them disappeared immediately after the presidential election.

Table 11.1 demonstrates the large number of third parties running candidates and appealing to voters. Although the Republican party was only the third party ever to make itself permanent (by replacing the Whigs), the others enjoyed an influence far beyond their electoral size. This was because large parts of their programs were adopted by one or both of the major parties, who sought to appeal to the voters mobilized by the new party, and so to expand their own electoral strength. The Democratic party, for example, became a great deal more liberal when it adopted most of the Progressive program early in the twentieth century. Many Socialists felt that President Roosevelt's New Deal had adopted most of their party's program, including old-age pensions, unemployment compensation, an agricultural marketing program, and laws guaranteeing workers the right to organize into unions.

This kind of third party influence explains their short lives. Their causes are usually eliminated by the ability of the major parties to absorb their programs and to draw their supporters into the mainstream. There are, of course, additional reasons for the short duration of most third parties. One is the usual limitation of their electoral support to one or two regions. Populist support, for example, was primarily midwestern. The 1948 Progressive party, with Henry Wallace as its candidate, polled nearly half its votes in the single state of New York. The American Independent party polled nearly 10 million popular votes and 45 electoral votes for George Wallace in 1968—the most electoral votes ever polled by a third-party candidate. But all of Wallace's electoral votes and the majority of his popular vote came from the Deep South states.

Americans usually assume that only the candidates nominated by one of the two major parties have any chance of winning an election. Thus, a vote cast for a third-party or independent candidate is often seen as a wasted vote. Voters who would prefer a third-party candidate may feel compelled to vote for the major-

TABLE 11.1
Parties and Candidates in 1992

In the 1992 presidential election, in addition to the Democratic and Republican nominees, twenty-one candidates appeared on the ballot in one or more states. Ross Perot came the closest to challenging the major-party candidates with nearly 19 percent of the popular vote. The remaining twenty candidates shared .79 percent of the votes cast with numerous write–ins. Many voters in 1992 told pollsters that they preferred "none of the above." However, in Nevada, where voters had an opportunity to mark this choice on their ballots, few actually did.

Candidate	Party	Vote Total	% Of Vote
Bill Clinton	Democrat	44,908,233	42.95%
George Bush	Republican	39,102,282	37.40
Ross Perot	Independent	19,721,433	18.86
Andre Marrou	Libertarian	291,612	0.28
James "Bo" Gritz	Populist/Am. First	98,918	0.09
Lenora Fulani	New Alliance	73,248	0.07
Howard Phillips	U.S. Taxpayers	42,960	0.04
John Hagelin	Natural Law	37,137	0.03
Ron Daniels	Independent	27,396	0.02
Lyndon LaRouche	Independent	25,863	0.02
James Mac Warren	Socialist Workers	22,883	0.00
Drew Bradford	Independent	4,749	0.00
Jack Herer	Grass roots	3,875	0.00
Helen Halyard	Workers League	3,050	0.00
John Quinn Brisben	Socialist	2,909	0.00
John Yiamouyiannis	Independent	2,199	0.00
Delbert Ehlers	Independent	1,149	0.00
Jim Boren	Apathy	956	0.00
Earl Dodge	Prohibition	935	0.00
Eugene Hem	Third Party	405	0.00
Isabelle Masters	Looking Back Group	327	0.00
Robert J. Smith	American	292	0.00
Gloria Estella La Riva	Workers World	181	0.00
Write-in		177,207	0.17
None of the above	Nevada	2,537	0.00
TOTAL		104,552,736	100.0%

Source: *Washington Post*, 18 January 1993.

party candidate whom they regard as the "lesser of two evils," to avoid wasting their vote in a futile gesture. Third-party candidates must struggle—usually without success—to overcome the perception that they cannot win. Thus, in 1992, many voters who favored Ross Perot gave their votes to George Bush or Bill Clinton on the presumption that Perot was not really electable.

As many scholars have pointed out, third-party prospects are also hampered by America's single-member-district plurality election system. In many other nations, several individuals can be elected to represent each legislative district. This is called a system of multimember districts. With this type of system, the candidates of

George Wallace
Courting Black Voters

George Wallace (b. 1919)

Born a farmer's son, George Corley Wallace exhibited drive and ambition from an early age in his pursuit of an education. He earned his way through college and law school by working odd jobs and boxing professionally. After service in the army in World War II, Wallace served as an assistant attorney general in 1946. The following year, he was elected to the state legislature at the age of twenty-eight. In 1958, he ran for Alabama governor, but he lost to an opponent who (in Wallace's words) "out-segged" him; that is, appeared to the electorate to be more strongly segregationist than Wallace. Wallace vowed this would not happen again, and four years later he was elected on a segregationist-economy platform. In his inaugural address, he proclaimed: "I say segregation now, segregation tomorrow, segregation forever!"

Wallace took his campaign nationwide, testing the presidential campaign waters in 1964. To everyone's surprise, he won more than a third of the votes cast in three northern state primaries. Four years later, Wallace mounted the most successful presidential third-party challenge since the 1920s. His American Independent party advocated tough treatment of criminals, election of federal judges, and an end to such programs as the open housing provision of the 1968 Civil Rights Act. In the fall campaign, Wallace received over 9.9 million votes, carrying forty-six electoral votes of five southern states. Four years later, Wallace was campaigning vigorously for the Democratic presidential nomination when he was struck down by an assassin's bullet, leaving him paralyzed from the waist down. Yet despite his paralysis, Wallace continued to campaign and govern from his wheelchair.

Despite the efforts of Wallace and others, blacks in the South began to accumulate political influence. The percentage of southern blacks who could now register and vote began to soar, and southern politicians who had run for office successfully on segregationist platforms in previous years found an increasingly hostile electorate.

Shrewd politician that he was, Wallace, too, could read the handwriting on the wall. In his 1982 gubernatorial bid, he openly courted the state's now large black vote. He apologized openly and repeatedly for his past, and he argued that, as a prominent national figure, he was the candidate best able to bring jobs and economic prosperity to the ailing Alabama economy. Wallace's apology for his segregationist past met with more than a little skepticism, but his economic appeal cut across racial lines since any jobs brought into the state would have to be open to whites and blacks, as job discrimination based on race was now illegal. Wallace was elected with the key help of nearly half of Alabama's black voters.

Source: Marshall Frady, *Wallace* (New York: New World Publishing Co., 1968).

weaker parties have a better chance of winning at least some seats. For their part,
voters are less concerned about wasting ballots and usually more willing to support
minor-party candidates.

Reinforcing the effects of the single-member district, plurality voting rules (as was noted in Chapter 10) generally have the effect of setting what could be called a high threshold for victory. To win a plurality race, candidates usually must secure many more votes than they would need under most European systems of proportional representation. For example, to win an American plurality election in a single-member district where there are only two candidates, a politician must win more than 50 percent of the votes cast. To win a seat from a European multimember district under proportional rules, a candidate may need to win only 15 or 20 percent of the votes cast. This high American threshold discourages minor parties and encourages the various political factions that might otherwise form minor parties to minimize their differences and remain within the major-party coalitions.[4]

It would, nevertheless, be incorrect to assert (as some scholars have maintained) that America's single-member plurality election system is the major cause of our historical two-party pattern. All that can be said is that American election law depresses the number of parties likely to survive over long periods of time in the United States. There is nothing magical about two. Indeed, the single-member plurality system of election can also discourage second parties. After all, if one party consistently receives a large plurality of the vote, people may eventually come to see their vote *even for the second party* as a wasted effort. This is partly what happened to the Republican party in the Deep South before World War II.

FUNCTIONS OF THE PARTIES

Parties perform a wide variety of functions. They are mainly involved in nominations and elections—providing the candidates for office, getting out the vote, and facilitating mass electoral choice. They also influence the institutions of government—providing the leadership and organization of the various congressional committees.

Nominations and Elections

Article I, Section 4, of the Constitution makes only a few provisions for elections. It delegates to the states the power to set the "times, places, and manner" of holding elections, even for U.S. senators and representatives. It does, however, reserve to Congress the power to make such laws if it chooses to do so. The Constitution has been amended from time to time to expand the right to participate in elections. Congress has also occasionally passed laws about elections, congressional districting, and campaign practices. But the Constitution and the laws are almost completely silent on nominations, setting only citizenship and age requirements

[4]See Maurice Duverger, *Political Parties* (New York: Wiley, 1954).

for candidates. The president must be at least thirty-five years of age, a natural-born citizen, and have been a resident of the United States for fourteen years. A senator must be at least thirty years of age, a U.S. citizen for at least nine years, and a resident of the state he or she represents. A member of the House must be at least twenty-five, a U.S. citizen for seven years, and a resident of the state he or she represents.

Nomination means selecting a single party candidate to run for each elective office. The nominating process can precede the election by many months, as it does when the many candidates for the presidency are eliminated from consideration through a grueling series of debates and state primaries until there is only one survivor in each party—the party's nominee.

Nomination is the parties' most serious and difficult business. When more than one person aspires to an office, the choice can divide friends and associates. In comparison to such an internal dispute, the electoral campaign against the opposition is almost fun, because there the fight is against the declared adversaries. In the course of American political history, the parties have used three modes of nomination—the caucus, the convention, and the primary election (see Process Box 11.2).

PROCESS BOX 11.2

Types of Nominating Processes

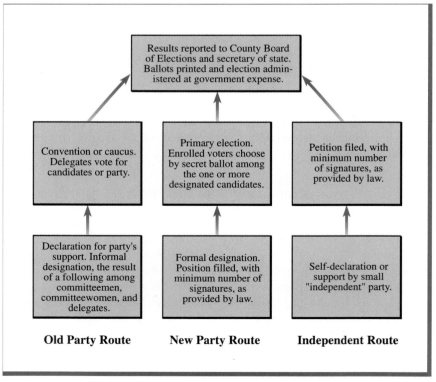

The Caucus   In the eighteenth and early nineteenth centuries, nominations were
informal, without rules or regulations. Local party leaders would simply gather all
the party activists, and they would agree on the person, usually from among themselves, who would be the candidate. The meetings where candidates were nominated were generally called *caucuses.* Informal nomination by caucus sufficed for
the parties until widespread complaints were made about cliques of local leaders or
state legislators dominating all the nominations and leaving no place for the other
party members who wanted to participate. Beginning in the 1830s, nominating
conventions were proposed as a reform that would enable the mass membership of
a party to express its will.

Nomination by Convention   A nominating convention is a formal caucus bound
by a number of rules that govern participation and nominating procedures. Conventions are meetings of delegates elected by party members from the relevant
county (county convention) or state (state convention). Delegates to each party's
national convention (which nominates the party's presidential candidate) are chosen by party members on a state by state basis, for there is no single national delegate selection process.

Historically, the great significance of the convention mode of nomination was
its effect on the presidential selection process and on the presidency itself. For
more than fifty years after America's founding, the nomination of presidential candidates was dominated by congressional caucuses, meetings of each party's congressional delegations which critics called "King Caucus." In the early 1830s,
when the major parties adopted the national nominating convention, they broke
the power of King Caucus. This helped to give the presidency a mass popular base
(see Chapter 6). Nevertheless, reformers of the early twentieth century regarded
nominating conventions as instruments of "boss rule." They proposed replacing
conventions with primaries, which provide for direct choice by the voters at an
election some weeks or months before the general election.

Nomination by Primary Election   In primary elections, party members select the
party's nominees directly rather than selecting convention delegates who then select the nominees. Primaries are far from perfect replacements for conventions,
since it is rare that more than 25 percent of the enrolled voters participate in them.
Nevertheless, they are replacing conventions as the dominant method of nomination.[5] At the present time, only a small number of states, including Connecticut,
Delaware, and Utah, provide for state conventions to nominate candidates for
statewide offices, and even these states combine them with primaries whenever a
substantial minority of delegates vote for one of the defeated aspirants.

Primary elections are of two types—closed and open. In a *closed primary,* participation is limited to individuals who have declared their affiliation by registering
with the party. In an *open primary,* individuals declare their party affiliation on the
actual day of the primary election. To do so, they simply go to the polling place

---

[5]For a discussion of some of the effects of primary elections see Peter F. Galderisi and Benjamin Ginsberg, "Primary Elections and the Evanescence of Third Party Activity in the United States," in *Do Elections Matter?,* ed. Benjamin Ginsberg and Alan Stone (Armonk, NY: M. E. Sharpe Publishers, 1986),
pp. 115–30.

Historically, the United States has remained a two-party system. Occasionally, however, a third-party candidate appears who captures the imagination of a significant segment of the voting population. Eugene V. Debs, a founder of the Socialist Party of America, polled an astonishing 6 percent (over 900,000) of the vote in his 1912 presidential bid, a reflection more of the need for reform in America than evidence of socialism's spread. Accused of encouraging resistance to the draft, the charismatic Debs ran his 1920 presidential campaign from prison, accumulating a remarkable 920,000 votes.

Occasionally a third-party candidate emerges who does not represent a disenfranchised constituency but arises out of a power struggle within a party. Republican Theodore Roosevelt, who became president in 1901 at the death of William McKinley, was elected to office with an impressive popular margin in 1904. Roosevelt ran on the Bull Moose ticket in 1912 against his chosen successor, Republican President William Howard Taft. Roosevelt and Taft split the Republican vote, allowing Democrat Woodrow Wilson to win the election.

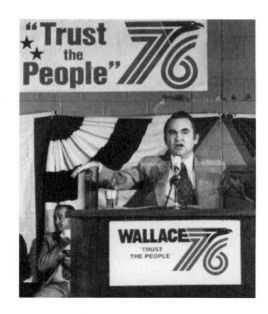

George Wallace, governor of Alabama, running on the American Independent party ticket, won 10 million votes, 13.5 percent of the total votes cast, in his 1968 bid for the presidency. Carrying the Deep South with his reputation as a pro-segregationist, he also appealed to conservative voters, with their growing fears of youthful unrest, the rise of militant leaders in the civil rights movement, and the growth of both the welfare system and the federal government.

When John Anderson ran as an independent in the 1980 election against Jimmy Carter and Ronald Reagan, both Republicans and Democrats feared that Anderson would draw votes from their candidate and help the other side. Ultimately, Anderson's candidacy did not affect the outcome of the election.

By pledging to "end politics as usual," independent candidate H. Ross Perot made an impressive showing in the 1992 election—the strongest of any third-party candidate in the nation's history. He gathered nearly 19 percent of the popular vote but failed to win any electoral college votes. Perot's success was due to the public's increasing frustration with the government's failure to seriously address the nation's deficit and troubled economy and their alienation from the established parties' often polarized political and social agendas.

and ask for the ballot of a particular party. The open primary allows each voter an opportunity to consider candidates and issues before deciding whether to participate and in which party's contest to participate. Open primaries, therefore, are less conducive to strong political parties. But in either case, primaries are more open than conventions or caucuses to new issues and new types of candidates.

Independent Candidates   The several types of nominating processes and the provisions for each are summarized by Process Box 11.2. This figure indicates that the convention and primary methods are not the only ways that candidates can get on the ballot. State laws extend the right of independent candidacy to individuals who do not wish to be nominated by political parties or who are unable to secure a party nomination.

Although nomination by a political party is complicated, the independent route to the ballot is even more difficult. Table 11.2 shows some of the special difficulties of getting on the ballot as an independent candidate in New York State. For almost all offices in all states, the law requires more signatures for independent nomination than for party designation. For example, the candidate for a party's nomination to Congress in New York must get 1,250 valid signatures within the congressional district, while the independent candidate must get 3,500 signatures.

Contested Nominations   Even though state laws favor party nomination, the task of the parties is not an easy one. Party organizations have grown weaker over the years, and the number of contested primaries—primaries where two or more designated candidates compete for the party's nomination—has increased. At the same time, the ability of the "regular" party leaders to win in such primaries has

TABLE 11.2
Getting on the Ballot in New York State

Office Sought	Number of Signatures Required for Nominating Petitions	
	Party Designation	*Independent Nomination*
Governorship or other statewide office	20,000 or 5% of enrolled voters of party, whichever is less	20,000 or 5% of registered voters, whichever is less
Mayoralty of large city*	2,000	5% of last election vote for governor in city
County office*	1,500	1,500
City council	500	1,500
Congress	1,250	3,500
State senate	1,000	3,000
State assembly	500	1,500

*Outside the city of New York. For New York City, 5,000 signatures are required.
Source: New York State Political Calendar, 1988–1989 (Albany, NY: Fort Orange Press, Inc.). Adapted by permission.

diminished. Regardless of who wins, a contested nomination is costly. Money that is spent on campaigning in the primaries is no longer available to spend in the general election against the opponent nominated by the other party. Moreover, contested primaries can be particularly bitter and the feud long-lasting because they are between members of the same party, who often consider opposition a personal affront.

But although contested nominations deplete party resources and interfere with party campaign strategy, they can be a sign of healthy politics because they expose parties to new or underrepresented interests. Indeed, parties have often been a channel for resolving important social conflicts. Contested nominations, especially contested primaries, can speed the resolution of such conflicts. Civil rights became a national issue in 1948 through a struggle within the Democratic party over the antidiscrimination commitment in its platform. In 1968, the Vietnam War was debated more by Democratic President Lyndon Johnson and antiwar Democratic Senator Eugene McCarthy than by Hubert Humphrey (who ultimately became the Demo-cratic presidential candidate) and Republican Richard Nixon. Any number of important local political issues have been resolved between candidates fighting each other for the nomination for mayor or district attorney or governor.

Many important advances in the participation of ethnic and racial minorities have begun through victories in local primaries. Party leaders once considered the nominating process to be their own personal property. In fact, the Democratic party in many southern states adopted rules excluding nonwhites from the primaries, on the grounds that political parties were the equivalent of private clubs (see Box 11.3). The Supreme Court did not invalidate all of these "white primaries" until 1944, when it held that primaries were an integral part of the electoral system and could not be left to private control.[6] The Court was recognizing a fact universally accepted well before 1944—that the nominating process is the first stage of the electoral process.

The Role of the Parties in Getting Out the Vote

The actual election period begins immediately after the nominations. Historically, this has been a time of glory for the political parties, whose popular base of support is fully displayed. All the paraphernalia of party committees and all the committee members are activated into local party work forces.

The first step in the electoral process involves voter registration. This aspect of the process takes place all year round. There was a time when party workers were responsible for virtually all of this kind of electoral activity, but they have been supplemented (and in many states virtually displaced) by civic groups such as the League of Women Voters, unions, and chambers of commerce.

Those who have registered have to decide on election day whether to go to the polling place, stand in line, and actually vote for the various candidates and referenda on the ballot. Political parties, candidates, and campaigning can make a big difference in convincing the voters to vote.

[6]Smith v. Allwright, 321 U.S. 649 (1944).

BOX 11.3
The White Primary in Texas

The Fifteenth Amendment provides that the right of American citizens to vote "shall not be denied or abridged by the United States or by any State on account of race, color, or previous condition of servitude." But during the decades following the amendment's ratification in 1870, southern states employed a variety of exclusionary devices such as literacy tests, poll taxes, and complicated registration laws to disenfranchise blacks. The "white primary" proved to be a particularly effective scheme for circumventing the Fifteenth Amendment because the South was virtually a one-party system. If black citizens could be precluded from participating in primary elections, they would be removed from electoral participation altogether since the Democratic nominee in the primary was all but assured of victory in the general election.

Texas's use of the white primary offers an illustrative case history. The Texas state legislature first attempted to disenfranchise blacks in the most blatant manner by enacting a law in 1923 that stated, ". . . in no event shall a negro be eligible to participate in a Democratic Party primary election held in the State of Texas and should a negro vote in a Democratic primary election such ballot shall be void and election officials are herein directed to throw out such ballot and not count the same."

State legislators soon realized, however, that their law was clearly unconstitutional under the Fifteenth Amendment. So four years later, the state legislature enacted a new law that seemed to remove the state of Texas from *direct* involvement in denying blacks the right to vote in primary elections. The 1927 law allowed the Executive Committee of the Democratic Party to prescribe the qualifications of party members "and shall in its own way determine who shall be qualified to vote or otherwise participate in such political party. . . ." To no one's surprise, the Texas Democratic party issued a resolution later that year declaring that "all white Democrats . . . and none other" would be permitted to vote in primary elections. Attorneys for Texas argued that the 1927 law was constitutional on the grounds that it was the Democratic party—a *private* organization—that had established voting requirements that barred blacks from voting, and not the state of Texas; since the Fifteenth Amendment was only explicitly directed at the federal and state governments, the Texas attorneys concluded that the law passed constitutional muster.

The NAACP, led by a young, aggressive lawyer named Thurgood Marshall, mounted a long litigation effort to expose the latent "state action" that legitimated the Democratic party's exclusion of black voters and that proved the unconstitutionality of the Texas law. In 1944, the U.S. Supreme Court decided in the case of *Smith* v. *Allwright* that Marshall and the NAACP were right. The court found that by enacting a law that allowed the Democratic party to prescribe voter requirements, the Texas legislature had transformed the Democratic party into "an agency of the state," which was then bound by the Fifteenth Amendment.

Source: Darlene Clark Hine, *Black Victory: The Rise and Fall of the White Primary in Texas* (Millwood, NY: KTO Press, 1979).

On any general election ballot, there are likely to be only two or three candidacies where the nature of the office and the characteristics and positions of the candidates are well known to voters. But what about the choices for judges, the state comptroller, the state attorney general, and many other elective positions? And what about referenda? This method of making policy choices is being used more and more as a means of direct democracy. A referendum may ask: Should there be a new bond issue for financing the local schools? Should there be a constitutional amendment to increase the number of county judges? The famous "Proposition 13" on the 1978 California ballot was a referendum to reduce local property taxes. It started a taxpayer revolt that spread to many other states. By the time it had spread, most voters knew where they stood on the issue. But the typical referendum question is one on which few voters have clear and knowledgeable positions. Parties and campaigns help most by giving information when voters must choose among obscure candidates and vote on unclear referenda.

The Parties' Influence on National Government

The ultimate test of the party system is its relationship to and influence on the institutions of government. Thus, it is important to examine the party system in relation to Congress and the president.

The Parties and Congress   Congress, in particular, depends more on the party system than is generally recognized. First, the speakership of the House is a party office. All the members of the House take part in the election of the Speaker. But the actual selection is made by the majority party. When the majority party caucus presents a nominee to the entire House, its choice is then invariably ratified in a straight party vote.

The committee system of both houses of Congress is also a product of the two-party system. Although the rules organizing committees and the rules defining the jurisdiction of each are adopted like ordinary legislation by the whole membership, all other features of the committees are shaped by parties. For example, each party is assigned a quota of members for each committee, depending upon the percentage of total seats held by the party. On the rare occasions when an independent or third-party candidate is elected, the leaders of the two parties must agree on whose quota this member's committee assignments will count against. Presumably the member will not be able to serve on any committee until the question of quota is settled.

As we saw previously in Chapter 5, the assignment of individual members to committees is a party decision. Each party has a "committee on committees" to make such decisions. Permission to transfer from one committee to another is also a party decision. Moreover, advancement up the committee ladder toward the chair is a party decision. Since the late nineteenth century, most advancements have been automatic—based upon the length of continual service on the committee. This seniority system has existed only because of the support of the two parties, and each party can depart from it by a simple vote. During the 1970s, both parties reinstituted the practice of reviewing each chairmanship—voting anew every two years on whether each chair would be continued. Few chairs actually have been removed, but notice has been served that the seniority system is no longer automatic and has thereby reminded everyone that all committee assignments are party decisions. Thus, although party leaders no longer can control the votes of many members, the party system itself remains an important factor.

The continuing importance of parties in Congress became especially evident during the first months of the Clinton administration in 1993. Congressional Democrats gave Clinton's economic proposals virtually unanimous support (see Chapter 5). The Democratic leadership was eager to contribute to a successful start by the first Democratic president in twelve years. Democratic unity, in turn, prompted an unprecedented display of partisan unity among Republican members of Congress as well. In April 1993, Senate Republicans responded to what they saw as Democratic "steamroller" tactics by staging a filibuster against Clinton's proposed economic stimulus package.

By remaining united, the forty-three Republican senators (joined by one Democrat) prevented the Senate from voting on the Clinton proposal and ended any chance of its enactment. With the Republicans united, a Democratic effort to end the filibuster could muster only fifty-six of the sixty votes needed for cloture. Republicans were concerned less with the substance of Clinton's spending proposal (though they did regard it as unnecessary and wasteful) than with their own isolation and weakness in the face of growing Democratic strength and confidence.[7] They hoped that by blocking this Clinton initiative they could demonstrate that they were a force with which the president would have to reckon.[8]

The high levels of congressional party unity achieved during this early period would have to be sustained in the face of constituency, interest group, and ideological pressures that often cut across party lines and oblige members of Congress to ignore their leaders' wishes. As a result, it was not surprising to see party unity weaken as the year went on. The Democrats were first to crumble. In the June 1993 vote on Clinton's economic program, more than thirty House Democrats, including eleven subcommittee chairs, deserted their party to vote with the Republicans. Giving the forces working against party unity in Congress, it is sometimes surprising when either party retains any cohesion at all.

The Parties and Election of the President: The Electoral College   The Constitution is silent on the selection of qualified candidates for president. The framers probably assumed that there would be a "favorite son" from each of several states and that the qualifications of each would be well known to at least some of the more prominent and well-traveled people elsewhere. In November every four years, the voters—who would vote only for electors, not directly for president—would presumably choose as electors these prominent and well-traveled people, who would exercise proper collective judgment in their choice of the best person for president. This is why the electors as a group came to be called the electoral college, although the Constitution does not use the term and the electors never meet nationwide as a group.

[7]Adam Clymer, "Republican Redux: Filibustering in Senate, G.O.P. Strives to Make Itself a Force to Deal With," *New York Times,* 5 April 1993, p. A14.

[8]David Broder, "Unity 'Doormat' Trips Democrats: Hill Republicans Turn Democrats' Hardball Tactics Into Rallying Point," *Washington Post,* 3 April 1993, p. 1.

The Twelfth Amendment provided that the electors would meet in their respective states following their election in November and that they would cast separate ballots for president and vice-president. The name of each person receiving
an electoral vote for president would be put on a list that would show the number
of electoral votes cast for each. The lists would be sent to the Senate to be counted
in a joint session of Congress. If no candidate received a majority of all electoral
votes, the names of the top three candidates would be submitted to the House,
where each state would be able to cast one vote, regardless of size. Whether a
state's vote would be decided by a majority, plurality, or some other fraction of the
state's delegates would be determined under rules established by the House. Thus,
the general election was to be a nominating process, and the real election was to
take place every four years in the House.

The last time the electoral college failed to produce a majority was in 1824,
when four candidates, John Quincy Adams, Andrew Jackson, Henry Clay, and
William H. Crawford, divided the electoral vote. The House of Representatives
eventually chose Adams over the others. After 1824, however, the two major political parties had begun to dominate presidential politics to such an extent that by
December of each election year only two candidates remained for the electors to
choose between. This freed the parties and the candidates from having to plan
their campaigns to culminate in Congress, and Congress very quickly ceased to
dominate the presidential selection process. Until the 1830s, the most important
candidates for president were nominated by caucuses of members of Congress.
But once the two major parties had practically eliminated the House's role in the
final selection of candidates, they created a means outside Congress altogether for
making the initial nominations. That means was the national convention, which
has given the president a popular base independent of Congress. Although the parties themselves have been weakened by the provisions in forty-seven states for
selecting convention delegates by primaries, the two-party system still keeps Congress out of the selection process and keeps the presidency independent of Congress.

Though it has not functioned as the framers anticipated, the electoral college
continues to be a part of the American presidential selection process. When Americans go to the polls on election day, they are technically not voting directly for
presidential candidates. Instead, voters within each state are choosing among slates
of electors selected by each state's party leadership and pledged, if elected, to support that party's presidential candidate. In each state, the slate that wins casts all the
state's electoral votes for its party's candidate. Each state is entitled to a number of
electoral votes equal to the number of the state's senators and representatives combined, for a total of 535 electoral votes for the fifty states. Occasionally, an elector
breaks his or her pledge and votes for the other party's candidate. For example, in
1976, when the Republicans carried the state of Washington, one Republican
elector refused to vote for Gerald Ford, the Republican presidential nominee.
Many states have now enacted statutes formally binding electors to their pledges,
but some constitutional authorities doubt whether such statutes are enforceable.

In each state, the electors whose slate has won proceed to the state's capital on
the Monday following the second Wednesday in December and formally cast their
ballots. These are sent to Washington, tallied by the Congress in January, and the
name of the winner is formally announced. On all but three occasions in Ameri-

can history, the electoral vote has simply ratified the nationwide popular vote. However, since electoral votes are won on a state-by-state basis, it is mathematically possible for a candidate who receives a nationwide popular plurality to fail to carry states whose electoral votes would add up to a majority. Thus, in 1876, Rutherford B. Hayes was the winner in the electoral college despite receiving fewer popular votes than his rival, Samuel Tilden. In 1888, Grover Cleveland received more popular votes than Benjamin Harrison but received fewer electoral votes.

The possibility that in some future election the electoral college will, once again, produce an outcome that is inconsistent with the popular vote has led to many calls for the abolition of this institution and the introduction of some form of direct popular election of the president. The 1992 Perot candidacy, for example, at one point opened the possibility of a discrepancy between the popular and electoral totals, and even raised the specter of an election decided in the House of Representatives. Efforts to introduce such a reform, however, are usually blocked by political forces that believe they benefit from the present system. For example, minority groups that are influential in large urban states with many electoral votes feel that their voting strength would be diminished in a direct, nationwide, popular election. At the same time, some Republicans believe that their party's usual presidential strength in the South and the West gives them a distinct advantage in the electoral college. There is little doubt, however, that an election resulting in a discrepancy between the electoral and popular outcomes would create irresistible political pressure to eliminate the electoral college and introduce direct popular election of the president.

Facilitation of Mass Electoral Choice

Parties facilitate mass electoral choice. As the late Harvard political scientist V. O. Key pointed out long ago, the persistence over time of competition between groups possessing a measure of identity and continuity is virtually a necessary condition for electoral control.[9] Party identity increases the electorate's capacity to recognize its options. Continuity of party division facilitates organization of the electorate on the long-term basis necessary to sustain any popular influence in the governmental process. In the absence of such identity and continuity of party division, the voter is, in Key's words, confronted constantly by "new faces, new choices," and little basis exists for "effectuation of the popular will."[10]

Even more significant, however, is the fact that party organization is generally an essential ingredient for effective electoral competition by groups lacking substantial economic or institutional resources. Party building has typically been the strategy pursued by groups that must organize the collective energies of large numbers of individuals to counter their opponents' superior material means or institutional standing. Historically, disciplined and coherent party organizations were generally developed first by groups representing the political aspirations of the

---

[9]V. O. Key, *Southern Politics* (New York: Random House, 1949), Chapter 14.
[10]Ibid.

working classes. Parties, French political scientist Maurice Duverger notes, "are always more developed on the Left than on the Right because they are always more necessary on the Left than on the Right."[11] In the United States, the first mass party was built by the Jeffersonians as a counterweight to the superior social, institutional, and economic resources that could be deployed by the incumbent Federalists. In a subsequent period of American history, the efforts of the Jacksonians to construct a coherent mass party organization were impelled by a similar set of circumstances. Only by organizing the power of numbers could the Jacksonian coalition hope to compete successfully against the superior resources that could be mobilized by its adversaries.

In the United States, the political success of party organizations forced their opponents to copy them in order to meet the challenge. It was, as Duverger points out, "contagion from the Left," that led politicians of the Center and Right to attempt to build strong party organizations.[12] These efforts were sometimes successful. In the United States during the 1830s, the Whig party, which was led by northeastern business interests, carefully copied the organizational techniques devised by the Jacksonians. The Whigs won control of the national government in 1840. But even when groups nearer the top of the social scale responded in kind to organizational efforts by their inferiors, the net effect nonetheless was to give lower-class groups an opportunity to compete on a more equal footing. In the absence of coherent mass organization, middle- and upper-class factions almost inevitably have a substantial competitive edge over their lower-class rivals. Even when both sides organize, the net effect is still to erode the relative advantage of the well-off. Parties of the Right, moreover, were seldom actually able to equal the organizational coherence of the working-class opposition. As Duverger and others have observed, middle- and upper-class parties generally failed to construct organizations as effective as those built by their working-class foes who typically commanded larger and more easily disciplined forces.

Although political parties continue to be significant in the United States, the role of party organizations in electoral politics has clearly declined over the past three decades. This decline, and the partial replacement of the party by new forms of electoral technology, is one of the most important developments in twentieth-century American politics.

WEAKENING OF PARTY ORGANIZATION

George Washington's warning against the "baneful effects of the spirit of party" was echoed by the representatives of social, economic, and political elites in many nations who saw their right to rule challenged by groups able to organize the collective energies and resources of the mass public.

[11]Duverger, *Political Parties,* p. 426.

[12]Ibid., Chapter 1.

Opposition to party politics was the basis for a number of the institutional re-forms of the American political process promulgated at the turn of the twentieth century during the so-called "Progressive era." Many Progressive reformers were undoubtedly motivated by a sincere desire to rid politics of corruption and to im-prove the quality and efficiency of government in the United States. But simulta-neously, from the perspective of middle- and upper-class Progressives and the fi-nancial, commercial, and industrial elites with which they were often associated, the weakening or elimination of party organization would also mean that power could more readily be acquired and retained by the "best men," that is, those with wealth, position, and education.

The list of anti-party reforms of the Progressive Era is a familiar one. The Aus-tralian ballot reform took away the parties' privilege of printing and distributing ballots and introduced the possibility of split-ticket voting. The introduction of nonpartisan local elections eroded grass-roots party organization. The extension of "merit systems" for administrative appointments stripped party organizations of their vitally important access to patronage and thus reduced their ability to recruit workers. The development of the direct primary reduced party leaders' capacity to control candidate nominations. These reforms obviously did not destroy political parties as entities, but taken together they did substantially weaken party organiza-tions in the United States. After the turn of the century, the organizational strength of American political parties gradually diminished. Between the two world wars, organization remained the major tool available to contending electoral forces, but in most areas of the country the "reformed" state and local parties that survived the Progressive era gradually lost their organizational vitality and coher-ence, and they became less effective campaign tools. Again, Progressive reform did not eliminate the political party as an entity. Most areas of the nation continued to boast Democratic and Republican party groupings. But reform did mean the elimination of the permanent mass organizations that had been the parties' princi-pal campaign weapons. In the new reformed legal and institutional environment of American politics, an environment that included merit systems, direct primaries, and nonpartisan elections, the chance that any group could construct and maintain an effective, large-scale mass organization was reduced.

High-Tech Politics

As a result of Progressive reform, American party organizations entered the twen-tieth century with rickety substructures. As the use of civil service, primary elec-tions, and the other Progressive innovations spread during the period between the two world wars, the strength of party organizations continued to be eroded. By the end of World War II, political scientists were already beginning to bemoan the absence of party discipline and "party responsibility" in the United States. This erosion of the parties' organizational strength set the stage for the introduction of new political techniques. These new methods represented radical departures from the campaign practices perfected during the nineteenth century. In place of man-power and organization, contending forces began to employ intricate electronic communications techniques to attract electoral support. This new political tech-nology includes five basic elements.

1. *Polling.* Surveys of voter opinion provide the information that candidates and
their staffs use to craft campaign strategies. Candidates employ polls to select issues,
to assess their own strengths and weaknesses, as well as those of the opposition, to
check voter response to the campaign, and to determine the degree to which various constituent groups are susceptible to campaign appeals. In recent years, pollsters have become central figures in most national campaigns. Indeed, Patrick
Caddell, who polled for the 1976 Carter campaign, became part of Carter's inner
circle of advisers and ultimately played a role in major policy decisions.[13] Virtually
all contemporary campaigns for national and statewide office as well as many local
campaigns make extensive use of opinion surveys. Republican pollsters were instrumental in persuading George Bush to select Dan Quayle as his running mate in
1988, arguing that their data showed Quayle to have strong appeal to the critically
important "baby boom" group of voters in their thirties and forties.

2. *The broadcast media.* Extensive use of the electronic media, television in particular, has become the hallmark of the modern political campaign. One commonly used broadcast technique is the thirty- or sixty-second television spot
advertisement—such as George Bush's "Willie Horton" ad in 1988 or Lyndon
Johnson's famous "daisy girl" ad in 1964—which permits the candidate's message
to be delivered to a target audience before uninterested or hostile viewers can psychologically, or physically, tune it out (see Box 11.4). Television spot ads and other
media techniques are designed to establish candidate name identification, to create
a favorable image of the candidate and a negative image of the opponent, to link
the candidate with desirable groups in the community, and to communicate the
candidate's stands on selected issues. These spot ads can have an important electoral
impact. Generally, media campaigns attempt to follow the guidelines indicated by
a candidate's polls. Advertisements seek to strike a responsive chord with voters or
reinforce existing loyalties. The broadcast media are now so central to modern
campaigns that most of a candidate's activities are tied to their media strategies.[14]
For example, a sizable percentage of most candidates' newspaper ads are now used
mainly to advertise radio and television appearances. Other candidate activities are
designed expressly to stimulate television news coverage. For instance, incumbent
senators running for re-election or for higher office almost always sponsor committee or subcommittee hearings to generate publicity. In recent years, Senate
hearings on hunger, crime, health, and defense have been used mainly to attract
television cameras.

The 1992 presidential election introduced three new media techniques: the talk
show interview, the "electronic townhall" meeting, and the infomercial. Candidates used television and radio talk show and interview programs such as "Larry
King Live," "Good Morning America," the "Rush Limbaugh" radio program, and
even Arsenio Hall's late-night TV program to reach mass audiences. From the perspective of the candidates, these television and radio appearances offered excellent
opportunities to appeal for the support of millions of potential voters. Because
these are entertainment programs, viewers are perceived to be more relaxed and,
hence, potentially more susceptible to candidates' appeals. Some programs allow

---

[13]Richard A. Joslyn, *Mass Media Elections* (New York: Random House, 1984).

[14]Larry J. Sabato, *The Rise of Political Consultants* (New York: Basic Books, 1981).

BOX 11.4
The Daisy Girl

On September 7, 1964, NBC TV's "Monday Night at the Movies" was interrupted by what came to be one of the most famous and controversial political commercials ever shown on American television. In this ad, a little girl with long, light brown hair stood in a field picking daisy petals. As she pulled the petals she counted 1-2-3, etc. As she counted, the voice of an announcer in the background counted backward, 10-9-8, and so on. As the counts continued, the announcer's voice became louder and the girl's voice more muted until the girl reached 10 and the announcer counted down to 0. At that point, a blinding nuclear explosion occurred destroying everything, with President Johnson saying, "These are the stakes. To make a world in which all of God's children can live or go into the dark. We must either love each other or we must die." The announcer then urged viewers to vote for President Johnson on November 3. The ad was cut after one use, but the practice of short spots continued.

Source: Photo courtesy of the Lyndon Baines Johnson Library.

listeners or viewers to call in, which gives candidates a chance to demonstrate that they are responsive to ordinary people and sympathetic to their problems.

Similarly, the "town meeting" format gave a candidate the chance to appear in a hall with a group of ordinary citizens, answer their questions, and listen to their ideas. Bill Clinton felt that he was very effective in this format and insisted that one of the presidential debates be organized as a town meeting. After the election, Clinton hosted a series of televised meetings on the economy and continued to hold town meetings to push his programs. He and his aides viewed these meetings as an excellent mechanism for bolstering public support.

Talk show appearances and town meetings, moreover, allowed candidates to avoid the twin problems usually associated with political use of the media—cost and filtering. Normally, candidates must spend hundreds of thousands—even millions—of dollars for the use of commercial television time, while press conferences and news program "sound-bite" appearances left candidates at the mercy of media interpretations and possibly unfriendly editing. The talk show format gave candidates a free opportunity to present themselves and their ideas—often in the company of a congenial host—to millions of Americans without the media filtering or

editorial revision that might undermine their presentations. For these reasons, during the 1992 campaign, talk show appearances came to be the preferred candidate campaign vehicle.[15] The Larry King program became one of Ross Perot's major campaign vehicles, while George Bush made good use of a conservative radio host, Rush Limbaugh. Probably the most unusual talk show appearance of the campaign was Bill Clinton's saxophone solo on the Arsenio Hall show. Political pundits were divided on the electoral value of Clinton's performance. Music critics, however, all seemed to agree that Clinton should stick to politics.

In addition to making talk show appearances, independent candidate Ross Perot purchased several thirty-minute network television slots to present detailed expositions of his ideas and programs. In the early days of television, candidates often scheduled fifteen- and even thirty-minute presentations. This format was later abandoned because of its cost and because only a candidate's strongest supporters would take the time to watch such a long presentation. In essence, candidates were paying a great deal of money to preach to the already committed.

In recent years, changes in television cost structures have made thirty-minute slots available at reasonable prices. At any rate, from billionaire Perot's perspective, the several million dollars that his lengthy infomercials cost was certainly not prohibitive. After all, Perot was prepared to spend more than $60 million of his own money to finance his presidential bid. To the surprise of many analysts, Perot was able to attract large audiences for his detailed discussions of the nation's budget deficit and other economic topics. Perhaps, the well-educated electorate of the 1990s is more willing than was the electorate of the 1950s to devote its time and attention to discourse and explanation. If so, we may see the thirty-second spot ad give way more and more to the thirty- or even sixty-minute infomercial in the years to come.

The most dramatic use of the electronic media in contemporary electoral politics is the televised debate. Televised presidential debates began with the 1960 Kennedy-Nixon clash. Today, candidates for many public offices hold debates during the weeks prior to the election. In 1992, the three leading presidential contenders, George Bush, Bill Clinton, and Ross Perot, debated on three occasions. Their respective running mates, Dan Quayle, Al Gore, and James Stockdale, met once. These presidential debates are held so late in the campaign season that they usually do not change many votes. Most viewers have already decided which candidate they will support and tend to use the debates to confirm their choice. Generally, viewers will perceive the candidate they already favor as the winner of the debate. This is especially true for viewers with strong partisan leanings. Republicans as a rule thought that George Bush was the stronger performer in the 1992 presidential debates, whereas Democrats were convinced that Bill Clinton was.

The debates do, however, allow candidates to reach the few viewers who have not fully made up their minds about the election. Moreover, the debates can enhance the credibility of lesser-known candidates. Thus, in 1960, little-known senator Jack Kennedy was able to use a solid debate performance to become a credible

[15]See Howard Kurtz, "The Talk Show Campaign," *Washington Post,* 28 October 1992, p. 1.

(and eventually victorious) candidate in a race against his much better-known and experienced rival, Richard Nixon. In 1992, the presidential debates gave a major boost to the candidacy of Ross Perot. The opportunity to appear on an equal footing with the Democratic and Republican nominees and to show that he could—at the very least—hold his own against them, gave Perot a chance to persuade uncommitted voters that he was a serious and credible candidate.

3. *Phone banks.* Through the broadcast media, candidates communicate with voters *en masse* and impersonally. Phone banks allow campaign workers to make personal contact with hundreds of thousands of voters. Personal contacts of this sort are thought to be extremely effective. Again, poll data serve to identify the groups that will be targeted for phone calls. Computers select phone numbers from areas in which members of these groups are concentrated. Staffs of paid or volunteer callers, using computer-assisted dialing systems and prepared scripts, then place calls to deliver the candidate's message. The targeted groups are generally those identified by polls as either uncommitted or weakly committed, as well as strong supporters of the candidate who are contacted simply to encourage them to vote. Phone banks are used extensively in pivotal contests. Before the 1980 Iowa caucuses, for example, Democratic and Republican presidential hopefuls placed a total of more than three million phone calls to Iowa's 1.7 million registered voters. During the same year, former President Carter was reported to have personally placed between twenty and forty calls every night to homes in key primary and caucus states. On some New Hampshire blocks, a dozen or more residents eventually received telephone calls from the president.[16]

4. *Direct mail.* Direct mail serves both as a vehicle for communicating with voters and as a mechanism for raising funds. The first step in a direct mail campaign is the purchase or rental of a computerized mailing list of voters deemed to have some particular perspective or social characteristic. Often sets of magazine subscription lists or lists of donors to various causes are employed. For example, a candidate interested in reaching conservative voters might rent subscription lists from *National Review, Human Events,* and *Conservative Digest,* or a candidate interested in appealing to liberals might rent subscription lists from *The New York Review of Books* or the *New Republic.* Considerable fine-tuning is possible. After obtaining the appropriate mailing lists, candidates usually send pamphlets, letters, and brochures describing themselves and their views to voters believed to be sympathetic. Different types of mail appeals are made to different electoral subgroups. Often the letters sent to voters are personalized. The recipient is addressed by name in the text and the letter appears actually to have been signed by the candidate. Of course, these "personal" letters are written and even signed by a computer. Probably the first campaign to make extensive use of direct mail advertising was Winthrop Rockefeller's successful bid to become Governor of Arkansas in 1966. Rockefeller's IBM 1401 and 360 computers—primitive and slow by contemporary standards—produced more than one million pieces of mail for the state's 500,000 voters.[17] In addition to use as a political advertising medium, direct mail has also become an important source of campaign funds. Computerized mail-

[16]Ibid., p. 218.
[17]James M. Perry, *The New Politics* (New York: Potter, 1968), Chapter 6.

PROCESS BOX 11.3
How to Run for Political Office

491

WEAKENING OF
PARTY
ORGANIZATION

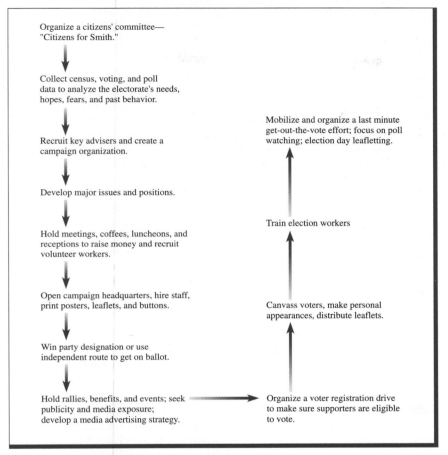

Organize a citizens' committee—
"Citizens for Smith."

Collect census, voting, and poll
data to analyze the electorate's needs,
hopes, fears, and past behavior.

Recruit key advisers and create a
campaign organization.

Develop major issues and positions.

Hold meetings, coffees, luncheons, and
receptions to raise money and recruit
volunteer workers.

Open campaign headquarters, hire staff,
print posters, leaflets, and buttons.

Win party designation or use
independent route to get on ballot.

Hold rallies, benefits, and events; seek
publicity and media exposure;
develop a media advertising strategy.

Mobilize and organize a last minute
get-out-the-vote effort; focus on poll
watching; election day leafletting.

Train election workers

Canvass voters, make personal
appearances, distribute leaflets.

Organize a voter registration drive
to make sure supporters are eligible
to vote.

ing lists permit campaign strategists to pinpoint individuals whose interests, background, and activities suggest that they may be potential donors to the campaign.
Letters of solicitation are sent to these potential donors. Some of the money raised
is then used to purchase additional mailing lists. Direct mail solicitation can be
enormously effective.[18]

5. *Professional public relations.* Modern campaigns and the complex technology
upon which they rely are typically directed by professional public relations consultants. Virtually all serious contenders for national and statewide office retain the
services of professional campaign consultants. Increasingly, candidates for local office, too, have come to rely upon professional campaign managers. Consultants
offer candidates the expertise necessary to conduct accurate opinion polls, produce
television commercials, organize direct mail campaigns, and make use of sophisticated computer analyses. A "full-service" firm will arrange

[18]Sabato, *Rise of Political Consultants,* p. 250.

advertising campaigns for radio, television, and newspapers, including layout, timing, and the actual placing of advertisements; public relations and press services, including the organization of public meetings, preparation and distribution of press releases and statements, and detailed travel arrangements for the candidate; research and presentation of issues, including preparation of position papers, speech writing, and arranging for consultations between candidates and outside experts in appropriate areas of public policy; fund-raising solicitations, both by mail and through testimonial dinners and other public events; public opinion sampling to test voter response to the campaign and voter attitudes on major issues; technical assistance on radio and television production, including the hiring of cameramen and recording studios for political films and broadcasts; campaign budgeting assistance designed to put campaign funds to the best possible use; use of data processing techniques to plan campaign strategy based on computer evaluations of thousands of bits of information; and mobilization of support through traditional door-to-door campaigns and telephone solicitation of voters.[19]

Several of the components of this "new" political technology were, of course, developed long before World War II. Professional public relations firms first became involved in electoral politics in 1934, when the firm of Whittaker and Baxter helped to defeat novelist Upton Sinclair's Socialist candidacy in the California gubernatorial race by charging that Sinclair was a Communist. The firm was hired by California business interests. Primitive opinion polls were used in American elections as early as 1824, and relatively sophisticated surveys were employed extensively during the 1880s and 1890s.

After the Second World War, however, the introduction of television and the computer provided the mechanisms that became the electronic heart of the modern campaign. These electronic innovations coincided with a growing realization on the part of politicians and activists that the capacity of traditional party organizations to mobilize voters had greatly diminished. As this realization spread, a small number of candidates began to experiment with new campaign methods. The initial trickle of political techniques were generally more effective than the more traditional campaign efforts that could be mounted by the now-debilitated party organizations.

In a number of well-publicized congressional, senatorial, and gubernatorial campaigns during the postwar years, candidates using the new campaign methods decisively defeated rivals who continued to rely on the older organizational techniques. The successful campaigns mounted by Richard Nixon, who relied on professional public relations in the 1948 California Senate race, and Jacob Javits, who made brilliant use of poll data in his 1948 New York congressional race, were very visible examples of the power of technology.

The number of technologically oriented campaigns increased greatly after 1971. The Federal Elections Campaign Act of that year prompted the creation of large numbers of political action committees (PACs) by a host of corporate and ideological groups. This development increased the availability of funds to political candidates—conservative candidates in particular—which meant in turn that the new technology could be used more extensively. Initially, the new techniques were

[19]Joslyn, *Mass Media Elections,* p. 33.

employed mainly by individual candidates who often made little or no effort to coordinate their campaigns with those of other political aspirants sharing the same party label. For this reason, campaigns employing the new technology sometimes came to be called "candidate-centered" efforts, as distinguished from the traditional party-coordinated campaign. Nothing about the new technology, however, precluded its use by political party leaders seeking to coordinate a number of campaigns. In recent years, party leaders, Republicans in particular, have learned to make good use of modern campaign technology. The difference between the old and new political methods is not that the latter is inherently candidate-centered while the former is strictly a party tool. The difference is, rather, a matter of the types of political resources upon which each method depends.

From Labor-Intensive to Capital-Intensive Politics

The displacement of organizational methods by the new political technology is, in essence, a shift from labor-intensive to capital-intensive competitive electoral practices. Campaign tasks were once performed by masses of party workers and some cash. These tasks now require fewer personnel but a great deal more money, for the new political style depends on polls, computers, and other electronic paraphernalia. Of course, even when manpower and organization were the key electoral tools, money had considerable political significance. Nevertheless, during the nineteenth century, national political campaigns in the United States employed millions of workers. Indeed, as many as 2.5 million individuals were employed in political work during the 1880s.[20] The direct cost of campaigns, therefore, was relatively low. For example, in 1860, Abraham Lincoln spent only $100,000—which was approximately twice the amount spent by his chief opponent, Stephen Douglas.

Modern campaigns depend heavily on money. Each element of the new political technology is enormously expensive. A sixty-second spot announcement on prime-time network television costs hundreds of thousands of dollars each time it is aired. Opinion surveys can be quite expensive. Polling costs in a state-wide race can easily reach or exceed the six-figure mark. Campaign consultants can charge substantial fees. A direct mail campaign can eventually become an important source of funds but is very expensive to initiate. The inauguration of a serious national direct mail effort requires at least $1 million in "front end cash" to pay for mailing lists, brochures, letters, envelopes, and postage.[21] While the cost of televised debates is covered by the sponsoring organizations and the television stations and is, thus, free to the candidates, even debate preparation requires substantial staff work and research, and money. It is the expense of the new technology that accounts for the enormous cost of recent American national elections. According to the nonpartisan Citizen's Research Foundation, an organization committed to campaign reform, total spending in the United States for all campaigning rose by

[20]M. Ostrogorski, *Democracy and the Organization of Political Parties* (New York: Macmillan, 1902).

[21]Timothy Clark, "The RNC Prospers, the DNC Struggles as They Face the 1980 Election," *National Journal,* 27 October 1980, p. 1619.

BOX 11.5
Federal Campaign Finance Regulation

Campaign Contributions

No individual may contribute more than $1,000 to any one candidate in any single election. Individuals may contribute as much as $20,000 to a national party committee and up to $5,000 to a political action committee. Full disclosure is required by candidates of all contributions over $100. Candidates may not accept cash contributions over $100.

Political Action Committees

Any corporation, labor union, trade association, or other organization may establish a political action committee (PAC). PACs must contribute to the campaigns of at least five different candidates and may contribute as much as $5,000 per candidate in any given election.

Presidential Elections

Candidates in presidential primaries may receive federal matching funds if they raise at least $5,000 in each of twenty states. The money raised must come in contributions of $250 and less. The amount raised by candidates in this way is matched by the federal government, dollar for dollar, up to a limit of $5 million. In the general election, major party candidates' campaigns are fully funded by the federal government. Candidates may spend no money beyond their federal funding. But independent groups may spend money on behalf of a candidate so long as their efforts are not directly tied to the official campaign. Minor party candidates may be entitled to partial federal funding.

Federal Election Commission (FEC)

The six-member FEC supervises federal elections, collects and publicizes campaign finance records, and investigates violations of federal campaign finance law.

13 percent from 1956 to 1960 (from $155 million to $175 million) and by 14 percent between 1960 and 1964 (to $200 million). The increase grew to 50 percent between 1964 and 1968 (to $300 million), and another 42 percent increase occurred between 1968 and 1972 (to $425 million). Expenditures exceeded the half-billion-dollar mark ($540 million) in 1976 and the billion-dollar mark in 1988 and 1992.

In recent years, Congress has sought to regulate campaign finance. The Supreme court, however, has limited the effect of this legislation by declaring unconstitutional any absolute limits on the freedom of individuals to spend their own money on campaigns.[22] The Federal Elections Campaign Act of 1971 imposes contribution limits and provides for full disclosure of all campaign receipts and expenditures (see Box 11.5). In 1990 and 1991, congressional efforts to strengthen campaign finance rules were blocked by partisan conflicts, with each party willing only to support rules that it saw helping its own interests and hurting the opposi-

[22]Buckley v. Valeo, 421 U.S. 1 (1976).

tion. Democrats, who benefit from incumbency, proposed public financing and
spending limits that would thwart challengers. Republicans, who raise most of
their money through direct mail, supported limits on the PAC spending upon
which Democrats depend for nearly 25 percent of their campaign funds. Republicans, by contrast, depend upon PACs for only 2 percent of their campaign funds.[23]

In 1993, President Clinton proposed a new set of campaign spending rules de-signed to limit the size of campaign contributions, to delimit campaign spending, and to provide congressional candidates with public funds to replace at least some of the private monies they are currently compelled to raise. His proposal would re-duce the influence of business interests, thereby strengthening liberal, public inter-est groups that depend less on money to secure political influence. In June 1993, the Senate passed a bill that contained some, but not all, of Clinton's proposals. The Senate bill contained provisions outlawing PAC contributions, introduced mechanisms for reducing campaign spending, and prohibited lobbyists from mak-ing contributions to senators they had lobbied within the preceding year. The bill provided only a limited role for public funding of campaigns. Designed to help in-cumbents rather than to serve only the interests of the Democratic party, the bill had some Republican support, whereas President Clinton's initial proposal had none.[24] Clinton's campaign finance reform is discussed more fully in Chapter 12.

Certainly "people power" is not irrelevant to modern political campaigns. Candidates continue to utilize the political services of tens of thousands of volun-teer workers. Nevertheless, in the contemporary era, even the recruitment of vol-unteer campaign workers has become a matter of electronic technology. Employ-ing a technique called "instant organization," paid telephone callers use phone banks to contact individuals in areas targeted by a computer (which they do when contacting potential voters, as we discussed before). Volunteer workers are re-cruited from among these individuals. A number of campaigns—Richard Nixon's 1968 presidential campaign was the first—have successfully utilized this technique.

The displacement of organizational methods by the new political technology has the most far-reaching implications for the balance of power among contending political groups. Labor-intensive organizational tactics allowed parties whose chief support came from groups nearer the bottom of the social scale to use the numer-ical superiority of their forces as a partial counterweight to the institutional and economic resources more readily available to the opposition. The capital-intensive technological format, by contrast, has given a major boost to the political fortunes of those forces whose sympathizers are better able to furnish the large sums now needed to compete effectively.[25] Indeed, the new technology permits financial re-sources to be more effectively harnessed and exploited than was ever before possible.

---

[23] *Congressional Quarterly Weekly Report,* 29 September 1990, p. 3089.

[24] See Richard L. Berke, "Clinton Unveils Plan to Restrict PAC Influence," *New York Times,* 8 May 1993; Helen Dewar and Kenneth Cooper, "Campaign Finance Bill Is Approved by Senate," *Washington Post,* 18 June 1993, p. A20.

[25] For discussions of the consequences, see Thomas Edsall, *The New Politics of Inequality* (New York: W.W. Norton, 1984). Also Thomas Edsall, "Both Parties Get the Campaign's Money—But the Boss Backs the GOP," *Washington Post National Weekly Edition,* 16 September 1986, p. 14; and Benjamin Ginsberg, "Money and Power: The New Political Economy of American Elections," in *The Political Economy,* ed. Thomas Ferguson and Joel Rogers (Armonk, NY: M.E. Sharpe Publishers, 1984).

Party Politics in America: Are Three Parties Better than Two?

Since the start of the Republic, party politics has almost always been dominated by two large parties. Yet the parties have been persistently criticized for their sameness and monopoly on the political system. Political scientist Theodore J. Lowi argues that the two-party system is beyond repair and that a three- or multiparty system is our most constructive alternative. In a classic defense of two-partyism, political parties expert E. E. Schattschneider argues that the present system suits an American public most comfortable with two large, diverse parties that emphasize compromise and moderation.

Lowi

Nothing about the present American party system warrants the respect it receives. Presidents need a party and have none. Voters need choices and continuity and rarely have either. Congress needs cohesion and has little. Although almost everyone recognizes that party organizations in the United States have all but disappeared . . . most people nevertheless assume that this is merely a momentary lapse and that the two-party system is the American way. But . . . it should be clear by now that big, modern, programmatic governments [like the U.S.] are not hospitable to two-party systems. . . . A two-party system simply cannot grapple with complex programmatic alternatives in a manner that is meaningful to large electorates. Modern programmatic governments do need political parties, just as much as traditional patronage governments needed them. It is not party systems but the two-party system in particular that no longer can suffice. No amount of tinkering by well-intentioned reformers can revive the two-party system. . . .

A multiparty system will seem alien on American soil only as long as the two-party system is taken as the only true, American way to govern. . . . The presence of other real parties with a real electoral base and a real presence in state legislatures, in Congress, and in the Electoral College, could clarify the policies, programs and the lines of accountability of the two major parties by reducing their need to appear to be all things to all people.[1]

Schattschneider

Does the fact that we have a two-party system make any difference? Most emphatically, it does! . . . What are the special qualities of American politics that result from the fact that we have a well-established two-party system?

First, the two-party system produces majorities automatically. Since there are only two major parties actually in the competition for power and these parties monopolize the vote, it is almost certain that one of them will get a majority. . . . The difficulty of assembling a majority is thus reduced very greatly. . . .

The second effect of the two-party system is the fact that it produces moderate parties. . . . The major party cannot afford to take an extreme stand, but neither is it condemned to futility . . . it is difficult to imagine anything more important than the tendency of the parties to avoid extreme policies. . . .

Minor party politicians, anxious to create new alternatives by breaking up the two-party system and trying to prove that the competition between the major parties is unreal, contend that the difference between the major parties is zero, while major party politicians have professed to see momentous alternatives between the great parties. . . . [But] the extravagant language of party orators, major and minor, deceives almost no one. . . . There seems to be ample moral authority in American civilization for a moderate party policy. The criticism most justly made of American major parties is not that they exhibit a tendency to be alike but rather that the moderate though significant differences between them are often too confused and ill defined to be readily understood.[2]

[1]Theodore J. Lowi, *The Personal President* (Ithaca, NY: Cornell University Press, 1985), pp. 203–4.

[2]E. E. Schattschneider, *Party Government* (New York: Holt, Rinehart, and Winston, 1942), pp. 84–93.

In a political process lacking strong party organizations, the likelihood that groups that do not possess substantial economic or institutional resources can acquire some measure of power is severely diminished. Dominated by the new technology, electoral politics becomes a contest in which the wealthy and powerful have a decided advantage.

Is the Party Over?

Of course, the Democratic and Republican parties still exist. The contemporary parties, however, differ from their predecessors. In recent decades, the Democrats and Republicans have become entrenched in distinct segments of the national governmental apparatus. The Democrats have a hold on Congress, federal social service, labor and regulatory agencies, and on government bureaucracies and non-profit organizations on the state and local levels that help administer national social programs. This entrenchment has its roots in Franklin D. Roosevelt's New Deal and Lyndon Johnson's Great Society programs that expanded the size and institutional capacities of the national government's domestic agencies. These developments have transformed the Democrats from a political force based upon state and local party machines into one grounded in Congress and the domestic state.

In 1993, the Democrats sought to entrench themselves still further in the domestic state apparatus. The three chief vehicles for this effort were President Clinton's economic proposals, health care reform proposals, and political reform initiatives. Clinton's economic package entailed substantial tax increases and cuts in military spending. In this way, the administration hoped to make additional revenues available for Democratic social programs and agencies that had been starved for funding through twelve years of Republican rule.

Clinton's health care reform proposals promised to create an enormous new set of agencies and institutions that would permit Democrats to substantially expand their influence over an area representing nearly 15 percent of the domestic economy while simultaneously attaching major constituency groups to the Democratic party.

Finally, Clinton proposed changes in campaign spending rules that would generally work to the advantage of liberal public interest groups and Democratic incumbents. He signed the "motor voter" bill, which potentially could bring larger numbers of mainly Democratic poor and minority voters to the polls. And he proposed reforms of the Hatch Act that would permit the heavily Democratic federal civil service to play a larger role in the political process.[26]

Taken together, these proposals represented a bold effort to ensure continuing Democratic control of the government. Adoption of these proposals would solidify the Democratic party's institutional base in the bureaucracies of the executive branch while making it all the more difficult for Republicans to dislodge the Democrats through electoral methods.

The Republicans, in turn, controlled the White House during the past quarter century, and still control the national security apparatus, sectors of the economy that benefit from military spending, and those segments of American society threatened by the welfare and regulatory state built by the Democrats. This was one of the major factors behind the efforts of the Reagan administration during the 1980s to increase levels of defense spending while reducing domestic social spending. In essence, Reagan sought to direct the flow of federal funds into agencies and institutions associated with the Republicans while reducing the flow of funds into those sectors of the government in which the Democrats were entrenched.

During the budget debates of the late 1980s and early 1990s, congressional Democrats sought to reverse this state of affairs by diminishing funding for the national security sector and increasing funding levels for the domestic social and regulatory sectors. Initially, Democratic efforts seemed to succeed. In the 1990 budget negotiations, congressional Democrats were able to defeat President Bush by producing a budget that opened the way for higher levels of social spending. Although the Persian Gulf War of 1991 increased the popular standing and prestige of the national security sector, the collapse of the Soviet Union made it more difficult for Republicans to argue for the continuation of Cold War levels of military spending. Until the end of the Bush administration, proponents of defense spending were able to block demands for sharp cuts in the military. Once Democrats were in control of the White House, however, they made it clear that levels of defense spending would drop significantly.

To a considerable extent, this competitive entrenchment of Republicans and Democrats has replaced mass electoral mobilization as a means of securing power

---

[26]Chuck Alston, "Democrats Flex New Muscle with Trio of Election Bills: Some Republicans Say That 'Motor Voter,' Campaign Finance and Hatch Act Bills Add Up to Permanent Power Grab," *Congressional Quarterly Weekly Report*, 20 March 1993, pp. 643–45.

in the United States today. This is one reason why high levels of partisan conflict coexist with low rates of voter participation in contemporary American politics. To today's parties, traditional electoral politics is only one arena of political combat. In between elections, the Democrats and Republicans engage in institutional struggles whose outcome is every bit as important to them as the verdict at the ballot box, but you will hear more about this in Chapter 14.

SUMMARY

Political parties seek to control government by controlling its personnel. Elections are one means to this end. Thus, parties take shape from the electorial process. The formal principle of party organization is this: For every district in which an election is held—from the entire nation to the local district, county, or precinct— there should be some kind of party unit.

The two-party system has dominated U.S. politics. Today, on individual issues, the two parties differ little from each other. In general, however, Democrats lean more to the Left on issues and Republicans more to the Right. Even though party affiliation means less to Americans than it once did, partisanship remains important. What ticket splitting there is occurs mainly at the presidential level.

Third parties are short-lived for several reasons. They have limited electoral support, the tradition of the two-party system is strong, and a major party often adopts their platform. Single-member districts with two competing parties also discourage third parties.

Nominating and electing are the basic functions of parties. Originally nominations were made in party caucuses, and individuals who ran as independents had a difficult time getting on the ballot. In the 1830s, dissatisfaction with the cliquish caucuses led to nominating conventions. Although these ended the "King Caucus" that had nominated the presidential candidates, and thereby gave the presidency a popular base, they too proved unsatisfactory. Primaries have now more or less replaced the conventions. There are both closed and open primaries. The former are more supportive of strong political parties than the latter. Contested primaries sap party strength and financial resources, but they nonetheless serve to resolve important social conflicts and recognize new interest groups. Winning by the top of a party ticket usually depends on the party regulars at the bottom getting out the vote. At all levels, the mass communications media are important. Mass mailings, too, are vital in campaigning. Thus, campaign funds are crucial to success.

Congress is organized around the two-party system. The House speakership is a party office. Parties determine the makeup of congressional committees, including their chairs, which are no longer based entirely on seniority.

In recent years, the role of parties in political campaigns has been partially supplanted by the use of new political technologies. These include the broadcast media, polling, professional public relations, phone banks, and direct mail fundraising and advertising. These techniques are enormously expensive and have led to a shift from a labor-intensive to a capital-intensive politics. This shift works to the advantage of political forces representing the well-to-do. The parties currently have also entrenched themselves in government agencies and sectors of the national economy.

FOR FURTHER READING

Broder, David. *The Party's Over.* New York: Harper & Row, 1971.

Chambers, William N., and Walter Dean Burnham. *The American Party Systems: Stages of Political Development.* New York: Oxford University Press, 1975.

Cooper, Joseph, and Louis Maisel. *Political Parties: Development and Decay.* Beverly Hills, CA: Sage Publications, 1978.

Goldman, Ralph. *The National Party Chairmen and Committees: Factionalism at the Top.* Armonk, NY: M. E. Sharpe, 1990.

Herrnson, Paul S. *Party Campaigning in the 1980s.* Cambridge, MA: Harvard University Press, 1988.

Hofstadter, Richard. *The Idea of a Party System: The Rise of Legitimate Opposition in the United States, 1780–1840.* Berkeley: University of California Press, 1970.

Kayden, Xandra, and Eddie Mahe, Jr. *The Party Goes On: The Persistence of the Two-Party System in the United States.* New York: Basic Books, 1985.

Lawson, Kay, and Peter Merkl. *When Parties Fail: Emerging Alternative Organizations.* Princeton: Princeton University Press, 1988.

LeBlanc, Hugh. *American Political Parties.* New York: St. Martin's Press, 1982.

Polsby, Nelson W. *Consequences of Party Reform.* New York: Oxford University Press, 1983.

Ranney, Austin. *Curing the Mischiefs of Faction.* Berkeley: University of California Press, 1975.

Sabato, Larry. *The Rise of Political Consultants.* New York: Basic Books, 1971.

Shafer, Byron, ed. *Beyond Realignment? Interpreting American Electoral Eras.* Madison, WI: University of Wisconsin Press, 1991.

Smith, Eric R.A.N. *The Unchanging American Voter.* Berkeley: University of California Press, 1989.

Sorauf, Frank J. *Party Politics in America.* Boston: Little, Brown, 1984.

Sundquist, James. *Dynamics of the Party System.* Washington, DC: Brookings Institution, 1983.

Wattenberg, Martin. *The Decline of American Political Parties 1952–1988.* Cambridge, MA: Harvard University Press, 1990.

12

Groups and Interests

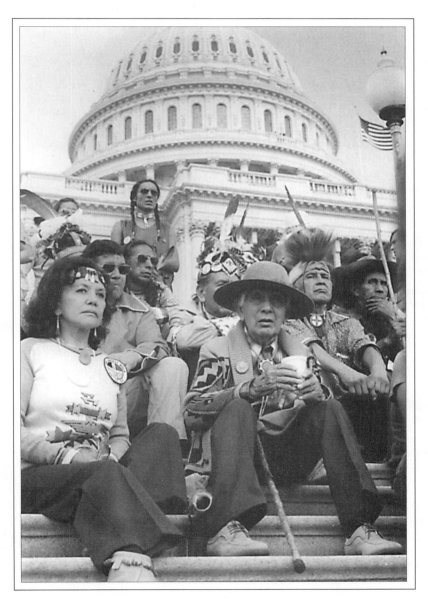

TIME LINE ON INTEREST GROUPS

EVENTS		INSTITUTIONAL DEVELOPMENTS
Early trade associations and unions formed (1820s and 1830s)		Term "lobbyist" is first used (1830)
Citizen groups and movements form—temperance (1820s), antislavery (1810–1830), women (1848), abolition (1850s)	**1850**	Local regulations restricting or forbidding manufacture and sale of alcohol (1830–1860); several states pass laws granting women control over their property (1839–1860s)
Civil War (1861–1865)		
		Lobbying is recognized in law and practice (1870s)
Development of agricultural groups, including the Grange (1860s–1870s)		Grangers successfully lobby for passage of "Granger laws" to regulate rates charged by railroads and warehouses (1870s)
American Federation of Labor (AFL) formed (1886)	**1880**	Beginnings of labor and unemployment laws (1880s)
Farmers' Alliances and Populists (1880s–1890s)		Election of candidates pledged to farmers (1890s)
Middle-class Progressive movement and trade associations (1890s)		Laws for direct primary, voter registration, regulation of business (1890s–1910s)
Growth of movement for women's suffrage (1890s)		Women's suffrage granted by Wyo., Colo., Utah, Idaho (1890s)
Renewal of women's movements—temperance (1890s) and suffrage (1914)	**1900**	
World War I (1914–1919)		Prohibition (Eighteenth) Amendment ratified (1919)
Teapot Dome scandal (1924)		Nineteenth Amendment gives women the vote (1920)
Growth of trade associations (1920s)		Corrupt practices legislation passed; lobbying registration legislation (1920s)
American Farm Bureau Federation (1920); farm bloc (1920s)		Farm bloc lobbies for farmers (1921–1923)
CIO is formed (1938)		Wagner National Labor Relations Act (1935)
U.S. enters W.W. II (1941–1945)	**1940**	Federal Regulation of Lobbying Act (1946)
Postwar wave of strikes in key industries (1945–1946)		Taft-Hartley Act places limits on unions (1947)

TIME LINE ON INTEREST GROUPS

EVENTS		INSTITUTIONAL DEVELOPMENTS
AFL and CIO merge (1955)	**1950**	
Senate hearings into labor racketeering (1950s)		Landrum-Griffin Act to control union corruption (1959)
Civil rights movement—boycotts, sit-ins, vote drives (1957), March on Washington (1963)		Passage of Civil Rights Acts of 1957, 1960, 1964, Voting Rights Act of 1965 (1960s)
National Organization of Women (NOW) formed (1966)		
Vietnam War: antiwar movement (1965–1973)	**1970**	End of draft (1971)
Watergate scandal (1972–1974)		Campaign spending legislation leads to PACs (1970s)
		Roe v. *Wade* (1973)
Pro-life and pro-choice groups emerge (post-1973)		
Public interest groups formed (1970s–1980s)		Consumer, environmental, health, and safety legislation (1970s)
		Ethics in Government Act (1978)
Moral Majority formed (late 1970s)		PACs help to elect conservative candidates (1980s)
Pentagon procurement scandal (1988)		Further regulation of lobbying (1980s)
The Keating Five investigation (1990–91)	**1990**	
Intense efforts by interest groups to influence Clinton health care and economic proposals (1993)		Proposals to restrict lobbying activities by blocking "revolving door," preventing lobbyists from contributing money to political candidates and restricting tax-deductibility of lobbying expenses. Proposals would mainly strike at corporate interests (1993)
Expanded use of new technologies for grass-roots lobby efforts (1993)		

*A*mericans often worry about the problem of special interests. Many believe that organized groups, pursuing special agendas, dominate the governmental and policy-making process. Senator Edward Kennedy once said that Americans sometimes feel they have the "best Congress money can buy." Certainly, a good deal of what Americans see and read about their nation's politics seems to confirm this pessimistic view.

For example, during the 1992 national elections, more than four thousand special-interest groups contributed more than $230 million to Democratic and Republican candidates. Many of the largest contributions came from industries whose members have extensive dealings with the federal government. Securities and investment interests donated more than $11 million to national political candidates. Lawyers and lobbyists contributed more than $13 million. Oil and gas companies and insurance interests each contributed nearly $10 million. Real estate concerns gave about $6 million.

Does this sea of special-interest money affect the behavior of our legislators? The answer often seems to be that it does. Take the case of the so-called Keating Five. In 1990, the Senate Ethics Committee investigated five senators on their activities on behalf of Charles H. Keating, Jr., head of the American Continental Corporation, which at one time owned the failed Lincoln Savings and Loan Association. In preceding years, Keating and his associates had raised over $1.3 million for the campaign committees and political causes of Senators Alan Cranston (D–Cal.), Dennis DeConcini (D–Ariz.), John Glenn (D–Ohio), John McClain (R–Ariz.), and Donald W. Riegle, Jr. (D–Mich.). When the Lincoln Savings and Loan was collapsing in 1987, these senators met with federal regulators and allegedly "offered a deal" on behalf of Keating's company, asking for leniency in exchange for the limiting of high-risk investments. Two years later, the government filed a fraud and racketeering suit against Keating, and soon afterward the senators were accused of having used their influence to aid a corrupt contributor. Arizona political activists were so incensed that they organized an ultimately unsuccessful "recall drive" against both of their senators.[1] However, Cranston retired from the Senate and Glenn was almost defeated in 1992. This case was a clear indication to many citizens that a handsome campaign contribution brought special attention.

The framers of the American Constitution feared the power that could be wielded by organized interests. Yet, they believed that interest groups thrived because of freedom—the freedom that all Americans enjoyed to organize and express their views. To the framers, this problem presented a dilemma, indeed the dilemma of freedom versus power that is central to our text. If the government were given the power to regulate or in any way to forbid efforts by organized interests to interfere in the political process, the government would in effect have the power to suppress freedom. The solution to this dilemma was presented by James Madison.

> Take in a greater variety of parties and interest [and] you make it less probable that a majority of the whole will have a common motive to invade the rights of other citizens. . . . [Hence the advantage] enjoyed by a large over a small republic.[2]

---

[1] *Congressional Quarterly Weekly Report*, 27 January 1990, pp. 211–16.

[2] Clinton Rossiter, ed., *The Federalist Papers* (New York: New American Library, 1861), No. 10, p. 83.

According to the Madisonian theory, a good constitution encourages multitudes of
interests so that no single interest can ever tyrannize the others. The basic assumption is that competition among interests will produce balance, with all the interests regulating each other.[3] Today, this Madisonian principle of regulation is called *pluralism.* According to pluralist theory, all interests are and should be free to compete for influence in the United States. Moreover, according to a pluralist doctrine, the outcome of this competition is compromise and moderation, since no group is likely to be able to achieve any of its goals without accommodating itself to some of the views of its many competitors.[4]

Certainly, there are tens of thousands of organized groups in the United States, ranging from civic associations to huge nationwide groups like the National Rifle Association, whose chief cause is opposition to gun registration, or Common Cause, a public interest group that advocates a variety of liberal political reforms. Despite the array of interest groups in American politics, however, we can neither be sure that all interests are represented nor that the results of this group competition are consistent with the common good. As we shall see, group politics is a political format that works more to the advantage of some types of interests than others.

In this chapter, we will examine some of the antecedents and consequences of interest group politics in the United States. First, we will seek to understand the character of the interests promoted by interest groups. Second, we will assess the growth of interest group activity in recent American political history, including the emergence of "public interest" groups. Finally, we will review and evaluate the strategies that competing groups use in their struggle for influence.

CHARACTER OF INTEREST GROUPS

Individuals form groups in order to increase the chance that their views will be heard and their interests treated favorably by the government. Interest groups are organized to influence governmental decisions. There are an enormous number of interest groups in the United States, and millions of Americans are members of one or more groups, at least to the extent of paying dues or attending an occasional meeting.

What Interests Are Represented

Interest groups come in as many shapes and sizes as the interests they represent. When most people think about interest groups, they immediately think of groups with a direct economic interest in governmental actions. These groups are generally supported by groups of producers or manufacturers in a particular economic sector. Examples of these types of groups include the National Petroleum Refiners

[3]Ibid.
[4]The best statement of the pluralist view is in David Truman, *The Governmental Process* (New York: Knopf, 1951), Chapter 2.

Association and the American Farm Bureau Federation. At the same time that broadly representative groups like these are active in Washington, specific companies, like Shell Oil, International Business Machines, and General Motors may be active on certain issues that are of particular concern to them.

Labor organizations are equally active lobbyists. The AFL-CIO, the United Mine Workers, and the Teamsters are all groups that lobby on behalf of organized labor. In recent years, lobbies have arisen to further the interests of public employees, the most significant among these being the American Federation of State, County, and Municipal Employees.

Professional lobbies like the American Bar Association and the American Medical Association have been particularly successful in furthering their own interests in state and federal legislatures. Financial institutions, represented by organizations like the American Bankers Association and the National Savings & Loan League, although often less visible than other lobbies, also play an important role in shaping legislative policy.

Recent years have witnessed the growth of a powerful public interest lobby purporting to represent interests whose concerns are not likely to be addressed by traditional lobbies. These groups have been most visible in the consumer protection and environmental policy areas, although public interest groups cover a broad range of issues. The National Resources Defense Council, the Union of Concerned Scientists, and Common Cause are all examples of public interest groups (see Box 12.1).

The perceived need for representation on Capitol Hill has generated a public sector lobby in the past several years, including the National League of Cities and the "research" lobby. The latter group comprises think tanks and universities who have an interest in obtaining government funds for research and support, and it includes such prestigious institutions as Harvard University, the Brookings Institution, and the American Enterprise Institute. Indeed, universities have expanded their lobbying efforts even as they have reduced faculty positions and course offerings.[5]

Organizational Components

Although there are many interest groups, most share certain key organizational components. First, all groups must attract and keep members. Usually, groups appeal to members not only by promoting political goals or policies they favor but also by providing them with direct economic or social benefits. Thus, for example, the American Association of Retired Persons (AARP), which promotes the interests of senior citizens, at the same time offers members a variety of insurance benefits and commercial discounts. Similarly, many groups whose goals are chiefly economic or political also seek to attract members through social interaction and good fellowship. Thus, the local chapters of many national groups provide their members with a congenial social environment while collecting dues that finance the national offices' political efforts.

Second, every group must build a financial structure capable of sustaining an

[5]Betsy Wagner and David Bowermaster, "B.S. Economics," *Washington Monthly* (November 1992), pp. 19–21.

BOX 12.1
Common Cause: A "People's Lobby"

The "new politics" of the 1970s and 1980s engendered a wide assortment of new-generation groups seeking to influence the political process. They include political action committees, single-issue groups, groups based on social issues, and organizations seeking to mobilize those who have not traditionally involved themselves in politics. One such new-generation group is Common Cause.

Founded in 1970 out of the foment that launched the decade, Common Cause was the brainchild of a group headed by John W. Gardner, a former foundation executive and HEW secretary under LBJ. Gardner decided to make Common Cause a "people's lobby" with broad grass-roots involvement. In the first six months of newspaper ads and mass mailings, the organization gained 100,000 members. By 1972, the membership included over a million people. Much of the impetus for the organization sprang from dissatisfaction with continued American involvement in Vietnam and growing disenchantment with the political turn of the government. The idea behind the organization was that it would serve as a political foil for special interests by using expressly political tactics (as opposed to simple educational or research efforts), especially lobbying. The organization would be run by an elected board, and would be guided in its direction by membership referenda on what issues to pursue.

Studies of early Common Cause membership revealed that it was composed of educated, upper-middle-class whites mostly from the East and West coasts. Anti-Vietnam sentiment was a key agenda item for the group at the outset. After the war wound down, however, the organization decided to emphasize procedural issues, such as campaign finance reform, corruption in government, and the like. Such a focus helped minimize ideological differences among the membership, as consensus could be more easily reached on "good government" issues. In this sense, Common Cause was following in the footsteps of Progressive era and other reformers.

Common Cause claims credit for enactment of federal election reform, helping to wind down the Vietnam War, enactment of many "good government" measures at the state level, reform of congressional procedures, blocking subsidies for a supersonic transport (SST), and cutbacks in the oil depletion allowance. Critics of the organization charge that it cloaks a liberal agenda in the guise of governmental improvement.

Founder John Gardner left the organization in 1977, to be followed by a succession of leaders, including Archibald Cox (former Watergate special prosecutor and Harvard Law School professor) and Fred Wertheimer, its current head. During the Reagan years, Common Cause found itself fighting rear-guard actions to protect reforms won in the previous decade. Its membership holds at about 250,000, with an annual budget of $6 to $8 million per year.

Source: Andrew S. McFarland, *Common Cause* (Chatham, NJ: Chatham House, 1984).

organization and funding the group's activities. Most interest groups rely on annual membership dues and voluntary contributions from sympathizers. Many also sell some ancillary service to members, such as insurance and vacation tours. Third, every group must have a leadership and decision-making structure. For some groups, this structure is very simple. For others, it can be quite elaborate and involve hundreds of local chapters that are melded into a national apparatus. Finally,

Cesar Chavez and Pat Robertson
Grassroots Populism

Grassroots politics takes many forms in America. One could scarcely find two more different grassroots activists than Cesar Chavez and Pat Robertson.

Cesar Chavez was the son of migrant farmers who harvested crops in Arizona and California. Chavez had long dreamed of organizing migrant workers, who typically labored under the most oppressive and exploitative circumstances. In 1962, he began to organize California grape pickers. In 1966, his group merged with another to form the United Farm Workers Organizing Committee. Shortly after the merger, they won their first big victory: wine grape growers recognized the UFWOC as the official bargaining agent for the workers. Renamed the United Farm Workers (UFW) in 1973, the organization attracted national attention, calling for boycotts on lettuce, grapes, and other produce as a means of forcing growers to make concessions concerning migrant worker safety, wages, and working conditions.

Chavez abhorred violence, finding success in nonviolent grassroots tactics such as picketing, marches, boycotts, fasting, and other legal direct-action methods borrowed from other movement leaders like Mahatma Gandhi and Martin Luther King, Jr. Chavez and his group won some important victories by turning national attention to the plight of migrant workers whose labors brought fresh produce to the rest of the country. In the 1980s, the UFW lost some organizing struggles to the Teamsters Union. Yet Chavez continued to exert key influence, engaging, for example, in a protracted fast in 1988 to draw attention to the use of pesticides considered harmful to both farm workers and consumers. The years of fasting took their toll, however, and Chavez died from heart failure in 1993.

Television evangelist turned presidential candidate Gordon M. "Pat" Robertson applied his own grassroots approach to Republican party politics in the 1980s and 1990s. The son of a United States senator, Pat Robertson at first turned his back on politics to start his own ministry. In the early 1970s, Robertson took over a run-down

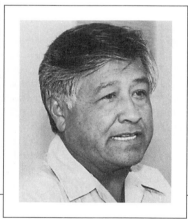

Cesar Chavez

most groups include an agency that actually carries out the group's tasks. This may be a research organization, a public relations office, a lobbying office in Washington or a state capital.

One example of a successful interest group is the National Rifle Association (NRA). Founded in 1871, the NRA claims a membership of over three million. It employs a staff of 350 and manages an operating budget of $5.5 million. Organized ostensibly to "promote rifle, pistol and shotgun shooting, hunting, gun collecting,

television station in Virginia in order to "claim it for the Lord." Within a decade, he had built a television ministry that reached about 30 million homes on the Christian Broadcasting Network (CBN) and grossed $200 million per year. Robertson's face became well known because of his television program "The 700 Club." Robertson's electronic grassroots support provided the basis for his move into national politics.

In 1987, Robertson announced that he would seek the Republican nomination for the presidency. Few considered his candidacy serious at first, but once again Robertson demonstrated what the *New York Times* called "awesome organizing ability." Emphasizing family values in his speeches, Robertson activated thousands of fundamentalist Christians, many of whom had never before been involved in politics. In the early party primaries and caucuses, where personal involvement counts the most, Robertson's supporters raised money from small donors and turned out for caucuses and primary elections. To the surprise of most pundits, Robertson finished second in the 1988 Iowa caucuses, and scored well in several primaries.

Yet much of what Robertson said aroused suspicion, including his assertions that only Christians and Jews were fit to govern, that both God and Satan had spoken directly to him, and that the world would end soon. He was labeled as quick-tempered and intolerant by critics, and in the long run his campaign faded. Despite his controversial views, Robertson has remained an important force in the Republican party, serving as a keynote speaker at its 1992 national convention. Robertson's fundamentalist Christian organizing tactics have subsequently spread to other Christian political organizations seeking to win local political races around the country.

As the accomplishments of both Chavez and Robertson illustrate, an individual or movement that can demonstrate its ability to rally significant numbers of motivated citizens to attract national attention or raise money can win important political concessions. Even in the modern media age, grassroots politics matters.

Source: Mark P. Petracca, ed., *The Politics of Interests* (Boulder, CO: Westview Press, 1992).

Pat Robertson

home firearm safety and wildlife conservation," the organization has been highly effective in recent decades in mobilizing its members to block any attempts to enact gun-control measures, even though such measures are supported by 80 percent of the Americans surveyed in opinion polls. The NRA provides numerous benefits to its members, like sporting magazines and discounts on various types of equipment, and it is therefore adept in keeping its members enrolled and active. Though the general public may support gun control, this support is neither organized nor very intense. This allows the highly organized NRA to prevail even though its views are those of a minority.

The Characteristics of Members

Membership in interest groups is not randomly distributed in the population. People with higher incomes, higher levels of education, and management or professional occupations are much more likely to become members of groups than those who occupy the lower rungs on the socioeconomic ladder.[6] Well-educated, upper-income business and professional people are more likely to have the time and the money, and to have acquired through the educational process the concerns and skills, needed to play a role in a group or association. Moreover, for business and professional people, group membership may provide personal contacts and access to information that can help advance their careers. At the same time, of course, corporate entities—businesses and the like—usually have ample resources to form or participate in groups that seek to advance their causes.

The result is that interest group politics in the United States tends to have a very pronounced upper-class bias. Certainly, there are many interest groups and political associations that have a working-class or lower-class membership—labor organizations or welfare-rights organizations, for example—but the great majority of interest groups and their members are drawn from the middle and upper-middle classes. In general, the "interests" served by interest groups are the interests of society's "haves." Even when interest groups take opposing positions on issues and policies, the conflicting positions they espouse usually reflect divisions among upper-income strata rather than conflicts between the upper and lower classes.

In general, to obtain adequate political representation, forces from the bottom rungs of the socioeconomic ladder must be organized on the massive scale associated with political parties. Parties can organize and mobilize the collective energies of large numbers of people who, as individuals, may have very limited resources. Interest groups, on the other hand, generally organize smaller numbers of the better-to-do. Thus, the relative importance of political parties and interest groups in American politics has far-ranging implications for the distribution of political power in the United States. As we saw in Chapter 11, political parties have declined in influence in recent years. Interest groups, on the other hand, as we shall see shortly, have become much more numerous, active, and influential.

THE PROLIFERATION OF GROUPS

Over the past twenty-five years, there has been an enormous increase both in the number of interest groups seeking to play a role in the American political process and in the extent of their opportunity to influence that process. This explosion of interest group activity has two basic origins—first, the expansion of the role of

---

[6]Kay Lehman Schlozman and John T. Tierney, *Organized Interests and American Democracy* (New York: Harper & Row, 1986), p. 60.

Ethel Andrus
The "Graying" of American Politics

Ethel Andrus (1885–1967)

During the early 1950s, Ethel Andrus, a retired high school principal, became active in the National Retired Teachers Association (NRTA). One of the major problems faced by NRTA members was the matter of health insurance. As elderly retirees, NRTA members found it difficult to obtain even minimal health insurance coverage at affordable rates. Yet, by very virtue of their age, NRTA members desperately needed such insurance. Andrus set about finding an insurance company that would provide NRTA members with adequate coverage at a more affordable group rate.

In 1955, Andrus finally found an insurance broker, Leonard Davis, who saw the possibility of profitably insuring older people and persuaded an insurer to take a chance. Davis was correct; insurance for the elderly proved to be a profitable venture.

In 1958, partly at the urging of Davis, who wanted to expand his insurance business beyond the NRTA's membership, Andrus founded the American Association of Retired Persons (AARP). By this time Andrus was concerned with far more than insurance. Because Americans were living longer, there were many more Americans over the age of sixty-five than ever before. Yet, the elderly were not recognized as a group with distinct needs and problems—problems involving health, economics, adjusting to retirement, abuse, crime, and so forth.

Andrus believed that elderly Americans did not need special sympathy or pity or government subsidies. Her belief was that the elderly could and should work together to develop dignity, pride, and self-reliance.

Since its founding, the AARP has moved beyond Andrus's conception. Today, the organization is among the most powerful lobbying groups in Washington. Through "telephone trees," AARP can mobilize a significant fraction of its 34 million members on behalf of issues of concern to the elderly such as Social Security, Medicare, and long-term health care. Recently, for example, the AARP leadership in New Jersey moved to protest cuts in Medicare spending. Using the telephone tree technique, the state AARP head called the state's eighteen district directors who, in turn, phoned 130 chapter presidents. The chapter presidents called their assistants, who phoned members. Within a day, tens of thousands of AARP members were calling the offices of New Jersey's two senators, Bill Bradley and Frank Lautenberg, to demand that they oppose cuts in Medicare. AARP chapters in all fifty states were doing much the same thing.

Few members of Congress are willing publicly to oppose AARP. Its members, most of whom are retired middle-income professionals, nearly all vote and have a great deal of time to write letters, attend rallies, and make their views known. Besides, what politician would like to be known as a granny basher? Thus, AARP has compelled politicians to treat senior citizens and their political demands with great respect. This is not the sort of self-reliance that Andrus envisioned for senior citizens, but it is surely conducive to dignity. Andrus died in 1967, before the organization she founded reached its present level of membership and influence in Washington.

government during this period; and second, the coming of age of a new and dynamic set of political forces in the United States—a set of forces that have relied heavily on "public interest" groups to advance their causes.

Expansion of Government

Modern governments' extensive economic and social programs have powerful politicizing effects, often sparking the organization of new groups and interests. The activities of organized groups are usually viewed in terms of their effects upon governmental action. But interest group activity is often as much a consequence as an antecedent of governmental programs. Even when national policies are initially responses to the appeals of pressure groups, government involvement in any area can be a powerful stimulus for political organization and action by those whose interests are affected. A *New York Times* report, for example, noted that during the 1970s, expanded federal regulation of the automobile, oil, gas, education, and health care industries impelled each of these interests to increase its efforts substantially to influence the government's behavior. These efforts, in turn, had the effect of spurring the organization of other groups to augment or counter the activities of the first.[7] Similarly, federal social programs have occasionally sparked political organization and action on the part of clientele groups seeking to influence the distribution of benefits and, in turn, the organization of groups opposed to the programs or their cost. For example, federal programs and court decisions in such areas as abortion and school prayer were the stimuli for political action and organization by fundamentalist religious groups. Thus, the expansion of government in recent decades has also stimulated increased group activity and organization.

One contemporary example of a proposed government program that sparked intensive organization and political action by affected interests is the case of health care reform. Soon after his election, President Clinton announced the formation of a health care task force charged with developing plans for a complete overhaul of the nation's medical-care system. Claiming that the escalating cost of health care represented a national social and economic crisis, Clinton and other Democratic strategists also believed that the creation of a vast federal health care program would provide them with the opportunity to link major constituency groups to the Clinton administration and the Democratic party for years to come. Health care, it was hoped, could do for the Clintonians what Social Security had done for Franklin Roosevelt and his Democratic party in the 1930s—it would provide millions of voters with an ongoing incentive to support the Democrats while providing the Democrats with a major new institutional base through which to manage the domestic economy.

Clinton's task force, led by First Lady Hillary Rodham Clinton, deliberated in secret. Indeed, for a time, even the composition of the group was secret. This secrecy, however, did not prevent hundreds of groups with interests in the health care field from mobilizing massive lobbying efforts. Major efforts were launched

[7]John Herbers, "Special Interests Gaining Power as Voter Disillusionment Grows," *New York Times,* 14 November 1978.

by various groups of physicians, the pharmaceutical industry, insurance companies,

nursing groups, mental health professionals, and even chiropractors. Every group claimed to speak for the public interest, although, curiously, each group's understanding of the public interest differed in some significant detail.

Major insurance companies, including Prudential, Aetna, and Cigna, organized as the Alliance for Managed Competition, enthusiastically supported what was generally seen as the president's preferred health care option. Large insurers liked the idea of managed competition because, as envisioned by the president, this system promised to give them virtually full control of the nation's health care system at the expense of physicians and smaller insurance concerns.[8] Indeed, the major insurers had worked for years to shape the health care debate by their involvement in the so-called Jackson Hole Group, which pioneered the notion of managed competition.

Smaller insurance companies, not surprisingly, sought to resist this effort by the giants to put them out of business. Their lobby group, called the Coalition for Health Insurance Choices, mounted a grass-roots campaign against managed competition.[9] In a similar vein, pharmaceutical manufacturers sponsored an advertising campaign designed to convince Americans that their own health could not be maintained without a healthy prescription-drug industry.[10] Pharmaceutical industry lobbyists also mounted a grass-roots effort aimed at members of Congress.

The administration denounced all these special interest activities. At one point, Clinton rejected a plea from the American Medical Association to be included in the health care reform planning process.[11] At the same time, however, the administration prepared its own public relations campaign to sell health care reform to the public and to Congress. Clinton presumed that congressional Republicans would bitterly oppose this major effort to expand the Democratic party's political base and institutional power. Clearly, Republicans would not accept the president's version of the public interest any more readily than he would accept the pharmaceutical manufacturers' corporate interests as *the* public interest.

New Politics Movement and Public Interest Groups

The second factor accounting for the explosion of interest group activity in recent years was the emergence of a new set of forces in American politics that can collectively be called the "New Politics" movement.

The New Politics movement is made up of upper-middle-class professionals and intellectuals for whom the civil rights and antiwar movements were formative experiences, just as the Great Depression and World War II had been for their

---

[8]Robin Toner, "Lobbyists Scurry for a Place on the Health-Reform Train," *New York Times,* 20 March 1993, p. 1.

[9]Alissa J. Rubin, "Special Interests Stampede to Be Heard on Overhaul," *Congressional Quarterly Weekly Report,* 1 May 1993, pp. 1081–1084.

[10]Howard Kurtz, "For Health Care Lobbies, a Major Ad Operation," *Washington Post,* 13 April 1993, p. D1.

[11]Robert Pear, "White House Shuns Bigger A.M.A. Voice in Health Changes," *New York Times,* 5 March 1993, p. 1.

Ralph Nader
Father of the Consumer Movement

Ralph Nader (b. 1934)

Perhaps the most startling fact about Ralph Nader's life of public service is that his profound impact on public policy has occurred despite the fact that he has never held public office, has no personal wealth, and does not have a well-known family name. In fact, Nader's life story resembles more than anything a Jimmy Stewart-like fictional hero in a Frank Capra movie.

Nader burst on the national scene at the age of thirty-two with the publication of *Unsafe at Any Speed,* a scathing indictment of the auto industry that criticized American carmakers for emphasizing profits and styling over safety and reliability. In the same year, Nader worked for enactment of the landmark National Traffic and Motor Vehicle Safety Act of 1966. This legislation set minimum safety standards for automobile design and construction, including such features as padded dashboards (unpadded dashes had produced severe brain damage injuries and decapitations) and collapsible steering columns (drivers were sometimes impaled on rigid columns).

Nader's activities have by no means been limited to auto safety, however. His investigations, and those of his associates, have encompassed such areas as gas pipeline safety standards, the condition of Native Americans, workplace safety, and food production standards. Nader no longer works alone. Investigations in these and other areas are carried on by several Nader-founded organizations, including the Center for the Study of Responsive Law, the Auto Safety Center, and the Public Interest Research Group. Nader

and his associates are credited with the enactment of such key legislation as the Wholesome Meat Act of 1967, the Natural Gas Pipeline Safety Act of 1968, the Radiation Control for Health and Safety Act of 1968, the Coal Mine Health and Safety Act of 1969, the Comprehensive Occupational Safety and Health Act of 1970.

Despite being considered the father of the consumer movement, Nader's own motivations are less aimed at protecting consumers per se, but rather at limiting what he sees as overweening corporate power. Nader argues that some corporate executives belong in jail for defrauding consumers, poisoning the food and water supply, and willfully manufacturing unsafe products. Nader and his organizations fund their activities from book sales, lecture fees, private donations, and foundation grants. The personal habits of this Harvard-trained lawyer are spartan. Nader works long hours, does not own a car, and lives in a modest residence.

One consumer expert noted that Nader "has done more as a private citizen for our country and its people than most public officials do in a lifetime." Nader critics might disagree. They would certainly agree, however, that Nader has been a potent force in national politics.

Source: Ralph Nader, *Unsafe at Any Speed: The Designed-in Dangers of the American Automobile* (New York: Grossman Publishers, 1966).

parents. The crusade against racial discrimination and the Vietnam War led these
young men and women to see themselves as a political force in opposition to the public policies and politicians associated with the nation's postwar regime. In more recent years, the forces of the New Politics have focused their attention on such issues as environmental protection, women's rights, and nuclear disarmament.

Members of the New Politics movement constructed or strengthened "public interest" groups, such as Common Cause, the Sierra Club, the Environmental Defense Fund, Physicians for Social Responsibility, the National Organization for Women, and the various organizations formed by consumer activist Ralph Nader. Through these groups, New Politics forces were able to influence the media, Congress, and even the judiciary, and enjoyed a remarkable degree of success during the late 1960s and early 1970s in securing the enactment of policies they favored while undermining the powers and prerogatives of many members of the postwar governing coalition. For example, opponents of the war in Vietnam ultimately succeeded in securing the withdrawal of American forces from Southeast Asia, and through the War Powers Act, the Foreign Commitments Resolution, the Arms Control Export Act, and stricter scrutiny of the CIA, they were able to impose limits on the president's ability to use American troops, intelligence operatives, and weapons to prop up anti-Communist regimes abroad. These acts placed restraints upon, although they did not entirely reverse, what had been a central thrust of American foreign policy during the era of the cold war. New Politics activists also played a major role in securing the enactment of environmental, consumer, and occupational health and safety legislation. This represented a dramatic change in the thrust of federal regulatory policy, whose primary function previously had been to restrict price competition in regulated industries, enabling firms in these industries to reap handsome profits and to pay above-market wages to their employees. In addition, environmental and community activists defeated numerous public works projects and, along with antinuclear activists, they have played an important role in restricting the growth of the multi-billion dollar nuclear power industry.

Environmental and consumer legislation in particular opened up avenues for participation by public interest groups in the political process. Turning frequently to the courts to enforce their assertions, public interest groups were frequently able to halt federally funded projects that they found objectionable.

One of the most significant examples of the use of this strategy was the controversy over completion of a dam being built by the Tennessee Valley Authority. The dam would have altered (and, in fact, destroyed) the habitat for a small fish known as the snail darter. The Endangered Species Act at the time prohibited federal agencies from engaging in actions that would "jeopardize the continued existence of an endangered or threatened species or . . . result in the adverse modification or destruction of [the species'] critical habitat." In a significance case, TVA v. Hill, the U.S. Supreme Court held that the act made it an unqualified duty for agencies to refrain from taking actions that would harm threatened or endangered species.[12]

---

[12]TVA v. Hill, 437 U.S. 153 (1978).

While environmentalists considered the case a major victory, the ultimate result was less satisfactory from their point of view. Concerned that the TVA project had been stopped midstream, so to speak, and wanting to insure that such a complete block might not hinder other projects, Congress amended the Endangered Species Act to soften the language and allow agencies to weigh the costs of protecting a species against the benefits to be gained from proceeding with certain kinds of projects.

New Politics groups sought to distinguish themselves from other interest groups—business groups, in particular—by styling themselves "public interest" organizations to suggest that they served the general good rather than their own selfish interest. These groups' claims to represent *only* the public interest should be viewed with caution, however. Quite often, goals that are said to be in the general or public interest are also or indeed primarily in the particular interest of those who espouse them. For example, environmental controls and consumer regulations not only serve a general interest in air and water quality and public safety, they also represent a way of attacking and weakening the New Politics movement's political rivals, especially big business and organized labor, by imposing restrictions on the manner in which goods can be produced, on capital investment, and on the flow of federal resources to these interests.

Private groups have also succeeded in cloaking their particular interests in the mantle of the public interest by allying themselves with public interest groups. One recent example is the case of cable television re-regulation. In 1987, Congress freed the television cable industry from local government price regulation. The result was a 61 percent increase in cable rates over the next three years. Public interest groups, led by the Consumer Federation of America (CFA), lobbied for the enactment of federal regulations governing cable prices and policies. Their efforts, however, were defeated by the cable industry. Then in 1991, consumer groups formed an alliance with the National Association of Broadcasters (NAB)—the powerful lobby group representing the television networks and local television stations. The NAB promised to support cable re-regulation in exchange for CFA support for a statutory provision that would require cable companies to pay local television stations for permission to transmit their programs. CBS President Laurence Tisch said that this provision would be worth one billion dollars to the broadcast industry. The NAB, in turn, mobilized the support of organized labor. Labor was willing to support the broadcasters because most television stations are unionized while most cable companies are not. For his part, Gene Kimmelman, legislative director of the CFA, called the alliance with broadcasters "a deal with the devil that was not a bad deal."[13]

In 1992, the alliance of consumer groups, broadcasters, and organized labor was able to overcome the lobbying power of the cable owners to secure the enactment of a bill re-regulating the cable industry and providing potentially enormous financial benefits to the broadcast industry. President Bush, however, responded to the cable owners and vetoed the bill. After a fierce battle, the cable television bill became the only one of Bush's forty-six vetoes to be overridden by Congress. The "deal with the devil" between public and private interests had prevailed.

[13]Mike Mills, "Bush Asks for a Sign of Loyalty; Congress Changes the Channel," *Congressional Quarterly Weekly Report,* 10 October 1992, pp. 3147–49.

This example underscores the often ambiguous character of claims that a policy serves the public interest. Whose interests truly prevailed in the case of cable television re-regulation? Who will ultimately provide the additional funds that will now flow into the coffers of the broadcast industry? The public interest is a concept that should be used cautiously. Claims that a group and its programs only serve some abstract public interest must always be viewed with a healthy measure of skepticism.[14]

STRATEGIES: THE QUEST FOR POLITICAL POWER

As we saw, people form interest groups in order to improve the probability that they and their interests will be heard and treated favorably by the government. The quest for political influence or power takes many forms, but among the most frequently used strategies are going public, lobbying, establishing access to key decision makers, using the courts, going partisan, and using bribery. These strategies do not exhaust all the possibilities, but they paint a broad picture of groups competing for power through the maximum utilization of their resources.

Going Public

Going public is a strategy that attempts to mobilize the widest and most favorable climate of opinion. Many groups consider it imperative to maintain this climate at all times, even when they have no issue to fight about. An increased use of this kind of strategy is usually associated with modern advertising. As early as the 1930s, political analysts were distinguishing between the "old lobby" of direct group representation before Congress and the "new lobby" of public relations professionals addressing the public at large to reach Congress.[15]

One of the best-known ways of going public is the use of institutional advertising. A casual scanning of important mass circulation magazines and newspapers will provide numerous examples of expensive and well-designed ads by the major oil companies, automobile and steel companies, other large corporations, and trade associations. The ads show how much these organizations are doing for the country, for the protection of the environment, or for the defense of the American way of life. Their purpose is to create and maintain a strongly positive association between the organization and the community at large in the hope that these favorable feelings can be drawn on as needed for specific political campaigns later on.

Going public is not limited to businesses or to upper-income professional groups. Rather, many groups resort to it because they lack the resources, the contacts, or the experience to use other political strategies.

[14]See Benjamin Ginsberg, *The Captive Public* (New York: Basic Books, 1986), Chapter 4. See also David Vogel, "The Public Interest Movement and the American Reform Tradition," *Political Science Quarterly,* 95 (Winter 1980), pp. 607–27.

[15]E. Pendleton Herring, *Group Representation before Congress* (New York: McGraw-Hill, 1936).

The sponsorship of boycotts, sit-ins, mass rallies, and marches by Martin Luther King's Southern Christian Leadership Conference (SCLC) and related organizations in the 1950s and 1960s is one of the most significant and successful cases of going public to create a more favorable climate of opinion by calling attention to abuses. The success of these events inspired similar efforts on the part of women. Organizations such as the National Organization for Women (NOW) used public strategies in their drive for legislation and in their efforts to gain ratification of the Equal Rights Amendment. In 1993, gay rights groups organized a mass rally in their effort to eliminate restrictions on military service and other forms of discrimination against individuals based on their sexual preference. Gay rights leaders met with President Clinton in mid-April 1993 and were assured of his support for a demonstration in Washington to be held at the end of the month.[16] Although President Clinton had campaigned actively for gay support during the election, he did not attend the march for fear of offending religious conservatives.

Organized labor sometimes uses the strike as a means of mobilizing public support, but it also has other means of going public. For example, in the 1970s, organized labor was weakened by Republican control of the White House. Its leaders were stunned in 1977 by their failure to push an important bill through Congress. This bill, known as the Common Situs Picketing Act, would have allowed a single union to close down a construction site by permitting workers from other unions to honor their picket lines. Victory on the measure seemed a sure bet: the act had been passed in the previous year, only to be vetoed by a Republican administration, and the 1976 election had put a Democrat in the White House and brought an overwhelming majority of Democrats into Congress. Despite warnings that sufficient votes had not been garnered and a last-minute appeal from House leader Tip O'Neill to pull the bill, a confident labor lobby pushed the bill to a vote—and lost.

Afterwards, union officials conceded that they had been out-politicked by the opposition and that they had miscalculated the political mood. The Carter administration was not willing to push the bill actively and jeopardize its tenuous relationship with the business community, and Congress was becoming edgy about catering to what might appear to be narrow union concerns. In the face of these problems, the labor lobby simply failed to do its job: it failed to drum up support by talking with House members (one congressman complained that he hadn't received a single visit from building trades officials), and it failed to pitch the bill broadly as a measure that would benefit more than simply the narrow interests of construction workers. The opposition, on the other hand, put together a massive lobbying campaign, flooding the House with letters and literature on the effects of the bill. In the face of such organized opposition, the labor lobby was forced to reassess the security of its position among House members.

Following their defeat, labor leaders decided to divert significant union money and time to grass-roots organizing and public relations aimed at nonunion laborers and the general public. The purpose of this campaign was to convince the American people and opinion leaders that labor's legislative goals were "not a power grab

---

[16]Ann Devroy, "Gay Rights Leaders Meet President in Oval Office: White House Tries to Play Down Session," *Washington Post*, 17 April 1993, p. 1.

PROCESS BOX 12.1

519

STRATEGIES:
THE QUEST
FOR POLITICAL
POWER

How Interest Groups Influence Congress

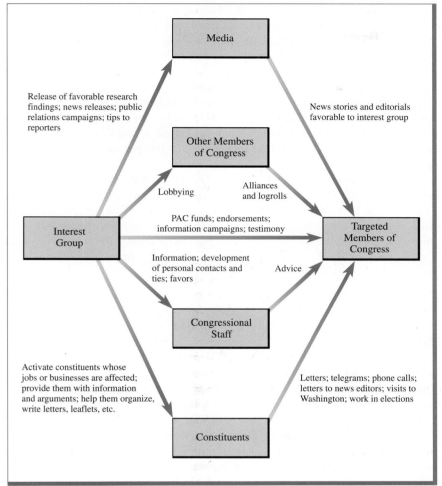

Release of favorable research findings; news releases; public relations campaigns; tips to reporters

News stories and editorials favorable to interest group

Media

Other Members of Congress

Lobbying

Alliances and logrolls

Interest Group

PAC funds; endorsements; information campaigns; testimony

Targeted Members of Congress

Information; development of personal contacts and ties; favors

Advice

Congressional Staff

Activate constituents whose jobs or businesses are affected; provide them with information and arguments; help them organize, write letters, leaflets, etc.

Letters; telegrams; phone calls; letters to news editors; visits to Washington; work in elections

Constituents

by labor leaders" but a positive good for American workers and for the public at large.[17]

Another form of going public is the grass-roots lobbying campaign. In such a campaign, a lobby group mobilizes its members and their families throughout the country to write to their representatives in support of the group's position. For example, in 1993 lobbyists for the Nissan Motor Company sought to organize a "grass-roots" effort to prevent President Clinton from raising tariffs on imported "mini-vans," including Nissan's Pathfinder model. Nissan's twelve hundred dealers across the nation, as well as their dealer's employees and family members, were urged to dial a toll-free number that would automatically generate a prepared

[17]"Labor Turning from Lobbying to New Political Tactics in Growing Struggle for Influence on Legislation," *New York Times,* 23 June 1977, p. 31.

mailgram opposing the tariff to the president and each dealer's senators. The mail-gram warned that the proposed tariff increase would hurt middle-class auto pur-chasers and small businesses, such as the dealers'.[18]

Among the most effective users of the grass-roots lobby effort in contemporary American politics is the religious Right. Networks of evangelical churches have the capacity to generate hundreds of thousands of letters and phone calls to Con-gress and the White House. For example, the religious Right was outraged when President Clinton announced soon after taking office that he planned to end the military's ban on the recruitment of homosexual soldiers. The Reverend Jerry Fal-well, an Evangelist leader, called upon viewers of his television program to dial a 900 number that would add their names to a petition urging Clinton to retain the ban on gays in the military. Within a few hours, 24,000 persons had called to sup-port the petition.[19]

Grass-roots lobbying campaigns have been so effective in recent years that a number of Washington consulting firms have begun to specialize in this area. Firms such as Bonner and Associates, for example, will work to generate grass-roots telephone campaigns on behalf of or in opposition to important legislative proposals. Such efforts can be very expensive. Reportedly, one trade association recently paid the Bonner firm three million dollars to generate and sustain a grass-roots effort to defeat a bill on the Senate floor.[20]

Lobbying

The First Amendment to the Constitution provides for the right to "petition the Government for a redress of grievances." But as early as the 1870s, "lobbying" became the common term for petitioning—and it is not an inaccurate one. Peti-tioning cannot take place on the floor of the House or Senate. Therefore, petition-ers must confront members of Congress in the lobbies, giving rise to the term "lobbying."

The Federal Regulation of Lobbying Act defines a lobbyist as "any person who shall engage himself for pay or any consideration for the purpose of attempting to influence the passage or defeat of any legislation of the Congress of the United States." Each lobbyist must register with the clerk of the House and the secretary of the Senate.

Lobbying involves a great deal of activity on the part of someone speaking for an interest. Lobbyists badger and buttonhole legislators, administrators, and com-mittee staff members with facts about pertinent issues and facts or claims about public support of them.[21] Lobbyists can serve a useful purpose in the legislative

---

[18]Michael Weisskopf and Steven Mufson, "Lobbyists in Full Swing on Tax Plan," *Washington Post,* 17 February 1993, p. 1.

[19]Michael Weisskopf, "Energized by Pulpit or Passion, the Public Is Calling," *Washington Post,* 1 February 1993, p. 1.

[20]Stephen Engelberg, "A New Breed of Hired Hands Cultivates Grass-Roots Anger," *New York Times,* 17 March 1993, p. A1.

[21]For discussions of lobbying, see Allan J. Cigler and Burdett A. Loomis, eds., *Interest Group Politics* (Washington, DC: Congressional Quarterly Press, 1983). See also, Jeffrey M. Berry, *Lobbying for the People* (Princeton, NJ: Princeton University Press, 1977).

and administrative process by providing this kind of information. In 1978, during debate on a bill to expand the requirement for lobbying disclosures, Democratic Senators Edward Kennedy of Massachusetts and Dick Clark of Iowa joined with Republican Senator Robert Stafford of Vermont to issue the following statement: "Government without lobbying could not function. The flow of information to Congress and to every federal agency is a vital part of our democratic system.[22] But they also added that there is a darker side to lobbying—one that requires regulation. The "Keating Five" scandal is a good example of this dark side.

The business of lobbying is uneven and unstable. Some groups send their own loyal members to Washington to lobby for them. These representatives usually possess a lot of knowledge about a particular issue and the group's position on it, but they have little knowledge about or experience in Washington or national politics. They tend not to remain in Washington beyond the campaign for their issue.

Other groups select lobbyists with a considerable amount of Washington wisdom. These professional lobbyists, who live in the Washington area, are either lawyers or former members of Congress or of government agencies. They seek to maintain close relationships with government agencies, members of Congress, and congressional staffers. These relationships often create misgivings about lobbying. For example, when Reagan aide Michael Deaver resigned in 1986 to become a professional lobbyist, members of the press and Congress charged that he was misusing his access to the president for private gain. Indeed, in 1988, a federal jury convicted Deaver of lying under oath about introducing a Korean trade offer to President Reagan and interceding with the White House on behalf of Trans World Airlines.

In 1992, President-elect Bill Clinton imposed stringent restrictions on future lobbying by members of his transition team. During the presidential campaign, Ross Perot had charged that both the Clinton and the Bush staffs included many professional lobbyists. One member of the Bush staff, as Perot noted, had often been employed as a lobbyist by Japanese firms. Perot suggested that it was inappropriate for someone who might be characterized as the agent of a foreign government to be involved in a presidential campaign.

After his inauguration, Clinton proposed tough new conflict-of-interest rules for members of his own and subsequent administrations that would limit future lobbying by government officials. Critics, however, noted that these proposals contained enough loopholes to permit the many former lobbyists appointed to official posts by Clinton to resume their lucrative careers after leaving office. For example, Clinton's rules would preclude such lobbyists as Howard Paster, on leave from the prominent Washington lobbying firm of Hill & Knowlton to work on the Clinton transition, from lobbying the White House for five years. However, Paster would be free to lobby Congress immediately after leaving the White House.[23]

A third type of lobbyist—the staff lobbyist—is clearly distinguishable from the amateur and from the paid professional. Staff lobbyists are usually professionals who work full time for a particular interest group. They have a number of duties,

---

[22]"The Swarming Lobbyists," *Time,* 7 August 1978, p. 15

[23]Jacob Weisberg, "Springtime for Lobbyists," *New Republic,* 1 February 1993, pp. 33–41.

INTEREST GROUPS IN
U. S. HISTORY

Interest groups have played a role in American politics since the founding. James Madison, in *The Federalist No. 10,* decried factions as evil but conceded they were inevitable in a true democracy. Instead of outlawing them, he proposed a system of checks and balances as a means of control. Many believed the Constitution itself was influenced by various economic interests of the time. Although interest groups always exist to some degree, they increase in visibility and power when the political, social, or economic environment of the country is disturbed or undergoing change.

During the period from 1830 to 1860, the first national organizations included many abolitionist groups, most notably the American Anti-Slavery Society. Founded in 1833, in response to increased abolitionist sentiment in the North, the group hoped to exploit the publicity gained by the British anti-slavery movement, which had that same year managed to induce Parliament to end slavery, with compensation to slave holders, throughout the British Empire. The Society's goal was to convince fellow citizens that slave holding was a heinous crime in the sight of God, and that the duty, safety, and best interests of all concerned required its immediate abandonment.

After the Civil War, another wave of national interest
groups emerged, representing mostly labor and business—
the result of expanding industrialization caused by the
postwar economic boom. In 1877, a series of wage cuts
provoked railroad workers and sympathizers across the
country to spontaneously strike. Without leadership,
however, the strike degenerated into mob violence: miles
of tracks and railroad cars were burned, rioting and
looting took the place of picketing and protesting. The
Great Railroad strike itself brought no results for workers,
but it demonstrated their potential strength. The Knights
of Labor—one of the first national unions to represent a
wide variety of labor forces—led many successful strikes
during the 1880s against the railroad industry.

The enormous social and economic changes in the United
States between 1900 and 1920—the rise of government
regulation, increased division of labor, immigration, and
improved communications systems—led to a new
proliferation of interest groups. One group, the National
Association of Manufacturers (NAM), initially created in
1895 to help expand business opportunities in foreign
trade, became a powerful institution in response to the rise
of organized labor. This group continues today to
successfully lobby the government to further their cause.

By far the largest explosion of interests groups has
occurred since the 1960s. This increase resulted from the
new politics movement, reflecting the social activism and
increased government activity of the period. The anti-war
movement, women's rights, civil rights, environmental,
and consumer groups surged in popularity. Also, changes
in campaign finance laws aided the rise of PACs as more
groups saw an opportunity to directly affect public policy.

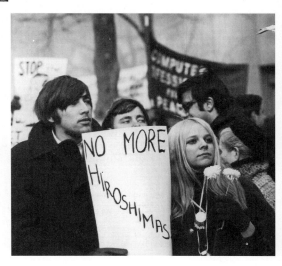

including part-time or full-time efforts in influencing the drafting or enactment of legislation.

The lobby industry in Washington is growing. At least eighteen hundred associations employing more than forty thousand persons are located in Washington. New groups are moving in all the time, relocating from Los Angeles, Chicago, and other important cities. More than two thousand individuals are registered with Congress as lobbyists, and many local observers estimate that the actual number of people engaged in important lobbying (part-time or full-time) is closer to fifteen thousand. In addition to the various unions, commodity groups, and trade associations, the important business corporations keep their own representatives in Washington.

Many groups—even those with reputations for being powerful—are constantly forming and reforming lobby coalitions in order to improve their effectiveness with Congress and with government agencies. The AFL and the CIO, for example, merged in 1955, largely for political advantage, despite many economic disagreements between them. In the 1970s, the venerable National Association of Manufacturers (NAM) tried vainly to work out a merger with the Chamber of Commerce of the United States. During that same period, more than two hundred top executives of some of America's most important business corporations—including AT&T, Boeing, Du Pont, General Motors, Mobile Oil, and General Electric—joined together in Washington to form a business roundtable, hoping it would coordinate their lobbying efforts on certain issues. In subsequent years, the roundtable worked effectively to promote business interests on labor law reform, tax policy, and consumer protection. In May 1993, Clinton proposed a set of rules that would prohibit lobbyists from making financial contributions to or raising funds on behalf of members of Congress, the president, or vice-president if they had lobbied these officials within the previous twelve months. This proposed reform was closely tied to Clinton's proposed campaign finance reforms to be discussed below.

Clinton also proposed that companies employing lobbyists be prohibited from deducting lobbying costs as business expenses from their federal taxes. This would, in effect, make it more difficult and costly for firms to employ lobbyists on behalf of their concerns. Not surprisingly, this proposal was bitterly resented by the lobbying industry, which saw it as a mortal threat to its own business interests. How did lobbying firms respond? By lobbying, of course. The American League of Lobbyists, a trade group representing the lobbying industry, quickly mobilized its members to conduct a vigorous campaign to defeat the proposal. One worried Washington lobbyist, however, observed, "This seems so self-serving, you wonder who is going to listen to us anyway."[24]

If enacted, Clinton's proposal would have the effect of reducing the influence of business groups in the policy process. This would, of course, work to the advantage of liberal public interest groups linked to the Democratic party. For this reason, a variety of business groups joined forces with the lobbying industry to oppose the administration's efforts.

---

[24]Michael Weisskopf, "Lobbyists Rally Around Their Own Cause: Clinton Move to Eliminate Tax Break Sparks Intense Hill Campaign," *Washington Post*, 14 May 1993, p. A16.

Gaining Access

525

STRATEGIES:
THE QUEST
FOR POLITICAL
POWER

Lobbying is an effort by outsiders to exert influence on Congress or government agencies by providing them with information about issues, support, and even threats of retaliation. Access is actual involvement in the decision-making process. It may be the outcome of long years of lobbying, but it should not be confused with lobbying. If lobbying has to do with "influence on" a government, access has to do with "influence within" it. Many interest groups resort to lobbying because they have insufficient access or insufficient time to develop it.

One interesting example of a group that had access but lost it and turned to lobbying and later to a strategy of "going public" is the dairy farmers. Through the 1960s, the dairymen were part of the powerful coalition of agricultural interests that had full access to the Congress and to the Department of Agriculture. During the 1960s, a series of disputes broke out between the dairy farmers and the producers of corn, grain, and other agricultural commodities over commodities prices. Dairy farmers, whose cows consume grain, prefer low commodities prices while grain producers obviously prefer to receive high prices. The commodities producers won the battle, and Congress raised commodities prices, in part, at the expense of the dairy farmers. In the 1970s, the dairy farmers left the agriculture coalition, set up their own lobby and political action groups, and became heavily involved in public relations campaigns and both congressional and presidential elections. The dairy farmers encountered a number of difficulties in pursuing their new "outsider" strategies. Indeed, the political fortunes of the dairy operations were badly hurt when they were accused of making illegal contributions to President Nixon's re-election campaign in 1972.

Access is usually a result of time and effort spent cultivating a position within the inner councils of government. This method of gaining access often requires the sacrifice of short-run influence. For example, many of the most important organized commodity interests in agriculture devote far more time and resources cultivating the staff and trustees of state agriculture schools and county agents back home than buttonholing members of Congress or bureaucrats in Washington.

Figure 12.1 is a sketch of some of the most important access patterns in recent American political history, Each pattern is almost literally a triangular shape, with one point in an executive branch program, another point in a Senate or House legislative committee or subcommittee, and a third point in some highly stable and well-organized interest group. The points in the triangular relationship are mutually supporting; they count as access only if they last over a long period of time. For example, access to a legislative committee or subcommittee requires that at least one member of it support the interest group in question. This member also must have built up considerable seniority in Congress. An interest cannot feel comfortable about its access to Congress until it has one or more of its "own" people with ten or more years of continuous service on the relevant committee or subcommittee.

It was often said that agriculture wrote its own ticket; this may be only a slight exaggeration of its political power until the 1980s. Agricultural interest groups often brought about great legislative successes without attracting much public attention. Their influence far exceeded their proportionate place in the American

FIGURE 12.1

The Iron Triangle in Defense

The emergence of an Iron Triangle was apparent very early in the relations of defense contractors and the federal government. Defense contractors are powerful actors in shaping defense policy, acting in concert with defense subcommittees in Congress and executive agencies concerned with defense.

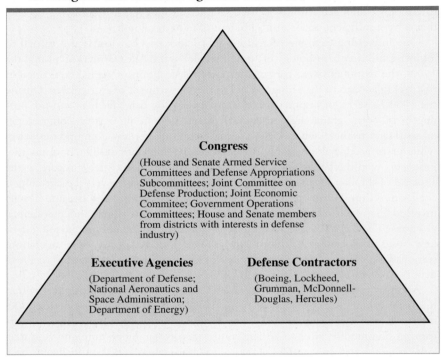

Congress

(House and Senate Armed Service
Committees and Defense Appropriations
Subcommittees; Joint Committee on
Defense Production; Joint Economic
Commitee; Government Operations
Committees; House and Senate members
from districts with interests in defense
industry)

Executive Agencies

(Department of Defense;
National Aeronautics and
Space Administration;
Department of Energy)

Defense Contractors

(Boeing, Lockheed,
Grumman, McDonnell-
Douglas, Hercules)

economy. Generally, agricultural interests managed to maintain high price supports even in inflationary periods. Also, tobacco farmers continued to get their special price supports even after tobacco was declared hazardous to health. After 1980, however, agriculture declined in political power as the economic fortunes of the industry waned and it was deserted by some of its former political allies. In recent years, the agricultural lobby found itself unable to maintain a united and coherent stand. The farm lobby has had to contend with internal disputes among competing sectors within its ranks as the pool of federal aid has shrunk. Disputes between sectors that would ordinarily have been kept as private matters now find themselves in the public eye: grain producers push for higher grain prices while poultry producers push for lower grain prices; cattle ranchers don't want programs that allow dairy farmers to slaughter their cows and then dump the beef into the cattle ranchers' market.

A very important example of access politics in action is the military-industrial complex—a notion put forth by President Eisenhower in his farewell address in

January 1961. The military-industrial complex is a pattern of relationships among

manufacturers, the Defense Department, and Congress that has emerged out of America's vast peacetime involvement in international military and economic affairs. More than four years before Eisenhower's farewell address, the House Armed Services Committee conducted a survey of the postmilitary careers of retired armed forces officers above the rank of major. The survey disclosed that more than 1,400 officers, including 261 at the rank of general or its equivalent in the navy, had left the armed forces directly for employment by one of the hundred leading defense contractors. [25] This same pattern was at the heart of the military procurement scandal that rocked the Reagan administration in 1988 when the news media and congressional investigators revealed that some defense contractors had systematically overcharged the Pentagon for military hardware and supplies.

During the Reagan and Bush administrations, the military-industrial complex became more closely linked to the Republican White House than to the Democratic Congress. Indeed, Republicans in the executive branch saw the military-industrial complex as an institutional base that could serve the Republican party in much the same way that the welfare and regulatory agencies of the domestic state served the Democrats. Thus, military and defense agencies, linked to industries and regions of the country that benefitted economically from high levels of defense spending, could enhance Republican political strength in the same way that domestic agencies, their clients in the public and not-for-profit sectors, and the beneficiaries of domestic spending programs strengthened the Democrats.

Between 1988 and 1990, the military-industrial complex was weakened by procurement scandals, budget cuts, and cost overruns that led to the cancellation of weapons projects such as the Navy's multi-billion dollar A-12 bomber. The successful performance of American military forces and, especially, of the technologically sophisticated new weapons systems used in the Persian Gulf War of 1991 provided an enormous boost for the political prestige of the entire national security sector. Televised accounts of the success of "smart bombs," cruise missiles, the radar-evading "Stealth" fighter, and anti-missile defenses such as the "Patriot" system, at least temporarily silenced congressional and other critics of the military-industrial complex who had argued for years that it built costly weapons that did not function properly. The political and economic collapse of the Soviet Union seemed to weaken arguments for continuing high levels of spending on expensive new weapons systems. Yet, despite the elimination of the major military threat to the United States—the threat that nominally justified enormous military outlays for nearly a half century—the country continued to spend hundreds of billions of dollars on defense. It was a tribute, in large part, to the political skill of the military-industrial complex that the United States continued to support a huge military force against a foe that no longer existed. But as the Clinton administration began to cut defense outlays to reduce the nation's budget deficit and free more funds for domestic programs, the military-industrial complex found itself losing

[25]U.S. Congress, House of Representatives, *Report of the Subcommittee for Special Investigations of the Committee on Armed Services,* 96th Congress, 1st session (Washington, DC: Government Printing Office, 1960), p. 7.

influence. Some wondered whether it would survive the end of the Cold War.[26]

Access politics through exchange of personnel is not limited to military-industrial relationships, however. It has spread to other areas, too, where it has also created "complexes." The spectacular expansion in federally assisted research and development programs has fostered the development of a government-science or government-university complex.

Changes in the manner in which federal aid is obtained for university research projects have generated a debate over the proper relationship between the federal government and private and public institutions of higher education in recent years. Federal financing of research programs and facilities at public and private universities for several decades has contributed significantly to research efforts, reaching a high in the 1960s and early 1970s. Traditionally, funds for research and development were either meted out by Congress to various agencies such as the National Science Foundation and, particularly, the Department of Defense, or these agencies solicited projects, subjecting them to a peer review process to determine what research proposals were worthy of funding.

Major research institutions had little quarrel with this system for many years, as the system tended to reward them consistently for various types of basic research. As federal funding dried up in the mid-1970s, however, the nature of the fight for funding has changed, setting off an intense competition debate. Rather than competing for funds from agencies through a peer review process, many universities have hired lobbyists and attempted to obtain direct appropriations from Congress via pork-barrel legislation. Appealing to members of the House and Senate with promises that funding for research facilities will attract industry, universities have been able to persuade members of Congress to request funds for particular research projects without having to endure a peer review selection process.

The grass-roots approach of agriculture and the personnel interchange approach of many businesses are not the only ways to engage in access politics. It is possible, although not easy, to buy access by securing the services of certain important Washington lawyers and lobbyists. These people can, for proper consideration, provide real access; not merely the more impersonal representation of the lobbyist. "Influence peddling" is the negative term for this sale or rental of access that goes on openly in Washington. Commerce Secretary Ron Brown, for example, was an important Washington lawyer-lobbyist, earning nearly one million dollars annually for his services to corporate clients and foreign governments, before joining the government. Brown's ties to a variety of corporate interests raised many questions about President Clinton's wisdom in appointing him—questions that Brown and his supporters angrily rebutted.[27]

The case of former defense secretary Clark Clifford is another example. After leaving the government, Clifford became one of the most important lawyers and lobbyists in Washington. In 1992, however, he was indicted by a federal grand jury for his role in the illegal takeover of Washington's First American Bank by a foreign banking corporation, the Luxembourg-based Bank of Credit and Commerce

---

[26]Thomas Ricks, "With Cold War Over, the Military-Industrial Complex Is Dissolving," *Wall Street Journal,* 20 May 1993, p. 1.

[27]William Raspberry, "Why Did Ron Brown Become a Target?" *Washington Post,* 20 January 1993, p. A21.

International (BCCI). Clifford was charged with lying to bank regulators about

BCCI's control of First American. A number of lobbyists and politicians have figured in the Justice Department's probe of fraud, illegal laundering of drug money, and bribery by BCCI. In 1993, Senator Orrin Hatch (R–Utah), who had defended the bank on the Senate floor even after bank officers pled guilty to federal money-laundering charges, came under investigation for his links to BCCI.[28]

Many retired or defeated members of Congress join or form Washington law firms and spend all their time either lobbying or funneling access. An even larger number of former government officials and congressional staff members remain in Washington in order to make a living from their expertise and their access. (Laws that limit the freedom of former government employees to take jobs in directly related private companies do not apply to employees of congressional committees.) The senior partnerships of Washington's top law firms are heavily populated with these former officials and staffers, and they practice law before the very commissions and committees on which they once served. There's an old saying about members of Congress—"they never go back to Pocatello"—and it is as true today as when it was coined.

Using the Courts (Litigation)

Interest groups sometimes turn to litigation when they lack access or when their satisfaction with government in general or with a specific government program is running low and they feel they have insufficient influence to change the situation. They can use the courts to affect public policy in at least three ways: (1) by bringing suit directly on behalf of the group itself, (2) by financing suits brought by individuals, or (3) by filing a companion brief as *amicus curiae* (literally "friend of the court") to an existing court case.

Among the most significant modern illustrations of the use of the courts as a strategy for political influence are those that accompanied the "sexual revolution" of the 1960s and the emergence of the movement for women's rights. Beginning in the mid-sixties, a series of cases were brought into the federal courts in an effort to force definition of a right to privacy in sexual matters. The effort began with a challenge to state restrictions on obtaining contraceptives for nonmedical purposes, a challenge that was effectively made in *Griswold* v. *Connecticut,* where the Supreme Court held that states could neither prohibit the dissemination of information about nor prohibit the actual use of contraceptives by married couples. That case was soon followed by *Eisenstadt* v. *Baird,* in which the Court held that the states could not prohibit the use of contraceptives by single persons any more than it could prohibit their use by married couples. One year later, the Court held, in the 1973 case of *Roe* v. *Wade,* that states could not impose an absolute ban on voluntary abortions. Each of these cases, as well as others, were part of the Court's enunciation of a constitutional doctrine of privacy.[29]

[28]Sharon Walsh, "Hatch's Links to BCCI Are Probed, Sources Say," *Washington Post,* 20 January 1993, p. A12.
[29]Griswold v. Connecticut, 381 U.S. 479 (1965). Eisenstadt v. Baird, 405 U.S. 438 (1972). Roe v. Wade, 410 U.S. 113 (1973).

The 1973 abortion case sparked a controversy that brought conservatives to the fore on a national level. These conservative groups made extensive use of the courts to whittle away the scope of the privacy doctrine. They obtained rulings, for example, that prohibit the use of federal funds to pay for voluntary abortions. And in 1989, right-to-life groups were able to use a strategy of litigation that significantly undermined the *Roe* v. *Wade* decision in the case of *Webster* v. *Reproductive Health Services* (see Chapter 4), which restored the right of states to place restrictions on abortion.[30]

Another extremely significant set of contemporary illustrations of the use of the courts as a strategy for political influence are those found in the history of the NAACP. The most important of these court cases was, of course, *Brown* v. *Board of Education of Topeka,* in which the U.S. Supreme Court held that legal segregation of the schools was unconstitutional.[31]

Business groups are also frequent users of the courts because of the number of government programs applied to them. Litigation involving large businesses is most mountainous in such areas as taxation, antitrust, interstate transportation, patents, and product quality and standardization. Often a business is brought to litigation against its will by virtue of initiatives taken against it by other businesses or by government agencies. But many individual businesses bring suit themselves in order to influence government policy. Major corporations and their trade associations pay tremendous amounts of money each year in fees to the most prestigious Washington law firms. Some of this money is expended in gaining access. A great proportion of it, however, is used to keep the best and most experienced lawyers prepared to represent the corporations in court or before administrative agencies when necessary.

Quite often the legal services desired by these corporations is precisely the converse of most litigation strategies: to keep them out of court. The willingness of corporate clients to compromise with government agencies in order to stay out of court helps to reinforce government policies and agency practices. A lobbyist for one of the more ideologically pro-business groups has observed that corporate bosses flinch from a real fight and "want to compromise before compromise is warranted."[32]

Many individual businesses bring suit themselves to influence government policy. Changes in federal regulatory policy will frequently generate a challenge by the business being regulated. This business will seek to have the regulatory policy, which almost inevitably will contain some ambiguity, interpreted by the courts in a manner that favors the business's position. Following passage of the Surface Mining Control and Reclamation Act of 1977, for example, coal companies launched a series of challenges not only to the constitutionality of the legislation but to its various provisions, hoping that the courts would limit the scope of agency regulatory authority in particular areas. Similarly, companies initiated challenges to the Federal Coal Leasing Amendments Act of 1976, under which the federal government asserted authority, among other things, to change the royalty terms of federal

[30]Webster v. Reproductive Health Services, 109 S. Ct. 3040 (1989).

[31]Brown v. Board of Education of Topeka, 347 U.S. 483 (1954).

[32]Quoted in "The Swarming Lobbyists."

coal leases when they came up for renewal. Even when the challenge is not particularly meritorious, companies can often benefit, as they can in litigation among
themselves, by tying up controversial matters for years in litigation and in the
meantime conducting business as usual. Alternately, when the agency's authority is
upheld, companies may be able to develop positions during litigation and obtain
concessions from the agencies that improve their bargaining positions within the
agencies after the litigation is concluded.

There is no paradox here. Many corporations and trade associations have to
worry about the impact of a major court case on their general political influence.
Individuals and small groups sometimes have greater impact on policy through litigation precisely because they do not need to worry about access or general influence with regard to other issues.

New Politics forces made very significant use of the courts during the 1970s
and 1980s, and judicial decisions were instrumental in advancing their goals. Facilitated by rules changes on access to the courts (standing is discussed in Chapter 8),
the New Politics agenda was clearly visible in court decisions handed down in several key policy areas. In the environmental policy area, New Politics groups were
able to force federal agencies to pay attention to environmental issues, even when
the agency was not directly involved in activities related to environmental quality.
Beginning with the U.S. Supreme Court's decision in *Citizens to Preserve Overton
Park, Inc.* v. *Volpe,* the federal courts allowed countless challenges to federal agency
actions under the National Environmental Policy Act (NEPA), brought by public
interest groups asserting that the agencies had failed to consider the adverse effects
of their actions upon the environment as required by NEPA.[33] While NEPA challenges have dropped off since the early 1980s, agencies have been much more
careful to give at least the appearance of having complied with the statute in federal actions as a result of the pressures imposed by New Politics groups.

While the skirmishes continued on the environmental front, consumer activists
were likewise realizing significant gains. Stung by harsh critiques in both the
Nader Report and the Report of the American Bar Association in 1969, the Federal Trade Commission (FTC) became very responsive to the demands of New
Politics activists. During the 1970s and 1980s, the FTC stepped up its activities
considerably, litigating a series of claims arising under regulations prohibiting deceptive advertising in cases ranging from false claims for over-the-counter drugs to
inflated claims about the nutritional value of children's cereal.

And while feminists and equal rights activists enjoyed enormous success in litigating discrimination claims under Title VII of the Civil Rights Act of 1964, antinuclear power activists succeeded in virtually shutting down the nuclear power
industry. Despite significant defeats, most notably *Duke Power Company* v. *Carolina
Environmental Study Group,* which upheld a federal statute limiting liability for
damages accruing from nuclear power plant accidents, challenges to power plant
siting and licensing regulations were instrumental in discouraging power companies from pursuing nuclear projects over the long term.[34]

Groups will also sometimes seek legislation designed to help them secure their

[33]Citizens to Preserve Overton Park, Inc. v. Volpe, 401 U.S. 402 (1971).
[34]Duke Power Co. v. Carolina Environmental Study Group, 438 U.S. 59 (1978).

PACs and Politics

T*he attempt to reform campaign finance laws in the early 1970s had an unintended effect: It prompted an explosion in the number and influence of Political Action Committees (PACs), organizations formed by corporations, unions, trade associations, and other entities to raise and distribute campaign contributions. Numbering now in the thousands, PACs are perfectly legal, yet are often condemned for corrupting the political process and providing incumbents with even more political advantages. (PACs rarely contribute to challengers since they have little chance of defeating incumbents.)*

Campaign finance expert Herbert Alexander defends PACs, arguing that the case against them is exaggerated. Public interest activist Fred Wertheimer summarizes the objections to PACs.

Alexander

Seen in historical perspective, political action committees represent a functional system for political fundraising that developed, albeit unintentionally, from efforts to reform the political process. PACs represent an expression of an issue politics that resulted from attempts to remedy a sometimes unresponsive political system. And they represent an institutionalization of the campaign fund solicitation process that developed from the enactment of reform legislation intended to increase the number of small contributors. . . . PAC supporters . . . should question the unarticulated assumptions at the basis of much anti-PAC criticism. Money is not simply a necessary evil in the political process. By itself money is neutral. . . . There is nothing inherently immoral or corrupting about corporate or labor contributions of money. . . . All campaign contributions are not attempts to gain special favors. . . . Money is not the sole, and often not even the most important, political resource. . . . Curbing interest group contributions will not free legislators of the dilemma of choosing between electoral necessity and legislative duty. . . . A direct dialogue between candidates and individual voters without interest group influence is not possible in a representative democracy. . . . The freedom to join in common cause with other citizens remains indispensable to our democratic system. The pursuit of self-interest is . . . a condition, not a problem.[1]

Wertheimer

The growth of PACs and the increased importance of PAC money have had a negative effect on two different parts of the political process—congressional elections and congressional decision making. First, PAC money tends to make congressional campaigns less competitive because of the overwhelming advantage enjoyed by incumbents in PAC fund-raising. The ratio of PAC contributions to incumbents over challengers in 1984 House races was 4.6 to 1.0; in the Senate, incumbents in 1984 enjoyed a 3.0 to 1.0 advantage in PAC receipts [comparable ratios hold for subsequent elections]. . . . The advantage enjoyed by incumbents is true for all kinds of PAC giving—for contributions by labor groups, corporate PACs, and trade and membership PACs. . . .

Second, there is a growing awareness that PAC money makes a difference in the legislative process, a difference that is inimical to our democracy. PAC dollars are given by special interest groups to gain special access and special influence in Washington. Most often PAC contributions are made with a legislative purpose in mind. . . .

Common Cause and others have produced a number of studies that show a relationship between PAC contributions and legislative behavior. The examples run the gamut of legislative decisions. . . .

PAC gifts do not guarantee votes or support. PACs do not always win. But PAC contributions do provide donors with critical access and influence; they do affect legislative decisions and are increasingly dominating and paralyzing the legislative process.[2]

[1]Herbert Alexander, "The Case for PACs." Public Affairs Council monograph (Washington, DC: 1983).
[2]Fred Wertheimer, "Campaign Finance Reform: The Unfinished Agenda," *The Annals of the American Academy of Political and Social Science 486* (July 1986), pp. 92–93.

aims through litigation. During the 1970s, for example, Congress fashioned legislation meant to make it easier for environmental and consumer groups to use the courts. Several regulatory statutes, such as the 1973 Endangered Species Act, contained "citizen suit" provisions, in effect, giving environmental groups the right to bring suits challenging the decisions of executive agencies and the actions of business firms in environmental cases even if the groups bringing suit were not being directly harmed by the governmental or private action in question. Such suits, moreover, could be financed by the expedient of "fee shifting"—that is, environmental or consumer groups could finance successful suits by collecting legal fees and expenses from their opponents.

In its decision in the 1992 case of *Lujan* v. *Defenders of Wildlife* (see Chapter 8), the Supreme Court seemed to question the constitutionality of citizen suit provisions. Justice Scalia indicated that such provisions violated Article III of the U.S. Constitution, which limits the jurisdiction of the federal courts to actual cases and controversies.[35] This means that only persons directly affected by a case can bring it before the court. If the Court continues to take this position, the capacity of public interest groups to employ a strategy of litigation will be diminished. Congress, however, has continued to write legislation designed to assist groups in achieving their aims through litigation.

An important recent product of this relationship between legislation and litiga-

[35]Lujan v. Defenders of Wildlife, 112 S. Ct. (1992); see also Linda Greenhouse, "Court Limits Legal Standing in Suits," *New York Times,* 13 June 1992, p. 12.

tion is the 1990 Americans with Disabilities Act (ADA), which took full effect in July 1992. The act resulted from the lobbying efforts of a host of public interest and advocacy groups and is aimed at allowing individuals with hearing, sight, or mobility impairments to participate fully in American life. Under the terms of this significant piece of legislation, businesses, private organizations, and local governmental agencies were required to make certain that their administrative procedures and physical plants did not needlessly deprive individuals with physical or emotional disabilities of access to the use of their facilities, or of employment and other opportunities.

Subsequently, the 1991 Civil Rights Act granted disabled individuals who believed that their rights under the ADA had been violated the right to sue for compensatory and punitive damages, as well as the right to demand a jury trial. In other words, this *legislation* encouraged individuals with disabilities to make use of *litigation* to secure their new rights and press their interests.

Hundreds of legal complaints were immediately filed. To make use of the opportunity for litigation, an advocacy group, the Disability Rights Litigation and Defense Fund, trained five thousand "barrier busters" to look for violators of the act and file law suits. Federal officials estimated that the ADA would generate approximately fifteen thousand discrimination cases every year—an estimate the act's critics consider much too low.[36]

Electoral Politics

Many groups seek to make use of electoral politics as a route to political influence. By far the most common electoral strategy employed by interest groups is that of giving financial support to the parties or to particular candidates. But such support can easily cross the threshold into outright bribery. Therefore, Congress has occasionally made an effort to regulate this strategy. Congress's most recent effort was the Federal Election Campaign Act of 1971 (as amended in 1974). This act limits campaign contributions and requires that each candidate or campaign committee itemize the full name and address, occupation, and principal business of each person who contributes more than $100. These provisions have been effective up to a point, considering the rather large number of embarrassments, indictments, resignations, and criminal convictions in the aftermath of the Watergate scandal.

The Watergate scandal, itself, was triggered by the illegal entry of Republican workers into the office of the Democratic National Committee in the Watergate apartment building. But an investigation quickly revealed numerous violations of campaign finance laws involving millions of dollars in unregistered cash from corporate executives to President Nixon's re-election committee. Many of these revelations were made by the famous Ervin Committee, whose official name and jurisdiction was the Senate Select Committee to Investigate the 1972 Presidential Campaign Activities.

Reaction to Watergate produced further legislation on campaign finance in 1974 and 1976, but the effect has been to restrict individual rather than interest

[36]See "Disabling America," *Wall Street Journal*, 24 July 1992, p. A10. See also, Gary Becker, "How the Disabilities Act Will Cripple Business," *Business Week*, 14 September 1992, p. 14.

TABLE 12.1
PAC Spending

Years	Contributions
1977–1978 (est.)	$ 77,800,000
1979–1980	131,153,384
1981–1982	190,173,539
1983–1984	266,822,476
1985–1986	339,954,416
1987–1988	364,201,275
1989–1990	372,100,000
1991–1992 (est.)	409,310,000

Source: Federal Election Commission

group campaign activity. Individuals may now contribute no more than $1,000 to any candidate for federal office in any primary or general election. A political action committee (PAC), however, can contribute $5,000, provided it contributes to at least five different federal candidates each year. Beyond this, the laws permit corporations, unions, and other interest groups to form PACs and to pay the costs of soliciting funds from private citizens for the PACs.

Electoral spending by interest groups has been increasing steadily despite the flurry of reform following Watergate. Table 12.1 presents a dramatic picture of the growth of PACs as the source of campaign contributions. The dollar amounts for each year indicate the growth in electoral spending. The number of PACs has also increased significantly—from 480 in 1972 to more than 4,000 in 1992 (see Table 12.2). Although the reform legislation of the early and mid-1970s attempted to reduce the influence of special interests over elections, the effect has been almost the exact opposite. Opportunities for legally influencing campaigns are now widespread.

Given the enormous costs of television commercials, polls, computers, and other elements of the new political technology (see Chapter 11), most politicians are eager to receive PAC contributions and are at least willing to give a friendly hearing to the needs and interests of contributors. It is probably not the case that most politicians simply sell their services to the interests that fund their campaigns. But there is considerable evidence to support the contention that interest groups' campaign contributions do influence the overall pattern of political behavior in Congress and in the state legislatures. Recently, for example, a lawsuit brought to light documents recording the activities of the General Electric Company's political action committee over a ten-year period. The PAC donated hundreds of thousands of dollars to congressional and senatorial campaigns for individuals who were or could be "helpful" to the company. One House member was given money because company officials felt that his help in protecting a $20 million GE project "alone justifies supporting him."[37]

---

[37]See Benjamin Ginsberg and John Green, "The Best Congress Money Can Buy," in *Do Elections Matter?*, ed. Benjamin Ginsberg and Alan Stone (Armonk, NY: M.E. Sharpe Publishers, 1986). See also Charles Babcock, "GE Files Offer Rare View of What PACs Seek to Buy on Capitol Hill," *Washington Post,* 1 June 1993, p. A10.

TABLE 12.2
Political Action Committee Growth: 1974–1992

As of:	Corpo-rate	Labor	Trade	Non-connected	Coop-erative	Corp. w/o stock	Total
12/31/74	89	201	318				608
12/31/76	433	224	489				1,146
12/31/77	550	234	438	110	8	20	1,360
12/31/78	785	217	453	162	12	24	1,653
12/31/79	950	240	514	247	17	32	2,000
12/31/80	1,206	297	576	376	42	56	2,551
12/31/81	1,329	318	616	531	41	68	2,901
12/31/82	1,469	380	651	723	47	103	3,371
12/31/83	1,538	378	645	793	51	122	3,525
12/31/84	1,682	394	698	1,053	52	130	4,009
12/31/85	1,710	388	695	1,003	54	142	3,992
12/31/86	1,744	384	745	1,077	56	151	4,157
12/31/87	1,775	364	865	957	54	145	4,165
12/31/88	1,816	354	786	1,115	59	138	4,268
12/31/89	1,796	349	777	1,060	59	137	4,178
12/31/90	1,795	346	774	1,062	59	136	4,172
12/31/91	1,738	338	742	1,083	57	136	4,094
12/31/92	1,735	347	770	1,145	56	142	4,195

Source: Federal Election Commission.

In May 1993, President Clinton introduced a set of proposals designed to diminish the impact of private contributions in political campaigns. Under the Clinton proposals, congressional candidates could voluntarily agree to spending limits that would, in turn, entitle them to public campaign funds. At the same time, contributions by individuals to political parties would be limited and contributions by PACs to campaigns would be curtailed. Table 12.3 outlines the Clinton plan.

Republicans immediately denounced the Clinton proposal as an effort to protect Democratic majorities in Congress by preventing challengers from raising enough money to have a chance of winning. Some Democrats were also wary of the Clinton plan, fearing that it would undermine their own campaign efforts.[38]

Beyond its direct implications for members of Congress, the Clinton plan would also restrict the influence of business firms and wealthy individuals who rely heavily on making campaign contributions to promote their political interests. The beneficiaries would be the various public interest groups who rely more on litigation, grass-roots lobbying, and electoral activism than on money to promote their interests. Such groups are, of course, to be found across the ideological and partisan spectrum. In general, however, the chief beneficiaries of the Clinton proposal would be the liberal, public interest groups tied to the Democratic party.

[38]Richard L. Berke, "Clinton Unveils Plan to Restrict PAC Influence," *New York Times,* 8 May 1993, p. 1.

TABLE 12.3

537

STRATEGIES:
THE QUEST
FOR POLITICAL
POWER

Campaign Finance: Clinton's Proposals

	Proposed	*Current*
Spending Limits	Voluntary limits would be placed on congressional campaign spending. Senate limits would vary, from $1.2 million to $5.5 million for general elections, depending on the state's population. House spending limits would be $600,000 in the two-year election period, but candidates could spend another 10 percent for fund-raising costs.	There are no spending limits in congressional campaigns.
Public Financing	Candidates who adhered to the spending limits would get vouchers to pay for television air time, postage, and printing. In the House, candidates could get vouchers to up to one-third of their spending limit. In the Senate, candidates could receive vouchers worth up to one-quarter of their spending limit.	Congressional candidates get no public funds in any form.
Soft Money	The big, unrestricted contributions that wealthy donors, corporations, and unions funnel through the political parties to help presidential campaigns would be eliminated. The parties could still accept large donations for funds that pay for building or non-administrative office costs.	Wealthy donors back candidates indirectly with large donations to parties.
Individual Donations	Individuals would be allowed to give federal candidates $60,000 per two-year election period. Within that limit, individuals each year can donate up to $25,000 to candidates, $20,000 to the national party committees, and another $20,000 for grassroots political activities in the states.	Individuals can give $30,000 each year to federal candidates.
Political Action Committees	House candidates could receive no more than one-third of their donations from PAC's and Senate candidates could collect up to 20 percent. The limit on how much a PAC can donate to a presidential candidate would drop to $1,000 from $5,000.	There are no caps on the amount candidates can receive from PAC's.
Lobbyists	Registered lobbyists, or those whose activities must be reported under the recent lobbying bill, may not contribute or solicit money for any member of Congress or the president or vice-president if they have lobbied the lawmaker or, in cases involving the president and vice-president, the executive branch, in the previous 12 months.	There are no special restrictions on lobbyists giving money.

Source: *New York Times,* 8 May 1993, p. 8.

Primarily for this reason, Republicans strongly opposed Clinton's reform efforts.

Financial support is not the only way that organized groups seek influence through electoral politics. Sometimes, activism can be even more important than campaign contributions. In recent years, for example, both opponents and proponents of abortion rights have been extremely active in national and local elections, providing political candidates with numerous campaign workers and activists. The willingness of pro- and anti-abortion groups to work vigorously in election campaigns helps to explain why the issue is far more important politically than its salience in public opinion polls might suggest.

In 1992, activists on both sides campaigned hard for the election of congressional candidates who supported their positions. In House races, abortion rights activists, organized in such groups as the Planned Parenthood Federation and Voters for Choice, helped secure the election of a number of sympathetic new legislators. Some observers calculated that backers of abortion rights gained as many as twenty votes in the House of Representatives. At the same time, opponents of abortion, led by the National Right to Life Committee, were pleased to see Georgia Democratic Senator Wyche Fowler defeated in a special runoff election by Republican Paul Coverdell. Fowler, a consistent supporter of abortion rights, had been vehemently opposed by anti-abortion forces.

Of course, abortion rights groups were especially pleased by the defeat of George Bush and the victory of Bill Clinton in the 1992 presidential contest. Since the late 1970s, Republican presidential strategy had involved opposition to abortion as a way of attracting the allegiance of conservative Catholics and fundamentalist Protestants. To this end, President Bush had supported legislative restrictions on abortion, endeavored to appoint federal judges known to be unfriendly to abortion, and signed a number of executive orders limiting abortion. These included the so-called gag rule, prohibiting abortion counseling in federally funded family planning clinics. President Clinton, who had been strongly supported by abortion rights forces, moved quickly to rescind the gag rule and other anti-abortion executive orders of the Bush era. With Clinton in office, abortion rights groups have pressed for the enactment of a "Freedom of Choice Act," that would outlaw most state restrictions on abortion.[39]

Using Bribery

The line between politics and corruption will always be difficult to draw. Most people will agree that it is better to seek power by currying favor than by using force or intimidation. When power is sought by outright purchase, however, the effect on the political system can be more demoralizing and disorienting than even the use of force.

The Washington bribery scandal, Koreagate, which came to light in the late 1970s, is a case in point. Originating with Korean businessman Tong Sun Park, a

[39]Julie Rovner, "Mixed Results on Both Sides Keep Spotlight on Abortion," *Congressional Quarterly Weekly Report,* 7 November 1992, pp. 3591–2.

web of legal and illegal favors was spun around at least two dozen members of the

House and Senate. Donations went to at least three former congressmen: $22,500
to Richard Hanna of California, and undisclosed amounts to Cornelius Gallagher
of New Jersey and Otto Passman of Louisiana. The wife of Edwin Edwards, a congressman who later became governor of Louisiana, received $10,000. Other con-
tributions included $4,650 to John Brademas of Indiana, deputy House majority
whip, and $4,000 to John McFall of California. Only a few indictments were ever
handed down as a result of congressional committee and grand jury investigations,
although suspicions of still more widespread and serious bribery efforts persisted.
Yet, it cannot be proven that Park or the Korean government got much for their
money. It may even be that Park was merely trying to buy access in illegal or suspicious ways rather than trying to pay bribes for specific favors.

Bribery is widepread in American society, but its true extent in national politics
is unknown—and because of its nature is likely to remain unknown. Some say
corruption from bribery is declining, and an occasional scandal like Watergate or
Koreagate is proof to them that it is being exposed and rooted out. Others insist
that such corruption is not declining, and they offer as evidence the same examples! Although the dispute between optimists and pessimists cannot be resolved, a
few general things can be said about bribery to keep the issue in proportion.

First, bribery is probably used more often to sustain friends than to convert opposition. An offer of a bribe to a member of the opposition is extremely risky. The
offer itself can be exposed, or it can be accepted with no intention of giving anything in return. The briber will certainly not bring suit for breach of contract.

Second, the offer of a bribe is frequently seen as evidence of weakness. Since
bribery is risky, it tends to be used only when all other tactics have been tried and
found wanting. Thus, the offer of a bribe can be counterproductive.

Third, bribery is only one of many forms of corruption, and corruption is not
limited to the political realm. For example, department stores build into their
prices a factor of at least 10 percent to cover losses from theft, and the Department
of Commerce estimates that employees account for the major portion of inventory
thefts.[40] One student of corruption in private industry estimates that theft, especially employee theft, accounts for 25 percent of all business losses.[41]

Fourth, bribery is probably limited to the narrowest of political issues: Who
will get a bridge or the contract to build it? Who gets a tax break, and how much
of one? How amicably and quickly can a case be settled before it gets to court or
to a commission? The bigger the issue—the more public it is, the larger the number of participants, the broader its scope—the less likely it is that bribery will be
employed as a strategy. With important issues, the stakes are big enough to make
people want to use bribery, but they generally would not do it because there
would be too many people to bribe, too much uncertainty, and too many advantages to be gained by the opposition from exposing the briber.

[40]Reported in "The Game Where Nobody Loses but Everybody Loses," *Forbes,* 16 April 1979, pp.
55–63.

[41]Mark Lipman, *Stealing* (New York: Harper Magazine Press, 1970).

GROUPS AND INTERESTS—THE DILEMMA

James Madison wrote that "liberty is to faction as air is to fire."[42] By this he meant that the organization and proliferation of interests was inevitable in a free society. To seek to place limits on the organization of interests, in Madison's view, would be to limit liberty itself. Madison believed that interests should be permitted to regulate themselves by competing with one another. So long as competition among interests was free, open, and vigorous there would be some balance of power among them and none would be able to dominate the political or governmental process.

There is considerable competition among organized groups in the United States. As we saw, cable television interests were recently defeated by an alliance of television networks and consumer groups after a fierce battle. Similarly, pro- and anti-abortion forces continue to be locked in a bitter struggle. Nevertheless, interest group politics is not as free of bias as Madisonian theory might suggest. Though the weak and poor do occasionally become organized to assert their rights, interest group politics is generally a form of political competition in which the wealthy and powerful are best able to engage.

Moreover, though groups sometimes organize to promote broad public concerns, interest groups more often represent relatively narrow, selfish interests. Small, self-interested groups are organized much more easily than large and more diffuse collectivities are. For one thing, the members of a relatively small group—say, bankers or hunting enthusiasts—are usually able to recognize their shared interests and the need to pursue them in the political arena. Members of large and more diffuse groups—say, consumers or potential victims of firearms—often find it difficult to recognize their shared interests or the need to engage in collective action to achieve them.[43] This is why causes presented as public interests by their proponents often turn out, upon examination, to be private interests wrapped in a public mantle.

Thus, we have a dilemma to which there is no ideal answer. To regulate interest group politics is, as Madison warned, to limit freedom and to expand governmental power. Not to regulate interest group politics, on the other hand, may be to ignore justice. Those who believe that there are simple solutions to the issues of political life would do well to ponder this problem.

SUMMARY

Efforts by organized groups to influence government and policy are becoming an increasingly important part of American politics. Such interest groups use a number of strategies to gain power.

---

[42]*The Federalist,* No. 10.

[43]Mancur Olson, *The Logic of Collective Action* (Cambridge, MA: Harvard University Press, 1971).

Going public is an effort to mobilize the widest and most favorable climate of opinion. Advertising is a common technique in this strategy. Others are boycotts, strikes, rallies, and marches.

Lobbying is the act of petitioning legislators. Lobbyists—individuals who receive some form of compensation for lobbying—are required to register in the House and Senate. In spite of an undeserved reputation for corruption, they serve a useful function, providing members of Congress with a vital flow of information.

Access is participation in government. Groups with access have less need for lobbying. Most groups build up access over time through great effort. They work years to get their members into positions of influence on congressional committees. Means of gaining access include the grass-roots approach of agriculture, the personnel-interchange approach of many businesses, and the use of influence peddling.

Litigation sometimes serves interest groups when other strategies fail. Groups may bring suit on their own behalf, finance suits brought by individuals, or file *amicus curiae* briefs.

Groups engage in electoral politics either by embracing one of the major parties, usually through financial support or through a nonpartisan strategy. Interest groups' campaign contributions now seem to be flowing into the coffers of candidates at a faster rate than ever before.

When all else fails, some groups try bribery. Although many believe bribery is widespread, it is nonetheless often a sign of weakness or an effort merely to sustain existing government support.

FOR FURTHER READING

Cigler, Allan J., and Burdett A. Loomis. *Interest Group Politics.* Washington, DC: Congressional Quarterly Press, 1983.

Day, Christine. *What Older Americans Think: Interest Groups and Aging Policy.* Princeton, NJ: Princeton University Press, 1990.

Goldfield, Michael. *The Decline of Organized Labor in the United States.* Chicago: University of Chicago Press, 1987.

Hansen, John Mark. *Gaining Access: Congress and the Farm Lobby, 1919–1981.* Chicago: University of Chicago Press, 1991.

Lowi, Theodore J. *The End of Liberalism.* New York: W. W. Norton, 1979.

McFarland, Andrew S. *Common Cause: Lobbying in the Public Interest.* Chatham, NJ: Chatham House, 1984.

Milbrath, Lester W. *Environmentalists: Vanguard for a New Society.* Albany, NY: State University of New York Press, 1984.

Moe, Terry M. *The Organization of Interests.* Chicago: University of Chicago Press, 1980.

Olson, Mancur, Jr. *The Logic of Collective Action: Public Goods and the Theory of Groups.* Cambridge, MA: Harvard University Press, 1971.

Paige, Connie. *The Right to Lifers.* New York: Summit, 1983.

Petracca, Mark, ed. *The Politics of Interests: Interest Groups Transformed.* Boulder, CO: Westview, 1992.

Pope, Jacqueline. *Biting the Hand That Feeds Them: Women on Welfare at the Grass Roots Level.* New York: Praeger, 1989.

Sabato, Larry. *PAC Power: Inside the World of Political Action Committees.* New York: W. W. Norton, 1984.

Scholzman, Kay Lehman, and John T. Tierney. *Organized Interests and American Democracy.* New York: Harper & Row, 1986.

Staggenborg, Suzanne. *The Pro-Choice Movement: Organization and Activism in the Abortion Conflict.* New York: Oxford University Press, 1991.

Stockman, David. *The Triumph of Politics.* New York: Harper & Row, 1986.

Truman, David. *The Governmental Process: Political Interests and Public Opinion.* New York: Knopf, 1951.

Vogel, David. *Fluctuating Fortunes.* New York: Basic Books, 1989.

13

The Media

TIME LINE ON THE MEDIA

EVENTS		INSTITUTIONAL DEVELOPMENTS
Alien and Sedition Acts attempt to silence opposition press (1798)	**1800**	Newspapers and pamphlets serve leaders (early 1800s)
New printing presses introduced, allowing cheaper printing of more newspapers (1820s–1840s)		Expansion of popular press; circulation of more newspapers, magazines, and books (1840s)
First transmission of telegraph message between cities (from Baltimore to Washington) (1844)		Nation begins to be linked by telegraph communications network (1840s)
Creation of Associated Press (AP) (1848)		
Completion of telegraph connections across country to San Francisco (1861)	**1850**	Advertising industry makes press financially free of parties; beginnings of an independent, nonpartisan press (1880s)
Publisher William R. Hearst sparks Spanish-American War (1898)		Circulation war between Hearst's *N.Y. Journal* and Pulitzer's *N.Y. World* leads to "yellow journalism"—sensationalized reporting (1890s)
Rise of large corporations and municipal corruption spark Progressive reform efforts (1880s–1890s)		Beginning of "muckraking"—exposure of social evils by journalists (1890s)
First radio news bulletins transmitted over radio; regular radio programs introduced (1920)	**1920**	Beginning of radio broadcasting (1920s)
NBC links radio stations into network (1926)		Regulation of broadcast industry begins with Federal Radio Commission (1927)
Great Depression (1929–1933)		*Near* v. *Minnesota*—Supreme Court holds that government cannot exercise prior restraint (1931)
Franklin D. Roosevelt uses radio "fireside chats" to assure the nation and restore confidence (1930s)		Federal Communications Act creates Federal Communications Commission (FCC) (1934)
Televised Senate hearings (1950s)	**1950**	Television is introduced (late 1940s–1950s)
Televised Kennedy-Nixon debate (1960)		Fairness doctrine governing TV coverage (1960s)

TIME LINE ON THE MEDIA

EVENTS	INSTITUTIONAL DEVELOPMENTS
John F. Kennedy uses televised news conference to mobilize public support for his policies (1961–1963)	Beginning of extended national television news coverage (1963)
"Daisy Girl" commercial helps defeat Goldwater and elect Lyndon Johnson president (1964)	*N.Y. Times* v. *Sullivan* asserts "actual malice" standard in libel cases involving public officials (1964)
Vietnam War; American officials in Vietnam leak information to the press (1960s–early 1970s)	Vietnam War first war to receive extended television coverage, which contributes to expansion of opposition to the war (1965–1973)
	TV spot ads become candidates' major weapons (1960s–1990s)
	Red Lion Broadcasting v. *U.S.* establishes "right of rebuttal" (1969)
Pentagon Papers on Vietnam War published by *N.Y. Times* and *Washington Post* (1971)	*N.Y. Times* v. *U.S.*—Supreme Court rules against prior restraint in *Pentagon Papers* case (1971)
Televised Watergate hearings (1973–1974)	
Unsuccessful libel suits by Israeli General Ariel Sharon against *Time* magazine (1984) and by General William Westmoreland against CBS News (1985)	FCC stops enforcing fairness doctrine (1985) Era of investigative reporting and critical journalistic coverage of government (1960s–1990s)
Televised Iran-Contra hearings (1987)	
Live coverage of Persian Gulf War (1990)	Military controlled media access throughout Persian Gulf conflict (1990)
Candidates make heavy use of talk show appearances in 1992 campaign; Ross Perot pioneers use of "infomercial"; Clinton uses televised town meetings during campaign and to sell programs after his election (1992–1993)	Politicians create new media formats to pitch themselves and their programs; era of permanent campaign (1992)

1970

1980

1990

The American news media are among the world's most free. Newspapers, news magazines, and the broadcast media regularly present information that is at odds with the government's claims, as well as editorial opinions sharply critical of the highest-ranking public officials. For example, even before Bill Clinton's inauguration in 1993, news commentators and editorial writers found reason to criticize the newly elected president. Clinton was accused of taking too much time to fill important governmental posts and appointing inexperienced individuals to major positions. He was charged with hypocrisy for sending his daughter to private school while claiming to support public education. Indeed, some commentators accused him of failing to live up to his campaign promises on taxes and the federal deficit even before his administration took office.[1]

During his first two months in office, President Clinton appeared to be gaining considerable media support. After the president's budget proposals were accepted by Congress, he was hailed as a political genius. One front page *Washington Post* story described the capital as "dazzled" by Clinton's acumen, and it approvingly quoted a Republican strategist who called Clinton "as formidable a political figure as I've seen in my lifetime."[2]

A few weeks later, however, the media had once again adopted a critical stance. In the wake of the Republican senatorial filibuster that defeated Clinton's proposed economic stimulus package, many commentators concluded that Clinton was inept after all. After his first hundred days in office, the president was accused of losing his focus, of disorganization, and of trying to do too many things at once. Suddenly, the capital was said to be more doubtful than dazzled. Not surprisingly, the president was reported to distrust and dislike the Washington press.[3]

Compared to its treatment of other recent presidents, though, the media are actually handling Clinton with kid gloves. Critical media coverage of the White House reached its apex during the Nixon administration. In this period, the three television networks frequently presented hostile assessments of presidential claims, actions, and speeches. Typically, a presidential address to the nation was followed by a half hour of network commentary purporting to correct inaccuracies and errors in the president's statements. These critical journalistic analyses led Nixon's vice-president, Spiro T. Agnew, to characterize television broadcasters as "nattering nabobs of negativism."

In this chapter, we will examine the role and increasing power of the media in American politics. First, we will look at the organization of the American news media. Second, we will discuss the factors that help to determine "what's news," that is, the factors that shape media coverage of events and personalities. Third, we will examine the scope of media power in politics. Finally, we shall address the

[1]Michael Kinsley, "Spare Change," *New Republic,* 1 February 1993, p. A8.

[2]David Von Drehle, "Beginner's Luck or President's Prowess? Dazzled Capitol Wonders if Clinton Can Keep Lighting Up the Board,"*Washington Post,* 26 March 1993, p. A1.

[3]See, for example, Thomas B. Edsall, "Clinton Loses Focus—and Time," *Washington Post,* 2 May 1993, p. C1; and Ann Devroy and Ruth Marcus, "White House Needs 'Tighter Coordination,' Clinton Concedes," *Washington Post,* 5 May 1993, p. A7. See also Jeffrey Birnbaum, "Resentful of Negative Coverage, Clinton Spurns the Media, but He May Need to Woo Them Back," *Wall Street Journal,* 15 April 1993, p. A16.

question of responsibility. To whom, if anyone, are the media accountable for the use of their formidable power?

547
ORGANIZATION
OF THE MEDIA

ORGANIZATION OF THE MEDIA

The United States boasts more than seven hundred television stations, approximately seventeen hundred daily newspapers, and nearly seven thousand radio stations. The great majority of these enterprises are locally owned and operated and present a good deal of news and many features with a distinctly local flavor. For example, for many months, viewers of the Syracuse, New York, evening news were informed that the day's "top story" concerned the proposed construction of a local garbage-burning steam plant. Similarly, in Seattle, Washington, viewers were treated to years of discussion about the construction of a domed athletic stadium, while audiences in Baltimore, Maryland, watched and read about struggles over downtown redevelopment. In all these cases, as in literally thousands of others, the local media focused heavily on a matter of particular local concern, providing local viewers, readers, and listeners with considerable information and viewpoints.

Yet, however much variation the American news media offer in terms of local coverage, there is far less diversity in the reporting of national events and issues. Most of the national news that is published by local newspapers is provided by the two wire services, the Associated Press and the United Press International. Although, as a result of Federal Communications Commission regulations, each television network may actually own no more than twelve local stations, more than five hundred of the nation's TV stations are affiliated with one of the three networks and carry its evening news reports. Dozens of others carry PBS (Public Broadcasting System) news. Several hundred local radio stations also carry network news or National Public Radio news broadcasts. At the same time, while there are only three national newspapers, the *Wall Street Journal*, the *Christian Science Monitor*, and *USA Today*, two other papers, the *New York Times* and the *Washington Post* are read by political leaders and other influential Americans throughout the nation. Such is the influence of these two "elite" newspapers that their news coverage sets the standard for virtually all other news outlets. Stories carried in the *New York Times* or the *Washington Post* influence the content of many other papers as well as the network news. Note how often this text, like most others, relies upon *New York Times* and *Washington Post* stories as sources for contemporary events.

National news is also carried to millions of Americans by the three major news magazines—*Time, Newsweek,* and *U.S. News & World Report.* Thus, while the number of TV and radio stations and daily newspapers reporting news in the United States is enormous, and while local coverage varies greatly from place to place, the number of sources of national news is actually quite small—two wire services, three broadcast networks, public radio and TV, two elite newspapers, three news magazines, and a scattering of other sources such as the national correspondents of a few large local papers, and the small independent radio networks. Beginning in the late 1980s, Cable News Network (CNN) became another major news source. The importance of CNN increased dramatically after its spectacular

coverage of the Persian Gulf War. At one point, CNN was able to provide live
coverage of American bombing raids on Baghdad, Iraq, after the major networks'
correspondents had been forced to flee to bomb shelters.

Nationalization of the News

In general, the national news media cover more or less the same sets of events, present similar information, and emphasize similar issues and problems (see Box 13.1).
Indeed, the national news services watch one another quite carefully. It is unlikely
that a major story carried by one will not soon find its way into the pages or programming of the others. As a result, we have developed in the United States
a rather centralized national news through which a relatively similar picture of

---

BOX 13.1
Nationalization of the News

L ocal newspapers throughout America generally offer their readers similar ac-
counts of the events of the day. On September 12, 1991, the front pages of the
Los Angeles Times and the *St. Louis Post-Dispatch* both highlighted stories on the tes-
timony of then Supreme Court nominee Clarence Thomas, Soviet troops leaving
Cuba, Israel granting freedom to 51 Arab prisoners, and the testimony of Clark M.
Clifford in a House hearing on the BCCI scandal.

events, issues, and problems is presented to the entire nation.[4] Nationalization

of the news began at the turn of the century, was accelerated by the development of radio networks in the 1920s and 1930s, and was brought to a peak by the creation of the television networks after the 1950s. This nationalization of news content has very important consequences for American politics.

Nationalization of the news has contributed greatly to the nationalization of politics and of political perspectives in the United States. Prior to the development of the national media and the nationalization of news coverage, the news traveled very slowly. Every region and city saw national issues and problems mainly through its own local lenses. Concerns and perspectives varied greatly from region to region, city to city, and village to village. Today, in large measure as a result of the nationalization of the media, residents of all parts of the country share similar ideas and perspectives.[5] They may not agree on everything, but they at least see the world in similar ways.

Regulation of the Broadcast Media

In some countries, the government controls media content. In other countries, the government owns the broadcast media (e.g., the BBC in Britain), but it does not tell the media what to say. In this country, the government neither owns nor controls the communication networks (although it does provide some funds for public radio and television), but it does regulate the broadcast media.

American radio and television are regulated by the Federal Communications Commission (FCC), an independent regulatory agency established in 1934. Radio and TV stations must have FCC licenses that must be renewed every five years. The basic rationale for licensing is that there must be some mechanism to allocate radio and TV frequencies to prevent broadcasts from interfering with and garbling one another. License renewals are almost always granted automatically by the FCC. Indeed, renewal requests are now filed by postcard.

But even though licensing is a routine administrative matter, the federal government has used its licensing power to impose several regulations that can affect the political content of radio and TV broadcasts. The first of these is the *equal time rule*. Under federal regulations, broadcasters must provide candidates for the same political office an equal opportunity to communicate their messages to the public. If, for example, a television station sells commercial time to a state's Republican gubernatorial candidate, it may not refuse to sell time to the Democratic candidate for the same position.

The second FCC regulation affecting the content of broadcasts is the *right of rebuttal*. This means that individuals must be given the opportunity to respond to personal attacks. In the 1969 case of *Red Lion Broadcasting Company v. FCC*, for example, the U.S. Supreme Court upheld the FCC's determination that a television station was required to provide a liberal author with an opportunity to respond to an attack from a conservative commentator that the station had aired.[6]

---

[4]See Leo Bogart, "Newspapers in Transition," *Wilson Quarterly,* special issue, 1982.

[5]See Benjamin Ginsberg, *The Captive Public* (New York: Basic Books, 1986).

[6]Red Lion Broadcasting Company v. FCC, 395 U.S. 367 (1969).

For many years, a third important federal regulation was the *fairness doctrine.* Under this doctrine, broadcasters who aired programs on controversial issues were required to provide time for opposing views. In 1985, the FCC stopped enforcing the fairness doctrine on the grounds that there were so many radio and television stations—to say nothing of newspapers and newsmagazines—that in all likelihood many different viewpoints were already being presented without having to require each station to try to present all sides of an argument. Critics of this FCC decision charge that in many media markets the number of competing viewpoints is small. Nevertheless, a congressional effort to require the FCC to enforce the fairness doctrine was blocked by the Reagan administration in 1987.

Freedom of the Press

Unlike the broadcast media, the print media are not subject to federal regulation. Indeed, the great principle underlying the federal government's relationship with the press is the doctrine of "no prior restraint." Beginning with the landmark 1931 case of *Near v. Minnesota*, the U.S. Supreme Court has held that, except under the most extraordinary circumstances, the First Amendment of the U.S. Constitution prohibits government agencies from seeking to prevent newspapers or magazines from publishing whatever they wish.[7] Indeed, in the case of *New York Times v. U.S.*, the so-called *Pentagon Papers* case, the Supreme Court ruled that the government could not even block publication of secret Defense Department documents furnished to the *New York Times* by a liberal opponent of the Vietnam War who had obtained the documents illegally.[8] In a 1990 case, however, the Supreme Court upheld a lower court order restraining Cable Network News (CNN) from broadcasting tapes of conversations between former Panamanian leader Manuel Noriega and his lawyer, supposedly recorded by the U.S. government. By a vote of 7–2 the Court held that CNN could be restrained from broadcasting the tapes until the trial court in the Noriega case had listened to the tapes and had decided whether their broadcast would violate Noriega's right to a fair trial. This case would seem to weaken the "no prior restraint" doctrine. But whether the same standard will apply to the print media has yet to be tested in the courts.[9]

But even though newspapers may not be restrained from publishing whatever they want, they may be subject to sanctions after the fact. Historically, newspapers were subject to the law of libel, which provided that newspapers that printed false and malicious stories could be compelled to pay damages to those they defamed. In recent years, however, American courts have greatly narrowed the meaning of libel and made it extremely difficult, particularly for politicians or other public figures, to win a libel case against a newspaper. The most important case on this topic is the 1964 U.S. Supreme Court case of *New York Times v. Sullivan,* in which the Court held that to be deemed libelous a story about a public official not only had to be untrue, but had to result from "actual malice" or "reckless disregard" for the

[7]Near v. Minnesota, 283 U.S. 697 (1931).

[8]New York Times v. U.S., 403 U.S. 731 (1971).

[9]Cable Network News v. Noriega, 1115 S. Ct. 451 (1990).

truth.[10] In other words, the newspaper had to deliberately print false and malicious
material. In practice, it is nearly impossible to prove that a paper deliberately printed false and damaging information and, as conservatives discovered in the 1980s, it is very difficult for a politician or other public figure to win a libel case. Libel suits against CBS News by General William Westmoreland and against *Time* magazine by Israeli General Ariel Sharon, both financed by conservative legal foundations who hoped to embarrass the media, were both defeated in court because they failed to show "actual malice." In the 1991 case of *Masson v. New Yorker Magazine,* this tradition was again affirmed when the Court held that fabricated quotations attributed to a public figure were libelous only if the fabricated account "materially changed" the meaning of what the person actually said.[11] For all intents and purposes, the print media can publish anything they want about a public figure.

NEWS COVERAGE

Because of the important role the media can play in national politics, it is vitally important to understand the factors that affect media coverage.[12] What accounts for the media's agenda of issues and topics? What explains the character of coverage—why does a politician receive good or bad press? What factors determine the interpretation or "spin" that a particular story will receive? Although a host of minor factors play a role, there are three major factors: (1) the journalists or producers of the news; (2) the sources or topics of the news; and (3) the audience for the news.

Journalists

First, media content and news coverage are inevitably affected by the views, ideals, and interests of those who seek out, write, and produce news and other stories. At one time, newspaper publishers exercised a great deal of influence over their papers' news content. Publishers such as William Randolph Hearst and Joseph Pulitzer became political powers through their manipulation of news coverage. Hearst, for example, almost singlehandedly pushed the United States into war with Spain in 1898 through his newspapers' relentless coverage of the alleged brutality employed by Spain in its efforts to suppress a rebellion in Cuba, then a Spanish colony. The sinking of the American battleship, *Maine,* in Havana Harbor under mysterious circumstances, gave Hearst the ammunition he needed to force a reluctant President McKinley to lead the nation into war. Today, few publishers have

---

[10]New York Times v. Sullivan, 376 U.S. 254 (1964).

[11]Masson v. New Yorker Magazine, 111 S. Ct. 2419 (1991).

[12]See the discussions in Gary Paul Gates, *Air Time* (New York: Harper & Row, 1978); Edward Jay Epstein, *News from Nowhere* (New York: Random House, 1973); Michael Parenti, *Inventing Reality* (New York: St. Martin's Press, 1986); Herbert Gans, *Deciding What's News* (New York: Vintage, 1980); and W. Lance Bennett, *News: The Politics of Illusion* (New York: Longman, 1986).

that kind of power. Most publishers are more concerned with the business end of the paper than its editorial content, although a few continue to impose their interests and tastes on the news.

More important than publishers, for the most part, are the reporters. Those who cover the news for the national media generally have a good deal of discretion or freedom to interpret stories and, as a result, have an opportunity to interject their views and ideals into news stories. For example, the personal friendship and respect that some reporters felt for Franklin Roosevelt and John Kennedy helped to generate a more favorable news coverage for these presidents. On the other hand, the personal dislike and distrust felt by many reporters for Richard Nixon was also communicated to the public. In the case of Ronald Reagan, the personal disdain that many national journalists felt for the president was communicated in stories suggesting that he was often asleep or inattentive when important decisions were made.

Journalists' preconceptions also have an effect on their perceptions of issues and events. In the late 1980s and early 1990s, sympathetic American media coverage of the Palestinian Intifada—organized protests against Israeli authorities—was, in part, the result of reporters' understanding of the issue as "civil rights" rather than what it actually was—civil war.[13] American journalists had grown up with the U.S. civil rights movement and were predisposed to understand Palestinian protestors as similar to African Americans demanding their constitutional rights as Americans. The truth of the matter, of course, is that Palestinians and Israelis are locked in mortal combat over control of land. Neither side is interested in civil rights in a territory controlled by the other. American reporters, however, saw the issue through American lenses rather than in the local context. Conservatives have, of course, long charged that the liberal biases of reporters and journalists result in distorted news coverage (see Figure 13.1).[14] A recent study has indicated that 44 percent of journalists consider themselves Democrats, while only 16 percent are Republicans. Most journalists deny that this results in biased news reporting.[15]

Sources of the News

News coverage is also influenced by the individuals or groups who are subjects of the news or whose interests and activities are actual or potential news topics. All politicians, for example, seek to shape or manipulate their media images by cultivating good relations with reporters as well as through news leaks and staged news events. Some politicians become extremely adept image-makers—or at least skilled at hiring publicists who are skillful imagemakers.

As we saw in Chapter 10, by using media consultants and "issues managers," many social, economic, and political groups vigorously promote their ideas and interests through speeches, articles, books, news releases, research reports, and other mechanisms designed to attract favorable media coverage. Typically, competing

[13]For a discussion, see Jim Lederman, *Battle Lines* (New York: Henry Holt, 1992).

[14]See Edith Efron, *The News Twisters* (Los Angeles: Nash Publishing, 1971).

[15]Michael Kinsley, "Bias and Baloney," *Washington Post,* 26 November 1992, p. A29.

FIGURE 13.1

553

NEWS
COVERAGE

Do Journalists Have a Liberal Bias?

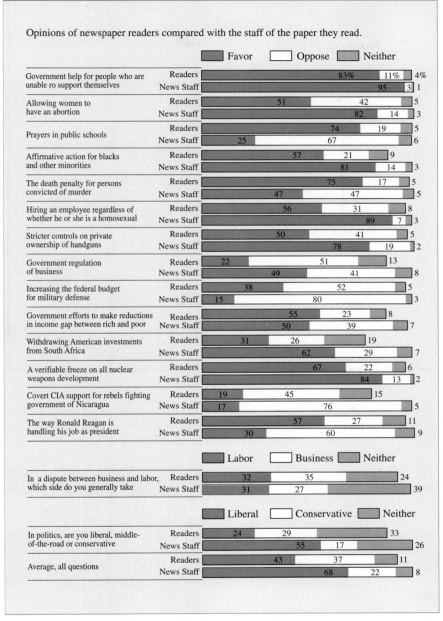

Opinions of newspaper readers compared with the staff of the paper they read.

	■ Favor □ Oppose ■ Neither
Government help for people who are unable to support themselves	Readers: Favor 83%, Oppose 11%, Neither 4% / News Staff: Favor 95, Oppose 3, Neither 1
Allowing women to have an abortion	Readers: 51, 42, 5 / News Staff: 82, 14, 3
Prayers in public schools	Readers: 74, 19, 5 / News Staff: 25, 67, 6
Affirmative action for blacks and other minorities	Readers: 57, 21, 9 / News Staff: 81, 14, 3
The death penalty for persons convicted of murder	Readers: 75, 17, 5 / News Staff: 47, 47, 5
Hiring an employee regardless of whether he or she is a homosexual	Readers: 56, 31, 8 / News Staff: 89, 7, 3
Stricter controls on private ownership of handguns	Readers: 50, 41, 5 / News Staff: 78, 19, 2
Government regulation of business	Readers: 22, 51, 13 / News Staff: 49, 41, 8
Increasing the federal budget for military defense	Readers: 38, 52, 5 / News Staff: 15, 80, 3
Government efforts to make reductions in income gap between rich and poor	Readers: 55, 23, 8 / News Staff: 50, 39, 7
Withdrawing American investments from South Africa	Readers: 31, 26, 19 / News Staff: 62, 29, 7
A verifiable freeze on all nuclear weapons development	Readers: 67, 22, 6 / News Staff: 84, 13, 2
Covert CIA support for rebels fighting government of Nicaragua	Readers: 19, 45, 15 / News Staff: 17, 76, 5
The way Ronald Reagan is handling his job as president	Readers: 57, 27, 11 / News Staff: 30, 60, 9

	■ Labor □ Business ■ Neither
In a dispute between business and labor, which side do you generally take	Readers: 32, 35, 24 / News Staff: 31, 27, 39

	■ Liberal □ Conservative ■ Neither
In politics, are you liberal, middle-of-the-road or conservative	Readers: 24, 29, 33 / News Staff: 55, 17, 26
Average, all questions	Readers: 43, 37, 11 / News Staff: 68, 22, 8

Source: *Los Angeles Times,* 11 August 1985, p. 12. Copyright, 1988, Los Angeles Times. Reprinted by permission. Three thousand editors and reporters and three thousand members of the general public were interviewed. Reporters and editors were substantially more liberal on a variety of social and political issues than their readers.

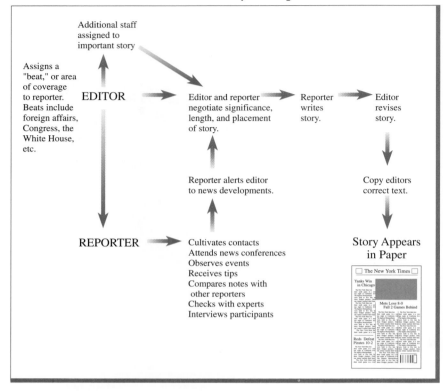

forces seek to present—and to persuade the media to present—their own interests as more general or "public" interests. In recent years, for example, liberals have been very successful in inducing the media to present their environmental, consumer, and political reform proposals as matters of the public interest. Indeed, the advocates of these goals are organized in "public interest" groups. Seldom do the national media ever question a public interest group's equation of its goals with the general interest of all.

The capacity of news sources and subjects to influence the news is hardly unlimited. Media consultants and issues managers may shape the news for a time, but it is generally not difficult for the media to penetrate the smoke screens thrown up by the news sources if they have a reason to do so. That reason is sometimes supplied by the third and most important factor influencing news content—the audience.

The Power of Consumers

The print and broadcast media are businesses that, in general, seek to show a profit. This means that like any other business, they must cater to the preferences of consumers. This has very important consequences for the content and character

of the news media.

Catering to the Upscale Audience In general, and especially in the political realm, the print and broadcast media and the publishing industry are not only responsive to the interests of consumers generally, but they are particularly responsive to the interests and views of the more "upscale" segments of the audience. The preferences of these audience segments have a profound effect upon the content and orientation of the press, of radio and television programming, and of books, especially in the areas of news and public affairs.[16] The influence of the upscale audience is a function of the economics of publishing and broadcasting. Books, especially books dealing with academic or intellectual issues, are purchased almost exclusively by affluent and well-educated consumers. As a result, the publishing industry caters to the tastes of this segment of the market.

For their part, newspapers, magazines, and the broadcast media depend primarily upon advertising revenues for their profits. These revenues, in turn, depend upon the character and size of the audience that they are able to provide advertisers for their product displays and promotional efforts. From the perspective of most advertisers and especially those whose products are relatively expensive, the most desirable audiences for their ads and commercials consist of younger, upscale consumers. What makes these individuals an especially desirable consumer audience is, of course, their affluence and their spending habits. Although they represent only a small percentage of the population, individuals under the age of fifty whose family income is in the 80th percentile or better account for nearly 50 percent of the retail dollars spent on consumer goods in the United States. To reach this audience, advertisers are particularly anxious to promote their products in the periodicals and newspapers and on the radio and television broadcasts that are known or believed to attract upscale patronage. Thus, advertisers flock to magazines like *The New Yorker, Fortune, Forbes, Architectural Digest,* and *Time.* Similarly, the pages of elite newspapers like the *New York Times* and the *Washington Post* are usually packed with advertisements for clothing, autos, computer equipment, stereo equipment, furs, jewelry, resorts and vacations, and the entire range of products and services that are such integral parts of the lifestyle of well-to-do business and professional strata.

Although affluent consumers do watch television programs and read periodicals whose contents are designed simply to amuse or entertain, the one area that most directly appeals to the upscale audience is that of news and public affairs. The affluent—who are also typically well-educated—are the core audience of news magazines, journals of opinion, books dealing with public affairs, serious newspapers like the *New York Times* and the *Washington Post,* and of broadcast news and weekend and evening public affairs programming. While other segments of the public also read newspapers and watch the television news, the level of interest in world events, national political issues, and the like, is closely related to the level of educa-

---

[16]See Tom Burnes, "The Organization of Public Opinion," in *Mass Communication and Society,* ed. James Curran (Beverly Hills, CA: Sage, 1979), pp. 44–230. See also David Altheide, *Creating Reality* (Beverly Hills, CA: Sage, 1976).

tion. As a result, upscale Americans are over-represented in the news and public affairs audience. The concentration of these strata in the audience makes news, politics, and public affairs potentially very attractive topics to advertisers, publishers, radio broadcasters, and television executives.

To attract audiences to their news and public affairs offerings, the media and publishing industries employ polls and other market research techniques, including the famous Nielsen and Arbitron rating services, analyses of sales, as well as a good deal of intuition to identify their audience's political interests, tastes, perspectives, and biases. The results of this research—and guesswork—affect the character, style, and content of the programming presented by the networks, as well as the topics of the books published by major houses and the stories and reports presented by the various periodicals. The media seeks to present material consistent with the interests or biases of important segments of the audience, and in a way that appeals to, or is at least not offensive to, the tastes or sensitivities of that audience.

Not surprisingly, given their general market power, it is the upper- and middle-class segment of the audience whose interests and tastes especially influence the media's news, public affairs, and political coverage. This is evident from the topics covered, the style of coverage, and in the case of network television, the types of reporters and newscasters who appear on the screen. First, the political and social topics given most extensive attention by the national media are mainly, albeit not exclusively, topics that appeal to the interests of well-educated professionals, executives, and intellectuals. In recent years, these topics have included the nuclear arms race, ecological and environmental matters, budgetary and fiscal questions, regulation of business and the economy, political changes in Russia and Eastern Europe, South African apartheid policies, attacks on Americans and American interests by terrorists and, of course, the fluctuations of the stock market, interest rates, the value of the dollar, the price of precious metals, and the cost of real estate. While many of these topics may, indeed, be of general importance and concern, most are of more interest to the upscale segments of the audience than to the lower-middle or working-class groups.

While these matters of concern to the upscale audience receive extensive media coverage, there are entire categories of events, issues, and phenomena of interest to lower-middle and working-class Americans that receive scant attention from the national print and broadcast media. For example, trade union news and events are discussed only in the context of major strikes or revelations of corruption. No network or national periodical routinely covers labor organizations. Religious and church affairs receive little coverage. The activities of veterans', fraternal, ethnic, and patriotic organizations are also generally ignored. Certainly, interpretations of economic events tend to reveal a class bias. For example, an increase in airline fares—a cost borne mainly by upper-income travelers—is usually presented as a negative development. Higher prices for commodities heavily used by the poor such as alcohol and cigarettes, on the other hand, are generally presented as morally justified.

The upscale character of the national media's coverage stands in sharp contrast to the topics discussed by syndicated afternoon television talk shows and the small number of news tabloids and major daily newspapers that seek to reach a blue-collar audience. These periodicals and programs feature some of the same events described by the national media. But from the perspective of these outlets and their viewers and readers, "public affairs" includes healthy doses of celebrity gossip, crime news, discussions of the occult, and sightings of UFOs. Also featured are ethnic, fraternal, patriotic, and religious affairs, and even demolition derbies. Executives, intellectuals, and professionals, as well as the journalists and writers who serve them may sneer at this blue-collar version of the news, but after all, are the stories of UFOs presented by the decidedly downscale *New York Post* any more peculiar than the stories of the UN told by the imperious *New York Times?*

The Media and Protest   While the media respond most to the upscale audience, groups who cannot afford the services of media consultants and issues managers can publicize their views and interests through protest. Frequently, the media are accused of encouraging protest and even violence as a result of the fact that they are instantly available to cover it, providing protesters with the publicity they crave. Clearly, protest and even violence can be important vehicles for attracting the attention and interest of the media, and thus they may provide an opportunity for media attention to groups otherwise lacking the financial or organizational resources to broadcast their views. During the 1960s, for example, the media coverage given to civil rights demonstrators and, particularly to the violence that Southern law enforcement officers in cities such as Selma and Birmingham directed against peaceful black demonstrators, at least temporarily increased white sympathy for the civil rights cause. This was, of course, one of the chief aims of Dr. Martin Luther King's strategy of nonviolence.[17] In subsequent years, the media turned their attention to antiwar demonstrations and, more recently, to anti-abortion demonstrations, antinuclear demonstrations, and even to acts of international terrorism designed specifically to induce the Western media to publicize the terrorists' causes. But while protest, disorder, and even terrorism can succeed in drawing media attention, these methods ultimately do not allow groups from the bottom of the social ladder to compete effectively in the media.

The chief problem with protest as a media technique is that, in general, the media upon which the protesters depend have considerable discretion in reporting and interpreting the events they cover. For example, should a particular group of protesters be identified as "freedom fighters" or "terrorists"? If a demonstration leads to violence, was this the fault of the protesters or the authorities? The answers to these questions are typically determined by the media, not by the protesters. This means that media interpretation of protest activities is more a reflection of the views of the groups and forces to which the media are responsive—as we have seen, usually segments of the upper-middle class—than it is a function of the wishes of the protesters themselves. It is worth noting that civil rights protesters received their most favorable media coverage when a segment of the white upper-middle class saw blacks as potential political allies. After the demise of this alliance, the media focused less on the brutal treatment of peaceful black demonstrators by bigoted law enforcement officials—the typical civil rights story of the 1960s—and

[17]David Garrow, *Protest at Selma* (New Haven, CT: Yale University Press, 1978).

Jessie Tarbox Bealson, a colleague of Jacob Riis, took this photograph of an immigrant family living in a one-room tenement. Riis's collection of photographs in the book *How the Other Half Lives* showed the terrible conditions in which many New York tenement dwellers lived during the 1880s. Its publication helped force landlords to improve their housing.

Lewis Hine was another photographer with a conscience. Concerned about hazards in the workplace, he concentrated on taking pictures of those who were least able to defend themselves: the children. While Hine once said, "If I could tell a story in words, I wouldn't have to lug a camera," his use of the camera led to stringent laws against child labor in the 1930s.

While civil rights protesters chose to take public actions, they did not know how far from their local city their actions would be seen. While demonstrating in Birmingham, Alabama, in 1963, protesters were attacked by police dogs, sprayed with tear gas and water hoses by the order of Police Commissioner Bull Conner. Partially as a result of worldwide viewing of increasingly violent reactions to the nonviolent protesters, pressure was put on the United States to live up to its claims to being a nation of "liberty and justice for all."

The media have increasingly covered more and more violent stories and shown at close range what they have found there. The graphic presentation of the conflict in Vietnam brought war into the homes of millions of Americans. Did this depiction of violence make viewers numb to violence or did it push Americans to take a stand on the issue of Vietnam? For one man, Nguyen Ngoc Loan, this famous photo of him killing a Vietcong prisoner at point-blank range followed him when he emigrated to Virginia and almost got him deported.

This image, captured on videotape on March 8, 1991, by a witness to the beating of Rodney King by Los Angeles police officers, received wide news coverage by all networks, bringing the issue of racism into the media's spotlight. Subsequently, this video was used as evidence by both the defense and the prosecution of the four officers placed on trial for police brutality. When the jury found the officers innocent, central Los Angeles erupted in rioting that lasted four days. The video, and the events following, changed again the way Americans view race and the protection of the law.

focused more on "black militants" when covering black protest activities. In the 1980s and early 1990s, the media generally portrayed African Americans as victims of Republican neglect. Thus, George Bush and the Republican administration, rather than the participants, received much of the blame for such events as the Los Angeles riots, sparked by the video of police officers beating an African American motorist.

Thus, the effectiveness of protest as a media strategy depends, in large measure, on the character of national political alignments and coalitions. If protesters are aligned with or potentially useful to more powerful forces, then protest can be an effective mechanism for the communication of the ideas and interests of the lower classes. If, on the other hand, the social forces to which the media are most responsive are not sympathetic to the protesters or their views, then protest is likely to be defined by the print and broadcast media as mindless and purposeless violence.

Occasionally, of course, segments of the upper social strata themselves engage in protest activities. Typically, upper-class protesters—student demonstrators and the like—have little difficulty securing favorable publicity for themselves and their causes. Witness the sympathetic coverage given anti-apartheid protests and antiwar protests, and the benign treatment afforded even upper-middle-class fringe groups like the "animal liberationists." First, upper-class protesters are often more skilled than their lower-class counterparts in the techniques of media manipulation. That is, they typically have a better sense—often as a result of formal courses on the subject—of how to package messages for media consumption. For example, it is important to know what time of day a protest should occur if it is to be carried on the evening news. Similarly, the setting, definition of the issues, and character of the rhetoric used, and so on, all help to determine whether a protest will receive favorable media coverage, unfavorable coverage, or no coverage at all. Moreover, upper-middle-class protesters can often produce their own media coverage through "underground" newspapers, college papers, student radio and television stations and, now, computer billboards. The same resources and skills that generally allow the upper-middle class to publicize their ideas are usually not left behind when segments of this class choose to engage in disruptive forms of political action.

MEDIA POWER IN AMERICAN POLITICS

The content and character of news and public affairs programming—what the media choose to present and how they present it—can have the most far-reaching political consequences. Media disclosures can greatly enhance—or fatally damage—the careers of public officials. Media coverage can rally support for—or intensify opposition to—national policies. The media can shape and modify, if not fully form public perceptions of events, issues, and institutions.

In recent American political history, the media have played a central role in at least four major events. First, the media were critically important factors in the civil rights movement of the 1950s and 1960s. Television photos showing peaceful civil rights marchers attacked by club-swinging police helped to generate sympathy among northern whites for the civil rights struggle and greatly increased the pressure on Congress to bring an end to segregation.[18] Second, the media were instrumental in compelling the Nixon administration to negotiate an end to the Vietnam War. Beginning in 1967, the national media portrayed the war as misguided and unwinnable and, as a result, helped to turn popular sentiment against continued American involvement.[19] So strong was the effect of the media, in fact, that when Walter Cronkite told television news viewers that the war was unwinnable, Johnson himself was reported to have said, "If I've lost Walter, then it's over. I've lost Mr. Average Citizen."[20]

Third, the media were central actors in the Watergate affair, which ultimately forced President Richard Nixon, landslide victor in the 1972 presidential election, to resign from office in disgrace. It was the relentless series of investigations launched by the *Washington Post,* the *New York Times,* and the television networks that led to the disclosures of the various abuses of which Nixon was guilty and ultimately forced Nixon to choose between resignation and almost certain impeachment. Finally, the media were crucial actors in the Iran-Contra investigations of the Reagan administration's dealings with the Iranian government and Nicaraguan Contra fighters, which seriously eroded President Reagan's power and standing during his last two years in office.

The Sources of Media Power

The power of the media stems from several sources. First, the media help to set the agenda for political discussion. Groups and forces that wish to bring their ideas before the public in order to generate support for policy proposals or political candidacies must somehow secure media coverage. If the media are persuaded that an idea is newsworthy, then they may declare it an "issue" that must be resolved or a "problem" to be solved, thus clearing the first hurdle in the policy-making process. On the other hand, if an idea lacks or loses media appeal, its chance of resulting in new programs or policies is diminished. Some ideas seem to surface, gain media support for a time, lose media appeal, and then resurface. Examples include repair of the "infrastructure," a topic that surfaced in the early 1980s, disappeared after 1983, and then reemerged in the press in the 1992 presidential campaign. Similarly, national health insurance excited media attention in the 1970s, all but disappeared during the 1980s, and became a major topic after 1992.

---

[18]Ibid.

[19]See Todd Gitlin, *The Whole World Is Watching* (Berkeley, CA: University of California Press, 1980).

[20]Quoted in George Brown Tindall, *America: A Narrative History,* 2nd ed. (New York: W. W. Norton, 1988), p. 1379.

Anthony Lewis and George Will
Journalists and the Political Process

The norms of journalism call for reporters to maintain some degree of "objectivity" about the subject on which they report. Reporters whose job is political commentary, such as Anthony Lewis of the *New York Times* and syndicated columnist George Will, have greater latitude to express their own opinions. Sometimes, their impact on politics can be greater than that of politicians.

Anthony Lewis began his career with the *Times* in 1948. After leaving the *Times* for a year to work for the Democratic National Committee, Lewis returned to the paper and in 1955 won the first of two Pulitzer Prizes for national reporting. His first Pulitzer was for a series of stories on a civilian employee of the U.S. Navy wrongfully accused of being a security risk. He received the second in 1963 for his coverage of the Supreme Court.

In 1969, Lewis became a columnist for the *Times*. His weekly opinion columns, found on the *Times's* op-ed page, have generally championed a variety of liberal causes and have been influential among liberals throughout the nation. Lewis has devoted particular attention to constitutional, legal, and criminal justice issues, including columns critical of the death penalty, the protection of the rights of the accused, and much criticism of the conservative direction of the Supreme Court in the 1980s and 1990s. His special interest in criminal and constitutional matters is reflected not only in his columns but in two highly praised books: *Gideon's Trumpet,* the story of the man whose lawsuit resulted in a Supreme Court ruling extending the right to counsel to the states; and *Make No Law,* an account

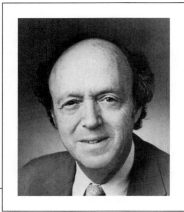

Anthony Lewis

The single most amusing example of an issue created and then dropped by the media remains Lincoln Steffens's "crime wave." Steffens, who later became a famous and influential journalist, began his career as a police reporter for the *New York Post* in the early 1900s. One quiet summer, Steffens began reading the police daily crime file and reporting all the crimes he found there. To compete, the reporters for all the other city papers began to follow suit. Soon, all the papers proclaimed that the city was in the grip of a crime wave of monstrous proportions and demanded that city officials take immediate action. Interestingly enough, during this "crime wave," the actual incidence of crime in the city was at a low point—only the number of newspaper stories about crime had increased. Police Commis-

of the famous *Sullivan* Supreme Court case, which extended greater legal protection to the media.

George Will began his career as a college professor trained in political philosophy. After a brief stint working for Republican Senator Gordon Allott, Will began writing a political column in the *Washington Post* in 1973. His columns came to be known for their dry wit and graceful style. Will was soon writing regularly for *Newsweek* and appearing regularly on television news and commentary shows.

Will's political slant is strongly conservative. He has staunchly supported a strong national defense, nuclear power, and term limits for members of Congress, and he has opposed abortion, affirmative action, and homosexual rights. In 1977, Will won the Pulitzer Prize for distinguished commentary.

Will's conservative leanings made him an ardent supporter of Ronald Reagan. During the 1980 presidential campaign, Will actually helped Reagan prepare for his debate with incumbent President Jimmy Carter, using a stolen copy of the Carter campaign's briefing book acquired by the Reagan campaign. After assisting Reagan before the debate, Will was asked in a television interview what he knew about Reagan's preparations for the debate with Carter. Will failed to mention his personal involvement, or the fact that the stolen briefing book was used to help Reagan prepare.

Unlike reporters, political commentators have much greater latitude to champion some political causes and attack others. Both Lewis and Will have placed greater emphasis on advocacy than on reporting.

Source: Eric Alterman, *Sound and Fury: The Washington Punditocracy and the Collapse of American Politics* (New York: Harper Collins, 1992).

George Will

sioner (and later U.S. President) Theodore Roosevelt ended the crime wave by blocking newspaper access to the police files. With their source of crime news removed, the reporters moved on to other topics.[21]

A second source of the media's power is their influence as interpreters and evaluators of events and political results. For example, media interpretations may often determine how people perceive an election outcome. In 1968, despite the growing strength of the opposition to his Vietnam War policies, incumbent President

[21]Lincoln Steffens, *The Autobiography of Lincoln Steffens* (New York: The Literary Guild, 1931), Chapter 14.

Lyndon Johnson won two-thirds of the votes cast in New Hampshire's Democratic presidential primary. His rival, Senator Eugene McCarthy, received less than one-third. The broadcast media, however, declared the outcome to have been a great victory for McCarthy, who was said to have done much better than "expected" (or at least expected by the media). His "defeat" in New Hampshire was one of the factors that persuaded Johnson to withdraw from the 1968 presidential race.

During the 1992 campaign, while being interviewed on "60 Minutes," Ross Perot ascribed his earlier decision to withdraw from the presidential campaign to his fear of a Republican "dirty tricks" campaign directed against him. Most media commentators reacted to Perot's assertion with incredulity and cited it as evidence that the Texan lacked the emotional stability needed by a president. Following that episode, they perceived that Perot's campaign was "losing momentum." Though Perot still received approximately 19 percent of the popular vote, the "60 Minutes" broadcast and the subsequent media reaction probably lost him substantial support in the electorate.

Of course, the influence of media interpretations extends beyond the electoral arena. For example, the national media portrayed the 1967 North Vietnamese Tet offensive as a staggering defeat for American military forces when, in fact, Tet was actually a crushing defeat for the North Vietnamese. The media's interpretation, however, turned Tet into a decisive political victory for North Vietnam and marked the beginning of the end of American involvement in the Vietnam War.

Finally, the media have a good deal of power to shape popular perceptions of politicians and political leaders. Most citizens will never meet George Bush or Bill Clinton or Al Gore. Popular perceptions and evaluations of these individuals are based upon their media images. Obviously, through public relations and other techniques, politicians seek to cultivate favorable media images. But the media have a good deal of discretion over how individuals are portrayed, or how they are allowed to portray themselves. For example, in 1976 candidate Jimmy Carter was portrayed favorably as a nuclear engineer, successful businessman, and populist. President Gerald Ford, by contrast, was portrayed as an incompetent and inexperienced bumbler. In point of fact, Ford was a graduate of the Yale Law School and minority leader of the House of Representatives, while Carter's background and experience in public affairs were much more limited. Ford, of course, had received favorable media coverage when he assumed office after Richard Nixon's resignation, but then he lost his standing with the media when he pardoned Nixon. Interestingly enough, the media came to change its collective mind about Jimmy Carter during the course of his term in office. After 1978, Carter was portrayed as having been an unsuccessful businessman and a mediocre engineer. In 1988, the media savaged Republican vice-presidential candidate Dan Quayle for avoiding the danger of serving in Vietnam by using family connections to obtain a place in the Indiana National Guard during the 1960s. In 1992, however, the media treated George Bush's charges that Bill Clinton had attempted to evade the draft as an inappropriate effort to divert popular attention from the "real" issues of the campaign.

In the case of political candidates, the media have considerable influence over whether or not a particular individual will receive public attention, whether or not a particular individual will be taken seriously as a viable contender, and whether

the public will perceive a candidate's performance favorably. Thus, if the media
find a candidate interesting, they may treat him or her as a serious contender even
though the facts of the matter seem to suggest otherwise. For example, in 1992,
the broadcast media found Ross Perot to be an incredible novelty. Here was a self-
made billionaire with oversized ears who was determined to challenge the American political establishment. Some members of the press treated Perot as a potential
Mussolini, while others portrayed him as a wealthy Harry Truman. Nevertheless,
from the beginning, Perot received enormous media attention, which helped
make his quixotic candidacy a serious threat to the two major parties.[22]

In a similar vein, the media may declare that a candidate has "momentum," a
mythical property that the media confer upon candidates they admire. Momentum
has no substantive meaning—it is simply a media prediction that a particular candidate will do even better in the future than in the past. Such media prophecies
can become self-fulfilling as contributors and supporters jump on the bandwagon
of the candidate possessing this "momentum." In 1992, when Bill Clinton's poll
standings surged in the wake of the Democratic National Convention (see Chapter
10), the media determined that Clinton had enormous momentum. In fact, nothing that happened during the remainder of the race led the media to change its
collective judgment. Even when George Bush's poll standing began to improve,
many news stories pointed to Bush's inability to gain momentum. While there is
no way to ascertain what impact this coverage had on the race, at the very least,
Republican contributors and activists must have been discouraged by the constant
portrayal of their candidate as lacking—and the opposition as possessing—this
magical "momentum."

Of course, what the media confer they can also take away. As noted earlier,
soon after his "momentum" carried Bill Clinton to victory in the 1992 election,
the new president became the target of fierce attacks by prominent members of
the national media. After a series of miscues during his first month in office, previously friendly commentators described Clinton as "incredibly inept," as "stum-
bling," and as a man with the "common sense of a gnat." Clinton went, according
to one prominent journalist, "from *Time*'s 'Man of the Year' to punching bag of
the week." Some analysts suggested that the media were trying to compensate for
their earlier enthusiastic support for Clinton.[23]

Media power to shape images is not absolute. Other image-makers compete
with and indeed do manipulate the media by planting stories and rumors and staging news events. Some politicians are so adept at communicating with the public
and shaping their own images that the media seem to have little effect upon them.
For example, for six years Ronald Reagan appeared to have the ability to project
such a positive image to millions of Americans that media criticism had little or no
effect upon his popularity. It was for this reason that the media came to refer to
Reagan as the "teflon-coated" president—criticism never seemed to "stick" (although eventually even Reagan's teflon coating chipped and cracked).

In 1991, President Bush's war policy in the Persian Gulf was predicated upon

---

[22]See Carl Bernstein, "The Idiot Culture," *New Republic,* 8 June 1992, pp. 22–28.

[23]Howard Kurtz, "Media Pounce on Troubles as Pendulum Swings Again," *Washington Post,* 1 February 1993, p. 1.

The Media: How Influential Are They?

*I*n *recent years there has emerged am important political argument over the real or imagined political power of the media. Commentators, politicians, and others routinely attribute vast influence to the American media; yet many who study the matter argue that claims about media power are exaggerated.*

Newspaper editor Michael J. O'Neill summarizes the thinking of many critics as he describes the media's reach and influence. On the basis of his study of media coverage of Congress, media analyst Stephen Hess argues that the media's actual power is less than most assume.

O'Neill

The extraordinary powers of the media, most convincingly displayed by network television and the national press, have been mobilized to influence major public issues and national elections, to help diffuse the authority of Congress and to disassemble the political parties—even to make Presidents or to break them. Indeed, the media now weigh so heavily on the scales of power that some political scientists claim we are upsetting the historic checks and balances invented by our forefathers. . . .

This is flattering, of course, because all newspapermen dream of being movers and shakers and the thought that we may actually be threatening the national government is inspirational. In several respects, it is also true. . . .

No longer are we just the messengers, observers on the sidelines, witch's mirrors faithfully telling society how it looks. Now we are deeply imbedded in the democratic process itself, as principal actors rather than bit players or mere audience. . . . Thanks mainly to television, we are often partners in the creation of news—unwilling and unwitting partners, perhaps, but partners nonetheless. . . .

In ways that Jefferson and Hamilton never intended nor could even imagine, Americans now have the whole world delivered to them every day, in pulsating, living color—all of life swept inside their personal horizon.[1]

Hess

There is no shortage of claims for the power of the press on Capitol Hill. . . . So many knowledgeable people, including senators, tell us that this is so that surely it must be so.

The most obvious reason why influence is attributed to the media is that the members of Congress, and especially their staffs, are incorrigible news junkies. . . .

The problem is that cause and effect are so difficult to match up. . . .

During the year I spent as an observer at the Senate, I did not see any cause and effect. I saw a lot of reporters writing stories. I saw a lot of bills being voted up or down. The stories often helped explain the votes, but I do not think the stories caused the votes. . . .

Ultimately, a lot more people and groups have an interest in noting the power of the press than in showing that media power sometimes may be akin to that of the Wizard of Oz. . . . There are also certain participants in the governmental process who must find it useful to blame "media power" for their own failures or frustrations. Books about the power that is will always sell better than those about the power that is not. And, finally, there are media researchers whose entitlements in the world of conference going and journal articles . . . will be in direct proportion to our colleagues' sense that we are writing about one of the real power players in public policy. This then becomes a collective bias of which readers should be aware. Beware.[2]

[1]Michael J. O'Neill, "The Power of the Press." A presidential address to the American Society of Newspaper Editors, 1982, reprinted in *The Mass Media: Opposing Viewpoints* (St. Paul, MN: Greenhaven Press, 1988), pp. 150–51.
[2]Stephen Hess, *The Ultimate Insiders: U.S. Senators and the National Media* (Washington, DC: Brookings Institution, 1986), pp. 100–112.

the assumption that if fighting lasted for more than a short period of time, critical news coverage would make it impossible to continue. In this case, its anticipation of the activities of the media shaped the reality of the Bush administration's military strategy. At the same time, the Bush administration imposed severe limits on press coverage of the war to limit the ability of the media to shape public perceptions on the basis of its own agenda. Journalists were not allowed free access to American or allied forces or to any part of the war zone. Instead, reporters and crews were provided with Pentagon reports, news briefings, and guided tours of the battlefield. This permitted the United States government to exercise a great deal of influence over the media's coverage of the war, and helped the government maintain a generally favorable flow of stories throughout the war. Indeed, reporters and cameras were even barred from the Dover Air Force Base in Delaware where the bodies of soldiers killed in the Persian Gulf were brought. The government feared the negative impact of news photos showing American casualties.

One of the few news sources not subject to Pentagon control was CNN correspondent Peter Arnett's live broadcasts from the Iraqi capital, Baghdad. The Iraqi government hoped to generate favorable publicity for its own cause in the United States by permitting CNN to broadcast scenes of destruction and photos of casualties produced by American bombing raids. The U.S. government was unhappy about Arnett's broadcasts, but could do nothing to stop them.

During the 1992 presidential campaign, candidates developed a number of techniques designed to take control of the image-making process away from journalists and media executives (as discussed in Chapters 10 and 11). Among the most important of these techniques were the many town meetings and television talk and entertainment show appearances that all the major candidates made. Frequent exposure on such programs as "Larry King Live," "Today," and even "Arsenio Hall" gave candidates an opportunity to shape and focus their own media images and to overwhelm any negative image that might be projected by the media. This strategy worked especially well for the independent candidate Ross Perot. By the end of the 1992 campaign, many journalists were depicting Perot as more than a bit of a kook. Nevertheless, Perot's numerous appearances on talk shows, in addition to his lengthy "infomercials," allowed him to maintain some—though not total—control over his media image.

Members of the national news media responded by aggressively investigating and refuting many of the candidates' claims. Each of the major television networks, for example, aired regular critical analyses of the candidates' speeches, television commercials, and talk-show appearances. "NBC Nightly News" frequently featured "Campaign Close–up" and "Ad Watch." Similarly, almost every night during the latter stages of the presidential campaign, "CBS Evening News" featured "Campaign 92 Reality Check." The PBS "MacNeil-Lehrer Newshour" regularly used its "Fact or Fiction" segment to probe candidates' assertions. Even the most innocuous photo opportunities came under media fire.

Thus, when George Bush appeared in Texas to witness American, Mexican, and Canadian representatives initial the North American Free Trade Agreement (NAFTA), NBC commentators dismissed the trip as election-year politics. CBS also told viewers that the trip was purely political and added a segment featuring a group of American workers who feared that the NAFTA agreement would threaten their jobs. CNN investigated and refuted a Clinton television commercial claiming that Bush's Labor secretary, Lynn Martin, had called job growth in Arkansas during Clinton's tenure as governor, "enormous." This was a claim that Clinton repeated during the presidential debates. CNN reporter Brooks Jackson revealed that what Martin actually said was Arkansas had low wages and dead-end jobs; she then went on to say, "If you say Arkansas's growth is enormous, if you are working from a low base, it's true."[24]

This type of political coverage serves the public interest by subjecting candidates' claims to scrutiny and refuting errors and distortions. At the same time, such critical coverage serves the interests of the news media by enhancing their own control over political imagery and perceptions and, thus, the power of the media vis-à-vis other political actors and institutions in the United States. We shall examine this topic next as we consider the development and significance of investigative reporting.

After his election, President Clinton returned to the town meeting and talk show format that had served him well during the campaign as a way of reaching the public without media intervention. The national media, however, were not prepared to accept the president's efforts to circumvent them and moved to reassert their own political "spin" control. For example, following Clinton's February 10, 1993, nationally televised town meeting on the economy, many major newspapers were sharply critical of the president's responses to questions posed by members of a Michigan studio audience and a group of callers from across the country. Clinton

---

[24]Alan Otten, "TV News Drops Kid-Glove Coverage of Election, Trading Staged Sound Bites for Hard Analysis," *Wall Street Journal,* 12 October 1992, p. A12.

was accused both of giving inadequate answers to questions and of screening participants to exclude hostile questioners. Some media commentators challenged the validity of the entire town meeting format, claiming that members of the general public—as distinguished from journalists—were not adequately prepared to confront the president. Commentators called for more events dominated by the media, such as press conferences, and fewer events like town meetings in which the role of the media was reduced.[25]

The Rise of Investigative Reporting

The political power of the news media has been greatly increased in recent years through the growing prominence of "investigative reporting"—a form of journalism in which the media adopt an adversary posture toward the government and public officials.

During the nineteenth century, American newspapers were completely subordinate to the political parties. Newspapers depended upon official patronage—legal notice and party subsidies—for their financial survival and were controlled by party leaders. (A vestige of that era survived into the twentieth century in such newspaper names as the *Springfield Republican* and the *St. Louis Globe-Democrat*.) At the turn of the century, with the development of commercial advertising, newspapers became financially independent. This made possible the emergence of a formally nonpartisan press.

Presidents were the first national officials to see the opportunities in this development. By communicating directly to the electorate through newspapers and magazines, Theodore Roosevelt and Woodrow Wilson established political constituencies for themselves independent of party organizations and strengthened their own power relative to Congress. President Franklin Roosevelt used the radio, most notably in his famous fireside chats, to reach out to voters throughout the nation and to make himself the center of American politics (see Box 13.2). FDR was also adept at developing close personal relationships with reporters that enabled him to obtain favorable news coverage despite the fact that in his day a majority of newspaper owners and publishers were staunch conservatives. Following Roosevelt's example, subsequent presidents have all sought to use the media to enhance their popularity and power. For example, through televised news conferences, President John F. Kennedy mobilized public support for his domestic and foreign policy initiatives.

During the 1950s and early 1960s, a few members of Congress also made successful use of the media—especially television—to mobilize national support for their causes. Senator Estes Kefauver of Tennessee became a major contender for the presidency and won a place on the 1956 Democratic national ticket as a result of his dramatic televised hearings on organized crime. Senator Joseph McCarthy of Wisconsin made himself a powerful national figure through his well-publicized investigations of alleged Communist infiltration of key American institutions.

[25]See Ann Devroy, "TV Public Puts Clinton on Defensive," *Washington Post,* 11 February 1993, p. 1. See also, Howard Kurtz, "Inaugurating a Talk Show Presidency," *Washington Post,* 12 February 1993, p. A4.

BOX 13.2
The First Fireside Chat
March 12, 1933

I want to talk for a few minutes with the people of the United States about banking—with the comparatively few who understand the mechanics of banking but more particularly with the overwhelming majority who use banks for the making of deposits and the drawing of checks. I want to tell you what has been done in the last few days, why it was done, and what the next steps are going to be. I recognize that the many proclamations from State capitols and from Washington, the legislation, the treasury regulations, etc., couched for the most part in banking and legal terms, should be explained for the benefit of the average citizen. I owe this in particular because of the fortitude and good temper with which everybody has accepted the inconvenience and hardships of the banking holiday. I know that when you understand what we in Washington have been about I shall continue to have your cooperation as fully as I have had your sympathy and help during the past week. . . .

After all, there is an element in the readjustment of our financial system more important than currency, more important than gold, and that is the confidence of the people. Confidence and courage are the essentials of success in carrying out our plan. You people must have faith; you must not be stampeded by rumors or guesses. Let us unite in banishing fear. We have provided the machinery to restore our financial system; it is up to you to support and make it work.

It is your problem no less than it is mine. Together we cannot fail.

These senators, however, were more exceptional than typical. Through the mid-1960s, the executive branch continued to generate the bulk of news coverage, and the media served as a cornerstone of presidential power.

The Vietnam War shattered this relationship between the press and the presidency. During the early stages of U.S. involvement, American officials in Vietnam who disapproved of the way the war was being conducted leaked information critical of administrative policy to reporters. Publication of this material infuriated the White House, which pressured publishers to block its release—on one occasion, President Kennedy went so far as to ask the *New York Times* to reassign its Saigon correspondent. The national print and broadcast media—the network news divisions, the national news weeklies, the *Washington Post* and the *New York Times*—discovered, however, that there was an audience for critical coverage among segments of the public skeptical of administration policy. As the Vietnam conflict dragged on, critical media coverage fanned antiwar sentiment. Moreover, growing opposition to the war among liberals encouraged some members of Congress, most notably Senator J. William Fulbright, chairman of the Senate Foreign Relations Committee, to break with the president. In turn, these shifts in popular and congressional sentiment emboldened journalists and publishers to continue to present critical news reports. Through this process, journalists developed a commitment to "investigative reporting," while a constituency emerged that would rally to the defense of the media when it came under White House attack.

This pattern, established during the Vietnam War, endured through the 1970s and into the 1980s. Political forces opposed to presidential policies, many members of Congress, and the national news media began to find that their interests often overlapped. Liberal opponents of the Nixon, Carter, Reagan, and Bush administrations welcomed news accounts critical of the conduct of executive agencies and officials in foreign affairs and in such domestic areas as race relations, the environment, and regulatory policy. In addition, many senators and representatives found it politically advantageous to champion causes favored by the antiwar, consumer, or environmental movements because, by conducting televised hearings on such issues, they were able to mobilize national constituencies, to become national figures, and in a number of instances to become serious contenders for their party's presidential nomination.

For their part, aggressive use of the techniques of investigation, publicity, and exposure allowed the national media to enhance their autonomy and carve out a prominent place for themselves in American government and politics. Increasingly, media coverage has come to influence politicians' careers, the mobilization of political constituencies, and the fate of issues and causes. Inasmuch as members of Congress and groups opposed to presidential policies in the 1970s and 1980s benefited from the growing influence of the press, they were prepared to rush to its defense when it came under attack. This constituency could be counted upon to denounce any move by the White House or its supporters to curb media influence as an illegitimate effort to manage the news, chill free speech, and undermine the First Amendment. It was the emergence of these overlapping interests, more than an ideological bias, that often led to a *de facto* alliance between liberal political forces and the national news media.

This confluence of interests was in evidence during the 1992 presidential campaign. Most journalists endeavored to be evenhanded in their coverage of the candidates. As we saw above, the media subjected all the major campaigns to regular scrutiny and criticism. However, as several studies have since indicated, during the course of the campaign the media tended to be more critical of Bush and more supportive of Clinton.[26] This was an almost inevitable outgrowth of the *de facto* alliance that developed over a number of years between the media and liberal forces. Like any long-standing relationship, this one tends to shape the attitudes and perceptions of the participants. Without any need for overt bias or sinister conspiracy, journalists tend naturally to provide more favorable coverage to liberal politicians and causes.

Thus, for example, writing in the *Washington Post*, noted print and television journalist Michael Kinsley angrily rejected charges that the media showed a liberal bias during the 1992 campaign. Kinsley admitted that the views of most journalists, including his own, were liberal. However, said Kinsley, this was not a bias. These views were merely "the sort of views a reasonable, intelligent person would hold."[27]

Thus, overlapping interests and perceptions, not conspiracies or overt biases,

[26]See, for example, Howard Kurtz, "Networks Stressed the Negative in Comments about Bush, Study Finds," *Washington Post,* 15 November 1992, p. A7. See also, Howard Kurtz, "Republicans and Some Journalists Say Media Tend to Boost Clinton, Bash Bush," *Washington Post,* 1 September 1992, p. A7.

[27]Kinsley, "Bias and Baloney."

Katharine Graham
The *Washington Post*

Katharine Graham (b. 1917)

An interest in public responsibility was a credo of Katharine Graham's family. Born into wealth, Katharine was taught by her parents to become involved in public affairs; education, civil rights, and free speech were all public causes that became family causes. Earning her bachelor's degree from the University of Chicago in 1938, Katharine worked on the newspaper her father had bought in 1933, the *Washington Post,* as well as on the *San Francisco News.*

In 1940, she married a successful lawyer, Philip Graham, who served in the military during World War II. After the war, Katharine's father offered her husband the position of associate publisher. Six months later, he became the *Post's* publisher. Under Philip Graham, the *Post* empire grew, acquiring other newspapers, radio and television stations, *Newsweek* magazine, and its own news service. Haunted by psychological problems, however, Graham committed suicide in 1963. Although she had been away from active involvement in the business for several years, Katharine agreed to succeed her husband as president of the company. Quoting her father's words, she expressed her philosophy for the news corporation—a philosophy that would be put to the sternest test ten years later: "The newspaper's duty is to its readers and to the public at large, and not to the private interests of the owner. In the pursuit of truth, the newspaper shall be prepared to make sacrifice of its material fortunes, if such cause be necessary for the public good."

In 1965, Graham appointed Ben Bradlee managing editor, and later executive editor, of the *Post,* as part of an effort to upgrade the quality of the paper. In 1969, Graham became the *Post's* publisher. Then in June 1972, two young, untested *Post* reporters— Bob Woodward and Carl Bernstein— uncovered information linking a break-in at the Democratic National Committee headquarters with the Republican White House of Richard Nixon. For the next year, the *Post* became virtually the only source of information on the growing scandal. Despite intense, relentless pressure from the White House, and the fact that no other newspapers were running the same information, Graham and Bradlee defended the stories of their two reporters after being convinced they were correct. Eventually, congressional investigations confirmed that President Nixon and his top aides had been involved in obstruction of justice, bribery, and a host of other crimes unprecedented for a presidential administration.

In the midst of Watergate, Graham became chair of the board of directors in 1973. She has continued to guide the corporation, and has served as a trustee of several universities, including her alma mater, and as president of the American Newspaper Publishers Association.

Source: Carl Bernstein and Bob Woodward, *All the President's Men* (New York: Simon and Schuster, 1974); Chalmers M. Roberts, *In the Shadow of Power: The Story of the Washington Post* (Cabin John, MD: Seven Locks Press, 1989).

have tended to link substantial segments of the media to liberal political groups in
the United States. This linkage is by no means necessarily permanent or absolute. It has, however, helped liberal forces in their political struggles over the past several decades. We shall return to the role of the media in politics in the next chapter.

MEDIA POWER AND RESPONSIBILITY

The free media comprise an institution absolutely essential to democratic government. We depend upon the media to investigate wrongdoing, to publicize and explain governmental actions, to evaluate programs and politicians, and to bring to light matters that might otherwise be known only to a handful of governmental insiders. In short, without free and active media, popular government would be virtually impossible. Citizens would have few means through which to know or assess the government's actions—other than the claims or pronouncements of the government itself. Moreover, without active—indeed, aggressive—media, citizens would be hard-pressed to make informed choices among competing candidates at the polls. Often enough, the media reveal discrepancies between candidates' claims and their actual records, and between the images that candidates seek to project and the underlying realities.

At the same time, the increasing decay of party organizations (see Chapter 11) has made politicians ever more dependent upon favorable media coverage. National political leaders and journalists have had symbiotic relationships, at least since FDR's presidency, but initially politicians were the senior partners. They benefited from media publicity, but they were not totally dependent upon it so long as they could still rely upon party organizations to mobilize votes. Journalists, on the other hand, depended upon their relationships with politicians for access to information, and would hesitate to report stories that might antagonize valuable sources. Newsmen feared exclusion from the flow of information in retaliation. Thus, for example, reporters did not publicize potentially embarrassing information, widely known in Washington, about the personal lives of such figures as Franklin Roosevelt and John F. Kennedy.

With the decline of party, the balance of power between politicians and journalists has been reversed. Now that politicians have become heavily dependent upon the media to reach their constituents, journalists no longer need fear that their access to information can be restricted in retaliation for negative coverage.

Freedom gives the media enormous power. The media can make or break reputations, help to launch or to destroy political careers, build support for or rally opposition against programs and institutions.[28] Wherever there is so much power, there exists at least the potential for its abuse or overly zealous use—the problem of freedom and power in a new and unexpected form. All things considered, free media are so critically important to the maintenance of a democratic society that

[28]See Martin Linsky, *Impact: How the Press Affects Federal Policymaking* (New York: W. W. Norton, 1986).

we must be prepared even to take the risk that the media will occasionally abuse their power. The forms of governmental control that would prevent the media from misusing their power would also certainly destroy our freedom.

SUMMARY

The American news media are among the world's most free. The print and broadcast media regularly present information and opinion critical of the government, political leaders, and policies.

The media help to determine the agenda or focus of political debate in the United States, to shape popular understanding of political events and results, and to influence popular judgments of politicians and leaders.

Over the past century, the media have helped to nationalize American political perspectives. Media coverage is influenced by the perspectives of journalists, the activities of news sources, and, most important, by the media's need to appeal to upscale audiences. The attention that the media give to protest and disruptive activities is also a function of audience factors.

Free media are essential ingredients of popular government.

FOR FURTHER READING

Altheide, David. *Creating Reality.* Beverly Hills, CA: Sage, 1976 .

Braestrup, Peter. *Big Story: How the American Press and Television Reported and Interpreted the Crisis of Tet 1968 in Vietnam and Washington.* Boulder, CO: Westview Press, 1977.

Cook, Timothy. *Making Laws and Making News: Media Strategies in the House of Representatives.* Washington, DC: Brookings Institution, 1989.

Dye, Thomas, and Harmon Ziegler. *American Politics in the Media Age.* Monterey, CA: Brooks/Cole, 1986.

Epstein, Edward. *News From Nowhere.* New York: Random House, 1973.

Gans, Herbert. *Deciding What's News.* New York: Pantheon, 1979.

Graber, Doris. *Mass Media and American Politics.* Washington, DC: Congressional Quarterly Press, 1989.

Grossman, Michael B., and Martha J. Kumar. *The Presidency and the Mass Media in the Age of Television.* Baltimore: Johns Hopkins University Press, 1981.

Hallin, Daniel C. *The Uncensored War.* Berkeley and Los Angeles: University of California Press, 1986.

Hess, Stephen. *Live From Capitol Hill: Studies of Congress and the Media.* Washington, DC: Brookings Institution, 1991.

Joslyn, Richard A. *Mass Media and Elections.* Reading, MA: Addison-Wesley, 1984.

Linsky, Martin. *Impact: How the Press Affects Federal Policymaking.* New York: W. W. Norton, 1986.

Nacos, Brigitte L. *The Press, Presidents and Crises.* New York: Columbia University Press, 1990.

Owen, Diana. *Media Messages in American Presidential Elections.* Westport, CT: Greenwood, 1991.

Paletz, David, and Robert M. Entman. *Media-Power-Politics,* New York: Free Press, 1981.

Patterson, Thomas W. *The Mass Media Election.* New York: Praeger, 1980.

Ranney, Austin. *Channels of Power: The Impact of TV on American Politics.* New York: Basic Books, 1983.

Robinson, Michael, and Margaret Sheehan. *Over the Wire and On TV: CBS and UPI in Campaign '80.* New York: Russell Sage Foundation, 1983.

Rubin, Richard L. *Press, Party and Presidency.* New York: W. W. Norton, 1981.

Winfield, Betty Houchin. *FDR and the News Media.* Urbana, IL: University of Illinois, 1990.

14

Politics and Government:
The Problem with the Process

TIME LINE ON POLITICS AND GOVERNANCE

EVENTS		INSTITUTIONAL DEVELOPMENTS
		Long-term decline in voter turnout begins (1890)
	1900	
McCarthy hearings (1950s)	**1950**	
	1960	Decay of political party organizations (1960s)
		Rise of activist and adversarial media (1968)
	1970	
Watergate hearings (1973–1974)		Legislative limits on presidential power: War Powers Resolution (1973); Budget and Impoundment Control Act (1974); Ethics in Government Act (1978)
	1980	Reagan's deficits impose budgetary limits on Congress; period of intense conflict between legislative and executive branches (1980–1992)
Iran-Contra affair (1986)		
Tower, Wright, Coelho and Frank revelations (1989)		
Clarence Thomas hearings (1990)	**1990**	
House post office and bank scandals (1992)		
Nannygate; Travelgate (1993)		Democratic control of both branches doesn't end gridlock (1993)

Over the preceding five chapters, we analyzed the disparate pieces of America's political process. We examined elections and political parties, evaluated the role of public opinion, and weighed the place of the media and interest groups in the workings of the American political system. Process can be meaningful in and of itself—witness the significance that many Americans attach to the right to participate in their government. Nevertheless, we study the American political process mainly because we believe that it has important consequences for American government and policy.

Having examined these parts of the contemporary American political process, let's try to step back and assess their impact on the institutions, policies, and governance of the United States. Unfortunately, as we shall see, in a number of important respects, America's current political process undermines our government's capacity to govern.

CAN THE GOVERNMENT GOVERN?

As we approach the twenty-first century, America faces many problems. Our capacity to compete successfully in world markets against other major industrial nations, most notably Japan and Germany, is open to question. America no longer seems able to provide enough jobs or an adequate standard of living for all of its citizens. Our dependence on foreign sources of energy is growing once again. Now that America is the world's largest debtor, its economy and economic policy are increasingly vulnerable to the wishes of foreign bondholders.[1] America's educational system is widely viewed as deserving failing marks. Millions of Americans lack adequate housing or health care. American cities are plagued by crime and drugs.

In such areas as health care, housing, crime, and education, the U.S. government has seemed unable to formulate or implement effective programs and policies. In other areas, the government, itself, is the cause of the nation's problems. For example, the long-term strength of the American economy is threatened by the $4 trillion national debt that is the fiscal legacy of the Reagan and Bush presidencies. Despite a general realization that the debt problem must be brought under control by some combination of tax increases and spending cuts, America's political leadership has been, thus far, incapable of swallowing the bitter medicine of fiscal discipline.

Shortly after entering office, President Clinton introduced a package of tax increases and spending cuts nominally designed to reduce the federal deficit by hundreds of millions of dollars. Many of the so-called cuts in spending, however, turned out to be changes in accounting procedures or unspecified "administrative savings" rather than actual reductions in federal outlays.[2] Even in some areas where real cuts were planned, such as in allocations for agricultural programs, congressional supporters of the interests affected were able to compel the president to restore the expenditures he had proposed eliminating.[3] Many experts doubted that the president's plans would actually result in substantial deficit reductions.[4] An excellent recent volume of essays published by Washington's prestigious Brookings Institution was aptly entitled, *Can the Government Govern?* The short answer to this complex question was a very clear "No!"[5]

One major reason for our present quandary is that over the past several decades an unhealthy and fundamentally undemocratic political process has developed in

---

[1]Douglas R. Sease and Constance Mitchell, "World's Bond Buyers Gain Huge Influence over U.S. Fiscal Plans," *Wall Street Journal*, 6 November 1992, p. 1.

[2]See Robert J. Samuelson, "Not-So-Serious Spending Cuts," *Washington Post*, 25 February 1993, p. A23.

[3]Eric Pianan and David Hilzenrath, "Budget Negotiators Soften Spending Cuts, Tax Rises," *Washington Post*, 1 April 1993, p. A6.

[4]See Allan Meltzer, "The Worst Kind of Short-Term Thinking," *Wall Street Journal*, 22 February 1993, p. A10.

[5]John Chubb and Paul Peterson, eds., *Can the Government Govern?* (Washington, DC: Brookings Institution, 1989).

580

POLITICS AND
GOVERNMENT:
THE PROBLEM
WITH THE
PROCESS

the United States. The framers of the Constitution believed that a strong government rested most securely upon a broad and active popular base. "I would raise the federal pyramid to a considerable altitude," said Pennsylvania delegate James Wilson. "Therefore, I would give it as broad a base as possible." As we saw in Chapter 1, concern for the new government's power and stability was a main reason that the framers established representative institutions and permitted political participation on the part of ordinary citizens. For much of U.S. history, the "federal pyramid," indeed, rested upon a relatively broad base of vigorous—often tumultuous—popular participation, with most major issues debated, fought, and ultimately resolved in the electoral arena. America's democratic politics, in turn, provided political leaders with a base of support from which to develop and implement programs, contend with powerful entrenched interests, and during times of crisis, such as the Civil War and World War II, ask their countrymen for the exertions and sacrifices needed in order for the nation to survive. As the framers had intended, democratic politics protected citizens' liberties *and* helped promote governance.

In recent decades, however, as noted in Chapter 10, popular participation in American political life has declined sharply. Despite a much ballyhooed increase in voter turnout, only 55 percent of eligible Americans bothered to vote in the 1992 presidential election. At the same time, the political parties that once mobilized voters and imparted a measure of unity to the scattered pieces of the American governmental structure have decayed (see Chapter 11), making it very difficult, if not impossible, to create a coherent government through the American electoral process.

Both reflecting and reinforcing these changes in the character of elections, the contending political forces in the United States have come to rely heavily on forms of political conflict that neither require nor encourage much in the way of citizen involvement. In recent years, many of the most important national political struggles have been fought largely outside the electoral arena rather than through competitive electoral contests. In fact, in contemporary America, electoral results themselves have at times been negated or reversed by political forces that were not satisfied with the outcomes.

America's contemporary political process—characterized by low voter turnout, weak parties, and the rise of a "politics by other means"—has narrowed the base upon which the "federal pyramid" rests and is the source of many of our government's present problems. As we shall see in this chapter, this political process is increasingly undemocratic, fragments political power, and fails to provide elected officials with the strong and stable political base they need to govern effectively. Most important, America's contemporary political patterns undermine the ability of elected officials to bring about or even to take account of the public good.

Let us now look critically at the pieces of America's political process and then consider their implications for our government's capacity to govern. We will first consider the declining importance of popular voting and the rise of new forms of political conflict in the United States. Second, we will see how these new forms of conflict undermine governance. Finally, we will attempt to ascertain why there are no easy solutions for America's current political problems. In particular, we will see why, despite their claims to the contrary, major political forces in the United States today are not interested in the one course of action that might restore the government's capacity to govern—the revitalization of the electoral process.

THE DECLINE OF VOTING AND THE RISE OF "POLITICS BY OTHER MEANS"

For most of U.S. history, elections were the main arenas of political combat. In recent years, however, elections have become less effective as ways of resolving political conflicts in the United States. Today's political struggles are frequently waged elsewhere, and crucial policy choices tend to be made outside the electoral realm. Rather than engage voters directly, contending political forces rely on such weapons of institutional combat as congressional investigations, media revelations, and judicial proceedings. In contemporary America, even electoral success fails to confer the capacity to govern, and political forces, even if they lose at the polls or do not even compete in the electoral arena, have been able to exercise considerable power.

Several trends in contemporary American political life bring sharply into focus the declining significance of the electoral arena. American elections in recent decades have been characterized by strikingly low levels of voter turnout and by a decline of political competition. Since 1900, turnout in national elections has declined by 25 percentage points. In the 1992 presidential election, only 55.9 percent of the eligible electorate went to the polls, and in the 1990 midterm congressional elections, voter turnout was a mere 33 percent. In other Western democracies, turnout normally exceeds 80 percent.

The extent to which genuine competition takes place in the electoral arena has also declined sharply in recent decades—especially in congressional races, which tend to be dominated by incumbents who are able to use the resources of their office to turn back any opponents who present themselves. In 1986, 1988, and 1990, 98 percent of the incumbents who sought another term were victorious.

In the 1992 general election, despite media claims of an anti-incumbent "mood" in the country, and despite nationwide redistricting, about 95 percent of those incumbents seeking re-election were successful. According to one estimate, there was effectively no opposition in more than three hundred House races.[6] The unusually large size of the 1992 freshman congressional class was due more to retirements and deaths among incumbents than to their defeat at the polls. Only sixteen incumbent members of Congress were actually defeated in the 1992 general election. Many modern-day congressional races are decided by more than a twenty-point margin; frequently, incumbents face no electoral challenge whatsoever.

---

[6]See Charles Babcock, "In Donating $230 Million, Interests Favored Bush, Hill Democrats," *Washington Post*, 23 October 1992, p. A19.

582

POLITICS AND
GOVERNMENT:
THE PROBLEM
WITH THE
PROCESS

Politics Outside the Electoral Arena

As competition in the electoral arena has declined, the significance of other forms of political combat has risen. Contemporary political struggles have come increasingly to involve the criminal justice system and the courts, the national security apparatus, and the mass media. Let us look at the political role played by each of these non-electoral institutions.

Criminal Indictments   One important substitute for competition in the electoral arena is the growing political use of a powerful non-electoral weapon—the criminal justice system. Between the early 1970s and the present, there was more than a tenfold increase in the number of indictments brought by federal prosecutors against national, state, and local officials. The data given in Figure 14.1 actually understate the extent to which public officials have been subjected to criminal proceedings in recent years, because they do not include those political figures (such as Ronald Reagan's attorney general, Edwin Meese, and former Democratic House Speaker Jim Wright) who were targets of investigations that did not result in indictments.

Many of the individuals indicted have been lower-level civil servants, but large numbers have been prominent political figures—among them more than a dozen members of Congress, several federal judges, and numerous state and local officials. Some of these indictments were initiated by Republican administrations, and their

FIGURE 14.1

Federal Indictments and Convictions of Public Officials, 1970–1990***

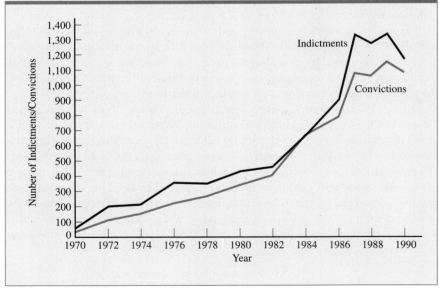

*Reporting procedures were modified in 1983, so pre- and post-1983 data are not strictly comparable.
Source: Annual reports of the U.S. Department of Justice, Public Integrity Section, 1971–1988; *Statistical Abstract of the United States* (Washington, DC: Government Printing Office, 1992), p. 195.

targets were primarily Democrats. At the same time, a substantial number of high-ranking Republicans in the executive branch—including former Defense Secretary Caspar Weinberger, former Assistant Secretary of State, Elliott Abrams, presidential aides Michael Deaver and Lyn Nofziger, and, of course, national security official Oliver North—were the targets of criminal prosecutions stemming from allegations or investigations initiated by Democrats. Weinberger and Abrams, along with several other figures in the Iran-Contra case, were pardoned by President George Bush in December 1992, just before he left office. In justifying the pardons, Bush charged that Democrats were attempting to criminalize policy differences.

There is no particular reason to believe that the level of political corruption or abuse of power in America actually increased tenfold over the past two decades; although it could be argued that this sharp rise reflects a heightened level of public concern about governmental misconduct. However, both the issue of government ethics and the growing use of criminal sanctions against public officials have been, as we shall see, closely linked to struggles for political power in the United States. In the aftermath of Watergate, institutions such as the office of special counsel were established and processes for ethics investigations created to investigate allegations of unethical conduct on the part of public figures. Since then political forces have increasingly sought to make use of these mechanisms to discredit their opponents. When scores of investigators, accountants, and lawyers are deployed to scrutinize the conduct of a John Tower, a Jim Wright, or a Caspar Weinberger, it is all but certain that something questionable will be found. The creation of these investigative processes, more than changes in the public's tolerance for government misconduct, explains why public officials are increasingly being charged with ethical and criminal violations.

The Judiciary   The growing use of criminal indictments as a partisan weapon has helped enhance the political importance of the judiciary. The prominence of the courts has been heightened by the sharp increase in the number of major policy issues that have been fought and decided in the judicial realm rather than in the arena of electoral politics.[7] The federal judiciary has become the main institution for resolving struggles over such issues as race relations and abortion, and it has also come to play a more significant role in deciding questions of social welfare and economic policy.[8] The number of suits brought by civil rights, environmental, feminist, and other liberal groups seeking to advance their policy goals increased dramatically during the 1970s and 1980s—reflecting the willingness and ability of these groups to fight their battles in the judicial arena. For example, as Figure 14.2 indicates, the number of civil rights cases brought in federal courts doubled during this period. After the emergence of a conservative majority on the Supreme Court in 1989, forces on the political Right began to use litigation to implement their own policy agenda. The growing political importance of the federal judiciary explains why Supreme Court confirmation battles, such as the struggle over the

[7]Jeremy Rabkin, *Judicial Compulsions* (New York: Basic Books, 1989).

[8]Martin Shapiro, "The Supreme Court's 'Return' to Economic Regulation," *Studies in American Political Development* 1 (1986), pp. 91–142.

584

POLITICS AND
GOVERNMENT:
THE PROBLEM
WITH THE
PROCESS

FIGURE 14.2

Civil Rights Cases Brought in Federal Courts

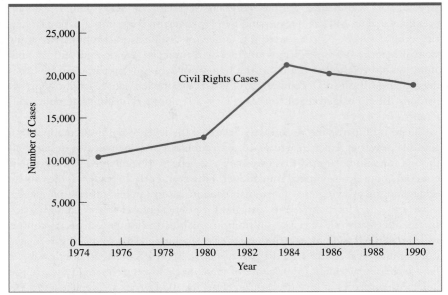

Source: *Statistical Abstract of the United States* (Washington, DC: Government Printing Office, 1988, 1989, 1992).

Clarence Thomas nomination, came to be so bitterly fought during the Reagan and Bush administrations.[9]

The National Security Apparatus   One of the best-documented examples of the use of the national security apparatus as a political weapon is the substantial expansion in the number of domestic counterintelligence operations directed against groups opposed to the policies of the executive branch during the 1960s and early 1970s. Such actions included wiretaps, surveillance, and efforts to disrupt the activities of the groups.[10] During the 1970s, congressional opposition brought a halt to these counterintelligence efforts; however, recent revelations indicate that in the 1980s, the FBI placed under surveillance groups opposing the Reagan administration's policies in Central America. His administration also relied on the national security apparatus to circumvent congressional opposition to its policies.

The Media   Another institution whose political significance has increased dramatically is the mass media. With the decline of political parties, politicians have become almost totally dependent on the media to reach their constituents, but this

[9]Martin Shefter, "Institutional Conflict Over Presidential Appointments: The Case of Clarence Thomas," *PS: Political Science & Politics* 25, no. 4 (December 1992), pp. 676–78.

[10]William Keller, *The Liberals and J. Edgar Hoover* (Princeton, NJ: Princeton University Press, 1989), Chapter 5.

585

THE DECLINE
OF VOTING AND
THE RISE OF
"POLITICS BY
OTHER MEANS"

Anita F. Hill
Sexual Harassment Becomes
an Issue

Anita F. Hill (b. 1956)

One of the most highly visible political struggles in recent years, involving the incendiary issues of race, sex, and ideology, occurred far away from the American voting booth. At the center of the controversy was a little-known law school professor from the University of Oklahoma, Anita Hill.

The initial confirmation hearings of Supreme Court nominee Clarence Thomas proceeded uneventfully in the late summer of 1991. The conservative African-American jurist revealed little about his predilections to the Senate Judiciary Committee, but no major obstacles seemed to obstruct his path to the high court. Before the committee had an opportunity to make a formal recommendation to the Senate, however, news leaked out that the committee had a deposition from a woman who had worked under Thomas at the Department of Education and the Equal Employment Opportunity Commission (EEOC) in the 1980s. In the deposition, she claimed she had been sexually harassed by Thomas over a period of years. That woman, Anita Hill (a Yale-trained lawyer, like Thomas) claimed that Thomas had repeatedly asked her out, had described the content of pornographic films to her, and had made repeated belligerent advances that she found upsetting and inappropriate.

When news of these charges leaked out, public pressure forced the committee to reopen the hearings. Hill's critics sought to discredit her testimony, suggesting she was in fact a scorned woman who had unsuccessfully pursued Thomas. They also questioned why, if the allegations were true, Hill maintained a professional relationship with Thomas for several years without reporting the incidents or simply leaving. Hill responded that she was intimidated, fearful, and in need of the job. She said that she had respected the work Thomas had done

at EEOC and simply did not consider reporting the advances. While some questioned Hill's honesty, her responses were consistent with the way women have typically responded to sexual harassment in the workplace.

Thomas hotly and categorically denied the accusations, claiming that he was being subjected to a "high-tech lynching." Both Thomas and Hill produced witnesses who supported their testimony, but Hill's credibility was hurt by the fact that no eyewitness ever heard or observed the alleged sexual advances. In a close vote, the Judiciary Committee recommended Thomas's confirmation to the Senate. The Senate subsequently approved Thomas by the narrowest ratification margin in history, 52 to 48.

The consequences of the hearings extended far beyond the Senate. The controversy provoked intense discussion and debate throughout the country. Greater attention and awareness was focused on the issue of sexual harassment. Many Americans were angered by the inquisitorial tone of the Judiciary Committee, especially since it was composed entirely of white middle-aged males. Women around the country who had previously taken no interest in politics became more interested and involved following the hearings. In the Senate, the number of women increased from two to six after the 1992 elections.

No final resolution to the conflicting stories emerged. Polls taken months after the incident indicated that more Americans believed Hill than they did Thomas. Yet Hill sought no special celebrity and she returned to her teaching job in Oklahoma.

586

POLITICS AND
GOVERNMENT:
THE PROBLEM
WITH THE
PROCESS

dependence has made politicians extremely vulnerable to attack by and through the media. At the same time, the development of techniques of investigative reporting and critical journalism, as we saw in Chapter 13, provided the modern news media with powerful weapons to use in political struggles.

The national media enhanced their autonomy and political power by aggressively investigating, publicizing, and exposing instances of official misconduct.[11] Conservative forces during the Nixon and Reagan years responded to media criticism by denouncing the press as biased and seeking to curb it. However, members of Congress and groups opposed to conservative presidential policies benefited from the growing influence of the press and, as noted in the preceding chapter, have been prepared to defend it when it comes under attack.

Revelation, Investigation, Prosecution

Taken together, the expanded political roles of the national news media and the federal judiciary has given rise to a major new weapon of political combat—revelation, investigation, and prosecution. The acronym for this, RIP, forms a fitting political epitaph for the public officials who have become its targets. The RIP weaponry was initially forged by opponents of the Nixon administration in their struggles with the White House, and through the Reagan years it was used primarily by congressional Democrats to attack their foes in the executive branch. In the 1980s, however, Republicans also began to wield the RIP weapon.

In 1972, after his re-election, President Nixon undertook to expand executive power at the expense of Congress by impounding funds appropriated for domestic programs and reorganizing executive agencies without legislative authorization. In addition, the White House established the so-called "plumbers" squad of former intelligence agents and mercenaries to plug leaks of information to Congress and the press, and (its opponents claimed) it sought to undermine the legitimacy of the federal judiciary by appointing unqualified justices to the Supreme Court. The administration's adversaries also charged that it tried to limit Congress's influence over foreign policy by keeping vital information from it, most notably, the "secret bombing" of Cambodia in 1973.

At the same time, Nixon sought to curtail the influence of the national news media. His administration brought suit against the *New York Times* in an effort to block publication of the Pentagon Papers and threatened, using the pretext of promoting ideological diversity, to compel the national television networks to sell the local stations they owned. The president's opponents denounced the administration's actions as abuses of power—which they surely were—and launched a full-scale assault upon Richard Nixon in the Watergate controversy.

The Watergate attack began with a series of revelations in the *Washington Post* linking the White House to a break-in at the Watergate Hotel headquarters of the Democratic National Committee. The *Post's* reporters were quickly joined by scores of investigative journalists from the *New York Times, Newsweek, Time,* and the television networks.

---

[11]Samuel P. Huntington, *American Politics: The Promise of Disharmony* (Cambridge, MA: Harvard University Press, 1981), pp. 203–10.

PROCESS BOX 14.1
The RIP Process

587
THE DECLINE
OF VOTING AND
THE RISE OF
"POLITICS BY
OTHER MEANS"

New appointment is proposed by the White House.

OPPONENTS

Opponents of the appointment do an extensive background check, trying to find any negative information that may exist.

Negative information discovered about the appointee is made public through leaks, rumors, and disclosures to reporters, TV news programs, and other media outlets.

In order to follow up on the leaks, the media do further investigations and the process picks up momentum, often resulting in additional negative information.

SUPPORTERS

Supporters martial evidence: the nominee's experience, judgment, knowledge, etc.

Positive information is disseminated through the media: public statements in support of nominee, etc., picked up by newspapers, TV news programs, and news magazines.

Supporters seek to refute damaging information by providing additional positive evidence and challenging media investigations and negative allegations.

Congressional hearings

Hostile questioning due to negative information in the media.

More negative information is uncovered and publicized by the media as momentum peaks.

Supporters are gradually silenced by momentum of negative information.

Supporters drop away, when accusations aimed at nominee prove to be accurate, particularly if the nominee has broken the law.

Nominee withdraws or is defeated.

As revelations of misdeeds by the Nixon White House proliferated, the administration's opponents in Congress demanded a full legislative investigation. In response, the Senate created a special committee, chaired by Senator Sam Ervin, to investigate White House misconduct in the 1972 presidential election. Investiga-

588

POLITICS AND
GOVERNMENT:
THE PROBLEM
WITH THE
PROCESS

tors for the Ervin committee uncovered numerous questionable activities on the part of Nixon's aides, and these were revealed to the public during a series of dramatic, nationally televised hearings.

Evidence of criminal activity unearthed by the Ervin committee led to congressional pressure for the appointment of a special prosecutor. Ultimately, a large number of high-ranking administration officials were indicted, convicted, and imprisoned. Impeachment proceedings were initiated against President Nixon, and when evidence linking him directly to the cover-up of the Watergate burglary was found, he was forced to resign from office. Thus, with the help of the RIP weaponry, the Nixon administration's antagonists achieved a total victory in their conflict with the president. Although no subsequent president has been driven from office, opponents of presidential administrations have since used the RIP process to attack and weaken their foes in the executive branch.

The RIP process became institutionalized when Congress adopted the 1978 Ethics in Government Act, which established procedures facilitating the appointment of special prosecutors to deal with allegations of wrongdoing in the executive branch. The act also defined as criminal several forms of influence peddling in which executive officials had traditionally engaged, such as lobbying former associates after leaving office. (Such activities are also traditional on Capitol Hill, but Congress chose not to impose the restrictions embodied in the act upon its own members and staff.) Basically, Congress created new crimes that executive branch officials could be charged with.

The extent to which the RIP process has come to be a routine feature of American politics became evident during the Iran-Contra conflict when Democrats charged that the Reagan administration had covertly sold arms to Iran and used the proceeds to provide illegal funding for Nicaraguan Contra forces, in violation of the Boland Amendment, which prohibited such help. After the diversion of funds to the Contras was revealed, it was universally assumed that Congress should conduct televised hearings and the judiciary should appoint an independent counsel to investigate the officials involved in the episode. Yet this procedure is really quite remarkable: The RIP process has criminalized ordinary policy differences. Officials who in other democracies would merely be compelled to resign from office are now threatened with criminal prosecution in the United States.

Revelations and investigations of misconduct by public figures have become an important vehicle for political competition in the United States. The primary means through which liberal political forces attacked the White House and mobilized support for themselves during the Reagan administration were the investigations of EPA administrator Anne Burford Gorsuch, Attorney General Edwin Meese, and Supreme Court nominee Robert Bork, as well as the hearings on the Iran-Contra affair.

During the early months of the Bush presidency, partisan warfare chiefly took the form of allegations of misconduct lodged by Democrats and Republicans against one another. Senate Democrats were able to block John Tower's confirmation as secretary of defense with charges that his record of alcohol abuse and sexual impropriety and his ties to defense contractors rendered him unfit to head the Defense Department. Republicans then drove Democratic House Speaker Jim Wright from office with accusations of financial misdeeds, including allegations that Wright and his wife had received large sums of money from a real estate de- *589*

THE DECLINE
OF VOTING AND
THE RISE OF
"POLITICS BY
OTHER MEANS"
veloper and had used inflated royalties from a book contract as a cover for exceed-
ing the limits in congressional rules on outside income. At roughly the same time,
charges of improper loans and investments compelled Democratic House whip
Tony Coelho to resign.

Congressional Democrats responded with allegations that Wright's chief ac-
cuser, Republican House whip Newt Gingrich, also reaped improper profits from
a book contract and engaged in dubious campaign fund-raising activities. Subsequently, House Democrats launched an investigation of Republican misuse of
funds in the Department of Housing and Urban Development under former secretary Samuel Pierce.

Later, House Republicans called upon Democratic Representative Barney
Frank to resign after embarrassing accounts of his personal life appeared in the
press. In 1991, Democrats savaged Bush's Supreme Court nominee, Clarence
Thomas, with sexual harassment charges while Republicans attacked the House
Democratic leadership with charges of mismanaging the House bank and post office. In 1992, Democrats called for an investigation of the Bush administration's
dealings with Iraq prior to the 1991 Persian Gulf War. They also demanded that a
special counsel be appointed to examine charges that the Bush administration had
improperly intervened in a case involving the Atlanta branch of Italy's Banca
Nazionale del Lavoro (BNL), a bank charged with having provided illegal loans to
Iraq during that nation's war with Iran.[12]

Divided Government: 1968–1992

The use of non-electoral means of political combat became more widely used during the 1980s and 1990s as a result of two decades of divided government. Since
1968 the Republicans have won all but two presidential elections, while the Democrats have dominated congressional races. As a result, rather than pinning its
hopes on defeating its opponent in the electoral arena, each party sought to
strengthen the institution it thought it could be sure of controlling while undermining the one associated with the enemy.

The Republicans reacted to their inability to win control of Congress by seeking to enhance the powers of the White House relative to the legislative branch.
As previously mentioned, President Nixon impounded billions of dollars already
appropriated by Congress and attempted, through various reorganization schemes,
to bring executive agencies under closer White House control while severing their
ties to the House and Senate. Presidents Reagan and Bush tolerated budget deficits
of unprecedented magnitude in part because these deficits precluded new congressional spending; they also sought to increase presidential authority over executive
agencies and diminish congressional authority by centralizing control over administrative rule making in the Office of Management and Budget. In addition, Reagan undertook to circumvent the legislative restrictions on presidential conduct

---

[12]George Lardner, Jr., "House Democrats Seek Independent Counsel to Probe Handling of BNL
Case," *Washington Post*, 16 October 1992, p. A17.

590

POLITICS AND
GOVERNMENT:
THE PROBLEM
WITH THE
PROCESS

embodied in the War Powers Act by sending American military forces abroad without congressional approval.

The Democrats, as we saw in Chapter 5, responded to the Republican presidential advantage by seeking to strengthen Congress while reducing the powers and prerogatives of the presidency—in sharp contrast to their behavior from the 1930s to the 1960s, when the Democratic party enjoyed an advantage in presidential elections. In the 1970s, Congress greatly enlarged its committee and subcommittee staffs, thus enabling the House and Senate to monitor and supervise closely the activities of executive agencies. Through the 1974 Budget and Impoundment Act, Congress increased its control over fiscal policy. It also enacted a number of statutory restrictions on presidential authority in the realm of foreign policy during the 1970s, including the Foreign Commitments Resolution and the Arms Export Control Act. Finally, congressional investigations, often conducted in conjunction with media exposés and judicial proceedings, were effective in constraining executive power. The most important example is the Iran-Contra affair, which represented the culmination of two decades of struggle over foreign policy.

No More Division?

Bill Clinton's victory in the 1992 presidential election, coupled with continued Democratic control of Congress, has at least temporarily ended America's experiment with divided partisan control of the national government. However, it remains to be seen whether this will bring an end to the politics of RIP. There is no a priori reason to believe it will. Clinton had campaigned as a centrist, or "New Democrat," but he and his supporters represented only one faction of the Democratic party. Given America's disjointed and decayed party structure, they have little or no capacity to control or discipline the other factions. Indeed, during the last Democratic administration, the presidency of Jimmy Carter, liberal Democrats who were dissatisfied with the president's handling of environmental, consumer, and economic policies, launched fierce RIP attacks against members of the president's staff.

Thus, it was hardly a surprise when factional conflicts broke out in the Democratic camp immediately after the 1992 election.[13] Nor was it surprising that even before Clinton's inauguration, the president-elect's cabinet appointees came under RIP attack. Clinton's commerce secretary designate, Ron Brown, was assailed for vigorously soliciting corporate and interest group contributions for an inaugural affair in his honor. Brown quickly canceled the event and was able to weather the storm because the host of Democratic politicians for whom he had raised funds over the years rallied to his defense.[14] At the same time, Clinton's first choice for attorney general, Zoë Baird, was attacked for employing as household workers a Peruvian couple who had entered the United States illegally and for not securing appropriate documentation or making Social Security payments for them. Baird

---

[13]See Thomas B. Edsall, "Cracks in the Clinton Coalition," *Washington Post*, 8 November 1992, p. C1. See also Elizabeth Drew, "The White House's New New Dealers," ibid.

[14]Paul Barrett and David Rogers, "Senate Support for Zoë Baird is Precarious," *Wall Street Journal*, 22 January 1992, p. A3.

made a large payment retroactively and paid a fine. Nevertheless, after two days of
hostile questioning by members of the Senate Judiciary Committee and a deluge
of letters and phone calls to members of Congress by individuals and groups
protesting the nomination, Baird asked the president to withdraw her name.
Clinton, eager to contain the damage from what came to be called the "Nanny-
gate" affair, hardly bothered to defend his nominee and quickly rescinded the
appointment.[15]

The campaign against Baird, according to some observers, was organized and
orchestrated not by Republicans but by Democratic liberals. Consumer advocate
Ralph Nader and other liberals objected to Baird's background as a corporate
lawyer and to her past support for tort law reforms that would restrict citizen suits
(see Chapter 8).[16] Some Republicans cheerfully joined the attack, happy to have
an opportunity to give Clinton a black eye.

Immediately after his inauguration, Clinton attempted to bolster his support
among the powerful liberal forces in the party by adopting a more liberal stance on
domestic social spending, as well as on gay rights, abortion, minority representation, and other causes championed by the Democratic Left. Campaign promises
such as welfare reform and the "middle-class tax cut," backed by the centrists, were
forgotten. Clinton and his team believed it had been Carter's failure to reach out
to the party's liberal wing after campaigning as a moderate that had led to the collapse of his presidency twelve years earlier.[17] But in shifting to the left, Clinton was
also echoing one of George Bush's tactics. Bush, a centrist, had felt compelled to
try to maintain the allegiance of forces on his party's right wing by championing
their views on abortion and other social issues.

By moving to the right, of course, Bush had alienated moderate Republicans.
In a similar way, as he sought to accommodate liberal forces, Clinton risked losing
the support of Democrats from other parts of the political spectrum. Liberals insisted that the president's health care reform package include a guarantee of funding for abortions for all women. This enraged conservatives, who then vowed to
oppose the entire plan.[18] His effort to end the military's ban on gay personnel engendered intense opposition within the armed services and among conservative
and even moderate Democrats. Democratic opposition was led by the powerful
chair of the Senate Armed Service Committee, Senator Sam Nunn of Georgia.
Clinton's efforts to conciliate liberals by expanding domestic spending programs
led to a revolt among conservative and moderate Democrats, who demanded the
imposition of caps on the growth of entitlement programs such as Medicare.[19]

---

[15]Ruth Marcus and David Broder, "President Takes Blame for Rushing Baird Selection," *Washington Post,* 23 January 1993, p. A1.

[16]Michael Isikoff and Ruth Marcus, "As Support for Baird Erodes, Senators Call for Withdrawal," *Washington Post,* 22 January 1993, p. 1. See also Seymour Martin Lipset, "Roosevelt Redux for the Democrats," *Wall Street Journal,* 21 January 1993, p. A14.

[17]Fred Barnes, "Back to Basics," *New Republic,* 17 May 1993, pp. 16–18. See also Michael Kelly, "New Democrats Say Clinton Has Veered Left and Left Them," *New York Times,* 23 May 1993, p. 20. See also Adam Clymer, "Single-Minded President," *New York Times,* 4 April 1993, p. 1.

[18]Dana Priest, "Health Plan Threatened by Abortion Coverage," *Washington Post,* 19 May 1993, p. 1.

[19]Eric Pianin, "Hill Democrats Press for Entitlement Caps," *Washington Post,* 18 May 1993, p. 1.

592

POLITICS AND
GOVERNMENT:
THE PROBLEM
WITH THE
PROCESS

The Senate's Democratic leadership became increasingly concerned that the administration's difficulties would, if unchecked, lead to a total collapse that could hurt Democratic senators and House members up for re-election in 1994. To prevent a complete disaster, Democratic Senate leaders took charge of the budget package in the Finance committee, and suggested that the president confine himself to enunciating broad principles while leaving it to Congress to develop the "details" of legislation.[20]

Clinton then surprised politicians in both parties by appointing David Gergen, who had formerly been a key advisor to three Republican presidents including Ronald Reagan, to the newly created position of presidential "counselor." The president hoped Gergen would reassure moderates and conservatives that the administration was moving back to the political center. While some politicians and commentators praised the Gergen appointment, for the most part, both the liberal and conservative camps charged Clinton (and Gergen) with deceit and opportunism. Liberals were dismayed that Clinton would give a key White House position to an individual who had played a central role in selling Ronald Reagan's program to the nation.[21]

Debate over the Gergen appointment had hardly ended when Clinton sparked a new controversy, and, again seeking to placate conservative and moderate Democrats, he withdrew his nomination of Lani Guinier, an African American law professor at the University of Pennsylvania, to head the civil rights division of the Justice Department.

Conservatives had strongly opposed the Guinier nomination and had mounted an RIP attack against her by writing press releases, reports, and op-ed pieces characterizing her as an extremist and labeling her "a quota queen." In the course of the Guinier nomination battle, her critics acknowledged that they were seeking to make use of the same techniques used so successfully by liberal forces over the preceding years. "There's no question," one critic said, "that in terms of tactics, the playbook was written by the left and we're playing by the rules of the game established over the last twelve years."[22]

Clinton initially accused Guinier's opponents of painting a misleading picture of her views. But once the president realized that a battle over the nomination was certain to alienate the conservatives and moderates he was again trying to court, Clinton abandoned the effort. Clinton's decision to withdraw the nomination was based on a political calculation similar to the one that had led to his attacks on Jesse Jackson and rap singer Sister Souljah during his campaign. The president concluded that, although they would be angered by his actions, African Americans and their liberal political allies ultimately would have no choice but to continue to support his administration. Whereas if he continued to alienate conservative

---

[20]David Broder, "Democrats Worrying: Clinton's Problems Raise Fears for 1994," *Washington Post,* 9 June 1993, p. 1. See also Ann Devroy and Eric Pianin, "Clinton Yields on Energy Tax," *Washington Post,* 9 June 1993, p. 1.

[21]See Ruth Marcus, "Clinton's New Spin Doctor Has Left a Trail of Blunt Diagnoses," *Washington Post,* 31 May 1993, p. A4; and "A History of Gergenism," *New York Times,* 2 June 1993, p. A18.

[22]Michael Isikoff, "Power Behind the Thrown Nominee: Activist with Score to Settle," *Washington Post,* 6 June 1993, p. A11.

Democrats, he would undermine his chances of winning their approval for his economic, health care, and political reform proposals.[23]

In the end, the president's handling of the Guinier nomination proved divisive and costly. As in the hiring of Gergen, Clinton's efforts to satisfy moderates and conservatives deeply offended liberal Democrats while doing little to placate the party's other wing. Civil rights leaders denounced the president for failing to even allow Guinier an opportunity to present her case to the Senate Judiciary Committee, which would have had to confirm the appointment. Conservatives, for their part, expressed disdain for the president's "waffling" and condemned him as an individual whose "only core principle is to bend to the strongest political force."[24]

The Media's Message In addition to the problems he faced from interest group opposition, partisan antagonism, and factional struggle in his own party, Clinton also found himself under attack from the national news media. As has often been noted, many of America's most prominent journalists tend to identify themselves as liberal Democrats, and many had implicitly or explicitly supported Clinton during the 1992 campaign. During his first two months in office, President Clinton continued to have considerable media support. After his initial budget proposals were accepted by Congress, he was hailed as a political genius. A few weeks later, however, the media began to adopt a considerably more critical stance. In the wake of the Republican senatorial filibuster that defeated Clinton's proposed economic stimulus package, many commentators concluded that Clinton was not experienced enough to manage the congressional process. After his first one hundred days in office, the president was accused of having lost his focus, of a lack of organization, and of trying to do too many things at once.[25]

Why did the president's relationship with the national media sour so quickly? There are essentially two reasons. First, as discussed in Chapter 13, the power of the news media in the United States is, in large measure, linked to the media's capacity to investigate and criticize. Investigative reporting and adversarial journalism are techniques that enhance the power and status of the media relative to other American political and social institutions. For this reason, any administration can expect a certain amount of critical coverage.

Second, the president and members of his staff responded to media criticism in ways that were guaranteed to antagonize journalists and generate even more hostility. For example, to avoid media questions, the president spurned press conferences in favor of "town meetings" with the public. Members of his staff helpfully observed that the president did not need the media and could reach "over their heads" to the American public. In a similar vein, large sections of the White House press office were declared "off-limits" to reporters, who then resented what they saw as another effort to block their access to legitimate news.

[23]Ruth Marcus, "Clinton Withdraws Nomination of Guinier," *Washington Post,* 4 June 1993, p. 1.

[24]Paul A. Gigot, "Guinier Is Going, No, She's Staying, No, Going . . . ," *Wall Street Journal,* 4 June 1993, p. A14.

[25]See, for example, Thomas B. Edsall, "Clinton Loses Focus—and Time," *Washington Post,* 2 May 1993, p. C1. But see also Jeffrey Birnbaum, "Resentful of Negative Coverage, Clinton Spurns the Media, but He May Need to Woo Them Back," *Wall Street Journal,* 15 April 1993, p. A16.

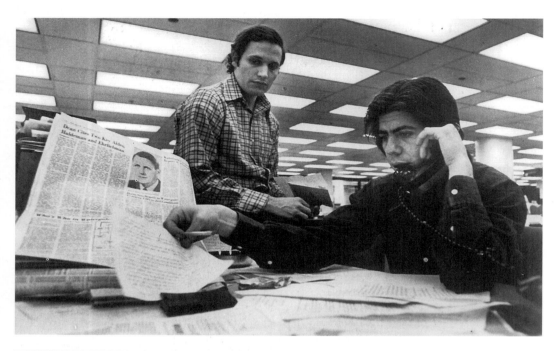

Persistent investigative reporting by *Washington Post* reporters Bob Woodward and Carl Bernstein linked the Nixon White House to the 1972 break-in at the Democratic campaign headquarters at the Watergate Hotel. The ensuing Senate investigation showed that the burglary was only a small part of a larger pattern of criminality and corruption in the Nixon administration. Richard Nixon was forced to resign and twenty-five of his officials were convicted and imprisoned. Revelation, investigation, and prosecution (RIP) had brought down a president and marked the start of a new political climate.

News reports of U.S. sales of weapons to Iran in exchange for hostages, and the use of profits from the sales to aid Nicaraguan Contra rebels in defiance of congressional legislation, created a scandal in 1986 reminiscent of Watergate. Several officials in the Reagan administration were prosecuted and one, Admiral John Poindexter, being sworn in here before the Senate, was sent to jail. However, the Reagan White House itself was not charged with any legal wrongdoing.

After investigating media reports of his alcohol abuse and marital infidelity, the Senate overwhelmingly rejected George Bush's nominee for secretary of defense, John Tower, in January 1989. The use of RIP weaponry by congressional Democrats against the Bush administration gave them an early victory in the endless jockeying for power between the two parties that would continue over the next four years.

In July 1989, Republicans were given the opportunity to retaliate. Reports by the media that House Speaker Jim Wright (D.-Tex.) and Representative Tony Coehlo (D.-Calif.) were using campaign finances inappropriately led to a Senate Ethics Committee investigation and both men were forced to resign. And in 1990, Representative Barney Frank (D.-Mass.), pictured here speaking to the press, was embarrassed by media reports of his involvement with a male prostitute that ultimately led to a reprimand by the House. RIP was increasingly being used as a weapon in partisan power disputes, in place of resolving such disputes in the electoral arena.

In 1992, President Bill Clinton nominated corporate lawyer Zoë Baird to the post of attorney general, the first woman ever selected for such a powerful position. When news stories exposed Baird's unlawful hiring of an illegal immigrant as a nanny, she was forced to withdraw from consideration. While Baird's illegal activities made it impossible for her to head the Justice Department, the group most opposed to her nomination, liberal Democrats, were less worried about her babysitter hiring practices than with how her policy decisions would affect their political agenda. As the RIP is used increasingly in everyday politics, groups use it to oppose one another regardless of party affiliation, leading to further governmental inaction. Should this trend continue, the process initially begun to protect the government may irrevocably cripple it.

596

POLITICS AND
GOVERNMENT:
THE PROBLEM
WITH THE
PROCESS

Once David Gergen joined the White House staff, he sought to develop a better relationship with the national media. He scheduled a White House cook-out for reporters, removed restrictions on media access to presidential press aides, and sought to schedule several traditional presidential press conferences to give journalists the opportunity they had been demanding to question the president. But the first of these news conferences ended rather badly. Clinton had just nominated Judge Ruth Bader Ginsburg to the U.S. Supreme Court, filling the vacancy created by Justice Byron White's pending retirement. Asked a question that seemed to imply criticism of his selection process, the president gave an angry response and stalked off, refusing to take any more questions.[26] (See Box 14.1.)

BOX 14.1

"The Ginsburg Nomination: The One-Question News Conference"

After remarks by Supreme Court nominee Ruth Bader Ginsburg, President Clinton took a question from Brit Hume of ABC News. The news conference opened and closed with this exchange:

Q: *"Mr. President, the result of the Guinier nomination, sir, and your apparent focus on Judge Breyer, and your turn, late it seems, to Judge Ginsburg may have created an impression, perhaps unfair, of a certain zigzag quality in the decision-making process here. I wonder, sir, if you could kind of walk us through it and perhaps disabuse us of any notion we might have along those lines. Thank you."*

A: *"I have long since given up the thought that I could disabuse some of you of turning any substantive decision into anything but a political process. How you could ask a question like that after the statement she just made is beyond me.*

"Goodbye. Thank you."

Sources: Cable News Network; news reports.

Reprinted from the *Washington Post*, 15 June 1993.

---

[26]Howard Kurtz, "One Question Too Many For Clinton," *Washington Post*, 15 June 1993, p. A13.

What came to be known as the "one-question news conference" drew angry responses from the national media. The next day, the nation's two most influential newspapers, the *New York Times* and the *Washington Post,* both published editorials praising Judge Ginsburg but sharply criticizing the White House for its selection process. The *Times* castigated the president for "an intemperate response to a reporter's question about his erratic selection process."[27] In its news coverage, the *Post* ridiculed the selection process as erratic and ultimately based on the president's personal rapport with the nominee—"personal karma," the *Post* called it—rather than reasoned judgment.[28]

Later that week, the White House scheduled a prime time press conference. The president hoped to use reporters' questions to review his administration's achievements. Two of the three national networks, however, refused to carry the news conference. Network executives saw the conference as simply another effort by David Gergen to manipulate the news.[29]

CAN DEMOCRATIC POLITICS FUNCTION WITHOUT VOTERS?

During the political struggles of the past decades, politicians sought to undermine the institution associated with their foes, disgrace one another on national television, force their competitors to resign from office, and in a number of cases, send their opponents to prison. Remarkably, one tactic that has not been so widely used is the mobilization of the electorate. Of course, Democrats and Republicans have continued to contest each other in national elections. Voter turnout even inched up in 1992. However, neither side has made much effort to mobilize new voters, to create strong local party organizations, or in general, to make full use of the electoral arena to defeat its enemies. The 1993 "Motor-Voter" Act is, at best, a very hesitant step in the direction of expanded voter participation. The act requires all states to allow voters to register by mail when they renew their driver's licenses (twenty-eight states already have similar mail-in procedures) and provides for the placement of voter registration forms in motor vehicle, public assistance, and military recruitment offices. This type of passive approach to registration still places the burden of action on the individual citizen and is not likely to result in many new

---

[27]"Mr. Clinton Picks a Justice," *New York Times,* 15 June 1993, p. A26.

[28]Ann Devroy and Ruth Marcus, "After 87 Days, Tortuous Selection Process Came Down to Karma," *Washington Post,* 15 June 1993, p. A11 and, "Judge Ginsburg's Nomination . . . And Getting There," *Washington Post,* 15 June 1993, p. A20.

[29]See Gwen Ifill, "Clinton, in Prime Time, Spurned by Two Networks," *New York Times,* 18 June 1993, p. A18.

598

POLITICS AND
GOVERNMENT:
THE PROBLEM
WITH THE
PROCESS

registrants, especially among the poor and uneducated. Mobilization requires more than the distribution of forms.[30]

It is certainly not true that politicians don't know how to mobilize new voters and expand electoral competition. Voter mobilization is hardly a mysterious process. It entails an investment of funds and organizational effort to actively register voters and bring them to the polls on election day. Occasionally, politicians demonstrate that they *do* know how to mobilize voters if they have a strong enough incentive. For example, a massive get-out-the-vote effort by Democrats to defeat neo-Nazi David Duke in the 1991 Louisiana Democratic gubernatorial primary led to a voter turnout of over 80 percent of those eligible—twice the normal turnout level of a Louisiana primary.

How extraordinary, then, that politicians who will stop at nothing in their efforts to "RIP" the opposition stop short of attempting to expand the electorate to overwhelm their foes in competitive elections. Why is this?

A large part of the answer to this question is that the decline of political party organizations over the past several decades strengthened politicians in both camps who were linked with and supported by the middle and upper-middle classes. Recall from Chapter 11 that party organization is an especially important instrument for enhancing the political influence of groups at the bottom of the social hierarchy–groups whose major political resource is numbers. Parties allowed politicians to organize the energies of large numbers of individuals from the lower classes to counter the superior financial and institutional resources available to those from the middle and upper classes.

The decline of party organization that resulted, in large measure, from the efforts of upper- and middle-class "reformers," over the years, undermined politicians such as union officials and Democratic and Republican "machine" leaders who had a stake in popular mobilization, while strengthening politicians with an upper-middle- or upper-class base. Recall the effects of registration laws, the elimination of patronage practices, and so forth, discussed in Chapter 11. As a result of these reforms, today's Democratic and Republican parties are dominated by different segments of the American upper-middle class. For the most part, contemporary Republicans speak for business and professionals from the private sector, while Democratic politicians and political activists are drawn from and speak for upper-middle-class professionals in the public and not-for-profit sector.

Both sides give lip service to the idea of fuller popular participation in political life. Politicians and their upper-middle-class constituents in both camps, however, have access to a variety of different political resources—the news media, the courts, universities, and interest groups, to say nothing of substantial financial resources. As a result, neither side has much need for or interest in political tactics that might, in effect, stir up trouble from below. Both sides prefer to compete for power without engaging in full-scale popular mobilization. This is a political process whose class bias is so obvious and egregious that, if it continues, Americans may have to begin adding a qualifier when they describe their politics

---

[30]For an excellent discussion see Steven J. Rosenstone and John Mark Hansen, *Mobilization, Participation and Democracy in America* (New York: Macmillan, 1993), Chapter 8.

as democratic. Perhaps the terms "semi–democratic," "quasi–democratic," or "neo–
democratic" are in order to describe a political process in which ordinary voters
have as little influence as they do in contemporary America.

POLITICS AND GOVERNANCE

The failure of political leaders to organize and mobilize strong popular bases leaves them weak and vulnerable to the institutions and interests, including the mass media, upon which they are now so dependent. Party politicians had stable, organized, popular followings that could be counted upon when their leaders came under fire. As Chicago's longtime machine mayor, Richard J. Daley, once said in response to media attacks, "When you've got the people behind you you don't need the media. . . . The media can kiss my ———!" Contemporary politicians seldom have well-organized popular followings. Lacking such a base of support, they seldom can afford Mayor Daley's indifference to his media image.

Contemporary American politics undermine governance in four ways. First, elections today fail to accomplish what must be the primary task of any leadership selection process: they fail to determine *who will govern.* An election should award the winners with the power to govern. Only in this way can popular consent be linked to effective governance. Under the fragmented system bequeathed to us by the Constitution's framers, seldom at any point in American history have all the levers of power been grasped by a unified and disciplined party or group.

Today, however, with the decay of America's political party organizations, this fragmentation has increased sharply. There are many victorious cliques and factions with little unity among them. During the Bush presidency, fragmentation and division led to a pattern of "gridlock" in which little or nothing could be accomplished in Washington. Deep factional divisions within the Democratic party, as we have seen, posed severe problems for the Clinton administration within its first few months in office, producing a paralysis not too different from the infamous gridlock of the Bush years. As we saw in Chapter 5, a number of conservative Democrats joined with the Republican opposition to oppose the president on issues ranging from the budget to the question of allowing gays in the military. Clinton was forced to change his proposals to accommodate this opposition within his own party. The budget eventually enacted by Congress and signed into law by the president in August 1993 bore little resemblance to Clinton's initial proposals. Congressional opponents forced Clinton to abandon his campaign promise to provide middle-class tax relief, as well as the bulk of his package of social and economic "investments." One journalist, sympathetic to Clinton's original goals, called the budget a "far cry" from Clinton's original proposals and hardly a long-term solution to the nation's problems.[31]

In addition to factional opposition, Clinton's efforts were hampered by the fact that many congressional Democrats have become "soloists," willing to give the ad-

---

[31]David Broder, "Some Victory," *Washington Post,* 10 August 1993, p. A15.

600

POLITICS AND
GOVERNMENT:
THE PROBLEM
WITH THE
PROCESS

ministration their support only in exchange for some set of tangible benefits for themselves and the interests they represent. In the absence of party organizations and mechanisms for enforcing party discipline, there is little to prevent legislators from demanding what amounts to immediate political payoffs in exchange for their support on important pieces of legislation. The result is that all legislation effectively becomes special-interest legislation filled with loopholes and special benefits. For example, the 1993 budget contains provisions requiring that cigarettes manufactured in the United States contain 75 percent domestically grown tobacco. This provision was inserted at the behest of Senator Wendell Ford of Kentucky for the benefit of his state's tobacco farmers. Similarly, Democratic Representative James Bilbray of Nevada agreed to support the budget only after securing a tax credit designed to offset the Social Security taxes paid on employees' tips by restaurant owners—an important constituency group in his district. Texas Democrat Solomon Ortiz traded his support of the president's budget for an enlarged share of defense conversion funds for his district. The list goes on and on.[32] No wonder columnist David Broder called the resulting budget a "pastiche of conflicting goals."[33] One Clinton administration official conceded that because the budget was "driven by politics not policy," it was "not the greatest package ever."[34]

Longstanding institutional rivalries also work to thwart governance. For example, the Senate's Democratic leadership was no more willing to give fellow Democrat Clinton the line-item veto than they had been to accede to similar requests from Republican presidents.

Second, contemporary governments are weak and unstable. Elected officials subjected to RIP attacks often find that their poll standing (today's substitute for an organized popular base) can evaporate overnight and their capacity to govern disappear with it. Thus, the Nixon administration was paralyzed for three years by the Watergate affair and the Reagan White House for two years by the Iran-Contra affair. Congress was nearly immobilized for a year by the Tower-Wright-Coelho-Frank imbroglio and for another year by the post office scandal. This is hardly a recipe for a strong government to solve America's long-term deficit and trade problems.

Third, because they lack a firm popular base, politicians seldom have the capacity to confront entrenched economic or political interest groups even when the public interest seems clear. For example, early in the Bush administration, the Treasury Department's plan for resolving the crisis in the savings and loan industry involved the imposition of a fee on S & L deposits. This idea was adamantly rejected by the industry and met overwhelming resistance on Capitol Hill, where thrift institutions enjoyed a good deal of influence. The administration was compelled to disown the Treasury plan and proposed, instead, a plan in which general tax revenues would finance the bulk of the cost of the $166 billion bailout. In this way, a powerful interest, the savings and loan industry, was able to shift the burden

---

[32]David Rogers and John Harwood, "No Reasonable Offer Refused as Administration Bargained to Nail Down Deficit Package in House," *Wall Street Journal,* 6 August 1983, p. A12.

[33]Broder, "Some Victory."

[34]Hobart Rowan, "It's Not Much of a Budget," *Washington Post,* 12 August 1993, p. A27.

of a major federal initiative designed for the industry's own benefit from itself to the general public. Moreover, to mask the impact that the bailout would have on the nation's budget deficit, it was largely financed through "off-budget" procedures—a ploy that over time adds billions of dollars to the cost of the bailout.

In a similar vein, after his election in 1992, President Clinton felt compelled to reassure the nation's business community and powerful banking and financial interests that his administration would be receptive to their needs. This was a major reason that Clinton—who had campaigned as a staunch opponent of business-as-usual in Washington—named Democratic National Committee chair Ron Brown to be his secretary of Commerce and Texas Democratic Senator Lloyd Bentsen to the post of secretary of the Treasury. Brown was a veteran Washington corporate lobbyist well known to the business community. Bentsen, as chair of the Senate Finance Committee, was noted for his close and cordial relationship with banking, finance, insurance, and real estate interests.[35] President Clinton was no more eager than his predecessor to confront these interests. Later, to secure the enactment of his tax proposals, Clinton felt compelled to give major tax concessions to a variety of interests including aluminum producers, real estate developers, multinational corporations, and the energy industry.[36]

Finally, the enhanced political power of non-electoral institutions means that the question of who will *not* govern is unlikely to be resolved in the electoral arena. The most important function of an election is to determine who will govern. At the same time, elections must also deprive the losing party of the power to prevent the winning party from governing effectively. Today, elections not only fail to determine who will govern but also do not definitively determine *who will not exercise power*. Given the political potency of non-electoral modes of political struggle, electoral defeat does not deprive the losing party of the power to undermine the programs and policies of the winner. Indeed, as we have seen, electoral verdicts can now be reversed outside the electoral arena.

As a result, even as the "winners" in the American electoral process do not acquire firm control of the government, so the "losers" are not deprived of power. Instead, "winners" and "losers" typically engage in a continuing struggle, which often distracts them from real national problems. For example, in 1991 and 1992, official Washington seemed much more concerned with several thousand dollars in bounced congressional checks than with several hundred billion dollars in debts.

More important, however, this struggle compels politicians to pay greater heed to the implications of policies for their domestic political battles than for collective national purposes. The Reagan and Bush administrations' tolerance of enormous budget deficits and their program of deregulation provide examples of this phenomenon. One important reason why Republican administrations were prepared to accept the economic risks of unprecedented deficits is the constraint these deficits imposed on congressional power. Similarly, the Republicans pressed for deregulation in part because the constellations of interests surrounding many regu-

---

[35]Jill Abramson and John Harwood, "Some Say Likely Choice of Bentsen, the Insider, for Treasury Post Could Send the Wrong Signals," *Wall Street Journal,* 9 December 1992, p. A26.

[36]David Hilzenrath, "Bentsen Signals White House's Willingness to Deal," *Washington Post,* 17 May 1993, p. A4.

602

POLITICS AND
GOVERNMENT:
THE PROBLEM
WITH THE
PROCESS

Ronald Reagan and Bill Clinton
Redefining the Role of Government

Debate over the size, scope, and power of the federal government dominated the American political agenda in the 1980s and 1990s. Ronald Reagan swept into office in 1980 in large part on the promise to reduce government. Yet twelve years after Reagan's election, Bill Clinton won the presidency based on his pledge to mobilize the resources of government to attack pressing domestic problems.

Ronald Reagan's career in politics extended back to his days as an actor, when he was elected president of the Screen Actors Guild in 1947. He began his political life as a Democrat but formally switched to the Republican party in 1962. He became an ardent supporter of conservative Republican Barry Goldwater's unsuccessful bid for the presidency in 1964. Two years later Reagan was elected governor of California, a position he held for eight years. In 1976, Reagan narrowly lost the Republican nomination to incumbent Gerald Ford. Four years later, he captured the nomination and the presidency on a crest of conservative enthusiasm for less government and stronger national defense spending, defeating beleaguered incumbent Jimmy Carter.

In his inaugural address, Reagan stated unequivocally that "government is not the solution to our problem; government is the problem." During his first term in office, Reagan won major revisions in fiscal policy and brought about the enormous increases in military spending that he sought. During his second term, however, most of Reagan's legislative efforts were blocked by Congress and his administration ended under the cloud of the Iran-Contra scandal. Whether viewed as successful or not, the Reagan administration redefined the American political agenda to one in which more would have to be done with less.

Although considered by many to be a supporter of big-government spending, Bill Clinton sought to adapt to the post–Reagan era of limited government by redefining the Democratic party while still drawing on the party's tradition of activism. Clinton's hum-

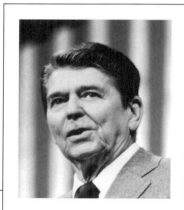

Ronald Reagan

latory policies are important Democratic bastions. This sort of political gamesmanship caused the administration to overlook potential costs and risks of their policies. The relaxation of regulatory restraints on financial institutions permitted many S & Ls to shift from their traditional role as home mortgage lenders into potentially more lucrative but dangerously speculative areas. We all now know the results.

Their concern for their institutional and political advantage can also affect the way officials respond to the initiatives of their opponents. For example, congres-

ble Arkansas roots belied his grand ambitions. A Rhodes scholar and graduate of Yale Law School, Clinton set his sights early on a political career. He became the nation's youngest governor when first elected in 1978. After an unexpected defeat in 1980, Clinton came back two years later to recapture the office, which he held until assuming the presidency.

Despite early political setbacks, Clinton proved to be a tenacious and durable campaigner for the 1992 presidential nomination. By the time he won the Democratic nomination, he stood even with his two rivals, George Bush and Ross Perot. From the end of the Democratic convention to election day, Clinton never trailed in the polls. Sensing that the mood of the country called for governmental leadership to address such pressing domestic problems as economic decline, revamping the nation's creaking health care system, and improving America's competitiveness, Clinton promised in his inaugural address to "resolve to make our Government a place for what Franklin Roosevelt called bold, persistent experimentation."

Once in office, Clinton introduced an ambitious package of proposals, including tax and spending increases, changes in America's health care system, and reform of campaign finance and lobbying practices. His proposals were initially greeted with enthusiasm by the media, the public, and members of his own party in Congress. Within several months, however, Clinton faced intense opposition from the Republicans, large segments of the media, and even from key congressional Democrats. Analysts asked whether Clinton's difficulties resulted from the president's own errors or whether they reflected some of the more systemic problems faced by America's government today. Is government the problem as Reagan suggests or the solution as Clinton contends? The debate continues. . . .

Source: John Chubb and Paul Peterson, eds., *Can Government Govern?* (Washington, DC: Brookings Institution, 1989).

Bill Clinton

sional Democrats regularly voted for lower levels of military spending than the two Republican administrations proposed, not because they were less committed to the nation's defense, but because the defense establishment has been an important institutional bastion of the Republicans. This reason also played a part in Democratic opposition to the 1991 Persian Gulf War.

Similarly, despite the continuing problem of America's huge budget deficit, the Clinton administration has been committed to increases in federal domestic spending. Like Reagan's and Bush's reasons for defense spending, domestic social spend-

604
POLITICS AND
GOVERNMENT:
THE PROBLEM
WITH THE
PROCESS

ing is politically necessary for the Clinton administration, whatever the long-term economic risks it may entail. Indeed, despite his reputation as a "policy wonk," Clinton quickly found that it was virtually impossible to focus on questions of policy effectiveness. Purely political considerations frequently had to come first.[37] In contemporary America, political struggle is constant, leaving little room for consideration of long-term public interests.

Electoral Mobilization and Governmental Power

What can be done to restore our government's capacity to govern? The most important implication of the political patterns we have observed is that good government is unlikely to result from an unhealthy politics. Rejuvenation of America's governmental capabilities would first and foremost require the revitalization of America's political process. In particular, we would need to revive the nation's crumbling electoral institutions.

Of course, the relationship between political patterns and governmental effectiveness is complex. Practices that severely undermine governmental capacities in some settings may not in others—witness the ability of Japan to thrive despite widespread political corruption in its government. But, political patterns sometimes emerge that seriously inhibit governments from pursuing collective purposes. For example, in Israel during the late 1980s, electoral stalemate between the Labor and Likud parties paralyzed the government. This stalemate prevented the government from responding effectively to the uprisings in the occupied territories and to diplomatic initiatives by the Palestine Liberation Organization, thereby threatening the close relationship with the United States, which is necessary for Israel's very survival.

Similar examples can be found in American history. In the United States during the early 1930s, prevailing party and factional conflict led the government to pursue policies that exacerbated rather than relieved the Depression. A notable example is the Smoot-Hawley Tariff of 1930. Congressional logrolling practices of the 1930s led to the adoption of the highest tariffs in American history. This provoked foreign retaliation, precipitated a virtual collapse of international trade, and helped turn what could have been an ordinary cyclical downturn into the most severe economic crisis of the modern era. Even more striking than the events of the early 1930s are those preceding the Civil War. Political paralysis and partisan deadlock during the James Buchanan administration prevented the government from responding to its own dismemberment as southern states seceded from the Union.

Historically, efforts to overcome political patterns that undermine governmental effectiveness have taken one of two forms in the United States: political demobilization or mobilization. Political demobilization involves attempts to free government from "political interference" by insulating decision-making processes, restricting political participation, or both. Mobilization consists of efforts by one

---

[37]See Jeffrey H. Birnbaum and Michael K. Frisby, "Clinton's Zigzags between Politics and Policy Explain Some Problems of His First 100 Days," *Wall Street Journal,* 29 April 1993, p. A16.

or another contender for power to overcome political stalemate and governmental

paralysis by bringing new voters into the electorate and strengthening their political base sufficiently to prevail over entrenched social and economic interests.

Demobilization and insulation were the paths followed by institutional reformers in the United States during the Progressive era. The Progressives, who spoke for a predominantly middle-class constituency, sought to cope with the problems of turn-of-the-century America by strengthening the institutions of national, state, and local government. Progressives undertook to strengthen executive institutions by promoting civil service reform, creating regulatory commissions staffed by experts, and transferring fiscal and administrative responsibilities from elected to appointed officials.[38] In addition, asserting that the intrusion of partisan considerations undermined governmental efficiency, the Progressives attacked state and local party organizations. They sponsored legislative investigations of ties between party leaders and businessmen as well as the criminal prosecution of politicians they deemed to be corrupt. The Progressives also supported the enactment of personal registration requirements for voting that served to reduce turnout among the poorly educated, immigrant, nonwhite, and working-class voters who had provided the various party organizations with their mass base.[39]

In the short run, the Progressive strategy of administrative reform did help improve the functioning of government in the United States. Government agencies penetrated by parties and rife with patronage are not well suited to performing the functions of a modern state. However, politicians are not in a position to prevail over entrenched social and economic forces when they lack the support of an extensive and well-organized mass constituency. In the long run, the Progressive strategy of insulation and demobilization weakened American government relative to powerful interests in society and helped produce the low rates of voter turnout that ultimately contributed to political stalemate in the United States today.

The second strategy—political mobilization—was used most effectively in the United States by the administrations of Abraham Lincoln and Franklin D. Roosevelt. To fight the Civil War and break the power of Southern slaveholders, the Lincoln administration vastly expanded the scope of the American national state. It raised an enormous army and created a national system of taxation, a national currency, and a national debt. The extraordinary mobilization of the electorate that brought the Republicans to power in 1860 enabled them to raise more than two million troops, to sell more than $2 billion in bonds to finance the military effort, and to rally popular support for the war. The higher levels of party organization and political mobilization in the North than in the South, as much as the superiority of Northern industry, help explain the triumph of the Union cause in the Civil War.[40]

[38]Stephen Skowronek, *Building a New American State* (New York: Cambridge University Press, 1982).

[39]Frances Fox Piven and Richard A. Cloward, *Why Americans Don't Vote* (New York: Pantheon, 1988), Chapter 3.

[40]Eric McKitrick, "Party Politics and the Union and Confederate War Efforts," in *The American Party Systems* ed. by William N. Chambers and Walter Dean Burnham (New York: Oxford University Press, 1967), pp. 117–51.

606
POLITICS AND
GOVERNMENT:
THE PROBLEM
WITH THE
PROCESS

Is America Declining?

T he end of the Cold War has resulted in important changes in the relationships among nations. While America seemed to emerge triumphantly from the eclipse of communism in the former Soviet Union and elsewhere, many have viewed America's changing role in the world as being in decline.

Foreign policy expert Edward N. Luttwak summarizes the concerns of many who fear that the United States is losing its economic competitive edge, to the point where we may one day resemble nations of the developing world, struggling to keep our economic heads above water. Newspaper editor Robert L. Bartley argues that the gloom-and-doomers ignore or distort the evidence indicating America's continued strength and resilience.

Luttwak

When will the United States become a third-world country? One estimate would place the date as close as the year 2020. A more optimistic projection might add another ten or fifteen years. Either way, if present trends simply continue, all but a small minority of Americans will be impoverished soon enough, left to yearn hopelessly for the lost golden age of American prosperity. . . .

The relentless erosion of the entire economic base of American society is revealed by undisputed statistics. . . . During the last 20 years—half a working lifetime—American "non-farm, non-supervisory" employees actually earned slightly less, year by year. As a matter of fact, by 1990 their real earnings . . . had regressed to the 1965 level. Will they regress further . . . to the 1955 level by the year 2000? It seems distinctly possible. . . .

Who are these poor unfortunates whose real earnings have been declining since 1965? Are they perhaps some small and peculiar minority? Not so . . . they numbered 74,888,000, or just over 81 percent of all non-farm employees—that is, more than eight out of ten of all Americans who are not self-employed, from corporate executives earning hundreds or even thousands of dollars per hour, to those working at the minimum wage.

Far from being a minority whose fate cannot affect the base of American society, then, they *are* the base of American society. . . .

How can the entire structure of American affluence and advancement from luxurious living to scientific laboratories *not* decline when the vast majority of all working Americans are earning less and less? And how can the U.S. not slide toward third world conditions if this absolute decline continues while in both Western Europe and East Asia real earnings continue to increase?[1]

Bartley

To the ordinary, everyday senses of mankind, America has not declined, it has prevailed. Its foe of two generations has collapsed and now even seeks to adopt American institutions of democracy and market economics.

Though to people who use their eyes and ears it is obvious that American influence in the world is on the rise, we have not been able to put the notion of decline behind us. For a segment of American opinion refuses to use its eyes and ears. Instead, proponents of decline confuse themselves with statistics they do not understand, or in some cases willingly distort. They invoke jingoism by turning international trade into some kind of combat, instead of a series of mutually beneficial arrangements among consenting adults. . . .

. . . Our dilemma is that all of us living in the 1990s have been taught from the cradle not to believe in dreams. We are cynical about politicians, and they live down to our expectations. . . . Instead of the promise of world cooperation led by the United States, we have the gloomy apostles of decline, alarmed because goods and capital move across lines someone drew on maps, trying to manufacture conflict out of the peaceful and mutually beneficial intercourse among peoples.

The last time the will of the West was tested, it rose to the challenge. In particular, the American electorate understood that the threat was Soviet Communism, not the military-industrial complex. With the more subtle test of a litany of decline coming out of Cambridge, Detroit, and Washington, there will again be confusion and apparent close calls, but in the end the delusion will not sell. Indeed, given any sort of intellectual and political leadership to frame the challenge, the American nation will rise to the rich opportunity before it.[2]

[1]Edward N. Luttwak, "Is America on the Way Down? Yes," *Commentary,* March 1992, pp. 15, 21.
[2]Robert L. Bartley, "Is America on the Way Down? No," *Commentary,* March 1992, pp. 22, 27.

In a similar vein, the Roosevelt administration permanently transformed the American institutional landscape, creating the modern welfare and regulatory state.[41] The support that the administration mobilized through party organizations and labor unions helped it contend with opposition to its programs both inside and outside the institutions of government. A marked increase in voter turnout, a realignment of some existing blocs of voters, and a revitalized Democratic party apparatus provided Roosevelt with the enormous majorities in the electoral college and Congress that allowed him to secure the enactment of his New Deal programs.[42] Worker mobilization through unions and strikes forced businessmen to accept the new pattern of industrial relations the administration was seeking to establish.[43]

[41]See the essays in Margaret Weir, Ann Orloff, and Theda Skocpol, eds., *The Politics of Social Policy in the United States* (Princeton, NJ: Princeton University Press, 1988).

[42]Kristi Andersen, *The Creation of a Democratic Majority, 1928–1936* (Chicago: University of Chicago Press, 1979).

[43]David Plotke, "The Wagner Act, Again: Politics and Labor, 1935–37," *Studies in American Political Development* 3 (1988), pp. 105–56.

608

POLITICS AND
GOVERNMENT:
THE PROBLEM
WITH THE
PROCESS

Electoral Mobilization in Contemporary Politics

The dangers facing the United States in the 1990s may not be as immediate as those it confronted on the eve of the Civil War or in the aftermath of the 1929 stock market crash. Nevertheless, America's political processes impede governmental responses to the challenges of today.

What could strengthen America's government? The answer lies in the realm of electoral organization and mobilization. As political scientists have been arguing for decades, stronger political parties could potentially diminish our electoral and governmental fragmentation and produce governments with greater unity and collective purpose than is currently possible. A bit of party discipline might go a long way toward enhancing the government's capacity to govern. A bit of party unity, moreover, might go a long way toward giving elected officials the strength to withstand attacks by their opposition.

Parties could certainly be strengthened through changes in campaign-funding rules, nominating rules, and ballot laws that might give party leaders greater control over campaign funds and candidate nominations. Unfortunately, one element of President Clinton's campaign finance reform package would have just the opposite effect. Clinton proposed prohibiting the use of so-called "soft money" (money contributed to the parties rather than to the candidates) in federal campaigns. Under present federal law, there is no restriction on the amount that wealthy individuals and interests can contribute to parties for voter registration, grass-roots organizing, and other partisan activities not directly linked to a particular candidate's campaign efforts. Critics charge that soft-money contributions allow wealthy donors unfair influence in the political process and, perhaps, this potential does exist. However, soft money also provides the national and state parties with the means to engage in voter registration and turn-out drives and to strengthen state and local party organizations. These are goals that should be encouraged rather than thwarted.[44]

Unfortunately, today's independent politicians have little stake in subjecting themselves to party control. Why, for example, should the currently autonomous members of Congress or of the state legislatures accept party control of nominations or campaign spending? The benefits of reforming the electoral system might accrue to the nation, but the costs would be borne by the very individuals who would have to agree to any package of reforms. As we noted in Chapter 11, nineteenth-century Progressives were able to undermine political parties precisely because they found elected representatives eager to free themselves from party discipline. The contemporary successors to those legislators are not eager to bind themselves again with the shackles their predecessors worked so hard to remove.

As for voter mobilization, were one of America's political parties to mobilize and forge organizational links to new voters, it might put itself in a position to prevail over entrenched interests and powerful social forces for the sake of achieving collective national purposes. Under such circumstances, the most debilitating fea-

[44] See Beth Donovan, "Much-Maligned 'Soft Money' Is Precious to Both Parties: Clinton Wants to Ban Its Use in Federal Campaigns; Scholars Say it Assists Grass-Roots Growth," *Congressional Quarterly Weekly Report,* 15 May 1993, pp. 1195–1200.

FIGURE 14.3
Percentage Reporting They Voted

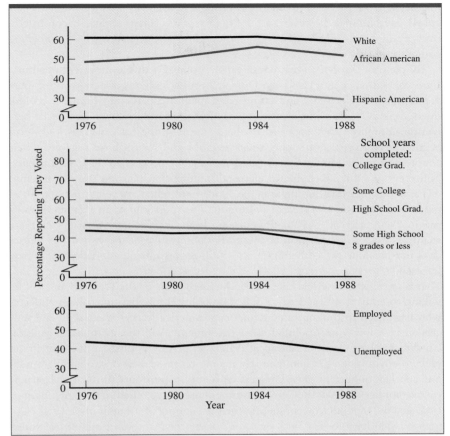

Source: *Statistical Abstract of the United States* (Washington, DC: Government Printing Office, 1993), p. 269.

ture of the contemporary American policy-making process—the government's lack of a firm base of support—might be contained.

For the Democrats, a strategy of mobilization presumably would involve a serious effort—going far beyond the Motor Voter Act—to bring into the electorate the tens of millions of working-class and poor Americans who at present stand entirely outside the political process. Figure 14.3 illustrates the large and long-standing differences in American voting-participation rates associated with race, education, and employment. Bringing citizens who currently do not vote into the Democratic party would probably require an organizational and programmatic focus on economic issues that unites poor, working-, and lower-middle-class voters and overcomes the racial and cultural issues that divide them.

Though it is generally assumed that only the Democrats could benefit from any substantial expansion of the electorate, it is important to note that mobilization is a

610

POLITICS AND
GOVERNMENT:
THE PROBLEM
WITH THE
PROCESS

strategy that the Republicans could employ as well.[45] Indeed, in the late 1970s and early 1980s, it was the GOP, through its alliance with conservative evangelicals, that made the more concerted effort to bring new voters into the electorate. Their efforts were limited, however and, thus, so was the party's ability to construct a base of support for conservatism large enough to pose a challenge to Democratic congressional hegemony.

By contrast, Europe's great conservative mobilizers of the nineteenth century, Otto von Bismarck and Benjamin Disraeli, brought millions of new working-class voters into the electorate and constructed extensive party organizations to link them securely to the conservative cause. By sponsoring factory and social legislation, moreover, they appealed to these voters on the basis of their long-term economic concerns, not simply their religious and nationalistic passions. Their counterpart in the United States, Abraham Lincoln, proceeded along similar lines. Nineteenth-century Republican electoral mobilization entailed the construction of party organizations throughout the North and relied on economic appeals as much as on the issues of slavery and union. The most important Republican slogan in 1860, after all, was "Vote yourself a farm, vote yourself a tariff." As these examples suggest, its position as the more conservative of the two major parties does not preclude the contemporary GOP from organizing a broad popular base for itself.

It is not likely, however, that either the Democrats or the Republicans will be willing to embark on the path of full-scale political mobilization. The politicians who have risen to the top in contemporary America learned their skills and succeeded in a low-voter-mobilization environment. And the weapons of political combat that have become central in American politics contribute to maintaining such an environment. When they rely mainly on these weapons to compete with one another, politicians provide voters with little opportunity or reason to participate in politics. Indeed, they give voters new reasons to refrain from participating.

Conversely, politicians competing for the support of a highly mobilized electorate would have to deal with questions of concern to tens of millions of voters and would find it impossible to focus on the issues of personal impropriety that loom so large in American politics today. Nor would they find themselves so vulnerable to such charges. In 1944, for example, when Republicans charged that Franklin Roosevelt had used government property for his personal benefit by sending a U.S. Navy destroyer to retrieve a pet he had left behind on the Aleutian Islands, the president ridiculed them for attacking "my little dog, Fala."[46] FDR's links to a mass constituency were too strong to be threatened by the GOP charges, and therefore he was in a position to dismiss them with a derisive quip. Lacking such support, elected officials today are much more vulnerable to any allegations of personal impropriety.

---

[45]James DeNardo, "Turnout and the Vote: The Joke's on the Democrats," *American Political Science Review* 70 (June 1980), pp. 406–20.

[46]John P. Diggins, *The Proud Decades: America in War and Peace, 1941–1960* (New York: W. W. Norton, 1988), p. 21.

In contrast to the immediate gains that politicians can realize today by resorting

to revelations and investigations to drive opponents from office, the path of voter mobilization would entail major risks for both parties. For the Republicans, expansion of the electorate could threaten an influx of poor voters who wouldn't seem likely to be supporters of the GOP. As for the Democrats, whatever the potential benefits to the party as a whole, an influx of millions of new voters would create serious uncertainties for current office holders at the local, state, and congressional levels. Moreover, various interests allied with the Democrats—notably upper-middle-class environmentalists, public interest lawyers, antinuclear activists, and the like—could not be confident of retaining their influence in a more fully mobilized electoral environment. Finally, though it is seldom openly admitted, the truth is that many members of both the liberal and the conservative camps are wary of fuller popular participation in American politics. Conservatives fear blacks, and liberals often have disdain for working- and lower-middle-class whites.

As long as these conditions persist, the path of electoral mobilization will not be taken. America's non-electoral political patterns, governmental incapacities, and economic difficulties will endure, and America will continue to pay the price of its undemocratic politics. This price is a government that cannot govern—surely a price the nation cannot afford to pay as it confronts the economic and social problems of the twenty-first century.

SUMMARY

As we approach the twenty-first century, America faces many problems. In such areas as health care, housing, crime, and education the U.S. government has been unable to formulate or implement effective programs or policies. In other areas, it is the government, itself, that seems to be the cause of the nation's difficulties. For example, the long-term strength of the American economy is threatened by the $4 trillion debt that is the fiscal legacy of the Reagan and Bush presidencies.

One major reason for our present dilemma is that an unhealthy and fundamentally undemocratic political process has developed in the United States over the past several decades. For much of American history, government rested on a relatively broad base of vigorous—often tumultuous—popular participation, with most major issues being debated, fought, and ultimately resolved in the electoral arena. America's democratic politics, in turn, provided political leaders with a base of support from which to develop and implement programs, contend with powerful, entrenched interests, and during times of crisis such as the Civil War and World War II, ask their countrymen for the exertions and sacrifices needed in order for the nation to survive.

In recent decades, however, popular participation in American political life has declined sharply. Despite a much ballyhooed increase in voter turnout, in the 1992 presidential election only 55 percent of eligible Americans bothered to vote. At the same time, the political parties that once mobilized voters and imparted a measure of unity to the scattered pieces of the American governmental structure have

612
POLITICS AND
GOVERNMENT:
THE PROBLEM
WITH THE
PROCESS

decayed, making it very difficult, if not impossible, to create a coherent government through the American electoral process.

Both reflecting and reinforcing these changes in the electoral process, contending political forces in the United States have come to rely heavily on forms of political conflict that neither require nor encourage much in the way of citizen involvement. In recent years, many of the most important national political struggles have been largely fought outside the electoral arena rather than through competitive electoral contests.

America's contemporary political process, characterized by low voter turnout, weak parties, and the rise of a "politics by other means," is the source of many of our government's present problems. This process is increasingly undemocratic, fragments political power, and fails to provide elected officials with the strong and stable political base needed to govern effectively. Most important, this process undermines the ability of elected officials to bring about, or even to take account of, the public good.

FOR FURTHER READING

Birnbaum, Jeffrey. *The Lobbyists* (New York: Times Books, 1992).

Calleo, David. *The Bankrupting of America* (New York: WIlliam Morrow, 1992).

Dionne, Jr., E.J. *Why Americans Hate Politics* (New York: Simon & Schuster, 1991).

Draper, Theodore. *A Very Thin Line: The Iran-Contra Affairs* (New York: Simon & Schuster, 1991).

Friedman, Benjamin. *Day of Reckoning: The Consequences of American Economic Policy Under Reagan and After* (New York: Random House, 1988).

Jackson, Brooks. *Honest Graft: Big Money and the American Political Process* (Washington, DC: Farragut Publishing, 1990 rev. ed.).

Johnson, Haynes. *Sleepwalking Through History* (New York: W. W. Norton, 1991).

Kernell, Samuel, ed. *Parallel Politics: Economic Policymaking in Japan and the United States* (Washington, DC: Brookings Institution, 1991).

Kurtz, Howard. *Media Circus* (New York: Times Books, 1993).

Kutler, Stanley. *The Wars of Watergate* (New York: W. W. Norton, 1990).

Phillips, Kevin. *Boiling Point: Democrats, Republicans and the Decline of Middle-Class Prosperity* (New York: Random House, 1993).

Rosenstone, Steven, and John Mark Hansen. *Mobilization, Participation and Democracy in America* (New York: Macmillan, 1993).

Sundquist, James L. *Constitutional Reform and Effective Government* (Washington, DC: Brookings Institution, 1992, rev. ed.).

Weaver, R. Kent, and Bert Rockman, eds. *Do Institutions Matter?* (Washington, DC: Brookings Institution, 1993).

Part 4
Governance

15

An Introduction to Public Policy

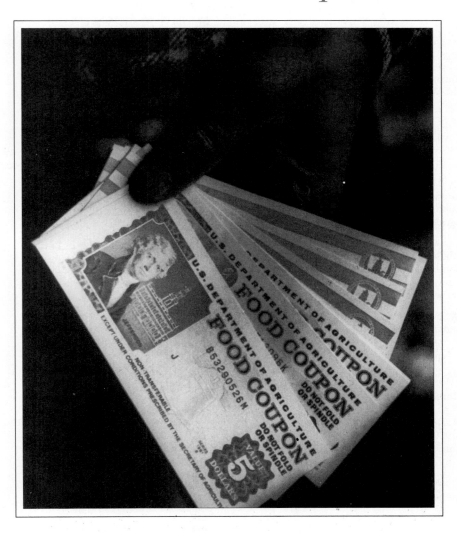

EVENTS		INSTITUTIONAL DEVELOPMENTS
Creation of first executive departments—state, treasury, war (1790s)		Constituent policies used to create structure of the executive branch (1790s)
Alexander Hamilton's *Report on Manufactures* expresses idea of policies as techniques for encouraging industry (1791)		Promotional policies used by national government to encourage American commerce (1800s)
Tariff duties enacted (1792)	**1800**	Regulatory policies reserved to states—policies regarding property, land use, education, morality, marriage, criminal conduct (1790s–1990s)
Territorial expansion, settlement of the West (1800s)		National government builds roads and makes land grants to farmers and railroads to promote western settlement (1800s)
Civil War (1861–1865)		After secession of southern states, national government adopts protective tariff, transcontinental railroad, Homestead Act (1862)
Growth of industry, corporations, railroads, and commercialization of agriculture (1860s–1890s)		National government's first regulatory policies enacted—Interstate Commerce Act (1887) and Sherman Antitrust Act (1890)
Abuses of workers, farmers, and consumers arise out of the new industrial system; progressives work for reform (1890s–1910s)	**1900**	National government enacts legislation to protect consumers—Meat Inspection Act and Pure Food and Drug Act (1906)
Wilbur and Orville Wright build and fly the first airplane (1903)		National government extends regulation to suits against businesses; Federal Trade Commission created (1914)
World War I (1914–1918) Railroads nationalized (1917)		First government mobilization of entire economy for war (1917–1920)
Railroads returned to private hands (1920); motor transportation emerges (1920s)		National government aids automobile industry through road building; encourages airline industry through federal subsidies (1920s and 1930s)
Franklin D. Roosevelt and the New Deal (1930s)	**1930**	National government's power to enact regulatory and redistributive policies recognized (1937)

TIME LINE ON PUBLIC POLICY

EVENTS		INSTITUTIONAL DEVELOPMENTS
U.S. enters World War II; conduct of war a management triumph (1941–1945)		Employment Act of 1946 commits national government to use of macroeconomic policies (1946)
Sputnik (1957)		First federal aid to education—National Defense Education Act (1958)
Executive Order by John Kennedy prohibits discrimination by firms receiving government contracts (1961)	**1960**	National government seeks through contracts and laws (Civil Rights Act of 1964) to eliminate racial discrimination (1960s)
Polluting of land and water by industry (1960s–1990s)		National government enacts "social regulation" programs to protect the environment, workers, and consumers (1965–1974)
Nixon imposes wage and price controls (1971)		National government tries to fight inflation through redistributive policies (1970s)
Deregulatory movement begins with Carter administration (1978)		Airline Deregulation Act (1978); Staggers Rail Deregulation Act (1980)
More deregulation of economy with Reagan and Bush, through administrative means rather than termination; but pro-regulation of morality, anti-abortion, etc. (1980s)	**1980**	Executive Order 12291 mandates presidential oversight of all regulatory proposals (1981)
		"Privatization" in earnest, with sale of Conrail and Amtrak (1988)
Public sentiment for some re-regulation mounts, favoring Democrats (1989–1992)		Bush vetoes extensively but accepts Clean Air Act (1990) and Americans with Disabilities Act (1991), and favors abortion regulation (1989–1992)
Clinton election supported by many industries demanding "more government" (1992)	**1990**	Clinton deregulates morality (gays in the military, abortion counseling) and supports moderate economic regulation (1993)

*I*nflation is a problem every administration—Democratic or Republican, pro-government or anti-government—must confront with timely and appropriate public policies. Everyone agrees that inflation is caused by too many dollars chasing too few goods. But people can disagree intensely about what particular anti-inflationary policy is in fact the timely and appropriate one. This makes inflation a good introduction to the public policy phenomenon.

Toward the end of the Vietnam War, inflationary pressure began to mount because President Lyndon Johnson had committed the United States to guns *and* butter—that is, to increased military expenditure without cutting domestic programs or raising taxes to pay for it. Wide public recognition of the problem led a Democratic Congress and a Republican president in 1970 to adopt the Economic Stabilization Act authorizing the president, through an agency of his choice in the executive branch, to *regulate* all wages, prices, rents, and interests in order to keep a ceiling on rates of increase. After more than two years of implementation, when almost everyone agreed that this regulatory approach had failed, the search for a new anti-inflationary policy resumed. By 1977, oil prices were becoming more important than war expenditures because of the dramatic increases in international oil prices imposed by the Organization of Petroleum Exporting Countries (OPEC). President Carter sought to control the inflationary effect of the "oil crisis" with his proposals to restrict oil importation from the Middle East using *tariffs* and *quotas.* He also proposed a **regulatory tax** on gasoline at the pump and on "gas-guzzler" automobiles, plus some new taxes on oil and natural gas. The argument for this strategy was that the taxes would so increase the price of gas and other forms of energy that people would consume less, thereby controlling inflation as well as striking a blow in favor of energy conservation. Since Congress only gave President Carter a small part of his requested policies, he attempted to reduce consumer spending in general by a **fiscal policy** of raising Social Security taxes imposed on employee earnings. These various policies raised a lot of revenue for the federal government but did not reduce the high rate of inflation by an acceptable amount. When President Reagan came into office in 1981, he was obliged to try another angle.

President Reagan replaced the oil import restrictions and selective taxes with an almost opposite policy, a general tax cut. His policies were called "supply-side economics" and were based on the theory that if tax cuts were deep enough and were guaranteed to endure, consumer confidence would rise, which would encourage individuals and corporations to invest more, therefore produce more, and cut inflation through an abundance of goods. President Reagan adopted another fiscal policy, an *investment tax credit,* a policy permitting investors to deduct from their taxes a portion of the cost of new machinery and other capital expenditures. President Reagan also adopted a new monetary policy, an effort to control the flow of money by getting the Federal Reserve to lower interest rates in order to encourage new investments rather than to keep interest rates high in order to discourage too much borrowing for consumption.[1] President Bush maintained the Reagan approach until the recession of 1990–91 convinced him that the problem for economic policy was for the moment not inflation but one of fighting off the increased deficits and of encouraging more economic growth.

By 1993, inflation rates had been so low for so long that the Clinton administration was able to relax the vigil on inflation and turn its attention toward policies that might increase the rate of economic growth. (As a general rule, Republicans are more sensitive to inflation, while Democrats are quicker to worry about general economic growth.) One of President Clinton's earliest successes was convinc-

---

[1]For more on fiscal and monetary policies on the role of the Federal Reserve in manipulating the interest rates, see Chapter 16 as well as later in this chapter.

ing Alan Greenspan, chairman of the Federal Reserve, that some new spending for
an "economic stimulus" would not "overheat" the economy to such an extent that the Federal Reserve would have to jump back in and raise interest rates. But despite Greenspan's approval, the Republicans in Congress, along with a few conservative Democrats, forced President Clinton to severely reduce his stimulus package from the requested $16 billion (which President Clinton already thought was pretty modest) to a minuscule figure of below a billion dollars. Inflation rates continued to run relatively low, toward 2 and 3 percent per year, compared to the "double-digit" inflation rates of the 1970s. But the large budgetary deficits, coupled with the reputation of a Democratic administration for "tax and spend" policies, once again ran up the flag of inflationary storm warnings. If inflation should in fact set in again, no one can say with any certainty which policy, if any, will be the appropriate one. All we can say is that no government will stand by and permit inflation to sap the vitality of the economy without trying to do something about it.

Absolute monarchs and warlords govern by their own discretion, with orders backed by military force. The purpose of constitutions and the "rule of law" is to put limits on the absolute discretion of such rulers by the requirement that even they be subject to law and that they must try to govern by stating "the intent of the state" in advance and in the form of law, which would spell out with some precision the obligations of citizens. In our time, these "intentions of the state" have come to be called *public policies*. The job of this and the succeeding three chapters is to step beyond the play of politics and governmental institutions to look at the *purposive* actions of government—the policies. First, we will discuss public order and control. Then we will provide an inventory of the controls that policy makers have to choose from when they draft policies. We will call these the "techniques of control" because they are means available to any government to get people to obey. Policies may be known by their goals, which are usually given fancy names by those who want them adopted. For example, a policy for "environmental protection" sounds like a pretty good idea, but it wouldn't mean very much if the policy as enacted by Congress said nothing more than "let there be clean air." A clean air policy has to include one or more of the "techniques of control"—that is, rules of conduct backed by specific rewards and punishments. Finally, we will discuss the techniques and the policies as they serve different interests and contribute to the power of different segments of society.

PUBLIC ORDER AND PUBLIC POLICY

Try as we may to have a system of limited government, where freedom and control are balanced, control has to be the first priority, because without a society that is predictable and relatively safe—which is all we mean by public order—our freedom would not count for much.

The most deliberate form of government control we call "public policy." **Public policy** can be defined simply as an officially expressed intention backed by a sanction, which can be a reward or a punishment. Thus, a public policy is a law, a rule, a statute, an edict, a regulation, an order. Today, the term "public policy" is the term of preference, probably because it conveys more of an impression of flexibility and compassion than other terms. But the citizen, especially the student of political science, should never forget that "policy" and "police" have common origins. Both derive from *polis* and *polity,* which refer to the political community. Consequently, it must be clearly understood that all public policies are coercive, even when they are motivated by the best and most beneficent of intentions. Because public policies are coercive, many people wrongly conclude that all public policies—all government—should be opposed. For us, the coercive element in public policy should instill not absolute opposition but a healthy respect for the risks as well as the good that may be inherent in any public policy.

TECHNIQUES OF CONTROL

Techniques of control are to policy makers roughly what tools are to a carpenter. There are a limited number of techniques; with each there is a logic or an orderliness; and there is an accumulation of experience helping us to understand when a certain technique is likely to work. There is no unanimous agreement on techniques, just as carpenters will disagree about the best tool for a task. But we offer here a workable elementary handbook of techniques that will be useful for analyzing the policies we will examine in succeeding chapters.

In this section, the important techniques have been grouped into three categories—promotional, regulatory, and redistributive policies—and the specifics of each will be discussed and explained in some detail. In the following section, the three categories will be analyzed for their effect on policy makers themselves, and a fourth category (constituent policy) will be introduced. Each category of policy is associated with a different kind of politics. In other words, since these techniques are different ways of using government, each type is likely to develop a distinctive pattern of power.

Promotional Techniques

Promotional techniques are the carrots of public policy. Their purpose is to encourage people to do something they might not otherwise do or to get people to do more of what they are already doing. Sometimes the purpose is merely to compensate people for something done in the past. Promotional techniques can be classified into at least three separate types—subsidies, contracts, and licenses.

Subsidies   Subsidies are simply government grants of cash or other valuable commodities, such as land. Although subsidies are often denounced as "give-aways," they have played a fundamental role in the history of government in the United States. As we discussed at length in Chapter 3, subsidies were the dominant form of public policy of both the national government and the state and local governments throughout the nineteenth century. The first planning document ever written for the national government, Alexander Hamilton's *Report on Manufactures,* was based almost entirely on Hamilton's assumption that American industry could be

Alexander Hamilton
The First American Planner

Alexander Hamilton (1757–1804)

Almost as soon as President Washington appointed him secretary of treasury, Alexander Hamilton was ordered by Congress to produce three reports to guide debate on the American economy.

In the first report, Hamilton had to counter the arguments made by a large number of American leaders that the public debt, swollen by war and speculation, was a burden that ought to be repudiated, especially since a large portion of our debt was held by foreigners. Hamilton responded with the argument that although the total debt, $79 million—almost $20 per capita—appeared to be a very large burden indeed, it was, properly treated, a blessing, not a burden. First, strict observance of debts was the only way a new nation could earn the respect and confidence of other nations. Second, a stably financed national debt would serve as collateral for making loans for public investment in roads and other capital expenditure. Third, interest payments on the public debt would be a monthly shot in the arm to the economy. Congress accepted Hamilton's approach, and within less than five years, the bonds of the United States enjoyed the highest credit rating of any bonds traded in Europe. A National Bank, designed in the second Hamilton report, was also established by Congress, although it was later terminated by President Andrew Jackson.

The third report, the Report on Manufactures, was important for its concept alone, that the United States could and should be an industrial na-

tion. This was heresy to the Jeffersonians. In the report, Hamilton proposed three types of policies for the national government. First, there had to be the proper funding of the debt, as covered in the first two reports. Second, there ought to be legislation providing for *"protecting duties—or duties on those foreign articles which are the rivals of the domestic ones intended to be encouraged* [italics in original]. That is to say, Hamilton favored protective tariffs. The revenue from high tariffs would then finance the third type of Hamiltonian policy: "pecuniary bounties," to stimulate and encourage new enterprises and to provide for the transportation of those commodities. Today, supporters tend to call these subsidies and public investments; critics tend to call them give-aways and pork-barrel. But by whatever name, Hamilton recognized that private capital or credit in our agricultural economy would be insufficient to generate manufactures without some kind of centralized public assistance. Judicious grants of money and public land to building of roads and canals would facilitate the establishment of larger and larger markets in agricultural and manufactured commodities and would tie the country together.

Sources: Charles H. Hession and Hyman Sardy, *Ascent to Affluence—A History of American Economic Development* (Boston: Allyn & Bacon, 1969); and Theodore J. Lowi, *Private Life and Public Order* (New York: W. W. Norton, 1968).

encouraged by federal subsidies and that these were not only desirable but constitutional.

The thrust of Hamilton's plan was not lost on later policy makers. Subsidies in the form of land grants were given to farmers and to railroad companies to encourage western settlement. Substantial cash subsidies have traditionally been given to commercial shipbuilders to help build the commercial fleet and to guarantee the use of the ships as military personnel carriers in time of war.

Subsidies have always been a technique favored by politicians because subsidies can be treated as "benefits" that can spread widely in response to many demands that might otherwise produce profound political conflict. Subsidies can, in other words, be used to buy off the opposition. So widespread is the use of the subsidy technique in government, in fact, that it takes encyclopedias to keep track of them all. Indeed, for a number of years, one company published an annual *Encyclopedia of U.S. Government Benefits,* a thousand-page guide to benefits "for every American—from all walks of life. . . . [R]ight now, there are thousands of other American Taxpayers who are missing out on valuable Government Services, simply because they do not know about them. . . . Start your own business. . . . Take an extra vacation. . . . Here are all the opportunities your tax dollars have made possible."[2]

Another secret of the popularity of subsidies is that those who receive the benefits do not perceive the controls inherent in them. In the first place, most of the resources available for subsidies come from taxation. (In the nineteenth century, there was a lot of public land to distribute, but that is no longer the case.) Second, the effect of any subsidy has to be measured somewhat indirectly in terms of what people *would be doing* if the subsidy had not been available. For example, many thousands of people settled in lands west of the Mississippi only because land subsidies were available. Hundreds of research laboratories exist in universities and corporations only because certain types of research subsidies from the government are available. And finally, once subsidies exist, the threat of their removal becomes a very significant technique of control. (More on this below under regulation.) But for the recipient, subsidy means promotion.

Contracting   Like any corporation, a government agency must purchase goods and services by contract. The law requires open bidding for a substantial proportion of these contracts because government contracts are extremely valuable to businesses in the private sector and because the opportunities and incentives for abuse are very great. But contracting is more than a method of buying goods and services. Contracting is also an important technique of policy because government agencies are often authorized to use their contracting power as a means of encouraging corporations to improve themselves, as a means of helping to build up whole sectors of the economy, and as a means of encouraging certain desirable goals or behavior, such as equal employment opportunity.

[2]Roy A. Grisham and Paul McConaughty, eds., *Encyclopedia of U.S. Government Benefits* (Union City, NJ: William H. Wise Co., 1972). The quote is taken from the dust jacket. A comparable guide published by the *New York Times* is called *Federal Aid for Cities and Towns* (New York: Quadrangle Books, 1972). It contains 1,312 pages of federal government benefits that cities and towns, rather than individuals, can apply for.

One of the outstanding examples of the use of contracting as a way of building

up an entire sector of the economy can be found in the relatively new (post-World War II) sector of the economy we call "research." Government contracts were one of the most important factors in the growing capacity of America's great universities to engage in scientific research. The research and development (R & D) divisions of the larger private corporations also owe their existence or a substantial proportion of their growth to government contracts. The latest and biggest government contract operation for science is the Superconducting Super Collider (SSC). This choice piece of patronage went to a consortium of universities in Texas, to be located twenty-five miles south of Dallas, in the form of a fifty-three-mile tunnel encircling the city of Waxahachie. The 1994 Clinton budget provided for "stretching out" the SSC project. Instead of the original cost of $8.2 billion for its completion by 1999, the "up front" expenditures will be reduced in the early years, and the project will be completed around 2003 at an estimated cost now of $10 billion or more.

Some research contracts are highly specific with regard to a particular research project; but many research contracts are either designed to enable the universities or corporations to build laboratories larger than the project requires, or designed to have loopholes to permit universities to do so. By this means, universities have been able to engage in "pure research" as an adjunct to the "contract research" for which the original contract was signed. The defense industry is another sector of the economy that owes its growth in size to the systematic use of government contracting, not only to acquire specified military goods and services but also to permit and encourage broader military research that might lead toward important technological innovations. For example, many university scientists supported the Strategic Defense Initiative (SDI, or "Star Wars") because the massive contracts for research finance expanded facilities.

The contracting power was of great significance for the Reagan and Bush administrations because of their commitment to "privatization." When a president says he wants to restore as much government as possible to the private sector, he may seek to terminate a government program and leave the activity to private companies to pick up. That would be true privatization. But in most instances true privatization is neither sought nor achieved. Instead, the government program is transferred to a private company to provide the service *under a contract with the government,* paid for by the government, and supervised by a government agency. In this case, privatization is only a euphemism. Government-by-contract has been around for a long time, and has always been seen by business as a major source of economic opportunity.

Licensing   A license is a privilege granted by a government to do something that it otherwise considers to be illegal. For example, state laws make medical practice and taxi driving without a license illegal. The states then create a board of doctors and a "hack bureau" to grant licenses respectively for the practice of medicine and for the operation of a cab for hire to all persons who have met the particular qualifications specified in the statute or by the agency. Licensing was used by kings to grant privileges to the favored few. Gourmet products in France still carry reference to the original license granted by a French monarch in the nineteenth century. It may mean nothing today except as a symbol of tradition and longevity. But it meant life or death to the company when the bottling of mineral water or the packaging of the cheese was illegal without the king's permission. Today in modern industrial societies licensing has also proved to be an effective technique. Like subsidies and contracting, licensing has two sides. One is the giveaway side, making the license a desirable object of patronage. The other side of licensing is the control or regulatory side, to be dealt with below.

Regulatory Techniques

If promotional techniques are the carrots of public policy, **regulatory techniques** can be considered the sticks. Regulation comes in several forms, but every regulatory technique shares a common trait: direct government control of conduct. The conduct may be regulated because people feel it is harmful to others, or threatens to be, such as drunk driving or false advertising. Or the conduct may be regulated because people think it's immoral, whether it is harming anybody or not, such as prostitution, gambling, or drinking. Because there are many forms of regulation, we have subdivided them here: (1) police regulation, through civil and criminal penalties, (2) administrative regulation, and (3) regulatory taxation.

Police Regulation   "Police regulation" is not a technical term, but we use it for this category because these techniques come closest to the traditional exercise of "police power"—the power traditionally reserved to the states (see Chapter 3). After a person's arrest and conviction, these techniques are administered by courts and, where necessary, penal institutions. They are regulatory techniques.

   Civil penalties usually refer to fines or some other form of material restitution (such as public service) for violating civil laws or such common law principles as negligence. Civil penalties can range from the $5 fine for a parking violation to a more onerous penalty for late payment of income taxes or to the much more onerous penalties for violating the antitrust laws against unfair competition or the environmental protection laws against pollution. **Criminal penalties** usually refer to imprisonment but can also involve heavy fines and the loss of certain civil rights and liberties, such as the right to vote or the freedom of speech.

   Although distinctions among types of penalties are relatively easy to make, this does not make the task of the legislator or judge any easier when the time comes to define a misdemeanor or felony and to decide on the appropriate penalty. For example, if the purpose of the law is deterrence—keeping other people from committing or repeating such crimes in the future—then a long prison sentence may be the only appropriate technique of control to apply against a professional bank robber, while the threat of brief sentences or mere public exposure may be a sufficient deterrent for those who might commit such "white-collar" crimes as embezzlement or insider trading. On the other hand, if the purpose of the policy is retribution rather than deterrence, then an entirely different technique of control or degree of punishment might be called for. For example, if retribution is the purpose of the policy, then punishment probably should be heavier for the white-collar criminal than for the habitual professional criminal, because the white-collar

criminal is not only taking the property of others but at the same time is undermining the credibility of the bank or business against which an embezzlement or
forgery or fraudulent stock deal took place. Thus, policy makers and students
should consider any technique of police regulation in light of the question: What
is the relationship between the technique of control and the policy it is supposed
to serve?

Administrative Regulation   Police regulation addresses conduct considered immoral. In order to eliminate such conduct, strict laws have been passed and severe
sanctions enacted. But what about conduct that is not considered morally wrong
but has harmful consequences? There is, for example, nothing morally wrong with
radio or television broadcasting. But broadcasting on a particular frequency or
channel is regulated by government because disorder would amount to virtual
chaos if everybody could broadcast on any frequency at any time.

This kind of conduct is thought of less as *policed* conduct and more as *regulated*
conduct. When conduct is said to be regulated, the purpose is rarely to eliminate
the conduct but rather to influence it toward more appropriate channels, toward
more appropriate locations, or toward certain qualified types of persons, all for the
purpose of minimizing injuries or inconveniences. This type of regulated conduct
is sometimes called *administrative regulation* because the controls are given over to
administrative agencies rather than to the police. As we have already seen in Chapter 7, each regulatory agency has extensive powers to keep a sector of the economy
under surveillance and also has powers to make rules dealing with the behavior of
individual companies and people. But these administrative agencies have fewer
powers of punishment than the police and the courts have, and the administrative
agencies generally rely on the courts to issue orders enforcing the rules and decisions made by the agencies.

Sometimes a government will adopt administrative regulation if an economic
activity is considered so important that it is not to be entrusted to competition
among several companies in the private sector. This is the rationale for the regulation of local or regional power companies. A single company, traditionally called a
"utility," is given an exclusive license (or franchise) to offer these services, but since
the one company is made a legal monopoly and is protected from competition by
other companies, the government gives an administrative agency the power to
"regulate" the quality of the services rendered, the rates charged for those services,
and the margin of profit for the company.

At other times, administrative regulation is the chosen technique because the
legislature decides that the economy needs protection from itself—that is, it may
set up a regulatory agency to protect companies from destructive or predatory
competition, on the assumption that economic competition is not always its own
solution. This is the rationale behind the Federal Trade Commission, which has
the responsibility of watching over such practices as price discrimination or pool-
ing agreements between two or more companies when their purpose is to eliminate competitors.

Most employers and companies will simply obey the law by regulating their
own conduct. But when the agency finds a company violating these laws, it can
order the business to "cease and desist." If the company should persist, the agency

can get a court order to enforce the agency order (a federal agency would go to the federal district court). If the behavior continues, the company can then be found in contempt of court and punished. By this means, a court order becomes a technique of control in administrative regulation. One of the most famous uses of administrative regulation involved the Justice Department and the courts in restraining the world's largest service corporation, AT&T. AT&T had been subject to administrative regulation since the 1920s when the government agreed to tolerate it as a monopoly as long as AT&T submitted to regulation of its rates and services. In 1948, the Antitrust Division brought suit against AT&T for building a monopoly in telephone equipment as well as services, and it sought to break AT&T into three separate companies. After eight years of litigation, in a 1956 "consent decree," AT&T agreed to limit itself to communication services if the government would drop the suit. This lasted over twenty-five years, until AT&T agreed in 1982 to spin off its twenty-five Bell operating companies in return for the termination of the 1956 decree—so that AT&T could get into the larger and more expansive information technology industry.[3]

Subsidies, licensing, and contracting are listed a second time on Table 15.1 because, although these techniques can be used strictly as promotional policies, they can also be used as techniques of administrative regulation. It all depends on whether the law sets serious conditions on eligibility for the subsidy, license, or contract. To put it another way, the threat of losing a valuable subsidy, license, or contract can be used by the government to improve compliance with the goals of regulation. For example, the threat of removal of the subsidies called "federal aid to education" has had a very significant influence on the willingness of schools to cooperate in the desegregation of their student bodies and faculties. For another example, social welfare subsidies (benefits) can be lowered to encourage or force people to take low-paying jobs, or they can be increased to placate people when they are engaging in political protest.[4]

An important social goal for which regulatory licensing has been a standard technique is the prevention of unqualified persons from practicing medicine. That power can, of course, be abused, as when medical licenses are issued merely to hold down the number of physicians so that they can charge higher fees. Other examples of regulatory licensing range from the allocation of channels for television companies, to the issuing of licenses for the export of wheat or to operate an automobile or restaurant, to the issuing of permits to hunt or fish in season. Table 15.2 demonstrates two important points—first, the extent of regulation by state governments; and second, the wide potential of regulation through licensing.

Like subsidies and licensing, government contracting can be an entirely different kind of technique of control when the contract or its denial is used as a reward or punishment to gain obedience in a regulatory program. For example, in 1961,

---

[3]Manly Irwin, "The Telecommunication Industry," in *The Structure of American Industry*, 7th ed., ed. Walter Adams (New York: Macmillan, 1986), pp. 262–66. See also the definitive study by Alan Stone, *Wrong Number* (New York: Basic Books, 1989).

[4]For an evaluation of the policy of withholding subsidies to carry out desegregation laws, see Gary Orfield, *Must We Bus?* (Washington, DC: Brookings Institution, 1978). For an evaluation of the use of subsidies to encourage work or to calm political unrest, see Frances Fox Piven and Richard Cloward, *Regulating the Poor: The Functions of Public Welfare* (New York: Random House, 1971).

TABLE 15.1

Highlights of Federal Government Policy in Selected Sectors
of Commerce and Industry

Technique	Agriculture Sector	Consumer Industries	Energy Industries	Communications Industries	Transportation Industries
Promotional	Grants to improve land productivity; education on how to do this; aids to facilitate marketing; government research and grants for university research.	Traditional tariffs against foreign competition; development of new products for the benefit of government research.	Tariffs and quotas against foreign sources; government research; public mineral resources; construction of dams; aid to develop new fuels.	Government-sponsored research; defense contracts; cash and services for satellite development.	Land and cash (for rail and shipping); mail contracts; highway building and airport construction; grants for public transit.
Regulatory	Control of uniform standards, measures, quality of products; support of increased prices by keeping down the amount of land under cultivation (the parity program); control of soil erosion; control of timber use on public lands.	Policing price discrimination and mergers; policing safety and advertising claims (drugs, cosmetics, and cigarettes); setting standards for safe products.	Control of rates; assignment of amounts to extract (oil and gas); licensing to enter market (atomic energy and oil-gas transport); rationing (being prepared for).	Licensing to control frequencies; policing access and "equal time"; regulating mergers and interlocking ownerships; policing telephone rate charges and services.	Antitrust regulation; policing rates and services; licensing entry and schedules of airlines; policing safety.
Redistributive	Credit extended on a below-market basis to protect farm mortgages and encourage expanded investment in farms.	Tax deductions for a high proportion of the business expenses of research, advertising, and building.	Tax allowance for depletion of resources to encourage exploration; tax allowance for conservation and conversion.	None in particular for these industries (only the usual tax breaks for investment).	Taxes on gasoline to finance part of highway construction and to discourage use of automobiles; reduced excise taxes to encourage purchase of automobiles.

The *consumer industries* include over-the-counter food, drugs, cigarettes, and cosmetics. The *energy industries* include oil, gas, coal, water, and atomic energy. The *communications industries* include telephone, radio and television, computer transmission, and satellite communication. The *transportation industries* include rail, air, truck, and water.

TABLE 15.2

Number of States That Regulate Occupations through Licensing

Licensed Occupation	Number of States	Licensed Occupation	Number of States
Abstractor	12	Acupuncturist	12
Aerial duster	8	Ambulance attendant	32
Auctioneer	24	Audiologist	30
Boiler inspector	26	Chauffeur	34
Collection agent	22	General contractor	20
Specialty contractor	5	Well driller	31
Driving instructor	40	Electrician	15
Elevator inspector	12	Funeral director	29
Employment agency	49	Engineer	49
Forester	12	Geologist	9
Guide	24	Hearing aid dealer	41
Landscape architect	35	Librarian	23
Marriage counselor	6	Masseur	15
Medical lab technician	8	Medical lab director	15
Midwife	28	Milk sampler	30
Mine foreman	19	Projectionist	6
Naturopath	11	Nursing home administrator	49
Occupational therapist	10	Occupational therapy assistant	6
Optician	19	Outfitter	4
Pest control applicator	23	Pesticide applicator	18
Pharmacist's assistant	17	Physical therapy assistant	21
Physician's assistant	25	Plumber	30
Polygraph examiners	21	Private detective	35
Private patrol agent	17	Psychologist	48
TV technician	4	Radiologic technician	10
Sanitarian	33	School bus driver	12
Securities agent	49	Harbor pilot	25
Shorthand reporter	13	Social worker	20
Soil tester	7	Surveyor	49
Tree surgeon	11	Veterinarian	16
Watchmaker	10	Watchman/guard	9
Weather modifier	21	Weighmaster	21

Sources: Frances S. Berry, "The States' Occupational Licensing Debate," *State Government News* 25 (May 1982), pp. 10–14; and Kenneth J. Meier, *Regulation: Politics, Bureaucracy, and Economics* (New York: St. Martin's Press, 1985) p. 176. Copyright © 1985 by St. Martin's Press, Inc. Reprinted by permission of St. Martin's Press, Incorporated.

three years before the passage of the historic Civil Rights Act of 1964, President Kennedy vowed that he could and would change the whole pattern of racial discrimination in the United States "with the stroke of a pen." Kennedy meant that he had a considerable amount of power to influence the employment practices of all the corporations seeking contracts from the national government to provide goods or services. Both Kennedy and Johnson issued executive orders, administered by the Office of Federal Contract Compliance in the Department of Labor, to prohibit discrimination by firms receiving government contracts.[5] The value of these contracts to many private corporations was so great that they were quite willing to alter if not eliminate racial discrimination in employment practices if that was the only way to qualify to bid for government contracts. Nowadays, it is common to see on employment ads the statement "We are an equal opportunity employer." Similarly, between 1977 and 1979, President Carter tried to use the contracting power to force major companies and unions to observe his wage and price guidelines as a means of fighting inflation.

Regulatory Taxation   Taxation is generally understood to be a fiscal technique, and it will be discussed as such below. But in many instances, the primary purpose of the tax is not to raise revenue but to discourage or eliminate an activity altogether by making it too expensive for most people. For example, since the end of Prohibition, although there has been no penalty for the production or sale of alcoholic beverages, the alcohol industry is not free from regulation. First, all alcoholic beverages have to be licensed, allowing only those companies that are "bonded" to put their product on the market. Beyond that, federal and state taxes on alcohol are made disproportionately high, on the theory that, in addition to the revenue gained, less alcohol will be consumed. For the same reasons, there was for many years a heavy tax on colored margarine, imposed through the lobbying efforts of the dairy industry, which sought to protect its market against the artificial spread.[6] We may be seeing a great deal more regulation by taxation, for at least the following reasons. First, it is a kind of hidden regulation, acceptable to people who in principle are against regulation. Second, it permits a certain amount of choice. For example, a heavy tax on gasoline or on smokestack and chemical industries (called an "effluent tax") will encourage drivers and these companies to regulate their own activities by permitting them to decide how much pollution they can afford. Third, advocates of regulatory taxation believe it to be more efficient than other forms of regulation, requiring less bureaucracy and less supervision.

Expropriation   People in the United States think of expropriation as a method used by revolutionary governments to eliminate capitalism or by postwar governments to punish property owners who collaborated with the enemy. Yet, ***expropriation***—seizing private property for a public use—is a widely used technique of control in the United States, especially in land-use regulation. Almost all public works, from highways to parks to government office buildings, involve the forceful taking of some private property in order to assemble sufficient land and the correct distribution of land for the necessary construction. The vast Interstate Highway Program required expropriation of thousands of narrow strips of private land. "Urban redevelopment" projects often require city governments to use the powers of seizure in the service of private developers, who actually build the urban pro-

---

[5]For an evaluation of Kennedy's use of this kind of executive power, see Carl M. Brauer, *John F. Kennedy and the Second Reconstruction* (New York: Columbia University Press, 1977), especially Chapter 3.

[6]For many years, margarine was sold in white, one-pound blocks, resembling lard, and was very unappetizing. An envelope of yellow food coloring accompanied the package, so that the consumer could take the trouble to make the margarine look a bit more like butter.

jects on the land that would be far too expensive if purchased on the open market. Private utilities that supply electricity and gas to individual subscribers are given powers to take private property whenever a new facility or a right-of-way is needed.

We generally call the power to expropriate **eminent domain**, and the eminent domain power is recognized as inherent in any government. The Fifth Amendment of the U.S. Constitution surrounds this expropriation power with important safeguards against abuse, so that government agencies in the United States are not permitted to use that power except through a strict due process, and they must offer "fair market value" for the land sought. Rarely in U.S. history has the government actually expropriated an entire company or sector of industries, as many countries do when they "nationalize" an industry. A significant exception would be nationalization of all the railroads during World War I; but these were returned to private hands in 1920. In 1970, the federal government nationalized several important railroads into the Amtrak system, but these were already on the verge of bankruptcy (and in the 1980s were "re-privatized"). The lack of nationalization should not, however, mask the frequency with which national, state, and local governments expropriate property for public uses.[7]

Forcing individuals to work for a public purpose is another form of expropriation. The draft of young men for the armed forces and court orders to strikers to return to work and to convicted felons to do community service are examples of the regular use of expropriation in the United States.

Redistributive (Macroeconomic) Techniques

Redistributive (or macroeconomic) techniques are usually of two types—fiscal and monetary—but they have a common purpose, to control people by manipulating the entire economy rather than by regulating people directly. (*Macroeconomic* refers to the economy as a system.) As observed earlier, regulatory techniques focus on individual conduct. For example: "Walking on the grass is not permitted," or "Membership in a union may not be used to deny employment, nor may a worker be fired for promoting union membership." In contrast, techniques are redistributive if they seek to control conduct more indirectly by altering the conditions of conduct or manipulating the environment of conduct.

Fiscal Techniques   Fiscal techniques of control are the government's taxing and spending powers. Personal and corporate income taxes, which raise most government revenues, are the most prominent examples. While the direct purpose of an income tax is to raise revenue, each tax has a different impact on the economy, and government can plan for that impact. For example, although the main reason favoring a significant increase in the Social Security tax (which is an income tax), under President Carter was to keep Social Security solvent, a big reason for it in the minds of many legislators was that it would reduce inflation by shrinking the

[7]For an evaluation of the politics of eminent domain, see Theodore J. Lowi and Benjamin Ginsberg, *Poliscide* (New York: Macmillan, 1976), p. 235 and *passim,* and especially Chapters 11 and 12, written by Julia and Thomas Vitullo-Martin.

The Federal Dollar: Where It Comes From, Where It Goes, and How (Fiscal Year 1993)

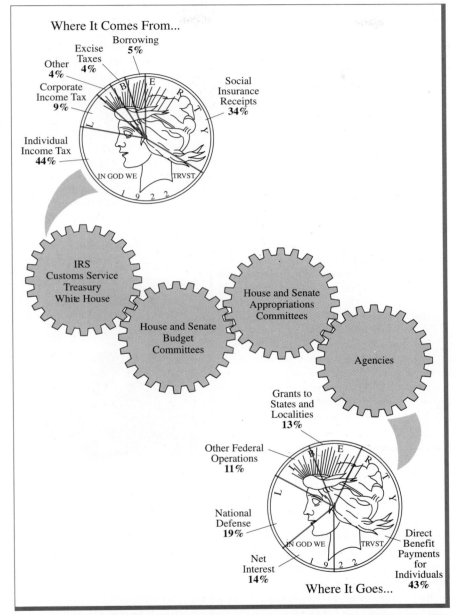

Where It Comes From...

Borrowing 5%

Excise Taxes 4%

Other 4%

Corporate Income Tax 9%

Social Insurance Receipts 34%

Individual Income Tax 44%

IRS
Customs Service
Treasury
White House

House and Senate Budget Committees

House and Senate Appropriations Committees

Agencies

Grants to States and Localities 13%

Other Federal Operations 11%

National Defense 19%

Net Interest 14%

Direct Benefit Payments for Individuals 43%

Where It Goes...

Source: Office of Management and Budget, *Budget of the United States Government,* Fiscal Year 1993 (Washington, DC: Government Printing Office, 1993), Supplement.

Paul Samuelson and Milton Friedman
Economists to Presidents

College professors who teach in the academic world rarely get the opportunity to influence the course of government policy. Two important exceptions to this principle are economists Paul Samuelson and Milton Friedman.

Considered by many to be one of the nation's foremost economic thinkers, Paul Samuelson helped formulate the important economic theories of the 1930s through the 1970s. As a student at Harvard University in the 1930s, Samuelson studied with the leading American proponent of Keynesian economics (named after British economist John Maynard Keynes), an economic theory that emphasizes government fiscal management of the economy through the manipulation of taxes and spending. The Keynesian approach is most well known for arguing that it is not always desirable to balance government budgets, especially when unemployment is high (as during the Great Depression of the 1930s). While Samuelson was identified with the Keynesian approach, he was also critical of some of the ways it was applied during Franklin Roosevelt's New Deal.

In 1940, Samuelson was appointed to the faculty at the Massachusetts Institute of Technology, where he became one of the nation's foremost economists. He authored the most well-known economics text in modern American publishing, *Economics,* and became a top advisor to Presidents John F. Kennedy and Lyndon Johnson. During the Kennedy administration, for example, Samuelson urged the government to accelerate spending to prod a sluggish economy; he did not, however, advocate the creation of new government-sponsored public works jobs as had been done during the depression.

If Samuelson was the guru of Demo-

Paul Samuelson

amount of money people had in their hands to buy more goods and services. Or if the concern is to fight a sluggish economy, the government can cut taxes for everyone, to increase "aggregate demand," or cut taxes primarily for higher-income people, to encourage new investment. No two presidents were programmatically further apart than Kennedy and Reagan, yet Kennedy adopted the latter method in 1961, and Reagan adopted both in 1981 and the latter in 1986.

President Clinton's commitment in his 1992 campaign for a "middle-class" tax cut was motivated by the goal of encouraging economic growth through increased consumption. Soon after the election, upon learning that the deficit would be far larger than had been earlier reported to him, he confessed he would have to break

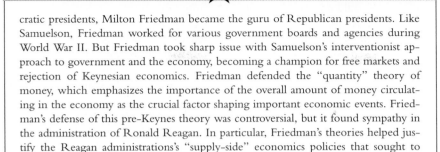

cratic presidents, Milton Friedman became the guru of Republican presidents. Like Samuelson, Friedman worked for various government boards and agencies during World War II. But Friedman took sharp issue with Samuelson's interventionist approach to government and the economy, becoming a champion for free markets and rejection of Keynesian economics. Friedman defended the "quantity" theory of money, which emphasizes the importance of the overall amount of money circulating in the economy as the crucial factor shaping important economic events. Friedman's defense of this pre-Keynes theory was controversial, but it found sympathy in the administration of Ronald Reagan. In particular, Friedman's theories helped justify the Reagan administrations's "supply-side" economics policies that sought to pump more money into the economy by lowering taxes.

In a different respect, however, Samuelson and Friedman expressed similar views that government deficits were not necessarily bad. In fact, according to Friedman, the idea that the escalating federal deficit and America's trade deficit were undermining national prosperity and borrowing from future generations was "simply rhetoric." What really mattered was the total amount the government spends, which was too much, according to Friedman. He noted that the federal debt is actually relatively small when it is figured as a percentage of the total national income.

Samuelson and Friedman each helped to influence a presidential administration and the course of government policy related to the economy. Because of their work and influence, Samuelson won the Nobel Prize for Economics in 1970 and Friedman won it in 1976.

Sources: Paul A. Samuelson and William D. Nordhaus, *Economics* (New York: McGraw-Hill, 1985); Milton Friedman, *Capitalism and Freedom* (Chicago: University of Chicago Press, 1962).

Milton Friedman

his promise of such a tax cut. Nevertheless, the idea of a middle-class tax cut is an example of a fiscal policy aimed at increased consumption, because of the theory that people in middle-income brackets tend to spend a high proportion of unexpected earnings or windfalls, rather than saving or investing them.

Monetary Techniques   Monetary techniques also seek to influence conduct by manipulating the entire economy through the supply or availability of money. The Federal Reserve Board (the Fed) can adopt what is called a "hard money policy" by increasing the interest rate it charges member banks (called the "discount rate"). In 1980, when inflation was at a historic high, the Fed permitted interest rates to reach a high of nearly 20 percent, in an attempt to rein it in. During the 1991 recession, however, the Fed permitted interest rates to drop well below 10 percent, hoping this would encourage people to borrow more to buy houses, etc. Another monetary policy is one of increasing or decreasing the "reserve requirement," which sets the actual proportion of deposited money that a bank must keep "on demand" as it makes all the rest of the deposits available as new loans.[8] A third important technique used by the Fed is "open market operations"—the buying and selling of Treasury securities to absorb excess dollars or to release more dollars into the economy.

Spending Power as Fiscal Policy   Perhaps the most important redistributive technique of all is the most familiar one—the "spending power"—which is a combination of subsidies and contracts. These techniques can be used for policy goals far beyond the goods and services bought and the individual conduct regulated. This is why subsidies and contracting show up again here, as techniques of fiscal policy.

One of the most important examples of the national government's use of purchasing power as a fiscal or redistributive technique is found in another of the everyday activities of the Federal Reserve Board. The Fed goes into the "open market" to buy and sell government bonds in order to increase or decrease the amount of money in circulation. By doing so, the Fed can raise or lower the prices paid for goods and the interest rate paid on loans. Sometimes the government wants to reach one sagging sector rather than the whole economy. For example, since the 1930s, the federal government has attempted to raise and to stabilize the prices of several important agricultural products, such as corn and wheat, by authorizing the Department of Agriculture to buy enormous amounts of these commodities and to store them if prices on the market fall below a fixed level. This endeavor is popularly referred to as the "parity program."[9] Moreover, this policy of using the purchasing power to support and stabilize agricultural prices continued in effect all through the Reagan administration ($26 billion in 1987) and into the Bush administration, despite the general opposition of both to government intervention, and especially to government spending. Cuts in the 1990 Reconciliation Act brought the 1991 estimated farm price support cost down from $54 billion to $40 billion.

Government has developed an historic stake in money, credit, and agriculture

---

[8]In 1989, President Bush proposed to Congress a significant increase in the legal reserve requirement for savings & loan companies, which are simply banks by another name. This would of course have an anti-inflationary effect, but we cannot cite it as a monetary policy because it was virtually forced on President Bush as a means of preventing these banks from engaging in the reckless investment activity of the previous decade, which had forced many into bankruptcy, eventually costing the American people $300 to $500 billion. Thus, in this case, the raising of the S & L reserve requirement is more an example of a regulatory policy. On the other hand, President Clinton's 1993 plan to relax certain banking regulations to help small businesses would be considered a monetary policy.

[9]The formulas for "parity" may be complicated, but the concept is simple. Parity means equality of rank or equality in treatment. Parity for agriculture has meant: (1) picking a year or group of years when farmers were doing fairly well, (2) calculating for that "base period" roughly how many bales of cotton or bushels of grain it took to buy a tractor or a basket of groceries, and then (3) calculating what price that farmer would have to receive today in order to buy the same type tractor or basket of groceries. Different programs seek to achieve parity in different ways, but they all involve government spending.

Techniques of Public Control: A Summary

Types of Techniques	Techniques	Definitions and Examples
Promotional techniques	Subsidies and grants of cash, land, etc.	Promotion of private activity through unconditional gifts or services that recipients consider "benefits."
	Contracting	Agreements with individuals or firms in the "private sector" to purchase goods or services.
	Licensing	Unconditional permission to do something that is otherwise illegal (franchise, permit).
Regulatory techniques	Criminal penalties	Heavy fines or imprisonment, loss of citizenship.
	Civil penalties	Less onerous fines, probation, exposure, restitution.
	Administrative regulation	Rate ceilings, quality standards, investigation, hearings and publicity, administrative adjudication, entry controls.
	Subsidies, contracting, and licensing as regulatory techniques	These become regulatory techniques when conditions are attached (e.g., contract refusal with firms that show no evidence of affirmative action in hiring).
	Regulatory taxation	Taxes whose main objective is not revenue but to keep consumption or production down (e.g., liquor, cigarette, gas taxes).
	Expropriation	"Eminent domain"—the power to take private property for public use. "Nationalization"—regulatory when used as sanction to enforce laws; a fiscal technique when used for planning, as in acquiring land for a highway.
Redistributive techniques	Fiscal use of taxes	Altering the quantity or distribution of money by changing tax rates or tax types (e.g., income v. sales tax).
	Fiscal use of budgeting	Deficit spending to pump money into the economy; creating a surplus through taxes to discourage consumption ("countercyclical" policies).
	Fiscal use of credit and interest (monetary techniques)	Manipulating interest rates and other investment conditions to affect demand in investment and consumption.
	Fiscal use of insurance I	Encouraging private investment by public sharing of part of the risk (e.g., mortgage insurance, loan guarantees).
	Fiscal use of insurance II	American welfare state; social insurance.

Americans value their freedoms. The nation was founded by individuals seeking freedoms unavailable in their homelands. It is not surprising, therefore, that Americans are committed to the institutions of government responsible for preserving individual rights and maintaining law and order. Public perception of the police is generally favorable. SWAT teams that apprehend berserk gunmen or rescue kidnapped children are viewed as heroes. While there are abuses of police power, most citizens are glad to know there are uniformed men and women walking around on whom they can depend in an emergency.

Not all police work provides the stuff of high drama, and sometimes the sight of a law officer is less than welcome. No one will argue that traffic cops aren't a necessary evil. But nobody likes getting a traffic ticket.

Whether or not to legalize drugs in the United States is a question over which legislators, theorists, and the American public grapple. Would drug use among Americans increase and would crime rates escalate following the legalization of drugs? Or, would the rate of drug-related crime fall because of legalization? Today, drug pushing and drug use remain illegal in the United States, and both continue to command a large portion of the country's time and resources in fighting them.

In keeping with the national fear of having our constitutional freedoms abrogated, various laws have been passed to protect the citizenry from overly zealous law enforcement agents. We worry that "Big Brother" may be watching us. Sometimes clandestine surveillance is employed as a method of crime prevention. This New York City police officer, a member of the city's Technical Assistance Response Unit, is "establishing visual surveillance on expected crime figures." If that means he's keeping his eyes on drug pushers or known racketeers, we applaud him.

In 1992, four police officers were acquitted of the brutal beating of a motorist, Rodney King, on the defense that they had acted according to established police procedures. The acquittal inflamed residents of South Central Los Angeles, who viewed it as a racial injustice because the officers were white and King was black. Their anger and frustration erupted into four days of rioting and looting. The slowness of the police to put down the rioting in the poor, mostly black and Latino section led to further charges of discrimination. In a federal trial, two of the officers were later found guilty of violating King's civil rights.

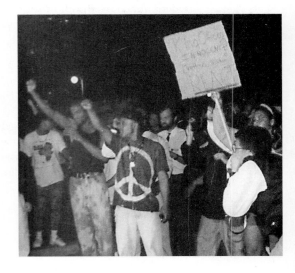

prices, just as it has in major public works and regulation—all seen as essential conditions of a stable and growing economy. As we shall see in the next chapter, policies dealing with these conditions are not likely to be discontinued during the administration of a single president. The final passage in David Stockman's book, confessing his frustration over President Reagan's inability (or lack of determination) to break out of the national government's commitment to established national government policies, states the difficulties that faced Reagan in this regard:

> The abortive Reagan Revolution proved the American electorate wants a moderate social democracy to shield it from capitalism's rougher edges.[10]

PUBLIC POLICY AND POLITICAL POWER

Public policy helps us understand government in action, or how government seeks to control the population. Public policy also helps us understand political power itself, because each of the techniques of control alters the costs and benefits of government as well as access to government. For example, when Congress incorporates one of the techniques of control into a statute, its intended purpose is to influence the society in some way. But the choice of technique also has unintended political consequences. This is why politicians can agree on a particular policy goal and disagree on the means or technique to be used to get there. In other words, policies shape politics: each type of policy (defined by the technique employed) tends to develop its own distinctive political pattern.

Table 15.4 mirrors Table 15.3, with the familiar division into promotional, regulatory, and redistributive policies. But added to Table 15.4 is a summary of the political characteristics most frequently associated with each of the policy categories. Thus, it can be said that each category is a sketch of a theory of political power. To understand the distribution of political power in the United States, we will describe and analyze these theories as they apply to the history of political development in the United States. We will find ultimately that power is not simply determined by wealth or social position; we will also find that power is not constant across all types of decisions and for all purposes. Power is segmented according to the *type of policy* at issue, thus there are four different ways that power is distributed.

Promotional Policy and Logrolling Politics

Promotional policies work largely through encouragement of individuals in the private sector. The government acts like any patron, such as a patron of the arts or a private foundation. A patronage policy simply authorizes a government agency to take whatever funds are budgeted to it and dispense them to individuals, com-

---

[10]David Stockman, *The Triumph of Politics* (New York: Harper & Row, 1986), p. 394

TABLE 15.4

639

PUBLIC POLICY
AND POLITICAL
POWER

Public Policies and Their Politics

Type of Policy	Explanation	Examples	Political Characteristics
Promotional Policy	Provides resources and facilities Not directly coercive	Public works Land grants Unconditional licensing Defense procurement and R & D	Clientele oriented Individualistic, logrolling Committee-centered structure, if any: the "complex"
Regulatory Policy	Imposes obligations and restrictions Directly coercive Uses sanctions to enforce standards of conduct	Antitrust Food and drug purity Protection of workers' rights to strike Licensing to enforce standards Reduction of racial discrimination	Pluralistic Group-dominated bargaining Congress-centered Coalitional structure, decentralized to "middle levels"
Redistributive Policy	Macropolicies Manipulates the structure Alters status or categories of people Controls "environment of conduct"	Income tax Social security Discount rate Deliberate deficit or surplus	Power elite, external base Large class interests or "peak associations" Ideological Executive-centered

panies, or groups to encourage new building, the provision of a particular service, or as an incentive for a private individual to take an initiative that he or she might not otherwise take. Sometimes these funds are distributed according to a contract for work to be done or goods to be bought, as in a contract with a private construction company to build a bridge. At other times, these funds are in the form of a grant to an individual to engage in research or to support an artistic project.

As we saw earlier in the chapter, promotional policy was the dominant type of policy adopted by Congress all during the nineteenth century, and it played an important role in our discussion of federalism in Chapter 3. These policies are called "pork-barrel" policies because they can be broken up into smaller pieces of resources and distributed to a maximum number of persons (i.e., voters) literally clamoring for a piece of the pork (i.e., government benefits). Just as "pork barrel" best describes these policies, so "logrolling" best describes the *politics* of these policies. **Logrolling** is a political relationship between two or more persons who have absolutely nothing in common. Their understanding is that "if you will support me on issue A, I will support you on any other issue you want; just tell me when and how you want me to vote. I don't need to know the particulars."[11] These logrolling relationships found a hospitable environment in Congress in the nineteenth century, and congressional committees and political parties flourished through their ability to gain and maintain political support through logrolling relationships. Indeed, Harvard political scientist Samuel Beer found that most of the nineteenth century was a period of "pork-barrel coalitions," where the members of these coalitions held no common interests but were joined together by the prospect of each member of the coalition being "able to get from the central government the action it needs."[12]

Drawing on these patterns of the past, we can make an informed guess about the power structure of politics in the category of promotional policy today. The following, by Stanford professor John Ferejohn, is a brief description of the pattern, written for today without any particular awareness of its nineteenth-century ancestry:

> . . . If a bill calling for improvements in a single district is [proposed], it will not pass since all the districts must pay and only one will benefit. Consequently, only an omnibus bill proposing expenditures in at least a majority of the districts has a chance of passage.[13]

"Omnibus" is the name given a bill or act that is composed of many sections with little substantive or logical connection among them. Each rivers and harbors bill, for example, is a collection of dozens of separate projects. Each project is of intense interest to one district and of little interest elsewhere. Supporters of each project agree to support all the other projects in return for the support their own project will receive. Thus, promotional policy has a distinctive pattern of power. Its distinctiveness will become clearer as we compare it to the three other categories.

Regulatory Policy and Pluralist Politics

As we have so often said, the key characteristic of regulatory policy is control of individual conduct by directly coercive techniques. Regulatory techniques are used to impose obligations, duties, or restrictions on conduct. The *politics* of regulation follows from this directly coercive character of regulatory *policy.*

---

[11] These policy categories and their associated political patterns were first laid out by Theodore J. Lowi, "American Business, Public Policy, Case Studies and Political Theory," *World Politics* 16, no. 4 (July 1964).

[12] Samuel Beer, "The Modernization of American Federalism," *Public Administration Review* 3, no. 2 (Fall 1973), p. 59, citing Lowi, "American Business, Public Policies, Case Studies and Political Theory."

[13] John Ferejohn, *Pork Barrel Politics—Rivers and Harbors Legislation, 1947–1968* (Stanford, CA: Stanford University Press, 1974), p. 235. See also Clem Miller, *Member of the House: Letters of a Congressman* (New York: Scribner's, 1962), especially pp. 16–17.

The best way to define the politics of regulatory policy, and distinguish it from

the politics of promotional policy, is to compare the politics of nineteenth-century
states to the politics of the nineteenth-century national government. Nineteenth-
century national government policies were almost exclusively promotional. And the
politics of the national government was very stable. It was dominated by political
parties, and the individual and sectional conflicts that emerged could be settled
peacefully, by logrolling, through the parties in Congress. The national government could expand and could subdivide government resources to meet the demands of individuals and groups. Thus political conflict could be bought off or
tabled until a future time. In contrast, the states in the nineteenth century were
doing all of the regulating, and the political patterns of the states were highly unstable, constantly upset by demonstrations, large social movements, and frequent
violence. In the less volatile moments, the politics of the states was dominated by
interest groups, especially corporate interest groups.[14]

Group politics is the essence of "pluralism," and pluralism is the key to the politics of modern regulatory policy. In the 1930s, when the national government
added a significant number of regulatory policies to its repertoire, it also added the
politics of regulatory policy. And this was the time when "pluralist theory" of
American political power became prominent.[15] Because pluralist politics was so
public and drew so much attention to itself, a false impression was conveyed that
the whole American system of politics was pluralistic. This belief was strengthened
by the resemblance of modern pluralist patterns to the theory of James Madison, as
set forth particularly in *The Federalist Papers, No. 10*. According to Madison, in
popular government, people divide into "factions," with each faction seeking its
own satisfaction without any regard for the public interest. As long as there are
many groups and no one group or coalition of groups can consistently dominate
all the others, power will not become too concentrated, and all groups will be
willing to conduct themselves within the constraints of the Constitution. Today
these factions are called groups, interests, and power centers, and the competition
among them leads to demands that formal government adopt policies to mediate
the conflicts. Groups seek to expand their power through lobbying Congress and
through forming larger coalitions with other groups, either to dominate the political parties by overpowering electoral support with economic force or by making
special arrangements with the parties.[16] Thus, while political parties and local dis-

---

[14]Good accounts of the politics of the states in the nineteenth century will be found in V. O. Key,
American State Politics (Westport, CT: Greenwood, 1983; orig. published 1965); Key, *Southern Politics in
State and Nation*, 2nd ed. (Knoxville, TN: University of Tennessee Press, 1984); Bernard Hyink et al.,
Politics and Government in California, 9th ed. (New York: Crowell, 1975); and Francis Fox Piven and
Richard Cloward, *Poor People's Movements* (New York: Pantheon, 1977). For studies of political vio-
lence that show the particular affinity of violence to state politics, see Phillip Taft and Phillip Ross,
"American Labor Violence: Its Causes, Character, and Outcome," in *The History of Violence in America,*
ed. Hugh Graham and Ted Robert Gurr (New York: Bantam Books, 1969); Robert Fogelson, "Violence as Protest," in *Proceedings of the Academy of Political Science* 29, no. 1, 1968; and on vigilantism, see
Lawrence Friedman, *A History of American Law* (New York: Simon and Schuster, 1973), pp. 318–22.

[15]For a brief intellectual history of the rise of pluralism as a theory and as an ideology, see Theodore J.
Lowi, *The End of Liberalism* (New York: W. W. Norton, 1979), Chapter 3.

[16]For the best theoretical statements of pluralism, see Robert A. Dahl, *A Preface to Democratic Theory*
(Chicago: University of Chicago Press, 1956); and Robert A. Dahl and Charles E. Lindblom, *Politics,
Economics and Welfare* (New York: Harper, 1953).

Regulation: Governmental Scalpel or Blunt Instrument?

Regulation has long been a key tool employed by government to advance public safety and welfare. Yet the rise of government regulation has also spawned intense criticism that such regulation has been more harmful than helpful. Editor Barry Crickmer argues against governmental regulatory efforts on the grounds that they are costly and ineffective. Political scientist Susan Tolchin and journalist Martin Tolchin argue that government regulation is unfairly blamed by big business for a variety of ills, and that regulation is in fact essential for the good of modern society.

Crickmer

Federal regulation is often called inflationary, irritating, costly, and even farcical. But that's not the worst that can be said of it. The worst is that it isn't working.

The development, methodology, philosophy, and results of federal intervention in the marketplace fit Sir Ernest Benn's definition of politics as "the art of looking for trouble, finding it everywhere, diagnosing it wrongly, and applying unsuitable remedies."

For all the billions of dollars the regulatory agencies have spent and the billions more they have caused to be spent, there is surprisingly little evidence that the world is any better off than it would have been without federal tinkering. . . .

The question is, why? Why has the direct and indirect expenditure of more than $100 billion a year on federal regulation failed to produce results commensurate with the effort? Or in some cases, any positive results at all?

Is the federal government trying to do the impossible? Or is it trying to do the possible in an impossible way? The answer is probably a little of both.

Many of the newer regulatory programs were ill-conceived and ill-considered. Typically, each got started after a single-interest pressure group succeeded in creating a wave of hysteria over an alleged crisis.

When this happens, most members of Congress quickly jump on the reform bandwagon. Those who don't may get crushed under its wheels. . . .

The news media—especially television—build pressure for quick fixes because they tend to focus on problems that can be presented dramatically, rather than on the comparatively dry analyses of possible solutions. . . .

In the words of [former] Washington Gov. Dixie Lee Ray, a former federal regulator herself: "The reality is that zero defects in products plus zero pollution plus zero risk on the job is equivalent to maximum growth of government plus zero economic growth plus runaway inflation. That's what we have."[1]

Tolchin and Tolchin

Regulation has become the national whipping boy. . . . The American automobile industry blamed its precipitous decline, not on its high prices, oversized cars, or shoddy products, but on the raft of government regulations intended to improve the safety and fuel efficiency of the vehicles and perhaps make them more marketable. . . .

By the late 1970s, complaints of excessive regulation had become management's all-purpose cop-out. Were profits too low? Blame regulation. Were prices too high? Blame regulation. Were inadequate funds and manpower earmarked for research and development? Blame regulation for sapping both funds and manpower. Was American industry unable to compete with foreign competitors? Blame regulation.

In a highly technological society such as ours, the need for increased regulation is manifest. It is inconceivable to think of "lessening the regulatory burden," as some put it, at a time when private industry has the power to alter our genes, invade our privacy, and destroy our environment. A single industrial accident . . . is capable of taking a huge toll in human life and suffering. Only the government has the power to create and enforce the social regulations that protect citizens from the awesome consequences of technology run amuck. Only the government has the ability to raise the national debate above the "balance sheet" perspective of American industry. This is not to dismiss the many socially conscious businessmen who are concerned with the public interest, but, unfortunately, they do not represent the political leadership of the business community. After all, the "bottom line" for business is making a profit, not improving the quality of the environment or the work place. Its primary obligation is to its shareholders, not to the community at large.[2]

[1]Barry Crickmer, "Regulation: How Much Is Enough?" *Nation's Business,* March 1980, pp. 26–33.
[2]Susan Tolchin and Martin Tolchin, *Dismantling America* (New York: Houghton Mifflin, 1983), pp. 3–5.

tricts have been at the very core of the politics of promotional policy, they have been far less important in the politics of regulatory policy. For example, groups organized around the steel interest, the cotton interest, small business, the trade unions, etc., cross electoral constituencies and therefore blur the lines of party politics and elections.

One important case study will help illustrate the politics of regulatory policy. In 1990, the Clean Air Act of 1970 came up for renewal. It had been renewed once (by requirement) in 1977, but when it was scheduled to be renewed in 1981, it failed because President Reagan and Congress had "incompatible basic objectives."[17] The 1970 act was kept alive for nine years by continuing resolutions until President Bush, promising to be the "Environmental President," took the initiative on renewal. However, other factors contributed to the adoption of the act, particularly a coalition of many of the largest regulated companies in the United States.

[17]Paul J. Quirk, "Divided Government and Cooperative Presidential Leadership," in Colin Campbell and Bert Rockman, *The Bush Presidency—First Appraisals* (Chatham, NJ: Chatham House), p. 86.

On Earth Day 1990, a major trade association, the Chemical Manufacturers Association, published its "Responsible Care Initiative," an environmental manifesto signed by 150 companies. Among those companies "taking the pledge" of greater care for the environment were Texaco, Du Pont, Dow, Mobil, Exxon, General Electric, and many other companies who were also on the EPA's list of factories whose emissions caused the highest risks of cancer. Why were they supporting clean air legislation? Not because they wanted stronger federal regulation but because an aroused public opinion had stimulated organized demands in many communities for the "right to know" about toxins polluting the air. These trade associations and companies were putting clean air legislation back on the federal agenda in order to head off increased local and state regulation and to weaken, if possible, the existing provisions in the national clean air regulations.

Once in Congress, the bill nearly died at the hands of a coalition made up of the automobile industry, electric utility companies, and East Coast coal industries (along with the quiet support of some of the aforementioned companies), led by the Democratic chair of the House Commerce Committee. This demonstrates how the politics of regulatory policy is an affair among groups and group coalitions and not a party or partisan affair.[18]

President Bush received a great deal of credit for the passage of the Clean Air Act of 1990, but let us briefly review the nature of that accomplishment. Bush's leadership consisted of putting together a coalition of interest groups just strong enough to overcome the opposition and get a minimal piece of clean air legislation adopted. He put together a working group with senior officials from several relevant agencies, and this group "consulted elaborately with congressional leaders and spokesmen for industry, environmental groups, and other interests."[19] Second, the Bush bill under consideration was definitely a minimalist bill, which "sought to strengthen environmental protection without imposing excessive costs on industry." It provided for the sale of "emission permits," which enabled companies to increase rather than decrease their emissions. Third, it increased the standards of technology that were to be involved but did not increase the strictness of the specific levels of pollution that were permitted. Finally, it set deadlines for compliance so far out beyond 1990 that many industries could look toward 2010 and 2020 as their deadline. "The new law gives us deadlines, but it's a non-law—making deadlines long enough so that they don't have any meaning."[20] The point here is not that George Bush pulled failure out of the jaws of victory, but that presidential leadership in the field of regulatory policy tends to be, at best, coalitional leadership, and that usually the outcome for the victorious coalition is the least common denominator of all the interests involved.

Redistributive Policy and Power Elite Politics

Redistributive policies are as coercive as regulatory policies but the coercion is imposed in a different way. Redistributive policies seek to control citizens by manip-

---

[18]See William Greider, *Who Will Tell the People* (New York: Simon and Schuster, 1992), pp. 126–131.

[19]Quirk, "Divided Government and Cooperative Presidential Leadership," p. 86.

[20]Quoted in Greider, *Who Will Tell the People,* p. 129.

ulating their environment rather than by attempting to control their conduct

directly. For example, a small percentage change in the interest rate can immediately affect millions of potential homeowners or investors; or, a change of the top income-tax rate from 30 percent to 36 percent can be equally effective. Yet in neither of these examples do citizens have to "do" anything to come within the jurisdiction of the law.

This kind of policy will almost certainly develop a different kind of political pattern, and case studies of policy making confirm this. The best theory describing the politics of redistributive policy is called the "power elite" theory. Offered by many social scientists as a general theory of power in a capitalist nation, it has turned out to be very weak as a general theory but quite strong and accurate as a theory limited to the politics of redistributive policy. According to the power elite theory, the most important decisions for the society are made by a small political elite, generally composed of individuals and families who enjoy the highest incomes and status of the society. These individuals and families tend to be drawn from (1) the corporate "command posts," (2) the occupants of the highest political positions, and (3) the highest echelons of the military, or the defense establishment. Although these may appear to be distinct sectors of society, power elite theory holds that they constitute a single elite, because these people tend to know each other, go to the same elite schools, and share a general consensus on long-range objectives for the society.[21]

The most recent policy decision involving the income tax—the Tax Reform Act of 1986, probably the most important reform in internal revenue taxation in fifty years—confirms the elitist structure of the politics of tax policy. The radical reduction in tax rates from a top bracket of 70 percent to a top bracket of 28–33 percent was made possible by the coming together of leading Democrats and Republicans. Each may have wanted the tax reform for different reasons, but they formed a single elite, led by President Reagan, "the most important player in tax reform. . . . Without his backing, tax reform could never have happened."[22] Lobbyists and the members of Congress representing special interests were unable to get together to defeat the tax reform that would eliminate so many advantages they cherished. As the authors of the definitive account of this decision wrote: "One of the most intriguing questions raised by the two-year tax debate in Congress was why the many powerful interest groups lined up in opposition [to the bill] never joined forces to defeat it."[23] This example fits the general pattern of politics for redistributive policies. The fact is that decisions such as those on basic tax policy are made in the executive branch in conjunction with a fairly stable national elite leadership. The struggle over the details of tax exemptions and implementation takes place in Congress. But this confirms an important distinction—that broad tax

---

[21]C. Wright Mills, *The Power Elite* (New York: Oxford University Press, 1956); Kenneth Prewitt and Alan Stone, *The Ruling Elites* (New York: Harper & Row, 1973); and G. William Domhoff, *Who Rules America Now?* (Englewood Cliffs, NJ: Prentice Hall, 1983).

[22]Jeffrey Birnbaum and Alan S. Murray, *Showdown at Gucci Gulch—Lawmakers, Lobbyists, and the Unlikely Triumph of Tax Reform* (New York: Random House, 1987), p. 286. In 1990, effective 1991, the law was changed to provide for three rates: 15 percent, 28 percent, and 31 percent. The last rate is for single individuals who earn taxable income over $49,200 and for joint filers with taxable income over $70,350.

[23]Ibid., p. 287.

PROCESS BOX 15.2

How Political Patterns Vary Among the Three Types of Policy

Promotional Policy

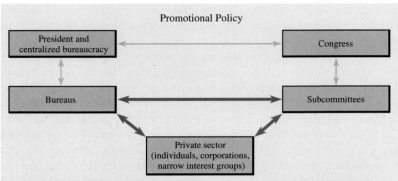

Logrolling politics; decentralized, committee-centered relations built on individualized demands;
narrow interests

Redistributive Policy

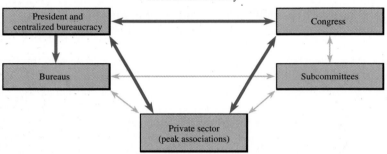

Power elite politics; few power centers, concentrate on executive branch; ideology strongest here;
interests broadest, society-wide

Regulatory Policy

President and centralized bureaucracy — Congress

Bureaus — Subcommittees

Private sector (regulated interests)

Pluralistic politics; many power centers, with conflictive, coalitional relationships; Congress-centered,
less logrolling, more direct compromise; private-sector- level interests overshadow ideology

← → Very important relationship
← → Moderately important relationship
← → Relatively unimportant relationship

principles are redistributive policy with an elitist power pattern, while loopholes are promotional policies with a different political pattern entirely.[24]

Constituent Policy and Bureaucratic Elite Politics

The constituent policy category is a step apart from the other three categories because constituent policies are concerned with the internal distribution of power among and within government institutions. This is why constituent policy was not included as part of Table 15.2.

Budgeting is the quintessential constituent policy. It attempts to provide a routine for allocating the billions of dollars appropriated each year by Congress. In 1921, the Bureau of the Budget was created, and Congress delegated budget-making authority to the executive. From then on it was called "the executive budget." This bureau became the Office of Management and Budget, OMB, in 1974. (For more on budgeting, see Chapters 5 and 7.)

The budget process is a "bottoms-up" affair that begins a good fifteen months in advance of the fiscal year. The process begins with agencies making requests for the next year's needs. These are accumulated by budget examiners, pared and adjusted to their understanding of presidential preferences, and then become the budget document that is sent to Congress in January of each year. Congress is expected to pull this together and make its appropriations by October 1. In the process, selected aspects of the budget become the foundation of "the president's program."[25]

The budgetary process is less important today than in the past mainly because Congress has, by law, placed a number of important programs, especially redistributive programs, outside the annual budget process altogether. These include the mandated expenditures in welfare entitlement programs and federal mortgage guarantees and deposit insurance. Even the $300–500 billion "bailout" of the savings and loans banks has been placed in an "off-budget" agency.[26]

---

[24]For case studies that confirm this "power elite" pattern in areas other than tax policy and for administrations other than Ronald Reagan's, see: Theodore J. Lowi, "Four Systems of Policy, Politics, and Choice," *Public Administration Review,* July/August 1972, pp. 290–310; Randall Ripley and Grace Franklin, *Congress, the Bureaucracy and Public Policy* (Belmont, CA: Brooks/Cole, 1991); David Price, *Who Makes the Laws?* (Cambridge, MA: Schenkman, 1972); and Theodore Marmor, *The Politics of Medicare,* rev. ed. (Chicago: Aldine Publishing, 1973).

[25]In late 1985, Congress was so embarrassed by the shocking growth in the deficit, that it adopted the Gramm-Rudman Act providing for a mandatory budget ceiling. The law mandated a balanced budget by 1991. To get there, the law provided that if an annual deficit exceeded a certain set amount (and that amount was to be decreased each year until 1991), an across-the-board cut of funds to all agencies would be implemented. The operative part of the Gramm-Rudman Act was declared unconstitutional on the grounds that the act authorized the comptroller general to implement the budget deficit and budget-cutting provisions. The comptroller general is an officer of Congress and was being ordered to do basically executive functions, which was a violation of the separation of powers, Bowsher v. Synar, 106 S. Ct. 3181 (1986). Even if the Court had not killed the operative feature of the Gramm-Rudman Act, however, Congress would have found ways to evade the spirit of the act.

[26]The best treatment of the decline of the budget is in Allen Schick, "The Budget as an Instrument of Presidential Policy," in *The Reagan Presidency and the Governing of America,* ed. Lester Salamon and Michael Lund (Washington, DC: Urban Institute Press, 1985), pp. 91–126. The classic work on budgeting is Aaron Wildavsky, *The New Politics of the Budgetary Process,* 5th ed. (New York: HarperCollins, 1992).

A brief account of President Reagan's use of OMB for deregulation will help to characterize the politics of constituent policy and to dramatize the difference between it and the politics of promotional, regulatory, and redistributive policy. In February 1981, President Reagan issued Executive Order 12291, which required that all proposals by agencies for new regulations be reviewed by OMB's Office of Information and Regulatory Affairs (OIRA). In the same executive order, OIRA was strengthened by the creation of the Task Force on Regulatory Relief, chaired by Vice-President George Bush.[27] Through this process, OMB could subject regulatory proposals to stringent cost-benefit analyses, could establish regulatory priorities, and could enforce these priorities.

Although President Reagan was genuinely committed to deregulation, he did not confront Congress with a single legislative proposal to terminate any regulatory agency or program. If he had tried to do so, he would have had to confront a House of Representatives controlled by the Democrats, and he would also have had to confront a wide array of interest groups who would have fought him in order to defend a particular program. The executive order and the process it set up required "presidential oversight of the regulatory process," and that gave President Reagan leverage to reduce rules and regulations without having to terminate any agencies.

One measure of Reagan's success was the significant reduction in the number of pages in the *Federal Register*. It had grown from 14,000 pages in 1960 to 60,000 in 1975, and to 87,000 pages in 1980. By 1987, the number had dropped to 49,600 pages.[28] Although not all material in the *Federal Register* is regulatory, a large proportion of it is, so that a reduction in the number of pages roughly indicates the considerable success of Reagan's deregulation strategy through "regulation management" rather than through any effort to get Congress to terminate legislation. In essence, President Reagan got what he wanted by avoiding the interest group process and Congress altogether.

Note, for example, the critical but fair characterization of Reagan's strategy provided by former assistant budget director and political science professor Harold Seidman:

> The Reagan administration devised a strategy for centralizing unprecedented decision-making power in the White House and reorganizing the executive branch without a significant change in the organization chart. It was a strategy focused on command relationships and processes rather than on formal structure; it was a strategy that, for the most part, could be implemented administratively and that was not dependent for success on enacting legislation.[29]

---

[27]George Bush perpetuated this arrangement by creation of the President's Council on Competitiveness chaired by Vice-President Dan Quayle. An excellent evaluation of this whole process will be found in Kirk Victor, "Quayle's Quiet Coup," *National Journal,* 6 July 1991, pp. 1676–80.

[28]The *Federal Register* (begun in 1935) is the daily publication of all official acts of Congress, the president, and the administrative agencies. A law or executive order is not legally binding until published in the *Federal Register.*

[29]Harold Seidman and Robert Gilmour, *Politics, Position, and Power* (New York: Oxford University Press, 1986), pp. 127, 131.

This description fits virtually the entire category of the politics of constituent policy. Top-ranking career officials can dominate the process through their com- mand of administrative routines, administrative processes, and administrative etiquette. This is itself a "power elite," but a very different kind of power elite, centered in the bureaucracy rather than in the society. President Reagan succeeded in taking control of regulation by using bureaucratic techniques and controlling the administrative elite rather than by proposing deregulation bills, which probably would have failed in Congress or would have otherwise cost him a very heavy political price in interest group support.

Dividing public policies into four functional categories—according to the different "techniques of control"—helps simplify policy analysis and makes some sense out of the myriad of specific policies and policy proposals that the vivid imaginations of members of Congress, bureaucrats, interest groups, academic scribblers, think tank experts, and many others can come up with. But beyond that, the four categories of policy also expose four quite distinct processes. This has implications for all of our ensuing analysis. More importantly, these distinctions have profoundly important consequences for the choices that presidents and other political leaders make in their efforts to make the political process work for the public interest.

SUMMARY

There are three reasons why students of political science study public policy. First, public policy helps us to understand government in action, or how government seeks to control the population through coercive and promotional means. Second, the proper study of public policy leads to a better understanding of political power itself: what classes of people enjoy the greater share of public benefits and how this comes about. A third reason of course is to prepare students for a role in actually making public policy. The first half of this chapter was concerned with the first reason. Some call this the study of "substantive policy." (This will also be the purpose of Chapters 16, 17, and 18.) The second half of this chapter was concerned with the second reason. Some call this "policy theory" or "the study of power structures" through the study of public policy.

First and foremost, then, the first part of the chapter provided an introduction to substantive policy with a handbook classification of the "techniques of control" that all policies embody. *Policy* was defined as the purposive and deliberate aspect of government in action. But if a policy is to come anywhere near to obtaining its stated goal (clean air, stable prices, equal employment opportunity), it must be backed up by some sanction, and that means some ability to reward or punish people and some ability to administer those sanctions. These are the "techniques of control," and the many techniques were presented in three categories: promotional techniques, regulatory techniques, and redistributive techniques.

The techniques of control, like any tools, are in themselves neutral. They can serve the policy goals of Democrats or Republicans, Left or Right. Whether the technique is appropriate to the goal is an individual judgment that must be made case by case.

The second part of the chapter addressed the question of where power lies in the American political system. We proposed the argument that there is not one "power structure" in America but at least four different distributions of power, one associated with each distinct category of public policy—promotional policy, regulatory policy, redistributive policy, and constituent policy. Each category has its own history, and a quite different theory of power is necessary to understand the politics of each.

Promotional policy, prominent from the very beginning of the republic, developed a decentralized but highly stable "power structure" throughout the nineteenth and early twentieth centuries. This power structure was once located in the political parties as well as in congressional committees, but with the decline of the parties, it now resides in the committees and subcommittees, through which individual members of Congress respond to groups from their constituencies "back home." Regulatory policy, in contrast, tends toward a truly pluralistic power structure, dominated by organized interest groups outside government; it is a politics of multiple elites. Redistributive policy has a power structure far more elitist than the pluralistic elitism of regulatory policy, and it is centered in the executive branch rather than in Congress, groups, or in electoral constituencies. Constituent policy is dominated by a technocratic elite.

There may be still another power structure for foreign policy. That question must be held until Chapter 18.

FOR FURTHER READING

Ackerman, Bruce, and William Hassler. *Clean Coal/Dirty Air*. New Haven, CT: Yale University Press, 1971.

Anderson, James. *Public Policymaking*. New York: Holt, Rinehart and Winston, 1979.

Blinder, Alan S. *Hard Heads, Soft Hearts—Tough-Minded Economics for a Just Society*. Reading MA: Addison-Wesley, 1987.

Chubb, John, and Paul Peterson, eds. *Can the Government Govern?* Washington, DC: Brookings Institution, 1988.

Gutmann, Amy, ed. *Democracy and the Welfare State*. Princeton, NJ: Princeton University Press, 1988.

Kettl, Donald F. *Deficit Politics: Public Budgeting in Its Institutional and Historical Context*. New York: Macmillan, 1992.

Kingdon, John W. *Agendas, Alternatives, and Public Policies*. Boston: Little, Brown, 1984.

Krasnow, Erwin, Lawrence Longley, and Herbert Terry. *The Politics of Broadcast Regulation*. New York: St. Martin's Press, 1982.

Martin, Cathie J. *Shifting the Burden: The Struggle over Growth and Corporate Taxation*. Chicago: University of Chicago Press, 1991.

Page, Benjamin. *Who Gets What from Government*. Berkeley and Los Angeles: University of California Press, 1983.

Peterson, Paul E., Barry G. Rabe, and Kenneth K. Wong, eds. *When Federalism Works*. Washington, DC: Brookings Institution, 1986.

Sabatier, Paul, and Daniel Mazmanian. *Can Regulation Work?* New York: Plenum Press, 1983.

Tatalovich, Raymond, and Byron Daynes, eds. *Social Regulatory Policy: Moral Controversies in American Politics.* Boulder, CO: Westview Press, 1988.

Weir, Margaret, Ann Shola Orloff, and Theda Skocpol, eds. *The Politics of Social Policy in the United States.* Princeton, NJ: Princeton University Press, 1988.

Wilson, James Q. *The Politics of Regulation.* New York: Basic Books, 1980.

16

Government and the Economy

EVENTS	INSTITUTIONAL DEVELOPMENTS
First Congress convenes (1789)	Constitution establishes power of Congress to make fiscal and monetary policies (1789)
Whiskey Rebellion quashed, establishing national power to tax (1794)	Tariffs and promotional policies used to encourage American industry (1800s)
Westward expansion (1800s)	*Gibbons* v. *Ogden* stipulates that states cannot pass laws that interfere with interstate commerce (1824)
Civil War—end of slavery and plantation economy in the South (1861–1865)	Income tax imposed (1861)
	Bureau of Internal Revenue created (1862)
Industrial development; large railroad companies; rise of large corporations, a large class of laborers, commercialized agriculture, and national trade associations (1860s–1890s)	Interstate Commerce Act to control monopolistic practices of the railroads; ICC established (1887)
	Sherman Antitrust Act to protect trade and commerce against monopolies (1890)
	Supreme Court declares income tax unconstitutional (1895)
	Sixteenth Amendment provides for income tax (1913)
World War I (1914–1919)	Federal Trade Act establishes Federal Trade Commission (1914)
Rise of motor and air transportation; establishment of principles of mass production; radio starts epoch of mass communication (1920s)	First government mobilization of the entire economy for war (1917–1920)
Stock market crash (1929)	
Great Depression (1929–1933)	
Franklin Roosevelt and the New Deal (1930s)	New Deal policies rescue banks, provide relief for unemployed, establish regulatory agencies to speed recovery of agriculture and business from Depression (1930s)

Timeline markers: 1800, 1890, 1930

EVENTS		INSTITUTIONAL DEVELOPMENTS
U.S. enters World War II (1941–1945)	**1940**	Price ceilings set by the Office of Price Administration; goods allocated through rationing—the first regulation of all Americans (1941); War Production Board created to oversee industrial conversion to war; Revenue Act broadens the tax base (1942); Payroll deductions for income taxes introduced (1943)
Postwar commitment to full employment through government programs (1946)		
Growth of government (1960s); Kennedy assassinated; Johnson assumes presidency (1963)	**1960**	Great Society programs—government spending to reduce poverty stimulates the economy (1965)
Vietnam War (1965–1973)		
Watergate scandal (1972–1974)		"Social Regulation"—the last great spurt of regulatory programs (1969–1974)
Carter and Congress move to deregulate certain industries (1978)	**1980**	Deregulation of securities (1975), railroads (1976 and 1980), airlines (1978–1981), banking (1980), motor carriers (1980)
Election of Ronald Reagan (1980)		Deregulation through management; vast tax cut; deficits mount (1980s)
Election of George Bush (1988)		Return to favor of some re-regulation; persistent deficits force Bush to break "no new taxes" pledge (1990)
Recession (1990–1992)	**1990**	
Election of Bill Clinton (1992)		
		Clinton's first budget calls for large tax increases and spending cuts to fight deficits (1993)

*W*e have seen in previous chapters that governments in America have always played a role in the U.S. economy. Unlike most other countries we must use governments in the plural because of federalism; but that should not mask the importance of government itself and of the many public policies that have promoted and regulated the American economy. Both the state and national governments have maintained public order and in so doing have enabled individuals and companies to function in a capitalistic economy that has encouraged both private ownership and public intervention in ways that have sustained massive economic growth.

Today the government ensures that the economy will never again collapse as it did during the Great Depression of 1929–1933. To do this, the government has established a capitalist "safety net" just as it established a welfare "safety net." Two agencies, the Federal Deposit Insurance Corporation (FDIC) and the Federal Savings and Loan Insurance Corporation (FSLIC), were established to insure deposits up to $100,000 that have been made in banks (FDIC) and savings and loan companies (FSLIC).

The capitalist safety net was put to its most serious test since the Depression when large numbers of Savings and Loan (S&L) companies collapsed in the late 1980s. Beginning in the late 1970s, the S&L's were caught in a crunch between the low interest on the mortgages they held and the high interest rates they were having to pay out on new deposits. This forced the banks to engage in higher risk ventures in hopes that the higher returns would bridge the gap. These high-risk ventures were made possible by the deregulation of the banking industry under the Reagan administration. Unfortunately, many of them did not pay off. But that was only one aspect of the crisis; there was also widespread fraud because the reduced government regulation had opened opportunities for what can only be called "looting" by some bank officials, who used deposits to make their own investments, gave large discounts and other favors to friends, and misappropriated bank funds for private use. There were also genuine crises, such as a long depression in midwestern agriculture, which brought down the largest number of S & L's, and the steadily falling price of oil, which impaired the ability of oil-rich but heavily indebted developing countries to meet their loan payments. The S & L system had taken a tremendous amount of abuse, and the losses eventually amounted to an estimated $300–$500 billion, which will need to be repaid by taxpayers over the next thirty years. But a panic was averted, because the safety net the American government had constructed under the capitalist system had worked. No campaign issue was made of the great S & L collapse or scandal in 1988 or 1992 because the Democratic party had supported S & L deregulation and the added safety net provisions, including the boost of deposit insurance up to $100,000; and several leading Democrats, including prominent senators, had been implicated in the scandals associated with the collapse.

The task in this chapter, and in Chapter 17, is neither to justify nor condemn government or any particular policy. Rather, the chapter accepts existing government action as a given, breaks it down into its policies, and evaluates their significance. Although we concentrate here on contemporary policies, review of national, state, and local government policies in the nineteenth century, as discussed in Chapters 3 and 4, is essential to a full understanding of policy and policy making in America.

National economic policies have been organized into three categories: (1) policies that protect public order and private property; (2) policies that control or influence markets; and (3) policies that are designed to defend or enhance the vitality of our capitalist economy. The chapter is divided accordingly, with a section on each.

POLICIES FOR PUBLIC ORDER AND PRIVATE PROPERTY

Some policies of public order are so old and so deeply imbedded in our society that they are hardly recognized as policies that at some point in the distant past had to be formulated, discussed, and adopted by a policy-making body. Americans, in particular, tend to overlook the fact that these were policies, because our federal Constitution authorizes state governments to enact most of them. This is federalism in action, and it makes the American approach to public order unique among modern governments.

We begin our economic policy chapter with public order policies for two reasons. First, these policies lay and maintain the foundations of the economy. Second, because so many of these policies are old and established state government policies, most people don't appreciate them as policies and go on believing that the U.S. economy was once "unregulated."

Federalism and Public Order Policies

Under the American federalist system, there is no national police force, there is no national criminal law, there is no national common law, there are no national property laws. The national government does have a few policies directly concerned with public order, however, most of which are mandated by the Constitution itself. These include laws against counterfeiting, against using the mails to defraud, and against crossing state lines to avoid arrest for a violation of state laws. A few other offenses against public order have simply been presumed to be interstate crimes against which federal statutes have been enacted, mainly in the twentieth century. Important examples include kidnapping, narcotics dealing, and political subversion. But virtually all of the multitudes of other policies dealing with public order and the foundations of the economy are left to the states and their local governments.

We have already seen in Chapters 3 and 4 that each state has its own body of criminal laws and that, although there is no longer a great deal of variation from state to state in what courts and legislatures decide to call a crime, there remain significant variations in the severity of the punishments for those crimes and in the techniques of control that states are prepared to utilize. For example, some states employ the death penalty as a deterrent against murder, while other states do not. Some states are a great deal more severe than others in their treatment of drug sales and usage. Some states are more restrictive than others about the sale of alcohol. Some states are far more restrictive about sexual practices and about divorce and other aspects of family and morality. And, thanks to *Webster* v. *Reproductive Health Services* (1989) and *Planned Parenthood of Southeastern Pennsylvania* v. *Casey* (1992), states again vary in the extreme on their abortion laws—from the most restrictive in Pennsylvania, Ohio, and Kentucky (which have notification requirements, waiting periods, etc.) to the lenient in Oregon and Washington (which have adopted abortion rights laws and provide adequate public funding for abortion aid), with all the other states varying in between.

Policies and Property

Another unique feature of the American approach to public order is the emphasis placed on *private property*. Private property is valued in most of the cultures of the world but not as centrally as in the United States, where we make it virtually a part of public order itself. And despite their importance, most of the laws protecting and extending property are state laws. The most important examples are, of course, laws against trespass and laws protecting and defending contracts.[1]

Not all the policies toward property are policies that regulate the conduct of people who would trespass or take property. Many policies positively encourage property ownership on the theory that property owners are better citizens and therefore more respectful of public order. One of the most important national policies in American history was **homesteading,** otherwise called "squatting," which was a method of permitting people to gain ownership of property by occupying public or unclaimed lands, living on the land for a specified period of time, and making certain minimal improvements on that land. This is an important aspect of national government subsidy policies, as discussed in Chapter 15. There has been in fact a movement since the 1980s to revive homesteading in urban areas, leading toward laws that would permit the homeless and the indigent to occupy abandoned urban apartments and houses and to improve them as a condition for the acquisition of ownership.

Many other policies encourage homeownership today (see Table 16.1), the most significant being that part of the Internal Revenue Code that permits homeowners to deduct interest on mortgage loans from their taxes. Three other very large federal agencies—the Federal Housing Administration (FHA), the Farmers Home Administration (FMHA), and the Veterans Administration (VA)—encourage homeownership by making mortgage loans available at interest rates below the market rate. The Farm Credit Administration (FCA) operates the extensive Farm Credit System, whose primary function is to make long-term and short-term loans to improve farm and rural real estate, loans available only to bona fide farm operators and farm-related companies who are members of the farm credit system. Many of these agencies make direct loans at below-market rates. Some of them (in particular the FHA and the VA) also insure or guarantee loans, so that private commercial banks have less risk and can charge proportionately lower interest rates.

The Reagan administration cut the federal housing programs more than any part of the domestic budget. Table 16.1 shows just how dramatic the break was; Carter's last housing budget was $33.4 billion, Reagan's first was $20.1 billion, and his second, $16.1 billion, which brought the authorization under Reagan to far less than half of Carter's average. President Bush favored programs that increased

---

[1]One of the few absolute prohibitions in the original Constitution was the prohibition in Article I, Section 10, which provides that "no state shall . . . pass any . . . law impairing the obligation of contracts." The Constitution protects contracts from state government interference. But in our time, most state policies and court decisions are pro-contract anyway.

659
MAKING AND
MAINTAINING A
NATIONAL
MARKET
ECONOMY

TABLE 16.1
Funding Federal Housing Policies
Fiscal years 1978–1993 (in billions of dollars)

Carter		Reagan		Bush		Clinton	
1978	$38.0	1982	$20.1	1990	$15.0	1992	$19.5
1979	31.1	1983	16.0	1991	23.7[†]	1993	21.8
1980	35.7	1984	17.9				
1981	33.4	1985	17.3[*]				
		1986	15.9				
		1987	14.7				
		1988	15.4				
		1989	13.6				

[*]The official figure for 1985 was $31.7 billion, but that was swollen by a one-time-only purchase, directed by Congress, of outstanding notes for public housing. It essentially distorts housing policy priorities and is therefore relegated to a footnote.
[†]Includes a $6.6 billion appropriation to maintain the number of people receiving rental vouchers.
Source:*Congressional Quarterly Weekly Report*, 2 January 1988, pp. 19–20; 2 April 1988, p. 893; and 1 February 1992, p. 240. Used by permission; Office of Management and Budget, *Budget of the United States Government* (Washington, DC: Government Printing Office, various years), Appendix.

home ownership by the poor and his housing secretary, Jack Kemp, gave the Bush program the affectionate name Homeownership and Opportunity for People Everywhere (HOPE). Although the 1993 budget contained a slight increase for housing policies over President Bush's last budget (see Table 16.1), President Clinton's program contained no genuinely new commitments in this area.

MAKING AND MAINTAINING A NATIONAL MARKET ECONOMY

Valuable as the states have been in fostering private property, their separate boundaries, their separate laws, and their separate traditions have also been a barrier to those enterprises seeking to expand beyond local markets. In fact, the protectionism of some states against others was precisely why our first constitution, the Articles of Confederation, was ultimately considered a failure and in need of replacement. Giving Congress the powers of Article I, Section 8, enabled the national government to provide a system of roads, canals, and communications that would foster a regional and ultimately a national market. In *Gibbons* v. *Ogden,* one of the most important cases the Supreme Court ever handed down, the states were told in no uncertain terms that they could not pass laws that would tend to interrupt or otherwise burden the free flow of commerce among the states.[2] In the

[2]Gibbons v. Ogden, 9 Wheaton 1 (1824). See also Chapter 3. This case was reaffirmed sixty years later even when the states were attempting to defend their own citizens from discriminatory charges by railroads for services rendered within their own state. The Supreme Court argued that the route of an interstate railroad could not be subdivided into its separate state segments for purposes of regulation, Wabash, St Louis and Pacific Railway Co. v. Illinois, 118 U.S. 557 (1886).

TABLE 16.2

Federalism and the Regulation of the U.S. Economy

	National Government and Economic Regulation	*State Governments and Economic Regulation*
Nineteenth Century		
Pre–Civil War	Fugitive slaves	Property ownership
Post–Civil War	Railroads	Monopolies
	Interstate trusts and monopolies	Price discrimination
		Contracts and their enforcement
		Apprenticeship
		The professions
		Compulsory education
		Public utilities
		Banking
		Slaves (in southern states)
		Agricultural markets
		Oil and gas extraction
		Coal mines
Twentieth Century		
Pre-1933	Unfair trade practices	All the nineteenth-century
	National banks	policies (except slavery)
	Impure food and drugs	plus:
Post-1933	Stock markets	Child labor
	Agricultural markets	Working conditions
	Trade unions	Equal employment
	Coal mines	opportunity
	Telecommunications	Equal education opportunity
	Natural gas transport	TV cable access
	Atomic energy	Local land use (zoning)
	Equal employment and other civil rights	Land conservation
		Building construction
	The environment	standards
	Consumer product safety	

twentieth century, one of the major reasons why Congress began to adopt national business regulatory policies was that the regulated companies themselves felt burdened by the inconsistencies among the states. These companies often preferred a single, national regulatory authority, no matter how burdensome, because they would have consistency throughout the United States and could thereby treat the nation as a single market.[3] Table 16.2 provides an historical overview of regulation in our federal system.

---

[3]Compare with Gabriel Kolko, *The Triumph of Conservatism* (New York: The Free Press, 1963), Chapter 6.

Promoting the Market

661

MAKING AND
MAINTAINING A
NATIONAL
MARKET
ECONOMY

During the nineteenth century, the national government was almost exclusively a promoter of markets. National roads and canals were built to tie states and regions together. National tariff policies promoted domestic markets by restricting imported goods; a tax on an import raised its price and weakened its ability to compete with similar domestic products. The national government also heavily subsidized the railroad. Until the 1840s, railroads were thought to be of limited commercial value. But by 1850, Congress was moved by the prophets and visionaries, and between 1850 and 1872 Congress granted over 100 million acres of public domain, and state and local governments pitched in an estimated $280 million in cash and credit. Before the end of the century, 35,000 miles of track existed—almost half the world's total.

In the twentieth century, traditional promotional techniques were expanded and some new ones were invented. For example, a great proportion of the promotional activities of the national government are now done indirectly through grants-in-aid. The national government offers grants to states on condition that the state (or local) government undertake a particular activity. Thus, in order to use motor transportation to improve national markets, a national highway system of 900,000 miles was built during the 1930s, based on a formula whereby the national government paid 50 percent of the cost if the state would provide the other 50 percent. Over twenty years, beginning in the late 1950s, the federal government constructed nearly 45,000 miles of interstate highways. This was brought about through a program whereby the national government agreed to pay 90 percent of the construction costs on the condition that each state provide for 10 percent of the costs of any portion of a highway built within its boundaries.[4] Typical examples within each major industrial sector of the country can be seen in Table 15.1 (p. 627). It is very significant that there are some kinds of U.S. government promotional policy in each of the major industrial sectors.

Regulating the Market

As the American economy prospered throughout the nineteenth century, some companies grew so large that they were recognized as possessing "market power." This meant that they were powerful enough to eliminate competitors and to impose conditions on consumers rather than catering to consumer demand. The growth of billion-dollar corporations led to collusion among companies to control prices, much to the dismay of smaller business people as well as ordinary consumers. Moreover, the expanding economy was more mechanized and this involved greater dangers to employees as well as to consumers.

Small businesses, laborers, farmers, and consumers all began to clamor for protective regulation. Although the states had been regulating businesses in one way or another all along, interest groups turned toward Washington as economic prob-

---

[4]The act of 1955 officially designated the interstate highways as the National System of Interstate and Defense Highways. It was indirectly a major part of President Eisenhower's defense program. But it was just as obviously a "pork barrel" policy as any rivers and harbors legislation.

lems appeared to be beyond the reach of the individual state governments. If markets were national, there would have to be national regulation.[5]

The first national regulatory policy was the Interstate Commerce Act of 1887, creating the first national independent regulatory commission, the Interstate Commerce Commission (ICC), designed to control the monopolistic practices of the railroads. Two years later, the Sherman Antitrust Act extended regulatory power to cover all monopolistic practices, including "trusts" or any other agreement between companies to eliminate competition. These were strengthened in 1914 with the enactment of the Federal Trade Act (creating the Federal Trade Commission, FTC) and the Clayton Act. The only significant addition of national regulatory policy beyond interstate regulation of trade, however, was the establishment of the Federal Reserve Board in 1912, giving it powers to regulate the banking industry along with its general monetary powers.

The modern epoch of comprehensive national regulation is not thought to have begun until the 1930s. Table 16.3 gives a birds-eye view of the number and variety of significant regulatory laws and programs enacted in the 1930s and during the second epoch of regulatory expansion in the 1970s. Most of the regulatory programs of the 1930s were established to regulate the conduct of companies within specifically designated sectors of American industry. For example, the jurisdiction of one agency was the securities industry; the jurisdiction of another was the radio (and eventually television) industry. Another was banking. Another was coal mining; still another was agriculture. When Congress turned once again toward regulatory policies, in the 1970s, it became still more bold, moving beyond the effort to regulate specific sectors of industry toward regulating some aspect of the entire economy. The scope or jurisdiction of such agencies as the Occupational Safety and Health Administration (OSHA), the Consumer Product Safety Commission (CPSC), and the Environmental Protection Agency (EPA) is as broad and as wide as the entire economy, indeed the entire society. This is why both defenders and critics of these 1970s programs have agreed to distinguish them from the New Deal agencies by calling the 1970s programs "new regulation" and "social regulation." This is a reasonable distinction as long as we do not forget the fact that all of these agencies are regulatory in that they use regulatory techniques to control some aspect of the conduct of individuals or companies. Another important area of social regulation is civil rights; this will be discussed in the next chapter.

Deregulation

Today, conservatives, as represented by Ronald Reagan and George Bush, are in principle opposed to government intervention in the economy.[6] They see govern-

---

[5]For an account of the relationship between mechanization and law, see Lawrence Friedman, *A History of American Law* (New York: Simon & Schuster, 1973), pp. 409–29.

[6]Actually, this point of view is better understood as nineteenth-century liberalism, or free-market liberalism, following the theories of Adam Smith. However, after the New Deal appropriated "liberal" for their pro-government point of view, the Republican anti-government wing got tagged with the conservative label. With Reagan, the label took on more popular connotations, while "liberal" became stigmatized as the "L-word."

663

MAKING AND
MAINTAINING A
NATIONAL
MARKET
ECONOMY

TABLE 16.3
Federal Regulation Programs—A Birds-eye View, 1887–1977

Formative Era

1887	Interstate Commerce Act (ICC)*	1935	Public Utility Holding Company Act
1890	Sherman Antitrust Act	1935	Federal Power Commission Act (FPC)
1912	Federal Reserve Act (Fed)	1935	National Labor Relations Act (NLRB)
1914	Federal Trade Act (FTC)		
1914	Clayton Act		
		1936	Federal Communications Act (FCC)
1933	Agricultural Adjustment Act (AAA)		
1933	National Industrial Recovery Act (NRA)	1938	Fair Labor Standards Act (FLSA)
		1938	Food, Drug, and Cosmetic Act (FDA)
1934	Securities and Exchange Act (SEC)	1938	Civil Aeronautics Act (CAB)

Era of the New Regulation, 1969–77**

1969	National Environmental Policy Act (EPA)	1973	Federal Mine Safety and Health Act (MSHA)
1970	Clean Air Act Amendments	1974	Commodity Futures Trading Act (CFTC)
1970	National Highway Traffic Safety Act (NHTSA)	1974	Employment Retirement Income Security Act (ERISA)
1970	Occupational Health and Safety Act (OSHA)	1974	Federal Energy Administration Act (FERA)
1970	Fair Credit Reporting Act		
1970	Economic Stabilization Act		
		1975	Nuclear Regulatory Act (NRC)
1972	Consumer Product Safety Act (CPSC)		
1972	Federal Election Campaign Act (FEC)	1976	Toxic Substance Control Act
1972	Federal Water Pollution Control Act Amendments	1977	Surface Mining Control and Reclamation Act (OSM)

*Abbreviations in parentheses are the names of agencies or commissions, where one was created.
**A selection or major action only. There are many additional programs, significant but more specialized.

ment not as part of the solution but as part of the problem. They adamantly oppose intervention by techniques of promoting commerce and are even more opposed to intervention through techniques of regulation, believing that markets would be bigger and healthier if not regulated at all.

The deregulation movement actually began under Presidents Ford and Carter. Their accomplishments include the Securities Act Amendment of 1975, the Railroad Revitalization Act of 1976, the Airline Deregulation Act of 1978, the Stag-

PROCESS BOX 16.1
How a Rule Becomes Law in a Regulatory Agency

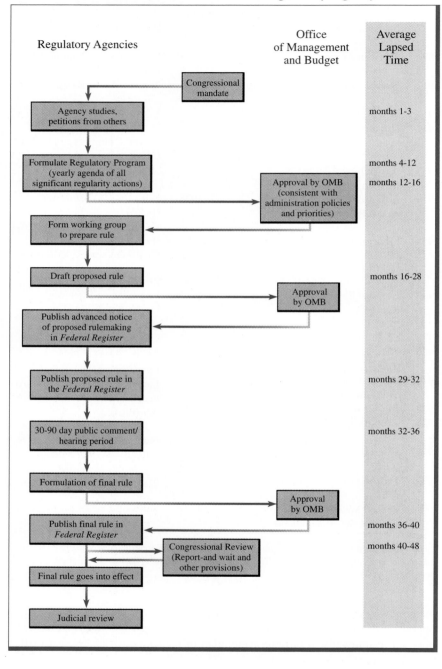

Regulatory Agencies

Office
of Management
and Budget

Average
Lapsed
Time

Congressional
mandate

Agency studies,
petitions from others

months 1-3

Formulate Regulatory Program
(yearly agenda of all
significant regularity actions)

months 4-12

Approval by OMB
(consistent with
administration policies
and priorities)

months 12-16

Form working group
to prepare rule

Draft proposed rule

months 16-28

Approval
by OMB

Publish advanced notice
of proposed rulemaking
in *Federal Register*

Publish proposed rule in
the *Federal Register*

months 29-32

30-90 day public comment/
hearing period

months 32-36

Formulation of final rule

Approval
by OMB

Publish final rule in
Federal Register

months 36-40

Congressional Review
(Report-and wait and
other provisions)

months 40-48

Final rule goes into effect

Judicial review

gers Rail Deregulation Act of 1980, the Depository Institution Deregulation and
Monetary Control Act of 1980, and the Motor Carrier Act of 1980.

In comparison with the reforms achieved by these presidents, it is surprising
that President Reagan proposed termination of only one regulatory program—the
old Interstate Commerce Commission—and this one late in his administration.
But this does not mean that the conservative deregulators in the Reagan and Bush
administrations were insincere. Reagan's approach is a good lesson in the relationship between executive management and legislative authority. President Reagan
almost immediately provided for an average 20 percent cut in the budgets of all
the regulatory agencies. While this cutback didn't have any significant effect on
the total budget of the federal government, because the regulatory agencies are
not very large, it certainly required severe reductions in agency staff and therefore
severe reductions in the level and vigor of regulatory activity by the federal
government.

Reagan's second approach to deregulation by management was his appointment
of people who were not in sympathy with the regulatory mission of the specific
agency. In fact, some of the members of these commissions were genuinely hostile
to the mission of their agency.[7] Another important approach President Reagan
took to the task of changing the direction of regulation was "presidential oversight." One of his first actions after taking office was Executive Order 12291, issued February 17, 1981, giving the Office of Management and Budget (OMB)
the authority to review all proposals by all executive branch agencies for new
regulations to be applied to companies or people within their jurisdiction (see
Chapter 15).

Although President Bush favored reviving some regulatory programs, he continued to rely on OMB review to keep the lid on regulation. In addition, Bush
exercised "presidential oversight" through the White House Council on Competitiveness, chaired by Vice-President Dan Quayle.[8] Under Quayle, the council
relaxed regulatory requirements when it believed the costs imposed on the regulated companies outweighed the benefits of the regulations to employees and the
public. For example, the council successfully eased HUD handicapped-access
rules, proposed a speed-up in FDA drug-approval procedures, and blocked EPA
plans for public input on stiffening rules for automobile anti-pollution devices.
The council and the EPA clashed often over proposed regulations because the
council was more sympathetic to the concerns of business and industry than to
those of conservationists.[9] Toward the end of the Bush administration, the federal
courts were beginning to limit the influence of the council.[10]

---

[7]For a good evaluation, see Kenneth J. Meier, *Regulation: Politics, Bureaucracy, and Economics* (New York:
St. Martin's Press, 1985), Chapters 4, 6, and 8; and George Eads and Michael Fix, "Regulatory Policy,"
in *The Reagan Experiment*, ed. John L. Palmer and Isabel Sawhill (Washington, DC: Urban Institute
Press, 1982), Chapter 5.

[8]The Council on Competitiveness was the successor to the Task Force on Regulatory Relief, which
was created by President Reagan's Executive Order 12291 and was originally chaired by Bush.

[9]Critics of the Bush administration's techniques charged that a combination of benefits for big business
and the council's virtually secret operations created an appearance of regulatory favors for large GOP
campaign contributors. See Bob Davis and Jill Abramson, "Many of Competitiveness Council's Beneficiaries Are Firms that Make Big Donations to the GOP" *Wall Street Journal*, 13 October 1992, p. A22.

[10]For background, see Keith Schneider, "Quayle's Council Is Set Back by Court Ruling" *New York
Times*, 15 July 1992, p. A14.

TABLE 16.4

Attitudes toward Government Regulation

	1948	*1952*	*1962*	*1974*	*1978*	*1979*	*1980*	*1987*
Too much	35%	49%	13%	28%	43%	47%	54%	38%
Right amount	27	29	27	38	23	23	19	32
Not enough, need more	23	7	29	24	25	24	19	23

Source: Various national polls as reported in Seymour Martin Lipset and William Schneider, *The Confidence Gap* (New York: The Free Press, 1983), pp. 222–28. Reprinted by permission. The 1974 figures are an average of Harris Polls between 1974 and 1977, during which there was "no clear trend." The 1987 figures are based on *Wall Street Journal* polls. Allowance has to be made for different ways in which the questions are asked, but the general pattern is an interesting one in any case.

The shrinkage of regulatory government in the past decade is solid evidence of the responsiveness of the national government to public opinion. Beginning in the 1970s, people did in fact grow weary of government regulation. They expressed this in their responses to opinion polls (see Table 16.4), and as early as the Ford and Carter administrations, the change in sentiment was already expressing itself in actual changes in government policy.

Public opinion began to shift toward the end of the Reagan administration. According to Table 16.4, anti-regulation attitude dropped from 54 percent in 1980 to 38 percent in 1987, with favorable and pro-regulatory attitude, taken together, expanding from 38 percent to 55 percent. Although no equivalent polls were taken after 1987, data does suggest that the trend continued. For example, one poll in mid-1992 found over 60 percent support for more regulation of guns and alcohol.[11] Another 1992 poll found that despite the many economic problems, Americans favored more environmental regulation even if forced to choose between the environment and economic growth.[12] Box 16.1 contains a selection of significant regulatory laws passed by Congress and signed by President Bush. President Clinton kept the re-regulation trend alive with his very first piece of legislation, the Family Leave Act, signed in a White House ceremony on February 4, 1993. Vetoed twice by President Bush, the law imposes an obligation on all companies with more than fifty employees to provide up to twelve weeks of unpaid leave for births or other family health emergencies.

There is no particular mystery as to why government gets into, out of, and back into regulatory policies.[13] One of the reasons is, of course, politics. The president may owe a particular debt to an interest group or a sector of the economy that can best be met by adding or subtracting a regulatory policy.[14] A second reason is

[11]The Gordon Black Poll, press release, Rochester, NY: The Gordon Black Corp., May 1992.

[12]Roper poll, reported in Faye Rice, "Next Steps for the Environment," *Fortune*, 19 October 1992, p. 98.

[13]For an excellent treatment of "why regulate," with a somewhat different listing of reasons, see Alan Stone, *Regulation and Its Alternatives* (Washington, DC: Congressional Quarterly Press, 1982), Chapters 3–5.

[14]See, for example, Martha Derthick and Paul Quirk, *The Politics of Deregulation* (Washington, DC: The Brookings Institution, 1985), pp. 33–34.

667

MAKING AND
MAINTAINING A
NATIONAL
MARKET
ECONOMY

BOX 16.1

Types of Re-Regulation
Regulatory Acts Signed Into Law by President Bush

PL 101–336* Extends to the disabled the rights already provided to women and racial and religious minorities under the 1964 Civil Rights Act.

PL 101–380 Significantly extends and stiffens liabilities of companies for oil spills, including compensation, clean-up, and prevention.

PL 101–433 Bans age discrimination in employee benefits, excluding benefits that are dependent on age-based cost differences.

PL 101–493 Renders non-mailable any sample of a drug or other hazardous substance that does not meet child-resistant purchasing requirements.

PL 101–500 Extends and strengthens regulations of refrigerated motor vehicles and cargo tanks in the transportation of hazardous materials.

PL 101–502 Strengthens regulations of vaccine-preventable diseases.

PL 101–535 Prescribes nutrition labeling for foods.

PL 101–549 Imposes strict new controls on toxic pollutants from industry and from automobile exhausts; mandates development of cleaner cars and fuels; and imposes first-ever limits on power plant emissions that cause acid rain.

PL 101–647 Stiffens penalties against white collar crime, including up to life imprisonment for S&L criminals.

PL 102–166 Refines and strengthens key job anti-discrimination laws, mainly by reversing a series of Supreme Court decisions and by expanding Title VIII of the 1964 Civil Rights Act.

PL 102–385 Regulates basic cable rates and services, requires cable programmers to deal fairly with competitors, and allows broadcasters to charge cable operators for their signals.

*PL = Public Law; 101 refers to the 101st Congress (1989–90); and 336 is the actual number given this particular act.

morality (see Box 16.2). A number of examples have already been given of federal and especially state regulations aimed at "criminalizing" conduct deemed immoral. Moreover, there are signs that *more* morals-based regulation may be forthcoming, because morality is quite clearly the strongest motivation regarding restrictions on abortion, on drug sales, and for establishing requirements for AIDS testing, smoking in public, labeling fatty foods, etc. Efficiency is a third reason for regulation, as well as for deregulation, based on the assumption that competition usually forces companies to be more efficient. Many people, mainly Democrats, believe that there should be more "anti-trust" regulation in an effort to keep companies from acquiring their competition or entering into collusive deals with one competitor to eliminate another. Others, mainly Republicans, believe that competition happens naturally if companies are left alone. A fourth reason for regulation is pure and simple convenience. Americans are quick to say "there ought to be a law" when people, places, or things stand in their way. Related to this is a somewhat more serious fifth reason for regulation, which is to reduce the risk of injury that may be recognized in certain actions or products. Most of the time it is diffi-

BOX 16.2
The Newark Factory Fire

The rise of industrialization and influx of immigration afforded great opportunity for economic entrepreneurs in the late 1800s and early 1900s. It was also a period of massive exploitation of the cheap, abundant labor force that had come to America to seek opportunity. And in the days before government regulation of working conditions or effective union organization, little attention was paid to minimally decent working conditions. Tragedies like the Newark Factory Fire were often the result.

In November 1910, a fire broke out at a Newark, New Jersey, factory. It was the factory's tenth fire in ten years. The factory produced a variety of goods, including textiles and explosives. Most of the factory's employees were girls and young women. The local fire chief reached the scene within three minutes of receiving the fire call. By then, however, most of the women trapped in the building had already succumbed to smoke or flames. Horrified bystanders watched helplessly as women jumped to their deaths to escape the fire.

The fire department's extension ladder refused to extend fully, only reaching the third floor of the four-story building. But the ladder was little help, as most of the employees were trapped at the other end of the building. No ladder could be used there, because that side of the building faced an alley crowded with a tree, a gateway, two steampipes that crossed twelve feet in the air, and a wire-laden telegraph pole. Girls who jumped were impaled on the gateway picket fence or tree branches. Some girls were saved by jumping into a fireman's net, until the net tore when three women hit the net at once. In the space of a few minutes, twenty-five girls were killed, and scores more injured.

A coroner's jury was convened after the fire to assess blame and bring charges, and most assumed that the building's operators would be charged. Although the jury concluded that no one was to blame, others believed that the employees lost their lives because the building was manifestly unsafe. Subsequent journalists' investigations revealed that the building had no fire alarm system. The workers in greatest peril—those working on the top floor—were the last to discover the fire. The only interior exit was a narrow, enclosed wooden stairway. The only provision for fire consisted of two small exterior fire escapes, which were difficult to access because the interior window ledges were four feet above the floor.

The Newark tragedy foreshadowed a more infamous one when the Triangle Shirtwaist Company building in New York was swept by a fire on its eighth, ninth, and tenth floors in March of 1911. In the space of a few minutes, 146 employees, mostly young women, were burned or crushed to death after leaping from the upper floors to avoid the flames. Despite the absence of proper fire escapes, the death toll might have been less had the factory owners not locked most of the doors as a means of keeping track of employees. The mounting toll of these and other senseless job-related deaths and injuries provided considerable impetus to the budding labor movement, and eventually spurred government efforts to regulate safety in the workplace.

Source: Harvey Swados, ed., *Years of Conscience* (Cleveland, OH: Meridian Books, 1962).

cult to draw a clear line between regulations aimed at eliminating injuries and inconveniences and regulations aimed at reducing the risk of such injuries and inconveniences. But these are practical matters, and regulations vary according to how many people feel a regulation will have the desired practical consequences. Finally, a sixth reason for regulation is equity, such as when a government program seeks to reduce racial discrimination in the workplace. (see Chapter 17)

With all of these reasons for regulating, it is quite unlikely that any president will significantly reduce the level of government regulation for long. There will be cycles of regulation and deregulation because legislatures and administrators are responsive to changes in attitudes and sentiments about what needs regulating and by how much. But it is truly unlikely that the overall level of (state and national) governmental regulation in the United States will be very significantly reduced.

MAINTAINING A CAPITALIST ECONOMY

When the 1980s were drawing to a close, no one, not even the boldest American booster, could have imagined that the 1990s would see the Communist world begin to embrace capitalism. However, Hungarians, Poles, Czechs, and Russians will soon discover, if they have not already, that capitalism doesn't just happen. It takes not only sustained, rational action and personal risk-taking on the part of business managers—it also takes a lot of government. Government and capitalism are not inherent foes; they depend on each other. The study of government policies toward our capitalist economy will thus enrich our understanding of capitalism and strengthen our grasp of the relation between freedom and power.

Our Constitution provides that Congress shall have the power:

> To lay and collect Taxes . . . to pay the Debts and provide for the common Defense and general Welfare . . . to borrow Money . . . to coin Money and regulate the Value thereof. . . .

These clauses of Article I, Section 8, are the constitutional sources of the fiscal and monetary policies of the national government. (Refer back to Table 15.3 on page 635.) Nothing is said, however, about *how* these powers can be used, although the way they are used will shape the economy. Most of the policies in the history of the United States have been distinctly capitalistic, that is, they have aimed at promoting investment and ownership by individuals and corporations in the private sector. That was true even during the first half of the nineteenth century, before anyone had a firm understanding of what capitalism was really all about.[15]

---

[15]The word "capitalism" did not come into common usage, according to the *Oxford English Dictionary*, until 1854. Words like "capital" and "capitalist" were around earlier, but a concept of capitalism as an economic system really comes to the forefront after the writings of Karl Marx in 1848.

THE SAVINGS AND LOAN CRISIS:
THE COST OF GREED

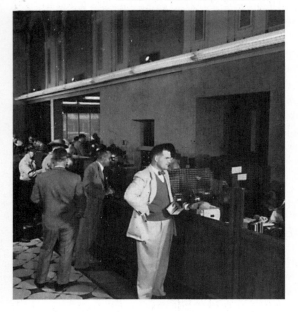

The original charter of the Savings and Loan industry, created in the 1930s, was to help millions of Americans buy affordable homes. For approximately forty years, local banks enjoyed a small but secure margin of profit by providing their communities with home loans that were FDIC insured.

By adhering to a policy that allowed its depositors to withdraw their money at any time, the thrift (S&L) industry was set up for a hard fall in the 1970s, when high inflation and rising interest rates caused many S&L depositors to look elsewhere to deposit their money. Money-market funds gave higher interest-rate returns than S&Ls, and therefore may have seemed like better investments for these depositors waiting to withdraw their money from Old Court Savings and Loan in Baltimore, Maryland.

The S&Ls could not legally invest in anything other than the home-building business, and by 1982 the industry was nearly bankrupt when Congress lifted the regulations and allowed S&Ls to invest in more high-risk, high-return business ventures. Because depositors' savings were guaranteed by the FDIC, many banks literally gambled with their depositors' money, investing in such speculative ventures as this amusement park in Colorado, which was built for $9.6 million yet sold for $800,000.

By 1987, many regulators began to realize that the S&L crisis was worsening and that legislation was needed to police the industry. The arguments in Washington over whether to regulate or deregulate raged on while the S&Ls continued to make bad business decisions and the crisis worsened. Some members of Congress who rallied against S&L-regulation legislation were also receiving large campaign contributions from S&L PACs. Democratic Senator Alan Cranston, from California, is reported to have received about $144,000 in campaign contributions from S&L interests during the 1980s. He resigned in 1992.

The lack of federal regulation led to a downright plundering of thrifts by slick investors such as Charles Keating. The "Keating Five," senators known for their political ties to the S&Ls, were subject to a Senate Ethics Committee investigation to determine whether or not they had deliberately blocked the investigation of Charles Keating. While the senators were not convicted of violating any federal laws, Keating himself was convicted of stealing $2.5 billion from American taxpayers.

Estimates have been made that Americans will have to pay over $500 billion in taxes for the Savings and Loan industry to be saved. Here the FDIC takes over a failed Texas bank, a familiar scene since the Savings and Loan scandal began.

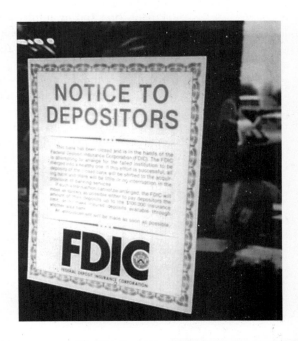

Monetary Policies—Banks, Credit, Insurance

With a very few exceptions cited below, banks in the United States are privately owned and locally operated. Until well into the twentieth century, the banks were regulated, if at all, by state legislatures. Each bank was granted a charter, giving it permission to make loans, hold deposits, and make investments. Although more than 25,000 banks continue to be state-chartered banks, they are less important than they used to be in the overall financial picture, as the most important banks now are members of the "federal system."

But banks did not become the core of American capitalism without intense political controversy. The Federalist majority in Congress, led by Alexander Hamilton, did in fact establish a Bank of the United States in 1791, but it was vigorously opposed by agrarian interests, led by Thomas Jefferson, based on the fear that the interests of urban, industrial capitalism would dominate such a bank. The Bank of the United States was terminated during the administration of Andrew Jackson, but the fear of a central, *public* bank still existed eight decades later, when Congress in 1913 established an institution—the Federal Reserve System—to integrate private banks into a single system. Yet even the "Fed" was not permitted to become a central bank. The "Fed" is a banker's bank. It charters national banks and regulates them in important respects.[16] The major advantage of belonging to the federal system is that each member bank can borrow money from the Fed, using as collateral the notes on loans already made. This enables them to expand their loan operations continually, as long as there is demand for new loans. This ability of a member bank to borrow money from the Fed is a profoundly important fiscal policy.[17] A bank's borrowing, say, $1,000 from the Fed is the equivalent of getting a fresh new $1,000 deposit from a new depositor. The bank, and therefore the economic system itself, is expanded to that extent. This sort of borrowing often occurs when an expanding region has an excess of demands for loans and some other less-expanding region has fewer demands and, therefore, a credit surplus. The Fed charges interest, called a "discount rate," on its loans to member banks.

Process Box 16.2 is an idealized illustration of the significance of the federal policy of permitting member banks to borrow money from the Fed. This is generally called the ***multiplier effect.*** As shown in the box, the original bank takes its new deposit of $1,000 and puts $200 of that in its reserves, assuming in this case that the "reserve requirement" sets 20 percent of all deposits as the amount to be held on reserve and "made payable on demand." This means that the bank can then make available $800 (80 percent of the new deposit) as new credit. In effect, this new credit was created by the first depositor. The second depositor then borrows the $800 of new credit created by the first depositor, and that becomes a new account on which the second depositor can draw. If the new customer takes the entire $800 and buys a refrigerator with it, then it is the appliance store owner

---

[16]Banks can choose between a state or a national charter. Under the state system, they are less stringently regulated and avoid the fees charged members of the Fed. But they also miss out on the advantages of belonging to the Federal Reserve System.

[17]This is usually called a "monetary" policy, but for purposes of simplicity, all monetary policies are grouped together as additional examples of the more general category of fiscal policy.

How Banks Create Money: The Multiplier Effect

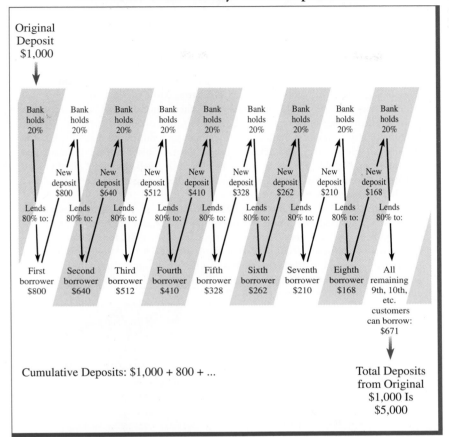

Original
Deposit
$1,000

| Bank holds 20% | Bank holds 20% | Bank holds 20% | Bank holds 20% | Bank holds 20% | Bank holds 20% | Bank holds 20% | Bank holds 20% | Bank holds 20% |

New deposit $800 — New deposit $640 — New deposit $512 — New deposit $410 — New deposit $328 — New deposit $262 — New deposit $210 — New deposit $168

Lends 80% to: (each)

| First borrower $800 | Second borrower $640 | Third borrower $512 | Fourth borrower $410 | Fifth borrower $328 | Sixth borrower $262 | Seventh borrower $210 | Eighth borrower $168 | All remaining 9th, 10th, etc. customers can borrow: $671 |

Cumulative Deposits: $1,000 + 800 + ...

Total Deposits
from Original
$1,000 Is
$5,000

who will deposit the $800, or a substantial proportion of it, in another account. (Even if it is at a different bank, the multiplier theory assumes a "closed banking system," which is actually part of the purpose of the Fed.) Either way, a substantial portion of the $800 goes into the banking system as an added deposit. Once again, 80 percent of this deposit can also be loaned out, and so on, as shown in Process Box 16.2. As long as each loan becomes a deposit in a bank within the system, the original $1,000 can expand toward a $5,000 increase in the monetary system. There is, of course, some slippage, and the multiplier would not produce the full $5,000 in the real world. But this spells out the general tendency.

The role of the Fed in the multiplier effect is one of the most important opportunities for government to influence the economy. If, for example, the economy is expanding too fast, the Fed can put on the brakes by raising the "reserve requirement" from 20 percent to 25 percent, thereby cutting the multiplier effect accord-

Carla Anderson Hills and Richard A. Gephardt
Battling Over Free Trade

A key issue in the 1992 presidential elections—international trade and the loss of American jobs—set free-trade advocates, such as Carla Anderson Hills, against advocates of protectionism, such as Richard Gephardt. Most policy makers agree that trade barriers between the United States and other nations should be lowered, but many fear that doing so will hurt too many American workers.

An attorney by training, Hills acquired extensive administrative experience in the Republican presidencies of Richard Nixon, Gerald Ford, Ronald Reagan, and George Bush. Notably, she was named secretary of the Department of Housing and Urban Development (HUD) under Ford in 1975, becoming the first female cabinet member in twenty years and the third ever.

In early 1989, President Bush named her to serve as U.S. trade representative, a cabinet-level position. She immediately championed Bush's efforts to lift trade restrictions between the United States and other nations. In 1990, for example, she defended the controversial decision to keep Japan off the list of nations labeled unfair trading partners, and in 1991, she promoted a free-trade agreement with Mexico as part of an administration plan to create a "hemispheric zone of free trade" to en-

courage economic development. This effort culminated in the completion of the North American Free Trade Agreement (NAFTA) in 1992 between the United States, Canada, and Mexico. The agreement called for eventual elimination of customs duties and other restrictions on the sale of goods and services across the three nations' borders.

Yet NAFTA encountered stiff opposition from those who feared that the elimination of such barriers would increase the loss of American jobs by accelerating the rate at

Carla Anderson Hills

ingly.[18] Conversely, it can set a lower reserve requirement to help boost a sagging economy.

The second fiscal policy available to the Fed is the discount rate. If the Fed significantly decreases the discount rate—i.e., the interest it charges member banks when they come for new credit—that can be a very good shot in the arm of a sagging economy. If the Fed adopts a policy of higher discount rates, that will serve as a brake on the economy if it is expanding too fast because the higher rate pushes

[18]This would mean that a member bank would have to hold $250 of the $1,000 deposit shown in Process Box 16.2, and that would shrink the multiplier toward $4,000 instead of $5,000.

which American companies moved to Mexico to take advantage of cheaper labor wages and less strict environmental regulations. House Majority Leader Richard Gephardt, a key critic of NAFTA, first took aim at such agreements in his 1988 run for the Democratic presidential nomination. The Missouri Democrat has long criticized Japan for what he views as their unfair trading practices—specifically for dumping their goods on the American market to drive out American competitors.

As a member of the House since 1976, Gephardt has become an expert on trade issues. His opposition to NAFTA centered on his concern that the agreement made no provision for the retraining of American workers who would lose their jobs to Mexico; it did not include any protections for the rights of Mexican workers; and it did not adequately address the need for environmental protection and cleanup. Hills argued that NAFTA would generate more jobs as a whole (in part because North America would be able to trade and compete more effectively with the rest of the world, thus enhancing the American economic picture), that it increased environmental protections, and that it would generally make America more competitive. Hills did admit, however, that some American economic sectors would be hurt, including glass producers and fruit and vegetable farming.

Despite a strong initial push to win approval of the NAFTA agreement, the 1992 presidential elections put a hold on the process. President Bill Clinton indicated qualified support for a NAFTA-type agreement, saying there was a need to renegotiate some parts of the agreement. The future trend will likely favor Hills's free-market approach, but congressional approval will depend on paying adequate attention to labor and environmental concerns.

Source: David C. Nice, *Federalism: The Politics of Intergovernmental Relations* (New York: St. Martin's Press, 1987).

Richard Gephardt

up interest rates charged by leading private banks to their prime customers (called the "prime rate"). For example, in mid-1982, the prime rate was a very high 16.5 percent, part of the anti-inflation campaign that had begun in the late seventies. A year later it had dropped to 10.5 percent, in an effort to boost the economy out of its deep recession. Through most of the 1980s, the discount rate and the prime rate tended downward as an economic booster, reaching a very low 8.75 percent in September 1987. It stayed well below the 10 percent level until 1989, when fear of inflation began to strengthen, and reached 11.5 percent early in 1989. At that point, a fear of recession—the opposite of inflation—convinced the Fed to drop its discount rate charges, and the prime rate followed accordingly, reaching a very low

6.0 percent in July 1992, just as the presidential election was heating up. Low discount and interest rates prevailed into 1993.

These methods of controlling the economy illustrate the influence of the national government on the private economy. But there are other types of influence. For example, the Home Loan Bank System,[19] the Farm Credit Administration, and the Small Business Administration operate as specialized banks. In other words, these are publicly operated banks, and they exist in order to make loans to qualified private-sector clients in competition with private banks. But the mission of these specialized banks is to promote private commerce through making credit available on a specialized basis. Another public but pro-capitalist mission is that of the Federal Deposit Insurance Corporation (FDIC) and the Federal Savings and Loan Insurance Corporation (FSLIC), which were discussed early in this chapter.

The federal government also provides other kinds of insurance to foster credit and encourage private capital investment. The most important is federal insurance of home mortgages through programs under the Federal Housing Administration (FHA) and the Veterans Administration (VA). These programs have enabled millions of families to finance the purchase of a house because they are only required to make moderate down payments and to pay moderate interest rates. Since federal insurance of loans and federal guarantees to banks for home mortgage loans reduce the risk to banks, the reduced risk enables banks to reduce interest rates, to spread far wider their willingness to hold low-interest mortgages for twenty and thirty years.

In brief, most of these monetary policies are aimed at encouraging a maximum of property ownership and a maximum of capital investment by individuals and corporations in the private sector. And all of these policies are illustrative of the interdependence of government and capitalism.

Taxation and the Capitalist Economy

All taxes discriminate. The public policy question is: How to raise revenue with a tax that provides the *desired* discrimination? The tariff was the most important tax policy of the nineteenth century. But the most important choice Congress *ever* made about taxation (and one of the most important policy choices it ever made about anything) was the decision to raise revenue by taxing personal and corporate incomes—the "income tax."[20] And the second most important choice Congress

---

[19]There is a separate but comparable system for all the savings and loan (S&L) associations: the Federal Home Loan Bank System, comprised of a Federal Home Loan Bank Board in Washington and eleven regional Federal Home Loan Banks. Created by Congress in the 1930s, these banks have power to borrow money at favorable rates and to relend the money to S&Ls, which pass along the savings to home buyers. Two additional agencies, the Federal National Mortgage Association (FNMA, or "Fannie Mae") and the General National Mortgage Association (GNMA, or "Ginnie Mae") provide a market for S&Ls to sell the mortgages they hold in order to finance new mortgages. This S&L system contributes to the "multiplier effect."

[20]The U.S. imposed an income tax during the Civil War, which remained in effect until 1872. In 1894, Congress enacted a modest 2 percent tax upon all incomes over $4,000. This $4,000 exemption in fact was fairly high, excluding all working-class people. But in 1895, the Supreme Court declared it unconstitutional, violating the provision of Article I, Section 9, that any direct tax would have to be proportional to population in each state, Pollock v. Farmers' Loan and Trust Company, 158 U.S. 601 (1895). In 1913, the Sixteenth Amendment was ratified, effectively reversing the *Pollock* case.

made was that the income tax be "progressive" or "graduated," with the heaviest
burden carried by those most able to pay. A tax is called *progressive* if the rate of taxation goes up with each income bracket. A tax is called *regressive* if people in lower income brackets pay a higher proportion of their income toward the tax than people in higher income brackets. For example, a sales tax is deemed regressive because everybody pays at the same rate, so that the proportion of total income paid in taxes goes down as the total income goes up. The Social Security tax is another example of a regressive tax. Current law applies a tax of 6.20 percent on the first $55,000 of income for the retirement program and an additional 1.45 percent on the first $130,200 of income for Medicare benefits, for a total of 7.65 percent "Social Security tax" (the law provides for automatic increases in the 1990s). This means that a person earning an income of $55,500 pays the *entire amount* of both the retirement and Medicare taxes, $4,246. But someone earning twice that income, $111,000, pays the same *amount* of tax—$4,246—but that represents only a 3.86 percent tax rate on the total income. The *rate* of the Social Security tax continues to go down as annual income moves above $130,200.

Although the primary purpose of the graduated income tax is, of course, to raise revenue, an important second objective is to collect revenue in such a way as to reduce the disparities of wealth between the lowest and the highest income brackets. We call this a *policy of redistribution.* Table 16.5 suggests that this tax policy has not been altogether effective because the difference between the lowest and highest brackets of income is about the same today as it was eighty years ago.

One reason for this is that there are many regressive taxes in the United States—such as Social Security taxes, state sales taxes, many federal excise taxes, and tariffs—and these neutralize to a large extent the impact of the progressive federal and

TABLE 16.5
Income Distribution in the United States (1910–1990)
The Proportion of Money Income Going to Each Quintile of the Population

Family Income Bracket	1910	1929	1934	1944	1950	1960	1970	1980	1990
Lowest fifth	8.3	5.4	5.9	4.9	4.5	4.8	5.4	5.1	4.6
Second fifth	11.5	10.1	11.5	10.9	12.0	12.2	12.2	11.6	10.7
Third fifth	15.0	14.4	15.5	16.2	17.4	17.8	17.6	17.5	16.7
Fourth fifth	19.0	18.8	20.4	22.2	23.5	24.0	23.8	24.3	24.0
Highest fifth	46.2	51.3	49.7	45.8	42.6	41.3	41.4	41.6	44.3
Gap between bottom and top fifth	39.7	45.9	43.8	40.9	38.1	36.5	35.5	36.5	39.7

Figures are not strictly comparable because of differences in calculating procedures.
Sources: Data for the period 1910–1950 are from Allan Rosenbaum, "State Government, Political Power, and Public Policy: The Case of Illinois" (Ph.D. diss., University of Chicago, 1974), Chapters 10–11. Used by permission. Figures for 1960–1990 are from U.S. Department of Commerce, Bureau of the Census. *Current Population Reports.* Series P-60 (Washington, DC: Government Printing Office, various issues).

state income taxes. Second, redistribution of wealth is not the *only* secondary policy behind the income tax. Another important secondary policy is the encouragement of the capitalist economy. When the tax law allows individuals or companies to deduct from their taxable income any money they can justify as an investment or as a "business expense," that is an incentive to individuals and companies to spend money to expand their production, their advertising, or their staff, and it reduces the income taxes they pay. These kinds of deductions are called incentives or "equity" by those who are able to save taxes from them. For others, they might be called "loopholes." The tax laws of 1981 actually closed a number of important loopholes. But others still exist—for example on home mortgages, including secondary homes, and on business expenses—and others will return, because there is a strong consensus among members of Congress that business people often need such incentives. They may differ on which incentives are best, but there is almost universal agreement in government that some incentives are justifiable.[21]

President Reagan embraced this theory to the fullest, calling it "supply-side economics," which holds that if people are suddenly allowed to retain a substantially larger amount of their income, and if they are reassured that this policy will be retained over an indefinite period of time, they will be much more likely to jump into the economy with more vigorous capital investment, which will eventually expand the economy for everybody. After a two-year recession, the economy did recover and expand. But there is no general agreement on whether the expansion was attributable to the 1981 and 1986 tax reforms or to the very large deficits that pumped money into the economy.

The persistence of large annual deficits put severe limits on the options of both Presidents Bush and Clinton. President Bush was forced to renege on his dramatic 1988 campaign promise, "Read my lips, no new taxes." President Clinton backed away from his 1992 "middle-class tax cut" campaign promise even before his 1993 transition was completed, and the stark reality of having to raise taxes occupied a large part of his 1993–94 legislative agenda. His goal had been equal sacrifice for everyone, beginning with increases in income taxes on the wealthy and taxing some social security retirement benefits.[22]

Some will argue that the deep income tax cuts of the 1980s, coupled with increasing Social Security taxes, sales taxes, and other regressive taxes in the 1990s are undemocratic in that they unfairly relieve those in the highest income brackets. Defenders of the Reagan-Bush approach argue that people in lower income brackets will not benefit from *any* taxing system if it discourages the wealthy from investing their resources, because an expanding economy is never regressive. They can also point to the fact that the income distribution in this century, as indicated by Table 16.5, has defied the prediction of Karl Marx that under capitalism "the

---

[21] For a systematic account of the role of government in providing incentives and inducements to business, see C. E. Lindblom, *Politics and Markets* (New York: Basic Books, 1977), Chapter 13. For a detailed account of the dramatic Reagan tax cuts and reforms, see Jeffrey Birnbaum and Alan Murray, *Showdown at Gucci Gulch—Lawmakers, Lobbyists, and the Unlikely Triumph of Tax Reform* (New York: Random House, 1987).

[22] For further background, see David E. Rosenbaum, "Cutting the Deficit Overshadows Clinton's Promise to Cut Taxes" *New York Times*, 12 January 1993, p. A1; and "Clinton Weighing Freeze or New Tax on Social Security" *New York Times*, 31 January 1993, p. A1.

rich get richer and the poor get poorer." Critics of the Reagan-Bush approach
look at those figures quite differently. They would argue that it is precisely because of the progressive income tax during the twentieth century that the gap between the income received by the lowest fifth of the population and the highest fifth of the population has remained stable and in fact actually shrank a bit. They would also argue there may be cause now for concern in the fact that the gap between the lowest fifth and the highest fifth grew slightly larger between 1970 and 1980 and then made a still larger jump between 1980 and 1990. Is the Reagan-Bush tax philosophy actually moving us closer to the validation of the Marxist hypothesis?

Government Spending and Capitalism

Modern monetary, fiscal, and tax policies are not the only techniques for influencing the economy and redistributing wealth. Government's spending power is another. President Franklin Roosevelt's practical instincts led him to this conclusion. He seemed to recognize from the beginning of the New Deal that, although money spent on roads, farms, parks, and art would accomplish good things and would put some people back to work, the more important reason for government spending was not the specific projects but the *aggregate amount spent*. If people were unemployed and couldn't buy anything, and if companies were pessimistic and would neither invest nor hire, then government spending to consume, to invest, and to hire would be a net gain for the economy. Budget deficits under these circumstances would be acceptable.[23] Then along came the great British economist John Maynard Keynes to give Roosevelt theoretical justification for what he was doing. Keynes argued that governments are now a significant economic force and they can use their power to make up for the imperfections of the capitalist system. Fiscal techniques, he argued, ought to be used as part of a "counter-cyclical" policy, in which, on the one hand, spending would be significantly increased (with "deficit spending") to fight deflationary sides of the business cycle, and, on the other hand, spending would be cut with tax rates kept high to produce budget surpluses, to fight the inflationary side of the business cycle.[24]

At least three serious weaknesses in the Keynesian approach to fiscal policy were exposed during the 1970s. First, although public spending can supplement private spending to produce higher demand and thereby heat up the economy, there is no guarantee that the public money will be spent on things that help produce higher productivity, higher employment, and prosperity. Public expenditure can merely inflate the economy.

Second, governments may not be able to increase spending quickly enough to reverse the declining employment or the pessimistic psychology among consumers and investors. New public works take time, arriving perhaps too late to boost the economy, perhaps just in time to inflate it.

---

[23]There is an ironic twist here. In the 1932 presidential election campaign, Roosevelt actually berated Hoover for being a big spender and producing budget deficits. He promised to balance the budget! President Bush's breaking of his "No new taxes" promise should be judged in this context.

[24]John Maynard Keynes, *The General Theory of Employment Interest and Money* (New York: Harcourt, Brace, 1936).

Does the Deficit Matter?

O ne important fiscal consequence of the Reagan and Bush presidencies was a vast increase in the national debt—from roughly $1 trillion to $4 trillion. While the economy prospered during most of this time, the enormity of the debt escalated fears that the country was heading for a long-term economic decline from which it could never extricate itself. Economist Benjamin M. Friedman summarizes the concern that deficit spending has borrowed too heavily against the future. Newspaper editor Robert L. Bartley expresses the views of many economists that the deficit's importance has been grossly exaggerated and that its political importance is far greater than its economic consequences.

Friedman

The radical course upon which United States economic policy was launched in the 1980s violated the basic moral principle that had bound each generation of Americans to the next since the founding of the republic: that men and women should work and eat, earn and spend, both privately and collectively, so that their children and their children's children would inherit a better world. Since 1980 we have broken with that tradition by pursuing a policy that amounts to living not just in, but for, the present. We are living well by running up our debt and selling off our assets. America has thrown itself a party and billed the tab to the future. The costs, which are only beginning to come due, will include a lower standard of living for individual Americans and reduced American influence and importance in world affairs. . . .

In short, our prosperity was a false prosperity, built on borrowing from the future. The trouble with an economic policy that artificially boosts consumption at the expense of investment, dissipates assets, and runs up debt is simply that each of these outcomes violates the essential trust that has always linked each generation to those that follow. We have enjoyed what appears to be a higher and more stable standard of living by selling our and our children's economic birthright. . . . Most individual Americans are working just as hard, and saving nearly as much, as their parents and grandparents did. What is different is economic policy. The tax and spending policies that the U.S. government has pursued throughout Ronald Reagan's presidency have rendered every citizen a borrower and every industry a liquidator of assets. The reason that the average American has enjoyed such a high standard of living lately is that since January 1981 our government has simply borrowed more than $20,000 on behalf of each family of four.[1]

Bartley

The deficit is not a meaningless figure, only a grossly overrated one. It measures something, but it does not measure the impulse of the economy. . . . In particular, the deficit has no detectable effect on interest rates; if it tends to raise interest rates, its effect is swamped by other more important variables. And if it doesn't affect interest rates, it can scarcely affect the sectors of the economy thought to depend on interest rates, investment, for example. Nor is what we call "the deficit" an appropriate or particularly meaningful measure

of the "burden we are leaving our grandchildren"; the federal government has
many other ways of imposing future burdens, which may or may not move in
tandem with its direct borrowing.

The fiscal health of the federal government certainly does matter, but the
government's impact on the economy is far too large and diffuse to measure
by any one number. . . . Yet we have increasingly made "the deficit" the centerpiece of economic policy, even writing it into law. Both the Gramm-
Rudman Act and the 1990 budget deal pretend to control the deficit, or some
convoluted version of it. Unable to do the right things on their own, our
politicians have conjured the deficit bogeyman with which to scare themselves. In symbolizing the bankruptcy of our political process, the deficit has
become a great national myth with enormous power. But behind this political
symbol, we need to understand the economic reality, or lack of it. Otherwise
the symbol may lead us to do dumb things, like trying to fight recessions by
increasing taxes.

In the advanced economic literature, the big debate is over whether
deficits matter *at all*. Professional economists have noticed that the much-
publicized deficits of the 1980s somehow didn't spell the end of the world, or
even the end of the economic boom.[2]

[1]Benjamin M. Friedman, *Day of Reckoning: The Consequences of American Economic Policy Under Reagan and After* (New York: Random House, 1988), pp. 4–6.
[2] Robert L. Bartley, *The Seven Fat Years and How to Do It Again* (New York: The Free Press, 1992), pp. 182–83.

Third, a very large and growing proportion of the annual federal budget is
mandated or, in the words of OMB, "relatively uncontrollable." Interest payments
on the national debt, for example, are determined by the actual size of the national
debt. Legislation has mandated payment rates for such programs as retirement
under Social Security, retirement for federal employees, unemployment assistance,
Medicare, and farm price supports. These payments go up with the cost of living;
they go up as the average age of the population goes up; they go up as national and
world agricultural surpluses go up. In 1970, 64 percent of the total federal budget
was "relatively uncontrollable"; in 1975, 72.8 percent fell into that category; and
by 1990, around 75 percent was in the uncontrollable category. Except for an early
effort by the Clinton administration to put a "cap" on the automatic cost of living
increases (COLAs) for Social Security benefits, there has been no significant effort
to bring down the extremely high percentage of federal expenditures that are
locked in. To do so would require fundamental revisions in the legislation that
mandated the expenditures in the first place.

The experience of the Reagan and Bush administrations suggests that spending
as fiscal policy works fairly well on the "up side" and almost not at all on the
"down side." In other words, it is politically easier to *expand* the budget to fight
deflation and recession than to *cut* it to fight inflation. The inability of presidents

John Maynard Keynes
Economic Revisionary

John Maynard Keynes (1883–1946)

John Maynard Keynes was born in 1883, the year Karl Marx died. A product of Eton and Cambridge University, an economist and mathematician, Keynes was a Cambridge professor, made a fortune for himself and for his university speculating in international currencies, became a director of the Bank of England, married a prima ballerina, led the intellectual Bloomsbury group and, among other books, wrote *The General Theory of Employment, Interest and Money*, which was to put him in a class with the nineteenth century's Karl Marx and John Stuart Mill and the eighteenth century's Adam Smith.

Until Keynes, the non-Socialist world was guided by Adam Smith's theory that the economy, if left to its own devices, would reach an equilibrium at full employment and maximum production. Keynes, on the other hand, began with the assumption that there was nothing self-perfecting about a free market economy. Neither the downward movements of wages nor of the rate of interest had the power to restore an economy to an equilibrium at full employment. To Keynes, the answer lay in the concept of "aggregate demand"; that is to say, the *total purchasing power* in the economy. For example, the wage reductions that come with unemployment do not necessarily lead to a restoration of employment; unemployment might merely reduce aggregate demand in the economy and as a consequence maintain the low level of employment. Moreover, interest rates could be re-duced to near zero and not necessarily trigger off a recovery if there was continuing reduction in consumer demand and a pessimistic psychology. Keynes's answer, brutally oversimplified, was to arrest the downward spiral of private expenditure by proportionate increases in public expenditure, financed by borrowing—in other words, by deliberate budget deficits.

Keynes tried to press his theory on president-elect Roosevelt in 1933 and went away intensely disappointed. But two things were about to happen that would convert Keynes's disappointment to triumph. First, the New Deal was going to put Keynes into practice without appreciating his theory. Second, the *General Theory* was about to become the accepted economics perspective among America's intellectuals.

The Keynesian revolution came to the Democrats in the 1940s. But the revolution would not be complete until 1955, when President Eisenhower's Economic Report to Congress was unselfconsciously based on Keynes: "Budget policies can help promote the objective of maximum production by wisely allocating resources *between private and public uses*" (italics added).

Sources: John Kenneth Galbraith, "Came the Revolution: Rise of an Orthodoxy," in the *New York Times Book Review,* 16 May 1965; and Robert L. Heilbroner, *The Worldly Philosophers* (New York: Simon & Schuster, Touchstone Edition, 1980).

or Congress to cut expenditures since 1982 has produced unprecedented budget deficits. These deficits actually helped pull the U.S. economy out of the 1982 recession—and that is ironic, because the 1983 recovery was a classic deficit-spending Keynesian recovery despite the fact that the Reagan administration was officially opposed to Keynesian economics. Once the economy had pulled out of that recession, the Reagan administration was unable to change course sufficiently to cut the deficits, let alone create a surplus. Extremely high interest rates (monetary policy) helped keep inflation low, but the continuing high deficits meant that in dealing with the next recession the government cannot use deficit spending as a recovery weapon. A recession did in fact begin late in 1990, and President Bush did not have any policy options to deal with it, except to leave it as his legacy to Bill Clinton. The true size of the deficit did not become a 1992 campaign issue, not only because it would have reflected badly on the Bush record, but also because it would have rendered less credible Clinton's promise to halve it by the end of his term. On the eve of his accession to office, Clinton described the final Bush/Darman deficit estimate as "an unsettling revelation." He then used the surprise revelation to justify breaking his campaign promise of a "middle-class tax cut" and to stress instead some new expenditure programs for a stronger economic stimulus to "grow us out of the deficit." But the widespread public sentiment for deficit reduction was reflected in the congressional revolt against Clinton's $30 billion expenditure package. He reduced it to $16 billion before presenting it to Congress, but with full awareness that only a small proportion of even that would be salvaged.

The Welfare State in a Capitalist Economy

Although most of the discussion of the welfare state is reserved for the next chapter, one important aspect of it needs to be introduced here. The architects of the original Social Security system in the 1930s were probably very well aware of the fact that a large welfare system can be very good fiscal policy. When the economy is declining and more people are losing jobs or are retiring early, welfare payments go up automatically. They can go up enough to maintain consumer demand, which can help counteract a deflationary psychology, thereby also helping maintain investment. Although such payments are no cure for the down side of the business cycle, the expansion of Social Security checks almost certainly makes the down side of the business cycle shorter and shallower. Conversely, during periods of full employment and/or high levels of government spending, when inflationary pressures can mount, welfare taxes take an extra bite out of consumer dollars, which tends to dampen inflation somewhat, because, to repeat, inflation is based upon "too many dollars chasing too few goods." Also, when there is close to full employment, fewer Social Security and unemployment checks go out. These countercyclical tendencies of our welfare state are also called "automatic stabilizers."

REFLECTIONS ON THE ROLE OF GOVERNMENT

With the exception of a few radical anarchists, all the people want some policies some of the time. And there is no way to predict what policies will be adopted, expanded, de-emphasized, or terminated. But whatever happens, at least two points can be stated with some confidence.

First, nothing about public policy is natural, inherent, or divine. Policies will continue to reflect the interests of those with influence. Second, above and beyond the political realities, important moral and ethical principles are involved, because each policy decision affects the balance between citizens' freedoms and government's power. All of the really important policies—including virtually all the examples in Chapters 15–18—are seen by their supporters as necessary, as a condition for their own freedom and safety. But this only confirms our contention that *freedom depends upon control,* even as freedom is threatened by control. My freedom depends upon the restraints of all other persons who might affect my actions. Although most of society's restraints are *self*-imposed—we call that civility, without which no society can work—many restraints are governmentally imposed. What would private property be worth without governmental restraints against trespass? What would freedom of contract be worth without laws making breach of contract more expensive than observance? The study of public policies is simply one more way of exploring the shifting balance between freedom and power. Good government is not created once and for all by establishing one position for all time between popular freedom and governmental control. The requirements of freedom are not constant. Policies must be designed and redesigned to meet new challenges.

SUMMARY

In the first section of this chapter, we discussed the national government's policies toward public order and private property, such as policies encouraging homesteading and homeownership. We then went on to describe the national government's making and maintaining of a national market economy through promotional techniques. Thus, we described how in the nineteenth century such promotional techniques as cash grants, land grants, and low-cost land sales by the national government helped lead to the making of a vast market in the United States. Government promotion policies continue in various forms today.

We then turned to regulatory policies, and here we found a mixed picture. Although all regulatory policies seek to control conduct by imposing restrictions or obligations on individuals, regulatory policies can serve three purposes in regard to the economy. Many regulatory policies can seek to promote the economy by imposing restrictions on companies thought to be hurtful to the economy. Thus, the whole point of antitrust policies has been to promote economic competition by restricting monopolistic practices. But other regulatory policies may actually be sought by the people being regulated. Thousands of farmers have wanted regulations imposed on the amounts of acreage they can cultivate because they feel that the only way to keep surpluses down and prices up is to impose regulation on themselves. Then other regulatory policies may seek to protect the consumer even if the regulation reduces competition, efficiency, or some other aspect of the private economy. Laws requiring companies to reduce air and water pollutants or laws keeping new drugs off the market can be extremely burdensome to the economy but are adopted on the theory that there are many dangers against which ordinary citizens are too limited in information or ability to defend themselves.

Levi, Margaret. *Of Rule and Revenue*. Berkeley and Los Angeles: University of California Press, 1988.

Lindblom, Charles. *Politics and Markets: The World's Political-Economic Systems*. New York: Basic Books, 1977.

Roberts, Paul C. *The Supply-Side Revolution*. Cambridge, MA: Harvard University Press, 1984.

Sanders, M. Elizabeth. *The Regulation of Natural Gas*. Phildadephia: Temple University Press, 1981.

Sawhill, Isabel. *Challenge to Leadership—Economic and Social Issues for the Next Decade*. Washington, DC: Urban Institute Press, 1988.

Stein, Herbert. *Governing the $5 Trillion Economy*. New York: Twentieth Century Fund, 1989.

Stone, Alan. *Wrong Number: The Breakup of AT&T*. New York: Basic Books, 1989.

Vogel, David. *Fluctuating Fortunes: The Political Power of Business in America*. New York: Basic Books, 1989.

17

Government and Society

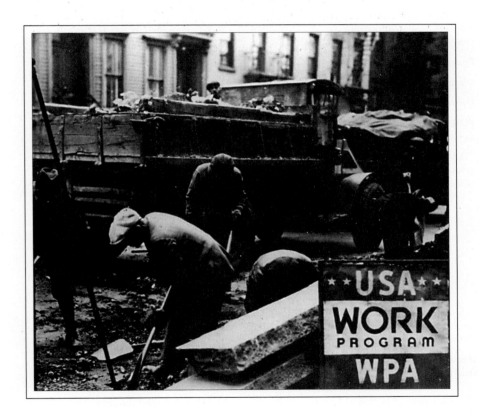

EVENTS	INSTITUTIONAL DEVELOPMENTS
Federalism and the new Constitution reserve most fundamental policies to the states (1787)	Land Ordinance of 1785 and Northwest Ordinance of 1787 provide public land for schools (1780s)
	U.S. Public Health Service created (1798)
Civil War (1861–1865)	Morrill Act establishes land grant colleges and universities (1862)
Industrial development; powerful railroads; large corporations (1860s–1890s)	Slavery abolished by the Thirteenth Amendment (1865)
Progressive era (1901–1917) **1900**	Pure Food and Drug Act and Meat Inspection Act to investigate and publicize abuses (1906)
World War I (1914–1919)	
Great Depression (1929–1933)	
FDR proposes New Deal legislation to Congress (1930s)	National Labor Relations (Wagner) Act guarantees right of labor to collective bargaining (1935); Social Security Act provides for unemployment and old-age insurance, as well as public welfare (1935); National Institutes of Health created (1937); Wagner-Steagall National Housing Act for public housing (1937); Food, Drug, and Cosmetic Act creates FDA (1938); Fair Labor Standards Act sets minimum wage, 40-hour week, and prohibits child labor under age 16 (1938)
FDR's overwhelming re-election gives mandate to the New Deal (1936)	
U.S. enters World War II; Armed forces provide first experiences with racial integration (1941–1945)	GI Bill of Rights for educational and vocational training (1944)
	National School Lunch Act (1946)
Postwar wave of strikes in key industries (1945–1946)	Housing Act provides for subsidized private housing (1949)
Sputnik launched by Soviet Union (1957) **1950**	National Defense Education Act (1958)
Civil Rights Movement (1950s and 1960s)	*Brown* v. *Board of Ed.*—Court rules against school segregation (1954)
Lyndon Johnson's War on Poverty (1964–1968)	Civil Rights Act establishes EEOC (1964); Food Stamp Act (1964); Elementary and Secondary Education Act (1965); Medicare and Medicaid established (1965)
"Confidence gap"; New Deal Coalition collapses; Richard Nixon elected (1968)	
	Voting Rights Act (1965)

TIME LINE ON GOVERNMENT AND SOCIETY

EVENTS		INSTITUTIONAL DEVELOPMENTS
Sustained Government growth plus administrative reorganization under Nixon (1968–1974)	**1970**	Civil Rights Act (1968)
		Indexing of welfare benefits (1972)
Watergate ends government growth (1974)		Equal Employment Opportunity Act provides that suits can be brought for patterns of employment discrimination (1972)
Energy crisis; rise of "stagflation" (1970s)		
		CETA for job training (1973)
		Supplemental Security Income (1974)
Ronald Reagan elected president; Republicans take control of Senate (1980)	**1980**	Reagan cuts health and housing programs (1981–1984); Congress restores some (1985–88)
Period of public reaction against social policies (1980s)		
Bush elected; continues in Reagan direction (1988)	**1990**	More civil rights, education, and welfare policies relegated to states (1990)
		Civil rights bill vetoed as a "quota bill," ultimately accepted (1992)
Clinton elected, promising new social agenda (1992)		Family Leave Act signed; health reform high on the agenda (1993)

*I*f there is one universally shared American ideal, it is the belief in ***equality of opportunity:*** freedom to use whatever talents and wealth we have to reach our fullest potential. This ideal is enshrined in the Declaration of Independence:

> We hold these truths to be self-evident, that all men are created equal, that they are endowed by their Creator with certain unalienable rights, that among these are Life, Liberty, and the Pursuit of Happiness.

What Thomas Jefferson, the Declaration's author, meant is that all individuals have the right to pursue happiness, in fact, an *equal* right to pursue happiness—or as we put it today, an equal opportunity.

But however much we may admire it, the ideal of equal opportunity raises questions and poses problems. First, and most important, equality of opportunity inevitably means *in*equality of results or outcomes. One of the reasons for this is obviously inequalities in talent. In the real world, talent is not the only differentiating factor. Another explanation is past inequality—the inequality of past generations visited upon the present one. This is generally called social class, or the class system. Inequality may result from poverty; lacking money for food may lead to inadequate nutrition, which may in turn explain reduced talent and reduced energies to compete. Educational opportunities also are limited by past inequalities. Since the quality of one's education and the status of one's school contribute to success, inadequate education is a tremendous disadvantage when looking for a job or a promotion. Also the etiquette of the work situation, which may appear to be trivial, is essential for entry into competitive opportunities. This etiquette ranges from the elemental ability to deal with others—to get to work on time, to follow the rules—all the way to esoteric rules that are drawn into the workplace from the more exclusive schools and clubs. There are many stories of individuals with superior talents who are denied opportunities because they are "greenhorns" and unaware of the more superficial rules of the game. All of these factors make up social class, and social class shapes opportunity and success, regardless of talent.

Finally, there is prejudice pure and simple. This includes racial and religious bias, ethnocentrism, and traditionalist attitudes toward the place of women. Some of these prejudices are caused by the class system, because social class separates people, and their ignorance of each other breeds anxiety and stereotyping.

As observed in Chapter 16, there is a great divide in America between rich and poor. However, one must be careful when making this statement. In the first place, overall economic growth has been so great during the twentieth century that the share received by the lowest income brackets is a much larger aggregate amount even if their percentage of the total has not improved. Second, many of the individuals who occupy the lowest brackets don't remain there for long. As libertarian writer George Gilder puts it,

> Statistical distributions . . . can misrepresent the economy. . . . This distribution appears permanent, and indeed, like [a] building, it will remain much the same year after year. But . . . people at the bottom will move up: Six decades [after three and one-half million Jewish immigrants arrived] the mean family income of Jews was almost double the national average. Meanwhile the once supreme British Protestants (WASPs) were passed in per capita earnings . . . not only by Jews and Orientals but also by Irish, Italians, Germans, and Poles . . . and the latest generation of black West Indians.[1]

But Gilder concedes that "a free society in which the distributions are widely seen as unfair cannot long survive."[2] And here's the rub. Although it is true that the composition of the lowest bracket is quite fluid in the United States, with a lot of people entering at the bottom and escaping after short periods, it is also true that the people in the bottom brackets are disproportionately composed of members of groups who have been deprived of opportunities to pursue their interests and their happiness.

---

[1]George Gilder, *Wealth and Poverty* (New York: Basic Books, 1981; Bantam Edition, 1982), pp. 11–12.
[2]Ibid., p. 11.

Andrew Carnegie
Wealth with a Social
Conscience

Andrew Carnegie (1835–1919)

Andrew Carnegie's life was inextricably enmeshed in the great industrial boom of the late nineteenth century. As a child in Scotland, Carnegie experienced first-hand the consequences of industrialization, vividly recalling later in life the night his father, a weaver, came home and announced mournfully to the family that he could no longer find work. His handloom weaving, performed at home, was no longer competitive with factory-produced linen. In 1848, the family immigrated to America.

Andrew Carnegie's rise to success was a classic example of the self-made man. He worked first as a bobbin boy in a factory before he landed a job in Pittsburgh as a telegraph message boy at the age of fourteen, earning the extravagant sum of $2.50 per week. Carnegie proved adept at telegraph operation and was soon the personal telegrapher for a rising executive of the Pennsylvania Railroad. Eventually, with the help of his boss, he rose in the company and succeeded him as a company superintendent. After the Civil War, Carnegie left the railroad and turned his attention to iron production, having recognized the potential for an American steel industry. Drawing on his considerable organizational and interpersonal skills—Carnegie was always a man of vast personal charms—he surrounded himself with the finest business people of the time. By concentrating on production rather than on stock-market manipulation, he built a steel empire that by 1900 was producing a quarter of the nation's steel, and controlled iron mines, coke ovens, shipping, and railroads. Unlike his competitors, Carnegie reinvested and built during economic hard times, when costs were lower, which put him ahead of the competition when good times returned.

Carnegie's business philosophy was ahead of its time. He encouraged employees to invest in the corporation, and actively developed talent from within the company. An avowed capitalist, Carnegie also recognized the evils of capitalism and proclaimed in a series of articles that the millionaire who grew wealthy from industry owed his fortune to the workers, and was thus obligated to return the money by using it for the public good. True to his philosophy, Carnegie donated millions to libraries, schools, churches, and a variety of institutions that still bear his name, from Carnegie Hall, to the Carnegie-Mellon Institute, to the Carnegie Institute for International Peace.

Yet Carnegie's enlightened approach to industrialism was marred by his ruthless suppression of labor unrest and union activities. The most famous of these incidents was the Homestead Strike of 1892, when Carnegie workers protesting a pay cut were violently suppressed by hired Pinkerton guards. Despite his stated preference for surrendering wealth for public purposes, when he died in 1919, he was one of the world's wealthiest men.

Source: Joseph F. Hall, *Andrew Carnegie* (New York: Oxford University Press, 1970).

For example, although many African Americans improved their economic situations in the past decades, *as a group* they remained economically deprived. Consequently, in 1991, 12.6 percent of all African American families earned less than $5,000 per year, compared to only 3.7 percent of all white families. Sadly, this has deteriorated even since 1970, when 9.9 percent of black families and 3.2 percent of white families occupied that lowly estate.[3] These inequalities of distribution apply not only to blacks but also to women and Hispanic Americans. For example, in 1991, the income of African American families was only 57 percent of the income of white families. The income of Hispanic American families was about 63 percent of that of white families. And families headed by a single female earned income of less than 59 percent of those headed by a single male.[4]

Even for members of minority groups who are "making it," the inequalities seem to plague them in occupations all the way up the ladder. For example, African American males in professional and technical jobs earned income on average nearly 30 percent less than whites in comparable jobs. African Americans in managerial, administrative, and sales positions earned only 65 percent of the incomes of white males in those same positions; and African Americans in skilled trades earned about 70 percent of what whites earned. The same kinds of inequality between males and females produced the cry of the feminist movement during the 1970s, "equal pay for equal work."

Let us now return to Thomas Jefferson and the Declaration of Independence. The main point of the passage from the Declaration quoted above was that individuals (men *and* women) have the right, the unalienable right, not to happiness itself, but at least to the *pursuit* of happiness. Now let's add the sentence immediately after that passage: "That to secure these rights, Governments are instituted among Men. . . ." There never seemed to be any doubt about the two points, first, that all Americans shared these rights equally, and second, that some government involvement would be necessary to reduce the barriers to the exercise of these rights.

There is no way to know precisely when the government ought to be called upon and what the government has to do to help individuals secure the right to pursue their own happiness by equalizing opportunities. This chapter is written on the assumption that *some* government involvement "to secure these rights" is inevitable, necessary, and constitutional. But this in no way implies that any *particular* policy is *inevitable* or that the government has made or will make the right policy choices. We recognize only that, in trying "to secure these rights," public policy will have to be directed at: (1) providing a floor or, as President Reagan had put it, a "safety net," for those who have, for whatever reason, found no place in the economy; and (2) finding ways of influencing the conduct, the rules, and the values in society that determine who shall be poor.

This neatly divides the chapter into two sections. The first section deals with *poverty*, the objective condition of having less of almost everything, and it deals with *dependency*, the objective condition of being unable to provide adequately for one's own survival. The second section deals with *inequality*, which is defined as

[3]Bureau of the Census, *Current Population Reports*, Series P-60, no. 180 (Washington, DC: Government Printing Office, 1992), Table 9.

[4]Ibid., Table 13.

the result of rules and practices in society that are so biased against certain groups

as to doom a higher proportion of the people in those groups to less of everything.

In brief, the first section deals with "who *is* poor?" Most of the public policies are called welfare policies, or cumulatively "the welfare state." The second section deals with "who shall be poor" and with policies oriented toward changing the social rules regarding the composition of that group. Most of these policies are civil rights policies.

THE WELFARE STATE

Americans have traditionally conceived of those living in poverty as two distinct classes, the "deserving poor" and the "undeserving poor." The deserving poor were the widows and orphans and others rendered dependent by some misfortune such as national disaster or injury in the course of honest labor. The undeserving poor were able-bodied persons unwilling to work, transients from their communities, or others of whom, for various reasons, the community did not approve. An extensive system of voluntary, private philanthropy developed during the nineteenth century on the basis of this tradition. Churches and related religious groups, ethnic and fraternal societies, communities and neighborhoods all gave money, goods, and services in one form or another. This was charity, and although most of it was private and voluntary, it was also thought of as a public obligation.

Government involvement in charity was very slight until the end of the nineteenth century, not only because of our preference for private and voluntary approaches, but also because there was confidence that all of the deserving poor could be taken care of by private efforts alone. Even as late as 1928, only 11.6 percent of all relief granted in fifteen of the largest cities came from public funds.[5]

This traditional approach crumbled in 1929 before the stark reality of the Depression. Some misfortune befell nearly everyone. Around 20 percent of the work force became unemployed, and few of these individuals had any monetary resources or the old family farm to fall back upon. Banks failed, wiping out the savings of millions who had been prudent enough or fortunate enough to have any. Thousands of businesses failed, throwing middle-class Americans onto the bread lines alongside unemployed laborers and dispossessed farmers. The Great Depression had finally proven to Americans that poverty could be a result of imperfections in the economic system rather than a result of individual irresponsibility. Americans held to their distinction between the deserving and the undeserving poor but significantly altered their standards regarding who was deserving and who was not.

Once poverty and dependency were accepted as problems inherent in the economy, a large-scale public policy approach became practical. Indeed, there was no longer any real question about whether the national government would assume a major responsibility for poverty; from that time forward, it was a question of how

[5]Merle Fainsod et al., *Government and the American Economy* (New York: W. W. Norton, 1959), p. 769, based on a WPA study by Ann E. Geddes.

TABLE 17.1
Growth of the Welfare State

	Welfare	Education	Health and Housing
State Era (1789–1935)	Private and local charity State child labor laws State unemployment and injury compensation State mothers' pensions	Northwest Ordinance of 1787 Local academies Local public schools State compulsory education laws Federal Morrill Act of 1862 for land grant colleges	Local public health ordinances
Federal Era (1935–Present)	Federal Social Security System Disability Insurance VISTA Supplemental Security Income Cost of Living Adjustment (indexing)	GI Bill National Defense Act of 1958 Elementary and Secondary Education Act of 1965 School desegregation Head Start	Public housing Hospital construction School lunch program Food stamps Medicare Medicaid

generous or restrictive the government was going to be about the welfare of the poor (see Table 17.1). The national government's efforts to improve the welfare of the poor can be divided into two responses. First, it instituted policies that attempted to change the economic rules about the condition of work for those who were working and could work. Second, it set in place policies seeking to change the economic rules determining the quality of life of those who could not (and in some cases, would not) work. The first response comes under the heading of policies for labor regulation. We dealt with some of these policies in Chapter 3, showing how the Constitution itself, especially the commerce clause, had to be interpreted in a fundamentally different way in order to reach into local plants and firms to improve the conditions and rewards of work. Since the adoption of the 1935 National Labor Relations (Wagner) Act, there have been revisions (e.g., the Taft-Hartley Act of 1947 and the Landrum-Griffin Labor Management Act of 1959), but no real change of the economic rules established in 1935. These rules were to protect laborers so that they could organize and bargain collectively with their employers rather than (according to the older economic rules) negotiating as individuals under vastly unequal conditions.

It is possible for public policies to go much further than the rules laid out under the Wagner Act, however. For example, rather than a minimum wage law, there could be a minimum annual income law. There could be laws giving workers virtual life tenure in their jobs, as enjoyed by many Japanese and European workers.

The right to sixty days notice before closing a plant, once thought radical, was adopted by Congress in August 1988. The next step could be worker participation in management decisions about closings or hiring and promotion and even owner- ship and investment.

The second response to welfare is the one that will most concern us in this section. These policies seek to change the economic rules regarding those who cannot work or who are, for whatever reason, outside the economic system. These policies make up the welfare state.

Foundations of the Welfare State

The foundations of the American welfare state were established by the Social Security Act of 1935. The 1935 act provided for two separate categories of welfare—*contributory* and *noncontributory*. Table 17.2 is an outline of the key programs in each of these categories.

Contributory Programs   Contributory programs are financed by taxation, which justifiably can be called "forced savings." These contributory programs are what most people have in mind when they refer to Social Security or social insurance. Under the original contributory program, old-age insurance, the employer and the employee were each required to pay equal amounts, which in 1937, were set at 1 percent of the first $3,000 of wages, to be deducted from the paycheck of each employee and matched by the same amount from the employer. This percentage increased over the years, so that the total contribution is now 7.65 percent but subdivided as follows: 6.20 percent on the first $55,500 for the Social Security benefits and an additional 1.45 percent on the first $130,200 for Medicare.[6]

Social Security is a rather conservative approach to welfare. In effect, the Social Security (FICA) tax, as a forced saving, sends a message that people cannot be trusted to save voluntarily in order to take care of their own needs. But in another sense, it is quite radical. Social Security is not real insurance; workers' contributions do not accumulate in a personal account like an annuity. Consequently, contributors do not receive benefits in proportion to their own contributions, and this means that there is a redistribution of wealth occurring. In brief, contributory Social Security mildly redistributes wealth from higher to lower income people, and it quite significantly redistributes wealth from younger workers to older retirees.

Noncontributory Programs: "Public Assistance"   Noncontributory programs are also known as public assistance programs. Historically, the two most important ones are aid to the aged, blind, and disabled—now grouped together as Supplemental Security Income (SSI)—and Aid to Families with Dependent Children (AFDC). Both programs are "means tested," requiring the applicant to show some definite need for assistance and an inability to provide for it. But both are "federal"

---

[6]Although on paper the employer is taxed, this is all part of "forced savings," because in reality the employer's contribution is nothing more than a mandatory wage or salary increase that the employee never sees or touches before it goes into the trust funds held exclusively for the contributory programs.

TABLE 17.2
Public Welfare Programs

Type of Program	Statutory Basis	Year Enacted	Number of Recipients in 1992 (in Millions)	Federal Outlays in 1992 (in Billions of Dollars)
Contributory (Insurance) System				
Old Age, Survivors and Disability Insurance	Social Security Act (SSA), Title II	1935	39.8	$280.6
Medicare	SSA Title XVIII	1965	34.2	$118.6
Unemployment Compensation	SSA Title III	1935	8.6	$36.7
Noncontributory (Public Assistance) Program				
Medicaid	SSA Title XIX	1965	25.3	$72.5
Food Stamps	Food Stamp Act	1964	21.5	$22.7
Aid to Families with Dependent Children	SSA Title IV	1935	11.5	$14.5
Supplemental Security Income (cash assistance for aged, blind, disabled)	SSA Title XVI	1974	5.0	$19.8
Housing Assistance to low-income families	National Housing Act	1937	2.5	$19.4
School Lunch Program	National School Lunch Act	1946	24.0	$6.3
Training and employment program	Job Training Partnership Act	1982	1.2	$5.8

Source: Office of Management and Budget, *Supplement to the Budget Of the United States Government, Fiscal Year 1993* (Washington, DC: Government Printing Office, 1993), pp. 107, 161–62; Bureau of the Census, *Statistical Abstract of the United States, 1992*, 112th ed. (Washington, DC: Government Printing Office, 1992), pp. 318–19, 356.

rather than national; grants-in-aid are provided by the national government to the states as incentives to establish the programs. Thus, from the beginning there could and would be considerable disparity in benefits from state to state. In 1974, Title XVI of the Social Security Act nationalized the first set of public assistance programs when it created SSI, providing uniform minimum benefits across the entire nation and including mandatory cost-of-living increases. States are allowed to be more generous if they wish, but no state is permitted to provide benefits below the

subsistence level provided by law. AFDC, on the other hand, continues to be operated by the states and, as a result, there continue to be substantial disparities among THE WELFARE
the states. For example, although the median "standard of need" for a family of STATE
three was $428 per month (55 percent of the poverty line), the AFDC benefits in
1990 ranged from $114 per month in Alabama to $647 in Alaska.[7]

During the 1970s, Medicaid and food stamps became the largest noncontributory welfare programs. Since eligibility for both of these is tied closely to AFDC,
however, all three must be evaluated more or less simultaneously. Table 17.2 identifies all the major welfare programs, together with the dates they were enacted,
and it provides some important data on the financing of each. This table also identifies still another important feature of the welfare state—the distinction between
benefits in the form of cash payments and benefits "in kind," such as food stamps
and medical services for the elderly and the poor. These in-kind benefits significantly increase the security of the poor. The cash income figures offered earlier in
this chapter and in Table 16.5 (see page 677) understate the real redistribution of
wealth in America in that they do not take into account in-kind benefits.

Welfare Today

Over the years, coverage has expanded and benefits have been increased in both
contributory and noncontributory programs and through cash and in-kind benefits. Congress increased Social Security benefits every two or three years during
the 1950s and 1960s. The biggest single expansion in contributory programs since
1935 was the establishment in 1965 of Medicare, which provides substantial medical services to elderly persons who are already eligible to receive old-age, survivors, and disability insurance under the original Social Security system. In 1972,
Congress decided to end the grind of biennial legislation by establishing "indexing," whereby benefits paid out under contributory programs would be tied to the
Cost of Living Index (COLA, also called the Consumer Price Index), so that benefits would increase automatically as the cost of living rose. But, of course, Social
Security taxes (contributions) also increased after almost every benefit increase.
This made Social Security, in the words of one observer, "a politically ideal program. It bridged partisan conflict by providing liberal benefits under conservative
financial auspices."[8] In other words, conservatives could more readily yield to the
demands of the well-organized and expanding constituency of elderly voters if
benefit increases were automatic; liberals could cement conservative support by
agreeing to finance the expanded benefits by increases in the regressive Social Security tax rather than out of the general revenues coming from the more progressive income tax.

The noncontributory public assistance categories also made their most significant advances during the 1960s. The largest single category of expansion was the

[7]Clarke E. Cochran, et al., *American Public Policy—An Introduction*, 2nd ed. (New York: St. Martin's
Press, 1993), pp. 222–23.

[8]Edward J. Harpham, "Fiscal Crisis and the Politics of Social Security Reform," in *The Attack on the
Welfare State,* ed. Anthony Champagne and Edward Harpham (Prospects Heights, IL: Waveland Press,
1984), p. 13.

Perhaps one of the nation's deepest wounds is the plight of the homeless population. Estimates of the numbers of homeless people nationwide vary from 300,000 to 3 million. The reasons why the numbers have grown so large range from the deinstitutionalization of mentally ill patients during the 1970s, to Reagan administration cuts of up to 75 percent in federal housing assistance, to the 1980s real estate boom during which developers eliminated more than half of all the nation's single-room-occupancy hotels in which many now-homeless people previously lived. To many city dwellers, the problem of homelessness is so large that it seems unsolvable. Imagine how many people daily rush past ironic images such as this man sleeping in a subway near the White House.

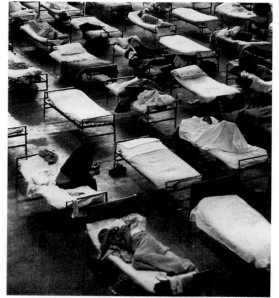

Photo Credit: Dith Pran/NY Times

In the country's major cities, such as New York, Chicago, and Los Angeles, the only shelter for some are the city-run shelters, with rows and rows of cots in large warehouse-like rooms. These shelters are noisy and violent and give no privacy.

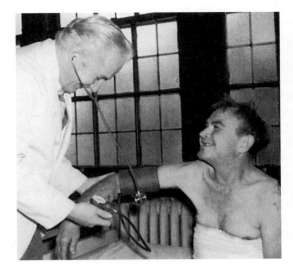

But most large cities do try to provide basic services for the homeless. Medical care is available in all the shelters, as well as showers, clean clothing, mental health referrals, and social services.

An increasing number of the homeless are families with a working parent who cannot find safe and affordable housing. Some private groups coordinate help for the homeless. The Red Cross has set up day-care centers to encourage homeless children to learn skills and to give them a warm environment, while also giving the children's parents a chance to work. But good, safe day care is not available for many of the poor, and funds are lacking for its growth.

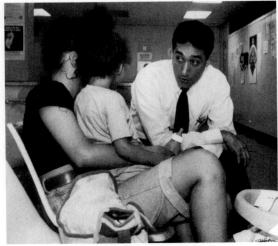

Henry G. Cisneros, Clinton's Secretary of Housing and Urban Development, immediately took an active interest in the problem of low-income housing. He has proposed a program that would place more people in permanent housing and provide more services to those with mental illnesses or drug addictions. Shortly after becoming secretary, he visited an interim housing program in New York where families lived while waiting for more permanent housing.

establishment in 1965 of Medicaid, which extended medical services to all low-income persons who had already established eligibility through "means testing" under AFDC. President Lyndon Johnson's War on Poverty was a commitment to expand virtually all of the other noncontributory, public assistance programs and also to establish a mechanism through the famous "Community Action Programs" (CAPs) in each city to bring the cash and in-kind benefits more directly and efficiently to the neighborhoods where they were most needed. These Community Action Programs also were good advertising for the other public assistance programs, encouraging more and more indigent persons to seek eligibility. We will return to these programs later in this chapter.

The expansion of all types of benefits and the expansion of the number of persons eligible to receive them added tremendously to the costs of noncontributory welfare programs. Meanwhile, important demographic changes were adding costs to the contributory programs and at the same time were reducing the amount of revenue raised by Social Security taxes. The most important demographic change

PROCESS BOX 17.1
The Web of Benefits and Controls for a Welfare Mother

was an increase in the number of elderly Americans relative to the number of individuals in the work force. Between the 1950s and the 1980s, the ratio between the two dropped from a high of eighteen workers for every one retired eligible beneficiary to four workers for every retired eligible beneficiary.[9] This obviously added greatly to the gap between welfare contributions and welfare obligations.

The period of expansion of Social Security and public assistance came to a sudden end in 1973, when the Board of Trustees of the Social Security Trust Fund published in their annual report a projection of an enormous deficit between contributions and benefits in the near future. This quickly was defined as a "fiscal crisis," with projections of insolvency by the end of the century. Both Presidents Ford and Carter sought long-term solutions, and in 1977, Congress adopted a series of increases extending over thirteen years, the final one taking effect January 1, 1990. Thus, during the 1980s, instead of a deficit, the Social Security Trust Fund began producing surpluses. In 1989, the Social Security surplus—contributions received in excess of benefits paid out—reached over $50 billion. The annual surplus was projected to go up to $200 billion by the year 2002—an accumulation of $4 billion "a week" in surpluses. Around the year 2020 the ratio of retirees to workers will require a drawing down of the surpluses. But by then, there will only be IOU's and not cash in the trust fund, because to avoid raising taxes, the Reagan and Bush administrations borrowed from the Social Security Trust Fund by selling it U.S. bonds—essentially IOUs. This could compromise the Social Security system in the future by producing high inflation, which, because of their fixed incomes, hurts the elderly most of all.

The Republicans came into power in the 1980s with welfare reform very high on the agenda of the planned "Reagan Revolution." They proceeded immediately, and with the cooperation of the Democrats, to cut the "rate of increase" of Old-Age Survivors Disability Insurance (OASDI) and Medicare. These are known as entitlement programs, because benefits can be terminated only by legislative action or by a due process judicial decision. The Reagan administration also succeeded in cutting the rate of increase of the public assistance, "need-based" programs. However, what is significant is how little was cut in either type of program and how quickly the welfare state once again began expanding (see Figure 17.1). After 1984, expenditures for public assistance programs again began to increase at a rate about equal to the rate of the general economic growth (the GNP). Moreover, no public assistance programs were terminated, despite Republican railings against them. Having discovered how extremely popular Social Security was in the United States, Reagan felt it necessary to make frequent public promises not to alter what he himself called "the safety net." Since President Bush was never so adamantly opposed to the principle of welfare, he included defense of the safety net in his promise of a "kinder, gentler society."

President Clinton was elected on a platform of "putting people first," but deficit realities significantly revised the meaning of his promise. His most positive proposal was for an increase in 1994 in the Earned Income Tax Credit (EITC) by

---

[9]From *Social Security Bulletins*, quoted in Gary Freeman and Paul Adams, "The Politics of Social Security," in *The Political Economy of Public Policy*, ed. Alan Stone and Edward Harpham (Beverly Hills, CA: Sage, 1982), p. 245.

FIGURE 17.1

Social Welfare Expenditures under Public Programs (1970–1989)

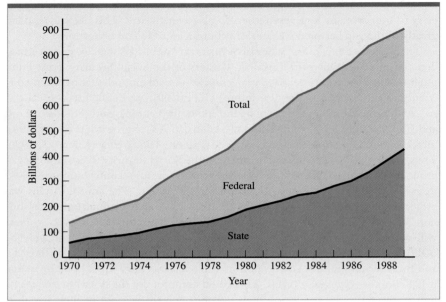

Source: Bureau of the Census, *Statistical Abstract of the United States, 1992*, 112th ed. (Washington, DC: Government Printing Office, 1992), p. 354.

which working households with children can file through their income tax returns for an income supplement if their annual earned incomes were below $20,000. But it was almost certain to fail because it involved too much revenue loss during a period of deficit reduction. Clinton's 1993–1994 agenda for Congress also included reductions in Social Security retirement benefits—raising taxes on benefits received and freezing or capping cost of living (COLA) increases. Even more conservatively, President Clinton also favored strengthening the enforcement of child-support laws and tying welfare benefits closer to work, or "workfare," requirements. This was all part of his effort to call on all classes of Americans to share the burden of deficit reduction while at the same time trying to confirm as strongly as possible the proposition that the welfare state is here to stay.

The Welfare State Evaluated

One great advantage to a large welfare system was identified in the previous chapter: it is good fiscal policy. When the economy is declining, welfare payments go up enough to help maintain consumer demand. In contrast, during inflationary periods, welfare taxes take an extra bite out of consumer dollars, thereby dampening inflation somewhat.

A second major point in favor of the American welfare system is that it meets the needs of capitalism. No one except the most extreme ideologue would claim that capitalism is perfect. The purpose of the welfare state is to identify the imperfections of capitalism and to cope with them.

Another point in favor of the welfare system is "forced saving" itself. Although it may seem harsh and paternalistic for a democracy, the requirement of a contribution serves to remind people that they must provide for themselves; and having done so, they can retain a sense of dignity when it comes their turn to collect.

A positive side of the noncontributory programs is the recognition that most recipients of this aid are dependent through no fault of their own. There are undoubtedly chiselers and abusers; but most of those on public assistance are young, white, and female, with dependent children. And many of them actually work, but at jobs that pay below subsistence wages.[10] Another positive feature is, of course, political. It would be risky for any country, especially a democracy, to permit hundreds of thousands of people to be cast adrift without a stake in the society or the political system.[11]

The most serious criticism of the contributory programs is that they do not reach the most needy—those who are unable to work long enough to qualify. The contributory system also discriminates heavily against low- and moderate-income retired people by setting severe limits on the amount of money they can earn over and above their welfare benefits.

Other criticism is aimed at the noncontributory programs, AFDC in particular. Critics on both the Left and the Right have argued that these programs can actually contribute to the very dependency they are seeking to eliminate. On the Right, the argument is that noncontributory programs discourage many capable people from taking low-paying jobs. This makes them lazy, and the jobs then go unfilled or to illegal aliens at still lower pay. Critics on the Left argue that AFDC, in particular, encourages dependency and broken homes by refusing aid to households if a breadwinner is present. It may encourage spouses to live apart, and parents may avoid marriage for fear of losing their eligibility.[12]

Most of these criticisms of the welfare system could be met by modest reforms. But there is one final problem that is inherent in any welfare system and is immune to reform: If welfare support is too generous, many able-bodied people will prefer welfare to work. If, on the other hand, welfare support is too skimpy, many genuinely dependent people will suffer, and some may die. Thus, there is no easy solution to the problem of support and work. Efforts to balance the two sides of this complex equation will always keep welfare on the policy agenda.

---

[10]John Schwarz and Thomas Volgy have carefully documented their findings that, at the beginning of the 1990s, 7.4 percent of all *fully employed* workers lived beneath the level of economic self-sufficiency. They also reported that 10.2 percent of white female heads of households and 21.8 percent of black female heads of households were in the same situation. Even with education through high school, 13.1 percent of the white women and 25.7 percent of the black women who headed their households, *fully employed*, lived beneath economic self-sufficiency. Thus, merely "getting a job" is not necessarily the appropriate answer. John E. Schwarz and Thomas J. Volgy, *The Forgotten Americans: Thirty Million Working Poor in the Land of Opportunity.* (New York: W. W. Norton, 1992), pp. 68–80.

[11]Frances Fox Piven and Richard Cloward, *The New Class War* (New York: Random House, 1982).

[12]From the Right, the most recent serious academic study is Lawrence M. Mead, *The New Policies of Poverty: The Nonworking Poor in America* (New York: Basic Books, 1992). From the Left, the best in our opinion is Schwarz and Volgy, *The Forgotten Americans.*

The War on Poverty:
Success or Failure?

*I*n the early 1960s, the federal government began a dramatic escalation in the scope and quantity of assistance it extended to the country's poor. President Lyndon Johnson led the charge against poverty in what he dubbed the War on Poverty. By the 1980s, federal leaders cut back on social welfare spending, arguing that such programs were harmful and too expensive.

At the root of this dispute is the question of whether the War on Poverty, and the programs it generated (most of which still exist in some form), were worth the expense. Social policy specialist Robert Rector argues that these efforts were misdirected and a failure, because they perpetuated rather than improved the conditions of poverty. Political scientist John E. Schwarz argues that the War on Poverty did succeed, in that it dramatically improved the lives of millions of Americans.

Rector

The War on Poverty has failed. Twenty-five years after the riots under Lyndon Johnson led to a massive expansion of urban welfare programs, the riots in Los Angeles [in 1992] show that the problems of the inner city have not been solved and have actually gotten worse.

This failure is not due to a lack of spending. In 1990 federal, state, and local governments spent $215 billion on assistance programs for low-income persons and communities. This figure includes only spending on programs for the poor and excludes middle-class entitlements such as Social Security and Medicare. Adjusting for inflation, total welfare spending in 1990 was five times the level of welfare spending in the mid-1960s when the War on Poverty began. Total welfare spending in the War on Poverty since its inception in 1964 has been $3.5 trillion (in constant 1990 dollars); an amount that exceeds the entire cost of World War II after adjusting for inflation.

The problem with the welfare state is not the level of spending, it is that nearly all of this expenditure actively promotes self-destructive behavior among the poor. Current welfare may best be conceptualized as a system that offers each single mother a "paycheck" . . . as long as she fulfills two conditions: 1) she does not work; and 2) she does not marry an employed male. . . .

. . . For over 40 years the welfare system has been paying for non-work and single parenthood and has obtained dramatic increases in both. But welfare that discourages work and penalizes marriage ultimately harms its intended beneficiaries.[1]

Schwarz

If we are to understand our present position, we must resolve the myriad misgivings. . . about the domestic programs of government, programs that played a major part in the nation's life. After 1960, government action expanded very rapidly on a variety of domestic fronts. Two crucial priorities of these years were the alleviation of poverty and the control of environmental pollution. In the attempt to meet these objectives, a multiplicity of programs arose or were

vastly expanded almost overnight, programs that demanded the largest increases of the post-Eisenhower era in the spending of tax money and the use
of governmental regulatory power. . . .

. . . The government's programs to attack poverty, though at times seriously
flawed, frequently were effective. They reduced poverty by more than half.
They alleviated some of the grimmest conditions attendant to poverty, and
they did so across the whole range of human needs pertaining to serious mal-
nutrition, inadequate medical care, and overcrowded housing. In providing
job training, they raised the economic fortunes of thousands of Americans. In
providing early education to low-income children, they increased the potential of a great number of these children for success in both school and later
employment. . . .

. . . The attack on poverty did assure that the benefits brought by the nation's
rapidly expanding economy would be shared by both the stronger and the
weaker groups. In 1980, one in fifteen Americans faced the desperation of
poverty, compared with about one in five Americans just a generation earlier.
This was accomplished, almost entirely, by the government. . . . Even the
most powerful alternative to the government's programs. . . would have been
unable to reduce poverty effectively unless accorded a level of funding from
the public treasury much the same as that which the government's programs
had involved.[2]

[1]Robert Rector, "Requiem for the War on Poverty: Rethinking Welfare after the L.A.
Riots," *Policy Review*, no. 61 (Summer 1992), pp. 40–46.
[2]John E. Schwarz, *America's Hidden Success: A Reassessment of Public Policy from Kennedy
to Reagan* (New York: W. W. Norton, 1988), pp. 19, 49–51.

Breaking Out of the Circle of Poverty

Poverty is a circle, a vicious circle. Many individuals break out of it, but they have
to overcome heavy odds. Although many policies may aim at breaking the circle
and others have a beneficial effect on the redistribution of opportunities, two types
of policies stand out as most effective: education policies and health policies.

Education Policies   Those who understand American federalism from Chapter 3
already are aware that most of the education of the American people is provided by
the public policies of state and local governments. What may be less appreciated is
the fact that these education policies—especially the policy of universal compulsory public education—are the most important single force in the distribution and
redistribution of opportunity in America.

Compared to state and local efforts, the role of *national* education policy pales in
comparison. With but three exceptions, the national government did not involve
itself at all in education for the first century of its existence as an independent re-

public. The first two of these exceptions were actually prior to the Constitution—the Land Ordinance of 1785 followed by the Northwest Ordinance of 1787. These provided for a survey of all the public lands in the Northwest Territory and required that four sections of the thirty-six sections in each township be reserved for public schools and their maintenance. It was not until 1862, with adoption of the Morrill Act, that Congress took a third step, establishing the land-grant colleges and universities. Later in the nineteenth century, more federal programs were created for the education of farmers and other rural residents. But the most important national education policies have come only since World War II: the GI Bill of Rights of 1944, the National Defense Education Act (NDEA) of 1958, the Elementary and Secondary Education Act of 1965 (ESEA), and various youth and adult vocational training acts since 1958. Note, however, that since the GI Bill was aimed almost entirely at post-secondary schooling, the national government did not really enter the field of elementary education until after 1957.[13]

What finally brought the national government into elementary education was embarrassment over the fact that the Soviets had beaten us into space with the launching of Sputnik. The national policy under NDEA was aimed specifically at improving education in science and mathematics. General federal aid for education did not come until ESEA in 1965, which allocated funds to school districts with substantial numbers of children from families who were unemployed or earning less than $2,000 a year. By the early 1970s, federal expenditures for elementary and secondary education were running over $4 billion per year, and rising, to its peak in 1980 at $4.8 billion.[14] Cuts by the Reagan administration of over 10 percent were substantial but not anywhere near the administration's goals. President Bush vowed, time after time, to be the "education president," and the Democratic majority in Congress was more than ready to help him. In truth, however, all of Bush's plans for improving elementary and secondary education depended on private financing or on state and local governments.

President Clinton's education program had a more national and public orientation, as might be expected of a Democratic president. It included more federal aid for preschool programs for needy children, national education standards coupled with teachers' incentives, and, at the post-secondary level, scholarship set-asides for minorities and an ambitious national service program available to all students to earn credit toward college tuition. However, a large part of President Clinton's public commitment to education rested with his programs for education outside the school system and outside the Department of Education, falling instead within the jurisdiction of the Labor Department. This emphasis, of course, is on an education directly attached to the job market. It reaches back to a program that was popular for a while in the 1970s, the Comprehensive Employment Training Program (CETA), which reached a peak budget of $10 billion in 1978. CETA, one of

---

[13]There were a couple of minor precedents. One was the Smith-Hughes Act of 1917, which made federal funds available to the states for vocational education at the elementary and secondary levels. Second, the Lanham Act of 1940 made federal funds available to schools in "federally impacted areas," that is, areas with an unusually large number of government employees and/or where the local tax base was reduced by large amounts of government-owned property.

[14]Office of Management and Budget, *Budget of the United States Government, Fiscal Year 1982* (Washington, DC: Government Printing Office, 1981), p. 427.

BOX 17.1
Like Taking Money from a Baby

The fates of Head Start and Social Security [in the 1991 budget] tell a story of a nation that treats its two most vulnerable populations—the young and the old—in wildly divergent ways.

A child in the United States is nearly twice as likely to be poor as a senior citizen—in large part because the federal government spends more than $4 on the elderly for every $1 it spends on children, studies show. This is novel in the nation's history and unique in the world: no other country has so large an age bias to its poverty rates nor so wild an age tilt in its allocation of resources.

"What we have done in this country in the past few decades is to socialize the cost of growing old and to privatize the cost of childhood," says Sylvia Hewlett, an economist. . . .

Here are some ways to measure the declining public investment in children:

—Eighty-two percent of the elderly who would be poor . . . are lifted out of poverty through government tax and transfer programs . . . only 32 percent of children who would be poor without government's help are lifted out of poverty because of it. . . .

—From 1978 to 1987, federal expenditures (adjusted for inflation) targeted on the elderly grew by 52 percent while expenditures targeted on children fell by 4 percent. . . .

—From 1965 to 1986 the share of all social welfare spending (including primary and secondary education, welfare, health programs, food stamps, Social Security, medicare, and medicaid) by all levels of government—federal, state, and local—targeted specifically at children declined from 37 percent to 24 percent, while the share allocated specifically to the elderly rose from 21 to 33 percent. . . .

Sixty-seven countries, including every industrialized society in the world except the United States, have some form of universal children's allowances. . . . These allowances are generally tax free and not means-tested. . . .

More than 100 countries also provide additional cash benefits to parents at the time of childbirth, with some nations providing a portion of the income lost from a parent's displacement from the labor force for six months or more after childbirth. A French married mother of three, for example, can stay at home until her youngest is three years old and receive the equivalent of minimum wage. (President Bush last year [1990] vetoed a family-leave bill that would have assured 12 weeks of unpaid leave at the time of child bearing.)* . . .

The nation's most successful anti-poverty program is not a children's program . . . it's Social Security. The political genius of that program has been that, even though it redistributes income from rich to poor and from workers to retirees, it also contains an element of the contribution-earned benefits plan. Thus, it avoids the stigma of welfare.

"We tend to see the elderly as deserving and children—or at least the parents of children—as undeserving," says Hewlett. . . . "And it doesn't help that more children and adults are black and brown."

Children's advocates say they don't want to get into a war with seniors or take away their benefits. They would just like to imitate some of their successes. . . .

*[Congress approved and President Clinton signed the same bill into law early in 1993— Editor's note.]

Excerpted from Paul Taylor, *Washington Post National Weekly Edition*, 4–10 March 1991, p. 31. Reprinted with permission.

PROCESS BOX 17.2

How State Priorities Change When Federal Spending Declines

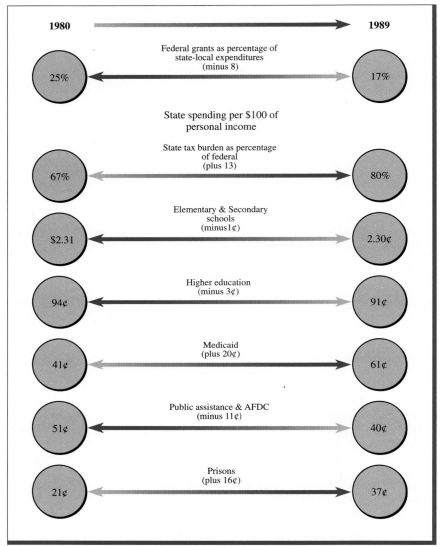

the earliest casualties of the Reagan administration, was actually replaced with the similar Job Training Partnership Act (JTPA) in 1982, albeit with a smaller budget. Like those earlier programs, the Clinton program made use of tax credits and direct subsidies to employers to set up apprentice-training jobs for young people and was to be part of a more ambitious national system that was called "lifelong learning." It was inspired by training programs that exist in some European countries, and it coupled national initiatives with community organizations and administration.

Health Policies   Until recent decades, no government in the United States—national, state, or local—concerned itself directly with individual health. But public
responsibility was always accepted for *public* health. Since early industrial cities
were very unhealthy—the mortality rate in our Atlantic seaboard cities exceeded
that of London!—public policies and public agencies were first organized to focus
on filth. The *germ* basis of disease was discovered and popularized after 1870, and
within twenty years, the followers of Louis Pasteur discovered the origins of such
communicable diseases as typhoid, leprosy, malaria, tuberculosis, cholera, diphthe-
ria, tetanus, bubonic plague, and dysentery.[15] The knowledge that these scourges
were carried and transmitted by "human carriers" led to segregation of individuals
rather than quarantine of whole areas. Hygiene laws replaced sanitation as the goal,
and the focus turned from police forces to public health agencies, from night sticks
to medicine, especially after the development and mandatory application of inocu-
lation. Medical education improved; but more important, it was being quickly absorbed and applied as a preventive measure in community situations rather than in
individual cures.[16] After New York City's newly created Board of Health was
credited with holding down a cholera epidemic in 1867, most states followed with
creation of statewide public health agencies. Within a decade, the results were obvious. For example, between 1884 and 1894, Massachusetts's rate of infant mortality dropped from 161.3 per 1,000 to 141.4 per 1,000.[17] Reductions in mortality
rates produced by local public health programs during the late nineteenth century
may be the most significant contribution ever made by government to human
welfare.

The U.S. Public Health Service (USPHS) has been in existence since 1798 but
was a small part of public health policy until after World War II. Beginning in
1937, but little noticed for twenty years, was the National Institutes of Health
(NIH), an agency within USPHS created to do biomedical research. Between
1950 and 1989, NIH expenditures by the national government increased from
$160 million to $7.1 billion—two-thirds of the nation's entire expenditure on
health research. Their research on the link between smoking and disease led to one
of the major public health campaigns in American history. Today, their focus has
turned to cancer and acquired immunodeficiency syndrome (AIDS). As with
smoking, this work on AIDS has resulted in massive public health education as
well as new products and regulations.

Other more recent commitments to the improvement of public health are the
numerous laws aimed at cleaning up and defending the environment (including
the creation in 1970 of the Environmental Protection Agency) and laws attempting to improve the health and safety of consumer products (regulated by the Consumer Product Safety Commission, created in 1972). Health policies aimed
directly at the poor are Medicaid and important nutritional programs, most particularly food stamps and the school lunch program.

During the early 1980s, the Reagan administration succeeded in cutting Med-

[15]Walter I. Trattner, *From Poor Law to Welfare State* (New York: Free Press, 1974), p. 116–17.

[16]Ibid., pp. 118–20.

[17]Morton Keller, *Affairs of State—Public Life in Nineteenth Century America* (Cambridge, MA: Belknap
Press of Harvard University Press, 1977), p. 500.

icaid by stiffening the eligibility requirements; Congress cooperated further by cutting the rate of increase in Medicaid. Public assistance to state and local governments was cut by 20 percent. But before Reagan's second term was over, most of the health budget, as with welfare, had "bottomed out" and was beginning to receive increased appropriations.

In 1992, federal grants to states for Medicaid were $70 billion, up from $44.9 billion in the fiscal year 1991 and $40.2 billion in the fiscal year 1990. It is estimated that the government will increase Medicaid expenditures to $79 billion in fiscal year 1993 and to $92 billion in fiscal year 1994. Federal programs for HIV/AIDS research, treatment, prevention, and income support had a budget of $5 billion in fiscal year 1993, a significant increase over the $2.9 billion spent in fiscal year 1990. President Clinton put greater emphasis on AIDS by appointing an "AIDS czar," Kristine Gebbie, and by giving the position of AIDS coordinator cabinet status for the first time.[18]

Perhaps President Clinton's most significant policy departure from his predecessors is in health policy. He campaigned against skyrocketing health costs and in favor of universal insurance coverage. Putting the two together became the responsibility of Hillary Rodham Clinton, who accepted her husband's appointment to chair his national task force on health care reform. Other members of the task force included Lloyd Bentsen (Treasury) and Donna Shalala (Health and Human Services), from the Right and Left wings, respectively, of the party.

Housing Policies   Through public housing for low-income families, which originated in 1937 with the Wagner-Steagall National Housing Act, and subsidized private housing after 1950, the percent of American families living in overcrowded housing was reduced from 20 percent in 1940 to 9 percent in 1970. Housing policies made an even greater contribution to reducing "substandard" housing, defined by the Census Bureau as dilapidated houses without hot running water and without some or all other plumbing. In 1940, almost 50 percent of American households lived in substandard housing. By 1950, this had been reduced to 35 percent; by 1975, to 8 percent.[19] Urban redevelopment programs and rent supplement programs have helped in a small way to give low-income families access to better neighborhoods and, through that, to better schools and working conditions.

Housing programs were heavily opposed by the Reagan administration, which succeeded in reducing housing benefits by 15 percent and in cutting the number of newly assisted households from an annual average of 300,000 in the late 1970s to 100,000 by 1984.[20] President Bush reversed both, concluding his administration with a $25 billion authorization for housing programs in his 1991 budget. Bush's HUD secretary, Jack Kemp, received a great deal of credit for cleaning up a major scandal inherited from Reagan, but the most important legacy he passed on to President Clinton and his HUD secretary, Henry Cisneros, was $7 billion in un-

---

[18]Office of Management and Budget, *Budget of the United States Government* (Washington, DC: Government Printing Office, 1990, 1993). See also "AIDS: Progress and Prospects," *Washington Post* 24 August 1992, p. A16.

[19]John E. Schwarz, *America's Hidden Success*, 2nd ed. (New York: W. W. Norton, 1988), pp. 41–42.

[20]For more details, see John L. Palmer and Isabel V. Sawhill, eds., *The Reagan Record* (Cambridge, MA: Ballinger Publishing Co., 1984), Appendix C, pp. 363–79.

spent authorization, about $3 billion of which was earmarked for housing.[21] Since
Cisneros is a former mayor (San Antonio) and Clinton is a former governor, all the mayors and governors in the country greeted the Clinton administration with optimism about a more cooperative federalism.

Drug Policies   During the 1980s, new, relatively inexpensive narcotics such as crack, a form of cocaine, had greatly increased the number of drug users and addicts in inner-city America. However, despite references to the need for education and treatment, Presidents Bush and Clinton continued the general American preference to treat drug abuse as a police problem. Although President Clinton's request for the 1993 anti-drug budget was $13.04 billion, only $100 million was earmarked for treatment and $130 million for education, and even that had little chance of surviving Congress's deficit-cutting mood. Including drug policies under welfare/health policy amounts to a profound public policy decision that has not yet happened.

INEQUALITY: WHO SHALL BE POOR?

Although the capitalist system has proven immensely productive, left to its own devices it produces dependency along with prosperity. The class of poverty in a capitalist economy is composed of everyone who cannot adapt to the demands and skills of commerce, the division of labor, relatively advanced literacy, highly organized working conditions, supervision, rules, and technology. Moreover, capitalism sets no limit upon how low wages will go—no limit except subsistence itself.[22]

But there are at least two redeeming features of capitalist poverty. First, capitalism has historically produced more goods at lower prices, so that, while a lower class always exists, the pie from which their share comes is larger. In other words, even if wages tend toward subsistence, the definition of subsistence itself has been moving upward. Second, and more to the point in this chapter, capitalist poverty is objective, neutral—a random harvest. If a disproportionate number of African Americans, Hispanic Americans, women, or other definable groups are found in poverty, or on the lower-income side of any given occupation, this is the result of

---

[21]Guy Gugliotta, "Cisneros: Bringing a Touch of the Cities to HUD," *Washington Post National Weekly Edition*, 18–24 January 1993, pp. 11–12.

[22]One of the earliest and most important economists, David Ricardo, formulated this in 1817 as the "iron law of wages." Ricardo argued that when economic relationships are finally reduced to wages and prices, competition for the available work will reduce the price of labor to the point below which it cannot go without endangering the physical survival of the worker. Yet, any effort to improve the income of workers, he argued, can only be temporarily successful, because it will produce more population by childbirth or immigration, producing eventually a "surplus of labor" that will push wages back down toward subsistence again. David Ricardo, *Principles of Political Economy and Taxation* (Totowa, NJ: Evman, Biblio Distribution Centre, 1978; orig. published 1817). See also Karl Polanyi, *The Great Transformation* (Boston: Beacon Press, 1957), Chapter 6. And compare with Alexis de Tocqueville, *Democracy in America*, Vol. 2 trans. Phillips Bradley (New York: Random House, Vintage, 1955), Chapter 22. Tocqueville argued that an upper class in a capitalist society will lack the common bonds of land and tradition that tied upper and lower classes together in pre-industrial society; thus, this "new aristocracy" would be limited by nothing but economic rationality, which Ricardo then goes on to argue will inevitably push all workers toward subsistence.

social rules that come from personal prejudices and traditions rather than from rational economic behavior.[23] If profit were the only motive, managers would hire the most efficient worker regardless of skin color, gender, etc. But since many employers do share or at least accept their community's social prejudices, the poverty class in America is disproportionately black and female. Those in poverty would remain impoverished if public policy did not intervene. This is what we mean by "changing the rules that determine who shall be poor."

Legislation and Administrative Action to Change the Rules

As we observed in Chapter 4, the right to equal protection of the laws could be established and, to a certain extent, implemented by the courts. But after a decade of very frustrating efforts, the courts and Congress ultimately came to the conclusion that the federal courts alone were not adequate to the task of changing the social rules and that legislation and administrative action would be needed.

Table 17.3 on pages 714 and 715 provides an overview of the efforts by Congress to use its legislative powers to help make equal protection of the laws a reality. As this table indicates, three civil rights acts were passed during the first decade after the 1954 Supreme Court decision in *Brown* v. *Board of Education*. But these acts were of only marginal importance. The first two, in 1957 and 1960, established that the Fourteenth Amendment of the Constitution, adopted almost a century earlier, could no longer be disregarded, particularly in regard to voting. The third, the Equal Pay Act of 1963, was more important, but it was concerned with women in the public sector and consequently did not touch the question of racial discrimination or discrimination in the private sector.

By far the most important piece of legislation passed by Congress concerning equal opportunity was the Civil Rights Act of 1964. It not only put some teeth in the voting rights provisions of the 1957 and 1960 acts but also went far beyond voting to attack discrimination in public accommodations, segregation in the schools, and at long last, the discriminatory conduct of employers in hiring, promoting, and laying off their employees. Discrimination against women was also included, extending the important 1963 provisions. The 1964 act seemed bold at the time, revolutionary to some, but it was enacted ten years after the Supreme Court had declared racial discrimination "inherently unequal" under the Fifth and Fourteenth Amendments. And it was enacted long after blacks had demonstrated that discrimination was no longer acceptable. The choice in 1964 was not between congressional action or inaction but between legal action and expanded violence.

The 1964 legislation declared discrimination by private employers and state governments (school boards, etc.) illegal, then went further to provide for admin-

---

[23]A very important study conducted in the 1950s confirmed in an unexpected way that capitalism is less prejudicial and discriminatory than the communities in which it operates. This study found that the mobility of employees upward from low status and humble origins is significantly higher in large, publicly traded corporations than in the more traditional family-owned companies, even when the family-owned company is large, as family-owned Ford was in the 1950s. W. Lloyd Warner and James C. Abegglen, *Occupational Mobility* (Minneapolis: University of Minnesota Press, 1955), pp. 168–69.

istrative agencies to help the courts implement these laws. Title IV of the 1964 act,
for example, authorized the executive branch, through the Justice Department, to
implement federal court orders to desegregate schools, and to do so without having to wait for individual parents to bring complaints. Title VI vastly strengthened
the role of the executive branch and the credibility of court orders by providing
that federal grants-in-aid to state and local governments for education must be
withheld from any school system practicing racial segregation. Title VI became the
most effective weapon for desegregating schools outside the South, because the situation in northern communities was more subtle and difficult to reach. In the
South, the problem was segregation by law coupled with overt resistance to the
national government's efforts to change the situation. In contrast, outside the
South, segregated facilities were the outcome of hundreds of thousands of housing
choices made by individuals and families. Once racial residential patterns emerged,
racial homogeneity, property values, and neighborhood schools and churches were
defended by realtors, neighborhood organizations, and the like. But local government agencies rarely took action even with announced intent to discriminate, and
the deliberate private discriminatory actions, even when coordinated, were not
documented. Thus, in order to eliminate discrimination nationwide, the 1964
Civil Rights Act: (1) gave the president through the Office for Civil Rights
(OCR) the power to withhold federal education grants,[24] and (2) gave the attorney general of the United States the power to initiate suits (rather than having to
await complaints) wherever there was a "pattern or practice" of discrimination.[25]

In the decade following the 1964 Civil Rights Act, the Justice Department
brought legal action against more than 500 school districts. During the same period, administrative agencies filed actions against 600 school districts, threatening
to suspend federal aid to education unless real desegregation steps were taken. At
the same time, the federal government filed more than 400 antidiscrimination suits
in federal courts against hotels, restaurants, taverns, gas stations, and other "public
accommodations" under Title II.[26]

Title VII, the fair employment title of the 1964 act, at last fulfilled goals that
proponents of racial equality had espoused since the 1940s. Title VII, declaring job
discrimination illegal, was written to cover all employers of more than fifteen employees, all governmental agencies, and also trade unions. Some of the powers to
enforce fair employment practices were delegated to the Justice Department's Civil
Rights Division and others to a new agency created in the 1964 act, the Equal
Employment Opportunity Commission (EEOC). It is also important to note the
use here of another "technique of control" identified in Chapter 15: by executive
order, these agencies had the power of the national government to revoke public

[24]For a thorough analysis of the OCR, see Jeremy Rabkin, "Office for Civil Rights," in *The Politics of Regulation,* ed. James Q. Wilson (New York: Basic Books, 1980), Chapter 9.

[25]As observed toward the end of Chapter 4, this was an accepted way of using quotas or ratios, to determine statistically that blacks or other minorities were being excluded from schools or jobs, and then
on the basis of that satistical evidence to authorize the Justice Department to bring suits in individual
cases and in "class action" suits as well. In most segregated situations outside the South, it is virtually
impossible to identify and document an intent to discriminate.

[26]For a review of these suits, see Richard Kluger, *Simple Justice* (New York: Random House, 1975),
p. 759 and Chapters 25 and 26.

TABLE 17.3

The Key Provisions of Federal Civil Rights Laws (1957–1991)

Civil Rights Act of 1957	Established the Commission on Civil Rights to monitor civil rights progress. Elevated the importance of the Civil Rights Division of the Department of Justice, headed by an assistant attorney general. Made it a federal crime to attempt to intimidate a voter or to prevent a person from voting.
Civil Rights Act of 1960	Increased the sanction against obstruction of voting or of court orders enforcing the vote. Established federal power to appoint referees to register voters wherever a "pattern or practice" of discrimination was found and declared by a federal court.
Equal Pay Act of 1963	Banned wage discrimination on the basis of sex in jobs requiring equal skill, effort, and responsibility. Exceptions involved employee pay differentials based on factors other than sex, such as merit or seniority.
Civil Rights Act of 1964	*Voting:* Title I made a sixth grade education (in English) a presumption to literacy.
	Public accommodations: Title II barred discrimination in any commercial lodging of more than five rooms for transient guests and in any service station, restaurant, theater, or commercial conveyance.
	Public schools: Title IV empowered the attorney general to sue for desegregation whenever he found a segregation complaint meritorious. Title VI authorized the witholding of federal aid to segregated schools.
	Private employment: Title VII outlawed discrimination in a variety of employment practices on the basis of race, religion, and sex (sex added for the first time in areas other than wage discrimination). Established the Equal Employment Opportunity Commission (EEOC) to enforce the law but required it to defer enforcement to state or local agencies for sixty days following each complaint.
Civil Rights Act of 1965	*Voting rights only:* Empowered the attorney general, with the Civil Service Commission, to appoint voting examiners to replace local registrars wherever he found fewer than 50 percent of the persons of voting age had voted in the 1964 presidential election and to suspend all literacy tests where they were used as a tool of discrimination.

contracts for goods and services and to refuse to engage in contracts for goods and services to any private company that could not guarantee that its rules for hiring, promotion, and firing were nondiscriminatory.

Although 1964 was the *most* important year, it was not the only important year for civil rights legislation. In 1965, Congress significantly strengthened legislation protecting voting rights by barring literacy and other tests as a condition for voting in six southern states,[27] by setting criminal penalties for interference with efforts to

---

[27]In 1970, this act was amended to outlaw for five years literacy tests as a condition for voting in all states.

Civil Rights Act of 1968	*Open housing:* Made it a crime to refuse to sell or rent a dwelling on the basis of race or religion, if a bona fide offer had been made, or to discriminate in advertising or in the terms and conditions of sale or rental. Administered by the Department of Housing and Urban Development, but the burden of proof is on the complainant, who must seek local remedies first, where they exist.
Amendments of 1970 to Voting Rights Act	Extended 1965 act and included some districts in northern states.
Equal Employment Opportunity Act of 1972	Increased coverage of the Civil Rights Act of 1964 to include public sector employees. Gave EEOC authority to bring suit against persons engaging in "patterns or practice" of employment discrimination.
Amendments of 1975 to Voting Rights Act	Extended 1965 act and broadened antidiscrimination measures to include protection for language minorities (e.g., Hispanics, Native Americans).
Amendments of 1978 to Civil Rights Act of 1964	Prohibited discrimination in employment on the basis of pregnancy or related disabilities. Required that pregnancy or related medical conditions be treated as disabilities eligible for medical and liability insurance.
Amendments of 1982 to Voting Rights Act	Extended 1965 act and strengthened antidiscrimination measures by requiring only proof of *effect* of discrimination, not *intent* to discriminate.
Americans with Disabilities Act of 1990	Extended to people with disabilities, protection from discrimination in employment and public accommodations similar to those given to women and racial, religious, and ethnic minorities by the 1964 Civil Rights Act. Required that public transportation systems, other public services, and telecommunications systems be accessible to those with disabilities.
Civil Rights Act of 1991	Reversed several Court decisions, beginning with *Wards Cove* (1989), that had made it harder for women and minorities to seek compensation for job discrimination. It put back on the employer the "burden of proof" to show that a discriminatory policy was a business necessity.

vote, and by providing for the replacement of local registrars with federally appointed registrars in counties designated by the attorney general as significantly resistant to registering eligible blacks to vote. The right to vote was further strengthened with ratification in 1964 of the Twenty-fourth Amendment abolishing the poll tax and in 1975 with legislation *permanently* outlawing literacy tests in all fifty states and by mandating bilingual ballots or oral assistance for Spanish, Chinese, Japanese, Koreans, Native Americans, and Eskimos. The Civil Rights Act of 1968, called "open housing legislation," prohibited discrimination in the sale or rental of most housing—covering over 80 percent of the nation's housing. Executive orders in 1965, 1967, and 1969 by Presidents Johnson and Nixon extended and reaffirmed nondiscrimination practices in employment and promotion in the federal government service. And in 1972, President Nixon and a Democratic Congress cooperated to strengthen the EEOC by giving it authority to initiate suits rather than wait for grievances; in 1972, Congress also enacted a law extending Title VI of the 1964 act to provide for withholding federal aid to education where there is a "pattern or practice" of sex discrimination.

In the long run, the laws extending and protecting voting rights could prove to be the most effective of all the great civil rights legislation, because the progress in black political participation produced by these acts has altered the shape of American politics. In 1965, in the seven states of the Old Confederacy covered by the Voting Rights Act, 29.3 percent of the eligible black residents were registered to vote, compared to 73.4 percent of the white residents (see Table 17.4). Mississippi was the extreme case, with 6.7 percent black and 69.9 percent white registration. In 1967, a mere two years after implementation of the voting rights laws, 52.1 percent of the eligible blacks in the seven states were registered, comparing favorably to 79.5 percent of the eligible whites, a gap of 27.4 points. By 1971–1972, the gap between black and white registration in the seven states was only 11.2 points, and in Mississippi the gap had been reduced to a narrow 9.4 points. In Chapter 10, there is an account of how white leaders in Mississippi attempted to dilute the influence of this growing black vote by gerrymandering districts to insure that no blacks would be elected to Congress. But the black voters changed Mississippi before Mississippi could change them. In 1988, 11 percent of all elected officials in Mississippi were black. This was up one full percentage point from 1987 and closely approximates the size of the national black electorate, which was just over 11 percent of the American voting age population. Mississippi's blacks had made significant gains (as was true in other Deep South states) as elected state and local

TABLE 17.4
Registration by Race and State in Southern States Covered by the Voting Rights Act

| | Before the Act* | | | After the Act* 1971–1972 | | |
	White	Black	Gap†	White	Black	Gap†
Alabama	69.2%	19.3%	49.9	80.7%	57.1%	23.6
Georgia	62.6	27.4	35.2	70.6	67.8	2.8
Louisiana	80.5	31.6	48.9	80.0	59.1	20.9
Mississippi	69.9	6.7	63.2	71.6	62.2	9.4
North Carolina	96.8	46.8	50.0	62.2	46.3	15.9
South Carolina	75.7	37.3	38.4	51.2	48.0	3.2
Virginia	61.1	38.3	22.8	61.2	54.0	7.2
TOTAL	73.4	29.3	44.1	67.8	56.6	11.2

*Available registration data as of March 1965 and 1971–72.
†The gap is the percentage point difference between white and black registration rates.
Source: U.S. Commission on Civil Rights, *Political Participation* (1968), Appendix VII: Voter Education Project, Attachment to Press Release, 3 October 1972.

representatives; and Mississippi was one of only eight states in the country in
which a black judge presided over the highest state court. (Four of the eight were
Deep South states.)[28]

Affirmative Action

As in Chapter 4, where we concluded with court efforts to go beyond antidiscrimination toward "affirmative action," so we end this legislative treatment of
equal protection with a discussion of affirmative action. Legislatively, affirmative
action is an effort to introduce consideration of inequality of *results* along with inequality of opportunity.

Most affirmative action comes not from new legislation but from more vigorous and positive interpretations of existing legislation arising out of feelings on the
part of many that compensatory actions are necessary to overcome the long years
of discrimination. President Johnson put the case emotionally in 1965: "You do
not take a person who, for years, has been hobbled by chains . . . and then say you
are free to compete with all the others, and still just believe that you have been
completely fair."[29] Consequently, one of the first affirmative action programs was
President Johnson's War on Poverty, begun in 1964. The aim was to help people in
underprivileged and ghetto neighborhoods form organizations with a leadership
that could speak for the people in those neighborhoods. The ultimate goal of these
"Community Action Programs" was to provide more assistance and at the same
time teach the poor how to organize to compete more effectively in political as
well as economic life.

The War on Poverty has been subjected to many valid criticisms, even from
those who were sympathetic to its goals. But experience with it does confirm the
proposition that some redistribution of political power must often precede redistribution of income toward the poor. The following excerpt illustrates the success of
a group of senior citizens who organized politically in order to gain economically:

> A new sort of political warlord is walking the ground that once belonged to the
> powerful Democratic county bosses in New York City. . . . Over 17 years of near ob-
> scurity [Assemblyman Viti J.] Lopez has built the prototype of the modern inner-city
> machine . . . potent enough to induce pilgrimage from mayors, senators, and a pres-
> idential candidate named Bill Clinton. . . . The organization, the Ridgewood Bush-
> wich [Brooklyn] Senior Citizens Council, employs 1,400 people through more than
> 50 grants budgeted at more than $33 million annually. [Such social service groups]
> managed to fill the vacuum left by the diminishing influence of county political
> bosses. . . . The strongest of the organizations have been able to wrest money from
> increasingly tight-fisted government agencies.[30]

---

[28]Joint Center for Political Studies, *Black Elected Officials: A National Roster—1988* (Washington, DC:
Joint Center for Political Studies Press, 1988), pp. 9–10. For a comprehensive analysis and evaluation of
the Voting Rights Act, see Bernard Grofman and Chandler Davidson, eds., *Controversies in Minority Voting—The Voting Rights Act in Perspective* (Washington, DC: Brookings Institution, 1992).

[29]From Lyndon B. Johnson, *The Vantage Point* (New York: Holt Rinehart and Winston, 1971), p. 166.

[30]Martin Gottleib, "Growth of a New-Age Political Machine: Social Service Grants Have Replaced
Party Bosses as the Path to Power," *New York Times*, 7 February 1993, p. 35.

W. E. B. DuBois and Booker T. Washington
Competing Paths to Equality

Two of the most important founders of the modern civil rights movement shared the same goal—equality for African Americans—but differed markedly on how best to achieve that goal.

William Edward Burghardt (better known as W. E. B.) DuBois, born in Massachusetts in 1868, entered the academic world via Fisk University and Harvard University, where his doctoral dissertation on the slave trade was the first volume published in the Harvard Historical Studies series. DuBois taught at many universities, wrote numerous books, and founded the National Association for the Advancement of Colored People (NAACP).

Booker T. Washington was born a Virginia slave in 1856. After the Civil War, Washington worked in coal mines and salt furnaces. In 1872, he was admitted to the Hampton Institute, an industrial school for blacks. Five years later he became a teacher there. In 1881, Washington established and headed the Tuskegee Institute in Alabama, a school modeled on Hampton that emphasized vocational trades for blacks, including farming, carpentry, mechanical skills, and teaching. Eventually Washington became a prominent political figure, and an adviser to Presidents Theodore Roosevelt and William H. Taft.

DuBois's philosophy of race relations emphasized the importance of black self-sufficiency and excellence, urging cultivation of a "talented tenth" that could excel and lead other blacks. And as early as 1903, he predicted that "the problem of the twentieth century is the problem of the color line." Washington, on the other hand, espoused the view that blacks should seek "through compromise, an emergence into

W. E. B. DuBois

Another confirmation comes from the 1965 riot in the Watts section of Los Angeles. A Senate committee investigation determined that the most important explanation for the riot came from the fact that large sums of federal War on Poverty money was *already authorized* for the Watts area but had never reached the groups, businesses, and individuals in the area because of the lack of government and committee organizations set up to receive and distribute the aid.[31]

---

[31]For a criticism of the administrative methods used, see Theodore J. Lowi, *The End of Liberalism* (New York: W. W. Norton, 1979), Chapter 8. For a very positive account of the impact, see Schwarz, *America's Hidden Success*, pp. 34–50. For more on the specifics and the significance of "redistributive" policies, see the first section of this chapter and portions of Chapters 15 and 16. See also Senate Subcom-

an economic, social, and cultural stability never quite equal to the white man's." This philosophy led Washington to state that blacks were better off by getting practical vocational education than by seeking college training. DuBois did not reject the need for vocational education, but he took sharp issue with Washington's willingness to accept an inferior and segregated status for blacks.

Not surprisingly, Washington's views found wider acceptance among white Americans, which won him influence among the nation's political leaders. Washington also promoted his views through his financial control of various black newspapers. Washington avoided any endorsement of controversial political causes, although he did funnel money secretly to support lawsuits to fight discrimination in the courts. Toward the end of his life, his influence declined, as the views of organizations such as the NAACP acquired greater respect.

DuBois never backed down from his advocacy of political and social equality. For many years, he worked for the NAACP and edited its publication called *The Crisis*. In 1950, he unsuccessfully ran for U.S. senator from New York on the American Labor party ticket. Disillusioned with American party politics, DuBois joined the Communist party and traveled extensively in China and the Soviet Union. In 1961, the aged man moved to Ghana, to direct the writing of the *Encyclopedia Africana*.

Both DuBois and Washington believed that their philosophies would ultimately help eradicate inequality. The course chosen by DuBois, however, more closely foreshadowed the civil rights struggles of years to come.

Sources: Booker T. Washington, *Up from Slavery* (New York: Corner House, 1971; orig. published in 1901); W. E. B. DuBois, *The Souls of Black Folk* (New York: Signet Classics, 1969; orig. published in 1903).

Booker T. Washington

Affirmative action also took the form of efforts by the agencies in the Department of Health, Education, and Welfare to shift their focus from "desegregation" to "integration." Federal agencies—sometimes with court orders and sometimes without them—required school districts to present plans for busing children across district lines, for pairing schools, for closing certain schools, and for redistributing faculties as well as students, under pain of loss of grants-in-aid from the federal government. The guidelines issued for such plans literally constituted preferential treatment to compensate for past discrimination, and without this legislatively as-

mittee on Executive Reorganization of the Senate Committee on Government Operations, *Federal Role in Urban Affairs*, 89th Cong. 2nd sess., 1966, pp. 748–79.

sisted approach to court integration orders, there would certainly not have been the dramatic increase in black children attending integrated classes. The yellow school bus became a symbol of hope for many and a signal of defeat for others. Important affirmative action has also taken place in higher education.

Affirmative action was also initiated in the area of employment opportunity. The Equal Employment Opportunity Commission often has required plans whereby employers must attempt to increase the number of their minority employees, and the Office of Federal Contract Compliance in the Department of Labor has used the threat of contract revocation for the same purpose.

The constitutionality of some of these legislative efforts at affirmative action has been upheld.[32] But affirmative action remains controversial, in fact one of the most important areas of controversy in domestic public policy. For nearly two decades, civil rights received high priority treatment by the federal government. But criticism mounted during the 1970s, and Ronald Reagan became "the first president in the post–World War II period to reverse this trend of an increasingly active government role in . . . redressing the consequences of past discrimination." The budgets and staff of key civil rights agencies were cut to the bone.[33] Busing was opposed. Government cases against school segregation, housing discrimination, and job discrimination dropped to a fraction of the cases brought under previous administrations.[34] And, although federal court decisions have upheld the use of statistics on the "effect" of discrimination as a basis for Justice Department initiatives in filing "pattern and practice" suits to open opportunities for minorities, the Justice Department under President Reagan virtually terminated such suits, focusing instead on individual cases where intent to discriminate could be proven.[35]

President Bush continued in the Reagan direction. He vetoed the Civil Rights Act of 1990 as a "quota bill" (although he accepted essentially the same bill in 1991). But most importantly, he "relentlessly" appointed known social conservatives to the federal courts "with the same energy that Ronald Reagan did."[36] And his single appointment to the Supreme Court, Clarence Thomas, to replace civil

---

[32]For example, Fullilove v. Klutznick, 448 U.S. 448 (1980). Here the Supreme Court upheld the "minority business enterprise" (MBE) provisions of the Public Works Employment Act of 1977, an affirmative action policy which required that 10 percent of federal funds granted for local public works projects must be used to procure services or supplies from businesses owned by minority group members. Although the Court was split in two or three directions, yielding no absolutely clear majority opinion, the decision did sustain the statute, upholding the objectives of the MBE as within Congress's power. For a discussion of the case, see Paul Brest and Sanford Levinson, *Processes of Constitutional Decision Making* (Boston: Little, Brown, 1983), pp. 541, 547. *Fullilove* was reaffirmed on June 8, 1990, in Metro Broadcasting v. FCC, 110 S. CT. 2997 (1990). However, in 1979, the Court returned to the position that any "rigid numerical quota" is suspect in City of Richmond v. J. A. Croson Co. 109 S. CT. 706 (1989); see Chapter 4.

[33]D. Lee Bawden and John L. Palmer, "Social Policy," in *The Reagan Record*, ed. John L. Palmer and Isabel Sawhill (Cambridge, MA: Ballinger, 1984), p. 201; see E. W. Kelley, *Policy and Politics in the U.S.* (Philadelphia: Temple University Press, 1987), p. 269. See also Harold Seidman and Robert Gilmour, *Politics, Position and Power*, 4th ed. (New York: Oxford University Press, 1986), pp. 130–35.

[34]Bawden and Palmer, "Social Policy." p. 206.

[35]Ibid.

[36]An observation by Nan Aron of the Liberal Alliance for Justice, quoted in Ruth Marcus, "Using the Bench to Bolster a Conservative Team," *Washington Post National Weekly Edition*, 25 February–3 March 1991, p. 31.

rights advocate Thurgood Marshall, had been an opponent of anything that had to do with affirmative action.

Since the Supreme Court has not declared affirmative action unconstitutional, many opportunities remain for civil rights groups to get new policies instituted, as well as more sympathetic agencies created. Although some outspoken African American intellectuals have argued that affirmative action programs will be counterproductive, most civil rights leaders and their organizations continue to be of the opinion that affirmative action programs are absolutely essential.[37] The issue can be understood as a struggle to change the rules determining who shall be poor, because poverty is almost surely the status to which people are doomed if they get no assistance to break out of the circle of poverty.

Madison set the tone for this chapter in *The Federalist,* No. 51, in prose that has more the character of poetry:

Justice is the end of government.
  It is the end of civil society.
  It ever has been and ever will be pursued
    Until it be obtained,
  Or until liberty be lost in the pursuit.

His words also connect this chapter with the theme of the book, freedom and power. Equality of opportunity has produced unequal results, and the unequal results of one generation can be visited upon later generations. Considerable inequality is acceptable unless the advantages are maintained through laws and rules that favor those already in positions of power, and through prejudices that tend to develop against any group that has for a long while been on the lower rungs of society. It is in this context that the more longstanding and extreme inequalities in the United States have been perceived as unjust. Yet, efforts to reduce the inequalities or to eliminate the consequences of prejudice can produce their own injustices if government intervention is poorly planned or is too heavy-handed.

SUMMARY

The capitalist system is the most productive type of economy on earth, but it is not perfect. Poverty amidst plenty continues. Many policies have emerged to deal with these imperfections. Some policies attempt to readjust and to tilt relations between management and labor.

The first section of this chapter discussed the welfare state, giving an account of how Americans came to recognize extremes of poverty and dependency and how Congress then attempted to reduce these extremes by policies that moderately redistribute opportunity.

---

[37]For discussion opposing affirmative action see Thomas Sowell, *Preferential Policies—An International Perspective* (New York: Morrow, 1990). For discussion in favor see Charles Willie, *Caste and Class Controversy on Race and Poverty—Round Two of the Willie-Wilson Debate,* 2nd ed. (Dix Hills, NY: General Hall, 1989).

Welfare state policies are subdivided into several categories. First there are the contributory programs. Virtually all employed persons are required to contribute a portion of their wages into welfare trust funds, and later on, when they retire or are disabled, they have a right, or entitlement, to draw upon those contributions. Another category of welfare is composed of noncontributory programs, also called "public assistance." These programs provide benefits and supports for people who can demonstrate need by passing a "means test." Noncontributory programs can involve cash benefits or "in-kind" benefits. All of the contributory programs are implemented through cash benefits.

The second section moved from the question of the economic rules of poverty ("who *is* poor?") to the social rules of inequality ("who *shall be* poor?"). Here we recognize that inequalities are not altogether the result of objective and random factors but, in a significant number of instances, they are the result of formal and informal rules that make advancement out of poverty particularly difficult for some social groups. Welfare policies exist to provide a general "safety net" for all who find themselves poor or dependent and to tilt the economy toward the lower brackets; civil rights policies are aimed at changing the social rules and deliberately lowering the barriers to advancement. Some civil rights policies were developed by the judiciary, and these were then followed by a variety of policies that originated in Congress but were implemented and expanded upon by several important administrative agencies.

The first civil rights policies were aimed at overcoming deliberate discrimination. Beginning with the most important, the Civil Rights Act of 1964, discrimination on the basis of race, gender, and several other characteristics was declared illegal, and victims of such discrimination were provided modest remedies. Significant progress was made in reducing the frequency of deliberately discriminatory conduct, but this only helped those who were already educated and had marketable skills. Their success in taking advantage of the civil rights laws served to increase the distance between them and the lower-income members of the same groups. Out of this problem arose the movement toward "affirmative action," aimed at compensating people for past discrimination even where no case can be made that they personally were victims of deliberate discrimination. This has produced a great deal of controversy: in fact, the struggle over discrimination against whole groups of people and the controversy over the permissibility of quotas and the constitutionality of "group rights" will affect the agenda of social policy for the next decade or more.

FOR FURTHER READING

Baumer, Donald C., and Carl E. Van Horn. *The Politics of Unemployment.* Washington, DC: Congressional Quarterly Press, 1985.

Brown, Michael, ed. *Remaking the Welfare State.* Philadelphia: Temple University Press, 1988.

Bullock, Charles, III, and Charles M. Lamb. *Implementation of Civil Rights Policy.* Monterey, CA: Brooks/Cole, 1984.

Derthick, Martha. *Agency Under Stress: The Social Security Administration in American Government.* Washington, DC: Brookings Institution, 1991.

Foreman, Christoper. *Signals from the Hill: Congressional Oversight and the Challenge of Social Regulation.* New Haven, CT: Yale University Press, 1988.

Forer, Lois G. *Criminals and Victims—A Trial Judge Reflects on Crimes and Punishment.* New York: W. W. Norton, 1980.

Gutman, Amy. *Democratic Education.* Princeton, NJ: Princeton University Press, 1987.

Katz, Michael. *In the Shadow of the Poorhouse: A Social History of Welfare in America.* New York: Basic Books, 1986.

Kronenfeld, Jennie Jacobs. *Controversial Issues in Health Care Policy.* Newbury Park, CA: Sage, 1993.

Lemann, Nicholas. *The Promised Land: The Great Black Migration and How It Shaped America.* New York: Knopf, 1991.

Levy, Frank. *Dollars and Dreams: The Changing American Income Distribution.* New York: W. W. Norton, 1988.

Light, Paul. *Artful Work: The Politics of Social Security Reform.* New York: Random House, 1985.

Marmor, Theodore R., Jerry L. Mashaw, and Phillip L. Harvey. *America's Misunderstood Welfare State.* New York: Basic Books, 1990.

Murray, Charles. *Losing Ground: American Social Policy, 1950–1980.* New York: Basic Books, 1984.

Piven, Frances Fox, and Richard A. Cloward. *Regulating the Poor.* New York: Pantheon, 1971.

Schwarz, John E. *America's Hidden Success: A Reassessment of Twenty Years of Public Policy.* New York: W. W. Norton, 1988.

Weicher, John C. *Maintaining the Safety Net: Income Redistribution Programs in the Reagan Administration.* Washington, DC: American Enterprise Institute, 1984.

Weir, Margaret, Ann Orloff, and Theda Skocpol. *The Politics of Social Policy in the United States.* Princeton, NJ: Princeton University Press, 1988.

18

Foreign Policy and World Politics

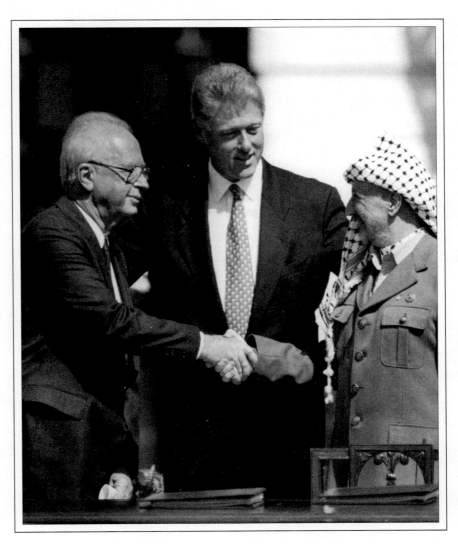

TIME LINE ON FOREIGN POLICY

EVENTS		INSTITUTIONAL DEVELOPMENTS
Treaties with Britain and Spain establish recognition of U.S. sovereignty (1795)		U.S. attempts to steer clear of foreign alliances; pursues neutrality policy (1790s)
Louisiana Purchase from France (1803)	**1800**	
War of 1812, despite American attempts to maintain neutrality (1812)		Monroe Doctrine to prevent further European colonization in Western Hemisphere (1823)
War with Mexico, ending in Mexico's giving up claim to Texas and ceding California and New Mexico to U.S. (1846–1848)		Manifest Destiny doctrine leads to war with Mexico (1840s); Mexican War first successful defensive war (1846–1848)
	1860	
Civil War (1861–1865)		
U.S. purchases Alaska from Russia; Midway Islands annexed (1867)		Unilateralism prevails (1870s–1890s)
First Inter-American Conference between U.S. and Latin American nations (1889–1890)		Reciprocal agreements between U.S. and Latin American nations (1890)
Spanish-American War; treaty leads to U.S. annexation of Puerto Rico, Guam, Philippines; Hawaii annexed (1898)		U.S. concern with world markets after closing of American frontier (1890s)
World War I (1914–1918)	**1900**	U.S. does not join the League of Nations (1919)
Unprecedented inflation and political instability in Germany (1920s)		Rogers Act recognizes foreign service officers as part of government career system (1924)
U.S. enters World War II (1941–1945)		U.N. established (1945)
Bretton Woods Conference (1944)		Foreign Service Act creates a professional diplomatic corps (1946)
Soviets have A-bomb (1949)		Cold War and containment— Truman Doctrine (1947); Marshall Plan (1947); Rio Treaty creating OAS (1947); NATO (1949); Mutual Security (1951); SEATO (1954)
Korean War (1950–1953)	**1950**	
Soviets launch Sputnik (1957); First U.S. satellite (1958)		U.S. and Soviets race to the moon (1957–1969)

TIME LINE ON FOREIGN POLICY

EVENTS		INSTITUTIONAL DEVELOPMENTS
Bay of Pigs Invasion (1961); Cuban Missile Crisis (1962)	**1960**	U.S. and Soviets face off in Cuba (1962)
		Nuclear Test-Ban Treaty (1963)
U.S. builds up troops in Vietnam (1965–1973)		Détente between U.S. and Soviet Union (1970s)
Nixon visits China (1972)		U.S.-Soviet Trade Agreement (1972)
Arab oil embargo (1973–1974)		End of U.S. military draft (1973)
U.S. intervenes in Chile (1974)		Termination of Bretton Woods System (1973)
Camp David Summit (1978)		Panama Canal Treaty (1978)
U.S. formally recognizes China (1979)		
Iranian hostage crisis (1979–1981)	**1980**	SALT II Agreement (1979–1981)
		SALT II repudiated (1981)
Grenada invasion (1983)		SDI ("Star Wars") commitment (1980s)
First Reagan-Gorbachev Summit (1985)		Policy of covert action in Latin America (1980s)
Iran-Contra affair (1986–1987)		INF Treaty 1988
Invasion of Panama by U.S.; Berlin Wall comes down (1989)		Soviet system collapses; NATO/Warsaw Pact withdrawals begin (1989)
Germany reunified (1990)	**1990**	Eastern Europe adopts capitalism (1990)
Iraq invades Kuwait (1990)		
Ethnic conflicts split U.S.S.R., Yugoslavia, and Czechoslovakia (1991–1993)		29-nation coalition under UN conducts blockade and war against Iraq; beginning of U.S. "new world order" role (1990–1991)
UN-sponsored humanitarian intervention in Somalia (1992)		Clinton-Yeltsin summit cements U.S./Russian ties (1993)
Crisis in Bosnia (1993–1995)		Clinton favors collective approach rather than leadership role in Bosnia but acts unilaterally against Iraq and takes lead in G7 economic talks (1993)
Israel signs peace treaty with PLO in Washington (1993)		

*E*ver since Franklin Roosevelt's dramatic "Hundred Days" in 1933, there has by tradition been a "honeymoon period," during which presidents address America's needs and Congress is expected to cooperate in a bipartisan spirit. Yet, for most presidents, the honeymoon is short, if there is one at all. The interruption in the happy marriage is usually foreign policy.

When President Bush assumed office on January 20, 1989, he proclaimed his commitment to a "kinder, gentler" society and gave America his plans for education, the drug epidemic, the plight of the disabled, and the "peace dividend." But within days of his inauguration, President Bush was off to the Far East, and he returned to a series of crises ranging from Nicaragua to NATO, from Khomeini's death to the collapse of the Berlin Wall. Even the good news of the end of the Cold War did not permit President Bush to turn to domestic policy.

President Clinton was by background and temperament a domestic president, and he marched into Washington with a bulging domestic portfolio. Yet within hours of his election in November, he discovered how sensitive foreign affairs can be. Having supported political asylum for Haiti's immigrants during his campaign, his election produced a whirlwind of boatbuilding on the island. Clinton was forced to reverse his stand before Florida became flooded with immigrants. It must have reminded him how easily foreign policy can trump domestic policy. Then President-elect Clinton felt obliged to give Bush's decision to send troops to Somalia an enthusiastic endorsement. There was also the agonizing dissolution of Yugoslavia and the question of whether America would have to follow the Somalia precedent with humanitarian aid and, quite possibly, military involvement in Bosnia. Then again, there was the instability of the Yeltsin regime and the possibility of Russia's collapse—potentially far more violent than Yugoslavia's.

Most American presidents have been domestic politicians who set out to make their place in the history books through domestic achievements. Despite their limited experience with foreign affairs, all postwar presidents have been confronted with major foreign policy issues as soon as they took the oath of office. They had to spend inordinate amounts of time on foreign policy throughout their tenure, and most of their legacy, for better and for worse, is in foreign policy.

This chapter will explore American foreign policy, the changing attitudes of presidents and other Americans toward world politics, and the place of America in world affairs. Although modern presidents cannot escape the demands of foreign policy and world politics, this has not always been the case in our nation's history, as we shall see in this chapter.

This chapter will begin with the world of nation-states and why nation-states present such a serious challenge to each other. From there, we trace out the history of America's place in the world of nation-states and how that history has influenced our contemporary foreign policies. Then we identify and evaluate the six basic instruments of American foreign policy. The last section of the chapter looks at actual roles we have attempted to play in world affairs.

THE SETTING: A WORLD OF NATION-STATES

A nation is a population of individuals bound to each other by a common past, a common language, or some other cultural ties that draw them together and distinguish them from other peoples. When such a nation has sufficient self-consciousness to organize itself also into a political entity, it is generally referred to as a nation-state. But, why form a nation-state? Hans Morgenthau, one of the most eminent students of the nation-state provides an answer:

> The most elementary function of the nation-state is the defense of the life of its citizens and of their civilization. A political organization that is no longer able to defend these values . . . must yield, either through peaceful transformation or violent destruction, to one capable of that defense.[1]

For at least two centuries, nation-states have effectively defended their populations; and the attraction to forming nation-states does not seem to have waned as a third century approaches. There were 54 nation-states at the beginning of the twentieth century. In 1945, when the United Nations (U.N.) was founded, there were 67, of which 51 were U.N. charter members. In 1979, 153 nation-states were recognized members of the United Nations. In 1990, there were 159.[2] Empires were broken up when their colonies sought independence in order to enjoy nation-state status. In the same spirit, many former colonies, as soon as their own independence was achieved, broke up into two or more nation-states. For example, India, having achieved independence from England, gave birth to two additional nation-states, Pakistan and Bangladesh. In 1991, seven new nation-states were added, and in 1992, eleven were formed and immediately given diplomatic recognition and U.N. membership status, bringing the total to 177. (One former nation-state—the Republic of China, or Taiwan—was divested of membership.) Most of these new states had been republics within the former Soviet Union, but others had been republics of Yugoslavia. In January 1993, one new nation-state was formed when Czechoslovakia was split into the Czech Republic and Slovakia bringing the total now to 178. More are sure to come in the near future.

All the signs seem to favor the existence of nation-states—despite their tendency to draw each other into war. But why has the principle of the nation-state tended to draw nations into war? As people form themselves into nation-states as a means of defense, they become unified only by isolating themselves from other nations. By doing so, each nation deprives itself of information about the motives and interests of other nations. Modern means of transportation and communication have made the world smaller but not better acquainted. Mutual ignorance has tended to breed hostility because each nation-state conducts its foreign policy on the assumption of what the experts call "the worst plausible case:" that every

---

[1]Hans J. Morgenthau, *The Purpose of American Politics* (New York: Knopf, 1960), pp. 169–70.

[2]*The Statesmen's Yearbook* (London: Macmillan, varying years).

country will pursue its interests at the expense of others. Note the following characterization by former Secretary of Defense Robert McNamara, one of the most important American policy makers of the 1960s and 1970s:

> In 1961 when I became Secretary of Defense, the Soviet Union had a very small operational arsenal of intercontinental missiles. However, it did possess the technology and industrial capacity to enlarge that arsenal. . . . We had no evidence that the Soviets did plan, in fact, fully to use that capability. But . . . a strategic planner must be conservative in his calculations; that is, he must prepare for the worst plausible case and not be content to hope and prepare merely for the most probable. . . . But the blunt fact remains that *if we had more accurate information about planned Soviet strategic forces,* we simply would not have needed to build as large a nuclear arsenal as we have today.[3]

The national purpose or national interest of the nation-state is said to be the maintenance of its *sovereignty.* Sovereignty can be defined as respect by other nations for the claim by a government that it has conquered its territory and is the sole authority over its population. Any threat to that claim is considered a failure of foreign policy.

The fragility of sovereignty was shown when Iraq occupied Kuwait in 1990, and it had to be restored by a large U.N. -sponsored military force. Then Iraq had its own sovereignty violated by the terms of the cease-fire, which required that it submit to regular U.N. inspections for possible violations of agreements not to develop atomic weapons and that it accept air surveillance by the U.S. and its allies. However, no nation-state is completely sovereign, with borders so respected that it is virtually impervious to external power. In 1973, even the most powerful nation-states, including the United States, were brutally reminded of this when the Organization of Petroleum Exporting Countries (OPEC), a political organization of several small, mainly Middle Eastern, states, adopted a common foreign policy to control world oil prices. This was well beyond a mere reminder that a global economy makes all countries interdependent. It made quite clear that "small states" can whittle away at the sovereignty of larger states, making it virtually impossible for the larger states to "go it alone" in foreign policy.

Obviously, sovereignty is something a country possesses as a matter of degree, in what we can call a "continuum." At one end of the continuum are the small and weak nation-states, commonly referred to as "satellites," because their own claim to sovereignty depends upon some powerful neighbor. At the other end of the continuum are those nation-states called the "powers," the "superpowers," and the "imperial powers." They have the resources to conduct their own foreign policy and to defend the sovereignty of one or more satellites.

In the middle of the continuum are middle-size states that are ungraciously called "client" states. These are states that have the capacity to carry out their own foreign policy most of the time but whose sovereignty in the long run still depends upon the interests of one or more of the major powers.[4]

---

[3]Robert McNamara, *The Essence of Security: Reflections in Office* (New York: Harper and Row, 1968), pp. 57–58. (Emphasis added.)

[4]There is at least one nation-state in the middle of the continuum that is not a client state, and this is

The power of a nation-state can be measured roughly according to the number and size of its satellites and clients. By that standard, the United States today is the greatest of the superpowers. However, for most of this century, the Soviet Union was virtually America's equal, and if the Russian republic can stabilize itself, it will probably return to some kind of superpower status early in the next century. The People's Republic of China is becoming a superpower. Japan already has become a superpower, even though it has no armed forces with international capacity. This may be a new phenomenon, an economic superpower. In that context, the oil-rich Arab states can achieve superpower status if they can maintain unity. We may see yet another economic superpower as the multi-state European Community becomes an integrated economic system.

Regardless of the status of each nation-state, all tend, in their foreign policies, to assume "the worst plausible case," as Secretary of Defense Robert McNamara put it a quarter of a century ago. In other words, each nation-state has to assume that its sovereignty is ultimately at risk of being encroached upon by one or more other nation-states. Just when we begin to doubt that nation-states view each other with the pessimistic perspective of "the worst plausible case," a dissatisfied dictator, such as Iraq's Saddam Hussein, will perceive an opportunity or a threat next door.

In addition to the tendency of nation-states to see other nation-states as predatory, democracies have a special problem in the conduct of foreign policy. Alexis de Tocqueville recognized this in the 1830s:

> Foreign policies demand scarcely any of those qualities which are peculiar to a democracy; they require, on the contrary, the perfect use of almost all those in which it is deficient. . . . A democracy can only with great difficulty regulate the details of an important undertaking, persevere in a fixed design, and work out its execution in spite of serious obstacles. It cannot combine its measures with secrecy or await their consequences with patience.[5]

The collapse of the Soviet system and the onset of the Gulf War changed the foreign policy agenda of the 1990s and beyond in profound and indeterminate ways. To call this period the "post–Cold War epoch" is only to admit ignorance about how nation-states will relate to each other without the "Old Order" principle of a bipolar world made up of the two superpowers, the Soviet Union and the United States. President Bush's evocation of a "New World Order" was an expression of hope, but not the articulation of a plan. The world of the 1990s will, in its own way, be just as challenging a test of American democracy as the world of de Tocqueville, or the world of the Cold War.

This chapter has no solution to the great foreign policy issues. Nonetheless, because the conduct of foreign policy is so complex and because there are particular problems facing a democracy as it formulates and puts into effect particular foreign

---

Switzerland, whose sovereignty is well guarded by most other states in order to maintain at least one spot on earth where diplomacy and business can take place no matter how chaotic international relations may be.

[5]*Democracy in America*, vol. 1, trans. Phillips Bradley (New York: Knopf, Vintage Books, 1945; orig. published 1835), p. 243.

policies, a well-balanced analysis of foreign policy problems is essential. Such an analysis must treat at least three dimensions of foreign policy, which will make up the three main sections of the chapter:

1. *Values.* What does the United States want? What are its national interests, if any? What counts as success?
2. *Instruments.* What tools are available for the conduct of foreign policy? What institutions, administrative arrangements, statutes, and programs have been established in order to enable the government to pursue our national interests?
3. *Roles.* How does the United States behave in world politics? Are its roles consistent with its values?

THE VALUES IN AMERICAN FOREIGN POLICY

When President Washington was preparing to leave office in 1796, he crafted with great care, and with the help of Hamilton and Madison, a farewell address that is one of the most memorable documents written by a government official or politician in all of American history. We have already had occasion to look at a portion of Washington's farewell address, because in it he gave some stern warnings against political parties. But Washington's greater concern was to warn the nation against foreign influence:

> History and experience prove that foreign influence is one of the most baneful foes of republican government. . . . The great rule of conduct for us in regard to foreign nations is, in extending our commercial relations to have with them as little *political* connection as possible. So far as we have already formed engagements let them be fulfilled with perfect good faith. Here let us stop. . . . There can be no greater error than to expect or calculate upon real favors from nation to nation. . . . Trust to temporary alliances for extraordinary emergencies . . . steer clear of permanent alliances with any portion of the foreign world. . . . Such an attachment of a small or weak toward a great and powerful nation dooms the former to be the satellite of the latter. [Emphasis in original.][6]

With the exception of a few leaders like Thomas Jefferson and Thomas Paine, who were eager to take sides with the French against all others, Washington was probably expressing sentiments shared by most Americans. In fact, during most of the nineteenth century, American foreign policy was to a large extent no foreign policy. But Americans were never isolationist if isolationism means the refusal to have any associations with the outside world. Americans were eager for trade and for the treaties and contracts facilitating trade. Americans were also expansionists, but their vision of expansionism was limited to filling up the American continent only.

There were of course domestic policies with important foreign policy implica-

---

[6]A full version of the text of the farewell address, along with a discussion of the contribution to it made by Hamilton and Madison, will be found in Daniel J. Boorstin, ed., *An American Primer* (Chicago: University of Chicago Press, 1966), vol. 1, pp. 192–210. The editing is by Richard B. Morris.

tions. For example, Congress gave subsidies to encourage shipbuilding so that
Americans could engage in coastal and international trade. And Congress imposed tariffs—taxes on imported goods. These were handy devices for raising revenue, because the persons being directly taxed were not even citizens who could vote against members of Congress. In addition to raising revenue, tariffs had the further advantage of protecting domestic competitors by artificially adding to the price of the imported goods.[7] There was also the famous Monroe Doctrine of 1823, which established the double principle that the European powers would not be permitted to colonize any territory or to intervene in the internal affairs of the existing nations in the Western Hemisphere. But note that it concerned itself strictly with *our* side of the Atlantic, and it was entirely defensive in nature. Moreover, it was a real foreign policy only to the extent that it was *in the interest of the European powers* to support and enforce it. At that time, America was still a client state.

What else was there of nineteenth-century foreign policy? We waged war against the British in 1812, but only after desperately trying to avoid getting involved with the British or their adversaries, the French. We waged war against Mexico in 1846, but this was a war to fill out the continent (as part of what we called our Manifest Destiny). Thus it was really a brutal extension of domestic policy, as was our policy toward Native Americans.

Three familiar historical factors help explain why Washington's sentiments became our tradition and the source of our foreign policy values. The first was the deep anti-statist ideology shared by most Americans in the nineteenth century, and on into the twentieth century. The second factor was federalism. The third was the United States's position in the world as a client state. The first two reinforced each other. Anti-statist means antagonism to central government. Federalism means preference for state government. Most nineteenth-century Americans recognized that if the United States became entangled in foreign affairs, national power would naturally grow at the expense of the states, and so would the presidency at the expense of Congress. Why? Because foreign policy meant having a professional diplomatic corps, professional armed forces with a general staff—and secrets. This meant professionalism, elitism, and remoteness from citizens. The third factor, being a client state, gave us the luxury of being able to keep our foreign policy to a minimum. Maintaining American sovereignty was in the interest of the European powers.

Legacy of the Traditional System

Two identifiable legacies flowed from the long tradition based on antistatism, with its fear of foreign policy and elitism, federalism, and client status. One of these legacies is the *intermingling* of domestic and foreign policy institutions. The second is *unilateralism*. Each of these will reveal a great deal more about the values behind today's conduct of foreign policy.

Intermingling of Domestic and Foreign Policy   Because the major European powers once policed the world, American political leaders could treat foreign pol-

[7]Frank W. Taussig, *The Tariff History of the United States* (New York: Capricorn Books, 1964), pp. 1–7.

American Foreign Policy:
Self-Interest or Idealism?

*W*ith *the end of the Cold War and the breakup of the Soviet Union, many foreign policy experts are reassessing America's role in the world community. Some argue that it is time to focus our attention and resources more directly on our own problems and needs. Others argue that this is no time for the United States to abandon its world leadership role.*

Economist Alan Tonelson defends what he labels an "interest-based" foreign policy for America. Such a position emphasizes placing American needs first and advocates foreign interventions only when they serve our interest. Foreign policy specialist Joshua Muravchik, on the other hand, rejects the realist view of Tonelson and others; he maintains that America has both a right and an obligation to extend democratic values around the world.

Tonelson

The United States cannot hope to achieve the desired level of security and prosperity by underwriting the security and prosperity of countries all over the world, and by enforcing whatever global norms of economic and political behavior this ambition requires. . . . It must therefore distinguish between what it must do that is absolutely essential for achieving this more modest set of objectives and those things it might do that are not essential. It must, in other words, begin to think in terms not of the whole world's well-being but rather of purely national interests. . . .

. . . An interest-based U.S. foreign policy would firmly subordinate international activism and the drive for world leadership to domestic concerns. Indeed, it would spring from new and more realistic ideas about what can be expected of a country's official foreign policy in the first place. . . . An interest-based approach would also reject the idea that meeting a set of global responsibilities can be the lodestar of U.S. foreign policy. . . . An interest-based foreign policy would acknowledge that the citizens of a democracy have every right to choose whatever foreign policy they please. . . .

The new foreign policy certainly would not preclude acting on principle. But it would greatly de-emphasize conforming to abstract standards of behavior. In fact, the new foreign policy would shy away from any overarching strategy of or conceptual approach to international relations. . . . Its only rule of thumb would be "whatever works" to preserve or enhance America's security and prosperity. . . . [1]

Muravchik

Although many state actions aim to defend interests, many do not. Some are motivated by altruism. The United States rushes aid to the victims of flood, famine, or other catastrophe wherever these occur for no motive other than human sympathy. Several other countries do the same. Various states offer asylum to the persecuted, provide good offices for the mediation of distant disputes, and even contribute troops to international peacekeeping forces, all for reasons that are essentially humanitarian. . . . The realists are left with the argument that it is wrong to foist our ways—that is, democracy—on others. In saying this the realists suddenly are arguing in moral terms. Their point, however, entails a logical fallacy. The reason it is wrong to impose something on others, presumably, is because it violates their will. But absent democracy, how can their will be known? Moreover, why care about violating people's will unless one begins with the democratic premise that popular will ought to be sovereign?

This argument implies that people prefer to be ruled by an indigenous dictator than to be liberated through foreign influence. The realists will have a hard time explaining this to the people of Panama who danced in the streets when U.S. invaders ousted dictator Manuel Noriega. . . .

The examples of Panama, Japan, Germany, the Dominican Republic, and Grenada notwithstanding, to foist democracy on others does not ordinarily mean to impose it by force. Nor does it mean to seek carbon copies of American institutions. . . . If individuals are obliged to abide by certain moral rules, can they be exempted from those rules when they act collectively with others in the name of the nation?[2]

[1]Alan Tonelson, "What Is the National Interest?" *The Atlantic*, July 1991, pp. 37, 39.
[2]Joshua Muravchik, *Exporting Democracy: Fulfilling America's Destiny* (Washington, DC: AEI Press, 1991), pp. 25, 34–36.

icy as a mere extension of domestic policy. The tariff is the best example. A tax on one category of imported goods as a favor to interests in one section of the country would directly cause friction elsewhere in the country. But the demands of those adversely affected could be met without directly compromising the original tariff, by adding a tariff to *still other goods* that would placate those who were complaining about the original tariff. In this manner, Congress was continually adding and adjusting tariffs on more and more classes of commodities. One student of the tariff reports that in the process the number of dutiable items, which began as just a handful in the 1830s, grew to many thousands by the 1930s.[8] Another important example of this intermingling is the Monroe Doctrine. As Ernest May, a Monroe Doctrine expert, put it, "the Monroe Doctrine [is] best explained in terms of domestic politics. . . . [It] was actually a by-product of an election campaign."[9] According to May, southern presidential candidate Henry Clay was using the threat of European intervention in Latin America as leverage against Massachusetts presidential candidate John Quincy Adams, who was then President Monroe's secretary of state.

[8]E. E. Schattschneider, *Politics, Pressures and the Tariff* (Englewood Cliffs, NJ: Prentice-Hall, 1935).
[9]Ernest May, *The Making of the Monroe Doctrine* (Cambridge, MA: Harvard University Press, 1975), p. x.

An important aspect of this intermingling of domestic and foreign affairs was amateurism. Americans refused to develop a tradition of a separate foreign service composed of professional people who spent much of their adult lives in foreign countries, learning foreign languages, absorbing foreign cultures, and developing a sympathy for foreign points of view. Instead, we tended to be highly suspicious of any American diplomat or entrepreneur who spoke sympathetically for any foreign viewpoint.[10] No systematic progress was made to create a professional diplomatic corps until after the passage of the Foreign Service Act of 1946. There was also an amateurism about our military services. Although we had distinguished military academies throughout our history, we resisted a professional army and rebelled against the development of a professional officer corps topped by a professional general staff. The Joint Chiefs of Staff (JCS) was not created until during World War II, and the curriculum of the military academies did not extend beyond ordinance and military etiquette until well after the war.

Even the great Woodrow Wilson was an amateur in foreign affairs. A leading Wilson biographer observed that Wilson was like most American leaders in ignoring the professionals in the State Department and distrusting the foreign service "because he thought that they, or many of them, were either aristocrats, the products of exclusive schools and a snobby society, or else sycophantic imitators of the wealthy class."[11]

No statement was ever more representative of American values than Wilson's "open covenants openly arrived at"—one of the Fourteen Points President Wilson included in his peace plan to end World War I. The idea behind this principle was that representatives of nations would get together and vote on decisions committing all nations to a course of action against any aggressor. And that was Wilson's hope for his pet project, the League of Nations—to render professional diplomacy unnecessary.

Unilateralism   Unilateralism, not isolationism, was the American posture toward the world. Isolationism means to try to cut off contacts with the outside, to be a self-sufficient fortress. We were never isolationist. Economically, culturally, and socially, we were always open and engaged. Unilateralism means to "go-it-alone." Americans have always been more likely to rally round the president in support of direct action rather than for a sustained, diplomatic venture. Unilateralism has meant distrust of diplomacy as well as diplomats.

The Great Leap—Thirty Years Late

The traditional era of United States foreign policy came to an end with World War I for several important reasons. First, the "balance of power" system[12] that

[10]E. E. Schattschneider, *Politics, Pressures and the Tariff.*

[11]Arthur S. Link, "Wilson the Diplomatist," in *The Philosophy and Politics of Woodrow Wilson*, ed. Earl Latham (Chicago: University of Chicago Press, 1958), p. 161.

[12]"Balance of power" is the primary foreign policy role played by the major European powers all during the nineteenth century, and it is a role available to the United States in contemporary foreign affairs, a role occasionally adopted but not on a world scale. This is the third of the four roles identified and discussed below.

had kept the major European powers from world war for 100 years[13] had collapsed. The most devastating of all wars up to that time had laid waste their economies, their empires, and in most cases, their political systems. Second, the United States was no longer a client state but in fact one of the great powers. Third, as shown in the earlier chapters, the United States was soon to shed its traditional domestic system of federalism with its national government of almost pure patronage policy. Thus, virtually all the conditions that contributed to the traditional system of American foreign policy had disappeared.

737
INSTRUMENTS
OF MODERN
AMERICAN
FOREIGN
POLICY

Yet, there was no discernible change in America's approach to foreign policy in the period between World War I and World War II. After World War I, as one foreign policy analyst put it, "the United States withdrew once more into its insularity. Since America was unwilling to use its power, that power, for purposes of foreign policy, did not really exist."[14] The Great Leap in foreign policy was finally made thirty years after conditions demanded it and only then after another world war, to which America's post–World War I behavior had undoubtedly contributed. This is not said with the intent merely to criticize—for who knows how different the world would have been if America had been more engaged in world affairs during the interwar years. The observation is made mainly to emphasize the strength of the traditional pattern, so strong as to resist change in the face of compelling conditions.

Habits of action and thought repeated generation after generation simply do not pass easily. Pressure for a new tradition came into direct conflict with the old. The new tradition required foreign entanglements; the old tradition feared them deeply. The new tradition required diplomacy; the old distrusted it. The new tradition required acceptance of antagonistic political systems; the old embraced democracy and anti-communism, even if the embrace required intervention into the internal affairs of other nations. The outcome was an effort to strike a balance between the old and the new.

The next section of this chapter identifies and analyzes the main instruments of foreign policy in the new, post–World War II tradition. But they can also be seen as five case studies in the balancing of the old tradition against the demands for a new tradition. Each is a dramatic illustration of how traditional values shaped the instruments we would use to fashion our new place in the world as the leading imperial power.

THE INSTRUMENTS OF MODERN AMERICAN FOREIGN POLICY

Just as we spoke of the techniques of control backing domestic policy, we speak here of instruments of foreign policy. Like a tool or technique, an instrument is

---

[13]The best analysis of what he calls the "100 years' peace" will be found in Karl Polanyi, *The Great Transformation* (New York: Rinehart and Company, 1944; Beacon paperback edition, 1957), pp. 5ff.

[14]John G. Stoessinger, *Crusaders and Pragmatists—Movers of Modern American Foreign Policy* (New York: W. W. Norton, 1985), pp. 21 and 34.

neutral, capable of serving many goals. There have been many instruments of American foreign policy, and we can deal here only with those instruments we deem to be most important in the modern epoch: diplomacy, the United Nations, the international monetary structure, economic aid, collective security, and military deterrence. Each will be evaluated for its utility in the conduct of American foreign policy, and each will be assessed in light of the history and development of American values.

Diplomacy

We begin this treatment of instruments with diplomacy because it is the instrument to which all other instruments must be subordinated, although they seldom are. In a world of nation-states in which each is proud of its nationhood and fiercely defensive of its sovereignty, the governments of all countries must accept each other or court violence. The *Oxford English Dictionary* defines diplomacy as "the management of international relations by negotiations; the method by which these relations are adjusted and managed by ambassadors and envoys." Diplomacy is simply the representation of a government to other foreign governments. Its purpose is to promote national values or interests by peaceful means. According to Hans Morgenthau, "A diplomacy that ends in war has failed in its primary objective."[15]

George Kennan, a former ambassador and distinguished foreign policy expert, recalled that when the first effort to create a modern foreign service was made by the Rogers Act of 1924, the State Department was still "a quaint old place with its law office atmosphere."[16] The Rogers Act recognized "foreign service officers" as members of a government career system based strictly on the merit principle—a system of stiff entrance examinations, probation, and orderly movement step by step through the ranks. But it took World War II and another important statute, the Foreign Service Act of 1946, to forge the foreign service into a fully professional diplomatic corps.

Diplomacy, by its very nature, is overshadowed by spectacular international events, dramatic initiatives, and meetings among heads of state or their direct personal representatives. The only U.S. career diplomat ever to win the Nobel Peace Prize, for example, was Ralph Bunche (who was also the first African American to win the prize). And even so, Bunche was at that time an employee of the United Nations staff rather than of the foreign service of the United States.

Diplomacy is as necessary as it is unnoticed. Only an occasional attack on diplomacy itself serves to remind us of its importance. One example is the November 1979 seizure of the U.S. embassy in Iran and the taking of diplomats as hostages. This serious affront to diplomacy was denounced by virtually every nation in the world, even by the Soviet Union. But the fact is that most countries going through genuine revolutions are distrustful of other countries, because of their diplomatic ties to the previous regime and because of the faith of the revolutionary leaders that the system they are creating is not only superior to all other

[15]Hans Morgenthau, *Politics Among Nations*, 2nd ed. (New York: Knopf, 1956), p. 505.

[16]George Kennan, *American Diplomacy, 1900–1945* (Chicago: University of Chicago Press, 1951), pp. 91–92.

systems in the world but is highly vulnerable. This is the origin of the *739*
INSTRUMENTS
OF MODERN
AMERICAN
FOREIGN
POLICY "Napoleonic role" to be discussed below.

That brings us back to the United States, whose distrust of diplomacy arises out of its own revolution. This distrust continues today, albeit in weaker form; impatience with or downright distrust of diplomacy has been built not only into all the other instruments to be discussed below but also into the modern presidential system itself.[17] So much personal responsibility has been heaped upon the presidency that it is difficult for presidents to entrust any of their authority or responsibility in foreign policy to professional diplomats stuck away in the State Department or in a far-away U.S. embassy. This distrust of diplomacy, coupled with the tradition of amateurism, has permitted presidents to use ambassadorial posts as patronage plums to reward prominent supporters in the presidential election campaign. This practice continues despite widespread complaints. The following report from the Reagan era is typical and could be leveled against every president:

> . . . The feeling . . . within the Foreign Service [is] that the Reagan White House has abused its prerogatives to name the president's ambassadors by filling 40% of the nation's 148 diplomatic missions around the world with political loyalists rather than career diplomats. Foreign service officers contend that the White House has unfairly blocked deserving professionals from promotion and devalued the quality of U.S. overseas representation.[18]

Given Bush's long career as a politician—even serving a term as chair of the Republican National Committee—the same general approach to the State Department was to be expected. Although President Bush promised to give friends or supporters no more than one-third of the total number of ambassadorships, before his first year was over he had made eighty-seven appointments, forty-eight of which (57 percent) were political contributors and only 43 percent were career foreign service officers. In comparison, at the same point in their terms, Presidents Reagan and Carter had appointed 37 percent of their friends in 1985 and 1977, respectively. In addition, the American Academy of Diplomacy (an organization of former Foreign Service and non-career ambassadors) rated the majority of Bush's political appointees as unqualified for their posts.[19] President Clinton was slower in making his appointments, filling a mere dozen ambassadorial posts during his first seven months in office. But his list of nominees and potential nominees also included a large proportion of friends and campaign contributors.[20]

Distrust of diplomacy has also produced a tendency among all recent presidents to turn frequently to military and civilian personnel outside the State Department to take on a special diplomatic role as direct personal representatives of the president. As discouraging as it is to those who have dedicated their careers to foreign service to have political hacks appointed over their heads, it is probably even more

---

[17]See Chapter 7 and Theodore J. Lowi, *The Personal President—Power Invested, Promise Unfulfilled* (Ithaca, NY: Cornell University Press, 1985), pp. 167–69.

[18]John M. Goshko, "Sticking It to the Foreign Service," *The Washington Post National Weekly Edition,* 25 May 1987, p. 6.

[19]*New York Times,* 7 November 1989.

[20]Elaine Sciolino, "Some Friends Fret as Clinton Is Slow in Choosing Envoys," *New York Times,* 3 June 1993, p. 1.

discouraging when they are displaced from a foreign policy issue as soon as relations with their country begin to heat up. When a special personal representative is sent abroad to represent the president, that envoy holds a status higher than the local ambassador, and the embassy becomes the envoy's temporary residence and base of operation. Despite the impressive professionalization of the American foreign service—with advanced training, competitive exams, language requirements, and career commitment—this practice of displacing career ambassadors with political appointees and with special personal presidential representatives continues.

The significance of diplomacy and its vulnerability to domestic politics may be better appreciated as we proceed to the other instruments. Diplomacy—which was invented, developed, and advanced by the Chinese, the Persians, the Romans, the European monarchs, and the British colonialists—was an instrument more or less imposed on the Americans as the prevailing method of dealing among nation-states in the nineteenth century. The other instruments to be identified and assessed below are instruments that Americans self-consciously crafted for themselves to take care of their own chosen place in the world affairs of the second half of the twentieth century. They are, therefore, more reflective of American culture and values than is diplomacy.

The United Nations

The utility of the United Nations to the United States as an instrument of foreign policy can too easily be underestimated. During the first decade or more after its founding in 1945, the United Nations was literally a direct servant of American interests. The most spectacular example of the United States's use of the United Nations as an instrument of American foreign policy was the official U.N. authorization and sponsorship of intervention in Korea with an international "peace-keeping force" in 1950. Thanks to the Soviet boycott of the United Nations at that time, depriving the U.S.S.R. of its ability to use its veto in the Security Council of the U.N., the United States was able to conduct the Korean War under the auspices of the United Nations.

The United States provided 40 percent of the U.N. budget in 1946 (its first full year of operation) and 28.8 percent of the billion-dollar U.N. budget of 1992.[21] Many Americans feel the United Nations does not give good value for the investment. But any evaluation of the United Nations must take into account the purpose for which the United States sought to create it: *power without diplomacy*. After World War II, when the United States could no longer remain aloof from foreign policy, the goal was to use our power to create an international structure that could be run with a minimum of regular diplomatic involvement—so that Americans

---

[21]In 1992 the Russian Federation contributed 9.4 percent; Germany, 8 percent; Japan, 11.9 percent; France, 5.7 percent; and Great Britain, 4.7 percent. The official U.N. budget of about a billion dollars is down significantly from the maximum $1.8 billion of 1988–89. But these numbers are not indicative of the U.N. scale of operation because they do not include U.S. and other contributions to specific U.N. operations and organizations. The following are examples of U.S. contributions (based on the 1990 budget): peace-keeping, $104 million; inter-American Organizations, $103 million; U.N. Children's Fund, $64 million; U.N. Development Program, $105 million; world food program, $163 million. See *The 1993 Information Please Almanac* (Boston: Houghton Mifflin, 1992), pp. 65 and 297–98.

could return to their normal domestic pursuits. This was the fulfillment of
Woodrow Wilson's dream of "open covenants openly arrived at": Debate instead
of diplomacy, votes instead of negotiation, international consensus and moral sua-
sion instead of intrigue and manipulation. Considered in this light, there is no
conceivable way the United Nations could have been a complete success.[22] It is
surprising that the United Nations can claim any successes at all, but it can.

The U.N. may have gained a new lease on life in the post–Cold War era, first
with its performance in the Gulf War and then with its role in Somalia. Although
President Bush's immediate reaction to Iraq's invasion of Kuwait was unilateral, he
quickly turned to the U.N. for sponsorship. The U.N. General Assembly initially
adopted resolutions condemning the invasion and approving the full blockage of
Iraq. Once the blockade was seen as having failed to achieve the unconditional
withdrawal demanded by the U.N., the General Assembly adopted further resolutions authorizing the twenty-nine nation coalition to use force if, by January 15,
1991, the resolutions were not observed. The Gulf War victory was a genuine
U.N. victory. The cost of the operation was estimated at $61.1 billion. First autho-
rized by the U.S. Congress, actual U.S. outlays were offset by pledges from the
other participants—the largest shares coming from Saudi Arabia ($15.6 billion),
Kuwait ($16 billion), Japan ($10 billion), and Germany ($6.5 billion). Final U.S.
costs were estimated at a maximum of $8 billion.[23]

The Gulf War was a special case because it was a clear case of invasion of one
country by another that also threatened the control of oil, which is of vital interest
to the industrial countries of the world. But in the case of Somalia, while the conflict violated the world's conscience, it did not threaten vital national interests
outside the country's region. The United States had propped up Somalia's government for years for purely Cold War purposes, but abandoned its dictatorial regime
in 1990 and left it to a chaotic civil war—with many war lords, tribal leaders, and
gangs of marauding youths. Late in 1992 thousands of American soldiers under
U.N. sponsorship were dispatched with almost no advance public preparation for a
limited military intervention to make the country safe enough for humanitarian
aid. One expert on diplomatic affairs characterized the operation as the affirmation of an important principle (and possibly a new U.N. precedent): "Once a
country utterly loses its ability to govern itself, it also loses its claim to sovereignty
and should become a ward of the United Nations."[24]

Somalia has been called a "war of conscience," and it was the first in which
U.N. troops were brought in strictly for humanitarian purposes.[25] The second be-

---

[22]One version of the purpose of the United Nations from the American perspective is the statement at
the time of its formation by the then Secretary of State Cordell Hull, who told an audience of wildly
applauding congressmen, "There will no longer be need for spheres of influence, for alliances, for balance of power, or any other of the special arrangements through which, in the unhappy past, the nations strove to safeguard their security or promote their interest." In other words, it would obviate
diplomacy. The quote is taken from John Lewis Gaddis, *The United States and the Origin of the Cold War,
1941–1947* (New York: Columbia University Press, 1972), pp. 30–31.

[23]There is in fact an ongoing dispute over a "surplus" of at least $2.2 billion, on the basis of which
Japan and others are expecting a bit of a rebate. *Report of the Secretary of Defense to the President and Congress* (Washington, DC: Government Printing Office, 1992), p. 26.

[24]Strobe Talbott, "America Abroad," *Time,* 14 December 1992, p. 35.

[25]"Defence in the 21st Century," *The Economist,* 5–11 September 1992, Special Insert, pp. 3–5.

came Bosnia, where Bosnian Serb and Croat troops were ejecting Muslims to prevent establishment of an independent state of Bosnia and Herzegovena. Throughout 1993, U.N. troops were employed as peacekeepers in an effort to maintain "safe havens" for Muslims, while diplomats searched for a peaceful solution.

Both of these interventions show the promise and the limits of the U.N. as an instrument of foreign policy in the post–Cold War era. Although the United States can no longer control U.N. decisions, as it could in the U.N.'s early days, the U.N. continues to function as a useful instrument of American foreign policy.

The International Monetary Structure

Fear of a repeat of the economic devastation that followed World War I brought the United States together with its allies (except the U.S.S.R.) to Bretton Woods, New Hampshire, in 1944 to create a new international economic structure for the postwar world. The result was actually two institutions, the International Bank for Reconstruction and Development (the World Bank) and the International Monetary Fund (IMF).

The World Bank was set up to finance long-term capital. Leading nations took on the obligation of contributing funds to enable the World Bank to make loans to capital-hungry countries. (The U.S. quota has been about one-third of the total.) The founders of the World Bank also provided that it could float bonds to raise capital and that it could insure or underwrite loans in order to encourage ventures by private investors.

The IMF was set up to provide for the short-term flow of money. After the war, the dollar was the chief means by which the currencies of one country would be "changed into" currencies of another country for purposes of making international transactions. A fund had to be set up to permit international exchanges to take place, permitting debtor countries with no international balances to make purchases and investments. The IMF was set up to work as an actual fund composed of both gold and the currencies of all the member countries. Dollars or other appropriate currencies would be lent to member countries to help them overcome temporary trade deficits without having to resort to draconian measures of contracting their demand for foreign goods and denying their own people consumer products. For many years after World War II, the IMF, along with U.S. foreign aid (see below), in effect constituted the only international medium of exchange.

After 1965, as a result of the Vietnam War and later of OPEC, the "dollar gap" that was the basis of World Bank and IMF operations became a dollar glut, where more dollars were available than nations needed or wanted for their international trade. The World Bank and the IMF declined in importance but continued to function in the face of the explosion in the amount of debt in the world. A major contribution to the problem in the 1970s was OPEC's accumulation of billions and billions of dollars with no place to put them. The answer was "recycling," where the oil-rich nations deposited their excess wealth in the banks of the big Western countries that bought most of the oil. These deposits, called "petrodollars," were then lent out by those private banks to developing countries, not only to modernize their economies but simply to pay their oil importation bills. The

743

INSTRUMENTS
OF MODERN
AMERICAN
FOREIGN
POLICY

TABLE 18.1
The World's Leading Debtor Nations in 1990 (in billions of dollars)

Nation	Debt	Nation	Debt
United States	$3,233	Morocco	24
Brazil	108	Yugoslavia	21
Mexico	94	Peru	19
Argentina	63	Chile	18
Nigeria	36	Colombia	17
Philippines	27	Côte d'Ivoire	16
Venezuela	26	Ecuador	12

Source: U.S. figure: *The World Almanac and Book of Facts, 1993* (New York: World Almanac, 1993), p. 128. All other figures are from OECD, *Financing and External Debt of Developing Countries, 1991* (Paris, 1992).

problem with having all these petrodollars to invest was that the private banks, which were completely unregulated, had a built-in incentive to encourage Third World countries to go further and further into debt. For example, every loan arranged by the bank received a commission of one-eighth of 1 percent. (On a $1 billion loan, this produced an automatic profit of $1.25 million.) The major banks were falling all over each other to encourage Third World countries to borrow more money. No wonder people turned around after about a decade and discovered that while the world was swimming in oil surpluses (by that time), it was also swimming in an even deeper sea of debt. Ironically, the world's greatest creditor, the United States, by the mid-1980s had become the world's heaviest debtor (see Table 18.1).[26]

During the past decade, the IMF returned to a position of enhanced importance through its efforts to reform some of the largest debtor nations, particularly those in the Third World, to bring them more fully into the global capitalist economy. The power of the IMF to set conditions on the loans it makes and to work with major private banks to refinance ("roll over") existing debt seems to have had a positive effect. For example, on August 20, 1982, Mexico announced that it would quit trying to repay its international debt, for the time being. This also meant no more borrowing. Exactly ten years later, in August 1992, "the Latin American debt saga [was], more or less, over. . . . Nowhere are the celebrations of life after debt bigger than on Wall Street. The re-emerging markets of Latin America had become hot business."[27] This modest but substantial reentry of Latin American countries into the world market is not due altogether to efforts of the IMF or the World Bank. But they helped pave the way for a trickle, then a flow, if not a flood, of Wall Street investment in Mexico and other countries.

Russia and thirteen other former Soviet republics were also invited to join the IMF and the World Bank with the expectation of receiving $10.5 billion from these two agencies, primarily for a rouble-stabilization fund. Each republic will get a permanent IMF representative, and the IMF is increasing its staff by at least 10

---

[26]A good discussion will be found in Stoessinger, *Crusaders and Pragmatists,* pp. 309–314.

[27]"Falling in Love Again," *The Economist,* 22 August 1992, p. 63.

percent to provide expertise in coping with the problems of these emerging capitalist economies. Although Boris Yeltsin insisted that "[Russians] do not intend to work to the direct dictation of the IMF," IMF and its policies would be sure to have an influence on the economic decisions of these newly emerging countries.[28]

Economic Aid

Commitment to rebuilding war-torn countries came as early as commitment to the basic postwar international monetary structure. This is the way President Franklin Roosevelt put the case in a press conference in November 1942, less than one year after we entered the war:

> Sure, we are going to rehabilitate [other nations after the war]. Why? . . . Not only from the humanitarian point of view . . . but from the viewpoint of our own pocketbooks, and our safety from future war.[29]

The particular form and timing for enacting American foreign aid was influenced by Great Britain's sudden decision in 1947 that it would no longer be able to maintain its commitments to Greece and Turkey. (Full proof that America would now have to *have* clients rather than *be* one.) Within three weeks of that announcement, President Truman recommended a $400 million direct aid program for Greece and Turkey, and by mid-May of 1947 Congress approved it. Since President Truman had placed the Greece-Turkey action within the larger context of a commitment to help rebuild and defend all countries the world over, wherever the leadership wished to develop democratic systems or to ward off communism, the Greek-Turkish aid was followed quickly by the historically unprecedented program that came to be known as the Marshall Plan, named in honor of Secretary of State (and former five-star general) George C. Marshall.[30]

The Marshall Plan—officially known as the European Recovery Plan (ERP)—was essential for the rebuilding of war-torn Europe. By 1952, the United States had spent over $34 billion for relief, reconstruction, and economic recovery of Western Europe. The emphasis was shifted in 1951, with passage of the Mutual Security Act, to building up European military capacity. Of the $48 billion appropriated between 1952 and 1961, over half went for military assistance, the rest for continuing economic aid. Over those years, the geographic emphasis also shifted, toward South Korea, Taiwan, the Philippines, Vietnam, Iran, Greece, and Turkey—that is, toward the rim of communism. In the 1960s, the emphasis shifted once again, toward what became known as the Third World. From 1962 to 1975, over $100 billion was sent, mainly to Latin America for economic assistance. Other countries of Africa and Asia were also brought in.[31]

---

[28]"IMF: Sleeve-Rolling Time," *The Economist*, 2 May 1992, pp. 98–99.

[29]Quoted in Gaddis, *The United States and the Origin of the Cold War, 1941–1947*, p. 21.

[30]The best account of the decision and its purposes will be found in Joseph Jones, *The Fifteen Weeks* (New York: Viking, 1955).

[31]Robert A. Pastor, *Congress and the Politics of U.S. Foreign Economic Policy* (Berkeley: University of California Press, 1980), pp. 256–80.

The importance of U.S. economic and military assistance to the economies of 745
INSTRUMENTS
OF MODERN
AMERICAN
FOREIGN
POLICY
the assisted countries and to their ability to resist "stomach communism" cannot
be denied. For example, for South Korea in the 1950s and 1960s and South Vietnam in the 1960s, U.S. foreign aid amounted to more than 10 percent of the
annual income of those two countries. Aid to India and Pakistan amounted to an
annual average of 2 percent and 3 percent, respectively, of their total annual income. American foreign aid to Israel and Egypt was of vital importance to their
economies and was an incentive for the establishment and maintenance of diplomatic relations between these two nations.

There has always been a conflict between whether aid would be used for economic development or military strength, and Table 18.2 demonstrates that a substantial proportion of foreign economic assistance has been in the form of direct
military aid. Although this aid seems to have reached its peak in the early 1970s,
that is slightly misleading, since all foreign grants and loans have become so permissive that each country is freer to allocate the assistance it receives to military
purchases if it decides to do so.

Many critics have argued that foreign aid is really aid for political and economic
elites, not for the people. Although this is to a large extent true, it needs to be understood in a broader context. If a country's leaders oppose distributing food or
any other form of assistance to its people, then there is little the United States, or
any aid organization, can do, short of terminating the assistance. Somalia was an
exception, but there have been many other cases where neither the United States
nor the U.N. were able to provide military protection for humanitarian economic
aid. Civil wars in Cambodia in the late 1970s and in Ethiopia and Sudan in the
1980s prevented thousands of starving families from receiving assistance while
goods piled up and rotted at nearby docks and airports. Elite greed has also interfered with economic aid. President Ferdinand Marcos of the Philippines skimmed
hundreds of millions of dollars worth of U.S. foreign aid before his abrupt removal

TABLE 18.2
U.S. Foreign Economic and Military Aid (1946–1990)

Period	Economic Aid	Military Aid	Total Economic and Military Aid	Annual Average
1946–1952	$ 31.1 billion	$ 10.5 billion	$ 41.6 billion	$ 5.94
1953–1961	24.1	19.3	43.4	5.42
1962–1969	33.4	16.9	50.3	6.3
1970–1979	26.9	38.8	65.7	6.57
1980–1988	82.0	43.2	125.2	13.91
1989–1990	10.8	4.9	15.7	7.85
Total 1946–1990	$208.3	$133.6	$345.5	

Source: *Statistical Abstract of the United States* (Washington, DC: Government Printing Office, 1992), p.
794. Economic aid shown here represents total U.S. economic aid: Agency for International Development, but also Food for Peace, Peace Corps, and subscriptions to World Bank and International Development Bank.

from office. Yet, needy people would probably be worse off if we cut off aid altogether. The lines of international communication must be kept open. That is why diplomacy exists, and foreign aid can facilitate diplomacy just as diplomacy is needed to help get foreign aid where it is most needed.

Another important criticism of U.S. foreign aid policy is that it has not been tied closely enough to U.S. diplomacy. The original Marshall Plan was set up as an independent program outside the State Department and had its own separate missions in each participating country. "ERP became a Second State Department."[32] This did not change until the program was reorganized as the Agency for International Development (AID) in the early 1960s and became part of the State Department. Meanwhile, the Defense Department always had principal jurisdiction over that substantial proportion of economic aid that went to military assistance. The Department of Agriculture has administered the commodity aid programs, such as Food for Peace. Each department has in effect been able to conduct its own foreign policy, leaving many foreign diplomats to ask, "Who's in charge here?"

That brings us back to the history of our efforts to balance traditional values with the modern needs of world leadership. Economic assistance is an instrument of American foreign policy, but it has been less effective than it might have been, because of the inability of American politics to overcome its traditional opposition to foreign entanglements and build a unified foreign policy—something that the older nation-states would call a foreign ministry. We have undoubtedly made progress, but foreigners often continue to wonder who is in charge.

Collective Security

In 1947, most Americans hoped that the United States could meet its world obligations through the United Nations and economic structures alone. But most foreign policy makers recognized that it was a vain hope even as they were permitting and encouraging Americans to believe it. They had anticipated the need for military entanglements at the time of the drafting of the original U.N. Charter by insisting upon language that recognized the right of all nations to provide for their mutual defense independently of the United Nations. And immediately after enactment of the Marshall Plan, the White House and State and Defense officials followed up with an urgent request to the Senate to ratify and to the House and Senate to finance mutual defense alliances.

At first quite reluctant to approve treaties providing for mutual security alliances, the Senate ultimately realized that the United States could not limit its peacetime involvement to purely economic matters and the U.N. As shown in Table 18.3, the first collective security agreement was the Rio Treaty (ratified by the Senate in September 1947), which created the Organization of American States (OAS). This was the model treaty, anticipating all succeeding collective security treaties by providing that an armed attack against any of its members "shall be considered as an attack against all the American states," including the United States. But since the OAS involved only the Western Hemisphere, it could be considered a modern implementation of the Monroe Doctrine. A more significant

---

[32]Quoted in Lowi, *The End of Liberalism*, p. 162.

TABLE 18.3
U.S. Collective Security (Multilateral) Treaties

Treaty	Date Signed	Treaty Terms	Members	
Rio Treaty (OAS)[a]	September 2, 1947	An armed attack against any American State "shall be considered as an attack against all the American States," and each one "undertakes to assist in meeting the attack."	Argentina Bolivia Brazil Chile Colombia Costa Rica Cuba[b] Dominican Republic Ecuador El Salvador	Guatemala Haiti Honduras Mexico Nicaragua Panama Paraguay Peru United States Uruguay Venezuela
North Atlantic Treaty (NATO)[c]	April 4, 1949	"The parties agree that an armed attack against one or more of them in Europe or North America shall be considered an attack against them all; and each party, will assist the . . . attacked by taking . . . such action as it deems necessary including the use of armed force."	Belgium Canada Denmark France[d] Germany[e] Greece[f] Iceland Italy	Luxembourg Netherlands Norway Portugal Spain Turkey[f] United Kingdom United States
ANZUS Treaty[g]	September 1, 1951	Each party recognizes that "an armed attack in the Pacific Area on any of the parties would be dangerous to its own peace and safety," and each party agrees that it will act "to meet the common danger in accordance with its own constitutional processes."	Australia New Zealand United States	
Southeast Asia Treaty (SEATO)[h]	September 8, 1954	Each party "recognizes that aggression by means of armed attack in the treaty area against any of the parties . . . would endanger its own peace and safety," and each will "in that event act to meet the common danger . . . "	Australia France New Zealand Pakistan Philippines	Thailand United Kingdom United States

[a]The Organization of American States (OAS), called for by the Rio Treaty, was established in April 1948, and includes the Caribbean states: Antigua and Barbuda, Bahamas, Barbados, Dominica, Grenada, Jamaica, St. Christopher and Nevis, St. Lucia, St. Vincent and the Grenadines, Suriname, Trinidad and Tobago.
[b]Suspended from the OAS in 1962.
[c]The North Atlantic Treaty Organization (NATO) was established in September 1950.
[d]Withdrew forces by 1967 but remains a NATO member.
[e]The Federal Republic of Germany joined in 1954 and maintained its membership, joined by East Germany, as a new united Germany in 1990.　[f]Joined in 1951.
[g]Abbreviation made up of the first letters of the names of the member nations.
[h]The Southeast Asia Treaty Organization (SEATO) was established in September 1954.
Sources: *The Cold War Years: American Foreign Policy since 1945* by Paul Y. Hammond and John Morton Blum, p. 256. Copyright © 1969 by Harcourt Brace Jovanovich, Inc., rearranged and printed with the permission of the publisher. Updated from U.S. Department of State, *Treaties in Force, 1989* (Washington, DC: Government Printing Office, 1989).

A NEW WORLD ORDER?

The tearing down of the Berlin Wall, the ultimate symbol of Soviet oppression, reunited East and West Germany, and marked the beginning of the end of Soviet dominance as a superpower. This shifting global balance of power has altered the stage of international politics considerably. Many threats to the new world order's promise of peace and cooperation exist and finding viable political solutions to these crises is difficult indeed.

Territorial aggression. During the Cold War, territorial disputes were viewed mostly as power plays between the satellite states of the United States and the Soviet Union. Fear of provoking these two military powers kept most nations from challenging each other's borders. Now, with the collapse of the Soviet Union, and Russia supporting U.S. policy, blatant acts of aggression similar to Iraq's invasion of Kuwait in August 1990 are more likely to occur. Although the United Nations coalition retaliated and defeated Iraq in the Gulf War, the UN's capacity to keep the peace is considerably less than was provided by the bipolar power balance of the Cold War era.

Arms control. While the United States and Russia dismantle their nuclear stockpiles, the proliferation of weapons among other countries has sustained the nuclear threat. Countries such as the United States and Germany have been trying to stimulate their sagging economies by selling off military hardware and technology. The countries of Asia now have the fastest growing military in the world, and some nations, such as China, admit to having nuclear capability. As it becomes more difficult to control the flow of arms in nations policed by the 1968 non-proliferation treaty, it is now the smaller powers that present the largest security concern.

Who is responsible for maintaining peace in the new world order? In Somalia, the former Soviet satellites, Eastern Europe, and Cambodia, the United Nations is playing an increasingly important role trying to resolve international crises as they occur. One suggestion has been made to create a new military division within the UN—either a voluntary unit that individuals from any country could join, or a permanent UN force from each country—to enable the UN to act more quickly in a crisis. But questions of "national interest" will always play a role in the decision to intervene, and it will still be necessary to balance one nation's needs with another's, making diplomacy an even more important part of any foreign policy.

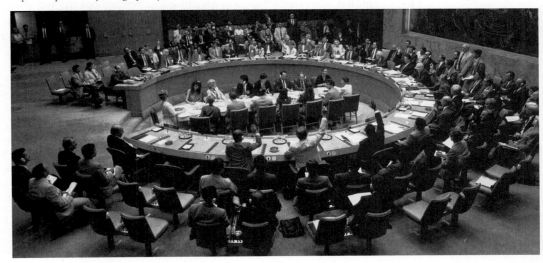

break with U.S. tradition against peacetime entanglements came with the North Atlantic Treaty (signed in April 1949), which created the North Atlantic Treaty Organization (NATO). ANZUS, a treaty tying Australia and New Zealand to the United States, was signed in September 1951. Three years later, the Southeast Asia Treaty created the Southeast Asia Treaty Organization (SEATO).

In addition to these *multilateral collective security treaties,* the United States entered into a number of *bilateral treaties*—treaties between two countries. The important ones are shown in Table 18.4. President Carter's reestablishment of full diplomatic relations with the People's Republic of China required cancellation of the treaty with the Republic of China (Taiwan). All other treaties continue in force. As one author observed, the United States has been a *producer* of security while most of its allies have been *consumers* of security.[33] This pattern has continued in the post–Cold War era, and its best illustration is the Persian Gulf War, where the United States provided the initiative, the leadership, and most of the armed forces, even though the allies were obliged to reimburse us for over 90 percent of the cost.

It is difficult to evaluate collective security and its treaties, because the purpose of collective security as an instrument of foreign policy is prevention, and success of this kind has to be measured according to what *did not* happen. The critics have argued that our collective security treaties posed a threat of encirclement to the U.S.S.R., forcing it to produce its own collective security, particularly in the Warsaw Pact.[34] Nevertheless, no one can deny the counterargument that the world enjoyed more than forty-five years without world war.

Both arguments are now obsolete. The Cold War as we knew it is over. The Warsaw Pact was formally terminated in 1991, East and West Germany were united, and the newly unified Germany elected to maintain membership in NATO, with the blessing of the Soviet Union. The end of the Cold War and of the Warsaw Pact produced an "identity crisis" in NATO and among its members, including the United States. Although the United States had always viewed NATO as a "profoundly political alliance," no one in U.S. foreign policy circles was ready to "sign off on its military activities."[35] Nevertheless, U.S. military forces within NATO changed their focus from containment of the Soviet Union to stabilization of a newly unified Germany.

NATO and the other mutual security organizations throughout the world are likely to survive in the post–Cold War epoch. But they are going to be less military alliances and more like economic associations to advance technology, reduce trade barriers, and protect the world environment. U.S. troops in Europe will be cut drastically in the 1990s, but some will remain in Germany, and they will, for the first time in the nearly half-century of NATO, serve under the supreme command of a European general.

---

[33]George Quester, *The Continuing Problem of International Politics* (Hinsdale, IL: Dryden Press, 1974), p. 229.

[34]The Warsaw Pact was signed in 1955 by the U.S.S.R., the German Democratic Republic (East Germany), Poland, Hungary, Czechoslovakia, Romania, Bulgaria, and Albania. Albania later dropped out.

[35]Norman, Kempster, "With No Cold War to Fight, NATO Faces an Identity Crisis," *Los Angeles Times,* 3 July 1990, p. H3.

TABLE 18.4
Bilateral Treaties between the United States and Individual Nations

Treaty	Date Signed	Treaty Terms	Members
Philippine Treaty	August 30, 1951	Each party recognizes that an "armed attack in the Pacific Area on either of the parties would be dangerous to its own peace and safety," and each party agrees that it will act "to meet the common dangers in accordance with its constitutional processes."	Philippines United States
Republic of Korea Treaty	October 1, 1953	Each party recognizes that "an armed attack in the Pacific Area on either of the parties . . . would be dangerous to its own peace and safety," and each party agrees to "act to meet the common danger in accordance with its constitutional processes."	Republic of Korea United States
Republic of China Treaty[*]	December 2, 1954	Each party recognizes that "an armed attack in the West Pacific Area directed against the territories of either of the parties would be dangerous to its own peace and safety" and that each would "act to meet the common danger in accordance with its constitutional processes." (The territory of the Republic of China is defined as "Taiwan and the Pescadores.")	Republic of China United States
Japanese Treaty[†]	January 19, 1960	Each party recognizes that "an armed attack against either party in the territories under the administration of Japan would be dangerous to its own peace and safety," and each party would "act to meet the common danger in accordance with its own constitutional provisions and processes."	Japan United States
Spanish Treaty	January 24, 1979	Each party is ready to prepare plans for action to be taken "in case of an attack against Spain or the United States in the context of a general attack against the West."	Spain United States

[*]The treaty was abrogated on January 1, 1980; but Congress in 1979 had passed a law (not written in the form of a defense agreement) requiring the United States "to maintain the capacity to resist any resort to force . . . that would jeopardize the security of Taiwan."

[†]Replaced the bilateral security treaty of 1951.

Sources: *The Cold War Years: American Foreign Policy since 1945* by Paul Y. Hammond and John Morton Blum, p. 256. Copyright ©1969 by Harcourt Brace Jovanovich, Inc., rearranged and printed with the permission of the publisher. Updated primarily from U.S. Department of States, *Treaties in Force, 1979* (Washington, DC: Government Printing Office, 1979), pp. 3031–3033.

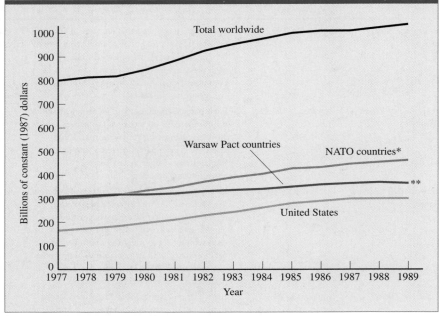

FIGURE 18.1
Military Expenditures through the End of the Cold War

*Excluding the United States.   **Dissolved 1991.
Source: *Statistical Abstracts, 1990* (Washington, DC: Government Printing Office, 1990), p. 334.

Military Deterrence

For the first century and a half of its existence as an independent republic, the United States held strongly to a "Minuteman" theory of defense: Maintain a small corps of professional officers, a few flagships, and a small contingent of marines; leave the rest of defense to the state militias; in case of war, mobilize as quickly as possible, taking advantage of the country's immense size and its separation from Europe to gain time to mobilize. The United States applied this policy as recently as post–World War I and was beginning to apply it after World War II, until the new policy of preparedness won out. The cycle of demobilization-remobilization was broken. With preparedness as the goal, peacetime defense expenditures grew steadily. Figure 18.1 compares this growth in the last twenty-two years of the Cold War for all the major powers, while Figure 18.2, Part 1, shows this growth for the United States.

However, the absolute size of the defense budget has not been the all-important consideration behind deterrence as an instrument of foreign policy. Figure 18.3 shows that, except for the late 1970s and early Reagan years, defense spending had actually declined as a percentage of gross national product since 1967; and Figure 18.1, Part 2 shows that, as a percentage of total federal outlays, national defense stayed fairly stable. Whether arms expenditures are motivated by a bilateral struggle, such as that between the United States and the Soviet Union, or by a variety

753

INSTRUMENTS
OF MODERN
AMERICAN
FOREIGN
POLICY

FIGURE 18.2

**Federal Budget Outlays for National Defense
(1975 to 1992 in 1982 dollars)**

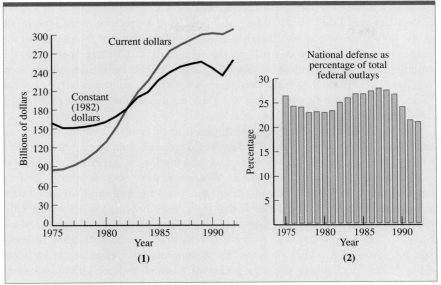

(1)

(2)

Source: *Statistical Abstracts, 1992* (Washington, DC: Government Printing Office, 1992), p. 330.

FIGURE 18.3

**Total Defense Spending
(As a Percentage of Gross National Product)**

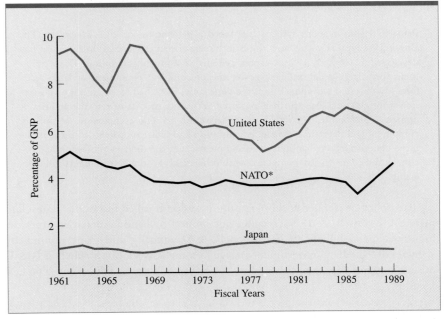

*Excluding the United States.

Source: U.S. Senate, Committee on the Budget, *Concurrent Resolution on the Budget for Fiscal Year 1989*
(Washington, DC: Government Printing Office, 1988), p. 138 and *Information Please Almanac, 1992.*

of struggles with many smaller potential aggressors, as in the post–Cold War era, the goal is not military dominance as such but *deterrence from any attack at all*. The Iraqi invasion of Kuwait proved that whatever had deterred the U.S.S.R. from aggression was not necessarily translatable into post-Cold War conflicts. The victory against Iraq may lead to technologies and policies of deterrence more appropriate to the post–Cold War world. But deterrence is still the name of the game, and the resumption and escalation of arms sales throughout the world, and especially in the Middle East since the Gulf War, suggests that the United States and other powers will have a real struggle to make deterrence work. There continues to be a kind of "arms race," but that race continues to be not for quantitative but for technologically qualitative superiority.

For over a century after Napoleon brought to the world the first mass citizen armies, military capacity in the Western world was measured quantitatively. Technology was, of course, always important. Technological superiority helped to make possible the domination of the Western powers over their non-Western colonies and of small U.S. armed contingents over the American Indians. But it was probably not until World War II that technology became the key to the military's value as an instrument of foreign policy. From then on, the technological tail began to wag the military dog. And it is not merely a question of adding technology by giving each soldier an automatic weapon and an electronic communications device. Technology means a policy of planned technological innovation. Probably the most important outcome of the Gulf War, especially from the military point of view, was that most of the expensive technology of the new weapons systems actually worked. This will likely enhance the credibility of military technology as the primary deterrent in the world.

The following observation, first made in 1960, is worth quoting at length for its applicability a generation later:

> Prior to 1940, weapons systems had lasted a generation, or even a century. The Brown Bess musket with which the British were armed at Waterloo in 1815 was first developed in 1690. By 1958, weapons systems were in rapid transition. The requirement for a large ready military power meant complete equipment of large ready forces with tested weapons. But at the same time, there had to be an improved version in production and a further improved version in process of research and development—each more costly than its predecessor. . . . The complexities of military equipment and operations demanded education and skills comparable to those in the more complicated civilian industries and professions; the military profession had become a skilled profession competing with other fields for the best in brains and leadership.[36]

The policy of planned technological innovation is called research and development (R & D). R & D is certainly not limited to national defense. American industries spend billions of dollars on R & D annually, and many nonmilitary agencies of the federal government engage in some R & D. But nowhere is R & D of such high priority as in the modern American military establishment. The U.S.

---

[36]G. A. Lincoln et al., "Mobilization and War," in *American Economic History*, ed. Seymour E. Harris (New York: McGraw-Hill, 1961), p. 232.

government and private industry together are spending about $150 billion a year *755*
INSTRUMENTS
OF MODERN
AMERICAN
FOREIGN
POLICY on R & D "covering everything from mapping the human genome to exploring the frontiers of physics. That is about 3 percent of America's gross domestic product, and about the same percentage that Japan and Germany spend." But there the similarity ends. Germany and Japan devote almost all of their R & D to civilian projects; the United States spends about 40 percent of its R & D on military projects. This came to nearly $60 billion in 1992, up from over $45 billion in 1988 and around $13 billion in 1980.[37]

There is also a hidden additional R & D military budget in the private manufacture of military hardware. We don't mean that this is a "cover-up." It is simply difficult to determine just where military R & D ends and manufacturing begins; nevertheless, it is certain that R & D takes a significant bite of each private defense production contract. Table 18.5 is a list of the top defense contractors and the value of their contracts with the Department of Defense for 1992. Immense companies like these are given defense contracts because the Defense Department assumes that big industries are more likely to engage in R & D as a natural and routine part of production and of competition for the next round of contracts. Ultimately, we are more concerned about the comparative number of scientists and engineers than with the comparative number of soldiers, or tanks and planes. This may not have been true at the start of the Cold War, but it certainly became true after 1957, when the Soviet Union embarrassed the United States with the launching of Sputnik, the first earth-orbiting satellite. Thirty-five years later education policy discourse continues to be moved by a concern for national power,

TABLE 18.5
The Top Ten Defense Contractors, 1992[*]

Company	Value of Contracts Received (billion)
McDonnell-Douglas	$9.3
Lockheed	7.5
General Electric	7.5
General Dynamics	6.0
Northrop	5.5
General Motors/Hughes Aircraft	5.3
Raytheon	5.1
Martin Marietta	5.0
Boeing	4.5
United Technologies	4.5

[*]Estimated 1992 military sales.
Source: *New York Times,* 17 January 1993, Section 3, page 6.

[37]The R & D budget totals include the following agencies: Department of Defense, Department of Energy (military related), and the National Aeronautics and Space Administration (NASA). See *Statistical Abstract of the United States, 1992* (Washington, DC: Government Printing Office, 1992), pp. 336, 595. The quote above and the 1992 figures come from Michael Lubell, "Getting the Right Mix on R&D," *New York Times,* 27 December 1992, sec. 3, p. 11.

military defense, and deterrence; and this has led to far greater stress on technical training. This phenomenon is worldwide, and it can be seen as a new expression of the arms race:

> Governments throughout the world are bullying educationalists to provide value-for-money, shifting expenditure from high-cost universities to low-cost polytechnics. . . . Governments have also moved their emphasis from education to training. A mixture of technological innovations and demographic trends is persuading governments to improve vocational qualifications of their workforces. The rise of information technology (IT) means that many of the lowliest shop-floor workers need to be able to operate a computer.[38]

The collapse of the Soviet Union as a superpower created an identity crisis for military deterrence, just as it did for collective security. Nearly two years before the collapse, a revision of deterrence policies was under way when Reagan and Gorbachev signed the 1987 Intermediate Nuclear Forces (INF) Treaty, which provided for an absolute reduction (toward zero) of medium-range intermediate nuclear missiles. The end of the Cold War raised public expectations for a "peace dividend" at last, after nearly a decade of the largest peacetime defense budget increases in U.S. history. Many defense experts, liberal and conservative, feared what they called a budget "free-fall," not only because deterrence was still needed but also because severe and abrupt cuts could endanger private industry in many friendly foreign countries as well as in the United States.

The Persian Gulf War brought both points dramatically into focus. First, the Iraqi invasion of Kuwait revealed the size, strength, and advanced modern technological base of not only the Iraq armed forces but of other countries, Arab and non-Arab, including the capability, then or soon, to make atomic weapons and other weapons of massive destructive power. Moreover, the demand for more-advanced weaponry was intensifying. The decisive victory of the United States and its allies in the Gulf War, far from discouraging the international arms trade, gave it fresh impetus. Following the Gulf War victory, *Newsweek* reported that "industry reps quickly realized that foreign customers would now be beating a path to their doors, seeking to buy the winning weaponry." The Soviet Union had led the list of major world arms sellers, and Russia and several other republics of the former Soviet Union have continued to make international arms sales, particularly since now there are "no ideological limitations" in the competition for customers.[39] The United States now probably leads the list of military weapons exporters, followed by France, Great Britain, and China. Note that these countrie. are also the five permanent members of the U.N. Security Council. The biggest buyers of military hardware are India, Japan, Saudi Arabia, and Syria. Iraq, second only to India before the Gulf War (and a major U.S. customer), will surely return as an important buyer if restrictions are lifted. Thus, some shrinkage of defense expenditure has been desirable but both Democrats and Republicans agree that this reduction must be guided by the continuing need to maintain U.S. and allied credibility as a deterrent to post–Cold War arms races.

[38]"Education: Trying Harder," *The Economist*, 21 November 1992, supplement pp. 3–4.
[39]"Arms for Sale," *Newsweek*, 8 April 1991, pp. 22–27.

757
INSTRUMENTS
OF MODERN
AMERICAN
FOREIGN
POLICY

Colin Powell
Soldier–Diplomat

Colin Powell (b. 1937)

Colin Powell followed one of the few career paths open to blacks in the years after World War II—military service. Powell enrolled as a cadet in the Reserve Officers' Training Corps (ROTC) while a student at City College of New York, and graduated at the top of his ROTC class in 1958. After receiving his commission, he served two tours of duty in Vietnam, and was injured and decorated both times.

In 1971, he earned a master's degree in business administration and was accepted in the highly competitive White House Fellowship program, where his quiet competence and efficiency earned the respect of Frank Carlucci and Caspar Weinberger, his superiors at the Office of Management and Budget. Powell returned to active military service in 1973, which included a tour in Korea, where he served as a battalion commander. He also served in the Carter administration as assistant to the deputy secretary of defense. In 1983, Powell was again called to serve in the Department of Defense (DOD), under President Reagan's defense secretary Caspar Weinberger. In that position, Powell became one of only five DOD officials informed of the covert effort to sell weapons to Iran in the scheme later labeled the Iran–Contra Affair. Yet Powell was one of the few individuals involved to emerge unscathed, because he had questioned the legality of the arms transfer, before the investigation began, and had been forthright in his testimony before Congress.

In June 1986 Powell returned to his preferred profession, active military service, in Germany. Six months later, Carlucci, who had been appointed Reagan's national security adviser, asked Powell to return to Washington to serve as his deputy. Powell declined several times, but reluctantly agreed after a direct request from Reagan. In this capacity, Powell oversaw the reorganization of the National Security Council called for by the Tower commission.

In November 1987, Carlucci was named secretary of defense, and Powell became national security adviser. In that position, Powell coordinated the implementation of the Intermediate-Range Nuclear Forces (INF) Treaty with the Soviet Union. In 1989, President Bush nominated him to be chairman of the Joint Chiefs of Staff, a position that perhaps best matched Powell's desire to remain in military service with his highly regarded ability to deal with Washington politics. In this position, Powell directed allied forces in the brief but militarily successful war with Iraq in early 1991. The swift victory only served to further polish Powell's image.

While he incurred the ire of some in the Bush administration for making known his early doubts about the wisdom of the military campaign, most people praised his handling of the war.

Source: Bob Woodward, *The Commanders* (New York: Simon and Schuster, 1991).

As to the second point, the end of the Cold War did not immediately open up equivalent opportunities for domestic uses of military production capacity. This has caused major changes and acute pains of readjustment for defense industries and any other industry with a large defense-industry component. Moreover, the conversion of these industries to domestic uses was not something the United States could do by itself within its own borders. Here is how the problem was expressed by the Office of Technology Assessment (OTA), an agency of Congress that has probably invested more time and resources into the study of R & D than any other agency:

> A comprehensive policy on international collaboration will be an integral part of deciding how to restructure the defense industries . . . how to allocate the burden of defense among the allied nations, and how to restructure the defense industries to do it. . . . Much weapons technology . . . is developed by large multinational companies with manufacturing facilities around the world. . . . Increasingly, international patterns of industrial development are making irrelevant much of the debate over U.S. defense production. If [we] pursued a strict policy of procuring only from U.S. companies, it would be difficult to specify exactly what a U.S. company is.[40]

Process Box 18.1 conveys a dramatic picture of the international relations involved in the production of one single weapons system, the F-16 fighter airplane. Another important example of an internationally produced weapon of the most advanced technological development is the involvement of the NATO countries in AWACS.[41] In a later report, OTA observed with increasing concern:

> The end of the Cold War and the accompanying decline in defense spending have . . . enhanced the economic motivations for international arms sales. . . . [Both] weapons and sophisticated military technology continue to proliferate. . . . This situation poses a major national policy dilemma—how to balance the use of arms exports as instruments of foreign policy, pressure by companies for greater and freer access to foreign markets, and the need to stem both a dangerous worldwide arms buildup and the increasing proliferation of the defense industry.[42]

All of this suggests that the threat of arms races and international conflicts exist even in the post–Cold War era. It also suggests that the United States is an important part of the problem as well as the most essential part of the solution. The only real hope for deterring the international use of arms—even without necessarily controlling the arms trade—will come from changes in the general political and economic environment. But such changes do not happen spontaneously. It takes effort, and such effort on an international scale must be understood as diplomacy. Try as we might, power without diplomacy can never be a permanent solution to the problem of controlling conflict among the distrustful nations of the world.

[40]U. S. Congress, Office of Technology Assessment, *Arming Our Allies: Cooperation and Competition in Defense Technology*, OTA-ICS-449 (Washington, DC: Government Printing Office, May 1990), pp. 10–11.

[41]Ibid., p. 10. AWACS is an acronym for Airborne Warning and Command System.

[42]U.S. Congress, Office of Technology Assessment, *OTA Report Brief*, (Washington, DC: Government Printing Office, June 1991), p. 1.

How the F-16 Is Produced
The International Relations of Defense

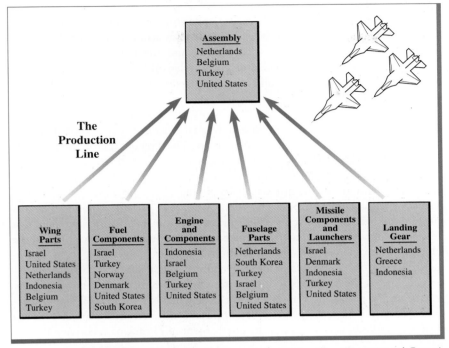

Source: U.S. Congress, Office of Technology Assessment, *Arming Our Allies: Cooperation and Competition in Defense Technology*, OTA-ICS-449 (Washington, DC: Government Printing Office, May 1990), pp. 42–43, which is an extremely elaborate diagram of at least seventy-five separate parts of the F-16. The information was provided by the main producer, General Dynamics Corporation.

ROLES NATIONS PLAY

Although each president has hundreds of small foreign fires to fight and can choose the instruments of policy in each particular situation, his primary foreign policy problem is choosing an overall *role* for the country in foreign affairs. Roles help us to define a situation in order to control the element of surprise in international relations. Surprise is in fact the most dangerous aspect of international relations, especially in a world made small and fragile by "smart weapons" technology.

Choosing a Role

Presidents have some freedom of choice in defining the role they would have our nation play. But each president is limited somewhat by the choices made by his predecessor and even more so by the way the presidency is constructed as well as by the relationship that the presidency has developed with the public (see Chapter 6 and later in this chapter). The modern presidency unintentionally pushes each occupant toward the power-without-diplomacy outlook we have already identified.

The problem of choosing a role can be understood by identifying from history a limited number of roles actually played by nation-states in the past. Four such roles will be drawn from history—the Napoleonic, the Holy Alliance, the economic expansionist, and the balance-of-power roles. Although the definitions will be exaggerations of the real world, they do capture in broad outline the basic choices available.

The Napoleonic Role The Napoleonic role takes its name from the role played by postrevolutionary France under Napoleon. The French at that time felt not only that their new democratic system of government was the best on earth but that France would not be safe until the system was adopted universally. If this meant intervention into the internal affairs of France's neighbors, and if that meant warlike reactions, then so be it. President Woodrow Wilson expressed a similar viewpoint when he supported our declaration of war in 1917 by his argument that "the world must be made safe for democracy." Obviously such a position can be adopted by any powerful nation as a rationalization for intervening at its convenience in the internal affairs of another country. But it can also be sincerely espoused, and in the United States it has from time to time enjoyed broad popular consensus. We played the Napoleonic role most recently in ousting Philippine dictator Ferdinand Marcos (February 1986), Panamanian leader Manuel Noriega (December 1989), and the Sandinista government of Nicaragua (February 1990).

The Holy Alliance Role The concept of the Holy Alliance emerged out of the defeat of Napoleon and the agreement by the leaders of Great Britain, Russia, Austria, and Prussia to preserve the social order against *all* revolution, including democratic revolution, at whatever cost. (Post-Napoleonic, Restoration France also joined it.) The Holy Alliance system made use of every kind of political instrument available—including political suppression, espionage, sabotage, and outright military intervention—to keep existing governments in power. The Holy Alliance role is comparable to the Napoleonic role in that each operates on the assumption that intervention into the internal affairs of other countries is justified for the maintenance of peace. But Napoleonic intervention is motivated by fear of dictatorship, and it can accept and even encourage revolution. In contrast, Holy Alliance intervention is antagonistic to political change *as such,* even when this means supporting a dictatorship. The following is a description of the original Holy Alliance pattern by the historian Paul Kennedy:

> . . . because the French Revolution had been such a frightening challenge. . . . Metternich and fellow conservatives now regarded any new developments with suspicion. An adventurist diplomacy. . . was as much to be frowned upon as a campaign for national self-determination or for constitutional reform. . . . Many of the military actions which did occur were initiated precisely to defend the existing socio-political order. . . . As for territorial changes within Europe, they could occur only after the agreement of the "Concert" of the Great Powers, some of which might need to be

compensated in one way or another. Unlike the age of Napoleon preceding it or the age of Bismarck [balance-of-power system] following it, therefore, the period 1815–1865. . . gave a basic, if precarious, stability to the existing states system.[43]

Because the Holy Alliance role became more important after the Cold War ended, illustrations of this role will be given toward the end of this chapter.

The Balance-of-Power Role   This role is basically an effort by the major powers to play off against each other so that no great power or combination of great and lesser powers can impose conditions on the others. The most relevant example is found in the nineteenth century, especially the latter half. Take the complex arrangement engineered by master balancer Otto von Bismarck, prime minister of Prussia:

> In the last weeks of 1886 and the early part of 1887, Bismarck was engaged in fostering four sets of negotiations: for the renewal of the Triple Alliance [Prussia, Austria, Italy] to safeguard Austria from a stab in the back by Italy; for an agreement primarily involving Austria and Britain, to preserve the *status quo* in the Balkans and the Near East; for an agreement centering around Britain, Italy, and Austria, to preserve the *status quo* in the Mediterranean; and for an agreement between [Prussia] and Russia . . . [in which] each agreed to remain neutral if the other became involved in war with a third power [except Prussia] against France, or by Russia against Austria.[44]

World War I was a consequence of the collapse of the "balance-of-power system."[45]

The feature of the balance-of-power role that is most distinct from the two previously identified roles is that this role accepts the political system of each country, asking no questions except whether the country will join an alliance and will use its resources to ensure that each country will respect the borders and interests of all the others.

The Economic Expansionist Role   This role, also called the capitalist role, shares with the balance-of-power role the attitude that the political system or ideology of a country is irrelevant; the only question is whether a country has anything to buy or sell and whether its entrepreneurs, corporations, and government agencies will honor their contracts. Governments and their armies are occasionally drawn into economic expansionist relationships in order to establish, reopen, or expand trade relationships, and to keep the lines of commerce open. But the role is political. The point can be made that the economic expansionist role was the role consistently played by the United States in Latin and Central America until the Cold War (perhaps in the 1960s and beyond) pushed us toward the Holy Alliance role in most of those countries.

[43]Paul Kennedy, *The Rise and Fall of the Great Powers* (New York: Vintage Books, 1987), pp. 159–60.

[44]Felix Gilbert et al., *The Norton History of Modern Europe* (New York: W. W. Norton, 1971), pp. 1222–24.

[45]For a comparison of the Holy Alliance role with the balance of power role see Karl Polanyi, *The Great Transformation*, pp. 5–11 and 259–62.

The collapse of the Soviet Union and the eagerness shown by the newly independent members of the former Communist bloc to join the free market have been acclaimed as the triumph of capitalism. And that may be only a modest exaggeration. However, like arms control, economic expansion does not happen spontaneously. In the past, economic expansion owed a great deal to military backing, because contracts do not enforce themselves, trade deficits are not paid automatically, and new regimes don't always honor the commitments made by regimes they replace. The only way to expand economic relationships is through diplomacy.

Roles For America Today

Although "making the world safe for democracy" was a popular expression of World War I, it was taken more seriously after World War II, when at last the United States was willing to play a more sustained part in foreign affairs. The Napoleonic role was most suited to our view of the postwar world. To create the world's ruling regimes in our own image would indeed give us the opportunity to return to our private pursuits, for if all or even most of the world's countries were governed by democratic constitutions, there would be no war since no democracy would ever attack another democracy—or so we assumed.

The emergence of the Soviet Union as a superpower was the overwhelming influence on American foreign policy thinking in the post–World War II era. The distribution of power in the world was "bipolar," and Americans saw the world separated in two, with an "Iron Curtain" dividing the Communist world from the free world. Immediately after the war, the American foreign policy goal had been "pro-democracy," a Napoleonic role dominated by the Marshall Plan and the genuine hope for a democratic world. This quickly shifted toward a Holy Alliance role, with "containment" as our primary foreign policy criterion.[46] Containment was fundamentally a Holy Alliance concept. According to foreign policy expert Richard Barnet, during the 1950s and 1960s, "the United States used its military or paramilitary power on an average of once every eighteen months either to prevent a government deemed undesirable from coming to power or to overthrow a revolutionary or reformist government considered inimical to America's interests."[47] Although Barnet did not refer to Holy Alliance, his description fits the model perfectly.

During the 1970s, the United States played the Holy Alliance role less frequently, not so much because of the outcome of the Vietnam War as because of the emergence of a multipolar world. In 1972, the United States accepted the People's Republic of China as the government of mainland China and broke forever its pure bipolar Cold War view of world power distribution. Other powers became politically important as well, including Japan, the European Economic Community (EC), India, and, depending on their own resolve, the countries making up the Organization of Petroleum Exporting Countries (OPEC). The United States

---

[46]The original theory of containment was articulated by former ambassador and scholar George Kennan in a famous article published under the pseudonym Mr. X, "The Sources of Soviet Conduct," *Foreign Affairs* 25 (1947), p. 556.

[47]Richard Barnet, "Reflections," *New Yorker*, 9 March 1987, p. 82.

experimented with all four of the previously identified roles, depending on which

was appropriate to a specific region of the world. In the Middle East, we tended to play an almost classic balance-of-power role, by appearing sometimes cool in our relations with Israel and by playing off one Arab country against another. President Nixon introduced balance-of-power considerations in the Far East by "playing the China card." In other parts of the world, particularly in Latin America, we tended to hold to the Holy Alliance role.

This multipolar phase lasted until 1989, when the Soviet Union collapsed and the Cold War ended. Soon thereafter the Warsaw Pact collapsed too, ending armed confrontation in Europe. With almost equal suddenness, armed suppression of minorities within Russia and Eastern Europe was relaxed, and the popular demand for "self-determination" produced several new nation-states and the demand for still more. On the one hand, it is indeed good to witness the reemergence of some twenty-five major nationalities after anywhere from forty-five to seventy-five years of suppression. On the other hand, policy makers with a sense of history are aware that this new world order bears a strong resemblance to the world of 1914. It was known then as Balkanization. Balkanization meant nationhood and self-determination. But it also meant war. The Soviet Union after World War I and Yugoslavia after World War II kept more than twenty-five nationalities from making war against each other for several decades until 1989. The world was caught unprepared for the dangers of a new disorder that the reemergence of these nationalities produced.

It should also be emphasized that the demand for nationhood has been emerging with new vigor in many other parts of the world—the Middle East, south and southeast Asia, South Africa. Perhaps this is *world Balkanization*. We should not overlook the reemergence of the spirit of nationhood among ethnic minorities in Canada and the United States.

Globalization of Markets   The collapse of the Cold War unleashed another dynamic factor, the globalization of markets; one could call it the globalization of capitalism. This is good news, but it has its problematic side because the free market can disrupt nationhood. Although globalization of markets is enormously productive, countries like to enjoy its benefits while attempting at the same time to prevent international economic influences from affecting local jobs, local families, and established class and tribal relationships.

This struggle between capitalism and nationhood produces a new kind of bipolarity in the world. The old world order was shaped by *external bipolarity*—of West versus East. This seems to have been replaced by *internal bipolarity*, wherein each country is struggling to make its own hard policy choices to preserve its cultural uniqueness while competing effectively in the global marketplace. The question is, What are the implications of internal bipolarity for the role or roles America is going to have to play in the post–Cold War world?

At first glance, it appears that America finally got what it wanted—a world that would run itself well enough without need for much U.S. foreign policy at all. But we have obviously been betrayed by events. U.S. foreign policy roles and priorities have not been shuffled very much, if at all. In fact, the Holy Alliance role seems to be more prominent than ever. There is, of course, one big difference—the absence of the Soviet Union and the current willingness of Russia to support rather than

George Kennan and Henry Kissinger
Architects of American Foreign Policy

Two of the most important and influential figures in American foreign policy never held elective office. Known more for their intellect than for their use of political power, both George Kennan and Henry Kissinger developed powerful paradigms for the conduct of American foreign policy.

George Kennan, a career foreign service officer and expert on the Soviet Union, has spent many years studying Soviet language and politics. While serving as second-in-command at the American embassy in Moscow at the end of World War II, Kennan was asked for advice about postwar Soviet intentions from policy makers in Washington. His response was an 8,000-word telegram in which he attacked America's spirit of cooperation with the Soviets. Kennan believed that the U.S.S.R. viewed the world as divided into two camps, socialist and capitalist, and that in such a "bipolar" world there could be no peaceful coexistence. Therefore, the United States had two choices: (1) resist Soviet efforts to undermine the Western coalition or (2) buy time until the Soviet Union changed from within.

This telegram became the blueprint for America's postwar policy in what has been labeled the Cold War. Fearing he had succeeded too well, however, Kennan published an article a year later in the journal *Foreign Affairs* under the pseudonym Mr. X, in which he argued that the U.S.S.R. was not out to dominate the world. Rather, he asserted, the Soviets wanted a ring of sympathetic nations around their country as a buffer against future attacks (remembering that over the centuries the Soviets had been attacked and devastated numerous times by invading armies). Kennan's conclusion to his article literally became American policy for the next two decades: "The main element of any United States policy toward the Soviet Union must be that of a long-term patient but firm and vigilant *containment* of Russian expansive tendencies" (emphasis added).

Like Kennan's, Henry Kissinger's path to foreign policy grew from intellect and

George Kennan

oppose American policies. During the Cold War era, the purpose of the Holy Alliance role was to keep regimes in power *as long as they did not espouse Soviet foreign policy goals*. In the post–Cold War world, the purpose of the Holy Alliance role is still to keep regimes in power, but only as long as they maintain general stability, keep their nationalities contained within their own borders, and encourage their economies to attain some level of participation in the global market.

Perhaps the first indication of post–Cold War American foreign policy conduct was President Bush's conciliatory approach to the dictatorial regime of the People's

experience. As a Harvard Ph.D. and professor, Kissinger wrote extensively in the 1950s and 1960s on American-Soviet policy and the role of nuclear weapons. Impressed with his ideas, foreign policy experts in the Eisenhower, Kennedy, and Johnson administrations sought Kissinger's advice as a so-called defense intellectual. In· 1969, Kissinger was selected by newly elected President Richard Nixon to serve as his national security adviser. Together, Nixon and Kissinger changed the shape of U.S. foreign policy. While taking a hard line on the Vietnam War, Kissinger orchestrated Nixon's historic trips to China and the Soviet Union in 1972, ushering in an era of "détente" between the superpowers. He was also instrumental in reaching an important agreement with the Soviets to limit nuclear arms, known as SALT I (the Strategic Arms Limitation Treaty). Kissinger sought to implement his long-standing belief in "power politics"—namely, that the only international relations that really matter are those between the world's big and powerful nations, and that the problems of smaller nations are best viewed in terms of how they affect the superpowers. While this philosophy was helpful in guiding improved U.S.-Soviet relations, it contributed to mistakes in Vietnam.

Through a combination of intellect and an unexcelled talent for bureaucratic politics, Kissinger dominated foreign policy making during the Nixon and Ford administrations (he was named secretary of state in 1973). After Ford's defeat in 1976, Kissinger began a consulting firm that helped provide access to top governmental and corporate leaders for his clients, which have included China and other nations. In contrast, George Kennan withdrew from public life, in part because of his disenchantment with the course of foreign policy in the 1950s and 1960s. As a scholar and researcher affiliated with the Institute for Advanced Study in Princeton, Kennan continued to garner respect for his intellect and perspectives on the policy he had helped create.

Source: Fred Kaplan, *The Wizards of Armageddon* (New York: Simon and Schuster, 1983).

Henry Kissinger

Republic of China following its brutal military suppression of the democratic student movement in Tiananmen Square in June 1989. Not only did the dictator Deng Xiaoping receive America's most ardent public embrace; China received our coveted "most favored nation" status despite repeated efforts by Congress to deny it until China reformed itself.[48] President Clinton continued this approach, again

---

[48]The 1974 Trade Act provides that nonmarket—namely, Communist—countries will not receive the trade concessions enjoyed by our best customers unless the president waives the restriction.

renewing China's "most favored nation" status in 1993, but with a promise to review it carefully after a year to be sure that political reform in China warranted another renewal.

Iraq offers probably the most meaningful example because our approach to Iraq's invasion of Kuwait was a genuine "concert of nations" approach. The concert in this case was the twenty-nine-nation alliance, under U.N. sponsorship, to remove Iraq's army from Kuwait. After the victory, President Bush initially took a Napoleonic position, urging the people of Iraq to "take matters into their own hands" and to force Hussein to "step aside." But once the uprisings began, President Bush backed away, thus revealing that the real intent had been to leave the existing military and party dictatorship in power, with or without Hussein.

Another indication of our post–Cold War role is the new arms race—that is, the international market in military products—and the growing importance of the Holy Alliance role in America's effort to produce a "new world order." The primary incentive in the international sale of military products is to keep our own defense industry alive and prosperous in the face of domestic defense budget cuts. We remain the biggest producer and exporter of advanced weaponry, but many other countries manufacture military materials, and a tremendous proportion of their military goods are for export. These countries are Brazil (over 80 percent for export); Italy (62 percent); Israel (47 percent); Spain (41 percent); the United Kingdom (40 percent); and Sweden (24 percent).[49] This means that each of these economies has a heavy stake in the international arms market. It also means that the United States and Russia in particular have a double stake in its maintenance, because they profit not only from their own exports but from royalties they earn on the exports of the other countries since most of the weapons and weapons components these smaller countries manufacture are *under license from the United States and Russia*.[50]

Until 1991, Iraq was the biggest importer of military goods. Between 1983 and 1988, the U.S. Arms Control and Disarmament Agency could identify $40 billion worth of arms bought by Iraq on the international market. And Iraq will almost certainly return in the near future to major status as a purchaser. Meanwhile, the largest importers are Saudi Arabia ($26 billion imported during the same five years), India ($15 billion during same period), Syria ($13 billion), and Iran ($12 billion). There were many other big-ticket importers.[51]

Why are these countries buying so much advanced military material? In some instances there are actual arms races. Just as the United States and the Soviet Union used weaponry as a deterrent against each other, so smaller but neighboring countries use their weaponry as a deterrent against one another. The value of weapons importation for these countries can be seen in the regular use the United States and the United Nations make of restrictions and embargoes on weapons as sanctions against misbehaving countries.

---

[49]See U.S. Congress, Office of Technology Assessment, *Global Arms Trade* (Washington, DC: Government Printing Office, June 1991).

[50]The license is a sale to a foreign company by, for example, a U.S. company, of the right to manufacture one of its products. This is subject to approval by the Departments of Defense and State.

[51]*Global Arms Trade*, pp. 4–7.

Another reason is that many of the most despotic regimes view a big military presence as an essential means of maintaining control of their own population. All too often, the United States has cooperated in this aspect of the arms trade, even encouraging it, as part of our Holy Alliance role. Supporting existing regimes was a key aspect of the original Holy Alliance of the nineteenth century and remains a key aspect of it in the post–Cold War world today. The United States will never wholly approve of despotic regimes and is rarely even comfortable with benevolent but undemocratic ones. But we find ourselves supporting distasteful regimes because we like world stability more than we dislike undemocratic regimes. And this attitude makes the Holy Alliance role a lot easier to play, because it is an attitude with which our European allies are historically comfortable.

A Holy Alliance role, however, will never relieve the United States of the need for diplomacy. In fact, diplomacy becomes all the more important because despotic regimes eventually fail and in the process attempt to thrust their problems on their neighbors. The dissolution of Yugoslavia and the inability of a concert of nations to stop the genocidal ethnic struggle there testify to the limits of the Holy Alliance role. This is not to argue that war is never justifiable or that peace can always be achieved by talk among professional diplomats or purchased by compromise or appeasement. It is only to argue that there are severe limits on how often a country like the United States can engage in Holy Alliances. When leaders in a democracy like ours engage in unilateral or multilateral direct action, with or without military force, they must have overwhelming justification. In all instances, the political should dominate the military. That is what diplomacy is all about. In 1952, the distinguished military career of General Douglas MacArthur was abruptly terminated when President Truman dismissed him for insubordination. At issue was MacArthur's unwillingness to allow the military in Korea to be subordinated to the politicians and the diplomats. His argument was "In war, there is no substitute for victory."[52] But he was overlooking the question and therefore missed the very point that should guide any foreign policy: Is there a substitute for war?

SUMMARY

This chapter began with a definition of the United States as a nation-state in a world of nation-states, whose ignorance of each other breeds distrust and hostility. The purpose of foreign policy is to defend national sovereignty against other nation-states that are conducting their foreign policy for the same purpose. The chapter was then divided into three sections, each devoted to one of the fundamental dimensions of foreign policy: values, instruments, and roles.

The first section, on values, traced out the history of American values that had a particular relevance to American perspectives on the outside world. We found that the American fear of a big national state applied to foreign as well as domestic governmental powers. The founders and the active public of the founding period all recognized that foreign policy was special, that the national government had

---

[52]Address to a joint session of Congress, 9 April 1951.

special powers in its dealings with foreigners, and that presidential supremacy was justified in the conduct of foreign affairs. The only way to avoid the big national government and presidential supremacy was to avoid the foreign entanglements that made foreign policy, diplomacy, secrecy, and presidential discretion necessary. Americans held on to their "antistatist" tradition until World War II, long after world conditions cried out for American involvement. And even as we made the "Great Leap" into involvement in world affairs, we held on tightly to the legacies of 150 years of tradition: the *intermingling* of domestic and foreign policy institutions, and *unilateralism,* the tendency to "go it alone" when confronted with foreign conflicts.

The second section looked at the instruments—that is, the tools—of American foreign policy. These are the basic statutes and the institutions by which foreign policy has been conducted after World War II had thoroughly thrust us into international engagements. Each of these instruments was presented in some detail: diplomacy, the United Nations, the international monetary structure, economic aid, collective security, and military deterrence. Although Republicans and Democrats look at the world somewhat differently, and although each president has tried to impose a distinctive flavor of his own on foreign policy, they have all made use of these basic instruments, and that has given foreign policies a certain continuity. When Congress created these instruments after World War II, the old tradition was still so strong that it moved Congress to try its best to create instruments that would do their international work with a minimum of diplomacy—a minimum of the human element. This is what we called power without diplomacy.

The third section concentrated on the role or roles the president and Congress have sought to play in the world. To help simplify the tremendous variety of tactics and strategies that foreign policy leaders can select, we narrowed the field down to four categories of roles nations play, suggesting that there is a certain amount of consistency and stability in the conduct of a nation-state in its dealings with other nation-states. These were labeled according to actual roles that diplomatic historians have identified in the history of major Western nation-states: the Napoleonic role, the Holy Alliance role, the balance-of-power role, and the economic expansionist role. These roles give meaning to a great number of the specific actions that American presidents and their representatives have taken in the world since World War II. And they are especially helpful in the analysis of the most recent presidents, because as the old tradition weakened, presidents were given more authority to operate with discretion throughout the world. Yet, the tactics available to a country's leadership must ultimately have some definable purpose. Otherwise, conduct would be unstable, unpredictable, and as great a danger to peace as aggression itself.

The final section attempted to identify and assess the role the United States was developing for itself in the post–Cold War era. Most of the signs and cases indicate that Holy Alliance was to be the role of choice. But whatever its advantages may be, Holy Alliance approaches will never allow the United States to have its domestic cake and eat it too. We are tied inextricably to the perils and ambiguities of international relationships, and diplomacy is still the monarch of all available instruments of foreign policy.

FOR FURTHER READING

Blechman, Barry M., and Stephen Kaplan. *Force Without War: U.S. Armed Forces as a Political Instrument*. Washington, DC: The Brookings Institution, 1978.

Bundy, McGeorge. *Danger and Survival: Choices about the Bomb in the First Fifty Years*. New York: Random House, 1989.

Chazan, Naomi. *Negotiating the Non-Negotiable: Jerusalem in the Framework of an Israeli-Palestinian Settlement*. Cambridge, MA: American Academy of Arts and Sciences, Occasional Paper No. 7, March 1991.

Crabb, Cecil V., and Kevin V. Mulcahy. *Presidents and Foreign Policymaking: From FDR to Reagan*. Baton Rouge, LA: Louisiana State University Press, 1986.

Feldman, Lily Gardner. *The Special Relationship between West Germany and Israel*. Boston and London: George Allen & Unwin, 1984.

Ferrell, Robert H. *American Diplomacy: The 20th Century*. New York: W. W. Norton, 1988.

Gilpin, Robert. *The Political Economy of International Relations*. Princeton, NJ: Princeton University Press, 1987.

Grandbard, Stephen, ed. "The Exit from Communism." *Daedalus* 1, No. 2 (Spring 1992).

Greenfeld, Liah. *Nationalism: Five Roads to Modernity*. Cambridge, MA: Harvard University Press, 1993.

Hilsman, Roger. *The Politics of Policymaking in Defense and Foreign Affairs*. Englewood Cliffs, NJ: Prentice-Hall, 1987.

Kennan, George F. *Around the Cragged Hill—A Personal and Political Philosophy*. New York: W. W. Norton, 1993.

Kennedy, Paul. *The Rise and Fall of the Great Powers: Economic Change and Military Conflict from 1500 to 2000*. New York: Random House, 1987.

LaFeber, Walter. *The American Age: United States Foreign Policy at Home and Abroad since 1750*. New York: W. W. Norton, 1989.

Macchiarola, Frank J., and Robert B. Oxnam, eds. *The China Challenge: American Policies in East Asia*. New York: Academy of Political Science, 1991.

U.S. Congress. *Report of the Congressional Committees Investigating the Iran-Contra Affair*. New York: Random House, 1988.

Wallace, William. *The Transformation of Western Europe*. London: Royal Institute of International Affairs, 1990.

Wessell, Nils H. *The New Europe—Revolution in East-West Relations*. New York: Academy of Political Science, 1991.

Wirls, Daniel. *Build Up: The Politics of Defense in the Reagan Era*. Ithaca, NY: Cornell University Press, 1992.

19

The State Of The Union

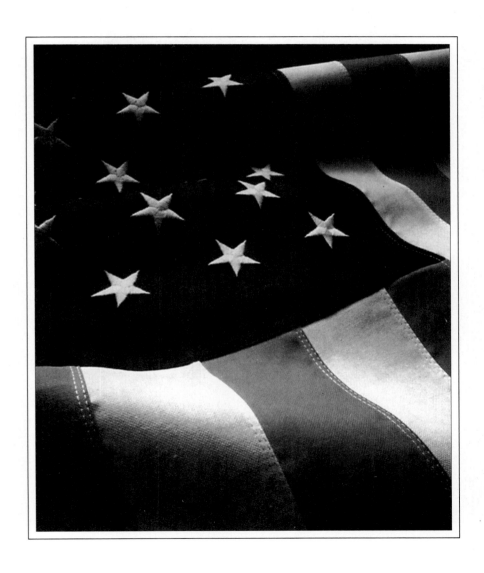

*I*n the autumn of 1989, the world began to change dramatically. Today we hear talk of a new world order, but in late 1989 we could see nothing but world disorder—a disorder both threatening and hopeful. Was the world, as well as America, in decline, or was America, as well as the world, a phoenix rising from the ashes?

An important and hopeful element of the new world disorder was the collapse of the Soviet empire. As the Berlin Wall tumbled down, the Iron Curtain was raised, revealing the Soviet military in retreat and the Soviet Union's Eastern European satellites drifting out of orbit. Then, in 1991, the failed coup against Gorbachev weakened what was left of the central government and gave the Baltic states, as well as several other republics, a chance to achieve their independence. The people of all these newly independent countries were expressing the hopes and desires that define for Americans "the pursuit of happiness." New constitutions were written, new governments were formed, and everywhere dramatic signs of economic freedom emerged. These new states looked to the West for their political and economic models.

AMERICA THE BEACON

In the late 1980s, a book entitled *The Rise and Fall of the Great Powers* explained why a decline of American influence in the world was all but inevitable. Within five years, however, not only had America reemerged as the world's preeminent military power but, perhaps more than ever, American democracy had become an example—a beacon—to the new nations of the world.

Despite America's many problems, there is much about the American democratic system that *is* worthy of emulation. Americans have not always been outstanding theorists of democracy, but, for 200 years, they have been among its foremost practitioners and have developed noteworthy ideas, institutions, and practices.

Foremost among these is the idea of constitutionalism. There are many good constitutions but only one principle of constitutionalism: to choose among instruments of government and then to set those choices slightly above majority rule and outside the immediate control of the people who are in power at a given moment in time. By this means, a people can set limits on the power of government and at the same time set limits on themselves.

Another American governmental institution worthy of emulation is our system of competing political parties. This is absolutely necessary for the American political system and for every system that wishes to maintain democracy. A *two*-party system is not sacred. What is necessary is some kind of competitive party system, one in which the parties enjoy control over the nomination and election process, and one in which the parties have the resources to mobilize voters without (and despite) government sponsorship. This is the best way to ensure democratic accountability and popular participation. Would that we could strengthen our party system!

The part of the American model most eligible for literal imitation is our provision in the Constitution for civil liberties and civil rights. But this must be properly understood. A mere listing of liberties and rights—"parchment guarantees"— is not enough. As we stressed so often in the text, the sphere of civil liberties and civil rights grows out of provisions and traditions that give individual citizens a specific cause of action if they feel their rights have been denied, and courts and other institutions that provide access to government for individual citizens and possess the power to act, utilizing a known set of enforceable remedies.

Freedom and Power

While the world is watching us, we must never cease watching ourselves—to make certain that America's democratic system continues to be worthy of emulation. In particular, we must make certain that, as a nation, we never forget that the chief problem or contradiction upon which our government is built is the problem of political freedom and governmental power. At what point does the power that we grant the government begin to pose a threat to our freedom and well-being? Can we indefinitely use government to improve our lot or does the government's power become more dangerous the more it grows?

During the first century of our own nation's history, Americans were profoundly distrustful of government. Our forebears were convinced that governmental power always posed a threat to their liberties. Given a choice, nineteenth-century Americans preferred freedom to government, and they were willing to forgo some of the benefits of government to ensure the preservation of liberty. In this spirit, they constructed and maintained a system of government whose powers were severely circumscribed. Federalism divided power between the state and the national governments and limited the scope of the national government's activities. Within the national structure, the principle of separation of powers dispersed authority among the three branches of government and between the two houses of Congress, thus using each institution to check and limit the powers of the others. The Constitution and the Bill of Rights placed restrictions on the range of governmental activity, prohibiting actions deemed to violate the fundamental liberties of the people. These limits and restraints meant that the national government was not as useful a servant as it might have been. For example, its capacity to promote the development of the economy was limited. It had little ability to provide assistance to the poor and needy. Even its capacity to provide for the common defense was limited.

During the course of the twentieth century, however, Americans constructed a larger and more powerful governmental apparatus—one capable of providing far more in the way of services and benefits than the institution they had inherited. By the close of the twentieth century, as we have seen, our national government has come to provide a vast array of services to Americans from every walk of life. The brief list of beneficiaries of federal programs given in Chapter 1 could be expanded for hundreds of pages.

It is difficult to deny that through these programs, and many others, Americans benefit from the activities and services of "big government." Opinion polls suggest that, despite some hostility to taxes, most Americans continue to support an extensive role for the national government. In fact, most would like government to do more rather than less in a variety of areas.

Of course, to make it possible for our government to provide the services we want, we have been forced to relax some of the constraints that bound and limited governmental actions. As we saw earlier, in order to give the national government more power to act, the restraints of federalism were weakened and the national government was allowed to exercise economic and police powers previously reserved to the states. To make the national government capable of more vigorous and decisive action both at home and abroad, a more powerful presidency and an enormous administrative bureaucracy were created and the separation of powers was weakened. To make it possible for the national government to provide the economic and social programs we desire, we have eagerly sought to justify governmental intervention in every area of our economy and society. Indeed, to face the challenges of the modern era, we may have no choice but to increase the strength and efficiency of our government and, so, provide it with an even greater capacity to intervene in our lives.

But despite the erosion of the restraints on governmental power, few Americans have perceived the growth of government over the past half century as posing a sustained threat to their liberties. As we saw in Chapter 1, the once-liberal theory that led Americans to agree with Jefferson that the best government was the one that governed least came to be supplanted by a democratic theory of state power. This democratic theory held that the contradiction between freedom and government could be resolved by strengthening democratic controls on government, and as long as the people controlled the government, what did it matter if government became more powerful? After all, if the government was simply the servant of the people, then its power was nothing more than its ability to serve them, and limits on its power were, in effect, limits on the citizens themselves.

Thus far, we *have* managed to have both a more powerful government and considerable freedom. Indeed, in many ways, Americans enjoy greater freedom now than ever before. Recall that judicial interpretations in recent years have expanded the scope of free speech, strengthened freedom of assembly, introduced a right to privacy, and limited the power of the police and prosecutors in dealing with criminal defendants. At the same time, the courts and Congress have strengthened the civil rights not only of African Americans but of *all* Americans. We are undeniably enjoying both the blessings of freedom and the benefits of government. But the success we have achieved should not lead us to believe that there is no problem at all. There is a contradiction between freedom and governmental power, and this contradiction is not eliminated by democratic control of government.

THE CONDITIONS FOR DEMOCRACY

Virtually everywhere in the world democratic controls seem to be associated with political liberty. Generally speaking, the same nations that possess democratic political institutions are also the most likely to respect basic civil liberties. For example, in one recent survey that sought to rank all nominally independent nations on a 1 (most free) to 7 (least free) scale on the basis of citizens' civil rights and liberties, all eighteen nations in the "most free" group were democracies. No nation that had a competitive electoral process ranked below the second scale position on civil liberties.[1] In another study, freedom of the press was found to be "complete" in thirty-three of forty nations with competitive electoral systems, while only six of thirty-six electorally uncompetitive nations could boast a completely free press.[2]

Such associations, however, do not tell the whole story. The history of the relationship between liberty and democratic practices suggests that democratic institutions are usually the result of rather than the cause of freedom. The citizens of the democracies are not free because they possess democratic controls; rather, they exercise democratic controls because they are free. A measure of liberty is a necessary precondition for the functioning of democratic processes. Governmental interference with speech, assembly, association, and the press precludes open and competitive policies.[3]

More fundamentally, democratic institutions are most likely to emerge and flourish where the public already possesses some freedom from governmental control. As we saw in Chapters 1 and 9, democratic elections are often introduced when governments are unable to compel the people's acquiescence. In a sense, elections are inaugurated in order to persuade a reluctant populace to surrender at least some of its freedom and allow itself to be governed. Thus, in the United States, the introduction of democratic institutions, as well as the adoption of formal constitutional guarantees of civil liberties, was in part prompted by the fact that the citizenry was free—born free, as Alexis de Tocqueville observed—and had the desire to remain so. Even several of the framers of the Constitution who were hostile to the principle of democracy nevertheless urged the adoption of democratic governmental forms on the grounds that the populace would otherwise refuse to accept the new government. John Dickinson, a prominent and well-to-do delegate from Delaware, asserted that limited monarchy was superior to any republican form of government. Unfortunately, however, limited monarchy was out of the question because of the "spirit of the times."[4] Similarly, senior Virginia delegate George Mason concluded that "notwithstanding the oppression and injustice experienced among us from democracy, the genius of the people is in favor of it, and the genius of the people must be consulted."[5] Subsequently, as we saw, the Constitution's proponents agreed to add the formal guarantees of civil liberties embodied in the Bill of Rights only when it appeared that the Constitution might otherwise not be ratified.[6] In effect, the public had to be persuaded to permit itself

---

[1]Raymond O. Gastil et al., *Freedom in the World: Political Rights and Civil Liberties* (New York: Freedom House, 1979).

[2]Arthur S. Banks and Robert B. Textor, *A Cross-Policy Survey* (Cambridge, MA: MIT Press, 1963).

[3]See Madison's discussion in *The Federalist Papers* No. 10, ed. Clinton Rossiter (New York: New American Library, 1937). See also Carl Cohen, *Democracy* (Athens: University of Georgia Press, 1971), Chapter 10.

[4]Max Farrand, ed., *The Records of the Federal Convention of 1787* (New Haven, CT: Yale University Press, 1966), vol. 1, p. 86.

[5]Ibid., p. 101.

[6]Forrest McDonald, *The Formation of the American Republic* (Baltimore, MD: Penguin, 1965), Chapter 8.

to be governed because it was, in fact, free to choose otherwise. Given the absence
of a national military force and the virtually universal distribution of firearms and
training in their use, the populace could not easily have been compelled to accept
a government it did not desire.

In general, democratic political practices are most likely to emerge and prosper in "free societies"—societies in which politically relevant resources are distributed outside the control of the central government. The importance of the distribution of military force is clear. When at some critical historical juncture rulers lacked the necessary force to govern, they tended to become much more concerned with citizens' rights.

Other resources are probably of even greater importance to the maintenance of freedom. An active private press coupled with a literate population, as in America, can, with information about government activities, stimulate resistance to those in power.[7] Broadly distributed reservoirs of private financial resources often help the formation of opposition. We are fortunate in the United States to possess a democratic form of government, but it is not a substitute for—and could not exist for long without—a significant measure of popular freedom.

One of the great problems facing the people in the new nations today is the development of personal freedom and independent resources on a scale sufficient to defend them from governmental power and to keep that power respectful of individuals. During forty-five years of Communist rule in Eastern Europe and the Soviet Union, governments did not redistribute wealth from the rich to the poor but actually redistributed resources from all the people to the government itself. This means that, for the near future, property, education, skill, and all the other resources that make for personal autonomy are too narrowly distributed to provide fertile ground for democratic processes. In other words, as a prerequisite to freedom, these governments must cooperate in the distribution and redistribution of resources to the people so that they have a stake in the new order and the ability to sustain some control over their governments. Will the new governments of Eastern Europe, and the former territories of the Soviet Union, be willing to do this?

FREEDOM OR POWER?

In the United States, constitutionally mandated controls on government offer some measure of protection for civil liberties and civil rights. The availability of governmental controls, however, if based on democratic processes, tends eventually to persuade citizens that they may enjoy the benefits of the state's power without risk to their freedom. Why, after all, should it be necessary to limit a servant's capacity to serve?

Unfortunately, despite democratic processes controlling government, individual freedom and governmental power inevitably conflict. This conflict does not necessarily mean deliberate and overt governmental efforts to abridge liberties. Typi-

---

[7]See Richard Hofstadter, *The Idea of a Party System* (Berkeley: University of California Press, 1969), Chapter 3.

cally, the erosion of citizens' liberties in the democracies is a more subtle, insidious, and often unforeseen result of routine administrative processes. As we saw earlier, federal agencies such as the Interstate Commerce Commission, the Civil Aeronautics Board, and the Federal Trade Commission have considerable control over who may enter the occupations and businesses that they regulate. The Food and Drug Administration has a good deal to say about what we may eat. The Federal Communications Commission has a measure of influence over what Americans see and hear over the airwaves. The Internal Revenue Service, in the mundane course of collecting taxes, makes decisions about what is and is not a religion, what is or is not political activity, whether given forms of education are or are not socially desirable, what types of philanthropy serve the public interest, and what sorts of information it should acquire about every citizen. The administration of tax policy is among the most intrusive activities of the federal government. Thus, congressional tax legislation and IRS regulations can have a critical effect upon every individual's business decisions, marital plans, childbirth and child-rearing decisions, vacation plans, and medical care. And housing policies, educational policies, and welfare programs, which are often directed by agencies given broad, discretionary mandates by Congress, affect the most minute details of citizens' lives.

Despite the availability of democratic institutions, Americans cannot expect to use the government's power without surrendering at least some of their freedom. This is the darkside of government. A government capable of solving our problems and maintaining America's place in the world is also a government capable of threatening our cherished liberties.

More than 150 years ago, Alexis de Tocqueville prophesied that Americans would someday become so convinced that they controlled the government that they would be willing to surrender their liberty to it. This would leave them, he warned, holding the ends of their own chains. For now, we possess both the blessing of freedom and the service of government. Let us hope we can keep them.

FOR FURTHER READING

Arendt, Hannah. *The Human Condition*. Chicago: University of Chicago Press, 1958.

Cnudde, Charles F., and Deane E. Neubauer. *Empirical Democratic Theory*. Chicago: Markham, 1969.

Laski, Harold. *Liberty in the Modern State*. London: Faber and Faber, 1930.

Locke, John. *The Second Treatise of Government*. Indianapolis: Bobbs-Merrill, 1972.

Love, Nancy S., ed. *Dogmas and Dreams: Political Ideologies in the Modern World*. Chatham, NJ: Chatham House, 1991.

McIlwain, Charles H. *Constitutionalism, Ancient and Modern*. Ithaca: Cornell University Press, 1947.

Mannheim, Karl. *Man and Society in an Age of Reconstruction*. London: Kegan Paul, Trench, Trubner and Co., 1940.

Mathiopoulos, Marjarita. *History and Progress: In Search of the European and American Mind*. New York: Praeger, 1989.

Mill, James. *An Essay on Government*. Cambridge, England: Cambridge University Press, 1937.

Mill, John Stewart. *On Liberty*. New York: W. W. Norton, 1975.

Schumpeter, Joseph A. *Capitalism, Socialism and Democracy*. New York: Harper & Row, 1950.

Shklar, Judith N. *American Citizenship—The Quest for Inclusion*. Cambridge, MA: Harvard University Press, 1990.

Thompson, Dennis P. *The Democratic Citizen*. Cambridge, England: Cambridge University Press, 1970.

Appendix

The Declaration of Independence

In Congress, July 4, 1776

When in the course of human events, it becomes necessary for one people to dissolve the political bands which have connected them with another, and to assume among the Powers of the earth, the separate and equal station to which the Laws of Nature and of Nature's God entitle them, a decent respect to the opinions of mankind requires that they should declare the causes which impel them to the separation.

We hold these truths to be self-evident, that all men are created equal, that they are endowed by their Creator with certain unalienable rights, that among these are Life, Liberty, and the pursuit of Happiness. That to secure these rights, Governments are instituted among Men, deriving their just powers from the consent of the governed. That whenever any Form of Government becomes destructive of these ends, it is the Right of the People to alter or to abolish it, and to institute new Government, laying its foundation on such principles and organizing its powers in such form, as to them shall seem most likely to effect their Safety and Happiness. Prudence, indeed, will dictate that Governments long established should not be changed for light and transient causes; and accordingly all experience hath shown, that mankind are more disposed to suffer, while evils are sufferable, than to right themselves by abolishing the forms to which they are accustomed. But when a long train of abuses and usurpations, pursuing invariably the same Object evinces a design to reduce them under absolute Despotism, it is their right, it is their duty, to throw off such Government, and to provide new Guards for their future security.—Such has been the patient sufferance of these Colonies; and such is now the necessity which constrains them to alter their former Systems of Government. The history of the present King of Great Britain is a history of repeated injuries and usurpations, all having in direct object the establishment of an absolute Tyranny over these States. To prove this, let Facts be submitted to a candid world.

He has refused his Assent to Laws, the most wholesome and necessary for the public good.

He has forbidden his Governors to pass Laws of immediate and pressing importance, unless suspended in their operation till his Assent should be obtained; and when so suspended, he has utterly neglected to attend to them.

He has refused to pass other Laws for the accommodation of large districts of people, unless those people would relinquish the right of Representation in the Legislature, a right inestimable to them and formidable to tyrants only.

He has called together legislative bodies at places unusual, uncomfortable, and distant from the depository of their public Records, for the sole purpose of fatiguing them into compliance with his measures.

He has dissolved Representative Houses repeatedly, for opposing with manly firmness his invasions on the rights of the people.

He has refused for a long time, after such dissolutions, to cause others to be elected; whereby the Legislative powers, incapable of Annihilation, have returned to the People at large for their exercise; the State remaining in the mean time exposed to all dangers of invasion from without, and convulsions within.

He has endeavored to prevent the population of these States; for that purpose obstructing the Laws of Naturalization of Foreigners; refusing to pass others to encourage their migrations hither, and raising the conditions of new Appropriations of Lands.

He has obstructed the Administration of Justice, by refusing his Assent to Laws for establishing Judiciary powers.

He has made Judges dependent on his Will alone, for the tenure of their offices, and the amount and payment of their salaries.

He has erected a multitude of New Offices, and sent hither swarms of Officers to harass our People, and eat out their substance.

He has kept among us, in times of peace, Standing Armies without the Consent of our legislature.

He has affected to render the Military independent of and superior to the Civil Power.

He has combined with others to subject us to a jurisdiction foreign to our constitution, and unacknowledged by our laws; giving his Assent to their Acts of pretended Legislation:

For quartering large bodies of armed troops among us:

For protecting them, by a mock Trial, from Punishment for any Murders which they should commit on the Inhabitants of these States:

For cutting off our Trade with all parts of the world:

For imposing taxes on us without our Consent:

For depriving us of many cases, of the benefits of Trial by jury:

For transporting us beyond Seas to be tried for pretended offences:

For abolishing the free System of English Laws in a neighboring Province, establishing therein an Arbitrary government, and enlarging its Boundaries so as to render it at once an example and fit instrument for introducing the same absolute rule into these Colonies:

For taking away our Charters, abolishing our most valuable Laws, and altering fundamentally the Forms of our Governments:

For suspending our own Legislatures, and declaring themselves invested with Power to legislate for us in all cases whatsoever.

He has abdicated Government here, by declaring us out of his Protection and waging War against us.

He has plundered our seas, ravaged our Coasts, burnt our towns, and destroyed the lives of our people.

He is at this time transporting large armies of foreign mercenaries to compleat the works of death, desolation, and tyranny, already begun with circumstances of Cruelty & perfidy scarcely paralleled in the most barbarous ages, and totally unworthy the Head of a civilized nation.

He has constrained our fellow Citizens taken Captive on the high Seas to bear Arms against their Country, to become the executioners of their friends and Brethren, or to fall themselves by their Hands.

He has excited domestic insurrections amongst us, and has endeavored to bring on the inhabitants of our frontiers, the merciless Indian Savages, whose known rule of warfare, is an undistinguished destruction of all ages, sexes, and conditions.

In every stage of these Oppressions We have Petitioned for Redress in the most humble terms: Our repeated Petitions have been answered only by repeated injury. A Prince, whose character is thus marked by every act which may define a Tyrant, is unfit to be the ruler of a free people.

Nor have We been wanting in attention to our British brethren. We have warned them from time to time of attempts by their legislature to extend an unwarrantable jurisdiction over us. We have reminded them of the circumstances of our emigration and settlement here. We have appealed to their native justice and magnanimity, and we have conjured them by the ties of our common kindred to disavow these usurpations, which, would inevitably interrupt our connections and correspondence. They too must have been deaf to the voice of justice and of consanguinity. We must, therefore, acquiesce in the necessity, which denounces our Separation, and hold them, as we hold the rest of mankind, Enemies in War, in Peace Friends.

WE, THEREFORE, the Representatives of the UNITED STATES OF AMERICA, in General Congress, Assembled, appealing to the Supreme Judge of the world for the rectitude of our intentions, do, in the Name, and by Authority of the good People of these Colonies, solemnly publish and declare, That these United Colonies are, and of Right ought to be FREE AND INDEPENDENT STATES; that they are Absolved from all Allegiance to the British Crown, and that all political connection between them and the State of Great Britain, is and ought to be totally dissolved; and that as Free and Independent States, they have full Power to levy War, conclude Peace, contract Alliances, establish Commerce, and to do all other Acts and Things which Independent States may of right do. And for the support of this Declaration, with a firm reliance on the Protection of Divine Providence, we mutually pledge to each other our Lives, our Fortunes, and our sacred Honor.

The foregoing Declaration was, by order of Congress, engrossed, and signed by the following members:

John Hancock

NEW HAMPSHIRE
Josiah Bartlett
William Whipple
Matthew Thornton

MASSACHUSETTS BAY
Samuel Adams
John Adams
Robert Treat Paine
Elbridge Gerry

RHODE ISLAND
Stephen Hopkins
William Ellery

CONNECTICUT
Roger Sherman
Samuel Huntington
William Williams
Oliver Wolcott

NEW YORK
William Floyd
Philip Livingston
Francis Lewis
Lewis Morris

NEW JERSEY
Richard Stockton
John Witherspoon
Francis Hopkinson
John Hart
Abraham Clark

PENNSYLVANIA
Robert Morris
Benjamin Rush
Benjamin Franklin
John Morton
George Clymer
James Smith
George Taylor

James Wilson
George Ross

DELAWARE
Caesar Rodney
George Read
Thomas M'Kean

MARYLAND
Samuel Chase
William Paca
Thomas Stone
Charles Carroll,
of Carrollton

VIRGINIA
George Wythe
Richard Henry Lee
Thomas Jefferson
Benjamin Harrison
Thomas Nelson, Jr.

Francis Lightfoot Lee
Carter Braxton

NORTH CAROLINA
William Hooper
Joseph Hewes
John Penn

SOUTH CAROLINA
Edward Rutledge
Thomas Heyward, Jr.
Thomas Lynch, Jr.
Arthur Middleton

GEORGIA
Button Gwinnett
Lyman Hall
George Walton

Resolved, That copies of the Declaration be sent to the several assemblies, conventions, and committees, or councils of safety, and to the several commanding officers of the continental troops; that it be proclaimed in each of the United States, at the head of the army.

The Articles of Confederation

*Agreed to by Congress November 15, 1977;
ratified and in force March 1, 1781*

To all whom these Presents shall come, we the undersigned Delegates of the States affixed to our Names send greeting. Whereas the Delegates of the United States of America in Congress assembled did on the fifteenth day of November in the Year of our Lord One Thousand Seven Hundred and Seventy seven, and in the Second Year of the Independence of America agree to certain articles of Confederation and perpetual Union between the States of Newhampshire, Massachusetts-bay, Rhodeisland and Providence Plantations, Connecticut, New-York, New-Jersey, Pennsylvania, Delaware, Maryland, Virginia, North-Carolina, South-Carolina and Georgia in the Words following, viz. "Articles of Confederation and perpetual Union between the states of Newhampshire, Massachusetts-bay, Rhodeisland and Providence Plantations, Connecticut, New-York, New-Jersey, Pennsylvania, Delaware, Maryland, Virginia, North-Carolina, South-Carolina and Georgia.

Art. I. The Stile of this confederacy shall be "The United States of America."

Art. II. Each state retains its sovereignty, freedom and independence, and every Power, Jurisdiction and right, which is not by this confederation expressly delegated to the United States, in Congress assembled.

Art. III. The said states hereby severally enter into a firm league of friendship with each other, for their common defence, the security of their Liberties, and their mutual and general welfare, binding themselves to assist each other, against all force offered to, or attacks made upon them, or any of them, on account of religion, sovereignty, trade, or any other pretence whatever.

Art. IV. The better to secure and perpetuate mutual friendship and intercourse among the people of the different states in this union, the free inhabitants of each of these states, paupers, vagabonds and fugitives from Justice excepted, shall be entitled to all privileges and immunities of free citizens in the several states; and the people of each state shall have free ingress and regress to and from any other state, and shall enjoy therein all the privileges of trade and commerce, subject to the same duties, impositions and restrictions as the inhabitants thereof respectively, provided that such restriction shall not extend so far as to prevent the removal of property imported into any state, to any other state of which the Owner is an inhabitant; provided also that no imposition, duties or restriction shall be laid by any state, on the property of the united states, or either of them.

If any Person guilty of, or charged with treason, felony, or other high misdemeanor in any state, shall flee from Justice, and be found in any of the united states, he shall upon demand of the Governor or executive power, of the state from which he fled, be delivered up and removed to the state having jurisdiction of his offence.

Full faith and credit shall be given in each of these states to the records, acts and judicial proceedings of the courts and magistrates of every other state.

Art. V. For the more convenient management of the general interests of the united states, delegates shall be annually appointed in such manner as the legislature of each state shall direct, to meet in Congress on the first Monday in November, in every year, with a power reserved to each state, to recall its delegates, or any of them, at any time within the year, and to send others in their stead, for the remainder of the Year.

No state shall be represented in Congress by less than two, nor by more than seven Members; and no person shall be capable of being a delegate for more than three years in any term of six years; nor shall any person, being a delegate, be capable of holding any office under the united states, for which he, or another for his benefit receives any salary, fees or emolument of any kind.

Each state shall maintain its own delegates in a meeting of the states, and while they act as members of the committee of the states.

In determining questions in the united states, in Congress assembled, each state shall have one vote.

Freedom of speech and debate in Congress shall not be impeached or questioned in any Court, or place out of Congress, and the members of congress shall be protected in their persons from arrests and imprisonments, during the time of their going to and from, and attendance on congress, except for treason, felony, or breach of the peace.

Art. VI. No state without the Consent of the united states in congress assembled, shall send any embassy to, or receive any embassy from, or enter into any conference, agreement, or alliance or treaty with any King, prince or state; nor shall any person holding any office or profit or trust under the united states, or any of them, accept of any present, emolument, office or title of any kind whatever from any king, prince or foreign state; nor shall the united states in congress assembled, or any of them, grant any title of nobility.

No two or more states shall enter into any treaty, confederation or alliance whatever between them, without the consent of the united states in congress assembled, specifying accurately the purposes for which the same is to be entered into, and how long it shall continue.

No state shall lay any imposts or duties, which may interfere with any stipulations in treaties, entered into by the united states in congress assembled, with any king, prince or state, in pursuance of any treaties already proposed by congress, to the courts of France and Spain.

No vessels of war shall be kept up in time of peace by any state, except such number only, as shall be deemed necessary by the united states in congress assembled, for the defence of such state, or its trade; nor shall any body of forces be kept up by any state, in time of peace, except such number only, as in the judgment of the united states, in congress assembled, shall be deemed requisite to garrison the forts necessary for the defence of such state; but every state shall always keep up a well regulated and disciplined militia, sufficiently armed and accoutred, and shall provide and constantly have ready for use, in public stores, a due number of field pieces and tents, and a proper quantity of arms, ammunition and camp equipage.

No state shall engage in any war without the consent of the united states in congress assembled, unless such state be actually invaded by enemies, or shall have received certain advice of a resolution being formed by some nation of Indians to invade such state, and the danger is so imminent as not to admit of a delay, till the united states in congress assssembled can be consulted; nor shall any state grant commissions to any ships or vessels of war, nor letters of marque or reprisal, except it be after a declaration of war by the united states in congress assembled, and then only against the kingdom or state and the subjects thereof,

against which war has been so declared, and under such regulations as shall be established by
the united states in congress assembled, unless such state be infested by pirates; in which case
vessels of war may be fitted out for that occasion, and kept so long as the danger shall continue, or until the united states in congress assembled shall determine otherwise.

Art. VII. When land-forces are raised by any state for the common defence, all officers
of or under the rank of colonel, shall be appointed by the legislature of each state respectively by whom such forces shall be raised, or in such manner as such state shall direct, and
all vacancies shall be filled up by the state which first made the appointment.

Art. VIII. All charges of war, and all other expences that shall be incurred for the common defence or general welfare, and allowed by the united states in congress assembled,
shall be defrayed out of a common treasury, which shall be supplied by the several states, in
proportion to the value of all land within each state, granted to or surveyed for any Person,
as such land and the buildings and improvements thereon shall be estimated according to
such mode as the united states in congress assembled, shall from time to time direct and appoint. The taxes for paying that proportion shall be laid and levied by the authority and direction of the legislatures of the several states within the time agreed upon by the united
states in congress assembled.

Art. IX. The united states in congress assembled, shall have the sole and exclusive right
and power of determining on peace and war, except in the cases mentioned in the sixth article—of sending and receiving ambassadors—entering into treaties and alliances, provided
that no treaty of commerce shall be made whereby the legislative power of the respective
states shall be restrained from imposing such imposts and duties on foreigners, as their own
people are subjected to, or from prohibiting the exportation of any species of goods or
commodities whatsoever—of establishing rules for deciding in all cases, what captures on
land or water shall be legal, and in what manner prizes taken by land or naval forces in the
service of the united states shall be divided or appropriated—of granting letters of marque
and reprisal in times of peace—appointing courts for the trial of piracies and felonies committed on the high seas and establishing courts for receiving and determining finally appeals
in all cases of captures, provided that no member of congress shall be appointed a judge of
any of the said courts.

The united states in congress assembled shall also be the last resort on appeal in all disputes and differences now subsisting or that hereafter may arise between two or more states
concerning boundary, jurisdiction or any other cause whatever; which authority shall always be exercised in the manner following. Whenever the legislative or executive authority
or lawful agent of any state in controversy with another shall present a petition to congress
stating the matter in question and praying for a hearing, notice thereof shall be given by
order of congress to the legislative or executive authority of the other state in controversy,
and a day assigned for the appearance of the parties by their lawful agents, who shall then be
directed to appoint by joint consent, commissioners or judges to constitute a court for hearing and determining the matter in question: but if they cannot agree, congress shall name
three persons out of each of the united states, and from the list of such persons each party
shall alternately strike out one, the petitioners beginning, until the number shall be reduced
to thirteen; and from that number not less than seven, nor more than nine names as congress shall direct, shall in the presence of congress be drawn out by lot, and the persons
whose names shall be so drawn or any five of them, shall be commissioners or judges, to
hear and finally determine the controversy, so always as a major part of the judges who shall
hear the cause shall agree in the determination: and if either party shall neglect to attend at
the day appointed, without shewing reasons, which congress shall judge sufficient, or being
present shall refuse to strike, the congress shall proceed to nominate three persons out
of each state, and the secretary of congress shall strike in behalf of such party absent or

refusing; and the judgment and sentence of the court to be appointed, in the manner before prescribed, shall be final and conclusive; and if any of the parties shall refuse to submit to the authority of such court, or to appear to defend their claim or cause, the court shall nevertheless proceed to pronounce sentence, or judgment, which shall in like manner be final and decisive, the judgment or sentence and other proceedings being in either case transmitted to congress, and lodged among the acts of congress for the security of the parties concerned: provided that every commissioner, before he sits in judgment, shall take an oath to be administered by one of the judges of the supreme or superior court of the state, where the cause shall be tried, "well and truly to hear and determine the matter in question, according to the best of his judgment, without favour, affection or hope of reward:" provided also that no state shall be deprived of territory for the benefit of the united states.

All controversies concerning the private right of soil claimed under different grants of two or more states, whose jurisdictions as they may respect such lands, and the states which passed such grants are adjusted, the said grants or either of them being at the same time claimed to have originated antecedent to such settlement of jurisdiction, shall on the petition of either party to the congress of the united states, be finally determined as near as may be in the same manner as is before prescribed for deciding disputes respecting territorial jurisdiction between different states.

The united states in congress assembled shall also have the sole and exclusive right and power of regulating the alloy and value of coin struck by their own authority, or by that of the respective states—fixing the standard of weights and measures throughout the united states—regulating the trade and managing all affairs with the Indians, not members of any of the states, provided that the legislative right of any state within its own limits be not infringed or violated—establishing and regulating post-offices from one state to another, throughout all the united states, and exacting such postage on the papers passing thro' the same as may be requisite to defray the expences of the said office—appointing all officers of the land forces, in the service of the united states, except regimental officers—appointing all the officers of the united states—making rules for the government and regulation of the said land and naval forces, and directing their operations.

The united states in congress assembled shall have the authority to appoint a committee, to sit in the recess of congress, to be denominated "A Committee of the States," and to consist of one delegate from each state; and to appoint such other committees and civil officers as may be necessary for managing the general affairs of the united states under their direction—to appoint one of their number to preside, provided that no person be allowed to serve in the office of president more than one year in any term of three years; to ascertain the necessary sums of Money to be raised for the service of the united states, and to appropriate and apply the same for defraying the public expences—to borrow money, or emit bills on the credit of the united states, transmitting every half year to the respective states an account of the sums of money so borrowed or emitted,—to build and equip a navy—to agree upon the number of land forces, and to make requisitions from each state for its quota, in proportion to the number of white inhabitants in such state; which requisition shall be binding, and thereupon the legislature of each state shall appoint the regimental officers, raise the men and cloath, arm and equip then in a soldier like manner, at the expence of the united states, and the officers and men so cloathed, armed and equipped shall march to the place appointed, and within the time agreed on by the united states in congress assembled: But if the united states in congress assembled shall, on consideration of circumstances judge proper that any state should not raise men, or should raise a smaller number than its quota, and that any other state should raise a greater number of men than the quota thereof, such extra number shall be raised, officered, cloathed, armed and equipped in the same manner as the quota of such state, unless the legislature of such state shall judge that such extra number cannot be safely spared out of the same, in which case they shall raise officer, cloath, arm and equip as many of such extra number as they judge can be safely

spared. And the officers and men so cloathed, armed and equipped, shall march to the place appointed, and within the time agreed on by the united states in congress assembled.

The united states in congress assembled shall never engage in a war, nor grant letters of marque and reprisal in time of peace, nor enter into any treaties or alliances, nor coin money, nor regulate the value thereof, nor ascertain the sums and expences necessary for the defence and welfare of the united states, or any of them, nor emit bills, nor borrow money on the credit of the united states, nor appropriate money, nor agree upon the number of vessels of war, to be built or purchased, or the number of land or sea forces to be raised, nor appoint a commander in chief of the army or navy, unless nine states assent to the same: nor shall a question on any other point, except for adjourning from day to day be determined, unless by the votes of a majority of the united states in congress assembled.

The congress of the united states shall have power to adjourn to any time within the year, and to any place within the united states, so that no period of adjournment be for a longer duration than the space of six Months, and shall publish the Journal of their proceedings monthly, except such parts thereof relating to treaties, alliances or military operations as in their judgment require secresy; and the yeas and nays of the delegates of each state on any question shall be entered on the Journal, when it is desired by any delegate; and the delegates of a state, or any of them, at his or their request shall be furnished with a transcript of the said Journal, except such parts as are above excepted to lay before the legislatures of the several states.

Art. X. The committee of the states, or any nine of them, shall be authorised to execute, in the recess of congress, such of the powers of congress as the united states in congress assembled, by the consent of nine states, shall from time to time think expedient to vest them with; provided that no power be delegated to the said committee, for the exercise of which, by the articles of confederation, the voice of nine states in the congress of the united states assembled is requisite.

Art. XI. Canada acceding to this confederation, and joining in the measures of the united states, shall be admitted into, and entitled to all the advantages of this union: but no other colony shall be admitted into the same, unless such admission be agreed to by nine states.

Art. XII. All bills of credit emitted, monies borrowed and debts contracted by, or under the authority of congress, before the assembling of the united states, in pursuance of the present confederation, shall be deemed and considered as a charge against the united states, for payment and satisfaction whereof the said united states and the public faith are hereby solemnly pledged.

Art. XIII. Every state shall abide by the determinations of the united states in congress assembled, on all questions which by this confederation are submitted to them. And the Articles of this confederation shall be inviolably observed by every state, and the union shall be perpetual; nor shall any alteration at any time hereafter be made in any of them; unless such alteration be agreed to in a congress of the united states, and be afterwards confirmed by the legislatures of every state.

AND WHEREAS it hath pleased the Great Governor of the World to incline the hearts of the legislatures we respectively represent in congress, to approve of, and to authorize us to ratify the said articles of confederation and perpetual union. KNOW YE that we the under-signed delegates, by virtue of the power and authority to us given for that purpose, do by these presents, in the name and in behalf of our respective constituents, fully and entirely ratify and confirm each and every of the said articles of confederation and perpetual union, and all and singular the matters and things therein contained: And we do further solemnly plight and engage the faith of our respective constituents, that they shall abide by the determination of the united states in congress assembled, on all questions, which by the said confederation are submitted to them. And that the articles thereof shall be inviolably observed by the states we respectively represent, and that the union shall be perpetual. In Witness whereof we have hereunto set our hands in Congress. Done at Philadelphia in the state of Pennsylvania the ninth Day of July in the Year of our Lord one Thousand seven Hundred and Seventy-eight and in the third year of the independence of America.

The Constitution of the United States of America

Annotated with references to the Federalist Papers

Federalist Paper Number and Author

[PREAMBLE]

84
(Hamilton)

We the People of the United States, in Order to form a more perfect Union, establish Justice, insure domestic Tranquility, provide for the common defence, promote the general Welfare, and secure the Blessings of Liberty to ourselves and our Posterity, do ordain and establish this Constitution for the United States of America.

ARTICLE I

Section 1

[LEGISLATIVE POWERS]

10, 45
(Madison)

All legislative Powers herein granted shall be vested in a Congress of the United States, which shall consist of a Senate and House of Representatives.

Section 2

[HOUSE OF REPRESENTATIVES, HOW CONSTITUTED, POWER OF IM-PEACHMENT]

39
(Madison)
45
(Madison)
52–53, 57
(Madison)
52
(Madison),
60
(Hamilton)

The House of Representatives shall be composed of Members chosen every second Year by the People of the several States, and the Electors in each State shall have the Qualifications requisite for Electors of the most numerous Branch of the State Legislature.

No Person shall be a Representative who shall not have attained to the Age of twenty-five Years, and been seven Years a Citizen of the United States, and who shall not, when elected, be an inhabitant of that State in which he shall be chosen.

54
(Madison)

Representatives and *direct Taxes*[1] shall be apportioned among the several States which may be included within this Union, according to their respective Num-

---

[1]Modified by Sixteenth Amendment.

A13

bers, *which shall be determined by adding to the whole Number of free Persons, including those bound to Service for a Term of Years,* and excluding Indians not taxed, *three-fifths of all other Persons.*[2] The actual Enumeration shall be made within three Years after the first Meeting of the Congress of the United States, and within every subsequent Term of ten Years, in such Manner as they shall by Law direct. The Number of Representatives shall not exceed one for every thirty Thousand, but each State shall have at Least one Representative; *and until such enumeration shall be made, the State of New Hampshire shall be entitled to chuse three, Massachusetts eight, Rhode-Island and Providence Plantations one, Connecticut five, New-York six, New Jersey four, Pennsylvania eight, Delaware one, Maryland six. Virginia ten, North Carolina five, South Carolina five, and Georgia three.*[3]

When vacancies happen in the Representation from any State, the Executive Authority thereof shall issue Writs of Election to fill such Vacancies.

The House of Representatives shall chuse their Speaker and other Officers; and shall have the sole Power of Impeachment.

Section 3

[THE SENATE, HOW CONSTITUTED, IMPEACHMENT TRIALS]

The Senate of the United States shall be composed of two Senators from each State, *chosen by the Legislature thereof,*[4] for six Years; and each Senator shall have one Vote.

Immediately after they shall be assembled in Consequence of the first Election, they shall be divided as equally as may be into three Classes. The Seats of the Senators of the first Class shall be vacated at the Expiration of the second Year, of the second Class at the Expiration of the fourth Year, and of the third Class at the Expiration of the sixth Year, so that one third may be chosen every second Year: *and if vacancies happen by Resignation, or otherwise, during the Recess of the Legislature of any State, the Executive thereof may make temporary Appointments until the next Meeting of the Legislature, which shall then fill such Vacancies.*[5]

No person shall be a Senator who shall not have attained to the Age of thirty Years, and been nine Years a Citizen of the United States, and who shall not, when elected, be an Inhabitant of that State for which he shall be chosen.

The Vice-President of the United States shall be President of the Senate, but shall have no Vote, unless they be equally divided.

The Senate shall chuse their other Officers, and also a President pro tempore, in the Absence of the Vice-President, or when he shall exercise the Office of President of the United States.

The Senate shall have the sole Power to try all Impeachments. When sitting for that Purpose, they shall be on Oath or Affirmation. When the President of the United States is tried, the Chief Justice shall preside: And no Person shall be convicted without the Concurrence of two-thirds of the Members present.

Judgment in Cases of Impeachment shall not extend further than to removal from Office, and disqualification to hold and enjoy any Office of honor, Trust or Profit under the United States: but the Party convicted shall nevertheless be liable and subject to Indictment, Trial, Judgment and Punishment, according to Law.

Margin references:
54 (Madison)
58 (Madison)
55–56 (Madison)
79 (Hamilton)
39, 45 (Madison), 60 (Hamilton), 62–63 (Madison) 59 (Hamilton)
68 (Hamilton)
62 (Madison), 64 (Jay)
39 (Madison), 65–67, 79 (Hamilton) 65 (Hamilton)
84 (Hamilton)

[2]Modified by Fourteenth Amendment.

[3]Temporary provision.

[4]Modified by Seventeenth Amendment.

[5]Ibid.

Section 4

[ELECTION OF SENATORS AND REPRESENTATIVES]

59–61
(Hamilton)

The Times, Places and Manner of holding Elections for Senators and Representatives, shall be prescribed in each State by the Legislature thereof; but the Congress may at any time by Law make or alter such Regulations, except as to the Places of chusing Senators.

The Congress shall assemble at least once in every Year, and such Meeting shall be on the first Monday in December, unless they shall by Law appoint a different Day.[6]

Section 5

[QUORUM, JOURNALS, MEETINGS, ADJOURNMENTS]

Each House shall be the Judge of the Elections, Returns and Qualifications of its own Members, and a Majority of each shall constitute a Quorum to do Business; but a smaller Number may adjourn from day to day, and may be authorized to compel the Attendance of absent Members, in such Manner, and under the Penalties as each House may provide.

Each House may determine the Rules of its Proceedings, punish its Members for disorderly Behavior and, with the Concurrence of two-thirds, expel a Member.

Each House shall keep a Journal of its Proceedings, and from time to time publish the same, excepting such Parts as may in their Judgment require Secrecy; and the Yeas and Nays of the Members of either House on any questions shall, at the Desire of one-fifth of the present, be entered on the Journal.

Neither House, during the Session of Congress, shall, without the Consent of the other, adjourn for more than three days, nor to any other Place than that in which the two Houses shall be sitting.

Section 6

[COMPENSATION, PRIVILEGES, DISABILITIES]

The Senators and Representatives shall receive a Compensation for their Services, to be ascertained by Law, and paid out of the Treasury of the United States. They shall in all Cases, except Treason, Felony and Breach of the Peace, be privileged from Arrest during their Attendance at the Session of their respective Houses, and in going to and returning from the same; and for any Speech or Debate in either House, they shall not be questioned in any other Place.

55
(Madison),
76
(Hamilton)

No Senator or Representative shall, during the time for which he was elected, be appointed to any civil Office under the authority of the United States, which shall have been created, or the Emoluments whereof shall have been encreased during such time; and no Person holding any Office under the United States, shall be a Member of either House during his Continuance in Office.

Section 7

[PROCEDURE IN PASSING BILLS AND RESOLUTIONS]

66
(Hamilton)

All Bills for raising Revenue shall originate in the House of Representatives; but the Senate may propose or concur with Amendments as on other Bills.

69, 73
(Hamilton)

Every Bill which shall have passed the House of Representatives and the Senate, shall, before it become a Law, be presented to the President of the United States; if he approve he shall sign it, but if not he shall return it, with his Objections to that House in which it shall have originated, who shall enter the Objec-

[6]Modified by Twentieth Amendment.

tions at large on their Journal, and proceed to reconsider it. If after such Reconsideration two-thirds of that House shall agree to pass the Bill, it shall be sent, together with the Objections, to the other House, by which it shall likewise be reconsidered, and if approved by two-thirds of that House it shall become a Law. But in all such Cases the Votes of both Houses shall be determined by Yeas and Nays, and the Names of the Persons voting for and against the Bill shall be entered on the Journal of each House respectively. If any Bill shall not be returned by the President within ten Days (Sundays excepted) after it shall have been presented to him, the Same shall be a Law, in like Manner as if he had signed it, unless the Congress by their Adjournment prevent its Return, in which Case it shall not be a Law.

69, 73
(Hamilton)

Every Order, Resolution, or Vote to which the Concurrence of the Senate and House of Representatives may be necessary (except on a question of Adjournment) shall be presented to the President of the United States; and before the Same shall take Effect, shall be approved by him, or being disapproved by him, shall be repassed by two-thirds of the Senate and House of Representatives, according to the Rules and Limitations prescribed in the Case of a Bill.

Section 8

[POWERS OF CONGRESS]

The Congress shall have Power

30–36
(Hamilton),
41
(Madison)

To lay and collect Taxes, Duties, Imposts and Excises, to pay the Debts and provide for the common Defence and general Welfare of the United States; but all Duties, Imposts and excises shall be uniform throughout the United States;

56
(Madison)

To borrow Money on the Credit of the United States;

42, 45, 56
(Madison)

To regulate Commerce with foreign Nations, and among the several States, and with the Indian Tribes;

32
(Hamilton),
42
(Madison)

To establish an uniform Rule of Naturalization, and uniform Laws on the subject of Bankruptcies throughout the United States;

42
(Madison)

To coin Money, regulate the Value thereof, and of foreign Coin, and fix the Standard of Weights and Measures;

42
(Madison)

To provide for the Punishment of counterfeiting the Securities and current Coin of the United States;

42
(Madison)

To establish Post Offices and post Roads;

42
(Madison)
43
(Madison)

To promote the Progress of Science and useful Arts, by securing for limited Times to Authors and Inventors the exclusive Right to their respective Writings and Discoveries;

81
(Hamilton)

To constitute Tribunals inferior to the supreme Court;

42
(Madison)

To define and Punish Piracies and Felonies committed on the high Seas, and Offences against the Law of Nations;

41
(Madison)

To declare War, grant Letters of Marque and Reprisal, and make Rules concerning Captures on Land and Water;

23, 24, 26
(Hamilton),

To raise and support Armies, but no Appropriation of Money to that Use shall be for a longer Term than two Years;

41
(Madison)

To provide and maintain a Navy;

To make Rules for the Government and Regulation of the land and naval forces;

29
(Hamilton)

To provide for calling for the Militia to execute the Laws of the Union, suppress Insurrections and repel Invasions;

29
(Hamilton),
56
(Madison)

To provide for organizing, arming, and disciplining, the Militia, and for governing such Part of them as may be employed in the Service of the United States, reserving to the States respectively, the Appointment of the Officers, and the Au-

32
(Hamilton),
43
(Madison)

To exercise exclusive Legislation in all Cases whatsoever, over such District (not exceeding ten Miles square) as may, by Cession of particular States, and the Acceptance of Congress, become the Seat of the Government of the United States, and to exercise like Authority over all Places purchased by the Consent of

43
(Madison)

the Legislature of the State in which the Same shall be, for the Erection of Forts, Magazines, Arsenals, dock-Yards, and other needful Buildings;—And

29, 33
(Hamilton)
44
(Madison)

To make all Laws which shall be necessary and proper for carrying into Execution the foregoing Powers, and all other Powers vested by this Constitution in the Government of the United States, or in any Department or Officer thereof.

Section 9

[SOME RESTRICTIONS ON FEDERAL POWER]

42
(Madison)

The Migration or Importation of such Persons as any of the States now existing shall think proper to admit, shall not be prohibited by the Congress prior to the Year one thousand eight hundred and eight, but a Tax or Duty may be imposed on such Importation, not exceeding ten dollars for each Person.[7]

83, 84
(Hamilton)

The privilege of the Writ of *Habeas Corpus* shall not be suspended, unless when in Cases of Rebellion or Invasion the public Safety may require it.

84
(Hamilton)

No Bill of Attainder or ex post facto Law shall be passed.

No Capitation, or other direct, Tax shall be laid, unless in Proportion to the Census or Enumeration herein before directed to be taken.[8]

No Tax or Duty shall be laid on Articles exported from any State.

32
(Hamilton)

No Preference shall be given by any Regulation of Commerce or Revenue to the Ports of one State over those of another; nor shall vessels bound to, or from, one State, be obliged to enter, clear, or pay Duties in another.

No Money shall be drawn from the Treasury, but in Consequence of Appropriations made by Law; and a regular Statement and Account of the Receipts and Expenditures of all public Money shall be published from time to time.

39
(Madison),
84
(Hamilton)

No Title of Nobility shall be granted by the United States: And no Person holding any Office of Profit or Trust under them, shall, without the Consent of the Congress, accept of any present, Emolument, Office or Title, of any kind whatever, from any King, Prince, or foreign State.

Section 10

[RESTRICTIONS UPON POWERS OF STATES]

33
(Hamilton),
44
(Madison)

No State shall enter into any Treaty, Alliance, or Confederation; grant Letters of Marque and Reprisal; coin Money; emit Bills of Credit; make any Thing but gold and silver Coin a Tender in Payment of Debts; pass any Bill of Attainder, ex post facto Law, or Law impairing the Obligation of Contracts, or grant any Title of Nobility.

32
(Hamilton),
44
(Madison)

No State shall, without the Consent of the Congress, lay any Imposts or Duties on Imports or Exports, except what may be absolutely necessary for executing its inspection Laws: and the net Produce of all Duties and Imposts, laid by any State on Imports or Exports, shall be for the Use of the Treasury of the United States; and all such Laws shall be subject to the Revision and Control of the Congress.

No State shall, without the Consent of Congress, lay any Duty of Tonnage, keep Troops, or Ships of War in time of Peace, enter into any Agreement or

[7]Temporary provision.

[8]Modified by Sixteenth Amendment.

Compact with another State, or with a foreign Power, or engage in War, unless actually invaded, or in such imminent Danger as will not admit of Delay.

ARTICLE II

Section 1

[EXECUTIVE POWER, ELECTION, QUALIFICATIONS OF THE PRESIDENT]

39
(Madison),
70, 71, 84
(Hamilton)
69, 71
(Hamilton)
39, 45
(Madison),
68, 77
(Hamilton)

The executive Power shall be vested in a President of the United States of America. *He shall hold his Office during the Term of four years and, together with the Vice-President, chosen for the same Term, be elected, as follows:*[9]

Each State shall appoint, in such Manner as the Legislature thereof may direct, a Number of Electors, equal to the whole Number of Senators and Representatives to which the State may be entitled in the Congress: but no Senator or Representative, or Person holding an Office of Trust or Profit under the United States, shall be appointed an Elector.

66
(Hamilton)

The electors shall meet in their respective States, and vote by ballot for two Persons, of whom one at least shall not be an Inhabitant of the same State with themselves. And they shall make a List of all the Persons voted for, and of the Number of Votes for each; which List they shall sign and certify, and transmit sealed to the Seat of the Government of the United States, directed to the President of the Senate. The President of the Senate shall, in the Presence of the Senate and House of Representatives, open all the Certificates, and the Votes shall then be counted. The Person having the greatest Number of Votes shall be the President, if such Number be a Majority of the whole Number of Electors appointed; and if there be more than one who have such Majority and have an equal Number of Votes, then the House of Representatives shall immediately chuse by Ballot one of them for President; and if no person have a Majority, then from the five highest on the List the said House shall in like Manner chuse the President. But in chusing the President, the Votes shall be taken by States, the Representation from each State having one Vote; A quorum for this Purpose shall consist of a Member or Members from two-thirds of the States, and a Majority of all the States shall be necessary to a Choice. In every Case, after the Choice of the President, the person having the greatest Number of Votes of the Electors shall be the Vice-President. But if there should remain two or more who have equal vote, the Senate shall chuse from them by Ballot the Vice-President.[10]

The Congress may determine the Time of chusing the Electors, and the Day on which they shall give their Votes; which Day shall be the same throughout the United States.

64 (Jay)

No Person except a natural born Citizen, or a Citizen of the United States, at the time of the Adoption of this Constitution, shall be eligible to the Office of President; neither shall any Person be eligible to that Office who shall not have attained to the Age of thirty-five Years, and been fourteen Years a Resident within the United States.

In Case of the Removal of the President from Office, or his Death, Resignation, or Inability to discharge the Powers and Duties of the said Office, the same shall devolve on the Vice-President, and the Congress may by Law provide for the Case of Removal, Death, Resignation, or Inability, both of the President and Vice-President, declaring what Officer shall then act as President, and such Officer shall act accordingly, until the Disability be removed, or a President shall be elected.

73, 79
(Hamilton)

The President shall, at stated Times, receive for his Services, a Compensation,

---

[9]Number of terms limited to two by Twenty-second Amendment.

[10]Modified by Twelfth and Twentieth Amendments.

which shall neither be encreased nor diminished during the Period for which he shall have been elected, and he shall not receive within that Period any other Emolument from the United States, or any of them.

Before he enter on the Execution of his Office, he shall take the following Oath or Affirmation:—"I do solemnly swear (or affirm) that I will faithfully execute the Office of President of the United States, and will to the best of my Ability, preserve, protect and defend the Constitution of the United States."

Section 2

[POWERS OF THE PRESIDENT]

69, 74
(Hamilton)

74
(Hamilton)
69
(Hamilton)
74
(Hamilton)
42
(Madison)
64 (Jay),
66
(Hamilton)
42
(Madison),
66, 69,
76, 77
(Hamilton)

The President shall be Commander in Chief of the Army and Navy of the United States, and of the Militia of the several States, when called into the actual Service of the United States; he may require the Opinion, in writing, of the principal Officer in each of the executive Departments, upon any Subject relating to the Duties of their respective Offices, and he shall have Power to grant Reprieves and Pardons for Offences against the United States, except in Cases of Impeachment.

He shall have Power, by and with the Advice and Consent of the Senate, to make Treaties, provided two-thirds of the Senators present concur; and he shall nominate, and by and with the Advice and Consent of the Senate, shall appoint Ambassadors, other public Ministers and Consuls, Judges of the Supreme Court, and all other Officers of the United States, whose Appointments are not herein otherwise provided for, and which shall be established by Law: but the Congress may by Law vest the Appointment of such inferior Officers, as they think proper, in the President alone, in the Courts of Law, or in the Heads of Departments.

67, 76
(Hamilton)

The President shall have Power to fill up all Vacancies that may happen during the Recess of the Senate, by granting Commissions which shall expire at the End of their next Session.

Section 3

[POWERS AND DUTIES OF THE PRESIDENT]

77
(Hamilton)
69, 77
(Hamilton)
77
(Hamilton)
69, 77
(Hamilton)
42
(Madison),
69, 77
(Hamilton)
78
(Hamilton)

He shall from time to time give to the Congress Information of the State of the Union, and recommend to their Consideration such Measures as he shall judge necessary and expedient; he may, on extraordinary Occasions, convene both Houses, or either of them, and in Case of Disagreement between them, with Respect to the Time of Adjournment, he may adjourn them to such Time as he shall think proper; he shall receive Ambassadors and other public Ministers; he shall take Care that the Laws be faithfully executed, and shall Commission all the Officers of the United States.

Section 4

[IMPEACHMENT]

39
(Madison),
69
(Hamilton)

The President, Vice-President and all civil Officers of the United States shall be removed from Office on Impeachment for, and Conviction of, Treason, Bribery, or other high Crimes and Misdemeanors.

ARTICLE III

Section 1

[JUDICIAL POWER, TENURE OF OFFICE]

81, 82
(Hamilton)

The judicial Power of the United States, shall be vested in one supreme Court, and in such inferior Courts as the Congress may from time to time ordain and establish. The Judges, both of the supreme and inferior Courts, shall hold their Offices during good Behavior, and shall, at stated Times, receive for their Services, a Compensation, which shall not be diminished during their Continuance in Office.

Section 2

[JURISDICTION]

The judicial Power shall extend to all Cases, in Law and Equity, arising under this Constitution, the Laws of the United States, and Treaties made, or which shall be made, under their Authority;—to all Cases affecting Ambassadors, other public Ministers and Consuls;—to all Cases of admiralty and maritime Jurisdiction;—to Controversies to which the United States shall be a party;—to Controversies between two or more States;—*between a State and Citizens of another State*;—between Citizens of different States,—between Citizens of the same State claiming Lands under Grants of different States, *and between a State*, or the Citizens thereof, *and foreign States, Citizens or Subjects.*[11]

In all Cases affecting Ambassadors, other public Ministers and Consuls, and those in which a State shall be Party, the supreme Court shall have original Jurisdiction. In all the other Cases before mentioned, the supreme Court shall have appellate Jurisdiction, both as to Law and Fact, with such Exceptions, and under such Regulations as Congress shall make.

The Trial of all Crimes, except in Cases of Impeachment, shall be by Jury; and such Trial shall be held in the State where the said Crimes shall have been committed; but when not committed within any State, the Trial shall be at such Place or Places as the Congress may by Law have directed.

Section 3

[TREASON, PROOF, AND PUNISHMENT]

Treason against the United States, shall consist only in levying War against them, or in adhering to their Enemies, giving them Aid and Comfort. No Person shall be convicted of Treason unless on the Testimony of two Witnesses to the same overt Act, or on Confession in open Court.

The Congress shall have Power to declare the Punishment of Treason, but no Attainder of Treason shall work Corruption of Blood, or Forfeiture except during the Life of the Person attained.

ARTICLE IV

Section 1

[FAITH AND CREDIT AMONG STATES]

Full Faith and Credit shall be given in each State to the public Acts, Records, and judicial Proceedings of every other State. And the Congress may by general Laws prescribe the Manner in which such Acts, Records and Proceedings shall be proved, and the Effect thereof.

Section 2

[PRIVILEGES AND IMMUNITIES, FUGITIVES]

The Citizens of each State shall be entitled to all Privileges and Immunities of Citizens in the several States.

---

[11]Modified by Eleventh Amendment.

A person charged in any State with Treason, Felony or other Crime, who shall flee from Justice, and be found in another State, shall on Demand of the executive Authority of the State from which he fled, be delivered up to be removed to the State having Jurisdiction of the Crime.

No person held to Service or Labour in one State, under the Laws thereof, escaping into another, shall, in Consequence of any Law or Regulation therein, be discharged from such Service or Labour, but shall be delivered up on Claim of the Party to whom such Service or Labour may be due.[12]

Section 3

[ADMISSION OF NEW STATES]

43
(Madison)

New States may be admitted by the Congress into this Union; but no new State shall be formed or erected within the Jurisdiction of any other State; nor any State be formed by the Junction of two or more States, or Parts of States, without the Consent of the Legislatures of the States concerned as well as of the Congress.

43
(Madison)

The Congress shall have Power to dispose of and make all needful Rules and Regulations respecting the Territory or other Property belonging to the United States; and nothing in this Constitution shall be so construed as·to Prejudice any Claims of the United States, or of any particular State.

Section 4

[GUARANTEE OF REPUBLICAN GOVERNMENT]

39, 43
(Madison)

The United States shall guarantee to every State in this Union a Republican Form of Government, and shall protect each of them against Invasion; and on Application of the Legislature, or of the Executive (when the Legislature cannot be convened) against domestic Violence.

ARTICLE V

[AMENDMENT OF THE CONSTITUTION]

39, 43
(Madison)
85
(Hamilton)

The Congress, whenever two-thirds of both Houses shall deem it necessary, shall propose Amendments to this Constitution, or, on the Application of the Legislatures of two-thirds of the several States, shall call a Convention for proposing Amendments, which, in either Case, shall be valid to all Intents and Purposes, as Part of this Constitution, when ratified by the Legislatures of three-fourths of the several States, or by Conventions in three-fourths thereof, as the one or the other Mode of Ratification may be proposed by the Congress; *Provided that no Amendment which may be made prior to the Year One thousand eight hundred and eight shall in any Manner affect the first and fourth Clauses in the Ninth Section of the first Ar-*

43
(Madison)

ticle;[13] *and that no State, without its Consent, shall be deprived of its equal Suffrage in the Senate.

ARTICLE VI

[DEBTS, SUPREMACY, OATH]

43
(Madison)

All Debts contracted and Engagements entered into, before the Adoption of this Constitution, shall be as valid against the United States under this Constitution, as under the Confederation.

[12]Repealed by the Thirteenth Amendment.

[13]Temporary provision.

27, 33
(Hamilton),
39, 44
(Madison)

This Constitution, and the Laws of the United States which shall be made in Pursuance thereof; and all Treaties made, or which shall be made, under the Authority of the United States, shall be the supreme Law of the Land; and the Judges in every State shall be bound thereby, any Thing in the Constitution or Laws of any State to the Contrary notwithstanding.

27
(Hamilton),
44
(Madison)

The Senators and Representatives before mentioned, and the Members of the several State Legislatures, and all executive and judicial Officers, both of the United States and of the several States, shall be bound by Oath or Affirmation, to support this Constitution; but no religious Test shall be required as a Qualification to any Office or public Trust under the United States.

ARTICLE VII

[RATIFICATION AND ESTABLISHMENT]

39, 40, 43
(Madison)

The Ratification of the Conventions of nine States, shall be sufficient for the Establishment of this Constitution between the States so ratifying the Same.[14]

Done in Convention by the Unanimous Consent of the States present the Seventeenth Day of September in the Year of our Lord one thousand seven hundred and Eighty seven and of the Independence of the United States of America the Twelfth. *In Witness* whereof We have hereunto subscribed our Names, G:[0] WASHINGTON—
*Presidt, and Deputy
from Virginia*

New Hampshire	JOHN LANGDON NICHOLAS GILMAN	Delaware	GEO READ GUNNING BEDFOR JUN
Massachusetts	NATHANIEL GORHAM RUFUS KING		JOHN DICKINSON RICHARD BASSETT JACO: BROOM
Connecticut	WM SAML JOHNSON ROGER SHERMAN	Maryland	JAMES MCHENRY DAN OF ST THOS. JENIFER
New York	ALEXANDER HAMILTON		DANL CARROLL
New Jersey	WIL: LIVINGSTON DAVID BREARLEY WM PATERSON JONA: DAYTON	Virginia	JOHN BLAIR— JAMES MADISON JR.
		North Carolina	WM BLOUNT RICHD DOBBS SPAIGHT HU WILLIAMSON
Pennsylvania	B FRANKLIN THOMAS MIFFLIN ROBT MORRIS GEO. CLYMER THOS. FITZSIMONS JARED INGERSOLL JAMES WILSON GOUV MORRIS	South Carolina	J. RUTLEDGE CHARLES COTESWORTH PINCKNEY CHARLES PINCKNEY PIERCE BUTLER
		Georgia	WILLIAM FEW ABR BALDWIN

[14]The Constitution was submitted on September 17, 1787, by the Constitutional Convention, was ratified by the conventions of several states at various dates up to May 29, 1790, and became effective on March 4, 1789.

Amendments to the Constitution

*Proposed by Congress and Ratified
by the Legislatures of the Several States,
Pursuant to Article V of the Original Constitution.*

Amendments I-X, known as the Bill of Rights, were proposed by Congress on September 25, 1789, and ratified on December 15, 1791. Federalist Papers *comments, mainly in opposition to a Bill of Rights, can be found in #84 (Hamilton).*

AMENDMENT I

[FREEDOM OF RELIGION, OF SPEECH, AND OF THE PRESS]

Congress shall make no law respecting an establishment of religion, or prohibiting the free exercise thereof; or abridging the freedom of speech, or of the press; or the right of the people peaceably to assemble, and to petition the Government for a redress of grievances.

AMENDMENT II

[RIGHT TO KEEP AND BEAR ARMS]

A well regulated Militia, being necessary to the security of a free State, the right of the people to keep and bear Arms, shall not be infringed.

AMENDMENT III

[QUARTERING OF SOLDIERS]

No Soldier shall, in time of peace be quartered in any house, without the consent of the Owner, nor in time of war, but in a manner to be prescribed by law.

AMENDMENT IV

[SECURITY FROM UNWARRANTABLE SEARCH AND SEIZURE]

The right of the people to be secure in their persons, houses, papers, and effects, against unreasonable searches and seizures, shall not be violated, and no Warrants shall issue, but upon probable cause, supported by Oath or affirmation, and particularly describing the place to be searched, and the persons or things to be seized.

AMENDMENT V

[RIGHTS OF ACCUSED PERSONS IN CRIMINAL PROCEEDINGS]

No person shall be held to answer for a capital, or otherwise infamous crime, unless on a presentment or indictment of a Grand Jury, except in cases arising in the land or naval forces, or in the Militia, when in actual service in time of War or in public danger; nor shall any person be subject for the same offence to be twice put in jeopardy of life or limb; nor shall be compelled in any Criminal Case to be a witness against himself, nor be deprived of life, liberty, or property, without due process of law; nor shall private property be taken for public use, without just compensation.

AMENDMENT VI

[RIGHT TO SPEEDY TRIAL, WITNESSES, ETC.]

In all criminal prosecutions, the accused shall enjoy the right to a speedy and public trial, by an impartial jury of the State and district wherein the crime shall have been committed, which district shall have been previously ascertained by law, and to be informed of the nature and cause of the accusation; to be confronted with the witnesses against him; to have compulsory process for obtaining Witnesses in his favor, and to have the Assistance of Counsel for his defence.

AMENDMENT VII

[TRIAL BY JURY IN CIVIL CASES]

In suits at common law, where the value in controversy shall exceed twenty dollars, the right of trial by jury shall be preserved, and no fact tried by a jury shall be otherwise re-examined in any Court of the United States, than according to the rules of the common law.

AMENDMENT VIII

[BAILS, FINES, PUNISHMENTS]

Excessive bail shall not be required, nor excessive fines imposed, nor cruel and unusual punishments inflicted.

AMENDMENT IX

[RESERVATION OF RIGHTS OF PEOPLE]

The enumeration in the Constitution, of certain rights, shall not be construed to deny or disparage others retained by the people.

AMENDMENT X

[POWERS RESERVED TO STATES OR PEOPLE]

The powers not delegated to the United States by the Constitution, nor prohibited by it to the States, are reserved to the States respectively, or to the people.

AMENDMENT XI

[*Proposed by Congress on March 4, 1794; declared ratified on January 8, 1798.*]

[RESTRICTION OF JUDICIAL POWER]

The Judicial power of the United States shall not be construed to extend to any suit in law or equity, commenced or prosecuted against one of the United States by Citizens of another State, or by Citizens or Subjects of any Foreign State.

AMENDMENT XII

[*Proposed by Congress on December 9, 1803; declared ratified on September 25, 1804.*]

[ELECTION OF PRESIDENT AND VICE-PRESIDENT]

The Electors shall meet in their respective states, and vote by ballot for President and Vice-President, one of whom, at least, shall not be an inhabitant of the same state with themselves; they shall name in their ballots the person voted for as President, and in distinct ballots the person voted for as Vice-President, and they shall make distinct lists of all persons voted for as President, and of all persons voted for as Vice-President, and of the number of votes for each, which lists they shall sign and certify, and transmit sealed to the seat of the government of the United States, directed to the President of the Senate;—The President of the Senate shall, in presence of the Senate and House of Representatives, open all the certificates and the votes shall then be counted;—The person having the greatest number of votes for President, shall be the President, if such number be a majority of the whole number of Electors appointed; and if no person have such majority, then from the persons having the highest numbers not exceeding three on the list of those voted for as President, the House of Representatives shall choose immediately, by ballot, the President. But in choosing the President, the votes shall be taken by states, the representation from each state having one vote; a quorum for this purpose shall consist of a member or members from two-thirds of the states, and a majority of all states shall be necessary to a choice. And if the House of Representatives shall not choose a President whenever the right of choice shall devolve upon them, before the fourth day of March next following, then the Vice-President, shall act as President, as in the case of the death or other constitutional disability of the President. The person having the greatest number of votes as Vice-President, shall be the Vice-President, if such a number be a majority of the whole number of Electors appointed, and if no person have a majority, then from the two highest numbers on the list, the Senate shall choose the Vice-President; a quorum for the purpose shall consist of two-thirds of the whole number of Senators, and a majority of the whole number shall be necessary to a choice. But no person constitutionally ineligible to the office of President shall be eligible to that of Vice-President of the United States.

AMENDMENT XIII

[*Proposed by Congress on January 31, 1865; declared ratified on December 18, 1865.*]

Section 1

[ABOLITION OF SLAVERY]

Neither slavery nor involuntary servitude, except as a punishment for crime whereof the party shall have been duly convicted, shall exist within the United States, or any place subject to their jurisdiction.

Section 2

[POWER TO ENFORCE THIS ARTICLE]

Congress shall have power to enforce this article by appropriate legislation.

AMENDMENT XIV

[*Proposed by Congress on June 13, 1866, declared ratified on July 28, 1868.*]

Section 1

[CITIZENSHIP RIGHTS NOT TO BE ABRIDGED BY STATES]

All persons born or naturalized in the United States, and subject to the jurisdiction thereof, are citizens of the United States and of the State wherein they reside. No state shall make or enforce any law which shall abridge the privileges or immunities of citizens of the

United States; nor shall any State deprive any person of life, liberty, or property, without due process of law; nor deny to any person within its jurisdiction the equal protection of the laws.

Section 2

[APPORTIONMENT OF REPRESENTATIVES IN CONGRESS]

Representatives shall be apportioned among the several States according to their respective numbers, counting the whole number of persons in each State, excluding Indians not taxed. But when the right to vote at any election for the choice of electors for President and Vice-President of the United States, Representatives in Congress, the Executive and Judicial officers of a State, or the members of the Legislature thereof, is denied to any of the male inhabitants of such State, being twenty-one years of age, and citizens of the United States, or in any way abridged, except for participation in rebellion, or other crime, the basis of representation therein shall be reduced in the proportion which the number of such male citizens shall bear to the whole number of male citizens twenty-one years of age in such State.

Section 3

[PERSONS DISQUALIFIED FROM HOLDING OFFICE]

No person shall be a Senator or Representative in Congress, or elector of President and Vice-President, or hold any office, civil or military, under the United States, or under any State, who, having previously taken an oath, as a member of Congress, or as an officer of the United States, or as a member of any State legislature, or as an executive or judicial officer of any State, to support the Constitution of the United States, shall have engaged in insurrection or rebellion against the same, or given aid or comfort to the enemies thereof. But Congress may by a vote of two-thirds of each House, remove such disability.

Section 4

[WHAT PUBLIC DEBTS ARE VALID]

The validity of the public debt of the United States, authorized by law, including debts incurred for payment of pensions and bounties for services in suppressing insurrection or rebellion, shall not be questioned. But neither the United States nor any State shall assume or pay any debt or obligation incurred in aid of insurrection or rebellion against the United States, or any claim for the loss or emancipation of any slave; but all such debts, obligations and claims shall be held illegal and void.

Section 5

[POWER TO ENFORCE THIS ARTICLE]

The Congress shall have power to enforce, by appropriate legislation, the provisions of this article.

AMENDMENT XV

[*Proposed by Congress on February 26, 1869; declared ratified on March 30, 1870.*]

Section 1

[NEGRO SUFFRAGE]

The right of citizens of the United States to vote shall not be denied or abridged by the United States or by any State on account of race, color, or previous condition of servitude.

Section 2

[POWER TO ENFORCE THIS ARTICLE]

The Congress shall have power to enforce this article by appropriate legislation.

AMENDMENT XVI

[*Proposed by Congress on July 12, 1909; declared ratified on February 25, 1913.*]

[AUTHORIZING INCOME TAXES]

The Congress shall have power to lay and collect taxes on incomes, from whatever source derived, without apportionment among the several States, and without regard to any census or enumeration.

AMENDMENT XVII

[*Proposed by Congress on May 13, 1912; declared ratified on May 31, 1913.*]

[POPULAR ELECTION OF SENATORS]

The Senate of the United States shall be composed of two Senators from each State, elected by the people thereof, for six years; and each Senator shall have one vote. The electors in each State shall have the qualifications requisite for electors of the most numerous branch of the State Legislature.

When vacancies happen in the representation of any State in the Senate, the executive authority of such State shall issue writs of election to fill such vacancies: Provided, That the Legislature of any State may empower the executive thereof to make temporary appointment until the people fill the vacancies by election as the Legislature may direct.

This amendment shall not be so construed as to affect the election or term of any Senator chosen before it becomes valid as part of the Constitution.

AMENDMENT XVIII

[*Proposed by Congress December 18, 1917; declared ratified on January 29, 1919.*]

Section 1

[NATIONAL LIQUOR PROHIBITION]

After one year from the ratification of this article the manufacture, sale, or transportation of intoxicating liquors within, the importation thereof into, or the exportation thereof from the United States and all territory subject to the jurisdiction thereof for beverage purposes is hereby prohibited.

Section 2

[POWER TO ENFORCE THIS ARTICLE]

The Congress and the several states shall have concurrent power to enforce this article by appropriate legislation.

Section 3

[RATIFICATION WITHIN SEVEN YEARS]

This article shall be inoperative unless it shall have been ratified as an amendment to the Constitution by the legislatures of the several states, as provided in the Constitution, within seven years from the date of the submission hereof to the states by the Congress.[15]

---

[15]Repealed by the Twenty-first Amendment

AMENDMENT XIX

[*Proposed by Congress on June 4, 1919; declared ratified on August 26, 1920.*]

[WOMAN SUFFRAGE]

The right of the citizens of the United States to vote shall not be denied or abridged by the United States or by any state on account of sex.

Congress shall have power, by appropriate legislation, to enforce this article by appropriate legislation.

AMENDMENT XX

[*Proposed by Congress on March 2, 1932; declared ratified on February 6, 1933.*]

Section 1

[TERMS OF OFFICE]

The terms of the President and Vice-President shall end at noon on the 20th day of January, and the terms of the Senators and Representatives at noon on the 3rd day of January, of the years in which such terms would have ended if this article had not been ratified; and the terms of their successors shall then begin.

Section 2

[TIME OF CONVENING CONGRESS]

The Congress shall assemble at least once in every year, and such meeting shall begin at noon on the 3rd day of January, unless they shall by law appoint a different day.

Section 3

[DEATH OF PRESIDENT-ELECT]

If, at the time fixed for the beginning of the term of the President, the President-elect shall have died, the Vice-President-elect shall become President. If a President shall not have been chosen before the time fixed for the beginning of his term, or if the President-elect shall have failed to qualify, then the Vice-President-elect shall act as President until a President shall have qualified; and the Congress may by law provide for the case wherein neither a President-elect nor a Vice-President-elect shall have qualified, declaring who shall then act as President, or the manner in which one who is to act shall be selected, and such person shall act accordingly until a President or Vice President shall have qualified.

Section 4

[ELECTION OF THE PRESIDENT]

The Congress may by law provide for the case of the death of any of the persons from whom the House of Representatives may choose a President whenever the right of choice shall have devolved upon them, and for the case of the death of any of the persons from whom the Senate may choose a Vice-President whenever the right of choice shall have devolved upon them.

Section 5

[AMENDMENT TAKES EFFECT]

Sections 1 and 2 shall take effect on the 15th day of October following ratification of this article.

Section 6

[RATIFICATION WITHIN SEVEN YEARS]

This article shall be inoperative unless it shall have been ratified as an amendment to the

Constitution by the legislatures of three-fourths of the several States within seven years from

the date of its submission.

AMENDMENT XXI

[Proposed by Congress on February 20, 1933; declared ratified on December 5, 1933.]

Section 1

[NATIONAL LIQUOR PROHIBITION REPEALED]

The eighteenth article of amendment to the Constitution of the United States is hereby repealed.

Section 2

[TRANSPORTATION OF LIQUOR INTO "DRY" STATES]

The transportation or importation into any State, Territory, or Possession of the United States for delivery or use therein of intoxicating liquors, in violation of the laws thereof, is hereby prohibited.

Section 3

[RATIFICATION WITHIN SEVEN YEARS]

This article shall be inoperative unless it shall have been ratified as an amendment to the Constitution by conventions in the several States, as provided in the Constitution, within seven years from the date of the submission hereof to the States by the Congress.

AMENDMENT XXII

[Proposed by Congress on March 21, 1947; declared ratified on February 26, 1951.]

Section 1

[TENURE OF PRESIDENT LIMITED]

No person shall be elected to the office of President more than twice, and no person who has held the office of President or acted as President for more than two years of a term to which some other person was elected President shall be elected to the Office of the President more than once. But this Article shall not apply to any person holding the office of President when this Article was proposed by the Congress, and shall not prevent any person who may be holding the office of President, or acting as President, during the term within which this Article becomes operative from holding the office of President or acting as President during the remainder of such term.

Section 2

[RATIFICATION WITHIN SEVEN YEARS]

This Article shall be inoperative unless it shall have been ratified as an amendment to the Constitution by the legislatures of three-fourths of the several states within seven years from the date of its submission to the States by the Congress.

AMENDMENT XXIII

[Proposed by Congress on June 21, 1960; declared ratified on March 29, 1961.]

Section 1

[ELECTORAL COLLEGE VOTES FOR THE DISTRICT OF COLUMBIA]

The District constituting the seat of Government of the United States shall appoint in such manner as the Congress may direct:

A number of electors of President and Vice-President equal to the whole number of Senators and Representatives in Congress to which the District would be entitled if it were a State, but in no event more than the least populous State; they shall be in addition to those appointed by the States, but they shall be considered, for the purposes of the election of President and Vice-President, to be electors appointed by a State; and they shall meet in the District and perform such duties as provided by the twelfth article of amendment.

Section 2

[POWER TO ENFORCE THIS ARTICLE]

The Congress shall have power to enforce this article by appropriate legislation.

AMENDMENT XXIV

[*Proposed by Congress on August 27, 1963; declared ratified on January 23, 1964.*]

Section 1

[ANTI-POLL TAX]

The right of citizens of the United States to vote in any primary or other election for President or Vice-President, for electors for President or Vice-President, or for Senator or Representative of Congress, shall not be denied or abridged by the United States or any State by reasons of failure to pay any poll tax or other tax.

Section 2

[POWER TO ENFORCE THIS ARTICLE]

The Congress shall have power to enforce this article by appropriate legislation.

AMENDMENT XXV

[*Proposed by Congress on July 7, 1965; declared ratified on February 10, 1967.*]

Section 1

[VICE-PRESIDENT TO BECOME PRESIDENT]

In case of the removal of the President from office or his death or resignation, the Vice-President shall become President.

Section 2

[CHOICE OF A NEW VICE-PRESIDENT]

Whenever there is a vacancy in the office of the Vice-President, the President shall nominate a Vice-President who shall take the office upon confirmation by a majority vote of both houses of Congress.

Section 3

[PRESIDENT MAY DECLARE OWN DISABILITY]

Whenever the President transmits to the President pro tempore of the Senate and the Speaker of the House of Representatives his written declaration that he is unable to discharge the powers and duties of his office, and until he transmits to them a written declaration to the contrary, such powers and duties shall be discharged by the Vice-President as Acting President.

Section 4

[ALTERNATE PROCEDURES TO DECLARE AND TO END PRESIDENTIAL DISABILITY]

Whenever the Vice-President and a majority of either the principal officers of the executive departments, or of such other body as Congress may by law provide, transmit to the President pro tempore of the Senate and the Speaker of the House of Representatives their written declaration that the President is unable to discharge the powers and duties of his office, the Vice-President shall immediately assume the powers and duties of the office as Acting President.

Thereafter, when the President transmits to the President pro tempore of the Senate and the Speaker of the House of Representatives his written declaration that no inability exists, he shall resume the powers and duties of his office unless the Vice-President and a majority of either the principal officers of the executive departments, or of such other body as Congress may by law provide, transmit within four days to the President pro tempore of the Senate and the Speaker of the House of Representatives their written declaration that the President is unable to discharge the powers and duties of his office. Thereupon Congress shall decide the issue, assembling within 48 hours for that purpose if not in session. If the Congress, within 21 days after receipt of the latter written declaration, or, if Congress is not in session, within 21 days after Congress is required to assemble, determines by two-thirds vote of both houses that the President is unable to discharge the powers and duties of his office, the Vice-President shall continue to discharge the same as Acting President; otherwise, the President shall resume the powers and duties of his office.

AMENDMENT XXVI

[*Proposed by Congress on March 23, 1971; declared ratified on June 30, 1971.*]

Section 1

[EIGHTEEN-YEAR-OLD VOTE]
    The right of citizens of the United States, who are eighteen years of age or older, to vote shall not be denied or abridged by the United States or by any State on account of age.

Section 2

[POWER TO ENFORCE THIS ARTICLE]
    The Congress shall have power to enforce this article by appropriate legislation.

AMENDMENT XXVII

[*Proposed by Congress on September 25, 1989; ratified on May 7, 1992.*]
    No law varying the compensation for the services of the Senators and Representatives shall take effect until an election of Representatives shall have intervened.

The Federalist Papers

NO 10: MADISON

Among the numerous advantages promised by a well-constructed Union, none deserves to be more accurately developed than its tendency to break and control the violence of faction. The friend of popular governments never finds himself so much alarmed for their character and fate as when he contemplates their propensity to this dangerous vice. He will not fail, therefore, to set a due value on any plan which, without violating the principles to which he is attached, provides a proper cure for it. The instability, injustice, and confusion introduced into the public councils have, in truth, been the mortal diseases under which popular governments have everywhere perished, as they continue to be the favorite and fruitful topics from which the adversaries to liberty derive their most specious declamations. The valuable improvements made by the American constitutions on the popular models, both ancient and modern, cannot certainly be too much admired; but it would be an unwarrantable partiality to contend that they have as effectually obviated the danger on this side, as was wished and expected. Complaints are everywhere heard from our most considerate and virtuous citizens, equally the friends of public and private faith and of public and personal liberty, that our governments are too unstable, that the public good is disregarded in the conflicts of rival parties, and that measures are too often decided, not according to the rules of justice and the rights of the minor party, but by the superior force of an interested and overbearing majority. However anxiously we may wish that these complaints had no foundation, the evidence of known facts will not permit us to deny that they are in some degree true. It will be found, indeed, on a candid review of our situation, that some of the distresses under which we labor have been erroneously charged on the operation of our governments; but it will be found, at the same time, that other causes will not alone account for many of our heaviest misfortunes; and, particularly, for that prevailing and increasing distrust of public engagements and alarm for private rights which are echoed from one end of the continent to the other. These must be chiefly, if not wholly, effects of the unsteadiness and injustice with which a factious spirit has tainted our public administration.

By a faction I understand a number of citizens, whether amounting to a majority or minority of the whole, who are united and actuated by some common impulse of passion, or of interest, adverse to the rights of other citizens, or to the permanent and aggregate interests of the community.

There are two methods of curing the mischiefs of faction: the one, by removing its causes; the other, by controlling its effects.

There are again two methods of removing the causes of faction: the one, by destroying the liberty which is essential to its existence; the other, by giving to every citizen the same opinions, the same passions, and the same interests.

It could never be more truly said than of the first remedy that it was worse than the dis-ease. Liberty is to faction what air is to fire, an aliment without which it instantly expires. But it could not be a less folly to abolish liberty, which is essential to political life, because it nourishes faction than it would be to wish the annihilation of air, which is essential to ani-mal life, because it imparts to fire its destructive agency.

The second expedient is as impracticable as the first would be unwise. As long as the rea-son of man continues fallible, and he is at liberty to exercise it, different opinions will be formed. As long as the connection subsists between his reason and his self-love, his opinions and his passions will have a reciprocal influence on each other; and the former will be ob-jects to which the latter will attach themselves. The diversity in the faculties of men, from which the rights of property originate, is not less an insuperable obstacle to a uniformity of interests. The protection of these faculties is the first object of government. From the pro-tection of different and unequal faculties of acquiring property, the possession of different degrees and kinds of property immediately results; and from the influence of these on the sentiments and views of the respective proprietors ensues a division of the society into dif-ferent interests and parties.

The latent causes of faction are thus sown in the nature of man; and we see them every-where brought into different degrees of activity, according to the different circumstances of civil society. A zeal for different opinions concerning religion, concerning government, and many other points, as well of speculation as of practice; an attachment to different leaders ambitiously contending for pre-eminence and power; or to persons of other descriptions whose fortunes have been interesting to the human passions, have, in turn, divided mankind into parties, inflamed them with mutual animosity, and rendered them much more disposed to vex and oppress each other than to co-operate for their common good. So strong is this propensity of mankind to fall into mutual animosities that where no substantial occasion presents itself the most frivolous and fanciful distinctions have been sufficient to kindle their unfriendly passions and excite their most violent conflicts. But the most common and durable source of factions has been the various and unequal distribution of property. Those who hold and those who are without property have ever formed distinct interests in society. Those who are creditors, and those who are debtors, fall under a like discrimination. A landed interest, a manufacturing interest, a mercantile interest, a moneyed interest, with many lesser interests, grow up of necessity in civilized nations, and divide them into differ-ent classes, actuated by different sentiments and views. The regulation of these various and interfering interests forms the principal task of modern legislation and involves the spirit of party and faction in the necessary and ordinary operations of government.

No man is allowed to be judge in his own cause, because his interest would certainly bias his judgment and, not improbably, corrupt his integrity. With equal, nay with greater rea-son, a body of men are unfit to be both judges and parties at the same time; yet what are many of the most important acts of legislation but so many judicial determinations, not in-deed concerning the rights of single persons, but concerning the rights of large bodies of citizens? And what are the different classes of legislators but advocates and parties to the causes which they determine? Is a law proposed concerning private debts? It is a question to which the creditors are parties on one side and the debtors on the other. Justice ought to hold the balance between them. Yet the parties are, and must be, themselves the judges; and the most numerous party, or in other words, the most powerful faction must be expected to prevail. Shall domestic manufacturers be encouraged, and in what degree, by restrictions on foreign manufacturers? are questions which would be differently decided by the landed and the manufacturing classes, and probably by neither with a sole regard to justice and the pub-lic good. The apportionment of taxes on the various descriptions of property is an act which seems to require the most exact impartiality; yet there is, perhaps, no legislative act in which greater opportunity and temptation are given to a predominant party to trample on the rules of justice. Every shilling with which they overburden the inferior number is a shilling saved to their own pockets.

It is in vain to say that enlightened statesmen will be able to adjust these clashing interests and render them all subservient to the public good. Enlightened statesmen will not always be at the helm. Nor, in many cases, can such an adjustment be made at all without taking into view indirect and remote considerations, which will rarely prevail over the immediate interest which one party may find in disregarding the rights of another or the good of the whole.

The inference to which we are brought is that the *causes* of faction cannot be removed and that relief is only to be sought in the means of controlling its *effects*.

If a faction consists of less than a majority, relief is supplied by the republican principle, which enables the majority to defeat its sinister views by regular vote. It may clog the administration, it may convulse the society; but it will be unable to execute and mask its violence under the forms of the Constitution. When a majority is included in a faction, the form of popular government, on the other hand, enables it to sacrifice to its ruling passion or interest both the public good and the rights of other citizens. To secure the public good and private rights against the danger of such a faction, and at the same time to preserve the spirit and the form of popular government, is then the great object to which our inquiries are directed. Let me add that it is the great desideratum by which alone this form of government can be rescued from the opprobrium under which it has so long labored and be recommended to the esteem and adoption of mankind.

By what means is this object attainable? Evidently by one of two only. Either the existence of the same passion or interest in a majority at the same time must be prevented, or the majority, having such coexistent passion or interest, must be rendered, by their number and local situation, unable to concert and carry into effect schemes of oppression. If the impulse and the opportunity be suffered to coincide, we well know that neither moral nor religious motives can be relied on as an adequate control. They are not found to be such on the injustice and violence of individuals, and lose their efficacy in proportion to the number combined together, that is, in proportion as their efficacy becomes needful.

From this view of the subject it may be concluded that a pure democracy, by which I mean a society consisting of a small number of citizens, who assemble and administer the government in person, can admit of no cure for the mischiefs of faction. A common passion or interest will, in almost every case, be felt by a majority of the whole; a communication and concert results from the form of government itself; and there is nothing to check the inducements to sacrifice the weaker party or an obnoxious individual. Hence it is that such democracies have ever been spectacles of turbulence and contention; have ever been found incompatible with personal security or the rights of property; and have in general been as short in their lives as they have been violent in their deaths. Theoretic politicians, who have patronized this species of government, have erroneously supposed that by reducing mankind to a perfect equality in their political rights, they would at the same time be perfectly equalized and assimilated in their possessions, their opinions, and their passions.

A republic, by which I mean a government in which the scheme of representation takes place, opens a different prospect and promises the cure for which we are seeking. Let us examine the points in which it varies from pure democracy, and we shall comprehend both the nature of the cure and the efficacy which it must derive from the Union.

The two great points of difference between a democracy and a republic are: first, the delegation of the government, in the latter, to a small number of citizens elected by the rest; secondly, the greater number of citizens and greater sphere of country over which the latter may be extended.

The effect of the first difference is, on the one hand, to refine and enlarge the public views by passing them through the medium of a chosen body of citizens, whose wisdom may best discern the true interest of their country and whose patriotism and love of justice will be least likely to sacrifice it to temporary or partial considerations. Under such a regulation it may well happen that the public voice, pronounced by the representatives of the people, will be more consonant to the public good than if pronounced by the people themselves, convened for the purpose. On the other hand, the effect may be inverted. Men of factious tempers, of local prejudices, or of sinister designs, may, by intrigue, by corruption, or by other means, first obtain the suffrages, and then betray the interests of the people. The question resulting is, whether small or extensive republics are most favorable to the election of proper guardians of the public weal; and it is clearly decided in favor of the latter by two obvious considerations.

In the first place it is to be remarked that however small the republic may be the representatives must be raised to a certain number in order to guard against the cabals of a few; and that however large it may be they must be limited to a certain number in order to guard against the confusion of a multitude. Hence, the number of representatives in the two cases not being in proportion to that of the constituents, and being proportionally greatest in the small republic, it follows that if the proportion of fit characters be not less in the large than in the small republic, the former will present a greater option, and consequently a greater probability of a fit choice.

In the next place, as each representative will be chosen by a greater number of citizens in the large than in the small republic, it will be more difficult for unworthy candidates to practise with success the vicious arts by which elections are too often carried; and the suffrages of the people being more free, will be more likely to center on men who possess the most attractive merit and the most diffusive and established characters.

It must be confessed that in this, as in most other cases, there is a mean, on both sides of which inconveniencies will be found to lie. By enlarging too much the number of electors, you render the representative too little acquainted with all their local circumstances and lesser interests; as by reducing it too much, you render him unduly attached to these, and too little fit to comprehend and pursue great and national objects. The federal Constitution forms a happy combination in this respect; the great and aggregate interests being referred to the national, the local and particular to the State legislatures.

The other point of difference is the greater number of citizens and extent of territory which may be brought within the compass of republican than of democratic government; and it is this circumstance principally which renders factious combinations less to be dreaded in the former than in the latter. The smaller the society, the fewer probably will be the distinct parties and interests composing it; the fewer the distinct parties and interests, the more frequently will a majority be found of the same party; and the smaller the number of individuals composing a majority, and the smaller the compass within which they are placed, the more easily will they concert and execute their plans of oppression. Extend the sphere and you take in a greater variety of parties and interests; you make it less probable that a majority of the whole will have a common motive to invade the rights of other citizens; or if such a common motive exists, it will be more difficult for all who feel it to discover their own strength and to act in unison with each other. Besides other impediments, it may be remarked that, where there is a consciousness of unjust or dishonorable purposes, communication is always checked by distrust in proportion to the number whose concurrence is necessary.

Hence, it clearly appears that the same advantage which a republic has over a democracy in controlling the effects of faction is enjoyed by a large over a small republic—is enjoyed by the Union over the States composing it. Does this advantage consist in the substitution of representatives whose enlightened views and virtuous sentiments render them superior to local prejudices and to schemes of injustice? It will not be denied that the representation of the Union will be most likely to possess these requisite endowments. Does it consist in the greater security afforded by a greater variety of parties, against the event of any one party being able to outnumber and oppress the rest? In an equal degree does the increased variety of parties comprised within the Union increase this security? Does it, in fine, consist in the greater obstacles opposed to the concert and accomplishment of the secret wishes of an unjust and interested majority? Here again the extent of the Union gives it the most palpable advantage.

The influence of factious leaders may kindle a flame within their particular States but will be unable to spread a general conflagration through the other States. A religious sect may degenerate into a political faction in a part of the Confederacy; but the variety of sects dispersed over the entire face of it must secure the national councils against any danger from that source. A rage for paper money, for an abolition of debts, for an equal division of property, or for any other improper or wicked project, will be less apt to pervade the whole body of the Union than a particular member of it, in the same proportion as such a malady is more likely to taint a particular county or district than an entire State.

In the extent and proper structure of the Union, therefore, we behold a republican remedy for the diseases most incident to republican government. And according to the degree of pleasure and pride we feel in being republicans ought to be our zeal in cherishing the spirit and supporting the character of federalist.   PUBLIUS

NO. 51: MADISON

To what expedient, then, shall we finally resort, for maintaining in practice the necessary partition of power among the several departments as laid down in the Constitution? The only answer that can be given is that as all these exterior provisions are found to be inadequate the defect must be supplied, by so contriving the interior structure of the government as that its several constituent parts may, by their mutual relations, be the means of keeping each other in their proper places. Without presuming to undertake a full development of this important idea I will hazard a few general observations which may perhaps place it in a clearer light, and enable us to form a more correct judgment of the principles and structure of the government planned by the convention.

In order to lay a due foundation for that separate and distinct exercise of the different powers of government, which to a certain extent is admitted on all hands to be essential to the preservation of liberty, it is evident that each department should have a will of its own; and consequently should be so constituted that the members of each should have as little agency as possible in the appointment of the members of the others. Were this principle rigorously adhered to, it would require that all the appointments for the supreme executive, legislative, and judiciary magistracies should be drawn from the same fountain of authority, the people, through channels having no communication whatever with one another. Perhaps such a plan of constructing the several departments would be less difficult in practice than it may in contemplation appear. Some difficulties, however, and some additional expense would attend the execution of it. Some deviations, therefore, from the principle must be admitted. In the constitution of the judiciary department in particular, it might be inexpedient to insist rigorously on the principle: first, because peculiar qualifications being essential in the members, the primary consideration ought to be to select that mode of choice which best secures these qualifications; second, because the permanent tenure by which the appointments are held in that department must soon destroy all sense of dependence on the authority conferring them.

It is equally evident that the members of each department should be as little dependent as possible on those of the others for the emoluments annexed to their offices. Were the executive magistrate, or the judges, not independent of the legislature in this particular, their

independence in every other would be merely nominal.

But the great security against a gradual concentration of the several powers in the same department consists in giving to those who administer each department the necessary constitutional means and personal motives to resist encroachments of the others. The provision for defense must in this, as in all other cases, be made commensurate to the danger of attack. Ambition must be made to counteract ambition. The interest of the man must be connected with the constitutional rights of the place. It may be a reflection on human nature that such devices should be necessary to control the abuses of government. But what is government itself but the greatest of all reflections on human nature? If men were angels, no government would be necessary. If angels were to govern men, neither external nor internal controls on government would be necessary. In framing a government which is to be administered by men over men, the great difficulty lies in this: you must first enable the government to control the governed; and in the next place oblige it to control itself. A dependence on the people is, no doubt, the primary control on the government; but experience has taught mankind the necessity of auxiliary precautions.

This policy of supplying, by opposite and rival interests, the defect of better motives, might be traced through the whole system of human affairs, private as well as public. We see it particularly displayed in all the subordinate distributions of power, where the constant aim is to divide and arrange the several offices in such a manner as that each may be a check on the other—that the private interest of every individual may be a sentinel over the public rights. These inventions of prudence cannot be less requisite in the distribution of the supreme powers of the State.

But it is not possible to give to each department an equal power of self-defense. In republican government, the legislative authority necessarily predominates. The remedy for this inconveniency is to divide the legislature into different branches; and to render them, by different modes of election and different principles of action, as little connected with each other as the nature of their common functions and their common dependence on the society will admit. It may even be necessary to guard against dangerous encroachments by still further precautions. As the weight of the legislative authority requires that it should be thus divided, the weakness of the executive may require, on the other hand, that it should be fortified. An absolute negative on the legislature appears, at first view, to be the natural defense with which the executive magistrate should be armed. But perhaps it would be neither altogether safe nor alone sufficient. On ordinary occasions it might not be exerted with the requisite firmness, and on extraordinary occasions it might be perfidiously abused. May not this defect of an absolute negative be supplied by some qualified connection between this weaker branch of the stronger department, by which the latter may be led to support the constitutional rights of the former, without being too much detached from the rights of its own department?

If the principles on which these observations are founded be just, as I persuade myself they are, and they be applied as a criterion to the several State constitutions, and to the federal Constitution, it will be found that if the latter does not perfectly correspond with them, the former are infinitely less able to bear such a test.

There are, moreover, two considerations particularly applicable to the federal system of America, which place that system in a very interesting point of view.

First. In a single republic, all the power surrendered by the people is submitted to the administration of a single government; and the usurpations are guarded against by a division of the government into distinct and separate departments. In the compound republic of America, the power surrendered by the people is first divided between two distinct governments, and then the portion allotted to each subdivided among distinct and separate departments. Hence a double security arises to the rights of the people. The different governments will control each other, at the same time that each will be controlled by itself.

Second. It is of great importance in a republic not only to guard the society against the oppression of its rulers, but to guard one part of the society against the injustice of the other part. Different interests necessarily exist in different classes of citizens. If a majority be united by a common interest, the rights of the minority will be insecure. There are but two methods of providing against this evil: the one by creating a will in the community independent of the majority—that is, of the society itself; the other, by comprehending in the society so many separate descriptions of citizens as will render an unjust combination of a majority of the whole very improbable, if not impracticable. The first method prevails in all governments possessing an hereditary or self-appointed authority. This, at best, is but a precarious security; because a power independent of the society may as well espouse the unjust views of the major as the rightful interests of the minor party, and may possibly be turned against both parties. The second method will be exemplified in the federal republic of the United States. Whilst all authority in it will be derived from and dependent on the society, the society itself will be broken into so many parts, interests and classes of citizens, that the rights of individuals, or of the minority, will be in little danger from interested combinations of the majority. In a free government the security for civil rights must be the same as that for religious rights. It consists in the one case in the multiplicity of interests, and in the other in the multiplicity of sects. The degree of security in both cases will depend on the number of interests and sects; and this may be presumed to depend on the extent of country and number of people comprehended under the same government. This view of the subject must particularly recommend a proper federal system to all the sincere and considerate friends of republican government, since it shows that in exact proportion as the territory of the Union may be formed into more circumscribed Confederacies, or States, oppressive combinations of a majority will be facilitated; the best security, under the republican forms, for the rights of every class of citizen, will be diminished; and consequently the stability and independence of some member of the government, the only other security, must be proportionally increased. Justice is the end of government. It is the end of civil society. It ever has been and ever will be pursued until it be obtained, or until liberty be lost in the pursuit. In a society under the forms of which the stronger faction can readily unite and oppress the weaker, anarchy may as truly be said to reign as in a state of nature, where the weaker individual is not secured against the violence of the stronger; and as, in the latter state, even the stronger individuals are prompted, by the uncertainty of their condition, to submit to a government which may protect the weak as well as themselves; so, in the former state, will the more powerful factions or parties be gradually induced, by a like motive, to wish for a government which will protect all parties, the weaker as well as the more powerful. It can be little doubted that if the State of Rhode Island was separated from the Confederacy and left to itself, the insecurity of rights under the popular form of government within such narrow limits would be displayed by such reiterated oppressions of factious majorities that some power altogether independent of the people would soon be called for by the voice of the very factions whose misrule had proved the necessity of it. In the extended republic of the United States, and among the great variety of interests, parties, and sects which it embraces, a coalition of a majority of the whole society could seldom take place on any other principles than those of justice and the general good; whilst there being thus less danger to a minor from the will of a major party, there must be less pretext, also, to provide for the security of the former, by introducing into the government a will not dependent on the latter, or, in other words, a will independent of the society itself. It is no less certain than it is important, notwithstanding the contrary opinions which have been entertained, that the larger the society, provided it lie within a practicable sphere, the more duly capable it will be of self-government. And happily for the *republican cause*, the practicable sphere may be carried to a very great extent by a judicious modification and mixture of the *federal principle*.

PUBLIUS

Glossary of Terms

absolutism A system of government in which the sovereign has unlimited powers; despotism.

administrative legislation Rules made by regulatory agencies and commissions.

affirmative action A policy or program designed to redress historic injustices committed against racial minorities and other specified groups by making special efforts to provide members of these groups with access to educational and employment opportunities.

agency representation The type of representation by which representatives are held accountable to their constituents if they fail to represent them properly; that is, constituents have the power to hire and fire their representative. This is the incentive for good representation when the personal backgrounds, views, and interests of the representative differ from their constituents'.

Aid to Families of Dependent Children (AFDC) The largest federal cash transfer program (as distinguished from assistance in kind). Federal funds, administered by the states, for children living with parents or relatives who fall below state standards of need.

amicus curiae "Friend of the court"; individuals or groups who are not parties to a lawsuit but who seek to assist the court in reaching a decision by presenting additional briefs.

appropriation The amounts approved by Congress in statutes (bills) that each unit or agency of government can spend.

area sampling A polling technique used for large cities, states, or the whole nation, when a high level of accuracy is desired. The population is broken down into small, homogeneous units, such as counties; then several units are randomly selected to serve as the sample.

Articles of Confederation America's first written constitution. Adopted by the Continental Congress in 1777, the Articles of Confederation and Perpetual Union were the formal basis for America's national government until 1789 when they were supplanted by the Constitution.

Australian ballot An electoral format that presents the names of all the candidates for any given office on the same ballot. Introduced at the turn of the century, the Australian ballot replaced the partisan ballot and facilitated split-ticket voting.

authoritarian government A system of rule in which the government recognizes no formal limits but may, nevertheless, be restrained by the power of other social institutions.

authorization   The process by which Congress enacts or rejects proposed statutes (bills) embodying the positive laws of government.

autocracy   A form of government in which a single individual—a king, queen, or dictator—rules.

automatic stabilizers   A category of public policy, largely fiscal and monetary, that automatically works against inflationary and deflationary tendencies in the economy.

balance of payments   Name for the "bottom line" in international trade. An excess of imports over exports is called "the international debt," which in the United States has been growing at a rate of over $100 billion per year.

balance of power   A system of political alignments by which stability can be achieved.

balance-of-power role   The strategy whereby many countries form alliances with one or more other countries in order to counterbalance the behavior of other, usually more powerful nation-states.

bandwagon effect   A situation wherein reports of voter or delegate opinion can influence the actual outcome of an election or a nominating convention.

bellwether districts   Towns or districts that are microcosms of the whole population or that have been found to be good predictors of electoral outcomes.

bicameralism   Having a legislative assembly composed of two chambers or houses; opposite of unicameralism.

bilateral treaty   Treaty made between two nations; contrast with multilateral treaty.

bill of attainder   A legislative act which inflicts guilt and punishment without a judicial hearing or trial, it is proscribed by Article I, Section 10, of the Constitution.

bill of information   Official opinion of a government prosecutor or district attorney that there is sufficient evidence of a crime to bring a case to trial; in some places the equivalent of an indictment by a grand jury.

Bill of Rights   The first ten amendments to the U.S. Constitution, ratified in 1791, they ensure certain rights and liberties to the people.

binding primary   Primary election in which the candidates for election as delegates to a presidential nominating convention pledge themselves to a certain candidate and are bound to vote for that person until released from the obligation.

bipartisan foreign policy   Based on the assumption that "politics stops at the water's edge," this is a strategy pursued by most presidents since World War II to coopt the opposition party leaders in order to minimize the amount of public criticism and the leakage of confidential information for political purposes.

bipartisanship   Close cooperation between two parties; usually an effort by the two major parties in Congress to cooperate with the president in making foreign policy.

bureaucracy   The complex structure of offices, tasks, rules, and principles of organization that are employed by all large-scale institutions to coordinate the work of their personnel effectively.

cabinet   The secretaries, or chief administrators, of the major departments of the federal government. Cabinet secretaries are appointed by the president with the consent of the Senate.

Calendar Wednesday   A procedure in the House whereby a committee chairman can bypass the Rules Committee and bring proposed legislation directly to the floor for consideration.

capitalism The economic system in which most of the means of production and distribution are privately owned and operated for profit.

categoric grants-in-aid Grants by Congress to states and localities, with the condition that expenditures be limited to a problem or group specified in the law.

caucus A normally closed meeting of a political or legislative group to select candidates, plan strategy, or make decisions regarding legislative matters.

certificate of convenience and necessity Permission granted by a regulatory agency to an individual or group to conduct a particular type of business; license.

checks and balances Mechanisms through which each branch of government is able to participate in and influence the activities of the other branches. Major examples include the presidential veto power over congressional legislation, the power of the Senate to approve presidential appointments, and judicial review of congressional enactments.

citizenship The duties, rights, and privileges of being a citizen of a political unit.

civil disobedience A form of direct action politics that involves the refusal to obey civil laws considered unjust. This is usually a nonviolent or passive resistance.

civil law A system of jurisprudence, including private law and governmental actions, to settle disputes that do not involve criminal penalties.

civil liberties Areas of personal freedom with which governments are constrained from interfering.

civil penalties Regulatory techniques in which fines or another form of material restitution is imposed for violating civil laws or common law principles, such as negligence.

civil rights Legal or moral claims that citizens are entitled to make upon the government.

clientele agencies Departments or bureaus of government whose mission is to promote, serve, or represent a particular interest.

client state A nation-state whose foreign policy is subordinated to that of another nation.

closed primary A primary election in which voters can participate in the nomination of candidates, but only of the party in which they are enrolled for a period of time prior to primary day.

closed rule Provision by the House Rules Committee limiting or prohibiting the introduction of amendments during debate.

closed shop A contract between an employer and a union in which the employer agrees to hire no worker who is not a bona fide member of that union. This was outlawed by the Taft-Hartley Act of 1947.

cloture rule Rule allowing a majority or two-thirds or three-fifths of the members in a legislative body to set a time limit on debate over a given bill.

coattail effect Result of voters casting their ballot for president or governor and "automatically" voting for the remainder of the party's ticket.

collective bargaining Negotiation between an employer and a union whose right to negotiate has been established by the vote of the employees; closely tied to the right to strike in case the bargaining process breaks down.

commerce power Power of Congress to regulate trade among the states and with foreign countries.

common law Law common to the realm in Anglo-Saxon history; judge-made law based on the precedents of previous lower court decisions.

concurrent power   Authority possessed by both state and national governments, such as the power to levy taxes.

confederation   League of independent states.

congressional veto   Legislative veto; a statutory arrangement under which Congress delegates power to an agency but requires the agency to submit its plans to Congress or to one of its committees for approval. See *legislative veto.*

conscription   Compulsory military service, usually for a prescribed period or for the duration of a war; "the draft."

conservative   Today this term refers to those who generally support the social and economic status quo and are suspicious of efforts to introduce new political formulae and economic arrangements. The belief that a large and powerful government poses a threat to citizens' freedoms.

constituency   The district comprising the area from which an official is elected.

constituent policy   Policies or programs that focus on the internal structure or operation of governmental agencies.

constitutionalism   An approach to legitimacy in which the rulers give up a certain amount of power in return for their right to utilize the remaining powers.

constitutional government   A system of rule in which formal and effective limits are placed on the powers of the government.

contracting power   The power of government to set conditions on companies seeking to sell goods or services to government agencies.

contract model   A theory asserting that governments originate from general agreements among members of the public about the necessity of dealing with common problems.

contributory programs   Social programs financed in whole or in part by taxation or other mandatory contributions by their present or future recipients. The most important example is Social Security, which is financed by a payroll tax.

control agencies   Agencies that have the power to intervene in the private sphere to regulate the conduct of individuals, groups, or corporations.

cooperative federalism   A type of federalism existing since the New Deal era in which grants-in-aid have been used strategically to encourage states and localities (without commanding them) to pursue nationally defined goals. Also known as intergovernmental cooperation.

cooptation   Strategy of bringing an individual into a group by joint action of the members of that group, usually in order to reduce or eliminate the individual's opposition.

correlational analysis   Analysis of two or more items that involve a mutual relationship; effort to determine the degree of relative correspondence between two sets of data.

coup d'état   Sudden, forcible overthrow of a government.

criminal law   The branch of law that deals with disputes or actions involving criminal penalties (as opposed to civil law), it regulates the conduct of individuals, defines crimes, and provides punishment for criminal acts.

criminal penalties   Regulatory techniques in which imprisonment or heavy fines and the loss of certain civil rights and liberties are imposed.

critical electoral realignment   The point in history when a new party supplants the ruling party, becoming in turn the dominant political force. In the United States, this has tended to occur roughly every 30 years.

debt limit Ceiling established by Congress upon the total amount of debt the government can accumulate. Can be changed by Congress as need requires.

debt service Interest paid on the public debt; an "uncontrollable" budget item because
the amount is determined by general interest rates.

de facto segregation Racial segregation that is not a direct result of law or government
policy but is, instead, a reflection of residential patterns, income distributions, or other
social factors.

deficit financing Usually refers to deficits that are deliberately incurred as part of an effort to fight off a deflationary phase of the business cycle. Deficits are financed by borrowing.

de jure segregation Racial segregation that is a direct result of law or official policy.

delegated powers Constitutional powers assigned to one governmental agency that are
exercised by another agency with the express permission of the first.

democratic government A system of rule that permits citizens to play a significant part
in the governmental process, usually through the selection of key public officials.

deregulation A policy of reducing or eliminating regulatory restraints on the conduct of
individuals or private institutions.

direct action A form of politics that uses informal channels to attempt to force rulers
into a new course of action, such as violent politics or civil disobedience.

discharge petition Procedure of the House whereby an absolute majority of the members can force a bill out of committee when the committee itself has refused to report
it out for consideration.

discount rate The interest rate charged by the Federal Reserve when commercial banks
borrow in order to expand their lending operations. An effective tool of monetary
policy.

double jeopardy Trial more than once for the same crime. The Constitution guarantees
that no one shall be subjected to double jeopardy.

dual federalism The system of government that prevailed in the United States from
1789 to 1937 in which most fundamental governmental powers were shared between
the federal and state governments.

due process The right of every citizen against arbitrary action by national or state governments.

economic expansionist role The strategy often pursued by many capitalist countries to
adopt foreign policies that will maximize the success of domestic corporations in their
dealings with other countries.

elastic clause See *necessary and proper clause.*

electoral college The presidential electors from each state who meet in their respective
state capitals after the popular election to cast ballots for president and vice president.

electorate All of the eligible voters in a legally designated area.

elite Those people at the top who exercise a major influence on decision making.

eminent domain The right of government to take private property for public use, with
reasonable compensation awarded for the property.

entitlement Eligibility for benefits by virtue of a category of benefits defined by law.
Category can only be changed by legislation. Deprivation of individual benefits can be
determined only through due process in court.

environmental impact statement   Since 1969, all federal agencies must file a statement demonstrating that a new program or project will not have a net negative impact on the human or physical environment.

equal time rule   The requirement that broadcasters provide candidates for the same political office an equal opportunity to communicate their messages to the public.

equality of opportunity   A universally shared American ideal that all have the freedom to use whatever talents and wealth they have to reach their fullest potential.

equity   Judicial process providing a remedy to a dispute where common law does not apply.

exclusive power   Power belonging exclusively to and exercised only by the national or state government.

executive agreement   An agreement between the president and another country which has the force of a treaty but does not require the Senate's "advice and consent."

executive privilege   The claim that confidential communications between a president and close advisers should not be revealed without the consent of the president.

ex post facto law   "After the fact" law; law that is retroactive and that has an adverse effect on someone accused of a crime. Under Article I, Sections 9 and 10, of the Constitution, neither the state nor the national government can enact such laws; this provision does not apply, however, to civil laws.

expressed power   The notion that the Constitution grants to the federal government only those powers specifically named in its text.

expropriation   Confiscation of property with or without compensation.

extraction-coercion cycle   A process of state-building in which governments use military force to extract money and other resources from the populace. These resources are then used to enhance the government's military power, which is used to extract more resources, and so on.

faction   Group of people with common interests, usually in opposition to the aims or principles of a larger group or the public.

fairness doctrine   A Federal Communications Commission requirement for broadcasters who air programs on controversial issues to provide time for opposing views.

federalism   System of government in which power is divided by a constitution between a central government and regional governments.

Federal Reserve System (Fed)   Consisting of twelve Federal Reserve Banks, the Fed facilitates exchanges of cash, checks, and credit; it regulates member banks; and it uses monetary policies to fight inflation and deflation.

filibuster   A tactic used by members of the Senate to prevent action on legislation they oppose by continuously holding the floor and speaking until the majority backs down. Once given the floor, Senators have unlimited time to speak, and it requires a vote of three-fifths of the Senate to end the filibuster.

first-strike capability   The number and power of nuclear weapons, plus delivery, that it would take to attack a major power with such extensive success that it would wipe out the capacity of the enemy to retaliate.

fiscal year   The yearly accounting period, which for the national government is October 1–September 30. The actual fiscal year is designated by the year in which it ends.

fiscal policy   Use of taxing, monetary, and spending powers to manipulate the economy.

food stamps   The largest in-kind welfare program, administered by the Department of Agriculture, providing coupons to individuals and families who satisfy a "needs test;" the food stamps can be exchanged for food at most grocery stores.

franchise   The right to vote; see *license, suffrage*.

full faith and credit clause   Article IV, Section 1, of the Constitution provides that each state must accord the same respect to the laws and judicial decisions of other states that it accords to its own.

gerrymandering   Apportionment of voters in districts in such a way as to give unfair advantage to one political party.

government   Institutions and procedures through which a territory and its people are ruled.

grants-in-aid   Programs through which Congress provides money to state and local governments on the condition that the funds be employed for purposes defined by the federal government.

Great Compromise   Agreement reached at the Constitutional Convention of 1787 that gave each state an equal number of senators regardless of its population, but linked representation in the House of Representatives to population.

Gross National Product (GNP)   An index of the total output of goods and services. A very imperfect measure of prosperity, productivity, inflation, deflation, but its regular publication influences business conditions as well as reflecting them.

habeas corpus   A court order demanding that the individual in custody be brought into court and shown the cause for detention. *Habeas corpus* is guaranteed by the Constitution and can be suspended only in cases of rebellion or invasion.

haphazard sampling   A type of sampling of public opinion which is an unsystematic choice of respondents.

Holy Alliance role   A strategy pursued by a superpower to prevent any change in the existing distribution of power among nation-states, even if this requires intervention into the internal affairs of the country in order to keep an authoritarian ruler from being overturned.

home rule   Power delegated by the state to a local unit of government to manage its own affairs.

homesteading   A national policy that permits people to gain ownership of property by occupying public or unclaimed lands, living on the land for a specified period of time, and making certain minimal improvements on that land. Also known as squatting.

ideology   The combined doctrines, assertions, and intentions of a social or political group that justify its behavior.

illusion of central tendency   The assumption that opinions are "normally distributed"—that responses to opinion questions are heavily distributed toward the center, as in a bell-shaped curve.

illusion of saliency   Impression conveyed by polls that something is important to the public when actually it is not.

impoundment   Efforts by presidents to thwart congressional programs that they cannot otherwise defeat by refusing to spend the funds that Congress has appropriated for them. Congress placed limits on impoundment in the Budget and Impoundment Control Act of 1974.

independent agencies   Agencies set up by Congress to be independent of direct presidential authority. Congress usually accomplishes this by providing the head or heads of the agency with a set term of office rather than allowing their removal at the pleasure of the president.

indexing   Periodic adjustments of welfare payments, wages, or taxes, tied to the cost of living.

indirect election   Provision for election of an official where the voters first select the delegates or "electors," who are in turn charged with making the final choice. The presidential election is an indirect election.

injunction   A court order requiring an individual or organization either to cease or to undertake some form of action to prevent a future injury or to achieve some desirable state of affairs.

in-kind benefits   Goods and services provided to needy individuals and families by the federal government, as contrasted with cash benefits. The largest in-kind federal welfare program is food stamps.

iron triangle   Name assigned by political scientists to the stable and cooperative relationships that often develop between a congressional committee or subcommittee, an administrative agency, and one or more supportive interest groups. Not all of these relationships are triangular, but the iron triangle is perhaps the most typical.

item veto   The power to veto specific provisions of a bill. Although some state governors possess this power, the President of the United States does not, and must accept or veto a bill in its entirety.

jingoism   Extreme or militant devotion to one's country.

Johnson rule   Senate rule, adopted while Lyndon Johnson was majority leader, providing that no senator could receive an assignment to a second major committee until all senators had received consideration for a major committee assignment.

judicial review   Power of the courts to declare actions of the legislative and executive branches invalid or unconstitutional. The Supreme Court asserted this power in *Marbury* v. *Madison*.

Kitchen Cabinet   An informal group of advisers to whom the president turns for counsel and guidance. Members of the official cabinet may or may not also be members of the Kitchen Cabinet.

laissez-faire   An economic theory first advanced by Adam Smith, it calls for a "hands off" policy by government toward the economy, in an effort to leave business enterprises free to act in their own self-interest.

legiscide   The diminution of congressional power through the enactment of statutes granting virtually unlimited discretion to the executive branch.

legislative clearance   The power given to the president to require all agencies of the executive branch to submit to him through the budget director all requests for new legislation along with estimates of their budgetary needs.

legislative intent   The supposed real meaning of a statute as it can be interpreted from the legislative history of the bill.

legislative supremacy   The preeminent position assigned to the Congress by the Constitution.

legislative veto A provision in a statute permitting Congress (or a congressional committee) to review and approve actions undertaken by the executive under authority of the statute. Although the U.S. Supreme Court held the legislative veto unconstitutional in the 1983 case of *Immigration and Naturalization Service* v. *Chadha*, Congress continues to enact legislation incorporating such a veto.

legitimacy Popular acceptance of a government and its decisions.

liberal A liberal today generally supports political and social reform; extensive governmental intervention in the economy; the expansion of federal social services; more vigorous efforts on behalf of the poor, minorities, and women; and greater concern for consumers and the environment.

license Permission to engage in some activity that is otherwise illegal, such as hunting or practicing medicine. Synonymous with franchise, permit, certificate of convenience and necessity.

line agency Department, bureau, or other unit of administration whose primary mission requires it to deal directly with the public; contrast with staff or overhead agency.

lobbying Strategy by which organized interests seek to influence the passage of legislation by exerting direct pressure on members of the legislature.

logrolling A legislative practice wherein reciprocal agreements are made between legislators, usually in voting for or against a bill. In contrast to bargaining, parties to logrolling have nothing in common but their desire to exchange support.

macroeconomic techniques Economic policies designed to control the economy through taxing and spending (fiscal policy) and manipulation of the supply of money and credit (monetary policy).

majority leader The elected leader of the party holding a majority of the seats in the House of Representatives or in the Senate. In the House, the majority leader is subordinate in the party hierarchy to the Speaker.

majority rule Rule by at least one vote more than half of those voting.

majority system A type of electoral system in which, to win a seat in the parliament or other representative body, a candidate must receive a majority of all the votes cast in the relevant district.

marketplace of ideas The public forum in which beliefs and ideas are exchanged and compete.

Marxism The system of thought developed by Karl Marx, it is predicated upon a history of class struggle between those who control production and distribution (the owners) and the workers, culminating in the overthrow of the owners, the redistribution of wealth and power, and the "withering away of the state."

Medicaid A federally financed, state-operated program for medical services to low-income people. Eligibility tied largely to AFDC.

Medicare National health insurance for the elderly and for the disabled.

military-industrial complex A concept coined by President Eisenhower in his farewell address, in which he was referring to the threats to American democracy that may arise from too close a friendship between major corporations in the defense industry and the Pentagon. This is one example of the larger political phenomenon of the "iron triangle."

minority leader The elected leader of the party holding less than a majority of the seats in the House or Senate.

Miranda rule   Principles developed by the Supreme Court in the 1966 case of *Miranda* v. *Arizona* requiring that persons under arrest be informed of their legal rights, including their right to counsel, prior to police interrogation.

monetary techniques   Efforts to regulate the economy through manipulation of the supply of money and credit. America's most powerful institution in the area of monetary policy is the Federal Reserve Board.

monopoly   The existence of a single firm in a market that divides all the goods and services of that market. Absence of competition.

multilateral treaty   A treaty among more than two nations.

multiple-member constituency   Electorate that selects all candidates at large from the whole district; each voter is given the number of votes equivalent to the number of seats to be filled.

multiple-member district   See *multiple-member constituency.*

multiplier effect   A fiscal policy permitting member banks to borrow money from the Federal Reserve System. Member banks put a certain percentage of this loan, the reserve requirement, into reserves, and make the remainder available for credit to customers. As this process continues, as long as each loan becomes a deposit in a bank within the system, the original loan from the Fed is multiplied dramatically. The Fed profoundly influences the economy by raising or lowering the reserve requirement.

Napoleonic role   Strategy pursued by a powerful nation to prevent aggressive actions against themselves by improving the internal state of affairs of a particular country, even if this means encouraging revolution in that country. Based on the assumption that countries with comparable political systems will never go to war against each other.

nationalism   The widely held belief that the people who occupy the same territory have something in common, that the nation is a single community.

nationalization   Government acquisition of a private enterprise that will then be operated as a government agency. Can take place either by confiscation or by eminent domain.

national supremacy   A principle, rooted in Article VI of the Constitution, which asserts that national law is superior to all other law.

nation-state   A political entity consisting of a people with some common cultural experience (nation) who also share a common political authority (state), recognized by other sovereignties (nation-states).

necessary and proper clause   Article I, Section 8, of the Constitution, it enumerates the powers of Congress and provides Congress with the authority to make all laws "necessary and proper" to carry them out; also referred to as the "elastic clause."

nomination   The process through which political parties select their candidates for election to public office.

nuclear freeze   A popular policy in the early 1980s to stop the testing, production, and deployment of nuclear weapons, leaving all sides with whatever capacity they had at the moment of the freeze. This became less attractive after the success of disarmament negotiations between President Reagan and Premier Gorbachev.

oligarchy   A form of government in which a small group of landowners, military officers, or wealthy merchants controls most of the governing decisions.

oligopoly   The existence of two or more competing firms in a given market, where price competition is usually avoided because they know that they would all lose from such competition. Rather, competition is usually through other forms, such as advertising, innovation, and obsolescence.

open market operations   A Federal Open Market Committee of the Fed buys and sells government securities, etc., to help finance government operations and to loosen or tighten the total amount of credit circulating in the economy.

open primary   A primary election in which the voter can wait until the day of the primary to choose which party to enroll in to select candidates for the general election: see *closed primary*.

ordinance   The legislative act of a local legislature or municipal commission. Puts the force of law under city charter but is a lower order of law than a statute of the national or state legislature.

overhead agency   A department, bureau, or other unit of administration whose primary mission is to regulate the activities of other agencies; it generally has no direct authority over the public. Contrast with line or auxiliary agency.

oversight   The effort by Congress, through hearings, investigations and other techniques, to exercise control over the activities of executive agencies.

parity (farm)   Price of selected farm products, partially guaranteed by government purchases and acreage allotments, to help farmers maintain purchasing power equal to a previous base period of good years.

partisanship   Loyalty to a particular political party.

party vote   A roll-call vote in the House or Senate in which at least 90 percent of the members of one party take a particular position and are opposed by at least 90 percent of the members of the other party. Party votes are rare today, although they were fairly common in the nineteenth century.

patriotism   Love of one's country; loyalty to one's country.

patronage   The resources available to higher officials, usually opportunities to make partisan appointments to offices and to confer grants, licenses, or special favors to supporters.

per curiam   Decision by an appellate court, without a written opinion, that refuses to review the decision of a lower court; amounts to a reaffirmation of the lower court's opinion.

petition   Right granted by the First Amendment to citizens to inform representatives of their opinions and to make pleas before government agencies.

plaintiff   The individual or organization who brings a complaint in court.

plebiscite   A direct vote by the electorate on an issue presented to them by a government.

pluralism   The theory that all interests are and should be free to compete for influence in the government. The outcome of this competition is compromise and moderation.

pluralist politics   Politics in which political elites actively compete for leadership, voters choose from among these elites, and new elites can emerge in quest of leadership.

plurality rule   Victory to the individual who gets the most votes in an election, not necessarily a majority of votes cast.

police power   Power reserved to the state to regulate the health, safety, and morals of its citizens.

policy of redistribution An objective of the graduated income tax—to raise revenue in such a way as to reduce the disparities of wealth between the lowest and the highest income brackets.

political socialization Induction of individuals into the political culture; learning how to accept authority; learning what is legitimate and what is not.

polity A society with an organized government; the "political system."

poll tax A state-imposed tax upon the voters as a prerequisite to registration, it was rendered unconstitutional in national elections by the Twenty-fourth Amendment and in state elections by the Supreme Court in 1966.

populism A late 1870s political and social movement of western and southern farmers that protested eastern business interests.

pork-barrel legislation Appropriations made by legislative bodies for local projects that are often not needed but that are created so that local representatives can carry their home district in the next election.

positive law Law made in and by legislatures self-consciously to fit an occasion; contrast with divine law, natural law, judge-made law.

power elite The group that is said to make the most important decisions in a particular community.

power-without-diplomacy Post-World War II foreign policy in which the goal was to use American power to create an international structure that could be run with a minimum of regular diplomatic involvement.

precedents Prior cases whose principles are used by judges as the bases for their decisions in present cases.

preferential primary Primary election in which the elected delegates to a convention are instructed, but not bound, to vote specifically for the presidential candidate preferred by the voters on a separate part of the ballot.

prior restraint An effort by a governmental agency to block the publication of material it deems libelous or harmful in some other way. In the United States, the courts forbid prior restraint except under the most extraordinary circumstances; censorship.

private bill A proposal in Congress to provide a specific person with some kind of relief, such as a special exemption from immigration quotas.

private law A system of jurisprudence designed to settle disputes between citizens who prefer the courts to the use of personal force.

privileges and immunities clause Article IV of the Constitution, it provides that the citizens of any one state are guaranteed the "privileges and immunities" of every other state, as though they were citizens of that state.

probability sampling A method used by pollsters to select a sample in which every individual in the population has a known (usually equal) probability of being selected as a respondent so that the correct weight can be given to all segments of the population.

procedural due process The Supreme Court's efforts to forbid any procedure that shocks the conscience or that makes impossible a fair judicial system. See *due process*.

progressive/regressive taxes A judgment made by students of taxation about whether a particular tax hits the upper brackets more heavily (progressive) or the lower brackets (regressive) more heavily.

promotional agencies See *clientele agencies*.

promotional techniques A technique of control that encourages people to do something they might not otherwise do, or continue an action or behavior. There are three types; subsidies, contracts, and licenses.

proportional representation   A multiple-member district system that allows each political party representation in proportion to its percentage of the vote.

public assistance program   A noncontributory social program providing assistance for the aged, poor, or disabled. Major examples include Aid to Families with Dependent Children (AFDC), and Supplemental Security Income (SSI).

public corporation   An agency set up by a government but permitted to finance its own operations by charging for its services or by selling bonds.

public law   Cases in private law, civil law, or criminal law in which one party to the dispute argues that a license is unfair, a law is inequitable or unconstitutional, or an agency has acted unfairly, violated a procedure, or gone beyond its jurisdiction.

public policy   A governmental law, rule, statute, or edict that expresses the government's goals and provides for rewards and punishments to promote their attainment.

quorum   The minimum number of members of a deliberative body who must be present in order to conduct business.

quota sampling   A type of sampling of public opinion which is used by most commercial polls. Respondents are selected whose characteristics closely match those of the general population along several significant dimensions, such as geographic region, sex, age, and race.

random sample polling   Polls in which respondents are chosen mathematically, at random, with every effort made to avoid bias in the construction of the sample.

rate regulation   Power delegated by the legislature to any regulatory agencies to set ceilings on how much railroads and other "common carriers" can charge for their services, based upon the best available estimates of a "fair return" on investments.

realigning eras   Periods during which major groups in the electorate shift their political party affiliations. Realigning eras have often been associated with long-term shifts in partisan control of the government and with major changes in public policy. One of the most important realigning eras was the period of the New Deal in the 1930s when President Franklin Roosevelt led the Democrats to a position of power that they have still not entirely relinquished.

reapportionment   The redrawing of election districts and the redistribution of legislative representatives due to shifts in population.

referendum   The practice of referring a measure proposed or passed by a legislature to the vote of the electorate for approval or rejection.

regulation   A particular use of government power, a "technique of control" in which the government adopts rules imposing restrictions on the conduct of private citizens.

regulation of entry   The purpose of licensing; permission to enter a trade or market. For example, medical licensing boards determine whether a person holding the MD degree can engage in the practice of medicine, or the FCC decides to permit a radio station to commence operation.

regulatory agencies   Departments, bureaus, or independent agencies whose primary mission is to eliminate or restrict certain behaviors defined as being evil in themselves or evil in their consequences.

regulatory tax   A tax whose primary purpose is not to raise revenue but to influence conduct—e.g., a heavy tax on gasoline to discourage recreational driving.

regulatory techniques   Techniques that government uses to control the conduct of the people.

redistribution   A particular use of government power, a "technique of control" in which the government adopts rules defining categories of individuals for purposes of conferring benefits or taking income or property.

representative democracy   A system of government that provides the populace with the opportunity to make the government responsive to its views through the selection of representatives, who, in turn, play a significant role in governmental decision making.

reserve requirement   The amount of liquid assets and ready cash that banks are required to hold to meet depositors' demands for their money. Ratio revolves above and below 20 percent of all deposits, with the rest being available for new loans.

revenue acts   Acts of Congress providing the means of raising the revenues needed by the government. The Constitution requires that all such bills originate in the House.

revenue sharing   A scheme to allocate national resources to the states according to a population and income formula.

revolution   A complete or drastic change of government and the rules by which government is conducted.

revolutionary politics   A form of politics that rejects the existing system of government entirely and attempts to replace it with a different organizational structure and a different ruling group.

right of rebuttal   A Federal Communications Commission regulation giving individuals the right to have the opportunity to respond to personal attacks made on a radio or TV broadcast.

roll-call vote   Each legislator's yes or no vote is recorded as the clerk calls the names of the members alphabetically.

satellites   Nation-states that are militarily, economically, and politically subordinate to other nations.

second-strike capacity   The number and power of nuclear weapons, plus delivery, that would be available after a first strike to wipe out the attacker. This is a measure of the "deterrent effect" of nuclear power.

select committee   A legislative committee established for a limited period of time and for a special purpose; not a standing committee.

selective polling   A sample drawn deliberately to reconstruct meaningful distributions of an entire constituency; not a random sample.

seniority   Priority or status ranking given to an individual on the basis of length of continuous service in an organization.

separation of powers   The division of governmental power among several institutions that must cooperate in decision making.

service agencies   Departments or other bureaus whose primary mission is to promote the interests of dependent persons or to deal with their problems.

single-member constituency   An electorate that is allowed to elect only one representative from each district; the normal method of representation in the United States.

single-member district   See *single-member constituency.*

sociological representation   A type of representation in which representatives have the same racial, ethnic, religious, or educational backgrounds as their constituents. It is based on the principle that if two individuals are similar in background, character, interests, and perspectives, then one could correctly represent the other's views.

sovereignty   Supreme and independent political authority.

Speaker of the House   The chief presiding officer of the House of Representatives. The Speaker is elected at the beginning of every Congress on a straight party vote. The Speaker is the most important party and House leader, and can influence the legislative agenda, the fate of individual pieces of legislation, and members' positions within the House.

special counsel   A prosecutor appointed under the terms of the Ethics in Government Act to investigate criminal misconduct by members of the executive branch.

split-ticket voting   The practice of casting ballots for the candidates of at least two different political parties in the same election. Voters who support only one party's candidates are said to vote a straight party ticket.

staff agency   An agency responsible for maintaining the bureaucracy, with responsibilities such as purchasing, budgeting, personnel management, planning.

standing   The right of an individual or organization to initiate a court case.

standing committee   A regular legislative committee that considers legislation within its designated subject area; the basic unit of deliberation in the House and Senate.

stare decisis   Literally "let the decision stand." A previous decision by a court applies as a precedent in similar cases until that decision is overruled.

state   A community that claims the monopoly of legitimate use of physical force within a given territory; the ultimate political authority; sovereign.

statute   A law enacted by a state legislature or by Congress.

Strategic Defense Initiative (SDI, or Star Wars)   A plan developed by the Reagan administration to construct a sophisticated system that would protect the United States against nuclear missile attack. Opponents forced the Reagan and Bush administrations substantially to scale back the initial, extremely expensive and ambitious plan.

subsidies   Governmental grants of cash or other valuable commodities such as land to individuals or organizations. Subsidies can be used to promote activities desired by the government, to reward political support, or to buy off political opposition.

substantive due process   A judicial doctrine used by the appellate courts, primarily before 1937, to strike down economic legislation the courts felt was arbitrary or unreasonable.

supremacy clause   Article VI of the Constitution, which states that laws passed by the national government and all treaties are the supreme laws of the land and superior to all laws adopted by any state or any subdivision.

suffrage   The right to vote; see also *franchise*.

Supplemental Security Income (SSI)   A program providing a minimum monthly income to people who pass a "needs test" and who are sixty-five years or older, blind, or disabled. Financed from general revenues rather than from Social Security Contributions.

systematic sampling   A method used in probability sampling to ensure that every individual in the population has a known probability of being chosen as a respondent. For example, by choosing every ninth name from a list.

Three-Fifths Compromise   Agreement reached at the Constitutional Convention of 1787 which stipulated that for purposes of the apportionment of congressional seats, every slave would be counted as three-fifths of a person.

ticket balancing   Strategy of party leaders to nominate candidates from each of the major ethnic, racial, and religious affiliations.

ticket splitting   The practice of voting for candidates of different parties on the same ballot.

totalitarian government   A system of rule in which the government recognizes no formal limits on its power and seeks to absorb or eliminate other social institutions that might challenge it.

treaty   A formal agreement between sovereign nations to create or restrict rights and responsibilities. In the U.S. all treaties must be approved by a two-thirds vote in the Senate. See also *executive agreement.*

trust   A method of avoiding competition in which two or more companies assign voting rights or actual stock to a common board of trustees to control marketing and other policies. A popular misuse of the term is to describe a single large corporation that dominates a particular market and pursues monopolistic pricing policies.

turnout   The percentage of eligible individuals who actually vote.

tyranny   Oppressive and unjust government that employs cruel and unjust use of power and authority.

uncontrollables   A term applied to budgetary items that are beyond the control of budgetary committees and can only be controlled by substantive legislative action by Congress itself. Some uncontrollables are actually beyond the power of the Congress, because the terms of payment are set in contracts, such as interest on the debt.

unilateralism   A foreign policy that seeks to avoid international alliances, entanglements, and permanent commitments in favor of independence, neutrality, and freedom of action.

urban renewal   An important urban policy of the national government during the 1950s in which large categories of grants-in-aid were made available to cities on condition that they develop plans for removing slums and for restoring property to more valuable uses, including new housing as well as new structures for business and civic affairs.

vested interests   Fixed or established interests; interests not varying with changing conditions; privileges respected or accepted by others.

veto   The president's constitutional power to turn down acts of Congress. A presidential veto may be overridden by a two-thirds vote of each house of Congress.

whip system   Primarily a communications network in each house of Congress, whips take polls of the membership in order to learn their intentions on specific legislative issues and to assist the majority and minority leaders in various tasks.

withholding tax   Deduction by employers of a specified percentage of all wages, paid to the government in advance to guarantee payment of taxes.

writ of *certiorari*   A decision concurred in by at least four of the nine Supreme Court justices to review a decision of a lower court; from the Latin "to make more certain."

Glossary of Court Cases

Abrams v. *United States* (1919)   The Supreme Court upheld the convictions of five Bolshevik sympathizers under the Espionage Act which made it an offense to intend interference in the war with Germany. Although the defendants actually opposed American intervention in the Russian Revolution, the Court imputed to them the knowledge that their actions would necessarily inpede the war effort against Germany. [See page 310.]

Argersinger v. *Hamlin* (1972)   The Court extended the right to counsel for those accused of misdemeanors. **[See page 114.]***

Arizona v. *Fulminante* (1991)   A bare majority of the Rehnquist Court held that coerced confessions may be used at trial if it could be shown that other evidence was also used to support a guilty verdict. But, the Court also held that in this case, the admission of a coerced confession was not "harmless error" and remanded the case for a new trial. **[See page 343.]**

Associated Press v. *National Labor Relations Board*   (1937)   A case resulting from New Deal legislation in which the Court ceased trying to restrict the national government from regulating local conditions. Here, the Court held that the labor relations of newspapers and press associations were also subject to the Labor Relations Act. **[See page 70.]**

Baker v. *Carr* (1962)   The Court held that the issue of malapportionment of election districts raised a justiciable claim under the Equal Protection Clause of the Fourteenth Amendment. The effect of the case was to force the reapportionment of nearly all federal, state, and local election districts nationwide. **[See page 337.]**

Barron v. *Baltimore* (1833)   This was one of the most significant cases ever handed down by the Court. Chief Justice John Marshall confirmed the concept of "dual citizenship," in that, each American is separately a citizen of the national government and of the state government. This meant that the Bill of Rights applied only nationally, and not to state or local laws. The consequences of this ruling were felt well into the twentieth century. **[See pages 104–105.]**

Benton v. *Maryland* (1969)   The Court ruled that double jeopardy was a right incorporated in the Fourteenth Amendment as a restriction on the states. **[See page 109.]**

Berkey Photo Inc. v. *Eastman Kodak Co.* (1979)   In a reminder of the limited place of juries within the judicial system, an appellate judge upheld a trial judge's decision to reduce a $120 million jury verdict award to $87 million, and further "remitted" the award to $900,000. **[See page 318.]**

*Additional text discussion of a case is indicated by page numbers in boldface type.

A55

Berman v. *Parker* (1954)   In this case, which involved a government effort to clear slum properties in the nation's capital to make way for new housing, the Court held that the government had a very broad constitutional sanction, under the concept of "eminent domain," to declare that the public interest required the taking of land from a private owner. **[See page 314.]**

Board of Education of Oklahoma City v. *Dowell* (1991)   This case, which restricted the use of court-ordered busing to achieve school integration, gave an early indication of the attitude of the new Bush Court. **[See page 343.]**

Bolling v. *Sharpe* (1954)   This case, which did not directly involve the Fourteenth Amendment because the District of Columbia is not a state, confronted the Court on the grounds that segregation is inherently unequal. Its victory in effect was "incorporation in reverse," with equal protection moving from the Fourteenth Amendment to become part of the Bill of Rights. **[See page 125.]**

Bowers v. *Hardwick* (1986)   In this case, the Supreme Court upheld a Georgia statute prohibiting sodomy, by ruling that the constitutional right of privacy protected the traditional family unit but not the conduct between homosexuals when that conduct offended "traditional Judeo-Christian values." **[See page 346.]**

Bowsher v. *Synar* (1986)   This was the second of two cases since 1937 in which the Court invalidated an act of Congress on constitutional grounds. In this case, the Court struck down the Gramm-Rudman Act mandating a balanced federal budget, ruling that it was unconstitutional to grant the comptroller general "executive" powers. **[See pages 83 and 245.]**

Brandenburg v. *Ohio* (1969)   The Court overturned an Ohio statute forbidding any person from urging criminal acts as a means of inducing political reform or from joining any association that advocated such activities, on the grounds that the statute punished "mere advocacy" and therefore violated the free speech provisions of the federal Constitution. **[See page 326.]**

Brown v. *Allen* (1952)   This case demonstrates how extremely difficult it is for state legislatures or Congress to summon up the majorities necessary to react against a Supreme Court decision. Justice Robert Jackson commented that "The Court is not final because it is infallible; the Court is infallible because it is final." [See page 324.]

Brown v. *Board of Education of Topeka, Kansas* (1954)   The Supreme Court struck down the "separate but equal" doctrine as fundamentally unequal. This case eliminated state power to use race as a criterion of discrimination in law and provided the national government with the power to intervene by exercising strict regulatory policies against discriminatory actions. **[See page 125.]**

Brown v. *Board of Education of Topeka, Kansas (Brown II)* (1955)   One year after *Brown* the Court issued a mandate for state and local boards to proceed "with all deliberate speed" to desegregate schools. **[See page 128.]**

Buckley v. *Valeo* (1976)   The Supreme Court limited congressional attempts to regulate campaign financing by declaring unconstitutional any absolute limits on the freedom of individuals to spend their own money on campaigns. **[See page 494.]**

Cable Network News v. *Noriega* (1990)   The doctrine of "no prior restraint" was weakened when the Supreme Court held that the Cable Network News could be restrained from broadcasting supposedly illegally obtained tapes of conversations between former Panamanian leader Manuel Noriega and his lawyer until the trial court had listened to the tapes and had determined whether such a broadcast would violate Noriega's right to a fair trial. **[See page 550.]**

Chicago, Burlington, and Quincy Railroad Company v. *Chicago* (1897) This case effectively overruled *Barron* by affirming that the due process clause of the Fourteenth
Amendment did prohibit states from taking property for a public use without just
compensation. **[See page 107.]**

Citizens to Preserve Overton Park, Inc. v. *Volpe* (1971) Beginning with the Supreme
Court's decision in this case, the federal courts allowed countless challenges to federal
agency actions under the National Environmental Policy Act (NEPA), brought by
public interest groups asserting that the agencies had failed to consider the adverse effects of their actions upon the environment as required by NEPA. **[See page 531.]**

City of Richmond v. *J. A. Croson Co.* (1989) In this case the Supreme Court held that
minority set-aside programs would have to redress specific instances of identified discrimination in order to avoid violating the rights of whites. [See page 137.]

The Civil Rights Cases (1883) The Court struck down the Civil Rights Act of 1875,
which attempted to protect blacks from discriminatory treatment by proprietors of
public facilities. It ruled that the Fourteenth Amendment applied only to discriminatory actions by state officials and did not apply to discrimination against blacks by private individuals. **[See page 107.]**

Coleman v. *Thompson* (1991) In this case, the Supreme Court cut away further at the
rights of an accused in holding that a defendant does not have a constitutional right to
counsel on appeal from a state habeas trial court judgement. **[See page 344.]**

Cooper v. *Aaron* (1958) In this historic case, the Supreme Court required that Little
Rock, Arkansas, desegregate its public schools by immediately complying with a lower
court's order, and warned that it is "emphatically the province and duty of the judicial
department to say what the law is." **[See page 130.]**

Dartmouth College v. *Woodward* (1819) In this case the Supreme Court held that one
who converts the property of another in good faith is entitled to an allowance for those
improvements. [See page 323.]

Doe v. *Bolton* (1973) Decided along with *Roe,* this case extended the decision in *Roe* by
striking down state requirements that abortions be performed in licensed hospitals;
that abortions be approved beforehand by a hospital committee; and that two physicians concur in the abortion decision. [See page 106.]

Dred Scott v. *Sandford* (1857) This was the infamous case in which Chief Justice Roger
Taney wrote that blacks were not citizens; that they "were never thought of or spoken
of except as property." In a vain attempt to settle the slavery issue, which was threatening to tear the country apart, the Court went further to rule that the Missouri Compromise was unconstitutional, and Congress could not bar slavery from the territories.
This ruling probably hastened the onset of the Civil War. **[See page 66.]**

Duke Power Co. v. *Carolina Environmental Study* (1978) The Supreme Court dealt antinuclear power activists a significant blow by upholding a federal statute limiting liability for damages accruing from nuclear power plant accidents. **[See page 531.]**

Duncan v. *Louisiana* (1968) The Court established the right to trial by jury in state criminal cases where the accused faces a serious charge and sentencing. [See page 109.]

Edwards v. *California* (1941) In an important case arising out of the Depression, the
Court struck down a California law prohibiting any person from knowingly bringing
nonresident indigents into the state, ruling that the measure had been designed in part
to limit interstate competition for jobs. [See page 345.]

Eisenstadt v. *Baird* (1972) The Court struck down state laws prohibiting the use of contraceptives by unmarried persons. **[See page 529.]**

Engel v. *Vitale* (1962)   In interpreting the separation of church and state doctrine, the Court ruled that organized prayer in the public schools was unconstitutional. **[See page 335.]**

Escobedo v. *Illinois* (1964)   The Supreme Court expanded the rights of an accused in this case by giving suspects the right to remain silent and the right to have counsel present during questioning. **[See page 335.]**

Frontiero v. *Richardson* (1973)   The Court rendered an important decision relating to the economic status of women when it held that the armed services could not deny married women fringe benefits, such as housing allowances and health care, that were automatically granted to married men. **[See page 339.]**

Fullilove v. *Klutznick* (1980)   The Court upheld the Public Works Employment Act of 1977, which required that at least 10 percent of federal funds for federal public works contracts be awarded to minority-owned businesses to remedy past discriminatory barriers, even if there was no evidence of deliberate discrimination by individual contractors. **[See page 720.]**

Garcia v. *San Antonio Metropolitan Transit Authority* (1985)   The question of whether the national government had the right to regulate state and local businesses was again raised in this case. The Court ruled that the national government had the right to apply minimum-wage and overtime standards to state and local government employees. This case overturned *National League of Cities* v. *Usery* (1976). [See page 228.]

G. E. v. *Gilbert* (1976)   In this case, the Court found no legislative requirement that pregnancy leaves be treated identically to other disability leaves. Congress effectively reversed the Court's decision by amending Title VII of the 1964 Civil Rights Act to require employers to provide benefits for pregnancy leaves similar to those for other temporary disability leaves. **[See page 322.]**

Gibbons v. *Ogden* (1824)   An early major case establishing the supremacy of the national government in all matters affecting interstate commerce, in which John Marshall broadly defined what Article I, Section 8, meant by "commerce among the several states." He affirmed that the federal government alone could regulate trade, travel, and navigation between the states. **[See page 69.]**

Gideon v. *Wainwright* (1963)   The Warren Court overruled an earlier case (*Betts* 1942) and established that "any person haled into court, who is too poor to have a lawyer, cannot be assured a fair trial unless counsel is provided for him." **[See page 109.]**

Gitlow v. *New York* (1925)   The Court ruled that the freedom of speech is "among the fundamental personal rights and 'liberties' protected by the due process clause of the Fourteenth Amendment from impairment by the states." **[See pages 107–108.]**

Griffin v. *Prince Edward County School Board* (1964)   The Supreme Court forced all the schools in Prince Edward County to reopen after they had been closed for five years to avoid desegregation. **[See page 130.]**

Griggs v. *Duke Power Company* (1971)   The Court held that although the statistical evidence did not prove intentional discrimination, and although the hiring requirements were race-neutral in appearance, their effects were sufficient to shift the burden of justification to the employer to show that his requirements were a "business necessity" that bore "a demonstrable relationship to successful performance." **[See page 134.]**

Griswold v. *Connecticut* (1965)   The Court ruled that the right to privacy included the right to marital privacy and struck down state laws restricting married persons' use of contraceptives and the circulation of birth control information. **[See pages 326 and 529.]**

Hague v. *Committee for Industrial Organization (CIO)* (1939)   The Court extended the concept of a public forum to include public streets and meeting halls and incorporated the freedom of assembly into the list of rights held to be fundamental and therefore binding on the states as well as on the national government. [See page 106.]

Hammer v. *Dagenhart* (1918)   The Court ruled unconstitutional the 1916 laws that banned goods made by children from interstate commerce. This was overturned in 1941 in *U. S.* v. *Darby.* **[See page 70.]**

Harris v. *New York* (1971)   In a ruling that limited the *Miranda* ruling, the Burger Court held that although a statement was inadmissable because of failure to give the Miranda warning, it could be used to impeach the defendant's testimony if the defendant took the stand. **[See page 114.]**

Herring v. *State* (1904)   In this perjury case, the Georgia Supreme Court declared that if the Fourth Amendment right to privacy means anything, it means that, "before Georgia can prosecute its citizens for making choices about the most intimate aspects of their lives, it must do more than assert that the choice they have made is an 'abominable crime not fit to be named among Christians.' " **[See page 346.]**

Hodgson v. *Minnesota* (1990)   In this case the Supreme Court upheld a Minnesota statute requiring parental notification before an abortion could be performed on a woman under the age of eighteen. **[See page 342.]**

Humphrey's Executor v. *United States* (1935)   The Court in this case made a distinction between "purely executive" officials—whom the president could remove at his discretion—and officials with "quasi-judicial and quasi-legislative" duties—who could be removed only for reasons specified by Congress. This decision limited the president's removal powers. [See page 215.]

Immigration and Naturalization Services (INS) v. *Chada* (1983)   This was the first of two cases since 1937 in which the Court invalidated an act of Congress on constitutional grounds. In this case the Court declared the legislative veto unconstitutional. **[See pages 83 and 306.]**

In re Agent Orange Product Liability Litigation (1983)   In this case, a federal judge in New York certified Vietnam War veterans as a class with standing to sue a manufacturer of herbicides for damages allegedly incurred from exposure to the defendants' product while they were in Vietnam. **[See page 353.]**

In re Debs (1895)   The Supreme Court upheld President Cleveland's power to obtain an injunction against the Pullman Strike, even in the absence of any statutory warrant, on the grounds that "the wrongs complained of by the President were such . . . as affect the public at large." **[See page 217.]**

In re Neagle (1890)   The Supreme Court held that the protection of a federal judge was a reasonable extension of the president's constitutional power to "take care that the laws be faithfully executed." **[See page 208.]**

In re Oliver (1948)   The Court incorporated the right to a public trial in the Fourteenth Amendment as a restriction on the states. **[See page 109.]**

Katz v. *United States* (1967)   In repudiation of the *Olmstead* doctrine, the Supreme Court declared that the Fourth Amendment "protects people, not places," and held that electronic surveillance conducted outside the judicial process, whether or not it involves trespass, is *per se* unreasonable. [See page 346.]

Katzenbach v. *McClung* (1964)   The Court gave an extremely broad definition to "interstate commerce" so as to allow Congress the constitutional authority to cover discrimination by virtually any local employer. Although the Court agreed that this case involved a strictly intrastate restaurant, they found a sufficient connection to interstate commerce resulting from the restaurant's acquisition of food and supplies so as to hold that racial discrimination at such an establishment would "impose commercial burdens of national magnitude upon interstate commerce." **[See page 134.]**

Kirchberg v. *Fenestra* (1981)   In a continuing effort to abolish gender lines in the law, the Court invalidated Louisiana's "head and master" rule that gave married men the sole right to dispose of property held jointly by both spouses. **[See page 339.]**

Lee v. *Weisman* (1992)   A bare majority of the Court ruled that prayers during a public school graduation ceremony amounted to a "state-sponsored and state-directed religious exercise" in violation of the First Amendment. [See page 344.]

Lochner v. *New York* (1905)   Seeking to protect business from government regulation, the Court invalidated a New York state law regulating the sanitary conditions and hours of labor of bakers on the grounds that the law interfered with liberty of contract. **[See page 71.]**

Loving v. *Virginia* (1967)   The Court invalidated a Virginia statute prohibiting interracial marriages, on the grounds that the statute violated guarantees of due process and equal protection contained in the Fourteenth Amendment of the Constitution. **[See page 326.]**

Lucas v. *South Carolina Growth Council* (1992)   The Court remanded this case to the state courts to determine whether the owner of a beachfront property had suffered economic loss by a zoning restriction aimed at preserving the beach and sand dunes. The Court's ruling recognized that a property owner is entitled to just compensation when a government's regulations diminish the value of private property, just as in an eminent domain proceeding. [See page 344.]

Lujan v. *Defenders of Wildlife* (1992)   The Court restricted the concept of standing by requiring that a party bringing suit against a government policy show that the policy is likely to cause them direct and imminent injury. **[See pages 355 and 533.]**

McGrain v. *Dougherty* (1927)   The Court unanimously affirmed Congress's power to compel a private individual to testify in its investigations and hearings. But it also required that the congressional committee show that its questions served a legislative purpose before compelling a witness to answer. [See page 189.]

Malloy v. *Hogan* (1964)   The Court ruled that the right of a person to remain silent and not incriminate himself applied to the states as well as to the federal government. This decision incorporated the Fifth Amendment into the Fourteenth Amendment. [See page 116.]

Mapp v. *Ohio* (1961)   The Court held that evidence obtained in violation of the Fourth Amendment ban on unreasonable searches and seizures would be excluded from trial. **[See page 112.]**

Marbury v. *Madison* (1803)   This was the landmark case in which Chief Justice Marshall established that the Court had the right to rule on the constitutionality of federal and state laws, although judicial review was not explicity granted by the Constitution. **[See page 325.]**

Martin v. *Hunter's Lessee* (1816)   In this case, the Supreme Court confirmed its congressionally conferred power to review and reverse state constitutions and laws whenever they are clearly in conflict with the U.S. Constitution, federal laws, or treaties. [See page 325.]

Martin v. *Wilks* (1989)   The Supreme Court further eased the way for employers to prefer white males when it held that any affirmative action program already approved by federal courts could be subsequently challenged by white males who alleged that the program discriminated against them. **[See page 138.]**

Masson v. *New Yorker Magazine* (1991)   The Supreme Court held that a successful libel claim must prove that an allegedly libelous author and/or publisher acted with requisite knowledge of falsity or reckless disregard as to truth or falsity in publishing the allegedly libelous material. [See page 551.]

McCulloch v. Maryland (1819)   This was the first and most important case favoring national control of the economy over state control. In his ruling, John Marshall established the "implied powers" doctrine enabling Congress to use the "necessary and
proper" clause of Article I, Section 8 to interpret its delegated powers. This case also
concluded that, when state law and federal law were in conflict, national law took
precedence. **[See pages 44–45 and 67.]**

Metro Broadcasting v. *FCC* (1990)   In one of its few efforts to continue some affirmative
action programs, the Rehnquist Court upheld two federal programs aimed at increasing minority ownership of broadcast licenses on the grounds that they serve the important governmental objective of broadcast diversity, and they are substantially related
to the achievement of that objective. **[See page 340.]**

Milliken v. *Bradley* (1974)   The Supreme Court severely restricted the *Swann* ruling
when it determined in this case that only cities found guilty of deliberate and *de jure*
segregation (segregation in law) would have to desegregate their schools. This ruling
exempted most northern states and cities from busing because school segregation in
northern cities is generally *de facto* segregation (segregation in fact) that follows from
segregated housing and other forms of private discrimination. **[See page 132.]**

Miranda v. *Arizona* (1966)   The Warren Court ruled that anyone placed under arrest
must be informed of the right to remain silent and to have counsel present during interrogation. **[See pages 335–336].**

Missouri ex rel. Gaines v. *Canada* (1938)   Rather than question the "separate but equal"
doctrine, the Court in this case ruled that Missouri had violated the equal protection
clause of the Fourteenth Amendment by not providing a law school for blacks. The
ruling reiterated that states must furnish "equal facilities in separate schools." **[See
page 121.]**

Missouri v. *Holland* (1920)   The Court recognized that a treaty could enlarge federal
power at the expense of the states, under the "supremacy clause" in Article VI. **[See
page 121.]**

Missouri v. *Jenkins* (1990)   The Court upheld the authority of a federal judge to order the
Kansas City, Missouri, school board to raise taxes to pay for a school plan to achieve
racial integration. **[See page 353.]**

Moore v. *Ogilvie* (1969)   In a significant relaxation of the original definition of mootness,
which generally made it impossible to challenge election rules, the Court began to
hear some such cases if the issue was likely to be repeated in later elections. [See page
316.]

Moran v. *McDonough* (1976)   In an effort to retain jurisdiction of the case until the
court's mandated school-desegregation plan had been satisfactorily implemented, District Court Judge Arthur Garrity issued fourteen decisions relating to different aspects
of the Boston school plan that had been developed under his authority and put into effect under his supervision. **[See page 353.]**

Morrison v. *Olson* (1988)   The Supreme Court upheld the constitutionality of the special
prosecutor law, which allows the attorney general to recommend that a panel of federal
judges appoint an independent counsel to investigate alleged wrongdoing by officials
of the executive branch. **[See pages 84 and 340.]**

Muskrat v. *United States* (1911)   The Court held that the case before it must be a real
controversy, with two adversarial parties; if one side is a straw man, the adversarial system cannot work. [See page 316.]

Myers v. *United States* (1926)   The Court upheld a broad interpretation of the president's
power to remove executive officers whom he had appointed, despite restrictions imposed by Congress. (Later limited by *Humphrey's* [1935]). [See page 215.]

NAACP v. *Alabama ex rel. Patterson* (1958) The Court recognized the right to "privacy in one's association" in its ruling protecting the NAACP from the state of Alabama using its membership list. **[See page 114.]**

NAACP v. *Button* (1963) The state of Virginia sued the NAACP in an attempt to restrict or eliminate its efforts to influence the pattern of cases by soliciting legal business in which they were not parties and had no pecuniary right or liability. The Supreme Court held that this strategy was protected by the First and Fourteenth Amendments, just as other forms of speech and petition are protected. **[See page 350.]**

National Labor Relations Board v. *Jones & Laughlin Steel Corporation* (1937) In a case involving New Deal legislation, the Court reversed its earlier rulings on "interstate commerce" and redefined it to permit the national government to regulate local economic and social conditions. **[See pages 70 and 226.]**

National League of Cities v. *Usery* (1976) Although in this case the Court invalidated a congressional act applying wage and hour regulations to state and local governments, it reversed its decision nine years later in *Garcia* v. *San Antonio Metropolitan Transit Authority* (1985). **[See page 83.]**

Near v. *Minnesota* (1931) In this landmark case, which established the doctrine of "no prior restraint," the Court held that, except under extraordinary circumstances, the First Amendment prohibits government agencies from seeking to prevent newspapers or magazines from printing whatever they wish. **[See page 550.]**

New York Times v. *Sullivan* (1964) In this case, the Supreme Court held that to be deemed libelous, a story about a public official not only had to be untrue, but had to result from "actual malice" or "reckless disregard" for the truth. In practice, this standard of proof is nearly impossible to reach. **[See pages 550–551.]**

New York Times v. *United States* (1971) In this case, the so-called *Pentagon Papers* case, the Supreme Court ruled that the government could not block publication of secret Defense Department documents that had been furnished to the *New York Times* by a liberal opponent of the Vietnam War who had obtained the documents illegally. **[See page 550.]**

New York v. *Quarles* (1984) The Supreme Court made a significant cutback in the area of criminal procedure when it ruled that statements obtained in violation of the *Miranda* requirements are admissible when those statements are responses to police questions asked out of concern for public safety. [See page 346.]

Nix v. *Williams* (1984) The Court held in this case that unlawfully obtained evidence is admissible at trial if it ultimately or inevitably would have been discovered by lawful means. [See page 339.]

Ohio v. *Akron Center for Reproductive Health* (1990) The Supreme Court upheld a state law requiring parental notification before an abortion could be performed on a woman under the age of eighteen. **[See page 342.]**

Olmstead v. *United States* (1928) The Supreme Court first confronted the issue of electronic surveillance in this case, which involved the wiretapping of a gang of rumrunners. The Court concluded that the Fourth Amendment was not applicable, because there had been no trespass of a constitutionally protected area nor a seizure of a physical object. [See page 346.]

Palko v. *Connecticut* (1937) The Court decided that double jeopardy was not a provision of the Bill of Rights protected at the state level. This was not reversed until 1969 in *Benton* v. *Maryland*. **[See page 108.]**

Panama Refining Company v. *Ryan* (1935) The Court ruled against a section of the National Industrial Recovery Act, a New Deal statute, as being an invalid delegation of legislative power to the executive branch. **[See page 83.]**

Payne v. *Tennessee* (1991)   The Supreme Court overruled some earlier decisions in holding that the Eighth Amendment does not erect a *per se* bar prohibiting a capital sentencing jury from considering "victim impact" evidence relating to the victim's personal characteristics and the emotional impact of the murder on the victim's family, nor does it preclude a prosecutor from arguing such evidence at a capital sentencing hearing. [See page 344.]

Penry v. *Lynaugh* (1989)   In this case the Supreme Court eased restrictions on the use of capital punishment by allowing states to execute mentally retarded murderers. **[See page 342.]**

Planned Parenthood of Southeastern Pennsylvania v. *Casey* (1992)   Abandoning *Roe's* assertion of a woman's "fundamental right" to choose abortion, a bare majority of the Court redefined it as a "limited or qualified" right subject to regulation by the states, so long as the states do not impose an "undue burden" on women. Specifically, the Court upheld portions of Pennsylvania's strict abortion law which included the requirement of parental notification for minors and a twenty-four hour waiting period. **[See pages 118 and 344.]**

Plessy v. *Ferguson* (1896)   The Court, in this now infamous case, held that the Fourteenth Amendment's "equal protection of the laws" was not violated by racial distinction as long as the "separate" facilities were "equal." **[See pages 109 and 120.]**

Plyler v. *Doe* (1982)   The Supreme Court invalidated on equal-protection grounds a Texas statute that withheld state funds from local school districts for the education of children who were illegal aliens and that further authorized the local school districts to deny enrollment to such children. [See page 350.]

Pollock v. *Farmers' Loan and Trust Company* (1895)   In this case involving the unconstitutionality of an income tax of 2 percent on all incomes over $4,000, the Supreme Court declared that any direct tax as such must be apportioned in order to be valid. **[See page 676.]**

Red Lion Broadcasting v. *FCC* (1969)   In upholding the fairness doctrine in this case, the Court differentiated between the broadcast media and the print media in regards to the First Amendment. The Court ruled that "a license permits broadcasting, but the licensee has no constitutional right to be the one who holds the license or to monopolize a radio frequency to the exclusion of his fellow citizens." **[See page 549.]**

Reed v. *Reed* (1971)   In this case, which made gender lines in the law illegitimate for the first time, the Supreme Court invalidated an Idaho probate statute that required courts to give preference to males over females as administrators of estates. **(See page 339.)**

Regents of the University of California v. *Bakke* (1978)   This case addressed the issue of qualification versus minority preference. The Court held that universities could continue to take minority status into consideration because a "diverse student body" contributing to a "robust exchange of ideas" is a "constitutionally permissible goal" on which a race-conscious university admissions program may be predicated. **[See pages 135–137.]**

Roe v. *Wade* (1973)   This is the famous case that rendered unconstitutional all state laws making abortion a crime, ruling that the states could not interfere in a woman's "right to privacy" and her right to choose to terminate a pregnancy. **[See pages 114 and 341.]**

Rust v. *Sullivan* (1991)   In the case, the Court upheld regulations of the Department of Health and Human Services that prohibited the use of Title X family planning funds for abortion counseling, referral, or activities advocating abortion as a method of family planning. **[See page 343.]**

Schechter Poultry Co. v. *United States* (1935)   The Court declared the National Industrial Recovery Act of 1933 unconstitutional on the grounds that Congress had delegated legislative power to the executive branch without sufficient standards or guidelines for presidential discretion. [See page 83.]

Schuttlesworth v. *Birmingham Board of Education* (1958)   This decision upheld a "pupil placement" plan purporting to assign pupils on various bases, with no mention of race. This case interpreted *Brown* v. *Board of Education* to mean that school districts must stop explicit racial discrimination but were under no obligation to take positive steps to desegregate. **[See page 130.]**

Scott v. *Illinois* (1979)   The Burger Court narrowed the virtually absolute right of defendants to legal counsel by identifying circumstances under which counsel need not necessarily be present. **[See page 338.]**

Shelley v. *Kraemer* (1948)   In this case, the Supreme Court ruled against the widespread practice of "restrictive covenants," declaring that although private persons could sign such covenants, they could not be judicially enforced since the Fourteenth Amendment prohibits any organ of the state, including the courts, from denying equal protection of its laws. **[See pages 123 and 330–331.]**

Sierra Club v. *Morton* (1972)   To have standing is to be the proper person to bring suit, and the basic requirement for standing is to show injury to oneself. In this case, the Court expanded the definition of injury from simply personal and/or economic harm to include such values as "aesthetic and environmental well being." [See page 316.]

The Slaughterhouse Cases (1873)   The Court ruled that the federal government was under no obligation to protect the "privileges and immunities" of citizens of a particular state against arbitrary action by that state's government. This was similar to the *Barron* case, except it was thought that the Fourteenth Amendment would now incorporate the Bill of Rights, applying it to the states. The Court however ruled that the Fourteenth Amendment was to "protect Negroes as a class" and had nothing to do with individual liberties. **[See page 107.]**

Smith v. *Allwright* (1944)   The Supreme Court struck down the southern practice of "white primaries," which legally excluded blacks from participation in the nominating process. The Court recognized that primaries could no longer be regarded as the private affairs of parties because parties were an integral aspect of the electoral process, and thus became an "agency of the State" prohibited from discriminating against blacks within the meaning of the Fifteenth Amendment. **[See pages 123 and 345.]**

Stanford v. *Kentucky* (1989)   The Supreme Court again eased restrictions on capital punishment by allowing states to execute murderers who were as young as sixteen at the time of the crime. **[See page 342.]**

Stanley v. *Georgia* (1969)   In reversing a conviction based on a Georgia statute, the Supreme Court held that mere private possession of obscene materials could not be made a crime even if the actual material itself was unprotected by the First and Fourteenth amendments. [See page 346.]

Steward Machine Company v. *Davis* (1937)   A case resulting from New Deal legislation in which the Court upheld the Social Security Act of 1935. **[See page 70.]**

Stone v. *Powell* (1976)   In this case, the Supreme Court ruled that where the state courts have concluded that an accused's Fourth Amendment rights had not been violated, federal courts should not exercise *habeas corpus* jurisdiction to review those findings. [See page 338–339.]

Swann v. *Charlotte-Mecklenburg Board of Education* (1971)   This case involved the most important judicial extension of civil rights in education after 1954. The Court held that state-imposed desegregation could be brought about by "busing," and under certain limited circumstances even racial quotas could be used as the "starting point in shaping a remedy to correct past constitutional violations." [See page 132.]

Sweatt v. *Painter* (1950)   The Court ruled in favor of a black student who refused to go to the Texas law school for blacks, arguing that it was inferior to the state school for whites. Although the Court still did not confront the "separate but equal" rule in this case, it did question whether any segregated facility could be equal. [See page 121.]

TVA v. *Hill* (1978)   In a significant case, the Court held that the Endangered Species Act made it an unqualified duty for governmental agencies to refrain from taking actions that would harm threatened or endangered species. Congress amended the act to allow agencies to weigh the costs of protecting a species against the benefits to be gained from proceeding with certain kinds of projects. **[See page 515.]**

United States v. *Curtiss–Wright Export Co.* (1936)   In this case the Court held that Congress may delegate a degree of discretion to the president in foreign affairs that might violate the separation of powers if it were in a domestic arena. **[See page 212.]**

United States v. *Darby Lumber Company* (1941)   The Court ruled that Congress could set minimum wage and hour requirements under the Fair Labor and Standards Act of 1938. This case invalidated *Hammer* v. *Dagenhart* (1918). **[See page 70.]**

United States v. *Harris* (1971)   Restricting the *Mapp* ruling somewhat, this case ruled that technical violations of search and seizure ought not to be used to free known criminals. **[See page 113.]**

United States v. *Leon* (1984)   In a further deterioration of the rights of an accused, the Supreme Court held that evidence obtained in reasonable reliance on a defective search warrant is admissible at trial. [See page 339.]

United States v. *Nixon* (1974)   The Court declared unconstitutional President Nixon's refusal to surrender subpoenaed tapes as evidence in a criminal prosecution. The Court argued that executive privilege did not extend to data in presidential files or tapes bearing upon criminal prosecution. **[See page 83.]**

United States v. *Pink* (1942)   The Court ruled that executive agreements have the same legal status as treaties, despite the fact that they do not require the "advice and consent" of the Senate. **[See page 212.]**

United States v. *S.C.R.A.P.* (1973)   In this case, the Court further defined issues of standing by holding that to have standing an individual must be among those injured and must show specific, personal, and substantial harm. [See page 316.]

United Steel Workers v. *Weber* (1979)   In rejecting the claim of a white employee who had been denied a place in a training program in which half the spots were reserved for black employees, the Supreme Court claimed that Title VII of the Civil Rights Act of 1964 did not apply to affirmative action programs voluntarily established by private companies. [See page 339.]

Wabash, St. Louis and Pacific Railway Company v. *Illinois* (1886)   The Supreme Court struck down a state law prohibiting rate discrimination by a railroad, arguing that the route of an interstate railroad could not be subdivided into its separate state segments for purposes of regulation. In response to the need for some form of regulation, Congress passed the Interstate Commerce Act of 1887, creating the Interstate Commerce Commission (ICC), the first federal administrative agency. **[See page 69.]**

Wards Cove v. *Atonio* (1989)   The Court held that the burden of proof of unlawful discrimination should be shifted from the defendant (the employer) to the plaintiff (the person claiming to be the victim of discrimination). **[See page 137.]**

Webster v. *Reproductive Health Services* (1989)   In upholding a Missouri law that restricted the use of public medical facilities for abortion, the Court opened the way for states to again limit the availability of abortions. **[See page 118.]**

West Coast Hotel Company v. *Parrish* (1937)   The Court upheld Washington state's minimum wage law, reversing its previous conservative rulings that had narrowly interpreted the right of contract and limited the right of states to enact social and economic regulation. **[See page 70.]**

Wickard v. *Filburn* (1942)   In this case, the Supreme Court established the "cumulative effect" principle. The Court held that Congress could control a farmer's production of wheat for home consumption because the cumulative effect of home consumption of wheat by many farmers might reasonably be thought to alter the supply-and-demand relationships of the interstate commodity market. [See page 228.]

Worcester v. *Georgia* (1832)   The Court ruled that states could not pass laws affecting federally recognized Indian nations, and therefore, Georgia had no right to trespass on the Cherokee's lands without their assent. To which President Andrew Jackson is reported to have replied, "John Marshall has made his decision, now let him enforce it." **[See page 351.]**

Youngstown Sheet and Tube Co. v. *Sawyer* (1952)   This case is also known as the *Steel Seizure* case. During the Korean War, when the United Steelworkers threatened to go on strike, President Truman seized the mills and placed them under military operation. He argued he had inherent power to prevent a strike that would interfere with the war. The Court ruled against him, however, saying that presidential powers must be authorized by statute and did not come from anything inherent in the presidency. [See page 83.]

Acknowledgments

CHAPTER 1
Page 3 Photo by New York City Police Department Photo Unit; **page 14** (top) Reproduced courtesy of the Trustees of the British Museum, (center) Warder Collection, (bottom) Warder Collection; **page 15** (top) MacArthur Library, (bottom) UPI/Bettmann Newsphotos; **page 21** Warder Collection.

CHAPTER 2
Page 25 Bettmann Archive; **page 31** Bettmann Archive; **page 40** (top) Courtesy of the Library of Congress, (bottom) Courtesy of the Library of Congress; **page 41** (top) Bettmann Archive, (center) Bettmann Archive, (bottom) Courtesy of the Library of Congress; **page 52** Bettmann Archive; **page 53** Bettmann Archive.

CHAPTER 3
Page 57 Architect of the Capitol; **page 66** Missouri Historical Society; **page 76** (top) Photo Researchers, Inc., (bottom) Photo by Nick Lawrence, Warder Collection; **page 77** (top from left to right), UPI/Bettmann Newsphotos, AP/Wide World Photos, Warder Collection, (bottom) © 1988 William R. Kiviat, Photo by Chris Edwards, *Trentonian;* **page 88** Reuters/Bettmann; **page 89** Lang Communications.

CHAPTER 4
Page 99 © 1985 Flip Schulke/Black Star; **page 110** (top) Bettmann Archive, (bottom left) © Jim Anderson 1983/Woodfin Camp, (bottom right) AP/Wide World Photos; **page 111** John Launois/Black Star, (bottom) AP/Wide World Photos; **page 116** Reuters/Bettmann; **page 117** UPI/Bettmann Newsphotos; **page 122** UPI/Bettmann Newsphotos; **page 126** © Bruce Roberts 1975/Rapho/Photo Researchers, Inc., (bottom) © Bettye Lane; **page 127** (top) AP/Wide World, (bottom) Reuters/Bettmann; **page 131** Warder Collection.

CHAPTER 5
Page 145 National Geographic photographer Thomas Nebbia, courtesy of U.S. Capitol Historical Society; **page 151** Courtesy of Carol Moseley-Braun; **page 172** (top) AP/Wide World Photos, (bottom) Ron Tarver, *Philadelphia Inquirer;* **page 173** (top) © 1992 Dennis Brack/Black Star, (bottom left) © 1992 Lisa Quinones/Black Star, (bottom right) Courtesy of Jay C. Kim; **page 176** Courtesy of Tom Foley; **page 177** Courtesy of Newt Gingrich; **page 190** Black Star.

CHAPTER 6
Page 203 Reuters/Bettmann; **page 210** UPI/Bettmann Newsphotos; **page 222** Courtesy of Culver Pictures, Inc.; **page 232** (top) Collection of the Library of Congress, (center) UPI/Bettmann Newsphotos, (bottom) UPI/Bettmann Newsphotos; **page 233** (top left) AP/Wide World Photos, (top right) UPI/Bettmann, (center) UPI/Bettmann Newsphotos, (bottom) Reuters/Bettmann; **page 248** Reuters/Bettmann; **page 249** Courtesy of the White House, Vice President's Office.

A68

Acknowledg-
ments

CHAPTER 7

Page 263 AP/Wide World; **page 268** Bettmann Archive; **page 269** Courtesy of the United States Senate, Office of the Secretary; **page 275** © 1993 Dennis Brack/Black Star; **page 284** (top) Reuters/Bettmann, (bottom) U.S. Government Printing Office: 1988–533-925; **page 285** (top) New York City Department of Health, (bottom) UPI/Bettmann Newsphotos.

CHAPTER 8

Page 309 Collection of the Supreme Court of the United States; **page 323** Warder Collection; **page 330** Warder Collection; **page 331** UPI/Bettmann; **page 332** (top) Jose R. Lopez, *New York Times,* (bottom) Photo by Harris and Ewing/Collection of the Supreme Court of the United States; **page 333** AP/Wide World Photos, (bottom) AP/Wide World Photos; **page 341** Jose R. Lopez, *New York Times.*

CHAPTER 9

Page 361 © Mark Antman, Image Works; **page 378** UPI/Bettmann Newsphotos; **page 379** AP/Wide World Photos; **page 382** (top) © 1989 Nita Winter, Image Works, (center) Jack Jurden, *Wilmington News Journal,* (bottom) © Mark Antman, Image Works; **page 383** (top) Reuters/Bettmann, (bottom) Reuters/Bettmann; **page 388** UPI/Bettmann Newsphotos.

CHAPTER 10

Page 405 AP/Wide World Photos; **page 434** (top) AP/Wide World Photos, (center) Franklin D. Roosevelt Library, (bottom) Courtesy of the LBJ Library, photo by Eric G. Iversen; **page 435** (top) AP/Wide World, bottom left Drawing by Herbert Block © 1985, from Herblock at Large, (Pantheon Books, 1987), used by permission, (bottom right) AP/WideWorld Photos; **page 442** Reuters/Bettmann; **page 443** Reuters/Bettmann; **page 448** UPI/Bettmann.

CHAPTER 11

Page 457 AP/Wide World Photos; **page 468 and 469** © 1993 Joe Dator and the Cartoon Bank, Inc.; **page 472** UPI/Bettmann Newsphotos; **page 476** (top left) Archives of Labor and Urban Affairs, Wayne State University, (top right) Courtesy of the Library of Congress, (bottom) © Alex Webb, Magnum Photos; **page 477** Cartoon by Steve Greenberg, *Seattle Post-Intelligencer,* (bottom) UPI/Bettmann Newsphotos.

CHAPTER 12

Page 501 Bettmann Archive; **page 508** AP/Wide World Photos; **page 509** AP/Wide World Photos; **page 511** Courtesy of the American Association of Retired Persons; **page 514** UPI/Bettmann; **page 522** (top) Bettmann Archive, (bottom) U.S. Military History Institute; **page 523** (top) Carnegie Library, (center) Warder Collection, (bottom) Warder Collection.

CHAPTER 13

Page 543 AP/Wide World Photos; **page 558** (top) Photo by Jessie Tarbox Beals, the Jacob A. Riis Collection, 1910, Museum of the City of New York; (bottom) Bettmann Archive; **page 559** (top) © 1963 Charles Moore/Black Star, (center) AP/Wide World Photos, (bottom) AP/Wide World Photos; **page 562** Courtesy of the *New York Times;* **page 563** Courtesy of the Free Press; AP/Wide World Photos.

CHAPTER 14

Page 577 © Smithsonian Institution; **page 585** UPI/Bettmann Newsphotos; **page 594** (top) UPI/Bettmann, (bottom) UPI/Bettmann Newsphotos; **page 595** (top) UPI/Bettmann Newsphotos, (center) AP/Wide World Photos, (bottom) AP/Wide World Photos; **page 602** Courtesy of the White House; **page 603** Courtesy of the White House.

CHAPTER 15

Page 615 © C. Gatewood, Image Works; **page 621** Warder Collection; **page 632** Donna Coveney/MIT; **page 633** UPI/Bettmann Newsphotos; **page 636** (top) © Brian Brainerd/*The Denver Post,* (bottom) Photo by Mike Lipack, © *New York Daily News,* photo courtesy of the New York City Police Foundation; **page 637** (top) Image Works, (center) Photo by Sheppard, *New York Daily News,* photo courtesy of the New York City Police Foundation, (bottom) AP/Wide World Photos.

CHAPTER 16

Page 653 UPI/Bettmann; **page 670** (top) Culver Pictures Inc., (bottom left) Bettmann Archives, (bottom right) Photo by Jon Durbin; **page 671** (top left) UPI/Bettmann Newsphotos, (top right) AP/Wide World Photos, (bottom) © Bob Daemmrich, Image Works; **page 674** © 1993 Carl Cox Photography; **page 675** Courtesy of Richard Gephart; **page 682** Bettmann Archive.

CHAPTER 17

Page 687 Bettmann Archive; **page 691** Courtesy of the Library of Congress; **page 698** (top) Photo by John Kaplan, (bottom) Dith Pran, *New York Times*; **page 699** (top) UPI/Bettmann Newsphotos, (center) © 1986 Richard Falco/Black Star, (bottom) Steve Berman, *New York Times*; **page 718** Warder Collection; **page 719** Warder Collection.

CHAPTER 18

Page 725 AP/Wide World Photos; **page 748** (top) UPI/Bettman Newsphotos, (bottom) United Nations Photos; **page 749** (top) © P. Perrin, Sygma, (bottom) Photo by Milton Grant, United Nation Photos; **page 757** AP/Wide World Photos; **page 764** AP/Wide World Photos; **page 765** Warder Collection.

CHAPTER 19

Page 771 Comstock Inc./Michael Stuckey.

INDEX

Page numbers in *italics* refer to illustrations.